Essentials of

W9-CSA-053

INESS LAW

EDITION 4

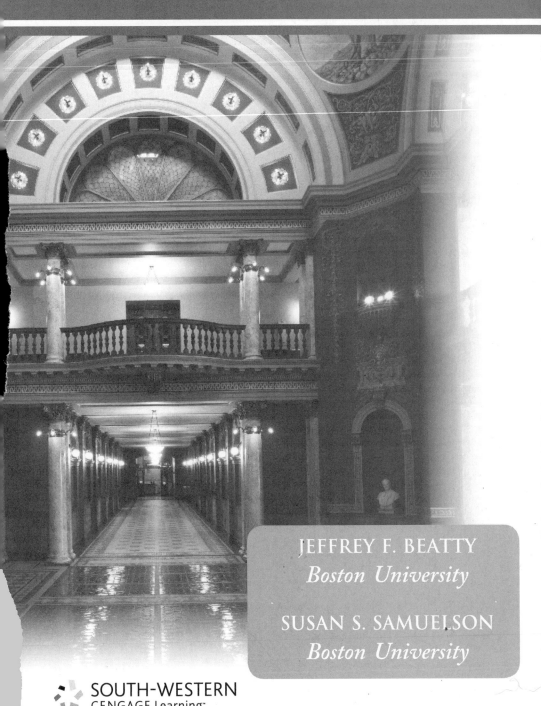

JEFFREY F. BEATTY
Boston University

SUSAN S. SAMUELSON
Boston University

SOUTH-WESTERN
CENGAGE Learning

l • Japan • Korea • Mexico • Singapore • Spain • United Kingdom • United States

SOUTH-WESTERN
CENGAGE Learning

Essentials of Business Law, Fourth Edition
Jeffrey F. Beatty and Susan S. Samuelson

VP/Editorial Director:
 Jack W. Calhoun

Editor-in-Chief:
 Rob Dewey

Senior Acquisitions Editor:
 Vicky True-Baker

Senior Developmental Editor:
 Laura Bofinger Ansara

Editorial Assistant:
 Patrick Ian Clark

Marketing Director:
 Lisa Lysne

Marketing Manager:
 Laura Stopa

Content Project Manager:
 Jacquelyn K Featherly

Senior Media Editor:
 Kristen Meere

Senior Manufacturing Buyer:
 Kevin Kluck

Production House/Compositor:
 Integra Software Service Pvt. Ltd.

Senior Rights Specialist:
 Mardell Glinski-Schultz

Senior Art Director:
 Michelle Kunkler

Cover and Internal Designer:
 Diane Gliebe/Design Matters

Cover Images:
 © Altrendo Travel/Getty Images, Inc.

© 2012, 2008 South-Western, a part of C

ALL RIGHTS RESERVED. No part of this w
may be reproduced, transmitted, stored or
graphic, electronic, or mechanical, including
recording, scanning, digitizing, taping, Web dis
information storage and retrieval systems, exce
or 108 of the 1976 United States Copyright Ac
permission of the publisher.

For product information and technolog
Cengage Learning Customer & Sales

For permission to use material fro
submit all requests online at **www.ce**
Further permissions questions
permissionrequest@ce

ExamView® and ExamView Pro® are register
Windows is a registered trademark of the M
under license. Macintosh and Power Macintc
Apple Computer, Inc. used herein under lice

Library of Congress Control Number: 201093
Student Edition ISBN 13: 978-0-538-47380-4
Student Edition ISBN 10: 0-538-47380-0

South-Western Cengage Learning
5191 Natorp Boulevard
Mason, OH 45040
USA

Cengage Learning products are represented
Nelson Education, Ltd.

For your course and learning solutions, visit v

Purchase any of our products at your local col
preferred online store **www.cengagebrain.com**

Printed in the United States of America
1 2 3 4 5 6 7 14 13 12 11 10

For Annabel, Daisy, and Arabella
j.f.b.

For Bill, Couper, Maisy, and Ned
s.s.s.

CONTENTS: OVERVIEW

CONTENTS

PREFACE

When we began work on the first edition of this textbook, our publisher warned us that our undertaking was risky because there were already so many law texts. Despite these warnings, we were convinced that there was a market for an Essentials book that was different from all the others. Our goal was to capture, in a book focusing on contracts and the Uniform Commercial Code (UCC), the passion and excitement of the law. Business law is notoriously complex, and as authors, we are obsessed with accuracy. Yet this intriguing subject also abounds with human conflict and hard-earned wisdom, forces that can make a law book sparkle.

Now, as the fourth edition goes to press, we think of the many unsolicited emails that we have received, such as this one that came in recently: "In terms of clarity, comprehensiveness, and vividness of style, I think it's probably the best textbook I've ever used in any subject." We are reminded of the students who have said to us, "I had no idea business law could be so interesting." We recall the faculty who have told us, "Until I read your book, I never really understood UCC 2-207," and "With your book, we have great class discussions." Comments such as these never cease to thrill us and to make us feel grateful that we persisted in our vision to write an Essentials of Business Law text like no other—a book that is precise and authoritative, yet a pleasure to read.

COMPREHENSIVE

Staying comprehensive means staying current. This fourth edition contains over 50 new cases. Almost all were reported within the last two or three years. We never include a new court opinion merely because it is recent, but the law evolves continually, and our willingness to toss out old cases and add important new ones ensures that this book— and its readers—remain on the frontier of legal developments.

Look, for example, at the important field of corporate governance. All texts cover Sarbanes-Oxley, executive compensation, and shareholder proposals. We present a clear path through this thicket of issues. Read the section in Chapter 30 about the election and removal of directors. Typically, students, whether undergraduates, MBA candidates, or executives, have a basic misconception about the process of removing a director from office. They think that it is easy. Once they understand the complexity of this process, their whole view of corporate governance changes. We want tomorrow's business leaders to anticipate the challenges that await them and then use their knowledge to avert problems.

This book also provides full coverage of rapidly evolving issues such as cyberlaw, international law, UCC revisions, and countless other topics. For example, Chapter 27 provides extensive coverage of the Restatement (Third) of Agency.

STRONG NARRATIVE

The law is full of great stories, and we use them. Your students and ours should come to class excited. Look at Chapter 3, on dispute resolution. No tedious list of next steps in litigation, this chapter teaches the subject by tracking a double-indemnity lawsuit. An executive is dead. Did he drown accidentally, obligating the insurance company to pay? Or did the businessman commit suicide, voiding the policy? The student follows the action from the discovery of the body, through each step of the lawsuit, to the final appeal. Students read stories and remember them. Strong narratives provide a rich context for the remarkable quantity of legal material presented. When students care about the material they are reading, they persevere. We have been delighted to find that they also arrive in class eager to question, discuss, and learn.

PRECISE

The great joy of using English accurately is the power it gives us to attack and dissect difficult issues, rendering them comprehensible to any lay reader. This text takes on the most complex legal topics of the day, yet it is appropriate for all college and graduate-level students. Accessible prose goes hand in hand with legal precision. We take great pride in walking our readers through the most serpentine mazes this tough subject can offer. UCC Section 2-207, on "battle of forms" conflicts, is hardly sexy material, but it is important. We spotlight the real-world need for Section 2-207 and then use pinpoint directions to guide our readers through its many switchbacks, arriving at a full understanding with sanity and good humor intact. (See Exhibit 10.2 on page 258.)

As we explore this extraordinary discipline, we lure readers along with quirky anecdotes and illustrative diagrams. (Notice that Exhibit 30.4 on page 767 clarifies the complex rules of the duty of care in the business judgment rule.) However, before the trip is over we insist that students:

• Gauge policy and political considerations,

• Grapple with legal and social history,

• Spot the nexus between disparate doctrines, and

• Confront tough moral choices

Beyond that, we ask students to figure out how to avoid the very problems that have generated our law.

AUTHORITATIVE

We insist, as you do, on a law book that is indisputably accurate. A professor must teach with assurance, confident that every paragraph is the result of exhaustive research and meticulous presentation. Dozens of tough-minded people spent thousands of hours reviewing this book, and we are delighted with the stamp of approval we have received from trial and appellate judges, working attorneys, scholars, and teachers.

We reject the cloudy definitions and fuzzy explanations that can invade judicial opinions and legal scholarship. To highlight the most important rules, we use bold print and then follow with vivacious examples written in clear, forceful English. We cheerfully venture into contentious areas, relying on very recent decisions. Can a creditor pierce the veil of a limited liability company (LLC)? What are the rights of an LLC member in the absence of an operating agreement? Where there is doubt about the current (or future) status of a doctrine, we say so. In areas of particularly heated debate, we footnote our work: We want you to have absolute trust in this book.

A BOOK FOR STUDENTS

We have written this book as if we were speaking directly to our students. We provide black letter law but we also explain concepts in terms that hook students. Over the years, we have learned how much more successfully we can teach when our students are intrigued. No matter what kind of a show we put on in class, *they are only learning when they want to learn.*

Every chapter begins with a story, either fictional or real, to illustrate the issues in the chapter and provide context. Chapter 33, on cyberlaw, begins with the true story of a college student who discovers nude pictures of himself online. These photos had been taken in the locker room without his knowledge. What privacy rights do any of us have? Does the Internet jeopardize them? Students want to know—right away.

Many of our students were not yet born when Ronald Reagan was president. They come to college with varying levels of preparation; many now arrive from other countries. We have found that to teach business law most effectively we must provide its context. For example, Chapter 26 describes how two celebrities, living a century apart, fared very differently under the bankruptcy laws of their time.

We also enjoy offering "nuts and bolts" information that grabs students: how much money corporate directors earn, how scam artists create car accidents in order to file fraudulent insurance claims, or where to incorporate.

Students respond enthusiastically to this approach. One professor asked a student to compare our book with the one the class was then using. This was the student's reaction: "I really enjoy reading the [Beatty & Samuelson] textbook and I have decided that I will give you this memo ASAP, but I am keeping the book until Wednesday so that I may continue reading. Thanks! :-)"

Along with other professors, we have used this text in courses for undergraduates and MBAs and Executive MBAs; the students ranging in age from 18 to 55. The book works, as some unsolicited comments indicate:

• An undergraduate wrote, "This is the best textbook I have had in college, on any subject."

- A business law professor stated that the "clarity of presentation is superlative. I have never seen the complexity of contract law made this readable."

- An MBA student commented, "I think the textbook is great. The book is relevant, easy to understand and interesting."

- A state supreme court justice wrote that the book is "a valuable blend of rich scholarship and easy readability. Students and professors should rejoice with this publication."

- A *Fortune 500* vice president, enrolled in an Executive MBA program, commented, "I really liked the chapters. They were crisp, organized and current. The information was easy to understand and enjoyable."

- An undergraduate wrote, "The textbook is awesome. A lot of the time I read more than what is assigned—I just don't want to stop."

HUMOR

Throughout the text we use humor—judiciously—to lighten and enlighten. Not surprisingly, students have applauded—but is wit appropriate? How dare we employ levity in this venerable discipline? We offer humor because we take law seriously. We revere the law for its ancient traditions, its dazzling intricacy, its relentless though imperfect attempt to give order and decency to our world. Because we are confident of our respect for the law, we are not afraid to employ some levity. Leaden prose masquerading as legal scholarship does no honor to the field.

Humor also helps retention. We have found that students remember a contract problem described in a fanciful setting and from that setting recall the underlying principle. By contrast, one widget is hard to distinguish from another.

NEW TO THIS EDITION

We have rewritten every chapter for this fourth edition to ensure coverage of rapidly evolving issues. Here are representative updates.

Does money buy happiness? Many students believe it does. Chapter 2, on ethics, includes a discussion of the latest research on the relationship between money and happiness. Far from making people happy, purchasing more stuff just puts them on the "hedonic treadmill"—struggling to buy more and more things so they can get that buyer's high, only to discover that they can never buy enough to maintain the thrill.

In Chapter 3, on dispute resolution, we offer an expanded look at the biggest recent change in litigation: the explosive rise of electronic discovery, and its consequences to business. In one recent case, a defendant had to pay 31 lawyers full time, for six months, just to wade through the e-ocean of documents and figure out which had to be supplied. In Chapter 5, on constitutional law, we take a new tack on the venerable issue of judicial review by examining the Supreme Court's news-grabbing decision in *Kennedy v. Louisiana*, on child rape.

One of the hottest topics in international law is extraterritoriality. Does the whistle-blower protection of Sarbanes-Oxley apply overseas? We examine both sides of the argument in Chapter 8 and provide a current Second Circuit case. In Chapter 10, on agreement in contracts, we take a fresh look at clickwraps and shrinkwraps. What if the plaintiff's online terms were not easily visible but the defendant knew of them? The court answers the question with a homely but effective metaphor about an apple stand.

Chapter 27, on agency law, is now based on the Restatement (Third) of Agency—an update from the Restatement (Second). As a result, there are significant changes in vocabulary. "Master/servant" has become "employer/employee," and a "partially disclosed" principal has become an "unidentified" principal.

Chapter 29, on starting a business, expands coverage on LLCs. There are now three cases involving LLCs. The chapter also takes a hard look at the practical differences between an LLC and a corporation and discusses how to decide which form to choose. Chapter 30, on corporations, uses the charter from Facebook.com as an example. Students will learn what choices Mark Zuckerberg made when he started Facebook in his dorm room.

Chapter 34, on intellectual property, describes the Patent and Trademark Office's new Peer-to-Patent system, which uses the online community to review patents. It also discusses the First Sale Doctrine in copyright law to help clarify for students when trading music is, and is not, legal. It includes a real email exchange between two Hollywood executives discussing in a humorous way the value of the fair use doctrine in copyright law. There are many real-life examples involving Barbie dolls, Prince songs, iPods, eBay, and the Lennon song "Imagine."

FEATURES

We chose the features for our book with great care. Each feature responds to an essential pedagogical goal. Here are some of those goals and the matching feature.

NEW FEATURE: EXAM STRATEGY

GOAL: To Help Students Learn More Effectively and to Prepare for Exams

In preparing this fourth edition, we asked ourselves: What do students want? The short answer is, a good grade in the course. How many times a semester does a student ask you, "What can I do to study for the exam?" We are happy to help them study and earn a good grade because that means they will also be learning.

About five times per chapter, we stop the action and give students a two-minute quiz. In the body of the text, again in the end-of-chapter review, and also in the Instructor's Manual, we present a typical exam question. Here lies the innovation: We guide the student in analyzing the issue. We teach the reader—over and over—how to approach a question: to start with the overarching principle, examine the fine point raised in the question, apply the analysis that courts use, and deduce the right answer. This skill is second nature to lawyers, but not to students. Without practice, too many students panic, jumping at a convenient answer, and leaving aside the tools they have spent the course acquiring. Let's change that. The students who have tried Exam Strategy love it.

YOU BE THE JUDGE

GOAL: Get Them Thinking Independently

When reading case opinions, students tend to accept the court's "answer." Judges, of course, try to reach decisions that appear indisputable, when in reality they may be controversial—or wrong. From time to time, we want students to think through the problem and reach their own answer. Virtually every chapter contains a "You Be the Judge" feature, providing the facts of the case and conflicting appellate arguments. The court's decision, however, appears only in the Instructor's Manual. Because students do not know the result, discussions tend to be free-flowing.

ECONOMICS AND THE LAW

Goal: Understand the Economic Impact of the Law

This feature helps students understand how laws do (or, in some cases, do not) make economic sense. For example, in Chapter 19 on ownership and risk (page 449), we look at cases of stolen art. Using economic principles, we examine the contrasting status of bona fide purchasers in the United States and in Europe. In Chapter 20, on product liability (page 473), we use this feature to explore a hidden irony in tobacco litigation: some economists conclude that smokers actually save money for their states because they die younger, thereby reducing the need for expensive nursing homes and pensions!

DEVIL'S ADVOCATE

GOAL: Challenge the Court's Conclusions

In this feature, we provide short critical commentary on a decision just reported. We are reminding students that the court's holding is the work of mortals. There is generally a very respectable counter-argument that at least some people will find more persuasive. Students should consider the opposing view and should practice formulating their own positions independent of the judges' reasoning. A student who concludes, after analyzing alternative views, that the court got it right understands the holding more comprehensively than one who never considered the other side.

For example, in Chapter 7 on crime, we include the famous Ewing case (page 186) on cruel and unusual punishment but follow it with a "Devil's Advocate" feature arguing against a sentence of 25 years to life in a recidivist shoplifting case.

ETHICS

GOAL: Make Ethics Real

We ask ethical questions about cases, legal issues, and commercial practices. Is it fair for one party to void a contract by arguing, months after the fact, that there was no consideration? What is a manager's ethical obligation when asked to provide a reference for a former employee? What is wrong with bribery? What is the ethical obligation of developed nations to dispose of toxic waste from computers? We do not have definitive answers, but we believe that asking the questions and encouraging discussion reminds students that ethics is an essential element of justice and of a satisfying life.

CASES

GOAL: Bring Case Law Alive

Each case begins with a summary of the facts followed by a statement of both the issue and the decision. Next comes a summary of the court's opinion. We have written this summary ourselves to make the judges' reasoning accessible to all readers while retaining the court's focus and the decision's impact. We cite cases using a modified bluebook form. In the principal cases in each chapter, we provide the state or federal citation, the regional citation, and the LEXIS or Westlaw citation. We also give students a brief description of the court. Because many of our cases are so recent, some will have only a regional reporter and a LEXIS or Westlaw citation.

EXAM REVIEW

GOAL: Encourage Students to Practice!

At the end of the chapter, we challenge the students with ten or more problems, including the following:

- *Internet Research Problem.* This question asks students to research an issue on the Internet.

- *You Be the Judge Writing Problem.* The students are given appellate arguments on both sides of the question and must prepare a written opinion.

- *Ethics.* This question highlights the ethical issues of a dispute and calls upon the student to formulate a specific, reasoned response.

- *CPA Questions.* For topics covered by the CPA exam, administered by the American Institute of Certified Public Accountants, the Exam Reviews include questions from previous CPA exams.

- *Role Reversal.* Students are asked to formulate their own test questions. Crafting questions is a good way to reinforce what they already understand and recognize areas that they need to review. In the "To the Student" section later in this preface, we guide students through the process of creating useful exam questions.

TEACHING MATERIALS

For more information about any of these ancillaries, contact your South-Western Legal Studies in Business Sales Representative for more details, or visit the Beatty and Samuelson *Essentials of Business Law*, *4e*, instructor's website at **http://login.cengage.com**.

INSTRUCTOR'S RESOURCE CD (IRCD)

(ISBN: 0-538-47355-X) The IRCD contains the Instructor's Manual in Microsoft Word, Microsoft PowerPoint lecture slides, and a Test Bank in Microsoft Word and in ExamView testing software.

INSTRUCTOR'S MANUAL

This manual includes special features to enhance class discussion and student progress:

- Exam Strategy problems. If your students would like more of these problems, there are additional examples in each chapter of the Instructor's Manual.

- Dialogues. These are a series of questions-and-answers on pivotal cases and topics. The questions provide enough material to teach a full session. In a pinch, you could walk into class with nothing but the manual and use the dialogues to conduct an exciting class.

- Action learning ideas: interviews, quick research projects, drafting exercises, classroom activities, commercial analyses, and other suggested assignments that get students out of their chairs and into the diverse settings of business law.

- Skits. Various chapters have lively skits that students can perform in class, with no rehearsal, to put legal doctrine in a real-life context.

- A chapter theme and a quote of the day.

- Additional cases and examples.

- Answers to "You Be the Judge" cases from the text and to the Exam Review questions found at the end of each chapter.

   The Instructor's Manual is located on the IRCD, or download it from the book's instructor website by logging on to **http://login.cengage.com.**

TEST BANK

The test bank offers hundreds of essay, short-answer, and multiple-choice problems and may be obtained on the IRCD.

ExamView—Computerized Testing Software

This testing software contains all of the test bank questions. This easy-to-use test creation software program is compatible with Microsoft Windows. Instructors can add or edit questions, instructions, and answers and select questions by previewing them on the screen, selecting them randomly, or selecting them by number. Instructors can also create and administer quizzes online, whether over the Internet, a local area network (LAN), or a wide area network (WAN). The ExamView testing software is available on the IRCD.

MICROSOFT POWERPOINT LECTURE REVIEW SLIDES

PowerPoint slides are available for use by instructors for enhancing their lectures. Find them on the IRCD or download from the book's instructor website by logging on to http://login.cengage.com.

BUSINESS LAW COURSEMATE

Cengage Learning's Business Law CourseMate brings course concepts to life with interactive learning, study, and exam preparation tools that support the printed textbook. CourseMate includes an interactive eBook, interactive teaching and learning tools—quizzes, flashcards, videos, Engagement Tracker, and more. Engagement Tracker is a first-of-its-kind tool that monitors student engagement in the course. This intuitive, online reporting tool makes it easy for you to evaluate use of study resources, monitor time-on-task, and track progress for the entire class or for individual students. Instantly see what concepts are the most difficult for your class and identify which students are at risk throughout the semester. For more information about how **CourseMate** can help you encourage engagement and assess student learning, contact your South-Western Legal Studies in Business Sales Representative.

BUSINESS LAW DIGITAL VIDEO LIBRARY

This dynamic video library features more that 60 video clips that spark class discussion and clarify core legal principles. The library is organized into five series: Legal Conflicts in Business (includes specific modern business and e-commerce scenarios); Ask the Instructor (presents straightforward explanations of concepts for student review); Drama of the Law (features classic business scenarios that spark classroom participation); Real World Legal (explores conflicts that arise in a variety of business environments), and LawFlix (contains clips from many popular films). Access is available as an optional package with a new textbook, or can be purchased at www.cengagebrain.com.

STUDENT GUIDE TO THE SARBANES-OXLEY ACT.

This brief overview for business students explains the Sarbanes-Oxley Act, what is required of whom, and how it might affect students in their business life. This guide is available as an optional package with the text or can be purchased at www.cengagebrain.com.

INTERACTION WITH THE AUTHORS

This is our standard: Every professor who adopts this book must have a superior experience. We are available to help in any way we can. Adopters of this text often call us or e-mail us to ask questions, obtain a syllabus, offer suggestions, share pedagogical concerns, or inquire about ancillaries. One of the pleasures of working on this project has been our discovery that the text provides a link to so many colleagues around the country. We value those connections, are eager to respond, and would be happy to hear from you.

TO THE STUDENT

WEBSITE ACCESS

To access additional course materials (including Business Law CourseMate), please visit **www.cengagebrain.com**. At the CengageBrain.com home page, search for the ISBN of your book (from the back cover) using the search box at the top of the page. This will take you to this book's product page where these resources can be found.

END-OF-CHAPTER REVIEW

Each Exam Review contains one Role Reversal feature in which we challenge you to create your own exam question. Your professor may ask you to submit the questions in writing or electronically or to prepare an overhead slide. The goal is to think creatively and accurately. The question should be challenging enough that the average student will need to stop and think but clear enough that there is only one answer. Questions can be formatted as essay, short answer, or multiple choice.

For a multiple-choice question, the first step is to isolate the single issue that you want to test. For example, in the unit on contract law, you do not want to ask a question that concerns five different aspects of forming an agreement. A good question will focus exclusively on one issue, for example, whether a job offer has to be in writing (some do; others do not). Create a realistic fact pattern that raises the issue. Provide one answer that is clearly correct. Add additional answers that might seem plausible but are definitely incorrect.

Some exam questions are very direct and test whether a student knows a definition. Other questions require deeper analysis. Here are two multiple-choice questions. The first is direct.

Question: Which contract is governed by the Uniform Commercial Code?

a. An agreement for an actor to appear in a movie for a $600,000 fee.

b. An agreement for an actor to appear in a movie for a fee of $600,000 plus 2% of box office.

c. An agreement for the sale of a house.

d. An agreement for the sale of 22,000 picture frames.

e. An agreement for the rental of an apartment.

As you will learn later on, the correct answer is (d) because the Code applies to the sale of goods, not to employment contracts or real estate deals.

The next question is more difficult, requiring the student to spot the issue of law involved (product liability), remember how damages are awarded in such cases (generally without regard to fault), and make a simple calculation.

Question: Lightweight Corp. manufactures strings of Christmas tree lights and sells 3.5 million sets per year. Every year, between 10 and 20 of the company's strings have a manufacturing defect that causes a consumer injury. Maxine receives a severe shock from a Lightweight string of lights. She sues. The evidence at trial is that: 1) Lightweight's safety record is the best in the industry; 2) all competing companies have a higher rate of injuries; 3) the lights that injured Maxine arrived at her house in the factory box, untouched by anyone outside of Lightweight; and 4) Maxine operated the lights properly. Maxine's medical bills amount to $200,000; her lost income is $100,000; and her pain and suffering amounts to $600,000. What is the probable outcome at trial?

a. Maxine will win $200,000.

b. Maxine will win $100,000.

c. Maxine will win $900,000.

d. Maxine will win nothing.

e. Lightweight might win damages for a frivolous lawsuit.

As you will learn, the correct answer is (c). Lightweight is responsible under product liability law regardless of its careful work and excellent record. Maxine is entitled to all of her damages. Notice that the same question could be used in essay format simply by deleting the multiple-choice answers.

Jeffrey F. Beatty   Susan S. Samuelson
                                   Phone: (617) 353-2033
                                   E-mail: ssamuels@bu.edu

ACKNOWLEDGMENTS

We are grateful to the following reviewers who gave such helpful comments as we updated this fourth edition:

Michael Chaplin
California State University, Northridge

Machiavelli W. Chao
University of California, Irvine

Patrizia Goldberg
Saddleback College

Michael A. Katz
Delaware State University

Sandra Leigh King
Northwood University, Cedar Hill

Byron Lilly
De Anza College

Richard Opie
Lakeshore Technical College

Thomas R. Rebhan
D'Youville College

THE LEGAL ENVIRONMENT

1

INTRODUCTION TO LAW

The Pagans were a motorcycle gang with a reputation for violence. Two of its rougher members, Rhino and Backdraft, entered a tavern called the Pub Zone, shoving their way past the bouncer. The pair wore gang insignia, in violation of the bar's rules. For a while, all was quiet, as the two sipped drinks at the bar. Then they followed an innocent patron toward the men's room, and things happened fast.

> For a while, all was quiet, as the two sipped drinks at the bar. Then they followed an innocent patron toward the men's room...

"Wait a moment," you may be thinking. "Are we reading a chapter on business law or one about biker crimes in a roadside tavern?" Both.

Law is powerful, essential, and fascinating. We hope this book will persuade you of all three ideas. Law can also be surprising. Later in the chapter we will return to the Pub Zone (with armed guards) and follow Rhino and Backdraft to the back of the pub. Yes, the pair engaged in street crime, which is hardly a focus of this text. However, their criminal acts will enable us to explore one of the law's basic principles, negligence. Should a pub owner pay money damages to the victim of gang violence? The owner herself did nothing aggressive. Should she have prevented the harm? Does her failure to stop the assault make her liable?

We place great demands on our courts, asking them to make our large, complex, and sometimes violent society into a safer, fairer, more orderly place. The Pub Zone case is a good example of how judges reason their way through the convoluted issues involved. What began as a gang incident ends up as a matter of commercial liability. We will traipse after Rhino and Backdraft because they have a lesson to teach anyone who enters the world of business.

THREE IMPORTANT IDEAS ABOUT LAW

POWER

The strong reach of the law touches us all. To understand something that powerful is itself power. Suppose, some years after graduation, you are a mid-level manager at Sublime Corp., which manufactures and distributes video games and related hardware and software. You are delighted with this important position in an excellent company—and especially glad you bring legal knowledge to the job. Sarah, an expert at computer-generated imagery, complains that Rob, her boss, is constantly touching her and making lewd comments. That is sexual harassment and your knowledge of *employment law* helps you respond promptly and carefully. You have dinner with Jake, who has his own software company. Jake wants to manufacture an exciting new video game in cooperation with Sublime, but you are careful not to create a binding deal. (*Contract law.*) Jake mentions that a similar game is already on the market. Do you have the right to market one like it? That answer you already know. (*Intellectual property law.*)

The next day a letter from the Environmental Protection Agency asks how your company disposes of toxic chemicals used to manufacture computer drives. You can discuss it efficiently with in-house counsel, because you have a working knowledge of *environmental law* and *administrative law*. You may think your corporation is about to surge ahead in its field, and you would like to invest in its stock. But wait! Are you engaging in insider trading? Your training in *securities law* will distinguish the intelligent investment from the felony.

It is not only as a corporate manager that you will confront the law. As a voter, investor, juror, entrepreneur, and community member, you will influence and be affected by the law. Whenever you take a stance about a legal issue, whether in the corporate office, in the voting booth, or as part of local community groups, you help to create the social fabric of our nation. Your views are vital. This book will offer you knowledge and ideas from which to form and continually reassess your legal opinions and values.

IMPORTANCE

Law is also essential. Every society of which we have any historical record has had some system of laws. Naturally, the systems have varied enormously.

An extraordinary example of a detailed written law comes from the Visigoths, a nomadic European people who overran much of present-day France and Spain during the fifth and sixth centuries A.D. Their code admirably required judges to be "quick of perception, clear in judgment, and lenient in the infliction of penalties." It detailed dozens of crimes. For example, a freeman who kidnapped the slave of another had to repay the owner with four slaves and suffer 100 lashes. If he did not have four slaves to give, the kidnapper was himself reduced to slavery. Sadly, the code explicitly permitted torture of slaves and lower-class freemen, while prohibiting it for nobles.[1] The Iroquois Native Americans, disregarded by many historians, in fact played a role in the creation of our own government. Five major nations made up the Iroquois group: the Mohawk, Cayuga, Oneida, Onondaga, and Seneca. Each nation governed itself as to domestic issues. But each nation also elected "sachems" to a League of the Iroquois. The league had authority over any matters that were common to all, such as relations with outsiders. Thus, by the fifteenth century, the Iroquois had solved the problem of *federalism:* how to

---

[1] S.P. Scott, *Visigothic Code (Forum Judicum)* (Littleton, CO: Fred B. Rothman & Co., 1982), pp. 3, 45.

have two levels of government, each with specified powers. Their system impressed Benjamin Franklin among others and influenced the drafting of our Constitution, with its powers divided between state and federal governments.[2] As European nations today seek to create a more united Europe, they struggle with the same problem.

The greatest of all Chinese lawgivers disliked written law altogether. Confucius, who lived from 551 to 479 B.C., understood law within a broader social perspective. He considered good rulers, strong family ties, and an enlightened nobility to be the surest methods to a good society. "As a judge, I decide disputes, for that is my duty; but the best thing that could happen would be to eliminate the causes for litigation!" Although he spoke 2,500 years ago, the distinction Confucius described is still critically important in our society: Which do we trust more—a written law or the people who enforce it?

FASCINATION

In 1835, the young French aristocrat Alexis de Tocqueville traveled through the United States, observing the newly democratic people and the qualities that made them unique. One of the things that struck de Tocqueville most forcefully was the American tendency to file suit: "Scarcely any political question arises in the United States that is not resolved, sooner or later, into a judicial question."[3] De Tocqueville got it right: For better or worse, we do expect courts to solve many problems.

Not only do Americans litigate—they watch each other do it. Every television season offers at least one new courtroom drama to a national audience breathless for more cross-examination. Almost all of the states permit live television coverage of real trials. The most heavily viewed event in the history of the medium was the O.J. Simpson murder trial. Nonetheless, cameras in the courthouse are still controversial. Federal courts generally prohibit them. Only a small (but growing) number of foreign countries allows coverage of some judicial proceedings, including Australia, Canada, France, Hong Kong, Israel, Italy, the Netherlands, Norway, the Philippines, and Spain. Proponents urge that televising trials increases awareness of social ills and reduces the chances of judicial unfairness. Opponents argue that the camera transforms a dignified search for truth into a carnival show of publicity gimmicks.

Regardless of where we allow cameras, it is an undeniable benefit of the electronic age that we can obtain information so quickly. From time to time we will mention Web sites of interest. Some of these are for nonprofit groups while others are commercial sites. We do not endorse or advocate on behalf of any group or company, but simply wish to alert you to what is out there. The commercial site of a cable television company devoted to trial broadcasts, **http://www.trutv.com/**, includes up-to-the-minute information on current cases, often including trial testimony, appeal briefs, and other timely data.

The law is a big part of our lives, and it is wise to know something about it. Within a few weeks, you will probably find yourself following legal events in the news with keener interest and deeper understanding. In this chapter we develop the background for our study. We look at where law comes from: its history and its present-day institutions. In the section on jurisprudence, we examine different theories about what "law" really means. And finally we see how courts—and students—analyze a case.

---

[2] Jack Weatherford, *Indian Givers* (New York: Fawcett Columbine, 1988), pp. 133–150.
[3] Alexis de Tocqueville, *Democracy in America* (1835), Vol. 1, Ch. 16.

ORIGINS OF OUR LAW

It would be nice if we could look up "the law" in one book, memorize it, and then apply it. But the law is not that simple, and *cannot* be that simple, because it reflects the complexity of contemporary life. In truth, there is no such thing as "the law." Principles and rules of law actually come from many different sources. Why is this so? In part because we inherited a complex structure of laws from England. We will see that by the time of the American Revolution, English law was already an intricate system.

Additionally, ours is a nation born in revolution and created, in large part, to protect the rights of its people from the government. The Founding Fathers created a national government but insisted that the individual states maintain control in many areas. As a result, each state has its own government with exclusive power over many important areas of our lives. To top it off, the Founders guaranteed many rights to the people alone, ordering national *and* state governments to keep clear. This has worked, but it has caused a multilayered system, with 50 state governments and one federal government all creating and enforcing law.

A summary of English legal history will show the origin of our legal institutions. This brisk survey will also demonstrate that certain problems never go away. Anglo-Saxon England, about 1,000 years ago, was a world utterly different from our own. Yet we can see uncanny foreshadowings of our own unfinished efforts to create a peaceful world.

ENGLISH ROOTS

England in the tenth century was a rustic agricultural community with a tiny population and very little law or order. Danes and Swedes invaded repeatedly, terrorizing the Anglo-Saxon peoples. Criminals were hard to catch in the heavily forested, sparsely settled nation. The king used a primitive legal system to maintain a tenuous control over his people.

England was divided into shires, and daily administration was carried out by a "shire reeve," later called a sheriff. The shire reeve collected taxes and did what he could to keep peace, apprehending criminals and acting as mediator between feuding families. Two or three times a year, a shire court met; lower courts met more frequently.

Contemporary Law: Mediation lives on. As we discuss in Chapter 3, on dispute resolution, lawsuits have grown ever more costly. Increasingly, companies are turning to mediation to settle disputes. The humble shire reeve's work is back in vogue.

Because there were so few officers to keep the peace, Anglo-Saxon society created an interesting method of ensuring public order. Every freeman (nonslave) belonged to a group of 10 freemen known as a "tithing," headed by a "tithingman." If anyone injured a person outside his tithing or interfered with the king's property, all 10 men of the tithing could be forced to pay.

Contemporary Law: Today, we still use this idea of collective responsibility. In a business partnership, all partners are personally responsible for the debts of the partnership. They could potentially lose their homes and all assets because of the irresponsible conduct of one partner. That liability has helped create new forms of business organization, including limited liability companies, which we discuss in Chapter 29 on business organizations.

When cases did come before an Anglo-Saxon court, the parties would often be represented either by a clergyman, by a nobleman, or by themselves. There were few professional lawyers. Each party produced "oath helpers," usually 12, who would swear that one version of events was correct. The court explicitly gave greater credence to oath helpers from the nobility.

Contemporary Law: The Anglo-Saxon oath helpers are probably forerunners of our modern jury of 12 persons. But as to who is telling the truth, that is a question that will never disappear. We deny giving a witness greater credence because of his or her status. But do we really? Some commentators believe that jurors are overly impressed with "expert witnesses," such as doctors or engineers, and ignore their own common sense when faced with such "pedigreed" people.

In 1066, the Normans conquered England. William the Conqueror made a claim never before made in England: that he owned all of the land. The king then granted sections of his lands to his favorite noblemen, as his tenants in chief, creating the system of feudalism. These tenants in chief then granted parts of their land to *tenants in demesne*, who actually occupied a particular estate. Each tenant in demesne owed fidelity to his lord (hence "landlord"). So what? Just this: land became the most valuable commodity in all of England, and our law still reflects that.

Contemporary Law: One thousand years later, American law still regards land as special. The statute of frauds, which we study in the section on contracts, demands that contracts for the sale or lease of property be in writing. And landlord-tenant law, vital to students and many others, still reflects its ancient roots. Some of a landlord's rights are based on the 1,000-year-old tradition that land is uniquely valuable.

In 1250, Henry de Bracton (1210-68) wrote a legal treatise that still influences us. *De Legibus et Consuetudinibus Angliae* (*On the Laws and Customs of England*), written in Latin, summarized many of the legal rulings in cases since the Norman Conquest. De Bracton was teaching judges to rule based on previous cases. He was helping to establish the idea of **precedent.** The doctrine of precedent, which developed gradually over centuries, requires that judges decide current cases based on previous rulings.

Contemporary Law: This vital principle is the heart of American common law. Precedent ensures predictability. Suppose a 17-year-old student promises to lease an apartment from a landlord, but then changes her mind. The landlord sues to enforce the lease. The student claims that she cannot be held to the agreement because she is a minor. The judge will look for precedent, that is, older cases dealing with the same issue, and he will find many holding that a contract generally may not be enforced against a minor. That precedent is binding on this case, and the student wins. The accumulation of precedent, based on case after case, makes up the **common law.**

During the next few centuries, judges and lawyers acquired special training and skills. Some lawyers began to plead cases full-time and gained unique skill—and power. They represented only those who could pay well.

Parliament passed an ever greater number of laws, generally called **statutes,** the word we still use to mean a law passed by a legislative body. Parliament's statutes swelled in number and complexity until they were unfathomable to anyone but a lawyer.

Contemporary Law: Our society still struggles with unequal access to legal talent. Rich people often fare better in court than poor. And many Americans regard law as byzantine and incomprehensible. A primary purpose of this text is to remove the mystique from the law and to empower you to participate in legal matters.

As lawyers became more highly skilled, they searched ever wider for ways to defeat the other side. One method was by attacking the particular writ in the case. The party bringing the case was called the plaintiff. His first task was to obtain a writ, which was a letter from the central government ordering a court to hear the case. Each type of lawsuit required a different writ. For example, a landlord's lawsuit against a tenant required one kind of writ, while a claim of assault needed a different one. If a court decided that the plaintiff's lawyer had used the wrong writ, it would dismiss the lawsuit. This encouraged lawyers for the defendant to attack the writ itself, claiming it was inappropriate. By doing that, they could perhaps defeat the case without ever answering who did what to whom.

Contemporary Law: This is the difference between procedure and substance, which will become clear during the course. Substantive rules of law state the rights of the parties. For example, it is substantive law that if you have paid the purchase price of land and accepted the deed, you are entitled to occupy the property. Procedural rules tell how a court should go about

---

Precedent

The obligation to decide current cases based on previous rulings.

Precedent = Common Law

Common law

Judge-made law.

(Actual laws)

Statute

A law passed by a legislative body.

(Constitutional laws made by legislatures, state legislatures & congress)

The constitution is known as a statute

(Mechanics - how to carry out the process)

settling disputes. For example, what evidence can be used to establish that you *did* pay for the property? How much evidence is necessary? Who may testify about whether you paid? Those are all issues of procedural law. To this day, lawyers attack procedural aspects of an opponent's case before dealing with the substantive rights.

Here is an actual case from more than six centuries ago, in the court's own language. The dispute illustrates that some things have changed but others never do. The plaintiff claims that he asked the defendant to heal his eye with "herbs and other medicines." He says the defendant did it so badly that he blinded the plaintiff in that eye.

THE OCULIST'S CASE (1329)

LI MS. HALE 137 (1), FO. 150, NOTTINGHAM[4]

CASE SUMMARY

Attorney Launde [for defendant]: Sir, you plainly see how [the plaintiff claims] that he had submitted himself to [the defendant's] medicines and his care; and after that he can assign no trespass in his person, inasmuch as he submitted himself to his care: but this action, if he has any, sounds naturally in breach of covenant. We demand [that the case be dismissed].

Excerpts from Judge Denum's Decision: I saw a Newcastle man arraigned before my fellow justice and me for the death of a man. I asked the reason for the indictment, and it was said that he had slain a man under his care, who died within four days afterwards. And because I saw that he was a [doctor] and that he had not done the thing feloniously but [accidentally] I ordered him to be discharged. And suppose a blacksmith, who is a man of skill, injures your horse with a nail, whereby you lose your horse: you shall never have recovery against him. No more shall you here.

Afterwards the plaintiff did not wish to pursue his case any more.

This case from 1329 is an ancient medical malpractice case. Defendant's lawyer makes a procedural argument. Attorney Launde does not deny that his client blinded the plaintiff. He claims that the plaintiff has brought the wrong kind of lawsuit. Launde argues that the plaintiff should have brought a case of "covenant," that is, a lawsuit about a contract.

Judge Denum decides the case on a different principle. He gives judgment to the defendant because the plaintiff voluntarily sought medical care. He implies that the defendant would lose only if he had attacked the plaintiff. As we will see when we study negligence law, this case might have a different outcome today. Note also the informality of the judge's ruling. He rather casually mentions that he came across a related case once before and that he would stand by that outcome. The idea of precedent is just beginning to take hold.

Sometimes a judge refused to hear a case, ruling that no such claims were legal. The injured party might then take his case to the Chancellor, in London, whose status in the king's council gave him unique, flexible powers. This *Court of Chancery* had no jury. The court's duty was to accomplish what "good conscience" required, that is, an *equitable* result, and so this more creative use of a court's power became known as **equity**.

Equity
A court's power to fashion a remedy, such as an injunction, which the common law does not provide.

[4] J. Baker and S. Milsom, *Sources of English Legal History* (London: Butterworth & Co., 1986).

Injunction:
A court order by which an individual is required to perform OR restrained from performing a particular act

Contemporary Law: In present-day America, judges still exercise equity powers, based on those cases the Chancery court accepted. For example, a court today might issue an injunction requiring a factory owner to stop polluting the air. The injunction (order to stop) is an equitable remedy. Only a judge can exercise equitable powers because, historically, Chancery had no jury. If a judge grants an injunction, she is said to be exercising equitable powers.

Parliament added statutes on more and more matters, at times conflicting with common law rulings of the various judges. What should a court do when faced with a statute that contradicts well-established precedent? In the seventeenth century, one of England's greatest judges, Lord Coke, addressed the problem. In *Dr. Bonhams Case*,[5] Lord Coke ruled that "when an Act of Parliament is against Common right and reason, or repugnant, or impossible to be performed, the Common Law will control it and adjudge such Act to be void."

Audacious man! In a decision of breathtaking strength, Lord Coke declared that a single judge could overrule the entire Parliament, based on what the judge might consider "common right and reason." This same tension carries on today between elected officials, such as state legislators, and courts, which sometimes declare acts of the legislatures void.

Of course, by the time Lord Coke was on the bench, in the seventeenth century, English common law had also spread across the ocean to the newly created colonies. We will pick up the story in America.

LAW IN THE UNITED STATES

The colonists brought with them a basic knowledge of English law, some of which they were content to adopt as their own. Other parts, such as religious restrictions, were abhorrent to them. Many had made the dangerous trip to America precisely to escape persecution, and they were not interested in recreating their difficulties in a new land. Finally, some laws were simply irrelevant or unworkable in a world that was socially and geographically so different. American law ever since has been a whitewater river created from two strong currents: One carries the ancient principles of English common law, the other, a zeal and determination for change.

During the nineteenth century, the United States changed from a weak, rural nation into one of vast size and potential power. Cities grew, factories appeared, and sweeping movements of social migration changed the population. Changing conditions raised new legal questions. Did workers have a right to form industrial unions? To what extent should a manufacturer be liable if its product injured someone? Could a state government invalidate an employment contract that required 16-hour workdays? Should one company be permitted to dominate an entire industry?

In the twentieth century, the rate of social and technological change increased, creating new legal puzzles. Were some products, such as automobiles, so inherently dangerous that the seller should be responsible for injuries even if no mistakes were made in manufacturing? Who should clean up toxic waste if the company that had caused the pollution no longer existed? If a consumer signed a contract with a billion-dollar corporation, should the agreement be enforced even if the consumer never understood it? New and startling questions will continue to confront us. Before we can begin to examine the answers, we need to understand the sources of contemporary law.

---

[5] Eng. Rep. 638 (C.P. 1610).

SOURCES OF CONTEMPORARY LAW

During the colonial period there were few trained lawyers and fewer law books in America. After the Revolution that changed, and law became a serious, professional career. The first great legal achievement was the adoption of the United States Constitution.

CONSTITUTIONS

United States Constitution

The United States Constitution, adopted in 1788 by the original 13 colonies, is the supreme law of the land.[6] Any law that conflicts with it is void. This Federal Constitution, as it is also known, does three basic things. First, it establishes the national government of the United States, with its three branches. The Constitution creates the Congress, with a Senate and a House of Representatives, and prescribes what laws Congress may pass. The same document establishes the office of the president and the duties that go with it. And it creates the third branch of government, the federal courts, describing what cases they may hear.

Second, the Constitution ensures that the states retain all power not given to the national government. This simple idea has meant that state governments play an important role in all of our lives. Major issues of family law, criminal law, property law, and many other areas are regulated predominantly by the various states.

Third, the Constitution guarantees many basic rights to the American people. Most of these rights are found in the amendments to the Constitution. The First Amendment guarantees the rights of free speech, free press, and the free exercise of religion. The Fourth, Fifth, and Sixth Amendments protect the rights of any person accused of a crime. Other amendments ensure that the government treats all people equally and that it pays for any property it takes from a citizen. Merely by creating a limited government of three branches and guaranteeing basic liberties to all citizens, the Constitution became one of the most important documents ever written.

State Constitutions

In addition to the Federal Constitution, each state has a constitution that establishes its own government. All states have an executive (the governor), a legislature, and a court system. Thus there are two entire systems of government affecting each of us: a federal government, with power over the entire country, and a state government, exercising those powers that the United States Constitution did not grant to the federal government. This is federalism at work.

STATUTES

The second important source of law is statutory law. The Constitution gave to the United States Congress the power to pass laws on various subjects. These laws are statutes, like those passed by the English Parliament. For example, the Constitution allows Congress to pass statutes about the military: to appropriate money, reorganize divisions, and close bases. You can find any federal statute, on any subject, at the Web site of the United States House of Representatives, which is **http://www.house.gov/**.

State legislatures also pass statutes. Each state constitution allows the legislature to pass laws on a wide variety of subjects. All state legislatures, for example, may pass statutes about family law issues such as divorce and child custody.

---

[6] The Constitution took effect in 1788, when nine of 13 colonies ratified it. Two more colonies ratified it that year, and the last of the 13 did so in 1789, after the government was already in operation. The complete text of the Constitution appears in Appendix A.

COMMON LAW

As we have seen, the common law originated in England as lawyers began to record decisions and urge judges to follow earlier cases. As judges started to do that, the earlier cases, called *precedent*, took on steadily greater importance. Eventually, judges were *obligated* to follow precedent. **The principle that precedent is binding on later cases is *stare decisis*, which means "let the decision stand."** *Stare decisis* makes the law predictable, and this in turn enables businesses and private citizens to plan intelligently.

Equity

Principles of equity, created by the Chancellor in England, traveled to the colonies along with the common law rules. All states permit courts to use equitable powers. An example of a contemporary equitable power is an *injunction,* a court order that someone stop doing something. Suppose a music company is about to issue a new album by a well-known singer, but a composer claims that the recording artist has stolen his song. The composer, claiming copyright violation, could seek an injunction to prevent the company from issuing the compact disc. Every state has a trial court that can issue injunctions and carry out other equitable relief. As was true in medieval England, there is no jury in an equity case.

[handwritten margin note: · gives courts the discretion to apply justice / provide a solution by issuing an injunction]

ADMINISTRATIVE LAW

In a society as large and diverse as ours, the executive and legislative branches of government cannot oversee all aspects of commerce. Congress passes statutes about air safety, but U.S. senators do not stand around air traffic towers, serving coffee to keep everyone awake. The executive branch establishes rules concerning how foreign nationals enter the United States, but presidents are reluctant to sit on the dock of the bay, watching the ships come in. Administrative agencies do this day-to-day work.

Most administrative agencies are created by Congress or by a state legislature. Familiar examples at the federal level are the Federal Communications Commission (FCC), which regulates most telecommunications; the Federal Trade Commission (FTC), which oversees interstate trade; and the Internal Revenue Service, whose feelings are hurt if it does not hear from you every April 15th. At the state level, regulators set insurance rates for all companies in the state, control property development and land use, and regulate many other issues.

OTHER SOURCES OF LAW

Treaties

The Constitution authorizes the president to make treaties with foreign nations. They must be ratified by a 2/3 vote in the Senate. When they are ratified, they are as binding upon all citizens as any federal statute. In 1994 the Senate ratified the North American Free Trade Agreement (NAFTA) with Mexico and Canada. NAFTA was controversial then and remains so today—but it is the law of the land.

Executive Orders

In theory all statutes must originate in Congress or a state legislature. But in fact executives also legislate by issuing executive orders. For example, in 1970 Congress authorized President Nixon to issue wage-price controls in an effort to stabilize the economy. This was a colossal grant of power, allowing the president personally to regulate the nation's economy. Critics charge that Congress should not give away the powers that the people have granted to it, and such delegations of authority have led to extensive lawsuits.

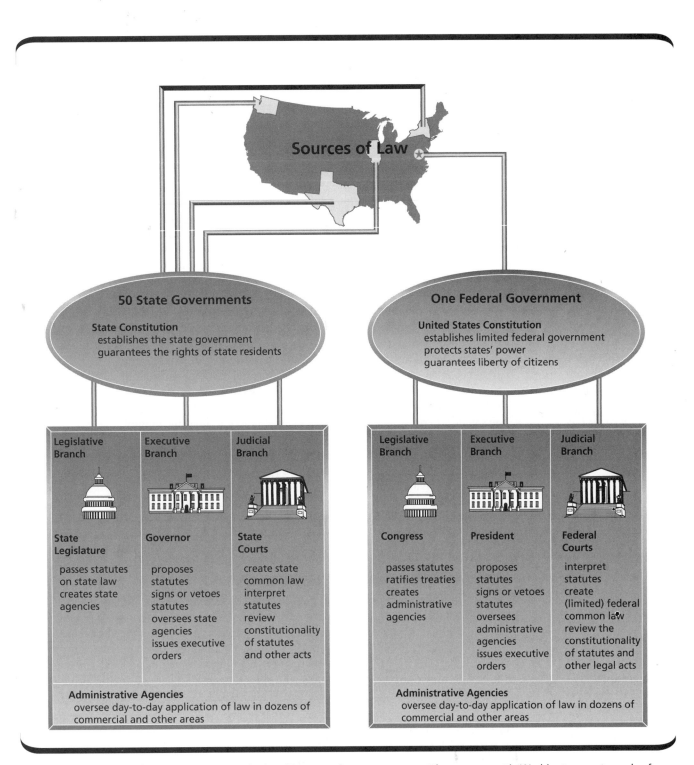

Federal Form of Government. Principles and rules of law come from many sources. The government in Washington creates and enforces law throughout the nation. But 50 state governments exercise great power in local affairs. And citizens enjoy constitutional protection from both state and federal government. The Founding Fathers wanted this balance of power and rights, but the overlapping authority creates legal complexity.

CLASSIFICATIONS OF LAW

We have seen where law comes from. Now we need to classify the law into different types. There are three main classifications that we use throughout the book: criminal and civil law, substantive and procedural law, and public and private law.

CRIMINAL AND CIVIL LAW

Criminal law
Criminal law prohibits or requires certain behavior.

It is a crime to embezzle money from a bank, to steal a car, to sell cocaine. **Criminal law** concerns behavior so threatening that society outlaws it altogether. Most criminal laws are statutes, passed by Congress or a state legislature. The government itself prosecutes the wrongdoer, regardless of what the bank president or car owner wants. A district attorney, paid by the government, brings the case to court. The injured party, for example the owner of the stolen car, is not in charge of the case, although she may appear as a witness. The government will seek to punish the defendant with a prison sentence, a fine, or both. If there is a fine, the money goes to the state, not to the injured party.

Civil law
Civil law regulates the rights and duties between parties.

Unless you committed a crime, the government will not prosecute the case

Civil law is different, and most of this book is about civil law. **The civil law regulates the rights and duties between parties.** Tracy agrees in writing to lease you a 30,000-square-foot store in her shopping mall. She now has a *legal duty* to make the space available. But then another tenant offers her more money, and she refuses to let you move in. Tracy has violated her duty, but she has not committed a crime. The government will not prosecute the case. It is up to you to file a civil lawsuit. Your case will be based on the common law of contract. You will also seek equitable relief, namely, an injunction ordering Tracy not to lease to anyone else. You should win the suit, and you will get your injunction and some money damages. But Tracy will not go to jail.

Some conduct involves both civil and criminal law. Suppose Tracy is so upset over losing the court case that she becomes drunk and causes a serious car accident. She has committed the crime of driving while intoxicated, and the state will prosecute. Tracy may be fined or imprisoned. She has also committed negligence, and the injured party will file a lawsuit against her, seeking money. We will again see civil and criminal law joined together when we return to the *Pub Zone* case, later in the chapter.

SUBSTANTIVE AND PROCEDURAL LAW

Substantive law
Substantive law defines the rights of the parties.

Procedural law
Procedural law establishes the processes for settling disputes.

We saw the distinction between substantive and procedural law in *The Oculists Case* and it remains important today. **Substantive law** defines the rights of people. Substantive law requires that a landlord who has signed a lease must deliver the store to her tenant. Most of this book concerns substantive law. **Procedural law** establishes the processes for settling disputes. Procedural law requires that to get an injunction against Tracy, you must first notify her in writing of your claims and the time and place of the hearing on the injunction.

PUBLIC AND PRIVATE LAW

Public law refers to the rights and obligations of governments as they deal with the nation's citizens. For example, when the Federal Trade Commission prohibits deceptive advertising, that is public law. Private law regulates the duties between individuals. Landlord-tenant law is private law.

JURISPRUDENCE

We have had a glimpse of legal history and a summary of the present-day sources of American law. But what *is* law? That question is the basis of a field known as **jurisprudence**. How do we distinguish a moral rule from a legal rule? What is the real nature of law? Can there be such a thing as an "illegal" law?

Jurisprudence
The philosophy of law.

LAW AND MORALITY

Law is different from morality, yet the two are obviously linked. There are many instances when the law duplicates what all of us would regard as a moral position. It is negligence to drive too fast in a school district, and few would dispute the moral value of that law. And similarly with contract law: If the owner of land agrees in writing to sell property to a buyer at a stated price, the seller must go through with the deal, and the legal outcome matches our moral expectations.

On the other hand, we have had laws that we now clearly regard as immoral. At the turn of the century, a factory owner could typically fire a worker for any reason at all—including, for example, his religious or political views. Today, things are different. It is immoral to fire a worker because she is Jewish—and the law now prohibits it.

Finally, there are legal issues where the morality is not so clear. You are walking down a country lane and notice a three-year-old child playing with matches near a barn filled with hay. Are you obligated to intervene? No, says the law, though many think that is preposterous. (See Chapter 4, on common law, for details.) A company buys property and then discovers, buried under the ground, toxic waste that will cost $300,000 to clean up. The original owner has gone bankrupt. Should the new owner be forced to pay for the cleanup? If the new owner fails to pay for the job, who will?

LEGAL POSITIVISM

This philosophy can be simply stated: Law is what the sovereign says it is. The **sovereign** is the recognized political power whom citizens obey, so in the United States, both state and federal governments are sovereign. A legal positivist holds that whatever the sovereign declares to be the law *is* the law, whether it is right or wrong.

Sovereign
The recognized political power, whom citizens obey.

The primary criticism of legal positivism is that it seems to leave no room for questions of morality. A law permitting a factory owner to fire a worker because she is Catholic is surely different from a law prohibiting arson. Do citizens in a democracy have a duty to consider such differences? Consider the following example.

Most states allow citizens to pass laws directly at the ballot box, a process called voter referendum. California voters often do this, and during the 1990s, they passed one of the state's most controversial laws. Proposition 187 was designed to curb illegal immigration into the state by eliminating social spending for undocumented aliens. Citizens debated the measure fiercely but passed it by a large margin. One section of the new law forbade public schools from educating illegal immigrants. The law obligated a principal to inquire into the immigration status of all children enrolled in the school and to report undocumented students to immigration authorities. Several San Diego school principals rejected the new rules, stating that they would neither inquire into immigration status nor report undocumented aliens. Their statements produced a heated response. Some San Diego residents castigated the school officials as lawbreakers, claiming that

- A school officer who knowingly disobeyed a law was setting a terrible example for students, who would assume they were free to do the same;

- The principals were advocating permanent residence and a free education for anyone able to evade our immigration laws; and

- The officials were scorning grass-roots democracy by disregarding a law passed by popular referendum.

Others applauded the principals' position, asserting that

- The referendum's rules would transform school officials from educators into border police, forcing them to cross-examine young children and their parents;

- The new law was foolish because it punished innocent children for violations committed by their parents; and

- Our nation has long respected civil disobedience based on humanitarian ideals, and these officials were providing moral leadership to the whole community.

Ultimately, no one had to decide whether to obey Proposition 187. A federal court ruled that only Congress had the power to regulate immigration and that California's attempt was unconstitutional and void. The debate over immigration reform—and ethics—did not end, however. Congress periodically considers proposals to cut social benefits for illegal immigrants.

Natural Law

St. Thomas Aquinas (1225–1274) answered the legal positivists even before they had spoken. In his *Summa Theologica*, he argued that an unjust law is no law at all and need not be obeyed. It is not enough that a sovereign makes a command. The law must have a moral basis.

> **St. Thomas Aquinas argued that an unjust law is no law at all...**

· Vague
What's morally right to you may not be morally right to someone else

Where do we find the moral basis that would justify a law? Aquinas says that "good is that which all things seek after." Therefore, the fundamental rule of all laws is that "good is to be done and promoted, and evil is to be avoided." This sounds appealing, but also vague. Exactly which laws promote good and which do not? Is it better to have a huge corporation dominate a market or many smaller companies competing? Did the huge company get that way by being better than its competitors? If Wal-Mart moves into a rural area, establishes a mammoth store, and sells inexpensive products, is that "good"? Yes, if you are a consumer who cares only about prices. No, if you are the owner of a Main Street store driven into bankruptcy. Maybe, if you are a resident who values small town life but wants lower prices.

Natural law debates are eternal. One of the greatest of the ancient Greek dramatists, Sophocles (496–406 B.C.), touches upon the subject in one of his famous plays, *Antigone*. Oedipus's two sons, Eteocles and Polyneices, have arranged to rule Thebes in rotation, but when Eteocles refuses to give up the throne, Polyneices and his many supporters attack the city. Both brothers are killed in the battle. Creon, who inherits the crown, declares that Eteocles will receive a hero's burial but that Polyneices must lie exposed in the dust. Anyone attempting to bury him will be executed. Antigone, the sister of the dead men, is horrified. Declaring that religious beliefs compel her to rescue her brother's soul from perpetual torment, she attempts to bury Polyneices. Antigone admits to Creon that she understood his ruling, but retorts, in the language of natural law:

[Your] order did not come from God. Justice,
That dwells with the gods below, knows no such law.

> I did not think your edicts strong enough
> To overrule the unwritten unalterable laws
> Of God and heaven, you being only a man.
> They are not of yesterday or to-day, but everlasting,
> Though where they came from, none of us can tell.[7]

Creon, a legal positivist, responds simply and forcefully that "Our country is our life." Any attack upon the city-state warrants death, as does any disobedience of its laws. Ultimately, he orders Antigone to her death and then, inevitably, regrets his decision.

Two thousand five hundred years later, we still debate the meaning and significance of natural law. Court cases and political debates about abortion, stem cell research, school prayer, evolution, and euthanasia all echo the themes disputed by Creon and Antigone.

What does natural law tell us about abortion? Abortion supporters, or those advocating free choice, will say that natural law protects a woman's reproductive rights and that it is violent and unnatural for any government to tell a woman what to do with her body. Opponents of abortion reach the opposite conclusion, arguing that no good can come from terminating the life of a fetus and that a law permitting abortion is no law at all. What do you think?

LEGAL REALISM

Legal realists take a very different tack. They claim it does not matter what is written as law. What counts is who enforces that law and by what process. All of us are biased by issues such as income, education, family background, race, religion, and many other factors. These personal characteristics, they say, determine which contracts will be enforced and which ignored, why some criminals receive harsh sentences while others get off lightly, and so on.

(Personal characteristics)

Judge Jones hears a multimillion dollar lawsuit involving an airplane crash. Was the airline negligent? The law is the same everywhere, but legal realists say that Jones's background will determine the outcome. If she spent 20 years representing insurance companies, she will tend to favor the airline. If her law practice consisted of helping the "little guy," she will favor the plaintiff.

Other legal realists argue, more aggressively, that those in power use the machinery of the law to perpetuate their control. The outcome of a given case will be determined by the needs of those with money and political clout. A court puts "window dressing" on a decision, they say, so that society thinks there are principles behind the law. A problem with legal realism, however, is its denial that any lawmaker can overcome personal bias. Yet clearly some do act unselfishly.

SUMMARY OF JURISPRUDENCE

Legal Positivism	Law is what the sovereign says.
Natural Law	An unjust law is no law at all.
Legal Realism	Who enforces the law counts more than what is in writing.

No one school of jurisprudence is likely to seem perfect. We urge you to keep the different theories in mind as you read cases in the book. Ask yourself which school of thought is the best fit for you.

---

[7] Sophocles, *Antigone*, translated by E.F. Watling in *Sophocles, The Theban Plays* (New York: Penguin, 1964).

WORKING WITH THE BOOK'S FEATURES

In this section we introduce a few of the book's features and discuss how you can use them effectively. We will start with *cases*.

ANALYZING A CASE

A law case is the decision a court has made in a civil lawsuit or criminal prosecution. Cases are the heart of the law and an important part of this book. Reading them effectively takes practice. Let us return to the Pub Zone tavern, which we visited in the chapter's opener, and see what we can learn about courts and the law.

KUEHN V. PUB ZONE

364 N.J. SUPER. 301, 835 A.2d 692
SUPERIOR COURT OF NEW JERSEY, APPELLATE DIVISION, 2003

CASE SUMMARY

Facts: Maria Kerkoulas owned the Pub Zone bar. She knew that several motorcycle gangs frequented the tavern. From her own experience tending bar, and conversations with city police, she knew that some of the gangs, including the Pagans, were dangerous and prone to attack customers for no reason. Kerkoulas posted a sign prohibiting any motorcycle gangs from entering the bar while wearing "colors," that is, insignia of their gangs. She believed that gangs without their colors were less prone to violence, and experience proved her right.

Rhino, Backdraft, and several other Pagans, all wearing colors, pushed their way past the tavern's bouncer and approached the bar. Although Kerkoulas saw their colors, she allowed them to stay for one drink. They later moved towards the back of the pub, and Kerkoulas believed they were departing. In fact, they followed a customer named Karl Kuehn to the men's room, where without any provocation they savagely beat him. Kuehn was knocked unconscious and suffered brain hemorrhaging, disc herniation, and numerous fractures of facial bones. He was forced to undergo various surgeries, including eye reconstruction.

Although the government prosecuted Rhino and Backdraft for their vicious assault, our case does not concern that prosecution. Kuehn sued the Pub Zone, and that is the case we will read. The jury awarded him $300,000 in damages. However, the trial court judge overruled the jury's verdict. He granted a judgment for the Pub Zone, meaning that the

tavern owed nothing. The judge ruled that the pub's owner could not have foreseen the attack on Kuehn, and had no duty to protect him from an outlaw motorcycle gang. Kuehn appealed, and the appeals court's decision follows:

Issue: *Did the Pub Zone have a duty to protect Kuehn from the Pagans' attack?*

Decision: Yes, the Pub Zone had a duty to protect Kuehn. The decision is reversed, and the jury's verdict is reinstated.

Reasoning: Whether a duty exists depends on the foreseeability of the harm, its potential severity, and the defendant's ability to prevent the injury. A court should also evaluate society's interest in the dispute.

A business owner generally has no duty to protect a customer from acts of a third party unless experience suggests that there is danger. However, if the owner could in fact foresee injury, she is obligated to take reasonable safety precautions.

Kerkoulas knew that the Pagans engaged in random violence. She realized that when gang members entered the pub, they endangered her customers. That is why she prohibited bikers from wearing their colors—a reasonable rule. Regrettably, the pub failed to enforce the rule. Pagans were allowed to enter wearing their colors, and the pub did not call the police. The pub's behavior was unreasonable and it is liable to Kuehn.

Analysis

Let's take it from the top. The case is called *Kuehn v. Pub Zone*. Karl Kuehn is the **plaintiff**, the person who is suing. The Pub Zone is being sued, and is called the **defendant**. In this example, the plaintiff's name happens to appear first but that is not always true. When a defendant loses a trial and files an appeal, *some* courts reverse the names of the parties.

The next line gives the legal citation, which indicates where to find the case in a law library. We explain in the footnote how to locate a book if you plan to do research.[8]

The *Facts* section provides a background to the lawsuit, written by the authors of this text. The court's own explanation of the facts is often many pages long, and may involve complex matters irrelevant to the subject covered in this book, so we relate only what is necessary. This section will usually include some mention of what happened at the trial court. Lawsuits always begin in a trial court. The losing party often appeals to a court of appeals, and it is usually an appeals court decision that we are reading. The trial judge ruled in favor of Pub Zone, but later, in the decision we are reading, Kuehn wins.

The *Issue* section is very important. It tells you what the court had to decide—and also why you are reading the case. In giving its decision, a court may digress. If you keep in mind the issue and relate the court's discussion to it, you will not get lost.

The *Decision* is the court's answer to the issue posed. A court's decision is often referred to as its *holding*. The court rules that the Pub Zone did have a duty to Kuehn. The appellate court *reverses* the trial court's decision, meaning that it declares the trial judge's ruling wrong and void. The appellate judges also reinstate the jury verdict. The appellate court could have *remanded* the case if the judges had wished, meaning to send it back down to the lower court for a new trial. If the appeals court had agreed with the trial court's decision, the judges would have *affirmed* the lower court's ruling, meaning to uphold it.

The *Reasoning* section explains why the court reached its decision. The actual written decision may be three paragraphs or 75 pages. Some judges offer us lucid prose, while others seem intent on torturing the reader. Judges frequently digress and often discuss matters that are irrelevant to the issue on which this text is focusing. For those reasons, we have taken the court's explanation and recast it in our own words. If you are curious about the full opinion, you can always look it up.

Let us examine the reasoning. The court begins with a set of guidelines concerning a business owner's duty. Whether a defendant has such a duty depends on the foreseeability and severity of the harm, whether the business person could have prevented it, and society's interest. The court emphasizes that a bar owner is not an ensurer of its patrons' safety. Not every assault in a pub results in the defendant's liability. The judges are emphasizing that courts do not reach decisions arbitrarily. They attempt to make thoughtful choices, consistent with earlier rulings, that make good sense for the general public.

Plaintiff
The person who is suing.

Defendant
The person being sued.

---

[8] If you want to do legal research, you need to know where to find particular legal decisions. A case citation guides you to the correct volume(s). The full citation of our case is *Kuehn v. Pub Zone*, 364 N.J. Super. 301, 835 A.2d 692. The string of numbers identifies two different books in which you can find the full text of this decision. The first citation is to "N.J. Super," which means the official court reporter of the state of New Jersey. New Jersey, like most states, reports its law cases in a series of numbered volumes. This case appears in volume 364 of the New Jersey Superior Court reporters. If you go to a law library and find that book, you can then turn to page 301 and—*voila!*—you have the case. The decision is also reported in another set of volumes, called the regional reporters. This series of law reports is grouped by geographic region. New Jersey is included in the Atlantic region, so our case appears in reporters dedicated to that region. The "A" stands for Atlantic. After a series of reporters reaches volume 999, a second set begins. Our case appears in volume 835 of the second set of the Atlantic reporters ("A.2d"), at page 692. In addition, most cases are now available online, and your professor or librarian can show you how to find them electronically.

Having laid out the ground rules, the court describes the key facts, from this case, that it will use to decide whether the Pub Zone had a duty to Kuehn. The judges note that the bar's owner knew that gang members were dangerous. The rule against wearing colors made sense. When Pagans entered wearing their insignia, the pub had a duty to protect its patrons. The pub's owner was still not obligated to guarantee the safety of its patrons, but she had to do a reasonable job of reacting to the foreseeable danger. All Kerkoulas reasonably had to do was enforce the pub's no-colors rule and telephone the police if gang members refused to obey it. When she failed to take those steps, she violated her duty to Kuehn and became liable. The court reversed the trial judge's decision and reinstated the jury's verdict.

Devil's Advocate

Each chapter has several cases. After some of them, a "Devil's Advocate" feature offers you a contrasting view of the legal issue. This is not part of the case, but is instead a suggestion of another perspective on the problem discussed. The authors take no position for or against the court's decision, but merely want you to consider an alternate view, and decide which analysis of the law makes more sense to you—that of the court or the Devil's Advocate. Is the following view persuasive?

Devil's Advocate

A court should not force small businesses to guarantee their customers' safety. Two or three violent men, whether motorcycle gang members or frustrated professors, could enter a grocery store or clothing retailer at any time and mindlessly attack innocent visitors. Random attacks are just that—random, unforeseeable. No merchant should be required to anticipate them. Send the criminals to jail, but do not place the burden on honest business people.

Exam Strategy

This feature gives you practice analyzing cases the way lawyers do—and the way *you* must on tests. Law exams are different from most others because you must determine the issue from the facts provided. Too frequently, students faced with a law exam forget that the questions relate to the issues in the text and those discussed in class. Understandably, students new to law may focus on the wrong information in the problem or rely on material learned elsewhere. Exam Strategy teaches you to figure out exactly what issue is at stake, and then analyze it in a logical, consistent manner. Here is an example, relating to the element of "duty," which the court discussed in the Pub Zone case.

EXAM *Strategy*

Question: The Big Red Traveling (BRT) Carnival is in town. Tony arrives at 8:00 p.m., parks in the lot—and is robbed at gun point by a man who beats him and escapes with his money. There are several police officers on the carnival grounds, but no officer in the parking lot at the time of the robbery. Tony sues, claiming that brighter lighting and more police in the lot would have prevented the robbery. There has never before been any violent crime—robbery, beating, or otherwise—at any BRT carnival. BRT claims it had no duty to protect Tony from this harm. Who is likely to win?

Strategy: Begin by isolating the legal issue. What are the parties disputing? They are debating whether BRT had a duty to protect Tony from an armed robbery, committed by a stranger. Now ask yourself: How do courts decide whether a business has a duty to prevent this kind of harm? The Pub Zone case provides our answer. A business owner is not an insurer of the visitor's safety. The owner generally has no duty to protect a customer from the criminal act of a third party, unless the owner knows the harm is occurring or could foresee it is about to happen. (In the Pub Zone case, the business owner *knew* of the gang's violent history, and could have foreseen the assault.) Now apply that rule to the facts of this case.

Result: There has never been a violent attack of any kind at a BRT carnival. BRT cannot foresee this robbery, and has no duty to protect against it. The carnival wins.

YOU BE THE JUDGE

Many cases involve difficult decisions for juries and judges. Often both parties have legitimate, opposing arguments. Most chapters in this book will have a feature called "You Be the Judge," in which we present the facts of a case but not the court's holding. We offer you two opposing arguments based on the kinds of claims the lawyers made in court. We leave it up to you to debate and decide which position is stronger or to add your own arguments to those given.

The following case is another negligence lawsuit, with issues that overlap those of the Pub Zone case. This time the court confronts murder in a high school. Distraught parents of the victims sued producers of a violent film and video games, claiming that the companies were partly responsible for the killings. Once again, the defendants asked the court to dismiss the case, claiming that they owed no duty to protect the victims—the same argument made by the Pub Zone. They pointed out, correctly, that a defendant owed a duty to a plaintiff only if it could foresee the harm that occurred. Could these defendants have foreseen what happened? You be the judge.

YOU *be the* JUDGE

JAMES V. MEOW MEDIA
300 F.3d 683
Sixth Circuit Court of Appeals, 2002

Facts: Michael Carneal was a 14-year-old freshman at Heath High School in Paducah, Kentucky. He carried a .22-caliber pistol and five shotguns into the school's lobby, where he shot into a crowd of students, killing three and wounding five more. He was arrested and convicted of murder.

An investigation revealed that Carneal regularly played violent video games, including "Doom," "Quake," "Redneck Rampage" and others. He also owned a copy of the movie *The Basketball Diaries*, in which a character played by Leonardo DiCaprio envisions murdering a teacher and several classmates.

The parents of the victims sued the producers of *The Basketball Diaries* and the video games, alleging that when the companies distributed such violent material to young people,

they knew or should have known that they were creating an unreasonable risk of harm to innocent people. The parents claimed that such games and movies made young people insensitive to violence, and more likely to commit such appalling acts.

The producers of the games and the movie claimed that they owed no duty to the victims. They argued that Carneal's actions were not foreseeable.

The trial court dismissed the case, ruling that Carneal's acts were unforeseeable. The producers had no duty to protect the victims. The parents appealed to the Court of Appeals.

You Be The Judge: Did the producers have a duty to protect the victims from harm caused by their products?

continued

Argument for the Parents: Your honors, the producers had a duty to the victims of this horrible assault because they should have foreseen what happened. In all likelihood, they *did* foresee it. These manufacturers do not merely churn out brutal, vivid material—they profit from it. That proves that they know their market. They do not blindly send this material into the world, hoping for the best. The producers create, advertise and distribute games and movies intending to sell them to young people. They know that many of their customers are adolescents, some of whom are going through periods of alienation, anger and potential violence. They also know that guns are easily available in our society. Into this combustible mix they toss a match—their movie, their games, all celebrating murder, all soaked in blood.

Each of these products depicts a protagonist engaging in gruesome conduct. Anyone can foresee that the movie and games will desensitize young people to violence, and make them more likely to act out what they have seen. The producers know that their efforts will cause innocent people to suffer, and some to die. Yet they carry on, contributing to bloodshed, earning a profit.

Because the producers could foresee the harm, they have a duty to protect against it. The producers failed in that duty. They are liable, and must pay the price.

Argument for the Producers: We agree that these shootings were a tragedy. However, while we share in the sympathy we do not share in the responsibility. The producers manufactured legal, commonplace items—video games and movies. Millions of young people played the games and watched the movie and never did anything violent or criminal.

It is absurd to suggest that we could have foreseen criminal conduct like this. How can a film producer anticipate every viewer's response to a movie? Perhaps a broken-hearted moviegoer will over-react to a painful scene in a love story. Maybe a high school student will empathize with the injustice inflicted on a movie character of his age. Does that mean we must ban movies about adolescence, or love? Are the producers expected to conduct psychological testing on patrons before admitting them to the cinema or selling them a video game?

Business people should expect that their customers are law-abiding citizens. Carneal was the rare exception: a troubled young man, determined upon violence. While his parents may bear some responsibility, and perhaps others close to him, it is preposterous to foist onto film and game producers the duty to control him.

The producers could not foresee that their customers would commit crimes, because most do not. The producers owed no duty to the victims or anyone else, and cannot be held responsible for these abnormal acts.

CHAPTER CONCLUSION

We depend upon the law to give us a stable nation and economy, a fair society, a safe place to live and work. These worthy goals have occupied Anglo-Saxon kings and twenty-first-century lawmakers alike. But while law is a vital tool for crafting the society we want, there are no easy answers about how to create it. In a democracy, we all participate in the crafting. Legal rules control us, yet *we* create *them*. A working knowledge of the law can help build a successful career—and a solid democracy.

EXAM REVIEW

1. **THE FEDERAL SYSTEM** Our federal system of government means that law comes from a national government in Washington, D.C., and from 50 state governments. (p. 11)

2. **LEGAL HISTORY** The history of law foreshadows many current legal issues, including mediation, partnership liability, the jury system, the role of witnesses, the special value placed on land, the idea of precedent, and the difference between substantive and procedural law. (p. 5)

3. **PRIMARY SOURCES OF LAW** The primary sources of contemporary law are

   - United States Constitution and state constitutions;

   - Statutes, which are drafted by legislatures;

   - Common law, which is the body of cases decided by judges, as they follow earlier cases, known as precedent; and

   - Administrative law, the rules and decisions made by federal and state administrative agencies. (p. 9)

EXAM Strategy

Question: The stock market crash of 1929 and the Great Depression that followed were caused in part because so many investors blindly put their money into stocks they knew nothing about. During the 1920s it was often impossible for an investor to find out what a corporation was planning to do with its money, who was running the corporation, and many other vital things. Congress responded by passing the Securities Act of 1933, which required a corporation to divulge more information about itself before it could seek money for a new stock issue. What kind of law did Congress create?

Strategy: What is the question seeking? The question asks you which *type* of law Congress created when it passed the 1933 Securities Act. What are the primary kinds of law? Administrative law consists of rules passed by agencies. Congress is not a federal agency. Common law is the body of cases decided by judges. Congress is not a judge. Statutes are laws passed by legislatures. Congress is a legislature. (See the "Result" at the end of this section.)

4. **OTHER SOURCES OF LAW** Other sources of contemporary law include

   - Treaties
   - Executive orders (p. 10)

5. **CRIMINAL LAW** Criminal law concerns behavior so threatening to society that it is outlawed altogether. Civil law deals with duties and disputes between parties, not with outlawed behavior. (p. 12)

(Verbal Contracts)

EXAM Strategy

Question: Bill and Diane are hiking in the woods. Diane walks down a hill to fetch fresh water. Bill meets a stranger, who introduces herself as Katrina. Bill sells a kilo of cocaine to Katrina, who then flashes a badge and mentions how much she enjoys her job at the Drug Enforcement Agency. Diane, heading back to camp with the water, meets Freddy, a motorist whose car has overheated. Freddy is late for a meeting where he expects to make a $30 million profit; he's desperate for water for his car. He promises to pay Diane $500 tomorrow if she will give him the pail of water, which she does. The next day, Bill is in jail and Freddy refuses to pay for Diane's water. Explain the criminal law/civil law distinction and what it means to Bill and Diane. Who will do what to whom, with what results?

Strategy: You are asked to distinguish between criminal and civil law. What is the difference? The criminal law concerns behavior that threatens society and is therefore outlawed. The government prosecutes the defendant. Civil law deals with the rights and duties between parties. One party files a suit against the other. Apply those different standards to these facts. (See the "Result" at the end of this section.)

6. **SUBSTANTIVE AND PROCEDURAL LAW** Substantive law defines the rights of people. Procedural law describes the processes for settling disputes. (p. 12)

7. **JURISPRUDENCE** Jurisprudence is concerned with the basic nature of law. Three theories of jurisprudence are

• Legal positivism: The law is what the sovereign says it is.

• Natural law: An unjust law is no law at all.

• Legal realism: Who enforces the law is more important than what the law says. (p. 13)

3. Result: The Securities Act of 1933 is a statute.

5. Result: The government will prosecute Bill for dealing in drugs. If convicted he will go to prison. The government will take no interest in Diane's dispute. However, if she chooses she may sue Freddy for $500, the amount he promised her for the water. In that civil lawsuit, a court will decide whether Freddy must pay what he promised; however, even if Freddy loses he will not go to jail.

ADDITIONAL QUESTIONS

1. Can one person really understand all of the legal issues mentioned at the beginning of this chapter? For example, can a business executive know about insider trading and employment law and environmental law and tort law and all of the others? Will a court really hold one person to such knowledge?

2. Why does our law come from so many different sources?

3. Union organizers at a hospital wanted to distribute leaflets to potential union members, but hospital rules prohibited leafleting in areas of patient care, hallways, cafeterias, and any areas open to the public. The National Labor Relations Board (NLRB) ruled that these restrictions violated the law and ordered the hospital to permit the activities in the cafeteria and coffee shop. The NLRB cannot create common law or statutory law. What kind of law was it creating?

4. Leslie Bergh and his two brothers, Milton and Raymond, formed a partnership to help build a fancy saloon and dance hall in Evanston, Wyoming. Later, Leslie met with his friend and drinking buddy, John Mills, and tricked Mills into investing in the saloon. Leslie did not tell Mills that no one else was investing cash or that the entire enterprise was already insolvent. Mills mortgaged his home, invested $150,000 in the saloon—and lost every penny of it. Mills sued all three partners for fraud. Milton and Raymond defended on the ground that they didn't commit the fraud, only Leslie did. The defendants lost. Was that fair? By holding them liable, what general idea did the court rely on? What Anglo-Saxon legal custom did the ruling resemble?

5. **ETHICS** Confucius did not esteem written laws, believing instead that good rulers were the best guarantee of justice. Does our legal system rely primarily on the rule of law or the rule of people? Which do you instinctively trust more? Legal realists argue that the "rule of law" is a misleading term. What point are they making, and how does it relate to Confucius's principles? Confucius himself was an extraordinarily wise man, full of wisdom about life and compassion for his fellow citizens. Since he was extraordinary, what does that tell us about other rulers by contrast? How does that affect Confucius's own views?

6. Tommy Parker may have been involved in some unsavory activities as an officer in a failed savings and loan institution. A federal agency, the Office of Thrift Supervision (OTS), ordered Tommy not to spend or waste any of his own assets while it was investigating him. Later, Tommy and his wife, Billie, got divorced and divided their property. On February 18, the OTS filed papers in court asking for an order that *Billie* not spend any of her assets. Billie received a copy of the papers on February 20, and the hearing took place on February 24, without Billie in attendance. The court ordered Billie not to spend any assets except for essential living expenses. Billie appealed, claiming that under court rules she was entitled to five days' notice before the hearing took place and that weekend days are not counted. She had had only two business days' notice. Assume that her counting of the days was correct (which it was). Explain the difference between procedural law and substantive law. Which type of law was Billie relying on? Should her appeal be granted?

7. Plaintiff Miss Universe, Inc., owns the trademark "Miss U.S.A." For decades, the company has produced the Miss U.S.A. beauty pageant, seen by many millions of people in the United States. William Flesher and Treehouse Fun Ranch began to hold a nude beauty pageant in California. They called this the "Miss Nude U.S.A." pageant. Most of the contestants were from California; the majority of states were not represented in the contest. Miss Universe sued Flesher and Treehouse, claiming that the public would be confused and misled by the similar names. The company sought an *equitable remedy* in this lawsuit. What does "equitable" mean? What equitable remedy did Miss Universe seek? Should it win?

8. **YOU BE THE JUDGE** WRITING PROBLEM Should trials be televised? Here are a few arguments to add to those in the chapter. You be the judge. **Arguments against Live Television Coverage**: We have tried this experiment and it has failed. Trials fall into two categories: Those that create great public interest and those that do not. No one watches dull trials, so we do not need to broadcast them. The few that are interesting have all become circuses. Judges and lawyers have shown that they cannot resist the temptation to play to the camera. Trials are supposed to be about justice, not entertainment. If a citizen seriously wants to follow a case, she can do it by reading the daily newspaper. **Arguments for Live Television Coverage**: It is true that some televised trials have been unseemly affairs, but that is the fault of the presiding judges, not the media. Indeed, one of the virtues of television coverage is that millions of people now understand that we have a lot of incompetent people running our courtrooms. The proper response is to train judges to run a tight trial by prohibiting the grandstanding in which some lawyers may engage. Access to accurate information is the foundation on which a democracy is built, and we must not eliminate a source of valuable data just because some judges are ill-trained.

9. In his most famous novel, *The Red and the Black*, the French author Stendhal (1783–1842) wrote: "There is no such thing as 'natural law': this expression is nothing but old nonsense. Prior to laws, what is natural is only the strength of the lion, or the need of the creature suffering from hunger or cold, in short, need." What do you think?

10. ***ROLE REVERSAL*** The Role Reversal feature challenges you to create your own exam question. The goal is to think creatively and accurately. Crafting questions is a good way to reinforce what you understand and recognize the areas you need to review. Your professor may ask you to submit the questions in writing or electronically or to prepare an overhead slide.

    The question should be challenging enough that the average student will need to stop and think, but clear enough that there is only one answer. Useful questions can be formatted as essay, short answer, or multiple choice. Notice that some exam questions are very direct, while others require deeper analysis. Here are two examples. The first focuses on a definition.

Question: Legal positivism is:

(a) A decision by an appeals court *affirming* the trial court.

(b) A decision by an appeals court *reversing* a trial court.

(c) A theory of jurisprudence insisting that the law is what the sovereign says it is.

(d) A theory of law requiring that current cases be decided based on earlier decisions.

(e) A theory of law requiring that current cases be decided by a majority vote of the judges.

As you know, the correct answer is "(c)."

The next question demands that the student spot the issue of law involved (foreseeability) and correctly apply it to the facts provided.

Question: Marvin asks Sheila, a qualified auto mechanic, to fix his engine, which constantly stalls (stops) while driving. When Marvin returns, Sheila informs him that the engine is now "Perfect—runs like a top." Marvin drives home along Lonesome Highway. Suddenly the car stalls. Sheila has not fixed it. Marvin pulls over and begins the long walk to the nearest telephone. A blimp flies overhead, advertising "Top" brand tires. Tragically, the blimp suddenly plummets to earth and explodes 20 feet from Marvin, seriously injuring him. Marvin sues Sheila. Sheila's best defense is that:

(a) The falling blimp is so bizarre that Sheila could never have foreseen it.

(b) Sheila made *reasonable efforts* to fix the engine.

(c) Marvin should have checked the engine himself.

(d) Marvin should have carried a cell phone with him in case of emergencies.

(e) Sheila is a qualified mechanic and her work is presumptively sufficient.

The correct answer is "(a)." Notice that the same facts could be used as an essay question, simply by deleting the multiple-choice answers. Now it is your turn for Role Reversal: draft a multiple-choice question focusing on *legal realism*.

INTERNET RESEARCH PROBLEM

Search online for two current cases that interest you: one civil, one criminal. Explain the different roles played by each type of law, and summarize the issues in the respective cases.

You can find further practice problems at www.cengagebrain.com. See the preface of this book for website access details.

C H A P T E R

2

BUSINESS ETHICS AND SOCIAL RESPONSIBILITY

Although Arthur worked hard as a waiter for much of his life, he never earned a lot of money. Now 79 years old, he spends 20 hours a week in a minimum wage job shelving books in a library in Chicago. His annual income is $18,000 a year. What kind of apartment could he possibly afford in Chicago? Luckily, the federal government subsidizes his rent so he pays only $350 a month for his small unit.

> **At age 79, Arthur pays $350 a month in a federally subsidized Chicago apartment. Now he faces eviction.**

Now Arthur faces eviction. Twenty years ago, his landlord, Sheldon, signed a contract with the government agreeing that, in return for a guaranteed subsidy, the rent in the building would be below market rate. That contract is about to expire. Sheldon could make more money for his investors by raising rents to the market rate or by selling the building to someone else who would do the same.

This issue affects more than just Arthur and the other tenants in his building. Across the country, landlords have taken more than a hundred thousand apartments out of the federal program so that they can raise rents. Shortages of affordable housing are widespread as decaying public housing projects are being torn down and the demand for subsidized apartments is rising. What should Sheldon do? On the one hand, he has an obligation to his investors. On the other hand, what about the needs of the elderly, who are often priced out of neighborhoods that they have lived in for years? What is best for other residents of the community? The elderly make good neighbors. Their presence tends to make city blocks more stable and safer.[1]

---

[1] From "Landlord's Dilemma: Help Poor Tenants or Seek More Profits" by Jonathan Eig, in *The Wall Street Journal*, July 1, 2001, p.1. Reprinted by permission of the Copyright Clearance Center.

Business is an enormously powerful tool that corporate managers can use to accomplish many goals. They may wish to earn a good living, even to become wealthy, but they can also use their business skills to cure the ill, feed the hungry, entertain the bored, and in many other ways affect their community, their country, and their world.

This book is primarily about the impact of law on business. But law is only one set of rules that governs business; ethics is another. **Ethics** is the study of how people ought to act. Law and ethics are often in harmony. Most reasonable people agree that murder should be prohibited. But law and ethics are not always compatible. In some cases, it might be *ethical* to commit an *illegal* act; in others, it might be *unethical* to be *legal*. Here are two examples in which law and ethics might conflict:

George Hart, a 75-year-old man confined to a wheelchair, robbed a bank in San Diego of $70 so that he could buy heart medicine. He entered a branch of the HomeFed Bank, where he had $4 in his account, and apologized while demanding $70 from a teller, threatening to blow up the bank if she did not comply. Hart was arrested minutes later when he tried to buy a $69 bottle of heart medicine at a nearby drugstore. Hart said he "hated to have to go to this extreme," but insisted he had tried every other way to find money to buy the medicine.[2]

In 1963, Martin Luther King, Jr., was arrested in Birmingham, Alabama, for leading illegal sit-ins and marches to protest laws that discriminated against African Americans. His *Letter from a Birmingham Jail* offered an eloquent defense of these actions. He described the burdens of being an African-American in the 1960s. How, when traveling, he was forced to sleep in his car because no hotel would take him. Or how his daughter cried when he told her that she was not allowed into the local amusement park. King argued he had no obligation to obey laws that permitted such wrongdoing. He quoted Saint Augustine: "an unjust law is not law at all."

Could one argue in the case of the bank robber that his actions, while illegal, were ethical? Would the argument be stronger if he had been stealing the money to help someone else? In the case of Martin Luther King, Jr., would it be reasonable to conclude not only that breaking the law was ethical, but also that *obeying* the law would have been *unethical?* Were local clergymen who criticized King behaving unethically by upholding these odious laws?

The other chapters of this book focus on legal issues, but this chapter concentrates on ethics. In all of the examples in this chapter, the activities are *legal*, but are they *ethical?*

Ethics
The study of how people ought to act.

WHY BOTHER WITH ETHICS?

Business schools teach students how to maximize the profitability of an enterprise, large or small. Does ethical behavior maximize profitability? Some people argue that, in the long run, ethical behavior does indeed pay. But they must mean the very long run, because to date there is little evidence that ethical behavior *necessarily* pays financially, either in the short or the long run.

For instance, when a fire destroyed the Malden Mills factory in Lawrence, Massachusetts, its 70-year-old owner, Aaron Feuerstein, could have shut down the business, collected the insurance money, and sailed off into retirement. But a layoff of the factory's 3,000 employees

---

[2] "Bank Robber in Wheelchair Has an Alibi: His Medicine," *New York Times*, Jan. 18, 1991, p. A16.

would have been a major economic blow to the region. So instead Feuerstein kept the workers on the payroll while he rebuilt the factory. These actions gained him a national reputation as a business hero. Many consumers promised to buy more of the company's patented Polartec fabric. In the end, however, the story did not have a fairy-tale ending: Five years after the fire, Malden Mills filed bankruptcy papers. The company was not able to pay off the loans it had incurred to keep the business going.

Likewise, many socially responsible funds are now available to the investor who wants to make ethical choices. The Amana Fund buys stocks that comply with Islamic laws. For example, it will not invest in holdings that earn interest, which is prohibited under Islamic law. The Ava Maria Fund is designed for Catholic investors, the Timothy Plan for evangelicals. The Sierra Fund focuses on environmentally friendly investments while the Women's Equity Fund chooses companies that promote women's interests in the workplace. On average, however, these socially responsible investments earn a lower return than standard index funds that mirror the performance of a stock index, such as the Standard & Poor's 500. (Generally index funds perform better than actively-managed funds for which managers pick individual stocks.)

It also appears that unethical behavior is no bar to financial success. The first antitrust laws in America were designed, at least in part, to restrain John D. Rockefeller's unethical activities. Yet, four generations later, his name is still synonymous with wealth and his numerous heirs can live comfortably on their inheritance from him.

If ethical behavior does not necessarily pay and unethical behavior sometimes does, why bother with ethics?

SOCIETY AS A WHOLE BENEFITS FROM ETHICAL BEHAVIOR

John Akers, the former chairman of IBM, argues that without ethical behavior, a society cannot be economically competitive. He puts it this way:

> Ethics and competitiveness are inseparable. We compete as a society. No society anywhere will compete very long or successfully with people stabbing each other in the back; with people trying to steal from each other; with everything requiring notarized confirmation because you can't trust the other fellow; with every little squabble ending in litigation; and with government writing reams of regulatory legislation, tying business hand and foot to keep it honest. That is a recipe not only for headaches in running a company, it is a recipe for a nation to become wasteful, inefficient, and noncompetitive. There is no escaping this fact: the greater the measure of mutual trust and confidence in the ethics of a society, the greater its economic strength.[3]

MONEY DOES NOT BUY HAPPINESS

Researchers who study happiness find that people expect material goods to make them happier than they actually do. Sure, you enjoy driving that snappy new car home from the dealership, but afterward your happiness quickly returns to its natural base level. People find themselves on the so-called "hedonic treadmill"—struggling to buy more and more things so they can get that buyer's high, only to discover that they can never buy enough to maintain the thrill. Almost no matter how much people earn, they feel they would be happier if their income were just a little bit higher. So what does make people happy in the long run? Good relationships, satisfying work, ties to the community—all available at no additional cost.

---

[3] David Grier, "Confronting Ethical Dilemmas," unpublished manuscript of remarks at the Royal Bank of Canada, Sept. 19, 1989.

PEOPLE FEEL BETTER WHEN THEY BEHAVE ETHICALLY

Every businessperson has many opportunities to be dishonest. Consider how one person felt when he resisted temptation:

> Occasionally a customer forgot to send a bill for materials shipped to us for processing.... It would have been so easy to rationalize remaining silent. After all, didn't they deserve to lose because of their inefficiency? However, upon instructing our staff to inform the parties of their errors, I found them eager to do so. They were actually bursting with pride.... Our honesty was beneficial in subtle ways. The "inefficient" customer remained loyal for years.... [O]ur highly moral policy had a marvelously beneficial effect on our employees. Through the years, many an employee visited my office to let me know that they liked working for a "straight" company.[4]

Profitability is generally not what motivates managers to care about ethics. Managers want to feel good about themselves and the decisions they have made; they want to sleep at night. Their decisions—to lay off employees, install safety devices in cars, burn a cleaner fuel— affect peoples' lives. When two researchers asked businesspeople why they cared about ethics, the answers had little to do with the profitability:

> The businesspeople we interviewed set great store on the regard of their family, friends, and the community at large. They valued their reputations, not for some nebulous financial gain but because they took pride in their good names.[5]

UNETHICAL BEHAVIOR CAN BE VERY COSTLY

Unethical behavior is a risky business strategy—it may lead to disaster. An engaged couple made a reservation, and put down a $1,500 deposit, to hold their wedding reception at a New Hampshire restaurant. Tragically, the bride died of asthma four months before the wedding. Invoking the terms of the contract, the restaurant owner refused to return the couple's deposit. In a letter to the groom, he admitted, "Morally, I would of course agree that the deposit should be returned." When newspapers reported this story, customers deserted the restaurant and it was forced into bankruptcy—over a $1,500 disagreement.[6] Unethical behavior does not always damage a business, but it certainly has the potential of destroying a company overnight. So why take the risk?

Even if unethical behavior does not devastate a business, it can cause other, subtler damage. In one survey, a majority of those questioned said that they had witnessed unethical behavior in their workplace and that this behavior had reduced productivity, job stability, and profits. Unethical behavior in an organization creates a cynical, resentful, and unproductive workforce.

ETHICAL BEHAVIOR IS MORE LIKELY TO PAY OFF

Although there is no *guarantee* that ethical behavior pays in the short or long run, there is evidence that the ethical company is more *likely* to win financially. Ethical companies tend to have a better reputation, more creative and cooperative employees and higher returns than those that engage in wrong doing.[7]

---

[4] Hugh Aaron, "Doing the Right Thing in Business," *Wall Street Journal*, June 21, 1993, p. A10.

[5] Amar Bhide and Howard H. Stevenson, "Why Be Honest if Honesty Doesn't Pay?" *Harvard Business Review*, Sept.–Oct. 1990, pp. 121–129, at 127.

[6] John Milne, "N.H. Restaurant Goes Bankrupt in Wake of Wedding Refund Flap," *Boston Globe*, Sept. 9, 1994, p. 25.

[7] For sources, see "Ethics: A Basic Framework," Harvard Business School case 9-307-059.

So why bother with ethics? Because society benefits when managers behave ethically. Because money does not buy happiness. Because ethical managers have happier, more satisfying lives. Because unethical behavior can destroy a business faster than a snake can bite. And because, in the end, ethical behavior is more likely to pay off.

WHAT IS ETHICAL BEHAVIOR?

It is one thing to decide, in theory, that being ethical is good; in practice, it can be much more difficult to make the right decisions. Supreme Court Justice Potter Stewart once said that he could not define pornography, but he knew it when he saw it. Many people feel the same way about ethics—that somehow, instinctively, they know what is right and wrong. In real life, however, ethical dilemmas are often not black and white, but many shades of gray. The purpose of this section is to analyze the following ethics checklist as an aid to managers in making tough decisions:

- What are the facts?

- What are the critical issues?

- Who are the stakeholders?

- What are the alternatives?

- What are the ethical implications of each alternative?

   - Is it legal?

   - How would it look in the light of day?

   - What are the consequences?

   - Does it violate important values?

   - What kind of world would this be if everyone behaved this way?

- Is more than one alternative right?

   - Which values are in conflict?

   - Which of these values are most important?

   - Can you find an alternative that is consistent with your values?

ANALYZING THE ETHICS CHECKLIST

WHAT ARE THE FACTS?

Although this question seems obvious, people often forget in the heat of battle to listen to (and, more importantly, to *hear*) all the different viewpoints. Instead of relying on hearsay and rumor, it is crucial to discover the facts, firsthand, from the people involved. There is always another side to the story. It may be easy to condemn a bank robber, until learning the money was needed to buy medicine.

WHAT ARE THE CRITICAL ISSUES?

In analyzing ethical dilemmas, expand your thinking to include *all* the important issues. Avoid a narrow focus that encompasses only one or two aspects. In the case of the New Hampshire restaurant that refused to refund a deposit, the owner focused on the narrow legal issue. His interpretation of the *contract* was correct. But if the owner had expanded his thinking to include consideration for his customers, he might have reached a different decision.

WHO ARE THE STAKEHOLDERS?

Stakeholders are all the people potentially affected by the decision. That list might include subordinates, bosses, shareholders, suppliers, customers, members of the community in which the business operates, society as a whole, or even more remote stakeholders, such as future generations. The interests of these stakeholders often conflict. Current shareholders may benefit from a company's decision to manufacture a product that contributes to global warming, while future generations are left to contend with a potential environmental nightmare.

WHAT ARE THE ALTERNATIVES?

The next step is to list the reasonable alternatives. A creative manager may find a clever solution that is a winner for everyone. What alternatives might be available to Sheldon, the landlord who faced a dilemma in the opening scenario?

WHAT ARE THE ETHICAL IMPLICATIONS OF EACH ALTERNATIVE?

Is the Alternative Legal?

Illegal may not always be synonymous with unethical, but, as a general rule, you need to think long and hard about the ethics of any illegal activities.

How Would the Alternative Look in the Light of Day?

If your activities were reported on the evening news, how would you feel? Proud? Embarrassed? Horrified? Undoubtedly, sexual harassment would be virtually eliminated if people thought that their parents, spouse, or partner would shortly see a video replay of the offending behavior.

What Are the Consequences of This Alternative?

Ask yourself: Am I hurting anyone by this decision? Which alternative will cause the greatest good (or the least harm) to the most people? For example, you would like to fire an incompetent employee. That decision will clearly have adverse consequences for him. But the other employees in your division will benefit and so will the shareholders of your company. Overall, your decision will cause more good than harm.

You should look with a particularly critical eye if an alternative benefits you while harming others. Suppose that you become CEO of a company whose headquarters are located in a distant suburb. You would like to move the headquarters closer to your home to cut your commuting time. Of course, such a decision would be expensive for shareholders and inconvenient for other employees. Do you simply impose your will on the company or consider the consequences for everyone?

Does the Alternative Violate Important Values?

In addition to consequences, consider fundamental values. It is possible to commit an act that does not harm anyone else, but is still the wrong thing to do. Suppose, for instance, that you are away from home and have the opportunity to engage in a one-night stand. You are absolutely certain that your spouse will never find out and your partner for the night will have no regrets or guilt. There would be no negative consequences, but you believe that infidelity is wrong, *regardless of the consequences*, so you resist temptation.

Some people question whether, as a diverse, heterogeneous society (not to mention, world), we have common values. But throughout history, and across many different cultures, common values do appear. The following values are almost universal:

- *Compassion* means being aware of and concerned about other people's feelings, desires, and needs. The compassionate person is able to imagine how he would feel in someone else's place.

- *Courage* is the strength to act in the face of fear and danger. Courage can require dramatic action (saving a buddy on a battlefield) or quiet strength (doing what you think is right, despite opposition from your boss).

- *Fairness* requires that decisions be made without fraud, prejudice or favoritism. The fair manager treats those he likes at work the same as those who are not his friends.

- *Integrity* means being sincere, honest, and loyal. If you have integrity, you do not criticize others behind their back or take credit for their ideas and efforts.

- *Responsibility* means being trustworthy and dependable. The responsible person meets her commitments, lives up to her promises and contributes to her community. People can count on her.

- *Self-control* is the ability to resist temptation. The person with self-control does not drink or eat too much, party too hard, watch too much television, or spend too much money.

Try compiling your own list of values and then check it periodically to see if you are living up to it in your business and personal life.

What Kind of World Would This Be if Everyone Behaved This Way?

Is this the kind of world in which you would want to live? Imagine that you could cheat on an exam without getting caught. You might gain some short-term benefit—a higher grade. But what would happen if everyone cheated? The professor would have to make the exams harder or curve everyone's grade down. If your school developed a reputation for cheating, you might not be able to find a job after graduation. Cheating works only if most people are honest. To take advantage of everyone else's honesty is contemptible.

Is More than One Alternative Right?

Thus far, the ethics checklist has served two purposes. It helps to clarify the issues at stake. It also filters out decisions that are downright wrong. Have you considered lying to a customer about product specifications? For a start, such an action violates principles of integrity, not to mention you would not want to live in a world in which everyone lied like this. Nor would you want your activity to be revealed on the front page of the local newspaper.

Often, the most difficult decisions arise not in cases of right versus wrong but in situations of right versus right.[8] President Harry Truman's decision to drop atomic bombs on two Japanese cities is a classic example of right versus right. He argued that if he had not ended the war by using nuclear weapons, more Americans and Japanese would have died during a land invasion. Looking simply at the consequences, he concluded that the terrible suffering by the Japanese people was justified because, ultimately, fewer people died overall. At the same time, none of us want to live in a world where nuclear weapons are used. Indeed, since the end of World War II, the United States has worked hard to ensure that no one else ever deploys nuclear weapons. The ethics checklist presents no clear-cut answer. In the end, Truman decided that the most right (or least wrong) choice was to end the war quickly.

Nuclear weapons make a dramatic example, but what about a more typical business decision? AT&T adopted a policy of cutting costs to maximize its stock price. To implement this policy, the company laid off 40,000 people, despite record profits. Even as workers suffered, shareholders benefited because the company's stock price rose in response to the layoff announcement. But is stock price the only issue? Does the company have an obligation to protect employee jobs? Is one right more important than another?

Which Values Are in Conflict?

There are many ways to justify a decision to lay off workers, even 40,000 of them. If managers avoid layoffs, then profits suffer, stock prices fall, companies merge, and executives lose their own jobs. In business school and on the job, managers learn how to analyze, compete, and win. Competing—and winning—are important. But what about other values, such as compassion and caring? Do the individual people affected by this decision matter, too?

Which of These Values Are Most Important?

Suppose that, growing up, you had seen family members or neighbors suffering through bouts of unemployment. That experience might have taught you that compassion is a high priority. Managers must determine which values are important in their own lives.

[handwritten note in margin:] What's most beneficial for one's company (stock prices) OR Ethical Values

Can You Find an Alternative That Is Consistent with Your Values?

The decision you make not only determines the kind of person you are now, but also sets your course for the future. Can you reach a decision that is consistent with the kind of person you are or want to be? Instead of announcing massive layoffs, some companies offer generous severance packages, retraining programs, and other voluntary methods of reducing the workforce. Shareholders may receive less benefit, but employees suffer less harm.

APPLYING THE ETHICS CHECKLIST: MAKING DECISIONS

An organization has responsibilities to customers, employees, shareholders, and society generally, both here and overseas. Employees also have responsibilities to their organizations. The purpose of this section is to apply the ethics checklist to actual business dilemmas. The

---

[8] For a thoughtful discussion of right versus right, see Joseph L. Badaracco, Jr., *Defining Moments: When Managers Must Choose between Right and Right* (Boston: Harvard Business School Press, 1997).

checklist does not lead to one particular solution; rather it is a method to use in thinking through ethics problems. The goal is for you to reach a decision that satisfies you.

ORGANIZATION'S RESPONSIBILITY TO SOCIETY

An organization
has responsibilities
to customers,
employees, shareholders,
and society...

FACTS

In the United States, teenagers routinely list alcohol commercials among their favorite advertisements. Adolescents who frequently see ads for alcohol are more likely to believe that drinkers are attractive, athletic, and successful. They are also more likely to drink, drink excessively, and drink in hazardous situations such as driving a car.

While Secretary of Health and Human Services, Louis W. Sullivan publicly denounced the test marketing of Uptown, a high-tar cigarette targeted at African Americans. He called it "contemptible that the tobacco industry has sought to increase their market" among minorities because this population was "already bearing more than its fair share of smoking-related illness and mortality." The comedian Jay Leno joked that R. J. Reynolds named the cigarette Uptown "because the word 'Genocide' was already taken."[9]

At a time when doctors are concerned that too many children are fat, one-third of all advertisements shown during children's television programs are for just the sort of foods that encourage obesity: those high in fat, sugar, and salt, but low in nutrition.

CRITICAL ISSUES

What are the obligations of advertising executives and marketing managers to those who see their ads? Is it ethical to entice teenagers into drinking or African Americans into smoking? If these ads sell product, is that justification enough?

STAKEHOLDERS

Ad designers are primarily responsible to their firms and the firms' clients. After all, designers are paid to sell product, not to make the world a better place. But what about the people who see the advertisements? Do the designers have any responsibility to them? Or to society as a whole?

ALTERNATIVES

Firms have at least four alternatives in dealing with issues of ethics in advertising. They can

- Ignore ethics and simply strive to create promotions that sell the most product, whatever the underlying message;

- Try, in a general way, to minimize racism, sexism, and other exploitation;

---

[9] Richard W. Pollay, Jung S. Lee, and David Carter-Whitney, "Separate, But Not Equal: Racial Segmentation in Cigarette Advertising," *Journal of Advertising*, Mar. 1992, vol. 21, no. 1, p. 45.

- Include, as part of the development process, a systematic, focused review of the underlying messages contained in their advertisements; or

- Refuse to create any ads that are potentially demeaning, insensitive, or harmful, recognizing that such a stand may lead to a loss of clients.

ETHICAL IMPLICATIONS

All of these alternatives are perfectly legal. And, far from the ad executives being embarrassed if the ads see the light of day, the whole purpose of ads is to be seen. As for the consequences, the ads may help clients sell their products. But the ads may also harm those who see them. A manager might question whether these ads violate fundamental values. Are they showing consideration for others? Do they encourage self-control? Are they creating the kind of world in which the managers want to live?

RIGHT VERSUS RIGHT

If you worked in an advertising agency or marketing department, you might feel a strong sense of loyalty to your company. But what about consideration for those who could be harmed by your ads? You must decide which values are important to you and look for solutions that enable you to live by these values.

EXAM *Strategy*

Question: Under Indian custom, many families pay a staggering dowry when their daughters marry. To avoid this burdensome debt, hundreds of thousands of pregnant women each year pay for an ultrasound to determine the gender of their fetus and then abort females. This practice has become such a problem that Indian law prohibits doctors from revealing a fetus's gender but many doctors violate the law. In some areas of India, fewer than 800 girls are born for every 1,000 boys. General Electric Co. is the largest seller of ultrasound machines in the Indian market. Indeed, there is some evidence that GE targets doctors in small towns where this problem is most severe. If you were the head of the Ultrasound Division of GE, what would you do?

Strategy: Begin by reviewing the ethics checklist. Stakeholders include GE shareholders and citizens of India. Are there alternatives? What could GE do to ensure that its machines are not used improperly? What are the consequences? Thousands of young men without mates could lead to an increase in prostitution and perhaps even lead to social unrest, with worldwide implications. Is GE being a responsible member of the world community? Do managers want to live in a world in which female fetuses are aborted because of their gender? Are some values in conflict? If so, which values are most important?

Result: That is for you to decide.

ORGANIZATION'S RESPONSIBILITY TO ITS CUSTOMERS

In this chapter's opening scenario, Sheldon faces a dilemma: Now that his contract with the federal government has expired, he can raise rents by as much as 500% in the apartment building that Sheldon lives in, which is home to 140 poor and elderly tenants. Moving would be difficult for the elderly tenants, especially since they are unlikely to find another apartment in the neighborhood. They might end up in homeless shelters. But what about Sheldon's partners? Is it fair to them if he decides to subsidize the rents of low-income tenants? Does he owe his partners the highest return on their investment?

What would you do if you were Sheldon? He is concerned about several important stakeholders—his partners and his tenants. What about the community? Does it benefit from having elderly members? Will the community be harmed if some of these elderly become homeless? How will Sheldon feel about himself if he puts these elderly tenants out on the street? Or if *The Wall Street Journal* runs a front-page article about his eviction plans? On the other hand, could he argue that it is the government's responsibility to house the poor and elderly? What decision would be best for Sheldon The tenants? His partners? The community?

ORGANIZATION'S RESPONSIBILITY TO ITS EMPLOYEES

When James Kilts became CEO of Gillette Co., the consumer products giant had been a mainstay of the Boston community for a hundred years. But the organization was going through hard times: Its stock was trading at less than half its peak price and some of its storied brands of razors were wilting under intense competitive pressure. In four short years, Kilts turned Gillette around—strengthening its core brands, cutting jobs, and paying off debt. With its stock up 61%, Kilts had added $20 billion in shareholder value.

Then suddenly Kilts sold Gillette to Procter & Gamble Co. for $57 billion. So short was Kilts's stay in Boston that he never moved his family from their home in Rye, New York. The deal was sweet for Gillette shareholders—the company's stock price went up 13% in one day. And tasty also for Kilts—his payoff was $153 million, including a $23.9 million reward from P&G for having made the deal and a "change in control" clause in his employment contract that was worth $12.6 million. In addition, P&G agreed to pay him $8 million a year to serve as vice chairman after the merger. When he retires, his pension will be $1.2 million per year. Moreover, two of his top lieutenants were offered payments totaling $57 million.

Any downside to this deal? Four percent of the Gillette workforce—6,000 employees—were fired. If the payouts to the top three Gillette executives were divided among these 6,000, each unemployed worker would receive $35,000. The loss of this many employees (4,000 of whom lived in New England) had a ripple effect throughout the area economy. Although Gillette shareholders certainly benefited in the short run from the sale, their profit would have been even greater without this $210 million payout to the executives. Moreover, about half the increase in Gillette revenues during the time that Kilts was running the show were attributable to currency fluctuations. A cheaper dollar increased revenue overseas. If the dollar had moved in the opposite direction, there might not have been any increase in revenue. Indeed, for the first two years after Kilts joined Gillette, the stock price declined. It was not until the dollar turned down that the stock price improved.

Some commentators have asked: (1) Do CEOs who receive sweeteners have too strong an incentive to sell their companies; and (2) Is it unseemly for them to be paid so much when many employees will lose their jobs? As one observer put it, "People think they are joining a company for the long haul and boom, the rug is pulled out from under them because the CEO wants a quick payday."[10] One study found that CEOs who receive sweeteners negotiate a lower sale price than those who do not.[11] But another commentator said of Kilts, "His

---

[10] Mark Maremont, "No Razor Here: Gillette Chief to Get A Giant Payday," *Wall Street Journal*, Jan. 31, 2005, p. 1.

[11] *Ibid.*

incentives were based on performance, and he performed. Look at his track record. There's a market for CEOs and he's one of the best."[12]

ORGANIZATION'S RESPONSIBILITY TO ITS SHAREHOLDERS

Staples, Inc. is the world's largest office products company. It also strives to be socially responsible. The company has prepared a document entitled "Staples Soul: It's what moves us" that reports on its corporate responsibility efforts. (This report is available at the company website.) For example, 20% of its energy consumption in the U.S. is from renewable sources. The company has reconfigured its fleet of vehicles to save 500,000 gallons of fuel a year. It donates to hundreds of worthy organizations. Suppose you were a shareholder of Staples, would you approve of these efforts?

Milton Friedman, a Nobel Laureate in economics, famously observed, "The one and only social responsibility of business is to increase its profits."[13] He argued that an executive should act for the benefit of the owners of the company. His primary responsibility is to them. If an individual wishes to support other responsibilities, such as a charity, a church, a city, or a country, let him do so with his own time and money, not that of the shareholders.

Look at some of the Staples corporate responsibility initiatives listed on its website. If you were a Staples shareholder, this would be your money. Is that how you would choose to spend it? For example, Staples stores are permitted to donate products to particular charitable organizations. Would it matter to you which organizations are chosen? Perhaps you would prefer to earn higher returns on your stock so that you could give money to other projects you consider more compelling. If the air needs to be cleaner or the schools richer, why shouldn't private donors or public institutions be responsible, not one company's shareholders?[14]

Reading deeper into the Staples Soul report, you would discover that the total giving to community organizations was $26 million out of $5.2 billion in revenue. Then you might have the opposite feeling—$26 million out of $5 billion? Should the company be *more* generous than that? Many religious organizations urge their members to tithe—to give 10% of their income to charity. How should companies balance their obligation to their shareholders and their world?

ORGANIZATION'S RESPONSIBILITY OVERSEAS

An American company's ethical obligations do not end at the border. What ethical duties does an American manager owe to stakeholders in countries where the culture and economic circumstances are very different?

Here is a typical story from Guatemala:

My father left home a long time ago. My mother supported me and my five brothers and sisters by selling tortillas and corn. Our house was a tin shack on the side of the road. We were crowded with all of us in one room, especially when it rained and the roof and sides leaked. There were hundreds of squatters in the neighborhood, but one day the police came and cleared us all out. The owners of the land said we couldn't come back unless we paid rent. How could we afford that? I was 12 and my

---

[12] *Ibid.*

[13] Milton Friedman, "The Social Responsibility of Business Is to Increase Its Profits," *New York Times Magazine*, Sept. 13, 1970, p. 32.

[14] See, for instance, David Henderson, "Misguided Virtue: False Notions of Corporate Social Responsibility," Hobart Paper 142, Institute of Economic Affairs, London, cited in *The Economist*, Nov. 17, 2001, p. 70.

mother said it was time for me to work. But most people won't hire children. Lots of other kids shine shoes or beg, but I heard that the maquila [clothing factory] was willing to hire children if we would work as hard as older people.

I can keep up with the grown-ups. We work from 6:00 in the morning to 6:30 at night, with half an hour break at noon. We have no other breaks the whole rest of the day. If I don't work fast enough, they hit me, not too hard, and threaten to fire me. Sometimes, if there is too much work to do, they'll lock the doors and not let us out until everything is finished.

I'm always really tired at the end of the day and in the morning, too. But I earn $30 a week and without that money, we would not have enough to eat. My mother hopes all of my brothers and sisters can get jobs in the factory, too.

Of course, I'd rather be in school where I could wear a uniform and have friends. Then I could get a job as a clerk at the medical clinic. I would find people's files and tell them how long before the doctor could see them.[15]

This description paints a distasteful picture indeed: children being beaten as they work 12-hour days. Should American companies (and consumers) buy goods that are produced in sweatshop factories? Jeffrey Sachs, a leading economist and adviser to developing nations, says, "My concern is not that there are too many sweatshops but that there are too few."[16] Why would he support sweatshops and child labor?

Historically, poor children have worked. Indeed, for many people and for many centuries, the point of having children was to create a supply of free labor to help support the family. In England in 1860, almost 40% of 14-year-old boys worked, and that was not just a few hours at Burger Box, but more likely 60 hours a week. That percentage is higher than in Africa or India today. For a child in a desperately poor family, the choice is not work or school, it is work, starvation, or prostitution.

Industrialization has always been the first stepping stone out of dire poverty—it was in England, it is now in the Third World. Eventually, higher productivity leads to higher wages. In China, factory managers have complained that their employees want to work even longer hours to earn more money. The results in China have been nothing short of remarkable: During the Industrial Revolution in England, per capita output doubled in 58 years. In China, it took only 10 years.

During the past 50 years, Taiwan and South Korea welcomed sweatshops. During the same period, India resisted what it perceived to be foreign exploitation. Although all three countries started at the same economic level, Taiwan and South Korea today have much lower levels of infant mortality and much higher levels of education than India.[17]

When governments or customers try to force Third World factories to pay higher wages, the factory owners typically either relocate to lower wage countries or mechanize, thereby reducing the need for workers. In either case, the local economy suffers.

The difference, however, between the twenty-first and the nineteenth centuries is that now there are wealthy countries able to help their poorer neighbors. In the nineteenth century, England was among the richest countries, so it was on its own to solve its economic problems. Is America ethically obligated to assist the people around the world who live in abject poverty? Already, owing to pressure from activists, many companies have introduced better conditions in their factories. Workers are less likely to be beaten. They can go to the bathroom without asking permission. They might even receive rudimentary medical care.

[15] Adapted from the *Boston Globe*, Jun 15, 1997.

[16] Allen R. Meyerson, "In Principle, A Case for More 'Sweatshops,'" *New York Times*, June 22, 1997, p. E5.

[17] The data in this and the preceding paragraph are from Nicholas D. Kristof and Sheryl WuDunn, "Two Cheers for Sweatshops," *New York Times Magazine*, Sept. 24, 2000, p. 70.

Manufacturing processes use fewer dangerous chemicals. Factories are cleaner, with better lighting and more ventilation. But hours are still long and wages low.

Companies argue that higher wages lead to increased prices, which, in their turn, drive away customers. Many of these sweatshops produce clothing. As a consumer, how much would be you willing to pay in higher clothing prices to eliminate sweatshops and child labor? As a taxpayer, how much are you willing to pay in taxes to subsidize Third World incomes so that sweatshops and child labor are no longer necessary?

EXAM *Strategy*

Question: Many of America's largest consumer product companies, such as Wal-Mart, Nike, and Land's End, buy fabric produced in China by Fountain Set Holdings Ltd. Chinese government investigators recently discovered that Fountain Set has contaminated a local river by dumping dye waste into it. What responsibility do U.S. companies have to ensure safe environmental practices by overseas suppliers?

Strategy: Look at the ethics checklist. Citizens of China are stakeholders of American companies. Although it is legal to buy fabric from a company that is polluting overseas, this is surely information that Nike would not want to be well-known. Does the company have values? What does its website say? Do any of us want to live in a world where Chinese children are poisoned so that our running shoes cost less?

Result: Do Wal-Mart and Nike have an obligation to source their products more carefully?

EMPLOYEES' RESPONSIBILITY TO THEIR ORGANIZATION

In the fall of 2008, the nation fell into its worst economic slump in a generation. The stock market lost half its value. Many companies cut salaries and laid off workers. The unemployment rate soared. Unable to pay their mortgages, families lost their homes. Fear and anxiety gripped the nation. Even people with secure jobs worried about the future.

Faced with a drop in advertising revenue, the New York Times Company cut the salaries of its non-union employees by 5 percent and furloughed them without pay for 10 days. It could not force such changes on the newsroom staff because they were unionized. Instead the company asked them to accept a similar reduction voluntarily. If the union did not agree, 60 to 70 of the 1,300 news staff would be laid off.

Suppose that you are a member of the Times union with enough seniority to be sure that you will not be laid off. You have a mortgage to pay and children in college. Money is tight. On the other hand, you know that if some of the younger staff are laid off, they may never find another job in journalism. All across the country, newspapers are closing and publishing houses are laying off workers. How will you vote in the secret union ballot?

CHAPTER CONCLUSION

Even employees who are ethical in their personal lives may find it difficult to uphold their standards at work if those around them behave differently. Managers wonder what they can do to create an ethical environment in their companies. To help foster a sense of ethics within their organizations, many U.S. companies have developed their own formal ethics codes. Many companies have also instituted formal ethics training programs for their employees.

In the end, however, the surest way to infuse ethics throughout an organization is for top executives to behave ethically themselves. Few employees will bother to "do the right thing" unless they observe that their bosses value and support such behavior. To ensure a more ethical world, managers must be an example for others, both within and outside their organizations.

EXAM REVIEW

1. **WHY BOTHER WITH ETHICS?** There are at least four reasons to be concerned about ethics in a business environment.

   - Society as a whole benefits from ethical behavior.
   - People feel better when they behave ethically.
   - Unethical behavior can be very costly.
   - Ethical behavior is more likely to pay off. (pp. 29–30)

2. **THE ETHICS CHECKLIST**
   - What are the facts?
   - What are the critical issues?
   - Who are the stakeholders?
   - What are the alternatives?
   - What are the ethical implications of each alternative?
     - Is it legal?
     - How would it look in the light of day?
     - What are the consequences?
     - Does it violate important values?
     - What kind of world would this be if everyone behaved this way?
   - Is more than one alternative right?
     - Which values are in conflict?
     - Which of these values are most important?
     - Can you find an alternative that is consistent with your values? (pp. 30–33)

EXAM Strategy

Question: Rap artist Ice-T and his band, Body Count, recorded a song called "Cop Killer," in which the singer gleefully anticipates slitting a policeman's throat. (The lyrics to this song are readily available on the Internet.) Time Warner, Inc., produced this song and other gangsta rap recordings with violent and sexually degrading lyrics. Recorded music was an important source of profits for the company, which was struggling with a $15 billion debt and a depressed stock price. If Time Warner renounced rap albums, its reputation in the music business—and future profits—might suffer. This damage could spill over into the multimedia market, which was crucial to Time Warner's future.

Strategy: Review the Ethics Checklist. The company was concerned about several important stakeholders—shareholders, consumers, suppliers (rap musicians), society. What are the alternatives? Would it be possible to work with rap musicians to tone down such hateful lyrics? Find other sources of music? Does this music violate important values? What about the artists' free speech rights? Are the Time Warner executives creating the kind of world in which they would want to raise their children? Do they care about anything other than profitability?

Result: You decide.

ADDITIONAL QUESTIONS

1. A Harvard Business School alumna told this story about her life as an MBA student in the 1980s:

   > During the spring of my first year, I took a Business Policy class. One of the young men in the class hung a bigger than life-size poster in the back of the room. It was a naked woman chained to a tree next to a Paul Bunyan-type man, fully clothed in a flannel jacket, with a chain saw. He was starting to de-limb her. The class broke up. The professor was standing there doubled over in laughter. There were 85 men guffawing away as if it were the funniest thing they'd ever seen. The women just sat there with their mouths open.

   Did this professor and these students behave ethically? What would you do if you were the professor? A male student? A female student?

2. Joya is the head of the personal insurance division of a large insurance company. Six months before, she was almost promoted to vice-president, but she lost out to Bill, a colleague from another division. Bill has now called a meeting to discuss who should be promoted to head the marine insurance division. In Joya's opinion, Ichiro is the most qualified person. However, she knows that Bill will not support him because he is Japanese and a relatively recent immigrant to the United States. Nonetheless, Joya is astonished at the meeting when Bill announces that the staff in the marine insurance division strongly object to Ichiro because of his drinking problem. Joya knows that Ichiro does not have a drinking problem and that the staff in his department think he would be a terrific choice. Based on Bill's false information, those at the meeting agree that the promotion should go to Jim, who happens to be a friend of Bill's. Joya knows that Jim is unpopular in his division because of his harsh, demanding style. She thinks

that his appointment as department head will be disastrous. At the end of the meeting, Bill says that he will report the sense of the meeting to the CEO. Joya knows the CEO (they exchange pleasantries when passing in the hallways), but they have no regularly scheduled meetings. Nor is Joya likely to have the opportunity to mention Bill's behavior in a casual way. She is concerned that if she reports that Bill is lying, the CEO will think she is causing trouble out of jealousy that Bill got the job she wanted. What should Joya do?

3. Executives were considering the possibility of moving their company to a different state. They wanted to determine if employees would be willing to relocate, but they did not want the employees to know the company was contemplating a move because the final decision had not yet been made. Instead of asking the employees directly, the company hired a firm to carry out a telephone survey. When calling the employees, these "pollsters" pretended to be conducting a public opinion poll and identified themselves as working for the new state's Chamber of Commerce. Has this company behaved in an ethical manner? Would there have been a better way to obtain this information?

4. Mark is an executive for a multinational office equipment company that would like to enter the potentially vast Chinese market. The official tariffs on office equipment imported into China are so high that these goods are uncompetitive in the local market. Mark discovers, however, that many companies sell their goods to importers offshore. These importers then negotiate "special" tariff rates with Chinese officials. Because these customs officials are under pressure to meet revenue targets, sometimes they are willing to negotiate lower, unofficial rates. What would you do if you were Mark?

5. H. B. Fuller Co. of St. Paul is a leading manufacturer of industrial glues. Its mission statement says the company "will conduct business legally and ethically." It has endowed a university chair in business ethics and donates 5% of its profits to charity. But now it is under attack for selling its shoemakers' glue, Resistol, in Central America. Many homeless children in these countries have become addicted to Resistol's fumes. So widespread is the problem that glue-sniffers in Central America are called "resistoleros." Glue manufacturers in Europe have added a foul-smelling oil to their glue that discourages abusers. Fuller fears that the smell may also discourage legitimate users. What should Fuller do?

6. According to the Electronic Industries Association, questionable returns have become the toughest problem plaguing the consumer electronics industry. Some consumers purchase electronic equipment to use once or twice for a special occasion and then return it—a radar detector for a weekend getaway or a camcorder to record a wedding. Or a customer might return a cordless telephone because he cannot figure out how it works. The retailer's staff lacks the expertise to help, so they refund the customer's money and ship the phone back to the manufacturer labeled as defective. Excessive and unwarranted returns force manufacturers to repackage and reship perfectly good products, imposing extra costs that squeeze their profits and raise prices to consumers. One retailer returned a cordless telephone that was two years old and had been chewed up by a dog. What ethical obligations do consumers and retailers have in these circumstances?

7. Six months ago, Todd, David, and Stacey joined a large, prestigious accounting firm in Houston. On paper, these three novices look similar and each graduated from a top MBA program. All three were assigned to work for the same client, a national restaurant chain. They quickly became friends and often lunched together. One day, a senior manager in the firm stopped by the conference room where Todd and David were

working to ask if they would like to join him for lunch at the posh Hunter Club nearby. David said, "Thanks, that'd be great, but we usually eat lunch with Stacey. Could she come, too?" The manager hemmed and hawed for a minute, shifted his weight from one foot to the other, and finally said, "The Hunter Club doesn't allow women at lunch." What should Todd and David do?

8. Genentech, Inc., manufactured Protropin, a genetically engineered version of the human growth hormone. This drug's purpose was to enhance the growth of short children. Protropin was an important product for Genentech, accounting for more than one-third of the company's total revenue of $217 million. Although the drug was approved for the treatment of children whose bodies made inadequate quantities of growth hormone, many doctors prescribed it for children with normal amounts of growth hormone who simply happened to be short. There was no firm evidence that the drug actually increased growth for short children with normal growth hormone. Moreover, many people questioned whether it is appropriate to prescribe such a powerful drug for cosmetic reasons, especially when the drug might not work. Nor was there proof that it was safe over the long term. Was Genentech behaving ethically? Should it have discouraged doctors from prescribing the drug to normal, short children?

9. **ROLE REVERSAL** Write one or two paragraphs that could be used as an essay question describing an ethical dilemma that you have faced in your own life.

INTERNET RESEARCH PROBLEM

Find on the Internet an example of a real-life ethical dilemma. How did the person involved solve it? What would you have done if you had been in that situation? Use the ethics checklist in this chapter to guide you.

You can find further practice problems at www.cengagebrain.com. See the preface of this book for website access details.

3

DISPUTE RESOLUTION

Tony Caruso had not returned for dinner, and his wife, Karen, was nervous. She put on some sandals and hurried across the dunes, a half mile to the ocean shore. She soon came upon Tony's dog, Blue, tied to an old picket fence. Tony's shoes and clothing were piled neatly nearby. Karen and friends searched frantically throughout the evening.

> **A little past midnight, Tony's body washed ashore, his lungs filled with water.**

A little past midnight, Tony's body washed ashore, his lungs filled with water. A local doctor concluded he had accidentally drowned.

Karen and her friends were not the only ones who were distraught. Tony had been partners with Beth Smiles in an environmental consulting business, Enviro-Vision. They were good friends, and Beth was emotionally devastated. When she was able to focus on business issues, Beth filed an insurance claim with the Coastal Insurance Group. Beth hated to think about Tony's death in financial terms, but she was relieved that the struggling business would receive $2 million on the life insurance policy.

Several months after filing the claim, Beth received this reply from Coastal: "Under the policy issued to Enviro-Vision, we are conditionally liable in the amount of $1 million in the event of Mr. Caruso's death. If his death is accidental, we are conditionally liable to pay double indemnity of $2 million. But pursuant to section H(5) death by suicide is not covered.

"After a thorough investigation, we have concluded that Anthony Caruso's death was an act of suicide, as defined in section B(11) of the policy. Your claim is denied in its entirety." Beth was furious. She was convinced Tony was incapable of suicide. And her company could not afford the $2 million loss. She decided to consult her lawyer, Chris Pruitt.

THREE FUNDAMENTAL AREAS OF LAW

This case is a fictionalized version of several real cases based on double indemnity insurance policies. In this chapter we follow Beth's dispute with Coastal from initial interview through appeal, using it to examine three fundamental areas of law: alternative dispute resolution, the structure of our court systems, and civil lawsuits.

When Beth Smiles meets with her lawyer, Chris Pruitt brings a second attorney from his firm, Janet Booker, who is an experienced **litigator,** that is, a lawyer who handles court cases. If they file a lawsuit, Janet will be in charge, so Chris wants her there for the first meeting. Janet probes about Tony's home life, the status of the business, his personal finances, everything. Beth becomes upset that Janet doesn't seem sympathetic, but Chris explains that Janet is doing her job: she needs all the information, good and bad.

LITIGATION VERSUS ALTERNATIVE DISPUTE RESOLUTION

Janet starts thinking about the two methods of dispute resolution: litigation and alternative dispute resolution. **Litigation** refers to lawsuits, the process of filing claims in court, and ultimately going to trial. **Alternative dispute resolution** is any other formal or informal process used to settle disputes without resorting to a trial. It is increasingly popular with corporations and individuals alike because it is generally cheaper and faster than litigation.

Litigation
The process of filing claims in court and ultimately going to trial.

Alternative dispute resolution
Any formal or informal process used to settle disputes without trial.

ALTERNATIVE DISPUTE RESOLUTION

Janet Booker knows that even after expert legal help, vast expense, and years of work, litigation may leave clients unsatisfied. If she can use alternative dispute resolution (ADR) to create a mutually satisfactory solution in a few months, for a fraction of the cost, she is glad to do it. We will look at different types of ADR and analyze their strengths and weaknesses.

NEGOTIATION

In most cases, the parties negotiate, whether personally or through lawyers. Fortunately, the great majority of disputes are resolved this way. Negotiation often begins as soon as a dispute arises and may last a few days or several years.

MEDIATION

Mediation is the fastest growing method of dispute resolution in the United States. Here, a neutral person, called a mediator, attempts to coax the two disputing parties toward a voluntary settlement. (In some cases, there may be two or more mediators, but we will use the singular.) Generally, the two disputants voluntarily enter mediation, although some judges order the parties to try this form of ADR before allowing a case to go to trial.

A mediator does not render a decision in the dispute, but uses a variety of skills to move the parties toward agreement. Often a mediator will shuttle between the antagonists, hearing their arguments, sorting out the serious issues from the less important, prompting the parties and lawyers alike to consider new perspectives, and looking for areas of agreement. Mediators must earn the trust of both parties, listen closely, try to diffuse anger and fear, and build the will to settle. Good mediators do not need a law degree, but they must have a sense of humor and low blood pressure.

Mediation has several major advantages. Because the parties maintain control of the process, the two antagonists can speak freely. They need not fear conceding too much, because no settlement takes effect until both parties sign. All discussions are confidential, further encouraging candid talk. This is particularly helpful in cases involving proprietary information that might be revealed during a trial.

Of all forms of dispute resolution, mediation probably offers the strongest "win–win" potential. Since the goal is voluntary settlement, neither party needs to fear that it will end up the loser. This is in sharp contrast to litigation, where one party is very likely to lose. Removing the fear of defeat often encourages thinking and talking that are more open and realistic than negotiations held in the midst of a lawsuit. Studies show that over 75% of mediated cases do reach a voluntary settlement. Such an agreement is particularly valuable to parties that wish to preserve a long-term relationship. Consider two companies that have done business successfully for 10 years but now are in the midst of a million dollar trade dispute. A lawsuit could last three or more years and destroy any chance of future trade. However, if the parties mediate the disagreement, they might reach an amicable settlement within a month or two and could quickly resume their mutually profitable business.

This form of ADR works for disputes both big and small. Two college roommates who cannot get along may find that a three-hour mediation session restores tranquility in the apartment. On a larger scale, consider the work of former U.S. Senator George Mitchell, who mediated the Anglo-Irish peace agreement, setting Northern Ireland on the path to peace for the first time in three centuries. Like most good mediators, Mitchell was remarkably patient. In an early session, Mitchell permitted the head of one militant party to speak without interruption—for seven straight hours. The diatribe yielded no quick results, but Mitchell believed that after Northern Ireland's tortured history, any nonviolent discussions represented progress.

ARBITRATION

In this form of ADR, the parties agree to bring in a neutral third party, but with a major difference: the arbitrator has the power to impose an award. The arbitrator allows each side equal time to present its case and, after deliberation, issues a binding decision, generally without giving reasons. Unlike mediation, arbitration ensures that there will be a final result, although the parties lose control of the outcome. Arbitration is generally faster and cheaper than litigation.

Parties in arbitration give up many rights that litigants retain, including discovery and class action. *Discovery*, as we see below, allows the two sides in a lawsuit to obtain, before trial, documentary and other evidence from the opponent. Arbitration permits both sides to keep secret many files that would have to be divulged in a court case, potentially depriving the opposing side of valuable evidence. A party may have a stronger case than it realizes, and the absence of discovery may permanently deny it that knowledge. A class action is a suit in which one injured party represents a large group of people who have suffered similar harm. For example, in an employment discrimination case, a large group of employees who claim similar injury might band together to bring the case, giving themselves much greater clout.

Arbitration eliminates this possibility, since injured employees face the employer one at a time. Finally, the fact that an arbitrator may not provide a written, public decision bars other plaintiffs, and society generally, from learning what happened.

Sometimes the parties agree *in advance* to arbitrate any disputes that may arise. For example, a consumer who purchases a computer or hires a real estate agent may sign an agreement requiring arbitration of any disputes; a customer opening an account with a stockbroker or bank—or health plan—may sign a similar form, often without realizing it. The good news is fewer lawsuits; the bad news is you might be the person kept out of court.

Assume that you live in Miami. Using the Internet, you order a $2,000 ThinkLite laptop computer, which arrives in a carton, loaded with six fat instructional manuals and many small leaflets. You read some of the documents and ignore others. For four weeks you struggle to make your computer work, to no avail. Finally, you telephone ThinkLite and demand a refund, but the company refuses. You file suit in your local court, at which time the company points out that buried among the hundreds of pages it mailed you was a *mandatory arbitration form.* This document prohibits you from filing suit against the company and states that if you have any complaint with the company, you must fly to Chicago; pay a $2,000 arbitrator's fee; plead your case before an arbitrator selected by the Laptop Trade Association of America; and, in the event you lose, pay ThinkLite's attorney's fees, which could be several thousand dollars. Is that mandatory arbitration provision valid? It is too early to say with finality, but thus far the courts that have faced such clauses have enforced them.[1]

To return to our hypothetical case, Janet Booker proposes to Coastal Insurance that they use ADR to expedite a decision in their dispute. Coastal rejects the offer. Coastal's lawyer, Rich Stewart, says that suicide is apparent. He does not want a neutral party to split the difference and award $1 million to Enviro-Vision. Janet reports this explanation to Beth, but adds that she does not believe it. She thinks that Coastal wants the case to drag on as long as possible in the hopes that Enviro-Vision will ultimately settle cheap.

It is a long way to go before trial, but Janet has to prepare her case. The first thing she thinks about is where to file the lawsuit.

COURT SYSTEMS

The United States has over 50 *systems* of courts. One nationwide system of *federal* courts serves the entire country. In addition, each *state* has its court system. The state and federal courts are in different buildings, have different judges, and hear different kinds of cases. Each has special powers and certain limitations.

STATE COURTS

The typical state court system forms a pyramid, as Exhibit 3.1 shows. You may use the Internet to learn the exact names and powers of the courts in your state. Go to **http://www.state.[two-letter abbreviation for state].us/**, and click on "agencies," "courts," or a similar link.

---

[1] See, e.g., Hill v. Gateway 2000, 105 F.3d 1147, 1997 U.S. App. LEXIS 1877 (7th Cir. 1997), upholding a similar clause.

State Supreme Court

Appellate Courts

Appeal Courts

General Civil Division

General Criminal Division

Small Claims Division

Juvenile Division

Land Division

Municipal Division

Probate Division

Domestic Relations Division

Trial Courts of General Jurisdiction

Trial Courts of Limited Jurisdiction

Exhibit 3.1   A trial court determines facts, while an appeals court ensures that the lower court correctly applied the law to those facts.

Trial courts

Determine the facts of a particular dispute and apply to those facts the law given by earlier appellate court decisions.

Trial Courts

Almost all cases start in trial courts, which are endlessly portrayed on television and in film. There is one judge and there will often (but not always) be a jury. This is the only court to hear testimony from witnesses and receive evidence. **Trial courts** determine the facts of a particular dispute and apply to those facts the law given by earlier appellate court decisions.

In the Enviro-Vision dispute, the trial court will decide all important facts that are in dispute. Did Tony Caruso die? Did he drown? Assuming he drowned, was his death accidental or suicide? Once the jury has decided the facts, it will apply the law to those facts. If Tony Caruso died accidentally, contract law provides that Beth Smiles is entitled to double indemnity benefits. If the jury decides he killed himself, Beth gets nothing.

Facts are critical. That may sound obvious, but in a course devoted to legal principles, it is easy to lose track of the key role that factual determinations play in the resolution of any dispute. In the Enviro-Vision case, we will see that one bit of factual evidence goes undetected, with costly consequences.

Jurisdiction refers to a court's power to hear a case. In state or federal court, a plaintiff may start a lawsuit only in a court that has jurisdiction over that kind of case. Some courts have very limited jurisdiction, while others have the power to hear almost any case.

Trial Courts of Limited Jurisdiction. These courts may hear only certain types of cases. Small claims court has jurisdiction only over civil lawsuits involving a maximum of, say, $2,500 (the amount varies from state to state). A juvenile court hears only cases involving minors. Probate court is devoted to settling the estates of deceased persons, though in some states it will hear certain other cases as well.

Trial Courts of General Jurisdiction. Trial courts of general jurisdiction, however, can hear a very broad range of cases. The most important court, for our purposes, is the general civil division. This court may hear virtually any civil lawsuit. In one day it might hear a $450 million shareholders' derivative lawsuit, an employment issue involving freedom of religion, and a foreclosure on a mortgage. Most of the cases we study start in this court.[2] If Enviro-Vision's case against Coastal goes to trial in a state court, it will begin in the trial court of general jurisdiction.

Appellate Courts

Appellate courts are quite different from trial courts. Three or more judges hear the case. There are no juries, ever. These courts do not hear witnesses or take new evidence. They hear appeals of cases already tried below. Appeals courts generally accept the facts given to them by trial courts and review the trial record to see if the court made errors of law.

Generally, an appeals court will accept a factual finding unless there was *no evidence at all* to support it. If the jury decides that Tony Caruso committed suicide, the appeals court will normally accept that fact, even though the appeals judges consider the jury's conclusion dubious. On the other hand, if a jury concluded that Tony had been murdered, an appeals court would overturn that finding if neither side had introduced any evidence of murder during the trial.

An appeals court reviews the trial record to make sure that the lower court correctly applied the law to the facts. If the trial court made an **error of law**, the appeals court may require a new trial. Suppose the jury concludes that Tony Caruso committed suicide, but votes to

Sidebar:

Writ: one must acquire a writ to bring a case to court

Jurisdiction
A court's power to hear a case.

Every court has their own/in charge of their own jurisdiction. To hear a particular aspect court cases on i.e. Taxes

Appeals courts
Generally accept the facts given to them by trial courts and review the trial record to see if the court made errors of law.

Error of law
A finding by an appellate court that a law was misapplied or misinterpreted.

---

[2] Note that the actual name of the court will vary from state to state. In many states it is called superior court because it has power superior to the courts of limited jurisdiction. In New York it is called supreme court (anything to confuse the layperson); in some states it is called court of common pleas; in Oregon and other states it is a circuit court. They are all civil trial courts of general jurisdiction. Within this branch, some states are beginning to establish specialized business courts to hear complex commercial disputes. At least one state has created a cybercourt for high-tech cases. Lawyers will argue their cases by teleconference and present evidence via streaming video.

award Enviro-Vision $1 million because it feels sorry for Beth Smiles. That is an error of law: if Tony committed suicide, Beth is entitled to nothing. An appellate court will reverse the decision. Or suppose that the trial judge permitted a friend of Tony's to state that he was certain Tony would never commit suicide. Normally, such opinions are not permissible in trial, and it was a legal error for the judge to allow the jury to hear it.

Court of Appeals.   The party that loses at the trial court may appeal to the intermediate court of appeals. The party filing the appeal is the **appellant.** The party opposing the appeal (because it won at trial) is the **appellee.**

This court allows both sides to submit written arguments on the case, called **briefs.** Each side then appears for oral argument, usually before a panel of three judges. The appellant's lawyer has about 15 minutes to convince the judges that the trial court made serious errors of law, and that the decision should be2 **reversed**, that is, nullified. The appellee's lawyer has the same time to persuade the court that the trial court acted correctly, and that the result should be **affirmed**, that is, permitted to stand.

State Supreme Court.   This is the highest court in the state, and it accepts some appeals from the court of appeals. In most states, there is no absolute right to appeal to the Supreme Court. If the high court regards a legal issue as important, it accepts the case. It then takes briefs and hears oral argument just as the appeals court did. If it considers the matter unimportant, it refuses to hear the case, meaning that the court of appeals' ruling is the final word on the case.[3]

In most states seven judges, often called justices, sit on the Supreme Court. They have the final word on state law.

FEDERAL COURTS

As discussed in Chapter 1, federal courts are established by the United States Constitution, which limits what kinds of cases can be brought in any federal court. See Exhibit 3.2. For our purposes, two kinds of civil lawsuits are permitted in federal court: federal question cases and diversity cases.

Federal Question Cases

A claim based on the United States Constitution, a federal statute, or a federal treaty is called a **federal question** case.[4] Federal courts have jurisdiction over these cases. If the Environmental Protection Agency orders Logging Company not to cut in a particular forest, and Logging Company claims that the agency has wrongly deprived it of its property, that suit is based on a federal statute and is thus a federal question. If Little Retailer sues Mega Retailer, claiming that Mega has established a monopoly, that claim is also based on a statute—the Sherman Antitrust Act—and creates federal question jurisdiction. Enviro-Vision's potential suit merely concerns an insurance contract. The federal district court has no federal question jurisdiction over the case.

Diversity Cases

Even if no federal law is at issue, federal courts have **diversity jurisdiction** when (1) the plaintiff and defendant are citizens of different states *and* (2) the amount in dispute

Appellant
The party filing the appeal.

Appellee
The party opposing the appeal

Briefs
Written arguments on the case.

Reversed
Nullified.

Affirmed
Permitted to stand.

Federal question
A case in which the claim is based on the United States Constitution, a federal statute, or a federal treaty.

Determines if cases go to Federal Courts

Diversity jurisdiction
(1) The plaintiff and defendant are citizens of different states *and* (2) The amount in dispute exceeds $75,000.

---

[3] In some states with smaller populations, there is no intermediate appeals court. All appeals from trial courts go directly to the state supreme court.

[4] 28 U.S.C. §1331 governs federal question jurisdiction and 28 U.S.C. §1332 covers diversity jurisdiction.

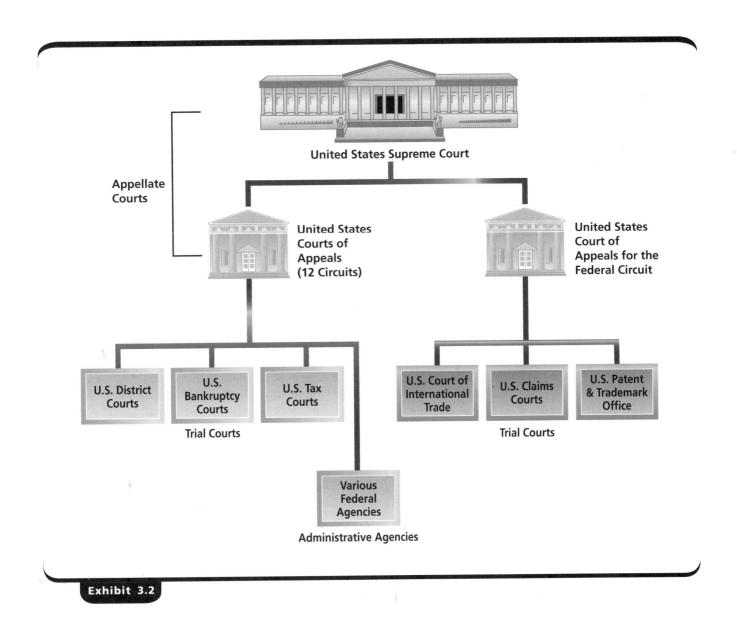

United States Supreme Court

Appellate Courts

United States Courts of Appeals (12 Circuits)

United States Court of Appeals for the Federal Circuit

U.S. District Courts

U.S. Bankruptcy Courts

U.S. Tax Courts

Trial Courts

U.S. Court of International Trade

U.S. Claims Courts

U.S. Patent & Trademark Office

Trial Courts

Various Federal Agencies

Administrative Agencies

Exhibit 3.2

exceeds $75,000. The theory behind diversity jurisdiction is that courts of one state might be biased against citizens of another state. To ensure fairness, the parties have the option of federal court.

Enviro-Vision is located in Oregon and Coastal Insurance is incorporated in Georgia.[5] They are citizens of different states and the amount in dispute far exceeds $75,000. Janet could file this case in United States District Court based on diversity jurisdiction.

[5] For diversity purposes, a corporation is a citizen of the state in which it is incorporated and the state in which it has its principal place of business.

Trial Courts

United States District Court.   This is the primary trial court in the federal system. The nation is divided into about 94 districts, and each has a district court. States with smaller populations have one district. States with larger populations have several districts; Texas is divided geographically into four districts.

Other Trial Courts.   There are other, specialized trial courts in the federal system. Bankruptcy Court, Tax Court, and the United States Court of International Trade all handle name-appropriate cases. The United States Claims Court hears cases brought against the United States, typically on contract disputes. The Foreign Intelligence Surveillance Court is a very specialized, secret court, which oversees requests for surveillance warrants against suspected foreign agents.

Judges.   The president of the United States nominates all federal court judges, from district court to Supreme Court. The nominees must be confirmed by the Senate.

Appellate Courts

United States Courts of Appeals.   These are the intermediate courts of appeals. As the map below shows, they are divided into "circuits," which are geographical areas. There are 11 numbered circuits, hearing appeals from district courts. For example, an appeal from the Northern District of Illinois would go to the Court of Appeals for the Seventh Circuit. You will find an interactive map of the District and Circuit Courts at **http://www.uscourts.gov**.

A twelfth court, the Court of Appeals for the District of Columbia, hears appeals only from the district court of Washington, D.C. This is a particularly powerful court because so many suits about federal statutes begin in the district court for the District of Columbia. Also in Washington is the thirteenth Court of Appeals, known as the Federal Circuit. It hears appeals from specialized trial courts, as shown in Exhibit 3.2.

Within one circuit there are many circuit judges, up to about 50 judges in the largest circuit, the Ninth. When a case is appealed, three judges hear the appeal, taking briefs and hearing oral argument.

United States Supreme Court.   This is the highest court in the country. There are nine justices on the Court. One justice is the chief justice and the other eight are associate justices. When they decide a case, each justice casts an equal vote. The chief justice's special power comes from his authority to assign opinions to a given justice. The justice assigned to write an opinion has an opportunity to control the precise language and thus to influence the voting by other justices. For a face-to-face meeting with Supreme Court justices, past and present, introduce yourself to **http://www.oyez.org**.

Writ of certiorari
A petition asking the Supreme Court to hear a case.

The Supreme Court has the power to hear appeals in any federal case and in certain cases that began in state courts. Generally, it is up to the Court whether or not it will accept a case. A party that wants the Supreme Court to review a lower court ruling must file a petition for a **writ of certiorari**, asking the Court to hear the case. The Court receives about 8,000 of these requests every year but currently accepts fewer than 100. Most cases accepted involve either an important issue of constitutional law or an interpretation of a major federal statute.

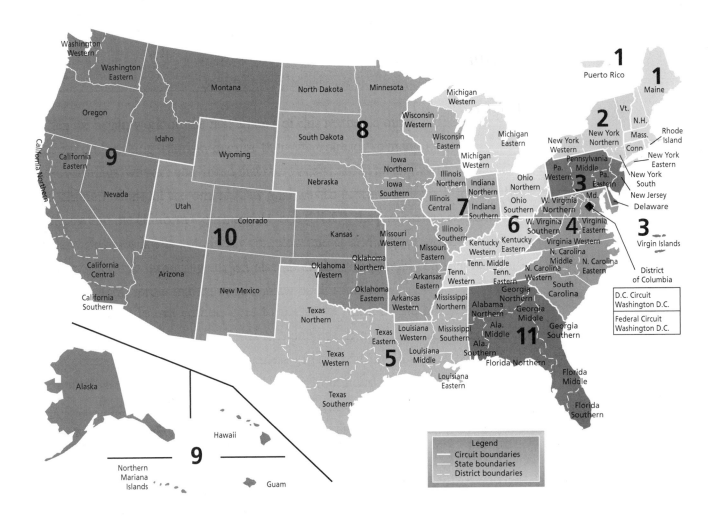

EXAM *Strategy*

Question: Mark has sued his neighbor, Janelle, based on the state common law of negligence. He is testifying in court, explaining how Janelle backed a rented truck out of her driveway and slammed into his Lamborghini, causing $82,000 in damages. Where is this taking place?

    (a) State appeals court.

    (b) United States Court of Appeals.

    (c) State trial court.

    (d) Federal District Court.

    (e) Either state trial court or Federal District Court.

Strategy: The question asks about trial and appellate courts, and also about state versus federal courts. One issue at a time, please. What are the different functions of trial and appellate courts? *Trial* courts use witnesses, and often juries, to resolve factual disputes. *Appellate* courts never hear witnesses and never have juries. Applying that distinction to these facts tells us whether we are in a trial or appeals court.

Next Issue: *State* trial courts may hear lawsuits on virtually any issue. *Federal District Courts* may only hear two kinds of cases: Federal question (those involving a statute or constitutional provision); or diversity (where the parties are from different states *and* the amount at issue is $75,000 or higher). Apply what we know to the facts here.

Result: We are in a trial court because Mark is testifying. Could we be in Federal District Court? No. The suit is based on state common law. This is not a diversity case because the parties live in the same state. We are in a state trial court.

LITIGATION

Janet Booker decides to file the Enviro-Vision suit in the Oregon trial court. She thinks that a state court judge may take the issue more seriously than a federal district court judge.

PLEADINGS

Pleadings

The documents that begin a lawsuit, consisting of the complaint, the answer, and sometimes a reply.

Complaint

A short, plain statement of the facts alleged and the legal claims made.

The documents that begin a lawsuit are called the **pleadings**. These consist of the complaint, the answer, and sometimes a reply.

Complaint

The plaintiff files in court a **complaint**, which is a short, plain statement of the facts she is alleging and the legal claims she is making. The purpose of the complaint is to inform the defendant of the general nature of the claims and the need to come into court and protect his interests.

Janet Booker files the complaint, as shown below. Since Enviro-Vision is a partnership, she files the suit on behalf of Beth, personally.

**STATE OF OREGON
CIRCUIT COURT**

Multnomah County

Civil Action No. _____

Elizabeth Smiles,
Plaintiff

JURY TRIAL DEMANDED

v.

Coastal Insurance Company, Inc.,
Defendant

COMPLAINT

Plaintiff Elizabeth Smiles states that:

1. She is a citizen of Multnomah County, Oregon.
2. Defendant Coastal Insurance Company, Inc., is incorporated under the laws of Georgia and has as its usual place of business 148 Thrift Street, Savannah, Georgia.
3. On or about July 5, 2010, plaintiff Smiles ("Smiles"), Defendant Coastal Insurance Co, Inc. ("Coastal") and Anthony Caruso entered into an insurance contract ("the contract"), a

copy of which is annexed hereto as Exhibit "A." This contract was signed by all parties or their authorized agents, in Multnomah County, Oregon.

4. The contract obligates Coastal to pay to Smiles the sum of two million dollars ($2 million) if Anthony Caruso should die accidentally.
5. On or about January 18, 2012, Anthony Caruso accidentally drowned and died while swimming.
6. Coastal has refused to pay any sum pursuant to the contract.
7. Coastal has knowingly, willingly and unreasonably refused to honor its obligations under the contract.

WHEREFORE, plaintiff Elizabeth Smiles demands judgment against defendant Coastal for all monies due under the contract; demands triple damages for Coastal's knowing, willing, and unreasonable refusal to honor its obligations; and demands all costs and attorney's fees, with interest.

ELIZABETH SMILES,
By her attorney,
[Signed]
Janet Booker
Pruitt, Booker & Bother
983 Joy Avenue
Portland, OR
October 18, 2012

Service

When she files the complaint in court, Janet gets a summons, which is a paper ordering the defendant to answer the complaint within 20 days. A sheriff or constable then *serves* the two papers by delivering them to the defendant. Coastal's headquarters are in Georgia, so the state of Oregon has required Coastal to specify someone as its agent for receipt of service in Oregon.

Answer

Once the complaint and summons are served, Coastal has 20 days in which to file an answer. Coastal's answer, shown below, is a brief reply to each of the allegations in the complaint. The answer tells the court and the plaintiff exactly what issues are in dispute. Since Coastal admits that the parties entered into the contract that Beth claims they did, there is no need for her to prove that in court. The court can focus its attention on the disputed issue: whether Tony Caruso died accidentally.

STATE OF OREGON
CIRCUIT COURT

Multnomah County   Civil Action No. 09-5626

Elizabeth Smiles,
Plaintiff
v.
Coastal Insurance Company, Inc.,
Defendant

ANSWER

Defendant Coastal Insurance Company, Inc., answers the complaint as follows:

1. Admit.
2. Admit.
3. Admit.
4. Admit.
5. Deny.
6. Admit.
7. Deny.

COASTAL INSURANCE COMPANY, INC.,
By its attorney,
[Signed]
Richard B. Stewart
Kiley, Robbins, Stewart & Glote
333 Victory Boulevard
Portland, OR
October 30, 2012

Default judgment

A decision that the plaintiff wins without a trial because the defendant failed to answer in time.

If the defendant fails to answer in time, the plaintiff will ask for a **default judgment**, meaning a decision that the plaintiff wins without a trial.

Counter-Claim

Counter-claim

A second lawsuit by the defendant against the plaintiff.

Sometimes a defendant does more than merely answer a complaint and files a **counter-claim**, meaning a second lawsuit by the defendant against the plaintiff. Suppose that after her complaint was filed in court, Beth had written a letter to the newspaper, calling Coastal a bunch of "thieves and scoundrels who spend their days mired in fraud and larceny." Coastal would not have found that amusing. The company's answer would have included a counter-claim against Beth for libel, claiming that she falsely accused the insurer of serious criminal acts. Coastal would have demanded money damages.

Reply

An answer to a counter-claim.

If Coastal counter-claimed, Beth would have to file a **reply**, which is simply an answer to a counter-claim. Beth's reply would be similar to Coastal's answer, admitting or denying the various allegations.

Class Actions

Class action

One plaintiff represents the entire group of plaintiffs, including those who are unaware of the lawsuit or even unaware they were harmed.

Suppose Janet uncovers evidence that Coastal denies 80 percent of all life insurance claims, calling them suicide. She could ask the court to permit a **class action**. If the court granted her request, she would represent the entire group of plaintiffs, including those who are unaware of the lawsuit or even unaware they were harmed. Class actions can give the plaintiffs much greater leverage, since the defendant's potential liability is vastly increased. In the back of her mind, Janet has thoughts of a class action, *if* she can uncover evidence that Coastal has used a claim of suicide to deny coverage to a large number of claimants.

Notice how potent a class action can be. From his small town in Maine, Ernie decides to get rich quickly. On the Internet he advertises "Energy Breakthrough! Cut your heating costs 15 percent for only $25." One hundred thousand people send him their money. In return, they receive a photocopied graph, illustrating that if you wear two sweaters instead of one, you will feel 15 percent warmer. Ernie has deceitfully earned $2,500,000 in pure profit. What can the angry homeowners do? Under the laws of fraud and consumer protection, they have a legitimate claim to their $25, and perhaps even to treble damages ($75). But few will sue, because the time and effort required would be greater than the money recovered.

Economists analyze such legal issues in terms of *efficiency*. The laws against Ernie's fraud are clear and well intended, but they will not help in this case because it is too expensive for 100,000 people to litigate such a small claim. The effort would be hugely *inefficient*, both for the homeowners and for society generally. The economic reality may permit Ernie to evade the law's grasp.

That is one reason we have class actions. A dozen or so "heating plan" buyers can all hire the same lawyer. This attorney will file court papers in Maine on behalf of *everyone*, nationwide, who has been swindled by Ernie—including the 99,988 people who have yet to be notified that they are part of the case. Now the con artist, instead of facing a few harmless suits for $25, must respond to a multimillion-dollar claim being handled by an experienced lawyer. Treble damages become menacing: three times $25 times 100,000 is no joke, even to a cynic like Ernie. He may also be forced to pay for the plaintiffs' attorney, as well as all costs of notifying class members and disbursing money to them. With one lawyer representing an entire class, the legal system has become fiercely efficient.

Congress recently passed a statute designed to force large, multi-state class actions out of state courts, into federal. Proponents of the new law complained that state courts often gave excessive verdicts, even for frivolous lawsuits. They said the cases hurt businesses while enriching lawyers. Opponents argued that the new law was designed to shield large corporations from paying for the harm they cause by sending the cases into a federal system that is often hostile to such suits.

Judgment on the Pleadings

A party can ask the court for a judgment based simply on the pleadings themselves, by filing a motion to dismiss. A **motion** is a formal request to the court that the court take some step or issue some order. During a lawsuit the parties file many motions. A **motion to dismiss** is a request that the court terminate a case without permitting it to go further. Suppose that a state law requires claims on life insurance contracts to be filed within three years, and Beth files her claim four years after Tony's death. Coastal would move to dismiss based on this late filing. The court might well agree, and Beth would never get into court.

Motion
A formal request to the court to take some step or issue an order.

Discovery

Few cases are dismissed on the pleadings. Most proceed quickly to the next step. **Discovery** is the critical, pre-trial opportunity for both parties to learn the strengths and weaknesses of the opponent's case.

The theory behind civil litigation is that the best outcome is a negotiated settlement and that parties will move toward agreement if they understand the opponent's case. That is likeliest to occur if both sides have an opportunity to examine most of the evidence the other side will bring to trial. Further, if a case does go all the way to trial, efficient and fair litigation cannot take place in a courtroom filled, like a piñata, with surprises. On television dramas,

Discovery
The pre-trial opportunity for both parties to learn the strengths and weaknesses of the opponent's case.

witnesses say astonishing things that amaze the courtroom (and keep viewers hooked through the next commercial). In real trials the lawyers know in advance the answers to practically all questions asked because discovery has allowed them to see the opponent's documents and question its witnesses. The following are the most important forms of discovery.

Interrogatories.   These are written questions that the opposing party must answer, in writing, under oath.

Depositions.   These provide a chance for one party's lawyer to question the other party, or a potential witness, under oath. The person being questioned is the **deponent.** Lawyers for both parties are present. During depositions, and in trial, good lawyers choose words carefully and ask questions calculated to advance their cause. A fine line separates ethical, probing questions from those that are tricky, and a similar line divides answers that are merely unhelpful from perjury.

Deponent
The person being questioned.

Production of Documents and Things.   Each side may ask the other side to produce relevant documents for inspection and copying; to produce physical objects, such as part of a car alleged to be defective; and for permission to enter on land to make an inspection, for example, at the scene of an accident.

Physical and Mental Examination.   A party may ask the court to order an examination of the other party, if his physical or mental condition is relevant, for example, in a case of medical malpractice.

Janet Booker begins her discovery with interrogatories. Her goal is to learn Coastal's basic position and factual evidence and then follow up with more detailed questioning during depositions. Her interrogatories ask for every fact Coastal relied on in denying the claim. She asks for the names of all witnesses, the identity of all documents, including electronic records, the description of all things or objects that they considered. She requests the names of all corporate officers who played any role in the decision and of any expert witnesses Coastal plans to call. Interrogatory No. 18 demands extensive information on all *other* claims in the past three years that Coastal has denied based on alleged suicide. Janet is looking for evidence that would support a class action.

Beth remarks on how thorough the interrogatories are. "This will tell us what their case is." Janet frowns and looks less optimistic: she's done this before.

Coastal has 30 days to answer Janet's interrogatories. Before it responds, Coastal mails to Janet a notice of deposition, stating its intention to depose Beth Smiles. Beth and Janet will go to the office of Coastal's lawyer, and Beth will answer questions under oath. But at the same time Coastal sends this notice, it sends 25 *other notices of deposition.* The company will depose Karen Caruso as soon as Beth's deposition is over. Coastal also plans to depose all seven employees of Enviro-Vision; three neighbors who lived near Tony and Karen's beach house; two policemen who participated in the search; the doctor and two nurses involved in the case; Tony's physician; Jerry Johnson, Tony's tennis partner; Craig Bergson, a college roommate; a couple who had dinner with Tony and Karen a week before his death; and several other people.

But there may be another reason that Coastal is doing this: the company wants to make this litigation hurt.

Beth is appalled. Janet explains that some of these people might have relevant information. But there may be another reason that Coastal is doing this: the company wants to make this litigation hurt. Janet will have to attend every one of these depositions. Costs will skyrocket.

Janet files a **motion for a protective order**. This is a request that the court limit Coastal's discovery by decreasing the number of depositions. Janet also calls Rich Stewart and suggests that they discuss what depositions are really necessary. Rich insists that all of the depositions are important. This is a $2 million case and Coastal is entitled to protect itself. As both lawyers know, **the parties are entitled to discover anything that could reasonably lead to valid evidence**.

Before Beth's deposition date arrives, Rich sends Coastal's answers to Enviro-Vision's interrogatories. The answers contain no useful information whatsoever. For example, Interrogatory No. 10 asked, "If you claim that Anthony Caruso committed suicide, describe every fact upon which you rely in reaching that conclusion." Coastal's answer simply says, "His state of mind, his poor business affairs, and the circumstances of his death all indicate suicide."

Janet calls Rich and complains that the interrogatory answers are a bad joke. Rich disagrees, saying that it is the best information they have so early in the case. After they debate it for 20 minutes, Rich offers to settle the case for $100,000. Janet refuses and makes no counteroffer.

Janet files a **motion to compel answers to interrogatories,** in other words, a formal request that the court order Coastal to supply more complete answers. Janet submits a **memorandum** with the motion, which is a supporting argument. Although it is only a few pages long, the memorandum takes several hours of online research and writing to prepare—more costs. Janet also informs Rich Stewart that Beth will not appear for the deposition, since Coastal's interrogatory answers are inadequate.

Rich now files *his* motion to compel, asking the court to order Beth Smiles to appear for her deposition. The court hears all of the motions together. Janet argues that Coastal's interrogatory answers are hopelessly uninformative and defeat the whole purpose of discovery. She claims that Coastal's large number of depositions creates a huge and unfair expense for a small firm.

Rich claims that the interrogatory answers are the best that Coastal can do thus far and that Coastal will supplement the answers when more information becomes available. He argues against Interrogatory No. 18, the one in which Janet asked for the names of other policyholders whom Coastal considered suicides. He claims that Janet is engaging in a fishing expedition that would violate the privacy of Coastal's insurance customers and provide no information relevant to this case. He demands that Janet make Beth available for a deposition.

These discovery rulings are critical because they will color the entire lawsuit. A trial judge has to make many discovery decisions before a case reaches trial. At times the judge must weigh the need of one party to see documents against the other side's need for privacy. One device a judge can use in reaching a discovery ruling is an **in camera inspection**, meaning that the judge views the requested documents alone, with no lawyers present, and decides whether the other side is entitled to view them.

E-Discovery.   The biggest change in litigation in the last decade is the explosive rise of electronic discovery. Companies send hundreds, or thousands, or millions of e-mails—every day. Many of the e-mails have attachments, sometimes hundreds of pages long. In addition, businesses large and small have vast amounts of data stored electronically. All of this information is potentially subject to discovery.

It is enormously time-consuming and expensive for companies to locate all of the relevant material, separate it from irrelevant or confidential matter, and furnish it. A firm may be obligated to furnish *millions* of e-mails to the opposing party. In one recent case, a defendant

Motion for a protective order

A request that the court limit discovery.

had to pay 31 lawyers full time, for six months, just to wade through the e-ocean of documents and figure out which had to be supplied and how to produce it. Not surprisingly, this data eruption has created a new industry: hi-tech companies that assist law firms in finding, sorting, and delivering electronic data.

Who is to say what must be supplied? What if an e-mail string contains individual e-mails that are clearly privileged (meaning a party need not divulge them), but others that are not privileged? May a company refuse to furnish the entire string? Many will try. However, some courts have ruled that companies seeking to protect e-mail strings must create a log describing every individual e-mail, and allow the court to determine which are privileged.[6]

When the cost of furnishing the data becomes burdensome, who should pay, the party seeking the information or the one supplying it? In a recent $4 million corporate lawsuit, the defendant turned over 3,000 e-mails and 211,000 other documents. But the trial judge noted that many of the e-mail attachments—sometimes 12 to an e-mail—had gone missing, and required the company to produce them. The defendant protested that finding the attachments would cost an additional $206,000. The judge ordered the company to do it, and bear the full cost.

The following case illustrates a common discovery problem: refusal by one side to appear for deposition. Did the defendant cynically believe that long delay would win the day, given that the plaintiff was 78 years old? What can a court do in such a case?

STINTON V. ROBIN'S WOOD, INC.

45 A.D.3d 203, 842 NYS2d 477
NEW YORK APP. DIV., 2007

CASE SUMMARY

Facts: Ethel Flanzraich, 78 years old, slipped and fell on the steps of property owned by Robin's Wood. She broke her left leg and left arm. Flanzraich sued, claiming that Robin's Wood caused her fall because its employee, Anthony Monforte, had negligently painted the stairs. In its answer to the complaint, Robin's Wood denied all of the significant allegations.

During a preliminary conference with the trial judge, the parties agreed to hold depositions of both parties on August 4. Flanzraich appeared for deposition but Robin's Wood did not furnish its employee, Monforte, nor did it offer any other company representative. The court then ordered the deposition of the defendant to take place the following April 2. Again, Robin's Wood produced neither Monforte nor anyone else. On July 16, the court ordered the defendant to produce its representative within 30 days. Once more, no one showed up for deposition.

On August 18—over *one year* after the original deposition date—Flanzraich moved to strike the defendant's answer, meaning that the plaintiff would win by default. The company argued that it had made diligent efforts to locate Monforte and force him to appear. However, all of the letters sent to Monforte were addressed care of Robin's Wood. Finally, the company stated that it no longer employed Monforte.

The trial judge granted the motion to strike the answer. That meant that Robin's Wood was liable for Flanraich's fall. The only remaining issue was damages. The court determined that Robin's Wood owed $22,631 for medical expenses, $150,000 for past pain and suffering, and $300,000 for future pain and suffering. One day later, Flanraich died, of other causes. Robin's Wood appealed.

Issue: *Did the trial court abuse its discretion by striking the defendant's answer?*

---

[6] *Universal Service Fund Telephone Billing Practices Litigation*, 232 F.R.D. 669 (D. Kan. 2005).

Decision: No, the trial court did not abuse its discretion. Affirmed.

Reasoning: Normally, a lawsuit must be decided on the evidence and reasonable conclusions. However, if a defendant fails to respond to discovery requests, and its failure is willful, extreme, and disrespectful of the court, a trial judge may strike the defendant's answer altogether.

Robin's Wood failed to comply with three orders to appear for deposition. The company never produced Monforte while he worked there. It failed to notify the plaintiff when Monforte left, and it made no effort to produce another employee for deposition. The company did everything it could to ensure that Flanzraich would never speak with its worker. Had the company at least produced another representative, Flanzraich could have learned where Monforte had gone, because the record indicates Robin's Wood knew his whereabouts.

These delays were particularly menacing to Flanzraich's case because she was elderly—a fact well known to the company. A trial judge may respond to such offensive conduct with appropriate orders.

In the Enviro-Vision case, the judge rules that Coastal must furnish more complete answers to the interrogatories, especially as to why the company denied the claim. However, he rules against Interrogatory No. 18, the one concerning other claims Coastal has denied. This simple ruling kills Janet's hope of making a class action of the case. He orders Beth to appear for the deposition. As to future depositions, Coastal may take any 10 but then may take additional depositions only by demonstrating to the court that the deponents have useful information.

Rich proceeds to take Beth's deposition. It takes two full days. He asks about Enviro-Vision's past and present. He learns that Tony appeared to have won their biggest contract ever from Rapid City, Oregon, but that he then lost it when he had a fight with Rapid City's mayor. He inquires into Tony's mood, learns that he was depressed, and probes in every direction he can to find evidence of suicidal motivation. Janet and Rich argue frequently over questions and whether Beth should have to answer them. At times Janet is persuaded and permits Beth to answer; other times she instructs Beth not to answer. For example, toward the end of the second day, Rich asks Beth whether she and Tony had been sexually involved. Janet instructs Beth not to answer. This fight necessitates another trip into court to determine whether Beth must answer. The judge rules that Beth must discuss Tony's romantic life only if Coastal has some evidence that he was involved with someone outside his marriage. The company lacks any such evidence.

Crucial Clue. Now limited to 10 depositions, Rich selects his nine other deponents carefully. For example, he decides to depose only one of the two nurses; he chooses to question Jerry Johnson, the tennis partner, but not Craig Bergson, the former roommate; and so forth. When we look at the many legal issues this case raises, his choices seem minor. In fact, unbeknownst to Rich or anyone else, his choices may determine the outcome of the case. As we will see later, Craig Bergson has evidence that is possibly crucial to the lawsuit. If Rich decides not to depose him, neither side will ever learn the evidence and the jury will never hear it. A jury can only decide a case based on the evidence presented to it. *Facts are elusive and often controlling.*

In each deposition, Rich carefully probes with his questions, sometimes trying to learn what he actually does not know, sometimes trying to pin down the witness to a specific version of facts so that Rich knows how the witness will testify at trial. Neighbors at the beach testify that Tony seemed tense; one testifies about seeing Tony, unhappy, on the beach with his dog. Another testifies he had never before seen Blue tied up on the beach. Karen Caruso admits that Tony had been somewhat tense and unhappy the last couple of months. She reluctantly discusses their marriage, admitting there were problems.

Other Discovery. Rich sends Requests to Produce Documents, seeking medical records about Tony. Once again, the parties fight over which records are relevant, but Rich gets most of what he wants.

Plaintiffs Discovery. Janet does less discovery than Rich because most of the witnesses she will call are friendly witnesses. She can interview them privately without giving any information to Coastal. With the help of Beth and Karen, Janet builds her case just as carefully as Rich, choosing the witnesses who will bolster the view that Tony was in good spirits and died accidentally.

She deposes all of the officers of Coastal who participated in the decision to deny insurance coverage. She is particularly aggressive in pinning them down as to the limited information they had when they denied Beth's claim.

Summary Judgment

Summary judgment

A ruling by the court that no trial is necessary because some essential facts are not in dispute.

When discovery is completed, both sides may consider seeking summary judgment. **Summary judgment** is a ruling by the court that no trial is necessary because some essential facts are not in dispute. The purpose of a trial is to determine the facts of the case, that is, to decide who did what to whom, why, when, and with what consequences. If there are no relevant facts in dispute, then there is no need for a trial.

Suppose Joe sues EZBuck Films, claiming that the company's new movie, *Lover Boy*, violates the copyright of a screenplay that he wrote, called *Love Man*. Discovery establishes that the two stories are suspiciously similar. But EZBuck's lawyer also learns that Joe sold the copyright for *Love Man* to HotShot Pix. EZBuck may or may not have violated a copyright, but there is no need for a trial because Joe *cannot win* even if there is a copyright violation. He does not own the copyright. The court will grant summary judgment for EZBuck.

In the following case, the defendant won summary judgment, meaning that the case never went to trial. And yet, this was only the beginning of trouble for that defendant, William Jefferson Clinton.

JONES V. CLINTON

990 F.SUPP. 657, 1998 U.S. DIST. LEXIS 3902
UNITED STATES DISTRICT COURT FOR THE EASTERN DISTRICT OF ARKANSAS, 1998

CASE SUMMARY

Facts: In 1991, Bill Clinton was governor of Arkansas. Paula Jones worked for a state agency, the Arkansas Industrial Development Commission (AIDC). When Clinton became president, Jones sued him, claiming that he had sexually harassed her. She alleged that, in May 1991, the governor arranged for her to meet him in a hotel room in Little Rock, Arkansas. When they were alone, he put his hand on her leg and slid it toward her pelvis. She escaped from his grasp, exclaimed, "What are you doing?" and said she was "not that kind of girl." She was upset and confused, and sat on a sofa near the door. She claimed that Clinton approached her, "lowered his trousers and underwear, exposed his penis and told her to kiss it." Jones was horrified, jumped up and said she had to leave. Clinton responded by saying, "Well, I don't want to make you do anything you don't want to do," and pulled his pants up. He added that if she got in trouble for leaving work, Jones should "have Dave call me immediately

and I'll take care of it." He also said, "You are smart. Let's keep this between ourselves." Jones remained at AIDC until February 1993, when she moved to California because of her husband's job transfer.

President Clinton denied all of the allegations. He also filed for summary judgment, claiming that Jones had not alleged facts that justified a trial. Jones opposed the motion for summary judgment.

Issue: *Was Clinton entitled to summary judgment or was Jones entitled to a trial?*

Decision: Jones did not make a claim of sexual harassment. Summary judgment granted for the president.

Reasoning: To establish this type of sexual harassment case, a plaintiff must show that her refusal to submit to unwelcome sexual advances resulted in specific harm to her job.

Jones received every merit increase and cost-of-living allowance for which she was eligible. Her only job transfer involved a minor change in working conditions, with no reduction in pay or benefits. Jones claims that she was obligated to sit in a less private area, often with no work to do, and was the only female employee not to receive flowers on Secretary's Day. However, even if these allegations were true, all were trivial and none was sufficient to create a sexual harassment suit. Jones demonstrated no specific harm to her job.

In other words, the court acknowledged that there were factual disputes but concluded that even if Jones proved each of her allegations, she would *still* lose the case because her allegations fell short of a legitimate case of sexual harassment. Jones appealed the case. Later the same year, as the appeal was pending and the House of Representatives was considering whether to impeach President Clinton, the parties settled the dispute. Clinton, without acknowledging any of the allegations, agreed to pay Jones $850,000 to drop the suit.

Janet and Rich each consider moving for summary judgment, but both correctly decide that they would lose. There is one major fact in dispute: Did Tony Caruso commit suicide? Only a jury may decide that issue. So long as there is *some evidence* supporting each side of a key factual dispute, the court may not grant summary judgment.

EXAM *Strategy*

Question: You are a judge. Mel has sued Kevin, claiming that while Kevin was drunk, he negligently drove his car down Mel's street, and destroyed rare trees on a lot that Mel owns, next to his house. Mel's complaint stated that three witnesses, at a bar, saw Kevin take at least eight drinks less than an hour before the damage was done. In Kevin's answer, he denied causing the damage and denied being in the bar that night.

Kevin's lawyer has moved for summary judgment. He proves that three weeks before the alleged accident, Mel sold the lot to Tatiana.

Mel's lawyer opposes summary judgment. He produces a security camera tape proving that Kevin was in the bar, drinking beer, 34 minutes before the damage was done. He produces a signed statement from Sandy, a landscape gardener who lives across the street from the scene. Sandy states that she heard a crash, hurried to the windows, and saw Kevin's car weaving away from the damaged trees. She is a landscape gardener and estimates the tree damage at $30,000–40,000. How should you rule on the motion?

Strategy: Do not be fooled by red herrings about Kevin's drinking or the value of the trees. Stick to the question: Should you grant summary judgment? Trials are necessary to resolve disputes about essential factual issues. Summary judgment is appropriate when there are no essential facts in dispute. Is there an essential fact not in dispute? Find it. Apply the rule. Being a judge is easy!

Result: It makes no difference whether Kevin was drunk or sober, whether he caused the harm or was at home in bed. Because Mel does not own the property, he cannot recover for the damage to it. He cannot win. You should grant Kevin's summary judgment motion.

Final Preparation

Well over 90 percent of all lawsuits are settled before trial. But the parties in the Enviro-Vision dispute are unable to compromise, so each side gears up for trial. The attorneys make lists of all witnesses they will call. They then prepare each witness very carefully, rehearsing the questions they will ask. It is considered ethical and proper to rehearse the questions, provided the answers are honest and come from the witness. It is unethical and illegal for a lawyer to tell a witness what to say. The lawyers also have colleagues cross-examine each witness, so that the witnesses are ready for the questions the other side's lawyer will ask.

This preparation takes hours and hours, for many days. Beth is frustrated that she cannot do the work she needs to for Enviro-Vision because she is spending so much time preparing the case. Other employees have to prepare as well, especially for cross-examination by Rich Stewart, and it is a terrible drain on the small firm. More than a year after Janet filed her complaint, they are ready to begin trial.

TRIAL

ADVERSARY SYSTEM

Our system of justice assumes that the best way to bring out the truth is for the two contesting sides to present the strongest case possible to a neutral fact finder. Each side presents its witnesses and then the opponent has a chance to cross-examine. The adversary system presumes that by putting a witness on the stand and letting both lawyers "go at" her, the truth will emerge.

The judge runs the trial. Each lawyer sits at a large table near the front. Beth, looking tense and unhappy, sits with Janet. Rich Stewart sits with a Coastal executive. In the back of the courtroom are benches for the public. On one bench sits Craig Bergson. He will watch the entire proceeding with intense interest and a strange feeling of unease. He is convinced he knows what really happened.

Janet has demanded a jury trial for Beth's case, and Judge Rowland announces that they will now impanel the jury.

RIGHT TO JURY TRIAL

Not all cases are tried to a jury. As a general rule, both plaintiff and defendant have a right to demand a jury trial when the lawsuit is one for money damages. For example, in a typical contract lawsuit, such as Beth's insurance claim, both plaintiff and defendant have a jury trial right whether they are in state or federal court. Even in such a case, though, the parties may *waive* the jury right, meaning they agree to try the case to a judge.

If the plaintiff is seeking an equitable remedy, such as an injunction, there is no jury right for either party. Equitable rights come from the old Court of Chancery in England, where there was never a jury. Even today, only a judge may give an equitable remedy.

VOIR DIRE

Voir dire
The process of selecting a jury.

The process of selecting a jury is called **voir dire**, which means "to speak the truth."[7] The court's goal is to select an impartial jury; the lawyers will each try to get a jury as favorable to their side as possible.

---

[7] Students of French note that *voir* means "to see" and assume that *voir dire* should translate, "to see, to speak." However, the legal term is centuries old and derives not from modern French but from Old French, in which *voir* meant "truth."

Potential jurors are questioned individually, sometimes by the judge and sometimes by the two lawyers, as each side tries to ferret out potential bias. Each lawyer may make any number of **challenges for cause**, claiming that a juror has demonstrated probable bias. For example, if a prospective juror in the Enviro-Vision case works for an insurance company, the judge will excuse her on the assumption that she would be biased in favor of Coastal. If the judge perceives no bias, the lawyer may still make a limited number of **peremptory challenges**, entitling him to excuse that juror for virtually any reason, which need not be stated in court. For example, if Rich Stewart believes that a juror seems hostile to him personally, he will use a peremptory challenge to excuse that juror, even if the judge sensed no animosity. The process continues until 14 jurors are seated. Twelve will comprise the jury; the other two are alternates who hear the case and remain available in the event one of the impaneled jurors is taken ill. In the next case, notice how determined the court is to ensure a fair jury.

Challenges for cause
A claim that a juror has demonstrated probable bias.

Peremptory challenges
The right to excuse a juror for virtually any reason.

PEREDA V. PARAJON

957 So.2d 1194
FLORIDA COURT OF APPEALS, 2007

CASE SUMMARY

Facts: Maria Parajon sued Diana Pereda for injuring her in a car accident. During *voir dire*, Parajon's lawyer asked the panel of prospective jurors these questions: "Is there anybody sitting on this panel now that has ever been under the care of a physician for personal injuries, whether you had a lawsuit or not? In other words, you may not have had any sort of lawsuit, but you slipped and fell—you had any accidents?"

Several of the prospective jurors raised their hands, allowing the lawyers to question more deeply into possible bias. However, Lisa Berg, a prospective juror who happened to be a lawyer, did not respond. Berg and others were seated as jurors, and ultimately awarded Parajon $450,000 for medical damages and pain and suffering.

After the trial, questioned in court by the judge, Berg admitted that three years earlier she had been injured in a car accident, hired a lawyer to sue, and settled out of court for $4,000. Asked about the settlement, Berg replied, "I think everyone always wants more money."

Parajon moved for a new trial but the judge denied the motion. Parajon appealed.

Issue: *Is Parajon entitled to a new trial based on Berg's failure to disclose her own personal injury lawsuit?*

Decision: Yes, Parajon is entitled to a new trial. Reversed and remanded for a new trial.

Reasoning: When a juror does not accurately answer questions during voir dire, a new trial is called for if the following three criteria are met:

First, the information is relevant and material to the case. Second, the juror concealed it. Third, the lawyers made a diligent effort to seek the information.

Berg's own car accident was relevant and material because it might have influenced her opinion in the case. As a lawyer herself, Berg knew that the question applied to her, and she deliberately chose not to answer it. The fact that other prospective jurors answered the question indicated that Parajon's lawyers made a diligent and reasonable attempt to get the information.

Although jury selection for a case can sometimes take many days, in the Enviro-Vision case the first day of the hearing ends with the jury selected. In the hallway outside the court, Rich offers Janet $200,000 to settle. Janet reports the offer to Beth and they agree to reject it. Craig Bergson drives home, emotionally confused. Only three weeks before his death, Tony had accidentally met his old roommate and they had had several drinks. Craig believes that what Tony told him answers the riddle of this case.

OPENING STATEMENTS

The next day, each attorney makes an opening statement to the jury, summarizing the proof he or she expects to offer, with the plaintiff going first. Janet focuses on Tony's successful life, his business and strong marriage, and the tragedy of his accidental death.[8]

Rich works hard to establish a friendly rapport with the jury. He expresses regret about the death. Nonetheless, suicide is a clear exclusion from the policy. If insurance companies are forced to pay claims never bargained for, everyone's insurance rates will go up.

BURDEN OF PROOF

In civil cases, the plaintiff has the burden of proof. That means that the plaintiff must convince the jury that its version of the case is correct; the defendant is not obligated to disprove the allegations.

The plaintiff's burden in a civil lawsuit is to prove its case by a **preponderance of the evidence**. It must convince the jury that its version of the facts is at least *slightly more likely* than the defendant's version. Some courts describe this as a "51–49" persuasion, that is, that plaintiff's proof must "just tip" credibility in its favor. By contrast, in a criminal case, the prosecution must demonstrate **beyond a reasonable doubt** that the defendant is guilty. The burden of proof in a criminal case is much tougher because the likely consequences are, too. See Exhibit 3.3.

PLAINTIFF'S CASE

Because the plaintiff has the burden of proof, Janet puts in her case first. She wants to prove two things. First, that Tony died. That is easy because the death certificate clearly demonstrates it and Coastal does not seriously contest it. Second, in order to win double indemnity damages, she must show that the death was accidental. She will do this with

Preponderance of the evidence

The plaintiff's burden of proof in a civil lawsuit.

Beyond a reasonable doubt

The government's burden of proof in a criminal prosecution.

Exhibit 3.3   *Burden of Proof.* In a civil lawsuit, a plaintiff wins with a mere preponderance of the evidence. But the prosecution must persuade a jury beyond a reasonable doubt in order to win a criminal conviction.

---

[8] Janet Booker has dropped her claim for triple damages against Coastal. To have any hope of such a verdict, she would have to show that Coastal had no legitimate reason at all for denying the claim. Discovery has convinced her that Coastal will demonstrate some rational reasons for what it did.

the testimony of the witnesses she calls, one after the other. Her first witness is Beth. When a lawyer asks questions of her own witness, it is **direct examination.** Janet brings out all the evidence she wants the jury to hear: that the business was basically sound, though temporarily troubled, that Tony was a hard worker, why the company took out life insurance policies, and so forth.

Then Rich has a chance to **cross-examine Beth**, which means to ask questions of an opposing witness. He will try to create doubt in the jury's mind. He asks Beth only questions for which he is certain of the answers, based on discovery. Rich gets Beth to admit that the firm was not doing well the year of Tony's death; that Tony had lost the best client the firm ever had; that Beth had reduced salaries; and that Tony had been depressed about business.

Rules of Evidence

The lawyers are not free simply to ask any question they want. The **law of evidence** determines what questions a lawyer may ask and how the questions are to be phrased, what answers a witness may give, and what documents may be introduced. The goal is to get the best evidence possible before the jurors so they can decide what really happened. In general, witnesses may only testify about things they saw or heard.

These rules are complex, and a thorough explication of them is beyond the scope of this chapter; however, they can be just as important in resolving a dispute as the underlying substantive law. Suppose a plaintiff's case depends upon the jury hearing about a certain conversation, but the rules of evidence prevent the lawyer from asking about it. That conversation might just as well never have occurred.

Janet calls an expert witness, a marine geologist, who testifies about the tides and currents in the area where Tony's body was found. The expert testifies that even experienced swimmers can be overwhelmed by a sudden shift in currents. Rich objects strenuously that this is irrelevant, because there is no testimony that there was such a current at the time of Tony's death. The judge permits the testimony.

Karen Caruso testifies that Tony was in "reasonably good" spirits the day of his death, and that he often took Blue for walks along the beach. Karen testifies that Blue was part Newfoundland. Rich objects that testimony about Blue's pedigree is irrelevant, but Janet insists it will show why Blue was tied up. The judge allows the testimony. Karen says that whenever Blue saw them swim he would instinctively go into the water and pull them to shore. Does that explain why Blue was tied up? Only the jury can answer.

Cross-examination is grim for Karen. Rich slowly but methodically questions her about Tony's state of mind and brings out the problems with the company, his depression, and tension within the marriage. Janet's other witnesses testify essentially as they did during their depositions.

Motion for Directed Verdict

At the close of the plaintiff's case, Rich moves for a **directed verdict,** that is, a ruling that the plaintiff has entirely failed to prove some aspect of her case. Rich is seeking to win without even putting in his own case. He argues that it was Beth's burden to prove that Tony died accidentally and that she has entirely failed to do that.

A directed verdict is permissible only if the evidence so clearly favors the defendant that reasonable minds could not disagree on it. If reasonable minds could disagree, the motion must be denied. Here, Judge Rowland rules that the plaintiff has put in enough evidence of accidental death that a reasonable person could find in Beth's favor. The motion is denied.

Direct examination
When a lawyer asks questions of her own witness.

Cross-examine
To ask questions of an opposing witness.

Directed verdict
A ruling that the plaintiff has entirely failed to meet his burden of proof.

DEFENDANT'S CASE

Rich now puts in his case, exactly as Janet did, except that he happens to have fewer witnesses. He calls the examining doctor, who admits that Tony could have committed suicide by swimming out too far. On cross-examination, Janet gets the doctor to acknowledge that he has no idea whether Tony intentionally drowned. Rich also questions several neighbors as to how depressed Tony had seemed and how unusual it was that Blue was tied up. Some of the witnesses Rich deposed, such as the tennis partner Jerry Johnson, have nothing that will help Coastal's case, so he does not call them.

Craig Bergson, sitting in the back of the courtroom, thinks how different the trial would have been had he been called as a witness. When he and Tony had the fateful drink, Tony had been distraught: business was terrible, he was involved in an extramarital affair that he could not end, and he saw no way out of his problems. He had no one to talk to and had been hugely relieved to speak with Craig. Several times Tony had said, "I just can't go on like this. I don't want to, anymore." Craig thought Tony seemed suicidal and urged him to see a therapist Craig knew and trusted. Tony had said that it was good advice, but Craig is unsure whether Tony sought any help.

This evidence would have affected the case. Had Rich Stewart known of the conversation, he would have deposed Craig and the therapist. Coastal's case would have been far stronger, perhaps overwhelming. But Craig's evidence will never be heard. Facts are critical. Rich's decision to depose other witnesses and omit Craig may influence the verdict more than any rule of law.

CLOSING ARGUMENT

Both lawyers sum up their case to the jury, explaining how they hope the jury will interpret what they have heard. Janet summarizes the plaintiff's version of the facts, claiming that Blue was tied up so that Tony could swim without worrying about him. Rich claims that business and personal pressures had overwhelmed Tony. He tied up his dog, neatly folded his clothes, and took his own life.

JURY INSTRUCTIONS

Judge Rowland instructs the jury as to its duty. He tells them that they are to evaluate the case based only on the evidence they heard at trial, relying on their own experience and common sense.

He explains the law and the burden of proof, telling the jury that it is Beth's obligation to prove that Tony died. If Beth has proven that Tony died, she is entitled to $1 million; if she has proven that his death was accidental, she is entitled to $2 million. However, if Coastal has proven suicide, Beth receives nothing. Finally, he states that if they are unable to decide between accidental death and suicide, there is a legal presumption that it was accidental. Rich asks Judge Rowland to rephrase the "legal presumption" part but the judge declines.

VERDICT

The jury deliberates informally, with all jurors entitled to voice their opinion. Some deliberations take two hours; some take two weeks. Many states require a unanimous verdict; others require only, for example, a 10–2 vote in civil cases.

This case presents a close call. No one saw Tony die. Yet even though they cannot know with certainty, the jury's decision will probably be the final word on whether he took his own life. After a day and a half of deliberating, the jury notifies the judge that it has reached a verdict. Rich Stewart quickly makes a new offer: $350,000. Beth hesitates but turns it down.

The judge summons the lawyers to court, and Beth goes as well. The judge asks the foreman if the jury has reached a decision. He states that it has: the jury finds that Tony Caruso drowned accidentally, and awards Beth Smiles $2 million.

MOTIONS AFTER THE VERDICT

Rich immediately moves for a **judgment** *non obstante veredicto* (JNOV), meaning a judgment notwithstanding the jury's verdict. He is asking the judge to overturn the jury's verdict. Rich argues that the jury's decision went against all of the evidence. He also claims that the judge's instructions were wrong and misled the jury.

Judge Rowland denies the JNOV. Rich immediately moves for a new trial, making the same claim, and the judge denies the motion. Beth is elated that the case is finally over—until Janet says she expects an appeal. Craig Bergson, leaving the courtroom, wonders if he did the right thing. He felt sympathy for Beth and none for Coastal. Yet now he is neither happy nor proud.

judgment *non obstante veredicto*
A judgment notwithstanding the jury's verdict.

APPEALS

Two days later, Rich files an appeal to the court of appeals. The same day, he phones Janet and increases his settlement offer to $425,000. Beth is tempted but wants Janet's advice. Janet says the risks of an appeal are that the court will order a new trial, and they would start all over. But to accept this offer is to forfeit over $1.5 million. Beth is unsure what to do. The firm desperately needs cash now. Janet suggests they wait until oral argument, another eight months.

Rich files a brief arguing that there were two basic errors at the trial: first, that the jury's verdict is clearly contrary to the evidence; and second, that the judge gave the wrong instructions to the jury. Janet files a reply brief, opposing Rich on both issues. In her brief, Janet cites many cases that she claims are **precedent**: earlier decisions by the state appellate courts on similar or identical issues. Although the following case is from a different jurisdiction, it is an example of the kind of case that she will rely on.

Precedent
Earlier decisions by the state appellate courts on similar issues.

HERNANDEZ V. MONTVILLE TOWNSHIP BOARD OF EDUCATION
354 N.J. SUPER. 467, 808 A.2d 128
SUPERIOR COURT OF NEW JERSEY, APPELLATE DIVISION, 2002

CASE SUMMARY

Facts: Victor Hernandez had worked for more than 20 years as a custodian at a public power plant. He had received training in health and safety rules from the Occupational Safety and Health Administration (OSHA).

Hernandez took a second job as night custodian at an elementary school. Shortly after he started work, the school board fired him for alleged poor job performance. Hernandez filed suit, claiming that the real reason for his termination was that he had repeatedly notified his superiors of health and safety violations in the schools, including missing bulbs in emergency exit lights and toilets that backed up for long periods, spilling foul matter on the floor. He argued that his termination violated the state's Conscientious Employee Protection Act (CEPA), which is designed to protect whistleblowers who report violations of health laws.

The jury awarded Hernandez $44,000 for lost wages and $150,000 for emotional distress. The jury had not been permitted to hear his claim for punitive damages (those designed to punish a defendant for exceptionally bad conduct). The trial judge then granted a judgment notwithstanding the verdict (JNOV) to the school board, meaning that Hernandez won nothing. The trial judge stated:

"Talk about trivial. By the time the jury went out, I should have concluded that the plaintiff simply had not made out a case, under the CEPA law, because he never disclosed or threatened to disclose to his supervisor an activity, policy, practice of an employer that the employee reasonably believed was in violation of law or a rule. There simply was none. But in addition to that, there isn't any other evidence adduced by anyone in the case that these things that he's complaining about ever occurred. I didn't believe anything [plaintiff] said. [This is] trivialization beyond belief."

Hernandez appealed.

Issue: *Did the trial court err by rejecting punitive damages, or by granting the JNOV?*

Decision: Yes, the trial court erred by rejecting punitive damages and by granting a JNOV.

Reasoning: Hernandez knew that various regulations and policies required that exit signs be lit and that toilets work properly. The school board's safety representative told Hernandez that federal regulations required washing facilities to be sanitary. The staff handbook repeatedly stressed the importance of safety.

Hernandez had a good work record until he began to complain about his safety concerns. There was ample evidence at trial that the school board's alleged reason for firing him was only a pretext, and that his whistleblowing actually caused the dismissal. Exit lights in fact were inoperable, and malfunctioning toilets exposed students to urine and feces. This was no "runaway jury," as the trial judge suggested, and it was error for the lower court to substitute its judgment for the jury's.

The trial court gave a JNOV in part because it found no corroboration of Hernandez's claims concerning unhealthy conditions. That was also an error. Where the jury finds a party's testimony credible, as it obviously did here, the trial judge must accept the evidence as true, and corroboration is not necessary.

The jury should have been allowed to consider Hernandez's claim for punitive damages. He asserted that all of his superiors lied under oath as to why he was fired. He also testified that a coworker warned him to "keep his mouth shut" about the safety problems or he would be terminated. The jurors' award of compensatory damages suggests that they believed Hernandez, and they should have had a chance to consider his request for punitive damages as well.

The JNOV is reversed and the compensatory damages verdict is reinstated. The case is remanded for a new trial on punitive damages, interest, and attorneys fees.

Eight months later, the lawyers representing Coastal and Enviro-Vision appear in the court of appeals to argue their case. Rich, the appellant, goes first. The judges frequently interrupt his argument with questions. Relying on decisions like *Hernandez*, they show little sympathy for his claim that the verdict was against the facts. They seem more sympathetic with his second point, that the instructions were wrong.

When Janet argues, all of their questions concern the judge's instructions. It appears they believe the instructions were in error. The judges take the case under advisement, meaning they will decide some time in the future—maybe in two weeks, maybe in five months.

APPEALS COURT OPTIONS

Modify
To affirm the outcome but with changes.

Reverse and remand
To nullify the lower decision and return the case for reconsideration or retrial.

The court of appeals can affirm the trial court, allowing the decision to stand. The court may **modify** the decision, for example, by affirming that the plaintiff wins but decreasing the size of the award. (That is unlikely here; Beth is entitled to $2 million or nothing.) The court might **reverse and remand**, nullifying the lower court's decision and returning the case to the lower court for a new trial. Or it could simply reverse, turning the loser (Coastal) into the winner, with no new trial.

What will it do here? On the factual issue it will probably rule in Beth's favor. There was evidence from which a jury could conclude that Tony died accidentally. It is true that there was also considerable evidence to support Coastal's position, but that is probably not enough to overturn the verdict. As we saw in the *Hernandez* case, if reasonable people could disagree on what the evidence proves, an appellate court generally refuses to change the jury's factual findings. The court of appeals is likely to rule that a reasonable jury *could* have found accidental death, even if the appellate judges personally suspect that Tony may have killed himself.

The judge's instructions raise a more difficult problem. Some states would require a more complex statement about "presumptions."[9]

What does a court of appeals do if it decides the trial court's instructions were wrong? If it believes the error rendered the trial and verdict unfair, it will remand the case, that is, send it back to the lower court for a new trial. However, the court may conclude that the mistake was **harmless error**, A trial judge cannot do a perfect job, and not every error is fatal. The court may decide the verdict was fair in spite of the mistake.

Janet and Beth talk. Beth is very anxious and wants to settle. She does not want to wait four or five months, only to learn that they must start all over. Janet urges that they wait a few weeks to hear from Rich: they don't want to seem too eager.

A week later, Rich telephones and offers $500,000. Janet turns it down, but says she will ask Beth if she wants to make a counter-offer. She and Beth talk. They agree that they will settle for $1 million. Janet then calls Rich and offers to settle for $1.7 million. Rich and Janet debate the merits of the case. Rich later calls back and offers $750,000, saying he doubts that he can go any higher. Janet counters with $1.4 million, saying she doubts she can go any lower. They argue, both predicting that they will win on appeal.

Rich calls, offers $900,000 and says, "That's it. No more." Janet argues for $1.2 million, expecting to nudge Rich up to $1 million. He doesn't nudge, instead saying, "Take it or leave it." Janet and Beth talk it over. Janet telephones Rich and accepts $900,000 to settle the case.

If they had waited for the court of appeals decision, would Beth have won? It is impossible to know. It is certain, though, that whoever lost would have appealed. Months would have passed waiting to learn if the state supreme court would accept the case. If that court had agreed to hear the appeal, Beth would have endured another year of waiting, brief writing, oral argument, and tense hoping. The high court has all of the options discussed: to affirm, modify, reverse and remand, or simply reverse.

Harmless error

A mistake by the trial judge that was too minor to affect the outcome.

CHAPTER CONCLUSION

No one will ever know for sure whether Tony took his own life. Craig Bergson's evidence might have tipped the scales in favor of Coastal. But even that is uncertain, since the jury could have found him unpersuasive. After two years, the case ends with a settlement and uncertainty—both typical lawsuit results. The missing witness is less common but not extraordinary. The vaguely unsatisfying feeling about it all is only too common and indicates why most parties settle out of court.

---

[9] Judge Rowland probably should have said, "The law presumes that death is accidental, not suicide. So if there were no evidence either way, the plaintiff would win because we presume accident. But if there is competing evidence, the presumption becomes irrelevant. If you think that Coastal Insurance has introduced some evidence of suicide, then forget the legal presumption. You must then decide what happened based on what you have seen and heard in court, and on any inferences you choose to draw." Note that the judge's instructions were different, though similar.

EXAM REVIEW

1. **ADR** Alternative dispute resolution is any formal or informal process to settle disputes without a trial. Mediation, arbitration, and other forms of ADR are growing in popularity. (p. 45)

2. **COURT SYSTEMS** There are many *systems* of courts, one federal and one in each state. A federal court will hear a case only if it involves a federal question or diversity jurisdiction. (p. 47)

3. **TRIAL AND APPELLATE COURTS** Trial courts determine facts and apply the law to the facts; appeals courts generally accept the facts found by the trial court and review the trial record for errors of law. (pp. 47–49)

EXAM Strategy

Question: Jade sued Kim, claiming that Kim promised to hire her as an in-store model for $1,000 per week for 8 weeks. Kim denied making the promise, and the jury was persuaded: Kim won. Jade has appealed, and now offers Steve as a witness. Steve will testify to the Appeals Court that he saw Kim hire Jade as a model, exactly as Jade claimed. Will Jade win on appeal?

Strategy: Before you answer, make sure you know the difference between trial and appellate courts. What is the difference? Apply that distinction here. (See the "Result" at the end of this section.)

4. **PLEADINGS** A complaint and an answer are the two most important pleadings, that is, documents that start a lawsuit. (p. 54)

5. **DISCOVERY** Discovery is the critical pre-trial opportunity for both parties to learn the strengths and weaknesses of the opponents case. Important forms of discovery include interrogatories, depositions, production of documents and objects, physical and mental examinations, and requests for admission. (p. 57)

6. **MOTIONS** A motion is a formal request to the court. (p. 57)

7. **SUMMARY JUDGMENT** Summary judgment is a ruling by the court that no trial is necessary because there are no essential facts in dispute. (p. 62)

8. **JURY TRIALS** Generally, both plaintiff and defendant may demand a jury in any lawsuit for money damages. (p. 64)

9. **VOIR DIRE** Voir dire is the process of selecting jurors in order to obtain an impartial panel. (p. 64)

EXAM Strategy

Question: You are a lawyer, representing the plaintiff in a case of alleged employment discrimination. The court is selecting a jury. Based on questions you have asked, you believe that juror number 3 is biased against your client. You explain this to the judge, but she disagrees. Is there anything you can do?

Strategy: The question focuses on your rights during *voir dire*. If you believe that a juror will not be fair, you may make two different types of challenge. What are they? (See the "Result" at the end of this section.)

10. **BURDEN OF PROOF** The plaintiffs burden of proof in a civil lawsuit is preponderance of the evidence, meaning that its version of the facts must be at least slightly more persuasive than the defendants. In a criminal prosecution, the government must offer proof beyond a reasonable doubt in order to win a conviction. (p. 66)

11. **RULES OF EVIDENCE** The rules of evidence determine what questions may be asked during trial, what testimony may be given, and what documents may be introduced. (p. 67)

12. **VERDICTS** The verdict is the jury's decision in a case. The losing party may ask the trial judge to overturn the verdict, seeking a judgment *non obstante veredicto* or a new trial. Judges seldom grant either. (p. 68)

13. **APPEALS** An appeals court has many options. The court may affirm, upholding the lower courts decision; modify, changing the verdict but leaving the same party victorious; reverse, transforming the loser into the winner; and/or remand, sending the case back to the lower court. (p. 69)

3. Result: Trial courts use witnesses to help resolve fact disputes. Appellate courts review the record to see if there have been errors of law. Appellate courts never hear witnesses, and they will not hear Steve. Jade will lose her appeal.

9. Result: You have already made a *challenge for cause*, claiming bias, but the judge has rejected your challenge. If you have not used up all of your *peremptory challenges*, you may use one to excuse this juror, without giving any reason.

ADDITIONAL QUESTIONS

1. You plan to open a store in Chicago, specializing in beautiful rugs imported from Turkey. You will work with a native Turk who will purchase and ship the rugs to your store. You are wise enough to insist on a contract establishing the rights and obligations of both parties and would prefer an ADR clause. But you want to be sensitive to different cultures and do not want a clause that will magnify a problem or alienate the parties. Is there some way you can accomplish all of this?

2. State which court(s) have jurisdiction as to each of these lawsuits:

   (a) Pat wants to sue his next-door neighbor, Dorothy, claiming that Dorothy promised to sell him the house next door.

   (b) Paula, who lives in New York City, wants to sue Dizzy Movie Theatres, whose principal place of business is Dallas. She claims that while she was in Texas on holiday, she was injured by their negligent maintenance of a stairway. She claims damages of $30,000.

   (c) Phil lives in Tennessee. He wants to sue Dick, who lives in Ohio. Phil claims that Dick agreed to sell him 3,000 acres of farmland in Ohio, worth over $2 million.

   (d) Pete, incarcerated in a federal prison in Kansas, wants to sue the United States government. He claims that his treatment by prison authorities violates three federal statutes.

3. Probationary schoolteachers sued the New Madrid, Missouri, school district, claiming that the school district refused to give them permanent jobs because of their union organizing activity. The defendant school district claimed that each plaintiff was refused a permanent job because of inferior teaching. During discovery, the plaintiffs asked for the personnel files of probationary teachers who *had* been offered permanent jobs. The school district refused to provide them, arguing that the personnel files did not indicate the union status of the teachers and therefore would not help the plaintiffs. The trial court ruled that the school district need not release the files. On appeal, the plaintiffs argue that this hindered their ability to prove the real reasons they had been fired. How should the appeals court rule?

4. Students are now suing schools for sexual harassment. The cases raise important issues about the limits of discovery. In a case in Petaluma, California, a girl claimed that she was harassed for years and that the school knew about it and failed to act. According to press reports, she alleges that a boy stood up in class and asked, "I have a question. I want to know if [Jane Doe] has sex with hot dogs." In discovery, the school district sought the parents' therapy records, the girl's diary, and a psychological evaluation of the girl. Should they get those things?

5. British discovery practice differs from that in the United States. Most discovery in Britain concerns documents. The lawyers for the two sides, called solicitors, must deliver to the opposing side a list of all relevant documents in their possession. Each side may then request to look at and copy those it wishes. Depositions are rare. What advantages and disadvantages are there to the British practice?

6. **ETHICS** Trial practice also is dramatically different in Britain. The parties' solicitors do not go into court. Courtroom work is done by different lawyers, called barristers. The barristers have very limited rights to interview witnesses before trial. They know the substance of what each witness intends to say but do not rehearse questions and

answers, as in the United States. Which approach do you consider more effective? More ethical? What is the purpose of a trial? Of pre-trial preparation?

7. Claus Scherer worked for Rockwell International and was paid over $300,000 per year. Rockwell fired Scherer for alleged sexual harassment of several workers, including his secretary, Terry Pendy. Scherer sued in United States District Court, alleging that Rockwell's real motive in firing him was his high salary.

8. Rockwell moved for summary judgment, offering deposition transcripts of various employees. Pendy's deposition detailed instances of harassment, including comments about her body, instances of unwelcome touching, and discussions of extramarital affairs. Another deposition, from a Rockwell employee who investigated the allegations, included complaints by other employees as to Scherer's harassment. In his own deposition, which he offered to oppose summary judgment, Scherer testified that he could not recall the incidents alleged by Pendy and others. He denied generally that he had sexually harassed anyone. The district court granted summary judgment for Rockwell. Was its ruling correct?

9. Lloyd Dace worked for ACF Industries as a supervisor in the punchpress department of a carburetor factory. ACF demoted Dace to an hourly job on the assembly line, and Dace sued, claiming that ACF discriminated on the basis of age. At trial, Dace showed that he had been 53 years old when demoted and had been replaced by a man aged 40. He offered evidence that ACF's benefits supervisor had attended the meeting at which his demotion was decided, and that the benefits supervisor was aware of the cost savings of replacing Dace with a younger man.

   At the end of Dace's case, ACF moved for a directed verdict and the trial court granted it. The judge reasoned that Dace's entire case was based on circumstantial evidence. He held that it was too speculative for the jury to infer age discrimination from the few facts that Dace had offered. Was the trial court correct?

10. **ROLE REVERSAL** Write a multiple-choice question that illustrates the unique significance of summary judgment: that there is no need for a trial because there are no essential facts in dispute.

INTERNET RESEARCH PROBLEM

You may be called for jury duty before long. Find a summary of the juror's responsibilities on the Internet. Some people try hard to get out of jury duty. Why is that a problem in a democratic society?

You can find further practice problems at www.cengagebrain.com. See the preface of this book for website access details.

CHAPTER 4

COMMON LAW, STATUTORY LAW AND ADMINISTRATIVE LAW

Jason observes a toddler wander onto the railroad tracks and hears a train approaching. He has plenty of time to pull the child from the tracks with no risk to himself, but chooses to do nothing. The youngster is killed. The child's family sues Jason for his callous behavior, and a court determines that Jason owes—nothing.

"Why can't they just fix the law?" students and professionals often ask, in response to Jason's impunity and countless other legal oddities. Their exasperation is understandable. This chapter cannot guarantee intellectual tranquility, but it should diminish the sense of bizarreness that law can instill. We will look at three sources of law: common law, statutory law, and administrative law. Most of the law you learn in the course comes from one of these sources. The substantive law will make more sense when you have a solid feel for how it was created.

> **Jason observes a toddler wander onto the railroad tracks and hears a train approaching.**

COMMON LAW

Jason and the toddler present a classic legal puzzle: What, if anything, must a bystander do when he sees someone in danger? We will examine this issue to see how the common law works.

The **common law** is judge-made law. It is the sum total of all the cases decided by appellate courts. The common law of Pennsylvania consists of all cases decided by appellate courts in that state. The Illinois common law of bystander liability is all of the cases on that subject decided by Illinois appellate courts. Two hundred years ago, almost all of the law was common law. Today, most new law is statutory. But common law still predominates in tort, contract, and agency law, and it is very important in property, employment, and some other areas.

We focus on appellate courts because they are the only ones to make rulings of law, as discussed in Chapter 3. In a bystander case, it is the job of the state's highest court to say what legal obligations, if any, a bystander has. The trial court, on the other hand, must decide *facts:* Was this defendant able to see what was happening? Was the plaintiff really in trouble? Could the defendant have assisted without peril to himself?

STARE DECISIS

Nothing perks up a course like Latin. *Stare decisis* means "let the decision stand." It is the essence of the common law. The phrase indicates that once a court has decided a particular issue, it will generally apply the same rule in future cases. Suppose the highest court of Arizona must decide whether a contract for a new car, signed by a 16-year-old, can be enforced against him. The court will look to see if there is **precedent**, that is, whether the high court of Arizona has already decided a similar case. The Arizona court looks and finds several earlier cases, all holding that such contracts may not be enforced against a minor. The court will apply that precedent and refuse to enforce the contract in this case. Courts do not always follow precedent but they generally do: *stare decisis*.

Two words explain why the common law is never as easy as we might like: *predictability* and *flexibility*. The law is trying to accommodate both goals. The need for predictability is apparent: people must know what the law is. If contract law changed daily, an entrepreneur who leased factory space and then started buying machinery would be uncertain if the factory would actually be available when she was ready to move in. Will the landlord slip out of the lease? Will the machinery be ready on time? The need for predictability created the doctrine of *stare decisis*.

Yet there must also be flexibility in the law, some means to respond to new problems and changing social mores. In this new millennium, we cannot be encumbered by ironclad rules established before electricity was discovered. These two ideas may be obvious but they also conflict: the more flexibility we permit, the less predictability we enjoy. We will watch the conflict play out in the bystander cases.

BYSTANDER CASES

This country inherited from England a simple rule about a **bystander's obligations: you have no duty to assist someone in peril unless you created the danger**. In *Union Pacific Railway Co. v. Cappier*,[1] through no fault of the railroad, a train struck a man, severing an arm and a leg. Railroad employees saw the incident happen but did nothing to assist him. By the time help arrived, the victim had died. In this 1903 case the court held that the railroad had no duty to help the injured man:

---

[1] 66 Kan. 649, 72 P. 281 (1903).

Margin notes:

Common law
Judge-made law.

(handwritten) Principles of theories developed over time

Stare decisis
"Let the decision stand," that is, the ruling from a previous case.

(handwritten) (Flexible) guideline
· follows precedent

Precedent
An earlier case that decided the issue.

(handwritten) Society — Law
As society changes, the law is constantly trying to change

OR if there is no connection between the 2 parties

Bystander laws vary in various jurisdictions (states) Including who is protected from liability and in what circumstances

With the humane side of the question courts are not concerned. It is the omission or negligent discharge of legal duties only which come within the sphere of judicial cognizance. For withholding relief from the suffering, for failure to respond to the calls of worthy charity, or for faltering in the bestowment of brotherly love on the unfortunate, penalties are found not in the laws of men but in [the laws of God].

As harsh as this judgment might seem, it was an accurate statement of the law at that time in both England and the United States: bystanders need do nothing. Contemporary writers found the rule inhumane and cruel, and even judges criticized it. But—*stare decisis*—they followed it. With a rule this old and well established, no court was willing to scuttle it. What courts did do was seek openings for small changes.

Eighteen years after the Kansas case of *Cappier*, the court in nearby Iowa found the basis for one exception. Ed Carey was a farm laborer, working for Frank Davis. While in the fields, Carey fainted from sunstroke and remained unconscious. Davis simply hauled him to a nearby wagon and left him in the sun for an additional four hours, causing serious permanent injury. The court's response:

It is unquestionably the well-settled rule that the master is under no legal duty to care for a sick or injured servant for whose illness or injury he is not at fault. Though not unjust in principle, this rule, if carried unflinchingly and without exception to its logical extreme, is sometimes productive of shocking results. To avoid this criticism [we hold that where] a servant suffers serious injury, or is suddenly stricken down in a manner indicating the immediate and emergent need of aid to save him from death or serious harm, the master, if present is in duty bound to take such reasonable measures as may be practicable to relieve him, even though such master be not chargeable with fault in bringing about the emergency.[2]

And this is how the common law changes: bit by tiny bit. In Iowa, a bystander could now be liable *if* he was the employer and *if* the worker was suddenly stricken and *if* it was an emergency and *if* the employer was present. That is a small change but an important one.

For the next 50 years, changes in bystander law came very slowly. Consider *Osterlind v. Hill*, a case from 1928.[3] Osterlind rented a canoe from Hill's boatyard, paddled into the lake, and promptly fell into the water. For *30 minutes* he clung to the side of the canoe and shouted for help. Hill heard the cries but did nothing; Osterlind drowned. Was Hill liable? No, said the court: a bystander has no liability. Not until half a century later did that same state supreme court reverse its position and begin to require assistance in extreme cases—a long time for Osterlind to hold on.[4]

In the 1970s, changes came more quickly.

TARASOFF V. REGENTS OF THE UNIVERSITY OF CALIFORNIA

17 Cal.3d 425, 551 P.2d 334, 131 Cal. Rptr. 14
SUPREME COURT OF CALIFORNIA, 1976

CASE SUMMARY

Facts: On October 27, 1969, Prosenjit Poddar killed Tatiana Tarasoff. Tatiana's parents claimed that two months earlier Poddar had confided his intention to kill Tatiana to Dr. Lawrence Moore, a psychologist employed by the University of California at Berkeley. They sued the university, claiming that Dr. Moore should have warned Tatiana and/or should have arranged for Poddar's confinement.

---

[2] Carey v. Davis, 190 Iowa 720, 180 N.W. 889 (1921).
[3] 263 Mass. 73, 160 N.E. 301 (1928).
[4] Pridgen v. Boston Housing Authority, 364 Mass. 696, 308 N.E.2d 467 (1974).

Issue: *Did Dr. Moore have a duty to Tatiana Tarasoff, and did he breach that duty?*

Decision: Yes, Dr. Moore had a duty to Tatiana Tarasoff.

Reasoning: Under the common law, one person generally owes no duty to control the conduct of another or to warn anyone who is in danger. However, courts make an exception when the defendant has a special relationship to a dangerous person or potential victim. A therapist is someone who has just such a special relationship with a patient.

It is very difficult to predict whether a patient presents a serious danger of violence, and no one can be expected to do a perfect job. A therapist must exercise only the reasonable degree of skill, knowledge, and care ordinarily possessed by others in the field. In this case, however, there is no dispute about whether Dr. Moore could have foreseen violence or predicted that Poddar would kill Tatiana. Once a therapist determines, or reasonably should determine, that a patient poses a serious danger of violence to someone, he must make reasonable efforts to protect the potential victim. The Tarasoffs have stated a legitimate claim against Dr. Moore.

The *Tarasoff* exception applies when there is some special relationship, such as therapist–patient. What if there is no such relationship? The 1983 case of *Soldano v. ODaniels*[5] arose when a patron in Happy Jack's bar saw Villanueva threaten Soldano with a gun. The patron dashed next door, into the Circle Inn bar, told the bartender what was happening, and urged him to call the police. The bartender refused. The witness then asked to use the phone to call the police himself, but the bartender again refused. Tragically, the delay permitted Villanueva to kill Soldano.

As in the earlier cases we have seen, this case presented an emergency. But the exception created in *Carey v. Davis* applied only if the bystander was an employer, and that in *Tarasoff* only for a doctor. In *Soldano* the bystander was neither. Should the law require him to act, that is, should it carve a new exception? Here is what the California court decided:

Many citizens simply "don't want to get involved." No rule should be adopted [requiring] a citizen to open up his or her house to a stranger so that the latter may use the telephone to call for emergency assistance. As Mrs. Alexander in Anthony Burgess' *A Clockwork Orange* learned to her horror, such an action may be fraught with danger. It does not follow, however, that use of a telephone in a public portion of a business should be refused for a legitimate emergency call.

We conclude that the bartender owed a duty to [Soldano] to permit the patron from Happy Jack's to place a call to the police or to place the call himself. It bears emphasizing that the duty in this case does not require that one must go to the aid of another. That is not the issue here. The employee was not the good samaritan intent on aiding another. The patron was.

Do these exceptions mean that the bystander rule is gone? *Parra v. Tarasco*[6] provides a partial answer. Ernesto Parra was a customer at the Jiminez Restaurant when food became lodged in his throat. The employees did not use the Heimlich maneuver or any other method to try to save him. Parra choked to death. Was the restaurant liable? No, said the Illinois Appeals Court. The restaurant had no obligation to do anything.

The bystander rule, that hardy oak, is alive and well. Various initials have been carved into its bark—the exceptions we have seen and a variety of others—but the trunk is strong and the leaves green. Perhaps someday the proliferating exceptions will topple it, but the process of the common law is slow and that day is nowhere in sight. In the meantime, it is nice to be reminded that even without a legal obligation, some citizens do choose to get involved.

[5] 141 Cal. App. 3d 443, 190 Cal. Rptr. 310, 1983 Cal. App. LEXIS 1539 (1983).
[6] 230 Ill. App. 3d 819, 595 N.E.2d 1186.

EXAM *Strategy*

Question: When Rachel is walking her dog, Bozo, she watches a skydiver float to earth. He lands in an enormous tree, suspended 45 feet above ground. "Help!" the man shouts. Rachel hurries to the tree and sees the skydiver bleeding profusely. She takes out her cell phone to call 911 for help, but just then Bozo runs away. Rachel darts after the dog, afraid that he will jump in a nearby pond and emerge smelling of mud. She forgets about the skydiver and takes Bozo home in a shopping bag. After bleeding for 3 hours, the skydiver expires.

The victim's family sues Rachel. She defends by saying she feared that Bozo would have an allergic reaction to mud, and that in any case she could not have climbed 45 feet up a tree to save the man. The family argues that the dog is not allergic to mud, that even if he is, a pet's inconvenience pales compared to human life, and that Rachel could have phoned for emergency help without climbing an inch. Please rule.

Strategy: The family's arguments might seem compelling, but are they relevant? Rachel is a bystander, someone who perceives another in danger. What is the rule concerning a bystander's obligation to act? Apply the rule to the facts of this case.

Result: A bystander has no duty to assist someone in peril unless she created the danger. Rachel did not create the skydiver's predicament. She had no obligation to do anything. Rachel wins.

STATUTORY LAW

Most new law is statutory law. Statutes affect each of us every day, in our business, professional, and personal lives. When the system works correctly, this is the one part of the law over which we the people have control. We elect the local legislators who pass state statutes; we vote for the senators and representatives who create federal statutes. If we understand the system, we can affect the largest source of contemporary law. If we live in ignorance of its strengths and pitfalls, we delude ourselves that we participate in a democracy.

As we saw in Chapter 1, there are many systems of government operating in the United States: a national government and 50 state governments. Each level of government has a legislative body. In Washington, D.C., Congress is our national legislature. Congress passes the statutes that govern the nation. In addition, each state has a legislature, which passes statutes for that state only. In this section we look at how Congress does its work creating statutes. State legislatures operate similarly, but the work of Congress is better documented and obviously of national importance.[7]

---

[7] See the chart of state and federal governments in Chapter 1. A vast amount of information about Congress is available on the Internet. The House of Representatives has a Web page at **http://www.house.gov/**. The Senate's site appears at **http://www.senate.gov/**. Each page provides links to current law, pending legislation, votes, committees, and more. If you do not know the name of your representative or senator (shame!), the Web page will provide that information. Most state legislatures have Web sites, which you can reach from links found at **http://www.ncsl.org/**. These sites typically permit you to read statutes, research legislative history, examine the current calendar, and note upcoming events. For example, the Web site **http://housegop.state.il.us/** brings you to the Republican caucus in the Illinois House of Representatives, while the site **http://www.housedem.state.il.us/** will take you to the same body's Democratic caucus. Many of these Web sites enable you to e-mail your local representatives.

BILLS

Congress is organized into two houses, the House of Representatives and the Senate. Either house may originate a proposed statute, which is called a **bill**. The bill must be voted on and approved by both houses. Once both houses pass it, they will send it to the president. If the president signs the bill, it becomes law and is then a statute. If the president opposes the bill, he will **veto** it, in which case it is not law.[8]

Committee Work

If you visit either house of Congress, you will probably find half a dozen legislators on the floor, with one person talking and no one listening. This is because most of the work is done in committees. Both houses are organized into dozens of committees, each with special functions. The House currently has about 25 committees (further divided into about 150 subcommittees) and the Senate has approximately 20 committees (with about 86 subcommittees). For example, the armed services committee of each house oversees the huge defense budget and the workings of the armed forces. Labor committees handle legislation concerning organized labor and working conditions. Banking committees develop expertise on financial institutions. Judiciary committees review nominees to the federal courts. There are dozens of other committees, some very powerful, because they control vast amounts of money, and some relatively weak. Few of us ever think about the House Agricultural Subcommittee on Specialty Crops. But if we owned a family peanut farm, we would pay close attention to the subcommittee's agenda, because those congressmen would pay close attention to us.

When a bill is proposed in either house, it is referred to the committee that specializes in that subject. Why are bills proposed in the first place? For any of several reasons:

- *New Issue, New Worry.* If society begins to focus on a new issue, Congress may respond with legislation. We consider below, for example, the congressional response to employment discrimination.

- *Unpopular Judicial Ruling.* If Congress disagrees with a judicial interpretation of a statute, the legislators may pass a new statute to modify or "undo" the court decision. For example, if the Supreme Court misinterprets a statute about musical copyrights, Congress may pass a new law correcting the Court's error. However, the legislators have no such power to modify a court decision based on the Constitution. When the Supreme Court ruled that lawyers had a right *under the First Amendment* to advertise their services, Congress lacked the power to change the decision.

- *Criminal Law.* Statutory law, unlike common law, is prospective. Legislators are hoping to control the future. And that is why almost all criminal law is statutory. A court cannot retroactively announce that it *has been* a crime for a retailer to accept kickbacks from a wholesaler. Everyone must know the rules in advance because the consequences—prison, a felony record—are so harsh.

DISCRIMINATION: CONGRESS AND THE COURTS

The civil rights movement of the 1950s and 1960s convinced most citizens that African Americans continued to suffer relentless discrimination in jobs, housing, voting, schools, and

---

[8] Congress may, however, attempt to override the veto. See the discussion following.

Bill
A proposed statute, submitted to Congress or a state legislature.

Veto
The power of the president to reject legislation passed by Congress.

other basic areas of life. Demonstrations and boycotts, marches and counter-marches, church bombings and killings persuaded the nation that the problem was vast and urgent.

In 1963 President Kennedy proposed legislation to guarantee equal rights to African Americans in these areas. The bill went to the House Judiciary Committee, which heard testimony for weeks. Witnesses testified that blacks were often unable to vote because of their race, that landlords and home sellers adamantly refused to sell or rent to blacks, that education was still grossly unequal, and that blacks were routinely denied good jobs in many industries. Eventually, the Judiciary Committee approved the bill and sent it to the full House.

The bill was dozens of pages long and divided into "titles," with each title covering a major issue. Title VII concerned employment. We will consider the progress of Title VII in Congress and in the courts. Here is one section of Title VII, as reported to the House floor:[9]

> Sec. 703(a). It shall be an unlawful employment practice for an employer—
>
> (1) to fail or refuse to hire or to discharge any individual, or otherwise to discriminate against any individual with respect to his compensation, terms, conditions, or privileges of employment, because of such individual's race, color, religion, or national origin; or
>
> (2) to limit, segregate, or classify his employees in any way which would deprive or tend to deprive any individual of employment opportunities or otherwise adversely affect his status as an employee, because of such individual's race, color, religion, or national origin.

DEBATE

The proposed bill was intensely controversial and sparked angry argument throughout Congress. Here are some excerpts from one day's debate on the House floor, on February 8, 1964:[10]

> MR. WAGGONNER. I speak to you in all sincerity and ask for the right to discriminate if I so choose because I think it is my right. I think it is my right to choose my social companions. I think it is my right if I am a businessman to run it as I please, to do with my own as I will. I think that is a right the Constitution gives to every man. I want the continued right to discriminate and I want the other man to have the right to continue to discriminate against me, because I am discriminated against every day. I do not feel inferior about it.
>
> I ask you to forget about politics, forget about everything except the integrity of the individual, leaving to the people of this country the right to live their lives in the manner they choose to live. Do not destroy this democracy for a Socialist government. A vote for this bill is no less.
>
> MR. CONTE. If the serious cleavage which pitted brother against brother and citizen against citizen during the tragedy of the Civil War is ever to be justified, it can be justified in this House and then in the other body with the passage of this legislation which can and must reaffirm the rights to all individuals which are inherent in our Constitution.
>
> The distinguished poet Mark Van Doren has said that "equality is absolute or no, nothing between can stand," and nothing should now stand between us and the passage of strong and effective civil rights legislation. It is to this that we are united in a strong bipartisan coalition today, and when the laws of the land proclaim that the 88th Congress acted effectively, judiciously, and wisely, we can take pride in our accomplishments as free men.

---

[9] The section number in the House bill was actually 704(a); we use 703 here because that is the number of the section when the bill became law and the number to which the Supreme Court refers in later litigation.

[10] The order of speakers is rearranged, and the remarks are edited.

Other debate was less rhetorical and aimed more at getting information. The following exchange anticipates a 30-year controversy on quotas:

MR. JOHANSEN. I have asked for this time to raise a question and I would ask particularly for the attention of the gentleman from New York [Mr. Goodell] because of a remark he made—and I am not quarreling with it. I understood him to say there is no plan for balanced employment or for quotas in this legislation.... I am raising a question as to whether in the effort to eliminate discrimination—and incidentally that is an undefined term in the bill—we may get to a situation in which employers and conceivably union leaders, will insist on legislation providing for a quota system as a matter of self-protection.

Now let us suppose this hypothetical situation exists with 100 jobs to be filled. Let us say 150 persons apply and suppose 75 of them are Negro and 75 of them are white. Supposing the employer... hires 75 white men and 25 Negroes. Do the other 50 Negroes or anyone of them severally have a right to claim they have been discriminated against on the basis of color?

MR. GOODELL. It is the intention of the legislation that if applicants are equal in all other respects there will be no restriction. One may choose from among equals. So long as there is no distinction on the basis of race, creed, or color it will not violate the act.

The debate on racial issues carried on. Later in the day, Congressman Smith of Virginia offered an amendment that could scarcely have been smaller—or more important:

Amendment offered by Mr. Smith of Virginia: On page 68, line 23, after the word "religion," insert the word "sex."

In other words, Smith was asking that discrimination on the basis of sex also be outlawed, along with the existing grounds of race, color, national origin, and religion. Congressman Smith's proposal produced the following comments:

MR. CELLER. You know, the French have a phrase for it when they speak of women and men. They say "vive la difference." I think the French are right. Imagine the upheaval that would result from adoption of blanket language requiring total equality. Would male citizens be justified in insisting that women share with them the burdens of compulsory military service? What would become of traditional family relationships? What about alimony? What would become of the crimes of rape and statutory rape? I think the amendment seems illogical, ill timed, ill placed, and improper.

MRS. ST. GEORGE. Mr. Chairman, I was somewhat amazed when I came on the floor this afternoon to hear the very distinguished chairman of the Committee on the Judiciary [Mr. Celler] make the remark that he considered the amendment at this point illogical. I can think of nothing more logical than this amendment at this point.

There are still many States where women cannot serve on juries. There are still many States where women do not have equal educational opportunities. In most States and, in fact, I figure it would be safe to say, in all States—women do not get equal pay for equal work. That is a very well known fact. And to say that this is illogical. What is illogical about it? All you are doing is simply correcting something that goes back, frankly to the Dark Ages.

The debate continued. Some supported the "sex" amendment because they were determined to end sexual bias. But politics are complex. Some *opponents* of civil rights supported the amendment because they believed that it would make the legislation less popular and cause Congress to defeat the entire Civil Rights bill.

That strategy did not work. The amendment passed, and sex was added as a protected trait. And, after more debate and several votes, the entire bill passed the House. It went to the Senate, where it followed a similar route from Judiciary Committee to full Senate. Much of the Senate debate was similar to what we have seen. But some senators raised a new issue, concerning §703(2), which prohibited *segregating or classifying* employees based on any of the protected categories (race, color, national origin, religion, or sex). Senator Tower was concerned that §703(2) meant that an employee in a protected category could never be given any sort of job test. So the Senate amended §703 to include a new subsection:

Sec. 703(h). Notwithstanding any other provision of this title, it shall not be an unlawful employment practice for an employer ... to give and to act upon the results of any professionally developed ability test provided that such test ... is not designed, intended or used to discriminate because of race, color, religion, sex or national origin.

With that amendment, and many others, the bill passed the Senate.

Conference Committee

Civil rights legislation had now passed both houses, but the bills were no longer the same due to the many amendments. This is true with most legislation. The next step is for the two houses to send representatives to a House–Senate Conference Committee. This committee examines all of the differences between the two bills and tries to reach a compromise. With the Civil Rights bill, Senator Tower's amendment was left in; other Senate amendments were taken out. When the Conference Committee had settled every difference between the two versions, the new, modified bill was sent back to each house for a new vote.

The House of Representatives and the Senate again angrily debated the compromise language reported from the Conference Committee. Finally, after years of violent public demonstrations and months of debate, each house passed the same bill. President Johnson promptly signed it. The Civil Rights Act of 1964 was law. See Exhibit 4.1.

Title VII of the Civil Rights Act obviously prohibited an employer from saying to a job applicant, "We don't hire blacks." In some parts of the country, that had been common practice; after the Civil Rights Act passed, it became rare. Employers who routinely hired whites only, or promoted only whites, found themselves losing lawsuits.

A new group of cases arose, those in which some job standard was set that appeared to be racially neutral, yet had a discriminatory effect. In North Carolina, the Duke Power Co. required that applicants for higher paying, promotional positions meet two requirements: they must have a high school diploma, and they must pass a standardized written test. There was no evidence that either requirement related to successful job performance. Blacks met the requirements in lower percentages than whites, and consequently whites obtained a disproportionate share of the good jobs.

Title VII did not precisely address this kind of case. It clearly outlawed overt discrimination. Was Duke Power's policy overt discrimination, or was it protected by Senator Tower's amendment, §703(h)? The case went all the way to the Supreme Court, where the Court had to interpret the new law.

STATUTORY INTERPRETATION

Courts are often called upon to interpret a statute, that is, to explain precisely what the language means and how it applies in a given case. There are three primary steps in a court's statutory interpretation:

- *Plain Meaning Rule.* When a statute's words have ordinary, everyday significance, the court will simply apply those words. Section 703(a)(1) of the Civil Rights Act prohibits firing someone because of her religion. Could an employer who had fired a Catholic because of her religion argue that Catholicism is not really a religion, but more of a social group? No. The word "religion" has a plain meaning and courts apply its commonsense definition.

- *Legislative History and Intent.* If the language is unclear, the court must look deeper. Section 703(a)(2) prohibits classifying employees in ways that are discriminatory. Does

(handwritten note at left: The statute means what it says)

(handwritten note at bottom left: using any ~~meanings~~ materials used/created during the process of making a legislative bill)

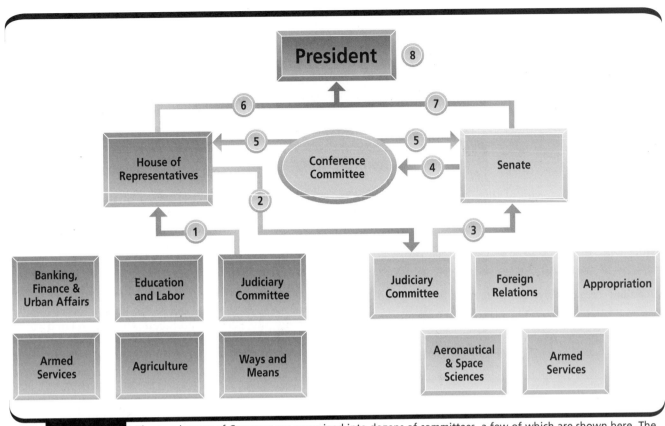

Exhibit 4.1 The two houses of Congress are organized into dozens of committees, a few of which are shown here. The path of the 1964 Civil Rights Act (somewhat simplified) was as follows: (1) The House Judiciary Committee approved the bill and sent it to the full House; (2) the full House passed the bill and sent it to the Senate, where it was assigned to the Senate Judiciary Committee; (3) the Senate Judiciary Committee passed an amended version of the bill and sent it to the full Senate; (4) the full Senate passed the bill with additional amendments. Since the Senate version was now different from the bill the House passed, the bill went to a Conference Committee. The Conference Committee (5) reached a compromise and sent the new version of the bill back to both houses. Each house passed the compromise bill (6 and 7) and sent it to the president, who signed it into law (8).

that section prevent an employer from requiring high school diplomas, as Duke Power did? The explicit language of the statute does not answer the question. The court will look at the law's history to determine the intent of the legislature. The court will examine committee hearings, reports, and the floor debates that we have seen.

- *Public Policy.* If the legislative history is unclear, courts will rely on general public policies, such as reducing crime, creating equal opportunity, and so forth. They may include in this examination some of their own prior decisions. Courts assume that the legislature is aware of prior judicial decisions, and if the legislature did not change those decisions, the statute will be interpreted to incorporate them.

Here is how the Supreme Court interpreted the 1964 Civil Rights Act.

GRIGGS V. DUKE POWER CO.

401 U.S. 424, 91 S.Ct. 849, 1971 U.S. LEXIS 134
UNITED STATES SUPREME COURT, 1971

CASE SUMMARY

Facts: See the discussion of the Duke Power Company's job requirements in the "Conference Committee" section above.

Issue: *Did Title VII of the 1964 Civil Rights Act require that employment tests be job-related?*

Decision: Yes, employment tests must be job-related.

Reasoning: Congress's goal in enacting Title VII is plain from its language: to achieve equality of opportunity and remove barriers that have favored whites. An employer may not use any practice, procedure, or test that perpetuates discrimination. This is true not only for overtly discriminatory behavior but also for conduct that appears fair yet has a discriminatory effect. The key is business necessity. An employment test or restriction that excludes blacks is prohibited unless it is required to do the particular job. In this case, neither the high school completion requirement nor the general intelligence test is related to job performance, and therefore neither is permissible.

And so the highest Court ruled that if a job requirement had a discriminatory impact, the employer could use that requirement only if it was related to job performance. Many more cases arose. For almost two decades courts held that, once workers showed that a job requirement had a discriminatory effect, the employer had the burden to prove that the requirement was necessary for the business. The requirement had to be essential to achieve an important goal. If there was any way to achieve that goal without discriminatory impact, the employer had to use it.

CHANGING TIMES

But things changed. In 1989, a more conservative Supreme Court decided *Wards Cove Packing Co. v. Atonio.*[11] The plaintiffs were nonwhite workers in salmon canneries in Alaska. The canneries had two types of jobs, skilled and unskilled. Nonwhites (Filipinos and native Alaskans) invariably worked as low-paid, unskilled workers, canning the fish. The higher paid, skilled positions were filled almost entirely with white workers, who were hired during the off-season in Washington and Oregon.

There was no overt discrimination. But plaintiffs claimed that various practices led to the racial imbalances. The practices included failing to promote from within the company, hiring through separate channels (cannery jobs were done through a union hall, skilled positions were filled out of state), nepotism, and an English language requirement. Once again the case reached the Supreme Court, where Justice White wrote the Court's opinion.

If the plaintiffs succeeded in showing that the job requirements led to racial imbalance, said the Court, the employer now only had to demonstrate that the requirement or practice

[11] 490 U.S. 642, 109 S.Ct. 2115, 1989 U.S. LEXIS 2794 (1989).

"serves, in a significant way, the legitimate employment goals of the employer.... [T]here is no requirement that the challenged practice be 'essential' or 'indispensable' to the employer's business." In other words, the Court removed the "business necessity" requirement of *Griggs* and replaced it with "legitimate employment goals."

VOTERS' ROLE

The response to *Wards Cove* was quick. Liberals decried it; conservatives hailed it. Everyone agreed that it was a major change that would make it substantially harder for plaintiffs to bring successful discrimination cases. Why had the Court changed its interpretation? Because the *Court* was different. The Court of the 1980s was more conservative, with a majority of justices appointed by Presidents Nixon and Reagan. And so, the voters' political preference had affected the high Court, which in turn changed the interpretation of a statute passed in response to voter concerns of the 1960s. See Exhibit 4.2.

Democrats introduced bills to reverse the interpretation of *Wards Cove*. President George H.W. Bush strongly opposed any new bill. He said it would lead to "quotas," that is, that employers would feel obligated to hire a certain percentage of workers from all racial categories to protect themselves from suits. This was the issue that Congressman Johansen had raised in the original House debate in 1964, but it had not been mentioned since.

Both houses passed bills restoring the "business necessity" holding of *Griggs*. Again there were differences, and a Conference Committee resolved them. After acrimonious debate, both houses passed the compromise bill in October 1990. Was it therefore law? No. President Bush immediately vetoed the bill. He said it would compel employers to adopt quotas.

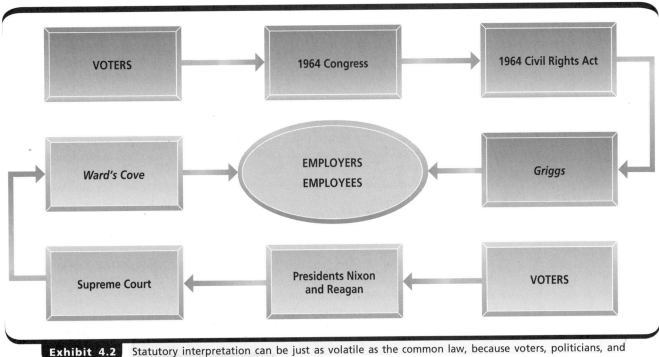

Exhibit 4.2 Statutory interpretation can be just as volatile as the common law, because voters, politicians, and courts all change over time.

CONGRESSIONAL OVERRIDE

When the president vetoes a bill, Congress has one last chance to make it law: an override. If both houses repass the bill, each by a two-thirds margin, it becomes law over the president's veto. Congress attempted to pass the 1990 Civil Rights bill over the Bush veto, but it fell short in the Senate by one vote.

Civil rights advocates tried again, in January 1991, introducing a new bill to reverse the *Wards Cove* rule. Again both houses debated and bargained. The new bill stated that, once an employee proves that a particular employment practice causes a discriminatory impact, the employer must "demonstrate that the challenged practice is job related for the position in question and consistent with business necessity."

Now the two sides fought over the exact meanings of two terms: "job related" and "business necessity." Each side offered definitions, but they could not reach agreement. It appeared that the entire bill would founder over those terms. So Congress did what it often does when faced with a problem of definition: it dropped the issue. Liberals and conservatives agreed not to define the troublesome terms. They would leave that task to courts to perform through statutory interpretation.

With the definitions left out, the new bill passed both houses. In November 1991, President Bush signed the bill into law. The president stated that the new bill had been improved and no longer threatened to create racial quotas. His opponents charged he had reversed course for political reasons, anticipating the 1992 presidential election.

And so, the Congress restored the "business necessity" interpretation to its own 1964 Civil Rights Act. No one would say, however, that it had been a simple process.

THE OTHER PLAYER: MONEY

No description of the legislative process would be complete, or even realistic, without mentioning money. Campaign contributions and spending have aroused controversy for decades. In 1971, Congress passed the Federal Election Campaign Act (FECA), which limited how much of his own money a federal candidate could spend. Three years later, the statute was amended to place two more limitations on federal campaigns: how much a campaign as a whole could spend, and how much anyone else could spend to promote a candidate. One goal was to reduce the power and influence of donors, who gave money expecting favors in return; another purpose was to permit candidates of modest means to compete with millionaire office seekers.

In 1976, the Supreme Court unsettled things in *Buckley v. Valeo*,[12] by ruling that mandatory *spending* limits violate the First Amendment. The Court permitted Congress to limit campaign *contributions*, from individuals and groups, but not to cap the amount that a candidate could spend. This decision was a windfall for wealthy candidates, who could now spend as much of their own money as they chose. It is no coincidence that most members of Congress are very rich. Once elected, they stay in office. In recent Senate elections, the average incumbent raised $11,317,025; the average challenger raised $1,814,844. The results were predictable: out of 30 incumbents, 23 were re-elected (77%).

During the first decade of this millennium, Congress has made several statutory attempts to curb campaign spending, with no success. A recent statute prohibited pre-election ads, paid for by corporations and unions, which mention candidates by name. The Supreme Court declared the statute an unconstitutional violation of free speech.[13]

Every recent election cycle has set a new record as the most expensive in history. Where does the money come from? Each party has industries that it depends upon for major support. Law firms, the entertainment industry, and educational organizations give heavily to the Democrats. Republicans receive equally strong support from insurers, commercial banks and the oil industry.

---

[12] 424 U.S. 1, 96 S.Ct. 612, 1976 U.S. LEXIS 16 (1976).

[13] Federal Election Commission v. Wisconsin Right to Life Inc., 127 S.Ct. 2652 (2007).

Sorting by zip code reveals that most campaign contributions come from large urban areas. A representative sample of zip codes that outpace others include no surprises: 10021 (New York City), 20007 (Washington, D.C.), 90210 (Beverly Hills), 85253 (Paradise Valley, AZ), 06831 (Greenwich, CT), 33480 (Palm Beach, FL), and so forth.[14]

EXAM *Strategy*

Question: Kelly Hackworth took a leave of absence from her job at Progressive Insurance, to care for her ailing mother. When she offered to return, Progressive refused to give her the same job or one like it. She sued, based on the Family Medical Leave Act, a federal statute that requires firms to give workers returning from family leave their original job or an equivalent one. However, the statute excludes from its coverage workers whose company employs "fewer than 50 people within 75 miles" of the worker's jobsite. Between Ms. Hackworth's job site in Norman, Oklahoma, and the company's Oklahoma City workplace (less than 75 miles away), Progressive employed 47 people. At its Lawton, Oklahoma facility, Progressive employed three more people – but Lawton was 75.6 miles (wouldn't you know it) away from Norman. Progressive argued that the job was not covered by the statute. Hackworth claimed that this distance should be considered "within 75 miles," thereby rendering her eligible for FMLA leave. Even if it were not, she urged, it would be absurd to disqualify her from important rights based on a disparity of six-tenths of a mile. Please rule.

Strategy: The question asks you to interpret a statute. How do courts do that? There are three steps: the plain meaning rule; legislative history; and public policy. Apply those steps to these facts.

Result: In this real case, the court ruled that the plain meaning of "within 75 miles" was *75 miles or less*. Lawton was not 75 miles or less from Norman. The statute did not apply and Ms. Hackworth lost.[15]

ADMINISTRATIVE LAW

Before beginning this section, please return your seat to its upright position. Stow the tray firmly in the seatback in front of you. Turn off any laptops, cell phones or other electronic devices. Sound familiar? Administrative agencies affect each of us every day in hundreds of ways. They have become the fourth branch of government. Supporters believe that they provide unique expertise in complex areas; detractors regard them as unelected government run amok.

Many administrative agencies are familiar. The Federal Aviation Agency, which requires all airlines to ensure that your seats are upright before takeoff and landing, is an administrative agency. The Internal Revenue Service haunts us every April 15. The Environmental Protection Agency regulates the water quality of the river in your town.

Rules/regulations/orders created by administrative agencies of government

To regulate the practices in industries day by day

Before beginning this section, please return your seat to its upright position.

---

[14] Election data from The Center for Responsive Politics, http://www.crp.org.

[15] Hackworth v. Progressive Casualty Ins. Co., 468 F.3d 722, 10th Cir. 2006 (10th Circuit Court of Appeals, 2006).

The Federal Trade Commission oversees the commercials that shout at you from your television set.

Other agencies are less familiar. You may never have heard of the Bureau of Land Management, but if you go into the oil and gas industry, you will learn that this powerful agency has more control over your land than you do. If you develop real estate in Palos Hills, Illinois, you will tremble every time the Appearance Commission of the City of Palos Hills speaks, since you cannot construct a new building without its approval. If your software corporation wants to hire an Argentine expert on databases, you will get to know the complex workings of Immigration and Customs Enforcement: no one lawfully enters this country without its nod of approval.

BACKGROUND

By the 1880s, the amazing iron horse crisscrossed America. But this technological miracle became an economic headache. Congress worried that the railroads' economic muscle enabled a few powerful corporations to reap unfair profits. The railroad industry needed closer regulation. Who would do it? Courts decide individual cases, they do not regulate industries. Congress itself passes statutes, but it has no personnel to oversee the day-to-day working of a huge industry. For example, Congress lacks the expertise to establish rates for freight passing from Kansas City to Chicago, and it has no personnel to enforce rates once they are set.

A new entity was needed. Congress passed the Interstate Commerce Act, creating the Interstate Commerce Commission (ICC), the first administrative agency. The ICC began regulating freight and passenger transportation over the growing rail system and continued to do so for over 100 years. Congress gave the ICC power to regulate rates and investigate harmful practices, to hold hearings, issue orders, and punish railroads that did not comply.

The ICC was able to hire and develop a staff that was expert in the issues that Congress wanted controlled. The agency had enough flexibility to deal with the problems in a variety of ways: by regulating, investigating, and punishing. And that is what has made administrative agencies an attractive solution for Congress: one entity, focusing on one industry, can combine expertise and flexibility. However, the ICC also developed great power, which voters could not reach, and thereby started the great and lasting conflict over the role of agencies.

During the Great Depression of the 1930s, the Roosevelt administration and Congress created dozens of new agencies. Many were based on social demands, such as the need of the elderly population for a secure income. Political and social conditions dominated again in the 1960s, as Congress created agencies, such as the Equal Employment Opportunity Commission, to combat discrimination.

Then during the 1980s the Reagan administration made an effort to decrease the number and strength of the agencies. For several years some agencies declined in influence, though others did not. In the new millennium, there is still controversy about how much power agencies should have, but there is no doubt that administrative agencies are a permanent part of our society.

CLASSIFICATION OF AGENCIES

Agencies exist at the federal, state, and local level. We will focus on federal agencies because they have national impact and great power. Most of the principles discussed apply to state and local agencies as well. Virtually any business or profession you choose to work in will be regulated by at least one administrative agency, and it may be regulated by several.

Executive-Independent

Some federal agencies are part of the executive branch while others are independent agencies. This is a major distinction. The president has much greater control of executive agencies for the simple reason that he can fire the agency head at any time. An executive agency will seldom diverge far from the president's preferred policies. Some familiar executive agencies are the Internal Revenue Service (part of the Treasury Department); the Federal Bureau of Investigation (Department of Justice); the Food and Drug Administration (Department of Health and Human Services); and the Nuclear Regulatory Commission (Department of Energy).

The president has no such removal power over independent agencies. The Federal Communications Commission (FCC) is an independent agency. For many corporations involved in broadcasting, the FCC has more day-to-day influence on their business than Congress, the courts, and the president combined. Other powerful independent agencies are the Federal Trade Commission, the Securities and Exchange Commission, the National Labor Relations Board, and the Environmental Protection Agency.

Enabling Legislation (legislation that creates a new government/administrative agency)

Congress creates a federal agency by passing **enabling legislation**. The Interstate Commerce Act was the enabling legislation that established the ICC. Typically, the enabling legislation describes the problems that Congress believes need regulation, establishes an agency to do it, and defines the agency's powers.

Gives appropriate officials the power/authority to implement and enforce the law

Critics argue that Congress is delegating to another body powers that only the legislature or courts are supposed to exercise. This puts administrative agencies above the voters. But legal attacks on administrative agencies invariably fail. Courts acknowledge that agencies have become an integral part of a complex economy. As long as there are some limits on an agency's discretion, a court will uphold its powers.

THE ADMINISTRATIVE PROCEDURE ACT

This act is a major limitation on how agencies do their work. Congress passed the Administrative Procedure Act (APA) in 1946 in an effort to bring uniformity and control to the many federal agencies. The APA regulates how federal agencies make rules, conduct investigations, hold meetings and hearings, reach decisions, and obtain and release information. How much power should agencies have? How much control should we impose on them? These are two of the major questions that businesses and courts face as we enter a new century.

Power of Agencies

Administrative agencies use three kinds of power to do the work assigned to them: they make rules, they investigate, and they adjudicate.

Rulemaking

One of the most important functions of an administrative agency is to make rules. In doing this, the agency attempts, prospectively, to establish fair and uniform behavior for all businesses in the affected area. **To create a new rule is to promulgate it**. Agencies promulgate two types of rules: legislative and interpretive.

Legislative Rules.   These are the most important agency rules, and they are much like statutes. Here, an agency creates law by requiring businesses or private citizens to act in a certain way. Suppose you operate a Web site for young shoppers, aged 10 to 18. Like most online merchants, you consider yourself free to collect as much data as possible about consumers. Wrong. The Federal Trade Commission, a federal agency, has promulgated detailed rules governing any site directed to young children. Before obtaining private data from these immature consumers, you must let them know exactly who you are, how to contact site operators, precisely what you are seeking, and how it will be used. You must also obtain verifiable parental consent before collecting, using, or disclosing any personal information. Failure to follow the rules can result in a substantial civil penalty. This modest legislative rule, in short, will be more important to your business than most statutes passed by Congress.

Interpretive Rules.   These rules do not change the law. They are the agency's interpretation of what the law already requires. But they can still affect all of us.

It's based on what/how an agency interprets a particular word/phrase

In 1977, Congress amended the Clean Air Act in an attempt to reduce pollution from factories. The act required the Environmental Protection Agency (EPA) to impose emission standards on "stationary sources" of pollution. But what did "stationary source" mean? It was the EPA's job to define that term. Obscure work, to be sure, yet the results could be seen and even smelled, because the EPA's definition would determine the quality of air entering our lungs every time we breathe. Environmentalists wanted the term defined to include every smokestack in a factory so that the EPA could regulate each one. The EPA, however, developed the "bubble concept," ruling that "stationary source" meant an entire factory, but not the individual smokestacks. As a result, polluters could shift emission among smokestacks in a single factory to avoid EPA regulation. Environmentalists howled that this gutted the purpose of the statute, but to no avail. The agency had spoken, merely by interpreting a statute.[16]

How Rules Are Made.   Corporations fight many a court battle over whether an agency has the right to issue a particular rule and whether it was promulgated properly. The critical issue is this: How much participation is the public entitled to before an agency issues a rule? There are two basic methods of rulemaking.[17]

Informal Rulemaking.   On many issues, agencies may use a simple "notice and comment" method of rulemaking. The agency must publish a proposed rule in advance and permit the public a comment period. During this period, the public may submit any objections and arguments, with supporting data. The agency will make its decision and publish the final rule.

For example, the Department of Transportation may use the informal rulemaking procedure to require safety features for all new automobiles. The agency must listen to objections from interested parties, notably car manufacturers, and it must give a written response to the objections. The agency is required to have rational reasons for the final choices it makes. However, it is not obligated to satisfy all parties or do their bidding.

Formal Rulemaking.   In the enabling legislation, Congress may require that an agency hold a hearing before promulgating rules. Congress does this to make the agency more accountable to the public. After the agency publishes its proposed rule, it must hold a public hearing. Opponents of the rule, typically affected businesses, may cross-examine the agency experts about the need for the rule and may testify against it. When the agency makes its final decision about the rule, it must prepare a formal, written response to everything that occurred at the hearing.

---

[16] An agency's interpretation can be challenged in court, and this one was.

[17] Certain rules may be made with no public participation at all. For example, an agency's internal business affairs and procedures can be regulated without public comment, as can its general policy statements. None of these directly affect the public, and the public has no right to participate.

When used responsibly, these hearings give the public access to the agency and can help formulate sound policy. When used irresponsibly, hearings can be manipulated to stymie needed regulation. The most famous example concerns peanut butter. The Food and Drug Administration (FDA) began investigating peanut butter content in 1958. It found, for example, that Jif peanut butter, made by Procter & Gamble, had only 75 percent peanuts and 20 percent of a Crisco-type base. P&G fought the investigation, and any changes, for years. Finally, in 1965, the FDA proposed a minimum of 90 percent peanuts in peanut butter; P&G wanted 87 percent. The FDA wanted no more than 3 percent hydrogenated vegetable oil; P&G wanted no limit.

The hearings dragged on for months. One day, the P&G lawyer objected to the hearing going forward because he needed to vote that day. Another time, when an FDA official testified that consumer letters indicated the public wanted to know what was really in peanut butter, the P&G attorney demanded that the official bring in and identify the letters—all 20,000 of them. Finally, in 1968, a decade after beginning its investigation, the FDA promulgated final rules requiring 90 percent peanuts but eliminating the 3 percent cap on vegetable oil.[18]

Investigation

Agencies do an infinite variety of work, but they all need broad factual knowledge of the field they govern. Some companies cooperate with an agency, furnishing information and even voluntarily accepting agency recommendations. For example, the U.S. Consumer Product Safety Commission investigates hundreds of consumer products every year and frequently urges companies to recall goods that the agency considers defective. Many firms comply. (For an up-to-the-minute report on dangerous products and company compliance, proceed carefully to **http://www.cpsc.gov**.)

Other companies, however, jealously guard information, often because corporate officers believe that disclosure would lead to adverse rules. To force disclosure, agencies use *subpoenas* and *searches*.

Subpoenas. A **subpoena** is an order to appear at a particular time and place to provide evidence. A **subpoena** *duces tecum* requires the person to appear and bring specified documents. Businesses and other organizations intensely dislike subpoenas and resent government agents plowing through records and questioning employees. What are the limits on an agency's investigation? The information sought:

- Must be *relevant* to a lawful agency investigation. The FCC is clearly empowered to investigate the safety of broadcasting towers, and any documents about tower construction are obviously relevant. Documents about employee racial statistics might indicate discrimination, but the FCC lacks jurisdiction on that issue and thus may not demand such documents.

- Must not be *unreasonably burdensome*. A court will compare the agency's need for the information with the intrusion on the corporation.

- Must not be *privileged*. The Fifth Amendment privilege against self-incrimination means that a corporate officer accused of criminal securities violations may not be compelled to testify about his behavior.

Subpoena
An order to appear at a particular place and time. A subpoena *duces tecum* requires the person to produce certain documents or things.

[18] For an excellent account of this high-fat hearing, see Mark J. Green, *The Other Government* (New York: W. W. Norton & Co., 1978), pp. 136–150.

In the following case, an agency's subpoena power conflicted with an important right of confidentiality.

DOE V. MARYLAND BOARD OF SOCIAL WORKERS

384 Md. 161, 862 A.2d 996
MARYLAND COURT OF APPEALS, 2004

CASE SUMMARY

Facts: "Ms. F." was a licensed social worker in Maryland. One of her clients, "John Doe," was convicted of child abuse and sex offenses involving his minor granddaughter. The Board of Social Work Examiners, an administrative agency, learned that Ms. F. had likely violated the law by failing to report the abuse. The agency began an investigation, and issued a subpoena *duces tecum* to Ms. F., demanding all treatment records for John Doe and his wife, Jane Doe, for the year in which the abuse occurred.

The Does ("Petitioners") sued, asking the court to quash the subpoena, that is, to nullify it. They claimed that a social worker–client privilege prohibited disclosure of their records. The intermediate court of appeals declared the subpoena valid. The Does appealed to the state's highest court.

Issue: *Was the subpoena valid?*

Decision: Yes, the subpoena was valid. Affirmed.

Reasoning: A state statute creates a confidentiality privilege for social workers and their clients similar to the one allowed doctors and patients, lawyers and clients, and so forth. The information contained in the social worker records is both confidential and privileged. The Board acknowledges the privilege but insists that its subpoena power creates an important exception, based on its need to supervise workers and protect clients. This court must weigh the competing claims.

The legislature established the Board to set reasonable standards of social work and to maintain and enforce those levels of service. But the Board's job becomes impossible if it is routinely denied access to a social worker's records. If there is evidence that a social worker failed to respond to evidence of child abuse, the Board should be able to investigate the case and, if necessary, discipline the worker. Anything less leaves the public at risk. No statutory or constitutional policy automatically bars the Board from obtaining such documents.

To do its job, the Board must be given access to these records. However, to maintain as much confidentiality as possible, the Board should ensure that the records are not given to any other parties.

Search and Seizure.   At times an agency will want to conduct a surprise **search** of an enterprise and **seize** any evidence of wrongdoing. May an agency do that? Yes, although there are limitations. When a particular industry is *comprehensively regulated*, courts will assume that companies know they are subject to periodic, unannounced inspections. In those industries, an administrative agency may conduct a search without a warrant and seize evidence of violations. For example, the mining industry is minutely regulated, with strict rules covering equipment, mining depths, and air quality. Mining executives understand that they are closely watched. Accordingly, the Bureau of Mines may make unannounced, warrantless searches to ensure safety.[19]

---

[19] Donovan v. Dewey, 452 U.S. 594, 101 S. Ct. 2534, 1980 U.S. LEXIS 58 (1981).

Adjudication

To **adjudicate** a case is to hold a hearing about an issue and then decide it. Agencies adjudicate countless cases. The FCC adjudicates which applicant for a new television license is best qualified. The Occupational Safety and Health Administration (OSHA) holds adversarial hearings to determine whether a manufacturing plant is dangerous.

Most adjudications begin with a hearing before an **administrative law judge** (ALJ). There is no jury. An ALJ is an employee of the agency but is expected to be impartial in her rulings. All parties are represented by counsel. The rules of evidence are informal, and an ALJ may receive any testimony or documents that will help resolve the dispute.

After all evidence is taken, the ALJ makes a decision. The losing party has a right to appeal to an appellate board within the agency. The appellate board has the power to make a *de novo* **decision**, meaning it may ignore the ALJ's decision. A party unhappy with that decision may appeal to federal court.

> **Adjudicate**
> To hold a formal hearing about an issue and then decide it.

> **Administrative law judge**
> An agency employee who acts as an impartial decision-maker.

> ***De novo* decision**
> The power of an appellate court or board to ignore a lower judge's ruling and make its own decision.

LIMITS ON AGENCY POWER

There are four primary methods of reining in these powerful creatures: statutory, political, judicial, and informational.

STATUTORY CONTROL

As discussed, the enabling legislation of an agency provides some limits. It may require that the agency use formal rulemaking or investigate only certain issues. The APA imposes additional controls by requiring basic fairness in areas not regulated by the enabling legislation.

[handwritten note: • Sets certain restrictions on agencies. Cannot get involved w/ or regulate beyond what the law denotes]

POLITICAL CONTROL

The president's influence is greatest with executive agencies. Congress, though, controls the purse. No agency, executive or independent, can spend money it does not have. An agency that angers Congress risks having a particular program defunded or its entire budget cut. Further, Congress may decide to defund an agency as a cost-cutting measure. In its effort to balance the budget, Congress abolished the Interstate Commerce Commission, transferring its functions to the Transportation Department.

Congress has additional control because it must approve presidential nominees to head agencies. Before approving a nominee, Congress will attempt to determine her intentions. And, finally, Congress may amend an agency's enabling legislation, limiting its power.

JUDICIAL REVIEW

An individual or corporation directly harmed by an administrative rule, investigation, or adjudication may generally have that action reviewed in federal court.[20] The party seeking

---

[20] In two narrow groups of cases, a court may not review an agency action. In a few cases, courts hold that a decision is "committed to agency discretion," a formal way of saying that courts will keep hands off. This happens only with politically sensitive issues, such as international air routes. In some cases, the enabling legislation makes it absolutely clear that Congress wanted no court to review certain decisions. Courts will honor that.

review, for example, a corporation, must have suffered direct harm; the courts will not listen to theoretical complaints about an agency action.[21] And that party must first have taken all possible appeals within the agency itself.[22]

Standard on Review

Suppose OSHA promulgates a new rule limiting the noise level within steel mills. Certain mill operators are furious because they will have to retool their mills in order to comply. After exhausting their administrative appeals, they file suit seeking to force OSHA to withdraw the new rule. How does a court decide the case? Or, in legal terms, what standard does a court use in reviewing the case? Does it simply substitute its own opinion for that of the agency? No, it does not. The standard a court uses must take into account:

Facts.   Courts generally defer to an agency's fact finding. If OSHA finds that human hearing starts to suffer when decibels reach a particular level, a court will probably accept that as final. The agency is presumed to have expertise on such subjects. As long as there is *substantial evidence* to support the fact decision, it will be respected.

Law.   Courts often—but not always—defer to an agency's interpretation of the law. This is due in part to the enormous range of subjects that administrative agencies monitor. Consider the following example. "Chicken catchers" work in large poultry operations, entering coops, manually capturing broilers, loading them into cages, and driving them to a processing plant where they … well, never mind. On one farm, the catchers wanted to organize a union, but the company objected, pointing out that *agricultural* workers had no right to do so. Were chicken catchers agricultural workers? The National Labor Relations Board, an administrative agency, declared that chicken catchers were in fact *ordinary* workers, entitled to organize. The Supreme Court ruled that courts were obligated to give deference to the agency's decision about chicken catchers. If the agency's interpretation was *reasonable* it was binding, even if the court itself might not have made the same analysis. The workers were permitted to form a union—though the chickens were not.

The following case contains vulgar language, so *please do not read it.*

---

[21] The law describes this requirement by saying that a party must have standing to bring a case. A college student who has a theoretical belief that the EPA should not interfere with the timber industry has no standing to challenge an EPA rule that prohibits logging in a national forest. A lumber company that was ready to log that area has suffered a direct economic injury: it has standing to sue.

[22] This is the doctrine of exhaustion of remedies. A lumber company may not go into court the day after the EPA publishes a proposed ban on logging. It must first exhaust its administrative remedies by participating in the administrative hearing and then pursuing appeals within the agency before venturing into court.

FOX TELEVISION STATIONS, INC. V. FEDERAL COMMUNICATIONS COMMISSION

2010 U.S. APP. LEXIS 14293
2d CIRCUIT COURT OF APPEALS, 2010

CASE SUMMARY

Facts: "People have been telling me I'm on the way out every year, right? So f*** 'em," said Cher, on a televised Billboard Music Awards ceremony. A year later, on the same program, Nicole Richie asked, "Have you ever tried to get cow s*** out of a Prada purse? It's not so f****** simple." The Federal Communications Agency (FCC), which regulates the broadcast industry, received complaints about this and other profanity on the airwaves.

The FCC declared that the above words were invariably indecent, explicit and shocking. Their utterance violated the Commission's decency standards. The Commission said it had the right to fine the networks for broadcasting such speech. The networks protested, arguing that the utterances were fleeting and isolated. They claimed that the Commission's precedent permitted such sporadic usage, that this new ruling was an arbitrary change of policy, and that it violated the networks' First Amendment free speech rights. The Commission disagreed, declaring that it had the right to prohibit even the occasional use of the words. The networks appealed to federal court.

Issue: *Did the FCC abuse its discretion by prohibiting even the occasional use of the words?*

Decision: Yes, the FCC arbitrarily abused its discretion and infringed upon First Amendment rights.

Reasoning: In the past, the Commission had not penalized the occasional use of four-letter words on live TV. Then it tightened its standard and declared that fleeting expletives could violate the Commission's indecency policy if the words were, "patently offensive". But the FCC failed to give a clear definition of "patently offensive", and it enforced its new rule unevenly. The FCC continued to allow profanity on the airwaves in some circumstances, such as outbursts of bad language during legitimate news interviews. The Commission also allowed words that it deemed to be artistic expression. Thus, it raised no complaint when an unedited version of the movie Saving Private Ryan contained a tremendous numbers of four-letter words.

The Second Circuit determined that the policy change had the effect of chilling speech, because broadcasters had no way to determine what the FCC might find patently offensive. The court struck down the FCC's new policy on fleeting expletives as unconstitutionally vague.

INFORMATIONAL CONTROL AND THE PUBLIC

We started this section describing the pervasiveness of administrative agencies. We should end it by noting one way in which all of us have some direct control over these ubiquitous authorities: information.

> A popular government, without popular information, or the means of acquiring it, is but a Prologue to a Farce or a Tragedy—or perhaps both. Knowledge will forever govern ignorance, and a people who mean to be their own Governors must arm themselves with the power which knowledge gives.
>
> *James Madison, President, 1809–1817*

Two federal statutes arm us with the power of knowledge.

Freedom of Information Act

Congress passed this landmark statute (known as "FOIA") in 1966. It is designed to give all of us, citizens, businesses, and organizations alike, access to the information that federal agencies are using. The idea is to avoid government by secrecy.

Any citizen or executive may make a "FOIA request" to any federal government agency. It is simply a written request that the agency furnish whatever information it has on the subject specified. Two types of data are available under FOIA. Anyone is entitled to information about how the agency operates, how it spends its money, and what statistics and other information it has collected on a given subject. People routinely obtain records about agency policies, environmental hazards, consumer product safety, taxes and spending, purchasing decisions, and agency forays into foreign affairs. A corporation that believes that OSHA is making more inspections of its textile mills than it makes of the competition could demand all relevant information, including OSHA's documents on the mill itself, comparative statistics on different inspections, OSHA's policies on choosing inspection sites, and so forth.

Second, all citizens are entitled to any records the government has *about them*. You are entitled to information that the Internal Revenue Service, or the Federal Bureau of Investigation, has collected about you.

FOIA does not apply to Congress, the federal courts, or the executive staff at the White House. Note also that, since FOIA applies to federal government agencies, you may not use it to obtain information from state or local governments or private businesses.

Exemptions.   An agency officially has 10 days to respond to the request. In reality, most agencies are unable to meet the deadline but are obligated to make good faith efforts. FOIA exempts altogether nine categories from disclosure. The most important exemptions permit an agency to keep confidential information that relates to national security, criminal investigations, internal agency matters such as personnel or policy discussions, trade secrets or financial institutions, or an individual's private life.

[handwritten margin note: There are 9 categories in which agencies do not need to provide citizens information!]

Privacy Act

This 1974 statute prohibits federal agencies from giving information about an individual to other agencies or organizations without written consent. There are exceptions, but overall this act has reduced the government's exchange of information about us "behind our back."

EXAM *Strategy*

Question: Builder wants to develop 1,000 acres in rural Montana, land that is home to the Kite Owl. The Environmental Protection Agency (EPA) rules that the Kite Owl is an endangered species, and prohibits development of the property. The developer appeals to court. The EPA based its decision on five statistical studies, and the opinions of three out of seven experts. The court looks at the same evidence and acknowledges that the EPA decision is carefully reasoned and fair. However, the judges believe that the other four experts were right: the owl is *not* endangered. Should the court permit development?

Strategy: What is the legal standard for deciding whether a court should affirm or reverse an agency decision? As long as there is *substantial evidence* to support the factual conclusions, and a *reasonable basis* for the legal conclusion, the court should not impose its judgment. Agencies are presumed to have special expertise in their areas. As the *Fox Television* case tells us, an agency ruling should generally be affirmed unless it is arbitrary and capricious. Apply that standard here.

Result: The EPA made a careful, reasoned decision. The court may disagree, but it should not impose its views. The court must affirm the agency's ruling and prohibit development.

CHAPTER CONCLUSION

"**Why can't they just fix the law?**" They can, and sometimes they do—but it is a difficult and complex task. "They" includes a great many people and forces, from common law courts to members of Congress to campaign donors to administrative agencies. The courts have made the bystander rule slightly more humane, but it has been a long and bumpy road. Congress managed to restore the legal interpretation of its own 1964 Civil Rights Act, but it took months of debate and compromising. The FDA squeezed more peanuts into a jar of Jif, but it took nearly a decade to get the lid on.

A study of law is certain to create some frustrations. This chapter cannot prevent them all. However, an understanding of how law is made is the first step toward controlling that law.

EXAM REVIEW

1. **COMMON LAW** The common law evolves in awkward fits and starts because courts attempt to achieve two contradictory purposes: predictability and flexibility. (p. 77)

2. **STARE DECISIS** *Stare decisis* means "let the decision stand," and indicates that once a court has decided a particular issue, it will generally apply the same rule in future cases. (p. 77)

3. **BYSTANDER RULE** The common law bystander rule holds that, generally, no one has a duty to assist someone in peril unless the bystander himself created the danger. Courts have carved some exceptions during the last 100 years, but the basic rule still stands. (p. 77)

4. **LEGISLATION** Bills originate in congressional committees and go from there to the full House of Representatives or Senate. If both houses pass the bill, the legislation normally must go to a Conference Committee to resolve differences between the two versions. The compromise version then goes from the Conference Committee back to both houses, and if passed by both, to the president. If the president signs the bill, it becomes a statute; if he vetoes it, Congress can pass it over his veto with a two-thirds majority in each house. (p. 81)

5. **STATUTORY INTERPRETATION** Courts interpret a statute by using the plain meaning rule; then, if necessary, legislative history and intent; and finally, if necessary, public policy. (p. 84)

EXAM Strategy

Question: Whitfield, who was black, worked for Ohio Edison. Edison fired him, but then later offered to rehire him. Another employee argued that Edison's original termination of Whitfield had been race discrimination. Edison rescinded its offer to rehire Whitfield. Whitfield sued Edison, claiming that the company was retaliating for the other employee's opposition to discrimination. Edison pointed out that Title VII of the 1964 Civil Rights Act did not explicitly apply in such cases. Among other things, Title VII prohibits an employer from retaliating against *an employee* who has opposed illegal discrimination. But it does not say anything about retaliation based on *another employee's* opposition to discrimination. Edison argued that the statute did not protect Whitfield.

Strategy: What three steps does a court use to interpret a statute? First, the plain meaning rule. Does that rule help us here? The statute neither allows nor prohibits Edison's conduct. The law does not mention this situation, and the plain meaning rule is of no help. Second step: Legislative history and intent. What did Congress intend with Title VII generally? With the provision that bars retaliation against a protesting employee? Resolving those issues should give you the answer to this question. (See the "Result" at the end of this section.)

6. **MONEY** Campaign contributions and spending are largely uncontrolled. (p. 88)

7. **ADMINISTRATIVE AGENCIES** Congress creates federal administrative agencies with enabling legislation. The Administrative Procedure Act controls how agencies do their work. (p. 89)

8. **RULEMAKING** Agencies may promulgate legislative rules, which generally have the effect of statutes, or interpretive rules, which merely interpret existing statutes. (p. 91)

9. **INVESTIGATION** Agencies have broad investigatory powers and may use subpoenas and, in some cases, warrantless searches to obtain information. (p. 93)

Question: When Hiller Systems, Inc., was performing a safety inspection on board the M/V *Cape Diamond*, an ocean-going vessel, an accident killed two men. The Occupational Safety and Health Administration (OSHA), a federal agency, attempted to investigate, but Hiller refused to permit any of its employees to speak to OSHA investigators. What could OSHA do to pursue the investigation? What limits would there have been on OSHA's actions?

Strategy: Agencies make rules, investigate and adjudicate. Which is involved here? Investigation. During an investigation, what power has an agency to force a company to produce data? What are the limits on that power? (See the "Result" at the end of this section.)

10. **ADJUDICATION** Agencies adjudicate cases, meaning that they hold hearings and decide issues. Adjudication generally begins with a hearing before an administrative law judge and may involve an appeal to the full agency or ultimately to federal court. (p. 95)

11. **AGENCY LIMITATIONS** The four most important limitations on the power of federal agencies are statutory control in the enabling legislation and the APA; political control by Congress and the president; judicial review; and the informational control created by the Freedom of Information Act and the Privacy Act. (p. 95)

2. Result: Congress passed Title VII as a bold, aggressive move to end race discrimination in employment. Further, by specifically prohibiting retaliation against an employee, Congress indicated it was aware that companies might punish those who spoke in favor of the very goals of Title VII. Protecting an employee from anti-discrimination statements made by a *co-worker* is a very slight step beyond that, and appears consistent with the goals of Title VII and the anti-retaliation provision. Whitfield should win, and in the real case, he did.[23]

9. Result: OSHA can issue a subpoena *duces tecum*, demanding that those on board the ship, and their supervisors, appear for questioning, and bring with them all relevant documents. OSHA may ask for anything that is (1) relevant to the investigation, (2) not unduly burdensome, and (3) not privileged. Conversations between one of the ship inspectors and his supervisor is clearly relevant; a discussion between the supervisor and the company's lawyer is privileged.

ADDITIONAL QUESTIONS

1. *ETHICS* Suppose you were on a state supreme court and faced with a restaurant-choking case. Should you require restaurant employees to know and employ the Heimlich maneuver to assist a choking victim? If they do a bad job, they could cause additional injury. Should you permit them to do nothing at all? Is there a compromise position? What social policies are most important?

2. *YOU BE THE JUDGE* WRITING PROBLEM An off-duty, out-of-uniform police officer and his son purchased some food from a 7-Eleven store and were still in the parking lot when a carload of teenagers became rowdy. The officer went to speak to them and the teenagers assaulted him. The officer shouted to his son to get the 7-Eleven clerk to call for help. The son entered the store, told the clerk that a police officer needed help, and told the clerk to call the police. He returned 30 seconds later and repeated the request, urging the clerk to say it was a Code 13. The son claimed that the clerk laughed at him and refused to do it. The policeman sued the store. **Argument for the Store:** We sympathize with the policeman and his family, but the store has no liability. A bystander is not obligated to come to the aid of anyone in distress unless the bystander created the peril, and obviously the store did not do so. The policeman should prosecute *and* sue those who attacked him. **Argument for the Police Officer:** We agree that in general a bystander has no obligation to come to the aid of one in distress.

---

[23] EEOC v. Ohio Edison, 7 F.3d 541 (6 Cir. 1993).

However, when a business that is open to the public receives an urgent request to call the police, the business should either make the call or permit someone else to do it.

3. You sign a two-year lease with a landlord for an apartment. The rent will be $1,000 per month. A clause in the lease requires payment on the first of every month. The clause states that the landlord has the right to evict you if you are even one day late with the payment. You forget to pay on time and deliver your check to the landlord on the third day of the month. He starts an eviction case against you. Who should win? If we enforce the contract, what social result does that have? If we ignore the clause, what effect does that have on contract law?

4. Federal antitrust statutes are complex, but the basic goal is straightforward: to prevent a major industry from being so dominated by a small group of corporations that they destroy competition and injure consumers. Does Major League Baseball violate the antitrust laws? Many observers say that it does. A small group of owners not only dominate the industry, but actually *own* it, controlling the entry of new owners into the game. This issue went to the United States Supreme Court in 1922. Justice Holmes ruled, perhaps surprisingly, that baseball is exempt from the antitrust laws, holding that baseball is not "trade or commerce." Suppose that a congressman dislikes this ruling and dislikes the current condition of baseball. What could he do?

5. Until recently, every state had a statute outlawing the burning of American flags. But in *Texas v. Johnson*,[24] the Supreme Court declared such statutes unconstitutional, saying that flag burning is symbolic speech, protected by the First Amendment. Does Congress have the power to overrule the Court's decision?

Background for Questions 6 through 8. The following three questions begin with a deadly explosion. In 1988, terrorists bombed Pan Am Flight 103 over Lockerbie, Scotland, killing all passengers on board. Congress sought to remedy security shortcomings by passing the Aviation Security Improvement Act of 1990, which, among other things, ordered the Federal Aviation Authority (FAA) to prescribe minimum training requirements and minimum staffing levels for airport security. The FAA promulgated rules according to the informal rulemaking process. However, the FAA refused to disclose certain rules, concerning training at specific airports. *Public Citizen, Inc. v. FAA.*[25]

6. Explain what "promulgated rules according to the informal rulemaking process" means.

7. A public interest group called Public Citizen, Inc., along with family members of those who had died at Lockerbie, wanted to know the details of airport security. What steps should they take to obtain the information? Are they entitled to obtain it?

8. The Aviation Security Improvement Act (ASIA) states that the FAA can refuse to divulge information about airport security. The FAA interprets this to mean that it can withhold the data in spite of FOIA. Public Citizen and the Lockerbie family members interpret FOIA as being the controlling statute, requiring disclosure. Is the FAA interpretation binding?

9. **ROLE REVERSAL** Draft a multiple-choice question that highlights the path of legislation from the first congressional committee to the president's desk.

---

[24] 491 U.S. 397, 109 S. Ct. 2533, 1989 U.S. LEXIS 3115 (1989).
[25] 988 F.2d 186, 1993 U.S. App. LEXIS 6024 (D.C. Cir. 1993).

INTERNET RESEARCH PROBLEM

Research some pending legislation in Congress. Go to the Web site of either the Senate or the House of Representatives. Choose some key words that interest you, and see what your government is doing. Read the summary of the bill, if one is provided, or go to the text of the bill, and scan the introduction. What do the sponsors of this bill hope to accomplish? Do you agree or disagree with their goals?

You can find further practice problems at www.cengagebrain.com. See the preface of this book for website access details.

CONSTITUTIONAL LAW

Suppose you want to dance naked in front of 75 strangers. Do you have the right to do it? May the police interrupt your show and insist that you don a few garments? You may consider these odd questions, as relatively few business law students contemplate a career as a nude dancer. Yet the answers to these questions will affect you every day of your life, even if you choose a more prosaic line such as investments or retailing (it is good to have a backup plan).

Suppose you want to dance naked in front of 75 strangers. Do you have the right to do it?

Consider a very different—yet related—question. To revitalize an economically depressed city, the local government attempts to seize houses from private owners, pay for them, and permit private developers to improve the area. The city might benefit, but is that fair to the original owners? Whose rights are more important? Or this one: A political protester is arrested for burning the American flag. May the state outlaw such conduct?

These seemingly unrelated questions all involve the same critical issue: power. Does your state have the power to prohibit nude dancing? If so, does that mean it could outlaw a campaign poster on your front lawn? Prohibit political protest? Take your house and turn it into a more upscale development?

Questions about regulating nude dancing affect all of us because the answers reveal how much control the government may exercise. Constitutional law is a series of variations on one vital theme: government power.

GOVERNMENT POWER

ONE IN A MILLION

The Constitution of the United States is the greatest legal document ever written. No other written constitution has lasted so long, governed so many, or withstood such challenge. This amazing work was drafted in 1787, when two weeks were needed to make the horseback ride from Boston to Philadelphia, a pair of young cities in a weak and disorganized nation. Yet today, when that trip requires less than two hours by jet, the same Constitution successfully governs the most powerful country on earth. This longevity is a tribute to the wisdom and idealism of the Founding Fathers.

The Constitution is not perfect. The original document contained provisions that were racist.[1] Other sections were unclear, and some needed early amendment. Overall, however, the Constitution has worked astonishingly well and has become the model for many constitutions around the world.

The Constitution is short and relatively easy to read. This brevity is potent. The Founding Fathers, also called the **Framers**, wanted it to last for centuries, and they understood that would happen only if the document permitted interpretation and "fleshing out" by later generations. The Constitution's versatility is striking, as we can see from the fact that the document can be used to resolve the crazy quilt of questions posed above. The *First Amendment* governs the two issues of nude dancing and flag burninig. Courts will use the *Takings Clause* to decide when a state's efforts to improve a community have unfairly injured property owners.

This chapter is organized around the issue of power. The first part provides an overview of the Constitution, discussing how it came to be and how it is organized. The second part describes the power given to the three branches of government. The third part is the flip side of power, explaining what individual rights the Constitution guarantees to citizens.

OVERVIEW

Thirteen American colonies gained independence from Great Britain in 1783. The new status was exhilarating. This was the first nation in modern history founded on the idea that the people could govern themselves, democratically. The idea was daring, brilliant, and fraught with difficulties. The states were governing themselves under the Articles of Confederation, but these articles gave the central government no real power. The government could not tax any state or its citizens and had no way to raise money. A government without the ability to raise money does not govern, it panhandles. The national government also lacked the power to regulate commerce between the states or between foreign nations and any state. This was disastrous. States began to impose taxes on goods entering from other states. The young "nation" was a collection of poor relations, threatening to squabble themselves to death.

By 1787 the articles were largely deemed a failure, and the states sent a group of 55 delegates to Philadelphia to amend them. These delegates—the Framers of our

---

[1] Two provisions explicitly endorsed slavery, belying the proposition that all people are created equal. The "Three-Fifths Clause," in Article I, section 2, required that for purposes of taxation and representation, a slave must be counted as three-fifths of a person. Article I, section 9, ensured that southern states would be permitted to continue importing slaves into the country at least until 1808.

Constitution—were not a true cross section of the populace. There were no women or blacks, artisans or small farmers. Most were wealthy; all were powerful within their states.

Rather than amend the old document, the Framers set out to draft a new one, to create a government that had never existed before. It was hard going. What structure should the government have? How much power? Representatives like Alexander Hamilton urged a strong central government. They were the *federalists.* The new government must be able to tax and spend, regulate commerce, control the borders, and do all things that national governments routinely do. But Patrick Henry and other *antifederalists* feared a powerful central government. They had fought a bitter war precisely to get rid of autocratic rulers; they had seen the evil that a distant government could inflict. The anti-federalists insisted that the states retain maximum authority, keeping political control closer to home.

Another critical question was how much power the *people* should have. Most of the aristocratic delegates had little love for the common people and feared that extending this idea of democracy too far would lead to mob rule. Anti-federalists again disagreed. The British had been thrown out, they insisted, to guarantee individual liberty and a chance to participate in the government. Power corrupted. It must be dispersed amongst the people to avoid its abuse.

How to settle these basic differences? By compromise, of course. **The Constitution is a series of compromises about power.** We will see many provisions granting power to one branch of the government while at the same time restraining the authority given.

SEPARATION OF POWERS

One method of limiting power was to create a national government divided into three branches, each independent and equal. Each branch would act as a check on the power of the other two, avoiding the despotic rule that had come from London. Article I of the Constitution created a Congress, which was to have legislative power. Article II created the office of president, defining the scope of executive power. Article III established judicial power by creating the Supreme Court and permitting additional federal courts.

Consider how the three separate powers balance one another: Congress was given the power to pass statutes, a major grant of power. But the president was permitted to veto legislation, a nearly equal grant. Congress, in turn, had the right to override the veto, ensuring that the president would not become a dictator. The president was allowed to appoint federal judges and members of his cabinet, but only with a consenting vote from the Senate.

FEDERALISM

The national government was indeed to have considerable power, but it would still be *limited power.* Article I, section 8, enumerates those issues on which Congress may pass statutes. If an issue is not on the list, Congress has no power to legislate. Thus Congress may create and regulate a post office because postal service is on the list. But Congress may not pass statutes regulating child custody in a divorce: that issue is not on the list. Only the states may legislate child custody issues.

INDIVIDUAL RIGHTS

The original Constitution was silent about the rights of citizens. This alarmed many who feared that the new federal government would have unlimited power over their lives. So in 1791 the first 10 amendments, known as the **Bill of Rights**, were added to the Constitution, guaranteeing many liberties directly to individual citizens.

In the next two sections, we look in more detail at the two sides of the great series of compromises: power granted and rights protected.

POWER GRANTED

CONGRESSIONAL POWER

Article I of the Constitution creates the Congress with its two houses. Representation in the House of Representatives is proportionate with a state's population, but each state elects two senators. The article establishes who is qualified to serve in Congress, setting only three requirements: age, citizenship, and residence.

Congress may perform any of the functions enumerated in Article I, section 8, such as imposing taxes, spending money, creating copyrights, supporting the military, declaring war, and so forth. None of these rights is more important than the authority to raise and spend money (the *power of the purse*), because every branch of government is dependent upon Congress for its money. One of the most important items on this list of congressional powers concerns trade.

Interstate Commerce

"The Congress shall have power to regulate commerce with foreign nations, and among the several states." This is the **Commerce Clause**. With it, the Framers were accomplishing several things in response to the commercial chaos that existed under the Articles of Confederation:

The Commerce Clause
Gives Congress the power to regulate commerce with foreign nations and among states.

1. ***International Commerce—Exclusive Power.*** As to international commerce, the Commerce Clause is clear: only the federal government may regulate it. The federal government must speak with one voice when regulating commercial relations with foreign governments.[2]

2. ***Domestic Commerce—Concurrent Power.*** As to domestic commerce, the clause gives *concurrent power*, meaning that both Congress and the states may regulate it. Congress is authorized to regulate trade between states; each state regulates business within its own borders. Conflicts are inevitable, and they are important to all of us: how business is regulated depends upon *who* does it.
   - ***Positive Aspect: Congressional Power.*** The Framers wanted to give power to Congress to bring coordination and fairness to trade between the states. This is the positive aspect of the Commerce Clause: **Congress is authorized to regulate interstate commerce**.

   - ***Negative or Dormant Aspect: A Limit on the States.*** The Framers also wanted to stop the states from imposing the taxes and regulations that were wrecking the nation's domestic trade. This is the negative, or dormant, aspect of the Commerce Clause: **The power of the states to regulate interstate commerce is severely restricted**.

Substantial Effect Rule

An early test of the Commerce Clause's positive aspect came in the depression years of the 1930s, in *Wickard v. Filburn*.[3] The price of wheat and other grains had fluctuated wildly, severely harming farmers and the national food market. Congress sought to stabilize prices by limiting the bushels per acre that a farmer could grow. Filburn grew more wheat than federal law allowed and was fined. In defense, he claimed that Congress had no right to regulate him. None of his wheat went into interstate commerce. He sold some locally and used the rest on his own farm as food for livestock and as seed. The Commerce Clause, Filburn claimed, gave Congress no authority to limit what he could do.

[2] *Michelin Tire Corp. v. Wages, Tax Commissioner*, 423 U.S. 276, 96 S.Ct. 535, 1976 U.S. LEXIS 120 (1976).
[3] 317 U.S. 111, 63 S.Ct. 82, 1942 U.S. LEXIS 1046 (1942).

The Supreme Court disagreed and held that **Congress may regulate any activity that has a substantial economic effect on interstate commerce**. Filburn's wheat affected interstate commerce because the more he grew for use on his own farm, the less he would need to buy in the open market of interstate commerce. Congress could regulate his farm. Since this ruling, most federal statutes based on the Commerce Clause have been upheld. Congress has used the Commerce Clause to regulate such diverse issues as the working conditions in a factory, discrimination in a motel, and the environmental aspects of coal mining.[4] Each of these has substantial effect on interstate commerce.

In *United States v. Lopez*,[5] however, the Supreme Court ruled that Congress had exceeded its power under the Commerce Clause. Congress had passed a criminal statute called the "Gun-Free School Zones Act," which forbade any individual from possessing a firearm in a school zone. The goal of the statute was obvious: to keep schools safe. Lopez was convicted of violating the act and appealed his conviction all the way to the high Court, claiming that Congress had no power to pass such a law. The government argued that the Commerce Clause gave it the power to pass the law, but the Supreme Court was unpersuaded.

> The possession of a gun in a local school zone is in no sense an economic activity that might, through repetition elsewhere, substantially affect any sort of interstate commerce. [Lopez] was a local student at a local school; there is no indication that he had recently moved in interstate commerce, and there is no requirement that his possession of the firearm have any concrete tie to interstate commerce. To uphold the Government's contentions here, we would have to pile inference upon inference in a manner that would bid fair to convert congressional authority under the Commerce Clause to a general police power of the sort retained by the States. [The statute was unconstitutional and void.]

Congress's power is great—but still limited.

State Legislative Power

The "dormant" or "negative" aspect of the Commerce Clause governs state efforts to regulate interstate commerce. **The dormant aspect holds that a state statute which discriminates against interstate commerce is almost always unconstitutional.** Here is an example, but please do not read it if you plan to drive later today. Michigan and New York permitted in-state wineries to sell directly to consumers. They both denied this privilege to out-of-state producers, who were forced to sell to wholesalers, who offered the wine to retailers, who sold to consumers. This created an impossible barrier for many small vineyards, which did not produce enough wine to attract wholesalers. Even if they did, the multiple resales drove their prices prohibitively high.

Local residents and out-of-state wineries sued, claiming that the state regulations violated the dormant Commerce Clause. The Supreme Court ruled that these statutes obviously discriminated against out-of-state vineyards; the schemes were illegal unless Michigan and New York could demonstrate an important goal that could not be met any other way. The states' alleged motive was to prevent minors from purchasing wine over the Internet. However, Michigan and New York offered no evidence that such purchases were really a problem. The Court said that minors seldom drink wine, and when they do, they seek instant gratification, not a package in the mail. States that allowed direct shipment to consumers reported no increase in purchases by minors. This discrimination against interstate commerce, like most, was unconstitutional.[6]

---

[4] *Maryland v. Wirts*, 392 U.S. 183, 88 S.Ct. 2017, 1968 U.S. LEXIS 2981 (1968); *Heart of Atlanta Motel v. United States*, 379 U.S. 241, 85 S.Ct. 348, 1964 U.S. LEXIS 2187 (1964); *Hodel v. Indiana*, 452 U.S. 314, 101 S.Ct. 2376, 1981 U.S. LEXIS 34 (1981).

[5] 514 U.S. 549, 115 S.Ct. 1624, 1995 U.S. LEXIS 3039 (1995).

[6] Granholm v. Heald, 544 U.S. 460, 1255 S.Ct. 1885 (2005).

DEVIL'S ADVOCATE Underage drinking is a serious problem. The Court should allow states wide leeway in their efforts to limit the harm. Even if the regulations are imperfect, they may help reduce the damage. ◆

Supremacy Clause

What happens when both the federal and state governments pass regulations that are permissible, but conflicting? For example, Congress passed the federal Occupational Safety and Health Act (OSHA) establishing many job safety standards, including those for training workers who handle hazardous waste. Congress had the power to do so under the Commerce Clause. Later, Illinois passed its own hazardous waste statutes, seeking to protect both the general public and workers. The state statute did not violate the Commerce Clause because it imposed no restriction on interstate commerce.

Each statute specified worker training and employer licensing. But the requirements differed. Which statute did Illinois corporations have to obey? Article VI of the Constitution contains the answer. **The Supremacy Clause** states that the Constitution, and federal statutes and treaties, shall be the supreme law of the land.

The Supremacy Clause
Makes the Constitution, and federal statutes and treaties, the supreme law of the land.

- If there is a conflict between federal and state statutes, the federal law **preempts** the field, meaning it controls the issue. The state law is void.

- Even in cases where there is no conflict, if Congress demonstrates that it intends to exercise exclusive control over an issue, federal law preempts.

Thus state law controls only when there is no conflicting federal law *and* Congress has not intended to dominate the issue. In the Illinois case, the Supreme Court concluded that Congress intended to regulate the issue exclusively. Federal law therefore preempted the field, and local employers were obligated to obey only the federal regulations.

EXAM *Strategy*

Question: Dairy farming was more expensive in Massachusetts than in other states. To help its farmers, Massachusetts taxed all milk sales, regardless of where the milk was produced. The revenues went into a fund that was then distributed to in-state dairy farmers. Discuss.

Strategy: By giving a subsidy to local farmers, the state is treating them differently than out-of-state dairies. This raises *Commerce Clause* issues. Does either the positive or the dormant aspect of that clause apply? The dormant aspect applies. What does it state? Apply that standard to theses facts.

Result: The dormant aspect holds that a state statute which discriminates against interstate commerce is almost always invalid. Massachusetts was subsidizing its farmers at the expense of those from other states. The tax violates the Commerce Clause and is void.

EXECUTIVE POWER

Article II of the Constitution defines the executive power. Once again the Constitution gives powers in general terms. The basic job of the president is to enforce the nation's laws. Three of his key powers concern appointment, legislation, and foreign policy.

Appointment

Administrative agencies play a powerful role in business regulation, and the president nominates the heads of most of them. These choices dramatically influence what issues the agencies choose to pursue and how aggressively they do it. For example, a president who believes that it is vital to protect our natural resources may appoint a forceful environmentalist to run the Environmental Protection Agency, whereas a president who dislikes federal regulations will choose a more passive agency head.[7]

Legislation

The president and his advisers propose bills to Congress. During the last 50 years, a vast number of newly proposed bills have come from the executive branch. Some argue that *too many* proposals come from the president and that Congress has become overly passive. When a president proposes controversial legislation on a major issue, such as Social Security reform, the bill can dominate the news—and Congress—for months or even years. The president, of course, also has the power to veto bills.[8]

Foreign Policy

The president conducts the nation's foreign affairs, coordinating international efforts, negotiating treaties, and so forth. The president is also the commander in chief of the armed forces, meaning that he heads the military. But Article II does not give him the right to declare war—only the Senate may do that. Thus a continuing tension between president and Congress has resulted from the president's use of troops overseas *without* a formal declaration of war. Once again, the Founding Fathers' desire to create a balanced government leads to uncertain application of the law.

JUDICIAL POWER

Article III of the Constitution creates the Supreme Court and permits Congress to establish lower courts within the federal court system.[9] Federal courts have two key functions: adjudication and judicial review.

Adjudicating Cases

The federal court system hears criminal and civil cases. All prosecutions of federal crimes begin in United States District Court. That same court has limited jurisdiction to hear civil lawsuits, a subject discussed in Chapter 3, on dispute resolution.

Judicial Review

One of the greatest "constitutional" powers appears nowhere in the Constitution. In 1803 the Supreme Court decided *Marbury v. Madison*.[10] Congress had passed a relatively minor statute that gave certain powers to the Supreme Court, and Marbury wanted the Court to use those powers. The Court refused. In an opinion written by Chief Justice John Marshall, the Court held that the statute violated the Constitution because Article III of the Constitution did not grant the Court those powers. The details of the case were insignificant, but the ruling was profound: because the statute violated the Constitution, said the Court, it was void. **Judicial review refers to the power of federal courts to declare a statute or governmental action unconstitutional and void.**

---

[7] For a discussion of administrative agency power, see Chapter 4, on administrative law.

[8] For a discussion of the president's veto power and Congress's power to override a veto, see Chapter 4, on statutory law.

[9] For a discussion of the federal court system, see Chapter 3, on dispute resolution.

[10] 5 U.S. (1 Cranch) 137 (1803).

This formidable grab of power has produced two centuries of controversy. The Court was declaring that it alone had the right to evaluate acts of the other two branches of government—the Congress and the executive—and to decide which were valid and which void. The Constitution nowhere grants this power. Undaunted, Marshall declared that "[I]t is emphatically the province and duty of the judicial department to say what the law is." In later cases, the Supreme Court expanded on the idea, holding that it could also nullify state statutes, rulings by state courts, and actions by federal and state officials. In this chapter we have already encountered an example of judicial review, for example, in the *Lopez case*, where the justices declared that Congress lacked the power to pass local gun regulations.

Is judicial review good for the nation? Those who oppose it argue that federal court judges are all appointed, not elected, and that we should not permit judges to nullify a statute passed by elected officials because that diminishes the people's role in their government. Those who favor judicial review insist that there must be one cohesive interpretation of the Constitution and the judicial branch is the logical one to provide it. The following example of judicial review shows how immediate and emotional the issue can be. This is a criminal prosecution for a brutal crime. Cases like this force us to examine two questions about judicial review. What is the proper punishment for such a horrible crime? Just as important, *who should make that decision*—appointed judges, or elected legislators?

KENNEDY V. LOUISIANA

128 S.CT. 2641
UNITED STATES SUPREME COURT, 2008

CASE SUMMARY

Facts: Patrick Kennedy raped his eight-year-old stepdaughter, referred to as L.H. A forensic expert testified that L.H.'s physical injuries were the most severe he had ever witnessed from a sexual assault. The jury also heard evidence that the defendant had raped another eight-year-old. Kennedy was convicted of aggravated rape, because the victim was under 12 years of age.

The jury voted to sentence Kennedy to death, which was permitted by the Louisiana statute. The state supreme court affirmed the death sentence, and Kennedy appealed to the United States Supreme Court. He argued that the Louisiana statute was unconstitutional. The Eighth Amendment prohibits cruel and unusual punishment, which includes penalties that are out of proportion to the crime. Kennedy claimed that capital punishment was out of proportion to rape, and violated the Eighth Amendment.

Issue: *Did the Louisiana statute violate the Constitution by permitting the death penalty in a case of child rape?*

Decision: Yes, the Louisiana statute violated the Eighth Amendment. Reversed.

Reasoning: Constitutional liberties create limits. States may define crimes and set punishments, but the penalties must not be excessive in light of evolving standards of decency in modern society. The death penalty requires special attention.

Only six states (Louisiana, Georgia, Montana, Oklahoma, South Carolina, and Texas) allow for a death sentence in cases of child rape. The other 44 states either do not have capital crimes or allow for the death penalty only when a defendant takes a life.

The majority of the Justices determined that the crime in this case, while horrific, was nonetheless not equivalent to murder in its "severity and irrevocability." It concluded that Louisiana's statute amounted to cruel and unusual punishment.

Dissent by Justice Alito: The court is wrong about the evolving standards of decency. In recent years, five states have passed laws that impose capital punishment in capital rape cases. They have acted in response to a significant increase in reports of the sexual abuse of children. These laws do not violate the Eighth Amendment.

Judicial Activism/Judicial Restraint.   The power of judicial review is potentially dictatorial. The Supreme Court nullifies statutes passed by Congress (*Marbury v. Madison, United States v. Lopez*) and executive actions. May it strike down any law it dislikes? In theory, no. The Court should nullify only laws that violate the Constitution. But of course that is circular, since it is the Court that will tell us which laws are violative.

Judicial activism

A court's willingness to be involved in major issues.

Judicial restraint

A court's attitude that it should leave lawmaking to legislators.

Judicial activism refers to a court's willingness, or even eagerness, to become involved in major issues and to decide cases on constitutional grounds. **Judicial restraint** is the opposite, an attitude that courts should leave lawmaking to legislators and nullify a law only when it unquestionably violates the Constitution.

From the 1950s through the 1970s, the Supreme Court took an active role, deciding many major social issues on constitutional grounds. The landmark 1954 decision in *Brown v. Board of Education*[11] ordered an end to racial segregation in public schools, not only changing the nation's educational systems but altering forever its expectations about race. The Court also struck down many state laws that denied minorities the right to vote. Beginning with *Miranda v. Arizona*,[12] the Court began a sweeping reappraisal of the police power of the state and the rights of criminal suspects during searches, interrogations, trials, and appeals. And in *Roe v. Wade*[13] the Supreme Court established certain rights to abortion, most of which remain after decades of continuous litigation and violence.

Beginning in the late 1970s, and lasting to the present, the Court has pulled back from its activism. Some justices believe that the Founding Fathers never intended the judicial branch to take so prominent a role in sculpting the nation's laws and its social vision. Simple numbers tell part of the story of a changing Court. Every year roughly 8,000 requests for review are made to the Court. In the early 1970s, the Supreme Court accepted almost 200 of these cases, but by 2000, it was taking fewer than 100. The Court's practice of judicial restraint means that major social issues will increasingly be left to state legislatures and Congress.

Exhibit 5.1 illustrates the balance among Congress, the president, and the Court.

PROTECTED RIGHTS

The amendments to the Constitution protect the people of this nation from the power of state and federal government. The First Amendment guarantees rights of free speech, free press, and religion; the Fourth Amendment protects against illegal searches; the Fifth Amendment ensures due process; the Sixth Amendment demands fair treatment for defendants in criminal prosecutions; and the Fourteenth Amendment guarantees equal protection of the law. We consider the First, Fifth, and Fourteenth Amendments in this chapter and the Fourth, Fifth, and Sixth Amendments in Chapter 7, on crime.

The "people" who are protected include citizens and, for most purposes, corporations. Corporations are considered persons and receive most of the same protections. The great majority of these rights also extend to citizens of other countries who are in the United States.

Constitutional rights generally protect only against governmental acts. The Constitution generally does not protect us from the conduct of private parties, such as corporations or other citizens.

---

[11] 347 U.S. 483, 74 S.Ct. 686, 1954 U.S. LEXIS 2094 (1954).
[12] 384 U.S. 436, 86 S.Ct. 1602, 1966 U.S. LEXIS 2817 (1966).
[13] 410 U.S. 113, 93 S.Ct. 705, 1973 U.S. LEXIS 159 (1973).

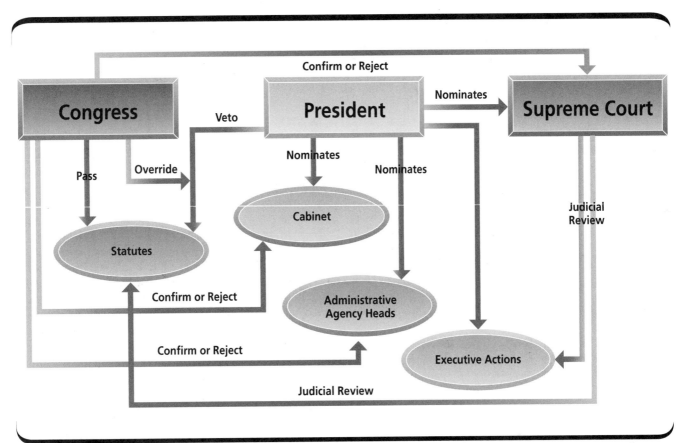

Exhibit 5.1   The Constitution established a federal government of checks and balances. Congress may pass statutes; the president may veto them; and Congress may override the veto. The president nominates cabinet officers, administrative heads, and Supreme Court justices, but the Senate must confirm his nominees. Finally, the Supreme Court (and lower federal courts) exercises judicial review over statutes and executive actions. Unlike the other checks and balances, judicial review is not provided for in the Constitution, but is a creation of the Court itself in *Marbury v. Madison*.

INCORPORATION

Constitutional protections apply to federal, state, and local governments. Yet that is not what the Bill of Rights explicitly states. The First Amendment declares that *Congress* shall not abridge the right of free speech. The Fourteenth Amendment explicitly limits the power only of state governments. But a series of Supreme Court cases has extended virtually all of the important constitutional protections to all levels of national, state, and local government. This process is called **incorporation** because rights explicitly guaranteed at one level are incorporated into rights that apply at other levels.

FIRST AMENDMENT: FREE SPEECH

The First Amendment states that "Congress shall make no law … abridging the freedom of speech…." In general, we expect our government to let people speak and hear whatever they choose. The Founding Fathers believed democracy would only work if the members of the electorate were free to talk, argue, listen, and exchange viewpoints in any way they wanted. The people could only cast informed ballots if they were informed. "Speech" also includes symbolic conduct, as the following case flamingly illustrates.

TEXAS V. JOHNSON

491 U.S. 397, 109 S.Ct. 2533, 1989 U.S. LEXIS 3115
UNITED STATES SUPREME COURT, 1989

CASE SUMMARY

Facts: Outside the Republican National Convention in Dallas, Gregory Johnson participated in a protest against policies of the Reagan administration. Participants gave speeches and handed out leaflets. Johnson burned an American flag. He was arrested and convicted under a Texas statute that prohibited desecrating the flag, but the Texas Court of Criminal Appeals reversed on the grounds that the conviction violated the First Amendment. Texas appealed to the United States Supreme Court.

Issue: *Does the First Amendment protect flag burning?*

Decision: Affirmed. The First Amendment protects flag burning.

Reasoning: The First Amendment literally applies only to "speech," but this Court has already ruled that the Amendment also protects written words and other conduct that will convey a specific message. For example, earlier decisions protected a student's right to wear a black armband in protest against American military actions. Judged by this standard, flag burning is symbolic speech.

Texas argues that its interest in honoring the flag justifies its prosecution of Johnson, since he knew that his action would be deeply offensive to many citizens. However, if there is a bedrock principle underlying the First Amendment, it is that the government may not prohibit the expression of an idea simply because society finds it offensive.

The best way to preserve the flag's special role in our lives is not to punish those who feel differently but to persuade them that they are wrong. We do not honor our flag by punishing those who burn it, because in doing so we diminish the freedom that this cherished emblem represents.

Flag burning is an issue that will not go away. For additional thoughts on the subject, fire up **http://www.esquilax.com** and click on "The Flag-Burning Page," an irreverent page that strongly supports the rights of free speech. To read an anti-flag burning Web page, extinguish all matches and go to **http://www.cfa-inc.org**.

Political Speech

Political speech

Protected unless it is intended and likely to create imminent lawless action.

Because the Framers were primarily concerned with enabling democracy to function, political speech has been given an especially high degree of protection. Such speech may not be barred even when it is offensive or outrageous. A speaker, for example, could accuse a U.S. senator of being insane and could use crude, violent language to describe him. The speech is still protected. **Political speech** is protected unless it is intended and likely to create imminent lawless action.[14] For example, suppose the speaker said, "The senator is inside that restaurant. Let's get some matches and burn the place down." Speech of this sort is not protected. The speaker could be arrested for attempted arson or attempted murder.

---

[14] *Brandenburg v. Ohio*, 395 U.S. 444, 89 S.Ct. 1827, 1969 U.S. LEXIS 1367 (1969).

Time, Place, and Manner

Even when speech is protected, the government may regulate the *time, place*, and *manner* of such speech. A town may require a group to apply for a permit before using a public park for a political demonstration. The town may insist that the demonstration take place during daylight hours and that there be adequate police supervision and sanitation provided. However, the town may not prohibit such demonstrations outright.

The Supreme Court is frequently called upon to balance the rights of the general public with the rights of those seeking to publicize their causes. In *Madsen v. Women's Health Center, Inc.,*[15] the Court ruled that a local judge could limit protesters' access to a family planning clinic. The protesters, opposed to abortion, had repeatedly blocked access to the clinic, harassed patients and doctors at the clinic and at their homes, and paraded with graphic signs and bullhorns. The Court upheld the order prohibiting the protesters from coming within 36 feet of the clinic and also the order that prohibited excessive noise. But the Court overturned a part of the order that had forbidden protesters from displaying graphic images that could be seen inside the clinic. The Court said that the proper remedy was for the clinic to close its curtains.

Morality and Obscenity

The regulation of morality and obscenity presents additional problems. Obscenity has never received constitutional protection. The Supreme Court has consistently held that it does not play a valued role in our society and has refused to give protection to obscene works. That is well and good, but it merely forces the question: What is obscene?

In *Miller v. California,*[16] the Court created a three-part test to determine if a creative work is obscene. The basic guidelines for the factfinder are:

- Whether the average person, applying contemporary community standards, would find that the work, taken as a whole, appeals to the prurient interest;

- Whether the work depicts or describes, in a patently offensive way, sexual conduct specifically defined by the applicable state law; and

- Whether the work, taken as a whole, lacks serious literary, artistic, political, or scientific value.

If the trial court finds that the answer to all three of those questions is "yes," it may judge the material obscene; the state may then prohibit the work. If the state fails to prove any one of the three criteria, though, the work is not obscene.[17] A United States District Court ruled that "As Nasty As They Wanna Be," recorded by 2 Live Crew, was obscene. The appeals court, however, reversed, finding that the state had failed to prove lack of artistic merit.[18]

What if sexual conduct is not obscene? Let's go back to the chapter's starting point, nude dancing.

---

[15] 511 U.S. 1016, 114 S.Ct. 1395, 1994 U.S. LEXIS 2671 (1994).
[16] 413 U.S. 15, 93 S.Ct. 2607, 1973 U.S. LEXIS 149 (1973).
[17] *Penthouse Intern Ltd. v. McAuliffe*, 610 F.2d 1353 (5th Cir. 1980).
[18] *Luke Records, Inc. v. Navarro*, 960 F.2d 134, 1992 U.S. App. LEXIS 9592 (11th Cir. 1992).

YOU *be the* JUDGE

BARNES V. GLEN THEATRE, INC.
501 U.S. 560, 111 S.Ct. 2456, 1991 U.S. LEXIS 3633
UNITED STATES SUPREME COURT, 1991

Facts: Indiana's public indecency statute prohibits any person from appearing nude in a public place. State courts have interpreted this to mean that a dancer in a theater or bar must wear pasties and a G-string. A nightclub called the Kitty Kat Lounge and several dancers who wished to perform nude filed suit, seeking an order that the statute was unconstitutional. The United States District Court ruled that the dancing was not expressive conduct and therefore was not entitled to First Amendment protection. The Court of Appeals reversed, declaring that it was nonobscene expressive conduct and thus protected by the First Amendment.

Indiana did not argue that the dancing was obscene. (If that were the issue, the *Miller* test would have determined the outcome.) Instead, Indiana claimed that its general police powers, including the power to protect social order, allowed it to enforce such a statute.

You Be the Judge: Does Indiana's public indecency statute violate the First Amendment?

Argument for Indiana: Your honors, the State of Indiana has no wish to suppress ideas or censor speech. We are not trying to outlaw eroticism or any other legitimate form of expression. We are simply prohibiting nudity in public. We have outlawed all public nudity, not just nightclub performances. Nudity on the beach, in the park, or anywhere in public is prohibited.

We do this to protect societal order, to foster a stable morality. It is well established that the police power of the state includes the right to regulate the public health, safety, and morals. Our citizens disapprove of people appearing in the nude in public places. The citizens of virtually all states feel the same. Decent dress has been a part of good society since time immemorial. Our voting public is entitled to have that standard upheld.

We also enforce this statute because experience has shown that nightclubs such as these are often associated with criminal behavior. Prostitution, illegal drugs, and violence appear too frequently in the vicinity. It is a reasonable step for the State to maintain control over the performances and the people they will attract.

Argument for Kitty Kat: It is apparent beyond debate that dance is expressive conduct. As an art form, it has existed for at least several thousand years. Eroticism, also, is not exactly news. Erotic dance is clearly expressive conduct. Indeed, the present dancing derives its strength from its eroticism. If the State did not consider it erotic, doubtless it would have left the dancers alone. This dancing is expressive conduct and deserves the full protection of the First Amendment.

Indiana is choosing a certain type of expression and outlawing it. The state has not outlawed all nudity, since quite obviously nudity in private is beyond the State's reach. Nor has it prohibited all nude performances. Testimony of police at trial indicated that no arrests have ever been made for nudity as part of a play or ballet. Nudity is no longer anything novel in musicals, ballets, stage plays, or film. Indiana permits nudity in all of them and enforces its moralizing law only against nightclubs.

This is an obvious value judgment on the part of the State. The State is saying that if you can afford to pay for a Broadway show that happens to have nudity, you are free to enjoy it; if your taste or pocketbook leads you to the Kitty Kat Lounge, we deny your right to witness nudity. If the State is allowed to make that appraisal, then it is free to censor any expression—artistic, political, or any other—that it finds inferior. It was *precisely* to prevent states from outlawing unpopular expression that the Founding Fathers added the First Amendment.

Commercial speech
Communication, such as advertisements, that has the dominant theme of proposing a business transaction.

Commercial Speech
This refers to **speech** that has a **dominant theme to propose a commercial transaction**. For example, most advertisements on television and in the newspapers are commercial speech. This sort of speech is protected by the First Amendment, but the government is permitted to regulate it more closely than other forms of speech. Commercial speech that is false or

misleading may be outlawed altogether. **The government may regulate other commercial speech, provided that the rules are reasonable, and directed to a legitimate goal.** The following case demonstrates the very different treatment given to this type of speech.

SALIB V. CITY OF MESA

133 P.3d 756 212 ARIZ. 446
ARIZONA COURT OF APPEALS, 2006.

CASE SUMMARY

Facts: Edward Salib owned a Winchell's Donut House in Mesa, Arizona. To attract customers, he displayed large signs in his store window. The city ordered him to remove the signs because they violated its Sign Code, which prohibited covering more than 30% of a store's windows with signs. Salib sued, claiming that the Sign Code violated his First Amendment free speech rights. The trial court gave summary judgment for Mesa, and the store owner appealed.

Issue: *Did Mesa's Sign Code violate the First Amendment?*

Decision: No, the Code placed a reasonable limit on commercial speech. Affirmed.

Reasoning: The First Amendment guarantees free speech rights to people and to organizations. The government, though, can restrict commercial speech in some circumstances. Regulators, for example, can ban false and misleading messages. They may also place limits on other advertisements if they pass the following three-part test:

First, the government has a substantial interest. Second, a restriction directly advances this interest. Third, the restriction is narrowly tailored to meet its goal.

In the case, the City of Mesa claimed a substantial interest in making its business district aesthetically pleasing. It argued that the Sign Code did in fact make the city more attractive. Mesa also claimed that its 30% standard was a narrow and reasonable compromise between its interest in city beautification and the rights of business owners.

The court agreed with Mesa's arguments and declined to second-guess the standard.

EXAM *Strategy*

Question: Maria owns a lot next to a freeway that passes through Tidyville. She has rented a billboard to Huge Mart, a nearby retailer, and a second billboard to Green, a political party. However, Tidyville prohibits off-premises signs (those not on the advertiser's property) that are visible from the freeway. Tidyville's rule is designed to make the city more attractive, to increase property values, and to eliminate distractions that may cause freeway accidents. Huge Mart and Green sue, claiming that Tidyville's law violates their First Amendment rights.

A   Huge Mart is likely to win; Green is likely to lose.

B   Green is likely to win; Huge Mart is likely to lose.

C   Huge Mart and Green are both likely to win.

D   Huge Mart and Green are both likely to lose.

E   I know the answer, I just can't think of it.

Strategy: What is the difference between the two cases? Huge Mart wants the billboard for commercial speech; Green wants it for a political message. What are the legal standards for commercial and political free speech? Apply those standards.

Result: The government may regulate commercial speech, provided that the rules are reasonable, and directed to a legitimate goal. Political speech is given much stronger protection, and can be prohibited only if it is intended and likely to create imminent lawless action. The regulation outlawing *advertising* will be upheld, but Tidyville will not be allowed to block political messages.

FIFTH AMENDMENT: DUE PROCESS AND THE TAKINGS CLAUSE

You are a third-year student in a combined business/law program at a major state university. You feel great about a difficult securities exam you took in Professor Watson's class. The Dean's Office sends for you, and you enter curiously, wondering if your exam was so good that the dean is awarding you a prize. Not quite. The exam proctor has accused you of cheating. Based on the accusation, Watson has flunked you. You protest that you are innocent and demand to know what the accusation is. The dean says that you will learn the details at a hearing, if you wish to have one. She reminds you that if you lose the hearing, you will be expelled from the university. Three years of work and your entire career are suddenly on the line.

> **Three years of work and your entire career are suddenly on the line.**

The hearing is run by Professor Holmes, who will make the final decision. Holmes is a junior faculty member in Watson's department. (Next year, Watson will decide Holmes's tenure application.) At the hearing, the proctor accuses you of copying from a student sitting in front of you. Both Watson and Holmes have already compared the two papers and concluded that they are strongly similar. Holmes tells you that you must convince him the charge is wrong. You examine the papers, acknowledge that there are similarities, but plead as best you can that you never copied. Holmes doesn't buy it. The university expels you, placing on your transcript a notation of cheating.

Have you received fair treatment? To answer that, we must look to the Fifth Amendment, which provides several vital protections. We will consider two related provisions, the Due Process Clause and the Takings Clause. Together, they state: "No person shall be… deprived of life, liberty, or property without due process of law; nor shall private property be taken for public use, without just compensation." These clauses prevent the government from arbitrarily taking the most valuable possessions of a citizen or corporation. We will discuss the civil law aspects of these clauses, but due process also applies to criminal law. The reference to "life" refers to capital punishment. The criminal law issues of this subject are discussed in Chapter 7, on crime.

In civil law proceedings, the government does have the right to take a person's liberty or property. But there are three important limitations:

- *Procedural Due Process.* Before depriving anyone of liberty or property, the government must go through certain procedures to ensure that the result is fair.

- *The Takings Clause.* When the government takes property for public use, such as to build a new highway, it has to pay a fair price.

- *Substantive Due Process.* Some rights are so fundamental that the government may not take them from us at all.

Takings Clause
Ensures that when any governmental unit takes private property for public use, it must compensate the owner.

Procedural Due Process

The government deprives citizens or corporations of their property in a variety of ways. The Internal Revenue Service may fine a corporation for late payment of taxes. The Customs Service may seize goods at the border. As to liberty, the government may take it by confining someone in a mental institution or by taking a child out of the home because of parental neglect. The purpose of **procedural due process** is to ensure that before the government takes liberty or property, the affected person has a fair chance to oppose the action.

There are two steps in analyzing a procedural due process case:

- Is the government attempting to take liberty or property?

- If so, how much process is due? (If the government is not attempting to take liberty or property, there is no due process issue.)

Is the Government Attempting to Take Liberty or Property?   Liberty interests are generally easy to spot: confining someone in a mental institution and taking a child from her home are both deprivations of liberty. A property interest may be obvious. Suppose that, during a civil lawsuit, the court **attaches** a defendant's house, meaning it bars the defendant from selling the property at least until the case is decided. This way, if the plaintiff wins, the defendant will have assets to pay the judgment. The court has clearly deprived the defendant of an important interest in his house, and the defendant is entitled to due process. However, a property interest may be subtler than that. A woman holding a job with a government agency has a "property interest" in that job, because her employer has agreed not to fire her without cause, and she can rely on it for income. If the government does fire her, it is taking away that property interest, and she is entitled to due process. A student attending any public school has a property interest in that education. If a public university suspends a law/business student, as described earlier, it is taking her property, and she, too, should receive due process.

How Much Process Is Due?   Assuming that a liberty or property interest is affected, a court must decide how much process is due. Does the person get a formal trial, or an informal hearing, or merely a chance to reply in writing to the charges against her? If she gets a hearing, must it be held before the government deprives her of her property, or is it enough that she can be heard shortly thereafter? **What sort of hearing the government must offer depends upon how important the property or liberty interest is and on whether the government has a competing need for efficiency.** The more important the interest, the more formal the procedures must be.

Neutral Factfinder.   Regardless of how formal the hearing, one requirement is constant: the factfinder must be neutral. Whether it is a superior court judge deciding a multimillion dollar contract suit or an employment supervisor deciding the fate of a government employee, the factfinder must have no personal interest in the outcome. In *Ward v. Monroeville*,[19] the plaintiff was a motorist who had been stopped for traffic offenses in a small town. He protested his innocence and received a judicial hearing. But the "judge" at the hearing was the town mayor. Traffic fines were a significant part of the town's budget. The motorist argued that the town was depriving him of procedural due process because the mayor had a financial interest in the outcome of the case. The United States Supreme Court agreed and reversed his conviction.

Attachment of Property.   As described earlier, a plaintiff in a civil lawsuit often seeks to attach the defendant's property. This protects the plaintiff, but it may also harm the defendant if, for example, he is about to close a profitable real estate deal. Attachments used to

Procedural due process
Ensures that before the government takes liberty or property, the affected person has a fair chance to oppose the action.

[handwritten note:] It only becomes a due process issue when the government is depriving anyone of their liberty or property

[handwritten note:] Where an individual is facing a deprivation of life, liberty or property, they are entitled to due process (notice of the charges against him/her, a hearing to oppose the action and a neutral judge)

---

[19] 409 U.S. 57, 93 S.Ct. 80, 1972 U.S. LEXIS 11 (1972).

be routine. In *Connecticut v. Doehr*, the Supreme Court required more caution.[20] Based on *Doehr*, when a plaintiff seeks to attach at the beginning of the trial, a court must look at the plaintiff's likelihood of winning. Generally, the court must grant the defendant a hearing *before* attaching the property. The defendant, represented by a lawyer, may offer evidence as to how attachment would harm him and why it should be denied.

Government Employment.   A government employee must receive due process before being fired. Generally, this means some kind of hearing, but not necessarily a formal court hearing. The employee is entitled to know the charges against him, to hear the employer's evidence, and to have an opportunity to tell his side of the story. He is not entitled to have a lawyer present. The hearing "officer" need only be a neutral employee. Further, in an emergency, where the employee is a danger to the public or the organization, the government may suspend with pay, before holding a hearing. It then must provide a hearing before the decision becomes final.

Academic Suspension.   There is still a property interest here, but it is the least important of those discussed. When a public school concludes that a student has failed to meet its normal academic standards, such as by failing too many courses, it may dismiss him without a hearing. Due process is served if the student receives notice of the reason and has some opportunity to respond, such as by writing a letter contradicting the school's claims.

    In cases of disciplinary suspension or expulsion, courts generally require schools to provide a higher level of due process. In the hypothetical situation at the beginning of this section, the university has failed to provide adequate due process.[21] The school has accused the student of a serious infraction. The school must promptly provide details of the charge and cannot wait until the hearing to do so. The student should see the two papers and have a chance to rebut the charge. Moreover, Professor Holmes has demonstrated bias. He appears to have made up his mind in advance. He has placed the burden on the student to disprove the charges. And he probably feels obligated to support Watson's original conclusion since Watson will be deciding his tenure case next year.

The Takings Clause

Florence Dolan ran a plumbing store in Tigard, Oregon. She and her husband wanted to enlarge it on land they already owned. But the city government said that they could expand only if they dedicated some of their own land for use as a public bicycle path and for other public use. Does the city have the right to make them do that? For an answer we must look to a different part of the Fifth Amendment.

    The **Takings Clause** is closely related to the Due Process Clause. **The Takings Clause prohibits a state from taking private property for public use without just compensation.** A town wishing to build a new football field may boot you out of your house. But the town must compensate you. The government takes your land through the power of **eminent domain**. Officials must notify you of their intentions and give you an opportunity to oppose the project and to challenge the amount the town offers to pay. But when the hearings are done, the town may write you a check and grind your house into goalposts, whether you like it or not.

    More controversial issues arise when a local government does not physically take the property but passes regulations that restrict its use. Tigard is a city of 30,000 in Oregon. The city developed a comprehensive land use plan for its downtown area in order to preserve green space, to encourage transportation other than autos, and to reduce its flooding problems. Under the plan, when a property owner sought permission to build in the downtown section,

---

Eminent domain

The power of the government to take private property for public use.

---

[20] 501 U.S. 1, 111 S.Ct. 2105, 1991 U.S. LEXIS 3317 (1991).
[21] See, e.g., *University of Texas Medical School at Houston v. Than*, 901 S.W.2d 926, 1995 Tex. LEXIS 105 (Tex. 1995).

the city could require some of her land to be used for public purposes. This has become a standard method of land use planning throughout the nation. States have used it to preserve coastline, urban green belts, and many environmental features.

When Florence Dolan applied for permission to expand, the city required that she dedicate a 15-foot strip of her property to the city as a bicycle pathway and that she preserve, as greenway, a portion of her land within a floodplain. She sued, and though she lost in the Oregon courts, she won in the United States Supreme Court. The Court held that Tigard City's method of routinely forcing all owners to dedicate land to public use violated the Takings Clause. The city was taking the land, even though title never changed hands.[22]

The Court did not outlaw all such requirements. What it required was that, **before a government may require an owner to dedicate land to a public use, it must show that this owner's proposed building requires this dedication of land.** In other words, it is not enough for Tigard to have a general plan, such as a bicycle pathway, and to make all owners participate in it. Tigard must show that it needs *Dolan's* land *specifically for a bike path and greenway*. This will be much harder for local governments to demonstrate than merely showing a city-wide plan. A related issue arose in the following controversial case. A city used eminent domain to take property on behalf of *private developers*. Was this a valid public use?

KELO V. CITY OF NEW LONDON, CONNECTICUT

545 U.S. 469, 125 S.CT. 2655
UNITED STATES SUPREME COURT, 2005

CASE SUMMARY

Facts: New London, Connecticut, was declining economically. The city's unemployment rate was double that of the state generally, and the population at its lowest point in 75 years. In response, state and local officials targeted a section of the city, called Fort Trumbull, for revitalization. Located on the Thames River, Fort Trumbull comprised 115 privately owned properties and 32 additional acres of an abandoned naval facility. The development plan included one section for a waterfront conference hotel and stores; a second one for 80 private residences; and one for research facilities.

The state bought most of the properties from willing sellers. However, nine owners of 15 properties refused to sell, and filed suit. The owners claimed that the city was trying to take land for private use, not public, in violation of the Takings Clause. The case reached the United States Supreme Court.

Issue: *Did the city's plan violate the Takings Clause?*

Decision: No, the plan was constitutional. Affirmed.

Reasoning: The Takings Clause allows for some transfers of real property from one private party to another, so long as the land will be used by the public. For example, land may be taken to allow for the construction of a railroad, even if private railroad companies will be the primary beneficiaries of the transfer.

New London's economic development plan aims to create jobs and increase the city's tax receipts. The Supreme Court has not previously considered this type of public use, but now determines that economic development is a legitimate public purpose. New London has not violated the Takings Clause.

Dissent by Justice O'Connor: Any public benefit in this case would be incidental and secondary. Under the majority's opinion, the government can now take private property for *any* purpose. This case will most likely benefit those with inside access to government officials, at the expense of small property owners.

---

[22] *Dolan v. City of Tigard*, 512 U.S. 374, 114 S.Ct. 2309, 1994 U.S. LEXIS 4826 (1994).

The Kelo decision was controversial, and in response some states passed statutes prohibiting eminent domain for private development.

Substantive Due Process

Substantive due process

Holds that certain rights are so fundamental that the government may not eliminate them.

This doctrine is part of the Due Process Clause, but it is entirely different from procedural due process and from government taking. During the first third of the twentieth century, the Supreme Court frequently nullified state and federal laws, asserting that they interfered with basic rights. For example, in a famous 1905 case, *Lochner v. New York*,[23] the Supreme Court invalidated a New York statute that had limited the number of hours that bakers could work in a week. New York had passed the law to protect employee health. But the Court declared that private parties had a basic constitutional right to contract. In this case, the statute interfered with the rights of the employer and the baker to make any bargain they wished. Over the next three decades, the Court struck down dozens of state and federal laws that were aimed at working conditions, union rights, and social welfare generally. This was called **substantive due process**[24] because the Court was looking at the underlying rights being affected, such as the right to contract, not at any procedures.

Critics complained that the Court was interfering with the desires of the voting public by nullifying laws that the justices personally disliked (judicial activism). During the Great Depression, however, things changed. Beginning in 1934, the Court completely reversed itself and began to uphold the types of laws it earlier had struck down. How does the Court now regard substantive due process issues? It treats economic and social regulations differently from cases involving fundamental rights.

Economic and Social Regulations.   Generally speaking, the Court will now *presume valid* any statute that regulates economic or social conditions. If the *Lochner* case were heard today, the legislation would be upheld. State or federal laws regulating wages, working conditions, discrimination, union rights, and any similar topics are presumed valid. The Court will invalidate such a law only if it is *arbitrary or irrational*. Almost all statutes have some minimal rationality, and most are now upheld.

Fundamental rights

Rights that are so basic that any governmental interference with them is suspect and likely to be unconstitutional.

Fundamental Rights.   The standard of review is different for laws that affect **fundamental** rights. The Constitution expressly provides some of these rights, such as the right of free speech, the right to vote, and the right to travel. Other rights do not explicitly appear in the Constitution, but the Supreme Court has determined that they are implied. One of the most important of these is the right to privacy. The Court has decided that the Bill of Rights, taken together, implies a right of privacy for all persons. This includes the right to contraception, to marriage, and, most controversially, to abortion.

Any law that infringes upon a fundamental right is presumed invalid and will be struck down unless it is necessary to a compelling government interest. For example, because it is a fundamental right, no state may outlaw abortion altogether. But the state may require a minor to obtain the consent of a parent or a judge. Although this infringes upon a fundamental right, the government has a compelling interest in regulating the welfare of minors, and this regulation is necessary to achieve that goal.

FOURTEENTH AMENDMENT: EQUAL PROTECTION CLAUSE

Shannon Faulkner wanted to attend The Citadel, a state-supported military college in South Carolina. She was a fine student who met every admission requirement that The Citadel set except one: she was not a man. The Citadel argued that its long and distinguished history

---

[23] 198 U.S. 45, 25 S.Ct. 539, 1905 U.S. LEXIS 1153 (1905).
[24] Be the first on your block to pronounce this word correctly. The accent goes on the first syllable: *substantive*.

demanded that it remain all male. The state government claimed that Ms. Faulkner had no need to attend this particular school. Faulkner responded that she was a citizen of the state and ought to receive the benefits that others got, including the right to a military education. Could the school exclude her on the basis of gender?

The Fourteenth Amendment provides that "No State shall…deny to any person within its jurisdiction the equal protection of the laws." This is the **Equal Protection Clause**, and it means that, generally speaking, **governments must treat people equally**. Unfair classifications among people or corporations will not be permitted. A notorious example of unfair classification would be race discrimination: permitting only white children to attend a public school violates the Equal Protection Clause.

Equal Protection Clause
Generally requires the government to treat people equally.

Yet clearly, governments do make classifications every day. Rich people pay a higher tax rate than poor people; some corporations are permitted to deal in securities, others are not. To determine which classifications are constitutionally permissible, we need to know what is being classified. There are three major groups of classifications. The outcome of a case can generally be predicted by knowing which group it is in.

- *Minimal Scrutiny: Economic and Social Relations.* Government actions that classify people or corporations on these bases are almost always upheld.
- *Intermediate Scrutiny: Gender.* Government classifications are sometimes upheld.
- *Strict Scrutiny: Race, Ethnicity, and Fundamental Rights.* Classifications based on any of these are almost never upheld.

Minimal Scrutiny: Economic and Social Regulation

Just as with the Due Process Clause, laws that regulate economic or social issues are presumed valid. They will be upheld if they are *rationally related to a legitimate goal*. This means a statute may classify corporations and/or people and the classifications will be upheld if they make any sense at all. The New York City Transit Authority excluded all methadone users from any employment. The United States District Court concluded that this violated the Equal Protection Clause by unfairly excluding all those who were on methadone. The court noted that even those who tested free of any illegal drugs and were seeking non-safety-sensitive jobs, such as clerks, were turned away. That, said the district court, was irrational.

Not so, said the United States Supreme Court. The Court admitted that the policy might not be the wisest. It would probably make more sense to test individually for illegal drugs rather than automatically exclude methadone users. But, said the Court, it was not up to the justices to choose the best policy. They were only to decide if the policy was rational. Excluding methadone users related rationally to the safety of public transport and therefore did not violate the Equal Protection Clause.[25]

Intermediate Scrutiny: Gender

Classifications based on gender must meet a tougher test than those resulting from economic or social regulation. Such laws must *substantially relate to important government objectives*. Courts have increasingly nullified government sex classifications as societal concern with gender equality has grown.

At about the same time Shannon Faulkner began her campaign to enter The Citadel, another woman sought admission to the Virginia Military Institute, an all-male state school. The Supreme Court held that Virginia had violated the Equal Protection Clause by excluding women from VMI. The Court ruled that gender-based government discrimination requires an

[25] *New York City Transit Authority v. Beazer*, 440 U.S. 568, 99 S.Ct. 1355, 1979 U.S. LEXIS 77 (1979).

"exceedingly persuasive justification," and that Virginia had failed that standard of proof. The Citadel promptly opened its doors to women.[26]

Today, over 800 high school girls wrestle competitively. Some join female clubs but others have no such opportunity and compete with boys—or seek to. Some schools allow girls to join the boys' wrestling team, but others refuse, citing moral reasons, concern for the girls' safety, and the possibility of sexual harassment. If a particular school has no female team, should girls be permitted to wrestle boys? Do they have an equal protection right to do so?

Strict Scrutiny: Race, Ethnicity, and Fundamental Rights

Any government action that intentionally discriminates against racial or ethnic minorities, or interferes with a fundamental right, is presumed invalid. In such cases, courts will look at the statute or policy with *strict scrutiny;* that is, courts will examine it very closely to determine whether there is compelling justification for it. The law will be upheld only if it is *necessary to promote a compelling state interest.* Very few meet that test.

- *Racial and Ethnic Minorities.* Any government action that intentionally discriminates on the basis of race or ethnicity is presumed invalid. For example, in *Palmore v. Sidoti,*[27] the state had refused to give child custody to a mother because her new spouse was racially different from the child. The practice was declared unconstitutional. The state had made a racial classification, it was presumed invalid, and the government had no *compelling need* to make such a ruling.

- *Fundamental Rights.* A government action interfering with a fundamental right also receives strict scrutiny and will likely be declared void. For example, New York State gave an employment preference to any veteran who had been a state resident when he entered the military. Newcomers who were veterans were less likely to get jobs, and therefore this statute interfered with the right to travel, a fundamental right. The Supreme Court declared the law invalid.[28]

EXAM *Strategy*

Question: Megan is a freshman at her local public high school; her older sister Jenna attends a nearby private high school. Both girls are angry because their schools prohibit them from joining their respective wrestling teams, where only boys are allowed. The two girls sue based on the U.S. Constitution. Discuss the relevant law and predict the outcomes.

Strategy: One girl goes to private and one to public school. Why does that matter? Now ask what provision of the Constitution is involved, and what legal standard it establishes.

Result: The Constitution offers protection from the *government.* A private high school is not part of the government, and Jenna has no constitutional case. Megan's suit is based on the Equal Protection Clause. This is gender discrimination, meaning that Megan's school must convince the court that keeping girls off the team *substantially relates to an important government objective.* The school will probably argue that wrestling with stronger boys will be dangerous for girls. However, courts are increasingly suspicious of any gender discrimination and are unlikely to find the school's argument persuasive.

[26] *United States v. Virginia*, 518 U.S. 515, 116 S.Ct. 2264, 1996 U.S. LEXIS 4259 (1996).
[27] 466 U.S. 429, 104 S.Ct. 1879, 1984 U.S. LEXIS 69 (1984).
[28] *Attorney General of New York v. Soto-Lopez*, 476 U.S. 898, 106 S.Ct. 2317, 1986 U.S. LEXIS 59 (1986).

PRIVATE REGULATIONS

All of the rights discussed thus far offer protection only from government action, not from the conduct of private citizens or corporations. Suppose it is Sunday morning. You are happily reading the newspaper, sipping coffee, while your nine-year-old niece, visiting for the weekend, plays hopscotch on your front walk. There is a knock at the front door. The Neighborhood Association has arrived with a stern message: "Get the kid out of the neighborhood; she's not allowed." Astonished and enraged, you call your lawyer. But her answer leaves you dazed: You may not have children in your house. "But this is America!" you shout. "The Constitution," she replies, "does not apply."

Like 50 million other Americans, you live in a *common interest development (CID)*. Yours happens to be a gated community of single-family homes, all of which were built by a developer. When you bought the house, you automatically joined the Neighborhood Association. Other CIDs take different forms: condominiums, co-ops, or retirement or vacation communities. They are increasingly common, and some observers predict that, soon, about 25% of all Americans will live in one.

Some CIDs ban children from living in the development or even visiting. Some prohibit signs on the lawns or windows; others outlaw pets, certain flowers, laundry drying in the sun, day care centers, or pickup trucks. But various features make CIDs attractive to prospective residents. CIDs are often gated or locked in other ways, so they may be safer than surrounding neighborhoods. The community collects its own fees and operates many services, such as water and sewer, road maintenance, garbage collection, and other work traditionally done by towns and cities. Because they are privately managed by boards elected by the residents, CIDs often do this work more promptly and efficiently than public agencies.

However, the price residents pay is more than cash: they do indeed forfeit constitutional rights. The Constitution protects citizens from government action, and the local CID is not a government. As the law currently stands, you are probably giving up constitutional protections when you enter a CID. If the Neighborhood Association demands that your niece leave, you will probably have to drive her home. Suppose the nasty Neighborhood Association official also notices that your cat looks heavy. "No cats over 20 pounds," he snarls. "Read the rules." The pet-weight rule is also probably enforceable: get that cat off the sofa and onto a treadmill, fast.

CHAPTER CONCLUSION

The legal battle over power never stops. The obligation of a state to provide equal educational opportunity for both genders relates to whether Tigard, Oregon, may demand some of Ms. Dolan's store lot for public use. Both issues are governed by one amazing document. That same Constitution determines what tax preferences are permissible, and even whether a state may require you to wear clothing. As social mores change in step with broad cultural developments, as the membership of the Supreme Court changes, the balance of power between federal government, state government, and citizens will continue to evolve. There are no easy answers to these constitutional questions because there has never been a democracy so large, so diverse, or so powerful.

EXAM REVIEW

1. **CONSTITUTION** The Constitution is a series of compromises about power. (p. 106)

2. **ARTICLES I, II AND III** Article I of the Constitution creates the Congress and grants all legislative power to it. Article II establishes the office of president and defines executive powers. Article III creates the Supreme Court and permits lower federal courts; the article also outlines the powers of the federal judiciary. (p. 106)

3. **COMMERCE CLAUSE** Under the Commerce Clause, Congress may regulate any activity that has a substantial effect on interstate commerce. (p. 107)

4. **INTERSTATE COMMERCE** A state may not regulate commerce in any way that will interfere with interstate commerce. (p. 107)

EXAM *Strategy*

Question: Maine exempted many charitable institutions from real estate taxes but denied this benefit to a charity that primarily benefited out-of-state residents. Camp Newfound was a Christian Science organization, and 95% of its summer campers came from other states. Camp Newfound sued Maine. Discuss.

Strategy: The state was treating organizations differently depending on what states their campers come from. This raised *Commerce Clause* issues. Did the positive aspect or dormant aspect of that clause apply? The dormant aspect applied. What does it state? Apply that standard to theses facts. (See the "Result" at the end of this section.)

5. **SUPREMACY CLAUSE** Under the Supremacy Clause, if there is a conflict between federal and state statutes, the federal law preempts the field. Even without a conflict, federal law preempts if Congress intended to exercise exclusive control. (p. 109)

6. **PRESIDENTIAL POWERS** The president's key powers include making agency appointments, proposing legislation, conducting foreign policy, and acting as commander in chief of the armed forces. (p. 109)

7. **FEDERAL COURTS** The federal courts adjudicate cases and also exercise judicial review, which is the right to declare a statute or governmental action unconstitutional and void. (p. 110)

8. **FREEDOM OF SPEECH** Freedom of speech includes symbolic acts. Political speech is protected unless it is intended and likely to create imminent lawless action. (p. 113)

9. **REGULATION OF SPEECH** The government may regulate the time, place, and manner of speech. (p. 114)

10. **OBSCENITY** Obscene speech is not protected. (p. 115)

11. **COMMERCIAL SPEECH** Commercial speech that is false or misleading may be outlawed; otherwise, regulations on this speech must be reasonable and directed to a legitimate goal. (p. 115)

EXAM Strategy

Question: A federal statute prohibits the broadcasting of lottery advertisements, except by stations that broadcast in states permitting lotteries. The purpose of the statute is to support efforts of states that outlaw lotteries. Truth Broadcasting operates a radio station in State A (a nonlottery state) but broadcasts primarily in State B (a lottery state). Truth wants to advertise State A's lottery but is barred by the statute. Does the federal statute violate Truth's constitutional rights?

Strategy: This case involves a particular kind of speech. What kind? What is the rule about that kind of speech? (See the "Result" at the end of this section.)

12. **PROCEDURAL DUE PROCESS** Procedural due process is required whenever the government attempts to take liberty or property. The amount of process that is due depends upon the importance of the liberty or property threatened. (p. 118)

EXAM Strategy

Question: Fox's Fine Furs claims that Ermine owes $68,000 for a mink coat on which she has stopped making payments. Fox files a complaint and also asks the court clerk to *garnish* Ermine's wages. A garnishment is a court order to an employer to withhold an employee's wages, or a portion of them, and pay the money into court so that there will be money for the plaintiff, if it wins. What constitutional issue does Fox's request for garnishment raise?

Strategy: Ermine is in danger of losing part of her income, which is property. The Due Process Clause prohibits the government (the court) from taking life, liberty or property without due process. What process is Ermine entitled to? (See the "Result" at the end of this section.)

13. **TAKINGS CLAUSE** The Takings Clause prohibits a state from taking private property for public use without just compensation. (p. 118)

14. **SUBSTANTIVE DUE PROCESS** A substantive due process analysis presumes that any economic or social regulation is valid, and presumes invalid any law that infringes upon a fundamental right. (p. 122)

15. **EQUAL PROTECTION CLAUSE** The Equal Protection Clause generally requires the government to treat people equally. Courts apply strict scrutiny in any equal protection case involving race, ethnicity, or fundamental rights; intermediate scrutiny to any case involving gender; and minimal scrutiny to an economic or social regulation. (p. 123)

16. **PRIVATE ACTION** Generally, constitutional rights protect citizens only from the action of the government, not from actions of private organizations such as common interest developments. (p. 125)

4. Result: The dormant aspect holds that a state statute which discriminates against interstate commerce is almost always invalid. Maine was subsidizing charities that served in-state residents, and penalizing those that attracted campers from elsewhere. The tax rules violated the Commerce Clause and was void.[29]

11. Result: An advertisement is *commercial* speech. The government may regulate this speech as long as the rules are reasonable and directed to a legitimate goal. The goal of supporting nonlottery states is reasonable, and there is no violation of Truth's free speech rights.[30]

12. Result: Ermine is entitled to notice of Fox's claim and to a hearing *before* the court garnishes her wages.[31]

ADDITIONAL QUESTIONS

1. Michigan's Solid Waste Management Act (SWMA) generally prohibited Michigan counties from accepting for disposal solid waste that had been generated outside that county. Fort Gratiot operated a sanitary landfill in St. Clair County, Michigan. The county denied Fort Gratiot permission to bring in solid waste from out of state, and Fort Gratiot sued. This case involves the negative, or dormant, aspect of the Commerce Clause. What is the difference between that aspect and the positive aspect? What is the evil that the dormant aspect is designed to avoid? How would you rule in this case?

2. **YOU BE THE JUDGE** WRITING PROBLEM Scott Fane was a CPA licensed to practice in New Jersey and Florida. He built his New Jersey practice by making unsolicited phone calls to executives. When he moved to Florida, the Board of Accountancy there prohibited him (and all CPAs) from personally soliciting new business. Fane sued. Does the First Amendment force Florida to forgo foreclosing Fane's phoning? **Argument for Fane:** The Florida regulation violates the First Amendment, which protects commercial

[29] *Camps Newfound/Owatonna, Inc. v. Town of Harrison, Maine,* 520 U.S. 564, 117 S.Ct. 1590 (1997).
[30] *United States v. Edge Broadcasting,* 509 U.S. 418, 113 S.Ct. 2696 (1993).
[31] *Sniadach v. Family Finance Corp.,* 395 U.S. 337 (1969).

speech. Fane was not saying anything false or misleading, but was just trying to secure business. This is an unreasonable regulation, designed to keep newcomers out of the marketplace and maintain steady business and high prices for established CPAs. **Argument for the Florida Board of Accountancy:** Commercial speech deserves—and gets—a lower level of protection than other speech. This regulation is a reasonable method of ensuring that the level of CPA work in our state remains high. CPAs who personally solicit clients are obviously in need of business. They are more likely to bend legal and ethical rules to obtain clients and keep them happy, and will lower the standards throughout the state.

3. President George H.W. Bush insisted that he had the power to send American troops into combat in the Middle East, without congressional assent. Yet before authorizing force in Operation Desert Storm, he secured congressional authorization. President Clinton stated that he was prepared to invade Haiti without a congressional vote. Yet he bargained hard to avoid an invasion, and ultimately American troops entered without the use of force. Why the seeming double-talk by both presidents?

4. In the early 1970s, President Nixon became embroiled in the Watergate dispute. He was accused of covering up a criminal break-in at the national headquarters of the Democratic Party. Nixon denied any wrongdoing. A United States District Court judge ordered the president to produce tapes of conversations held in his office. Nixon knew that complying with the order would produce damaging evidence, probably destroying his presidency. He refused, claiming executive privilege. The case went to the Supreme Court. Nixon strongly implied that even if the Supreme Court ordered him to produce the tapes, he would refuse. What major constitutional issue did this raise?

5. **ETHICS** In the landmark 1965 case of *Griswold v. Connecticut*, the Supreme Court examined a Connecticut statute that made it a crime for any person to use contraception. The majority declared the law an unconstitutional violation of the right of privacy. Justice Black dissented, saying, "I do not to any extent whatever base my view that this Connecticut law is constitutional on a belief that the law is wise or that its policy is a good one. [It] is every bit as offensive to me as it is to the majority. [There is no criticism by the majority of this law] to which I cannot subscribe—except their conclusion that the evil qualities they see in the law make it unconstitutional." What legal doctrines are involved here? Why did Justice Black distinguish between his personal views on the statute and the power of the Court to overturn it? Should a federal court act as a "superlegislature," nullifying statutes with which it disagrees? If a court aggressively takes on social issues, what dangers—and what advantages—does that present to society?

6. You begin work at Everhappy Corp. at the beginning of November. On your second day at work, you wear a political button on your overcoat, supporting your choice for governor in the upcoming election. Your boss glances at it and says, "Get that stupid thing out of this office or you're history, chump." You protest that his statement (a) violates your constitutional rights and (b) uses a boring cliché. Are you right?

7. Gilleo opposed American participation in the war in the Persian Gulf. She displayed a large sign on her front lawn that read, "Say No to War in the Persian Gulf, Call Congress Now." The city of Ladue prohibited signs on front lawns and Gilleo sued. The city claimed that it was regulating "time, place, and manner." Explain that statement, and decide who should win.

8. David Lucas paid $975,000 for two residential lots on the Isle of Palms near Charleston, South Carolina. He intended to build houses on them. Two years later the South Carolina legislature passed a statute that prohibited building seaward of a certain line,

and Lucas's property fell in the prohibited zone. Lucas claimed that his land was now useless and that South Carolina owed him its value. Explain his claim. Should he win?

9. This case concerns unequal taxes on property. In Pennsylvania, a county tax commissioner appraises land, meaning that he sets a value for the land, and the owner then pays real estate taxes based on that value. A commissioner valued land at its sales price, whenever it was sold. If land did not sell for many years, he made little or no adjustment in its appraised value. As a result, some property was assessed at 35 times as much as neighboring land. A corporate landowner sued. What constitutional issue is raised? What should the outcome be?

10. **ROLE REVERSAL** Write an exam question that distinguishes between these three important Fifth Amendment protections: procedural due process, the Takings Clause, and substantive due process.

INTERNET RESEARCH PROBLEM

Online, find a book that was formerly censored. Find another volume that is currently banned, either in the United States or elsewhere. How have changing mores affected censorship? Will the book that is currently outlawed someday be legal?

You can find further practice problems at www.cengagebrain.com. See the preface of this book for website access details.

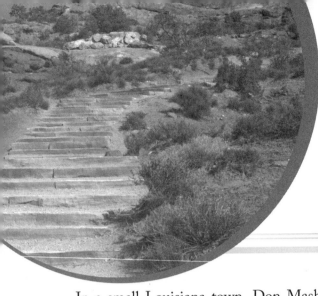

TORTS

In a small Louisiana town, Don Mashburn ran a restaurant called Maison de Mashburn. The *New Orleans States-Item* newspaper reviewed his eatery, and here is what the article said:

"'Tain't Creole, 'tain't Cajun, 'tain't French, 'tain't country American, 'tain't good. I don't know how much real talent in cooking is hidden under the mélange of hideous sauces which make this food and the menu a travesty of pretentious amateurism but I find it all quite depressing. Put a yellow flour sauce on top of the duck, flame it for drama and serve it with some horrible multi-flavored rice in hollowed-out fruit and what have you got? A well-cooked duck with an ugly sauce that tastes too sweet and thick and makes you want to scrape off the glop to eat the plain duck. [The stuffed eggplant was prepared by emptying] a shaker full (more or less) of paprika on top of it. [One sauce created] trout à la green plague [while another should have been called] yellow death on duck."

> 'Tain't Creole, 'tain't Cajun, 'tain't French, 'tain't country American, 'tain't good.

Mashburn sued, claiming that the newspaper had committed libel, damaging his reputation and hurting his business.[1] Trout à la green plague will be the first course on our menu of tort law.

[1] *Mashburn v. Collins*, 355 So. 2d 879 (La. 1977).

Tort

A violation of a duty imposed by the civil law.

This odd word *tort* is borrowed from the French, meaning "wrong." **A tort is a violation of a duty imposed by the civil law.** When a person breaks one of those duties and injures another, it is a tort. The injury could be to a person or her property. Libel is one example of a tort, in which, for example, a newspaper columnist falsely accuses someone of being an alcoholic. A surgeon who accidentally removes the wrong kidney from a patient commits a different kind of tort, called negligence. A con artist who tricks you out of money with a phony offer to sell you a boat commits fraud, yet another tort.

Because tort law is so broad, it takes awhile to understand its boundaries. To start with, we must distinguish torts from two other areas of law: criminal law and contract law.

It is a crime to steal a car, to embezzle money from a bank, to sell cocaine. As discussed in Chapter 1, society considers such behavior so threatening that the government itself will prosecute the wrongdoer, whether or not the car owner or bank president wants the case to go forward.

In a tort case, it is up to the injured party, the plaintiff, to seek compensation. She must hire her own lawyer, who will file a lawsuit. Her lawyer must convince the court that the defendant breached some legal duty and ought to pay money damages to the plaintiff. The plaintiff has no power to send the defendant to jail. Bear in mind that a defendant's action might be both a crime and a tort. The con artist who tricks you out of money with a fake offer to sell you a boat has committed the tort of fraud. You may file a civil suit against him and will collect money damages if you can prove your case. The con artist has also committed the crime of fraud. The state will prosecute, seeking to imprison and fine him.

A tort is also different from a contract dispute. A contract case is based on an agreement two people have already made. For example, Deirdre claims that Raul promised to sell her 10,000 pairs of sneakers at a good price but has failed to deliver them. She files a contract lawsuit. In a tort case, there is usually no "deal" between the parties. Don Mashburn had never met the restaurant critic who attacked his restaurant and obviously had never made any kind of contract. The plaintiff in a tort case claims that the law itself creates obligations that the defendant has breached.

DIFFERENCES BETWEEN CONTRACT, TORT, AND CRIMINAL LAW

	Type of Obligation		
	Contract	**Tort**	**Criminal Law**
How the obligation is created	The parties agree on a contract, which creates duties for both.	The civil law imposes duties of conduct on all.	The criminal law prohibits certain conduct.
How the obligation is enforced	Suit by plaintiff.	Suit by plaintiff.	Prosecution by government.
Possible result	Money damages for plaintiff.	Money damages for plaintiff.	Punishment for defendant, including prison and/or fine.
Example	Raul contracts to sell Deirdre 5,000 pairs of sneakers at $50 per pair but fails to deliver them. Deirdre buys the sneakers elsewhere for $60 per pair and receives $50,000, her extra expense.	A newspaper falsely accuses a private citizen of being an alcoholic. The plaintiff sues and wins money damages to compensate for her injured reputation.	Leo steals Kelly's car. The government prosecutes Leo for grand theft, and the judge sentences him to two years in prison. Kelly gets nothing.

Tort law itself is divided into categories. We begin by considering **intentional torts**—that is, harm caused by a deliberate action. Then we will examine **negligence** and **strict liability**, which are injuries caused by neglect.

INTENTIONAL TORTS

DEFAMATION

Defamation refers to false statements that harm someone's reputation. Defamatory statements can be written or spoken. Written defamation is **libel.** Suppose a newspaper accuses a local retail store of programming its cash registers to overcharge customers, when the store has never done so. That is libel. Oral defamation is **slander.** If Professor Wisdom, in class, refers to Sally Student as a drug dealer, and Sally has never sold anything stronger than Arm & Hammer, he has slandered her.

There are four elements to a defamation case. **An element is a fact that a plaintiff must prove to win a lawsuit.** In *any* kind of lawsuit, the plaintiff must prove *all* of the elements to prevail. The elements in a defamation case are:

- *Defamatory Statement.* These are words likely to harm another person's reputation. When Professor Wisdom accuses Sally of dealing drugs, that will clearly harm her reputation.

- *Falseness.* The statement must be false. If Sally Student actually sold marijuana to a classmate, then Professor Wisdom has a defense to slander.

- *Communicated.* The statement must be communicated to at least one person other than the plaintiff. If Wisdom speaks only to Sally and accuses her of dealing drugs, there is no slander.

- *Injury.* In slander cases, the plaintiff generally must show some injury. Sally's injury would be a lower reputation in the school, embarrassment, and humiliation. But in libel cases, the law is willing to assume injury. Because libel is written and more permanent, courts award damages even without proof of injury.[2]

OPINION

Opinion is generally a valid defense in a defamation suit because it cannot be proven true or false. Suppose that a television commentator says, "Frank Landlord certainly does less than many rich people do for our community." Is that defamation? Probably not. Who are the "rich people"? How much do they do? How do we define "does less"? These vague assertions indicate the statement is one of opinion. Even if Frank works hard feeding homeless families, he will probably lose a defamation case.

A related defense involves cases in which a supposed statement of fact should not be taken literally. "Reverend Wilson's sermons go on so long, many parishioners suffer brain death before receiving communion." Brain death is a tragic fact of medical science, but this author obviously exaggerates to express her opinion. No defamation.

---

[2] When defamation by radio and television became possible, the courts chose to consider it libel, analogizing it to newspapers because of the vast audience. This means that in broadcasting cases, a plaintiff generally does not have to prove damages.

Intentional torts
Harm caused by a deliberate action.

Negligence
Injuries caused by neglect and oversight rather than by deliberate conduct.

Strict liability
A type of tort lawsuit which does not require a plaintiff to prove the element of fault.

Libel
Written defamation.

Slander
Oral defamation.

Element
A fact that a plaintiff must prove to win a lawsuit.

Opinion
Generally a valid defense in a defamation suit because it cannot be proven true or false.

Mr. Mashburn, who opened the chapter suing over his restaurant review, lost his case. The court held that a reasonable reader would have understood the statements to be opinion only. "A shaker full of paprika" and "yellow death on duck" were not to be taken literally but were merely the author's expression of his personal dislike.

What about a crude description of a college official that appears in the school's newspaper?

YOU *be the* JUDGE

YEAGLE V. COLLEGIATE TIMES

255 VA. 293, 497 S.E.2d 136, 1998 VA. LEXIS 32
Virginia Supreme Court, 1998

Facts: Sharon Yeagle was assistant to the Vice President of Student Affairs at the Virginia Polytechnic Institute and State University. The state had an academic honors program called the Governor's Fellows Program, and one of Yeagle's duties was to help students apply. The school newspaper, the *Collegiate Times*, published an article describing the university's success at placing students in the Fellows Program. The article included a block quotation in larger print, attributed to Yeagle. Underneath Yeagle's name was the phrase "Director of Butt Licking."

Yeagle sued the *Collegiate Times*, alleging that the vulgar phrase defamed her. The trial court dismissed the case, ruling that no reasonable person would take the words literally, and that the phrase conveyed no factual information. Yeagle appealed to the Virginia Supreme Court.

You Be the Judge: Was the phrase defamatory, or was it deliberate exaggeration that no reasonable person would take literally?

Argument for Yeagle: The disgusting phrase that the *Collegiate Times* used to describe Ms. Yeagle is defamatory for several reasons. The conduct described by the words happens to be a crime in Virginia, a violation of the state sodomy statute. Thus the paper is accusing her of criminal offenses that she has never committed.

If, however, defendants argue that the phrase must be interpreted figuratively, then the newspaper has accused Ms. Yeagle of currying favor, or directing others to do so, in a uniquely degrading fashion. The *Collegiate Times* is informing its readers that she performs her job in a sleazy, unprofessional manner evidently because she cannot succeed by merit. The paper is suggesting that she is devoid of integrity and capable of achieving goals only by devious, deviant methods.

Finally, the *Collegiate Times* is holding Ms. Yeagle up to ridicule and scorn, for no legitimate reason, and with the sole purpose of harming her reputation. Ms. Yeagle should have had a chance to present her case in court and let a jury decide just how funny the article was.

Argument for *Collegiate Times*: Statements are only defamatory if a reasonable reader would understand them as asserting facts that can be proven true or false. There is no such statement in this case, and no defamation. No reasonable reader, after finishing an article about the Fellows Program, would believe that Ms. Yeagle was actually the director as described, or even that there is such a job. From the bluntness of the phrase, it is obvious that the words are hyperbole and have no meaning that can be proven true or false.

The paper chose to inject humor into its coverage of a mundane issue, for the entertainment of its readers. What Ms. Yeagle really objects to is the vulgarity of the phrase, and to that claim the paper pleads guilty. The *Collegiate Times* acknowledges that the phrase is off-color and might offend a few readers. There are two responses. First, the great majority of the paper's readers appreciate lively language that is at times irreverent. Second, vulgarity is not defamation. Freedom of speech is more important than the hurt feelings of an overly sensitive reader. For anyone who is quick to take offense, the proper recourse is not to file suit, but to put down the paper.

Public Personalities

The rules of the game change for those who play in public. Public officials and public figures receive less protection from defamation. An example of a **public official** is a police chief. A **public figure** is a movie star, for example, or a multimillionaire playboy constantly in the news. In the landmark case *New York Times Co. v. Sullivan*[3] the Supreme Court ruled that the free exchange of information is vital in a democracy and is protected by the First Amendment to the Constitution. A public official or public figure can win a defamation case only by proving actual malice by the defendant. **Actual malice means that the defendant knew the statement was false or acted with reckless disregard of the truth.** If the plaintiff merely shows that the defendant newspaper printed incorrect statements, even very damaging ones, he loses. In the *New York Times* case, the police chief of Birmingham, Alabama, claimed that the *Times* falsely accused him of racial violence in his job. He lost the suit because he could not prove that the *Times* had acted with actual malice. If he had demonstrated that the *Times* knew its accusation was false, he would have won.

Online Defamation

Kenneth Zeran awoke one day to learn he had become notorious. An unidentified person had posted a message on an AOL bulletin board advertising "Naughty Oklahoma T-Shirts." The shirts featured deeply offensive slogans relating to the 1995 bombing of a federal building in Oklahoma City, in which hundreds of innocent people died. Those interested in purchasing such a T-shirt were instructed to call "Ken" at Zeran's home telephone number. Zeran had nothing to do with the posting or the T-shirts. He was quickly inundated with phone messages from furious callers, some of whom made death threats.

Zeran could not change his number because he ran his business from his home. A radio station in Oklahoma City learned of the alleged offer and angrily urged its listeners to call Zeran, which they did. Over the next few days, additional similar messages were posted, and before long Zeran was receiving an abusive call every two minutes. Zeran phoned AOL on the first day. The company promised to remove the messages immediately but did not promptly delete the postings or close the responsible account. Zeran sued AOL for defamation—and lost.

The court held that AOL was immune from a defamation suit based on a third-party posting, based on the Communications Decency Act (CDA). Section 230 of the CDA creates this immunity for any Internet service provider. The court held that it would be impossible for a service provider to screen each of its millions of postings and that was why Congress prohibited suits such as Zeran's.

PRIVILEGE

Defendants receive additional protection from defamation cases when it is important for them to speak freely. **Absolute privilege** exists in courtrooms and legislative hearings. Anyone speaking there, such as a witness in a trial, can say anything at all and never be sued for defamation. Courts extend an absolute privilege in those few instances when candor is essential to a functioning democracy.[4]

Qualified privilege exists when two people have a legitimate need to exchange information. Suppose Trisha Tenant lives in a housing project. She honestly believes that her

Absolute privilege
A witness testifying in a court or legislature may never be sued for defamation.

Qualified privilege
Exists between two people who have a legitimate need to exchange information.

---

[3] 376 U.S. 254, 84 S.Ct. 710, 1964 U.S. LEXIS 1655 (1964).
[4] A witness who lies is guilty of perjury but not liable for slander.

To protect the common good!

neighbor is selling guns illegally. She reports this to the manager of the project, who investigates and discovers the guns were toys, being sold legally. Trisha is not liable for slander because she had a good faith reason to report this and the manager needed to hear it. As long as Trisha acts in good faith and talks only to someone who ought to know about the activity, she is protected by qualified privilege.

EXAM *Strategy*

Question: Raymond, a billionaire businessman widely known in the state, is running for the U.S. Senate. A newspaper reports that Raymond received $150,000 from an organization with "proven links to terrorist groups." The story came from a woman working in Raymond's own campaign, and two other witnesses, all three of whom had proven reliable in the past. Raymond, leading in the polls by 18%, plummets in popularity and loses the election. Raymond sues the paper. Outcome?

Strategy: First, determine the injury that Raymond has suffered. His reputation has been damaged. Second, ask what tort protects reputation. Defamation. Third, apply the elements to these facts.

Result: The newspaper's story, very likely to harm reputation, was widely communicated and did injure Raymond. But we don't know whether the article was true or false. Do we need to know? Usually we do, because a defendant is only liable for false statements. However, notice that a public personality must also prove *actual malice*. Was Raymond a public figure? Yes, he was a prominent billionaire and Senate candidate. There was no actual malice. The paper acted in good faith, using three credible sources. Raymond loses his lawsuit.

FALSE IMPRISONMENT

False imprisonment
The intentional restraint of another person without reasonable cause and without consent.

False imprisonment is the intentional restraint of another person without reasonable cause and without consent. A bank teller became seriously ill and wanted to go to the doctor, but the bank forbade her to leave until she made a final tally of her accounts. Officials barred her from leaving the bank. That was false imprisonment. The restraint was unreasonable because her accounts could have been verified later.[5]

False imprisonment cases most commonly arise in retail stores, which sometimes detain employees or customers for suspected theft. Most states now have statutes governing the detention of suspected shoplifters. **Generally, a store may detain a customer or worker for alleged shoplifting provided there is a reasonable basis for the suspicion and the detention is done reasonably.** To detain a customer in the manager's office for 20 minutes and question him about where he got an item is lawful. To chain that customer to a display counter for three hours and humiliate him in front of other customers is unreasonable, and false imprisonment.

INTENTIONAL INFLICTION OF EMOTIONAL DISTRESS

What should happen when a defendant's conduct hurts a plaintiff emotionally but not physically? Most courts allow a plaintiff to recover for emotional injury that a defendant intentionally caused.

[5] *Kanner v. First National Bank of South Miami*, 287 So.2d 715, 1974 Fla.App. LEXIS 8989 (Fla. Dist. Ct. App. 1974).

The intentional infliction of emotional distress **results from extreme and outrageous conduct that causes serious emotional harm**. A credit officer was struggling vainly to locate Sheehan, who owed money on his car. The officer phoned Sheehan's mother, falsely identified herself as a hospital employee, and said she needed to find Sheehan because his children had been in a serious auto accident. The mother provided Sheehan's whereabouts, which enabled the company to seize his car. But Sheehan spent seven hours frantically trying to locate his supposedly injured children, who in fact were fine. The credit company was liable for the intentional infliction of emotional distress.[6]

By contrast, a muffler shop, trying to collect a debt from a customer, made six phone calls over three months, using abusive language. The customer testified that this caused her to be upset, to cry, and to have difficulty sleeping. The court ruled that the muffler shop's conduct was neither extreme nor outrageous and sent the customer home for another sleepless night.[7]

The following case arose in a setting that guarantees controversy: an abortion clinic.

Intentional infliction of emotional distress
Results from extreme and outrageous conduct that causes serious emotional harm.

JANE DOE AND NANCY ROE V. LYNN MILLS

212 MICH.APP. 73, 536 N.W.2d 824, 1995 Mich.App. LEXIS 313
MICHIGAN COURT OF APPEALS, 1995

CASE SUMMARY

Facts: Late one night, an anti-abortion protestor named Robert Thomas climbed into a dumpster located behind an abortion clinic. He found documents indicating that Doe and Roe (not their real names) were soon to have abortions at the clinic. Thomas gave the information to Lynn Mills. She and another woman created signs, using the women's names, indicating that they were about to undergo abortions and urging them not to "kill their babies." Doe and Roe sued, claiming intentional infliction of emotional distress. The trial court gave summary judgment for the defendants, stating that they had a right to express their views on abortion. The plaintiffs appealed.

Issue: Have the plaintiffs made a valid claim of intentional infliction of emotional distress?

Decision: Reversed. The plaintiffs have made a valid claim of intentional infliction of emotional distress.

Reasoning: A defendant is liable for the intentional infliction of emotional distress only when his conduct is outrageous in character, extreme in degree, and utterly intolerable in a civilized community. Petty insults and annoyances are not enough. A good test is whether the average member of the community would respond to the defendant's conduct by exclaiming, "Outrageous!"

As the trial court noted, the defendants have a constitutional right to protest against abortion. However, the plaintiffs are not objecting to peaceful protest but to defendants' efforts to publicize matters that are purely personal. This is much more than trivial insult or annoyance. The defendants' behavior might well cause the average member of the community to shout, "Outrageous!" The plaintiffs are entitled to a trial on their claim. A jury should decide whether the defendants have committed this tort.

---

[6] _Ford Motor Credit Co. v. Sheehan_, 373 So.2d 956, 1979 Fla.App. LEXIS 15416 (Fla. Dist. Ct. App. 1979).
[7] _Midas Muffler Shop v. Ellison_, 133 Ariz. 194, 650 P.2d 496, 1982 Ariz.App. LEXIS 488 (Ariz. Ct. App. 1982).

ADDITIONAL INTENTIONAL TORTS

Battery
An intentional touching of another person in a way that is unwanted or offensive.

Battery is an intentional touching of another person in a way that is unwanted or offensive. There need be no intention to *hurt* the plaintiff. If the defendant intended to do the physical act, and a reasonable plaintiff would be offended by it, battery has occurred.

Suppose an irate parent throws a chair at a referee during his daughter's basketball game, breaking the man's jaw. It is irrelevant that the father did not intend to injure the referee. But a parent who cheerfully slaps the winning coach on the back has not committed battery, because a reasonable coach would not be offended.

Assault
Occurs when a defendant does some act that makes a plaintiff fear an imminent battery.

Assault occurs when a defendant does some act that makes a plaintiff fear an imminent battery. It is assault even though the battery never occurs. Suppose Ms. Wilson shouts "Think fast!" at her husband and hurls a toaster at him. He turns and sees it flying at him. His fear of being struck is enough to win a case of assault, even if the toaster misses.

Fraud
Injuring another person by deliberate deception.

Fraud is injuring another person by deliberate deception. It is fraud to sell real estate knowing that there is a large toxic waste deposit underground of which the buyer is ignorant. Later in this chapter, a plaintiff claims that for many years, a cigarette manufacturer fraudulently suggested its product was safe, knowing its assurances were deadly lies. Fraud is a tort that typically occurs during contract negotiation, and it is discussed in more detail in Unit 2 on contracts.

DAMAGES

COMPENSATORY DAMAGES

Mitchel Bien, who is deaf, enters the George Grubbs Nissan dealership, where folks sell cars aggressively—*very* aggressively. Maturelli, a salesman, and Bien communicate by writing messages back and forth. Maturelli takes Bien's own car keys, and the two then test drive a 300ZX. Bien says he does not want the car, but Maturelli escorts him back inside and fills out a sales sheet. Bien repeatedly asks for his keys, but Maturelli only laughs, pressuring him to buy the new car. Minutes pass. Hours pass. Bien becomes frantic, writing a dozen notes, begging to leave, threatening to call the police. Maturelli mocks Bien and his physical disabilities. Finally, after four hours, the customer escapes.

> **Bien becomes frantic, writing a dozen notes, begging to leave, threatening to call the police.**

Bien sues for the intentional infliction of emotional distress. Two former salesmen from Grubbs testify they have witnessed customers cry, yell, and curse as a result of the aggressive tactics. Doctors state that the incident has traumatized Bien, dramatically reducing his confidence and self-esteem and preventing his return to work even three years later.

The jury awards Bien damages. But how does a jury calculate the money? For that matter, why should a jury even try? Money can never erase pain or undo a permanent injury. The answer is simple: money, however inexact and ineffective, is the only thing a court has to give.

Compensatory damages
Money intended to restore a plaintiff to the position he was in before the injury.

A successful plaintiff generally receives **compensatory damages**, meaning an amount of money that the court believes will restore him to the position he was in before the defendant's conduct caused an injury. Here is how compensatory damages are calculated.

Single-recovery principle
Requires a court to settle the matter once and for all, by awarding a lump sum for past and future expenses.

First, a plaintiff receives money for medical expenses that he has proven by producing bills from doctors, hospitals, physical therapists, and psychotherapists. Bien receives all the money he has paid. If a doctor testifies that Bien needs future treatment, he will offer evidence of how much that will cost. **The single-recovery principle requires a court to settle the matter once and for all, by awarding a lump sum for past and future expenses.** A plaintiff may not return in a year and say, "Oh, by the way, there are some new bills."

Second, the defendants are liable for lost wages. The court takes the number of days or months that Bien missed work and multiplies that times his salary. If Bien is currently unable to work, a doctor estimates how many more months he will miss work, and the court adds that to his damages.

Third, a plaintiff is paid for pain and suffering. Bien testifies about how traumatic the four hours were and how the experience has affected his life. He may state that he now fears shopping, suffers nightmares, and seldom socializes. To bolster the case, a plaintiff uses expert testimony, such as the psychiatrists who testified for Bien. Awards for pain and suffering vary enormously, from a few dollars to many millions, depending on the injury and depending on the jury. In some lawsuits, physical and psychological pain are momentary and insignificant; in other cases, the pain is the biggest part of the verdict. In Bien's case, the jury returns with its verdict: $573,815, calculated as follows.[8]

Past medical	$ 70.00
Future medical	$ 6,000.00
Past rehabilitation	$ 3,205.00
Past lost earning capacity	$ 112,910.00
Future lost earning capacity	$ 34,650.00
Past physical symptoms and discomfort	$ 50,000.00
Future physical symptoms and discomfort	$ 50,000.00
Past emotional injury and mental anguish	$ 101,980.00
Future emotional injury and mental anguish	$ 200,000.00
Past loss of society and reduced ability to socially interact with family, former fiancée, and friends and hearing (i.e., nondeaf) people in general	$ 10,000.00
Future loss of society and reduced ability to socially interact with family, former fiancée, and friends and hearing people	$ 5,000.00
TOTAL	**$ 573,815.00**

[handwritten annotation: general damages VS. special damages → Pain and Sufferings (Subjective) → Lost wages/ medical expenses (objective)]

PUNITIVE DAMAGES

Here we look at a different kind of award, one that is more controversial and potentially more powerful: punitive damages. The purpose is not to compensate the plaintiff for harm, because compensatory damages will have done that. **Punitive damages** are intended to punish the defendant for conduct that is extreme and outrageous. Courts award these damages in

Punitive damages

Intended to punish the defendant for conduct that is extreme and outrageous.

[8] The compensatory damages are described in *George Grubbs Enterprises v. Bien*, 881 S.W.2d 843, 1994 Tex.App. LEXIS 1870 (Tex.Ct.App. 1994). In addition to the compensatory damages described, the jury awarded $5 million in punitive damages. The Texas Supreme Court reversed the award of punitive damages, but not the compensatory. Id., 900 S.W.2d 337, 1995 Tex. LEXIS 91 (Tex. 1995). The high court did not dispute the appropriateness of punitive damages, but reversed because the trial court failed to instruct the jury properly as to how it should determine the assets actually under the defendants' control, an issue essential to punitive damages but not compensatory.

relatively few cases. When an award of punitive damages is made, it is generally in a case of intentional tort, although they occasionally appear in negligence suits.

The idea behind punitive damages is that certain behavior is so unacceptable that society must make an example of it. A large award of money should deter the defendant from repeating the mistake and others from ever making it. This is social engineering in an extreme form. Predictably, some believe punitive damages represent the law at its most avaricious,[9] while others attribute to them great social benefit. Large verdicts make headlines, but in fact punitive damages are rare and generally modest.

When plaintiffs suffer serious personal injuries, high awards may occur. However, when a plaintiff has suffered only economic harm and no personal injury, a court will not permit such a high award.

The United States Supreme Court has declared that in awarding punitive damages, a court must consider three "guideposts":

- The reprehensibility of the defendant's conduct;

- The ratio between the harm suffered and the award; and

- The difference between the punitive award and any civil penalties used in similar cases.[10]

The Court has refused to provide a definitive ratio between compensatory and punitive damages but has given additional guidance to lower courts:

- The trial court generally should not permit a punitive award more than nine times higher than the compensatory damages.

- The trial court may not use the defendant's wealth as an excuse to award an unreasonably high award.

Despite the Supreme Court guidelines, dramatic cases may still lead to very large awards, as the following case illustrates.

WILLIAMS V. PHILIP MORRIS INCORPORATED

93 OR.APP. 527, 92 P.3d 126
COURT OF APPEALS OF OREGON, 2004

CASE SUMMARY

Facts: Jesse Williams smoked three packs of Marlboros a day—and died of lung cancer. Philip Morris sold Marlboros and controlled about half the cigarette market in the United States. Mayola Williams, Jesse's widow, sued the tobacco company, claiming fraud. She argued that for decades, Philip Morris knew its cigarettes were addictive and knew they caused illness and death, but it deceived the public to boost its profits. The jury awarded her $21,485 in economic damages, $800,000 in pain and suffering—and $79.5 million in punitive damages. Then the Supreme Court established the guidelines described above, and the case was sent back to the Oregon appellate court for reconsideration.

Issue: Was the punitive damage award excessive?

Decision: No, the award was not excessive.

Reasoning: From the trial evidence, the jury could reasonably have found these facts. Philip Morris sold Jesse Williams

---

[9] Lawyers normally take personal injury cases on a contingency basis, meaning that they receive no money upfront from their client. Their fee will be a percentage of the plaintiff's judgment if she wins. Lawyers often take about one third of the award. But if the defendant wins, the plaintiff's lawyer will have worked several years for no pay.

[10] *BMW of North America, Inc. v. Gore*, 517 U.S. 559, 116 S.Ct. 1589, 1996 U.S. LEXIS 3390 (1996).

a product that the company knew was dangerous and potentially fatal. Despite realizing the grave risks of smoking, Philip Morris engaged in an extensive campaign to convince the public that there was no conclusive evidence that tobacco was harmful. The company claimed that more research was necessary, while carefully avoiding such studies. Instead, Philip Morris used its research to determine the optimum dose of nicotine. While publicly denying that nicotine was addictive, the company worked hard to make its products as addictive as possible.

The Supreme Court has declared that "few awards exceeding a single-digit ratio will satisfy due process." This award surpasses that ratio. However, it is hard to conceive of more appalling conduct for a longer period of time than that of Philip Morris. A punitive damages award of $79.5 million does not violate the Due Process Clause under the Supreme Court's guidelines because it is reasonable and proportionate to the wrong inflicted on Jesse Williams, as well as the wider public of this state. The punitive damages found by the jury are reinstated.

TORT REFORM AND *EXXON VALDEZ*

Some people believe that jury awards are excessive and need statutory reform, while others argue that the evidence demonstrates punitive awards are rare and modest in size. About one-half of the states have passed limits. The laws vary, but many work this way. A jury is permitted to award whatever it considers fair for economic damages, meaning lost wages and medical expenses. However, noneconomic damages (pain and suffering), together with any punitive award, may not exceed a prescribed limit, such as three times the economic damages, or sometimes a flat cap, such as $250,000 total. These restrictions can drastically lower the total verdict.

In the famous *Exxon Valdez* case, the Supreme Court placed a severe limit on a certain type of punitive award. It is unclear how influential the decision will be because the case arises in the isolated area of maritime law. Nonetheless, the justices wrote at length about punitive awards, and the decision may reverberate in future holdings. This is what happened.

Captain Joseph Hazelwood's negligence caused the *Exxon Valdez* to run aground off the coast of Alaska. The ship dumped 11 million gallons of oil into the sea, damaging 3,000 square miles of vulnerable ecosystem. The oil spill forced fishermen into bankruptcy, disrupted entire communities, and killed hundreds of thousands of birds and marine animals. A decade later, many of the damaged species had not recovered. The jury decided that Exxon had been reckless by allowing Hazelwood to pilot the ship when the company knew he was an alcoholic. The jury awarded compensatory damages to the plaintiffs, and punitive damages of $5 billion. Exxon appealed.

Almost two decades after the accident, the Supreme Court ruled. The justices discussed punitive damages in general, noting that much of the criticism of punitive awards appeared overstated. The court declared there had been no major increase in how frequently juries gave punitive damages. In the unusual cases where jurors made such awards, the sums were modest. The problem, declared the justices, was the unpredictability of punitive damages. The median ratio of punitive to compensatory awards was just 0.62:1. If the plaintiff received compensatory damages of $100,000 and *if* the jury made a punitive award, the latter would be only $62,000. However, the mean ratio was 2.90:1 (compensatory damages of $100,000 translate to a punitive award of $290,000). This suggested that a few juries were awarding dramatically higher punitive damages, and that these outlier cases rendered the system unpredictable and unfair.

Based on that analysis, the court ruled that in maritime cases the ratio should be no higher than 1:1. The court approved the jury's compensatory award of $507 million, then reduced the punitive award from $5 billion to $507 million. Supporters of the court's decision stated that it would allow businesses to make plans based on predictable outcomes. Opponents said that the justices ignored the jury's finding of reckless behavior and calamitous environmental harm.

BUSINESS TORTS

In this section, we look at intentional torts that occur in a commercial setting: interference with a contract, interference with a prospective advantage, and the rights to privacy and publicity. Patents, copyrights, and trademarks are discussed in Chapter 34, on intellectual property, as are Lanham Act violations.

TORTIOUS INTERFERENCE WITH BUSINESS RELATIONS

Competition is the essence of business. Successful corporations compete aggressively, and the law permits and expects them to. But there are times when healthy competition becomes illegal interference. This is called tortious interference with business relations. It can take one of two closely related forms: interference with a contract or interference with a prospective advantage.

Tortious Interference with a Contract

Tortious interference with a contract exists only if the plaintiff can establish the following four elements:

- There was a contract between the plaintiff and a third party;
- The defendant knew of the contract;
- The defendant improperly induced the third party to breach the contract or made performance of the contract impossible; and
- There was injury to the plaintiff.

Tortious interference with a contract

The defendant improperly induced a third party to breach a contract with the plaintiff.

There is nothing wrong with two companies bidding against each other to buy a parcel of land, and nothing wrong with one corporation doing everything possible to convince the seller to ignore all competitors. But once a company has signed a contract to buy the land, it is improper to induce the seller to break the deal. The most commonly disputed issues in these cases concern elements one and three: Was there a contract between the plaintiff and another party? Did the defendant *improperly* induce a party to breach it?

Texaco v. Pennzoil.   One of the largest verdicts in the history of American law came in a case of contract interference. Pennzoil made an unsolicited bid to buy 20 percent of Getty Oil at $112.50 per share, and the Getty board approved the agreement. Before the lawyers for both sides could complete the paperwork, Texaco appeared and offered Getty stockholders $128 per share for the entire company. Getty officers turned their attention to Texaco, but Pennzoil sued, claiming tortious interference. Texaco replied that it had not interfered because there was no binding contract.

The jury bought Pennzoil's argument, and they bought it big: $7.53 billion in actual damages, and $3 billion more in punitive damages. After appeals and frantic negotiations, the two parties reached a settlement. Texaco agreed to pay Pennzoil $3 billion as settlement for having wrongfully interfered with Pennzoil's agreement to buy Getty.

Tortious Interference with a Prospective Advantage

Tortious interference with a prospective advantage is an awkward name for a tort that is simply a variation on interference with a contract. The difference is that, for this tort, there need be no contract; the plaintiff is claiming outside interference with an expected economic relationship. Obviously, the plaintiff must show more than just the hope of a profit. **A plaintiff who has a definite and reasonable expectation of obtaining an economic advantage may sue a corporation that maliciously interferes and prevents the relationship from developing.**

Tortious interference with a prospective advantage

Malicious interference with a developing economic relationship.

Suppose that Jump Co. and Block Co. both hope to purchase a professional basketball team. The team's owners reject the offer from Block. They informally agree to a price with Jump but refuse to make a binding deal until Jump leases a stadium. Block owns the only stadium in town and refuses to lease to Jump, meaning that Jump cannot buy the team. Block has interfered with Jump's prospective advantage.[11]

Privacy and Publicity

We live in a world of dazzling technology, and it is easier than ever—and more profitable—to spy on someone. For example, the Web page **http://www.thesmokinggun.com** specializes in publishing revealing data about celebrities. Does the law protect us? What power do we have to limit the intrusion of others into our lives and to prohibit them from commercially exploiting information about us?

Intrusion

Intrusion into someone's private life is a tort if a reasonable person would find it offensive. Peeping through someone's windows or wiretapping his telephone are obvious examples of intrusion. In a famous case involving a "paparazzo" photographer and Jacqueline Kennedy Onassis, the court found that the photographer had invaded her privacy by making a career out of photographing her. He had bribed doormen to gain access to hotels and restaurants she visited, had jumped out of bushes to photograph her young children, and had driven power boats dangerously close to her. The court ordered him to stop.[12] Nine years later the paparazzo was found in contempt of court for again taking photographs too close to Ms. Onassis. He agreed to stop once and for all—in exchange for a suspended contempt sentence.

Intrusion
A tort if a reasonable person would find the invasion of her private life offensive.

Commercial Exploitation

This right prohibits the use of someone's likeness or voice for commercial purposes. For example, it would be illegal to run a magazine ad showing actress Gwyneth Paltrow holding a can of soda without her permission. The ad would imply that she endorses the product. Someone's identity is her own, and it cannot be exploited unless she permits it.

Negligence

Party time! A fraternity at the University of Arizona welcomed new members, and the alcohol flowed freely. Several hundred people danced and shrieked and drank, and no one checked for proof of age. A common occurrence—but one that ended tragically. A minor student drove away, intoxicated, and slammed into another car. The other driver, utterly innocent of wrongdoing, was gravely injured.

The drunken student was obviously liable, but his insurance did not cover the huge medical bills. The injured man also sued the fraternity. Should that organization be legally responsible? The question leads to other similar issues. Should a restaurant that serves an intoxicated adult be liable for resulting harm? If *you* give a party, should you be responsible for any damage caused by your guests?

---

[11] Or, to rephrase it, Jump, having courted the owners, must now jump into court and block Block's attempt to bounce Jump off its court. For a case with similar facts, see *Fishman v. Estate* of Wirtz, 807 F.2d 520 (7th Cir. 1986).

[12] *Galella v. Onassis*, 487 F.2d 986, 1973 U.S.App. LEXIS 7901 (2d Cir. 1973).

These are moral questions—but very practical ones, as well. They are typical issues of negligence law. In this contentious area, courts continually face one question: *When someone is injured, how far should responsibility extend?*

We might call negligence the "unintentional" tort because it concerns harm that arises by accident. A person, or perhaps an organization, does some act, neither intending nor expecting to hurt anyone, yet someone is harmed. Should a court impose liability? The fraternity members who gave the party never wanted—or thought—that an innocent man would suffer terrible damage. But he did. Is it in society's interest to hold the fraternity responsible?

Before we can answer this question, we need some background knowledge. Things go wrong all the time, and society needs a means of analyzing negligence cases consistently and fairly.

To win a negligence case, the plaintiff must prove five elements:

• *Duty of Due Care.* The defendant had a duty of due care to this plaintiff.

• *Breach.* The defendant breached her duty.

• *Factual Cause.* The defendant's conduct actually caused the injury.

• *Foreseeable Harm.* It was foreseeable that conduct like the defendant's might cause this type of harm.

• *Injury.* The plaintiff has actually been hurt.

DUTY OF DUE CARE

The first issue may be the most difficult in all of tort law: Did the defendant have a duty of due care *to the injured person?* The test is generally "foreseeability." **If the defendant could have foreseen injury to a particular person, she has a duty to him**. If she could not have foreseen the harm, there is usually no duty. Let us apply this principle to the fraternity case.

HERNANDEZ V. ARIZONA BOARD OF REGENTS

177 ARIZ. 244, 866 P.2d 1330, 1994 ARIZ. LEXIS 6
ARIZONA SUPREME COURT, 1994

CASE SUMMARY

Facts: At the University of Arizona, the Epsilon Epsilon chapter of Delta Tau Delta fraternity gave a welcoming party for new members. The fraternity's officers knew that the majority of its members were under the legal drinking age, but they permitted everyone to consume alcohol. John Rayner, who was under 21 years of age, left the party. He drove negligently and caused a collision with an auto driven by Ruben Hernandez. At the time of the accident, Rayner's blood alcohol level was 0.15, exceeding the legal limit. The crash left Hernandez blind, severely brain damaged, and quadriplegic.

Hernandez sued Rayner, who settled the case, based on the amount of his insurance coverage. The victim also sued the fraternity, its officers and national organization, all fraternity members who contributed money to buy alcohol, the university, and others. The trial court granted summary judgment for all defendants, and the court of appeals affirmed. Hernandez appealed to the Arizona Supreme Court.

Issue: Did the fraternity and the other defendants have a duty of due care to Hernandez?

Decision: Reversed and remanded. The defendants did have a duty of due care to Hernandez.

Reasoning: Historically, Arizona and most states have considered that *consuming* alcohol led to liability, but not *furnishing* it. However, the common law also has had a longstanding rule that a defendant could be liable for supplying some object to a person who is likely to endanger others. Giving a car to an intoxicated youth would be an example of such behavior; the youth might easily use the object (the car) to injure other people.

There is little difference between giving a car to an intoxicated youth and giving alcohol to a young person with a car. Both acts involve minors who, because of their age and inexperience, are likely to endanger third parties. Moreover, furnishing alcohol to a minor violates several state statutes. As a result, most states have concluded that a defendant who serves intoxicating drinks to a minor is legally responsible for resulting harm to third parties. Arizona now joins that majority. The defendants did have a duty of due care to Hernandez and to the public in general.

ECONOMICS AND THE LAW

Economists often analyze legal issues by looking at **externalities: costs or benefits of one person's activity that affect someone else**. For example, a factory that pollutes the air imposes negative externalities, because the sullied atmosphere makes life unpleasant and unhealthy for those who live nearby. By contrast, a corporation that landscapes its headquarters to include a duck pond with waterfall creates positive externalities, by making the neighborhood more attractive for local residents.

Bars and restaurants can generate negative externalities because innocent people may be injured or killed by drivers who become intoxicated in those establishments. **Dram shop laws** are a response. These acts make liquor stores, bars, and restaurants liable for serving drinks to intoxicated customers who later cause harm. (Historically, a dram was a small serving of alcohol.) These statutes force a financial dilemma on such firms. The more a tavern or café encourages its customers to drink, the greater its revenue—but also the larger its risk of a liability lawsuit. The goal of dram shop laws is to force businesses serving liquor to consider these externalities. In states without a dram shop statute, the threat of a lawsuit is removed and the establishment has an incentive to maximize alcohol consumption, despite the external costs.

Do dram shop acts work? Yes, answer the authors of one economic study. In states with such statutes, bars monitor underage drinking more aggressively, refuse drinks earlier to an intoxicated customer, check the references of their own employees more carefully, and prohibit their workers from drinking on the job. These economists conclude that dram shop laws are a promising way to reduce drunk driving accidents.[13] ◆

CRIME AND TORT: LANDOWNER'S LIABILITY

Regrettably, a major concern of tort law today is how to respond to injury caused by criminals. If a criminal assaults and robs a pedestrian in a shopping mall, that act is a crime and may be prosecuted by the state. But prosecution leaves the victim uncompensated. The assault is also an intentional tort, and the victim could file a civil lawsuit against the criminal. But most violent criminals have no assets. Given this economic frustration and the flexibility of the common law, it is inevitable that victims of violence look elsewhere for compensation, as they did in the following tragic case.

---

[13] Sloan, Liang, Stout, and Whetten-Goldstein, "Liability, Risk Perceptions, and Precautions at Bars," *Journal of Law and Economics*, 2000, vol. 43, p. 473.

WIENER V. SOUTHCOAST CHILDCARE CENTERS, INC.

32 CA.4TH. 1138, 88 P.3d 517, 12 CAL.RPTR.3d 615
SUPREME COURT OF CALIFORNIA, 2004,

CASE SUMMARY

Facts: Southcoast operated a child-care facility on a busy street corner property that it leased from First Baptist Church. A four-foot-high chain link fence enclosed the playground located adjacent to the sidewalk and street. Steven Abrams intentionally drove his large Cadillac through the fence, onto the playground, and into a group of children, causing horrific carnage. He killed two children and injured many others. Abrams was convicted of first-degree murder.

Parents of killed and injured youngsters sued Southcoast and the church, alleging that the defendants knew the fence was inadequate to protect the children. The trial judge granted summary judgment for the defendants, ruling that Southcoast and the others owed no duty to prevent such harm. The appellate court reversed, and Southcoast appealed to the state's highest panel.

Issue: Did Southcoast have a duty to the plaintiffs to prevent this kind of harm?

Decision: No, Southcoast had no duty to the plaintiffs.

Reasoning: The parents allege that Southcoast and the church knew that the chain link fence was inadequate to protect their children. There had, in fact, been a few earlier accidents. According to one neighbor, when a mail-truck driver fell out of his truck, the vehicle took off, bounced over the curb, and drove through the fence before striking a tree inside the yard. No one was injured. Neighbors testified that other traffic incidents occurred near the premises involving vehicles that hit the curb.

The parents argue that it makes no difference whether the driver who killed the children acted negligently or with criminal intent. The risk of harm from an unsafe fence was the same, and the two defendants owed a duty to make the fence stronger.

In fact, the law treats third-party criminal acts differently from ordinary negligence. A court must find heightened foreseeability before holding a defendant liable for the criminal acts of third parties. It is difficult or impossible to predict when a criminal might strike. And if a criminal decides on a particular goal or victim, it is very hard to remove his every means of achieving that goal.

Abrams's brutal criminal act was unforeseeable. Southcoast had never been the target of violence before. The attack was outrageous and bizarre. It was impossible for anyone to anticipate a perpetrator committing premeditated murder against the children. Southcoast and the church owed no duty to the children.

The case is reversed, and summary judgment is granted for the defendants.

EXAM *Strategy*

Question: Compare the *Weiner* decision with a case from Chapter 1: *Kuehn v. Pub Zone*, on pages **16**. Both are negligence cases in which the harm is caused by criminal conduct. However, the two cases have opposite outcomes. Why is that?

Strategy: What standard did the *Pub Zone* court use to decide that the bar owner was liable? Who won? Apply the same standard to the *Weiner* case. Who should win?

Result: The *Pub Zone* court declared that a property owner was not an ensurer against criminal acts but would be liable if the violent conduct was *foreseeable*, based on experience. Maria Kerkoulas knew from earlier incidents that gang members wearing insignia presented a danger to patrons, and she was liable when violence erupted. In the *Weiner* case, the court used the same standard, but found there was no history of violence at the day care center. Harm to the children was unforeseeable. The law was the same in both cases, but different facts led to contrasting results.

BREACH OF DUTY

The second element of a plaintiff's negligence case is **breach of duty**. Courts apply the reasonable person standard: **a defendant breaches his duty of due care by failing to behave the way a reasonable person would under similar circumstances**. Reasonable "person" means someone of the defendant's occupation. A taxi driver must drive as a reasonable taxi driver would. A heart surgeon must perform bypass surgery with the care of a trained specialist in that field.

Two medical cases illustrate the reasonable person standard. A doctor prescribes a powerful drug without asking his 21-year-old patient about other medicines she is currently taking. The patient suffers a serious drug reaction from the combined medications. The physician is liable for the harm. A reasonable doctor always checks current medicines before prescribing new ones.

On the other hand, assume that an 84-year-old patient dies on the operating table in an emergency room. While the surgeon was repairing heart damage, the man had a fatal stroke. If the physician followed normal medical procedures and acted with reasonable speed, he is not liable. A doctor must do a reasonable professional job but cannot guarantee a happy outcome.

Crime and Tort: Negligent Hiring

In a recent one-year period, more than 1,000 homicides and two million attacks occurred in the workplace. Companies must beware because they can be liable for hiring or retaining violent employees. A mailroom clerk with a previous rape and robbery conviction followed a secretary home after work and fatally assaulted her. Even though the murder took place off the company premises, the court held that the defendant would be liable if it knew or should have known of the mail clerk's criminal history.[14] In other cases, companies have been found liable for failing to check an applicant's driving record, to contact personal references, and to search criminal records.

What can an employer do to diminish the likelihood of workplace violence? Many things.

- Evaluate the workplace for unsafe physical features. Install adequate lighting in parking lots and common areas, hire security guards if necessary, and use closed-circuit television and identification cards.

- Ensure that the company uses thorough prehire screening, contacts all former employers, and checks all references and criminal records. Nursing homes have paid huge sums for negligently hiring convicted assailants who later attack elderly residents.

- Respond quickly to dangerous behavior. In many cases of workplace violence, the perpetrator had demonstrated repeated bizarre, threatening, or obsessive behavior on the job, but his supervisors had not taken it seriously.

Negligence Per Se

In certain areas of life, courts are not free to decide what a "reasonable" person would have done, because the state legislature has made the decision for them. **When a legislature sets a minimum standard of care for a particular activity, in order to protect a certain group of people, and a violation of the statute injures a member of that group, the defendant has committed negligence per se**. A plaintiff who can show negligence per se need not prove breach of duty.

In Minnesota, the state legislature became alarmed about children sniffing glue and passed a statute prohibiting the sale to a minor of any glue containing toluene. About one month later, 14-year-old Steven Zerby purchased glue containing toluene from a store in his

---

[14] *Gaines v. Monsanto*, 655 S.W.2d 568, 1983 Mo. LEXIS 3439 (Mo.Ct.App. 1983).

hometown. Steven inhaled the glue and died from injury to his central nervous system. A reasonable person might have made the same error, but that is irrelevant: the clerk violated the statute, and the store was liable.[15]

FACTUAL CAUSE AND FORESEEABLE HARM

A plaintiff must also show that the defendant's breach of duty caused the plaintiff's harm. Courts look at two issues to settle causation: Was the defendant's behavior the *factual cause* of the harm? Was *this type of harm foreseeable?*[16]

Factual Cause

Nothing mysterious here. **If the defendant's breach physically led to the ultimate harm, it is the factual cause.** Suppose that Dom's Brake Shop tells Customer his brakes are now working fine, even though Dom knows that is false. Customer drives out of the shop, cannot stop at a red light, and hits Bicyclist crossing at the intersection. Dom is liable to Bicyclist. Dom's unreasonable behavior was the factual cause of the harm. Think of it as a row of dominoes. The first domino (Dom's behavior) knocked over the next one (failing brakes), which toppled the last one (the cyclist's injury).

Suppose, alternatively, that just as Customer is exiting the repair shop, Bicyclist hits a pothole and tumbles off her cycle, avoiding Customer's auto. Bicyclist's injuries stem from her fall, not from the auto. Customer's brakes still fail, and Dom has breached his duty to Customer, but Dom is not liable to Bicyclist. She would have been hurt anyway. This is a row of dominoes that veers off to the side, leaving the last domino (cyclist's injury) untouched. No factual causation.

Foreseeable Type of Harm

For the defendant to be liable, the *type of harm* must have been reasonably foreseeable. In the case just discussed, Dom could easily foresee that bad brakes would cause an automobile accident. He need not have foreseen exactly what happened. He did not know there would be a cyclist nearby. What he could foresee was this general type of harm involving defective brakes.

By contrast, assume the collision of car and bicycle produces a loud crash. Two blocks away, a pet pig, asleep on the window ledge of a twelfth-story apartment, is startled by the noise, awakens with a start, and plunges to the sidewalk, killing a veterinarian who was making a house call. If the vet's family sues Dom, should it win? Dom's negligence was the factual cause: it led to the collision, which startled the pig, which flattened the vet. Most courts would rule, though, that Dom is not liable. The type of harm is too bizarre. Dom could not reasonably foresee such an extraordinary chain of events, and it would be unfair to make him pay for it. (See Exhibit 6.1.)

Another way of stating that Dom is not liable to the vet's family is by calling the falling pig a *superseding cause.* When one of the "dominoes" in the row is entirely unforeseeable, courts will consider it a superseding cause, letting the defendant off the hook. Negligence cases often revolve around whether the chain of events leading from the defendant's conduct to the injury was broken by a superseding cause.

---

[15] *Zerby v. Warren*, 297 Minn. 134, 210 N.W.2d 58 (1973).

[16] Courts often refer to these two elements, grouped together, as *proximate cause* or *legal cause*. But, as many judges acknowledge, those terms have created confusion, so we use *factual cause* and *foreseeable type of harm*, the issues on which most decisions ultimately focus.

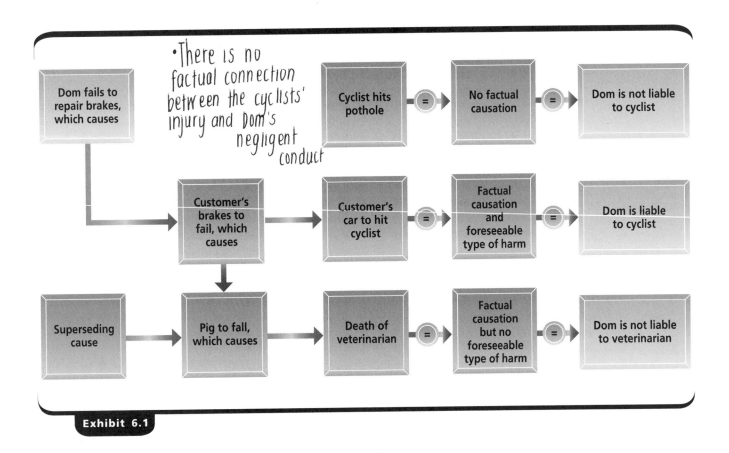

Exhibit 6.1

EXAM *Strategy*

Question: Jenny asked a neighbor, Tom, to water her flowers while she was on vacation. For three days, Tom did this without incident, but on the fourth day, when he touched the outside faucet, he received a violent electric shock that shot him through the air, melted his sneakers and glasses, set his clothes on fire, and seriously burned him. Tom sued, claiming that Jenny had caused the damage when she negligently repaired a second-floor toilet. Water from the steady leak had flooded through the walls, soaking wires and eventually causing the faucet to become electrified. You are Jenny's lawyer. Use one (and only one) element of negligence law to move for summary judgment.

Strategy: The four elements of negligence we have examined thus far are: duty to this plaintiff, breach, factual cause and foreseeable type of injury. Which element seems to be most helpful to Jenny's defense? Why?

Result: Jenny is entitled to summary judgment because this was not a foreseeable type of injury. Even if she did a bad job of fixing the toilet, she could not possibly have anticipated that her poor workmanship could cause *electrical* injuries—and violent ones—to anybody.

Res Ipsa Loquitur

Normally, a plaintiff must prove factual cause and foreseeable type of harm in order to establish negligence. But in a few cases, a court may *infer* that the defendant caused the harm, under the doctrine of *res ipsa loquitur* ("the thing speaks for itself"). Suppose a pedestrian is walking along a sidewalk when an air-conditioning unit falls on his head from a third-story window. The defendant, who owns the third-story apartment, denies any wrongdoing, and it may be difficult or impossible for the plaintiff to prove why the air conditioner fell. In such cases, many courts will apply *res ipsa loquitur* and declare that the **facts imply that the defendant's negligence caused the accident**. If a court uses this doctrine, then the defendant must come forward with evidence establishing that it did not cause the harm.

Because *res ipsa loquitur* dramatically shifts the burden of proof from plaintiff to defendant, it applies only when (1) the defendant had exclusive control of the thing that caused the harm, (2) the harm normally would not have occurred without negligence, and (3) the plaintiff had no role in causing the harm. In the air conditioner example, most states would apply the doctrine and force the defendant to prove she did nothing wrong.

Injury

Finally, a plaintiff must prove that he has been injured. In some cases, injury is obvious. For example, Ruben Hernandez, struck by the intoxicated fraternity member, obviously suffered grievous harm. In other cases, though, injury is unclear. **The plaintiff must persuade the court that he has suffered a harm that is genuine, not speculative**.

Among the most vexing are suits involving future harm. Exposure to toxins or trauma may lead to serious medical problems down the road—or it may not. A woman's knee is damaged in an auto accident, causing severe pain for two years. She is clearly entitled to compensation for her suffering. After two years, all of her troubles may cease. Yet there is a chance that in 15 years the trauma will lead to painful arthritis. A court must decide today the full extent of present and *future* damages.

The following case examines a different issue: may a plaintiff recover damages because of the *emotional* injury suffered when a relative is harmed?

RA V. SUPERIOR COURT

154 CAL.APP. 4TH 142, 64 CA.RPTR.3d 539
CALIFORNIA COURT OF APPEALS, 2007

CASE SUMMARY

Facts: Michelle Ra and her husband, Phil Ra, were shopping in an Armani Exchange in Old Town, Pasadena. Michelle was looking at merchandise in the women's section while Phil examined men's sweaters, about 10 or 15 feet away. Michelle was not facing her husband when she heard a loud bang. A large, overhead store sign had fallen, striking Phil and seriously injuring him. Michelle turned, saw her husband bent over in pain, and hurried to him. Ten days later, Michelle suffered a miscarriage, which she attributed to the accident.

The Ras sued Armani for negligence in permitting the sign to fall, and also for the emotional distress suffered by Michelle. This case concerns only Michelle's claim. The trial court granted summary judgment to the store, declaring that Michelle had not made out a valid claim of bystander recovery because she had not seen the accident occur. She appealed.

Issue: *May a bystander recover for emotional distress caused by an accident that she did not see?*

Decision: A bystander may not recover for emotional distress caused by an accident unless she witnessed it. Summary judgment affirmed.

Reasoning: Michelle testified that when she heard the crash, "I was not sure if he was involved, but I knew the sound came from the direction—the part of the store he was in."

To recover for negligent infliction of emotional distress as a bystander, a plaintiff must prove she (1) is closely related to the injury victim; (2) is present at the scene of the event and is aware it is injuring the victim; and (3) as a result suffers serious emotional distress. Someone who hears an accident but does not then know it is causing injury to a relative does not have a viable bystander claim for emotional distress, even if she learns the truth moments later.

It is the trauma caused by *witnessing* the injury to a close relative that gives rise to a lawsuit. Michelle did not witness the accident and cannot prevail.

Damages

The plaintiff's damages in a negligence case are generally compensatory damages. In unusual cases, a court may award punitive damages—that is, money intended not to compensate the plaintiff but to punish the defendant. We discussed both forms of damages earlier in this chapter.

DEFENSES

Contributory and Comparative Negligence

Joe is a mental patient in a hospital. The hospital knows he is dangerous to himself and others, but it permits him to wander around unattended. Joe leaves the hospital and steals a gun. Shawn drives by Joe, and Joe waves the gun at him. Shawn notices a police officer a block away. But instead of informing the cop, Shawn leans out his window and shouts, "Hey, knucklehead, what are you doing pointing guns at people?" Joe shoots and kills Shawn.

Shawn's widow sues the hospital for negligently permitting Joe to leave. But the hospital, in defense, claims that Shawn's foolishness got him killed. Who wins? It depends on whether the state in which the suit is heard uses a legal theory called **contributory negligence**. This used to be the law throughout the nation, but it remains in effect in only a few states. It means that, even assuming the defendant is negligent, **if the plaintiff is even *slightly* negligent himself, he recovers nothing**. So if Shawn's homicide occurs in a contributory negligence state, the hospital is not liable regardless of how negligent it was.

Critics attacked the rule as unreasonable. A plaintiff who was 1 percent negligent could not recover from a defendant who was 99 percent negligent. So most states threw out the contributory negligence rule, replacing it with comparative negligence. **In a comparative negligence state, a plaintiff may generally recover even if she is partially negligent**. A jury will be asked to assess the relative negligence of plaintiff and defendant.

Suppose we are in a comparative negligence state, and the jury believes the hospital was 80 percent responsible for Shawn's death, and Shawn himself was 20 percent responsible. It might conclude that the total damages for Shawn's widow are $2 million, based on Shawn's pain in dying and the widow's loss of his income. If so, the hospital would owe $1.6 million, or 80 percent of the damages. (See Exhibit 6.2.)

Today, most states have adopted some form of comparative negligence. Critics of comparative negligence claim that it rewards a plaintiff for being careless. Suppose, they say, a driver speeds to beat an approaching train, and the railroad's mechanical arm fails to

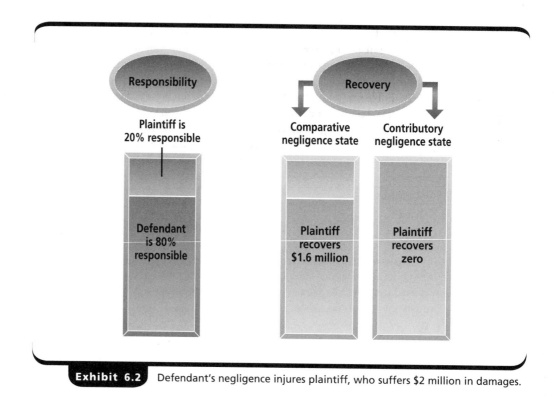

Exhibit 6.2   Defendant's negligence injures plaintiff, who suffers $2 million in damages.

operate. Why should we reward the driver for his foolishness? In response to this complaint, some comparative negligence states do not permit a plaintiff to recover anything if he was more than 50 percent responsible for his injury.

Assumption of the Risk

Duck! That was a close call—the baseball nearly knocked your ear off. If it had, the team would owe you ... nothing. Here at the ballpark, there is always a slight chance of injury, and you are expected to realize it. Wherever there is an obvious hazard, a special rule applies. **Assumption of the risk: A person who voluntarily enters a situation that has an obvious danger cannot complain if she is injured**. If you are not willing to tolerate the risk of being hurt by a batted ball, stay home and watch the game on television. And while you are here—pay attention, will you?

Suppose that Good Guys, a restaurant, holds an ice-fishing contest on a frozen lake, to raise money for accident victims. Margie grabs a can full of worms and strolls to the middle of the lake to try her luck but slips on the ice and suffers a concussion. When she returns to consciousness, Margie should not bother filing suit—she assumed the risk.

STRICT LIABILITY

Some activities are so naturally dangerous that the law places an especially high burden on anyone who engages in them. A corporation that produces toxic waste can foresee dire consequences from its business that a stationery store cannot. This higher burden is **strict liability**. There are two main areas of business that incur strict liability: *ultrahazardous activity* and *defective products*. Defective products are discussed in Chapter 20 on product liability.

ULTRAHAZARDOUS ACTIVITY

Ultrahazardous activities include using harmful chemicals, operating explosives, keeping wild animals, bringing dangerous substances onto property, and a few similar activities where the danger to the general public is especially great. **A defendant engaging in an ultrahazardous activity is virtually always liable for any harm that results**. Plaintiffs do not have to prove duty or breach or foreseeable harm. Recall the deliberately bizarre case we posed earlier of the pig falling from a window ledge and killing a veterinarian. Dom, the mechanic whose negligence caused the car crash, could not be liable for the veterinarian's death because the plunging pig was a superseding cause. But if the pig was jolted off the window ledge by Sam's Blasting Co., which was doing perfectly lawful blasting for a new building down the street, Sam is liable. Even if Sam took extraordinary care, it will do him no good at trial. The "reasonable person" rule is irrelevant in a strict liability case.

Dangerous nature of what you're doing

CHAPTER CONCLUSION

This chapter has been a potpourri of sin, a bubbling cauldron of conduct best avoided. Although tortious acts and their consequences are diverse, two generalities apply. First, the boundaries of torts are imprecise, the outcome of a particular case depending to a considerable extent upon the factfinder who analyzes it. Second, the thoughtful executive and the careful citizen, aware of the shifting standards and potentially vast liability, will strive to ensure that his or her conduct never provides that factfinder an opportunity to give judgment.

EXAM REVIEW

1. **TORT** A tort is a violation of a duty imposed by the civil law. (p. 132)

EXAM Strategy

Question: Keith is driving while intoxicated. He swerves into the wrong lane and causes an accident, seriously injuring Caroline. Which statement is true?

(a) Caroline could sue Keith, who might be found guilty in her suit.

(b) Caroline and the state could start separate criminal cases against Keith.

(c) Caroline could sue Keith, and the state could prosecute Keith for drunk driving.

(d) The state could sue Keith but only with Caroline's consent.

(e) The state could prosecute Keith and sue him at the same time, for drunk driving.

Strategy: What party prosecutes a criminal case? The government does, not the injured party. What is the result in a criminal case? Guilt or innocence. What about a tort lawsuit? The injured party brings a tort suit. The defendant may be found liable but never guilty. (See the "Result" at the end of this section.)

2. **DEFAMATION** Defamation involves a false statement, likely to harm another's reputation, which is uttered to a third person and causes an injury. Opinion and privilege are valid defenses. Public personalities can win a defamation suit only by proving actual malice. (pp. 133–135)

3. **FALSE IMPRISONMENT** False imprisonment is the intentional restraint of another person without reasonable cause and without consent. (p. 136)

4. **INTENTIONAL INFLICTION OF EMOTIONAL DISTRESS** The intentional infliction of emotional distress involves extreme and outrageous conduct that causes serious emotional harm. (p. 137)

5. **BATTERY** Battery is an intentional touching of another person in a way that is offensive. Assault involves an act that makes the plaintiff fear an imminent battery. (p. 138)

6. **COMPENSATORY DAMAGES** Compensatory damages are the normal remedy in a tort case. In unusual cases, the court may award punitive damages to punish the defendant. (pp. 138–139)

7. **TORTIOUS INTERFERENCE** Tortious interference with business relations involves the defendant harming an existing contract or a prospective relationship that has a definite expectation of success. (p. 142)

8. **UNREASONABLE INTRUSION** The related torts of privacy and publicity involve unreasonable intrusion into someone's private life or unfair commercial exploitation by using someone's name, likeness, or voice without permission. (pp. 143)

9. **NEGLIGENCE** The five elements of negligence are duty of due care, breach, factual causation, foreseeable type of harm, and injury. (pp. 143–144)

10. **DUTY** If the defendant could foresee that misconduct would injure a particular person, he probably has a duty to her. (p. 144)

11. **DUTY OF DUE CARE** A defendant breaches his duty of due care by failing to behave the way a reasonable person would under similar conditions. (p. 147)

12. **NEGLIGENCE** Employers may be liable for negligent hiring or retention of employees. (p. 147)

EXAM Strategy

Question: A supervisor reprimanded an employee for eating in a restaurant when he should have been at work. Later, the employee showed up at the supervisor's office and shot him. Although the employee previously had been violent, management withheld this information from supervisory personnel. Discuss.

Strategy: An employer must do a *reasonable* job of hiring and retaining employees. (See the "Result" at the end of this section.)

13. **NEGLIGENCE PER SE** If a legislature sets a minimum standard of care for a particular activity in order to protect a certain group of people, and a violation of the statute injures a member of that group, the defendant has committed negligence per se. (p. 147)

14. **FACTUAL CAUSE** If an event physically leads to the ultimate harm, it is the factual cause. (p. 148)

15. **FORESEEABLE TYPE OF HARM** For the defendant to be liable, the type of harm must have been reasonably foreseeable. (p. 148)

16. **GENUINE HARM** The plaintiff must persuade the court that he has suffered a harm that is genuine, not speculative. (p. 150)

17. **CONTRIBUTORY VS. COMPARATIVE NEGLIGENCE** In a contributory negligence state, a plaintiff who is even slightly responsible for his own injury recovers nothing; in a comparative negligence state, the jury may apportion liability between plaintiff and defendant. (p. 151)

18. **STRICT LIABILITY.** A defendant is strictly liable for harm caused by an ultrahazardous activity or a defective product. Strict liability means that if the defendant's conduct led to the harm, the defendant is liable, even if she exercised extraordinary care. (p. 152)

EXAM Strategy

Question: Marko owned a cat and allowed it to roam freely outside. In the three years he had owned the pet, the animal had never bitten anyone. The cat entered Romi's garage. When Romi attempted to move it outside, the cat bit her. Romi underwent four surgeries, was fitted with a plastic finger joint, and spent more than $39,000 in medical bills. She sued Marko, claiming both strict liability and ordinary negligence. Assume that state law allows a domestic cat to roam freely. Evaluate both of Romi's claims.

Strategy: Negligence requires proof that the defendant breached a duty to the plaintiff by behaving unreasonably, and that the resulting harm was foreseeable. Was it? When would harm by a domestic cat be foreseeable? A defendant can be strictly liable for keeping a wild animal. Apply that rule as well. (See the "Result" at the end of this section.)

---

1. Result: (a) is wrong because a defendant cannot be found guilty in a civil suit. (b) is wrong because a private party has no power to prosecute a criminal case. (c) is correct. (d) is wrong because the state will prosecute Keith, not sue him. (e) is wrong for the same reason.

12. Result: This employer *may* have been liable for negligently hiring a previously violent employee, and *certainly* did an unreasonable job retaining him, without advising his supervisor of the earlier violence. The assault was easily foreseeable, and the employer is liable.

18. Result: If Marko's cat had bitten or attacked people in the past, this harm was foreseeable and Marko is liable. If the cat had never done so, and state law allows domestic animals to roam, Romi probably loses her suit for negligence. Her strict liability case definitely fails: a house cat is not a wild animal.

ADDITIONAL QUESTIONS

1. Benzaquin had a radio talk show in Boston. On the program, he complained about an incident earlier in the day, in which state trooper Fleming had stopped his car, apparently for lack of a proper license plate and safety sticker. Even though Benzaquin explained that the license plate had been stolen and the sticker had fallen onto the dashboard, Fleming refused to let him drive the car away, and Benzaquin and his daughter and two young grandsons had to find other transportation. On the show, Benzaquin angrily recounted the incident, then made the following statements about Fleming and troopers generally: "arrogants wearing troopers' uniforms like tights"; "little monkey, you wind him up and he does his thing"; "we're not paying them to be dictators and Nazis"; "this man is an absolute barbarian, a lunkhead, a meathead." Fleming sued Benzaquin for defamation. Comment.

2. Caldwell, carrying a large purse, was shopping in a K-Mart store. A security guard observed her look at various small items such as stain, hinges, and antenna wire. On occasion she bent down out of sight of the guard. The guard thought he saw Caldwell put something in her purse. Caldwell removed her glasses from her purse and returned

them a few times. After she left, the guard approached her in the parking lot and said that he believed she had store merchandise in her purse but was unable to say what he thought was put there. Caldwell opened the purse, and the guard testified he saw no K-Mart merchandise in it. The guard then told Caldwell to return to the store with him. They walked around the store for approximately 15 minutes, while the guard said six or seven times that he saw her put something in her purse. Caldwell left the store after another store employee indicated she could go. Caldwell sued. What kind of suit did she file, and what should the outcome be?

3. Fifteen-year-old Terri Stubblefield was riding in the back seat of a Ford Mustang II when the car was hit from behind. The Mustang was engulfed in a ball of fire, and Terri was severely burned. She died. Terri's family sued Ford, alleging that the car was badly designed—and that Ford knew it. At trial, Terri's family introduced evidence that Ford knew the fuel tank was dangerous and that it could have taken measures to make the tank safe. There was evidence that Ford consciously decided not to remedy the fuel tanks in order to save money. The family sought two different kinds of damages from Ford. What were they?

4. ***ETHICS*** In the *Stubblefield* case in Question 3, the jury awarded $8 million in punitive damages to the family. Ford appealed. Should the punitive damages be affirmed? What are the obligations of a corporation when it knows one of its products may be dangerous? Is an automobile company ethically obligated to make a *totally safe* car? Should we require a manufacturer to improve the safety of its cars if doing so will make them too expensive for many drivers? What would you do if you were a mid-level executive and saw evidence that your company was endangering the lives of consumers to save money? What would you do if you were on a *jury* and saw such evidence?

5. Caudle worked at Betts Lincoln-Mercury dealer. During an office party, many of the employees, including President Betts, were playing with an electric auto condenser, which gave a slight electric shock when touched. Some employees played catch with the condenser. Betts shocked Caudle on the back of his neck and then chased him around, holding the condenser. The shock later caused Caudle to suffer headaches, to pass out, and eventually to require surgery on a nerve in his neck. Even after surgery, Caudle had a slight numbness on one side of his head. He sued Betts for battery. Betts defended by saying that it was all horseplay and that he had intended no injury. Please rule.

6. ***YOU BE THE JUDGE*** WRITING PROBLEM Johnny Carson was for many years the star of a well-known television program, *The Tonight Show*. For about 20 years, he was introduced nightly on the show with the phrase, "Here's Johnny!" A large segment of the television watching public associated the phrase with Carson. A Michigan corporation was in the business of renting and selling portable toilets. The company chose the name "Here's Johnny Portable Toilets," and coupled the company name with the marketing phrase, "The World's Foremost Commodian." Carson sued, claiming that the company's name and slogan violated his right to commercial exploitation. Who should win? **Argument for Carson:** The toilet company is deliberately taking advantage of Johnny Carson's good name. He worked hard for decades to build a brilliant career and earn a reputation as a creative, funny, likable performer. No company has the right to use his name, his picture, or anything else closely identified with him, such as the phrase "Here's Johnny." The pun is personally offensive and commercially unfair. **Argument for Here's Johnny Portable Toilets:** Johnny Carson doesn't own his first name. It is available for anyone to use for any

purpose. Further, the popular term *john*, meaning toilet, has been around much longer than Carson or even television. We are entitled to make any use of it we want. Our corporate name is amusing to customers who have never heard of Carson, and we are entitled to profit from our brand recognition.

7. Jason Jacque was riding as a passenger in a car driven by his sister, who was drunk and driving 19 mph over the speed limit. She failed to negotiate a curve, skidded off the road, and collided with a wooden utility pole erected by the Public Service Company of Colorado (PSC). Jacque suffered severe brain injury. He sued PSC for negligently installing the pole too close to the highway at a dangerous curve where an accident was likely to happen. The trial court gave summary judgment for PSC, ruling that PSC owed no duty to Jacque. He appealed. Please rule.

8. Ryder leased a truck to Florida Food Service; Powers, an employee, drove it to make deliveries. He noticed that the door strap used to close the rear door was frayed, and he asked Ryder to fix it. Ryder failed to do so in spite of numerous requests. The strap broke, and Powers replaced it with a nylon rope. Later, when Powers was attempting to close the rear door, the nylon rope broke and he fell, sustaining severe injuries to his neck and back. He sued Ryder. The trial court found that Powers's attachment of the replacement rope was a superseding cause, relieving Ryder of any liability, and granted summary judgment for Ryder. Powers appealed. How should the appellate court rule?

9. A new truck, manufactured by General Motors Corp. (GMC), stalled in rush hour traffic on a busy interstate highway because of a defective alternator, which caused a complete failure of the truck's electrical system. The driver stood nearby and waved traffic around his stalled truck. A panel truck approached the GMC truck, and immediately behind the panel truck, Davis was driving a Volkswagen fastback. Because of the panel truck, Davis was unable to see the stalled GMC truck. The panel truck swerved out of the way of the GMC truck, and Davis drove straight into it. The accident killed him. Davis's widow sued GMC. GMC moved for summary judgment, alleging (1) no duty to Davis, (2) no factual causation, and (3) no foreseeable harm. Comment.

10. A prison inmate bit a hospital employee. The employee sued the state for negligence and lack of supervision, claiming a fear of AIDS. The plaintiff had tested negative for HIV three times, and there was no proof that the inmate was HIV positive. Comment on the probable outcome.

11. **ETHICS** Swimming pools in private homes often have diving boards, but those in public parks, hotels, and clubs rarely do. Why is that? Is it good or bad?

12. There is a collision between cars driven by Candy and Zeke, and both drivers are partly at fault. The evidence is that Candy is about 25 percent responsible, for failing to stop quickly enough, and Zeke about 75 percent responsible, for making a dangerous turn. Candy is most likely to win:

   a. A lawsuit for battery;

   b. A lawsuit for negligence, in a comparative negligence state;

   c. A lawsuit for negligence, in a contributory negligence state;

   d. A lawsuit for strict liability; or

   e. A lawsuit for assault.

13. Van Houten owned a cat and allowed it to roam freely outside. In the three years he had owned it, it had bitten 10 people. The cat entered Pritchard's garage. Pritchard attempted to move it outside his garage, and the cat bit him. As a direct result of the bite, Pritchard underwent four surgeries, was fitted with a plastic finger joint, and spent more than $39,000 in medical bills. He sued Van Houten, claiming both strict liability and ordinary negligence. Evaluate his claims.

14. ***ROLE REVERSAL*** Write a multiple-choice question about defamation in which one and only one element is missing from the plaintiff's case. Choose a set of answers that forces the student to isolate the missing element.

INTERNET RESEARCH PROBLEM

Take a look at **http://response.restoration.noaa.gov/**. What are some of the long-term problems associated with oil spills? View some of the photos in the "gallery." Are punitive damages for oil spills appropriate or excessive?

You can find further practice problems at www.cengagebrain.com. See the preface of this book for website access details.

CHAPTER

7

CRIME

Crime can take us by surprise. Stacey tucks her nine-year-old daughter, Beth, into bed. Promising her husband, Mark, that she will be home by 11:00 PM, she jumps into her car and heads back to Be Patient, Inc. She puts a compact disc in the player of her $85,000 sedan and tries to relax. Be Patient is a health care organization that owns five geriatric hospitals. Most of its patients use Medicare, and Stacey supervises all billing to their largest client, the federal government.

A major crime has occurred during the 90 minutes Stacey was at her desk, but she will never report it to the police.

She parks in a well-lighted spot on the street and walks to her building, failing to notice two men, collars turned up, watching from a parked truck. Once in her office, she goes straight to her computer and works on billing issues. Tonight's work goes more quickly than she expected, thanks to new software she helped develop. At 10:30 she emerges from the building with a quick step and a light heart, walks to her car—and finds it missing.

A major crime has occurred during the 90 minutes Stacey was at her desk, but she will never report it to the police. It is a crime that costs Americans countless dollars each year, yet Stacey will not even mention it to friends or family. Stacey is the criminal.

When we think of crime, we imagine the drug dealers and bank robbers endlessly portrayed on television. We do not picture corporate executives sitting at polished desks. "Street crimes" are indeed serious threats to our security and happiness. They deservedly receive the attention of the public and the law. (For a look at the FBI's 10 most wanted list, see http://www.fbi.gov.) But when measured only in dollars, street crime takes second place to white-collar crime, which costs society *tens of billions* of dollars annually.

The hypothetical about Stacey is based on many real cases and is used to illustrate that crime does not always dress the way we expect. Her car was never stolen; it was simply towed. Two parking bureau employees, watching from their truck, saw Stacey park illegally and did their job. It is Stacey who committed a crime—Medicare fraud. Stacey has learned the simple but useful lesson that company profits rise when she charges the government for work Be Patient has never done. For months she billed the government for imaginary patients. Then she hired a computer hacker to worm into the Medicare computer system and plant a "Trojan horse," a program that seemed useful to Medicare employees but actually contained a series of codes opening the computer to Stacey. Stacey simply entered the Medicare system and altered the calculations for payments owed to Be Patient. Every month, the government paid Be Patient about $10 million for imaginary work. Stacey's scheme was quick and profitable—and a distressingly common crime.

What do we do about cases like these? These questions involve multifarious fact issues and important philosophical values. In this chapter, we look first at the big picture of criminal law and then focus on that part of it that most affects business—white-collar crime. We examine four major issues:

- *Crime, Society, and Law.* What makes conduct criminal? We enumerate the basic elements that the prosecution must establish to prove that a crime has been committed, and also some of the most common defenses.

- *Crimes That Harm Business.* We look at specific crimes, such as fraud and embezzlement, that cost businesses enormous sums every year.

- *Crimes Committed by Business.* We analyze "white-collar crimes," which are generally committed by businesspeople and may be directed at consumers, other businesses, or the government.

- *Criminal Process and Constitutional Protections.* We examine how the Bill of Rights protects citizens subjected to search, interrogation, and trial. And we pay a final visit to Stacey.

CRIME, SOCIETY, AND LAW

CIVIL LAW/CRIMINAL LAW

Most of this book concerns the civil law—the rights and liabilities that exist between private parties. As we have seen, if one person claims that another has caused her a civil injury, she must file a lawsuit and convince a court of her damages.

The **criminal law** is different. Conduct is criminal when society outlaws it. When a state legislature or Congress concludes that certain behavior threatens the population generally, it passes a statute forbidding that behavior, in other words, declaring it criminal. Medicare fraud,

Criminal law
Prohibits conduct threatening to the people and social stability.

which Stacey committed, is a crime because Congress has outlawed it. Money laundering is a crime because Congress concluded it was a fundamental part of the drug trade and prohibited it.

Prosecution

Suppose the police arrest Roger and accuse him of breaking into a video store and stealing 25 video cameras, videos, and other equipment. The owner of the video store is the one harmed, but **it is the government that prosecutes crimes**. The local prosecutor will decide whether or not to charge Roger and bring him to trial.

Jury Right

The facts of the case will be decided by a judge or jury. A criminal defendant has a right to a trial by jury for any charge that could result in a sentence of six months or longer. The defendant may demand a jury trial or may waive that right, in which case the judge will be the factfinder.

Punishment

In a civil lawsuit, the plaintiff seeks a verdict that the defendant is liable for harm caused to her. But in a criminal case, the government asks the court to find the defendant **guilty** of the crime. The government wants the court to punish the defendant. If the judge or jury finds the defendant guilty, the court will punish him with a fine and/or a prison sentence. The fine is paid to the government, not to the injured person (although the court will sometimes order **restitution**, meaning that the defendant must reimburse the victim for harm suffered). It is almost always the judge who imposes the sentence. If the jury is not persuaded of the defendant's guilt, it will **acquit** him, that is, find him not guilty.

Felony/Misdemeanor

A **felony** is a serious crime, for which a defendant can be sentenced to one year or more in prison. Murder, robbery, rape, drug dealing, money laundering, wire fraud, and embezzlement are felonies. A **misdemeanor** is a less serious crime, often punishable by a year or less in a county jail. Public drunkenness, driving without a license, and simple possession of one marijuana cigarette are considered misdemeanors in most states.

Punishment

Why punish a defendant? Sometimes the answer is obvious. If a defendant has committed armed robbery, we want that person locked up. Other cases are not so apparent.

You are the judge in charge of sentencing Jason. He is a 61-year-old minister who has devoted 40 years to serving his community, leading his church, and helping to rehabilitate schools. Fifteen years ago he founded a children's hospital and has raised enormous sums to maintain it. He has labored with local government to rebuild abandoned housing and established a center for battered women. Jason suffers from a terminal illness and will die in three to four years. But the jury has just found that in his zeal to get housing built, Jason took kickbacks from construction firms run by gangsters. The construction companies padded their bills, some of which were paid with state and city money. They kicked back a small amount of this illegal profit to Jason, who gave the money to his charities. Jason thought of himself as Robin Hood, but the law regards him as a felon. You can fine Jason and/or sentence him to prison for a maximum of five years.

Guilty
A court's finding that a defendant has committed a crime.

Restitution
A court order that a guilty defendant reimburse the victim for the harm suffered.

Felony
A serious crime, for which a defendant can be sentenced to one year or more in prison.

Misdemeanor
A less serious crime, often punishable by less than a year in a county jail.

A flood of letters urges you to allow Jason to continue raising money and helping others. You need to understand the rationale of punishment. Over the past several centuries, philosophers in many countries—and judges in this country—have proposed various reasons for punishing the guilty.

Restraint

A violent criminal who appears likely to commit more crimes must be physically restrained. Here there is no pretense of prison being anything but a cage to protect the rest of society. (An online group that sees little good and much evil in our system of incarceration gives examples of perceived abuses at **http://www.prisonactivist.org.**) In Jason's case, there is clearly no reason to restrain him.

Deterrence

Imprisonment may deter future crimes in two ways. **Specific deterrence** is intended to teach *this defendant* that crime carries a heavy price tag, in the hope that he will never do it again. **General deterrence** is the goal of demonstrating to *society generally* that crime must be shunned. Notice that both ideas of deterrence are utilitarian; that is, they are means to an end. Specific and general deterrence both assume that by imprisoning someone, the law achieves a greater good for everyone. Jason almost certainly requires no specific deterrence. Is general deterrence a reason to imprison him?

> **Specific deterrence**
> Is intended to teach *this defendant* that crime carries a heavy price tag.

> **General deterrence**
> Is the goal of demonstrating to *society generally* that crime must be shunned.

Retribution

The German philosopher Immanuel Kant (1724–1804) rejected the idea of deterrence. He argued that human beings were supremely important and as a result must always be treated as ends in themselves, *never as a means to an end.* Kant would argue that, if deterrence were legitimate, then it would be all right to torture prisoners—even innocent prisoners—if this deterred massive amounts of crime.

For Kant, there is only one valid reason to punish: the prisoner deserves it. This is the idea of **retribution**—giving back to the criminal precisely what he deserves. A moral world, said Kant, requires that the government administer to all prisoners a punishment exactly equal to the crime they committed. A murderer must be put to death (even if he is dying from an illness and would live only a few days); an executive who bribes a government official must suffer a punishment equal to the harm he caused. To Kant, all of Jason's good deeds would be irrelevant, as would his terminal illness. If three years is the appropriate imprisonment for the crime of fraud, then he must serve three years, even if he dies in prison, even if it stops him from raising $10 million for charity.

> **Retribution**
> Giving back to the criminal precisely what he deserves.

Related to the idea of retribution is **vengeance**. When a serious crime has occurred, society wants the perpetrator to suffer. If we punish no one, people lose faith in the power and effectiveness of government and may take the law into their own hands.

Rehabilitation

To rehabilitate someone is to provide training so that he may return to a normal life. Most criminal justice experts believe that little or no rehabilitation occurs in a prison, though other forms of punishment may achieve this worthy goal.

Jason's Case.   What is your decision? Restraint and specific deterrence are unnecessary. You may imprison him for general deterrence or for retribution. Should you let him go free so that he can raise more money for good causes? In a similar case, a federal court judge decided that general deterrence was essential. To allow someone to go free, he said, would be to send a message that certain people can get away with crime. The judge sentenced the defendant to a prison term, though he shortened the sentence based on the defendant's age and ill health.[1]

THE PROSECUTION'S CASE

In all criminal cases, the prosecution faces several basic issues.

Conduct Outlawed

Virtually all crimes are created by statute. The prosecution must demonstrate to the court that the defendant's alleged conduct is indeed outlawed by a statute. Returning to Roger, the alleged video thief, the state charges that he stole video cameras from a store, a crime clearly defined by statute as burglary.

Burden of Proof

Beyond a reasonable doubt

The very high burden of proof in a criminal trial, demanding much more evidence and certainty than required in a civil trial.

In a civil case, the plaintiff must prove her case by a preponderance of the evidence.[2] But in a criminal case, the government must prove its case **beyond a reasonable doubt**. This is because the potential harm to a criminal defendant is far greater. Roger, the video thief, can be fined and/or sent to prison. The stigma of a criminal conviction will stay with him, making it more difficult to obtain work and housing. Therefore, in all criminal cases, if the jury has any significant doubt at all that Roger stole the video cameras, it *must* acquit him. This high standard of proof in a criminal case reflects a very old belief, inherited from English law, that it is better to set 10 guilty people free than to convict a single innocent one. We will see that our law offers many protections for the accused.

Actus Reus

Actus reus

The guilty act.

Actus reus means the "guilty act." **The prosecution must prove that the defendant voluntarily committed a prohibited act.** Suppose Mary Jo files an insurance claim for a stolen car, knowing that her car was not stolen. That is insurance fraud, and mail fraud if she sent documents through the Post Office. Filing the claim is the *actus reus:* Mary Jo voluntarily filled out the insurance claim and mailed it. At a bar, Mary Jo describes the claim to her friend, Chi Ling, who laughs and replies, "That's great. It'll serve the company right." Has Chi Ling committed a crime? No. There is no *actus reus*, because Chi Ling has done nothing illegal. Her cynical attitude may contribute to higher premiums for all of us, but criminal law punishes acts, not thoughts or omissions.

Mens Rea

Mens rea

A guilty state of mind.

The prosecution must also show **mens rea**, a "guilty state of mind," on the defendant's part. This is harder to prove than *actus reus*—it requires convincing evidence about something that is essentially psychological. Precisely what "state of mind" the prosecution must prove varies, depending on the crime. We will discuss the exact *mens rea* requirement for various crimes later in the chapter. In general, however, there are four mental states that a prosecutor may be required to prove, depending on the crime:

General intent

The defendant intended to do the prohibited physical action (the *actus reus*).

General Intent.   Most crimes require a showing of **general intent**, meaning that the defendant intended to do the prohibited physical action (the *actus reus*). Suppose Miller, a customer in a bar, picks up a bottle and smashes it over the head of Bud. In a trial for criminal

---

[1] *United States v. Bergman*, 416 F.Supp. 496, 1976 U.S. Dist. LEXIS 14577 (S.D.N.Y. 1976).

[2] See the earlier discussion in Chapter 3, on dispute resolution.

assault, the *mens rea* would simply be the intention to hit Bud. The prosecution need not show that Miller intended serious harm, only that he intended the blow.

How will a prosecutor prove what was in Miller's mind? By circumstantial evidence: a witness will describe how Miller picked up the bottle and what he did with it. A jury is free to conclude that Miller intended physical contact since there would be no other reason for his action.

Specific Intent.   Some crimes require the prosecution to prove that the defendant willfully intended to do something beyond the physical act. For example, burglary requires proof that the defendant entered a building at night and intended to commit a felony inside, such as stealing property.

Reckless or Negligent Conduct.   For a few crimes, the prosecution is concerned more with the defendant's irresponsible conduct than with what the defendant was thinking. **Criminal recklessness** means consciously disregarding a substantial risk of injury. A pedestrian who jokingly points a gun at another commits criminal recklessness. The danger of the gun going off is obvious, and the defendant is guilty even if no shot is fired. A slightly lesser crime, **criminal negligence**, refers to gross deviations from reasonable conduct. A hunter who sees movement and shoots at it, without bothering to determine whether the target is a turkey or a professor, commits criminal negligence.

Strict Liability.   In strict liability cases, the prosecution must only prove *actus reus*. If the defendant committed the act, he is guilty, regardless of mental state or irresponsibility. For example, in an effort to improve the environment, many states now hold corporate defendants strictly liable for discharging certain pollutants into the air. If an oil refinery discharges toxic fumes, it is strictly liable, regardless of what efforts it may have taken to control emissions. Thus, strict liability crimes are the easiest for a prosecutor to prove and potentially the most dangerous to corporations.

DEFENSES

A criminal defendant will frequently dispute the facts that link her to the crime. For example, she might claim mistaken identity (that she merely resembles the real criminal) or offer an alibi (that she can prove she was elsewhere when the crime was committed). In addition, a defendant may offer **legal defenses**. Many of these are controversial, as we will see.

Insanity

A defendant who can prove that he was **insane** at the time of the criminal act will be declared not guilty. This reflects the moral basis of our criminal law. Insane people, though capable of great harm, historically have not been considered responsible for their acts. A defendant found to be insane will generally be committed to a mental institution. If and when that hospital determines he is no longer a danger to society, he will, in theory, be released. Some people applaud this as deeply humane, while others see it as muddled thinking that allows guilty people to walk free. The most common test for insanity is the M'Naghten Rule.

M'Naghten Rule.   The defendant must show (1) that he suffered a serious, identifiable mental disease and that because of it (2) he did not understand the nature of his act or did not know that it was wrong. Suppose Jerry, a homeless man, stabs Phil. At trial, a psychiatrist testifies that Jerry suffers from chronic schizophrenia, that he does not know where he is or what he is doing, and that when he stabbed Phil he believed he was sponging down his pet giraffe. If the jury believes the psychiatrist, it may find Jerry not guilty by reason of insanity.

What if the alleged mental defect is a result of the defendant's own behavior? You be the judge. (Those of you with Bieber Fever will be relieved to know that the killer in the next case is not Justin Bieber.)

YOU *be the* JUDGE

BIEBER V. PEOPLE

856 P.2d 811, 1993 COLO. LEXIS 630
Supreme Court of Colorado, 1993

Facts: Donald Bieber walked up to a truck in which William Ellis was sitting and shot Ellis, whom he did not know, in the back of his head. He threw Ellis's body from the truck and drove away. Shortly before and after the killing, Bieber encountered various people in different places. He sang "God Bless America" and the "Marine Hymn" to them and told them he was a prisoner of war and was being followed by communists. He told people he had killed a communist on "War Memorial Highway." The police arrested him.

Bieber had a long history of drug abuse. As a teenager, he began using drugs, including amphetamines. As an adult, he continued his heavy drug use, while making money selling drugs. Several years before the homicide, Bieber voluntarily sought treatment for mental impairment, entering a hospital and saying he thought he was going to hurt someone. He was later released into a long-term drug program.

Bieber was charged with first degree murder. He pleaded not guilty by reason of insanity. An expert witness testified that he was insane, suffering from "amphetamine delusional disorder" (ADD), a recognized psychiatric illness resulting from long-term use of amphetamines and characterized by delusions. At trial, Bieber's attorney argued that he was not intoxicated at the time of the crime but that he was insane due to ADD. The trial court refused to instruct that Bieber could be legally insane due to ADD, and the jury found Bieber guilty of first degree murder. He appealed.

You Be the Judge: May a jury find that a defendant with ADD is legally insane?

Argument for Bieber: Your honors, Mr. Bieber acknowledges the rule that someone who becomes voluntarily intoxicated and commits an offense is liable for the crime. That rule is irrelevant here, since Mr. Bieber was not intoxicated at the time of this homicide. He was insane.

The state of Colorado has long held that insanity is a valid defense to a criminal charge. It is morally and legally proper to distinguish between people who commit a crime out of viciousness and those who suffer serious mental illness. Mr. Bieber suffered from amphetamine delusional disorder, a serious psychotic illness recognized by the American Psychiatric Association. There was overwhelming evidence that he was out of control and did not know what he was doing at the time of the homicide.

The fact that ADD is brought about by years of amphetamine use should make no difference in an insanity case. This man's reason was destroyed by a serious illness. He should not be treated the same as a cold-blooded killer.

Argument for the State: Your honors, there is no qualitative difference between a person who drinks or takes drugs knowing that he or she will be momentarily "mentally defective" as an immediate result and one who drinks or takes drugs knowing that he or she may be "mentally defective" as an eventual, long-term result. In both cases, the person is aware of the possible consequences of his or her actions. We do not believe that in the latter case, such knowledge should be excused simply because the resulting affliction is more severe.

It is a matter of common knowledge that the excessive use of liquor or drugs impairs the perceptual, judgmental, and volitional faculties of the user. Also, because the intoxication must be "self-induced," the defendant necessarily must have had the conscious ability to prevent this temporary incapacity from coming into being at all. Self-induced intoxication by its very nature involves culpability.

As a matter of public policy, therefore, we must not excuse a defendant's actions, which endanger others, based upon a mental disturbance or illness that he or she actively and voluntarily contracted. There is no principled basis to distinguish between the short-term and long-term effects of voluntary intoxication by punishing the first and excusing the second. If anything, the moral blameworthiness would seem to be even greater with respect to the long-term effects of many, repeated instances of voluntary intoxication occurring over an extended period of time. We ask that you affirm.

Jury Role. The insanity defense creates fear and confusion in the public, but most experts believe the concern is unwarranted. A Connecticut study showed that the defense was invoked in only one-tenth of 1% of criminal prosecutions in that state, and that in over 90% of *those* cases it still failed. Juries are reluctant to acquit based on insanity, probably fearing that the defendant will soon be back on the streets. But just the opposite is true. Most defendants acquitted by reason of insanity spend more time in a mental hospital than convicts spend in prison for the same act.

Entrapment

You go to a fraternity party where you meet a pledge named Joey. After a drink or two, Joey asks if you can get him some marijuana. You tell him you never use drugs. A week later you accidentally meet Joey in the cafeteria and he repeats the question, promising a very large profit if you will supply him with an ounce. You again say "no thanks." About once a week Joey bumps into you, in the school hallways, in the bookstore, at parties. He continues to ask you to "get him some stuff," and his offers grow more lucrative. Finally, after six requests, you speak to someone who is reputed to deal in drugs. You buy an ounce, then offer it to Joey at a large markup. Joey gratefully hands over the money, takes your package—and flashes his badge in your face, identifying himself as an undercover agent of the State Police. You are speechless, which is fine, since Joey informs you that you have the right to remain silent.

Drugs are a deadly serious problem in our society, involved directly or indirectly in more than half of all street crime. We need creative police efforts. Has this one gone too far? The issue is entrapment. **When the government induces the defendant to break the law, the prosecution must prove beyond a reasonable doubt that the defendant was predisposed to commit the crime.**

If the government cannot prove predisposition, the defendant is not guilty. In other words, the goal is to separate the cases where the defendant was innocent before the government tempted him from those where the defendant was only too eager to break the law.

Most courts would agree that the state police officer entrapped the student. The seller said "no" five times. Unless the government has other evidence that the defendant was involved in dealing drugs, there appears to be no predisposition, and the entrapment defense is valid.

CRIMES THAT HARM BUSINESS

Three major crimes involve taking money from businesses: larceny, fraud, and embezzlement. In each case the criminal ends up with money or property that belongs to someone else.

LARCENY

It is holiday season at the mall, the period of greatest profits—and the most crime. At the Foot Forum, a teenager limps in wearing ragged sneakers and sneaks out wearing Super Rags, valued at $145. Down the aisle at a home furnishing store, a man is so taken by a $375 power saw that he takes it. Sweethearts swipe sweaters, pensioners pocket produce. All are committing larceny.

Larceny is the trespassory taking of personal property with the intent to steal it. "Trespassory taking" means that someone else originally has the property. The Super Rags are personal property (not real estate), they were in the possession of the Foot Forum, and the teenager deliberately left without paying, intending never to return the goods. That is larceny. By contrast, suppose Fast Eddie leaves Bloomingdale's in New York, descends to the subway system, and jumps over a turnstile without paying. Larceny? No. He has "taken" a service— the train ride—but not personal property.

Every day in the United States, over $25 million in merchandise is stolen from retail stores. Economists estimate that *12 cents out of every dollar* spent in retail stores covers the cost of shoplifting. Some criminal experts believe that drug addicts commit over half of all shoplifting to support their habits. Stores have added electronic surveillance, security patrols, and magnetic antitheft devices, but the problem will not disappear. We revisit this issue later, in the Ewing case, where we examine the heavy penalty one state has imposed on repeat offenders.

FRAUD

Robert Dorsey owned Bob's Chrysler in Highland, Illinois. He ordered cars from the manufacturer, the First National Bank of Highland paid Chrysler, and Dorsey—supposedly—repaid the loans as he sold autos. Dorsey, though, began to suffer financial problems, and the bank suspected he was selling cars without repaying his loans. A state investigator notified Dorsey that he planned to review all dealership records. One week later a fire engulfed the dealership. An arson investigator discovered that an electric iron, connected to a timer, had been placed on a pile of financial papers doused with accelerant.

The saddest part of this true story is that it is only too common. Some experts suggest that 1% of corporate revenues are wasted on fraud alone. Dorsey was convicted and imprisoned for committing two crimes that cost business billions of dollars annually—fraud and arson.[3]

Fraud refers to various crimes, all of which have a common element: **the deception of another person for the purpose of obtaining money or property from him**. Robert Dorsey's precise violation was bank fraud, a federal crime. It is bank fraud to use deceit to obtain money, assets, securities, or other property under the control of any financial institution. The maximum penalty is a fine of $1 million and/or a prison term of 30 years.[4]

Wire fraud and **mail fraud** are additional federal crimes, involving the use of interstate mail, telegram, telephone, radio, or television to obtain property by deceit.[5] For example, if Marsha makes an interstate phone call to sell land that she does not own, that is wire fraud.

Insurance fraud is another common crime. A Ford suddenly swerves in front of a Toyota, causing it to brake hard. A Mercedes, unable to stop, slams into the Toyota, as the Ford races away. Regrettable accident? No: a "swoop and squat" fraud scheme. The Ford and Toyota drivers were working together, hoping for an accident. The "injured" Toyota driver now goes to a third member of the fraud team—a dishonest doctor—who diagnoses serious back and neck injuries and predicts long-term pain and disability. The driver files a claim against the Mercedes's driver, whose insurer may be forced to pay tens or even hundreds of thousands of dollars for an accident that was no accident. Insurance companies investigate countless cases like this each year, trying to distinguish the honest victim from the criminal.

Finally, Stacey, the hospital executive described in the chapter's introduction, committed a fourth type of fraud. **Medicare fraud** includes using false statements, bribes, or kickbacks to obtain Medicare payments from the federal or state government.[6]

Fraud

Deception used to obtain money or property.

---

[3] *United States v. Dorsey*, 27 F.3d 285, 1994 U.S.App. LEXIS 15010 (7th Cir. 1994).
[4] 18 U.S.C. §1344.
[5] 18 U.S.C. §§1341–1346.
[6] 18 U.S.C. §§1320 et seq. (1994).

EXAM *Strategy*

Question: Eric mails glossy brochures to 25,000 people, offering to sell them a one-month time-share in a stylish apartment in Las Vegas. The brochure depicts an imposing building, an opulent apartment, and spectacular pools. To reserve a space, customers need only send in a $2,000 deposit. Three hundred people respond, sending in the money. In fact, there is no such building. Eric, planning to flee with the cash, is arrested and prosecuted. His sentence could be as long as 20 years. (1) With what crime is he charged? (2) Is this a felony or misdemeanor prosecution? (3) Does Eric have a right to a jury trial? (4) Describe the burden of proof, *actus reus*, and *mens rea* in this case.

Strategy: (1) Eric is deceiving people, and that should tell you the *type* of crime. (2, 3) The potential 20-year sentence determines whether Eric's crime is a misdemeanor or felony, and whether or not he is entitled to a jury trial. (4) We know that the government has the burden of proof in a criminal prosecutions—but *how much* evidence must it offer? Finally, distinguish *actus reus* from *mens rea*.

Result: A felony is one in which the sentence could be a year or more. The potential penalty here is 20 years, so the crime is a felony. Eric has a right to a jury, as does any defendant whose sentence could be six months or longer. The prosecution must prove its case beyond a reasonable doubt, a much higher burden than that in a civil case. The *actus reus* in this case is mailing 25,000 brochures about a nonexistent building. The *mens rea* is Eric's guilty knowledge that the brochure is intended to swindle people.

ARSON

Robert Dorsey, the Chrysler dealer, committed a second serious crime. **Arson** is the malicious use of fire or explosives to damage or destroy any real estate or personal property. It is both a federal and a state crime. Dorsey used arson to conceal his bank fraud. Most arsonists hope to collect on insurance policies. Every year thousands of buildings burn, particularly in economically depressed neighborhoods, as owners try to make a quick kill or extricate themselves from financial difficulties. We involuntarily subsidize their immorality by paying higher insurance premiums.

Arson
The malicious use of fire or explosives to damage or destroy real estate or personal property.

EMBEZZLEMENT

This crime also involves illegally obtaining property, but with one big difference: the culprit begins with legal possession. **Embezzlement** is the fraudulent conversion of property already in the defendant's possession.

Professor Beach, in North Dakota, asks his work-study student, Sandy, to drive his car to the repair shop. Sandy drives halfway and then hears on the car radio a forecast of snow. "I don't like snow," she thinks. Sandy turns south and never stops until she reaches Key West, Florida. "This is nicer," she murmurs. Sandy is innocent of larceny because she took the car keys with Beach's permission, but guilty of embezzlement because she converted the auto to her own use.

Wherever money abounds, embezzlement tempts. Banks are prime targets. A loan officer embezzled money simply by creating false loans and taking the money for himself. He paid off earlier loans by taking out new ones and managed to stay ahead of the game until he had embezzled over $5 million. He was eventually caught by a suspicious teller.[7]

Embezzlement
The fraudulent conversion of property already in the defendant's possession.

---

[7] *Peoples State Bank v. American Casualty Co. of Reading, Mich.*, No. Ed-8425-11, *Lawyers Weekly*, May 17, 1993, p. 6A.

COMPUTER CRIME

Christopher Maxwell, a 21-year-old computer expert, wanted to earn commissions by installing ad-ware onto the computers of unsuspecting owners. And he did! To accomplish his task, he hacked into thousands of computers around the world. He used botnet software to spread his ad-ware. Botnet uses zombie computers (those compromised by the invasion) to spread the virus, using common commands and infrastructure. Christopher's plan worked, and he earned about $100,000 doing it.

But the virus caused enormous harm. A hospital lost computer service and was forced to use runners to transport vital medical information from one department to another. The virus seized control of more than 400 Defense Department computers. An educational district's system was shut down, stopping online instruction in every school, and costing $50,000 in repairs. The other flaw in Christopher's plan was its end result: After his arrest, he pleaded guilty to a felony charge of intentionally damaging computers. At sentencing, he begged the judge to grant him probation, urging that he was a 21-year-old boy with a good heart, who had no idea of the harm that he might cause. The judge's eyes remained dry. She declared that he was a self-centered young man who was sophisticated enough to know what he wanted—and understand the harm he would cause. She sentenced him to 37 months in prison followed by 3 years supervised release.

The ascent of the Internet inevitably brings with it new forms of crime. Various federal statutes criminalize this behavior.

- The **Computer Fraud and Abuse Act** prohibits using a computer to commit theft, espionage, trespass, fraud, and damage to another computer.[8]

- The **Access Device Fraud Act** outlaws the fraudulent use of cards, codes, account numbers, and other devices to obtain money, goods, or services.[9] For example, it is a violation of this act to reprogram a cellular telephone so that calls are charged to an improper account.

- The **Identity Theft and Assumption Deterrence Act** bars the use of false identification to commit fraud or other crime.[10] A waiter who uses stolen credit card numbers to buy airline tickets has violated this act. The Federal Trade Commission receives about 100,000 complaints of identity theft every year, so you should guard identifying data carefully.

- The **Wire and Electronic Communications Interception Act** makes it a crime to intercept most wire, oral, and electronic communications.[11] (This law does not prohibit recording your own conversations.) We *warned* you not to tape your roommate's conversations!

Identity Theft

Identity theft is growing explosively. How do thieves get personal information?

- Steal records at work by hacking into company files or bribing coworkers.

- Rummage through trash or mailboxes.

- Pose as a landlord or employer with a valid interest in your credit.

- "Skim," which means to use an electronic device to record your personal information when you are using a credit card for a proper purpose, such as paying at a retail store.

---

[8] 18 U.S.C. §1030.
[9] 18 U.S.C. §1029.
[10] 18 U.S.C. §1028.
[11] 18 U.S.C. §2511.

- "Phish," which means to contact you by phone or e-mail, posing as a legitimate company attempting to correct a problem with your account.

    What do thieves do with private data?

- Open new credit card accounts and purchase "big ticket" items.

- Open a new bank account and write bad checks.

- Use credit cards and checks to drain your bank account.

- Give your name to police during an investigation, meaning that when the thieves fail to appear in court, a warrant will issue for *your* arrest.

    How should an identity theft victim respond?

- Place a fraud alert on your credit reports, by phoning one of three credit companies (Equifax, 800–525-6285; Experian, 888-397-3742; TransUnion, 800-680-7289).

- Close any account that is potentially affected.

- Notify the local police.

- File a complaint with the Federal Trade Commission. You may do this online, at **http://www.consumer.gov**.

    The following case illustrates the devious nature of identity thieves, and the harm they cause.

UNITED STATES V. DRAGON

472 F.3d 501
THIRD CIRCUIT COURT OF APPEALS, 2006

CASE SUMMARY

Facts: Shalon Dragon was convicted of identity theft and sentenced to 44 months in prison. He appealed, claiming his punishment was too harsh. The appellate decision provides a vivid glimpse of the crime and the lives of those engaged in it.

Issue: *Did Dragon's identity theft warrant this sentence?*

Decision: Yes, the punishment fit the crime. Affirmed.

Reasoning: Durham obtained the personal information of 45 hospital patients from a contact he had at Mount Sinai Medical Center. Dragon and Durham then obtained false identification cards from photo stores in New York City, reflecting the patients' names and identifying information. They used the false identification to charge merchandise and gift cards to the real account-holder at Macy's stores in New Jersey, New York, and Pennsylvania.

After hearing from Dragon's counsel, Dragon himself, and the government, the District Court imposed a sentence of 44 months. The District Court commented on the complexity of the fraud scheme and the harm caused to victims of identity theft. The District Court twice acknowledged Dragon's request for leniency. It first stated, "Mr. Dragon, you're right you're a young man, but you're a young man that's found a pretty nifty way to get extra cash with very little danger to yourself." In imposing a higher sentence, the District Court emphasized Dragon's long history of fraudulent criminal conduct and the fact that Dragon had been given "a second chance" by various courts "over and over again." In light of his failure to take advantage of this past leniency, the District Court found it necessary to sentence Dragon "to a serious term of imprisonment."

CRIMES COMMITTED BY BUSINESS

A corporation can be found guilty of a crime based on the conduct of any of its **agents**, who include anyone undertaking work on behalf of the corporation. An agent can be a corporate officer, an accountant hired to audit a statement, a sales clerk, or almost any other person performing a job at the company's request.

If an agent commits a criminal act within the scope of his employment and with the intent to benefit the corporation, the company is liable.[12] This means that the agent himself must first be guilty. The normal requirements of *actus reus* and *mens rea* apply. If the agent is guilty, the corporation is, too.

Critics believe that the criminal law has gone too far. It is unfair, they argue, to impose *criminal* liability on a corporation, and thus penalize the shareholders, unless high-ranking officers were directly involved in the illegal conduct. The following case concerns a corporation's responsibility for a death caused by its employee.

COMMONWEALTH V. ANGELO TODESCA CORP.

446 MASS. 128, 842 N.E.2d 930
SUPREME JUDICIAL COURT OF MASSACHUSETTS, 2006

CASE SUMMARY

Facts: Brian Gauthier, an experienced truck driver, worked for Todesca, a paving company. After about a year driving a particular 10-wheel tri-axle dump truck, Gauthier noticed that the back-up alarm had stopped working. When he reported this, the company mechanic realized that the old alarm needed replacement. The mechanic had none in stock, so the company instructed Gauthier to drive the truck without the alarm.

About a month later, Gauthier and other Todesca drivers were delivering asphalt to the work site on a highway at the entrance to a shopping mall. A police officer directed the construction vehicles and the routine mall traffic. A different driver asked the officer to "watch our backs" as the trucks backed through the intersection. All of the other trucks were equipped with back-up alarms. When it was Gauthier's turn to back up, he struck the police officer, killing him.

The state charged the Todesca corporation with motor vehicle homicide, and the jury found the company guilty. The trial judge imposed a fine—of $2,500. The court of appeals reversed the conviction, and the prosecution appealed to the state's highest court.

Issue: *Could the company be found guilty of motor vehicle homicide?*

Decision: Yes, the company was guilty of motor vehicle homicide. Affirmed.

Reasoning: The defendant maintains that a corporation never can be criminally liable for motor vehicle homicide because a corporation cannot "operate" a vehicle. We disagree. A corporation can act only through its agents. By the defendant's reasoning, a corporation never could be liable for any crime. A corporation can no more serve alcohol to minors, or bribe government officials, than operate a vehicle negligently. Only human agents are capable of these actions. Nevertheless, we consistently have held that a corporation may be criminally liable for such acts when performed by corporate employees acting within the scope of their employment and on behalf of the corporation.

Gauthier's truck was not equipped with a functioning backup alarm, and he knew the alarm was missing.

---

[12] *New York Central & Hudson River R.R. Co. v. United States*, 212 U.S. 481, 29 S.Ct. 304, 1909 U.S. LEXIS 1832 (1909). And note that what counts is the intention to benefit, not actual benefit. A corporation will not escape liability by showing that the scheme failed.

The defendant had a written safety policy mandating that all its trucks be equipped with such alarms. An employee's violation of his employer's rules, intended to protect the safety of third persons, is evidence of the employee's negligence, for which the employer may be held liable.

Gauthier never informed the victim that his truck did not have an alarm. The jury could have inferred that the victim, a veteran police officer, knew that the defendant routinely equipped its trucks with backup alarms. The victim expected to hear a backup alarm and would have, almost right in his ear—had the truck been properly maintained.

PUNISHING A CORPORATION

Fines

The most common punishment for a corporation is a fine, as demonstrated in the Todesca case. This makes sense in that the purpose of a business is to earn a profit, and a fine, theoretically, hurts. But most fines are modest by the present standards of corporate wealth. In the Todesca prosecution, does a $2,500 fine force corporate leaders to be more cautious, or does it teach them that cutting corners makes economic sense, because the penalties will be a tolerable cost of doing business?

Sometimes the fines are stiffer. British Petroleum was found guilty of two serious environmental violations. In Alaska, the company's failure to inspect and clean pipelines caused 200,000 gallons of crude oil to spill onto the tundra. In Texas, the company's failure to follow standard procedures for ensuring safe refineries caused a catastrophic explosion that killed 15 people and injured 170 more. The total fine for both criminal violations was $62 million.[13] Is that too much – or not enough?

Compliance Programs

The **Federal Sentencing Guidelines** are the detailed rules that judges must follow when sentencing defendants convicted of crimes in federal court. The guidelines instruct judges to determine whether, at the time of the crime, the corporation had in place a serious **compliance program**, that is, a plan to prevent and detect criminal conduct at all levels of the company. A company that can point to a detailed, functioning compliance program may benefit from a dramatic reduction in the fine or other punishment meted out. Indeed, a tough compliance program may even convince federal investigators to curtail an investigation and to limit any prosecution to those directly involved, rather than attempting to get a conviction against high-ranking officers or the company itself.

To persuade prosecutors or judges that it seriously intended to follow the law, a company must demonstrate a thorough and effective compliance plan:

- The program must be reasonably capable of reducing the prospect of criminal conduct.

- Specific, high-level officers must be responsible for overseeing the program.

- The company must not place in charge any officers it knows or should have known, from past experience, that are likely to engage in illegal conduct.

- The company must effectively communicate the program to all employees and agents.

- The company must ensure compliance by monitoring employees in a position to cheat and by promptly disciplining any who break the law.

Federal Sentencing Guidelines
The detailed rules that judges must follow when sentencing defendants convicted of crimes in federal court.

Compliance program
A plan to prevent and detect criminal conduct at all levels of the company.

---

[13] Source: **http://epa.gov/**.

SELECTED CRIMES COMMITTED BY BUSINESS

Workplace Crimes

The workplace can be dangerous. Working on an assembly line exposes factory employees to fast-moving machinery. For a roofer, the first slip may be the last. The invisible radiation in a nuclear power plant can be deadlier than a bullet. The most important statute regulating the workplace is the federal **Occupational Safety and Health Act of 1970 (OSHA)**,[14] which sets safety standards for many industries.[15] May a state government go beyond standards set by OSHA and use the criminal law to punish dangerous conditions? In *People v. ONeill*,[16] the courts of Illinois answered that question with a potent "yes," permitting a *murder prosecution* against corporate executives. Notice that whereas Wisconsin prosecuted RKI *Corporation* for vehicular homicide, Illinois brought this case against the corporate executives themselves.

Film Recovery Systems was an Illinois corporation in business to extract silver from used X-ray film and then resell it. Steven O'Neill was president of Film Recovery, Charles Kirschbaum was its plant manager, and Daniel Rodriguez the foreman. To extract the silver, workers at Film Recovery soaked the X-ray film in large, open, bubbling vats that contained sodium cyanide.

A worker named Stefan Golab became faint. He left the production area and walked to the lunchroom, where workers found him trembling and foaming at the mouth. He lost consciousness. Paramedics were unable to revive him. They rushed him to a hospital, where he was pronounced dead on arrival. The Cook County medical examiner determined that Golab died from acute cyanide poisoning caused by inhalation of cyanide fumes in the plant.

Illinois indicted Film Recovery and several of its managers for murder. The indictment charged that O'Neill and Kirschbaum committed murder by failing to disclose to Golab that he was working with cyanide and other potentially lethal substances and by failing to provide him with appropriate and necessary safety equipment.

The case was tried to a judge without a jury. Workers testified that O'Neill, Kirschbaum, and other managers never told them they were using cyanide or that the fumes they inhaled could be harmful; that management made no effort to ventilate the factory; that Film Recovery gave the workers no goggles or protective clothing; that the chemicals they worked with burned their skin; that breathing was difficult in the plant because of strong, foul orders; and that workers suffered frequent dizziness, nausea, and vomiting.

The trial judge found O'Neill, Kirschbaum, and others guilty of murder. Illinois defines murder as performing an act that the defendant *knows will create a strong probability of death* in the victim, and the judge found they had done that. He found Film Recovery guilty of involuntary manslaughter. Involuntary manslaughter is *recklessly* performing an act that causes death. He sentenced O'Neill, Kirschbaum, and Rodriguez to 25 years in prison.

The defendants appealed, contending that the verdicts were inconsistent. They argued, and the Illinois Court of Appeals agreed, that the judge had made contradictory findings. Murder required the specific intent of *knowing there was a strong probability of death*, whereas the manslaughter conviction required *reckless* conduct. The appeals court reversed the convictions and remanded for a new trial.

Moments before the new trial was to start, O'Neill, Kirschbaum, and Rodriguez all pleaded guilty to involuntary manslaughter. They received sentences of three years, two years, and four months, respectively.

---

[14] 29 U.S.C. §§651 et seq. (1982).
[15] See Chapter 28, on employment law.
[16] 194 Ill.App.3d 79, 550 N.E.2d 1090, 1990 Ill.App. LEXIS 65 (Ill.App.Ct. 1990).

RICO

The **Racketeer Influenced and Corrupt Organizations Act (RICO)**[17] is one of the most powerful and controversial statutes ever written. Congress passed the law primarily to prevent gangsters from taking money they earned illegally and investing it in legitimate businesses. But RICO has expanded far beyond the original intentions of Congress and is now used more often against ordinary businesses than against organized criminals. Some regard this wide application as a tremendous advance in law enforcement, but others view it as an oppressive weapon used to club ethical companies into settlements they should never have to make.

RICO creates both criminal and civil law liabilities. The government may prosecute both individuals and organizations for violating RICO. For example, the government may prosecute a mobster, claiming that he has run a heroin ring for years. It may also prosecute an accounting firm, claiming that it lied about corporate assets in a stock sale to make the shares appear more valuable than they really were. If the government proves its case, the defendant can be hit with large fines and a prison sentence of up to 20 years. RICO also permits the government to seek forfeiture of the defendant's property. A court may order a convicted defendant to hand over any property or money used in the criminal acts or derived from them.

RICO creates civil liability as well. The government, organizations, and individuals all have the right to file civil lawsuits, seeking damages and, if necessary, injunctions. For example, shareholders claiming that they were harmed by the accounting firm's lies could sue the firm for money lost in buying and selling the stock. RICO is powerful (and for defendants, frightening) in part because a civil plaintiff can recover **treble damages**, that is, a judgment for three times the harm actually suffered, and can also recover attorney's fees.

What is a violation of this law? **RICO prohibits using two or more racketeering acts to accomplish any of these goals: (1) investing in or acquiring legitimate businesses with criminal money; (2) maintaining or acquiring businesses through criminal activity; or (3) operating businesses through criminal activity.**

What does that mean in English? It is a two-step process to prove that a person or an organization has violated RICO. We will assume that this is a criminal prosecution, though the steps are similar in a civil lawsuit.

- The prosecutor must show that the defendant committed two or more **racketeering acts**, which are any of a long list of specified crimes: embezzlement, arson, mail fraud, wire fraud, and so forth. Thus, if a gangster ordered a building torched in January and then burned a second building in October, that would be two racketeering acts. If a stockbroker told two customers that Bronx Gold Mines was a promising stock, when she knew that it was worthless, that would be two racketeering acts.

- The prosecutor must show that the defendant used these racketeering acts to accomplish one of the three *purposes* listed above. If the gangster committed two arsons and then used the insurance payments to buy a dry cleaning business, that would violate RICO. If the stockbroker gave fraudulent advice and used the commissions to buy advertising for her firm, that would violate RICO.

Money Laundering

Money laundering consists of taking the proceeds of certain criminal acts and either (1) using the money to promote crime, or (2) attempting to conceal the source of the money.[18]

Racketeer Influenced and Corrupt Organizations Act (RICO)
A powerful federal statute, originally aimed at organized crime, now used in many criminal prosecutions and civil lawsuits.

Racketeering acts
Any of a long list of specified crimes, such as embezzlement, arson, mail fraud, wire fraud, and so forth.

Money laundering
Using the proceeds of criminal acts either to promote crime or conceal the source of the money.

[17] 18 U.S.C. §§1961–1968.
[18] 18 U.S.C. §§1956 et seq.

Money laundering is an important part of major criminal enterprises. Successful criminals earn enormous sums, and they strive to filter their profits back into the flow of commerce so that their crimes go undetected. Laundering is an essential part of the corrosive traffic in drugs. Profits, all in cash, mount so swiftly that the most difficult step for a successful dealer can be to use the money without attracting the government's attention. However, as the following case illustrates, it is not only drug dealers who seek to launder their wrongfully obtained cash. But, really . . . a minister?

UNITED STATES v. KENNARD

472 F.3d 851
11TH CIRCUIT COURT OF APPEALS, 2006

CASE SUMMARY

Facts: The Reverend Abraham Kennard bilked hundreds of churches and other nonprofits out of millions of dollars. He set up the Network International Investment Corporation, and then approached churches and other nonprofit organizations that needed funds for capital improvements. Kennard made a simple offer: for every $3,000 in membership fees that an organization paid into the Network, they would receive $500,000 in grants. He told investors that the grants were possible because he had lined up famous investors who would provide tens of millions of dollars in financing. The Network would also be profiting from its own Christian resorts from around the country. Victims believed Kennard: More than 1,600 churches and other nonprofits around the nation paid in over $8.7 million.

Kennard deposited the money in an escrow account of his attorney, Scott Cunningham, and from there transferred the money to various locations, including the bank account of Promotional Time International, Inc., which was controlled by Abraham's brother, Laboyce Kennard.

Needless to say, the "investors" never received their money. Abraham was prosecuted and found guilty of various crimes. This case concerns Laboyce Kennard, who was convicted of money laundering. He appealed, arguing there was insufficient proof he knowingly laundered money.

Issue: *Was there sufficient evidence that Laboyce knowingly laundered money?*

Decision: Yes, there was sufficient evidence that Laboyce knowingly laundered money. Affirmed.

Reasoning: This case demonstrates two important truths: "The love of money is the root of all evil," and "There's a sucker born every minute."

To convict Laboyce on the money laundering conspiracy charge, the government had to prove that some agreement existed to launder the proceeds of Abraham's church fraud, and that Laboyce knowingly and voluntarily participated in that agreement. Conspiracy may be proven by circumstantial evidence.

Laboyce made most of the account withdrawals, generally in cash. He went with Abraham to a Network meeting in Charlotte, N.C., at which Abraham gave Network members fake, oversized disbursement checks instead of the grant money that they had been promised. Two months later, Laboyce videotaped Abraham conducting a sham groundbreaking ceremony for one of the Christian resorts that Abraham had promised Network would build, the plan being to show the video to members in an attempt to forestall their complaints. Laboyce later "worked security" for Abraham at a July Network meeting in Orlando, where those in attendance reacted angrily to Abraham's announcement that their grants would again be delayed. And in October, Laboyce attended a meeting at which Abraham informed him that an FBI investigation of Network had led to the seizure of Cunningham's escrow account. All of this evidence is enough for a jury to find beyond a reasonable doubt that Laboyce knowingly participated in the conspiracy to launder the proceeds of the fraud.

EXAM *Strategy*

Question: Explain the difference between embezzlement and money laundering. Give an example of each.

Strategy: Both crimes involve money illegally obtained, but they are very different. As to embezzlement, how did the criminal obtain the funds? In a laundering case, to what use is the criminal trying to put the cash?

Result: Embezzlement refers to fraudulently taking money that is already in the defendant's possession. For example, if a financial advisor, *lawfully entrusted* with his client's funds for investing, uses some of the cash to buy himself a luxurious yacht, he has embezzled the client's money. Money laundering consists of taking *illegally obtained* money and either using the funds to promote additional crimes or attempting to *conceal* the source of the cash. In the preceding case, the defendant laundered money when he took "investment" funds and transferred them, first to the lawyer's account, and then to various other banks, trying to disguise their origin.

Other Crimes

Additional crimes that affect business appear elsewhere in the text. An increasing number of federal and state statutes are designed to punish those who harm the environment. Antitrust violations, in which a corporation establishes a monopoly, can lead to criminal prosecutions. Finally, securities fraud is a crime and can lead to severe prison sentences. (See Chapter 31, on securities regulation.)

ECONOMICS AND THE LAW

Reputational Penalty. Businesses convicted of criminal conduct often pay more than just a fine. Many economists have concluded that companies suffer significant reputational penalties as well. Studies indicate that several negative consequences generally follow a criminal conviction.

First, stock prices fall significantly, reducing shareholder wealth. The angry shareholders may seek compensation from the executives who committed the crime. Second, executives are often forced out of the offending company.

Finally, business relationships often suffer, especially for crimes such as fraud or overcharging in a contract. Suppose that Integrity Motors promises to sell to PlaneMaker 1,000 aircraft engines that have been tested for quality control. When too many of the engines fail, the state government convicts Integrity of falsifying test results. PlaneMaker will never buy another engine from Integrity, and other aircraft manufacturers may also turn away from the convicted company. One study concluded that these reputational penalties are much more likely to occur when the crime is committed against customers, as in the fraud case, rather than against the general public, as in a case of environmental damage.[19] ◆

---

[19] Alexander, "On the Nature of the Reputational Penalty for Corporate Crime: Evidence," *Journal of Law and Economics*, 1999, vol. 42, p. 489.

CONSTITUTIONAL PROTECTIONS

The police arrest Jake and charge him with armed robbery and rape. They claim that he entered a convenience store, took all the money from the cash register, robbed the clerk of her wristwatch, and then raped her. Jake refuses to talk, but the police are absolutely certain he is guilty. The community is outraged and wants a conviction. Should the police be allowed to question Jake for hours without stopping? May they lock him in a walk-in freezer? Beat him? After 5 hours of interrogation, followed by 10 hours in a freezer and a severe beating, Jake confesses. He tells the police where to find the money and the clerk's watch. Does his guilt render the police conduct acceptable?

> Jake refuses to talk, but the police are absolutely certain he is guilty.

These are issues of **criminal procedure**. We are no longer looking at the elements of particular crimes, as we have thus far, but at the *process of investigating, interrogating, and trying* a criminal defendant. The first 10 amendments to the United States Constitution, known as the Bill of Rights, control the behavior of all law enforcement officers.[20] In this section, we look at some of the protections that these amendments offer.

Criminal procedure
The process of investigating, interrogating, and trying a criminal defendant.

THE CRIMINAL PROCESS

In order to understand constitutional safeguards, we need to know how the police do their work. The exact steps will vary from case to case, but the summary in Exhibit 7.1 highlights the important steps.

Informant

Yasmin is a secretary to Stacey, the Be Patient executive who opened this chapter. On her lunch break, Yasmin gets up the courage to telephone an FBI office and speaks to Moe, an agent. She reports that Stacey routinely charges the government for patients who do not exist. Moe arranges to interview Yasmin at her apartment that evening. He tape-records everything she says, including her own job history, her duties at Be Patient, and how she knows about the fraud. Yasmin has not only seen the false bills, she has entered some of them on computers. The next day, Moe prepares an **affidavit** for Yasmin to sign, detailing everything she told him. An affidavit is simply a written statement signed under oath.

Affidavit
A written statement signed under oath.

Warrant

Moe takes Yasmin's affidavit to a United States magistrate, an employee of the federal courts who is similar to a judge. Moe asks the magistrate to issue search warrants for Be Patient's patient records. A search warrant is written permission from a neutral official, such as the magistrate, to conduct a search. **A warrant must specify with reasonable certainty the place to be searched and the items to be seized.** This warrant application names all five of Be Patient's hospitals and asks to look through their admission notes, surgery and doctor reports, and discharge data. It states that the records will be copied so that they can be compared with the bills the government has received.

---

[20] As discussed in Chapter 5, on constitutional law, most of the protections as written apply only to state government or the federal government. But through the process of incorporation, almost all important criminal procedure rights have been expanded to apply to federal, state, and local governments.

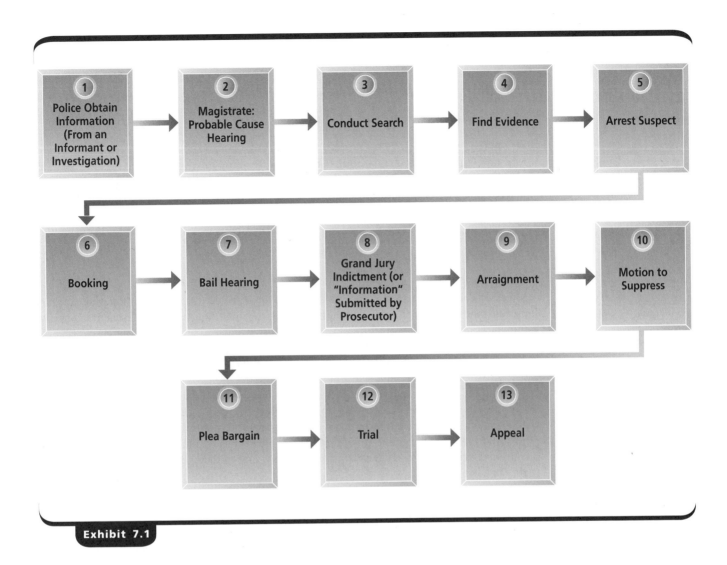

Exhibit 7.1

Probable Cause

The magistrate will issue a warrant only if there is probable cause. **Probable cause** means that based on all of the information presented, it is likely that evidence of crime will be found in the place to be searched. The magistrate will look at Yasmin's affidavit to determine (1) whether the informant (Yasmin) is reliable and (2) whether she has a sound basis for the information. If Yasmin is a five-time drug offender whose information has proven wrong in the past, the warrant should not issue. Here, Yasmin's career record is good, she has no apparent motive to lie, and she is in an excellent position to know what she is talking about. The magistrate issues the warrant, specifying exactly what records may be examined.

Probable cause

Means it is likely that evidence of crime will be found in the place to be searched.

Search and Seizure

Armed with the warrants, Moe and other agents arrive at the various hospitals, show the warrants, and take away the appropriate records. The **search** may not exceed what is described in the warrant. Even if Moe suspects that Dr. Narkem is illegally drugging certain patients, he may not seize test tube samples from the lab. He may take only the records described in the warrant.

The agents cart the records back to headquarters and enter the data on a computer. The computer compares the records of actual patients with the bills submitted to the government and indicates that 10% of all bills are for fictional patients. Moe summarizes the new data on additional affidavits and presents the affidavits to the magistrate, who issues **arrest warrants**, authorizing the FBI to arrest Stacey and others involved in the overbilling.

Arrest

Moe arrives at Be Patient and informs Stacey that she is under arrest. He reads her the *Miranda* warnings, discussed later in this chapter. He drives Stacey to FBI headquarters where she is **booked**; that is, her name, photograph, and fingerprints are entered in a log, along with the charges. She is entitled to a prompt **bail hearing**. A judge or magistrate will set an amount of bail that she must pay in order to go free pending the trial. The purpose of bail is to ensure that Stacey will appear for all future court hearings.

Indictment

Grand jury

A group of ordinary citizens that decides whether there is probable cause the defendant committed the crime and should be tried.

Indictment

The government's formal charge that the defendant has committed a crime and must stand trial.

Moe turns all of his evidence over to Larry, the local prosecutor for the United States. Larry presents the evidence to a **grand jury**, which is a group of ordinary citizens, like a trial jury. But the grand jury holds hearings for several weeks at a time, on many different cases. It is the grand jury's job to determine whether there is probable cause that this defendant committed the crime with which she is charged. Larry shows the computer comparison of the bills with the actual patient lists, and the grand jury votes to indict Stacey. An **indictment** is the government's formal charge that the defendant has committed a crime and must stand trial. The grand jury is persuaded that there is probable cause that Stacey billed for 1,550 nonexistent patients, charging the government for $290 million worth of services that were never performed. The grand jury indicts her for (1) Medicare fraud, (2) mail fraud, (3) several computer crimes, and (4) RICO violations.[21] It also indicts Be Patient, Inc., and other employees.

Arraignment

Stacey is ordered back to court. A clerk reads her the formal charges of the indictment. The judge asks whether Stacey has a lawyer, and of course she does. If she did not, the judge would urge her to get one quickly. If a defendant cannot afford a lawyer, the court will appoint one to represent her free of charge. The judge now asks the lawyer how Stacey pleads to the charges. Her lawyer answers that she pleads not guilty to all charges.

Discovery

During the months before trial, both prosecution and defense will prepare the most effective case possible. There is less formal discovery than in civil trials. The prosecution is obligated to hand over any evidence favorable to the defense that the defense attorney requests. The defense has a more limited obligation to inform the prosecution. In most states, for example, if the defense will be based on an alibi, counsel must explain the alibi to the government before trial. In Stacey's case, most of the evidence is data that both sides already possess.

---

[21] In federal court, when the defendant is charged with a felony, formal charges may be made only by indictment. In many state court cases, the prosecutor is not required to seek an indictment. Instead, she may file an **information**, which is simply a formal written accusation. In state courts, most cases now begin by information.

Motion to Suppress

If the defense claims that the prosecution obtained evidence illegally, it will move to suppress it. A **motion to suppress** is a request that the court exclude certain evidence because it was obtained in violation of the Constitution. We look at those violations later.

Plea Bargaining

Sometime before trial the two attorneys will meet to consider a plea bargain. A **plea bargain** is an agreement between prosecution and defense that the defendant will plead guilty to a reduced charge, and the prosecution will recommend to the judge a relatively lenient sentence. Based on the RICO violations alone, Stacey faces a possible 20-year prison sentence, along with a large fine and a devastating forfeiture order. The government makes this offer: Stacey will plead guilty to 100 counts of mail fraud; Be Patient will repay all $290 million and an additional $150 million in fines; the government will drop the RICO and computer crime charges and recommend to the judge that Stacey be fined only $1 million and sentenced to three years in prison. In the federal court system, about 75% of all prosecutions end in a plea bargain. In state court systems the number is often higher.

Stacey agrees to the government's offer. The judge accepts the plea, and Stacey is fined and sentenced accordingly. A judge need not accept the bargain, but usually does.

Trial and Appeal

When there is no plea bargain, the case must go to trial. The mechanics of a criminal trial are similar to those for a civil trial, described in Chapter 3, on dispute resolution. It is the prosecution's job to convince the jury beyond a reasonable doubt that the defendant committed every element of the crime charged. The defense counsel will do everything possible to win an acquittal. In federal courts, prosecutors obtain a conviction in about 80% of cases; in state courts, the percentage is slightly lower. Convicted defendants have a right to appeal, and again, the appellate process is similar to that described in Chapter 3.

THE FOURTH AMENDMENT

The Fourth Amendment prohibits the government from making illegal searches and seizures. This amendment protects individuals, corporations, partnerships, and other organizations.

In general, the police must obtain a warrant before conducting a search. There are six exceptions to this rule, in which the police may **search without a warrant**:

- *Plain View.* Police may search if they see a machine gun, for example, sticking out from under the front seat of a parked car.

- *Stop and Frisk.* If police have an articulable reason for suspecting that someone may be armed and dangerous, they may pat him down.

- *Emergencies.* If police pursue a store robber and catch him, they may search him.

- *Automobiles.* If police have lawfully stopped a car and observe evidence of other crimes in the car, such as burglary tools, they may search.

- *Lawful Arrest.* Police may always search a suspect they have arrested.

- *Consent.* If someone in lawful occupancy of a home gives consent to a search, the police may do so.

Motion to suppress
A request that the court exclude certain evidence because it was obtained in violation of the Constitution.

Plea bargain
An agreement in which the defendant pleads guilty to a reduced charge, and the prosecution recommends to the judge a relatively lenient sentence.

Apart from those six cases, a warrant is required. If the police search without one, they have violated the Fourth Amendment. Even a search conducted with a warrant can violate the amendment. **A search with a warrant violates the Fourth Amendment if:**

- There was no probable cause to issue the warrant;

- The warrant does not specify the place to be searched and the things sought; or

- The search extends beyond what is specified in the warrant.

Exclusionary Rule

Under the exclusionary rule, evidence obtained illegally may not be used at trial against the victim of the search. If the police conduct a warrantless search that is not one of the six exceptions, any evidence they find will be excluded from the trial.

Suppose when Yasmin called the FBI, Moe simply drove straight to one of Be Patient's hospitals and grabbed patient records. Moe lacked a warrant, and his search would be illegal. Stacey's lawyer would file a **motion to suppress** the evidence. Before the trial starts, the judge would hold a hearing. If he agreed that the search was illegal, he would **exclude** the evidence, that is, refuse to allow it in trial. The government could go forward with the prosecution only if it had other evidence.[22]

Is the exclusionary rule a good idea? The Supreme Court created the exclusionary rule to ensure that police conduct legal searches. The theory is simple: if police know in advance that illegally obtained evidence cannot be used in court, they will not be tempted to make improper searches.

Opponents of the rule argue that a guilty person may go free because one police officer bungled. They are outraged by cases like *Coolidge v. New Hampshire*.[23] Pamela Mason, a 14-year-old babysitter, was brutally murdered. Citizens of New Hampshire were furious, and the state's attorney general personally led the investigation. Police found strong evidence that Edward Coolidge had done it. They took the evidence to the attorney general, who personally issued a search warrant. The search of Coolidge's car uncovered incriminating evidence, and he was found guilty of murder and sentenced to life in prison. But the United States Supreme Court reversed the conviction. The warrant had not been issued by a neutral magistrate. A law officer may not lead an investigation and simultaneously decide what searches are permissible.

After the Supreme Court reversed Coolidge's conviction, New Hampshire scheduled a new trial, attempting to convict him with evidence lawfully obtained. Before the trial began,

---

[22] There are two important exceptions to the exclusionary rule:

Inevitable Discovery Exception. Suppose that Moe's search of Be Patient is declared illegal. But then officials in the Medicare office testify that they were already aware of Be Patient's fraud, had already obtained some proof, and were about to seek a search warrant for the same records that Moe took. If the court believes the testimony, it will allow the evidence to be used. The inevitable discovery exception permits the use of evidence that would inevitably have been discovered even without the illegal search.

Good Faith Exception. Suppose the police use a search warrant believing it to be proper, but it later proves to have been defective. Is the search therefore illegal? No, said the Supreme Court in *United States v. Leon*, 468 U.S. 897, 104 S. Ct. 3405, 1984 U.S. LEXIS 153 (1984). As long as the police reasonably believed the warrant was valid, the search is legal. It would violate the Fourth Amendment if, for example, it was later shown that the police knew the affidavit used to obtain the warrant was filled with lies. In such a case, the search would be illegal and the evidence obtained would be excluded.

[23] 403 U.S. 443, 91 S.Ct. 2022, 1971 U.S. LEXIS 25 (1971).

Coolidge pleaded guilty to second degree murder. He was sentenced and remained in prison until his release 27 years later.

In fact, very few people do go free because of the exclusionary rule. For example, a study by the General Accounting Office showed that suppression motions were filed in 10.5% of all federal prosecutions. But in 80 to 90% of those motions, the judge declared that the search was legal. Evidence was actually excluded in only 1.3% of all prosecutions. And in about one-half of *those* cases, the court convicted the defendant on other evidence. Only in 0.7% of all prosecutions did the defendant go free after the evidence was suppressed. Other studies reveal similar results.[24]

The Revised Patriot Act

In response to the devastating attacks of September 11, 2001, Congress passed a sweeping antiterrorist law known as the Patriot Act. The statute was designed to give law enforcement officials greater power to investigate and prevent potential terrorist assaults. The bill raced through Congress nearly unopposed. Proponents hailed it as a vital weapon for use against continuing lethal threats. Opponents argued that the hastily passed law would not provide serious benefits but did threaten the liberties of the very people it purported to shield. Supporters responded that its most controversial sections would expire unless reenacted by Congress.

In an early legal test, a federal judge permitted the government to use secret evidence in its effort to freeze the assets of Global Relief Foundation, a religious organization suspected of terrorist activity. The group, which claimed to be purely humanitarian, asserted that it could hardly defend itself against unseen evidence. Finding "acute national security concerns," the judge allowed the government to introduce the evidence in private, without the foundation ever seeing it.

In a particularly controversial section, the law permitted the FBI to issue a **national security letter** (NSL) to communications firms such as Internet service providers and telephone companies. An NSL typically demanded that the recipient furnish to the government its customer records, and that the recipient never divulge to anyone what it has done. NSLs could be used to obtain access to subscriber billing records, phone, financial, credit and other information—even records of books taken from libraries. A federal court declared this provision an unconstitutional violation of rights under the Fourth Amendment (illegal searches) and the First Amendment (free speech).

In response, Congress revised and reauthorized the Patriot Act, but a year later, the same court found the revised NSL provisions unconstitutional. The court was deeply concerned with the government's power to invade the privacy of innocent Americans. Evidence indicated that between 2003 and 2005, the FBI had issued over 143,000 NSLs. The trial judge declared:

> Through the use of NSLs, the government can unmask the identity of internet users engaged in anonymous speech in online discussions. It can obtain an itemized list of all of the emails sent and received by the target of the NSL, and it can then seek information on individuals communicating with that person. It may even be able to discover the websites an individual has visited and queries submitted to search engines. In light of the seriousness of the potential intrusion into the individual's personal affairs and the significant possibility of a chilling effect on speech and association—particularly of expression that is critical of the government or its policies—a compelling need exists to ensure that the use of NSLs is subject to the safeguards of public accountability, checks and balances, and separation of powers that our Constitution prescribes.

[24] See the discussion in *United States v. Leon* (Justice Brennan, dissenting), cited at footnote 22.

In addition, the court worried that allowing NSLs without adequate judicial review created a dangerous precedent for removing judicial oversight from vital issues of liberty.

> The Constitution was designed so that the dangers of any given moment would never suffice as justification for discarding fundamental individual liberties or circumscribing the judiciary's unique role under our governmental system in protecting those liberties and upholding the rule of law. It is the judiciary's independent function to uphold the Constitution even if to do so may mean curtailing Congress's efforts to confer greater freedom on the executive to investigate national security threats.[25]

EXAM *Strategy*

Question: Police bang down the door of Mary Beth's apartment, enter without her permission and search the apartment. They had no warrant. The officers discover a machine used to manufacture fake driver's licenses, and over 75 freshly minted licenses, all with Mary Beth's picture but each with a different name and identification number. She is arrested and prosecuted. (1) What crime will the government charge Mary Beth with? (2) What motion will the defense lawyer make before trial? (3) Please rule on the defendant's motion.

Strategy: What crime focuses on identification documents? The defendant's motion is based on the police conduct. What was wrong with that conduct, and what are the consequences?

Result: Mary Beth is engaging in identity theft. The machine and licenses have no lawful purpose. The police violated the Fourth Amendment, because they lacked a warrant for the search. The defendant is moving to suppress the machine and the licenses. Under the exclusionary rule, a court should suppress that evidence.

THE FIFTH AMENDMENT

The Fifth Amendment includes three important protections for criminal defendants: due process, double jeopardy, and self-incrimination.

Due Process

Due process requires fundamental fairness at all stages of the case. The basic elements of due process are discussed in Chapter 5, on constitutional law. In the context of criminal law, due process sets additional limits. The requirement that the prosecution disclose evidence favorable to the defendant is a due process rule. Similarly, if a witness says that a tall white male robbed the liquor store, it would violate due process for the police to place the male suspect in a lineup with four short women and two rabbits.

Due process
Requires fundamental fairness at all stages of the case.

Double Jeopardy

The prohibition against **double jeopardy** means that a criminal defendant may be prosecuted only once for a particular criminal offense. The purpose is to guarantee that the government may not destroy the lives of innocent citizens with repetitive prosecutions. Assume that

Double jeopardy
A criminal defendant may be prosecuted only once for a particular criminal offense.

---

[25] *Doe v. Gonzalez*, 500 Fed.Supp.2d 379 (SDNY, 2007).

Roger, the video thief, goes to trial. But the police officer cannot remember what the suspect looked like, and the jury acquits. Later, the prosecutor learns that a second witness actually *videotaped* Roger hauling VCRs from the store. Too late. The Double Jeopardy Clause prohibits the state from retrying Roger for the same offense.

Self-Incrimination

The Fifth Amendment bars the government from forcing any person to testify against himself. In other words, the police may not use mental or physical coercion to force a confession out of someone. (This clause applies only to people; corporations and other organizations are not protected.) Society does not want a government that engages in torture. Such abuse might occasionally catch a criminal, but it would grievously injure innocent people and make all citizens fearful of the government that is supposed to represent them. Also, confessions that are forced out of someone are inherently unreliable. The defendant may confess simply to end the torture. So Jake, the rape-robbery suspect who confessed at the beginning of this section, will never hear his confession used against him in court. Unless the police have other evidence, he will walk free.

When the FBI arrests Stacey for Medicare fraud, she may refuse to answer any questions. The privilege against self-incrimination covers any statement that might help to prosecute her. So, if the FBI agent asks Stacey, "Did you commit Medicare fraud?" she will refuse to answer. If the agent asks, "What are your duties here?" she will also remain silent.

Miranda

In *Miranda v. Arizona*,[26] the Supreme Court ruled that a confession obtained from a custodial interrogation may not be used against a defendant unless he was first warned of his Fifth Amendment rights. A "custodial interrogation" means that the police have prevented the defendant from leaving (usually by arresting him) and are asking him questions. If they do that, and obtain a confession from the defendant, they may use that confession in court only if they first warned him of his Fifth Amendment rights. He must be told that:

- He has the right to remain silent;

- Anything he says can be used against him at trial;

- He has the right to a lawyer; and

- If he cannot afford a lawyer, the court will appoint one for him.

Exclusionary Rule (Again).   If the police fail to give these warnings before interrogating a defendant, the exclusionary rule prohibits the prosecution from using any confession. The rationale is the same as for Fourth Amendment searches: suppressing the evidence means that the police will not attempt to get it illegally. But remember that the confession is void only if it results from custodial questioning. Suppose a policeman, investigating a bank robbery, asks a pedestrian if he noticed anything peculiar. The pedestrian says, "You mean after I robbed the bank?" Result? No custodial questioning, and the confession *may* be used against him.

---

[26] 384 U.S. 436, 86 S.Ct. 1602, 1966 U.S. LEXIS 2817 (1966).

THE SIXTH AMENDMENT

The Sixth Amendment guarantees the **right to a lawyer** at all important stages of the criminal process. Stacey, the hospital administrator, is entitled to have her lawyer present during custodial questioning and all court hearings. Because of this right, the government must **appoint a lawyer** to represent, free of charge, any defendant who cannot afford one.

THE EIGHTH AMENDMENT

The Eighth Amendment prohibits cruel and unusual punishment. The most dramatic issue litigated under this clause is the death penalty. The Supreme Court has ruled that capital punishment is not inherently unconstitutional. Most state statutes bifurcate a capital case, so that the jury first considers only guilt or innocence, and then, if the defendant is found guilty, deliberates on the death penalty. As part of that final decision, the jury must consider aggravating and mitigating circumstances that may make the ultimate penalty more or less appropriate.[27] However, other "cruel and unusual" issues are now coming to the forefront.

EWING V. CALIFORNIA

538 U.S. 11, 123 S.CT. 1179, 155 L.Ed.2d 108
UNITED STATES SUPREME COURT, 2003

CASE SUMMARY

Facts: California passed a "three strikes" law, dramatically increasing sentences for repeat offenders. A defendant with two or more serious convictions, who was convicted of a third felony, had to receive an indeterminate sentence of life imprisonment. Such a sentence required the defendant to actually serve a minimum of 25 years, and in some cases much more.

Gary Ewing, on parole from a nine-year prison term, stole three golf clubs worth $399 each, and was prosecuted. Because he had prior convictions, the crime, normally a misdemeanor, was treated as a felony. Ewing was convicted and sentenced to 25 years to life. He appealed, claiming that the sentence violated the Eighth Amendment.

Issue: *Did Ewing's sentence violate the Eighth Amendment?*

Decision: No, the sentence did not violate the Eighth Amendment. Affirmed.

Reasoning: States have a valid interest in deterring and jailing habitual criminals. Nothing in the Eighth Amendment prohibits the California legislature from choosing this method of protecting the public. Recidivism is a serious public safety concern nationwide. According to a recent report, 67 percent of former inmates released from state prison were charged with a serious new crime within three years. Property offenders like Ewing were even likelier to commit a new crime than those who served time for violent crimes.

Ewing had already been convicted of numerous misdemeanors and felonies, and he had served nine terms of incarceration. He committed most of his crimes while on parole or probation. His previous convictions included serious crimes, such as robbery and residential burglary. By imposing a three strikes sentence, the State is not merely punishing the

[27] *Gregg v. Georgia*, 428 U.S. 153, 96 S.Ct. 2909, 1976 U.S. LEXIS 82 (1976).

"triggering" offense. The State is also deciding to treat more harshly someone whose repeated criminal acts demonstrate that he is incapable of conforming to the norms of society.

Unquestionably the sentence is a long one, and the three strikes law has generated controversy. But criticism of the statute should be directed to the State legislature. Federal courts do not sit as a "super-legislature," second-guessing policy choices made by elected officials. The three strikes law represents a rational legislative judgment, entitled to judicial deference, that repeat offenders who have committed serious crimes must be incapacitated.

Ewing's sentence of 25 years to life is not grossly disproportionate and therefore does not violate the Eighth Amendment.

DEVIL'S ADVOCATE Are we really going to send Ewing to prison for a minimum of 25 years—for *shoplifting?* It is true that Ewing is a recidivist, and undoubtedly a state is entitled to punish chronic troublemakers more harshly than first-time offenders. However, this still seems excessive. In California, a first-time offense of "arson causing *great bodily injury*" incurs a maximum nine-year sentence. A first-time offender convicted of voluntary manslaughter receives a sentence of no more than 11 years. Only a first-time murderer receives a penalty equal to Ewing's—25 years to life. It is unfair to Ewing to equate his property crimes with a homicide, and foolish for society to spend this much money locking him up. ◆

The Eighth Amendment also outlaws excessive fines. Forfeiture is the most controversial topic under this clause. **Forfeiture** is a *civil* law proceeding that is permitted by many different *criminal* statutes. Once a court has convicted a defendant under certain criminal statutes—such as RICO or a controlled substance law—the government may seek forfeiture of property associated with the criminal act. *How much* property can the government take? To determine if forfeiture was fair, courts generally look at three factors: whether the property was used in committing the crime, whether it was purchased with proceeds from illegal acts, and whether the punishment is disproportionate to the defendant's wrongdoing. Neal Brunk pleaded guilty to selling 2.5 ounces of marijuana, and the government promptly sought forfeiture of his house on 90 acres, worth about $99,000. The court found forfeiture was legitimate, because Brunk had used drug money to buy the land, and then sold narcotics from the property.[28] By contrast, Hosep Bajakajian attempted to leave the United States without reporting $375,000 cash to customs officials as the law requires. The government demanded forfeiture of the full sum, but the Supreme Court ruled that seizure of the entire amount would be grossly disproportionate to the minor crime of failing to report cash movement.[29]

CHAPTER CONCLUSION

Business crime appears in unexpected places, with surprising suspects. A corporate executive aware of its protean nature is in the best position to prevent it. Classic fraud and embezzlement schemes are often foiled with commonsense preventive measures. Federal Sentencing Guidelines make it eminently worthwhile for corporations to establish aggressive compliance programs. Sophisticated computer and money laundering crimes can be thwarted only with determination and the cooperation of citizens and police agencies. We can defeat business crime if we have the knowledge and the will.

---

[28] *U.S. v. Brunk*, 2001 U.S. App. LEXIS 7566 (4th Cir. 2001).
[29] *U.S. v. Bajakajian*, 524 U.S. 321, 118 S.Ct. 2028, 1998 U.S. LEXIS 4172 (1998).

EXAM REVIEW

1. **PUNISHMENT RATIONALE** The rationales for punishment include restraint, deterrence, retribution, and rehabilitation. (p. 162)

2. **GOVERNMENT'S BURDEN** In all prosecutions, the government must establish that the defendant's conduct was outlawed, that the defendant committed the *actus reus*, and that he had the necessary *mens rea*. The government must prove its case beyond a reasonable doubt. (p. 164)

EXAM Strategy

Question: Arnie owns a two-family house in a poor section of the city. A fire breaks out, destroying the building and causing $150,000 damage to an adjacent store. The state charges Arnie with arson. Simultaneously, Vickie, the store owner, sues Arnie for the damage to her property. Both cases are tried to juries, and the two juries hear identical evidence of Arnie's actions. But the criminal jury acquits Arnie, while the civil jury awards Vickie $150,000. How did that happen?

Strategy: The opposite outcomes are probably due to the different burdens of proof in a civil and criminal case. Make sure you know that distinction. (See the "Result" at the end of this section.)

3. **DEFENSES** In addition to factual defenses, such as mistaken identity or alibi, a defendant may offer various legal defenses, including insanity, entrapment, and duress. (p. 165)

4. **LARCENY** Larceny is the trespassory taking of personal property with the intent to steal. (p. 167)

5. **FRAUD** Fraud refers to a variety of crimes, all of which involve the deception of another person for the purpose of obtaining money or property. (p. 168)

EXAM Strategy

Question: National Medical Enterprises (NME) is a large for-profit hospital and health corporation. One of its hospitals, Los Altos Hospital, in Long Beach, California, paid one doctor $219,275, allegedly for consulting work. In fact, the government alleged, the payment was in exchange for the doctor's referring to the hospital a large number of Medicare patients. Other NME hospitals engaged in similar practices, said the government. *Specifically* what crime is the government accusing NME of committing?

Strategy: This case involves making money by deceit—your signal that it is a case of fraud. Check to find out exactly what type of fraud it is. (See the "Result" at the end of this section.)

6. **ARSON** Arson is the malicious use of fire or explosives to damage or destroy real estate or personal property. (p. 169)

7. **EMBEZZLEMENT** Embezzlement is the fraudulent conversion of property already in the defendant's possession. (p. 169)

8. **COMPUTER CRIME** Computer crime statutes prohibit computer trespass and fraud; wrongful use of cards, codes, and identification; and most intercepting or taping of conversations. (p. 170)

9. **CORPORATE LIABILITY** If a company's agent commits a criminal act within the scope of her employment and with the intent to benefit the corporation, the company is liable. (p. 172)

10. **RICO** RICO prohibits using two or more racketeering acts to invest in legitimate business or carry on certain other criminal acts. RICO permits civil lawsuits as well as criminal prosecutions. (p. 175)

EXAM Strategy

Question: Cheryl is a bank teller. She figures out a way to steal $99.99 per day in cash without getting caught. She takes the money daily for eight months and invests it in a catering business she is starting with Floyd, another teller. When Floyd learns what she is doing, he tries it, but he is caught in his first attempt. He and Cheryl are both prosecuted.

(a) Both are guilty only of larceny.

(b) Both are guilty of larceny and violating RICO.

(c) Both are guilty of embezzlement; Cheryl is also guilty of violating RICO.

(d) Both are guilty of embezzlement and violating RICO.

(e) Both are guilty of larceny and violating RICO.

Strategy: You need to know the difference between larceny and embezzlement. What is it? Once you have that figured out, focus on RICO. The government must prove two things: First, that the defendant committed crimes more than once—how many times? Second, that the defendant used the criminal proceeds for a specific purpose—what? (See the "Result" at the end of this section.)

11. **MONEY LAUNDERING** Money laundering consists of taking profits from a criminal act and either using them to promote crime or attempting to conceal their source. (p. 175)

12. **FOURTH AMENDMENT** The Fourth Amendment prohibits the government from making illegal searches and seizures. (p. 181)

13. **FIFTH AMENDMENT** The Fifth Amendment requires due process in all criminal procedures and prohibits double jeopardy and self-incrimination. (p. 184)

14. **SIXTH AMENDMENT** The Sixth Amendment guarantees criminal defendants the right to a lawyer. (p. 186)

15. **EXCLUSIONARY RULE** Information obtained in violation of the Fourth, Fifth, or Sixth Amendment is generally excluded from trial. (p. 182)

16. **EIGHTH AMENDMENT** The Eighth Amendment prohibits excessive fines and cruel and unusual punishments. (p. 186)

2. Result: The plaintiff offered enough proof to convince a jury *by a preponderance of the evidence* that Arnie had damaged her store. However that same evidence, offered in a criminal prosecution, was not enough to persuade the jury *beyond a reasonable doubt* that Arnie had lit the fire.

5. Result: This is Medicare fraud. When Congress creates a specific offense (Medicare fraud) within an existing criminal area (fraud), we know that the particular crime is widespread.

10. Result: Cheryl and Floyd both committed embezzlement, which refers to fraudulently taking money that was properly in their possession. Floyd did it once, but a RICO conviction requires two or more racketeering acts—Floyd has not violated RICO. Cheryl embezzled dozens of times, and invested the money in a legitimate business. She is guilty of embezzlement and RICO; the correct answer is (c).

ADDITIONAL QUESTIONS

1. *YOU BE THE JUDGE* WRITING PROBLEM An undercover drug informant learned from a mutual friend that Philip Friedman "knew where to get marijuana." The informant asked Friedman three times to get him some marijuana, and Friedman agreed after the third request. Shortly thereafter, Friedman sold the informant a small amount of the drug. The informant later offered to sell Friedman three pounds of marijuana. They negotiated the price and then made the sale. Friedman was tried for trafficking in drugs. He argued entrapment. Was Friedman entrapped? **Argument for Friedman**: The undercover agent had to ask three times before Friedman sold him a small amount of drugs. A real drug dealer, predisposed to commit the crime, leaps at an opportunity to sell. If the government spends time and money luring innocent people into the commission of crimes, all of us are the losers. **Argument for the Government**: Government officials suspected Friedman of being a sophisticated drug dealer, and they were right. When he had a chance to buy three pounds, a quantity only a dealer would purchase, he not only did so, but bargained with skill, showing a working knowledge of the business. Friedman was not entrapped—he was caught.

2. ***ETHICS*** Nineteen-year-old David Lee Nagel viciously murdered his grandparents, stabbing them repeatedly and slitting their throats, all because they denied him use of the family car. He was tried for murder and found not guilty by reason of insanity. He has lived ever since in mental hospitals. In 1994 he applied for release. The two psychiatrists who examined him stated that he was no longer mentally ill and was a danger neither to society nor to himself. Yet the Georgia Supreme Court refused to release him, seemingly because of the brutality of the killings. Comment on the court's ruling. What is the rationale for treating an insane defendant differently from others? Do you find the theory persuasive? If you do, what result must logically follow when psychiatrists testify that the defendant is no longer a danger? Should the brutality of the crime be a factor in deciding whether to prolong the detention? If you do not accept the rationale for treating such defendants differently, explain why not.

3. Federal law requires that all banks file reports with the IRS any time a customer engages in a cash transaction in an amount over $10,000. It is a crime for a bank to "structure" a cash transaction, that is, to break up a single transaction of more than $10,000 into two or more smaller transactions (and thus avoid the filing requirement). In *Ratzlaf v. United States*, 510 U.S. 135, 114 S.Ct. 655, 1994 U.S. LEXIS 936 (1994), the Supreme Court held that in order to find a defendant guilty of structuring, the government must prove that he specifically intended to break the law, that is, that he knew what he was doing was a crime and meant to commit it. Congress promptly passed a law "undoing" Ratzlaf. A bank official can now be convicted on evidence that he structured a payment, even with no evidence that he knew it was a crime. The penalties are harsh. (1) Why is structuring so serious? (2) Why did Congress change the law about the defendant's intent?

4. Conley owned video poker machines. They are outlawed in Pennsylvania, but he placed them in bars and clubs. He used profits from the machines to buy more machines. Is he guilty of money laundering?

5. Northwest Telco Corp. (Telco) provides long-distance telephone service. Customers dial a general access number, then enter a six-digit access code and then the phone number they want to call. A computer places the call and charges the account. On January 10, 1990, Cal Edwards, a Telco engineer, noticed that Telco's general access number was being dialed exactly every 40 seconds. After each dialing, a different six-digit number was entered, followed by a particular long-distance number. This continued from 10 P.M. to 6 A.M. Why was Edwards concerned?

6. Under a new British law, a police officer must now say the following to a suspect placed under arrest: "You do not have to say anything. But if you do not mention now something which you later use in your defense, the court may decide that your failure to mention it now strengthens the case against you. A record will be made of anything you say and it may be given in evidence if you are brought to trial." What does a police officer in the United States have to say, and what difference does it make at the time of an arrest?

7. After graduating from college, you work hard for 15 years, saving money to buy your dream property. Finally, you spend all your savings to buy a 300-acre farm with a splendid house and pool. Happy, an old college friend, stops by. She is saving her money to make a down payment on a coffee shop in town. You let her have a nice room in your big house for a few months, until she has the funds to make her down payment. But odd acquaintances stop by almost daily for short visits, and you realize

that Happy is saving money from marijuana sales. You are unhappy with this, but out of loyalty you permit it to go on for a month. Why is that a big mistake?

8. **ROLE REVERSAL** Write a short-answer question that focuses on the elements of a RICO violation.

INTERNET RESEARCH PROBLEM

On the Internet, find a current crime that might victimize you. What steps should you take to avoid harm?

You can find further practice problems at www.cengagebrain.com. See the preface of this book for website access details.

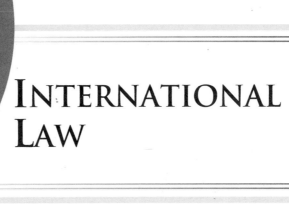

INTERNATIONAL LAW

The day after Anfernee graduates from business school, he opens a shop specializing in sports caps and funky hats. Sales are brisk, but Anfernee is making little profit because his American-made caps are expensive. Then an Asian company offers to sell him identical merchandise for 45% less than the American suppliers charge. Anfernee is elated, but quickly begins to wonder. Why is the new price so low? Are the foreign workers paid a living wage? Could the Asian company be using child labor? The sales representative expects Anfernee to sell no caps except his. Is that legal? He also requests a $50,000 cash "commission" to smooth the export process in his country. That sounds suspicious. The questions multiply without end. Will the contract be written in English or a foreign language? Must Anfernee pay in dollars or some other currency? The foreign company wants a letter of credit. What does that mean? What law will govern the agreement? If the caps are defective, how will disputes be resolved—and where?

> **A dozen developing countries with a total population 10 times that of the U.S. account for 40% of all export opportunities.**

Anfernee should put this lesson under his cap: the world is now one vast economy, and negotiations quickly cross borders. Transnational business grows with breathtaking speed. The United States now exports more than $800 billion worth of goods each year, and an additional $330 billion worth of services. Leading exports include industrial machinery, computers, aircraft and other transportation equipment, electronic equipment, and chemicals.

Here are the nations that trade the most goods with the United States, as of 2007:[1]

Rank	Country	Exports (in billions of U.S. dollars)	Imports (in billions of U.S. dollars)	Total, All Trade (in billions of U.S. dollars)	Percent of Total Trade
	Total, All Countries	1,061.4	1,791.8	2,853.3	100.0%
	Total, Top 15 Countries	750.4	1,325.2	2,075.6	72.7%
1	Canada	229.1	288.7	517.8	18.1
2	China	58.3	295.8	354.2	12.4
3	Mexico	126.3	194.1	320.4	11.2
4	Japan	57.4	133.6	191.0	6.7
5	Germany	45.5	86.3	131.8	4.6
6	United Kingdom	46.4	52.5	98.9	3.5
7	South Korea	31.6	44.1	75.7	2.7
8	France	25.2	38.5	63.7	2.2
9	Taiwan	23.6	35.2	58.7	2.1
10	Netherlands	29.8	16.8	46.6	1.6
11	Brazil	22.0	23.6	45.6	1.6
12	Venezuela	9.5	35.5	45.0	1.6
13	Italy	12.9	32.1	44.9	1.6
14	Singapore	23.9	17.0	40.9	1.4
15	Saudi Arabia	9.0	31.5	40.5	1.4

The end is nowhere in sight. A dozen developing countries with a total population 10 times that of the United States account for 40% of all export opportunities. In China alone roughly 300 million people have entered the economic middle class—and the rank of potential consumers.

Who are the people who do all of this trading? Anfernee's modest sports cap concern is at one end of the spectrum. At the other are multinational enterprises (MNEs), that is, companies doing business in several countries simultaneously.

---

[1] United States Census Bureau. Data is year-to-date through November, 2007.

MNEs and Power

An MNE can take various forms. It may be an Italian corporation with a wholly owned American subsidiary that manufactures electrical components in Alabama and sells them in Brazil. Or it could be a Japanese company that licenses a software company in India to manufacture computer programs for sale throughout Europe. One thing is constant: the power of these huge enterprises. Each of the top 10 MNEs earns annual revenue greater than the gross domestic product of *two-thirds of the worlds nations*. Over 200 MNEs have annual sales exceeding $1 billion and more cash available at any one time than the majority of countries do. Money means power. This corporate might can be used to create jobs, train workers, and build life-saving medical equipment. Such power can also be used to corrupt government officials, rip up the environment, and exploit already impoverished workers. International law is vital.

Trade Regulation

Nations regulate international trade in many ways. In this section we look at export and import controls that affect trade out of and into the United States. **Exporting** is shipping goods or services out of a country. The United States, with its huge farms, is the world's largest exporter of agricultural products. **Importing** is shipping goods and services into a country. The United States suffers trade deficits every year because the value of its imports exceeds that of its exports, as the following table demonstrates.

Exporting
Shipping goods or services out of a country.

Importing
Shipping goods or services into a country.

U.S. INTERNATIONAL TRADE IN GOODS AND SERVICES (IN MILLIONS OF DOLLARS)

	BALANCE			EXPORTS			IMPORTS		
Year	Total	Goods	Services	Total	Goods	Services	Total	Goods	Services
1980	−19,407	−25,500	6,093	271,834	224,250	47,584	291,241	249,750	41,491
1990	−80,864	−111,037	30,173	535,233	387,401	147,832	616,097	498,438	117,659
2000	−378,344	−452,414	74,070	1,070,980	771,994	298,986	1,449,324	1,224,408	224,916
2006	−758,522	−838,271	79,749	1,445,703	1,023,109	422,594	2,204,225	1,861,380	342,845

Source: United States Census Bureau

Export Controls

You and a friend open an electronics business, intending to purchase goods in this country for sale abroad. A representative of Interlex stops in to see you. Interlex is a Latin American electronics company, and the firm wants you to obtain for it a certain kind of infrared dome. The representative explains that this electronic miracle helps helicopters identify nearby aircraft. You find a Pennsylvania company that manufactures the domes, and you realize that you can buy and sell them to Interlex for a handsome profit. Any reason not to? As a matter of fact, there is.

All nations limit what may be exported. In the United States, several statutes do this. The **Export Administration Act of 1985**[2] is one. This statute balances the need for free trade, which is essential in a capitalist society, with important requirements of national security. The statute permits the federal government to restrict exports if they endanger national security, harm foreign policy goals, or drain scarce materials.

The Secretary of Commerce makes a **Controlled Commodities List** of those items that meet any of these criteria. No one may export any commodity on the list without a license, and the license may well be denied. A second major limitation comes from the **Arms Export Control Act**.[3] This statute permits the president to create a second list of controlled goods, all related to military weaponry. Again, no person may export any listed item without a license.

The Arms Export Control Act (AECA) will prohibit you from exporting the infrared domes to the overseas company. They are used in the guidance system of one of the most sophisticated weapons in the American defense arsenal. Foreign governments have attempted to obtain the equipment through official channels, but the American government has placed the domes on the list of restricted military items. When a U.S. citizen did send such goods overseas, he was convicted and imprisoned.[4]

IMPORT CONTROLS

Tariffs

Tariffs are the most widespread method of limiting what may be imported into a nation. **A tariff is a tax imposed on goods when they enter a country.** Tariffs are also called *duties*. Nations use tariffs primarily to protect their domestic industries. Because the company importing the goods must pay this duty, the importer's costs increase, making the merchandise more expensive for consumers. This renders domestic products more attractive. High tariffs unquestionably help local industry, but they proportionately harm local buyers. Consumers benefit from zero tariffs, because the unfettered competition drives down prices.

Tariffs change frequently and vary widely from one country to another. For manufactured goods, the United States imposes an average tariff of less than 4%, about the same as that in the European Union. However, major trading partners around the world set tariffs of 10 to 30% for identical items, with those duties generally being highest in developing countries. Foodstuffs show even greater diversity. For agricultural products, average tariffs are about 25% in North America, 30% in the European Union, 39% in South America, 75% in Sub-Saharan Africa, and 113% in South Asia. You can export potatoes to Israel duty free, but the same produce sent to Norway will cost you a tariff of 476%. Rice is welcome in Iceland, but not in Japan, where the duty is 648%. Tariffs count.[5]

As we will see later in the chapter, regional trade treaties have changed the tariff landscape. Two-thirds of all U.S. products entering Mexico are duty free. Almost all trade between Canada and the United States is done with zero tariffs, which is partly why the two nations do more bilateral commerce than any others in the world.

Classification.   The U.S. Customs Service[6] imposes tariffs at the point of entry into the United States. A customs official inspects the merchandise as it arrives and **classifies** it, in other

Goods
Things that can be moved.

Classification
Before imposing a tariff, the Customs Service decides the precise nature of imported merchandise.

[2] 50 U.S.C. §2402 (1994).
[3] 22 U.S.C. §2778 (1994).
[4] *United States v. Tsai*, 954 F.2d 155, 1992 U.S.App. LEXIS 601 (3d Cir. 1992).
[5] World Bank; Economic Research Service, United States Department of Agriculture.
[6] The Customs Service is part of the United States Customs and Border Protection, which is itself a division of the Department of Homeland Security.

words, decides precisely what the goods are. This decision is critical because the tariff will vary depending on the classification.

Disputes at this stage typically involve an importer claiming that the Customs Service has imposed the wrong classification. The goods in the following case were not designed to hold money—but that is what the case was really about.

AVENUES IN LEATHER, INC. v. U.S.

423 F.3d 1326
COURT OF APPEALS FOR THE FEDERAL CIRCUIT, 2005

CASE SUMMARY

Facts: Avenues in Leather (Avenues) imported Presentation Calcu-Folios. What are they, you ask? It took two courts to supply the answer.

Calcu-Folios are 13 inches tall, 11 inches wide and 1.5 inches deep. They are made of paperboard covered with plastic. A padded handle is fitted to the spine. The goods are zippered on three sides, and contain an interior sleeve, several small pockets, a solar-powered calculator, and a three-ring binder.

The Customs Service (Customs) classified the merchandise under tariff Heading 4202, which covers "Trunks, suitcases, vanity cases, attaché cases, briefcases, school satchels, and similar containers." Avenues argued the Calcu-Folios should be classified under Heading 4820, which applies to "Binders, folders, file covers, memorandum pads, letter pads, and similar articles."

That distinction might sound pretty dull (in fact, it *is* pretty dull), but of course the real difference is profit and loss. Heading 4820 carries a tariff of about 3%, while Heading 4202 imposes a 20% rate. Avenues filed suit and the Court of International Trade agreed with the company, awarding the lower duty. Customs appealed.

Issue: *Was the Calcu-Folio properly classified as a briefcase or a binder?*

Decision: The Calcu-Folio was a binder and should have received the lower tariff rate. Affirmed.

Reasoning: The Calcu-Folio's designer testified that the article was designed as an aid for taking and organizing notes. Customs submitted dictionary definitions of "briefcase" to argue that the merchandise was classifiable as a briefcase or similar container. It also introduced evidence that the items had been marketed as business travel goods, useful for carrying non-paper personal objects.

While the Calcu-Folios may be used to organize and protect small, flat items, they have an internal capacity of only 1 inch. They cannot carry newspapers, books, and other objects normally carried in briefcases.

The Court of International Trade correctly concluded that the Calcu-Folios are neither classifiable as a form of briefcase nor as a "similar container" under Heading 4202.

Valuation.   After classifying the imported goods, customs officials impose the appropriate duty *ad valorem*, meaning "according to the value of the goods." In other words, the service must determine the value of the merchandise before it can tax a percentage of that value. This step can be equally contentious, since goods will have different prices at each stage of manufacturing and delivery. The question is supposed to be settled by the **transaction value** of the goods, meaning the price actually paid for the merchandise when sold for export to the United States (plus shipping and other minor costs). But there is often room for debate, so importers use customs agents to help negotiate the most favorable valuation.

Ad valorem
Customs officials impose duties "according to the value of of the goods."

Duties for Dumping and Subsidizing

Dumping

Selling merchandise at one price in the domestic market and at a cheaper, unfair price in an international market.

Dumping means selling merchandise at one price in the domestic market and at a cheaper, unfair price in an international market. Suppose a Singapore company, CelMaker, makes cellular telephones for $20 per unit and sells them in the United States for $12 each, vastly undercutting domestic American competitors. CelMaker may be willing to suffer short-term losses in order to drive out competitors for the American market. Once it has gained control of that market, it will raise its prices, more than compensating for its initial losses. And CelMaker may get help from its home government. Suppose the Singapore government prohibits foreign cellular phones from entering Singapore. CelMaker may sell its phones for $75 at home, earning such high profits that it can afford the temporary losses in America.

In the United States, the Commerce Department investigates suspected dumping. If the Department concludes that the foreign company is selling items at **less than fair value**, and that this harms an American industry, it will impose a **dumping duty** sufficiently high to put the foreign goods back on fair footing with domestic products.

Subsidized goods are also unfair. Suppose the Singapore government permits CelMaker to pay no taxes for 10 years. This enormous benefit will enable the company to produce cheap phones and undersell competitors. Again, the United States imposes a tariff on subsidized goods, called **countervailing duties**. If CelMaker sells phones for $15 that would cost an unsubsidized competitor $21 to make, it will pay a $6 countervailing duty on every phone entering the United States.

Nontariff Barriers

Quota

A limit on the quantity of a particular good that may enter a nation.

All countries use additional methods to limit imports. A **quota** is a limit on the quantity of a particular good that may enter a nation. For example, the United States, like most importing nations, has agreements with many developing nations, placing a quota on imported textiles. In some cases, textile imports from a particular country may grow by only a small percentage each year. Without such a limit, textile imports from the developing world would increase explosively because costs are so much lower there. As part of the GATT treaty (discussed later in this chapter), the wealthier nations pledged to increase textile imports from the developing countries, but whether that has occurred is open to dispute.

An **import** ban means that particular goods are flatly prohibited. Some nations prohibit alcohol imports for religious reasons. The United States bars the importation of narcotic drugs. Virtually all countries from time to time halt certain goods for political purposes, for example, to protest the behavior of the exporting country. The United States has increasingly used economic sanctions in an effort to advance its foreign policy goals. During one three-year period, it threatened or imposed sanctions 60 times, against 35 nations. Sanctions were aimed at Colombia for permitting drug trafficking; the Netherlands, Switzerland, and other European nations for trading with Cuba; and Taiwan for environmental violations. Proponents of such sanctions consider them essential components of an ethical foreign policy. Opponents regard them as hypocritical attempts at moral superiority.

Money and politics are a volatile mix, as demonstrated by all recorded history from 3000 B.C.E. to the present. As long as nations have existed, they have engaged in disputes about quotas and import bans. And that is why more than 100 countries negotiated and signed the GATT treaty, the subject of the next section.

GENERAL AGREEMENT ON TARIFFS AND TRADE (GATT)

What is GATT? The greatest boon to American commerce in a century. Or, the worst assault on the American economy in 200 years. It depends on whom you ask. Let's start where everyone agrees.

GATT is the General Agreement on Tariffs and Trade. This massive international treaty has been negotiated on and off since the 1940s to eliminate trade barriers and bolster commerce. GATT has already had considerable effect. In 1947 the worldwide average tariff on industrial goods was about 40%. Now it is about 4% (although agricultural duties still average over 40%). The world's economies have exploded over those six decades. Proponents of GATT applaud the agreement. Opponents scoff that both lower duties and higher trade would have arrived without GATT.

The most recent round of bargaining took seven hard years. Finally, in 1994, the United States and 125 other countries signed the treaty. A **signatory**, that is, a nation that signs a treaty, is still not bound by the agreement until it is **ratified**, that is, until the nation's legislature votes to honor it. In the United States, Congress voted to ratify GATT. If the latest round of cuts is fully implemented, average duties in all signatories should drop to about 3.7%. Further, nearly half of all trade in industrial goods will be duty free, at least in developed countries. That must be good—or is it?

GATT
The General Agreement on Tariffs and Trade.

Signatory
A nation that signs a treaty.

Ratification
A vote by a nation's legislature to honor a treaty.

Trade

Leading supporters of GATT suggest that its lower tariffs vastly increase world trade. The United States is one of the biggest beneficiaries because for decades this country has imposed lower duties than most other nations. American companies for once compete on equal footing. A typical American family's annual income has increased due to the more vigorous domestic economy, and at the same time many goods are less expensive because they enter with low duties.

But opponents claim that the United States now competes against nations with unlimited pools of exploited labor. These countries dominate labor-intensive industries such as textiles, clothing, and manufacturing, and are steadily taking jobs from millions of American workers. It is unfair for U.S. companies to struggle against competitors in countries with no labor standards and dirt-cheap pay. Because domestic job losses come in low-end employment, those put out of work are precisely those least able to find a new job. The chasm between rich and poor is widening, leaving us all the losers.

EXAM *Strategy*

Question: California producers of sea salt protest to the American government that they cannot compete with the same product imported from China. How do the California producers want the United States government to respond? May the U.S. government legally oblige?

Strategy: Domestic producers who cannot compete with foreign competition typically ask their government to impose higher tariffs on the imported goods. However, the whole point of GATT, and the WTO, is to avoid trade wars. There are two instances in which the U.S. government is free to levy increased duties on the Chinese goods. What are they?

Result: When a company *dumps* goods, it sells them overseas at an artificially low price, generally to destroy competition and gain a foothold. That is illegal, and the domestic (U.S.) government may impose dumping duties to protect local producers. Subsidized goods—those supported by foreign company's government—are also illegal. If the United States government can demonstrate illegal subsidies, it will impose countervailing duties designed to give all producers an equal chance.

World Trade Organization and the Environment

**World Trade
Organization (WTO)**

Created by GATT to stimulate
international commerce and
resolve trade disputes.

GATT created the **World Trade Organization** (WTO) to stimulate international commerce and resolve trade disputes. The WTO is empowered to hear arguments from any signatory nation about tariff violations or nontariff barriers. This international "court" may order compliance from any nation violating GATT and may penalize countries by imposing trade sanctions. Proponents say that it is high time to have one international body to resolve complex issues impartially and create an international body of trade law that corporations can rely on when planning business.

Here is how the WTO decides a trade dispute. Suppose that the United States believes that Brazil is unfairly restricting trade. The United States uses the WTO offices to request a consultation with Brazil's trade representative. In the majority of cases, these discussions lead to a satisfactory settlement. If the consultation does not resolve the problem, the United States asks the WTO's Dispute Settlement Body (DSB) to form a panel, which consists of three nations uninvolved in the dispute. After the panel hears testimony and arguments from both countries, it releases its report. The DSB generally approves the report, unless either nation appeals. If there is an appeal, the WTO Appellate Body hears the dispute and generally makes the final decision, subject to approval by the entire WTO. No single nation has the power to block final decisions. If a country refuses to comply with the WTO's ruling, affected nations may retaliate by imposing punitive tariffs. (The official Web site of the WTO, http://www.wto.org/, includes libraries on all sorts of international trade topics, from goods and services to dispute settlement and legal texts.)

The following case forced the WTO to weigh the merits of two important, competing goals: environmental protection and trade growth.

UNITED STATES—IMPORT PROHIBITION OF CERTAIN SHRIMP AND SHRIMP PRODUCTS

WT/DS58/R15 WTO PANEL, 1998

CASE SUMMARY

Facts: Sea turtles are migratory animals that live throughout the world. The United States recognizes the animals as an endangered species. Studies showed that the greatest threat to the turtles around the world came from shrimp fishermen inadvertently catching the animals in their nets. The federal government responded by requiring any importers to certify that shrimp had been caught using turtle excluder devices (TEDs), which keep the animals out of the nets.

India, Pakistan, Malaysia, and Thailand filed complaints with the WTO, claiming that the United States had no right to impose its environmental concerns on world trade. The United States argued that Article XX of the WTO Agreement permitted trade restrictions based on environmental concerns. Article XX states in part:

Nothing in this Agreement shall be construed to prevent the adoption or enforcement by any Member of measures:

(b) necessary to protect human, animal, or plant life or health;
(g) relating to the conservation of exhaustible natural resources if such measures are made effective in conjunction with restrictions on domestic production or consumption;

The Dispute Settlement Body appointed a panel to hear the dispute and make recommendations.

Issue: Did Article XX permit the United States to impose environmental restrictions on shrimp importers?

Decision: No, Article XX did not permit the United States to impose its restrictions on shrimp importers.

Reasoning: The WTO Agreement acknowledges the importance of sustainable development of the world's resources, done in a way that preserves and protects the environment. However, a different section of the Agreement emphasizes the reduction of trade barriers and discrimination in international trade. The central focus of the Agreement is the promotion of economic development through trade.

If one member were allowed to adopt measures such as the shrimp regulations, other members would have the right to pass different, or even conflicting, rules. It could become impossible for a shrimp producer to comply with the inconsistent demands.

The United States may be right in claiming that the sea turtles are a shared global resource. However, such a common interest would be better addressed through negotiated international agreements, rather than unilateral actions that place a heavy commercial burden on other members. The Panel recommends that the Dispute Settlement Body ask the United States to bring this measure into conformity with its obligations under the WTO Agreement.

The United States appealed the panel's decision to the WTO's Appellate Body.

UNITED STATES—IMPORT PROHIBITION OF CERTAIN SHRIMP AND SHRIMP PRODUCTS

AB-1998–4 WTO APPELLATE BODY, 1998

CASE SUMMARY

Issue: Should the Panel's recommendation be enforced?

Decision: Yes, the Panel's recommendation should be enforced.

Reasoning: The United States requires the use of approved TEDs on all domestic shrimp vessels. It is acceptable for a nation to impose a uniform policy on its domestic industry, regardless of any hardships. However, the shrimp policy goes further, requiring other WTO members to adopt regulations that are essentially identical or suffer exclusion from the U.S. market.

The preservation of the environment is of great significance to members of the WTO. However, no nation has the right to use environmental policy to discriminate against other members. It is not acceptable, in international trade, for one WTO member to use an economic embargo to force its regulations on other members. The United States should have engaged other nations in serious negotiations designed to create multilateral agreements that would protect sea turtles. It failed to do so and thus violated the WTO agreement.

Environmental groups attacked the ruling, declaring that the WTO paid lip service to the environment but ensured further killing of an important endangered species. Trade supporters applauded it. In addition to the trade versus environment tension, there is a second conflict: rich versus poor. Critics of the shrimp regulations claim that it is unseemly for a wealthy nation to punish subsistence fishermen because of environmental concerns. Their opponents argue that we all share this planet, and long-term growth for each of us depends upon living in harmony with limited resources and fragile ecosystems. Which of the competing goals is more important to you?

ETHICS   **Child labor** is an even more wrenching issue. The practice exists to some degree in all countries and is common throughout the developing world. The International Labor Organization, an affiliate of the United Nations, estimates that 120 million children between the ages of 5 and 14 work full time, and 130 million more labor part time. As the world generally becomes more prosperous, this ugly problem has actually increased. Children in developing countries typically work in agriculture and domestic work, but many toil in mines and others in factories, making rugs, glass, clothing, and other goods. The rug industry illustrates the international nature of this tragedy. In the 1970s, the Shah of Iran banned child labor in rug factories, but many manufacturers simply packed up and moved to southern Asia. Today, in India and Pakistan, tens of millions of children, some as young as four, toil in rug workrooms, seven days a week, 12 hours a day. Many, shackled to the looms they operate, are essentially slaves, working for pennies a day or, in some cases, for no money at all.

Child labor raises compelling moral questions—and economic ones as well. No American company can compete with an industry that uses slave labor. As discussed earlier, the United States is relatively quick to impose trade sanctions in response to moral issues. In 1997, Congress passed a statute prohibiting the import of goods created by forced or indentured child labor. The first suit under the new law targeted the carpet factories of southern Asia and sought an outright ban on most rugs from that area. Is this statute humane legislation or cultural imperialism dressed as a nontariff barrier? Should the voters of this country or the WTO decide the issue? In answering such difficult questions, we must bear in mind that child labor is truly universal. The United Farm Workers union estimates that 800,000 underage children help their migrant parents harvest U.S. crops—work that few Americans are willing to do.

Our response to such a troubling moral issue need not take the form of a statute or lawsuit. Duke University is one of the most popular names in sports apparel, and the school sells about $20 million worth of T-shirts, sweatshirts, jackets, caps, and other sportswear bearing its logo. To produce its clothing, the university licenses about 700 companies in the United States and 10 foreign countries. In response to the troubling issue of child labor, Duke adopted a code of conduct that prohibits its manufacturers from using forced or child labor and requires all of the firms to pay a minimum wage, permit union organizing, and maintain a safe workplace. The university plans to monitor the companies producing its apparel and terminate the contract for any firm that violates its rules. ◆

Intellectual Property

Some foreign countries, particularly developing nations, have long ignored U.S. copyrights and patents. GATT changes things. It allows this country to halt duty-free imports from, and assess tariffs against, a nation that refuses to honor American copyrights or patents.

WTO Summary

It will be many years before we can fairly evaluate GATT and the WTO. In all likelihood, some of the most extreme claims will prove false, and the agreement's effects will evolve somewhere in the middle. Unquestionably, some industries will suffer, forcing workers into unemployment. Others will discover and exploit lucrative opportunities. Perhaps the final cost/benefit analysis of the WTO will be decided not by the letter of its rulings but by the spirit and goodwill of those who implement them.

REGIONAL AGREEMENTS

Many regional agreements also regulate international trade. We will briefly describe some that affect the United States.

The European Union

The **European Union (EU)** used to be known as the Common Market. The original six members—Belgium, France, Luxembourg, the Netherlands, West Germany, and Italy—have been joined by twenty-one additional countries. See the map on the following page.

The EU is one of the world's most powerful associations, with a prosperous population of nearly half a billion people. Its sophisticated legal system sets Union-wide standards for tariffs, dumping, subsidies, antitrust, transportation, and many other issues. The first goals of the EU were to eliminate trade barriers between member nations, establish common tariffs with respect to external countries, permit the free movement of citizens across its borders, and coordinate its agricultural and fishing policies for the collective good. The EU has largely achieved these goals. Most but not all of the EU countries have adopted a common currency, the euro. During the next decade the union will focus on further economic integration and effective coordination of foreign policy.

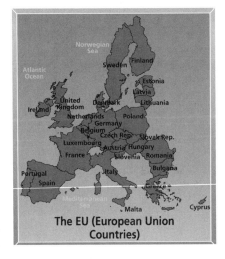

The EU (European Union Countries)

NAFTA

In 1993, the United States, Canada, and Mexico signed the **North American Free Trade Agreement** (NAFTA). The principal goal was to eliminate almost all trade barriers, tariff and nontariff, between the three nations. Like GATT, this trilateral (three-nation) compact has been controversial, and there will probably never be agreement on NAFTA's value because the treaty has enriched some while impoverishing others. Unquestionably, trade between the three nations has increased enormously. Mexico now exports more goods to the United States than do Germany, Britain, and Korea combined. Opponents of the treaty argue that NAFTA costs the United States jobs and lowers the living standards of American workers by forcing them to compete with low-paid labor. For example, Swingline Staplers closed a factory in Queens, New York, after 75 years of operation and moved to Mexico. Instead of paying its American workers $11.58 per hour, Swingline will pay Mexican workers 50 cents an hour to do the same job. Proponents contend that although some jobs are lost, many others are gained, especially in fields with a future, such as high technology. They claim that as new jobs invigorate the Mexican economy, consumers there will be able to afford American goods for the first time, providing an enormous new market.

North American Free Trade Agreement (NAFTA)
A treaty eliminating almost all trade barriers, tariff and nontariff, between the United States, Canada, and Mexico.

ASEAN

The Association of Southeast Asian Nations consists of 10 countries: Brunei Darussalam, Cambodia, Indonesia, Laos, Malaysia, Myanmar, the Philippines, Singapore, Thailand, and Vietnam. The group's population of about 500 million produces a combined gross domestic product of $737 billion and total trade of $720 billion. ASEAN seeks to eliminate tariffs, accelerate economic growth, and promote peace and stability in the region.

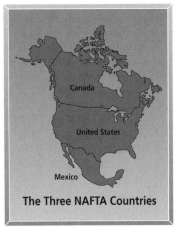

The Three NAFTA Countries

Mercosur

Brazil, Argentina, Uruguay, and Paraguay formed Mercosur to improve commerce among the four South American nations. Bolivia, Chile, Colombia, Ecuador, and Peru are associate members, with limited rights. The organization represents the fourth largest economic entity in the world, after the EU, the United States, and Japan. The Mercosur nations have a combined population of over 250 million, and a GDP of more than $1 trillion. Almost all trade barriers between the four nations have been eliminated, and the organization has established a broad social agenda focusing on education, labor, culture, the environment, justice, and consumer protection.

INTERNATIONAL SALES AGREEMENTS

Cowboy boots are hot in France. Big Heel, Inc., your small company in Austin, Texas, makes superb boots with exquisite detailing, and you realize that France could be a bonanza. Your first decision is how to produce and sell the boots in France. For our purposes, Big Heel has three choices:

- *Direct Sales.* You can continue to manufacture the boots in Tucson and sell them directly to French retailers.

- *Indirect Sales.* You can manufacture the boots in Tucson and use a French distributor to wholesale them to French stores.

- *Licensing.* You can license a French manufacturer to make Big Heel boots in France and wholesale them.

DIRECT SALES

You must focus on two principal issues: the sales contract and letters of credit.

You decide to sell the boots directly. Le Pied D' Or, a new, fast-growing French chain of shoe stores, is interested in buying 10,000 pairs of your boots, at about $ 300 per pair. You must focus on two principal issues: the sales contract and letters of credit. You are wise enough to know that you must have a written contract—$3 million is a lot of money for Big Heel.

This is a contract for the sale of goods. **Goods** are things that can be moved, such as boots, airplanes, pencils, and computers. A sale of goods is governed by different law than the sale of real estate (e.g., a house) or securities (e.g., a share of stock) or services (e.g., accounting).

What Law Governs the Sale of Goods?

Potentially, three conflicting laws could govern your boot contract: Arizona law, French law, and an international treaty. Each is different, and it is therefore essential to negotiate which law will control.

Because this contract is for the sale of goods, your local law is the Arizona **Uniform Commercial Code (UCC)**. The UCC is discussed throughout Units 2 and 3, on contracts and commercial transactions. This statute has taken the common law principles of contract and modified them to meet the needs of contemporary business. Article 2 of the UCC governs the sale of goods. American business lawyers are familiar with the UCC and will generally prefer that it govern. French law is based on **Roman law** and the **Napoleonic Code** and is obviously different. French lawyers and business executives are naturally partial to it. How to compromise? Perhaps by using a neutral law.

The **United Nations Convention on Contracts for the International Sale of Goods (CISG)** is the result of 50 years of work by various international groups, all seeking to create a uniform, international law on this important subject. Finally, in 1980, a United Nations conference adopted the CISG, though it became the law in individual nations only if and when they adopted it. The United States and most of its principal trading partners have adopted this important treaty. The United Kingdom is a notable exception.

The CISG applies automatically to any contract for the sale of goods between two parties, from different countries, each of which is a signatory. France and the United States have both signed. Thus the CISG automatically applies to the Big Heel–Pied D' Or deal unless the parties *specifically opt out*. If the parties want to be governed by other law, they must state very clearly that they exclude the CISG and elect, for example, the UCC.

Should the parties allow the CISG to govern? They can make an intelligent choice by first understanding how the CISG differs from other law. Here are a few key differences between the CISG and the UCC:

- *Must the contract be written?* Under the UCC, a contract for the sale of goods valued at $500 or more generally must be written to be enforceable. But the CISG does not require a writing for any contract. Be advised that discussions you consider informal or preliminary might create a contract under the CISG.

- *When is an offer irrevocable?* The UCC declares that an offer is irrevocable only if it is in writing and states that it will be held open for a fixed period. But the CISG makes some offers irrevocable even if unwritten.

- *What if an acceptance includes new terms?* Under the UCC, an acceptance generally creates a contract, even if it uses new terms. But the CISG insists on an acceptance that is a "mirror image" of the offer. Almost anything else constitutes a rejection.

- *What remedies are available?* The UCC entitles a plaintiff only to money damages for breach of a sales contract. But the CISG permits many plaintiffs to seek specific performance of the contract, that is, to force the other party to perform the contract.

Choice of Forum

The parties must decide not only what law governs, but where disagreements will be resolved. The French and American legal systems are dramatically different. In a French civil lawsuit, generally neither side is entitled to depose the other or to obtain interrogatories or even documents, in sharp contrast to the American system where such discovery methods dominate litigation. American lawyers, accustomed to discovery to prepare a case and advance settlement talks, are unnerved by the French system. Similarly, French lawyers are dismayed at the idea of spending two years taking depositions, exchanging paper, and arguing motions, all at great expense. At trial, the contrasts grow. In a French civil trial, there is generally no right to a jury. The rules of evidence are more flexible (and unpredictable), neither side employs its own expert witnesses, and the parties themselves never appear as witnesses.

Choice of Language and Currency

The parties must select a language for the contract and a currency for payment. Language counts because legal terms seldom translate literally. Currency is vital because the exchange rate may alter between the signing and payment. Suppose the Argentine peso falls 30% against the dollar in one week. An Argentine company that contracted on Monday to pay $1 million for U.S. aircraft engines will suddenly have to pay 30% more in pesos to meet its contractual obligations. To avoid such calamities, companies engaged in international commerce often purchase from currency dealers a guarantee to obtain the needed currency at a future date for a guaranteed price. Assuming that Big Heel insists on being paid in U.S. dollars, Pied D'Or could obtain a quote from a currency dealer as to the present cost of obtaining $3 million at the time the boots are to be delivered. Pied D'Or might pay a 5% premium for this guarantee, but it will have insured itself against disastrous currency changes.

Choices Made.   The parties agree that the contract price will be paid in U.S. dollars. Pied D'Or is unfamiliar with the UCC and absolutely refuses to make a deal unless either French law or the CISG governs. Your lawyer, Susan Fisher, recommends accepting the CISG, provided that the contract is written in English and that any disputes will be resolved in Arizona courts. Pied D'Or balks at this, but Fisher presses hard, and ultimately those are the terms agreed upon. Fisher is delighted with the arrangement, pointing out that the CISG provisions can all be taken into account as the contract is written, and that by using Texas courts to settle any dispute, Big Heel has an advantage in terms of familiarity and location.

Letter of Credit

Because Pied D'Or is new and fast growing, you are not sure it will be able to foot the bill. Pied D'Or provides a letter of reference from its bank, La Banque Bouffon, but this is a small bank in Pleasanterie, France, unfamiliar to you. You need greater assurance of payment, and Fisher recommends that payment be made by **letter of credit**. Here is how the letter will work.

Letter of credit
A commercial device used to guarantee payment in international trade, usually between parties that have not previously worked together.

Big Heel demands that the contract include a provision requiring payment by confirmed, irrevocable letter of credit. Le Pied D'Or agrees. The French company now contacts its bank, La Banque Bouffon, and instructs Bouffon to issue a letter of credit to Big Heel. The letter of credit is a promise *by the bank itself* to pay Big Heel, if Big Heel presents certain documents. Banque Bouffon, of course, expects to be repaid by Pied D'Or. The bank is in a good position to assess Pied D'Or's creditworthiness, since it is local and can do any investigating it wants before issuing the credit. It may also insist that Pied D'Or give Bouffon a mortgage on property, or that Pied D'Or deposit money in a separate Bouffon account. Pied D'Or is the **account party** on the letter of credit, and Big Heel is the **beneficiary**.

But at Big Heel you are still not entirely satisfied about getting paid because you don't know anything about Bouffon. That is why you have required a *confirmed* letter of credit. Bouffon will forward its letter of credit to Big Heel's own bank, the Bandito Trust Company of Tucson. Bandito examines the letter and then *confirms* the letter. This is *Bandito's own guarantee* that it will pay Big Heel. Bandito will do this only if it knows, through international banking contacts, that Bouffon is a sound bank. The risk has now been spread to two banks, and at Big Heel, you are confident of payment.

You get busy, make excellent boots, and pack them. When they are ready, you truck them to Galveston, where they are taken alongside a ship, *Le Fond de la Mer*. Your agent presents the goods to the ship's officials, along with customs documents that describe the goods. *Le Fond de la Mer*'s officer in turn issues your agent a **negotiable bill of lading**. This document describes *exactly* the goods received—their quantity, color, quality, and anything else important.

You now take the negotiable bill of lading to Bandito Trust. You also present to Bandito a **draft**, which is simply a formal order to Bandito to pay, based on the letter of credit. Bandito will look closely at the bill of lading, which must specify *precisely* the goods described in the letter of credit. Why so nitpicky? Because the bank is dealing only in paper. It never sees the boots. Bandito is exchanging $3 million of its own money based on instructions in the letter of credit. The bank should pay only if the bill of lading indicates that *Le Fond de la Mer* received exactly what is described in the letter of credit. Bandito will decide whether the bill of lading is *conforming* or *nonconforming*. If the terms of both documents are identical, the bill of lading is conforming and Bandito must pay. If the terms vary, the bill of lading is nonconforming and Bandito will deny payment. Thus, if the bill of lading indicated 9,000 pairs of boots and 1,000 pairs of sneakers, it is nonconforming and Big Heel would get no money.

Bandito concludes that the documents are conforming, so it issues a check to Big Heel for $3 million. In return, you endorse the bill of lading and other documents over to the Bandito Bank, which endorses the same documents and sends them to Banque Bouffon. Bouffon makes the same minute inspection and then writes a check to Bandito. Bouffon then demands payment from Le Pied D'Or. Pied D'Or pays its bank, receiving in exchange the bill of lading and customs documents. Note that payment in all stages is now complete, though the boots are still rolling on the high seas. Finally, when the boots arrive in Le Havre, Pied D'Or trucks roll up to the wharf and, using the bill of lading and customs documents, collect the boots. See Exhibit 8.1.

Exhibit 8.1

Good news: They fit! Not all customers walk away in such comfort, though, as the following case indicates.

CENTRIFUGAL CASTING MACHINE CO., INC. V. AMERICAN BANK & TRUST CO.

966 F.2d 1348, 1992 U.S.App. LEXIS 13089
TENTH CIRCUIT COURT OF APPEALS, 1992

CASE SUMMARY

Facts: Centrifugal Casting Machine Co. (CCM) entered into a contract with the State Machinery Trading Co. (SMTC), an agency of the Iraqi government. CCM agreed to manufacture cast iron pipe plant equipment for a total price of $27 million. The contract specified payment of the full amount by confirmed irrevocable letter of credit. The Central Bank of Iraq then issued the letter, on behalf of SMTC (the "account party") to be paid to CCM (the "beneficiary"). The Banca Nazionale del Lavorov (BNL) confirmed the letter.

Following Iraq's invasion of Kuwait on August 2, 1990, President George H.W. Bush issued two executive orders blocking the transfer of property in the United States in which Iraq held any interest. In other words, no one could use, buy, or sell any Iraqi property or cash. When CCM attempted to draw upon the letter of credit, the U.S. government intervened. The government claimed that like all Iraqi money in the United States, this money was frozen by the executive order. The United States District Court rejected the government's claim, and the government appealed.

Issue: *Is CCM entitled to be paid pursuant to the letter of credit?*

Decision: Affirmed. CCM is entitled to payment.

Reasoning: The United States claims that it is freezing Iraqi assets to punish international aggression. That is a legitimate foreign policy argument. However, no court has the power to rewrite basic principles of international trade.

A letter of credit has unique value for two reasons. First, the bank that issues the letter is substituting its credit for that of the account party. Because the bank is promising to pay with its own funds, the beneficiary is confident of receiving its money.

Second, the bank's obligation to pay on the letter of credit is entirely separate from the underlying bargain between the account party and the beneficiary. The bank must pay, even if the beneficiary has breached the contract, the account party has gone bankrupt, or a crisis such as war blocks completion of the deal. The money in this case came from an issuing bank that was obligated to pay, not from Iraq, and the government may not seize it. Any other ruling would undermine all letters of credit.

EXAM *Strategy*

Question: In an international contract for the sale of goods, Seller is to be paid by a confirmed irrevocable letter of credit. Buyer claims that the goods are defective, and threatens to sue. If the parties are going to end up in court anyway, why bother with a letter of credit?

Strategy: A confirmed letter of credit is unique because the seller is assured of payment as soon as it presents a proper bill of lading to the appropriate local bank—regardless of the quality of the goods. Seller would much rather defend this lawsuit against Buyer than sue for its money in foreign courts.

Result: There *may* be a lawsuit, but Seller is not worried. It is Buyer who must sue, probably in Seller's home country. Buyer now risks substantial time and cash for an uncertain outcome. When the parties discuss a settlement, as surely they will, Seller is holding a big advantage—the cash.

INDIRECT SALES THROUGH A DISTRIBUTOR

You might also have decided that Big Heel would be better off doing business through a French shoe distributor, on the theory that the local company would have superior market knowledge and easier access to valuable retailers. The questions you face regarding choice of law, forum, and method of payment are identical to those you face in direct sales; they must be worked out in advance. But there is one additional problem that deserves close attention.

Suppose you choose Voleurs Freres, a French fashion distributor, to do all of Big Heel's work in France. Voleurs Freres will be an **exclusive dealer**, meaning that it will take on no other accounts of cowboy boots. In return you will give it an **exclusive distributorship**, indicating that no other French distributors will get a chance at Big Heel boots. This is a common method of working. Voleurs Freres benefits because no one else in France may distribute the valuable boots. Big Heel in turn need not worry that Voleurs Freres will devote more energy to a competing boot. It is a tidy relationship, but does it violate antitrust laws?

Antitrust laws make it illegal to restrain trade and capture an entire market. The United States and the EU both have strong antitrust laws that can potentially be applied domestically and in foreign countries.

Antitrust laws
Make it illegal to restrain trade and capture an entire market.

EU Antitrust Law

The European Union law is found in Articles 85 and 86 of the Treaty of Rome. From the American point of view, the former is more important. **Article 85 outlaws any agreement, contract, or discussion that distorts competition within EU countries.** In other words, any attempt to gain a market edge by *avoiding* competition is going to be suspect. Suppose three Italian cosmetic firms agree to act in unison to increase earnings. They set common prices for makeup and agree that none will undersell the others. This greatly reduces competition, leaving the consumer with fewer options and more expensive products. Their deal violates Article 85.

Will Big Heel's contract with Voleurs Freres violate Article 85? There is no quick answer. You will need to do a careful market analysis and consult with French lawyers, who undoubtedly will have many questions. How popular are Big Heel boots in Europe? How many competitors would like to distribute them? How many other boot companies want Voleurs Freres to sell *their* products? Does the exclusive arrangement between Big Heel and Voleurs Freres diminish competition? Will consumers pay more because of the contract? These questions are a nuisance and an expense, but it is easier and cheaper to make the inquiry now than to face years of antitrust litigation.

American Antitrust Law

In the United States, the primary antitrust law is the Sherman Act. This statute controls anticompetitive conduct that harms the American market. It will probably not affect the Big Heel–Voleurs Freres contract, since that deal is likely to have consequences only in Europe. But it is important to understand the Sherman Act when facing foreign competition. In effect, this statute is the American counterpart to Article 85. Any conduct that eliminates competition in the United States and enables one company, or group of companies, to control a market probably violates this law. And "any conduct" means that anticompetitive acts taking place in a foreign country may still violate the Sherman Act. A company doing business in the United States **may sue a competitor based on its conduct in a foreign country**, provided the local firm can show (1) that the foreign competitor *intends* to affect the U.S. market, and (2) that the foreign conduct has a *direct and substantial effect* on the U.S. market.

Let's look again at the Italian cosmetics makers. Suppose they decide to act in unison in the United States. They set common prices and agree not to compete with each other. That agreement is illegal. It violates the Sherman Act *even if all arrangements were made in Milan*. The companies intend to affect the U.S. market. When an American cosmetics firm demonstrates that the agreement caused it direct and substantial harm, the company may file suit in the United States against all three Italian corporations and expect to recover large damages.

Extraterritoriality

The United States has many statutes designed to protect employees, such as those that prohibit discrimination on race, religion, gender and so forth. Do these laws apply overseas? This is an issue of **extraterritoriality—the power of one nation to impose its laws in other countries**.[7] Many American companies do business through international **subsidiaries—**foreign companies which they control. The subsidiary may be incorporated in a nation that denies workers the protection they would receive in the United States. What happens when an employee of a foreign subsidiary argues that his rights under an American statute have been violated? You make the call.

YOU *be the* JUDGE

CARNERO V. BOSTON SCIENTIFIC CORPORATION
433 F.3d 1
First Circuit Court of Appeals, 2006

Facts: Boston Scientific (BSC) was an American company that manufactured medical equipment. The company had its headquarters in Massachusetts, but did business around the world through foreign subsidiaries. One of the company's subsidiaries was Boston Scientific Argentina (BSA), and it was there that Ruben Carnero began working. His employment contract stated he would work at BSA's headquarters in Buenos Aires and be paid in pesos. Argentine law was to govern the contract. Four years later, Carnero took an assignment to work as Country Manager for a different BSC subsidiary, Boston Scientific Do Brasil (BSB). Carnero frequently traveled to Massachusetts to meet with company executives, but did most of his work in South America.

About a year later, BSB fired Carnero, and BSA soon did the same. Carnero claimed that the companies terminated him in retaliation for his reporting to BSC executives that the Argentine and Brazilian subsidiaries inflated sales figures and engaged in other accounting fraud. Carnero filed suit in Massachusetts, alleging that his firing violated an American statute, the Sarbanes-Oxley Act of 2002 (SOX).

Congress passed that law in response to the massive fraud cases involving Enron, Arthur Andersen and others. The law was passed primarily to protect investors, but included a "whistleblower" provision. That section was designed to guard employees who informed superiors or investigating officials of fraud within the company. The law allows injured employees reinstatement and back pay.

BSC argued that SOX did not apply overseas and the District Court agreed, dismissing the case. Carnero appealed.

Issue: *Does SOX protect a whistleblower employed overseas by a subsidiary of an American company?*

Argument for Carnero: Congress passed SOX because the American people were appalled by the massive fraud in some major corporations, and the resulting harm to employees, investors, the community and the economy. The whistleblower protection is designed to encourage honest employees to come forward and report wrongdoing—an act

---

[7] Extraterritoriality can also refer to exemption from local laws. For example, ambassadors are generally exempt from the law of the nation in which they serve.

continued

that no employee wants to do, and one which has historically led to termination. Mr. Carnero knew his report would be poorly received but believed he had an ethical obligation to protect his company. For that effort he was fired, and now Boston Scientific attempts to avoid liability using the technicality of corporate hierarchy.

Yes, Mr. Carnero was employed by BSB and BSA. But both of those companies are owned and operated by Boston Scientific. It is the larger company, with headquarters in the United States, which calls the shots. That is why executives in Massachusetts frequently asked Mr. Carnero to report to them—and why he brought them his unhappy news.

A whistleblower deserves gratitude and a pay raise. Mr. Carnero may well have saved his employer from massive losses and public disgrace. Would Boston Scientific like to wind up as Enron did—the company in bankruptcy court, its executives in prison? If Boston Scientific is too petty to acknowledge Mr. Carnero's contribution, the company should at least honor the purpose and intent of SOX by protecting his job.

Argument for Boston Scientific: First, we do not know whether there have been any accounting irregularities or not. Second, the fact that Mr. Carnero is employed by companies incorporated in Argentina and Brazil is more than a technicality. He is asking an American court to go into two foreign countries—sovereign nations with good ties to the United States—and investigate accounting and employment practices of companies incorporated and operating there. The very idea is offensive. No nation can afford to treat its allies and trading partners with such contempt.

If the United States can impose its whistleblowing law in foreign countries, may those nations impose their rules and values here? Suppose that a country forbids women to do certain work. May companies in those nations direct American subsidiaries to reject all female job applicants? Neither the citizens nor courts of this country would tolerate such interference for a moment.

Mr. Carnero's idea is also impractical. How would an American court determine why he was fired? Must the trial judge here subpoena Brazilian witnesses and demand documentary evidence from that country?

Finally, the SOX law does not apply overseas because Congress never said it did. The legislators—well aware that American corporations operate subsidiaries abroad—made no mention of those companies when they passed this statute.

International Comity

A related principle is **international comity**. "Comity" refers to "concomitant jurisdiction," meaning that two courts have the right to hear a particular case. When those two courts are in different nations, the laws of the two countries may conflict. **In the event of a conflict, international comity requires one court to respect the other legal system and decline to hear a suit if it would more logically be resolved in the foreign country.**

> **International comity**
> Requires one court to reject a lawsuit that would more logically be resolved in another nation.

Licensing a Foreign Manufacturer

Big Heel has a third option when selling abroad, which is to license a French manufacturer to produce Big Heel boots. It should do this only if it is convinced the manufacturer will maintain sufficiently high standards. Even so, there are two major issues.

First, Big Heel must ensure that all of its patents and trademarks are protected. In fact, France will honor both forms of American intellectual property, and there should be no problems. But some nations may ignore American intellectual property rights, and no company should establish a licensing arrangement without investigating. As mentioned above, the WTO should increase respect worldwide for the intellectual property rights created by all nations.

Second, if Big Heel grants an exclusive license to any French manufacturer, it could encounter exactly the same antitrust problems as those discussed above. It must analyze both EU and American antitrust law before taking the risk.

INVESTING ABROAD

Foreign investment is another major source of international commerce. Assume that Ambux is an American communications corporation that decides to invest in a growing overseas market. The president of Ambux is particularly interested in building telephone systems in the former republics of the Soviet Union, reasoning that these economies offer great opportunity for growth. She wants you to report to her on the most important issues concerning possible investment in Uzbekistan and other former Soviet republics. You quickly realize that such an investment presents several related issues:

- Repatriation of profits
- Expropriation
- Sovereign immunity
- Act of State doctrine
- Foreign corrupt practices

REPATRIATION OF PROFITS

Repatriation of profits occurs when an investing company pulls its earnings out of a foreign country and takes them back home. If Ambux builds a telephone system in Uzbekistan, it will plan to make money and then repatriate the profit to its headquarters in the United States. But Ambux must not assume an automatic right to do so. Many countries impose a much higher tax on repatriated profits than on normal income in order to keep the money in domestic commerce. Others bar repatriation altogether. Developing countries in particular want the money for further growth, and they tend to regard repatriation of rapidly earned profit as a close relative of exploitation. Thus, before Ambux invests anywhere, it must ensure that it can repatriate profits or be prepared to live with any limitations the foreign country might impose.

Fortunately, investing in Uzbekistan is relatively secure. Uzbekistan and the United States have signed a trade treaty guaranteeing unlimited repatriation for American investors. This treaty should suffice. But Ambux might still feel cautious. Uzbekistan is a new nation, and the mechanisms for actually getting the money out of Uzbekistan banks may be slow or faulty. The solution is to get a written agreement from the Minister of Commerce explicitly permitting Ambux to repatriate all profits and providing a clear mechanism to do it through the local banks.

EXPROPRIATION

Nationalize
The government assumes ownership of a business or industry.

Expropriation
The process by which a government takes property owned by foreign investors.

Many nations, both developed and developing, **nationalize** property, meaning that they declare the national government to be the new owner. For example, during the 1940s and 1950s, Great Britain nationalized its coal, steel, and other heavy industries. The state assumed ownership and paid compensation to the previous owners. In the United States, nationalization is rare, but local governments often take land by eminent domain, to be used for roads or other public works. The United States Constitution requires that the owners be fairly compensated.

When a government takes property owned by foreign investors, it is called **expropriation**. Again, this practice is common and legal, provided there is adequate compensation. The U.S. government historically has acknowledged that the expropriation of American interests is legal, provided the host government pays the owners *promptly and fully, in dollars*. But if compensation is inadequate or long delayed, or made in a local currency that is hard to exchange, the taking is **confiscation**.

The courts of almost all nations concede that confiscation is illegal. But it can be difficult or impossible to prevent because courts of the host country may be partial to their own government. And any attempt to obtain compensation in an American court will encounter two separate problems: sovereign immunity and the Act of State doctrine.

Sovereign Immunity

Sovereign immunity holds that the courts of one nation lack the jurisdiction (power) to hear suits against foreign governments. Most nations respect this principle. In the United States, the **Foreign Sovereign Immunities Act (FSIA)** states that American courts generally cannot entertain suits against foreign governments. This is a difficult hurdle for a company to overcome when seeking compensation for foreign expropriation. There are three exceptions.

Waiver. A lawsuit is permitted against a foreign country that waives its immunity, that is, voluntarily gives up this protection. Suppose the Czech government wishes to buy fighter planes from an American manufacturer. The manufacturer might insist on a waiver in the sales contract, and the Czech Republic might be willing to grant one to get the weapons it desires. If the planes land safely but the checks bounce, the manufacturer may sue.

Commercial Activity. A plaintiff in the United States can sue a foreign country engaged in commercial activity, as opposed to political. Suppose the government of Iceland hires an American ecology-consulting firm to help its fishermen replenish depleted fishing grounds. Since fishing is a for-profit activity, the contract is commercial, and if Iceland refuses to pay, the company may sue in American courts.

Violation of International Law. A plaintiff in this country may sue a foreign government that has confiscated property in violation of international law, provided that the property either ends up in the United States or is involved in commercial activity that affects someone in the United States. Suppose a foreign government confiscates a visiting American ship, with no claim of right, and begins to use it for shipping goods for profit. Later, the ship carries some American produce. The taking was illegal, and it now affects American commerce. The original owner may sue.

Investment Insurance

Companies eager to do business abroad but anxious about expropriation should consider publicly funded insurance. In 1971, Congress established the **Overseas Private Investment Corporation (OPIC)** to insure U.S. investors against overseas losses due to political violence and expropriation. OPIC insurance is available to investors at relatively low rates for investment in almost any country. The agency has had remarkable success at no cost to the U.S. government. Every year, OPIC participates in overseas ventures worth many billions of dollars, earning insurance fees that have paid the agency's entire budget and left a substantial surplus.

Should Ambux investigate OPIC insurance before investing in Uzbekistan? Absolutely. While the Uzbekistan government has the best of intentions with respect to foreign investment, the nation is young and the government has no track record. A government can change course as quickly as a gnat, and often with less planning. Why take unnecessary risks?

Confiscation
The process by which a government takes property without fair payment.

Foreign Sovereign Immunities Act (FSIA)
States that American courts generally cannot entertain suits against foreign governments.

FOREIGN CORRUPT PRACTICES ACT

The Foreign Corrupt Practices Act (FCPA)[8] makes it illegal for an American business-person to give "anything of value" to any foreign official in order to influence an official decision. It is sad but true that in many countries bribery is routine and widely accepted. When Congress investigated foreign bribes to see how common they were, more than 450 U.S. companies admitted paying hundreds of millions of dollars in bribes to foreign officials. Legislators concluded that such massive payments distorted competition between American companies for foreign contracts, interfered with the free market system, and undermined confidence everywhere in our way of doing business. The statutory response was simple: foreign bribery is illegal, plain and simple. The FCPA has two principal requirements:

- *Bribes.* The statute makes it illegal for U.S. companies and citizens to bribe foreign officials to influence a governmental decision. The statute prohibits giving anything of value and also bars using third parties as a conduit for such payments.

- *Record Keeping.* All publicly traded companies—whether they engage in international trade or not—must keep detailed records that prevent hiding or disguising bribes. These records must be available for U.S. government officials to inspect.

Not all payments violate the FCPA. A **grease or facilitating payment is legal**, provided the company is paying a foreign official only to expedite performance of a routine function. Grease payments are common in many foreign countries to obtain a permit, process governmental papers, or obtain utility service. For example, the cost of a permit to occupy an office building might be $100, but the government clerk suggests that you will receive the permit faster (within this lifetime) if you pay $150, one-third of which he will pocket. Such small payments are legal. Further, a payment **does not violate the FCPA if it was legal under the written laws** of the country in which it was made. Since few countries establish written codes *permitting* officials to receive bribes, this defense is unlikely to help many Americans who hand out gifts.

The following case is a classic example of bribery. Not much loyalty within Owl Securities. Why is that? What does it teach us?

UNITED STATES V. KING

354 F.3d 859
EIGHTH CIRCUIT COURT OF APPEALS, 2004

CASE SUMMARY

Facts: Owl Securities and Investments, Ltd., hoped to develop a large port in Limon, Costa Rica. The project included docks, housing, recreational facilities, an airport, and more. Richard King was one of Owl's largest investors, and Stephen Kingsley its CEO. The government charged King with attempting to bribe Costa Rican officials to obtain land and other concessions needed for their project. At trial, several of Owl's officers, including Kingsley, Richard Halford, and Albert Reitz, testified

---

[8] 15 U.S.C. §§78 et seq.

against King. A jury convicted King of violating the FCPA. He received a 30-month sentence and a fine of $60,000. He appealed.

Issue: *Was there sufficient evidence that King had violated the FCPA?*

Decision: Yes, there was abundant evidence to support the conviction. Affirmed.

Reasoning: The tape recordings alone prove King's knowledge of the proposed payment. The following exchanges are just a small sample of what the jury heard:

Kingsley: Well you've always known about the closing cost fees and that.

King: I've known what?

Kingsley: You've known about the closing costs.

King: The 1 million dollars?

Kingsley: Yeah.

King: I've known about that for five years, yeah…

[A later tape recording:]

Kingsley: Yeah, what, um, what Pablo had said, was why just pay, pay off the current politicians. Pay off the future ones.

King: That's right. Because we're gonna have to work with them anyway.

Kingsley: And so what he was saying was double, you know, give them more money. Buy the opposition. If you buy the current party and the opposition, then it doesn't matter who's in because there's only two parties.

King: The thing that really worries me is that, uh, if the Justice Department gets a hold of. Finds out how many people we've been paying off down there. Uh, or even if they don't. Are we gonna have to spend the rest of our lives paying off these petty politicians to keep them out of our hair? I can just see us, every, everyday some politician on our doorstep down there wanting a hand out for this or that…. Think we could pay the top people enough, that the rest of the people won't bother us any. That's what I'm hoping this million and a half dollars does. I'm hoping it pays enough top people…

[A later recording:]

Kingsley: Now Pablo's continued to talk to the politicians. They know about the toll, closing costs, call it what you will.

King: Does everybody agree to what we talked about recently?

Kingsley: Yeah, a million into escrow for the toll.

King: And then we get the property and then we do the (unintelligible)?

Kingsley: Um hum. Yeah now let me I'll, I'll, I'll come on to that because I'll explain how we work through that. Uh, essentially once the politicians see the money in escrow, they'll move. That's what it comes down to (clears throat). Pablo's gonna send a list, an e-mail with a list of politicians already paid off and the ones he's gonna pay off.

King: Isn't that awfully dangerous?

Kingsley: No, e-mail's probably the most secure form of communication.

King: From what I read it's not, number one, and number two, there's got to be a better way.

Transparency International, a nonprofit agency based in Germany, publishes a "Corruption Perception Index," gauging how much dishonesty businesspeople and scholars encounter in different nations. In 2004 the agency listed 145 nations on its index. The highest-ranking countries (perceived *least* corrupt) were Finland, New Zealand, Denmark, Iceland, Singapore, Sweden, Switzerland, Norway, Australia, and the United Kingdom. The agency listed the United States as the 17th least corrupt. The countries ranking lowest (perceived *most* corrupt) were Cote d'Ivoire, Georgia, Indonesia, Tajikstan, Turkmenistan, Azerbaijan, Paraguay, Chad, Myanmar, Nigeria, Bangladesh, and Haiti. The full index is available from Transparency International at **http://www.transparency.org**.

But corruption is a two-sided coin. Of the more than 200 nations in the world, very few aggressively prevent their nationals from bribing foreign officials. Further, in some countries, a bribe paid to a foreign official may be treated as a tax deduction!

American executives have long complained that the FCPA puts their companies at a competitive disadvantage, and political leaders have lobbied for an international agreement. Finally, the efforts are reaching fruition. The Organization for Economic Cooperation and Development (OECD) produced a "Convention of Combatting Bribery of Foreign Public Officials in International Business Transactions." About 36 of the world's largest trading nations have ratified the Convention.

The Convention requires signatories to enact criminal penalties for offering or giving bribes to foreign officials. The Convention also compels signatories to enact record-keeping laws that will prevent companies from disguising bribes. The Convention has various weaknesses, and it remains to be seen whether signatories will implement it aggressively, but the agreement is clearly a bold step on an ethical path.

EXAM *Strategy*

Question: Splash is a California corporation that develops resorts. Lawrence, a Splash owner-executive, is hoping to land a $700 million dollar contract with a developing country in Southeast Asia. He seeks your advice. "I own a beach house in Australia, worth about $2 million. If I give it to a certain government official in the Asian country, I know that will close the resort deal. If I don't, someone else will, and my company loses out. Do you think that's wrong? Should I do it?" Please advise him.

Strategy: Lawrence has phrased his question in terms of ethics, which is important. But there is more involved. What law governs his proposed conduct? Is Lawrence legally safe, given that the land is foreign and the contract will be signed overseas?

Result: If Lawrence gives anything of value (such as a house) to secure a government contract, he has violated the FCPA. It makes no difference where the property is located or the deal signed. He could go to jail, and his company could be harshly penalized. Ethically, his gift would exacerbate corruption in a developing nation, and mean that the agreement was determined by a bribe, not the merits of Splash. Other companies might do a superior job employing local workers, constructing an enduring resort and protecting the environment, all for less money.

CHAPTER CONCLUSION

Overseas investment, like sales abroad, offers potentially great rewards but significant pitfalls. A working knowledge of international law is essential to any entrepreneur or executive seriously considering foreign commerce. Issues such as choice of law, currency protection, antitrust statutes, and expropriation can mean the difference between profit and loss. As the WTO lowers barriers, international trade will increase, and your awareness of these principles will grow still more valuable.

EXAM REVIEW

1. **EXPORT RESTRICTIONS** Several statutes restrict exports from the United States that would harm national security, foreign policy, or certain other goals. (p. 195)

2. **TARIFFS** A tariff is a tax imposed on goods entering a country. The Customs Service classifies goods when they enter the United States and imposes appropriate tariffs. (p. 196)

Question: Sports Graphics, Inc. imports "Chill" brand coolers from Taiwan. Chill coolers have an outer shell of vinyl, with handles and pockets, and an inner layer of insulation. In a recent lawsuit, the issue was whether "Chill" coolers were "luggage" or "articles used for preparing, serving or storing food or beverages," as Sports Graphics claimed. Who was the other party to the dispute, why did the two sides care about this, and what arguments did they make?

Strategy: The Customs Service (the other party) classifies goods and then imposes an appropriate *ad valorem* tax. What is at stake, of course, is money. (See the "Result" at the end of this section.)

3. **DUMPED AND SUBSIDIZED IMPORTS** Most countries, including the United States, impose duties for goods that have been dumped (sold at an unfairly low price in the international market) and for subsidized goods (those benefiting from government financial assistance in the country of origin). (p. 198)

4. **GATT** The General Agreement on Tariffs and Trade (GATT) is lowering the average duties worldwide. Proponents see it as a boon to trade; opponents see it as a threat to workers and the environment. (p. 199)

5. **WTO** GATT created the World Trade Organization (WTO), which resolves disputes between signatories to the treaty. (p. 200)

Question: In a recent WTO case, several nations claimed that American laws concerning shrimp fishing were unfair and illegal. The case demonstrated a conflict between two important values. What were the values? In your view, which is more important? Who won and why?

Strategy: Make sure you understand the *Shrimp Products* case in the text. (See the "Result" at the end of this section.)

6. **CISG** A sales agreement between an American company and a foreign company may be governed by the UCC, by the law of the foreign country, or by the United Nations Convention On Contracts For The International Sale Of Goods (CISG). The CISG differs from the UCC in several important respects. (p. 204)

7. **LETTERS OF CREDIT** A confirmed, irrevocable letter of credit is an important means of facilitating international sales contracts, because the seller is assured of payment by a local bank as long as it delivers the specified goods. (p. 206)

EXAM *Strategy*

Question: Flyby Knight (FK) contracts to sell 12 helicopters to Air Nigeria, for $8 million each. Payment is to be made by letter of credit, issued by the Bank of Nigeria, confirmed by Citibank in New York, and due when the confirming bank receives a bill of lading indicating all helicopters are on board ship, ready for sailing to Nigeria. FK loads the aircraft on board ship, and the next day delivers the bill of lading to Citibank. The same day, Air Nigeria informs FK that its inspectors onboard ship have discovered serious flaws in the rotator blades and the fuel lines. Air Nigeria states it will neither accept nor pay for the helicopters. Is FK entitled to its $96 million?

(a) FK is entitled to no money.

(b) FK is entitled to no money *provided* Air Nigeria can prove the helicopters are defective.

(c) Air Nigeria is obligated to pay FK the full price.

(d) Bank of Nigeria is obligated to pay FK the full price.

(e) Citibank is obligated to pay FK the full price.

Strategy: Payment is to be made by confirmed letter of credit. Ask yourself what that means. In such a case, the confirming bank is obligated to pay the seller, when the bank receives a bill of lading indicating that conforming goods have been delivered. What about the fact that the goods seem defective? That is irrelevant. It is precisely to avoid long distance arguments over such problems that sellers insist on these letters. (See the "Result" at the end of this section.)

8. **ANTITRUST LAW** Antitrust laws exist in the United States, the European Union (EU), and other countries. International merchants must be careful not to make agreements that would distort competition. (p. 209)

9. **EXTRATERRITORIALITY** This refers to the power of one nation to impose its laws in other countries. (p. 210)

10. **COMITY** International comity requires a local court to respect the legal system of a foreign country and dismiss a lawsuit if the dispute would more logically be resolved in the other nation. (p. 211)

11. **REPATRIATION** A foreign government may restrict repatriation of profits. (p. 212)

12. **EXPROPRIATION** Expropriation refers to a government taking property owned by foreign investors. U.S. courts regard this as lawful, provided the country pays the American owner promptly and fully, in dollars. (p. 212)

13. **SOVEREIGN IMMUNITY** Sovereign immunity means that, in general, American courts lack jurisdiction to hear suits against foreign governments, unless the foreign nation has waived immunity, is engaging in commercial activity, or has violated international law. (p. 213)

14. **FOREIGN CORRUPT PRACTICES ACT (FCPA)** The FCPA makes it illegal for an American business person to bribe foreign officials. (p. 214)

2. Result: Customs evidently claimed the goods were luggage, with a higher tariff than food storage articles. Customs argued that the handles and portability made the articles luggage. But Sports Graphics prevailed, convincing the court that the primary purpose of the containers was the storage of food. The lawsuit reduced the company's tariff from 20% to 3.4%.

5. Result: Small nations sued, claiming that American regulations made it difficult or impossible for them to fish, devastating their economic growth. The United States argued that vital environmental concerns mandated such rules. The WTO found in favor of the small nations, ruling that before the United States imposed its environmental standards on other countries, it must engage in multinational negotiations, seeking an acceptable compromise. Environmentalists argued that the decision was short-sighted, and contributed to the destruction of an endangered species. Supporters of the decision responded that long-term environmental concerns sound patronizing and hollow to people with empty stomachs.

7. Result: When Citibank receives the bill of lading, indicating delivery of the helicopters, it is obligated to pay. The correct answer is (e).

ADDITIONAL QUESTIONS

1. Arnold Mandel exported certain high-technology electronic equipment. Later, he was in court arguing that the equipment he shipped should not have been on the Department of Commerce's Commodity Control List. What items may be on that list, and why does Mandel care?

2. **ETHICS** Hector works in Zoey's importing firm. Zoey overhears Hector on the phone say, "O.K., 30,000 ski parkas at $80 per parka. You've got yourself a deal. Thanks a lot." When Hector hangs up, Zoey is furious, yelling, "I told you not to make a deal on those Italian ski parkas without my permission! I think I can get a better price elsewhere." "Relax, Zoey," replies Hector. "I wanted to lock them in, to be sure we had some in case your deal fell through. It's just an oral contract, so we can always back out if we need to." Is that ethical? How far can a company go to protect its interests? Does it matter that another business might make serious financial plans based on the discussion? Apart from the ethics, is Hector's idea smart?

3. **YOU BE THE JUDGE** WRITING PROBLEM Continental Illinois National Bank issued an irrevocable letter of credit on behalf of Bill's Coal Co. for $805,000, with the Allied Fidelity Insurance Co. as beneficiary. Bill's Coal Co. then went bankrupt. Allied then presented to Continental documents that were complete and conformed to the letter of credit. Continental refused to pay. Since Bill's Coal was bankrupt, there was no way Continental would collect once it had paid on the letter. Allied filed suit. Who should win? **Argument for Allied Fidelity:** An irrevocable letter of credit serves one purpose: to assure the seller that it will be paid if it performs the contract. Allied has met its obligation. The company furnished documents demonstrating compliance with the agreement. Continental *must* pay. Continental's duty to pay is an independent obligation, unrelated to the status of Bill's Coal. The bank issued this letter knowing the rules of the game and expecting to make a profit. It is time for Continental to honor its word. **Argument for Continental Bank:** In this transaction, the bank was merely a middleman, helping to facilitate payment of a contract. Allied has fulfilled its obligations under the contract, and we understand the company's desire to be paid. Regrettably, Bill's Coal is bankrupt. No one is going to be paid on this deal. Allied should have researched Bill's financial status more thoroughly before entering into the agreement. While we sympathize with Allied's dilemma, it has only itself to blame and cannot expect the bank to act as some sort of insurance company for a deal gone awry.

4. Jean-François, a French wine exporter, sues Bob Joe, a Texas importer, claiming that Bob Joe owes him $2 million for wine. Jean-François takes the witness stand to describe how the contract was created. Where is the trial taking place?

5. The Kyrgyz Republic is one of the new nations that broke away from the old Soviet Union. In September 1994, the government of Kyrgyzstan made two independent announcements: (1) it was abolishing all taxes on repatriation; (2) the government was resigning and would shortly be replaced. Explain the significance of these announcements for an American company considering a major investment in Kyrgyzstan.

6. The Instituto de Auxilios y Viviendas is a government agency of the Dominican Republic. Dr. Marion Fernandez, the general administrator of the Instituto and Secretary of the Republic, sought a loan for the Instituto. She requested that Charles Meadows, an American citizen, secure the Instituto a bank loan of $12 million. If he obtained a loan on favorable terms, he would receive a fee of $240,000. Meadows secured a loan on satisfactory terms, which the Instituto accepted. He then sought his fee, but the Instituto and the Dominican government refused to pay. He sued the government in United States District Court. The Dominican government claimed immunity. Comment.

7. Blondek and Tull were two employees of an American company called Eagle Bus. They hoped that the Saskatchewan provincial government would award Eagle a contract for buses. To bolster their chances, they went to Saskatchewan and paid $50,000 to two government employees. Back in the United States, they were arrested and charged with a crime. Suppose they argue that even if they did something illegal, it occurred in Canada, and that is the only nation that can prosecute them. Comment on the defense.

8. Richard Johnson, an American citizen, was a highly trained electrical engineer who had worked for Hughes Aircraft and Norcroft Corp. He strongly believed in the cause of the Provisional Irish Republican Army (PIRA), which at the time was attacking British civilian and military targets in Northern Ireland and England. Johnson researched and developed explosives to be exported to Ireland and used by the PIRA. Christina Reid,

an electrical engineer, worked with Johnson on IRA projects. She served as a courier of electronic components for remote-control bombs that the two sent to Northern Ireland. What legal problems did they risk by engaging in these transactions?

9. ***ROLE REVERSAL*** Draft an essay or short-answer question that involves a dispute brought to the WTO on one of these issues: dumping, nontariff barriers, or intellectual property.

INTERNET RESEARCH PROBLEM

Read about the worldwide problem of sweatshops. Is this a serious issue? If so, what role should the law play in its resolution? What can one student do about it?

You can find further practice problems at www.cengagebrain.com. See the preface of this book for website access details.

CONTRACTS

CHAPTER 9

INTRODUCTION TO CONTRACTS

In Marina del Rey, California, Cassandra sits on the sunny deck of her waterside condominium, sipping a mocha latte while watching spinnakers fill with the warm Pacific wind. She has just received an offer of $1.7 million to buy her condominium. Cassandra has decided to counteroffer for $1.9 million. She is in high spirits because she assumes that at the very worst she has $1.7 million guaranteed, and that represents a huge profit to her. Cassandra plans to buy a cheaper house in North Carolina and invest her profits so that she can retire early. She opens the newspaper, notices a headline "Hard Body Threatens Suit," and turns the page, thinking that a corporate lawsuit in Ohio is of no concern to her. She is mistaken and may learn some hard lessons about contract law.

> **She opens the newspaper, notices a headline "Hard Body Threatens Suit," and turns the page…**

A year earlier, Jerusalem Steel had signed a contract with Hard Body, a manufacturer of truck and bus bodies. Jerusalem was to deliver 20,000 tons of steel to Hard Body's plant in Joy, Ohio. Hard Body relied on the contract, hiring 300 additional workers even before the steel was delivered, so that the plant would be geared up and ready to produce buses when the metal arrived. To help deal with the new workers, Hard Body offered a mid-level personnel job to Nicole. Hard Body told Nicole, "Don't worry, we expect your job to last forever." Nicole, in turn, relied on that statement to quit her old job in Minneapolis, move to Joy, and sign an agreement with Jasper to purchase his house for $450,000. Based on that sales contract, Jasper phoned his offer to Cassandra's real estate agent for $1.7 million. See Exhibit 9.1.

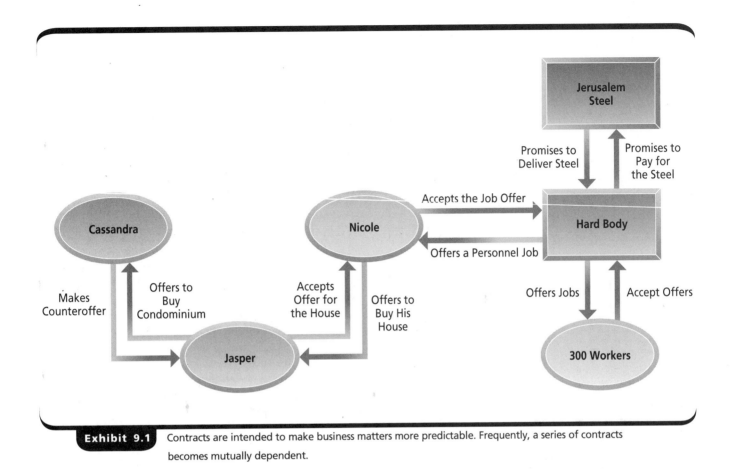

Exhibit 9.1   Contracts are intended to make business matters more predictable. Frequently, a series of contracts becomes mutually dependent.

But in the year since Jerusalem signed its contract, the price of the specified steel has gone up 60%. Jerusalem now refuses to deliver the steel unless the price is renegotiated. Hard Body has insisted on the original contract price. Hard Body cannot afford to buy steel at the current price, which would make its deal to produce buses unprofitable. If Hard Body receives no steel, does it have a valid lawsuit against Jerusalem? May the company force Jerusalem to deliver the steel? If it cannot get steel, may Hard Body lay off the newly hired workers? May the company fire Nicole, or does she have a job for life? If Nicole loses her paycheck, will the law force her to buy a house she no longer wants? Jasper will never get such a good price from anyone else because with no work at Hard Body, property prices in Joy will plummet. May Jasper refuse to buy Cassandra's condo, or is he committed for $1.7 million?

CONTRACTS

THE PURPOSE OF A CONTRACT

Throughout this unit on contracts, we will consider issues like those raised in the Cassandra–Hard Body story. This long chain of mutually dependent people and companies exemplifies not only the law of contracts but the *purpose* of contracts. Parties enter into contracts attempting to control their future. **Contracts exist to make business matters more predictable.** Most contracts work out precisely as the parties intended because the parties fulfill their obligations. Most—but not all. In this unit, we will study contracts that have gone wrong. We look at these errant deals to learn how to avoid the problems they manifest.

JUDICIAL ACTIVISM VERSUS JUDICIAL RESTRAINT

Judicial restraint

A court's reluctance to interfere with the terms of a contract.

We will see that courts *generally but not always do what we expect.* In most contract cases, judges do their best simply to enforce whatever terms the parties have agreed to. Even if the contract results in serious harm to one party, a court will typically enforce it. This is **judicial restraint**—a court taking a passive role and requiring the parties to fulfill whatever obligations they agreed to, whether the deal was wise or foolish. Judges often say that it is not their job to rewrite a deal that the parties crafted. For example, if a real estate developer contracts with a builder to erect 10 expensive homes, but the housing market collapses before construction begins, the developer is still obligated to pay the builder for the houses, even though the expense will cause him devastating losses. Judicial restraint makes the law **less flexible but more predictable.**

Judicial activism

A court's willingness to change or ignore a contract that it perceives as unjust.

On the other hand, courts sometimes practice **judicial activism**. In contract law, this means that a court will ignore certain provisions of a contract, or an entire agreement, if the judge believes that enforcing the deal would be unjust. Further, a court may be willing to artificially create a contract where none existed, if the judge believes that is the only way to avoid injustice. Since judicial activism is always phrased in terms of "doing justice," it has an initial appeal. For example, when one party deceives the other with a misleading contract, it may be appropriate for a court to rewrite the agreement. But when a court practices judicial activism, it may diminish our ability to control our own future—which is the whole point of creating a contract. Judicial activism makes the law **more flexible but less predictable.** In this unit on contracts, we look at many examples of both judicial activism and restraint.

ISSUES (AND ANSWERS)

The chain of contracts connecting Jerusalem Steel and Cassandra illustrates various contract problems. We consider each problem in detail in this unit, but here we briefly identify the issues and summarize the answers. A contract has four elements:

- *Agreement.* One party must make a valid offer, and the other party must accept it.

- *Consideration.* There has to be bargaining that leads to an *exchange* between the parties.

- *Legality.* The contract must be for a lawful purpose.

- *Capacity.* The parties must be adults of sound mind.

The chapters that follow cover each of the elements in sequence. Contract cases often raise several other important issues, which we examine in later chapters:

- *Consent.* Neither party may trick or force the other into the agreement.

- *Written Contracts.* Some contracts must be in writing to be enforceable.

- ***Third Party Interests.*** Some contracts affect people other than the parties themselves.

- ***Performance and Discharge.*** If a party fully accomplishes what the contract requires, his duties are discharged.

- ***Remedies.*** A court will award money or other relief to a party injured by a breach of contract.

When we apply these principles to the problem at this chapter's beginning, we see that Jerusalem Steel is almost certainly bound by its agreement. A rise in price is generally no excuse to walk away from a contract. Hard Body has made the bargain precisely to protect itself in case of a price rise. These are issues of offer and acceptance, consideration, and discharge. Can Hard Body force Jerusalem to deliver the steel? Probably not, as we learn in Chapter 17, on remedies. But Hard Body might be able to block Jerusalem from delivering the steel anywhere else. And Hard Body almost certainly is entitled to money damages if it is forced to buy steel at higher prices. If Hard Body is unable to obtain steel in the rising market, may it lay off its workers? Very likely, as Chapter 10, on agreement, indicates. Can it fire Nicole? The statement about expecting her job to last forever almost certainly creates no lifetime employment. In fact, even if Nicole has begun her job, the company can probably terminate her. What about the fact that she quit her job in reliance on this one? That raises an issue called *promissory estoppel,* which we discuss later in this chapter; it may or may not help Nicole, depending on the facts.

Must Nicole go through with her purchase of Jasper's house? Probably, as Chapters 14 and 17, on written contracts and remedies, will demonstrate. Do Jasper and Cassandra have a contract? No, because the agreement must be in writing to be enforceable. Even if there is no settled price, is Cassandra safe in assuming she has $1.7 million guaranteed? Not at all, as Chapter 10, on agreement, shows. If Cassandra had read this unit, she would be faxing a written contract to Jasper rather than waiting for her latte to cool.

All Shapes and Sizes

Some contracts are small. If you agree to sell your bicycle to your roommate for $75 at the end of the academic year, that is an enforceable agreement. But contracts can also be large. Lockheed Martin and Boeing spent years of work and millions of dollars competing for a Defense Department aircraft contract. Why the fierce effort? The deal was potentially good for 25 years and *$200 billion.* Lockheed won. The company earned the right to build the next generation of fighter jets—3,000 planes, with different varieties of the aircraft to be used by each of the American defense services and some allied forces as well. (Boeing promptly set to work designing and building unpiloted aircraft, which it believes will soar to the cutting edge of flight.)

At other times we may be stunned to learn that a contract we are relying on does not exist. Jerome Howard was the agent for hip-hop artist Domino. Howard was delighted that his contract gave him a long-term relationship with an artist whose most recent album sold at "platinum" levels. But Domino was unhappy with the arrangement and walked away from it—legally. Howard was not licensed by the state of California to work as a music agent. His contract with Domino was void.

Societal interests can shape contract law. For example, federal law requires that landowners clean up toxic waste on their property, a process that can cost millions of dollars. Suppose Klene Corp. wants to sell land that might have toxic chemicals underground. May Klene include a provision in its sales contract shifting the cost of any cleanup to the buyer? No, and yes. Regardless of what the contract says, federal statutes prohibit Klene from abandoning its own responsibility to clean up the waste. Yet the contract could make the buyer equally liable.

In turn, contract law can shape society. For example, some states cap the interest rate that a mortgage company may charge. Because of the cap, mortgage companies may not find it profitable to lend money to the most credit-risky customers, meaning that those people will be unable to borrow money. Other states place no cap at all on mortgage rates. This enables low-income borrowers to obtain funds. But it also means they pay astronomical interest rates, sometimes over 50 percent. The result? Many end up losing their homes. This is a typical problem at the intersection of public policy and contract law.

Many contracts involve public issues. The Lockheed agreement concerns government agencies deciding how to spend taxpayer money for national defense. Other contracts concern intensely private matters. Mary Beth Whitehead signed a contract with William and Elizabeth Stern, of New Jersey. For a fee of $10,000, Whitehead agreed to be impregnated with Mr. Stern's sperm, carry the baby to term, and then deliver it to the Sterns for adoption. But when little Melissa was born, Whitehead changed her mind and fled to Florida with the baby. The Sterns sued for breach of contract. Surrogacy contracts now lead to over 500 births per year. Are the contracts immoral? Should they be illegal? Are there limits to what one person may pay another to do? The New Jersey Supreme Court, the first to rule on the issue, declared the contract illegal and void. The court nonetheless awarded Melissa to the Sterns, saying that it was in the child's best interest to live with them. Inevitably, legislators disagree about this emotional issue. Some states have passed statutes permitting surrogacy. Others prohibit the enforcement of some or all surrogacy contracts. A few states have gone further, making paid surrogacy a crime. As usual, the law will develop more slowly than technology. At times we enter contracts without knowing it. Suppose you try to book a flight using your frequent flyer miles, but the airline tells you the terms of the frequent flyer program have changed and you must earn more mileage. According to the Supreme Court, you may well have an enforceable agreement based on the terms the airline quoted when you earned the miles.[1]

CONTRACTS DEFINED

Contract law is a study in promises. Is Nicole entitled to a lifetime job at Hard Body? Is Jasper obligated to buy Cassandra's condominium? Contract law determines which promises to enforce. **A contract is a promise that the law will enforce.**

As we look more closely at the elements of contract law, we will encounter some intricate issues. This is partly because we live in a complex society, which conducts its business in an infinite variety of ways. It is also due to the constant tug between predictability and fairness, described above. Remember, though, that we are usually interested in answering three basic questions of common sense, all relating to promises:

- Is it certain that the defendant promised to do something?

- If she did promise, is it fair to make her honor her word?

- If she did not promise, are there unusual reasons to hold her liable anyway?

DEVELOPMENT OF CONTRACT LAW

Courts have not always assumed that promises are legally significant. As English judges were developing the common law in the twelfth and thirteenth centuries, they seldom used the term "contract," focusing instead on other issues in the case. Suppose a farmer and a horse dealer orally

[1] *American Airlines, Inc. v. Wolens*, 513 U.S. 219, 115 S.Ct. 817, 1995 U.S. LEXIS 690 (1995).

agreed that the dealer would deliver two draught horses to the farmer by April 1, and the farmer agreed to pay £100 for each. If the horse dealer never made any effort to fulfill his promise, the farmer could *not* sue. Even if he lost a year's crop because of the dealer's incompetence, he recovered nothing. The dealer's promise was never binding unless he made it *in writing and affixed a seal* to the document. This was seldom done, and therefore most promises were unenforceable.

The common law changed very slowly, but by the fifteenth century courts began to allow some suits based on a broken promise. There were still major limitations. Suppose a merchant hired a carpenter to build a new shop, and the carpenter failed to start the job on time. Now courts would permit the suit but only if the merchant had paid some money to the carpenter. If the merchant made a 10% down payment, the contract would be enforceable. But if the merchant merely *promised* to pay when the building was done, and the carpenter never began work, the merchant could recover nothing.

In 1602, English courts began to enforce *mutual promises*, that is, deals in which neither party gave anything to the other but both promised to do something in the future. Thus, if a farmer promised to deliver a certain quantity of wheat to a merchant and the merchant agreed on the price, both parties were now bound by their promise, even though there had been no down payment. This was a huge step forward in the development of contract law, but many issues remained. Consider the following employment case from 1792, which raises issues of public policy that still challenge courts today.

DAVIS V. MASON

COURT OF KING'S BENCH
MICHAELMAS TERM, 33d GEORGE III, P. 118 (1792)

CASE SUMMARY

Facts: Mason was a surgeon/apothecary in the English town of Thetford. Davis wished to apprentice himself to Mason. The two agreed that Davis would work for Mason and learn his profession. They further agreed that if Davis left Mason's practice, he would not set up a competing establishment within 10 miles of Thetford at any time within 14 years. Davis promised to pay £200 if he violated the agreement not to compete.

Davis began working for Mason in July 1789. In August 1791, Mason dismissed Davis, claiming misconduct, though Davis denied it. Davis then established his own practice within 10 miles of Thetford. Mason sued for the £200.

Davis admitted promising to pay the money. But he claimed that the agreement should be declared illegal and unenforceable. He argued that 14 years was unreasonably long to restrict him from the town of Thetford, and that 10 miles was too great a distance. (Ten miles in those days might take the better part of a day to travel.) He added an additional policy argument, saying that it was harmful to the public

health to restrict a doctor from practicing his profession: if the people needed his service, they should have it. Finally, he said that his "consideration" was too great for this deal. In other words, it was unfair that he should pay £200, because he did not receive anything of that value from Mason.

Issue: *Was the contract too unreasonable to enforce?*

Decision: No. The parties made a reasonable agreement. Judgment for the plaintiff.

Reasoning: Both Mason and Davis made promises, and each expected to benefit from the agreement. Davis stood to learn a trade, and Mason secured protection from competition in the future. Davis alleges that the contract was unreasonable, but how long is too long? How far is too far? This line is difficult to draw, and I will not even try. The people of Thetford will suffer no harm because other doctors have the right to practice medicine there without restriction.

Davis must pay the £200.

Noncompetition agreement

A contract in which one party agrees not to compete with another.

The contract between Davis and Mason is called a **noncompetition agreement.** Today they are more common than ever, and frequently litigated. The policy issues that Davis raised have never gone away. Two hundred years later, a group of stockbrokers brought a class action suit, alleging that their employer had forced them to pay an excessive fee for taking their skills elsewhere.

You may well be asked to sign a noncompetition agreement sometime in your business or professional life. We look at the issue in detail in Chapter 11, on consideration. But note that in 1792 the court did in fact enforce the contract. In other words, the mutual promises seemed reasonable, and the court ordered the parties to live up to the deal.

That outcome was typical of contract cases for the next 100 years. Contracts were generally bargained between business people of roughly equal knowledge and power, and the law expected them to know what they were doing. Courts took a *laissez-faire* approach, declaring that parties had *freedom to contract* and would have to live with the consequences. Lord Kenyon saw Davis and Mason as equals, entering a bargain that made basic sense, and he had no intention of rewriting it. After 500 years of evolution, courts had come to regard promises as almost sacred. The law had gone from ignoring most promises to enforcing nearly all.

By the early twentieth century, bargaining power in business deals had changed dramatically. Farms and small businesses were yielding place to huge corporations in a trend that accelerated throughout the century. In the twenty-first century, multinational corporations span many continents, wielding larger budgets and more power than many of the nations in which they do business. When such a corporation contracts with a small company or an individual consumer, the latter may have little or no leverage. Courts increasingly looked at the basic fairness of contracts. In other words, they were more willing to play an *activist* role.

Noncompetition agreements are no longer automatically enforced. Courts may alter them or ignore them entirely because the parties have such unequal power and because the public may have an interest in letting the employee go on to compete. Davis's argument—that the public is entitled to as many doctors as it needs—is frequently more successful in court today than it was before Lord Kenyon.

It is not only the unequal bargaining power that causes courts to look closely at contracts. The issue of toxic waste illustrates how the public interest may be "read into" a contract. Environmental statutes assume that the public interest requires holding all owners of property liable to clean up toxic waste. So even when the seller of polluted land writes a contract placing cleanup responsibility on the buyer, the courts will simply ignore the provision, holding that the seller remains liable. This is socially sensible, because it ensures that our world will be cleaned up, but it diminishes a party's ability to control its future.

Legislatures and the courts limit the effect of promises in other ways. Suppose you purchase a lawn mower with an attached tag, warning you that the manufacturer is not responsible in the event of any malfunction or injury. You are required to sign a form acknowledging that the manufacturer has no liability of any kind. That agreement is clear enough—but a court will not enforce it. The law holds that the manufacturer *has* warranted the product to be good for normal purposes, regardless of any language included in the sales agreement. If the blade flies off and injures a child, the manufacturer is liable. This is socially responsible, but again, it interferes with a private agreement.

The law has not come full circle back to the early days of the common law. Courts still enforce the great majority of contracts. But the possibility that a court will ignore an agreement means that any contract is a little less certain than it would have been a century ago. That is all the more reason to understand contract principles and avoid agreements that fall afoul of the law.

TYPES OF CONTRACTS

BILATERAL AND UNILATERAL CONTRACTS

In a **bilateral contract**, both parties make a promise. A producer says to Gloria, "I'll pay you $2 million to star in my new romantic comedy, *A Promise for a Promise*, which we are shooting three months from now in Santa Fe." Gloria says, "It's a deal." That is a bilateral contract. Each party has made a promise to do something. The producer is now bound to pay Gloria $2 million, and Gloria is obligated to show up on time and act in the movie. The vast majority of contracts are bilateral contracts. They can be for services, such as this acting contract; they can be for the sale of goods, such as 1,000 tons of steel, or for almost any other purpose. When the bargain is a promise for a promise, it is a bilateral agreement.

In a unilateral contract, one party makes a promise that the other party can accept only by doing something. These contracts are less common. Suppose the movie producer says to Leo, "I'll give you a hundred bucks if you mow my lawn this weekend." Leo is not promising to do it. If he mows the lawn, he has accepted the offer and is entitled to his hundred dollars. If he spends the weekend at the beach, neither he nor the producer owes anything.

Bilateral contract
A promise made in exchange for another promise.

EXPRESS AND IMPLIED CONTRACTS

In an **express contract**, the two parties explicitly state all important terms of their agreement. The vast majority of contracts are express contracts. The contract between the producer and Gloria is an express contract, because the parties explicitly state what Gloria will do, where and when she will do it, and how much she will be paid. Some express contracts are oral, as that one was, and some are written. They might be bilateral express contracts, as Gloria's was, or unilateral express contracts, as Leo's was. Obviously, it is good business sense always to make express contracts, and wise to put them in writing. We emphasize, however, that many oral contracts are fully enforceable.

In an implied contract, the words and conduct of the parties indicate that they intended an agreement. Suppose every Friday, for two months, the producer asks Leo to mow his lawn, and loyal Leo does so each weekend. Then for three more weekends, Leo simply shows up without the producer asking, and the producer continues to pay for the work done. But on the 12th weekend, when Leo rings the doorbell to collect, the producer suddenly says, "I never asked you to mow it. Scram." The producer is correct that there was no express contract, because the parties had not spoken for several weeks. But a court will probably rule that the conduct of the parties has *implied* a contract. Not only did Leo mow the lawn every weekend, but the producer even paid on three weekends when they had not spoken. It was reasonable for Leo to assume that he had a weekly deal to mow and be paid. Naturally, there is no implied contract thereafter.

Today, the hottest disputes about implied contracts continue to arise in the employment setting. Many corporate employees have at-will contracts with their companies. This means that the employees are free to quit at any time and the company has the right to fire them at any time, for virtually any reason. Courts routinely enforce at-will contracts. But often a company provides its workers with personnel manuals that guarantee certain rights. The legal issue is whether the handbook implies a contract guaranteeing the specified rights. What is your opinion?

Express contract
An agreement with all important terms explicitly stated.

Implied Contract
· A contract that arises from the parties' conduct and/or assumed intentions

YOU *be the* JUDGE

DEMASSE V. ITT CORPORATION
194 ARIZ. 500, 984 P.2d 1138
Supreme Court of Arizona, 1999

Facts: Roger DeMasse and five others were employees-at-will at ITT Corporation, where they started working at various times between 1960 and 1979. Each was paid an hourly wage.

ITT issued an employee handbook, which it revised four times over two decades.

The first four editions of the handbook stated that within each job classification, any layoffs would be made in reverse order of seniority. The fifth handbook made two important changes. First, the document stated that "nothing contained herein shall be construed as a guarantee of continued employment. ITT does not guarantee continued employment to employees and retains the right to terminate or layoff employees."

Second, the handbook stated that "ITT reserves the right to amend, modify or cancel this handbook, as well as any or all of the various policies [or rules] outlined in it." Four years later, ITT notified its hourly employees that layoff guidelines for hourly employees would be based not on seniority but on ability and performance. About ten days later, the six employees were laid off, though less senior employees kept their jobs. The six employees sued.

You Be the Judge: Did ITT have the right to unilaterally change the layoff policy?

Argument for the workers: It is true that all of the plaintiffs were originally employees-at-will, subject to termination at the company's whim. However, things changed when the company issued the first handbook. ITT chose to include a promise that layoffs would be based on seniority. Long-term workers and new employees all understood the promise and relied on it. The company put it there to attract and retain good workers. The policy worked. Responsible employees understood that the longer they remained at ITT, the safer their job was. Company and employees worked together for

many years with a common understanding, and that is a textbook definition of an implied contract.

Once a contract is formed, whether express or implied, it is binding on both sides. That is the whole point of a contract. If one side could simply change the terms of an agreement on its own, what value would any contract have? The company's legal argument is a perfect symbol of its arrogance: It believes that because these workers are mere hourly workers, they have no rights, even under contract law. The company is mistaken. Implied contracts are binding, and ITT should not make promises it does not intend to keep.

Argument for ITT: Once an at-will employee, always one. ITT had the right to fire any of its employees at any time—just as the workers had the right to quit whenever they wished. That never changed, and in case any workers forgot it, the company reiterated the point in its most recent handbook. If the plaintiffs thought layoffs would happen in any particular order, that is their error, not ours.

All workers were bound by the terms of whichever handbook was then in place. For many years, the company had made a seniority-layoff promise. Had we fired a senior worker during that period, he or she would have had a legitimate complaint—and that is why we did not do it. Instead, we gave everyone four years' notice that things would change. Any workers unhappy with the new policies should have left to find more congenial work.

Why should an employee be allowed to say, "I prefer to rely on the old, outdated handbooks, not the new one"? The plaintiffs' position would mean that no company is ever free to change its general work policies and rules. Since when does an at-will employee have the right to dictate company policy? That would be disastrous for the whole economy—but fortunately it is not the law.

ETHICS   Other than the workers and the company, who are the stakeholders? What *alternatives* were available to DeMasse? What are the most important *values* involved in this dispute? If there are conflicting values, which are most important? ◆

EXECUTORY AND EXECUTED CONTRACTS

A contract is **executory** when one or more parties has not fulfilled its obligations. Recall Gloria, who agrees to act in the producer's film beginning in three months. The moment Gloria and the producer strike their bargain, they have an executory bilateral express contract.

A contract is **executed** when all parties have fulfilled their obligations. When Gloria finishes acting in the movie and the producer pays her final fee, their contract will be fully executed.

Executory contract
An agreement in which one or more parties has not yet fulfilled its obligations.

Executed contract
An agreement in which all parties have fulfilled their obligations.

EXAM *Strategy*

Question: Abby has long coveted Nicola's designer handbag, because she saw one of them in *Brainless, the Movie*. Finally, Nicola offers to sell her friend the bag for $350 in cash. "I don't have the money right now," Abby replies, "but I'll have it a week from Friday. Is it a deal?" Nicola agrees to sell the bag on that day. Use three terms to describe the contract.

Strategy: An express contract is one whose terms are explicitly stated. If that has not happened there may still be an implied agreement. In a bilateral contract, both parties make a promise, but in a unilateral agreement, only one side does so. Finally, an executory contract is one with unfulfilled obligations, while an executed agreement is one with nothing left to be done.

Result: Nicola promised to sell the bag for $350 cash, and Abby agreed to pay. The terms were explicit and complete, so this is an express contract. Because both parties made a promise, this a bilateral agreement. The deal is not yet completed, meaning that they have an executory contract.

VALID, UNENFORCEABLE, VOIDABLE, AND VOID AGREEMENTS

A **valid contract** is one that satisfies all of the law's requirements. A court will enforce it. The contract between Gloria and the producer is a valid contract, and if the producer fails to pay Gloria, she will win a lawsuit to collect the unpaid fee.

An **unenforceable agreement** occurs when the parties intend to form a valid bargain but a court declares that some rule of law prevents enforcing it. Suppose Gloria and the producer orally agree that she will star in his movie, which he will start filming in 18 months. The statute of frauds requires that this contract be in writing, because it cannot be completed within one year. If the producer signs up another actress two months later, Gloria has no claim against him.

A **voidable contract** occurs when the law permits one party to terminate the agreement. This happens, for example, when the other party has committed fraud or misrepresentation. Suppose that Klene Corp. induces Smart to purchase 1,000 acres of land by telling Smart that there is no underground toxic waste, even though Klene knows that just under the topsoil lies an ocean of bubbling purple sludge. Klene is committing fraud. Smart may void the contract, that is, terminate it and owe nothing. If, for some reason, Smart still considers the land a bargain, he may go through with the sale. Klene has no power to void the contract.

A **void agreement** is one that neither party can enforce, usually because the purpose of the deal is illegal or because one of the parties had no legal authority to make a contract. When Jerome Howard agreed to represent the rapper Domino, the agreement was void from the start because Howard was not a licensed agent. He had no legal right to obtain employment for entertainers and therefore no lawful ability to sign a contract saying he would.

Voidable contract
An agreement that may be terminated by one of the parties.

Void agreement
A contract that neither party can enforce, because the bargain is illegal or one of the parties had no legal authority to make it.

REMEDIES CREATED BY JUDICIAL ACTIVISM

Now we turn away from true contracts and consider two remedies created by judicial activism: promissory estoppel and quasi-contract. We emphasize that these remedies are exceptions. Most of the agreements that courts enforce are the express contracts that we have already studied. Nonetheless, the next two remedies are still pivotal in some lawsuits. In each case, a sympathetic plaintiff can demonstrate an injury. The harm has occurred in a setting where a contract might well have been made. But the crux of the matter is this: *there is no contract.* The plaintiff cannot claim that the defendant breached the contract, because none ever existed. The plaintiff must hope for more "creative" relief.

The two remedies can be confusingly similar. The best way to distinguish them is this:

- In promissory estoppel cases, the defendant made a promise that the plaintiff relied on.

- In quasi-contract cases, the defendant did not make any promise, but did receive a *benefit* from the plaintiff.

PROMISSORY ESTOPPEL

A fierce fire swept through Dana and Derek Andreason's house in Utah, seriously damaging it. The good news was that agents for Aetna Casualty promptly visited the Andreasons and helped them through the crisis. The agents reassured the couple that all of the damage was covered by their insurance, instructed them on which things to throw out and replace, and helped them choose materials for repairing other items. The bad news was that the agents were wrong: the Andreasons' policy had expired six weeks before the fire. When Derek Andreason presented a bill for $41,957 worth of meticulously itemized work that he had done under the agents' supervision, Aetna refused to pay.

The Andreasons sued—but not for breach of contract. There *was* no contract, that was exactly the problem. The insurance contract had expired. So they sued Aetna under the legal theory of promissory estoppel: Even when there is no contract, a plaintiff may use **promissory estoppel** to enforce the defendant's promise if he can show that:

- The defendant made a promise knowing that the plaintiff would likely rely on it;

- The plaintiff did rely on the promise; and

- The only way to avoid injustice is to enforce the promise.

Promissory estoppel

A *possible* remedy for an injured plaintiff in a case with no valid contract, where the plaintiff can show a promise, reasonable reliance, and injustice.

Is enforcing the promise the only way to avoid injustice?

Aetna made a promise to the Andreasons, namely, its assurance that all of the damage was covered by insurance. The company knew that the Andreasons would rely on that promise, which they did by ripping up a floor that might have been salvaged, throwing out some furniture, and buying materials to repair the house. Is enforcing the promise the only way to avoid injustice? Yes, ruled the Utah Court of Appeals.[2] The Andreasons' conduct was reasonable and based entirely on what the Aetna agents told them. Under promissory estoppel, the Andreasons received virtually the same amount they would have obtained had the insurance contract been valid.

---

[2] *Andreason v. Aetna Casualty & Surety Co.*, 848 P.2d 171, 1993 Utah App. LEXIS 26 (Utah App. 1993).

Promissory estoppel is an important development of twentieth-century law. The doctrine provides opportunities for a court to do justice where no contract exists. Clearly, this is judicial activism, helping people by crafting new remedies. But, as is true whenever the rules are "bent," it means that the outcome of a particular case is less predictable.

There was plenty of romance in the following case. Was there an enforceable promise?

NORTON V. HOYT

278 F.Supp.2d 214
UNITED STATES DISTRICT COURT FOR THE DISTRICT OF RHODE ISLAND, 2003

CASE SUMMARY

Facts: Gail Norton sued Russell Hoyt, and this is what she alleged. The two met when Norton, who was single, worked as an elementary school teacher. Hoyt told her he was also single, and they began an affair. She later learned that he was married, but he assured her he was getting a divorce, and they continued their relationship.

Six years later, Hoyt, who was rich, convinced Norton to quit her job so that they could travel together. The couple lived lavishly, spending time in Newport, Rhode Island, where Hoyt was part of the yachting crowd, in London, the Bahamas, and other agreeable places. Hoyt rented Norton an apartment, bought her cars, and repeated his promises to divorce his wife and marry his lover. He never did either.

After 23 years, Hoyt ended the relationship. Norton became ill and saw various doctors for anxiety, depression, headaches, stomach maladies, and weight loss. During one joint therapy session, Hoyt told Norton and the psychiatrist that he would continue to support her with $80,000 a year. But he did not.

Norton sued, claiming promissory estoppel. Hoyt moved for summary judgment. In ruling on the motion, the court assumed that Norton's allegations were true.

Issue: *Was Norton entitled to support, based on promissory estoppel?*

Decision: No. Norton failed to establish promissory estoppel.

Reasoning: Norton did not establish a clear, unambiguous promise. She claimed that Hoyt promised to take care of her for life. But what does "take care of for life" mean? It could refer to emotional closeness, social pleasures, or financial support.

Even assuming, for the sake of argument, that there was a clear, unconditional promise, Norton's reliance was unreasonable. It is true that the couple discussed wedding plans, but Norton knew that Hoyt was married and that he spent time with his wife and children. She and Hoyt never presented themselves as husband and wife. Friends and family knew of their complicated living arrangement. Further, Norton knew that Hoyt had lied to her about his marital status, had never fulfilled his promise of marriage, and was committing adultery by spending time with her. At some point between year 1 of their affair and year 23, she should have grasped that reliance on Hoyt's promises was badly misplaced. Her conduct was unreasonable, and she cannot establish promissory estoppel.

Hoyt's motion for summary judgment is granted.

DEVIL'S ADVOCATE Why should one person be able to make repeated promises over two decades and escape all responsibility? Even if Hoyt's precise words varied, each of his promises involved long-term emotional and financial security for Norton. Norton was naïve, but Hoyt was dishonest. The law should be a tool for teaching people like him a lesson. ◆

Why have we chosen to illustrate an important point of law—promissory estoppel—with a case that fails? Because that is the typical outcome. Plaintiffs allege promissory estoppel very frequently, but seldom succeed. They do occasionally win, as the Andreasons demonstrated earlier, but courts are skeptical of these claims. The lesson is clear: Before you rely on a promise, negotiate a binding contract.

QUASI-CONTRACT

Don Easterwood leased over 5,000 acres of farmland in Jackson County, Texas, from PIC Realty for one year. The next year he obtained a second one-year lease. During each year, Easterwood farmed the land, harvested the crops, and prepared the land for the following year's planting. Toward the end of the second lease, after Easterwood had harvested his crop, he and PIC began discussing the terms of another lease. While they negotiated, Easterwood prepared the land for the following year, cutting, plowing, and disking the soil. But the negotiations for a new lease failed, and Easterwood moved off the land. He sued PIC Realty for the value of his work preparing the soil.

Easterwood had neither an express nor an implied contract for the value of his work. How could he make any legal claim? By relying on the legal theory of a quasi-contract: Even when there is no contract, a court may use **quasi-contract** to compensate a plaintiff who can show that:

- The plaintiff gave some benefit to the defendant;

- The plaintiff reasonably expected to be paid for the benefit and the defendant knew this; and

- The defendant would be unjustly enriched if he did not pay.

If a court finds all of these elements present, it will generally award the value of the goods or services that the plaintiff has conferred. The damages awarded are called **quantum meruit**, meaning that the plaintiff gets "as much as he deserves." The court is awarding money that it believes the plaintiff *morally ought to have*, even though there was no valid contract entitling her to it. This again is judicial activism, with the courts inventing a "quasi" contract where no true contract exists. The purpose is justice, the term is contradictory.

Don Easterwood testified that in Jackson County, it was quite common for a tenant farmer to prepare the soil for the following year but then be unable to farm the land. In those cases, he claimed, the landowner compensated the farmer for the work done. Other witnesses agreed that this was the local custom. The court ruled that indeed there was no contract, but that all elements of quasi-contract had been satisfied. Easterwood gave a benefit to PIC because the land was ready for planting. Jackson County custom caused Easterwood to assume he would be paid, and PIC Realty knew it. Finally, said the court, it would be unjust to let PIC benefit without paying anything. The court ordered PIC to pay the fair market value of Easterwood's labors.

Almost all courts would agree with the result in the Easterwood case. But, once again, if a court "invents" a contract where none existed, it may have opened the door to an infinite variety of claims. When is the enrichment "unjust"? When would a defendant "reasonably know that the plaintiff expects compensation"? In the following case, the defendant knew nothing at all about what doctors did for him—how could he?

Quasi-contract

A *possible* remedy for an injured plaintiff in a case with no valid contract, where the plaintiff can show benefit to the defendant, reasonable expectation of payment, and unjust enrichment.

Quantum meruit

"As much as he deserves"—the damages awarded in a quasi-contract case.

NOVAK V. CREDIT BUREAU COLLECTION SERVICE

877 N.E.2d 1253
IND.APP., 2007.

CASE SUMMARY

Facts: David Novak was unconscious. He suffered a brain aneurysm, a weakness in the brain's blood vessels that can be life-threatening. An ambulance took him to Saint Regional Medical Center, where doctors operated successfully. He remained in the hospital for two months and was discharged, able to go about life's normal activities.

Novak did not pay the Medical Center's bill. The hospital assigned its claim to a credit bureau, meaning that the credit bureau acquired the right to sue Novak for the full debt—which it promptly did.

The trial court found that because Novak had been unconscious, he could not give consent to the treatment. The medical services had been necessary to avoid serious injury or death. When Novak recovered, he remained in the hospital and participated in his own recovery without objecting to the services he received. Based on all of that, the trial court gave judgment to the credit bureau on a theory of quasi-contract. Novak appealed.

Issue: *Was the credit bureau entitled to damages based on quasi-contract?*

Decision: Yes, the bureau was entitled to damages based on quasi-contract. Affirmed.

Reasoning: Novak argues that the credit bureau is entitled to nothing because he never expressly or impliedly requested medical services. However, the real issue in a case of quasi-contract is whether the plaintiff supplied a benefit under circumstances in which compensation is essential to avoid unjust enrichment.

A plaintiff who has supplied services to the defendant, although acting without the defendant's consent, is entitled to restitution if he expected to charge for his work, the services were necessary to prevent serious bodily harm, and it was impossible for the defendant to give consent.

The hospital saved Novak's life, and its doctors assumed they would be paid. Novak could not give consent because he was unconscious. Novak would be unjustly enriched if he received these vital services for free.

FOUR THEORIES OF RECOVERY

Theory	Did the Defendant Make a Promise?	Is There a Contract?	Description
Express Contract	Yes	Yes	The parties intend to contract and agree on explicit terms.
Implied Contract	Not explicitly	Yes	The parties do not formally agree, but their words and conduct indicate an intention to create a contract.
Promissory Estoppel	Yes	No	There is no contract, but the defendant makes a promise that she can foresee will induce reliance; the plaintiff relies on it; and it would be unjust not to enforce the promise.
Quasi-Contract	No	No	There is no intention to contract, but the plaintiff gives some benefit to the defendant, who knows that the plaintiff expects compensation; it would be unjust not to award the plaintiff damages.

EXAM *Strategy*

Question: The table above lists the different theories a plaintiff may use to recover damages in a contract dispute. In the following examples, which one will each plaintiff use in trying to win the case? (1) Company pays all employees 10% commission on new business they develop. Company compensates the employee when the new customer pays its first bill. After Leandro obtains three new clients, Company fires him. When the new customers pay their bill, Company refuses to pay Leandro a commission because he is no longer an employee. Leandro sues. (2) Burt agrees in writing to sell Red 100 lobsters for $15 each, payable by credit card, in exactly 30 days. When the lobsters fail to arrive, Red sues. (3) Company handbook, given to all new hires, states that no employee will be fired without a hearing and an appeal. Company fires Delores without a hearing or appeal. She sues.

Strategy: In (1) the Company never promised to pay a commission to nonemployees, so there is no contract. However, the Company *benefited* from Leandro's work. In (2) the parties have *clearly stated all terms* to a simple sales agreement. In (3) the Company and Delores never negotiated termination, but *the handbook suggests* that all employees have certain rights.

Result: (1) is a case of quasi-contract, because the company benefited and should reasonably expect to pay. (2) is an express contract because all terms are clearly stated. (3) is an implied contract, similar to the *DeMasse* case, based on the handbook.

SOURCES OF CONTRACT LAW

COMMON LAW

We have seen the evolution of contract law from the twelfth century to the present. Express and implied contracts, promissory estoppel, and quasi-contract were all crafted, over centuries, by appellate courts deciding one contract lawsuit at a time. In this country, the basic principles are similar from one state to another, but there have been significant differences concerning most important contract doctrines.

In part because of these differences, the twentieth century saw the rise of a major source of contract law: the Uniform Commercial Code, and also the influential Restatement of Contracts.

UNIFORM COMMERCIAL CODE

Business methods changed quickly during the first half of the last century. Executives used new forms of communication, such as telephone and wire, to make deals. Transportation speeded up. Corporations routinely conducted business across state borders and around the world. Executives, lawyers, and judges wanted a body of law for commercial transactions that reflected modern business methods and provided uniformity throughout the United States. That desire gave birth to the Uniform Commercial Code (UCC), created in 1952. The drafters intended the UCC to facilitate the easy formation and enforcement of contracts in a fast-paced world. The Code governs many aspects of commerce, including the sale and leasing of goods, negotiable instruments, bank deposits, letters of credit, investment securities, secured transactions, and other commercial matters. Every state has adopted at least part of the UCC to govern commercial transactions within that state. For our purposes in studying contracts, the most important part of the Code is Article 2. The entire UCC is available online at **http://www.law.cornell.edu/**

UCC Article 2 governs the sale of goods. "Goods" means anything movable, except for money, securities, and certain legal rights. Goods include pencils, commercial aircraft, books, and Christmas trees. Goods do not include land or a house, because neither is movable. They also do not include stock certificates. A contract for the sale of 10,000 sneakers is governed by the UCC; a contract for the sale of a condominium in Marina del Rey is governed by the California common law and its statute of frauds. Thus, when analyzing any contract problem as a student or business executive, you must note whether the agreement concerns the sale of goods. Most of the time the answer is clear, and you will immediately know whether the UCC or the common law governs. In some cases, as in a mixed contract for goods and services, it is not so obvious. **In a mixed contract, the UCC governs only if the primary purpose was the sale of goods.** In the following case, the court had to decide the primary purpose.

FALLSVIEW GLATT KOSHER CATERERS, INC. v. ROSENFELD

2005 WL 53623
CIVIL COURT, CITY OF NEW YORK, 2005

CASE SUMMARY

Facts: During the Jewish holidays, Fallsview Glatt Kosher Caterers organized programs at Kutcher's Country Club, where it provided all accommodations, food, and entertainment.

Fallsview sued Willie Rosenfeld, alleging that he had requested accommodations for 15 members of his family, agreeing to pay $24,050, and then failed to appear or pay.

Rosenfeld moved to dismiss, claiming that even if there had been an agreement, it was never put in writing. Under UCC Section 2-201, any contract for the sale of goods worth $500 or more can be enforced only if it is in writing and signed. Fallsview argued that the agreement was not for the sale of goods, but for services. The company claimed that because the contract was not governed by the UCC, it should be enforced even with no writing.

Issue: *Was the agreement one for the sale of goods, requiring a writing, or for services, enforceable with no writing?*

Decision: The agreement was for services. The defendant's motion to dismiss is denied.

Reasoning: Rosenfeld contends that the predominant purpose of the contract was the service of Kosher food. He urges that the hotel accommodations and entertainment were merely incidental benefits. This conclusion is compelled, he suggests, by the very nature of the Passover holiday. The

essential religious obligation during this eight-day period is to eat only food that is "Kosher for Passover." It is the desire to obtain acceptable nourishment that causes customers to participate in such programs.

Fallsview countered by offering the court a schedule of activities available during the Passover program. These included tennis, racquetball, swimming, Swedish massage, "make over face lift show," "trivia time," aerobics, bingo, ice skating, dancing, "showtime," "power walk," arts and crafts, day camp, ping-pong, Yiddish theater, board games, horse racing, horseback riding, wine tasting, and indoor bocce. The activities were provided, along with accommodation and food, for an all-inclusive price. It is apparent that the activities and accommodations were a major part of the program, and that services were a more important aspect of the agreement than were goods.

Fallsview also argues that if, as Rosenfeld claims, hotel reservations are for the sale of goods, then all such contracts made via telephone or the Internet would be unenforceable, leaving the hospitality industry in an impossible situation. That may or may not be true, but it does indicate how important it is not to carelessly apply a statutory provision to contracts beyond its scope. UCC Section 2-201 was never meant to cover an agreement involving such a full slate of accommodations and activities.

The common law governs contracts for services, employment, real estate and certain other things, and so each chapter in this unit will analyze the relevant common law principles—of offer and acceptance, consideration, and so forth. But the sale of goods is obviously a major element in business nationwide, and therefore each chapter will also discuss appropriate aspects of the Code.

UCC Article 2 Alert.   For more than a decade, the drafters of the UCC analyzed and debated significant revisions to Article 2 (and other articles). In 2003, they completed their work on Article 2, and the new version has many significant changes. However, the proposed changes will not become law until state legislatures choose to adopt them. As this book goes to press, no state has adopted the recommended changes. All references in this text are to the existing Article 2.

EXAM *Strategy*

Question: Leila agrees to pay Kendrick $35,000 to repair windmills. Confident of this cash, Kendrick contracts to buy Derrick's used Porsche for $33,000. Then Leila informs Kendrick she does not need his help and will not pay him. Kendrick tells Derrick that he no longer wants the Porsche. Derrick sues Kendrick, and Kendrick files suit against Leila. What law or laws govern these lawsuits?

Strategy: Always be conscious of whether a contract is for services or the sale of goods. Different laws govern. To make that distinction, you must understand the term "goods." If you are clear about that, the question is easily answered.

Result: *Goods* means anything movable, and a Porsche surely qualifies. The UCC will control Derrick's suit. Repairing windmills is a service. Kendrick's lawsuit is governed by the common law of contracts.

RESTATEMENT (SECOND) OF CONTRACTS

In 1932 the American Law Institute (ALI), a group of lawyers, scholars, and judges, drafted the Restatement of Contracts, attempting to codify what its members regarded as the best rulings of contract law. Where courts had disagreed, for example, about when to enforce promissory estoppel, the drafters of the Restatement chose what they considered the wisest decisions. The Restatement was a treatise and never became the law anywhere. But because of the eminence of those who wrote it, the Restatement influenced many courts as they decided contract cases.

In 1979, the ALI issued a new version, the Restatement (Second) of Contracts. This revised version naturally reflects the changes in society, business, and judicial decisions in the half century since the first edition. Like its predecessor, the Restatement (Second) is not the law anywhere, and in this respect it differs from the common law and the UCC. But the Restatement (Second) influences lawyers as they draft contracts and judges as they decide cases; we, too, will seek its counsel throughout the chapters on contracts.

CHAPTER CONCLUSION

Contracts govern countless areas of our lives, from intimate family issues to multibillion dollar corporate deals. Understanding contract principles is essential for a successful business or professional career and is invaluable in private life. This knowledge is especially important because courts no longer rubber-stamp any agreement that two parties have made. If we know the issues that courts scrutinize, the agreement we draft is likelier to be enforced. We thus achieve greater control over our affairs—the very purpose of a contract.

EXAM REVIEW

A contract is a promise that the law will enforce. Contracts are intended to make business matters more predictable. Analyzing a contract generally involves inquiring into some or all of these issues:

1. **SUBJECT** What is the subject of the agreement?

   - If the contract is for the sale of goods, UCC Article 2 governs.
   - If the contract is for services, employment, or real estate, the common law governs. (p. 238)

> **EXAM Strategy**
>
> **Question:**   Honeywell, Inc., and Minolta Camera Co. had a contract providing that Honeywell would give to Minolta various technical information on the design of a specialized camera lens. Minolta would have the right to use the information in its cameras provided that Minolta also used certain Honeywell parts in its cameras. Honeywell delivered to Minolta numerous technical documents, computer software, and test equipment, and Honeywell engineers met with Minolta engineers at least 20 times to discuss the equipment. Several years later, Honeywell sued, claiming that Minolta had taken the design information but failed to use Honeywell parts in its cameras. Minolta moved to dismiss, claiming that the UCC required lawsuits concerning the sale of goods to be filed within four years of the breach and that this lawsuit was too late. Honeywell answered that the UCC did not apply and that therefore Minnesota's six-year statute of limitations governed. Who is right?
>
> **Strategy:**   Like many contracts, this one involves both goods, which are governed by the UCC, and services, controlled by the common law. We decide which of those two laws governs by using the predominant purpose test. Was this contract primarily about selling goods, or about providing services? (See the "Result" at the end of this section.)

2. **INTENT** Did the parties intend to contract?

   - If the parties formally agreed and stated explicit terms, there is probably an express contract.
   - If the parties did not formally agree but their conduct, words, or past dealings indicate they intended a binding agreement, there may be an implied contract. (p. 231)

3. **ENFORCEABILITY** If there is an agreement, is there any reason to doubt its enforceability?

- An unenforceable agreement is one with a legal defect, such as an oral agreement that the law requires to be in writing.
- A voidable contract occurs when one party has committed fraud, giving the other party the right to terminate the agreement, or when one party lacks capacity to make the contract and may escape liability.
- A void agreement means that the law will ignore the deal regardless of what the parties want, typically because the purpose of the deal is illegal. (p. 233)

EXAM Strategy

Question: Yasmine is negotiating to buy Stewart's house. She asks him what condition the roof is in. "Excellent," he replies. "It is only 2 years old, and should last 25 more." In fact, Stewart knows that the roof is 26 years old and has had a series of leaks. The parties sign a sales contract for $600,000. A week before Yasmine is to pay for the house and take possession, she discovers the leaks, and learns that the mandatory new roof will cost $35,000. At the same time, she learns that the house has increased in value by $60,000 since she signed the agreement. What options does Yasmine have?

Strategy: You know intuitively that Stewart's conduct is as shabby as his roof. What is the legal term for his deception? Fraud. Does fraud make an agreement void or voidable? Does it matter? (See the "Result" at the end of this section.)

4. **OTHER REMEDIES** If there is no contract, are there other reasons to give the plaintiff damages?

- A claim of promissory estoppel requires that the defendant made a promise knowing that the plaintiff would likely *rely*, and the plaintiff did so. It would be wrong to deny recovery.
- A claim of quasi-contract requires that the defendant received a benefit, knowing that the plaintiff would expect compensation, and it would be unjust not to grant it. (p. 234)

EXAM Strategy

Question: The Hoffmans owned and operated a successful small bakery and grocery store. They spoke with Lukowitz, an agent of Red Owl Stores, who told them that for $18,000, Red Owl would build a store and fully stock it for them. The Hoffmans sold their bakery and grocery store and purchased a lot on which Red Owl was to build the store. Lukowitz then told Hoffman that the price had gone up to $26,000. The Hoffmans borrowed the extra money from relatives, but then Lukowitz informed them that the cost would be $34,000. Negotiations broke off and the Hoffmans sued. The court determined that there was no contract because too many details had not been worked out—the size of the store, its design, and the cost of constructing it. Can the Hoffmans recover any money?

Strategy: Because there is no contract, the Hoffmans must rely on either promissory estoppel or quasi-contract. Promissory estoppel focuses on the defendant's promise and the plaintiff's reliance. Those suing in quasi-contract must show that the defendant received a benefit for which it should reasonably expect to pay. Does either fit here? (See the "Result" at the end of this section.)

1. Result: The primary purpose of this agreement was not the sale of goods, but rather the exchange of technical data, ideas, designs and so forth. The common law governs the contract, and Honeywell's suit may go forward.

3. Result: Indeed it does matter. Stewart's fraud makes the contract voidable by Yasmine. She has the right to terminate the agreement and pay nothing. However, she may go through with the contract if she prefers. The choice is hers—but not Stewart's.

4. Result: Red Owl received no benefit from the Hoffmans' sale of their store or purchase of the lot. However, Red Owl did make a promise and expected the Hoffmans to rely on it, which they did. The Hoffmans won their claim of promissory estoppel.

ADDITIONAL QUESTIONS

1. What is the purpose of a contract?

2. Pennsylvania contracted with Envirotest Systems, Inc., an Arizona company, to build 86 automobile emissions inspection stations in 25 counties, and operate them for seven years. This contract is worth hundreds of millions of dollars to Envirotest. But suddenly Pennsylvania legislators opposed the entire system, claiming that it would lead to long delays and high expenses for motorists. These lawmakers urged that Pennsylvania simply stop construction of the new system. Was Pennsylvania allowed to get out of the contract because its legislators concluded the whole system is unwise?

3. Central Maine Power Co. made a promotional offer in which it promised to pay a substantial sum to any homeowner or builder who constructed new housing heated with electricity. Motel Services, Inc., which was building a small housing project for the city of Waterville, Maine, decided to install electrical heat in the units in order to qualify for the offer. It built the units and requested payment for the full amount of the promotional offer. Is Central Maine obligated to pay? Why or why not?

4. Interactive Data Corp. hired Daniel Foley as an assistant product manager at a starting salary of $18,500. Over the next six years Interactive steadily promoted Foley until he became Los Angeles branch manager at a salary of $56,116. Interactive's officers repeatedly told Foley that he would have his job as long as his performance was adequate. In addition, Interactive distributed an employee handbook that specified "termination guidelines," including a mandatory seven-step pre-termination procedure. Two years later Foley learned that his recently hired supervisor, Robert Kuhne, was under investigation by the FBI for embezzlement at his previous job. Foley reported this to Interactive officers. Shortly thereafter, Interactive fired Foley. He sued, claiming that Interactive could only fire him for good cause, after the seven-step procedure. What kind of a claim is he making? Should he succeed?

5. **ETHICS** You want to lease your automobile to a friend for the summer but do not want to pay a lawyer to draw up the lease. Joanna, a neighbor, is in law school. She is not licensed to practice law. She offers to draft a lease for you for $100, and you unwisely accept. Later, you refuse to pay her fee and she sues to collect. Who will win the lawsuit, and why? Apart from the law, was it morally right for the law student to try to help out by drafting the lease? Was she acting helpfully, or foolishly, or fraudulently? Is it just for you to agree to her fee and then refuse to pay it? What is society's interest in

this dispute? Should a court be more concerned with the ethical issue raised by the conduct of the two parties or with the social consequences of this agreement?

6. Describe the role each of the following plays in contract law: the common law, the UCC, and the Restatement (Second) of Contracts.

7. **YOU BE THE JUDGE** WRITING PROBLEM John Stevens owned a dilapidated apartment that he rented to James and Cora Chesney for a low rent. The Chesneys began to remodel and rehabilitate the unit. Over a four-year period, they installed two new bathrooms, carpeted the floors, installed new septic and heating systems, and rewired, replumbed, and painted. Stevens periodically stopped by and saw the work in progress. The Chesneys transformed the unit into a respectable apartment. Three years after their work was done, Stevens served the Chesneys with an eviction notice. The Chesneys counterclaimed, seeking the value of the work they had done. Are they entitled to it? **Argument for Stevens:** Mr. Stevens is willing to pay the Chesneys exactly the amount he agreed to pay: nothing. The parties never contracted for the Chesneys to fix up the apartment. In fact, they never even discussed such an agreement. The Chesneys are making the absurd argument that anyone who chooses to perform certain work, without ever discussing it with another party, can finish the job and then charge it to the other person. If the Chesneys expected to get paid, obviously they should have said so. If the court were to allow this claim, it would be inviting other tenants to make improvements and then bill the landlord. The law has never been so foolish. **Argument for the Chesneys:** The law of quasi-contract was crafted for cases exactly like this. The Chesneys have given an enormous benefit to Stevens by transforming the apartment and enabling him to rent it at greater profit for many years to come. Stevens saw the work being done and understood that the Chesneys expected some compensation for these major renovations. If Stevens never intended to pay the fair value of the work, he should have stopped the couple from doing the work or notified them that there would be no compensation. It would be unjust to allow the landlord to seize the value of the work, evict the tenants who did it, and pay nothing.

8. Explain the difference between judicial restraint and judicial activism in contract law.

9. **ROLE REVERSAL** Write a multiple-choice question that requires use of the predominant factor test to determine whether a contract is one for goods or services.

INTERNET RESEARCH PROBLEM

Search for a case concerning either "implied contract" or "quasi-contract." What are the details of the dispute? Who won and why?

You can find further practice problems at www.cengagebrain.com. See the preface of this book for website access details.

AGREEMENT

Interior. A glitzy café, New York. Evening. Bob, a famous director, and Katrina, a glamorous actress, sit at a table, near a wall of glass looking onto a New York sidewalk that is filled with life and motion. Bob sips a margarita while carefully eyeing Katrina. Katrina stares at her wine glass.

BOB (smiling confidently): *Body Work* is going to be huge—for the right actress. I know a film that's gonna gross a hundred million when I'm holding one. I'm holding one.

KATRINA (perking up at the mention of money): It is quirky. It's fun. And she's very strong, very real.

BOB: She's you. That's why we're sitting here. We start shooting in seven months.

KATRINA (edging away from the table): I have a few questions. That nude scene.

BOB: The one on the toboggan run?

KATRINA: *That* one was O.K. But the one in the poultry factory—very explicit. I don't work nude.

BOB: It's not really nude. Think of all those feathers fluttering around.

KATRINA: It's nude.

BOB: We'll work it out. This is a romantic comedy, not tawdry exploitation. Katrina, we're talking $2.5 million. A little accommodation, please. We'll give you $600,000 up front, and the rest deferred, the usual percentages.

KATRINA: Bob, my fee is $3 million. As you know. That hasn't changed.

KATRINA picks up her drink, doesn't sip it, places it on the coaster, using both hands to center it perfectly. He waits, as she stares silently at her glass.

> I should talk with my agent. I'd need something in writing about the nude scene …

BOB: We're shooting in Santa Fe, the weather will be perfect. You have a suite at the Excelsior plus a trailer on location.

KATRINA: I should talk with my agent. I'd need something in writing about the nude scene, the fee, percentages—all the business stuff. I never sign without talking to her.

BOB shrugs and sits back.

KATRINA (made anxious by the silence): I love the character, I really do.

BOB: You and several others love her. (That jolts her.) Agents can wait. I have to put this together fast. We can get you the details you want in writing. *Body Work* is going to be bigger than *Sex in the City*.

That one hooks her. She looks at Bob. He nods reassuringly. Bob sticks out his hand, smiling. Katrina hesitates, lets go of her drink, and SHAKES HANDS, looking unsure. Bob signals for the check.

Do Bob and Katrina have a deal? *They* seem to think so. But is her fee $2.5 million or $3 million? What if Katrina demands that all nude scenes be taken out, and Bob refuses? Must she still act in the film? Or suppose her agent convinces her that *Body Work* is no good even with changes. Has Katrina committed herself? What if Bob auditions another actress the next day, likes her, and signs her? Does he owe Katrina her fee? Or suppose Bob learns that the funding has fallen apart and there will be no film. Is Katrina entitled to her money?

Bob and Katrina have acted out a classic problem in *agreement*, one of the basic issues in contract law. Their lack of clarity means that disputes are likely and lawsuits possible. Similar bargaining goes on every day around the country and around the world, and the problems created are too frequently resolved in court. Some of the negotiating is done in person; more is done over the phone, by fax, by e-mail—or all of them combined. This chapter highlights the most common sources of misunderstanding and litigation so that you can avoid making deals you never intended—or "deals" that you cannot enforce.

There almost certainly is no contract between Bob and Katrina. Bob's offer was unclear. Even if it was valid, Katrina counteroffered. When they shook hands, it is impossible to know what terms each had in mind.

MEETING OF THE MINDS

As courts dissect a negotiation that has gone awry, they examine the intent of the parties. The parties can form a contract only if they had a **meeting of the minds**. This requires that they (1) understood each other and (2) intended to reach an agreement.

Keep in mind that judges must make *objective assessments* of the respective intent of each party. A court will not try to get inside Katrina's head and decide what she was thinking as she shook hands. It will look at the handshake *objectively*, deciding how a reasonable person would interpret the words and conduct. Katrina may honestly have meant to conclude a deal for $3 million with no nude scenes, while Bob might in good faith have believed he was committing himself to $2.5 million and absolute control of the script. Neither belief will control the

Meeting of the minds
A situation in which the parties understand each other and intend to reach an agreement.

outcome. A reasonable person observing their discussion would not have known what terms they agreed to, and hence there is no agreement.

OFFER

Bargaining begins with an offer. An offer is a serious matter because it permits the other party to create a contract by accepting. An **offer** is an act or statement that proposes definite terms and permits the other party to create a contract by accepting those terms.

The person who makes an offer is the **offeror**. The person to whom he makes that offer is the **offeree**. The terms are annoying but inescapable because, like handcuffs, all courts use them. In most contract negotiations, two parties bargain back and forth, maybe for minutes, perhaps for months. Each may make several offers, revoke some proposals, suggest counter-offers, and so forth. For our purposes, the offeror remains the one who made the first offer, and the offeree is the one who received it.

Two questions determine whether a statement is an offer:

- Did the offeror *intend* to make a bargain?

- Are the terms of the offer definite?

Offer
An act or statement that proposes definite terms and permits the other party to create a contract by accepting those terms.

Offeror
The person who makes an offer.

Offeree
The person to whom an offer is made.

Three elements (offer)
· Intent
· Clear
· Communicated

PROBLEMS WITH INTENT

Zachary says to Sharon, "Come work in my English language center as a teacher. I'll pay you $500 per week for a 35-hour week, for six months starting Monday." This is a valid offer. Zachary intends to make a bargain and his offer is definite. If Sharon accepts, the parties have a contract that either one can enforce. By contrast, we will consider several categories of statements that are *generally not* valid offers.

Invitations to Bargain

An invitation to bargain is not an offer. Suppose Martha telephones Joe and leaves a message on his answering machine, asking if Joe would consider selling his vacation condo on Lake Michigan. Joe faxes a signed letter to Martha saying, "There is no way I could sell the condo for less than $150,000." Martha promptly sends Joe a cashier's check for that amount. Does she own the condo? No. Joe's fax was not an offer. It is merely an invitation to bargain. Joe is indicating that he would be happy to receive an offer from Martha. He is not promising to sell the condo for $150,000 or for any amount.

Price Quotes

A price quote is generally not an offer. If Imperial Textile sends a list of fabric prices for the new year to its regular customers, the list is not an offer. Once again, the law regards it merely as a solicitation of offers. Suppose Ralph orders 1,000 yards of fabric, quoted in the list at $40 per yard. Ralph is making the offer, and Imperial may decline to sell at $40, or at any price, for that matter.

This can be an expensive point to learn. Leviton Manufacturing makes electrical fixtures and switches. Litton Microwave manufactures ovens. Leviton sent a price list to Litton, stating what it would charge for specially modified switches for use in Litton's microwaves. The price letter included a statement greatly limiting Leviton's liability in

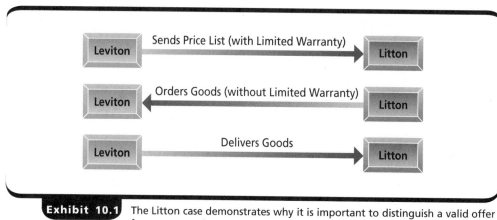

Exhibit 10.1 The Litton case demonstrates why it is important to distinguish a valid offer from a mere price quote. Leviton's price list (including a limited warranty) was not an offer. When Litton ordered goods (with no limit to the warranty), it was making an offer, which Leviton accepted by delivering the goods. The resulting contract did not contain the limited warranty that Leviton wanted, costing that company a $4 million judgment.

the event of any problem with the switches. Litton purchased thousands of the switches and used them in manufacturing its microwaves. But consumers reported fires due to defects in the switches. Leviton claimed that under the contract it had no liability. But the court held that the price letter was not an offer. It was a request to receive an offer. Thus the contract ultimately formed did not include Leviton's liability exclusion. Litton won over $4 million.[1] See Exhibit 10.1.

Letters of Intent

Letter of intent

A letter that summarizes negotiating progress.

In complex business negotiations, the parties may spend months bargaining over dozens of interrelated issues. Because each party wants to protect itself during the discussions, ensuring that the other side is serious without binding itself to premature commitments, it may be tempting during the negotiations to draft a **letter of intent**. The letter *might* help distinguish a serious party from one with a casual interest, summarize the progress made thus far, and assist the parties in securing necessary financing. But a letter of intent contains a built-in danger: one party may not consider it binding. Yet if it is not a contract, what is it?

The case involves a very common situation that you will encounter at some point in your life. A homeowner has negotiated to sell her house to buyers. The parties put the terms in writing and sign the document, so they must have a deal ... or do they? It's up to you.

---

[1] *Litton Microwave Cooking Products v. Leviton Manufacturing Co., Inc.*, 15 F.3d 790, 1994 U.S.App. LEXIS 1876 (8th Cir. 1994).

YOU *be the* JUDGE

COCHRAN V. NORKUNAS
398 Md. 1, 919 A.2d 700
Court of Appeals of Maryland, 2007

Facts: Eileen Norkunas owned a house in Baltimore, Maryland. Two couples, the Groves and the Cochrans, expressed their interest in buying the house. Assisted by their real estate agent, the two couples drafted a handwritten letter, stating:

> Letter of Intent
>
> We, Rebecca Cochran, Robert Cochran, Hope Grove and Robert Grove, Buyers—offer to buy 835 McHenry Street, Baltimore, Md. 21230 for $162,000. Payment by $5,000 check, this date and $157,000 by certified or cashiers funds not later than April 17, 2004.
>
> A standard form Maryland Realtors contract will be delivered to Seller within 48 hours. Seller to pay only 1/2 normal transfer taxes and a 3% commission to Long & Foster. All other costs of closing to be paid by buyers.
>
> The contract will contain a financing requirement for buyers, but buyers will guarantee closing and not invoke the financing contingency.
>
> We will delete the standard home inspection contingency.

The name of the seller, each buyer, and the agent was included, along with a space to sign. All parties did sign. Norkunas accepted the buyers' check for $5,000 but never deposited it. A few days later, the agent sent Norkunas a pack of documents, including a "Residential Contract of Sale," published by the state association of realtors, and several other documents. The Residential Contract form incorporated all of the terms from the letter of intent and included various other provisions. Norkunas signed the Contract but never returned it to the buyers. About a week later, Norkunas informed the buyers she would not sell the property and was taking it off the market.

The buyers sued, claiming that the letter of intent entitled them to the house. At Norkunas's deposition, she acknowledged that she never telephoned the buyers or their agent to express dissatisfaction with any contract terms in the Contract or other documents.

The trial court gave summary judgment to the buyers, but the intermediate appeals court reversed, declaring that the letter of intent was not binding. The buyers appealed to the state's highest court.

You Be the Judge: Did the letter of intent create a binding contract?

Argument for the Buyers: We understand that contract terms must be clear and complete, and that the parties must agree on them. That is exactly what we have here. In the letter, the parties agreed on the property to be sold, the price, the down payment, method and date of final payment, what standard form contract we would all sign, and which provisions of it would not apply. What else is there? Nothing.

What we have here is a seller who changed her mind. That does happen in life, but it does not give a party to a signed agreement the right to just walk away from the bargain. In fact, that is exactly why people enter into contracts—so that each side knows it can depend upon the agreement. If the seller suddenly gets cold feet, she has no right to back out.

The agreed upon terms were being transferred from one piece of paper to another. That is no excuse to breach a clearly understood agreement.

Argument for the Seller: There is one important issue: Did the parties intend to create a binding agreement? If they did not, nothing else matters and there is no contract.

The letter's first paragraph states that the buyers *offer* to buy the house. The next paragraph states that a standard form contract *will be delivered* to the seller. The letter goes on to discuss financing provisions that will appear in the final contract. The buyers' agent later sent a packet of documents to Ms. Norkunas, hoping she would agree to all terms.

It is clear from the letter and the packet of documents that the parties did not consider the letter to be a final agreement. The letter outlined the next steps they would take in an effort to reach a binding contract. The buyers sent Ms. Norkunas a packet of material, which she was free to accept or reject. She promptly notified the buyers that there was no deal. The buyers' disappointment is understandable but no basis for a contract suit.

Advertisements

Mary Mesaros received a notice from the United States Bureau of the Mint, announcing a new $5 gold coin to commemorate the Statue of Liberty. The notice contained an order form stating:

VERY IMPORTANT—PLEASE READ: YES, Please accept my order for the U.S. Liberty Coins I have indicated. I understand that all sales are final and not subject to refund. Verification of my order will be made by the Department of the Treasury, U.S. Mint. If my order is received by December 31, I will be entitled to purchase the coins at the Pre-Issue Discount price shown.

Mesaros ordered almost $2,000 worth of the coins. But the Mint was inundated with so many requests for the coin that the supply was soon exhausted. Mesaros and thousands of others never got their coins. This was particularly disappointing because the market value of the coins doubled shortly after their issue. Mesaros sued on behalf of the entire class of disappointed purchasers. Like most who sue based on an advertisement, she lost.[2] **An advertisement is generally not an offer.** An advertisement is merely a request for offers. The consumer makes the offer, whether by mail, as above, or by arriving at a merchant's store ready to buy. The seller is free to reject the offer.

Note that while the common law regards advertisements as mere solicitations, consumers do have protection from those shopkeepers intent upon deceit. Almost every state has some form of **consumer protection statute.** These statutes outlaw false advertising. For example, an automobile dealer who advertises a remarkably low price but then has only one automobile at that price has probably violated a consumer protection statute because the ad was published in bad faith, to trick consumers into coming to the dealership. The United States Mint did not violate any consumer protection statute because it acted in good faith and simply ran out of coins.

Auctions

It is the property you have always dreamed of owning—and it is up for auction! You arrive bright and early, stand in front, bid early, bid often, bid higher, bid highest of all—it's yours! For five seconds. Then, to your horror, the auctioneer announces that none of the bids were juicy enough and he is withdrawing the property. Robbery! Surely he cannot do that? But he can. Auctions are exciting and useful, but you must understand the rules.

Every day auctions are used to sell exquisite works of art, real estate, property confiscated from drug dealers, and many other things. Auctions for the sale of goods are governed by UCC Section 2-328; auctions for real estate are governed by the common law. The rules are similar and straightforward. **Placing an item up for auction is *not* an offer, it is merely a request for an offer.** The *bids* are the offers. If and when the hammer falls, the auctioneer has accepted the offer.

The important thing to know about a particular auction is whether it is conducted with or without reserve. Most auctions are *with reserve*, meaning that the items for sale have a minimum price. The law assumes that an auction is with reserve unless the auctioneer clearly states otherwise. The auctioneer will not sell anything for less than its reserve (minimum price). So when the bidding for your property failed to reach the reserve, the auctioneer was free to withdraw it.

The rules are different in an auction *without reserve*. Here there is no minimum. Once the first bid is received, the auctioneer must sell the merchandise to the highest bidder.

---

[2] *Mesaros v. United States*, 845 F.2d 1576, 1988 U.S.App. LEXIS 6055 (Fed.Cir. 1988).

EXAM *Strategy*

Question: Ahn and Chet are both unhappy. (1) Ahn, an interior designer, is working on a hotel project. In the annual catalog of a furniture wholesaler, she sees that sofa beds cost $3,000. Based on the catalog, she sends an order for 100 sofa beds to the wholesaler. The wholesaler notifies Ahn that the price has gone up to $4,000. (2) At an estate auction, held without reserve, Chet is high bidder on a rare violin. The seller considers Chet's bid too low and refuses to sell. Both Ahn and Chet sue, but only one will win. Which plaintiff will win, and why?

Strategy: (1) A contract requires an offer and an acceptance. When the furniture wholesaler sent out its catalog, did it make an offer that Ahn could accept? (2) Chet was high bidder. At some auctions, the high bidder is merely making an offer, but at others, he wins the item. Which kind of auction was this?

Result: (1) A price quote is generally not an offer. Ahn's order for 100 sofas was the offer, and the company was free to reject it. Ahn loses. (2) Most auctions are with reserve, meaning that the high bidder is merely making an offer. However, this one was without reserve. Chet gets the violin.

PROBLEMS WITH DEFINITENESS

It is not enough that the offeror intends to enter into an agreement. **The terms of the offer must be definite.** If they are vague, then even if the offeree "accepts" the deal, a court does not have enough information to enforce it and there is no contract.

You want a friend to work in your store for the holiday season. This is a definite offer: "I offer you a job as a sales clerk in the store from November 1 through December 29, 40 hours per week at $10 per hour." But suppose, by contrast, you say: "I offer you a job as a sales clerk in the store from November 1 through December 29, 40 hours per week. We will work out a fair wage once we see how busy things get." Your friend replies, "That's fine with me." This offer is indefinite, and there is no contract. What is a fair wage? $5 per hour? Or $15 per hour? How will the determination be made? There is no binding agreement.

The following case presents a problem with definiteness, concerning a famous television show. You want to know what happened? Go to the place. See the guy. No, not the guy in hospitality. Our friend in waste management. Don't say nothing. Then get out.

BAER V. CHASE

392 F.3d 609
Third Circuit Court of Appeals, 2004

CASE SUMMARY

Facts: David Chase was a television writer-producer with many credits, including a detective series called *The Rockford Files*. He became interested in a new program, set in New Jersey, about a "mob boss in therapy," a concept he eventually developed into *The Sopranos*. Robert Baer was a prosecutor in New Jersey who wanted to write for television. He submitted a *Rockford Files* script to Chase, who agreed to meet with Baer.

When they met, Baer pitched a different idea, concerning "a film or television series about the New Jersey Mafia." He did not realize Chase was already working on such an idea. Later that year, Chase visited New Jersey. Baer arranged meetings for Chase with local detectives and prosecutors, who provided the producer with information, material, and personal stories about their experiences with organized crime. Detective Thomas Koczur drove Chase and Baer to various New Jersey locations and introduced Chase to Tony Spirito. Spirito shared stories about loan sharking, power struggles between family members connected with the mob, and two colorful individuals known as Big Pussy and Little Pussy, both of whom later became characters on the show.

Back in Los Angeles, Chase wrote and sent to Baer a draft of the first *Sopranos* teleplay. Baer called Chase and commented on the script. The two spoke at least four times that year, and Baer sent Chase a letter about the script.

When *The Sopranos* became a hit television show, Baer sued Chase. He alleged that on three separate occasions, Chase had agreed that if the program succeeded, Chase would "take care of" Baer, and would "remunerate Baer in a manner commensurate to the true value of his services." This happened twice on the phone, Baer claimed, and once during Chase's visit to New Jersey. The understanding was that if the show failed, Chase would owe nothing. Chase never paid Baer anything.

The district court dismissed the case, holding that the alleged promises were too vague to be enforced. Baer appealed.

Issue: *Was Chase's promise definite enough to be enforced?*

Decision: No. The promise was too indefinite to be enforced. Affirmed.

Reasoning: To create a binding agreement, the offer and acceptance must be definite enough that a court can tell what the parties were obligated to do. The parties need to agree on all the essential terms; if they do not, there is no enforceable contract.

One of the essential terms is price. The agreement must either specify the compensation to be paid or describe a method by which the parties can calculate it. The duration of the contract is also basic: How long do the mutual obligations last?

There is no evidence that the parties agreed on how much Chase would pay Baer, or when, or for what period. The parties never defined what they meant by the "true value" of Baer's services, or how they would determine it. The two never discussed the meaning of "success" as applied to *The Sopranos*. They never agreed on how "profits" were to be calculated. The parties never discussed when the alleged agreement would begin or end.

Baer argues that the courts should make an exception to the principle of definiteness when the agreement concerns an "idea submission." The problem with his contention is that there is not the slightest support for it in the law. There is no precedent whatsoever for ignoring the definiteness requirement, in this type of contract or any other.

ETHICS Was it fair for Chase to use Baer's services without compensation? Did Baer really *expect* to get paid, or was he simply hoping that his work would land him a job? Has either party violated the Golden Rule? What are the most important *values* involved? ◆

EXAM *Strategy*

Question: Niels owned three adjoining parcels of land in Arizona ranging from 60 to 120 acres. Hannah wanted to buy one. The two had dinner in Chicago and then sketched this agreement: "Binding Contract: Niels agrees to sell one of his three Arizona lots to Hannah. Within fourteen days, the parties will meet on the land, decide which lot Hannah is buying, and settle on a price. If they cannot agree on a price, they will decide a fair method of doing so. Both parties agree to be bound by this contract." Each signed. When they meet in Arizona, Niels refuses to sell any land, and Hannah sues. What will happen?

Strategy: Do not be fooled by wording such as "Binding Contract." Focus on the legal issues: Was there a meeting of the minds? Niels and Hannah *thought* they had a contract—but courts make an objective assessment, not subjective. Did Niels make an offer? Were the terms definite?

Result: Both parties believed they had a binding deal, and both parties were wrong. There are two primary issues—which lot is being sold and how much will it cost—and neither is specified. How are they to select a lot? What is a "fair method" of determining price? Other issues are not touched upon: When will the deal close, how will payment be made, what happens if Hannah cannot finance the purchase? The terms are too vague. The parties never reached a meeting of the minds, and Hannah will lose her suit.

UCC AND OPEN TERMS

Throughout this unit, we witness how the Uniform Commercial Code makes the law of sales more flexible. There are several areas of contract law where imperfect negotiations may still create a binding agreement under the Code, even though the same negotiations under the common law would have yielded no contract. "Open terms" is one such area.

Yuma County Corp. produced natural gas. Yuma wanted a long-term contract to sell its gas so that it could be certain of recouping the expenses of exploration and drilling. Northwest Central Pipeline, which operated an interstate pipeline, also wanted a deal for 10 or more years so it could make its own distribution contracts, knowing it would have a steady supply of natural gas in a competitive market. But neither Yuma nor Northwest wanted to make a long-term *price* commitment, because over a period of years the price of natural gas could double—or crash. Each party wanted a binding agreement without a definitive price. If their negotiations had been governed by the common law, they would have run smack into the requirement of definiteness—no price, no contract. But because this was a sale of goods, it was governed by the UCC.

UCC Section 2-204(3).   Even though one or more terms are left open, a contract for sale does not fail for indefiniteness if the parties have intended to make a contract and there is a reasonably certain basis for giving an appropriate remedy.

Thus a contract for the sale of goods may be enforced when a key term is missing. Business executives may have many reasons to leave open a delivery date, a price, or some other term. But note that the parties must still have *intended* to create a contract. The UCC will not create a contract where the parties never intended one.

In some cases the contract will state how the missing term is to be determined. Yuma County and Northwest drafted a contract with alternative methods of determining the price. In the event that the price of natural gas was regulated by the Federal Energy Regulatory Commission (FERC), the price would be the highest allowed by the FERC. If the FERC deregulated the price (as it ultimately did), the contract price would be the average of the two highest prices paid by different gas producers in a specified geographic area.

If the contract lacks a method for determining missing terms, the Code itself contains **gap-filler provisions**, which are rules for supplying missing terms. Some of the most important gap-filler provisions of the Code follow.

Gap-filler provisions
UCC rules for supplying missing terms.

Open Price

In general, if the parties do not settle on a price, the Code establishes a *reasonable price*. This will usually be the market value or a price established by a neutral expert or agency. (UCC Section 2-305.)

The quantity is missing
"As much as you require" Under the common law, there is no contract
But, there is
under UCC

Output contract
An agreement that obligates the seller to sell all of his output to the buyer, who agrees to accept it.

(Delivery of goods)

Requirements contract
An agreement that obligates a buyer to obtain all of his needed goods from the seller.

Output and Requirements Provisions

An **output contract** obligates the seller to sell all of his output to the buyer, who agrees to accept it. For example, a cotton grower might agree to sell all of his next crop to a textile firm. A **requirements contract** obligates a buyer to obtain all of his needed goods from the seller. A vineyard might agree to buy all of its wine bottles from one supplier. Output and requirements contracts are by definition incomplete, since the exact quantity of the goods is unspecified. The Code requires that in carrying out such contracts, both parties act in good faith. Neither party may suddenly demand a quantity of goods (or offer a quantity of goods) that is disproportionate to their past dealings or their reasonable estimates. (UCC Section 2-306.)

Delivery, Time, and Payment

The Code provides terms for each of these issues. In general, the place of delivery is the seller's business. The time for shipping goods is usually a reasonable time, based on the normal trade practice. And payment is normally due when and where the buyer receives the goods. For each of these issues, the Code offers alternative provisions for cases with unusual facts. (UCC Sections 2-308 through 2-310.)

Warranties

Warranties are a source of frequent conflict between the parties because when something goes wrong, the costs can be enormous. Parties frequently enter a contract without agreeing on the warranty provisions, so the Code often supplies the terms. We consider warranty in detail in Chapter 20, on warranties and products liability. To summarize here, we can mention two important warranties that the Code implies. One is an **implied warranty of merchantability**, which means that the goods must be of at least average, passable quality in the trade. Ten thousand pairs of sneakers must be such that a typical shoe store would accept them. The other is an **implied warranty of fitness for a particular purpose**. If the seller knows that the buyer plans to use the goods for a particular purpose, the seller generally is held to warrant that the goods are in fact fit for that purpose. If an engine manufacturer knows that the buyer is going to use 10,000 engines in outboard motors, the Code normally considers that the manufacturer is warranting the engines for that purpose. (UCC Sections 2-312 through 2-317.)

Implied warranty of merchantability
A warranty that goods must be of at least average, passable quality in the trade.

Implied warranty of fitness for a particular purpose
A warranty requiring that if the seller knows that the buyer plans to use the goods for a particular purpose, the seller generally is held to warrant that the goods are in fact fit for that purpose.

TERMINATION OF OFFERS

As we have seen, the great power that an offeree has is to form a contract by accepting an offer. But this power is lost when the offer is terminated, which can happen in four ways: revocation, rejection, expiration, or operation of law.

To prevent the offeree from Revoking an offer
Option (another exchange of promise)
• Buys time

Termination by Revocation

In general, the offeror may revoke the offer any time before it has been accepted. **Revocation is effective when the offeree receives it.** Douglas County, Oregon, sought bids on a construction job involving large quantities of rock. The Taggart Co. discovered a local source of supply with cheap rock and put in a bid. Shortly thereafter, Taggart discovered that the local rock was no longer for sale. Taggart hand-delivered a written revocation of its bid. Later, the county opened all bids and accepted Taggart's low offer—but lost the case. By delivering its revocation, Taggart terminated the county's power to accept.[3]

---

[3] *R. J. Taggart, Inc. v. Douglas County*, 31 Or.App. 1137, 572 P.2d 1050, 1977 Ore.App. LEXIS 2868 (Or.Ct.App. 1977).

Firm Offers and Revocability

Some offers cannot be revoked. A **firm offer** is one that by its own terms will be held open for a given period. Bonnie writes Clyde on January 2 and says, "I offer to sell you X for $1 million. This offer will be valid until February 2." Suppose Bonnie changes her mind on January 5 and wants to revoke. May she? It depends on "X."

Common Law Rule.   **Under the common law, revocation of a firm offer is effective if the offeree receives it before he accepts.** Suppose Bonnie was offering to sell her ranch for that sum. On January 5 she faxed Clyde a revocation and he received it. On January 10 he mailed her an acceptance. Result? No contract—the revocation was effective.

Option Contract.   With an option contract, an interested purchaser buys the right to have the offer held open. **The offeror may not revoke an offer during the option period.** Suppose Clyde is interested in Bonnie's ranch, but needs three weeks to learn whether he can finance the purchase. They agree that Clyde will pay $25,000 for Bonnie to hold open her offer until February 2. Clyde arranges financing on January 20, but later that day Bonnie notifies him she is selling to someone else. Result? Clyde can enforce *his* contract. Bonnie had no power to revoke because Clyde had purchased an option.

Sale of Goods.   Once again, the UCC has changed the law on the sale of goods. A writing, signed by a *merchant*, offering to hold open an offer for a stated period, may not be revoked. The open period may not exceed three months. Thus, if Bonnie is a merchant, and the "X" she is offering to sell Clyde is 10,000 theatrical costumes, she may not revoke any time before February 2. (UCC Section 2-205.)

Termination by Rejection

If an offeree rejects an offer, the rejection immediately terminates the offer. Suppose a major accounting firm telephones you and offers a job, starting at $80,000. You respond, "Nah. I'm gonna work on my surfing for a year or two." The next day you come to your senses and write the firm, accepting its offer. No contract. Your rejection terminated the offer and ended your power to accept.

Counteroffer.   Frederick faxes Kim, offering to sell a 50 percent interest in the Fab Hotel in New York for only $135 million. Kim faxes back, offering to pay $115 million. Moments later, Kim's business partner convinces her that Frederick's offer was a bargain, and she faxes an acceptance of his $135 million offer. Does Kim have a binding deal? No. **A counteroffer is a rejection.** When Kim offered $115 million, she rejected Frederick's offer. Her original fax created a new offer, for $115 million, which Frederick never accepted. The parties have no contract at any price.

Termination by Expiration

Quentin calls you and offers you a job as best boy on his next motion picture. He tells you, "I've got to know by tomorrow night." If you call him in three days to accept, you are out of the picture. **When an offer specifies a time limit for acceptance, that period is binding.**

If the offer specifies no time limit, the offeree has a reasonable period in which to accept. A reasonable period varies, depending upon the type of offer, previous dealings between the parties, and any normal trade usage. "Trade usage" means the customary practices in a particular industry. When the parties are bargaining face to face, any offer made will normally be valid only during that discussion. Neither party may call the next day to accept. Similarly, if the offer concerns a speculative item, such as commodities futures, the offer will be open very briefly. By contrast, if a used car wholesaler faxes an offer to sell 50 used cars for $5,000 each,

Firm offer
An offer that by its own terms will be held open for a given period.

· Sale of goods
· A contract signed
     between merchants

Once you reject a contract, the offer is no longer on the table · the offer doesn't exist anymore. Unless the offeror chooses to make the deal again and the local custom is to respond within three days, an acceptance faxed within two days creates a contract.

Termination by Operation of Law

In some circumstances, the law itself terminates an offer. **Death or mental incapacity of the offeror terminates an offer, whether the offeree knows of the change or not.** Arnie offers you a job as an assistant in his hot-air balloon business. Before you can even accept, Arnie tumbles out of a balloon at 3,000 feet. The offer terminates along with Arnie.

Destruction of the subject matter terminates the offer. A used car dealer offers to sell you a rare 1938 Bugatti for $475,000 if you bring cash the next day. You arrive, suitcase stuffed with century notes, just in time to see Arnie drop 3,000 feet through the air and crush the Bugatti. The dealer's offer is terminated.

· If an offeror dies, the offer dies with him (only an offer can be terminated, not a contract)

(house burns down or horse dies - terminates any offer made)

ACCEPTANCE

As we have seen, when there is a valid offer outstanding, the offeree can create a contract by accepting. **The offeree must say or do something to accept.** Silence, though golden, is not acceptance. Marge telephones Vick and leaves a message on his answering machine: "I'll pay $75 for your law textbook from last semester. I'm desperate to get a copy, so I will assume you agree unless I hear from you by 6:00 tonight." Marge hears nothing by the deadline and assumes she has a deal. She is mistaken. Vick neither said nor did anything to indicate that he accepted.

> ### Silence, though golden, is not acceptance.

only a contract After he performs an action

(may not have to necessarily say anything)

When the offer is for a bilateral contract, the offeree generally must accept by making a promise. An employer calls you and says, "If you're able to start work two weeks from today, we can pay you $5,000 per month. Can you do it?" That is an offer for a bilateral contract. You must accept by promising to start in two weeks. If you make the promise, both sides are contractually bound from the moment you agree. You do not, however, have the option to think it over for two weeks and then show up.

When the offer is for a unilateral contract, the offeree must accept by performing. A newspaper telephones you: "If you write us a 5,000-word article on iguanas that can play bridge, and get it to us by Friday at noon, we'll pay you $750." The newspaper does not want a promise, it wants the article. If your work is ready on time, you get paid. If you never write a word, neither party owes the other anything.

With some offers it is unclear whether the offeror wants acceptance by promise or performance. **If the offer is ambiguous, the offeree may accept by either a promise or performance.** A contractor offered to lease a Link-Belt construction crane from a dealer for two months for $6,500 per month. The contractor signed and mailed a written lease that required him to insure the crane. The dealer read the lease, did not sign it, but delivered the crane. The crane was promptly destroyed. Was the contractor liable? Yes. The written lease invited acceptance by promise or by performance. The dealer accepted by delivering the crane, and the liability clause (requiring the contractor to obtain insurance) was part of their contract.[4] The rule is the same in cases involving the sale of goods. (UCC Section 2-206.)

---

[4] *Anderson Excavating v. Certified Welding,* 769 P.2d 887, 1988 Wyo. LEXIS 185 (Wyo. 1988).

MIRROR IMAGE RULE

If only he had known! A splendid university, an excellent position as department chair—gone. And all because of the mirror image rule.

Ohio State University wrote to Philip Foster offering him an appointment as a professor and chair of the art history department. His position was to begin July 1, and he had until June 2 to accept the job. On June 2, Foster telephoned the Dean and left a message accepting the position, *effective July 15.* Later, Foster thought better of it and wrote the university, accepting the school's starting date of July 1. Too late! Professor Foster never did occupy that chair at Ohio State. The court held that since his acceptance varied the starting date, it was a counteroffer. And a counteroffer, as we know, is a rejection.[5]

Was it sensible to deny the professor a job over a mere 14-day difference? Sensible or not, that is the law. The common law **mirror image rule** requires that acceptance be on precisely the same terms as the offer. If the acceptance contains terms that add or contradict the offer, even in minor ways, courts generally consider it a counteroffer. The rule worked reasonably well in the nineteenth century, when parties would write an original contract and exchange it, penciling in any changes. But now that businesses use standardized forms to purchase most goods and services, the rule creates enormous difficulties. Sellers use forms they have prepared, with all conditions stated to their advantage, and buyers employ their own forms, with terms they prefer. The forms are exchanged in the mail or electronically, with neither side clearly agreeing to the other party's terms.

The problem is known as the "battle of forms." Once again, the UCC has entered the fray, attempting to provide flexibility and common sense for those contracts involving the sale of goods. But for contracts governed by the common law, such as Professor Foster's, the mirror image rule is still the law.

Mirror image rule
A principle in contract law that requires that acceptance be on precisely the same terms as the offer.

(Counter-offer)
• Rejecting someone's previous offer

UCC AND THE BATTLE OF FORMS

UCC Section 2-207 dramatically modifies the mirror image rule for the sale of goods. Under this provision, an acceptance that adds additional or different terms will often create a contract. The rule is intricate, but it is important to understand its basic features because most goods are bought and sold with standardized forms. Exhibit 10.2 illustrates UCC Section 2-207.[6]

Additional or Different Terms

One basic principle of the common law of contracts remains unchanged: the key to creation of a contract is a valid offer that the offeree *intends* to accept. If there is no intent to accept, there is no contract. The big change brought about by UCC Section 2-207 is this: **an offeree who accepts may include in the acceptance terms that are additional to or different from those in the offer.** Thus, even with additional or different terms, the acceptance may well create a contract.

(Sale of goods)
between merchants

> *Example A.* Wholesaler writes to Manufacturer, offering to buy "10,000 wheelbarrows at $50 per unit. Payable on delivery, 30 days from today's date." Manufacturer writes back, "We accept your offer of 10,000 wheelbarrows at $50 per unit, payable on delivery. Interest at normal trade rates for unpaid balances." Manufacturer clearly intends to form a contract. The company has added a new term, but there is still a valid contract.

---

[5] *Foster v. Ohio State University*, 41 Ohio App.3d 86, 534 N.E.2d 1220, 1987 Ohio App. LEXIS 10761 (Ohio Ct.App. 1987).

[6] *Article 2 Alert.* There has been great dissatisfaction with Section 2-207 because it is hard to understand and even harder to apply. Under the proposed revisions, Section 2-206 would determine whether a contract exists. If the parties did make an enforceable deal, a simplified Section 2-207 would determine its provisions, based primarily on any terms that both parties explicitly agreed to, along with Code gap-filler terms. Some of the confusing concepts, such as "material alteration," will probably be deleted.

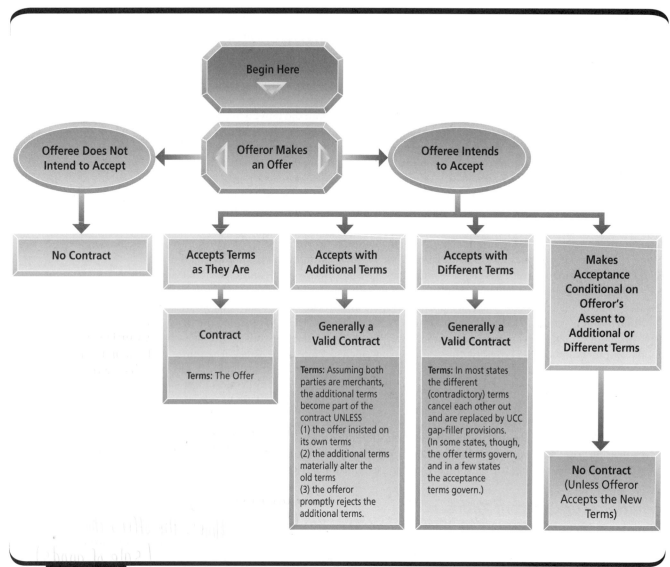

Exhibit 10.2   UCC Section 2-207.

However, if the offeree states that her acceptance is *conditioned on the offerors assent* to the new terms, there is no contract.

Example B. Same offer as above. Manufacturer adds the interest rate clause and states, "Our acceptance is conditional upon your agreement to this interest rate." Manufacturer has made a counteroffer. There is no contract, yet. If Wholesaler accepts the counteroffer, there is a contract; if Wholesaler does not accept it, there is no contract.

Additional terms are those that bring up new issues, such as interest rates, not contained in the original offer. Additional terms in the acceptance are considered proposals to add to the contract. Assuming that both parties are merchants, **the additional terms will generally become**

part of the contract. Thus, in Example A, the interest rate will become a part of the binding deal. If Wholesaler is late in paying, it must pay whatever interest rate is current.

In three circumstances, the additional terms in the acceptance *do not* become part of the contract:

- If the original offer *insisted on its own terms*. In other words, if Wholesaler wrote, "I offer to buy them on the following terms and *no other terms*," then the Manufacturer is not free to make additions.

- If the additional terms *materially alter* the original offer. Suppose Manufacturer wrote back, "We accept your offer for 10,000 wheelbarrows. Delivery will be made within 180 days, unless we notify you of late delivery." Manufacturer has changed the time from 30 days to 180 days, with a possible extension beyond that. That is a material alteration, and it will not become part of the contract. By contrast, Manufacturer's new language concerning "interest at normal trade rates" was not a material alteration, and therefore that interest rate becomes part of the contract.

- If the offeror receives the additional terms and *promptly objects* to them.

Different terms are those that contradict terms in the offer. For example, if the seller's form clearly states that no warranty is included, and the buyer's form says the seller warrants all goods for three years, the acceptance contains different terms. An acceptance may contain different terms and still create a contract. But in these cases, courts have struggled to decide what the terms of the contract are. **The majority of states hold that different (contradictory) terms cancel each other out.** Neither term is included in the contract. Instead, the neutral terms from the Code itself are "read into" the contract. These are the gap-filler terms discussed above. If, for example, the forms had contradictory warranty clauses (as they almost always do), the different terms would cancel each other out, and the warranty clauses from the UCC would be substituted.[7]

Here is a typical UCC Section 2-207 case in which the court must decide whether additional language "materially alters" the contract. The result is very different from what it would have been under the common law.

BAYWAY REFINING CO. V. TOSCO CORP.

215 F.3d 219
Second Circuit Court of Appeals, 2000

CASE SUMMARY

Facts: Bayway Refining and Oxygenated Marketing and Trading A.G. (OMT) were both in the business of buying and selling petroleum products. Bayway agreed to sell OMT 60,000 barrels of gasoline, and OMT faxed a confirmation letter stating that the document represented the full understanding of the parties. The next day, Bayway faxed its own confirmation letter, which stated that the document canceled and superseded any other correspondence. Bayway's fax *incorporated by reference* the company's own "General Terms and Conditions." Those general terms did not accompany the fax, but were available for OMT to examine if it wished. One of those terms stated that the buyer would be responsible for any federal taxes.

---

[7] Not all states follow this rule, however. Some courts have held that when the acceptance contains terms that contradict those in the offer, the language in the offer should be final. A few courts have ruled that the terms in the acceptance should control.

OMT, which never objected to the "general terms," received the gasoline but refused to reimburse Bayway for the federal taxes, which amounted to $464,035. Bayway sued. OMT claimed that the tax clause *materially altered* the contract and, under Section 2-207, never became part of the agreement. The district court gave summary judgment for Bayway, and OMT appealed.

Issue: *Was the tax clause a material alteration or was it part of the contract?*

Decision: The tax clause was not a material alteration of the contract. Affirmed.

Reasoning: It is OMT's burden to prove that the additional terms were a "material alteration," creating surprise and/or hardship.

OMT's officers asserted they were amazed by Bayway's addition to the agreement and called it a "contract by ambush." However, OMT cannot demonstrate that reasonable petroleum executives would have been shocked. Two industry experts offered unchallenged testimony that buyers routinely pay all taxes resulting from a petroleum transaction. One authority said he could not recall a single instance to the contrary. Common sense supports this view because federal taxes are imposed only when a petroleum buyer is not registered with the government. OMT's decision not to register created the tax obligation.

Finally, there is no true hardship to OMT. If this tax burden were ongoing, for many future transactions, the argument might be stronger. However, the obligation is a one-time expense, routine in the industry and created by OMT's own failure to register. There was no material alteration of the agreement.

EXAM *Strategy*

Question: Elaine faxes an offer to Raoul. Raoul writes, "I accept. Please note, I will charge 2% interest per month for any unpaid money." He signs the document and faxes it back to Elaine. Do the two have a binding contract?

Strategy: Slow down, this is trickier than it seems. Raoul has added a term to Elaine's offer. We must take two steps to decide whether there is a contract. In a contract for services, acceptance must mirror the offer, but not so in an agreement for the sale of goods.

Result: If this is an agreement for services, there is no contract. However, if this agreement is for goods, the additional term *may* become part of an enforceable contract.

Question: Assume that Elaine's offer concerns goods. Is there an agreement?

Strategy: Under UCC 2-207, an additional term will become part of a binding agreement for goods except in three instances. What are the three exceptions?

Result: Raoul's extra term will be incorporated in a binding contract unless: (1) Elaine's offer made clear she would accept no other terms; (2) Raoul's interest rate is a material alteration of the offer (almost never the case for interest rates); or (3) Elaine promptly rejects the interest rate.

Clickwraps and Shrinkwraps. You want to purchase Attila brand software and download it to your computer. You type in your credit card number and other information, agreeing to pay $99. Attila also requires that you "read and agree to" all of the company's terms. You click "I agree," without having read one word of the terms. Three frustrating weeks later, tired of trying to operate defective Attilaware, you demand a refund and threaten to sue. The company breezily replies that you are barred from suing because the terms you agreed to included an arbitration clause. To resolve any disputes, you must travel to Attila's hometown, halfway across the nation, use an arbitrator that the company chooses, pay one-half the arbitrator's fee, and also pay Attila's legal bills if you should lose. The agreement makes it financially impossible for you to get your money back. Is that contract enforceable?

You have entered into a "clickwrap" agreement. Similar agreements, called "shrink-wraps," are packaged inside many electronic products. A shrinkwrap notice might require that before inserting a purchased CD into your computer, you must read and agree to all terms in the brochure. Clickwraps and shrinkwraps often include arbitration clauses. They frequently limit the seller's liability if anything goes wrong, saying that the manufacturer's maximum responsibility is to refund the purchase price (even if the software destroys your hard drive).

Many courts that have analyzed these issues have ruled that clickwrap and shrinkwrap agreements are indeed binding, even against consumers. The courts have emphasized that sellers are entitled to offer a product on any terms they wish, and that shrinkwrap and clickwrap are the most efficient methods of including complicated terms in a small space. Think before you click![8]

However, some courts have *refused* to enforce such contracts against a consumer, stating that the buyer never understood or agreed to the shrinkwrapped terms. The court in the following case works hard to balance the competing interests, and in the process demonstrates that this new area of law is very much in flux.

SPECHT V. NETSCAPE COMMUNICATIONS CORPORATION

306 F.3d 17
Second Circuit Court of Appeals, 2002

The offeree MUST know that the offer exists (lost dog award $100)

CASE SUMMARY

Facts: A group of plaintiffs sued Netscape, claiming that two of the company's products illegally captured private information about files that they downloaded from the Internet. The plaintiffs alleged that this was electronic eavesdropping, in violation of two federal statutes.

From Netscape's Web page, the plaintiffs had downloaded SmartDownload, a software plug-in that enabled them to download the company's Communicator software. The Web page advertised the benefits of Smart-Download, and near the bottom of the screen was a tinted button labeled "Download." The plaintiffs clicked to download. If, instead of downloading, they had scrolled further down, they would have seen an invitation to "review and agree to the terms of the Netscape SmartDownload software license agreement." By clicking the appropriate button, they would have

been sent to a series of linked pages, and finally arrived at a license agreement. Among the terms was an agreement to arbitrate any dispute. In other words, a consumer downloading SmartDownload was in theory giving up the right to file suit if anything went wrong, and agreeing to settle the dispute by arbitration. However, the plaintiffs never reviewed the license terms.

In the district court, Netscape moved to dismiss the case and compel arbitration. Netscape claimed that the plaintiffs had forfeited any right to sue based on the license agreement. The district court denied the company's motion, ruling that the plaintiffs had not agreed to the terms of the license. Netscape appealed.

Issue: *Had the plaintiffs agreed to arbitrate their claims?*

Decision: No, the plaintiffs did not agree to arbitration.

---

[8] *ProCD, Inc. v. Zeidenberg*, 86 F.3d 1447 (7th Cir. 1996), is the leading case to enforce shrinkwrap agreements (and, by extension, clickwraps). *Klocek v. Gateway*, 104 F.Supp. 1332 (D.Kan. 2000), is one of the few cases to reject such contracts. *Klocek*, however, was dismissed for failure to reach the federal court $75,000 jurisdictional level.

Reasoning: Netscape contends that if the plaintiffs had scrolled down to the next screen, they would have discovered the license terms. This means that they were on notice of those terms and effectively agreed to them.

When a contract is based on paper documents, courts often find that notice like this does bind the parties. If one document adequately advises a party that the agreement includes terms detailed in a *second* document, the terms can be enforceable. The same principle sometimes applies in the world of e-commerce, when pages contain pop-up screens and hyperlinks to other sites. The question in this case is whether the plaintiffs received sufficient notice of the licensing terms. Did they give real consent to those terms?

What the plaintiffs saw was a screen filled with praise for a fast, free plug-in called SmartDownload. The plaintiffs were urged to "Download Now!" At the very bottom was a "Download" button. There was no immediately visible notice that license terms were detailed elsewhere, or that the company required assent to the terms.

The company claims that the position of the scroll bar notified the plaintiffs that there was additional information below the download button. This is unrealistic. A reasonable person would not conclude from the scroll bar position that important licensing terms were referred to farther down. When consumers are urged to download free software at the click of a button, a reference to license terms placed on a submerged screen is not enough to put them on notice of those terms. The plaintiffs never assented to the terms.

The lower court denied the motion to compel arbitration. That order is affirmed.

The plaintiffs in *Specht* won because they knew nothing about the arbitration clause and were unlikely to discover it on the company's Web site. Notice what happens when a user *does* know about terms posted online. Register.com was a registrar of internet domain names, meaning that it issued domain names to people and companies establishing a new Web site. The company was legally obligated to make available to the public, for free, the names and contact information of its customers. Register was also in the business of assisting owners, for a fee, to develop their Web sites.

Verio, Inc. competed in the site development business. Verio's automated software program (robot) would search Register.com daily, seeking information about new sites. *After* Verio obtained contact information, a notice would appear on the Register site, stating:

By submitting a query, you agree that under no circumstances will you use this data to support the transmission of mass unsolicited, commercial advertising or solicitation via email.

In fact, though, Verio used the contact information for exactly that purpose, sending mass e-mailings to owners of new Web sites, soliciting their development business. Register sued. Verio defended by stating it was not bound by the notice because the notice did not appear until after it had obtained the information. Verio argued that when it sent the queries, it was unaware of any restrictions on use of the data. The court was unpersuaded, and explained its reasoning with a simple but telling metaphor:

The situation might be compared to one in which plaintiff P maintains a roadside fruit stand displaying bins of apples. A visitor, defendant D, takes an apple and bites into it. As D turns to leave, D sees a sign, visible only as one turns to exit, which says "Apples—50 cents apiece." D does not pay for the apple. D believes he has no obligation to pay because he had no notice when he bit into the apple that 50 cents was expected in return. D's view is that he never agreed to pay for the apple. Thereafter, each day, several times a day, D revisits the stand, takes an apple, and eats it. D never leaves money.

P sues D in contract for the price of the apples taken. D defends on the ground that on no occasion did he see P's price notice until after he had bitten into the apples. D may well prevail as to the first apple taken. D had no reason to understand upon taking it that P was demanding the payment. In our view, however, D cannot continue on a daily basis to take apples for free, knowing full well that P is offering them only in exchange for 50 cents in compensation, merely because the sign demanding payment is so placed that on each occasion D does not see it until he has bitten into the apple.

Register.com won its case. Verio was prohibited from using the contact information for mass e-mailings because it had actual knowledge of the restrictions placed on its use.[9]

COMMUNICATION OF ACCEPTANCE

The offeree must communicate his acceptance for it to be effective. The questions that typically arise concern the medium, the manner, and the time of acceptance.

Medium and Manner of Acceptance

The "medium" refers to whether acceptance is done in person or by mail, telephone, e-mail, or fax. The "manner" refers to whether the offeree accepts by promising, by making a down payment, by performing, and so forth. **If an offer demands acceptance in a particular medium or manner, the offeree must follow those requirements.** Suppose a newly incorporated town offers a power company the right to provide electrical service to the residents. The offer states that the power company must accept in writing, and the writing must be delivered to the town's offices by a given date. If the power company orally notifies the town of its acceptance and begins its preparations for delivering electrical service, it has no contract.

If the offer does not specify a type of acceptance, the offeree may accept in any reasonable manner and medium. We have already seen that an offer generally may be accepted by performance or by a promise, unless it specifies a particular method. The same freedom applies to the medium. If Masako faxes Eric an offer to sell 1,000 acres in Montana for $800,000, Eric may accept by mail or fax. Both are routinely used in real estate transactions, and either is reasonable. The same rule applies for the sale of goods.[10] If Masako e-mails Eric an offer to sell 20,000 pairs of jeans for $20 each, he may write, fax, or e-mail his reply.

Time of Acceptance: The Mailbox Rule

An acceptance is generally effective upon dispatch, meaning the moment it is out of the offeree's control. When Masako faxes her offer to sell land to Eric, and he mails his acceptance, the contract is binding the moment he puts the letter into the mail. In most cases, this **mailbox rule** is just a detail. But it becomes important when the offeror revokes her offer at about the same time the offeree accepts. Who wins? Suppose Masako's offer has one twist:

Mailbox rule
Acceptance is generally effective when it is sent.

- On Monday morning, Masako faxes her offer to Eric.

- On Monday afternoon, Eric writes "I accept" on the fax.

- On Tuesday morning, Eric mails his acceptance.

- On Tuesday afternoon, Masako faxes Eric a revocation of her offer.

- On Thursday morning, Eric's acceptance arrives at Masako's office.

Outcome? Eric has an enforceable contract. Masako's offer was effective when it reached Eric. His acceptance was effective on Tuesday morning, when he mailed it. Nothing that happens later, such as Masako's attempt to revoke, can "undo" the contract.

---

[9] *Register.Com v. Verio, Inc.*, 353 F.3d 393 (2d Cir. 2004).
[10] UCC Section 2-206(1)(a).

SOLDAU V. ORGANON, INC.

860 F.2d 355, 1988 U.S.APP. LEXIS 14757
UNITED STATES COURT OF APPEALS FOR THE NINTH CIRCUIT, 1988

CASE SUMMARY

Facts: Organon fired John Soldau. Then the company sent to him a letter offering to pay him double the normal severance pay, provided Soldau would sign a full release, that is, a document giving up any and all claims he might have against Organon. The release was included with the letter. Soldau signed it, dated it, and took it to the nearest post office, where he deposited it in the mailbox. When he returned home, Soldau discovered in the mail a check from Organon for the double severance pay. He hustled back to the post office, where he persuaded a postal clerk to open the mailbox and retrieve the release he had posted. He then cashed Organon's check and finally filed a suit against the company, alleging that his firing was age discrimination.

The federal district court gave summary judgment for Organon, ruling that Soldau's acceptance of the proposed release was effective when he mailed it, creating a contract. He appealed.

Issue: *Did Soldau create a contract by mailing the release?*

Decision: Affirmed. Soldau created an enforceable contract.

Reasoning: Soldau argues that federal law should govern this case, not California law. In fact, it makes no difference because both court systems use the "mailbox" rule. Acceptance is effective when dispatched. The U.S. Supreme Court adopted the rule almost 100 years ago. Since then, every court, treatise, and commentator has approved the rule, both in the United States and most common-law countries. The mailbox rule offers a reasonable method of balancing the risks between two parties. Leaving it as a settled principle creates certainty in contract formation.

The moment Soldau put the envelope in the mailbox, the company became obligated to give him double severance pay, and he gave up any right to file suit.

CHAPTER CONCLUSION

The law of offer and acceptance can be complex and even baffling. Yet for all its fault, the law is not the principal source of dispute between parties unhappy with negotiations. Most litigation concerning offer and acceptance comes from *lack of clarity* on the part of the people negotiating. Letters of intent are often an effort to "have it both ways," that is, to ensure the other side's commitment without accepting a corresponding obligation. Similarly, the "battle of the forms" is caused by corporate officers seeking to make a deal and hurry things forward without settling details. These, and the many other examples discussed, are all understandable given the speed and fluidity of the real world of business. But the executive who insists on clarity is likelier in the long run to spend more time doing business and less time in court.

EXAM REVIEW

1. **MEETING OF THE MINDS** The parties can form a contract only if they have a meeting of the minds, which requires that they understand each other and intend to reach an agreement. (p. 246)

EXAM Strategy

Question: Norv owned a Ford dealership and wanted to expand by obtaining a BMW outlet. He spoke with Jackson and other BMW executives on several occasions. Norv now claims that those discussions resulted in an oral contract that requires BMW to grant him a franchise, but the company disagrees. Norv's strongest evidence of a contract is the fact that Jackson gave him forms on which to order BMWs. Jackson answered that it was his standard practice to give such forms to prospective dealers, so that if the franchise were approved, car orders could be processed quickly. Norv states that he was "shocked" when BMW refused to go through with the deal. Is there a contract?

Strategy: A court makes an *objective* assessment of what the parties did and said to determine whether they had a meeting of the minds and intended to form a contract. Norv's "shock" is irrelevant. Do the order forms indicate a meeting of the minds? Was there additional evidence that the parties had reached an agreement? (See the "Result" at the end of this section.)

2. **OFFER** An offer is an act or statement that proposes definite terms and permits the other party to create a contract by accepting those terms. (p. 247)

3. **OTHER STATEMENTS** Invitations to bargain, price quotes, and advertisements are generally not offers. A letter of intent may or may not be an offer, depending upon the exact language and whether it indicates that the parties have reached an agreement. (pp. 247–250)

Question: "Huge selection of Guernsey sweaters," reads a newspaper ad from Stuffed Shirt, a clothing retailer. "Regularly $135, today only $65." Waldo arrives at Stuffed Shirt at 4:00 that afternoon, but the shop clerk says there are no more sweaters. He shows Waldo a newly arrived Shetland sweater that sells for $145. Waldo sues, claiming breach of contract and violation of a consumer protection statute. Who will prevail?

(a) Waldo will win the breach of contract suit and the consumer protection suit.

(b) Waldo will lose the breach of contract suit but might win the consumer protection suit.

(c) Waldo will lose the consumer protection suit but should win the breach of contract suit.

(d) Waldo will win the consumer protection suit only if he wins the contract case.

(e) Waldo will lose both the breach of contract suit and the consumer protection suit.

Strategy: Waldo assumes that he is accepting the store's offer. But did Stuffed Shirt make an offer? If not, there cannot be a contract. Does the consumer protection statute help him? (See the "Result" at the end of this section.)

4. **DEFINITENESS** The terms of the offer must be definite, although under the UCC the parties may create a contract that has open terms. (p. 251)

5. **TERMINATION** An offer may be terminated by revocation, rejection, expiration, or operation of law. (p. 254)

EXAM Strategy

Question: Rick is selling his espresso coffee maker. He sends Tamara an email, offering to sell the machine for $350. Tamara promptly emails back, offering to buy the item for $300. She hears nothing from Rick, so an hour later Tamara stops by his apartment, where she learns that he just sold the machine to his roommate for $250. She sues Rick. Outcome?

(a) Tamara will win because her offer was higher than the roommate's.

(b) Tamara will win because Rick never responded to her offer.

(c) Tamara will win because both parties made clear offers, in writing.

(d) Tamara will lose because she rejected Rick's offer.

(e) Tamara will lose because her offer was not definite.

Strategy: A valid contract requires a definite offer and acceptance. Rick made a valid offer. When Tamara said she would buy the machine for a lower amount, was that acceptance? If not, what was it? (See the "Result" at the end of this section.)

---

6. **SILENCE.** The offeree must say or do something to accept. Silence is not acceptance. (p. 256)

7. **MIRROR IMAGE AND UCC 2-207** The common law mirror image rule requires acceptance on precisely the same terms as the offer. Under the UCC, an offeree may often create a contract even when the acceptance includes terms that are additional to or different from those in the offer. (p. 257)

8. **CLICKWRAPS** Clickwrap and shrinkwrap agreements are generally enforceable. (p. 260)

9. **MANNER OF ACCEPTANCE** If an offer demands acceptance in a particular medium or manner, the offeree must follow those requirements. If the offer does not specify a type of acceptance, the offeree may accept in any reasonable manner and medium. (p. 263)

10. **MAILBOX RULE** An acceptance is generally effective upon dispatch, meaning from the moment it is out of the offeree's control. (p. 263)

---

1. Result: The order forms are neither an offer nor an acceptance. Norv has offered no evidence that the parties agreed on price, date of performance, or any other key terms. There is no contract. Norv allowed eagerness and optimism to replace common sense.[11]

3. Result: An advertisement is not an offer, but merely a solicitation of one. It is Waldo who is making the offer, which the store may reject. Waldo loses his contract case, but he may win under the consumer protection statute. The correct answer is B. If Stuffed Shirt proclaimed "Huge selection" when there were only five sweaters, the store was deliberately misleading consumers, and Waldo wins. However, if there was indeed a large selection, and Waldo arrived too late, he is out of luck.

5. Result: Tamara made a counteroffer of $300. A counteroffer is a rejection. Tamara rejected Rick's offer and simultaneously offered to buy the coffee maker at a lower price. Rick was under no obligation to sell to Tamara at any price. He will win Tamara's suit.

ADDITIONAL QUESTIONS

1. The town of Sanford, Maine, decided to auction off a lot it owned. The town advertised that it would accept bids through the mail, up to a specified date. Arthur and Arline Chevalier mailed in a bid that turned out to be the highest. When the town refused to sell them the lot, they sued. Result?

2. Arturo hires Kate to work in his new sporting goods store. "Look," he explains, "I can only pay you $9.00 an hour. But if business is good a year from now, and you're still here, I'm sure I can pay you a healthy bonus." Four months later, Arturo terminates Kate. She sues. (a)Kate will win her job back, plus the year's pay and the bonus. (b)Kate will win the year's pay and the bonus. (c)Kate will win only the bonus. (d)Kate will win only her job back. (e)Kate will win nothing.

3. The Tufte family leased a 260-acre farm from the Travelers Insurance Co. Toward the end of the lease, Travelers mailed the Tuftes an option to renew the lease. The option arrived at the Tuftes' house on March 30, and gave them until April 14 to accept. On April 13, the Tuftes signed and mailed their acceptance, which Travelers received on April 19. Travelers claimed there was no lease and attempted to evict the Tuftes from the farm. May they stay?

4. Northrop is a huge defense firm, and Litronic manufactures electronic components such as printed wire boards. Northrop requested Litronic to submit an offer on certain printed boards. Litronic sent its offer form, stating a price and including its pre-printed warranty clause, which limited its liability to 90 days. Northrop orally accepted the offer, then sent its own purchase order form, which contained a warranty clause holding the seller liable with no time limit. Six months after the goods were

---

[11] Based on *Arnold Pontiac-GMC, Inc. v. General Motors Co.*, 786 F.2d 564 (3 Cir. 1986).

delivered Northrop discovered they were defective. Northrop sued, but Litronic claimed it had no liability. Was there a contract? If not, why not? If there was a contract, what were its warranty terms?

5. Consolidated Edison Co. of New York (Con Ed) sought bids from General Electric Co. (GE) and others to supply it with two huge transformers. Con Ed required that the bids be held open for 90 days. GE submitted a written bid and included a clause holding the bid open for 90 days. During that period, Con Ed accepted GE's bid, but GE refused to honor it. Is there a contract?

6. The Dukes leased land from Lillian Whatley. Toward the end of their lease, they sent Ms. Whatley a new contract, renewing the lease for three years and giving themselves the option to buy the land at any time during the lease for $50,000. Ms. Whatley crossed out the clause giving them an option to buy. She added a sentence at the bottom, saying, "Should I, Lillian Whatley, decide to sell at end [sic] of three years, I will give the Dukes the first chance to buy." Then she signed the lease, which the Dukes accepted in the changed form. They continued to pay the rent until Ms. Whatley sold the land to another couple for $35,000. The Dukes sued. Are the Dukes entitled to the land at $50,000? At $35,000?

7. **YOU BE THE JUDGE** WRITING PROBLEM Academy Chicago Publishers (Academy) approached the widow of author John Cheever about printing some of his unpublished stories. She signed a contract, which stated:

2. The Author will deliver to the Publisher on a mutually agreeable date one copy of the manuscript of the Work as finally arranged by the editor and satisfactory to the Publisher in form and content....

5. Within a reasonable time and a mutually agreeable date after delivery of the final revised manuscript, the Publisher will publish the Work at its own expense, in such style and manner and at such price as it deems best, and will keep the Work in print as long as it deems it expedient.

Within a year, Academy had located and delivered to Mrs. Cheever more than 60 unpublished stories. But she refused to go ahead with the project. Academy sued for the right to publish the book. The trial court ruled that the agreement was valid; the appeals court affirmed; and the case went to the Illinois Supreme Court. Was Academy's offer valid, and was the contract enforceable? **Argument for Mrs. Cheever:** The agreement is too vague to be enforceable. None of the essential terms are specified: the number of stories, their length, who selects them, the date of publication, the size or cost of the book, or anything else. There is no contract. **Argument for Academy:** Mrs. Cheever wanted to publish this book and agreed in writing to help Academy do so. Both parties understood the essential nature of the book and were willing to permit some flexibility, to ensure a good edition. She has no right to back out now.

8. Rebecca, in Honolulu, faxes a job offer to Spike, in Pittsburgh, saying, "We can pay you $55,000 per year, starting June 1." Spike faxes a reply, saying, "Thank you! I accept your generous offer, though I will also need $3,000 in relocation money. See you June 1. Can't wait!" On June 1, Spike arrives, to find that his position is filled by Gus. He sues Rebecca. (a)Spike wins $55,000. (b)Spike wins $58,000. (c)Spike wins $3,000. (d)Spike wins restitution. (e)Spike wins nothing.

9. **ROLE REVERSAL** Write a multiple-choice question focusing on the mailbox rule.

INTERNET RESEARCH PROBLEM

Search the Internet for an auction with a ring selling for over $500. Find a site that is new to you. Is the site reliable? Who is actually selling the item? If you were to pay for the ring, would you receive it? If you were unhappy with your purchase, what remedies would you have? How can you ascertain the Web site's reliability?

You can find further practice problems at www.cengagebrain.com. See the preface of this book for website access details.

CHAPTER 11

CONSIDERATION

We have all made promises that we soon regretted. Mercifully, the law does not hold us accountable for everything we say. Yet some promises must be enforced. Which ones? The doctrine of consideration exists for one purpose: to distinguish promises that are binding from those that are not. Which of these four promises should a court enforce?

PROMISE ONE. In a delirious burst of affection, Professor Parsley says to a class of 50 students, "You've been a great class all semester. Next week I'm going to mail each of you a check for $1,000." But that night, the professor reconsiders and decides that her class is actually a patch full of cabbage heads whose idea of work is getting out of bed before noon. The following day, in class, Parsley announces that she has changed her mind. Mike, a student, sues for his $1,000. Should a court enforce the professor's promise?

You've been a great class all semester. Next week I'm going to mail each of you a check for $1,000.

PROMISE TWO. After class, Parsley promises a student, Daisy, a part-time job as a researcher for the rest of the semester. "You can start on Monday," she says, "and we'll work out pay and all the details then." "You mean I can give up my job at Burger Bucket?" asks an elated Daisy. "Sure thing," chirps the prof. But on Monday, Parsley informs Daisy that she has lost the funding for her research and can offer no job. Daisy is unable to get back her position at Burger Bucket and sues Parsley.

PROMISE THREE. Professor Parsley announces in class that she will be selling her skis at the end of the semester for $450. After class, Arabella says she would like to buy the skis but can only afford to pay $250. Parsley frowns and mutters, "They're worth a lot more than that." But Arabella looks so heartbroken that Parsley adds, "OK, what the heck. You can have them May 15." On that date Arabella shows up with the cash, but Parsley explains that another student offered her the full $450 for the skis and she sold them. Arabella purchases a nearly identical pair for $475 and sues Parsley.

PROMISE FOUR. The professor makes no promise at all. In fact, she announces in class that she will be unable to attend the next session because her favorite racehorse, Preexisting Duty, is running in the third race at the local track and she wants to be there. The students are crushed at the idea of missing a class. Sam wails, "Don't do this to us, Professor! I'll pay you twenty bucks if you'll be here to teach us." Other students chime in, and in a groundswell of tears and emotion, the students promise a total of $1,000 if Parsley will do her job. She agrees. When she arrives to teach the next class, 50 suddenly sullen students refuse to pay, and she sues.

Society could enforce *all* promises in the interests of simple morality. Or should it enforce only those where the two sides engaged in some bargaining? Does it matter whether someone relied on a promise? Should the outcome be different if someone is promising to do what she is already obligated to do? These are important policy questions, affecting promises for a hundred dollars and deals for a billion; their answers lie in the law of consideration.

A BARGAIN AND AN EXCHANGE

Consideration is a required element of any contract. **Consideration means that there must be bargaining that leads to an exchange between the parties.** "Bargaining" indicates that each side is obligating itself in some way *to induce the other side to agree.* Generally, a court will enforce one party's promise only if the other party did something or promised something in exchange. Without an exchange of mutual obligations, there is usually no deal.

How would the four Parsley examples in the introduction work out? In the first case, Mike loses. There is no consideration because the students neither bargained for Parsley's promise nor gave anything in exchange for it. In the second case, there is also no contract because none of the terms were definite. What were Daisy's hours, her salary, her duties? Daisy cannot sue on a contract, but she does have a claim of promissory estoppel, the one major exception to the rule of consideration. Because Daisy relied on Parsley's promise, a court may give her some compensation. In case three, Arabella should win. A bargain and an exchange occurred. The professor promised to sell the skis at a given price, then broke her promise. Arabella will probably recover $225, the difference between the contract price and what she was forced to pay for substitute skis. Finally, in the fourth case, the professor loses. Clearly, bargaining and an exchange took place, but the professor only promised to do something that she was already obligated to do. The law does not respect such a promise.

We will look more deeply into these issues. First, a case to demonstrate the basic rule: there must be bargaining and an exchange.

KELSOE V. INTERNATIONAL WOOD PRODUCTS, INC.

588 So.2d 877, 1991 Ala. LEXIS 1014
Supreme Court of Alabama, 1991

CASE SUMMARY

Facts: Carol Kelsoe worked at International Wood Products. One day, her supervisor, Rene Hernandez, promised Kelsoe 5% of the company's stock. But he never gave her the shares, and she sued. The trial court gave a directed verdict for International Wood, and Kelsoe appealed.

Issue: *Is Hernandez's promise binding?*

Decision: Affirmed. Hernandez's promise was not binding.

Reasoning: On behalf of International Wood, Hernandez promised Kelsoe 5% of the company's stock. The real nature of that promise, though, becomes clear from Kelsoe's own testimony:

Q. [by the lawyer for International Wood:] Ms. Kelsoe, you were compensated for your work at International Wood, weren't you?[1]

A. Yes, sir, I received a check.

Q. Were you pleased with your compensation?

A. Yes, sir.

Q. Did you think you were compensated well enough for the work you did?

A. I worked long hours, long hours.

Q. My question was, did you think that you were adequately compensated for the work you did?

A. Yes, sir.

Q. Ms. Kelsoe, you never entered an agreement with Mr. Hernandez; "Mr. Hernandez, if I work long and hard and do this," and then he said, "I'll give you 5 percent of the corporation," did you?

A. No, sir.

Q. You never had that kind of a bargain, did you?

A. No, sir.

Q. And all the time, all the work you did was part of your normal job?

A. Yes, sir.

Q. And then [on] March 8th, you were getting a little reward that you didn't really expect, weren't you?

A. Yes, sir.

Q. You didn't expect to get that 5 percent, but it was nice, wasn't it?

A. Yes, sir.

Q. And you didn't expect it, though, did you?

A. No, sir.

Q. And you had no reason to expect it?

A. No, sir.

Q. And you just kept right on from March 8th doing your work, didn't you?

A. That's correct.

Q. And you didn't stay on [at] International Wood Products, you didn't commit yourself to Mr. Hernandez, "I'll stay on forever," did you? Or, "I'll stay on for five years in return for this?" You left yourself free to quit at any time, didn't you?

A. Yes, sir, that's correct.

Q. He just up one day and surprised you and said, here is 5 percent of this corporation?

A. Yes, sir.

Consideration is an essential element of a contract. There must have been an act, forbearance, detriment, or return promise that was bargained for and given in exchange for the promise. Hernandez's promise to give his employee stock was made as a friendly gesture, based on her past work. Kelsoe gave no consideration, and Hernandez's promise was legally unenforceable. The directed verdict was proper.

---

[1] International Wood's lawyer is cross-examining Ms. Kelsoe, so he is permitted to ask leading questions.

ETHICS   Because Kelsoe had given no consideration, International Wood was legally permitted to escape from its promise. Was that ethical? Use the ethics checklist from Chapter 2. Should a corporation honor all commitments to employees? What policy would create the best workforce? What harm might befall a company that fulfilled all promises? What decision would you have made if you were Hernandez's boss and had the power to award the stock to Kelsoe or deny it? ◆

When trying to enforce a defendant's promise, the plaintiff must show that she did something or promised something in exchange for that promise. What sort of action or promise is good enough? It need not be much. **Consideration can be anything that someone might want to bargain for.** As we explore this idea, we need to use two more legal terms: **promisor,** meaning the person who makes the promise, and **promisee,** the person to whom the promise is made. In consideration cases, a court is typically trying to determine whether the promisee should be able to enforce the promise, and the decision will depend upon whether the promisee gave consideration.

The thing bargained for can be another promise or action. Usually, the thing bargained for is another promise. In the *Kelsoe* case, suppose Hernandez had said, "I will give you 5% of our stock if you'll promise not to quit for three years," and Kelsoe had agreed to stay. Her promise would be consideration, making Hernandez's promise enforceable. They would have had a typical bilateral contract. (See Exhibit 11.1.)

The thing bargained for can be an action, rather than a promise. Suppose Professor Parsley says to Wade, "If you plow my driveway by tonight, I'll pay you $150." Her offer seeks an action, not a promise. If Wade plows the driveway, his work is consideration and the parties have a binding contract.

Promisor

The person who makes a promise.

Promisee

The person to whom a promise is made.

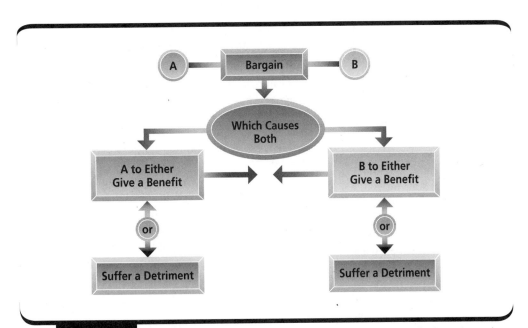

Exhibit 11.1   There is consideration to support a contract when *A* and *B* bargain, and their bargaining causes both *A* and *B* either to give a benefit to the other or to suffer a detriment.

The thing bargained for can be a benefit to the promisor or a detriment to the promisee. If Hernandez had asked Kelsoe to stay on at International Wood, her promise to do so would have been a benefit to the company. That is consideration.

Suppose Professor Parsley says to the class, "You're all in terrible shape. I offer $25 to anyone who enters next week's marathon and finishes the race." "No way," shouts Joanne. "But I'll do it for $100." Parsley agrees and Joanne completes the entire race. Her running was of no particular benefit to Parsley, but it was clearly a detriment to Joanne, so Parsley owes her $100.

The thing bargained for can be a promise to do something or a promise to refrain from doing something. Megan promises to deliver 1,000 canoes in two months if Casey agrees to pay $300 per canoe. Megan's promise is consideration. Leroy, who runs a beauty parlor, offers Chloe $75,000 not to open a beauty parlor within 30 miles. Chloe's promise *not* to compete is consideration.

The most famous of all consideration lawsuits began in 1869, when a well-meaning uncle made a promise to his nephew. Ever since *Hamer v. Sidway* appeared, generations of American law students have dutifully inhaled the facts and sworn by its wisdom; now you, too, may drink it in.

HAMER V. SIDWAY

124 N.Y. 538, 27 N.E. 256, 1891 N.Y. LEXIS 1396
NEW YORK COURT OF APPEALS, 1891

CASE SUMMARY

Facts: This is a story with two Stories. William Story wanted his nephew to grow up healthy and prosperous. In 1869, he promised the 15-year-old boy (also William Story) $5,000 if the lad would refrain from drinking liquor, using tobacco, swearing, and playing cards or billiards for money until his twenty-first birthday. (In that wild era—can you believe it?—the nephew had a legal right to do all those things.) The nephew agreed and, what is more, he kept his word. When he reached his twenty-first birthday, the nephew notified his uncle that he had honored the agreement. The uncle congratulated the young man and promised to give him the money, but he said he would wait a few more years before handing over the cash, until the nephew was mature enough to handle such a large sum. The uncle died in 1887 without having paid, and his estate refused to honor the promise. Because the nephew had transferred his rights in the money, it was a man named Hamer who eventually sought to collect from the uncle's estate. The estate argued that since the nephew had given no consideration for the uncle's promise, there was no enforceable contract. The trial court found for the plaintiff, and the uncle's estate appealed.

Issue: *Did the nephew give consideration for the uncle's promise?*

Decision: Yes, the nephew's conduct was valid consideration and the contract must be enforced.

Reasoning: The uncle's estate argues that the conduct, far from harming the boy, actually aided him. Because it is wise to avoid tobacco, alcohol, and gambling, the nephew's decision to give up those vices could never be consideration for a contract. The agreement could be enforced only if the behavior somehow benefited the uncle—which it did not. The estate's argument, however, is unpersuasive. Courts do not and should not ask whether agreed-on behavior actually helps anyone. What matters is simply this: Did one party do something or refrain from doing something at the request of the other party? If so, that conduct or forbearance is consideration, and the contract is enforceable.

Before making the agreement, the nephew had lawfully used alcohol and tobacco. When his uncle promised him $5,000, the nephew gave up the various activities, restricting his freedom of action for several years. Because the nephew did what his uncle requested, the contract must be enforced whether or not anyone benefited.

ADEQUACY OF CONSIDERATION

Gold can make people crazy. At the turn of the twentieth century, John Tuppela joined the gold rush to Alaska. He bought a mine and worked it hard, a disciplined man in an unforgiving enterprise. Sadly, his prospecting proved futile and mental problems overwhelmed him. In 1914, a court declared him insane and locked him in an institution in Portland, Oregon. Four years later, Tuppela emerged and learned to his ecstasy that gold had been discovered in his mine, now valued at over half a million dollars. Then the bad news hit: a court-appointed guardian had sold the mine for pennies while Tuppela was institutionalized. Destitute and forlorn, Tuppela turned to his lifelong friend, Embola, saying, "If you will give me $50 so I can go to Alaska and get my property back, I will pay you $10,000 when I win my property." Embola accepted the offer, advancing the $50.

After a long and bitter fight, Tuppela won back his mine, though a guardian would still supervise his assets. Tuppela asked the guardian to pay the full $10,000 to Embola, but the guardian refused. Embola sued, and the issue was whether his $50 was *adequate consideration* to support Tuppela's promise of $10,000. A happy ending: Embola won and recovered his money.

Courts seldom inquire into the adequacy of consideration. Although the difference between Embola's $50 and Tuppela's $10,000 was huge, it was not for a court to decide whether the parties had made an intelligent bargain. Embola undertook a risk and his $50 *was valid consideration*. The question of adequacy is for the parties as they bargain, not for the courts.

Law professors often call this the "peppercorn rule," a reference to a Civil War era case[2] in which a judge mused, "What is a valuable consideration? A peppercorn." Even the tiniest benefit to a plaintiff counts, so long as it has a measureable value.

·EXAM *Strategy*

Question: 50 Cent has been rapping all day, and he is very thirsty. He pulls his Ferrari into the parking lot of a convenience store. The store turns out to be closed, but luckily for him, a Pepsi machine sits outside. While walking over to it, he realizes that he has left his wallet at home. Frustrated, he whistles to a ten-year-old kid who is walking by. "Hey, kid!" he shouts. "I need to borrow fifty cents!" "I know you are!" the kid replies. Fiddy tries again. "No, no, I need to *borrow* fifty cents!" The kid walks over. "Well, I'm not going to just give you my last fifty cents. But maybe you can sell me something." 50 Cent can't believe it, but he really is very thirsty. He takes off a Rolex, which is his least expensive bling. "How about this?" "Deal," the kid says, handing over two quarters. Does consideration exist to support this agreement?

Strategy: Even in extreme cases, courts rarely take an interest in *how much* consideration is given, or whether everyone got a "good deal." Even though the Rolex is worth thousands of times more than the quarters, the quarters still count under the peppercorn rule.

Result: After this transaction, 50 Cent may have second thoughts. If he sues the kid to get his Rolex back, many interesting issues might arise, but let's focus on consideration. The kid and 50 Cent each delivered a benefit. So, consideration exists to support this deal, and 50 Cent would not get his watch back by making a consideration argument.

---

[2] *Hobbs v. Duff*, 23 Cal. 596 (1863).

MUTUALITY OF OBLIGATIONS

Generally, both sides must be committed to the agreement to make it enforceable. Though courts will not inquire into the adequacy of consideration, they will insist that it be genuine. In some cases, a party appears to make a commitment but actually does not. The result: no contract. Here we examine the major issues concerning mutuality.

ILLUSORY PROMISE

Annabel calls Jim and says, "I'll sell you my bicycle for 325 bucks. Interested?" Jim says, "I'll look at it tonight in the bike rack. If I like what I see, I'll pay you three and a quarter in the morning." At sunrise, Jim shows up with the $325, but Annabel refuses to sell. Can Jim enforce their deal? No. He said he would buy the bicycle *if he liked it*, keeping for himself the power to get out of the agreement for any reason at all. He is not committing himself to do anything, and the law considers his promise illusory, that is, not really a promise at all. **An illusory promise is not consideration.** Because he has given no consideration, there is no contract and *neither party* can enforce the deal. Is the promise in the following case illusory?

YOU *be the* JUDGE

CULBERTSON V. BRODSKY
788 S.W.2d 156, 1990 Tex. App. LEXIS 1008
Texas Court of Appeals, 1990

Facts: Sam Culbertson had some Texas real estate to sell. He and Frederick Brodsky signed an option contract. Brodsky was to deliver a check for $5,000, representing "earnest money," to a bank. The bank would hold the check in escrow for 60 days. During that period, the bank would not cash it. Brodsky could inspect the property and perform engineering studies to determine whether the real estate could be used for his purposes. If he decided that the land was of no use to him, he could terminate the agreement and demand return of his earnest money. Ultimately, Brodsky decided that he did want to buy the land, but Culbertson refused to sell, claiming that Brodsky gave no consideration to support their contract. The trial court gave judgment for Brodsky, ordering Culbertson to convey the land. Culbertson appealed.

You Be the Judge: Did Brodsky give valid consideration that makes Culbertson's promise enforceable?

Argument for Culbertson: Your honors, Mr. Brodsky made a very sly promise, since it was in fact no promise at all. Brodsky insisted on keeping the right to terminate this phony agreement at any time, for any reason. Mr. Culbertson was expected to leave the property off the market for 60 valuable days while Brodsky took his own sweet time to inspect the land, perform engineering tests, make feasibility calculations, reconsider his position, and ultimately decide whether he had any interest in the property. If he decided for any reason that he no longer wanted the land, Brodsky could simply walk away from the deal. Please note that he didn't even lose the use of the $5,000. The bank was not permitted to cash the check until Brodsky made up his mind. No money ever left Brodsky's account—indeed, no money even had to be in his account, unless and until he decided to exercise his option.

A true option contract provides something for each party. The landowner is obligated to hold the property open for the buyer, but the buyer pays a fee for this privilege. Here, Brodsky was obligated to pay nothing and do nothing. He made no promise at all, and we urge that no contract resulted.

Argument for Brodsky: Your honors, it is rather disingenuous of Mr. Culbertson to pose as an injured party here. He is, in fact,

continued

a sophisticated property owner. He voluntarily entered into a contract with Mr. Brodsky for one reason: it was in his own interest. He concluded that the best way to "land" Mr. Brodsky was first to "hook" him with an option contract. He wanted Mr. Brodsky to show serious interest, and demanded earnest money. He got it. He insisted that Mr. Brodsky's check be held in escrow. He got it. Culbertson hoped that by getting this degree of commitment, Mr. Brodsky would perform the necessary tests on the land and conclude that he wanted to buy it. And that is *precisely what happened*. Mr. Brodsky, in total good faith, performed his tests, decided the land was what he had wanted, and exercised the option that Culbertson had sold him. But Culbertson decided to back out of the deal—presumably to sell elsewhere.

Now Culbertson comes into court and relies on a technical rule of contract law to try to weasel out of a good faith deal. The law of consideration was never intended to permit such chicanery.

SALES LAW: REQUIREMENTS AND OUTPUT CONTRACTS

You decide to open a "novelty T-shirt" business. You will buy plain white T-shirts from a wholesaler and then arrange for them to be printed with funny pictures and quotes. You will sell them to the public from a small booth you rent in a popular shopping mall. Your single biggest expense will be the wholesale cost of the T-shirts. How many will you need? You *think* that sales will soar, and you will need hundreds each week. But what if business lags? You do not want to overstock. Your solution may be a requirements contract.

In a requirements contract, the buyer agrees to purchase 100% of her goods from one seller. The seller agrees to sell the buyer whatever quantity she reasonably needs. The quantity is not stated in the contract, though it may be estimated, based on previous years or best calculations.

The common law regarded requirements contracts as void because the buyer held all the power. She could purchase a vast quantity or none at all. She was making no commitment, and hence was giving no consideration. Common law courts refused to enforce requirements contracts, as well as their counterpart, output contracts. **In an output contract, the seller guarantees to sell 100% of its output to one buyer, and the buyer agrees to accept the entire quantity.** For example, a timber company might agree to sell all of its wood products to a lumber wholesaler. The common law frowned because now it was the seller who was making no real commitment.

The problem with the common law rule was that many merchants valued these contracts. Consider the utility of requirements contracts. From the buyer's viewpoint, a requirements contract provides flexibility. The buyer can adjust purchases based on consumer demands. The agreement also guarantees her a source of goods in a competitive market. For a seller, the requirements agreement will ensure him at least this one outlet and will prevent competitors from selling to this buyer. The contract should enable the seller to spend less on marketing, and may enable him to predict sales more accurately. Output contracts have similar value.

The UCC responded in a forthright fashion: **Section 2-306 expressly allows output and requirements contracts in the sale of goods**.[3] However, the Code places one limitation on how much the buyer may demand (or the seller may offer):

---

[3] UCC Section 2-306(2) permits a related type of contract, the exclusive dealing agreement. Here, either a buyer or a seller of goods agrees to deal exclusively with the other party. The results are similar to an output or requirements agreement. Once again, one party is receiving a guarantee in exchange for a promise that the common law would have considered illusory. Under the Code, such a deal is enforceable.

A term which measures the quantity by the output of the seller or the requirements of the buyer means such actual output or requirements as may occur *in good faith*, …

The "good faith" phrase is critical. In requirements contracts, courts have ruled that it is the "good faith" that a buyer brings to the deal that represents her consideration.[4] In other words, by agreeing to act in good faith, she actually is limiting her options. Since she is obligating herself, the deal becomes binding. Beware that this is not just word play. A buyer *must make its requirement demands in good faith*, based on the expectations the parties had when they signed the deal.

Suppose, in your T-shirt business, you and the wholesaler agree on a two-year requirements contract with a fixed price of three dollars per T-shirt and an estimate of 150 T-shirts per week. If business is slow the first two months, you are permitted to purchase only 25 T-shirts per week in the event that is all you are selling. Should sales suddenly boom and you need 200 per week, you may also require that many. Both of those demands are made in good faith. But suppose the price of cotton skyrockets and the wholesale cost of T-shirts everywhere suddenly doubles. You have a two-year guaranteed price of three dollars per T-shirt. Could you demand 2,000 T-shirts per week, knowing that you will be able to resell the shirts to other retailers for a big profit? No. That is not acting in good faith based on the original expectations of the parties. The wholesaler is free to ignore your exorbitant demand. The legal requirement has come full circle: your good faith is valid consideration and makes the deal enforceable—but it is binding on you, too.

EXAM *Strategy*

Question: Will bought simple wood furniture and custom painted it for sale to interior designers. He entered into a written agreement to buy all of the furniture he needed, for two years, from Wood Knot, Inc. Wood Knot agreed to supply Will with all the furniture he requested. During the second year, Will's business grew, and he requested 28% more furniture than in the first year. Wood Knot would not deliver unless Will would pay a higher price per unit, which Will would not. Will sued. What kind of a contract was this? Will Will win? Why or why not?

Strategy: Because this agreement did not specify the quantity of goods being sold, we know that it was either a requirements contract or an output contract. Review the difference between the two. Which was this agreement? These contracts are now legal, with one major limitation. What is that limitation? Apply it here.

Result: This was a requirements contract, because Will agreed to purchase all of his furniture from Wood Knot. Under the UCC, requirements contracts are enforceable, provided the buyer makes his demands in good faith. Will's increased order was a result of his booming business. Indeed, he entered into this agreement to protect his ability to grow his company. He made the request in good faith, the contract is enforceable, and yes—Will will win.

PAST CONSIDERATION

In *Kelsoe v. International Wood Products, Inc.* (discussed earlier in this chapter), International Wood's manager, Hernandez, promised employee Carol Kelsoe some shares of the company stock, but never delivered them. She sued and lost, because there had been no bargaining and no exchange. Yet Hernandez must have had some reason for making the promise. Presumably,

---

[4] *Famous Brands, Inc. v. David Sherman Corp.*, 814 F.2d 517, 1987 U.S. App. LEXIS 3634 (8th Cir. 1987).

it was because of Kelsoe's good work for the company in years past. Could she claim the previous work as consideration? No.

Past consideration is generally no consideration. It all goes back to our basic definition of consideration, which requires bargaining and an exchange of obligations. If one party makes a promise based on what the other party has already done, there is no exchange, and there will usually be no enforceable contract.

• Any act that was performed prior to the contract is not a consideration

DEMENTAS V. ESTATE OF TALLAS

95 UTAH ADV. REP. 28, 764 P.2d 628, 1988 UTAH APP. LEXIS 174
UTAH COURT OF APPEALS, 1988

CASE SUMMARY

Facts: Jack Tallas came to the United States from Greece in 1914. He lived in Salt Lake City for nearly 70 years, achieving great success in insurance and real estate. When he died, he left a large estate. During the last 14 years of his life, Tallas was a close friend of Peter Dementas, who helped him with numerous personal and business chores. Two months before his death, Tallas met with Dementas and dictated a memorandum to him, in Greek, stating:

> PETER K. DEMENTAS, is my best friend I have in this country and since he came to the United States he treats me like a father and I think of him as my own son. He takes me in his car grocery shopping. He drives me to the doctor and also takes me every week to Bingham to pick up my mail, collect the rents and manage my properties. For all the services Peter has given me all these years, I owe to him the amount of $50,000 (Fifty Thousand Dollars). I will shortly change my will to include him as my heir.

Tallas signed the memorandum, but he did not in fact alter his will to include Dementas. The estate refused to pay, and Dementas sued. The trial was entertaining, thanks to Judge Dee, whose remarks included: "It's hearsay, I agree, but its damn good hearsay, and I want to hear it." Urging a lawyer to hurry up, the judge snapped, "Go on to your next question. This witness—who is supposed to be one witness for 15 minutes—is now into the second day, and we've still got the same witness. ... At the rate we're going, I will have long retired and been happily fishing in Wyoming." Finally hearing something worthwhile from the witness, he interrupted, "Wait a minute. Wait. Wait. Wait. Now, the factfinder has finally got a fact. He said, 'I did it a lot of times.' I've identified a fact in a day

and a half. Let's go to the next witness and see if we can find another one in this case."

Unfortunately for Dementas, when the testimony ground to a halt, Judge Dee ruled that there was no consideration to support Tallas's promise. Dementas appealed.

Issue: *Was there consideration to make Tallas's promise enforceable?*

Decision: Affirmed. There was no consideration to support the promise.

Reasoning: Consideration refers to a legal detriment that has been bargained for and exchanged for a promise. Any detriment, no matter how economically inadequate, will support a promise. The trial judge correctly stated: "If Tallas thought it was worth 50,000 bucks to get one ride to Bingham, that's Tallas' decision. The only thing you can't do is take it with you."

On the other hand, services performed before the promise is made, with no intention of inducing that promise, are not consideration. This is so because no bargaining has taken place. No one has said, if you will do this for me, I will do that for you.

Some courts, finding the rule too harsh, have created a "moral obligation" exception. When the past services were rendered with the expectation of future payment, a court may enforce the promise to pay. However, even if Utah had adopted the moral obligation rule, Dementas would still lose. He performed his services gratuitously, not with any expectation that Tallas would later pay him. Dementas gave no consideration for Tallas's statement, so the promise may not be enforced.

Exception: Economic Benefit

As the *Dementas* court mentions, there is a modest trend in the law in favor of enforcing promises based on past consideration *if that consideration was an economic benefit that was rendered with the expectation of payment.* The Restatement (Second) of Contracts Section 86 suggests that promises based on past consideration may be enforceable "to the extent necessary to avoid injustice." But as we can see from the *Kelsoe* and *Dementas* cases, the courts are loathe to carve exceptions into this venerable rule.

PREEXISTING DUTY

A promise to do something the promisor is already obligated to do is not consideration. In the chapter opener, Professor Parsley agrees to show up for the next class if the students pay her $1,000. *They promise to pay.* They are adults, they understood the deal, the cost is only $20 per student, and they strike the bargain. When she arrives to teach, she is entitled to—nothing. Parsley has given no consideration for the $1,000. She was already obligated to teach the class. The students, having paid their tuition, were already entitled to her instruction. Because *her* promise to teach is no consideration, the students are not bound by *their* promise to pay her.

Of course, exceptions are the spice of law, and the preexisting duty rule provides us with a rack full. Courts have created these exceptions because a rigid application of the rule might interfere with legitimate business goals.

> Of course,
> exceptions are
> the spice of law...

Exception: Additional Work

When a promisor agrees to do something above and beyond what he is obligated to do, his promise is generally valid consideration. Cecil has promised to build a fabulous swimming pool/cabana for Nathalie for $250,000. When the work is half complete, he offers to build the cabana out of sea shells, rather than pine wood. If Nathalie agrees to a new price of $300,000 for the pool complex, she is obligated to pay, because Cecil's extra work is valid consideration for her promise.

Exception: Modification

If both parties agree that a modification is necessary, the surest way to accomplish that is to rescind the original contract and draft a new one. **To rescind means to cancel.** Thus, if neither party has completed its obligations, the agreement to rescind will terminate each party's rights and obligations under the old contract. This should be done in writing. Then the parties sign the new agreement. Courts will *generally* enforce a rescission and modification provided both parties voluntarily entered into it, in good faith. If one side, determined to earn greater profits, unfairly coerces the other into the changes, the modification is invalid.

Once again the UCC has changed the common law, making it easier for merchants to modify agreements for the sale of goods. UCC Section 2-209 provides:

- An agreement modifying a contract within this Article needs no consideration to be binding.

- A signed agreement which excludes modification or rescission except by a signed writing cannot be otherwise modified or rescinded.

Here is how these two provisions work together. Mike's Magic Mania agrees to deliver 500 rabbits and 500 top hats to State University, for the school's Sleight of Hand 101 course.

[handwritten margin notes:]
- Mutual Recission (Both parties mutually end the contract)
- Unilateral Recission (Breaching the contract) or by Court

The goods, including 100 cages and 1,000 pounds of rabbit food, are to arrive no later than September 1, in time for the new semester, with payment on delivery. By September 20 no rabbits have appeared, in or out of hats. The university buys similar products from another supply house at a 25% steeper price, and sues MMM for the difference. Mike claims that in early September the dean had orally agreed to permit delivery in October. The dean is on sabbatical in Tahiti and cannot be reached for comment. Is the alleged modification valid?

Under the common law, the modification would have been void, because MMM gave no consideration for the extended delivery date. However, this is a sale of goods, and under UCC Section 2-209, an oral modification may be valid even without consideration. Unfortunately for Mike, though, the original agreement included a clause forbidding oral modification. Any changes had to be in writing, signed by both parties. Mike never obtained such a document. Even if the dean did make the oral agreement, the university wins.

The following case arose in a setting that is traumatic and lamentably common: a home owner could not make his mortgage payments. Foreclosure loomed. Did the parties agree to save the home?

YOU *be the* JUDGE

CITIZENS TRUST BANK V. WHITE
274 Ga.App. 508, 618 S.E.2d 9
Georgia Court of Appeals, 2005

Facts: Herbert White owned a house in Atlanta. He refinanced his home through Citizens Trust Bank, but fell behind on his loan payments. He owed about $43,000. The Bank notified White that it intended to foreclose. After some delays, the Bank sent White a formal notice that it would sell his house at a foreclosure sale on the courthouse steps, on May 7. The finance agreement provided that if the Bank foreclosed, White owed the full amount.

On that date, White arrived and offered the Bank $35,000 to stop the foreclosure. The Bank's collection manager, D.J. Hughlett, accepted the money, and drafted a letter, which he and White signed:

Citizens Trust Bank agrees to postpone the foreclosure [based on] a payment of $33,000.00 in certified funds and a possible $2,000.00 from the account of Cora White Cummings on the above-referenced property. Our Attorney William A. Broughman will forward to you a written agreement, for your signature, to consummate this transaction. The payoff balance as of 11:05 AM is $7,986.43. If his sister pays the $2,000.00 the balance will be $5,986.43.

White did pay the extra $2,000. Hughlett decided that the signed letter was a forbearance agreement with White, so he did not bother to send an additional document. Hughlett believed that White would pay the balance within 30 days, but White never did so. The Bank sent a new foreclosure notice, and did in fact sell the house.

White sued the Bank, claiming that it had breached its agreement not to foreclose. The jury agreed, awarding White $250,000 in compensatory damages. The Bank appealed, arguing that White gave no consideration for the agreement, because he was already obligated to pay the full balance.

You Be the Judge: Was the signed letter an enforceable contract?

Argument for the Bank: Mr. White fell behind on his mortgage payments. As soon as the Bank notified him that it was foreclosing, his full debt became due. When he offered to pay a percentage of that debt, he was fulfilling a preexisting duty. He was *legally obligated* to pay the $35,000 that he "offered," along with the full balance due. A promise to do what the promisor is required to do is never consideration. Without consideration, there is no contract.

The jury made an emotional decision based on sympathy for the debtor. That leads to bad policy and bad law.

continued

The policy is poor because if everyone were allowed to default without suffering a loss, no bank would lend money and most citizens could never buy a house. The law is even worse, because the case should not have gone to a jury. The trial judge should have dismissed the suit based on the pre-existing duty rule.

Argument for Mr. White: There were two parties to this agreement, and both believed they had a binding agreement. The Bank's officer agreed to postpone foreclosure. He also promised to forward a formal document confirming the understanding, but did not do so. And why did he send no other document? Because he believed the Bank had already agreed to halt any foreclosure effort. He was right.

Mr. White paid 80% of the balance due. It is wrong of the Bank to take the money, then break its promise. Furthermore, it is absurd to foreclose based on such a modest debt. The legal argument about consideration is nonsense. Mr. White's consideration was a check for $35,000.

The jury award indicates a group of average citizens who were angry about what the Bank did. The verdict should be affirmed.

EXAM *Strategy*

Question: Star Struck, a Hollywood talent agency, employs Puneet as one of its young agents, and Max as a part-time delivery boy. Puneet's contract is for one year. She earns $5,000 per month, payable on the last day of each month. After she has worked at the firm for four months, a Star Struck executive says to her, "We are having cash flow problems. We cannot pay you this month, and will probably fall about two months behind. However, if you will agree to do Max's job for the next few months, we can pay you on time." Puneet cheerfully agrees to the deal. However, after a few weeks of the extra labor, Puneet confesses that she is overwhelmed, and can no longer do Max's job. Star Struck fires her. Puneet sues. Was there a binding agreement for Puneet to do Max's work?

Strategy: Star Struck made an offer to Puneet and she accepted it. But a contract needs more than offer and acceptance. Both parties must give consideration. Had they done more than they were required to do under their preexisting duty?

Result: A promise to do what the promisor is already obligated to do is no consideration. Star Struck was required to pay Puneet every month, so its "offer" included no consideration. Without consideration, there can be no agreement. Puneet was not obligated to do Max's job, and she will win this lawsuit.

Exception: Unforeseen Circumstances

Hugo has a deal to repair major highways. Hugo hires Hal's Hauling to cart soil and debris. Hal's trucks begin work, but after crossing the work site several times they sink to their axles in sinister, sucking slime. Hal demands an additional 35% payment from Hugo to complete the job, pointing out that the surface was dry and cracked and that neither Hal nor Hugo was aware of the subsurface water. Hal howls that he must use different trucks with different tires and work more slowly to permit the soil to dry. Hugo hems and haws and finally agrees. But when the hauling is finished, Hugo refuses to pay the extra money. Is Hugo liable?

Yes. When unforeseen circumstances cause a party to make a promise regarding an unfinished project, that promise is generally valid consideration. Even though Hal is only promising to finish what he was already obligated to do, his promise is valid consideration because neither party knew of the subsoil mud. Hal was facing a situation quite different from what the parties anticipated. It is almost as though he were undertaking a new project. Hal has given consideration and Hugo is bound by his promise to pay extra money.

SETTLEMENT OF DEBTS

You claim that your friend Felicity owes you $90,000, but she refuses to pay. Finally, when you are desperate, Felicity offers you a cashier's check for $60,000—provided you accept it as full settlement. To get your hands on some money, you agree and cash the check. The next day you sue Felicity for $30,000. Who wins? First, an ethical question.

ETHICS Even if you think you have a chance of winning, is it right to accept the money as full settlement and then sue for the balance? From the Chapter 2 ethics checklist: Which values are in conflict? Which of these values are most important? Under what circumstances would you feel ethically correct in suing for the balance? When would you consider it wrong? ◆

As to the legal outcome, it will depend principally upon one major issue: Was Felicity's debt liquidated or unliquidated?

LIQUIDATED DEBT

A **liquidated debt** is one in which there is no dispute about the amount owed. A loan is a typical example. If a bank lends you $10,000, and the note obligates you to repay that amount on June 1 of the following year, you clearly owe that sum. The debt is liquidated.

In cases of liquidated debt, if the creditor agrees to take less than the full amount as full payment, her agreement is not binding. The debtor has given no consideration to support the creditor's promise to accept a reduced payment, and therefore the creditor is not bound by her word. The reasoning is simply that the debtor is already obligated to pay the full amount, so no bargaining could reasonably cause the creditor to accept less. If Felicity's debt to you is liquidated, your agreement to accept $60,000 is not binding, and you will successfully sue for the balance.

Liquidated debt
A debt in which there is no dispute about the amount owed.

Must give something in exchange for something you don't already owe

Exception: Different Performance
There is one important exception to this rule. If the debtor offers a *different performance* to settle the liquidated debt, and the creditor agrees to take it as full settlement, the agreement is binding. Suppose that Felicity, instead of paying $60,000, offers you five acres in Alaska and you accept. When you accept the deed to the land, you have given up your entire claim, regardless of the land's precise value.

UNLIQUIDATED DEBT: ACCORD AND SATISFACTION

A debt is **unliquidated** for either of two reasons: (1) the parties dispute whether any money is owed, or (2) the parties agree that some money is owed but dispute how much. When a debt is unliquidated, for either reason, the parties may enter into a binding agreement to settle for less than what the creditor demands.

Such a compromise will be enforced if:

Unliquidated debt
A debt that is disputed because the parties disagree over its existence or amount.

- The debt is unliquidated and

- The parties agree that the creditor will accept as full payment a sum less than she has claimed; and

- The debtor pays the amount agreed upon.

Accord and satisfaction

A completed agreement to settle a debt for less than the sum claimed.

This agreement is called an **accord and satisfaction**. The accord is the agreement to settle for less than the creditor claims. The satisfaction is the actual payment of that compromised sum. An accord and satisfaction is valid consideration to support the creditor's agreement to drop all claims. Each party is giving up something: the creditor gives up her full claim, and the debtor gives up his assertion that he owed little or nothing.

Accord and Satisfaction by Check

Most accord and satisfaction agreements involve payment by check. UCC Section 3-311 governs these agreements, using the same common law rules described above.[5] The Code specifies that when the debtor writes "full settlement" on the check, a creditor who cashes the check generally has entered into an accord and satisfaction. If Felicity's debt is unliquidated, and she gives you a check with "full payment of all debts" written on the face in bold letters, the moment you deposit the check you lose any claim to more money. What happens if the debtor makes such a notation but the creditor changes it? A massage therapist learned the answer and felt sore for days.

HENCHES V. TAYLOR

138 WASH. APP. 1026, 2007 WL 1241525
WASHINGTON COURT OF APPEALS, 2007

CASE SUMMARY

Facts: Jim Henches, a licensed massage therapist, treated Benjamin Taylor after he was injured in a car accident. When all treatments were finished, Henches billed Taylor for more than $7,000. Taylor's insurance company claimed the bill was exorbitant, and paid only $2,625, for 24 massage treatments.

Henches continued to send bills to Taylor, not only for the balance due, but for additional time spent consulting with Taylor's other health care providers, preparing to testify in Taylor's personal injury lawsuit, and attempting to collect his debts. In response to a bill for $11,945.86, Taylor's lawyer James Harris sent Henches a letter, stating:

I have reviewed your billing statements and am having a difficult time understanding a number of charges you

included. By my calculations, the amount owed to you is approximately $5,243.45. I have enclosed a check for that amount as payment in full to settle Mr. Taylor's account with you.

The letter was accompanied by a check with "final payment" written on the notation line. Henches filed suit, seeking the full balance. Then he wrote "attorney/fee" on the check, over the word "final," and deposited the check.

The trial court gave summary judgment to Taylor, ruling that deposit of the check constituted accord and satisfaction. Henches appealed.

Issue: *Was there an accord and satisfaction, discharging the debt?*

---

[5] A check is legally an instrument, which is why this section comes from Article 3 of the Code. For a full discussion of instruments, see Chapters 22–24.

Decision: Yes, depositing the check created an accord and satisfaction. Affirmed.

Reasoning: An accord and satisfaction exists when three circumstances arise. Parties have a legitimately disputed debt. They agree that a partial payment of the debt will settle the dispute. Finally, the defendant accepts the partial payment.

In this case, the defendant easily established the first and third elements. The parties had a genuine dispute over the costly treatments, and Henches deposited the check. But

Henches claimed that he had not agreed to accept the check as full payment of the debt. In the end, his own actions contradicted his argument.

When he wrote "attorney/fee" over the word "final," Henches indicated that he knew that Taylor intended for the check to be a final settlement. If an amount is in dispute and the defendant offers partial payment as full settlement, then accepting this money counts as full satisfaction, no matter what else the plaintiff may do. When Henches deposited the check, he lost the ability to seek any further payment.

UCC Exceptions

The Code creates two exceptions for accord and satisfaction cases involving checks. The first exception concerns "organizations," which typically are businesses. The general rule of Section 3-311 is potentially calamitous to them, since a company that receives thousands of checks every day is unlikely to inspect all notations. A consumer who owes $12,000 on a credit card might write "full settlement" on a $200 check, potentially extinguishing the entire debt through accord and satisfaction. Under the exception, if an organization notifies a debtor that any offers to settle for less than the debt claimed must be made to a particular official, and the check is sent to anyone else in the organization, depositing the check generally does *not* create an accord and satisfaction. Thus a clerk who deposits 900 checks daily for payment of MasterCard debts will not have inadvertently entered into dozens of accord and satisfaction agreements.

The second exception allows a way out to most creditors who have inadvertently created an accord and satisfaction. If, within 90 days of cashing a "full payment" check, the creditor offers repayment of the same amount to the debtor, there is no accord and satisfaction. Homer claims that Virgil owes him $7 million, but foolishly cashes Virgil's check for $3 million, without understanding that "paid in full" means just what it says. Homer has created an accord and satisfaction. But if he promptly sends Virgil a check for $3 million, he has undone the agreement and may sue for the full amount.

CHAPTER CONCLUSION

This ancient doctrine of consideration is simple to state but subtle to apply. The parties must bargain and enter into an exchange of promises or actions. If they do not, there is no consideration and the courts are unlikely to enforce any promise made. A variety of exceptions modify the law, but a party wishing to render its future more predictable—the purpose of a contract—will rely on a solid bargain and exchange.

EXAM REVIEW

1. **CONSIDERATION** A promise is normally binding only if it is supported by consideration, which requires a bargaining and exchange between the parties. (p. 271)

EXAM Strategy

Question: An aunt saw her eight-year-old nephew enter the room, remarked what a nice boy he was, and said, "I would like to take care of him now." She promptly wrote a note, promising to pay the boy $3,000 upon her death. Her estate refused to pay. Is it obligated to do so?

Strategy: A contract is enforceable only if both parties have given consideration. The consideration might be a detriment to the promisor or a benefit to the promisee. The aunt's consideration is apparent: a promise to pay her nephew $3,000. That was a detriment to her *and* a benefit to the nephew. Did the nephew give consideration? (See the "Result" at the end of this section.)

2. **NATURE OF CONSIDERATION** The "thing" bargained for can be another promise or an action—virtually anything that a party might seek. It can create a benefit to the promisor or a detriment to the promisee. (p. 273)

3. **ADEQUACY** The courts will seldom inquire into the adequacy of consideration. (p. 275)

4. **ILLUSORY PROMISES** An illusory promise is not consideration. (p. 276)

EXAM Strategy

Question: Eagle ran convenience stores. He entered into an agreement with Commercial Movie in which Commercial would provide Eagle with videotape cassettes for rental. Eagle would pay Commercial 50% of the rental revenues. If Eagle stopped using Commercial's service, Eagle could not use a competitor's services for 18 months. The agreement also provided: "Commercial shall not be liable for compensation or damages of any kind, whether on account of the loss by Eagle of profits, sales or expenditures, or on account of any other event or cause whatsoever." Eagle complied with the agreement for two years but then began using a competitor's service, and Commercial sued. Eagle claimed that the agreement was unenforceable for lack of consideration. Please rule.

Strategy: In this case, both parties seem to have suffered a detriment by making a promise. But there is a flaw in the "promise" that Commercial made. Commercial can never be liable to Eagle—no matter what happens. Has Commercial suffered a detriment by making this promise? Has Eagle gained a benefit from the promise? (See the "Result" at the end of this section.)

5. **REQUIREMENT AND OUTPUT CONTRACTS** Under sales law, requirement and output contracts are valid. Although one side controls the quantity, its agreement to make demands *in good faith* is consideration. (p. 278)

6. **PAST CONSIDERATION** Past consideration is generally no consideration. (p. 278)

7. **PREEXISTING DUTY** Under the doctrine of preexisting duty, a promise to do something that the promisor is already legally obligated to perform is generally not consideration. (p. 280)

8. **LIQUIDATED DEBT** A liquidated debt is one in which there is no dispute about the amount owed. For a liquidated debt, a creditor's promise to accept less than the full amount is not binding. (p. 283)

9. **UNLIQUIDATED DEBT** For an unliquidated debt, if the parties agree that the creditor will accept less than the full amount claimed and the debtor performs, there is an accord and satisfaction and the creditor may not claim any balance. (p. 283)

10. **"FULL PAYMENT" NOTATIONS** In most states payment by a check that has a "full payment" notation will create an accord and satisfaction unless the creditor is an organization that has notified the debtor that full payment offers must go to a certain officer. (p. 284)

EXAM Strategy

Question: When White's wife died he filed a claim with Boston Mutual for $10,000 death benefits under her insurance policy. The insurer rejected the claim, saying that his wife had misrepresented her medical condition in the application form. The company sent White a check for $478.75, which it said represented "a full refund of all applicable premiums paid" for the coverage. White deposited the check. Had the parties reached an accord and satisfaction?

Strategy: The UCC permits parties to enter into an accord and satisfaction by check. The debtor must make clear that the check is offered in full payment of a disputed debt. Debtor's generally do that by writing "Final Settlement" or "Accepted as Full Payment of All Debts" or some similar notation on the check. Had the insurance company complied with that requirement? (See the "Result" at the end of this section.)

---

1. Result: The nephew gave no consideration. He did not promise to do anything. He suffered no detriment, nor did he do anything that would benefit his aunt. Without consideration from both parties, there is no enforceable contract. The estate wins.

4. Result: Commercial's promise was illusory. The company was free to walk away from the deal at any time. Commercial could never be held liable. The company has suffered no detriment. Nor has Eagle gained any benefit, because he cannot rely on Commercial to fulfill its promise. Commercial gave no consideration, and there was no binding contract for either party to enforce.

10. Result: The insurer merely stated that its check was a refund of premiums. Nowhere did the company indicate that the check was full payment of its disputed obligation. The company should have made it clear that it would not pay any benefits, and that this payment was all that it would offer. There was no accord and satisfaction.

ADDITIONAL QUESTIONS

1. ***YOU BE THE JUDGE*** WRITING PROBLEM Elio Pino took out a health insurance policy with the Union Bankers Insurance Co. Eighteen months later he became ill, suffered medical expenses, and filed a claim for benefits. Union Bankers wrote Pino this letter:

> Dear Mr. Pino:
>
>   While servicing your claim, we learned that the medical facts on the application for this policy were not complete. If we had known the complete health history, we couldn't have issued this insurance. We must place you and ourselves back where we were when you applied for the policy and consider that the insurance was never in effect. (We are refunding the premiums you've paid us.)

Pino deposited the refund check, which was much less than his claim, and then sued for the full claim. Bankers Insurance argued that Pino had entered into an accord and satisfaction. The trial court gave summary judgment for the insurer, and Pino appealed. Did Pino enter into an accord and satisfaction by cashing the insurance company check? **Argument for Pino:** The insurance company has its contract law wrong. The company attempted to rescind the contract. Then it termed its unilateral act an accord and satisfaction. The company's attempts fail: a rescission requires the agreement of both parties; an accord and satisfaction needs a clear statement that the creditor is accepting the check as full payment. Neither occurred. **Argument for Union Bankers Insurance Co.:** This is classic accord and satisfaction. The company informed Mr. Pino that it regarded his application as false and offered him a partial payment as full settlement. He deposited the check, creating an accord and satisfaction, and has no claim for any more money.

2. ***CPA QUESTION*** For there to be consideration, there must be:

    (a) A bargained-for detriment to the promisor(ee) or a benefit to the promisee(or)

    (b) A manifestation of mutual assent

    (c) Genuineness of assent

    (d) Substantially equal economic benefits to both parties

3. American Bakeries had a fleet of over 3,000 delivery trucks. Because of the increasing cost of gasoline, the company was interested in converting the trucks to propane fuel. It signed a requirements contract with Empire Gas, in which Empire would convert "approximately 3,000" trucks to propane fuel, as American Bakeries requested, and would then sell all required propane fuel to run the trucks. But American Bakeries changed its mind and never requested a single conversion. Empire sued for lost profits. Who won?

4. ***CPA QUESTION*** Which of the following requires consideration in order to be binding on the parties?

   (a) Modification of a contract involving the sale of real estate

   (b) Ratification of a contract by a person after reaching the age of majority

   (c) A written promise signed by a merchant to keep an offer to sell goods open for 10 days

   (d) Modification of a sale of goods contract under the UCC

5. Tindall operated a general contracting business in Montana. He and Konitz entered into negotiations for Konitz to buy the business. The parties realized that Konitz could succeed with the business only if Tindall gave support and assistance for a year or so after the purchase, especially by helping with the process of bidding for jobs and obtaining bonds to guarantee performance. Konitz bought the business and Tindall helped with the bidding and bonding. Two years later, Tindall presented Konitz with a contract for his services up to that point. Konitz did not want to sign but Tindall insisted. Konitz signed the agreement, which said: "Whereas Tindall sold his contracting business to Konitz and thereafter assisted Konitz in bidding and bonding without which Konitz would have been unable to operate, NOW THEREFORE Konitz agrees to pay Tindall $138,629." Konitz later refused to pay. Comment.

6. CeCe Hylton and Edward Meztista, partners in a small advertising firm, agreed to terminate the business and split assets evenly. Meztista gave Hylton a two-page document showing assets, liabilities, and a bottom line of $35,235.67, with one half due to each partner. Hylton questioned the accounting, and asked to see the books. Meztista did not permit Hylton to see any records, and refused to answer her phone calls. Instead, he gave her a check in the amount of $17,617.83, on which he wrote "Final payment/payment in full." Hylton cashed the check, but wrote on it, "Under protest—cashing this check does not constitute my acceptance of this amount as payment in full." Hylton then filed suit, demanding additional monies. Meztista claimed that the parties had made an accord and satisfaction. What is the best argument for each party? Who should win?

7. ***ETHICS*** Melnick built a house for Gintzler, but the foundation was defective. Gintzler agreed to accept the foundation if Melnick guaranteed to make future repairs caused by the defects. Melnick agreed but later refused to make any repairs. Melnick argued that his promise to make future repairs was unsupported by consideration. Who will win the suit? Is either party acting unethically? Which one, and why?

8. ***ROLE REVERSAL*** Write a short-answer question that focuses on one of these consideration issues: illusory promise, preexisting duty, or accord and satisfaction.

INTERNET RESEARCH PROBLEM

UCC Section 2-209 concerns contract modification. Find the full section online. Write a clear one- or two-paragraph explanation of subsections (1) and (2). Explain what these subsections mean (in English) and how they work together.

You can find further practice problems at www.cengagebrain.com. See the preface of this book for website access details.

LEGALITY

Soheil Sadri, a California resident, did some serious gambling at Caesar's Tahoe casino in Nevada. And lost. To keep gambling, he wrote checks to Caesar's and then signed two memoranda pledging to repay money advanced. After two days, with his losses totaling more than $22,000, he went home. Back in California, Sadri stopped payment on the checks and refused to pay any of the money he owed Caesar's. The casino sued. In defense, Sadri claimed that California law considered his agreements illegal and unenforceable. He was unquestionably correct about one thing: a contract that is illegal is void and unenforceable.

> **A contract that is illegal is void and unenforceable.**

CONTRACTS THAT VIOLATE A STATUTE

In this chapter, we examine a variety of contracts that may be void. Illegal agreements fall into two groups: those that violate a statute, and those that violate public policy.

WAGERS

Gambling is big business. Almost all states now permit some form of wagering, whether casinos to race tracks to lotteries, and they eagerly collect the billions of dollars in revenue generated. Supporters urge that casinos create jobs and steady income, boost state coffers, and take business away from organized crime. Critics argue that naïve citizens inevitably lose money they can ill afford to forfeit, and that addicted gamblers destroy families and weaken the fabric of communities. With citizens and states divided over the ethics of gambling, it is inevitable that we have conflicts such as the dispute between Sadri and Caesar's. The basic rule, however, is clear: **a gambling contract is illegal unless it is specifically authorized by state statute**.

In California, as in many states, gambling on credit is not allowed. In other words, it is illegal to lend money to help someone wager. But in Nevada, gambling on credit is legal, and debt memoranda such as Sadri's are enforceable contracts. Caesar's sued Sadri in California (where he lived). The result? The court admitted that California's attitude toward gambling had changed, and that bingo, poker clubs, and lotteries were common. Nonetheless, the court denied that the new tolerance extended to wagering on credit:

There is a special reason for treating gambling on credit differently from gambling itself. Having lost his or her cash, the pathological gambler will continue to play on credit, if extended, in an attempt to win back the losses. This is why enforcement of gambling debts has always been against public policy in California and should remain so, regardless of shifting public attitudes about gambling itself. If Californians want to play, so be it. But the law should not invite them to play themselves into debt. The judiciary cannot protect pathological gamblers from themselves, but we can refuse to participate in their financial ruin.[1]

Caesar's lost and Sadri kept his money. However, do not become too excited at the prospect of risk-free wagering. Casinos responded to cases like *Sadri* by changing their practices. Most now extend credit only to a gambler who agrees that disputes about repayment will be settled in *Nevada* courts. Because such contracts are legal in that state, the casino is able to obtain a judgment against a defaulting debtor and—yes—enforce that judgment in the gambler's home state. In *your* home state.

Despite these more restrictive casino practices, Sadri's dispute is a useful starting place from which to examine contract legality because it illustrates two important themes.

First, morality is a significant part of contract legality. In refusing to enforce an obligation that Sadri undeniably had made, the California court relied on the human and social consequences of gambling and on the ethics of judicial enforcement of gambling debts. Second, "void" really means just that: a court will not intercede to assist either party to an illegal agreement, even if its refusal leaves one party obviously shortchanged.

INSURANCE

Another market in which "wagering" unexpectedly pops up is that of insurance. You may certainly insure your own life for any sum you choose. But may you insure someone else's life?

---

[1] *Metropolitan Creditors Service of Sacramento v. Sadri*, 15 Cal. App. 4th 1821, 1993 Cal. App. LEXIS 559, 19 Cal.Rptr.2d 646 (Cal. Ct. App. 1993).

Anyone taking out a policy on the life of another must have an insurable interest in that person. The most common insurable interest is family connection, such as spouses or parents. Other valid interests include creditor-debtor status (the creditor wants payment if the debtor dies), and business association (an executive in the company is so valuable, the firm will need compensation if something happens to him). If there is no insurable interest there is generally no contract. But should that rule *always* be enforced?

YOU *be the* JUDGE

CHEM V. NEW YORK LIFE INSURANCE COMPANY
168 F.3d 498
Ninth Circuit Court of Appeals, 1999

Facts: Thuan Wu was an insurance agent. An acquaintance named Suulan Chem asked Wu to purchase an insurance policy on the life of her young son, Michael. Wu purchased a short-term policy through Surety Life Insurance. Later, without telling Chem, he renewed the contract, and bought additional policies on Michael's life through New York Life and three other companies. The policies totaled $750,000. On each one, Wu named Suulan Chem as the principal beneficiary and himself as the secondary beneficiary. Wu's plan was grotesque and simple: murder the boy and his mother, collect the money.

Wu gave orders to confederates, who kidnapped and slew the eight-year-old boy. Chem was never killed. Wu was convicted of first-degree murder.

Chem sought to collect the $750,000, but all of the companies refused to pay. She sued. The court dismissed the case, ruling that Wu, who took out the policies without Chem's knowledge, had no insurable interest in Michael's life. Chem appealed.

You Be the Judge: Are the insurance policies void for lack of insurable interest?

Argument for Chem: There is no law that requires a court to ignore basic fairness. When Wu applied for these policies, not one company inquired into his insurable interest in Michael's life. Not one company asked about his relationship with Suulan, or with Michael, or why he named himself secondary beneficiary. Not one company wondered why it was Wu making the application instead of Suulan. Each insurer was happy to take the money, and issue a policy with Suulan Chem as principal beneficiary. If asked at the time, each company would have said, "These are valid, enforceable contracts." Only when it was time to pay up did the companies become interested in Wu's role.

Obviously, Suulan has a legitimate insurable interest in the life of her son. She is the named beneficiary. It is time to pay her. Yet the companies, oblivious to the murder of a young boy and the grief of a mother, suddenly argue that the contracts for which they happily accepted premiums have been void all along. The law should never endorse such callous hypocrisy.

Argument for New York Life and the other insurers: The companies deeply regret Suulan Chem's appalling loss, but the criminal is Thuan Wu.

Wu was the applicant and he had no insurable interest in Michael's life. As a result, each of these contracts was void from the start. In other words, as a matter of law there never were any contracts. None of the insurers were at any time obligated to Suulan Chem or anyone else. Once a contract is void, that is the end of the matter. No words, actions—or even tragedies—can transform a void contract into a valid one.

Sadly, this case demonstrates exactly why courts demand an insurable interest. The law is designed to assure that someone taking an insurance policy on the life of another *wants the person to live*. Life insurance is supposed to compensate financially for a loss that everyone hopes never occurs. Without the requirement of insurable interest, some would be tempted to take out policies as a crude wager, hoping that the insured would die. Others would plan to murder the insured. Had Wu understood the law, Michael would still be alive.

EXAM *Strategy*

Question: Jimenez sold Breton a used motorcycle for $5,500, payable in weekly install-ments. Jimenez then purchased an insurance policy on Breton's life, worth $320,000 if Breton died in an accident. Breton promptly died in a collision with an automobile. The insurance company offered only $5,500, representing the balance due on the motorcycle. Jimenez sued, demanding $320,000. Make an argument that the insurance company should win.

Strategy: The issue is whether Jimenez had an insurable interest in Breton's life. If he had no interest, he cannot collect on an insurance policy. If he had an interest, what was it? For how much money?

Result: Jimenez's had an interest in Breton's life to insure payment of the motorcycle debt—$5,500. Beyond that, this policy represented a wager by Jimenez that Breton was going to die. Contracts for such wagers are unenforceable. Jimenez is entitled only to $5,500.[2]

LICENSING STATUTES

You sue your next-door neighbor in small claims court, charging that he keeps a kangaroo in his backyard and that the beast has disrupted your family barbecues by leaping over the fence, stealing salad, and even punching your cousin in the ear. Your friend Foster, a graduate student from Melbourne, offers to help you prepare the case, and you agree to pay him 10 percent of anything you recover. Foster proves surprisingly adept at organizing documents and arguments. You win $1,200 and Foster demands $120. Must you pay? The answer is determined by the law of licensing.

States require licenses for anyone who practices a profession, such as law or medicine, works as a contractor or plumber, and for many other kinds of work. These licenses are required in order to protect the public. States demand that an electrician be licensed because the work is potentially dangerous to a homeowner: the person doing the work must know an amp from a watt. **When a licensing requirement is designed to protect the public, any contract made by an unlicensed worker is unenforceable.** Your friend Foster is unlicensed to practice law. Even though Foster did a fine job with your small claims case, he cannot enforce his contract for $120.

States use other licenses simply to raise money. For example, most states require a license to open certain kinds of retail stores. This requirement does not protect the public, because the state will not investigate the store owner the way it will examine a prospective lawyer or electrician. The state is simply raising revenue. **When a licensing requirement is designed merely to raise revenue, a contract made by an unlicensed person is generally enforceable.** Thus, if you open a stationery store and forget to pay the state's licensing fee, you can still enforce a contract to buy 10,000 envelopes from a wholesaler at a bargain price.

Many cases, such as the following one, involve contractors seeking to recover money for work they did without a license.

---

[2] *Jimenez v. Protective Life Insurance Co.*, 8 Cal. App. 4th 528 (Cal. App. 1992).

AUTHENTIC HOME IMPROVEMENTS V. MAYO

2006 WL 2687533
DISTRICT OF COLUMBIA SUPERIOR COURT, 2006

CASE SUMMARY

Facts: Authentic Home Improvements (Authentic) performed work on Diane Mayo's home, but she sued for return of the money she had paid. In court, Authentic's owner acknowledged that he did not have a contractor's license when the company began the work, but expected soon to obtain it. The court ordered Authentic to refund Mayo the entire sum she had paid, and the company agreed. Later, however, Authentic returned to court, stating that things had changed. The license had in fact been issued soon after work began. Authentic argued that it should not be obligated to return Mayo's money, and was in fact entitled to its full fee for the work accomplished.

Issue: *Did the new license entitle Authentic to its home improvement fee?*

Decision: No, the new license did not change the outcome. Original ruling upheld.

Reasoning: Consumers lose billions each year on fraudulent home improvement schemes. For this reason, courts strictly interpret licensing requirements for contractors. Even when homeowners knowingly hire a contractor who lacks a license and then benefit from his work, they are not required to pay him.

Authentic Home Improvements lacked a license when the work on Mayo's home started. The relevant statute plainly requires a license in hand before a job begins. A driver cannot drive a car without license plates merely because she expects delivery of her plates soon, and the same principle applies here.

Authentic remains obligated to refund Mayo's money.

USURY

(handwritten margin note: rates/ Prohibits interests (charging excessively high on loans))

(handwritten margin note: Statutes regulate the amount of interest that could be charged on a loan)

Henry Paper and Anthony Pugliese were real estate developers. They bought a $1.7 million property in West Palm Beach, Florida, intending to erect an office building. They needed $1 million to start construction but were able to raise only $800,000. Walter Gross, another developer, agreed to lend them the final $200,000 for 18 months at 15% interest. Gross knew the partners were desperate for the money, so at the loan closing, he demanded 15% equity (ownership) in the partnership, in addition to the interest. Paper and Pugliese had no choice but to sign the agreement. The two partners never repaid the loan, and when Gross sued, the court ruled they need never pay a cent. It pays to understand usury.

Usury laws prohibit charging excess interest on loans. A lender who charges a usurious rate of interest may forfeit the illegal interest, or all interest, or, in some states, the entire loan. Florida permits interest rates of up to 18% on loans such as Gross's. A lender who charges more than 18% loses the right to collect any interest. A lender who exceeds 25% interest forfeits the entire debt. Where was the usury? Just here: when Gross insisted on a 15% share of the partnership, he was simply extracting additional interest and disguising it as partnership equity. The Paper–Pugliese partnership had equity assets of $600,000. A 15% equity, plus interest payments of 15% over 18 months, was the equivalent of a per annum interest rate of 45%. Gross probably thought he had made a deal that was too good to be true. And in the state of Florida, it was. He lost the entire debt.[3]

---

[3] *Jersey Palm-Gross, Inc. v. Paper*, 639 So.2d 664, 1994 Fla. App. LEXIS 6597 (Fla. Ct. App. 1994).

CONTRACTS THAT VIOLATE PUBLIC POLICY

In the preceding section, we saw that courts refuse to enforce contracts that violate a statute. In this section we examine cases in which no statute applies but where a *public policy* prohibits certain contracts. In other words, we focus primarily on the common law.

RESTRAINT OF TRADE

Free trade is the basis of the American economy, and any bargain that restricts it is suspect. Most restraint of free trade is barred by antitrust law. But it is the common law that still regulates one restriction on trade: agreements to refrain from competition. Some of these agreements are legal, some are void.

To be valid, an agreement not to compete must be ancillary to a legitimate bargain. "Ancillary" means that the noncompetition agreement must be part of a larger agreement. Suppose Cliff sells his gasoline station to Mina and the two agree that Cliff will not open a competing gas station within five miles anytime during the next two years. Cliff's agreement not to compete is ancillary to the sale of his service station. His noncompetition promise is enforceable. But suppose that Cliff and Mina already had the only two gas stations within 35 miles. They agree between themselves not to hire each other's workers. Their agreement might be profitable to them, because each could now keep wages artificially low. But their deal is ancillary to no legitimate bargain, and it is therefore void. Mina is free to hire Cliff's mechanic despite her agreement with Cliff.

The two most common settings for legitimate noncompetition agreements are the sale of a business and an employment relationship.

Sale of a Business

Kory has operated a real estate office, Hearth Attack, in a small city for 35 years, building an excellent reputation and many ties with the community. She offers to sell you the business and its goodwill for $300,000. But you need assurance that Kory will not take your money and promptly open a competing office across the street. With her reputation and connections, she would ruin your chances of success. You insist on a noncompete clause in the sale contract. In this clause, Kory promises that for one year, she will not open a new real estate office or go to work for a competing company within a 10-mile radius of Hearth Attack. Suppose, six months after selling you the business, Kory goes to work for a competing real estate agency two blocks away. You seek an injunction to prevent her from working. Who wins?

When a noncompete agreement is ancillary to the sale of a business, it is enforceable if reasonable in time, geographic area, and scope of activity. In other words, a court will not enforce a noncompete agreement that lasts an unreasonably long time, covers an unfairly large area, or prohibits the seller of the business from doing a type of work that she never had done before. Measured by this test, Kory is almost certainly bound by her agreement. One year is a reasonable time to allow you to get your new business started. A 10-mile radius is probably about the area that Hearth Attack covers, and realty is obviously a fair business from which to prohibit Kory. A court will probably grant the injunction, barring Kory from her new job.

If, on the other hand, the noncompetition agreement had prevented Kory from working anywhere within 200 miles of Hearth Attack, and she started working 50 miles away, a court would refuse to enforce the contract. The geographic restriction is unreasonable, since Kory

> With her reputation and connections, she would ruin your chances of success.

never previously did business 50 miles away, and Hearth Attack is unlikely to be affected if she works there now.

Employment

When you sign an employment contract, the document may well contain a noncompete clause. Employers have legitimate worries that employees might go to a competitor and take with them trade secrets or other proprietary information. Some employers, though, attempt to place harsh restrictions on their employees, perhaps demanding a blanket agreement that the employee will never go to work for a competitor. Once again, courts look at the reasonableness of restrictions placed on an employee's future work. Because the agreement now involves the very livelihood of the worker, a court scrutinizes the agreement more closely.

trade secrets / confidential information

A noncompete clause in an employment contract is generally enforceable only if it is essential to the employer, fair to the employee, and harmless to the general public. Judges invariably enforce these agreements to protect trade secrets and confidential information. They may protect customer lists that have been expensive to produce. Courts rarely restrain an employee simply because he wants to work for a competitor, and they disfavor agreements that last too long or apply in a very wide area. The following chart summarizes the factors that courts look at in all types of noncompetition agreements.

THE LEGALITY OF NONCOMPETITION CLAUSES ("NONCOMPETES")

Type of Noncompetition Agreement	When Enforceable	
Not ancillary to a sale of business or employment	Never	
Ancillary to a sale of business	If reasonable in time, geography, and scope of activity	
Ancillary to employment	Contract is *more* likely to be enforced when it involves: • Trade secrets or confidential information: these are almost always protected • Customer lists developed over extended period of time and carefully protected • Limited time and geographical scope • Terms essential to protect the employer's business	Contract is *less* likely to be enforced when it involves: • Employee who already had the skills when he arrived, or merely developed general skills on the job • Customer lists that can be derived from public sources • Excessive time or geographical scope • Terms that are unduly harsh on the employee or contrary to public interest

Suppose that Gina, an engineer, goes to work for Fission Chips, a silicon chip manufacturer that specializes in defense work. She signs a noncompete agreement promising never to work for a competitor. Over a period of three years, Gina learns some of Fission's proprietary methods of etching information onto the chips. She acquires a great deal of new expertise about chips generally. And she periodically deals with Fission Chip's customers, all of whom are well-known software and hardware manufacturers. Gina accepts an offer from WriteSmall, a competitor. Fission Chips races into court, seeking an injunction that would prevent Gina from (1) working for WriteSmall; (2) working for any other competitor; (3) revealing any of Fission's trade secrets; (4) using any of the general expertise she acquired at Fission Chips; and (5) contacting any of Fission's customers.

This injunction threatens Gina's career. If she cannot work for a competitor, or use her general engineering skills, what *will* she do? And for exactly that reason, no court will grant such a broad order. The court will allow Gina to work for competitors, including WriteSmall. It will order her not to use or reveal any trade secrets belonging to Fission. She will, however, be permitted to use the general expertise she has acquired, and she may contact former customers since anyone could get their names from the yellow pages.

Was the noncompete in the following case styled fairly, or was the employee clipped?

KING V. HEAD START FAMILY HAIR SALONS, INC.

886 So.2d 769
SUPREME COURT OF ALABAMA, 2004

CASE SUMMARY

Facts: Kathy King was a single mother supporting a college-age daughter. For 25 years, she had worked as a hairstylist. For the most recent 16 years, she had worked at Head Start, which provided haircuts, coloring, and styling for men and women. King was primarily a stylist, though she had also managed one of the Head Start facilities.

King quit Head Start and began working as manager of a Sports Clips shop, located in the same mall as the store she just left. Sports Clip offered only haircuts, and primarily served men and boys. Head Start filed suit, claiming that King was violating the noncompetition agreement that she had signed. The agreement prohibited King from working at a competing business within a two-mile radius of any Head Start facility for 12 months after leaving the company. The trial court issued an injunction enforcing the noncompete. King appealed.

Issue: *Was the noncompetition agreement valid?*

Decision: The agreement was only partly valid.

Reasoning: Head Start does business in 30 locations throughout Jefferson and Shelby counties. Virtually every hair-care facility in those counties is located within 2 miles of a Head Start business, and is thus covered by the noncompetition agreement. The contract is essentially a blanket restriction, entirely barring King from this business.

King must work to support herself and her daughter. She is 40 years old and has worked in the hair-care industry for 25 years. She cannot be expected at this stage in life to learn new job skills.

Enforcing the noncompetition agreement would inflict a grave hardship on her. The contract cannot be permitted to impoverish King and her daughter. On the other hand, Head Start is entitled to some of the protection that it sought in this agreement. The company has a valid concern that if King is permitted to work anywhere she wants, she could take away many customers from Head Start. The trial court should fashion a more reasonable geographic restriction, one that will permit King to ply her trade while ensuring that Head Start does not unfairly lose customers. For example, the lower court could prohibit King from working within 2 miles of the Head Start facility where she previously worked, or some variation on that idea.

Reversed and remanded.

EXAM *Strategy*

Question: Caf-Fiend is an expanding chain of coffeehouses. The company offers to buy Bessie's Coffee Shop, in St. Louis, on these terms: Bessie will manage the store, as Caf-Fiend's employee, for one year after the sale. For four years after the sale, Bessie will not open a competing restaurant anywhere within 12 miles. For the same four years, she will not work anywhere in the United States for a competing coffee retailer. Are the last two terms enforceable against Bessie?

Strategy: This contract includes two noncompete clauses. In the first, Bessie agrees not to open a competing business. Courts generally enforce such clauses if they are reasonable in time, geography, and scope of activity. Is this clause reasonable? The second clause involves employment. Courts take a dimmer view of these agreements. Is this clause essential to protect the company's business? Is it unduly harsh for Bessie?

Result: The first restriction is reasonable. Caf-Fiend is entitled to prevent Bessie from opening her own coffeehouse around the corner and drawing her old customers. The second clause is unfair to Bessie. If she wants to move from St. Louis to San Diego and work as a store manager, she is prohibited. It is impossible to see how such employment would harm Caf-Fiend —but it certainly takes away Bessie's career options. The first restriction is valid, the second one unenforceable.

EXCULPATORY CLAUSES

You decide to capitalize on your expert ability as a skier and open a ski school in Colorado, "Pike's Pique." But you realize that skiing sometimes causes injuries, so you require anyone signing up for lessons to sign this form:

> I agree to hold Pike's Pique and its employees entirely harmless in the event that I am injured in any way or for any reason or cause, including but not limited to any acts, whether negligent or otherwise, of Pike's Pique or any employee or agent thereof.

The day your school opens, Sara Beth, an instructor, deliberately pushes Toby over a cliff because Toby criticized her color combinations. Eddie, a beginning student, "blows out" his knee attempting an advanced racing turn. And Maureen, another student, reaches the bottom of a steep run and slams into a snowmobile that Sara Beth parked there. Maureen, Eddie, and Toby's family all sue Pike's Pique. You defend based on the form you had them sign. Does it save the day?

Exculpatory clause
A contract provision that attempts to release one party from liability in the event the other is injured.

Its an attempt to release a party from being held liable from any damages/injuries caused

The form on which you are relying is an **exculpatory clause**, that is, one that attempts to release you from liability in the event of injury to another party. Exculpatory clauses are common. Ski schools use them and so do parking lots, landlords, warehouses, and day-care centers. All manner of businesses hope to avoid large tort judgments by requiring their customers to give up any right to recover. Is such a clause valid? Sometimes. Courts frequently—but not always—ignore exculpatory clauses, finding that one party was forcing the other party to give up legal rights that no one should be forced to surrender.

An exculpatory clause is generally unenforceable when it attempts to exclude an intentional tort or gross negligence. When Sara Beth pushes Toby over a cliff, that is the intentional tort of battery. A court will not enforce the exculpatory clause. Sara Beth is clearly liable.[4] As to

---

[4] Note that Pike's Pique is probably not liable, under agency law principles that preclude an employer's liability for an employee's intentional tort.

the snowmobile at the bottom of the run, if a court determines that was gross negligence (carelessness far greater than ordinary negligence), then the exculpatory clause will again be ignored. If, however, it was ordinary negligence, then we must continue the analysis.

An exculpatory clause is generally unenforceable when the affected activity is in the public interest, such as medical care, public transportation, or some essential service. Suppose Eddie goes to a doctor for surgery on his damaged knee, and the doctor requires him to sign an exculpatory clause. The doctor negligently performs the surgery, accidentally leaving his cuff links in Eddie's left knee. The exculpatory clause will not protect the doctor. Medical care is an essential service, and the public cannot give up its right to demand reasonable work.

But what about Eddie's suit against Pike's Pique? Eddie claims that he should never have been allowed to attempt an advanced maneuver. His suit is for ordinary negligence, and the exculpatory clause probably *does* bar him from recovery. Skiing is a recreational activity. No one is obligated to do it, and there is no strong public interest in ensuring that we have access to ski slopes.

An exculpatory clause is generally unenforceable when the parties have greatly unequal bargaining power. When Maureen flies to Colorado, suppose that the airline requires her to sign a form contract with an exculpatory clause. Because the airline almost certainly has much greater bargaining power, it can afford to offer a "take it or leave it" contract. The bargaining power is so unequal, though, that the clause is probably unenforceable. Does Pike's Pique have a similar advantage? Probably not. Ski schools are not essential and are much smaller enterprises. A dissatisfied customer might refuse to sign such an agreement and take her business elsewhere. A court probably will not see the parties as grossly unequal.

An exculpatory clause is generally unenforceable unless the clause is clearly written and readily visible. Thus, if Pike's Pique gave all ski students an eight-page contract, and the exculpatory clause was at the bottom of page seven in small print, the average customer would never notice it. The clause would be void.

In the following case, the court focused on the public policy concerns of exculpatory clauses used in a very common setting.

RANSBURG V. RICHARDS

770 N.E.2d 393
INDIANA COURT OF APPEALS, 2002

CASE SUMMARY

Facts: Barbara Richards leased an apartment at Twin Lakes, a complex owned by Lenna Ransburg. The written lease declared that:

- Twin Lakes would "gratuitously" maintain the common areas.
- Richards's use of the facilities would be "at her own risk."
- Twin Lakes was not responsible for any harm to the tenant or her guests, anywhere on the property (including the parking lot), even if the damage was caused by Twin Lakes' negligence.

It snowed. As Richards walked across the parking lot to her car, she slipped and fell on snow-covered ice. Richards sued Ransburg, who moved for summary judgment based on the exculpatory clause. The trial court denied Ransburg's motion and she appealed.

Issue: *Was the exculpatory clause valid?*

Decision: The exculpatory clause was void. The lower court's order is affirmed.

Reasoning: When deciding whether an agreement is legal, courts start with a presumption that a contract has been freely bargained by the parties and should be enforced as they wrote it. However, in some cases, the public's interest takes precedence. Several factors suggest that Ransburg's exculpatory clause should not be enforced. A tenant must live somewhere. He has few meaningful choices. He can accept this landlord or go to another landlord who charges the same rent and asks the tenant to sign the same standard form lease. A tenant's urgent need for housing means that he has almost no bargaining power with a landlord.

In addition, this clause, if ratified by the law, will be included in virtually all leases. The rental industry is enormous. A court's interpretation of this exculpatory provision would then affect thousands of tenants who were never party to the contract. Finally, it is important to encourage landlords to maintain their properties in good condition and take reasonable steps to avoid personal injuries. An exculpatory clause has the opposite effect.

Courts should not be used as instruments of inequity and unfairness. The law is not so primitive that it sanctions every injustice other than brute force and downright fraud. This exculpatory clause seeks to immunize Ransburg from damages caused by her negligence. The clause is contrary to public policy and void.

Dissenting Judge's Reasoning: The majority ignores the plain meaning of the exculpatory clause and violates the well-settled right of the parties to agree to such a provision and have it enforced. The majority has unilaterally altered the economic equation in countless residential leases across the state.

ECONOMICS AND THE LAW Judicial rejection of exculpatory clauses may have a hidden cost, as the dissenting judge in the *Ransburg* case suggests. Presumably, the landlord and tenant each attempted to negotiate the most favorable rent possible, based on the local real estate market. The landlord may have offered a slightly lower rent because of the exculpatory clause. She assumed she could never be found liable for damages. When the court threw the clause out the window, it very effectively notified landlords all across the state that they had better fix up their rental property or obtain more insurance. Landlords probably passed on the increased costs to their tenants, in the form of higher rent. So the court's decision is likely to result in rental units that are safer but more expensive. Some tenants may be pushed down to less desirable apartments, or squeezed out of the market altogether. A judicial ruling that is essentially pro-consumer could leave some families out in the cold. ◆

Bailment Cases

Bailment

Giving possession and control of personal property to another person.

Bailor

One who creates a bailment by delivering goods to another.

Bailee

A person who rightfully possesses goods belonging to another.

Exculpatory clauses are very common in bailment cases. **Bailment** means giving possession and control of personal property to another person. The person giving up possession is the **bailor**, and the one accepting possession is the **bailee**. When you leave your laptop computer with a dealer to be repaired, you create a bailment. The same is true when you check your coat at a restaurant or lend your Matisse to a museum. Bailees often try to limit their liability for damage to property by using an exculpatory clause.

Judges are slightly more apt to enforce an exculpatory clause in a bailment case, because the harm is to property and not person. But courts will still look at many of the same criteria we have just examined to decide whether a bailment contract is enforceable. In particular, when the bailee is engaged in an important public service, a court is once again likely to ignore the exculpatory clause. The following contrasting cases illustrate this.

In *Weiss v. Freeman*,[5] Weiss stored personal goods in Freeman's self-storage facility. Freeman's contract included an exculpatory clause relieving it of any and all liability. Weiss's goods were damaged by mildew and she sued. The court held the exculpatory clause valid. The court considered self-storage to be a significant business, but not as vital as medical care or housing. It pointed out that a storage facility would not know what each customer stored and therefore could not anticipate the harm that might occur. Freedom of contract should prevail, the clause was enforceable, and Weiss got no money.

In *Gardner v. Downtown Porsche Audi*,[6] Gardner left his Porsche 911 at Downtown for repairs. He signed an exculpatory clause saying that Downtown was "Not Responsible for Loss or Damage to Cars or Articles Left in Cars in Case of Fire, Theft, or Any Other Cause Beyond Our Control." Due to Downtown's negligence, Gardner's Porsche was stolen. The court held the exculpatory clause void. It ruled that contemporary society is utterly dependent upon automobile transportation and Downtown was therefore in a business of great public importance. No repair shop should be able to contract away liability, and Gardner won. (This case also illustrates that using 17 uppercase letters in one sentence does not guarantee legal victory.)

EXAM *Strategy*

Question: Shauna flew a World War II fighter aircraft as a member of an exhibition flight team. While the team was performing in a delta formation, another plane collided with Shauna's aircraft, causing her to crash land, leaving her permanently disabled. Shauna sued the other pilot and the team. The defendants moved to dismiss, based on an exculpatory clause that Shauna had signed. The clause was one paragraph long, and stated that Shauna knew team flying was inherently dangerous and could result in injury or death. She agreed not to hold the team or any members liable in case of an accident. Shauna argued that the clause should not be enforced against her if she could prove the other pilot was negligent. Please rule.

Strategy: The issue is whether the exculpatory clause is valid. Courts are likely to declare such clauses void if they concern vital activities like medical care, exclude an intentional tort or gross negligence, or if the parties had unequal bargaining power.

Result: This is a clear, short clause, between parties with equal bargaining power, and does not exclude an intentional tort or gross negligence. The activity is unimportant to the public welfare. The clause is valid. Even if the other pilot was negligent, Shauna will lose, meaning the court should dismiss her lawsuit.

UNCONSCIONABLE CONTRACTS

Gail Waters was young, naive, and insecure. A serious injury when she was 12 years old left her with an annuity, that is, a guaranteed annual payment for many years. When Gail was 21, she became involved with Thomas Beauchemin, an ex-convict, who introduced her to drugs. Beauchemin suggested that Gail sell her annuity to some friends of his, and she agreed. Beauchemin arranged for a lawyer to draw up a contract, and Gail signed it. She received $50,000 for her annuity, which at that time had a cash value of $189,000 and was worth, over its

[5] 1994 Tenn. App. LEXIS 393 (Tenn. Ct. App. 1993).
[6] 180 Cal.App.3d 713, 225 Cal. Rptr. 757, 1986 Cal. App. LEXIS 1542 (Cal. Ct. App. 1986).

remaining 25 years, $694,000. Gail later decided this was not a wise bargain. Was the contract enforceable? That depends on the law of unconscionability.

An unconscionable contract is one that a court refuses to enforce because of fundamental unfairness. Historically, a contract was considered unconscionable if it was "such as no man in his senses and not under delusion would make on the one hand, and as no honest and fair man would accept on the other."[7] The two factors that most often led a court to find unconscionability were (1) **oppression**, meaning that one party used its superior power to force a contract on the weaker party, and (2) **surprise**, meaning that the weaker party did not fully understand the consequences of its agreement.

Oppression

One party uses its superior power to force a contract on the weaker party.

When one party has superior bargaining power over the weaker party

These cases have always been controversial because it is not easy to define oppression and unfair surprise. Further, anytime a court rejects a contract as unconscionable, it diminishes freedom of contract. If one party can escape a deal based on something as hard to define as unconscionability, then no one can rely as confidently on any agreement. This is another of the public policy issues we have seen throughout the law of contracts. As an English jurist said in 1824, "public policy is a very unruly horse, and when once you get astride it you never know where it will carry you."[8] With the creation of the Uniform Commercial Code (UCC), the law of unconscionability got a boost. The Code explicitly adopts unconscionability as a reason to reject a contract.[9] Although officially the Code applies only to the sale of goods, its unconscionability section has proven influential in other cases as well, and courts today are more receptive than they were 100 years ago to a contract defense of fundamental unfairness.

Gail Waters won her case. The Massachusetts high court ruled:

> Beauchemin introduced the plaintiff to drugs, exhausted her credit card accounts to the sum of $6,000, unduly influenced her, suggested that the plaintiff sell her annuity contract, initiated the contract negotiations, was the agent of the defendants, and benefited from the contract between the plaintiff and the defendants. The defendants were represented by legal counsel; the plaintiff was not. The cash value of the annuity policy at the time the contract was executed was approximately four times greater than the price to be paid by the defendants. For payment of not more than $50,000 the defendants were to receive an asset that could be immediately exchanged for $189,000, or they could elect to hold it for its guaranteed term and receive $694,000.
>
> The defendants assumed no risk and the plaintiff gained no advantage. We are satisfied that the disparity of interests in this contract is so gross that the court cannot resist the inference that it was improperly obtained and is unconscionable.[10]

Adhesion Contracts

Adhesion contracts

Standard form contracts prepared by one party and presented to the other on a "take it or leave it" basis.

unequal bargaining power

A related issue concerns **adhesion contracts**, which are standard form contracts prepared by one party and given to the other on a "take it or leave it" basis. We have all encountered them many times when purchasing goods or services. When a form contract is vigorously negotiated between equally powerful corporations, the resulting bargain is generally enforced. However, when the contract is simply presented to a consumer, who has no ability to bargain, it is an adhesion contract and subject to an unconscionability challenge.

---

[7] *Hume v. United States*, 132 U.S. 406, 411, 10 S.Ct. 134, 1889 U.S. LEXIS 1888 (1889), quoting *Earl of Chesterfield v. Janssen*, 38 Eng. Rep. 82, 100 (Ch. 1750).

[8] *Richardson v. Mellish*, 2 Bing. 229, 103 Eng. Rep. 294, 303 (1824).

[9] UCC Section 2-302.

[10] *Waters v. Min Ltd.*, 412 Mass. 64, 587 N.E.2d 231, 1992 Mass. LEXIS 66 (1992).

WORLDWIDE INSURANCE V. KLOPP

603 A.2d 788, 1992 DEL. LEXIS 13
SUPREME COURT OF DELAWARE, 1992

CASE SUMMARY

Facts: Ruth Klopp had auto insurance with Worldwide. She was injured in a serious accident that left her with permanent neck and back injuries. The other driver was uninsured, so Klopp filed a claim with Worldwide under her "uninsured motorist" coverage. Her policy required arbitration of such a claim, and the arbitrators awarded Klopp $90,000. But the policy also stated that if the arbitrators awarded more than the statutory minimum amount of insurance ($15,000), either side could appeal the award and request a full trial. Worldwide appealed and demanded a trial.

In the trial court, Klopp claimed that the appeal provision was unconscionable and void. The trial court agreed and entered judgment for the full $90,000. Worldwide appealed.

Issue: *Is the provision that requires arbitration and then permits appeal by either party void as unconscionable?*

Decision: Affirmed. The contract provision is unconscionable.

Reasoning: Worldwide contends that the arbitration provision is clear and unambiguous, but Klopp argues that it is grossly unfair. State policy favors the use of arbitration to resolve disputes, but it rejects any part of a contract of adhesion that is unconscionable.

This contract binds both parties to a low award, one that an insurance company would be unlikely to appeal anyway. Either party may appeal a high award, but common sense suggests that only the insurer would do so. The policy enables the insurer to avoid a high arbitration award that may have been perfectly fair.

This policy promotes litigation and provides an arbitration "escape hatch" that favors insurance companies. The provision is unconscionable and void.

Unconscionability and Sales Law

As mentioned above, the drafters of the UCC reinforced the principle of unconscionability by including it in the Code.

Section 2-302 provides:

If the court as a matter of law finds the contract or any clause of the contract to have been unconscionable at the time it was made the court may refuse to enforce the contract, or it may enforce the remainder of the contract without the unconscionable clause, or it may so limit the application of any unconscionable clause as to avoid any unconscionable result.

In Code cases, the issue of unconscionability often arises when a company attempts to limit the normal contract law remedies. Yet the Code itself allows such limitations, provided they are reasonable.

Section 2-719 provides in part:

[A contract] may provide for remedies in addition to or in substitution for those provided [by the Code itself]*and may limit or alter the measure of damages recoverable...* as by limiting the buyer's remedies to return of the goods and repayment of the price...

In other words, the Code includes two potentially competing sections. Section 2-719 permits a seller to insist that the buyer's only remedy for defective goods is return of the purchase price. But Section 2-302 says that *any unconscionable* provision is unenforceable. In lawsuits concerning defective goods, the seller often argues that the buyer's only remedies are those stated in the agreement, and the buyer responds that the contract limitation is unconscionable.

Electronic Data Systems (EDS) agreed to create complex software for Chubb Life America at a cost of $21 million. Chubb agreed to make staggered payments over many months, as work proceeded. The contract included a limitation on remedies, stating that if EDS became liable to Chubb, its maximum liability would be equal to two monthly payments.

EDS's work was woefully late and completely unusable, forcing Chubb to obtain its software elsewhere. Chubb sued, claiming $40 million in damages, based on money paid to EDS and funds spent purchasing alternative goods. EDS argued that the contract limited its liability to two monthly payments, a fraction of Chubb's damage. Chubb of course responded that the limitation was unconscionable.

The court noted that both parties were large, sophisticated corporations. As they negotiated the agreement, the companies both used experienced attorneys and independent consultants. This was no contract of adhesion presented to a meek consumer, but an allocation of risk resulting from hard bargaining. The court declared that the clause was valid and EDS owed no more than two monthly payments.[11]

CHAPTER CONCLUSION

It is not enough to bargain effectively and obtain a contract that gives you exactly what you want. You must also be sure that the contract is legal. What appears to be an insurance contract might legally be an invalid wager. Unintentionally forgetting to obtain a state license to perform a certain job could mean you will never be paid for it. Bargaining a contract with a noncompete or exculpatory clause that is too one-sided may lead a court to ignore it. Legality is many faceted, sometimes subtle, and always important.

EXAM REVIEW

Illegal contracts are void and unenforceable. Illegality most often arises in these settings:

1. **WAGERING** A purely speculative contract—whether for gambling or insurance—is likely to be unenforceable. (p. 291)

2. **LICENSING** When the licensing statute is designed to protect the public, a contract by an unlicensed plaintiff is generally unenforceable. When such a statute is designed merely to raise revenue, a contract by an unlicensed plaintiff is generally enforceable. (p. 293)

[11] *Colonial Life Insurance Co. v. Electronic Data Systems Corp.*, 817 F. Supp. 235, 1993 U.S. Dist. LEXIS 4123 (D.N.H. 1993).

EXAM Strategy

Question: James Wagner agreed to build a house for Nancy Graham. Wagner was not licensed as a contractor, and Graham knew it. When the house was finished, Graham refused to pay the final $23,000, and Wagner sued. Who will prevail?

Strategy: A licensing statute designed to protect the public is strictly enforced, but that is not true for one intended only to raise revenue. What was the purpose of this statute? (See the "Result" at the end of this section.)

---

3. **USURY** Excessive interest is generally unenforceable and may be fatal to the entire debt. (p. 294)

EXAM Strategy

Question: McElroy owned 104 acres worth about $230,000. He got into financial difficulties and approached Grisham, asking to borrow $100,000. Grisham refused, but ultimately the two reached this agreement: McElroy would sell Grisham his property for $80,000, and the contract would include a clause allowing McElroy to repurchase the land within two years for $120,000. McElroy later claimed the contract was void. Is he right?

Strategy: Loans involving usury do not always include a clearly visible interest rate. You may have to do some simple math to see the interest being charged. McElroy wanted to borrow $100,000, but instead sold his property, with the right to repurchase. If he did repurchase, how much interest would he have effectively paid? (See the "Result" at the end of this section.)

---

4. **NONCOMPETE** A noncompete clause in the sale of a business must be limited to a reasonable time, geographic area, and scope of activity. In an employment contract, such a clause is considered reasonable—and enforceable—only to protect trade secrets, confidential information, and customer lists. (p. 295)

EXAM Strategy

Question: The purchaser of a business insisted on putting this clause in the sales contract: The seller would not compete, for five years, "anywhere in the United States, the continent of North America, or anywhere else on earth." What danger does that contract represent *to the purchaser?*

Strategy: This is a noncompete clause based on the sale of a business. Such clauses are valid if reasonable. Is this clause reasonable? If it is unreasonable, what might a court do? (See the "Result" at the end of this section.)

5. **EXCULPATORY CLAUSES** These clauses are generally void if the activity involved is in the public interest, the parties are greatly unequal in bargaining power, or the clause is unclear. In other cases they are generally enforced. (p. 298)

6. **UNCONSCIONABILITY** Oppression and surprise may create an unconscionable bargain. An adhesion contract is especially suspect when it is imposed by a corporation on a consumer or small company. Under the UCC, a limitation of liability is less likely to be unconscionable when both parties are sophisticated corporations. (p. 301)

2. Result: This statute was designed to protect the public. Wagner was unlicensed and cannot enforce the contract. Graham wins.

3. Result: By selling at $80,000 and repurchasing at $120,000, McElroy would be paying $40,000 in interest on an $80,000 loan. The 50% rate is usurious. The court prohibited Graham from collecting the interest.

4. Result: "Anywhere else on earth"? This is almost certainly unreasonable. It is hard to imagine a purchaser who would legitimately need such wide-ranging protection. In some states, a court might rewrite the clause, limiting the effect to the seller's state, or some reasonable area. However, in other states a court finding a clause unreasonable will declare it void in its entirety—enabling the seller to open a competing business next door.

ADDITIONAL QUESTIONS

1. At a fraternity party, George mentions that he is going to learn to hang glide during spring break. Vicki, a casual friend, overhears him, and the next day she purchases a $100,000 life insurance policy on George's life. George has a happy week of hang gliding, but on the way home he is bitten by a parrot and dies of a rare tropical illness. Vicki files a claim for $100,000, but the insurance company refuses to pay.

   (a) Vicki will win $100,000 but only if she mentioned animal bites to the insurance agent.

   (b) Vicki will win $100,000 regardless of whether she mentioned animal bites to the insurance agent.

   (c) Vicki will win $50,000.

   (d) Vicki will win nothing.

2. For 20 years, Art's Flower Shop relied almost exclusively on advertising in the yellow pages to bring business to its shop in a small West Virginia town. One year the yellow pages printer accidentally omitted to print Art's ad, and Art's suffered an enormous drop in business. Art's sued for negligence and won a judgment of $50,000 from the jury, but the printing company appealed, claiming that under an exculpatory clause in the contract, the company could not be liable to Art's for more than the cost of the ad, about $910. Art's claimed that the exculpatory clause was unconscionable. Please rule.

3. Brockwell left his boat to be repaired at Lake Gaston Sales. The boat contained electronic equipment and other personal items. Brockwell signed a form stating that Lake Gaston had no responsibility for any loss to any property in or on the boat. Brockwell's electronic equipment was stolen and other personal items were damaged, and he sued. Is the exculpatory clause enforceable?

4. **ETHICS** Richard and Michelle Kommit traveled to New Jersey to have fun in the casinos. While in Atlantic City, they used their MasterCard to withdraw cash from an ATM conveniently located in the "pit," which is the gambling area of a casino. They ran up debts of $5,500 on the credit card and did not pay. The Connecticut National Bank sued for the money. What argument should the Kommits make? Which party, if any, has the moral high ground here? Should a casino offer ATM services in the gambling pit? If a credit card company allows customers to withdraw cash in a casino, is it encouraging them to lose money? Do the Kommits have any ethical right to use the ATM, attempt to win money by gambling, and then seek to avoid liability?

5. Guyan Machinery, a West Virginia manufacturing corporation, hired Albert Voorhees as a salesman and required him to sign a contract stating that if he left Guyan he would not work for a competing corporation anywhere within 250 miles of West Virginia for a two-year period. Later, Voorhees left Guyan and began working at Polydeck Corp., another West Virginia manufacturer. The only product Polydeck made was urethane screens, which comprised half of 1 percent of Guyan's business. Is Guyan entitled to enforce its noncompete clause?

6. KwikFix, a Fortune 500 company, contracts with Allied Rocket, another huge company, to provide the software for Allied's new Jupiter Probe rocket for $14 million. The software is negligently designed, and when the rocket blasts off from Cape Kennedy, it travels only as far as Fort Lauderdale. Allied Rocket sues for $200 million and proves that as a result of the disaster it lost a huge government contract, worth at least that much, which KwikFix was aware of. KwikFix responds that its contract with Allied included a clause limiting its liability to the value of the contract. Is the contract clause valid?

   (a) The clause is unenforceable because it is unconscionable.

   (b) The clause is unenforceable because it is exculpatory.

   (c) The clause is enforceable because both parties are sophisticated corporations.

   (d) The clause is enforceable because $200 million is an unconscionable claim.

7. 810 Associates owned a 42-story skyscraper in midtown Manhattan. The building had a central station fire alarm system, which was monitored by Holmes Protection. A fire broke out and Holmes received the signal. But Holmes's inexperienced dispatcher misunderstood the signal and failed to summon the fire department for about nine minutes, permitting tremendous damage. 810 sued Holmes, which defended based on an exculpatory clause that relieved Holmes of any liability caused in any way. Holmes's dispatcher was negligent. Does it matter *how* negligent he was?

8. **YOU BE THE JUDGE** WRITING PROBLEM Oasis Waterpark, located in Palm Springs, California, sought out Hydrotech Systems, Inc., a New York corporation, to design and construct a surfing pool. Hydrotech replied that it could design the pool and sell all the necessary equipment to Oasis, but could not build the pool because it was not licensed in California. Oasis insisted that Hydrotech do the construction work

because Hydrotech had unique expertise in these pools. Oasis promised to arrange for a licensed California contractor to "work with" Hydrotech on the construction; Oasis also assured Hydrotech that it would pay the full contract price of $850,000, regardless of any licensing issues. Hydrotech designed and installed the pool as ordered. But Oasis failed to make the final payment of $110,000. Hydrotech sued. Can Hydrotech sue for either breach of contract or fraud (trickery)? **Argument for Oasis:** The licensing law protects the public from incompetence and dishonesty. The legislature made the section strict: no license, no payment. If the court were to start picking and choosing which unlicensed contractors could win a suit, it would be inviting incompetent workers to endanger the public and then come into court and try their luck. That is precisely the danger the legislature seeks to avoid. **Argument for Hydrotech:** This is not the kind of case the legislature was worried about. Hydrotech has never solicited work in California. Hydrotech went out of its way to avoid doing any contracting work, informing Oasis that it was unlicensed in the state. Oasis insisted on bringing Hydrotech into the state to do work. If Oasis has its way, word will go out that any owner can get free work done by hiring an *unlicensed* builder. Make any promises you want, get the work done to your satisfaction, and then stiff the contractor—you'll never have to pay.

9. ***ROLE REVERSAL*** Write one multiple-choice question with two noncompete clauses, one of which is valid and the other void.

INTERNET RESEARCH PROBLEM

Choose any state, and research its gambling laws. Does the state permit lotteries? Horse racing? Casino gambling? Online wagering? Are the state's policies cohesive? Should gambling *contracts* be enforceable?

You can find further practice problems at www.cengagebrain.com. See the preface of this book for website access details.

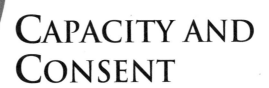

CAPACITY AND CONSENT

For Kevin Green, it was love at first sight. She was sleek, as quick as a cat, and a beautiful deep blue. He paid $4,600 cash for the used Camaro. The car soon blew a gasket, and Kevin demanded his money back. But the Camaro came with no guarantee, and the dealer refused. Kevin repaired the car himself. Next, some unpleasantness on the highway left the car a worthless wreck. Then he sued the dealer, seeking a refund of his purchase price. The dealer pointed out that it was not responsible for the accident, and that the car had no warranty of any kind. Yet the trial court awarded Kevin the full $4,600. How can this be? Should Kevin receive the full purchase price for a demolished car?

She was sleek, as quick as a cat, and a beautiful deep blue.

According to the trial court, the automobile dealer made a basic mistake of law. It ignored *legal capacity*. Kevin Green was only 16 years old when he bought the car, and a minor, said the court, has the right to cancel any agreement he made anytime he wants to, for any reason. We will see how the appellate court resolved the case, as we examine two related issues: capacity and consent.

Capacity concerns the legal ability of a party to enter a contract. Someone may lack capacity because of his young age or mental infirmity. Consent refers to whether a contracting party truly understood what he was getting into and whether he made the agreement voluntarily. Consent issues arise in cases of fraud, mistake, duress, and undue influence.

CAPACITY

Capacity is the legal ability to enter into a contract. An adult of sound mind has the legal capacity to contract. Generally, any deal she enters into will be enforced if all elements we have seen—agreement, consideration, and so forth—are present. But two groups of people usually lack legal capacity: minors and those with a mental impairment.

MINORS

A minor is someone under the age of 18. Because a minor lacks legal capacity, she normally can create only a voidable contract. **A voidable contract may be canceled by the party who lacks capacity.** Notice that *only the party lacking capacity* may cancel the agreement. So a minor who enters into a contract generally may choose between enforcing the agreement or negating it. The other party, however, has no such right. Voidable contracts are very different from those that are void, which we examined in Chapter 12, on legality. A *void* contract is illegal from the start and may not be enforced by either party. A *voidable* contract is legal, but permits one party to escape.

Disaffirmance

Disaffirm
To give notice of refusal to be bound by an agreement.

A minor who wishes to escape from a contract generally may **disaffirm** it; that is, he may notify the other party that he refuses to be bound by the agreement. There are several ways a minor may disaffirm a contract. He may simply tell the other party, orally or in writing, that he will not honor the deal. The minor also has the option of filing a suit to **rescind** the contract, that is, to have it cancelled. Or he may disaffirm a contract simply by refusing to perform his obligations under it.

Rescind
Cancellation of a contract.

Kevin Green was 16 when he signed a contract with Star Chevrolet. Since he was a minor, the deal was voidable. When the Camaro blew a gasket and Kevin informed Star Chevrolet that he wanted his money back, he was disaffirming the contract. He happened to do it because the car suddenly seemed a poor buy, but notice that he could have disaffirmed for any reason at all, such as deciding that he no longer liked Camaros. When Kevin disaffirmed, he was entitled to his money back. If Star Chevrolet had understood the law of capacity, it would have towed the Camaro away and returned Kevin's $4,600. At least Star would have had a repairable automobile.

Restitution

Restitution
Restoring an injured party to its original position.

A minor who disaffirms a contract must return the consideration he has received, to the extent he is able. Restoring the other party to its original position is called **restitution**. The consideration that Kevin Green received in the contract was, of course, the Camaro. If Star Chevrolet had delivered a check for $4,600, Kevin would have been obligated to return the car.

What happens if the minor is not able to return the consideration because he no longer has it or it has been destroyed? Most states hold that the minor is still entitled to his money back. A minority of states refuse to rescind a contract when the minor cannot return the consideration. Star appealed to the Mississippi Supreme Court, arguing that the state should join those that refuse disaffirmance when a minor cannot make restitution.

STAR CHEVROLET CO. V. GREEN

473 So.2d 157, 1985 Miss. LEXIS 2141
SUPREME COURT OF MISSISSIPPI, 1985

CASE SUMMARY

Facts: The facts are summarized in the opening paragraph of this chapter.

Issue: *Is Kevin Green entitled to disaffirm the contract with Star Chevrolet even though the Camaro has been destroyed?*

Decision: Affirmed. Green is entitled to disaffirm the contract.

Reasoning: Sound public policy permits a minor to disaffirm a contract. The goal is to protect a young person from his own impetuous conduct and to discourage aggressive adults from taking advantage of youthful inexperience. The simple way for an adult to avoid the harsh consequences of this rule is to refrain from contracts with those under 18.

When a minor disaffirms an agreement, he must return any portion of the property still in his possession. However, the young person need not return or pay for anything he has sold, destroyed, or otherwise lost.

Kevin Green had the automobile when he notified Star Chevrolet that he was disaffirming the contract. If Star had offered Kevin the full purchase price, as the law required, the young man would have been obligated to return the vehicle. The car dealer failed to do that, though, and the auto was demolished.

We award Kevin $3,100, representing his $4,600 purchase price minus $1,500, which was the salvage value of the car when he delivered it to his insurance company.

ETHICS   As the Mississippi court tells us, the rule permitting a minor to disaffirm a contract is designed to discourage adults from making deals with innocent children. The rule is centuries old. But is this rule workable in our consumer society? There are entire industries devoted to (and dependent upon) minors. Think of children's films, and music, and toys. Does this rule imperil retailers? Who are the *stakeholders*? What are the *consequences*? ◆

Timing of Disaffirmance/Ratification

A minor may disaffirm a contract anytime before she reaches age 18. She also may disaffirm within a reasonable time *after* turning 18. Suppose that 17-year-old Betsy signs a contract to buy a $3,000 stereo. The following week, she picks up the system and pays for it in full. Four months later, she turns 18, and two months after that, she disaffirms the contract. Her disaffirmance is effective. In most states, she gets 100 percent of her money back. In some cases minors have been entitled to disaffirm a contract several *years* after turning 18. But the minor's right to disaffirm ends if she later ratifies the contract.

Ratification

Words or actions indicating an intention to be bound by a contract.

If a minor enters into a contract and then, after turning 18, ratifies the deal, she loses her right to disaffirm and the agreement becomes fully enforceable. **Ratification** is made by any words or action indicating an intention to be bound by the contract. Suppose Betsy, age 17, buys her stereo on credit, promising to pay $150 per month. She has made only four payments by the time she turns 18, but after reaching her majority, she continues to pay every month for six more months. Then she attempts to disaffirm. Too late. Her payment of the monthly bill for six months as an adult ratified the contract she entered into as a minor. She is now fully obligated to pay the entire $3,000, on the agreed-upon schedule.

Exception: Necessaries

A necessary is something essential to the minor's life and welfare. **On a contract for necessaries, a minor must pay for the value of the benefit received.** In other words, the minor may still disaffirm the contract and return whatever is unused. But he is liable to pay for whatever benefit he obtained from the goods while he had them. Food, clothing, housing, and medical care are necessaries. Thus a 16-year-old who seeks emergency medical care and signs an agreement to pay for it is probably liable for the full bill. She has received the benefit of the services and must pay. A car, in most states, is *not* considered to be a necessary. Star Chevrolet argued that Kevin's Camaro ought to be considered a necessary, but the Mississippi court followed the general rule and held that it was not.

Exception: Misrepresentation of Age

The rules change somewhat if a minor lies about his age. Sixteen-year-old Dan is delighted to learn from his friend Betsy that a minor can buy a fancy stereo system, use it for a year or so, and then get his money back. Dan drops into SoundBlast and asks to buy a $9,000 surround-sound system. The store clerk says that the store no longer sells expensive systems to punks. Dan produces a fake driver's license indicating that he is 19, and the clerk sells him the system. Two years later, Dan drives up to SoundBlast and unloads the system, now in shambles. He asks for his $9,000 back. Is he still permitted to disaffirm?

States have been troubled by this problem, and there is no clear rule. A few states will still permit Dan to disaffirm the contract entirely. The theory is that a minor must be saved from his own poor judgment, including his foolish lie. Many states, though, will prohibit Dan from disaffirming the contract. They take the reasonable position that the law was intended to protect childhood innocence, not calculated deceit.

MENTALLY IMPAIRED PERSONS

You are a trial court judge. Don wants you to rule that his father, Cedric, is mentally incompetent and, on behalf of Cedric, to void a contract he signed. Here is the evidence:

Cedric is a 75-year-old millionaire who keeps $300,000 stuffed in pillowcases in the attic. He lives in a filthy house with a parrot, whom he calls the Bishop, an iguana named Orlando, and a tortoise known as Mrs. Sedgely. All of the pets have small beds in Cedric's grungy bedroom, and each one eats at the food-encrusted dining table with its master. Cedric pays college students $50 an hour to read poetry to the animals, but forbids reading any sonnets, which he regards as "the devil's handiwork." Don has been worried about Cedric's bizarre behavior for several years and has urged his father to enter a nursing home. Last week, when Don stopped in to visit, Cedric became angry at him, accusing his son of "dissing" the Bishop and Mrs. Sedgely, who were, according to Cedric, enjoying a fifteenth-century Castilian poem that Jane, a college student, was reading. Don then blurted out that Cedric was no longer able to take care of himself. Cedric snapped back, "I'll show you how capable I am." On the back of a 40-year-old menu, he scratched out a contract, promising to give Jane "$100,000 today and $200,000 one year from today if she agrees to feed, house, and care for the Bishop, Orlando, and Mrs. Sedgely for the rest of their long lives." Jane promptly signed the agreement. Don urges that the court, on Cedric's behalf, declare the contract void. How will you rule? Courts often struggle when deciding cases of mental competence.

A person suffers from a mental impairment if by reason of mental illness or defect he is unable to understand the nature and consequences of the transaction.[1] The mental impairment can be insanity that has been formally declared by a court or mental illness that has never been ruled on but is now evident. The impairment may also be due to some other mental illness, such as schizophrenia, or to mental retardation, brain injury, senility, or any other cause that renders the person unable to understand the nature and consequences of the contract.

A party suffering a mental impairment generally creates only a voidable contract. The impaired person has the right to disaffirm the contract just as a minor does. But again, the contract is voidable, not void. The mentally impaired party generally has the right to full performance if she wishes.[2]

The law presumes that an adult is mentally competent. As always, courts respect the freedom to contract. Anyone seeking to avoid a contract because of mental impairment has the burden of proving the infirmity, since "mental incompetence" could be a very handy way out of a deal gone sour.

How will a court evaluate Cedric's mental status? Of course, if there had already been a judicial determination that he was insane, any contract he signed would be voidable. Since no judge has issued such a ruling about Cedric, the court will listen to doctors or therapists who have evaluated him and to anyone else who can testify about Cedric's recent conduct. Finally, the court may choose to look at the contract itself, to see if it is so lopsided that no competent person would agree to it.

How will Don fare in seeking to preserve Cedric's wealth? Poorly. Unless Don has more evidence than we have heard thus far, he is destined to eat canned tuna while Jane and the Bishop dine on caviar. Cedric is unclean, decidedly eccentric, and possibly unwise. But none of those characteristics proves mental impairment. Neither does leaving a fortune to a poetry reader. If Don could produce evidence from a psychiatrist that Cedric, for example, was generally delusional or could not distinguish a parrot from a religious leader, that would persuade a court of mental impairment. But on the evidence presented thus far, Mrs. Sedgely and friends will be living well.[3]

Intoxication

Similar rules apply in cases of drug or alcohol intoxication. When one party is so intoxicated that he cannot understand the nature and consequences of the transaction, the contract is voidable. Toby's father gives him a new Jaguar sports car for his birthday, and foolish Toby celebrates by getting drunk. Amy, realizing how intoxicated he is, induces Toby to promise in writing that he will sell his car to her the next day for $1,000. Toby may probably void the contract and keep his auto.

---

[1] Restatement (Second) of Contracts Section 15.
[2] As mentioned below, in many states, it is the law that if a court has actually judged someone legally insane, a contract he enters into is entirely void, not just voidable.
[3] For a similar case, see *Harwell v. Garrett*, 239 Ark. 551, 393 S.W.2d 256, 1965 Ark. LEXIS 1033 (1965).

Restitution

A mentally infirm party who seeks to void a contract must make restitution. If a party succeeds with a claim of mental impairment, the court will normally void the contract but will require the impaired party to give back whatever she got. Suppose Danielle buys a Rolls-Royce and promises in writing to pay $3,000 per month for five years. Three weeks later she seeks to void the contract on the grounds of mental impairment. She must return the Rolls. If the car has depreciated, Danielle normally will have to pay for the decrease in value. What happens if restitution is impossible? Generally, courts require a mentally infirm person to make full restitution if the contract is to be rescinded. If restitution is impossible, the court will not rescind the agreement unless the infirm party can show bad faith by the other. This is because, unlike minority, which is generally easy to establish, mental competence may not be so apparent to the other person negotiating.

Reality of Consent

Smiley offers to sell you his house for $300,000, and you agree in writing to buy. After you move in, you discover that the house is sinking into the earth at the rate of six inches per week. In 12 months, your only access to the house will be through the chimney. You sue, asking to rescind. You argue that when you signed the contract, you did not truly consent because you lacked essential information. In this section we look at four claims that parties make in an effort to rescind a contract based on lack of valid consent: (1) misrepresentation or fraud, (2) mistake, (3) duress, and (4) undue influence.

Misrepresentation and Fraud

Misrepresentation

A factually incorrect statement made during contract negotiations.

Misrepresentation occurs when a party to a contract says something that is factually wrong. "This house has no termites," says a homeowner to a prospective buyer. If the house is swarming with the nasty pests, the statement is a misrepresentation. The misrepresentation might be innocent or fraudulent. If the owner believes the statement to be true and has a good reason for that belief, he has made an **innocent misrepresentation**. If the owner knows that it is false, the statement is **fraudulent misrepresentation**. To explain these concepts, we will assume that two people are discussing a possible deal. One is the "maker," that is, the person who makes the statement that is later disputed. The other is the "injured person," the one who eventually claims to have been injured by the statement. In order to rescind the contract, the injured person must show that the maker's statement was *either* fraudulent *or* a material misrepresentation. She does not have to show both. Innocent misrepresentation and fraud each make a contract voidable and permit the injured party to rescind. **To rescind a contract based on misrepresentation or fraud, a party must show three things: (1) there was a false statement of fact; (2) the statement was fraudulent or material; and (3) the injured person justifiably relied on the statement.**

Element One: False Statement of Fact

The injured party must show a false statement of fact. Notice that this does not mean the statement was a lie. If a homeowner says that the famous architect Stanford White designed his house, but Bozo Loco actually did the work, it is a false statement. The owner might have a good reason for the error. Perhaps a local history book identifies the house as a Stanford White. Or his words might be an intentional lie. In either case, it is a false statement of fact.

An opinion, though, is not a statement of fact. A realtor says, "I think land values around here will be going up 20 or 30 percent for the foreseeable future." That statement is pretty enticing to a buyer, but it is not a false statement of fact. The maker is clearly stating her own opinion, and the buyer who relies on it does so at his peril. Although there are exceptions, most opinions are no basis to rescind a contract. A close relative of opinion is something called "puffery."

Puffery.   Get ready for one of the most astonishing experiences you've ever had! This section on puffery is going to be the finest section of any textbook you have ever read! You're going to find the issue intriguing, the writing dazzling, and the legal summary succinct and literally unforgettable!! "But what happens," you might wonder, "if this section fails to astonish? What if I find the issue dull, the writing mediocre, and the legal summary incomprehensible? Can I sue for misrepresentation?" No. The promises we made were mere puffery. A statement is puffery when a reasonable person would realize that it is a sales pitch, representing the exaggerated opinion of the seller. Puffery is not a statement of fact. Because puffery is not factual, it is never a basis for rescission.

Consumers filed a class action against Intel Corporation, claiming fraud. They asserted that Intel advertised its "Pentium 4" computer chip as the "best" in the market, when in fact it was no faster than the Pentium III chip. The Illinois Supreme Court dismissed the claims, asserting that no reasonable consumer would make a purchase relying solely on the name "Pentium 4." Even if the consumers could show that Intel plotted to persuade the market that the Pentium 4 was the finest processor, they are demonstrating nothing but puffery.

[Saying that the Pentium 4 is "better" or "best"] could mean that the Pentium 4 is cheaper, smaller, more reliable, of higher quality, better for resale, more durable, creates less heat, uses less electricity, is more compatible with some versions of software, or is simply the latest in a temporal line of processors. Because the term "better" as a mere suggestion in the name "Pentium 4" is not capable of precise measuring, it is mere puffery and therefore not actionable. That is true even if Intel specifically set out to show the market that the Pentium 4 was the best processor to date.[4]

Courts have found many similar phrases to be puffery, including "high-quality," "expert workmanship," and "you're in good hands with us."

That brings us to the end of the section on puffery. The writing was pretty poor, but you still may not sue.

Element Two: Fraud or Materiality

This is the heart of the case. The injured party must demonstrate that the statement was fraudulent *or* material:

- The statement was *fraudulent* if the maker intended to induce the other party to contract, either knowing that her words were false or uncertain that they were true.

- The statement was *material* if the maker expected the other party to rely on her words in reaching an agreement.

Material:
An error made by the defendant that would be a significant/important influence to a buyer's decision

Consider the examples in the following chart. In case 1, the homeowner tells a prospective buyer that the heating system works perfectly, when he knows that it barely functions, leaving some rooms suitable only for penguins. The words are fraudulent.

In case 2, the homeowner is not lying when he says his cliff house is built on solid bedrock, but he is making a statement without being certain of its truth. This is also fraud.

---

[4] *Barbara's Sales, Inc. v. Intel Corp.*, 879 N.E.2d 910 (Ill. 2007).

By contrast, in case 3, there is no fraud because the homeowner is acting in good faith. He says that the roof is six years old because half a dozen years ago the previous owner said it was new. In fact, the roof is 25 years old and will soon need replacement. The homeowner's statement is a *material misrepresentation* because it is incorrect and the owner expects the buyer to rely on it.

Finally, in case 4, the homeowner says that the swimming pool is 30 feet long because he measured it himself. But he did the job incorrectly, and the pool is only 29 feet. This is another misrepresentation, but is it *material?* No. An error of a foot or so would not influence a reasonable purchaser, and this buyer has failed to prove her case.

THE DIFFERENCE BETWEEN FRAUD AND MISREPRESENTATION

Statement. In each case, the words are false.	Owner's Belief	Legal Result	Explanation
1. "The heating system is perfect."	Owner knows this is false.	Fraud.	Owner knew the statement was false and intended to induce the buyer to enter into a contract.
2. "The house is built on solid bedrock."	Owner has no idea what is under the surface.	Fraud.	Owner was not certain the statement was true and intended to induce the buyer to enter into a contract.
3. "The roof is only six years old."	Owner has a good reason to believe the statement is true.	Material misrepresentation.	Owner acted in good faith, but the statement is material because owner expects the buyer to rely on it.
4. "The pool is 30 feet long."	Owner has a good reason to believe the statement is true.	Not a material misrepresentation.	Although this is a misrepresentation, it is not material, since a reasonable buyer would not make a decision based on a one-foot error in the pool length.

Element Three: Justifiable Reliance

The injured party must also show that she actually did rely on the false statement and that her reliance was reasonable. Suppose the seller of a gas station lies through his teeth about the structural soundness of the building. The buyer believes what he hears but does not much care, because he plans to demolish the building and construct a day-care center. There was fraud but no reliance, and the buyer may not rescind.

The reliance must be justifiable—that is, reasonable. If the seller of wilderness land tells Lewis that the area is untouched by pollution, but a large lake is permanently covered with six inches of thick red scum, Lewis is not justified in relying on the seller's statements. If he goes forward with the purchase, he may not rescind.

No Duty to Investigate   Lewis must act reasonably and keep his eyes open as he walks around the "wilderness" property. But he has no duty to undertake an investigation of what he is told. In other words, if the seller states that the countryside is pure and the lake looks crystal clear, Lewis is not obligated to take water samples and have them tested by a laboratory. A party to a contract has no duty to investigate the other party's factual statements. In the following case, a group of buyers not only alleged fraud, but claimed that the misleading statements were part of a well-orchestrated scam.

HOFFMAN V. STAMPER

867 A.2d 276
COURT OF APPEALS OF MARYLAND, 2005

CASE SUMMARY

Facts: Nine plaintiffs in Baltimore sued various defendants, claiming fraud in an elaborate "flipping" scheme. The plaintiffs alleged that Robert Beeman purchased dilapidated houses in poor sections of Baltimore, searched for unsophisticated, low-income buyers, and promised them a renovated home for a mere $500 down payment. Beeman had the buyers sign contracts for greatly inflated prices. Working with a mortgage company officer named Joyce Wood, he obtained 100 percent financing through the Department of Housing and Urban Development, needing only an appraisal to obtain the money. Arthur Hoffman supplied the necessary appraisal at exactly the sales price, and the buyers took possession—only to find that no repairs had been made.

The jury awarded all nine plaintiffs diverse amounts for their economic losses, plus $145,000 each for emotional harm and $200,000 each in punitive damages. Most of the defendants appealed. This part of the appeal focuses on the appraiser, Hoffman.

Issue: *Did Hoffman commit fraud?*

Decision: Yes, he committed fraud. Affirmed.

Reasoning: Hoffman earned 99 percent of his income from appraisals that he did for Joyce Wood's mortgage company. He knew that if the appraisal did not match the contract price, the deal would fall through.

The clear and convincing evidence showed a similar pattern in all of Hoffman's appraisals. He knew that Beeman had purchased the properties only months earlier for a fraction of the appraisal value. Hoffman justified the extraordinary price inflation by assuming major improvements had been made or would be made, when in fact he knew, or could easily have discovered, that no such repairs were ever made. He also tried to legitimize the appraisals by comparing the houses being sold to "comparable" properties, which in fact were located in much better neighborhoods and were not remotely similar.

For example, Beeman purchased the house at 17 N. Kresson Street for $14,500. Less than three weeks later, he sold the property for $52,000. Hoffman's appraisal stated that the residence had originally been in poor condition but was now in good condition. But that could not have been true because the same document listed defects that still had to be repaired: rotted wood on the front porch, a collapsing ceiling, paint chipping throughout the house, gutters and downspouts requiring replacement, defective windows that needed replacement, and so forth. Hoffman described the property as being in a residential district, when in fact it was surrounded by industrial properties and fronted a road with very heavy truck traffic.

The same pattern occurred time and again. Hoffman's actions, deliberate and knowing, clearly constituted fraud.

Plaintiff's Remedy for Misrepresentation or Fraud
Both innocent and fraudulent misrepresentation permit the injured party to rescind the contract. In other words, the injured party who proves all three elements will get her money back. She will, of course, have to make restitution to the other party. If she bought land and now wants to rescind, she will get her money back but must return the property to the seller.

But the injured party is not forced to rescind the deal if it makes financial sense to go forward with it. After signing a contract to buy a new house, Nancy learns that the building has a terrible heating system. A new one will cost $12,000. If the seller told her the system was "like new," Nancy may rescind the deal. But it may be economically harmful for her to do so. She might have sold her old house, hired a mover, taken a new job, and so forth. She has the option of fully performing the contract and moving into the new house. What are her other remedies? That will depend on whether the misstatement ("the system is like new") was fraudulent or simply a material misrepresentation.

If the maker's statement is fraudulent, the injured party generally has a choice of rescinding the contract or suing for damages. If the seller's mistake was fraudulent, Nancy will generally be allowed to carry out the contract and sue for damages. She could move into the new house and sue for the difference between what she got and what was promised, which is probably about $12,000, the cost of replacing the heating system. But if the seller's mistake was innocent, and Nancy can prove only material misrepresentation, she has no remedy other than rescission. If she chooses to go forward with the contract, she must accept the house the way she finds it.

Finally, in some states, a party injured by fraud may both rescind *and* sue for damages. In these states, Nancy could rescind her contract, get her deposit back, and then sue the seller for any damages she has suffered. Her damages might be, for example, a lost opportunity to buy another house or wasted moving expenses.

SALE OF GOODS

This last option—rescinding and still suing for damages—is available in all states when the contract is for the sale of goods. **UCC Section 2-721 permits a party to rescind a contract and then sue for damages, whether the misrepresentation was fraudulent or innocent.**

Ted Seaton bought a car (a Chevy Camaro—what else?) from Lawson Chevrolet. It was a demonstrator that had a few thousand miles on it but was supposedly in like-new condition. In fact, a salesman had wrecked the car, which had then been substantially rebuilt. Lawson knew this but did not tell Seaton. After Seaton bought the car for $13,000, he discovered the fraud and sued. Seaton won rescission, getting back his $13,000. But this was the sale of goods, so Seaton was entitled to seek money damages as well. The court awarded him $20,000 punitive damages, based upon Lawson's deliberate deceit.[5] See Exhibit 13.1.

Special Problem: Silence

We know that a party negotiating a contract may not misrepresent a material fact. The house seller may not say that "the roof is in great shape" when she sleeps under an umbrella to avoid rain. But what about silence? Suppose the seller knows the roof is in dreadful condition, but the buyer never asks. Does the seller have an affirmative obligation to disclose what she knows?

This is perhaps the hottest topic today in the law of misrepresentation. In 1817 the United States Supreme Court laid down the general rule that a party had no duty to disclose, even when he knew that the other person was negotiating under a mistake.[6] In other words, the Court was reinforcing the old rule of *caveat emptor*, "let the buyer beware." But social attitudes about fairness have changed. Today, a seller who knows something that the buyer does not know is often required to divulge it. The Restatement (Second) of Contracts offers guidance:

Nondisclosure of a fact amounts to misrepresentation only in these four cases: (1) where disclosure is necessary to *correct a previous assertion;* (2) where disclosure would correct a *basic*

---

[5] *Seaton v. Lawson Chevrolet-Mazda, Inc.*, 821 S.W.2d 137, 1991 Tenn. LEXIS 440 (Tenn. 1991).
[6] *Laidlaw v. Organ*, 15 U.S. 178, 1817 U.S. LEXIS 396 (1817).

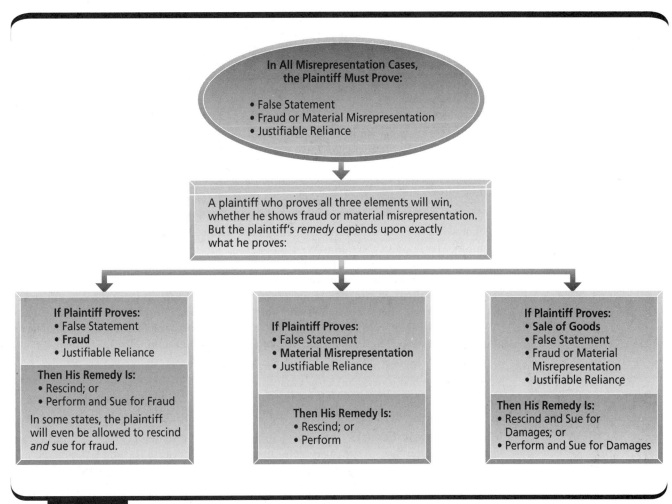

In All Misrepresentation Cases, the Plaintiff Must Prove:

- False Statement
- Fraud or Material Misrepresentation
- Justifiable Reliance

A plaintiff who proves all three elements will win, whether he shows fraud or material misrepresentation. But the plaintiff's *remedy* depends upon exactly what he proves:

If Plaintiff Proves:
- False Statement
- **Fraud**
- Justifiable Reliance

Then His Remedy Is:
- Rescind; or
- Perform and Sue for Fraud

In some states, the plaintiff will even be allowed to rescind *and* sue for fraud.

If Plaintiff Proves:
- False Statement
- **Material Misrepresentation**
- Justifiable Reliance

Then His Remedy Is:
- Rescind; or
- Perform

If Plaintiff Proves:
- **Sale of Goods**
- False Statement
- Fraud or Material Misrepresentation
- Justifiable Reliance

Then His Remedy Is:
- Rescind and Sue for Damages; or
- Perform and Sue for Damages

Exhibit 13.1

mistaken assumption that the other party is relying on; (3) where disclosure would correct the other party's *mistaken understanding about a writing;* or (4) where there is *a relationship of trust* between the two parties.[7]

To Correct a Previous Assertion.   During the course of negotiations, one party's perception of the facts may change. When an earlier statement later appears inaccurate, the change generally must be reported.

W. R. Grace & Co. wanted to buy a natural-gas field in Mississippi. An engineer's report indicated large gas reserves. On the basis of the engineering report, the Continental Illinois National Bank committed to a $75 million nonrecourse production loan. A "nonrecourse loan" meant that Continental would be repaid only with revenues from the gas field. After Continental committed but before it had closed on the loan, Grace had an exploratory well drilled and struck it rich—with water. The land would never produce any gas. Without informing Continental of the news, Grace closed the $75 million loan. When Grace failed to repay,

---

[7] Restatement (Second) of Contracts Section 161.

> She also knew that a reasonable buyer might avoid a haunted house, fearing grisly events...

Continental sued and won. A party who learns new information indicating that a previous statement is inaccurate must disclose the bad news.[8]

To Correct a Basic Mistaken Assumption. When one party knows that the other is negotiating with a mistaken assumption about an important fact, the party who knows of the error must correct it. Jeffrey Stambovsky agreed to buy Helen Ackley's house in Nyack, New York, for $650,000. Stambovsky signed a contract and made a $32,500 down payment. Before completing the deal, he learned that in several newspaper articles Ackley had publicized the house as being haunted. Ackley had also permitted the house to be featured in a walking tour of the neighborhood as "a riverfront Victorian (*with ghost*)." Stambovsky refused to go through with the deal and sued to rescind. He won. The court ruled that Ackley sold the house knowing Stambovsky was ignorant of the alleged ghosts. She also knew that a reasonable buyer might avoid a haunted house, fearing grisly events—or diminished resale value. Stambovsky could not have discovered the apparitions himself, and Ackley's failure to warn permitted him to rescind the deal.[9]

A seller generally must report any latent defect he knows about that the buyer should not be expected to discover himself. As social awareness of the environment increases, a buyer potentially worries about more and more problems. We now know that underground toxic waste, carelessly dumped in earlier decades, can be dangerous or even lethal. Accordingly, any property seller who realizes that there is toxic waste underground must reveal that fact.

To Correct a Mistaken Understanding about a Writing. Suppose the potential buyer of a vacation property has a town map showing that the land he wants to buy has a legal right of way to a beautiful lake. If the seller of the land knows that the town map is out of date, and that there is no such right of way, she must disclose her information.

A Relationship of Trust. Maria is planning to sell her restaurant to her brother Ricardo. Maria has a greater duty to reveal problems in the business because Ricardo assumes she will be honest. **When one party naturally expects openness and honesty, based on a close relationship, the other party must act accordingly.** If the building's owner has told Maria he will not renew her lease, she must pass that information on to Ricardo.

As mentioned above, most courts require a property seller to disclose hidden defects. What happens if an owner, rather than disclosing information, sells the property "as is"? The following case provides insight.

HESS v. CHASE MANHATTAN BANK, USA, N.A.

220 S.W.3d 758
MISSOURI SUPREME COURT, 2007

CASE SUMMARY

Facts: Billy Stevens owned a paint company. On several occasions, he ordered employees to load a trailer with 55-gallon paint drums, and pallets of old paint cans, and dump them on property he owned. This illegal dumping saved Stevens the cost of proper disposal. Later, employees notified the Environmental Protection Agency of what Stevens

[8] *FDIC v. W.R. Grace & Co.*, 877 F.2d 614, 1989 U.S.App. LEXIS 8905 (7th Cir. 1989).
[9] *Stambovsky v. Ackley*, 169 A.D.2d 254, 572 N.Y.S.2d 672, 1991 N.Y.App.Div. LEXIS 9873 (N.Y.App. Div. 1991).

had done, and the EPA began an investigation. (Stevens later served time for environmental crimes.)

Stevens defaulted on his mortgage to the land. While Chase Manhattan Bank was in the process of foreclosing, it learned that the EPA was investigating the property for contamination. Chase foreclosed and put the property up for sale "as is." Several buyers expressed interest. The bank did not inform any of them of the ongoing EPA investigation. Dennis Hess bought the property for $52,000.

After Hess bought the land, he discovered the illegal waste and sued Chase for failing to disclose the EPA's investigation. The jury awarded Hess $52,000 and Chase appealed.

Issue: *Did Chase have a duty to disclose to Hess the ongoing investigation?*

Decision: Yes, Chase had a duty to disclose the investigation. Affirmed.

Reasoning: Buyers of "as-is" properties must exercise ordinary diligence before making the purchase. Sellers of such properties need not disclose anything that buyers could discover during a reasonable inspection. Chase argued that because old paint cans were strewn about the property, Hess should have known that the previous owner had dumped hazardous waste there.

Hess responded that even though the paint cans were visible, he had no way of knowing that the EPA was investigating the land. He claimed that he would not have purchased the property if Chase had notified him of the government inquiry. Hess also presented evidence that two other potential buyers who were aware of the paint cans had made offers on the land. But both testified that they would not have done so if they had known about the EPA investigation.

Chase was wrong to conceal its superior knowledge because Hess had no reasonable chance to discover *the EPA action* during his inspection of the property. Chase's silence amounted to fraud, and Missouri law does not allow a disclaimer like "as is" to protect a defendant from liability for fraud.

Hess may rescind the contract and recover the $52,000 purchase price.

EXAM *Strategy*

Question: Mako is selling his country house for $400,000. Guppy, an interested buyer, asks whether there is sufficient water from the property's well. Mako replies, "Are you kidding? Watch this." He turns on the tap, and the water flows bountifully. Mako then shows Guppy the well, which is full. Guppy buys the property, but two weeks later, the well runs dry. In fact, Mako knew the water supply was inadequate, and had the well filled by a tanker truck while the property was being sold. A hydrologist tells Guppy it will cost $100,000 to dig a better well, with no guarantee of success. Guppy sues Mako. What remedy should Guppy seek? Who will win?

Strategy: Is this a case of innocent misrepresentation or fraud? Fraud. Therefore, Guppy may seek two remedies: damages, or rescission. Make sure that you understand the difference. To win, Guppy must show a false statement of fact, fraud, and reliance.

Result: When Mako responded to Guppy's question by demonstrating the apparent abundance of water, he made a false statement. This was fraud (not innocent misrepresentation), because Mako knew the well was inadequate. Guppy reasonably relied on the demonstration. Guppy will win. He can elect to rescind the contract (return the property to Mako and get his money back) or choose damages (the cost of digging a proper well). Given the uncertain nature of well digging, he is probably wise to rescind.

MISTAKE

Most contract principles come from appellate courts, but in the area of "legal mistake" a cow wrote much of the law. The cow was Rose 2d of Aberlone, a gentle animal that lived in Michigan in 1886. Rose's owner, Hiram Walker & Sons, had bought her for $850. After a few years, the company concluded that Rose could have no calves. As a barren cow she was worth much less, so Walker contracted to sell her to T. C. Sherwood for $80. But when Sherwood came to collect Rose, the parties realized she was pregnant. Walker refused to part with the happy mother, and Sherwood sued. Walker defended, claiming that both parties had made a mistake and that the contract was voidable.

Mistake can occur in many ways. It may be a basic error about the quality of the thing being sold, as in Rose's case. It could be an erroneous prediction about future prices, such as an expectation that oil prices will rise. It might be a mechanical error, such as a builder offering to build a new home for $300 when he clearly meant to bid $300,000. Some mistakes lead to voidable contracts, others create enforceable deals. The first distinction is between bilateral and unilateral mistakes.

Bilateral Mistake

Bilateral mistake

Occurs when both parties negotiate based on the same factual error.

A **bilateral mistake** occurs when both parties negotiate based on the same factual error. Sherwood and Walker both thought Rose was barren, both negotiated accordingly, and both were wrong. The Michigan Supreme Court gave judgment for Walker, the seller, permitting him to rescind the contract because the parties were both wrong about the essence of what they were bargaining for.

If the parties contract based on an important factual error, the contract is voidable by the injured party. Sherwood and Walker were both wrong about Rose's reproductive ability, and the error was basic enough to cause a tenfold difference in price. Walker, the injured party, was entitled to rescind the contract. Note that the error must be *factual*. Suppose Walker sold Rose thinking that the price of beef was going to drop, when in fact the price rose 60 percent in five months. He made a mistake, but it was simply a business prediction that proved wrong. Walker would have no right to rescind.

Conscious Uncertainty.   No rescission is permitted where one of the parties knows he is taking on a risk—that is, he realizes there is uncertainty about the quality of the thing being exchanged. Rufus offers 10 acres of mountainous land to Priscilla. "I can't promise you anything about this land," he says, "but they've found gold on every adjoining parcel." Priscilla, panting with gold lust, buys the land, digs long and hard, and discovers—mud. She may not rescind the contract. She understood the risk she was assuming, and there was no mutual mistake.

Unilateral Mistake (no relief by the court)

Unilateral mistake

Occurs when only one party enters a contract under a mistaken assumption.

Sometimes only one party enters a contract under a mistaken assumption, a situation called **unilateral mistake**. In these cases, it is more difficult for the injured party to rescind a contract. This makes sense, since in a bilateral error neither side really knew what it was getting into, and rescission seems a natural remedy. But with unilateral mistake, one side may simply have made a better bargain than the other. As we have seen throughout this unit on contracts, courts are unwilling to undo an agreement merely because someone made a foolish deal. Nonetheless, if her proof is strong enough, the injured party in a case of unilateral mistakes still may rescind the contract.

To rescind for unilateral mistake, a party must demonstrate that she entered the contract because of a basic factual error and that either (1) enforcing the contract would be unconscionable or (2) the nonmistaken party knew of the error.[10]

Courts are suspicious of unilateral mistake. A contractor who makes a computational error in making a bid may obtain rescission; others seeking this remedy generally fail. Town obtains five bids for construction of a new municipal swimming pool. Four are between $100,000 and $111,000. Fred's bid is for $82,000. His offer includes a figure of $2,000 for excavation work, while the others have allotted about $20,000 for that work. Fred has inadvertently dropped a zero, resulting in a bid that is $18,000 too low. Town officials accept Fred's offer. When he sues to rescind, Fred wins. Town officials knew that the work could not be done that cheaply, and it would be unfair to hold Fred to a mathematical error that the other side perceived.[11]

In contrast, suppose that Rebecca sues Pierce, whose bad driving caused an accident, and Amy, who owned the car that Pierce was operating. While the case is pending, Amy's insurance company, Risknaught, pays Rebecca a $700,000 settlement. Later, the state's supreme court rules that Pierce was an unauthorized driver and an owner's insurer is never liable in such a case. Risknaught seeks to rescind its settlement, claiming unilateral mistake as to its liability. The company loses. Risknaught was aware that an appellate ruling might establish new precedent. The insurer settled based on a decision calculated to minimize its risk.[12]

In the following case an automobile dealer made a mistake—how often does *this* happen?—in the customer's favor.

DONOVAN V. RRL CORPORATION

26 Cal.4th 261, 27 P.3d 702, 109 Ca.Rptr.2d 807
Supreme Court of California, 2001

CASE SUMMARY

Facts. Brian Donovan was in the market for a used car. As he scanned the Costa Mesa *Daily Pilot*, he came upon a "Pre-Owned Coup-A-Rama Sale!" at Lexus of Westminster. Of the 16 cars listed in the ad (with vehicle identification numbers), one was a sapphire blue Jaguar XJ6 Vanden Plas, priced at $25,995.

Brian drove to a Jaguar dealership to do some comparison shopping. Jaguars of the same year and mileage cost about $8,000 to $10,000 more than the auto at the Lexus agency. The next day, Brian and his wife hurried over to the Coup-A-Rama event, spotted the Jaguar (which had the correct VIN) and asked a salesperson if they might test drive it. Pleased with the ride, Brian said to the salesman, "O.K. We will take it at your price, $26,000." This figure startled the sales representative, who glanced at the newspaper ad Brian showed him, and responded, "That's a mistake."

As indeed it was. The Lexus agency had paid $35,000 for the Jaguar and intended to sell it for about $37,000. Brian was adamant. "No, I want to buy it at your advertised price, and I will write you a check right now." The sales manager was called in, and he refused to sell the car for less than $37,000.

It turned out that the *Daily Pilot*'s typographical and proofreading errors had caused the mistake, although the Lexus dealership had failed to review the proof sheet, which would have revealed the error before the ad went to press.

Brian sued. The trial court found that unilateral mistake prevented enforcement of the contract. The appellate court reversed, and Donovan appealed to the state's highest court.

---

[10] Restatement (Second) of Contracts Section 153.

[11] See examples provided in Restatement (Second) of Contracts Section 153.

[12] See, e.g., *AID Hawai'i Ins. Co. v. Bateman*, 82 Haw. 453, 923 P.2d 395 (Haw. 1996).

The state supreme court first ruled that there *was* in fact a contract between the parties. Generally, a newspaper advertisement is merely a solicitation for an offer, and does not permit the customer to form a contract by accepting. (See Chapter 10, on agreement.) However, a California statute generally holds automobile dealers to the terms of their offers. The court then went on to examine the mistake.

Issue: *Did the Lexus dealer's mistake entitle it to rescind the contract?*

Decision: Yes, the mistake entitled the dealership to rescind.

Reasoning: The price is a "basic assumption" of a contract. A significant mistake about that price may permit one party to rescind an agreement. The injured party must show that the error is so severe that it would be unfair to enforce the bargain.

Measured by this standard, the Lexus dealership's price error was a material mistake. A sales price of $25,995 would require the dealer to sell the Lexus for $12,000 less than it intended. That is a 32% error, creating a bonanza for Donovan and a large loss for the seller.

Donovan argues that a dealer is able to monitor its ads and must be strictly held to the terms that it publishes. However, if a court were to enforce this rule, it would mean that a dealer who inadvertently advertised a $75,000 car for $75 would be stuck with the bargain. That is too harsh.

There is no evidence that the Lexus dealership knew of the misprint or intended to mislead customers. Nothing indicated that the dealer routinely permitted such errors to appear in the press. It was the *Daily Pilot* that made the mistake. The dealership should not suffer a large loss because of that error. The judgment in favor of the dealership is affirmed.

EXAM *Strategy*

Question: Joe buys an Otterhound named Barky from Purity Dog Shop. He pays $2,500 for the puppy, the high cost due to the certificate Purity gives him, indicating that the puppy's parents were both AKC champions (elite dogs). Two months later, Joe sells the hound to Emily for $2,800. Joe and Emily both believe that Barky is descended from champions. Then a state investigation reveals that Purity has been cheating and its certificates are fakes. Barky is a mixed-breed dog, worth about $100. Emily sues Joe. Who wins?

Strategy: Both parties are mistaken about the kind of dog Joe is selling, so this is an instance of bilateral mistake. What is the rule in such cases?

Result: If the two sides agree based on an important factual error, the contract is voidable by the injured party. A mutt is entirely different from a dog that might become a champion. The parties erred about the essence of their deal. Joe's good faith does not save him, and Emily is entitled to rescind.

DURESS

Duress
An improper threat made to force another party to enter into a contract.

True consent is also lacking when one party agrees to a contract under **duress**. If kindly Uncle Hugo signs over the deed to the ranch because Niece Nelly is holding a Colt .45 to his head, Hugo has not consented in any real sense, and he will have the right to rescind the contract. **If one party makes an improper threat that causes the victim to enter into a contract, and the victim had no reasonable alternative, the contract is voidable.**[13] The key issues are, thus, whether there was an improper threat and whether the victim had a reasonable alternative.

On a Sunday morning, Bancroft Hall drove to pick up his daughter Sandra, who had slept at a friend's house. The Halls are black and the neighborhood was white. A suspicious

---

[13] Restatement (Second) of Contracts Section 175(1).

neighbor called the police, who arrived, aggressively prevented the Halls from getting into their own car, and arrested the father. The officers took Hall to the police station for booking but eventually realized there might be some problems with the arrest, since neither of the Halls had violated any law or done anything wrong whatsoever. An officer told Hall that he could leave immediately if he signed a full release (stating that he had no claims of any kind against the police), but that if he refused to sign it, he would be detained for a bail hearing. Hall signed the release but later filed suit for false arrest, false imprisonment, battery, and civil rights violations. The police defended based on the release.

The court held that the release was voidable because Hall had signed it under duress. The threat to detain Hall for a bail hearing was clearly improper because he had committed no crime. He also had no reasonable alternative to signing. The Halls' suit went to trial, where the jury awarded them compensatory and punitive damages, plus attorney's fees, totaling over $525,000.[14]

ECONOMIC DURESS

If improper threats can permit one party to rescind a contract, then why not *economic* intimidation? Many plaintiffs have posed that question over the last half century, and courts have grudgingly yielded. Today, in most but not all states, economic duress can also be used to void a contract. But economic duress sounds perilously close to hard competition, in other words—business. The free market system is expected to produce tough competition. A smart, aggressive executive may bargain fiercely. How do we distinguish economic duress from successful business tactics? Courts have created no single rule to answer the question, but they do focus on certain issues.

In analyzing a claim of economic duress, courts look at whether there exists:

- Acts that have no legitimate business purpose
- Greatly unequal bargaining power
- An unnaturally large gain for one party
- Financial distress to one party

Is the following case one of duress or hard bargaining?

YOU *be the* JUDGE

IN RE RLS LEGAL SOLUTIONS, L.L.C.
2005 WL 171381
TEXAS COURT OF APPEALS, 2005

Facts: Amy Maida sued her employer, RLS Legal Solutions, for various claims relating to her job. RLS asked that the case be dismissed, because Maida had signed an arbitration agreement. Maida had in fact signed the contract while already working at MLS.

However, she responded that the agreement should not be enforced because she had signed it under economic duress. At trial, she was asked whether she had found the agreement acceptable:

[14] *Halls v. Ochs*, 817 F.2d 920, U.S.App. LEXIS 5822 (1st Cir. 1987).

continued

I did not. The arbitration clause was going to allow me not to be able to be in a position that I needed to be in now, and that is, to have someone represent me to help me where I feel like the company did me wrong.

After I refused to agree to this arbitration clause, I was told that my payroll checks would not be direct deposited into my account until I signed the agreement and that I would not be paid until I signed the agreement. I had received my paychecks by direct deposit for three years. [RLS did in fact stop the direct deposit payment of Maida's salary.]

I needed my paycheck to meet my financial responsibilities since I am a single family income household provider. I had no way to pay my mortgage, vehicle note, car and homeowner's insurance as well as any household bills.

Maida testified that after signing and returning the agreement, she received a manual check. Maida said that when she asked why she had not been paid by direct deposit as usual, she was told her paycheck would be held until she signed the agreement.

RLS argued that Maida had eventually received every paycheck to which she was entitled, had suffered no losses, and was free to leave RLS at any time if she found her employment terms unacceptable.

The trial court refused to dismiss the case or order arbitration, and RLS appealed.

You Be the Judge: Did Maida sign the arbitration under economic duress?

Argument for RLS: Your honors, it is hard to take seriously a claim of economic duress when the plaintiff has not lost one cent and was never forced to sign anything. RLS runs a business, not a community center. To stay competitive, we constantly revise our commercial practices, and this was one such change. We did not ask for some bizarre or inappropriate change: Arbitration is a widely favored method of settling disputes, quicker and cheaper *for all parties*. Maida signed. Yes, we stopped direct deposit of her check, but we paid her. We were not obligated to pay her in any particular fashion, or even to continue her employment. If she wanted to stay with us, she had to play by our rules.

Argument for Maida: The company could offer an arbitration contract to all workers. But that is distinct from forcing such agreements down employees' throats, which is what they did here. RLS knows that its workers depend on prompt payment of payroll checks to avoid falling quickly into debt. The company offered Maida the arbitration agreement, she rejected it, and they responded by stopping direct deposit of her check. Knowing that she was the sole provider for her family, the firm intended to subject her to intolerable economic pressure. It worked. However, the court should have no part of this coercion. The two sides had hugely differing bargaining power, and RLS attempted to use financial distress to obtain what it could not by persuasion.

UNDUE INFLUENCE

(usually voidable)

"Special Relationship"

She was single and pregnant. A shy young woman in a large city with no family nearby, she needed help and support. She went to the Methodist Mission Home of Texas where she found room and board, support—and a lot of counseling. Her discussions with a minister and a private counselor stressed one point: that she should give up her baby for adoption. She signed the adoption papers, but days later she decided she wanted the baby after all. Was there any ground to rescind? She claimed *undue influence*, in other words, that the Mission Home so dominated her thinking that she never truly consented. Where one party has used undue influence, the contract is voidable at the option of the injured party. There are two elements to the plaintiff's case. **To prove undue influence, the injured party must demonstrate:**

- A relationship between the two parties either of trust or of domination, and

- Improper persuasion by the stronger party.[15]

In other words, a party seeking to rescind based on undue influence must first show that the parties had some close bond, either because one would normally have trusted and relied on

---

[15] Restatement (Second) of Contracts Section 175(1).

the other or because one was able to dominate the other. Second, the party seeking to rescind must show improper persuasion, which is an effort by the stronger party to coerce the weaker one into a decision that she otherwise would not have made.

In the Methodist Mission case, the court held that the plaintiff had been young and extremely vulnerable during the days following the birth of her child. The mission's counselor, to whom she turned for support, had spent day after day forcefully insisting that the young woman had no moral or legal right to keep her child. The harangue amounted to undue influence. The court voided the adoption agreement.[16] In the following case, the age difference is reversed.

SEPULVEDA V. AVILES

762 N.Y.S.2d 358, 308 A.D.2d 1
NEW YORK SUPREME COURT, APPELLATE DIVISION, 2003

CASE SUMMARY

Facts: Agnes Seals owned and lived in a ten-unit apartment building on East 119th Street in New York City. When she was 80 years old, a fire damaged much of the building's interior, leaving Seals physically and mentally unable to care for the property. Shortly after the fire, she met David Aviles, a 35-year-old neighbor. Aviles convinced Seals to sell him the building, promising to care for her for the rest of her life. She sold him the building for $50,000, taking a down payment of $10,000, with the rest to be paid over time. At the closing, Seals was represented by an attorney, Martin Freedman, whom she had never met before, and who had been referred to her by Aviles's lawyer (with whom he shared office space).

Three years later, Seals died. Her will left her entire estate to Elba and Victor Sepulveda, but the building had been Seals's principal asset. The Sepulvedas sued Aviles, asking the court to set aside the sale of the building, claiming that Aviles had used undue influence to trick Seals into a sale that was not in her interest. The jury found that Aviles had not used undue influence, and the Sepulvedas appealed.

Issue: *Did Aviles use undue influence to obtain the apartment building?*

Decision: Yes, Aviles used undue influence.

Reasoning: The jury's verdict was completely at odds with the evidence. A social worker testified that at the time of the sale, Seals was traumatized by the fire, housebound, and utterly dependent on others for her daily needs. Sister Lachapelle, a second neutral witness, confirmed this. They both stated that Aviles promised to take care of Seals if she would sell him the building. At the closing, Seals was represented by a lawyer she had never met before, recommended to her by Aviles.

A medical expert testified that in his opinion, Seals suffered from severe Alzheimer's disease at the time of the sale. Aviles testified that at the time of the sale, Seals was coherent and lucid, but the expert testimony is far more persuasive than Aviles's self-serving, lay opinion.

At trial, Aviles admitted that he made unfettered use of Seals's funds and credit cards. In a particularly brazen example, he wrote Seals monthly checks for payment on the house, and then had her endorse the checks back to him. Aviles deposited the checks in his account, having effectively paid nothing for the house. The sale was a sham.

Aviles clearly and repeatedly used undue influence to bring about the sale and then avoid his payments for the building. The jury's verdict that there was no undue influence was based on a wildly unreasonable interpretation of the evidence. The case is reversed and remanded for a new trial.

---

[16] *Methodist Mission Home of Texas v. N A B*, 451 S.W.2d 539, 1970 Tex.App. LEXIS 2055 (Tex.Civ. App. 1970).

CHAPTER CONCLUSION

An agreement between two parties may not be enough to make a contract enforceable. A minor or a mentally impaired person may generally disaffirm contracts. Even if both parties are adults of sound mind, courts will insist that consent be genuine. Misrepresentation, mistake, duress, and undue influence all indicate that at least one party did not truly consent. As the law evolves, it imposes an increasingly greater burden of *good faith negotiating* on the party in the stronger position. Do not bargain for a contract that is too good to be true.

EXAM REVIEW

1. **VOIDABLE CONTRACT** Capacity and consent are different contract issues that can lead to the same result: a voidable contract. A voidable agreement is one that can be canceled by a party who lacks legal capacity or who did not give true consent. (p. 310)

2. **DISAFFIRMANCE** A minor (someone under the age of 18) generally may disaffirm any contract while she is still a minor or within a reasonable time after reaching age 18. (p. 310)

EXAM Strategy

Question: John Marshall and Kirsten Fletcher decided to live together. They leased an apartment, each agreeing to pay one-half of the rent. When he signed the lease, Marshall was 17. Shortly after signing the lease, Marshall turned 18, and two weeks later, he moved into the apartment. He paid his half of the rent for two months and then moved out because he and Fletcher were not getting along. Fletcher sued Marshall for one-half of the monthly rent for the remainder of the lease. Who wins?

Strategy: Marshall was clearly a minor when he signed the lease, and could have rescinded the agreement at that time. However, after he turned 18, he moved in and began to pay rent. What effect did that have on his contract obligation? (See the "Result" at the end of this section.)

3. **RESTITUTION** A minor who disaffirms must make restitution; that is, she must return to the other party whatever consideration she received, such as goods that she purchased. If she cannot make restitution because the goods are damaged or destroyed, in most (but not all) states the minor is still entitled to disaffirm and receive her money. (p. 310)

4. **MENTAL IMPAIRMENT** A mentally impaired person may generally disaffirm a contract. In this case, though, he generally must make restitution. (p. 312)

5. **FRAUD AND MISREPRESENTATION** Both fraud and material misrepresentation are grounds for disaffirming a contract. The injured party must prove:

   (a) A false statement of fact; and
   (b) Fraud or materiality; and
   (c) Justifiable reliance. (p. 314)

Question: Ron buys 1,000 "Smudgy Dolls" for his toy store. Karen, the seller, tells him the dolls are in perfect condition, even though she knows their heads are defectively attached. Ron sells all of the products but then has 1,000 angry customers with headless dolls. Ron sues Karen, seeking rescission of the contract and punitive damages. What is the likely outcome?

   (a) Ron will be able to rescind, based on fraud, but he cannot recover punitive damages as well.

   (b) Ron will be able to rescind, based on fraud, and may also obtain punitive damages.

   (c) Ron may win a case of misrepresentation, but not one of fraud.

   (d) Ron will lose unless he can show that Karen intended to harm Ron's business.

   (e) Ron will win only if he can show that both parties were mistaken about a basic assumption.

Strategy: Karen knew her statement was false, so this is a case of fraud. Ron must prove a false statement of fact; fraud or materiality; and reliance. Can he do so? Notice also that this is a contract for the sale of goods, giving the plaintiff additional remedies. (See the "Result" at the end of this section.)

---

6. **SILENCE** Silence amounts to misrepresentation only in four instances:

   (a) Where disclosure is necessary to *correct a previous assertion*
   (b) Where disclosure would correct a *basic mistaken assumption* on which the other party is relying
   (c) Where disclosure would correct the other party's *mistaken understanding about a writing;* or Where there is a *relationship of trust* between the two parties. (p. 318)

---

7. **MISTAKE** In a case of bilateral mistake, either party may rescind the contract. In a case of unilateral mistake, the injured party may rescind only upon a showing that enforcement would be unconscionable or that the other party knew of her mistake. (p. 322)

---

8. **DURESS** If one party makes an improper threat that causes the victim to enter into a contract, and the victim had no reasonable alternative, the contract is voidable. (p. 324)

Question: Andreini's nerve problem diminished the use of his hands. Dr. Beck operated, but the problem grew worse. A nurse told the patient that Beck might have committed a serious error, exacerbating the problem. Andreini returned for a second operation, which Beck assured him would correct the problem. But after Andreini had been placed in a surgical gown, shaved, and prepared for surgery, the doctor insisted that he sign a release relieving Beck of liability for the first operation. Andreini did not want to sign it, but Beck refused to operate until he did. Later, Andreini sued Beck for malpractice. A trial court dismissed Andreini's suit based on the release. You are on the appeals court. Will you affirm the dismissal or reverse?

Strategy: Adreini is claiming physical duress. Did Beck act *improperly* in demanding a release? Did Adreini have a *realistic alternative?* (See the "Result" at the end of this section.)

9. **ECONOMIC DURESS** Cases of economic duress are more common but harder to win. Courts will look at the parties' motives, their respective bargaining power, any unnaturally large gains, and resulting financial distress. (p. 325)

10. **UNDUE INFLUENCE** Once again the injured party may rescind a contract, but only upon a showing of a special relationship and improper persuasion. (p. 326)

2. Result: A minor can disaffirm a contract. However, if he turns 18 and then ratifies the agreement, he is fully liable. When he paid the rent, Marshall ratified the contract, and he is fully liable.

5. Result: Karen made a false statement of fact, knowing it was wrong. Ron reasonably relied on her. Karen has committed fraud, so the answer is either "a" or "b." Because this case is governed by the UCC, Ron is entitled to rescind the agreement and also to seek punitive damages. The correct answer is "b." "C" is wrong because Karen's misstatement was not innocent. "D" is incorrect because Karen's attitude towards Ron's business is irrelevant. "E" focuses on mutual mistake.

8. Result: The Utah Supreme Court reversed the trial court, so you probably should as well. Beck forced Adreini to sign under duress. The threat to withhold surgery was improper, and Adreini had no reasonable alternative.

ADDITIONAL QUESTIONS

1. Raymond Barrows owned a 17-acre parcel of undeveloped land in Seaford, Delaware. For most of his life Mr. Barrows had been an astute and successful businessman, but by the time he was 85 years old, he had been diagnosed as "very senile and confused 90 percent of the time." Glenn Bowen offered to buy the land. Barrows had no idea of its value, so Bowen had it appraised by a friend, who said it was worth $50,000. Bowen drew up a contract, which Barrows signed. In the contract, Barrows agreed to sell the land for $45,000, of which Bowen would pay $100 at the time of closing; the remaining $44,900 was due whenever Bowen developed the land and sold it. There was no time limit on Bowen's right to develop the land nor any interest due on the second payment. Comment.

2. On television and in magazines, Maurine and Mamie Mason saw numerous advertisements for Chrysler Fifth Avenue automobiles. The ads described the car as "luxurious," "quality-engineered," and "reliable." When they went to inspect the car, the salesman told them the warranty was "the best…comparable to Cadillacs and Lincolns." After the Masons bought a Fifth Avenue, they began to have many problems with it. Even after numerous repairs, the car was unsatisfactory and required more work. The Masons sued, seeking to rescind the contract based on the ads and the dealer's statement. Will they win?

3. Kerry finds a big green ring in the street. She shows it to Leroy, who says, "Wow. That could be valuable." Neither Kerry nor Leroy knows what the ring is made of or whether it is valuable. Kerry sells the ring to Leroy for $100, saying, "Don't come griping if it turns out to be worth two dollars." Leroy takes the ring to a jeweler who tells him it is an unusually perfect emerald, worth at least $75,000. Kerry sues to rescind.

   a. Kerry will win based on fraud.

   b. Kerry will win based on mutual mistake.

   c. Kerry will win based on unilateral mistake.

   d. Kerry will lose.

4. The McAllisters had several serious problems with their house, including leaks in the ceiling, a buckling wall, and dampness throughout. They repaired the buckling wall by installing I-beams to support it. They never resolved the leaks and the dampness. When they decided to sell the house, they said nothing to prospective buyers about the problems. They stated that the I-beam had been added for reinforcement. The Silvas bought the house for $60,000. Soon afterwards, they began to have problems with leaks, mildew, and dampness. Are the Silvas entitled to any money damages? Why or why not?

5. **ETHICS** Sixteen-year-old Travis Mitchell brought his 19-year-old Pontiac GTO into M&M Precision Body and Paint for body work and a paint job. M&M did the work and charged $1,900, which Travis paid. Travis later complained about the quality of the work and M&M did some touching up, but Travis was still dissatisfied. Travis demanded his $1,900 back, but M&M refused to give it back since all of the work was "in" the car and Travis could not return it to the shop. The state of Nebraska, where this occurred, follows the majority rule on this issue. Does Travis get his money? What is the common law rule? Who *ought* to win? Is the common law rule fair? What is the rationale for the rule?

6. Roy Newburn borrowed money and bought a $49,000 truck from Treadwell Ford. A few months later the truck developed transmission problems. Newburn learned that the truck had 170,000 more miles on it than the odometer indicated. The company admitted the mileage and promised to install a new transmission free. Treadwell did install the new transmission, but when Newburn came to pick up the truck, Treadwell demanded that he sign a general release absolving the dealership of any claims based on the inaccurate mileage. Treadwell refused to turn over the truck until Newburn finally signed. The truck broke down again, and delays cost Newburn so much income that he fell behind on his loan payments and lost the truck. He sued Treadwell, which defended based on the release. Is the release valid?

7. ***YOU BE THE JUDGE*** WRITING PROBLEM Susan Gould was appointed to a three-year probationary position as a teacher at Sewanhaka High School. Normally, after three years, the school board either grants tenure or dismisses the teacher. The Sewanhaka school board notified Gould she would not be rehired. To keep the termination out of her file, Gould agreed to resign. In fact, because Gould had previously taught at a different New York school, state law required that she be given a tenure decision after only two years. If the board failed to do that, the teacher was automatically tenured. When she learned this, Gould sued to rescind her agreement to resign. Is Gould entitled to rescind the contract (i.e., her agreement to resign)? **Argument for Gould:** Both parties assumed that Gould was on probation and could be dismissed after three years. Neither party understood that after three years, Gould actually *had* tenure under New York State law. Gould would never have resigned had she understood she was entitled to tenure. The misunderstanding goes to the essence of the resignation agreement, and she should be permitted to rescind. **Argument for the School Board:** The school board has done nothing wrong here. It is unfair to penalize the school system for an honest mistake. If Gould is serious about her career, she should understand the tenure process and should take the trouble to inform the board about unusual rules that pertain to her case. She failed to do that, causing both parties to negotiate under a misperception, and she must bear the loss.

8. Morell bought a security guard business from Conley, including the property on which the business was located. Neither party knew that underground storage tanks were leaking and contaminating the property. After the sale, Morell discovered the tanks and sought to rescind the contract. Should he be allowed to do so?

9. ***ROLE REVERSAL*** Write a short-essay question that includes one instance each of puffery, misrepresentation, and fraud.

INTERNET RESEARCH PROBLEM

Online, find a new lawsuit alleging undue influence. Analyze the plaintiff's claims. Assuming he can prove those facts, are they sufficient for him to prevail? Was there a relationship of trust or domination? Improper persuasion?

You can find further practice problems at www.cengagebrain.com. See the preface of this book for website access details.

WRITTEN CONTRACTS

Oliver and Perry were college roommates, two sophomores with contrasting personalities. They were sitting in the cafeteria with some friends, Oliver chatting away, Perry slumped on a plastic bench. Oliver suggested that they buy a lottery ticket, as the prize for that week's drawing was $13 million. Perry muttered, "Nah. You never win if you buy just one ticket." Oliver bubbled up, "O.K., we'll buy a ticket every week. We'll keep buying them from now until we graduate. Come on, it'll be fun. This month, I'll buy the tickets. Next month, you will, and so on." Other students urged Perry to do it and, finally, grudgingly, he agreed. The two friends carefully reviewed their deal. Each party was providing consideration—namely, the responsibility for purchasing tickets during his month. The amount of each purchase was clearly defined at one dollar. They would start that week and continue until graduation day, two and a

Perry moved out of their dorm room into a suite at the Ritz and refused to give Oliver one red cent.

half years down the road. Finally, they would share equally any money won. As three witnesses looked on, they shook hands on the bargain. That month, Oliver bought a ticket every week, randomly choosing numbers, and won nothing. The next month, Perry bought a ticket with equally random numbers—and won $52 million. Perry moved out of their dorm room into a suite at the Ritz and refused to give Oliver one red cent. Oliver sued, seeking $26 million, and the return of an Eric Clapton compact disc that he had loaned Perry. If the former friends had understood the statute of frauds, they would never have slid into this mess.[1]

---

[1] Based loosely on *Lydon v. Beauregard* (Middlesex Sup. Ct., Mass., Dec. 22, 1989), reported in Paul Langher, "Couple Lose Suit to Share $2.8M Prize," *Boston Globe*, Dec. 23, 1989, p. 21.

The rule we examine in this chapter is not exactly news. Parliament passed the original statute of frauds in 1677. The purpose was to prevent lying (fraud) in civil law suits. Jury trials of that era invited perjury. Neither the plaintiff nor the defendant was permitted to testify, meaning that the jury never heard from the people who really knew what had happened. Instead, the court heard testimony from people who claimed to have witnessed the contract being created. A plaintiff might concoct a fraudulent claim of contract, knowing that he would never be subjected to aggressive cross-examination, and then bribe witnesses to support his case. A powerful earl, seeking to acquire 300 acres of valuable land owned by a neighboring commoner, might claim that the neighbor had orally promised to sell his land. Although the claim was utterly false, the earl would win if he could bribe enough "reputable" witnesses to persuade the jury.

To provide juries with more reliable evidence that a contract did or did not exist, Parliament passed the statute of frauds. The statute required that in six types of cases, a contract would be enforced only if it were in writing. Almost all states of this country later passed their own statutes making the same requirements. It is important to remember, as we examine the rules and exceptions, that Parliament and the state legislatures all had a commendable, straightforward purpose in passing their respective statutes of fraud: *to provide a court with the best possible evidence of whether the parties intended to make a contract.*

Ironically, the British government has repealed the writing requirement for most contracts. Parliament concluded that the old statute, far from preventing wrongdoing, was *helping* people commit fraud. A wily negotiator could orally agree to terms and then, if the deal turned unprofitable, walk away from the contract, knowing it was unenforceable without written evidence.

Thus far, no state in this country has entirely repealed its statute of frauds. Instead, as we have often seen in the common law, courts have carved exceptions into the original statute to prevent unfairness. Some scholars have urged state legislatures to go further and repeal the law altogether. Other commentators defend the statute of frauds as a valuable tool for justice. They argue that, among other benefits, the requirement of a writing cautions people to be careful before making—or relying on—a promise. For now, the statute of frauds is a vital part of law. Sadly, Oliver will learn this the hard way.

The statute of frauds: A plaintiff may not enforce any of the following agreements, unless the agreement, or some memorandum of it, is in writing and signed by the defendant.

The agreements that must be in writing are those:

- For any interest in **land**
- That **cannot be performed within one year**
- To pay the **debt of another**
- Made by an **executor of an estate**
- Made **in consideration of marriage**; and
- For the **sale of goods worth $500 or more**.

UNENFORCEABLE

In other words, when two parties make an agreement covered by any one of these six topics, it must be in writing to be enforceable. Oliver and Perry made a definite agreement to purchase lottery tickets during alternate months and share the proceeds of any winning ticket. But their agreement was to last two and one-half years. As the second item on the list indicates, a contract must be in writing if it cannot be performed within one year. The good news is, Oliver gets back his Eric Clapton disc. The bad news is he gets none of the lottery money. Even though three witnesses saw the deal made, it is unlikely to be enforced in any state. Perry the pessimist will probably walk away with all $52 million.[2]

But Not Void

Note that although the Oliver–Perry agreement is unenforceable, it is not void. Suppose that Perry does the right thing, agreeing to share the winnings with Oliver. Over the next 20 years, as he receives the winnings, Perry gives one-half to his friend. But then, having squandered his own fortune, Perry demands the money back from Oliver, claiming that the original contract violated the statute of frauds. Perry loses. **Once a contract is fully executed, it makes no difference that it was unwritten.** The statute of frauds prevents the enforcement of an executory contract, that is, one in which the parties have not fulfilled their obligations. But the contract is not *illegal*. Once both parties have fully performed, neither party may demand rescission.

> **ETHICS**   The law permits Perry to keep all of the lottery money. Is that fair? Does Perry have a moral right to deny Oliver his half-share, when we know the two friends had agreed? Is the statute of frauds serving a useful purpose here? Remember that Parliament passed the original statute of frauds believing that a written document would be more reliable than the testimony of alleged witnesses. If we permitted Oliver to enforce the oral contract, based on his testimony and that of the witnesses, would we simply be inviting other plaintiffs to conjure up lottery "contracts" that had never been made? ◆

Contracts That Must Be in Writing

Agreements for an Interest in Land

A contract for the sale of any interest in land must be in writing to be enforceable. Notice the phrase "interest in land." This means *any legal right* regarding land. A house on a lot is an interest in land. A mortgage, an easement, and a leased apartment are all interests in land. As a general rule, leases must therefore be in writing, although most states have created an exception for short-term leases. A short-term lease is often one for a year or less, although the length varies from state to state.

Kary Presten and Ken Sailer were roommates in a rental apartment in New Jersey, with a view of the Manhattan skyline. The lease was in Sailer's name, but the two split all expenses. Then the building became a "cooperative," meaning that each tenant would have the option of buying the apartment.[3] Sailer learned he could buy his unit for only $55,800 if he promptly

"Joint Tenant"

---

[2] Perry might also raise *illegality* as a defense, claiming that a contract for gambling is illegal. That defense is likely to fail. Courts appear to distinguish between the simple purchase of a legal lottery ticket, which friends often share, and the more traditional—and socially dangerous—gambling contracts involving horse racing or casino betting. See, e.g., *Pando v. Fernandez*, 118 A.D.2d 474, 499 N.Y.S.2d 950, 1986 N.Y.App.Div. LEXIS 54345 (N.Y.App.Div. 1986), finding no illegality in an agreement to purchase a lottery ticket, even where the purchaser was a minor! Since an illegality defense would probably fail Perry, it is all the more unfortunate that Oliver did not jot down their agreement in writing.

[3] Technically, the residents of a "co-op" do not own their apartments. They own a share of the corporation that owns the building. Along with their ownership shares, residents have a right to lease their unit for a modest fee.

paid a $1,000 fee to maintain his rights. He mentioned to Presten that he planned to buy the unit, and Presten asked if he could become half owner. Sailer agreed and borrowed the $1,000 from Presten to pay his initial fee. But as the time for closing on the purchase came nearer, Sailer realized that he could sell the apartment for a substantial profit. He placed an ad in a paper, and promptly received a firm offer for $125,000. Sailer then told Presten that their deal was off, and that he, Sailer, would be buying the unit alone. He did exactly that, and Presten filed suit. Regrettably, the outcome of Presten's suit was only too easy to predict.

A cooperative apartment is an interest in land, said the court. This agreement could be enforced only if put in writing and signed by Sailer. The parties had put nothing in writing, and therefore Presten was out of luck. He was entitled to his $1,000 back, but nothing more. The apartment belonged to Sailer, who could live in it or sell it for a large, quick profit.[4]

Suppose that you are interested in buying five expensive acres in a fast-growing rural area. There is no water on the property, and the only way to bring public water to it is through land owned by the neighbor, Joanne, who agrees to sell you an easement through her property. An easement is a legal right that an owner gives to another person to make some use of the owner's land. In other words, Joanne will permit you to dig a 200-foot trench through her land and lay a water pipe there in exchange for $15,000. May you now safely purchase the five acres? Not until Joanne has signed the written easement. You might ignore this "technicality," since Joanne seems friendly and honest. But you could then spend $300,000 buying your property, only to learn that Joanne has changed her mind. She might refuse to go through with the deal unless you pay $150,000 for the easement. Without her permission to lay the pipe, your new land is worthless. Avoid such nightmares: get it in writing.

Exception: Full Performance by the Seller

If the seller completely performs her side of a contract for an interest in land, a court is likely to enforce the agreement even if it was oral. Adam orally agrees to sell his condominium to Maggie for $150,000. Adam delivers the deed to Maggie and expects his money a week later, but Maggie fails to pay. Most courts will allow Adam to enforce the oral contract and collect the full purchase price from Maggie.

Exception: Part Performance by the Buyer

The buyer of land may be able to enforce an oral contract if she paid part of the purchase price *and either* entered upon the land *or* made improvements to it. Suppose that Eloise sues Grover to enforce an alleged oral contract to sell a lot in Happydale. She claims they struck a bargain in January. Grover defends based on the statute of frauds, saying that even if the two did reach an oral agreement, it is unenforceable. Eloise proves that she paid 10 percent of the purchase price and that in February she began excavating on the lot, to build a house, and that Grover knew of the work. Eloise has established part performance and will be allowed to enforce her contract.

This exception makes sense if we recall the purpose of the statute of frauds: to provide the best possible evidence of the parties' intentions. The fact that Grover permitted Eloise to enter upon the land and begin building on it is compelling evidence that the two parties had reached an agreement. But be aware that most claims of part performance fail. Merely paying a deposit on a house is not part performance. A plaintiff seeking to rely on part performance must show partial payment *and* either entrance onto the land *or* physical improvements to it.

---

[4] *Presten v. Sailer*, 225 N.J. Super. 178, 542 A.2d 7, 1988 N.J. Super. LEXIS 151 (N.J. Super. Ct. App. Div. 1988).

Exception: Promissory Estoppel

The other exception to the writing requirement is our old friend promissory estoppel. **If a promisor makes an oral promise that should reasonably cause the promisee to rely on it, and the promisee does rely, the promisee may be able to enforce the promise,** despite the statute of frauds, if that is the only way to avoid injustice. This exception potentially applies to any contract that must be written, such as those for land, those that cannot be performed within one year, and so forth.

Maureen Sullivan and James Rooney lived together for seven years, although they never married. They decided to buy a house. The parties agreed that they would be equal owners, but Rooney told Sullivan that in order to obtain Veterans Administration financing he would have to be the sole owner on the deed. They each contributed to the purchase and maintenance of the house, and Rooney repeatedly told Sullivan that he would change the deed to joint ownership. He never did. When the couple split up, Sullivan sued, seeking a 50 percent interest in the house. She won. The agreement was for an interest in land and should have been in writing, said the court. But Rooney had clearly promised Sullivan that she would be a half owner, and she had relied by contributing to the purchase and maintenance. The statute of frauds was passed to *prevent* fraud, not to enable one person to mislead another and benefit at her expense.[5]

In the following case, the defendant seems to have acknowledged *in court* that she agreed to sell her property. Does that satisfy the statute of frauds?

BAKER V. DAVES

83 ARK.APP. 145, 119 S.W.3d 53
COURT OF APPEALS OF ARKANSAS, 2003

CASE SUMMARY

Facts: Tommy and Eleanor Daves had a daughter, Lisa Baker. The Daves gave Lisa a deed to a 2-acre property with a house on it, keeping for themselves a *life interest* in the parcel. In other words, the Daves each had a half interest in the land for the rest of their lives; they could live in the house and use the land any way they wished. When they died, the property returned to their daughter.

Tommy and Eleanor divorced, and settled their affairs amicably. In court, with Lisa watching from the second row, their lawyers informed the court of an agreement that all three parties had allegedly made to sell the 2-acre property. Lisa would be reimbursed for taxes and insurance she had paid during the two years she owned the property, and the Daveses would split the rest of the money.

After the agreement was announced, Lisa put the property on the market but then withdrew it, and refused to sell. Tommy Daves sued his daughter. Lisa defended based on the Statute of Frauds, saying she had never agreed in court to the deal, and never signed any contract to sell. The trial court acknowledged that Lisa had signed nothing, but found that the courtroom statements proved the parties had formed a binding contract. The judge ordered Lisa to sell the house, and she appealed.

Issue: *Was Lisa obligated to sell the house?*

Decision: No, Lisa was not obligated to sell the house. Reversed and remanded.

Reasoning: In the trial court, the lawyers for Tommy and Eleanor Daves summarized what they considered to be an agreement to sell the property:

Attorney for Eleanor Daves: The parties have a joint life estate in 2.2 acres of property and a house on Vimy Ridge Road in Alexander, Arkansas. The parties have agreed to

---

[5] *Sullivan v. Rooney,* 404 Mass. 160, 533 N.E.2d 1372, 1989 Mass. LEXIS 49 (1989).

sell the house and 2.2 acres and split the proceeds. They have agreed that Mr. Daves will contact a real estate agency.

Attorney for Tommy Daves: They have a life estate. It was placed in her daughter's name and the daughter is the title owner. She is going to cooperate in listing the property for sale. They are actually selling the property, not just the life estate.

Attorney for Eleanor Daves: The daughter has agreed to sell her interest in the property as well as the life estate of the two parties.

Tommy Daves argues that because Lisa was in court while the statements were made, she implicitly agreed to them, and is bound by the oral contract that was formed. Lisa argues that she made no such agreement.

Lisa Baker was not a party to the divorce proceedings. She was not represented by counsel during the trial. The trial court never asked whether she had heard the purported agreement or whether she agreed to it. In the absence of clear evidence that Lisa orally agreed in court to sell the property, the statute of frauds must control this case. There is no written evidence of a contract, and Lisa is not bound by any alleged oral agreement.

Recall that the Statute of Frauds was created to prevent lying in contract cases. Is Lisa Baker relying on a "legal technicality" to evade a legitimate contract? She was silent during the court session in which two lawyers stated she had agreed to sell. She actually put her house on the market. Judge Crabtree thinks that is clear evidence of an agreement. Is he right, or are there policy reasons to conclude that her behavior is not enough to prove a contract?

EXAM *Strategy*

Question: Aditi and Danielle, MBA students, need an apartment for next September. They find a lovely two-bedroom unit that the owner is rehabbing. The students can see that the owner is honest, his workmanship excellent. The owner agrees to rent them the apartment beginning September first, for $1,200 per month for one year. "Come back at the end of August. By then my work will be done and I'll have the papers to sign." Aditi asks, "Should we sign something now, to be sure?" The landlord laughs and replies, "I trust you. You don't trust me?" They both trust him, and shake hands on the deal. When the students return in August, the landlord has rented it to Danielle's former boyfriend, for $1,400 per month. Aditi and Danielle sue. Who wins?

Strategy: Under the Statute of Frauds, a contract for the sale of any interest in land must be in writing to be enforceable. What does "any interest" mean? Does the statute of frauds apply to this case?

Result: An "interest" means any legal right. A lease is an interest in land, meaning that the students cannot enforce this agreement unless it is in writing, signed by the owner—and it is not. The students need to look for a new apartment.

AGREEMENTS THAT CANNOT BE PERFORMED WITHIN ONE YEAR

Contracts that cannot be performed within one year are unenforceable unless they are in writing. This one-year period begins on the date the parties make the agreement. The critical phrase here is "*cannot be performed* within one year." If a contract *could* be completed within one year, it need not be in writing. Betty gets a job at Burger Brain, throwing fries in oil. Her boss tells her she can have Fridays off for as long as she works there. That oral contract is enforceable, whether Betty stays one week or fifty-seven years. It *could* have been performed within one year if, say, Betty quit the job after six months. Therefore it does not need to be in writing.[6]

If the agreement will *necessarily* take longer than one year to finish, it must be in writing to be enforceable. If Betty is hired for three years as manager of Burger Brain, the agreement is unenforceable unless put in writing. She cannot perform three years of work in one year.

Type of Agreement	Enforceability
Cannot be performed within one year. *Example:* An offer of employment for three years.	Must be in writing to be enforceable.
Might be performed within one year, although could take many years to perform. *Example:* "As long as you work here at Burger Brain you may have Fridays off."	Enforceable whether it is oral or written, since the employee might quit working a month later.

The following case starts with a notorious diet pill and ends with a paralegal suing her boss. Which argument carries greater weight?

YOU *be the* JUDGE

SAWYER V. MILLS
295 S.W.3d 79
SUPREME COURT OF KENTUCKY, 2009

Facts: Barbara Sawyer, a paralegal, worked for attorney Melbourne Mills, assisting him in a class action lawsuit against the makers of a popular diet drug called Fen-Phen. Mills promised Sawyer a large bonus "when the ship comes in," but never specified how much he would pay her. Mills successfully settled the Fen-Phen case for millions of dollars, and later met with Sawyer and her husband to discuss her bonus. The Sawyers secretly recorded the conversation.

The Sawyers asked Mills for a $1 million bonus, to be paid as a lump sum. Mills refused. However, the parties kept talking and Mills eventually agreed to pay Sawyer $1 million, plus $65,000 for a luxury automobile. Payments were to be made in monthly installments of $10,000, for 10 years. Mills also agreed to sign a

[6] This is the majority rule. In most states, for example, if a company hires an employee "for life," the contract need not be in writing because the employee could die within one year. "Contracts of uncertain duration are simply excluded [from the statute of frauds]; the provision covers only those contracts whose performance cannot possibly be completed within a year." Restatement (Second) of Contracts Section 130, Comment a, at 328 (1981). See, e.g., *Mackay v Four Rivers Packing Co.*, 2008 WL 427789 (Id. 2008). However, a few states disagree. The Illinois Supreme Court ruled that a contract for lifetime employment is enforceable only if written. *McInerney v. Charter Golf, Inc.*, 176 Ill.2d 482, 680 N.E.2d 1347, 1997 Ill. LEXIS 56 (Ill. 1997).

continued

document confirming his promise. Sawyer's lawyer drafted the writing but Mills never signed it. He did pay nine monthly installments, along with an extra payment of $100,000.

At trial, jurors heard the tape recording, which confirmed the oral agreement. The jury concluded that the parties had reached a binding agreement, and awarded Sawyer $900,000. However, the court granted a judgment notwithstanding the verdict for Mills. He ruled that the agreement was barred by the Statute of Frauds. Sawyer appealed.

You Be the Judge: Does the Statute of Frauds prevent enforcement of Mills's promise?

Argument for Sawyer: The Statute of Frauds exists to make sure that a plaintiff does not come into court and allege an oral promise that never existed. The fear of fraudulent claims is legitimate, but obviously does not apply in this case. We *know* that Mills agreed to pay a million dollars because we can *hear* him make the promise. We know the exact terms of the agreement, we know it was a reasonable arrangement based on years of work and a

massive settlement. We even hear Mills agree to sign a document confirming his promise.

The Statute of Frauds was designed to prevent fraud— not encourage it. Mills's tiresome, technical arguments did not fool the jurors. After hearing—literally—the evidence, the jury knew there had been a deal and awarded Sawyer her fair share. Let's stop playing legal games, start doing justice, and restore the verdict.

Argument for Mills: This is a simple case. The plaintiffs allege an oral contract for 10 years' worth of installment payments. In other words, *if* there was an agreement, it was for 10 years' duration. Sawyer's own lawyer drafted a contract—never signed—for compensation lasting a full decade. Under the Statute of Frauds, an agreement that cannot be performed within one year is unenforceable unless written and signed. End of case.

If our legislature wanted to encourage secret tape recordings and deception, it could have included an exception to the Statute of Frauds, giving tricky plaintiffs a reward for bad faith negotiating. However, the legislators wisely have made no such exception. The alleged oral contract is worthless.

PROMISE TO PAY THE DEBT OF ANOTHER
When one person agrees to pay the debt of another as a favor to that debtor, it is called a collateral promise, and it must be in writing to be enforceable. D. R. Kemp was a young entrepreneur who wanted to build housing in Tuscaloosa, Alabama. He needed $25,000 to complete a project he was working on, so he went to his old college professor, Jim Hanks, for help. The professor said he would see what he could do about getting Kemp a loan. Professor Hanks spoke with his good friend Travis Chandler, telling him that Kemp was highly responsible and would be certain to repay any money loaned. Chandler trusted Professor Hanks but wanted to be sure of his money. Professor Hanks assured Chandler that if for any reason Kemp did not repay the loan, he, Hanks, would pay Chandler in full. With that assurance, Chandler wrote out a check for $25,000, payable to Kemp, never having met the young man.

Kemp, of course, never repaid the loan. (Thank goodness he did not; this textbook has no use for people who do what they are supposed to.) Kemp exhausted the cash trying to sustain his business, which failed anyway, so he had nothing to give his creditor. Chandler approached Professor Hanks, who refused to pay (naturally!), and Chandler sued. The outcome was easy to predict. Professor Hanks had agreed to repay Kemp's debt *as a favor to Kemp*, making it a collateral promise. Chandler had nothing in writing, and that is exactly what he got from his lawsuit—nothing.

EXCEPTION: THE LEADING OBJECT RULE
There is one major exception to the collateral promise rule. When the promisor guarantees to pay the debt of another and *the leading object of the promise is some benefit to the promisor himself*, then the

contract will be enforceable even if unwritten. In other words, if the promisor makes the guarantee not as a favor to the debtor, but out of self-interest, the statute of frauds does not apply.

Robert Perry was a hog farmer in Ohio. He owed $26,000 to Sunrise Cooperative, a supplier of feed. Because Perry was in debt, Sunrise stopped giving him feed on credit and began selling him feed on a cash-only basis. Perry also owed money to Farm Credit Services, a loan agency. Perry promised Farm Credit he would repay his loans as soon as his hogs were big enough to sell. But Perry couldn't raise hogs without feed, which he lacked the money to purchase. Farm Credit was determined to bring home the bacon, so it asked Sunrise Cooperative to give Perry the feed on credit. Farm Credit orally promised to pay any debt that Perry did not take care of. When Perry defaulted on his payments to Sunrise, the feed supplier sued Farm Credit based on its oral guarantee. Farm Credit claimed the promise was unenforceable, based on the statute of frauds. But the court found in favor of Sunrise. The *leading object* of Farm Credit's promise to Sunrise was self-interest, and the oral promise was fully enforceable.[7]

PROMISE MADE BY AN EXECUTOR OF AN ESTATE

This rule is merely a special application of the previous one, concerning the debt of another person. An executor is the person who is in charge of an estate after someone dies. The executor's job is to pay debts of the deceased, obtain money owed to him, and disburse the assets according to the will. In most cases, the executor will use only the estate's assets to pay those debts. The statute of frauds comes into play only when an executor promises to pay an estate's debts with her *own* funds. **An executor's promise to use her own funds to pay a debt of the deceased must be in writing to be enforceable.** Suppose Esmeralda dies penniless, owing Tina $35,000. Esmeralda's daughter, Sapphire, is the executor of her estate. Tina comes to Sapphire and demands her $35,000. Sapphire responds, "There is no money in mamma's estate, but don't worry, I'll make it up to you with my own money." Sapphire's oral promise is unenforceable. Tina should get it in writing while Sapphire is feeling generous.

PROMISE MADE IN CONSIDERATION OF MARRIAGE

Barney is a multimillionaire with the integrity of a gangster and the charm of a tax collector. He proposes to Li-Tsing, who promptly rejects him. Barney then pleads that if Li-Tsing will be his bride, he will give her an island he owns off the coast of California. Li-Tsing begins to see his good qualities and accepts. After they are married, Barney refuses to deliver the deed. Li-Tsing will get nothing from a court either, because **a promise made in consideration of marriage must be in writing to be enforceable**.

WHAT THE WRITING MUST CONTAIN

Each of the five types of contract described above must be in writing in order to be enforceable. What must the writing contain? It may be a carefully typed contract, using precise legal terminology, or an informal memorandum scrawled on the back of a paper napkin at a business lunch. The writing may consist of more than one document, written at different times, with each document making a piece of the puzzle. But there are some general requirements: **the contract or memorandum**

---

[7] *Sunrise Cooperative v. Robert Perry*, 1992 Ohio App. LEXIS 3913 (Ohio Ct.App., 1992).

- **Must be signed by the defendant, and**
- **Must state with reasonable certainty the name of each party, the subject matter of the agreement, and all of the essential terms and promises.**[8]

SIGNATURE

A statute of frauds typically states that the writing must be "signed by the party to be charged therewith," that is, the party who is resisting enforcement of the contract. Throughout this chapter we refer to that person as the defendant, since when these cases go to court, it is the defendant who is disputing the existence of a contract.

Judges define "signature" very broadly. Using a pen to write one's name, though sufficient, is not required. A secretary who stamps an executive's signature on a letter fulfills this requirement. Any other mark or logo placed on a document to indicate acceptance, even an "X," will likely satisfy the statute of frauds. Electronic commerce creates new methods of signing—and new controversies, discussed in the Cyberlaw feature later in the chapter.

REASONABLE CERTAINTY (Terms)

[handwritten margin note: • The parties involved • The subject matter • The price / amount of quantity]

Suppose Garfield and Hayes are having lunch, discussing the sale of Garfield's vacation condominium. They agree on a price and want to make some notation of the agreement even before their lawyers work out a detailed purchase and sales agreement. A perfectly adequate memorandum might say, "Garfield agrees to sell Hayes his condominium at 234 Baron Boulevard, apartment 18, for $350,000 cash, payable on June 18, 2005, and Hayes promises to pay the sum on that day." They should make two copies of their agreement and sign both. Notice that although Garfield's memo is short, it is *certain* and *complete*. This is critical because problems of vagueness and incompleteness often doom informal memoranda.

Vagueness

Ella Hayden owned valuable commercial property on a highway called Route 9. She wrote a series of letters to her stepson Mark, promising that several of the children, including Mark, would share the property. One letter said: "We four shall fairly divide on the Route 9 property. [sic]" Other letters said: "When the Route 9 Plaza is sold you can take a long vacation," and "The property will be sold. You and Dennis shall receive the same amount." Ella Hayden died, without leaving Mark anything. He sued, but got nothing. The court ruled:

> The above passages written by Ms. Hayden do not recite the essential elements of the alleged contract with reasonable certainty. The writings do not state unequivocally or with sufficient particularity the subject matter to which the writings relate, nor do they provide the terms and conditions of alleged promises made which constitute a contract. The alleged oral contract between Ms. Hayden and Mr. Hayden cannot be identified from the passages from Ms. Hayden's letters quoted above when applied to existing facts. In sum, Mr. Hayden's cause of action seeking an interest in the Route 9 property is foreclosed by the statute of frauds.[9]

---

[8] Restatement (Second) of Contracts Section 131.
[9] *Hayden v. Hayden*, Mass. Lawyers Weekly No. 12-299-93 (Middlesex Sup.Ct. 1994).

Incompleteness

During Ronald McCoy's second interview with Spelman Memorial Hospital, the board of directors orally offered him a three-year job as assistant hospital administrator. McCoy accepted. Spelman's CEO, Gene Meyer, sent a letter confirming the offer, which said:

> To reconfirm the offer, it is as follows: 1. We will pay for your moving expenses. 2. I would like you to pursue your Master's Degree at an area program. We will pay 100% tuition reimbursement. 3. Effective September 26 you will be eligible for all benefits. 4. A starting salary of $48,000 annually with reviews and eligibility for increases at 6 months, 12 months and annually thereafter. 5. We will pay for the expenses of 3 trips, if necessary, in order for you to find housing. 6. Vacation will be for 3 weeks a year after one year, however, we do allow for this to be taken earlier. [Signed] Gene Meyer.

Spelman Hospital fired McCoy less than a year after he started work, and McCoy sued. The hospital's letter seems clear, and it is signed by an authorized official. The problem is, it is incomplete. Can you spot the fatal omission? The court did.

To satisfy the statute of frauds, an employment contract—[or] its memorandum or note— must contain all essential terms, including duration of the employment relationship. Without a statement of duration, an employment at will is created which is terminable at any time by either party with no liability for breach of contract. McCoy's argument that the letter constituted a memorandum of an oral contract fails because the letter does not state an essential element, duration. The letter did not state that Spelman was granting McCoy employment for any term— only that his salary would be reviewed at six months, twelve months and "annually thereafter."[10]

These two lawsuits demonstrate the continuing force of the statute of frauds. In either case, if the promisor had truly wanted to make a binding commitment, he or she could have written the appropriate contract or memorandum in a matter of minutes. Great formality and expense are unnecessary. But the document *must be clear and complete,* or it will fail.

Because some merchants make dozens or even hundreds of oral contracts every year, the drafters of the UCC wanted to make the writing requirement less onerous for the sale of goods, to which we now turn.

EXAM *Strategy*

Question: Major Retailer negotiated a lease with Owner of a strip mall, the tenancy to begin August first. Retailer's lawyer then drafted a lease accurately reflecting all terms agreed to, including the parties, exact premises, condition of the store, dates of the lease, and monthly rent of $18,000. Retailer signed the lease and delivered it to Owner on July 1st. On July 20, Owner leased the same space to a different tenant for $23,000 per month. Retailer sued, claiming that the parties had a binding deal, and the Owner had breached his agreement in order to obtain higher rent. Who will win?

Strategy: To comply with the Statute of Frauds, a writing must state all essential terms. This lease appears to do that. However, there is another thing the writing must contain. What is it?

Result: The writing must be signed by the party claiming that there is no contract, that is, by the defendant. Owner never signed the lease. This lease does not comply with the Statute of Frauds, and the Retailer will lose his case.

---

[10] *McCoy v. Spelman Memorial Hospital,* 845 S.W.2d 727, 1993 Mo.App. LEXIS 105 (Mo.Ct.App. 1993).

SALE OF GOODS

The UCC requires a writing for the sale of goods worth $500 or more. This is the sixth and final contract that must be in writing, although the Code's requirements are easier to meet than those of the common law. **UCC Section 2-201,** the statute of frauds section, has three important elements:

1. The basic rule

2. The merchants' exception

3. Special circumstances

UCC SECTION 2-201(1)—THE BASIC RULE

A contract for the sale of goods worth $500 or more is not enforceable unless there is some writing, signed by the defendant, indicating that the parties reached an agreement. The key difference between the common law rule and the UCC rule is that the Code does not require all of the terms of the agreement to be in writing. The Code looks for something simpler: *an indication that the parties reached an agreement.* The two things that *are* essential are the signature of the defendant and the quantity of goods being sold. The quantity of goods is required because this is the one term for which there will be no objective evidence. Suppose a short memorandum between textile dealers indicates that Seller will sell to Buyer "grade AA 100% cotton, white athletic socks." If the writing does not state the price, the parties can testify at court about what the market price was at the time of the deal. If the writing says nothing about the delivery date, the court will assume a reasonable delivery date, say, 60 days. But how many socks were to be delivered? 100 pairs or 100,000? The court will have no objective evidence. The quantity must be written. (A basic sale of goods contract appears at **http://www.lectlaw.com**)

> The key difference between the common law rule and the UCC rule is that the Code does not require all of the terms of the agreement to be in writing.

Writing	Result
"Confirming phone conversation today, I will send you 1,000 reams of paper for laser printing, usual quality & price. [Signed,] Seller."	This memorandum satisfies UCC Section 2-201(1), and the contract may be enforced against the seller. The buyer may testify as to the "usual" quality and price between the two parties, and both sides may rely on normal trade usage.
"Confirming phone conversation today, I will send you best quality paper for laser printing, $3.25 per ream, delivery date next Thursday. [Signed,] Seller."	This memorandum is not enforceable because it states no quantity.

UCC SECTION 2-201(2)—THE MERCHANTS' EXCEPTION

When both parties are "merchants," that is, business people who routinely deal in the goods being sold, the Code will accept an even more informal writing. **Within a reasonable time of making an oral contract, if one merchant sends a written confirmation to the other, and the**

confirmation is definite enough to bind the *sender herself*, then the merchant who receives the confirmation will *also* be bound by it unless he objects in writing within 10 days. This exception dramatically changes the rules from the common law. It only applies between two merchants, since the drafters of the Code assumed that experienced merchants are able to take care of themselves in fast-moving negotiations. The critical difference is this: a writing may create a binding contract even when it is not signed by the defendant.

Madge manufactures "beanies," that is, silly caps with plastic propellers on top. Rachel, a retailer, telephones her and they discuss the price of the beanies, shipping time, and other details. Madge then faxes Rachel a memo: "This confirms your order for 2,500 beanies at $12.25 per beanie. Colors: blue, green, black, orange, red. Delivery date: 10 days. [Signed] Madge." Rachel receives the fax, reads it while negotiating with another manufacturer, and throws it in the wastebasket. Rachel buys her beanies elsewhere and Madge sues. Rachel defends, claiming there is no written contract because she, Rachel, never signed anything. Madge wins, under UCC Section 2-201(2). Both parties were merchants, because they routinely dealt in these goods. Madge signed and sent a confirming memo that could have been used to hold her, Madge, to the deal. When Rachel read it, she was not free to disregard it. Obviously, the intelligent business practice would have been to promptly fax a reply saying, "I disagree. We do not have any deal for beanies." Since Rachel failed to respond within 10 days, Madge has an enforceable contract.

A merchant must send a confirming memo within a *reasonable* time. But how long is that? A few days certainly qualifies. Could 13 months be quick enough?

SETON CO. V. LEAR CORP.

198 Fed.Appx. 496, 2006 WL 2860774
Sixth Circuit Court of Appeals, 2006

CASE SUMMARY

Facts: General Motors hired Lear Corporation to supply all of the leather seats for its trucks and SUVs. In October 1998, Lear reached an agreement with Seton Company to provide Lear with the actual cut-to-pattern leather, which Lear would then assemble. Seton agreed to give Lear certain rebates, based on the size of the orders. Despite the great value of this contract, the parties initially put nothing in writing. (Note to students: Later in life, if you negotiate a multimillion dollar deal and fail to put it in writing, your grade in this course will be *retroactively lowered!*)

Both parties performed the contract satisfactorily for about a year. Then they agreed to a slight modification in the rebates. All was still well. In the fall of 1999, Lear asked Seton to send a written summary of the agreement, including the modified rebates. In November 1999, Seton sent a one-page memorandum to Lear, summarizing the agreement. It stated: "Lear is to award Seton the entire [truck and SUV program] cut to pattern business for the

life of the program." The letter ended with a request that Lear "kindly return with acknowledgement signature," but Lear did not do so.

For two more years, the parties worked together amicably. Then Seton became anxious that Lear was planning to take its business elsewhere. In January 2002, Seton sent a letter, requesting that Lear affirm its commitment to deal exclusively with Seton for the life of the GMC program. Lear responded that there had never been any such agreement. Seton filed suit.

At trial, Lear claimed that no contract had ever been signed. Seton replied that its memo summarizing the agreement created a valid contract, under the "merchant exception" rule. The jury agreed with Seton and awarded the company $34 million. Lear appealed.

Issue: *Did Seton's memorandum create a contract under the merchant exception?*

Decision: Yes, the confirming memo between merchants created a contract under the UCC. Affirmed.

Reasoning: Lear argued that the November letter was not a written confirmation of an existing contract, but rather an offer of a new contract. The company emphasized that the phrase "kindly return with acknowledgement signature" was evidence that there was no final agreement. But the jury disagreed. It was clearly influenced by Seton's argument that the letter referred to a prior agreement between Lear and Seton executives. Also, although the letter asked for a signature, it did not *require* one. For these reasons, the letter amounted to more than a mere offer.

The UCC does require, however, that merchants send any confirmatory memo within a reasonable length of time. Lear contended that the letter could not count as a written confirmation because it arrived 13 months after the first discussion of the deal with Seton, but the jury disagreed, probably because the relationship between the companies had been casual and friendly for a long time.

UCC Section 2-201(3)—Special Circumstances

An oral contract *may* be enforceable, even without a written memorandum, if:

- **The seller is specially manufacturing the goods for the buyer,** *or*

- **The defendant admits in court proceedings that there was a contract,** *or*

- **The goods have been delivered or they have been paid for.**

In these three special circumstances, a court may enforce an oral contract even without a memorandum.

Specially Manufactured Goods

If a seller, specially manufacturing goods for the buyer, begins work on them before the buyer cancels, and the goods cannot be sold elsewhere, the oral contract is binding. Bernice manufactures solar heating systems. She phones Jason and orders 75 special electrical converter units designed for her heating system, at $150 per unit. Jason begins manufacturing the units, but then Bernice phones again and says she no longer needs them. Bernice is bound by the contract. The goods are being manufactured for her and cannot be sold elsewhere. Jason had already begun work when she attempted to cancel. If the case goes to court, Jason will win.

Admissions in Court

When the defendant admits in court proceedings that the parties made an oral contract, the agreement is binding. Rex sues Sophie, alleging that she orally agreed to sell him five boa constrictors that have been trained to stand in a line and pass a full wine glass from one snake to the next. Sophie defends the lawsuit, but during a deposition she says, "OK, we agreed verbally, but nothing was ever put in writing, and I knew I didn't have to go through with it. When I went home, the snakes made me feel really guilty, and I decided not to sell." Sophie's admission under oath dooms her defense.

Goods Delivered or Paid For

If the seller has delivered the goods, or the buyer has paid for them, the contract may be enforced even with nothing in writing. Malik orally agrees to sell 500 plastic chairs to University for use in its cafeteria. Malik delivers 300 of the chairs, but then University notifies him that it will not honor the deal. Malik is entitled to payment for the 300 chairs, though not for the other 200. Conversely, if University had sent a check for one-half of the chairs, it would be entitled to 250 chairs.

Electronic Contracts and Signatures.   E-commerce has grown at a dazzling rate, and U.S. enterprises buy and sell tens of billions of dollars worth of goods and services over the Internet. What happens to the writing requirement, though, when there is no paper? The present statute of frauds requires some sort of "signing" to ensure that the defendant committed to the deal. Today, an "electronic signature" could mean a name typed (or automatically included) at the bottom of an e-mail message, a retinal or vocal scan, or a name signed by electronic pen on a writing tablet, among others.

Are electronic signatures valid? Yes. State legislatures and Congress are struggling to craft a cohesive law, and the job is incomplete, but here are the rules so far:

- *The Uniform Electronic Transaction Act (UETA).* This law was drafted by the National Conference of Commissioners on Uniform State Laws, who also draft the UCC. As this book goes to press, UETA is the law in 48 states and territories. UETA declares that a contract or signature may not be denied enforceability simply because it is in electronic form. In other words, the normal rules of contract law apply, but one party may not avoid such a deal merely because it originated in cyberspace.

- *The Electronic Signatures in Global and National Commerce Act (E-Sign).* This federal statute, which applies in any state that has not adopted UETA, also declares that contracts will not be denied enforcement simply because they are in electronic form, or signed electronically.

With cyberlaw in its early stages, how can an executive take advantage of the Internet's commercial opportunities while protecting his company against losses unique to the field?

First, acknowledge the risks, which include lost or intercepted communications, fraudulently altered documents, and difficulties authenticating the source of an offer or acceptance. Second, be cautious about "electronic signatures." Assume that any commitments you make electronically can be enforced against you. Paradoxically, if the contract is important, do not assume that the other party's promises, if made electronically, are enforceable unless your lawyer has given you assurance. If in doubt, get a hard copy, signed in ink.

EXAM *Strategy*

Question: Beasley is a commercial honey farmer. He orally agrees to sell 500,000 pounds of honey to Grizzly at $1 per pound. Grizzly immediately faxes Beasley a signed confirmation, summarizing the deal. Beasley receives the fax but ignores it, and never responds to Grizzly. Five days later, Beasley sells his honey to Brown for $1.15 per pound. Grizzly sues Beasley for breach of contract. Beasley claims that he signed nothing and was free to sell his honey anywhere he wanted. Who will win?

Strategy: Honey is a moveable thing, meaning that this contract is governed by the UCC. Under the Code, contracts for the sale of goods worth $500 or more must be in writing. However, the merchant exception changes things when both parties are merchants. Beasley and Grizzly are both merchants. Apply the merchant exception.

Result: Beasley breached the contract. Within a reasonable time after making the agreement, Grizzly sent a memo to Beasley confirming it. Beasley had 10 days either to object in writing, or be held to the agreement. Beasley will lose this lawsuit because he ignored the faxed confirmation.

Parol Evidence

Tyrone agrees to buy Martha's house for $800,000. The contract obligates Tyrone to make a 10 percent down payment immediately and pay the remaining $720,000 in 45 days. As the two parties sign the deal, Tyrone discusses his need for financing. Unfortunately, at the end of 45 days, he has been unable to get a mortgage for the full amount. He claims that the parties orally agreed that he would get his deposit back if he could not obtain financing. But the written agreement says no such thing, and Martha disputes the claim. Who will win? Probably Martha, because of the parol evidence rule. To understand this rule, you need to know two terms. **Parol evidence refers to anything (apart from the written contract itself) that was said, done, or written before the parties signed the agreement or as they signed it.** Martha's conversation with Tyrone about financing the house was parol evidence because it occurred as they were signing the contract. The other important term is **integrated contract**, which means a writing that the parties intend as the final, complete expression of their agreement. Now for the rule.

The parol evidence rule: When two parties make an integrated contract, neither one may use parol evidence to contradict, vary, or add to its terms. Negotiations may last for hours, weeks, or even months. Almost no contract includes everything that the parties said. When parties consider their agreement integrated, any statements they made before or while signing are irrelevant. If a court determines that Martha and Tyrone intended their agreement to be integrated, it will prohibit testimony about Martha's oral promises.

One way to avoid parol evidence disputes is to include an *integration clause*. That is a statement clearly proclaiming that this writing is the full and final expression of the parties' agreement, and that anything said before signing or while signing is irrelevant. For example, an art dealer may say to a prospective buyer, "Watteau's paintings have increased in value 10 percent every year for the last decade. They're going to continue to climb, I know it." Perhaps the dealer shows the customer an article on Watteau that claims that his paintings are still undervalued. When it is time to sign the contract, the dealer will not want these statements included, since they were meaningless puffery, and he has no intention of being bound by them. The dealer will include an integration clause, stating that the buyer is not relying on any promises, statements, or documents of any kind made or examined during negotiations, and that the written agreement is the complete expression of their contract.

In the following case, learned people learned about parol evidence the hard way.

Integrated contract
A writing that the parties intend as the final, complete expression of their agreement.

[handwritten note: The Laws attempt to protect the written contract/document]

[handwritten note: Extrinsic "outside of" Evidence outside of/not included in the written document]

Mayo v. North Carolina State University

608 S.E.2d 116
North Carolina Court of Appeals, 2005

CASE SUMMARY

Facts: Dr. Robert Mayo was a tenured faculty member of the engineering department at North Carolina State University (NCSU), and director of the school's nuclear engineering program. In July, he informed his department chair, Dr. Paul Turinsky, that he was leaving NCSU effective September 1. Turinsky accepted the resignation.

In October, after Mayo had departed, Phyllis Jennette, the university's payroll coordinator, informed him that he had been overpaid. She explained that for employees who worked 9 months but were paid over 12 months, the salary checks for July and August were in fact prepayments for the period beginning that September. Because Mayo had not worked after September 1, the checks for July and August were overpayment. When he refused to refund the money, NCSU sought to claim it in legal proceedings. The first step was a hearing before an administrative agency.

At the hearing, Turinsky and Brian Simet, the university's payroll director, explained that the "prepayment" rule was a basic part of every employee's contract. However, both acknowledged that the prepayment rule was not included in any of the documents that formed Mayo's contract, including his appointment letter, annual salary letter, and policies adopted by the university's trustees. The university officials used other evidence, outside the written documents, to establish the prepayment policy.

Based on the additional evidence, the agency ruled that NCSU was entitled to its money. However, Mayo appealed to court, and the trial judge declared that he owed nothing, ruling that the university was not permitted to rely on parol evidence to establish its policy. NCSU appealed.

Issue: *May NCSU rely on parol evidence to establish its prepayment rule?*

Decision: No, neither party may use parol evidence to explain the terms of the agreement.

Reasoning: When the parties intend a written document to be the final, integrated expression of their agreement, neither side may introduce parol evidence that changes, adds to, or contradicts any of the written terms. However, if the writing is

not intended as a full integration of the agreement, or if the writing is ambiguous, then parol evidence is allowed.

Brian Simet, the university's payroll director, argued that the prepayment rule was a basic part of every employee's contract. However, during the agency hearing, he acknowledged that the rule was "not stated anywhere specifically."

The department chair, Dr. Turinsky, testified that Professor Mayo's employment agreement consisted only of his appointment letter, his annual salary letter, and the policies adopted and amended by the school's Board of Governors and its Board of Trustees. The language in each of these documents is unambiguous and says nothing about the supposed "prepayment rule." Dr. Turinsky also stated that he had never heard of the prepayment rule until September, after Professor Mayo left the school.

It appears that the parties intended these documents to be the final, integrated expression of Professor Mayo's employment agreement. Because the documents are complete and unambiguous, parol evidence must be excluded.

Professor Mayo owes the university nothing based on the alleged overpayment. Affirmed.

EXCEPTION: AN INCOMPLETE OR AMBIGUOUS CONTRACT

If a court determines that a written contract is incomplete or ambiguous, it will permit parol evidence. Suppose that an employment contract states that the company will provide "full health coverage for Robert Watson and his family." Three years later, Watson divorces and remarries, acquiring three stepchildren, and a year later, his second wife has a baby. Watson now has two children by his first marriage and four by the second. The company refuses to insure Watson's first wife or his stepchildren. A court will probably find that the health care clause is ambiguous. A judge cannot determine exactly what the clause means from the contract itself, so the parties will be permitted to introduce parol evidence to prove whether or not the company must insure Watson's extended family.[11]

MISREPRESENTATION OR DURESS

A court will permit parol evidence of misrepresentation or duress. To encourage Annette to buy his house, Will assures her that no floodwaters from the nearby river have ever come within two miles of the house. Annette signs a contract, which is silent about flooding and includes an integration clause stating that neither party is relying on any oral statements made during negotiations. When Annette moves in, she discovers that the foundation is collapsing due to earlier flooding, and that Will knew of the flooding and the damage. Despite the integration clause, a court will probably allow Annette to testify about Will's misrepresentations.[12]

[11] See, e.g., *Eure v. Norfolk Shipbuilding & Drydock Corp., Inc.*, 561 S.E.2d 663 (Va. 2002).
[12] *Lindberg v. Roseth*, 137 Idaho 222, 46 P.3d 518 (2002).

CHAPTER CONCLUSION

Some contracts must be in writing to be enforceable, and the writing must be clear and unambiguous. Drafting the contract need not be arduous. The disputes illustrated in this chapter could all have been prevented with a few carefully crafted sentences. It is worth the time and effort to write them.

EXAM REVIEW

1. **THE STATUTE OF FRAUDS** Six types of contract are enforceable only if written:

   - **LAND** The sale of any interest in land (p. 335)

   - **ONE YEAR** An agreement that cannot be performed within one year (p. 338)

EXAM Strategy

CPA Question: Able hired Carr to restore Able's antique car for $800. The terms of their oral agreement provided that Carr was to complete the work within 18 months. Actually, the work could be completed within one year. The agreement is:

(a) Unenforceable because it covers services with a value in excess of $500

(b) Unenforceable because it covers a time period in excess of one year

(c) Enforceable because personal service contracts are exempt from the statute of frauds

(d) Enforceable because the work could be completed within one year

Strategy: This is a subtle question. Notice that the contract is for a sum greater than $500. But that is a red herring. Why? The contract also might take 18 months to perform. But it *could* be finished in less than a year. (See the "Result" at the end of this section.)

   - **DEBT OF ANOTHER** A promise to pay the debt of another. (p. 340)

EXAM Strategy

Question: Donald Waide had a contracting business. He bought most of his supplies from Paul Bingham's supply center. Waide fell behind on his bills, and Bingham told Waide that he would extend no more credit to him. That same day, Donald's father, Elmer Waide, came to Bingham's store, and said to Bingham that he would "stand good" for any sales to Donald made on credit. Based on Elmer's statement, Bingham again gave Donald credit, and Donald ran up $10,000 in goods before Bingham sued Donald and Elmer. What defense did Elmer make and what was the outcome?

Strategy: This was an oral agreement, so the issue is whether the promise had to be in writing to be enforceable. Review the list of six contracts that must be in writing. Is this agreement there? (See the "Result" at the end of this section.)

   - **EXECUTORS** A promise made by an executor of an estate (p. 341)

   - **MARRIAGE** A promises made in consideration of marriage; and (p. 341)

   - **GOODS** The sale of goods worth $500 or more (p. 344)

EXAM Strategy

Question: James River-Norwalk, Inc., was a paper and textile company that needed a constant supply of wood. James River orally contracted with Gary Futch to supply wood for the company, and Futch did so for several years. The deal was worth many thousands of dollars but nothing was put in writing. Futch actually purchased the wood for his own account and then resold it to James River. After a few years, James River refused to do more business with Futch. Did the parties have a binding contract?

Strategy: If this is a contract for services, it is enforceable without anything in writing. However, if it is one for the sale of goods, it must be in writing. Clearly what James River wanted was the wood, and it did not care where Futch found it. (See the "Result" at the end of this section.)

---

2. **CONTENTS** The writing must be signed by the defendant and must state the name of all parties, the subject matter of the agreement, and all essential terms and promises. (p. 341)

---

3. **MERCHANTS** A contract or memorandum for the sale of goods may be less complete than those required by the common law.
   - The basic UCC rule requires only a memorandum signed by the defendant, indicating that the parties reached an agreement and specifying the quantity of goods.
   - Between merchants even less is required. If one merchant sends written confirmation of a contract, the merchant who receives the document must object within 10 days or be bound by the writing.
   - In the following special circumstances, no writing may be required: the goods are specially manufactured; one party admits in litigation that there was a contract; or one party pays for part of the goods or delivers some of the goods. (p. 344)

---

4. **PAROL EVIDENCE** When an integrated contract exists, neither party may generally use parol evidence to contradict, vary, or add to its terms. Parol evidence refers to anything (apart from the written contract itself) that was said, done, or written before the parties signed the agreement or as they signed it. (p. 348)

---

1. "One Year" Result: (d) A contract for the sale of goods worth $500 or more must be in writing—but this is a contract for *services*, not the sale of goods. The $500–$800 discrepancy is irrelevant. The contract *can* be completed within one year, and thus falls outside the Statute of Frauds. This is an enforceable agreement.

1. "Debt of Another" Result: Elmer made a promise to pay the debt of another. He did so as a favor to his son. This is a collateral promise. Elmer never signed any such promise, and the agreement cannot be enforced against him.

1. "Goods" Result: James River was buying wood, and this is a contract for the sale of goods. With nothing in writing, signed by James River, Futch has no enforceable agreement.

ADDITIONAL QUESTIONS

1. Richard Griffin and three other men owned a grain company called Bearhouse, Inc., which needed to borrow money. First National Bank was willing to loan $490,000, but insisted that the four men sign personal guaranties on the loan, committing themselves to repaying up to 25 percent of the loan each if Bearhouse defaulted. Bearhouse went bankrupt. The bank was able to collect some of its money from Bearhouse's assets, but it sued Griffin for the balance. At trial, Griffin wanted to testify that before he signed his guaranty, a bank officer assured him that he would only owe 25 percent of *whatever balance was unpaid,* not 25 percent of the total loan. How will the court decide whether Griffin is entitled to testify about the conversation?

2. When Deana Byers married Steven Byers, she was pregnant with another man's child. Shortly after the marriage Deana gave birth. The marriage lasted only two months, and the couple separated. In divorce proceedings, Deana sought child support. She claimed that Steven had orally promised to support the child if Deana would marry him. Steven claims he never made the promise. Comment on the outcome.

3. **CPA QUESTION** Two individuals signed a contract that was intended to be their entire agreement. The parol evidence rule will prevent the admission of evidence offered to:

   (a) Explain the meaning of an ambiguity in the written contract

   (b) Establish that fraud had been committed in the formation of the contract

   (c) Prove the existence of a contemporaneous oral agreement modifying the contract

   (d) Prove the existence of a subsequent oral agreement modifying the contract

4. Lonnie Hippen moved to Long Island, Kansas, to work in an insurance company owned by Griffiths. After he moved there, Griffiths offered to sell Hippen a house he owned, and Hippen agreed in writing to buy it. He did buy the house and moved in, but two years later Hippen left the insurance company. He then claimed that at the time of the sale, Griffiths had orally promised to buy back his house at the selling price if Hippen should happen to leave the company. Griffiths defended based on the statute of frauds. Hippen argued that the statute of frauds did not apply because the repurchase of the house was essentially part of his employment with Griffiths. Comment.

5. **ETHICS** Jacob Deutsch owned commercial property. He orally agreed to rent it for six years to Budget Rent-A-Car. Budget took possession, began paying monthly rent, and over a period of several months expended about $6,000 in upgrading the property. Deutsch was aware of the repairs. After a year, Deutsch attempted to evict Budget. Budget claimed it had a six-year oral lease, but Deutsch claimed that such a lease was worthless. Please rule. Is it ethical for Deutsch to use the statute of frauds in attempting to defeat the lease? Assume that, as landlord, you had orally agreed to rent premises to a tenant, but then for business reasons preferred not to carry out the deal. Would you evict a tenant if you thought the statute of frauds would enable you to do so? How should you analyze the problem? What values are most important to you?

6. Landlord owned a clothing store and agreed in writing to lease the store's basement to another retailer. The written lease, which both parties signed, (1) described the

premises exactly, (2) identified the parties, and (3) stated the monthly rent clearly. But an appeals court held that the lease did not satisfy the statute of frauds. Why not?

7. **YOU BE THE JUDGE** WRITING PROBLEM Harrison Epperly operated United Brake Systems in Indianapolis, Indiana, and wanted to open a similar store in Nashville. He offered Kenneth Jarrett a job as manager, promising six months severance pay if the store was not profitable in six months, and 49 percent ownership if he managed the new store for 10 years. Jarrett agreed, but the two men never put the deal in writing. Under Jarrett's management, the Nashville branch grew dramatically. After four years of renting space, the company purchased the land and buildings it used. Epperly periodically acknowledged his promise to make Jarrett 49 percent owner of the Nashville branch, and from time to time he mentioned the arrangement to other workers. But after 10 years, Epperly sold United Brake, which had grown to 23 branches, to another company for $11 million. Jarrett sued Epperly for 49 percent of the Nashville branch. The trial court awarded Jarrett $812,000. Epperly appealed. Is Jarrett's contract with Epperly barred by the statute of frauds? **Argument for Epperly:** This alleged contract is unenforceable for two reasons. First, the agreement includes real estate, namely, the valuable land and buildings the company uses. A contract for the sale of any interest in land is unenforceable unless written. Second, the contract could not have been performed within one year. If there was a deal, then by Jarrett's own words the parties intended it to last 10 years. Ten years' work cannot be performed in one year. **Argument for Jarrett:** The agreement had nothing to do with land. Jarrett and Epperly agreed that Mr. Jarrett would obtain a 49 percent ownership of the *Nashville branch*. At the time they made that agreement, the Nashville branch had no real estate. There is no rule saying that a valid contract becomes invalid because a corporation acquires some land. The "not in one year" argument also misses the point. The primary obligation was to open the branch and manage it for six months. If it was not profitable, Mr. Jarrett would immediately receive six months' severance pay, and the contract would be fully performed by both parties in less than a year. Finally, Epperly made a binding commitment and Mr. Jarrett relied. Promissory estoppel prohibits Mr. Epperly from using deceit to profit.

8. Mast Industries and Bazak International were two textile firms. Mast orally offered to sell certain textiles to Bazak for $103,000. Mast promised to send documents confirming the agreement, but never did. Finally, Bazak sent a memorandum to Mast confirming the agreement, describing the goods, and specifying their quantity and the price. Bazak's officer signed the memo. Mast received the memo but never agreed to it in writing. When Mast failed to deliver the goods, Bazak sued. Who won?

9. **ROLE REVERSAL** Write a multiple-choice question that focuses on the merchants' exception to the statute of frauds.

INTERNET RESEARCH PROBLEM

Online, find a residential tenancy lease. Is it important for a lease to be in writing? Who probably drafted the lease, a landlord or a tenant? How can you tell? Should any other provisions be included? Is this lease fair? What provisions would you change?

You can find further practice problems at www.cengagebrain.com. See the preface of this book for website access details.

CHAPTER

15

THIRD PARTIES

A copy of Howdy Doody sold at auction for $113,000. Christopher then claimed ownership of Howdy Doody and refused to give him to the museum.

During television's formative days, Howdy Doody was one of the medium's biggest stars. His acting was wooden—as were his head and body—but for 13 years, Howdy and an assorted group of puppets starred in one of the most popular children's programs of all time. Rufus Rose maintained and repaired the puppets.

When Howdy took his last double-jointed bow (to a chorus of toddler wails), NBC permitted Rose temporarily to keep the various puppets. Six years later, NBC became concerned that Rose was inadequately maintaining them. The network wanted Howdy and friends moved to a safe, public location. Rose claimed the puppets were in good shape and wanted payment for the maintenance he had provided. The two parties agreed in writing that Rose would give Howdy and the other stars of the show (including Dilly Dally and Flub-A-Dub) to a puppet museum at the Detroit Institute of Arts (DIA). NBC agreed to pay the puppeteer for his work. The company permitted Rose to keep some of the minor puppets from the program, provided they were not used for commercial purposes.

When Rose died, his son Christopher took possession of the famous puppet. At about that time, a copy of Howdy Doody sold at auction for $113,000. Christopher then claimed ownership of Howdy Doody and refused to give him to the museum.

The DIA wanted its famous puppet, but the museum had never been a party to the agreement between NBC and Rose. Did the DIA have any rights to Howdy? The museum filed suit, making a third party claim.

The basic pattern in third party law is quite simple. Two parties make a contract, and their rights and obligations are subject to the rules that we have already studied: offer and acceptance, consideration, legality, and so forth. However, sometimes their contract affects a *third party*, one who had no role in forming the agreement itself. The two contracting parties may intend to benefit a third person. Those are cases of *third party beneficiary*. In other cases, one of the contracting parties may actually transfer his rights or responsibilities to a third party, raising issues of *assignment* or *delegation*. We consider the issues one at a time.

THIRD PARTY BENEFICIARY

The two parties who make a contract always intend to benefit themselves. Oftentimes their bargain will also benefit someone else. **A third party beneficiary is someone who was not a party to the contract but stands to benefit from it.** Many contracts create third party beneficiaries. In the chapter's introduction, NBC and Rufus Rose contracted to give Howdy Doody to the Detroit Institute of Arts. The museum stood to benefit from this agreement.

As another example, suppose a city contracts to purchase from Seller 20 acres of an abandoned industrial site in a rundown neighborhood, to be used for a new domed stadium. The owner of a pizza parlor on the edge of Seller's land might benefit enormously. A once marginal operation could become a gold mine of cheese and pepperoni.

When the two contracting parties fulfill their obligations and the third party receives her benefit, there is no dispute to analyze. If Christopher Rose had walked Howdy Doody into the puppet museum, and if the city completed the stadium, there would be no unhappy third parties. Problems arise when one of the parties fails to perform the contract as expected. The issue is this: *May the third party beneficiary enforce the contract?* The museum had no contract with the Rose family. Is the museum entitled to the puppet? The pizza parlor owner was not a party to the contract for the sale of the stadium land. If the city breaks its agreement to buy the property, should the owner recover profits for unsold sausage and green pepper?

The outcome in cases like these depends upon the intentions of the two contracting parties. If they intended to benefit the third party, she will probably be permitted to enforce their contract. If they did not intend to benefit her, she probably has no power to enforce the agreement. The Restatement uses a bit more detail to analyze these cases. We must first recall the terms "promisor" and "promisee." The **promisor** is the one who makes the promise that the third party beneficiary is seeking to enforce. Parts of the contract may not interest her, so the Restatement looks only at the relevant promise, not at the entire contract. The **promisee** is the other party to the contract.

According to the Restatement (Second) of Contracts Section 302: A beneficiary of a promise is an **intended beneficiary** and may enforce a contract if the parties intended her to benefit *and if either* (a) enforcing the promise will satisfy a duty of the promisee to the beneficiary, or (b) the promisee intended to make a gift to the beneficiary.

Any beneficiary who is not an intended beneficiary is an **incidental beneficiary**, and may not enforce the contract. In other words, a third party beneficiary must show two things in order to enforce a contract that two other people created. First, she must show that the two contracting parties were aware of her situation and knew that she would receive something of value from their deal. Second, she must show that the promisee wanted to benefit her for one of two reasons: either to satisfy some duty owed or to make her a gift.

If the promisee is fulfilling some duty, the third party beneficiary is called a **creditor beneficiary**. Most often, the "duty" that a promisee will be fulfilling is a debt already owed to

---

Promisor
The party who makes the promise that a third party seeks to enforce.

Promisee
The party *to whom* a promise is made.

Intended beneficiary
Someone who may enforce a contract made between two other parties.

Incidental beneficiary
Someone who might have benefited from a contract between two others but has no right to enforce that agreement.

[Handwritten margin notes:]

"Alienability" (The right to transfer legal rights)

• Third parties can't breach a contract b/c they have no obligations to fulfill

("Coincidence" It just so happened)

Wasn't party A's or party B's intent to have party C benefit

Party A owes money to party C (Meant to settle a debt)

(BOTH can sue if the money isn't paid)

the beneficiary. If the promisee is making a gift, the third party is a **donee beneficiary**.[1] So long as the third party is either a creditor or a donee beneficiary, she may enforce the contract. If she is only an incidental beneficiary, she may not.

We will apply this rule to the dispute over Howdy Doody. Like most contracts, the deal between NBC and Rufus Rose had two promises: Rose's agreement to give the puppet to the museum, and NBC's promise to pay for the work done on Howdy. The promise that interests us was the one concerning Howdy's destination in Detroit. Rose was the promisor and NBC was the promisee.

Did the two parties intend to benefit the museum? Yes, they did. NBC wanted Howdy to be displayed to the general public, and in a noncommercial venue. Rose, who wanted payment for work already done, was happy to go along with the network's wishes. Did NBC owe a duty to the museum? No. Did the network intend to make a gift to the museum? Yes. The museum wins! The Detroit Institute of Arts was an intended third party beneficiary, and is entitled to Howdy Doody.[2] See Exhibit 15.1.

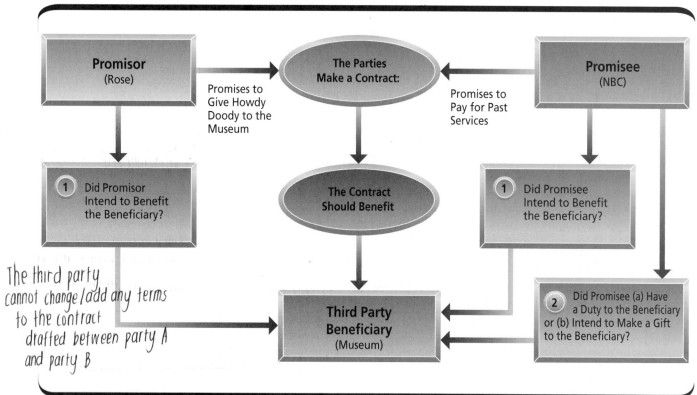

The third party cannot change/add any terms to the contract drafted between party A and party B

Exhibit 15.1   *The issue:* May a third party beneficiary enforce a contract to which it was not a party?

The answer: A third party beneficiary may enforce a contract if (1) the parties intended to benefit it and *either* (2) (a) enforcing the promise will satisfy a duty of the promisee to the beneficiary or (2)(b) the promisee intended to make a gift to the beneficiary.

In this case: Rose and NBC both intended to benefit the museum. The promisee (NBC) intended to make a *gift* to the museum. The museum is therefore an intended third party beneficiary, entitled to the puppet.

---

[1] "Donee" comes from the word "donate," meaning "to give."
[2] *The Detroit Institute of Arts Founders Society v. Rose*, 127 F.Supp.2d 117 (D.Conn. 2001).

By contrast, the pizza parlor owner will surely lose. A stadium is a multimillion dollar investment, and it is most unlikely that the city and the seller of the land were even aware of the owner's existence, let alone that they intended to benefit him. He probably cannot prove either the first element or the second element, and certainly not both.

In the following case, a dazzling diamond loses its luster. Who is entitled to sue?

SCHAUER V. MANDARIN GEMS OF CALIFORNIA, INC.

2005 WL 5730
COURT OF APPEAL OF CALIFORNIA, 2005

CASE SUMMARY

Facts: Sarah Schauer and her fiancé, Darin Erstad, went shopping for an engagement ring, first at Tiffany and Cartier, then at Mandarin Gems, where they were captivated by a 3.01 carat diamond with a clarity grading of "S11." Erstad bought the ring the same day for $43,121. Later, Mandarin supplied Erstad with a written appraisal, again rating the ring as an S11 and valuing it at $45,500. Paul Lam, a certified gemologist, signed the appraisal.

Diamonds may last forever, but this marriage was short-lived. The divorce decree gave each party the right to keep whatever personal property they currently held, meaning that Schauer could keep the ring. She had the ring appraised by the Gem Trade Laboratory, which gave it a poorer clarity rating and a value of $20,000.

Schauer sued Mandarin for misrepresentation and breach of contract, but the jeweler defended by saying that it had never contracted with her, and that she was not a third party beneficiary of the company's agreement with Erstad. The trial court dismissed Schauer's suit, and she appealed.

Issue: *Does Schauer have any right to sue for breach of contract?*

Decision: Yes, she is entitled to sue. Reversed and remanded.

Reasoning: A true third party beneficiary may enforce a contract made by others unless they rescinded the agreement. Persons who expect to incidentally or remotely benefit from a bargain may not enforce it.

A plaintiff claiming status as a third party beneficiary must demonstrate that the promisor understood that the promisee intended to benefit the third party. It is not necessary that both parties intended to benefit the third party.

Schauer alleged that she and Erstad went shopping for an engagement ring. They were together when they looked at the ring, and they explained to the jeweler that Erstad was buying the diamond to give to Schauer as an engagement ring. The jeweler *must* have understood that Erstad was entering into a sales contract intending to benefit Schauer.

Schauer has alleged facts that, if found to be true, establish her as a third party beneficiary. She is entitled to proceed with her contract claim against Mandarin Gems.

EXAM *Strategy*

Question: Mr. Inspector examines houses and gives its reports to potential buyers. Mr. Inspector contracts with Greenlawn, a real estate agent, to furnish reports on houses that Greenlawn is selling. The agreement allows the agent to give the reports to potential buyers. Greenlawn gives Molly one of Mr. Inspector's reports and, relying upon it, she buys a house. Although the report states that the house is structurally sound, it turns out that chronic roof leaks have caused water to seep into the walls, causing rot. Molly sues Mr. Inspector. The inspector requests summary judgment, claiming that he had no contract with Molly.

Strategy: Mr. Inspector is right in saying he had no agreement with Molly. To prevail, Molly must demonstrate she is a third party beneficiary of the contract between the other two. A third party beneficiary may enforce a contract if the parties intended to benefit her and either (a) enforcing the promise will satisfy a duty of the promisee to the beneficiary or (b) the promisee intended to make a gift to the beneficiary.

Result: Greenlawn used the inspection summaries as sales tools. When Greenlawn assured a potential buyer that she could rely upon a report, the real estate agent took on a duty to deliver reliable information. Mr. Inspector understood that. The two parties intended to benefit Greenlawn's buyers. Molly may sue Mr. Inspector for breach of his contract with the agent. Mr. Inspector's motion for summary judgment is denied.

Assignment and Delegation

Assignment
Transferring contract *rights*.

(money $)

Delegation
Transferring contract *duties*.

(What kind of rights could be assigned/delegated ?)

A contracting party may transfer his rights under the contract, which is called an **assignment** of rights. Or a party may transfer her duties pursuant to the contract, which is a **delegation** of duties. Frequently, a party will make an assignment and delegation simultaneously, transferring both rights and duties to a third party.

Statutory and common law, the Restatement (Second) of Contracts, and the UCC all govern various aspects of assignments. For our purposes, the Restatement serves as a good summary of common law provisions. The UCC rules are generally similar, although we note some differences later on. Our first example is a sale of goods case, governed by the UCC, but the outcome would be the same under the Restatement.

Lydia needs 500 bottles of champagne. Bruno agrees to sell them to her for $10,000, payable 30 days after delivery. He transports the wine to her. Bruno happens to owe Doug $8,000 from a previous deal, so he says to Doug, "I don't have the money, but I'll give you my claim to Lydia's $10,000." Doug agrees. Bruno then *assigns* to Doug *his rights* to Lydia's money, and in exchange Doug gives up his claim for $8,000. Bruno is the **assignor, the one making an assignment**, and Doug is the **assignee, the one receiving an assignment**.

Why would Bruno offer $10,000 when he owed Doug only $8,000? Because all he has is a *claim* to Lydia's money. Cash in hand is often more valuable. Doug, however, is willing to assume some risk for a potential $2,000 gain.

Obligor
The one obligated to do something.

Bruno notifies Lydia of the assignment. Lydia, who owes the money, is called the **obligor**, that is, the one obligated to do something. At the end of 30 days, Doug arrives at Lydia's doorstep, asks for his money, and gets it, since Lydia is obligated to him. Bruno has no claim to any payment. See Exhibit 15.2.

Lydia bought the champagne because she knew she could sell it at a profit. She promptly agrees to sell and deliver the 500 bottles to Coretta, at a mountaintop wilderness camp. Lydia has no four-wheel drive cars, so she finds Keith, who is willing to deliver the bottles for $1,000. Lydia *delegates her duty* to Keith to deliver the bottles to Coretta. Keith is now obligated to deliver the bottles to Coretta, the **obligee**, that is, the one who has the obligation coming to her. As we see later, Lydia also remains obligated to Coretta, the obligee, to ensure that the bottles are delivered. See Exhibit 15.3.

Obligee
The one to whom an obligation is due.

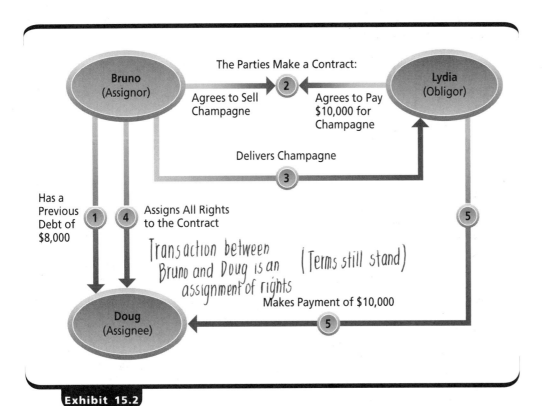

Exhibit 15.2

Exhibit 15.3

EXAM *Strategy*

Question: Hasannah, an art dealer, signs a contract with Jason. Hasannah will deliver a David Hockney painting to Jason's house. Jason may keep it for 30 days and then either return it or pay Hasannah $2 million. Hasannah delivers the painting. Hasannah finds a better building to house her gallery and agrees to buy it from Shannon. She and Shannon sign a contract allowing Shannon to receive Jason's payment, if he keeps the picture. Hasannah then notifies Jason to pay Shannon the $2 million. Identify the obligor, the assignor, and the assignee.

Strategy: The obligor is the one obligated to do something. The assignor makes an assignment and the assignee receives it.

Result: Jason is obligated either to return the picture or pay $2 million for it. He is the obligor. Hasannah is entitled to the money, but assigns her right to Shannon. Hasannah is the assignor and Shannon the assignee.

Assignment and delegation can each create problems. We will examine the most common ones.

ASSIGNMENT

What Rights Are Assignable?

Most contract rights are assignable, but not all. Disputes sometimes arise between the two contracting parties about whether one of the parties could legally assign her rights to a third party. The Restatement (Second) of Contracts Section 317(2) sums up the assignability of rights this way:

> **Any contractual right may be assigned unless assignment**
>
> (a) would substantially change the obligor's rights or duties under the contract; or
>
> (b) is forbidden by law or public policy; or
>
> (c) is validly precluded by the contract itself.[3]

(Usually rights to Money)

contract

(the law explicitly excludes the assignment of a particular right)

Substantial Change. Subsection (a) prohibits an assignment if it would substantially change the obligor's situation. For example, Bruno is permitted to assign to Doug his rights to payment from Lydia because it makes no difference to Lydia whether she writes a check to one or the other. But suppose Erica, who lives on a one-quarter acre lot in Hardscrabble, hires Keith to mow her lawn once per week for the summer, for a total fee of $700. Erica pays up front, before she leaves for the summer. May she assign her right to weekly lawn care to Lloyd, who enjoys a three-acre estate in Halcyon, 60 miles distant? No. The extra travel and far larger yard would dramatically change Keith's obligations, and Erica has no right to make the assignment.

Assignment is also prohibited when the obligor is agreeing to perform **personal services**. The close working relationship in such agreements makes it unfair to expect the obligor to work with a stranger. Warner, a feature film director, hires Mayer to be his assistant on a film to

---

[3] Restatement (Second) of Contracts Section 317(2). And note that UCC Section 2-210 is, for our purposes, nearly identical.

be shot over the next 10 weeks. Warner may not assign his right to Mayer's work to another director.

Public Policy.   Some assignments are prohibited by public policy. For example, someone who has suffered a personal injury may not assign her claim to a third person. Vladimir is playing the piano on his roof deck when the instrument rolls over the balustrade and drops 35 stories, striking Wanda and bruising her elbow. Wanda has a valid tort claim against Vladimir, but she may not assign the claim to her father, Arturo. As a matter of public policy, all states have decided that the sale of personal injury claims would create an unseemly and unethical bazaar.

Contract Prohibition.   Finally, one of the contracting parties may try to prohibit assignment in the agreement itself. For example, most landlords include in the written lease a clause prohibiting the tenant from assigning the tenancy without the landlord's written permission. How much leeway does a landlord have in rejecting a proposed assignment? The following case provides the answer.

TENET HEALTHSYSTEM SURGICAL, L.L.C. v. JEFFERSON PARISH HOSPITAL SERVICE DISTRICT No. 1

426 F.3d 738
FIFTH CIRCUIT COURT OF APPEALS, 2005

CASE SUMMARY

Facts: MSC, Inc. owned the Marrero Shopping Center, and leased space to Tenet Healthsystem for use in outpatient surgery and general medical practice. The lease allowed Tenet to assign the lease with the consent of the lessor and stated that consent would not be unreasonably withheld.

Two years later, MSC sold the shopping center to West Jefferson Medical Center, which owned an adjacent hospital and wanted the space for expansion. A few months after that, Tenet went out of business and requested permission from West Jefferson to assign its lease to Pelican Medical, which intended to use the space for an occupational medical clinic. West Jefferson denied permission, stating that Pelican would be performing work not permitted under the original lease, and also because Pelican would compete with West Jefferson.

Tenet sued, claiming that West Jefferson was unreasonably withholding permission to assign. The trial court granted summary judgment for West Jefferson. Tenet appealed.

Issue: *Did West Jefferson unreasonably withhold permission to assign the lease?*

Decision: Yes, West Jefferson withheld consent for an improper reason. Reversed and remanded.

Reasoning: Tenet the tenant used the office space for nothing more than minor surgery. Pelican proposed to offer many medical services in the space, but none were unusual. West Jefferson objected primarily because it did not want to lose patients to Pelican. This is a reasonable economic concern, but nonetheless it is not a factor that a landlord may consider in approving a lease assignment. In this situation, a landlord must make an objective assessment that is not related to its own personal circumstances. Thus, it may consider only whether the new tenant is financially responsible, will adequately maintain the property, and will use the premises for a legal business.

Tenet's lease allowed for "general medical and physician's offices." Pelican did not propose to provide any services not covered by that definition. There was no indication that Pelican would miss lease payments or damage the property. West Jefferson may have acted as a reasonable business in defending its own interests, but it acted wrongfully in its role as landlord

"Equal Dignities"

How Rights Are Assigned

Writing.   In general, an assignment may be written or oral, and no particular formalities are required. However, when someone wants to assign rights governed by the statute of frauds, she must do it in writing. Suppose City contracts with Seller to buy Seller's land for a domed stadium and then brings in Investor to complete the project. If City wants to assign to Investor its rights to the land, it must do so in writing.

Consideration.   An assignment can be valid with or without consideration, but the lack of consideration may have consequences. Two examples should clarify this. Recall Bruno, who sells champagne to Lydia and then assigns to Doug his right to payment. In that case there *is* consideration for the assignment. Bruno assigns his rights only because Doug cancels the old debt, and his agreement to do that is valid consideration. **An assignment for consideration is irrevocable.** Once the two men agree, Bruno may not telephone Doug and say, "I've changed my mind, I want Lydia to pay me after all." Lydia's $10,000 now belongs to Doug.

But suppose that Bruno assigns his contract rights to his sister Brunhilde as a birthday present. This is a **gratuitous assignment,** that is, one made as a gift, for no consideration. **A gratuitous assignment is generally revocable if it is oral and generally irrevocable if it is written.** If Bruno orally assigns his rights to Brunhilde, but then changes his mind, telephones Lydia, and says, "I want you to pay me, after all," that revocation is effective and Brunhilde gets nothing. But if Bruno puts his assignment in writing and Brunhilde receives it, Bruno has given up his right to the money.

> **Gratuitous assignment**
> An assignment made as a gift, for no consideration.

Notice to Obligor.   The assignment is valid from the moment it is made, regardless of whether the assignor notifies the obligor. But an assignor with common sense will immediately inform the obligor of the assignment. Suppose Maude has a contract with Nelson, who is obligated to deliver 700 live frogs to her shop. If Maude (assignor) assigns her rights to Obie (assignee), Maude should notify Nelson (obligor) the same day. If she fails to inform Nelson, he may deliver the frogs to Maude. Nelson will have no further obligations under the contract, and Maude will owe Obie 700 frogs.

Rights of the Parties after Assignment

Once the assignment is made and the obligor notified, the assignee may enforce her contractual rights against the obligor. If Lydia fails to pay Doug for the champagne she gets from Bruno, Doug may sue to enforce the agreement. The law will treat Doug as though he had entered into the contract with Lydia.

But the reverse is also true. **The obligor may generally raise all defenses against the assignee that she could have raised against the assignor.** Suppose Lydia opens the first bottle of champagne—silently. "Where's the pop?" she wonders. There is no pop because all 500 bottles have gone flat. Bruno has failed to perform his part of the contract, and Lydia may use Bruno's nonperformance as a defense against Doug. If the champagne was indeed worthless, Lydia owes Doug nothing.

Assignors Warranty.   The law implies certain warranties (assurances) on the part of the assignor. Unless the parties expressly agree to exclude them, the assignor warrants that (1) the rights he is assigning actually do exist, and (2) there are no defenses to the rights other than those that would be obvious, like nonperformance. But the assignor *does not* warrant that the obligor is solvent. Bruno is impliedly warranting to Doug that Lydia has no defenses to the contract, but he is not guaranteeing Doug that she has the money to pay, or that she will pay.

Differences under the UCC

As we mentioned, the Code's provisions regarding assignment, found in Section 2-210, are very similar to the Restatement section quoted above. Assignments are common in sales contracts. The UCC favors them and tends to limit contractual clauses that prohibit assignment. Thus, if a contract states in general terms that assignment is prohibited, the Code will limit that language to mean only that a party may not delegate his duties; assignment of the party's *rights* will still be allowed. If a contracting party wants to prohibit assignment of rights, it must specifically say so.[4]

Article 9 of the UCC governs the assignment of security interests. A **security interest** is a legal right in personal property that assures payment. When an automobile dealer sells you a new car on credit, the dealer will keep a security interest in your car. If you do not make your monthly payments, the dealer retains a right to drive your car away, and that authority is called a security interest. (See Chapter 25 for a full discussion.)

Companies that sell goods often prefer to assign their security interests to some other firm, such as a bank or finance company. The bank is the assignee. Just as we saw with the common law, the assignee of a security interest generally has all of the rights that the assignor had. And the obligor (the buyer) may also raise all of the defenses against the assignee that she could have raised against the assignor.

According to UCC Section 9-404, the obligor on a sales contract may generally assert any defenses against the assignee that arise from the contract, and any other defenses that arose before notice of assignment. The Code's reference to any defenses that arise from the contract means that if the assignor breached his part of the deal, the obligor may raise that as a defense. Suppose a dealer sells you a new Porsche on credit, retaining a security interest. He assigns the security interest to the bank. The car is great for the first few weeks, but then the roof slides onto the street, both doors fall off, and the engine implodes. You refuse to make any more monthly payments. When the bank sues you, you may raise as a defense the automobile's defects, just as you could have raised them against the dealer itself. Where the Code talks about other defenses that arose before notice of assignment, it refers, for example, to fraud. Suppose the dealer knew that before you bought the Porsche, it had been smashed up and rebuilt. If the dealer told you it was brand new, that was fraud, and you could raise the defense against the bank.

A contract may prohibit an obligor from raising certain defenses against an assignee. Sometimes a seller of goods will require the buyer to sign a contract that permits the seller to assign *and* prohibits the buyer from raising defenses against the assignee that he could have raised against the seller. University wants to buy a computer system on credit from Leland for $85,000. Leland agrees to the deal but insists that the contract permit him to assign his rights to anyone he chooses. He also wants this clause: "University agrees that it will not raise against an assignee any defenses that it may have had against Leland." This clause is sometimes called a *waiver clause*, because the obligor is waiving (giving up) rights. Courts may also refer to it as an *exclusion clause*, since the parties are excluding potential defenses. Leland wants a waiver clause because it makes his contract more valuable. As soon as University signs the agreement, Leland can take his contract to Krushem Collections, a finance company. Krushem might offer Leland $70,000 cash for the contract. Leland can argue, "You have to pay $80,000 for this. You are guaranteed payment by University, since they cannot raise any defenses against you, even if the

Security interest
A legal right in personal property that assures payment.

(handwritten notes in margin):
(Subsequent assignment of the same rights)
Revocation of Assignments
1. U.S. Rule
   "Time"
2. English Rule

---

[4] UCC Section 2-210(3).

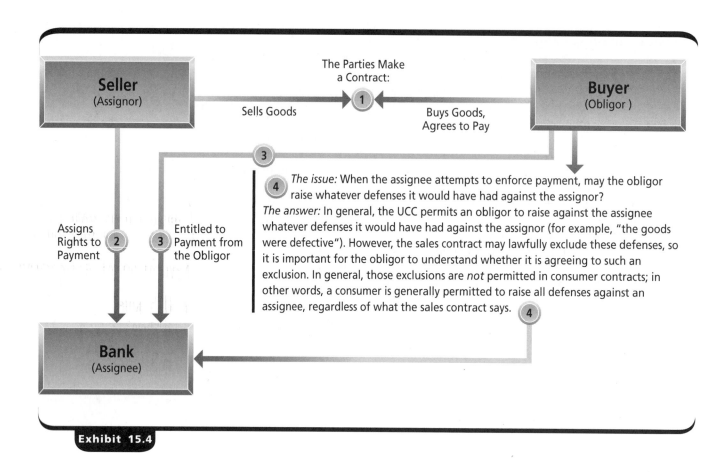

The issue: When the assignee attempts to enforce payment, may the obligor raise whatever defenses it would have had against the assignor?

The answer: In general, the UCC permits an obligor to raise against the assignee whatever defenses it would have had against the assignor (for example, "the goods were defective"). However, the sales contract may lawfully exclude these defenses, so it is important for the obligor to understand whether it is agreeing to such an exclusion. In general, those exclusions are *not* permitted in consumer contracts; in other words, a consumer is generally permitted to raise all defenses against an assignee, regardless of what the sales contract says.

Exhibit 15.4

computer system collapses in the first half-hour." Leland gets cash and need not worry about collecting payments. Krushem receives the full value of the contract, with interest, spread out over several years.

Under UCC Section 9-403, an agreement by a buyer (or lessee) that he will not assert against an assignee any claim or defense that he may have against the seller (or lessor) is generally enforceable by the assignee if he took the assignment in good faith, for value, without notice of the potential defenses. In other words, Leland's waiver clause with University is enforceable. If Leland assigns the contract to Krushem Collections and the system proves worthless, Krushem is still entitled to its monthly payments from University. The school must seek its damages against Leland—a far more arduous step than simply withholding payment.

These waiver clauses are generally *not* valid in consumer contracts. If Leland sold a computer system to a consumer (an individual purchasing it for her personal use), the waiver would generally be unenforceable. See Exhibit 15.4.

In the following case, one side pushes the waiver rule to its extreme. Can an assignee recover for money advanced…when the money was never advanced? You be the judge.

YOU *be the* JUDGE

WELLS FARGO BANK MINNESOTA V. BROOKSAMERICA MORTGAGE CORPORATION

419 F. 3d 107 Second Circuit Court of Appeals, 2005

Facts: Michael Brooks desperately needed financing for his company, BrooksAmerica, so he agreed to a sale-leaseback agreement with Terminal Marketing Company. Terminal would pay BrooksAmerica $250,000, and in exchange would obtain title to BrooksAmerica's computers and office equipment. BrooksAmerica would then lease the equipment for three years, for $353,000. The equipment would never leave BrooksAmerica's offices.

The contract included a "hell or high water clause," stating that BrooksAmerica's obligation to pay was "absolute and unconditional." Another clause permitted Terminal to assign its rights without notice to BrooksAmerica, and stated that the assignee took its rights "free from all defenses, setoffs or counterclaims."

Brooks also signed a "Delivery and Acceptance Certificate," stating that BrooksAmerica had received the $250,000 (even though no money had yet changed hands), and reaffirming BrooksAmerica's absolute obligation to pay an assignee, despite any defenses BrooksAmerica might have.

Terminal assigned its rights to Wells Fargo, which had taken about 2,000 other equipment leases from Terminal. Terminal never paid any portion of the promised $250,000. Brooks refused to make the required payments (about $10,000 per month) and Wells Fargo sued. Brooks acknowledged that Wells Fargo paid Terminal for the assignment.

Both parties moved for summary judgment. The trial court ruled in favor of Wells Fargo, and Brooks appealed.

You Be the Judge: Is Wells Fargo entitled to its monthly lease payments despite the fact that BrooksAmerica never received financing?

Argument for BrooksAmerica: We acknowledge the general validity of UCC 9-403. However, in this case Wells Fargo makes an absurd argument. Neither Terminal nor any assignee has a right to enforce a financing contract when Terminal failed to deliver the financing. There is no valid contract to enforce here, because Terminal never paid the $250,000 owed to BrooksAmerica. "Good faith" required Wells Fargo to make sure that Terminal had performed. A simple inquiry would have informed Wells Fargo that Terminal was entitled to no money. This entire transaction is a sham, and section 9-403 was never drafted to encourage financial swindles.

Argument for Wells Fargo: Under UCC 9-403, an assignee such as Wells Fargo may enforce a waiver of defenses clause if the assignment was taken in good faith, for value, and free of knowledge of any claims or defenses. Wells Fargo meets that test.

The "simple inquiry" argument has two flaws. First, section 9-403 does not require one. The UCC requires good faith, not an investigation. Second, Wells Fargo *did* investigate, by checking the contract and the Delivery Certificate. We have done more than required.

Rebuttal for BrooksAmerica: The trial court *penalized* BrooksAmerica for acting in good faith. Mr. Brooks signed the Delivery Certificate assuming that any reasonable company would promptly deliver the money it had promised. Unfortunately Terminal does not operate at the same ethical level—a fact that Wells Fargo should know from its earlier assignments.

Rebuttal for Wells Fargo: We have taken thousands of equipment leases as assignees. In this case, we examined the contract and the Delivery Certificate, and assumed that BrooksAmerica had received its money. If Terminal had not paid, why did Mr. Brooks sign a certificate stating he had received his cash? We are entitled to payment. Any dispute between BrooksAmerica and Terminal is for those parties to resolve.

DELEGATION OF DUTIES

Garret has always dreamed of racing stock cars. He borrows $250,000 from his sister, Maybelle, in order to buy a car and begin racing. He signs a promissory note in that amount, in other words, a document guaranteeing that he will repay Maybelle the full amount, plus interest, on a monthly basis over 10 years. Regrettably, during his first race, on a Saturday night, Garret discovers that he has a speed phobia. He finishes the race at noon on Sunday and quits the business. Garret transfers the car and all of his equipment to Brady, who agrees in writing to pay all money owed to Maybelle. For a few months Brady sends a check, but he is killed while watching bumper cars at a local carnival. Maybelle sues Garret, who defends based on the transfer to Brady. Will his defense work?

Garret has assigned his rights in the car and business to Brady and that is entirely legal. But more important, he has *delegated his duties* to Brady. Garret was the **delegator** and Brady was the **delegatee**. In other words, the promissory note he signed was a contract, and the agreement imposed certain *duties* on Garret, primarily the obligation to pay Maybelle $250,000 plus interest. Garret had a right to delegate his duties to Brady, but delegating those duties did not relieve Garret of his own obligation to perform them. When Maybelle sues, she will win. Garret, like many debtors, would have preferred to wash his hands of his debt, but the law is not so obliging.

Most duties are delegable. But delegation does not by itself relieve the delegator of his own liability to perform the contract.

Garret's delegation to Brady was typical in that it included an assignment at the same time. If he had merely transferred ownership, that would have been only an assignment. If he had convinced Brady to pay off the loan without getting the car, that would have been merely a delegation. He did both at once. See Exhibit 15.5.

What Duties Are Delegable

The rules concerning what duties may be delegated mirror those about the assignment of rights. And once again, the common law, as summarized by the Restatement, agrees with the UCC.

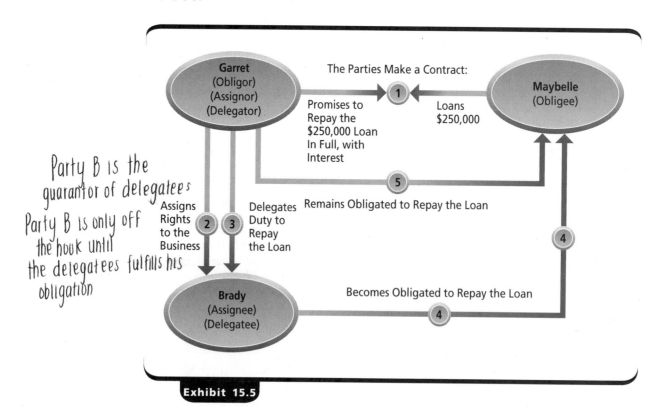

Party B is the guarantor of delegatees

Party B is only off the hook until the delegatees fulfills his obligation

Exhibit 15.5

An obligor may delegate his duties unless

1. delegation would violate public policy, or
2. the contract prohibits delegation, or ↘ Example=fireman
3. the obligee has a substantial interest in personal performance by the obligor.[5]

Public Policy.   Delegation may violate public policy, for example, in a public works contract. If City hires Builder to construct a subway system, state law may prohibit Builder from delegating his duties to Beginner. The theory is that a public agency should not have to work with parties that it never agreed to hire.

Contract Prohibition.   It is very common for a contract to prohibit delegation. We saw in the assignment section that courts may refuse to enforce a clause that limits one party's ability to assign its contract rights. That does not hold true with delegation. The parties may forbid almost any delegation, and the courts will enforce the agreement. Hammer, a contractor, is building a house and hires Spot as his painter, including in his contract a clause prohibiting delegation. Just before the house is ready for painting, Spot gets a better job elsewhere and wants to delegate his duties to Brush. Hammer may refuse the delegation even if Brush is equally qualified.

Substantial Interest in Personal Performance.   Suppose Hammer had omitted the "nondelegation" clause from his contract with Spot. Could Hammer still refuse the delegation on the grounds that he has a substantial interest in having Spot do the work? No. Most duties are delegable. There is nothing so special about painting a house that one particular painter is required to do it. But some kinds of work do require personal performance, and obligors may not delegate these tasks. The services of lawyers, doctors, dentists, artists, and performers are considered too personal to be delegated. There is no single test that will perfectly define this group, but generally when the work will test the *character, skill, discretion, and good faith of the obligor*, she *may not* delegate her job.

> The services of lawyers, doctors, dentists, artists, and performers are considered too personal to be delegated.

EXAM *Strategy*

Question: Parker is a well-known actress. She agrees to act in Will's play for four weeks, for $30,000 per week. A week before rehearsals are to begin, Parker notifies Will that she cannot appear, because a film producer has offered her over $1 million to start shooting immediately. She has arranged for Claire, another well-known actress, to appear in her place. Will objects. Parker claims, correctly, that their agreement does not prohibit her from making this substitution. Is Parker allowed to do this?

Strategy: Parker is attempting to delegate her duties. Under the Restatement, delegation is allowed unless (1) it would violate public policy, (2) it is prohibited by the contract, or (3) the obligee has a substantial interest in the obligor's personal performance.

---

[5] Restatement (Second) of Contracts Section 318. And see UCC Section 2-210, establishing similar limits.

Result: This is hardly a matter of public concern, and the contract does not speak to the issue. However, acting is a very personal kind of work. The actor must be right for the part, interact smoothly with other cast members, work well with the director, and help draw the audience. Will is entitled to have Parker perform the work, and she may not delegate her role.

....

Improper Delegation and Repudiation.   Sometimes parties delegate duties they should not. Suppose Spot, having agreed not to delegate his painting job, is so tempted by the higher offer from another contractor that he delegates the work anyway. Hammer informs Spot he will not allow Brush on the job site. If Spot still refuses to work, he has **repudiated** the agreement; in other words, he has formally notified the other side he will not perform his side of the contract. Hammer will probably sue him. On the other hand, if Hammer allows Brush up the ladder and Brush completes the job, Hammer has no claim against anybody.

Novation

As we have seen, a delegator does not get rid of his duties merely by delegating them. But there is one way a delegator can do so. A **novation** is a three-way agreement in which the obligor transfers all rights and duties to a third party. The obligee agrees to look only to that third party for performance.

Recall Garret, the forlorn race car driver. When he wanted to get out of his obligations to Maybelle, he should have proposed a novation. He would assign all rights and delegate all duties to Brady, and Maybelle would agree that *only Brady* was obligated by the promissory note, releasing Garret from his responsibility to repay. Why would Maybelle do this? She might conclude that Brady was a financially better bet than Garret and that this was the best way to get her money. Maybelle would prefer to have both people liable. But Garret might refuse to bring Brady into the deal until Maybelle permits a novation. In the example given, Garret failed to obtain a novation, and hence he and Brady (or Brady's estate) were *both* liable on the promissory note.

Since a novation has the critical effect of releasing the obligor from liability, you will not be surprised to learn that two parties to a contract sometimes fight over whether some event was a simple delegation of duties or a novation. Here is one such contest.

Novation
A three-way agreement in which the obligor transfers all rights and duties to a third party.

ROSENBERG V. SON, INC.

491 N.W.2d 71, 1992 N.D. LEXIS 202
SUPREME COURT OF NORTH DAKOTA, 1992

CASE SUMMARY

Facts: The Rosenbergs owned a Dairy Queen in Grand Forks, North Dakota. They agreed in writing to sell the Dairy Queen to Mary Pratt. The contract required her to pay $10,000 down and $52,000 over 15 years, at 10 percent interest. Two years later, Pratt assigned her rights and delegated her duties under the sales contract to Son, Inc. The agreement between Pratt and Son contained a "Consent to Assignment" clause that the Rosenbergs signed. Pratt then moved to Arizona and had nothing further to do with the Dairy Queen. The Rosenbergs never received full payment for the Dairy Queen. They sued Mary Pratt.

The trial court gave summary judgment for Pratt, finding that she was no longer obligated on the original contract. The Rosenbergs appealed.

Issue: *Did Pratt obtain a novation relieving her of her duties under the original sales contract?*

Decision: Reversed and remanded. Pratt did not obtain a novation.

Reasoning: One party to a contract does not escape liability simply by delegating duties and assigning rights. To relieve itself of all responsibility, a party must obtain a novation, meaning an agreement from the other side that all liability has now passed on to a third person.

It is apparent from the language of this agreement that the parties intended only an assignment, not a novation. The document made no mention of discharging Pratt from her duties. In fact, the agreement included a clause in which Son indemnified Pratt; the only reason for such a provision was that Pratt remained liable to the Rosenbergs.

The assignment did not become a novation merely because Rosenberg signed it. A creditor may permit assignment without releasing the original obligor. That is what happened here, and Pratt remains liable to the Rosenbergs.

It appears that Mary Pratt, moving to Arizona, honestly thought she was not only out of the ice cream business but relieved of any debt to the Rosenbergs. This lawsuit undoubtedly came as a cold shock. What should she have done to avoid the dispute?

CHAPTER CONCLUSION

A moment's caution! That is what enables contracting parties to anticipate and realistically appraise any rights and responsibilities of third parties.

EXAM REVIEW

1. **THIRD PARTY BENEFICIARY** A third party beneficiary is an intended beneficiary and may enforce a contract if the parties intended her to benefit from the agreement and if either (1) enforcing the promise will satisfy a debt of the promisee to the beneficiary, or (2) the promisee intended to make a gift to the beneficiary. The intended beneficiary described in (1) is a *creditor beneficiary*, while (2) describes a *donee beneficiary*. Any beneficiary who meets neither description is an *incidental beneficiary* and has no right to enforce the contract. (p. 355)

2. **ASSIGNMENT AND DELEGATION** An assignment transfers the assignor's contract rights to the assignee. A delegation transfers the delegator's duties to the delegatee. (p. 358)

3. **RIGHTS ASSIGNABLE** A party generally may assign contract rights unless doing so would substantially change the obligor's rights or duties, is forbidden by law, or is validly precluded by the contract. (p. 360)

Question: Angelo Zavarella and Yvette Rodrigues were injured in an automobile accident allegedly caused by a vehicle belonging to Truck Equipment of Boston. Travelers Insurance Co. paid insurance benefits to Zavarella and Rodrigues, who then assigned to Travelers their claims against Truck Equipment. Travelers sued Truck Equipment, which moved to dismiss. What is Truck Equipment's claim that the case should be dismissed, and how would you rule?

Strategy: Travelers is claiming to be the assignee of the plaintiffs' claims. Any contractual right may be assigned except in the three instances listed above. Does one of those prohibitions apply? (See the "Result" at the end of this section.)

4. **ENFORCEMENT** Once the assignment is made and the obligor notified, the assignee may enforce her contractual rights against the obligor. The obligor, in turn, may generally raise all defenses against the assignee that she could have raised against the assignor. (p. 363)

5. **UCC AND WAIVERS** Under the UCC, the assignee may generally enforce a waiver that prohibits the obligor from raising defenses. This is not true, however, in most consumer contracts. (p. 363)

6. **DUTIES DELEGABLE** Duties are delegable unless delegation would violate public policy, the contract prohibits delegation, or the obligee has a substantial interest in personal performance by the obligor. (p. 365)

Question: Pizza of Gaithersburg, Maryland, owned five pizza shops. Pizza arranged with Virginia Coffee Service to install soft drink machines in each of its stores and maintain them. The contract made no mention of the rights of either party to delegate. Virginia Coffee delegated its duties to the Macke Co., leading to litigation between Pizza and Macke. Pizza claimed that Virginia Coffee was barred from delegating because Pizza had a close working relationship with the president of Virginia Coffee, who personally kept the machines in working order. Was the delegation legal?

Strategy: Any contractual duty may be delegated except in the three instances listed above. Does one of those prohibitions apply? (See the "Result" at the end of this section.)

7. **DISCHARGE** Unless the obligee agrees otherwise, delegation does not discharge the delegator's duty to perform. (p. 368)

8. **NOVATION** A *novation* is a three-way agreement in which the obligor delegates all duties to the delegatee and the obligee agrees to hold only the delegatee responsible. (p. 368)

EXAM Strategy

Question: Mardy, a general contractor, is building a house. He contracts with Plumbco to do all plumbing work for $120,000. Before Plumbco begins the work, it notifies Mardy in writing that Leo will be doing the work instead. Mardy does not respond. When Leo fails to perform, Mardy sues Plumbco. Plumbco is

(a) Liable.

(b) Liable only if Plumbco agreed to remain responsible for the job.

(c) Not liable because Mardy failed to repudiate the delegation.

(d) Not liable because Plumbco validly delegated its duties.

(e) Not liable because the parties entered into a novation.

Strategy: Delegation does not by itself relieve the delegator of his own liability to perform the contract. In a novation, the obligee agrees to look only to the third party for performance. Was this a delegation or a novation? (See the "Result" at the end of this section.)

---

3. Result: Truck Equipment's winning argument was one sentence long: claims for personal injury may not be assigned. Such assignments would transform accident claims into commercial commodities, and encourage assignees to exaggerate the gravity of the harm.

6. Result: There is no public policy issue involved. The contract is silent as to delegation. And Pizza's only legitimate interest was in seeing that installation and maintenance were adequate. There is no reason to believe that Virginia Coffee would perform the work better than others. The duty was delegable and Virginia Coffee wins.

8. Result: When Plumbco announced that Leo would do the work, Mardy did not respond. Mardy certainly did not agree to look exclusively to Leo for performance. There has not been a novation, and Plumbco remains liable on the contract. The correct answer is (a).

ADDITIONAL QUESTIONS

1. Intercontinental Metals Corp. (IMC) contracted with the accounting firm of Cherry, Bekaert & Holland to perform an audit. Cherry issued its opinion about IMC, giving all copies of its report directly to the company. IMC later permitted Dun & Bradstreet to examine the statements, and Raritan River Steel Co. saw a report published by Dun & Bradstreet. Relying on the audit, Raritan sold IMC $2.2 million worth of steel on credit, but IMC promptly went bankrupt. Raritan sued Cherry, claiming that IMC was not as sound as Cherry had reported, and that the accounting firm had breached its contract with IMC. Comment on Raritan's suit.

2. *CPA QUESTION* Yost contracted with Egan for Yost to buy certain real property. If the contract is otherwise silent, Yost's rights under the contract are:

(a) Assignable only with Egan's consent

(b) Nonassignable because they are personal to Yost

(c) Nonassignable as a matter of law

(d) Generally assignable

3. Woodson Walker and Associates leased computer equipment from Park Ryan Leasing. The lease said nothing about assignment. Park Ryan then assigned the lease to TCB as security for a loan. Park Ryan defaulted on its loan, and Walker failed to make several payments on the lease. TCB sued Walker for the lease payments. Please rule on two issues:

(a) Was the assignment valid, given the fact that the original lease made no mention of it?

(b) If the assignment was valid, may Walker raise defenses against TCB that it could have raised against Park Ryan?

4. Nationwide Discount Furniture hired Rampart Security to install an alarm in its warehouse. A fire would set off an alarm in Rampart's office, and the security company was then supposed to notify Nationwide immediately. A fire did break out, but Rampart allegedly failed to notify Nationwide, causing the fire to spread next door and damage a building owned by Gasket Materials Corp. Gasket sued Rampart for breach of contract, and Rampart moved for summary judgment. Comment.

5. C. Gaston Whiddon owned Gaston's LP Gas Co., Inc. Curtis Dufour purchased the company. Since Whiddon had personally operated the company for many years, Dufour was worried about competition from him and insisted on a noncompetition clause in the sales contract. The clause stated that Whiddon would not "compete with Gaston's LP Gas Co. anywhere south of Interstate Highway 20 for nine years." Three years later, the Herring Gas Co. offered to buy all of Dufour's gas business, assuming that Whiddon would not be a competitor for six more years. Dufour sold all of the assets to Herring, keeping the actual corporation "Gaston's LP Gas Co." for himself. What mistake in drafting have Dufour and Herring made?

6. **CPA QUESTION** One of the criteria for a valid assignment of a sales contract to a third party is that the assignment must:

(a) Not materially increase the other party's risk or duty

(b) Not be revocable by the assignor

(c) Be supported by adequate consideration from the assignee

(d) Be in writing and signed by the assignor

7. **ETHICS** A century and a half ago an English judge stated: "All painters do not paint portraits like Sir Joshua Reynolds, nor landscapes like Claude Lorraine, nor do all writers write dramas like Shakespeare or fiction like Dickens. Rare genius and extraordinary skill are not transferable." What legal doctrine is the judge describing? What is the ethical basis of this rule?

8. **YOU BE THE JUDGE** WRITING PROBLEM David Ricupero suspected his wife Polly of having an affair, so he taped her phone conversations and, based on what he heard, sued for divorce. David's lawyer, William Wuliger, had the recorded conversations transcribed for use at trial. The parties settled the divorce out of court and signed an agreement that included this clause:

Except as herein otherwise provided, each party hereto completely and forever releases the other and his attorneys from any and all rights each has or may have…to any property, privileges, or benefits accruing to either by virtue of their marriage, or conferred by the Statutory or Common Law of Ohio or the United States of America.

After the divorce was final, Polly sued William Wuliger for invasion of privacy and violation of federal wiretapping law. Wuliger moved to dismiss the case based on the clause quoted. Polly argued that Wuliger was not a party to the divorce settlement and had no right to enforce it. May Wuliger enforce the waiver clause from the Ricuperos' divorce settlement? **Argument for Wuliger:** The contract language demonstrates that the parties intended to release one another and their attorneys from any claims. That makes Wuliger an intended third party beneficiary, and he is entitled to enforce the agreement. If Polly did not want to release Wuliger from such claims, she was free not to sign the agreement. **Argument for Polly Ricupero:** A divorce agreement settles the affairs between the couple. That is all it is ever intended to do, and the parties here never intended to benefit a lawyer. Wuliger is only an incidental beneficiary and cannot use this contract to paper over his violation of federal wiretapping law.

9. Judith and John Brooks hired Wayne Hayes to build a house. The contract required Hayes to "provide all necessary labor and materials and perform all work of every nature whatsoever to be done in the erection of the residence." Hayes hired subcontractors to do all of the work. One of Hayes's employees checked on the work site daily, but neither Hayes nor any of his employees actively supervised the building. The Brookses were aware of this working arrangement and consented to it. The mason negligently installed the fireplace, ultimately leading to a serious fire. The Brookses sued Hayes for breach of contract. Hayes contended that when the Brookses approved of his hiring of subcontractors to do all work, that created a novation, relieving him of any liability. Discuss.

10. ***ROLE REVERSAL*** Write a short-answer question that highlights the difference between an assignment and a novation.

INTERNET RESEARCH PROBLEM

Go online to find a standard apartment lease. What does the lease say about subletting? Suppose you intend to rent an apartment next year, live there during the school year, and then sublet over the summer. May you do so?

You can find further practice problems at www.cengagebrain.com. See the preface of this book for website access details.

PERFORMANCE AND DISCHARGE

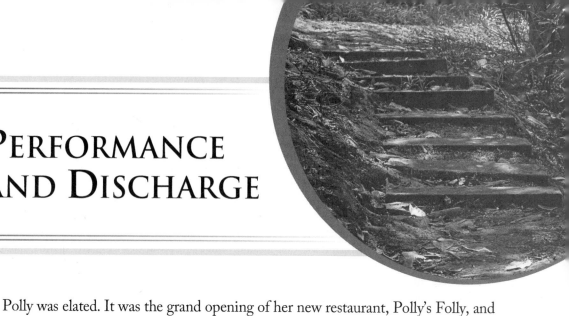

Polly was elated. It was the grand opening of her new restaurant, Polly's Folly, and everything was bubbling. The wait staff hustled and Caesar, the chef, churned out succulent dishes. Polly had signed a contract promising him $1,000 per week for one year, "provided Polly is personally satisfied with his cooking." Polly was determined that her Folly would be a glorious one. Her three-year lease would cost $6,000 per month, and she had signed an advertising deal with Billboard Bonanza for the same period. Polly had also promised Eddie, a publicity agent, a substantial monthly fee, to begin as soon as the restaurant was 80 percent booked for one month. Tonight, with candles flickering at packed tables, Polly beamed.

Polly disliked a veal dish and gagged on one of Caesar's soups. She fired her chef.

After a week, Polly's smiles were a bit forced. Some of Caesar's new dishes had been failures, including a grilled swordfish that was hard to pierce and shrimp jambalaya that was too spicy for the owner. The restaurant was only 60 percent full, and the publicity agent yelled at Caesar for costing him money, though the chef pointed out that most of his dishes were very popular. Later that month, Polly disliked a veal dish and gagged on one of Caesar's soups. She fired her chef.

Then troubles gushed forth—literally. A water main burst in front of Polly's restaurant, flooding the street. The city embarked on a two-month repair job that ultimately took four times that long. The street was closed to traffic, and no one could park within blocks of the Folly. For several months, Polly bravely served food, but patronage dropped steadily as hungry customers refused to deal with the bad parking and construction noise. Finally, behind on the rent and in debt to everyone, Polly closed her doors for good.

DISCHARGE

Grimly, the court doors swung open, offering a full menu of litigation. Polly's landlord sued for three years' rent, and Billboard Bonanza demanded its money for the same period. Caesar claimed his year's pay. Eddie, the agent, insisted on some money for his hard work.

Polly defended vigorously, seeking to be *discharged* from her various contracts. A party is **discharged** when she has no more duties under a contract. In each lawsuit, Polly asked a court to declare that her obligations were terminated and that she owed no money.

Most contracts are discharged by full performance. In other words, the parties generally do what they promise. Suppose, before the restaurant opened, Walter had promised to deliver 100 sets of cutlery to Polly and she had promised to pay $20 per set. Walter delivered the goods on time, and Polly paid on delivery. The parties got what they expected, and that contract was fully discharged.

Sometimes the parties discharge a contract by agreement. For example, the parties may agree to **rescind** their contract, meaning that they terminate it by mutual agreement.[1] If Polly's landlord believed he could get more rent from a new tenant, he might agree to rescind her lease. But he was dubious about the rental market and refused to rescind.

Discharge
A party is discharged when she has no more duties under the contract.

Rescind
To terminate a contract.

DEFENSES THAT DISCHARGE

At times a court may discharge a party who has not performed. When things have gone amiss, a judge must interpret the contract and issues of public policy to determine who in fairness should suffer the loss. In the lawsuits brought by the landlord and Billboard Bonanza, Polly argued a defense called "commercial impracticability," claiming that she should not be forced to rent space that was useless to her or buy advertising for a restaurant that had closed. From Polly's point of view, the claim was understandable. But we can also respect the arguments made by the landlord and the advertiser, that they did not cause the burst water main. Claims of commercial impracticability are difficult to win, and Polly lost against both of these opponents. Though she was making no money at all from the restaurant, the court found her liable in full for the lease and the advertising contract.[2]

Polly's argument against Caesar raised another issue of discharge. Caesar claimed that his cooking was good professional work and that all chefs make occasional mistakes, especially in a new restaurant. But Polly responded that they had a "personal satisfaction" contract. Under such contracts, "good" work may not suffice if it fails to please the promisee. Polly won this argument, and Caesar recovered nothing.

As to Eddie's suit, Polly raised a defense called "condition precedent," meaning that some event had to occur before she was obligated to pay. Polly claimed that she owed Eddie money only if and when the restaurant was 80 percent full, and that had never happened. The court agreed and discharged Polly on Eddie's claim.

We will analyze each of these issues, and begin with a look at conditions.

---

[1]The parties could also decide that one party's duties will be performed by someone else, a modification called a **novation**. Or they could create an **accord and satisfaction**, in which they agree that one party will substitute a new kind of performance in place of his contract obligations. See Chapter 15, on third parties, and Chapter 11, on consideration.
[2]Based on *Luminous Neon v. Parscale*, 17 Kan.App.2d 241, 836 P.2d 1201, 1992 Kan. App. LEXIS 572 (Kan. Ct. App. 1992).

Intentional breach is always a (small or large) material breach

BOTH parties may rescind or excuse or waive the condition before it happens

CONDITIONS

Condition

An event that must occur before a party becomes obligated under a contract.

My duty to perform depends on whether or not the condition happened

Even after a condition is removed, the party STILL has a duty to perform

Parties often put conditions in a contract. A **condition** is an event that must occur before a party becomes obligated under a contract. Polly agreed to pay Eddie, the agent, a percentage of her profits, but with an important condition: 80% of the tables had to be booked for a month. Unless and until those tables were occupied, Polly owed Eddie nothing. That never happened, or, in contract language, the *condition failed*, and so Polly was discharged.

Conditions can take many forms. Alex would like to buy Kevin's empty lot and build a movie theater on it, but the city's zoning law will not permit such a business in that location. Alex signs a contract to buy Kevin's empty lot in 120 days, *provided that* within 100 days the city re-zones the area to permit a movie theater. If the city fails to re-zone the area by day 100, Alex is discharged and need not complete the deal. As another example, Friendly Insurance issues a policy covering Vivian's house, promising to pay for any loss due to fire, but only if Vivian furnishes proof of her damages within 60 days of the damage. If the house burns down, Friendly becomes liable to pay. But if Vivian arrives with the proof 70 days after the fire, she collects nothing. Friendly, though it briefly had a duty to pay, was discharged when Vivian failed to furnish the necessary information on time.

HOW CONDITIONS ARE CREATED

Express Conditions

The parties may expressly state a condition. Alex's contract with Kevin expressly discharged all obligations if the city failed to re-zone within the stated period. Notice that **no special language is necessary to create the condition.** Phrases such as "provided that" frequently indicate a condition, but neither those nor any other words are essential. As long as the parties *intended* to create a condition, a court will enforce it.

Because informal language can create a condition, the parties may dispute whether they intended one or not. Sand Creek Country Club, in Indiana, was eager to expand its clubhouse facilities and awarded the design work to CSO Architects. The club wanted the work done quickly but had not secured financing. The architects sent a letter confirming their agreement:

> It was our intent to allow Mr. Dan Moriarty of our office to start work on your project as early as possible in order to allow you to meet the goals that you have set for next fall. Also, it was the intent of CSO to begin work on your project and delay any billings to you until your financing is in place. As I explained to you earlier, we will continue on this course until we reach a point where we can no longer continue without receiving some payment.

The club gave CSO the go-ahead to begin design work, and the architects did their work and billed Sand Creek for $33,000. But the club, unable to obtain financing, refused to pay. Sand Creek claimed that CSO's letter created a *condition* in their agreement, namely, that the club would have to pay only if and when it obtained financing. The court was unpersuaded and ruled that the parties had never intended to create an express condition. The architects were merely delaying their billing as a convenience to the club. It would be absurd, said the court, to assume that CSO intended to perform $33,000 worth of work for free.[3]

---

[3]*Sand Creek Country Club, Ltd. v. CSO Architects, Inc.*, 582 N.E.2d 872, 1991 Ind. App. LEXIS 2151 (Ind.Ct.App. 1991).

Implied Conditions

At other times, the parties say nothing about a condition, but it is clear from their agreement that they have implied one. Charlotte orally rents an apartment to Hakan for one year and promises to fix any problems in the unit. It is an implied condition that Hakan will promptly notify Charlotte of anything needing repair. Although the parties have not said anything about notice, it is only common sense that Hakan must inform his landlord of defects since she will have no other way to learn of them.

Conditions in the Outfield.   Professional sports contracts are often full of conditions. Assume that the San Francisco Giants want to sign Tony Fleet to play center field, a key position. The club considers him a fine defensive player but a dubious offensive performer. The many conditional clauses in his contract reflect hard bargaining over a questionable athlete. The Giants guarantee Fleet $500,000, a modest salary by today's standards. If the speedy outfielder appears in 110 games (out of 162 total), his pay increases to $900,000, and if he plays in 120 games, he earns $1 million. Additional conditional payments relate to a "Gold Glove" award, which coaches and managers throughout the league award annually to the top defensive performers. If Fleet receives even one vote for a Gold Glove, he earns an extra $100,000, and an additional $200,000 if he wins the award. The Giants insist on an option to re-sign Fleet for the following season for $800,000 (he has no say in the matter), but if the center fielder only plays in 100 games, the team loses that right, leaving Fleet free to negotiate for higher pay with other teams.

TYPES OF CONDITIONS

Courts divide conditional clauses into three categories: (1) condition precedent, (2) condition subsequent, and (3) concurrent conditions.[4] But what they have in common is more important than any of their differences. The key to all conditional clauses is this: **if the condition does not occur, one party will probably be discharged without performing**.

Condition Precedent

In this kind of condition, an event *must occur before* a duty arises. Polly's contract with Eddie concerned a condition precedent. Polly had no obligation to pay Eddie anything *unless and until* the restaurant was 80 percent full for a month. Since that never happened, she was discharged.

Condition Subsequent

The only difference here is that the condition must occur *after* the particular duty arises. If the condition does not occur, the duty is discharged. Vivian's policy with Friendly Insurance contains a condition subsequent. As soon as the fire broke out, Friendly became obligated to pay for the damage. But if Vivian failed to produce her proof of loss on time, Friendly's obligation was discharged.

Precedent/Subsequent Distinction—Who Cares?

The difference between condition precedent and condition subsequent is important for one reason: it tells us *who must prove* whether the condition occurred. If the parties agreed to a condition precedent, the plaintiff has the burden to prove that the condition happened, and hence that the defendant was obligated to perform. But with a condition subsequent, it is the defendant who must prove that the condition occurred, relieving him of any obligation.

---

[4]The Restatement (Second) of Contracts has officially abandoned the terms "condition precedent" and "condition subsequent." See Restatement Sections 224 et seq. But courts routinely use the terms, so it is difficult to avoid the old distinctions.

CONDITION PRECEDENT AND CONDITION SUBSEQUENT COMPARED

	Condition Created	Does Condition Occur?	Duty Is Determined	Result
Condition Precedent	"Fee to be paid when restaurant is filled to 80% capacity for one month."	Condition DOES occur: restaurant is packed.	Duty arises: Polly owes Eddie his fee.	Polly pays the fee.
		Condition DOES NOT occur: restaurant is empty.	Duty never arises: Polly is discharged.	Polly pays nothing.

	Condition Created	Duty Is Determined	Does Condition Occur?	Result
Condition Subsequent	"Vivian must give proof of loss within 60 days."	Fire damages property, and Friendly Insurance becomes obligated to pay Vivian.	Condition DOES occur: Vivian proves her losses within 60 days.	Friendly pays Vivian for her losses.
			Condition DOES NOT occur: Vivian fails to prove her losses within 60 days.	Friendly is discharged and owes nothing

Concurrent Conditions

Here, both parties have a duty to perform *simultaneously*. Renee agrees to sell her condominium to Tim on July 5. Renee agrees to furnish a valid deed and clear title to the property on that date, and Tim promises to present a cashier's check for $600,000. The parties have agreed to concurrent conditions. Each performance is the condition for the other's performance. If Renee arrives at the Registry of Deeds and can only say, "I'm pretty darn sure I own that property," Tim need not present his check; similarly, if Tim arrives only with an "IOU" scribbled on the back of a candy wrapper, Renee has no duty to hand over a valid deed.

EXAM *Strategy*

Question: Roberto wants to buy Naomi's house for $350,000, and is willing to pay a 20% down payment, which satisfies Naomi. However, he needs a $250,000 mortgage in order to complete the purchase, and is not certain he can obtain one. Naomi is worried that Roberto might change his mind about buying the house, and then use alleged financing problems to skip out of the deal. How can the two parties protect themselves?

Strategy: Both parties should use conditional clauses in the sales agreement. Naomi must force Roberto to do his best to obtain a mortgage. How? Roberto's clause should protect him if he cannot obtain a sufficient mortgage. How?

Result: Naomi should demand the 20% down payment. Further, her conditional clause should state that Roberto forfeits the down payment unless he demonstrates that, within two weeks, he has applied in good faith for a mortgage to at least three banks. Roberto should insist that if he promptly and fully applies to three banks, but fails to obtain a mortgage, his down payment is refunded.

Public Policy

At times a court will refuse to enforce an express condition on the grounds that it is unfair and harmful to the general public. In other words, a court might agree that the parties created a conditional clause but conclude that permitting its enforcement would hurt society. Did the insurance contract in the following case harm society? You be the judge.

YOU *be the* JUDGE

ANDERSON V. COUNTRY LIFE INS. CO.

180 Ariz. 625, 886 P.2d 1381, 1994 Ariz. App. LEXIS 240
Arizona Court of Appeals, 1994

Facts: On November 26, a Country Life Insurance agent went to the house of Donald and Anna Mae Anderson. He persuaded the Andersons to buy a life insurance policy and accepted a check for $1,600. He gave the Andersons a "conditional receipt for medical policy," dated that day. The form stated that the Andersons would have a valid life insurance policy with Country Life, effective November 26, but only when all conditions were met. The most important of these conditions was that the Country Life home office accept the Andersons as medical risks. The Andersons were pleased with the new policy and glad that it was effective that same day.

It was not. Donald Anderson died of a heart attack a few weeks later. Country Life declined the Andersons as medical risks and refused to issue a policy. Anna Mae Anderson sued. Country Life pointed out that medical approval was a condition precedent. In other words, the company argued that the policy would be effective as of November 26, but only if it later decided to make the policy effective. Based on this argument, the trial court gave summary judgment for Country Life. Ms. Anderson appealed, claiming that the conditional clause was a violation of public policy.

You Be the Judge: Did the conditional clause violate public policy?

Argument for Ms. Anderson: Your honors, this policy is a scam. This so-called "conditional receipt for medical policy" is designed to trick customers and then steal their money. The company leads people to believe they are covered as of the day they write the check. But they aren't covered until *much later*, when the insurer gets around to deciding the applicant's medical status.

The company gets the customer's money right away and gives nothing in exchange. If the company, after taking its time, decides the applicant is not medically fit, it returns the money, having used it for weeks or even months to earn interest. If, on the other hand, the insurance company decides the applicant is a good bet, it then issues the policy effective for weeks or months *in the past, when coverage is of no use*. No one can die retroactively, your honors. The company is being paid for a period during which it had no risk.

This is a fraud and a disgrace, and the company should pay the benefits it owes.

Argument for Country Life: Your honors, is Country Life supposed to issue life insurance policies without doing a medical check? That is the road to bankruptcy and would mean that no one could obtain this valuable coverage. Of course we do a medical inquiry, as quickly as possible. It's in our interest to get the policy decided one way or the other.

The policy clearly stated that coverage was effective *only when approved by the home office*, after all inquiries were made. The Andersons knew that as well as the agent. If they were covered immediately, why would the company do a medical check? Country Life resents suggestions that this policy is a scam, when in reality it is Ms. Anderson who is trying to profit from a tragedy that the company had nothing to do with.

The facts of this case are unusual. Obviously, most insureds do not die between application and acceptance. It would be disastrous for society to rewrite every insurance policy in this state based on one very sad fact pattern. The contract was clear and it should be enforced as written.

> **ETHICS**   Imagine that you are a young insurance agent, eager to do a good job and advance your career. Your company urges you to sell insurance with "conditional receipts" such as the one used by Country Life. Would you do it? From the Chapter 2 ethics checklist: What values are in conflict? Which of these values are most important? ◆

PERFORMANCE

Caitlin has an architect draw up plans for a monumental new house, and Daniel agrees to build it by September 1. Caitlin promises to pay $900,000 on that date. The house is ready on time, but Caitlin has some complaints. The living room was supposed to be 18 feet high, but it is only 17 feet; the pool was to be azure, yet it is aquamarine; the maid's room was not supposed to be wired for cable television, but it is. Caitlin refuses to pay anything for the house. Is she justified? Of course not, it would be absurd to give her a magnificent house for free when it has only tiny defects. And that is how a court would decide the case. But in this easy answer lurks a danger. Technically, Daniel did breach the contract, and yet the law allows him to recover the full contract price, or virtually all of it. Once that principle is established, how far will a court stretch it? Suppose the living room is only 14 feet high, or 12 feet, or 5 feet? What if the foundation has a small crack? A vast and dangerous split? What if Daniel finishes the house a month late? Six months late? Three years late? At some point a court will conclude that Daniel has so thoroughly botched the job that he deserves little or no money. But where is that point? That is a question that businesses—and judges—face everyday.

The more complex a contract, the more certain that at least one party will perform imperfectly. Every house ever built has some defects. A delivery of a thousand bushels of apples is sure to include a few rotten ones. A custom-designed computer system for a huge airline is likely to have some glitches. The cases raise several related doctrines, all concerning how well a party *performed* its contract obligations.

STRICT PERFORMANCE AND SUBSTANTIAL PERFORMANCE

Strict Performance

When Daniel built Caitlin's house with three minor defects, she refused to pay, arguing that he had not *strictly performed* his obligations. She was right, yet she lost anyway. Courts dislike strict performance because it enables one party to benefit without paying and sends the other one home empty-handed. A party is generally not required to render **strict performance** unless the contract expressly demands it and such a demand is reasonable. Caitlin's contract never suggested that Daniel would forfeit all payment if there were minor problems. Even if Caitlin had insisted on such a clause, few courts would have enforced it because the requirement would be unreasonable.

Strict performance

Requires one party to perform its obligations precisely, with no deviation from the contract terms.

There are cases where strict performance does make sense. Marshall agrees to deliver 500 sweaters to Leo's store, and Leo promises to pay $20,000 cash on delivery. If Leo has only $19,000 cash and a promissory note for $1,000, he has failed to perform, and Marshall need not give him the sweaters. Leo's payment represents 95 percent of what he promised, but there is a big difference between cash and a promissory note.

Substantial Performance

Daniel, the house builder, won his case against Caitlin because he fulfilled most of his obligations, even though he did an imperfect job. Courts often rely on the substantial performance doctrine, especially in cases involving services as opposed to those concerning the sale of goods or land. In a contract for services, a party that **substantially performs** its obligations will receive the full contract price, minus the value of any defects. Daniel receives $900,000, the contract price, minus the value of a ceiling that is one foot too low, a pool the wrong color, and so forth. It will be for the trial court to decide how much those defects are worth. If the court decides the low ceiling is a $10,000 damage, the pool color worth $5,000 and the cable television worth $500, then Daniel receives $884,500.

On the other hand, a party that fails to give substantial performance may get nothing. **A party that fails to perform substantially receives nothing on the contract itself and will only recover the value of the work, if any.** If the foundation cracks in Caitlin's house and the walls collapse, Daniel will not receive his $900,000. In such a case, he collects only the market value of the work he has done, which is probably zero.

When is performance substantial? There is no perfect test, but courts look at these issues:

- How much benefit has the promisee received?

- If it is a construction contract, can the owner use the thing for its intended purpose?

- Can the promisee be compensated with money damages for any defects?

- Did the promisor act in good faith?

In the following case, did the newspaper substantially perform?

Substantial performance
Occurs when one party fulfills enough of its contract obligations to warrant payment.

STRATEGIC RESOURCES GROUP v. KNIGHT-RIDDER, INC.

870 So.2d 846
COURT OF APPEAL OF FLORIDA, 2003

CASE SUMMARY

Facts: Brighton Homes developed residential housing in the Miami area. The company contracted with Knight-Ridder to run advertisements in the *Miami Herald* newspaper. The contract required Brighton to designate the size of each ad and stated that Knight-Ridder would print them and "bill for the exact space published." The agreement also permitted Knight-Ridder to "revise, alter, or reject any advertisement for any reason, but no change in advertising copy will be made without the customer's prior consent."

Brighton assigned to Strategic Resources Group all rights the developer might have for overpayments made to Knight-Ridder. Strategic then sued Knight-Ridder, claiming that for three years, the newspaper had routinely printed ads that were 3.83 percent smaller than the copy submitted by Brighton. Strategic sought $83,000 in damages. The trial court found that such reductions were standard in the newspaper industry, that Knight-Ridder had in fact made them, and that the size difference was noticeable only if measured

with a ruler. Declaring that Knight-Ridder had substantially performed, the trial court gave summary judgment to the news company, and Strategic appealed.

Issue: *Did Knight-Ridder substantially perform its advertising contract?*

Decision: Yes, Knight-Ridder substantially performed. Affirmed.

Reasoning: For six years, Knight-Ridder ran these advertisements without a single complaint from its customer. Brighton never asked for advertising proofs before publication, nor did it measure the ads when they appeared in print. Indeed, the size reduction was hard to discern in a side-by-side comparison. Even after Brighton discovered the reduction, it continued to do business with Knight-Ridder, using similar advertisements under the same terms. Brighton clearly received the benefit of the bargain.

Strategic argues that the doctrine of substantial performance does not apply to the payment of money. However, the focus of this contract was not on payment of money but rather on Knight-Ridder's obligation to print advertisements that substantially complied with Brighton's expectation. The newspaper did what it was supposed to.

Strategic also contends that the breach of contract is intentional and that the doctrine therefore should not apply.

Although Knight-Ridder deliberately reduced the size of the ads, it did not intentionally breach the agreement. The newspaper relied on the contract, which authorized it to "revise, alter, or reject any advertisement." Yes, the better practice would have been for Knight-Ridder to notify its customer of the size reduction. In fact, though, Brighton would have consented to the minor adjustment because it was receiving substantially what it wanted.

EXAM *Strategy*

Question: Jade owns a race track. She hires Trevor to resurface it, for $180,000, paying $90,000 down. When the project is completed, Jade refuses to pay the balance and sues Trevor for her down payment. He counterclaims for the $90,000 still due. At trial, Trevor proves that all of the required materials were applied by trained workers in an expert fashion, the dimensions were perfect, and his profit margin very modest. The head of the national drag racing association testifies that his group considers the strip unsafe. He noticed puddles in both asphalt lanes, found the concrete starting pads unsafe, and believed the racing surface needed to be ground off and reapplied. His organization refuses to sanction races at the track until repairs are made. Who wins the suit?

Strategy: When one party has performed imperfectly, we have an issue of substantial performance. To decide whether Trevor is entitled to his money, we apply four factors: (1) How much benefit did Jade receive? (2) Can she use the racing strip for its intended purpose? (3) Can Jade be compensated for defects? (4) Did Trevor act in good faith?

Result: Jade has received no benefit whatsoever. She cannot use her drag strip for drag racing. Compensation will not help Jade—she needs a new strip. Trevor's work must be ripped up and replaced. Trevor may have acted in good faith, but he failed to deliver what Jade bargained for. Jade wins all of the money she paid. (As we will see in the next chapter, she may also win additional sums for her lost profits.)

PERSONAL SATISFACTION CONTRACTS

" IF I don't like it,
I won't pay for it"
Enforceable only if its
included in the contract

(objective test/reasonable
person test)

Sujata, president of a public relations firm, hires Ben to design a huge multimedia project for her company, involving computer software, music, and live actors, all designed to sell frozen bologna sandwiches to supermarkets. His contract guarantees him two years' employment, provided all of his work "is acceptable in the sole judgment of Sujata." Ben's immediate supervisor is delighted with his work and all his colleagues are impressed—all, that is, but Sujata. Three months later, she fires him, claiming that his work is "uninspired." Does she have the right to do that?

This is a **personal satisfaction contract**, in which the promisee makes a personal, subjective evaluation of the promisor's performance. Employment contracts may require personal satisfaction of the employer; agreements for the sale of goods may demand that the buyer be personally satisfied with the product; and deals involving a credit analysis of one party may insist that his finances be satisfactory to the other party. In resolving disputes like

Ben and Sujata's, judges must decide: When is it fair for the promisee to claim that she is *not* satisfied? May she make that decision for any reason at all, even on a whim?

A court applies a subjective standard only if assessing the work involves personal feelings, taste, or judgment and the contract explicitly demanded personal satisfaction. A "subjective standard" means that the promisee's personal views will greatly influence her judgment, even if her decision is foolish and unfair. Artistic or creative work, or highly specialized tasks designed for a particular employer, may involve subtle issues of quality and personal preference. Ben's work combines several media and revolves around his judgment. Accordingly, the law applies a subjective standard to Sujata's decision. Since she concludes that his work is uninspired, she may legally fire him, even if her decision is irrational.

Note that the promisee, Sujata, has to show two things: that assessing Ben's work involves her personal judgment *and* that their contract explicitly demands personal satisfaction. If the contract were vague on this point, Sujata would lose. Had the agreement merely said, "Ben will at all times make his best efforts," Sujata could not fire him.

In all other cases, a court applies an objective standard to the promisee's decision. In other words, the objective standard will be used if assessing the work does not involve personal judgment *or if* the contract failed to explicitly demand personal satisfaction. An objective standard means that the promisee's judgment of the work must be reasonable. Suppose Sujata hires Leila to install an alarm system for her company, and the contract requires that Sujata be "personally satisfied." Leila's system passes all tests but Sujata claims, "It just doesn't make me feel secure. I know that some day it's going to break down." May Sujata refuse to pay? No. Even though the contract used the phrase "personally satisfied," a mechanical alarm system does not involve personal judgment and taste. Either the system works or it does not. A reasonable person would find that Leila's system is just fine and therefore, under the objective standard, Sujata must pay. The law strongly favors the objective standard because the subjective standard gives unlimited power to the promisee.

• Personal Satisfaction of third party

> **Either the system works or it does not.**

Good Faith

The parties to a contract must carry out their obligations in good faith. The Restatement (Second) of Contracts Section 205 states: **"Every contract imposes upon each party a duty of good faith and fair dealing in its performance and its enforcement."** For its part, the UCC establishes a similar requirement for all contracts governed by the Code.[5] The difficulty, of course, is applying this general rule to the infinite problems that may arise when two people, or companies, do business. How far must one side go to meet its good faith burden? The Restatement emphasizes that the parties must remain faithful to the "agreed common purpose and justified expectations of the other party." Two examples should illustrate.

Marvin Shuster was a physician in Florida. Three patients sued him for alleged malpractice. Shuster denied any wrongdoing and asked his insurer to defend the claims. But the insurance company settled all three claims without defending and with a minimum of investigation. Shuster had to pay nothing, but he sued the insurance company claiming that it acted in bad faith. The doctor argued that the company's failure to defend him caused emotional suffering and

---

[5]UCC Section 1-203 states: "Every contract or duty within this Act imposes an obligation of good faith in its performance or enforcement." The present Code defines good faith as "honesty in fact." The proposed revision to Article 1 broadens the requirement to "honesty in fact and the observance of reasonable commercial standards of fair dealing," but thus far that is the law in only a few states.

meant that it would be impossible for him to obtain new malpractice insurance. The Florida Supreme Court found that the insurer acted in good faith. The contract clearly gave all control of malpractice cases to the company. It could settle or defend as it saw fit. Here, the company considered it more economical to settle quickly, and Shuster should have known, from the contract language, that the insurer might choose to do so.[6]

In the following case, one party to a contract played its cards very close to its chest. Too close?

Brunswick Hills Racquet Club Inc. v. Route 18 Shopping Center Associates

182 N.J. 210 864 A.2d 387
Supreme Court of New Jersey, 2005

CASE SUMMARY

Facts: Brunswick Hills Racquet Club (Brunswick) owned a tennis club on property that it leased from Route 18 Shopping Center Associates (Route 18). The lease ran for 25 years, and Brunswick had spent about $1 million in capital improvements. The lease expired March 30, 2002. Brunswick had the option of either buying the property or purchasing a 99-year lease, both on very favorable terms. To exercise its option, Brunswick had to notify Route 18 no later than September 30, 2001, and had to pay the option price of $150,000. If Brunswick failed to exercise its options, the existing lease automatically renewed as of September 30, for 25 more years, but at more than triple the current rent.

In February, 2000—19 months before the option deadline—Brunswick's lawyer, Gabriel Spector, wrote to Rosen Associates, the company that managed Route 18, stating that Brunswick intended to exercise the option for a 99-year lease. He requested that the lease be sent well in advance so that he could review it. He did not make the required payment of $150,000.

In March, Rosen replied that it had forwarded Spector's letter to its attorney, who would be in touch. In April, Spector again wrote, asking for a reply from Rosen or its lawyer.

Over the next six months, Spector continually asked for a copy of the lease, or information, but neither Route 18's lawyer nor anyone else provided any data. In January 2001, Spector renewed his requests for a copy of the lease. Route 18's lawyer never replied. Sadly, in May 2001, after a long illness, Spector died. In August 2001, Spector's law partner, Arnold Levin, wrote to Rosen, again stating Brunswick's

intention to buy the 99-year lease and requesting a copy of all relevant information. He received no reply, and the September deadline passed.

In February 2002, Route 18's lawyer dropped the hammer, notifying Levin that Brunswick could not exercise its option to lease because it had failed to pay the $150,000 by September 30, 2001.

Brunswick sued, claiming that Route 18 had breached its duty of good faith and fair dealing. The trial court found that Route 18 had no duty to notify Brunswick of impending deadlines and gave summary judgment for Route 18. The appellate court affirmed, and Brunswick appealed to the state supreme court.

Issue: *Did Route 18 breach its duty of good faith and fair dealing?*

Decision: Yes, Route 18 breached its duty of good faith and fair dealing.

Reasoning: Courts generally should not tinker with precisely drafted agreements entered into by experienced business-people. Nonetheless, every party to a contract is bound by a duty of good faith and fair dealing in its performance. Good faith is conduct that conforms to community standards of decency and reasonableness. Neither party may do anything that will prevent the other from receiving the contract benefits.

Route 18 and its agents acted in bad faith. Nineteen months before the deadline, Brunswick Hills notified the landlord that it intended to exercise its option to purchase

[6]*Shuster v. South Broward Hospital Dist. Physicians Prof. Liability Ins. Trust*, 591 So.2d 174, 1992 Fla. LEXIS 20 (Fla. 1992).

a 99-year lease. Brunswick Hills mistakenly believed that its payment was not due until closing. During that year and a half, Route 18 engaged in a pattern of evasion, sidestepping every request by Brunswick Hills to move forward on closing the lease. After Spector's death, Route 18's lawyer continued to play possum despite the obvious risk to Brunswick Hills. Route 18 acknowledged that it did not want the lease payment because the long-term lease was not in its financial interest.

Neither a landlord nor its attorney is required to act as his brother's keeper. However, there are ethical norms that apply even in the harsh world of commercial transactions. All parties must behave in good faith and deal fairly with the other side. Brunswick Hills' repeated letters and calls to close the lease placed an obligation on Route 18 to respond in a timely, honest manner. The company failed to do that, and Brunswick Hills is entitled to exercise the 99-year lease.

EXAM *Strategy*

Question: Sun operates an upscale sandwich shop in New Jersey, in a storefront that she leases from Ricky for $18,000 per month. The lease, which expires soon, allows Sun to renew for five years, at $22,000 per month. Ricky knows, but Sun does not, that Prada will open a store on the same block in a year. The dramatic increase in pedestrian traffic will render Sun's space more valuable. Ricky says nothing about Prada, Sun declines to renew, and Ricky leases the space for $40,000. Sun sues Ricky, claiming he breached his duty of good faith and fair dealing. Based on the *Brunswick Hills* case, how would the New Jersey Supreme Court rule?

Strategy: In the *Brunswick Hills* case, the court, on the one hand, criticized the defendant for cynically evading the plaintiff's efforts to renew. However, the court also said, "We do not expect a landlord or even an attorney to act as his brother's keeper in a commercial transaction." Using those opposing themes as guidelines, examine the court's decision and predict the ruling in Sun's suit.

Result: *Brunswick Hills* begins: "Courts generally should not tinker with a finely drawn and precise contract entered into by experienced business people." Sun's lease imposes no responsibility on Ricky to report on neighborhood changes or forecast profitability. Further, Sun made no requests to Ricky about the area's future. Sun is asking Ricky to be "her brother's keeper," and neither this court nor any other will do that. She loses.

TIME OF THE ESSENCE CLAUSES

> Go, sir, gallop, and don't forget that the world was made in six days. You can ask me for anything you like, except time.
>
> *Napoleon, to an aide, 1803*

Generals are not the only ones who place a premium on time. Ask Gene LaSalle. The Seabreeze Restaurant agreed to sell him all of its assets. The parties signed a contract stating the price and closing date. Seabreeze insisted on a clause saying, "Seabreeze considers that time is of the essence in consummating the proposed transaction." Such clauses are common in real estate transactions and in any other agreement where a delay would cause serious damage to one party. LaSalle was unable to close on the date specified and asked for an extension. Seabreeze refused and sold its assets elsewhere. A Florida court affirmed that Seabreeze acted legally.

[handwritten margin note:] Failure to act within the time required constitutes a breach of contract

[handwritten margin note:] Must be explicitly stated in the contract

Time of the essence clauses

Provisions that generally make contract dates strictly enforceable.

A **time of the essence clause** will generally make contract dates strictly enforceable. Seabreeze regarded a timely sale as important, and LaSalle agreed to the provision. There was nothing unreasonable about the clause, and LaSalle suffered the consequences of his delay.[7]

Suppose the contract had named a closing date but included no time of the essence clause. If LaSalle offered to close three days late, could Seabreeze sell elsewhere? No. **Merely including a date for performance does not make time of the essence.** Courts dislike time of the essence arguments because even a short delay may mean that one party forfeits everything it expected to gain from the bargain. If the parties do not clearly state that prompt performance is essential, then both are entitled to reasonable delays.

BREACH

[handwritten margin note: Right at the time the contract is breached, the contract ends and the statute of limitations begins (the time period of when the party has the right to cause of action) — May sue or do nothing]

When one party breaches a contract, the other party is discharged. The discharged party has no obligation to perform and may sue for damages. Edwin promises that on July 1 he will deliver 20 tuxedos, tailored to fit male chimpanzees, to Bubba's circus for $300 per suit. After weeks of delay Edwin concedes he hasn't a cummerbund to his name. Bubba is discharged and obviously owes nothing. In addition, he may sue Edwin for damages. If Bubba is forced to pay $350 elsewhere to obtain similar tuxedos, he will recover the difference in cost. Twenty tuxedos, at $50 extra per suit, means that Bubba will get $1,000 from Edwin.

MATERIAL BREACH

As we know, parties frequently perform their contract duties imperfectly, which is why courts accept substantial performance rather than strict performance, particularly in contracts involving services. In a more general sense, **courts will only discharge a contract if a party committed a** *material* **breach.** A material breach is one that substantially harms the innocent party and for which it would be hard to compensate without discharging the contract. Suppose Edwin fails to show up with the tuxedos on June 1, but calls to say they will arrive under the big top the next day. He has breached the agreement. Is his breach material? No. This is a trivial breach, and Bubba is not discharged. When the tuxedos arrive, he must pay.

The following case raises the issue in the context of a major college sports program.

O'BRIEN v. OHIO STATE UNIVERSITY

2007 WL 2729077
OHIO COURT OF APPEALS, 2007

CASE SUMMARY

Facts: The Ohio State University (OSU), experiencing a drought in its men's basketball program, brought in a highly regarded coach, Jim O'Brien, to turn things around. He did. In only his second year, he guided the team to its best record ever.

---

[7] *Seabreeze Restaurant, Inc. v. Paumgardhen*, 639 So.2d 69, 1994 Fla. App. LEXIS 4546 (Fla. Dist. Ct. App. 1994).

The team played in the most prestigious postseason tournament, that run by the National Collegiate Athletic Association (NCAA), and won a berth in the "final four." O'Brien was named national coach of the year. OSU's athletic director promptly offered the coach a new, multiyear contract, worth about $800,000 per year.

O'Brien also wanted job security. So Section 5.1 of the contract included these termination provisions. The University could fire O'Brien *for cause* if (a) there was a material breach of the contract by the coach, or (b) O'Brien's conduct subjected the school to NCAA sanctions. OSU could also terminate O'Brien *without cause*, but in that case it had to pay him the full salary owed.

O'Brien began recruiting a talented 21-year-old Serbian player named Alex Radojevic. While getting to know the young man, O'Brien discovered two things. First, it appeared that Radojevic had been paid to play briefly for a Yugoslavian team, meaning that he was ineligible to play in the NCAA. Second, it was clear that Radojevic's family had suffered terribly during the strife in the Balkans.

O'Brien concluded that Radojevic would never play for OSU or any major college. He also decided to loan Radojevic's mother some money. Any such loan would violate an NCAA rule if done to recruit a player, but O'Brien believed the loan was legal since Radojevic could not play in the NCAA anyway. Several years later, the university learned of the loan and realized that O'Brien had never reported it. Hoping to avoid trouble with the NCAA, OSU imposed sanctions on itself. The university also fired the coach, claiming he had lied, destroyed the possibility of postseason play, and harmed the school's reputation.

O'Brien sued, claiming he had not materially breached the contract. The trial court awarded the coach $2.5 million, and the University appealed.

Issue: *Did O'Brien materially breach the contract?*

Decision: No, he did not materially breach his contract. Affirmed.

Reasoning: Ohio State suffered no substantial damage. The Buckeyes played poorly in the weeks leading up to the announcement of the ban on postseason play, and they were unlikely to receive an NCAA bid.

The university's reputation was not significantly harmed because Radojevic never played for the school. Also, Ohio State promptly recruited a top coach to replace O'Brien. Moreover, OSU presented no evidence that O'Brien lied about the payment, tried to conceal it, or even knew that it was wrong.

Violations of NCAA rules are common. A minor violation is not necessarily a material breach. Coach O'Brien remained entitled to his $2.5 million award.

[Author's note: Since reading this case, I have been wracking my brain to come up with a small rule that I might break and then collect $2.5 million. Maybe something with parking. They are real sticklers for parking here at the University of Texas.]

ANTICIPATORY BREACH (anticipatory repudiation)

Sally will receive her bachelor's degree in May and already has a job lined up for September, a two-year contract as window display designer for Surebet Department Store. The morning of graduation, she reads in the paper that Surebet is going out of business that very day. Surebet has told Sally nothing about her status. Sally need not wait until September to learn her fate. Surebet has committed an **anticipatory breach by making it unmistakably clear that it will not honor the contract**. Sometimes a promisor will actually inform the promisee that it will not perform its duties. At other times, as here, the promisor takes some step that makes the breach evident. Sally is discharged and may immediately seek other work. She is also entitled to file suit for breach of contract. The court will treat Surebet's anticipatory breach just as though the store had actually refused to perform on September 1.

A breach of contract committed prior to the time of the required performance

STATUTE OF LIMITATIONS

A party injured by a breach of contract should act promptly. A **statute of limitations** begins to run at the time of injury and will limit the time within which the injured party may file suit. Statutes of limitation vary from state to state and even from issue to issue within a state.

Statute of limitations

A statutory time limit within which an injured party must file suit.

In some states, for example, an injured party must sue on oral contracts within three years, on a sale of goods contract within four years, and on some written contracts within five years. Failure to file suit within the time-limits discharges the party who breached the contract. Always consult a lawyer promptly in the case of a legal injury. We have seen the overlap of tort and contract in cases such as fraud, and statutes of limitations for tort are generally shorter than for contract. Further, some related areas of law, such as employment discrimination, have statutes of limitation that are numbered in days, not years. Do not wait, mate.

IMPOSSIBILITY

"Your honor, my client wanted to honor the contract. He just couldn't. *Honest*." This plea often echoes around courtrooms, as one party seeks discharge without fulfilling his contract obligations. Does the argument work? It depends. If performing a contract was truly impossible, a court will discharge the agreement. But if honoring the deal merely imposed a financial burden, the law will generally enforce the contract.

TRUE IMPOSSIBILITY (objective impossibility) - no one can do it

These cases are easy—and rare. **True impossibility means that something has happened making it utterly impossible to do what the promisor said he would do.** Francoise owns a vineyard that produces Beaujolais Nouveau wine. She agrees to ship 1,000 cases of her wine to Tyrone, a New York importer, as soon as this year's vintage is ready. Tyrone will pay $50 per case. But a fungus wipes out her entire vineyard. Francoise is discharged. It is theoretically impossible for Francoise to deliver wine from her vineyard, and she owes Tyrone nothing.

Meanwhile, though, Tyrone has a contract with Jackson, a retailer, to sell 1,000 cases of any Beaujolais Nouveau wine at $70 per case. Tyrone has no wine from Francoise, and the only other Beaujolais Nouveau available will cost him $85 per case. Instead of earning $20 per case, Tyrone will lose $15. Does this discharge Tyrone's contract with Jackson? No. It is possible for him to perform, just undesirable. He must fulfill his agreement.

True impossibility is generally limited to these three causes:

Example: Madonna

- *Destruction of the Subject Matter,* as happened with Francoise's vineyard.

- *Death of the Promisor in a Personal Services Contract.* When the promisor agrees personally to render a service that cannot be transferred to someone else, her death discharges the contract. Producer hires Josephine to write the lyrics for a new Broadway musical, but Josephine dies after writing only two words: "Act One." The contract was personal to Josephine and is now discharged. Neither Josephine's estate nor Producer has any obligation to the other. But notice that most contracts are not for personal services. Suppose that Tyrone, the wine importer, drowns in a bathtub filled with cheap gin. His contract to sell wine to Jackson is not discharged because anyone can deliver the required wine. Tyrone's estate remains liable on the deal with Jackson.

- *Illegality.* Charley, a Silicon Valley entrepreneur, wants to capitalize on his computer expertise. He contracts with Construction Co. to build a factory in Iran that will manufacture computers for sale in that country. Construction Co. fails to build the factory on time and Charley sues. Construction Co. defends by pointing out that the president of the United

Personal services contracts
Permit the promisee to make a subjective evaluations of the promisor's performance.

States has issued an executive order barring trade between the U. S. and Iran. Construction Co. wins; the executive order discharged the contract.

COMMERCIAL IMPRACTICABILITY AND FRUSTRATION OF PURPOSE

It is rare for contract performance to be truly impossible, but common for it to become a financial burden to one party. Suppose Bradshaw Steel in Pittsburgh agrees to deliver 1,000 tons of steel beams to Rice Construction in Saudi Arabia at a given price, but a week later the cost of raw ore increases 30 percent. A contract once lucrative to the manufacturer is suddenly a major liability. Does that change discharge Bradshaw? Absolutely not. Rice signed the deal *precisely to protect itself against price increases.* As we have seen, the primary purpose of contracts is to enable the parties to control their future.

Yet there may be times when a change in circumstances is so extreme that it would be unfair to enforce a deal. What if a strike made it impossible for Bradshaw to ship the steel to Saudi Arabia, and the only way to deliver would be by air, at five times the sea cost? Must Bradshaw fulfill its deal? What if war in the Middle East meant that any ships or planes delivering the goods might be fired upon? Other changes could make the contract undesirable for *Rice.* Suppose the builder wanted steel for a major public building in Riyadh, but the Saudi government decided not to go forward with the construction. The steel would then be worthless to Rice. Must the company still accept it?

None of these hypotheticals involves true impossibility. It is physically possible for Bradshaw to deliver the goods and for Rice to receive. But in some cases it may be so dangerous or costly or pointless to enforce a bargain that a court will discharge it instead. Courts use the related doctrines of commercial impracticability and frustration of purpose to decide when a change in circumstances should permit one side to escape its duties.

Commercial impracticability means some event has occurred that neither party anticipated and *fulfilling the contract would now be extraordinarily difficult and unfair to one party.* If a shipping strike forces Bradshaw to ship by air, the company will argue that neither side expected the strike and that Bradshaw should not suffer a fivefold increase in shipping cost. Bradshaw will probably win the argument.

(Really extreme)

Frustration of purpose means some event has occurred that neither party anticipated and *the contract now has no value for one party.* If Rice's building project is canceled, Rice will argue that the steel now is useless to the company. Frustration cases are hard to predict. Some states would agree with Rice, but others would hold that it was Rice's obligation to protect itself with a government guarantee that the project would be completed. Courts consider the following factors in deciding impracticability and frustration claims:

- *Mere financial difficulties will never suffice to discharge a contract.* Barbara and Michael Luber divorced, and Michael agreed to pay alimony. He stopped making payments and claimed that it was impracticable for him to do so, because he had hit hard times and simply did not have the money. The court dismissed his argument, noting that commercial impracticability requires some objective event that neither party anticipated, not merely the financial deterioration of one party.[8]

- *The event must have been truly unexpected.* Wayne Carpenter bought land from the state of Alaska, intending to farm it and agreeing to make monthly payments. The sales contract

---

[8]*Luber v. Luber*, 418 Pa. Super. 542, 614 A.2d 771, 1992 Pa. Super. LEXIS 3338 (Pa. Super. Ct. 1992).

stated that Alaska did not guarantee the land for agriculture or any other purpose. Carpenter struggled to farm the land but failed; as soon as the ground thawed, the water table rose too high for crops. Carpenter abandoned the land and stopped making payments. Alaska sued and won. The high court rejected Carpenter's claim of impracticability since the "event"—bad soil—was not unexpected. Alaska had warned that the land might prove unworkable, and Carpenter had no claim for commercial impracticability.[9]

- *If the promisor must use a different means to accomplish her task, at a greatly increased cost, she probably does have a valid claim of impracticability.* If a shipping strike forces Bradshaw to use a different means of delivery—say, air—and this multiplies its costs several times, the company is probably discharged. But a mere increase in the cost of raw materials, such as a 30 percent rise in the price of ore, will almost never discharge the promisor.

- *A force majeure* clause is significant but not necessarily dispositive. To protect themselves from unexpected events, companies sometimes include a *force majeure* clause, allowing cancellation of the agreement in case of extraordinary and unexpected events. A typical clause might permit the seller of goods to delay or cancel delivery in the event of "acts of God, fire, labor disputes, accidents or transportation difficulties." A court will always consider a *force majeure* clause, but may not enforce it if one party is trying to escape from routine financial problems.

- *The UCC permits discharge only for major, unforeseen disruptions.* **UCC Section 2-615** endorses commercial impracticability as a ground for discharge, but emphasizes that mere cost increases will not justify discharge, nor will simple inconvenience or financial loss.

CHAPTER CONCLUSION

Negotiate carefully. A casually written letter may imply a condition precedent that the author never intended. The term "personal satisfaction" should be defined so that both parties know whether one party may fire the other on a whim. Never assume that mere inconvenience or financial loss will discharge contractual duties.

EXAM REVIEW

1. **CONDITIONS** A condition is an event that must occur before a party becomes obligated. It may be stated expressly or implied, and no formal language is necessary to create one. (p. 376)

[9]*State v. Carpenter*, 869 P.2d 1181, 1994 Alaska LEXIS 23 (Alaska 1994).

EXAM Strategy

Question: Stephen Krogness, a real estate broker, agreed to act as an agent for Best Buy Co., which wanted to sell several of its stores. The contract provided that Best Buy would pay Krogness a commission of 2% for "a sale to any prospect submitted directly to Best Buy by Krogness." Krogness introduced Corporate Realty Capital (CRC) to Best Buy, and the parties negotiated but could not reach agreement. CRC then introduced Best Buy to BB Properties (BB). Best Buy sold several properties to BB for $46 million. CRC acted as the broker. Krogness sought a commission of $528,000. Is he entitled to it?

Strategy: This contract contains a conditional clause. What is it? What must occur before Best Buy is obligated to pay Krogness? Did that event happen? (See the "Result" at the end of this section.)

2. **SUBSTANTIAL PERFORMANCE** Strict performance, which requires one party to fulfill its duties perfectly, is unusual. In construction and service contracts, substantial performance is generally sufficient to entitle the promisor to the contract price, minus the cost of defects in the work. (p. 380)

3. **PERSONAL SATISFACTION** Personal satisfaction contracts are interpreted under an objective standard, requiring reasonable ground for dissatisfaction, unless the work involves personal judgment *and* the parties intended a subjective standard. (p. 382)

4. **GOOD FAITH** Good faith performance is required in all contracts. (p. 383)

5. **TIME OF THE ESSENCE** Time of the essence clauses result in strict enforcement of contract deadlines. (p. 385)

EXAM Strategy

Question: Colony Park Associates signed a contract to buy 44 acres of residential land from John Gall. The contract stated that closing would take place exactly one year later. The delay was to enable Colony Park to obtain building permits to develop condominiums. Colony Park worked diligently to obtain all permits, but delays in sewer permits forced Colony Park to notify Gall it could not close on the agreed date. Colony Park suggested a date exactly one month later. Gall refused the new date and declined to sell. Colony Park sued. Gall argued that since the parties specified a date, time was of the essence and Colony Park's failure to buy on time discharged Gall. Please rule.

Strategy: A time of the essence clause generally makes a contract date strictly enforceable. Was there one in this agreement? (See the "Result" at the end of this section.)

6. **MATERIAL BREACH** A material breach is the only kind that will discharge a contract; a trivial breach will not. (p. 386)

7. **IMPOSSIBILITY** True impossibility means that some event has made it impossible to perform an agreement. It is typically caused by destruction of the subject matter, the death of an essential promisor, or intervening illegality. (p. 388)

EXAM Strategy

Question: Omega Concrete had a gravel pit and factory. Access was difficult, so Omega contracted with Union Pacific Railroad (UP) for the right to use a private road that crossed UP property and tracks. The contract stated that use of the road was solely for Omega employees and that Omega would be responsible for closing a gate that UP planned to build where the private road joined a public highway. In fact, UP never constructed the gate; Omega had no authority to construct the gate. Mathew Rogers, an Omega employee, was killed by a train while using the private road. Rogers's family sued Omega, claiming that Omega failed to keep the gate closed as the contract required. Is Omega liable?

Strategy: True impossibility means that the promisor cannot do what he promised to do. Is this such a case? (See the "Result" at the end of this section.)

8. **COMMERCIAL IMPRACTICABILITY** Commercial impracticability means that some unexpected event has made it extraordinarily difficult and unfair for one party to perform its obligations. (p. 389)

9. **FRUSTRATION OF PURPOSE** Frustration of purpose may occur when an unexpected event renders a contract completely useless to one party. (p. 389)

1. Result: The conditional clause requires Best Buy to pay a commission for "a sale to any prospect submitted directly to Best Buy by Krogness." Krogness did not in fact introduce BB Properties to Best Buy. The condition has not occurred and Best Buy is under no obligation to pay.

5. Result: Merely including a date for performance does not make time of the essence. A party that considers a date critical must make that clear. This contract did not indicate that the closing date was vital to either party, so a short delay was reasonable. Gail was ordered to convey the land to Colony Park.

7. Result: There was no gate, and Omega had no right to build one. This is a case of true impossibility. Omega was not liable.

ADDITIONAL QUESTIONS

1. **ETHICS** Commercial Union Insurance Co. (CU) insured Redux, Ltd. The contract made CU liable for fire damage, but stated that the insurer would not pay for harm caused by criminal acts of any Redux employees. Fire destroyed Redux's property. CU claimed that the "criminal acts" clause was a condition precedent, but Redux asserted it was a condition subsequent. What difference does it make, and who is legally right? Does the insurance company's position raise any ethical issues? Who drafted the contract? How clear were its terms?

2. Evans built a house for Sandra Dyer, but the house had some problems. The garage ceiling was too low. Load-bearing beams in the "great room" cracked and appeared to be steadily weakening. The patio did not drain properly. Pipes froze. Evans wanted the money promised for the job, but Dyer refused to pay. Comment.

3. Stephen Muka owned U.S. Robotics. He hired his brother Chris to work in the company. His letter promised Chris $1 million worth of Robotics stock at the end of one year, "provided you work reasonably hard & smart at things in the next year." (We should all have such brothers.) Chris arrived at Robotics and worked the full year, but toward the end of the year Stephen died. His estate refused to give Chris the stock, claiming their agreement was a personal satisfaction contract and only Stephen could decide whether Chris had earned the reward. Comment.

4. Ken Ward was an Illinois farmer who worked land owned by his father-in-law, Frank Ruda. To finance his operation, he frequently borrowed money from Watseka First National Bank, paying back the loans with farming profits. But Ward fell deeper and deeper into debt and Watseka became concerned. When Ward sought additional loans, Watseka insisted that Ruda become a guarantor on all of the outstanding debt, and the father-in-law agreed. The new loans had an acceleration clause, permitting the bank to demand payment of the entire debt if it believed itself "insecure," that is, at risk of a default. Unfortunately, just as Ward's debts reached more than $120,000, Illinois suffered a severe drought, and Ward's crops failed. Watseka asked Ruda to sell some of the land he owned to pay back part of the indebtedness. Ruda reluctantly agreed but never did so. Meanwhile, Ward decreased his payments to the bank because of the terrible crop. Watseka then "accelerated" the loan, demanding that Ruda pay off the entire debt. Ruda defended by claiming that Watseka's acceleration at such a difficult time was bad faith. Who won?

5. Loehmann's clothing stores, a nationwide chain with headquarters in New York, was the anchor tenant in the Lincoln View Plaza Shopping Center in Phoenix, Arizona, with a 20-year lease from the landlord, Foundation Development, beginning in 1978. Loehmann's was obligated to pay rent the first of every month and to pay common area charges four times a year. The lease stated that if Loehmann's failed to pay on time, Foundation could send a notice of default, and that if the store failed to pay all money due within 10 days, Foundation could evict. On February 23, 1987, Foundation sent to Loehmann's the common area charges for the quarter ending January 31, 1987. The balance due was $3,500. Loehmann's believed the bill was in error and sent an inquiry on March 18, 1987. On April 10, 1987, Foundation insisted on payment of the full amount within 10 days. Foundation sent the letter to the Loehmann's store in Phoenix. On April 13, 1987, the Loehmann's store received the bill and, since it was not responsible for payments, forwarded it to the New York office. Because the

company had moved offices in New York, a Loehmann's officer did not see the bill until April 20. Loehmann's issued a check for the full amount on April 24 and mailed it the following day. On April 28 Foundation sued to evict; on April 29 the company received Loehmann's check. Please rule.

6. ***CPA QUESTION*** Nagel and Fields entered into a contract in which Nagel was obligated to deliver certain goods by September 10. On September 3, Nagel told Fields that he had no intention of delivering the goods. Prior to September 10, Fields may successfully sue Nagel under the doctrine of:

   (a) Promissory estoppel

   (b) Accord and satisfaction

   (c) Anticipatory breach

   (d) Substantial performance

7. ***YOU BE THE JUDGE*** WRITING PROBLEM Kuhn Farm Machinery, a European company, signed an agreement with Scottsdale Plaza Resort, of Arizona, to use the resort for its North American dealers' convention during March 1991. Kuhn agreed to rent 190 guest rooms and spend several thousand dollars on food and beverages. Kuhn invited its top 200 independent dealers from the United States and Canada and about 25 of its own employees from the United States, Europe, and Australia, although it never mentioned those plans to Scottsdale.

   On August 2, 1990, Iraq invaded Kuwait and on January 16, 1991, the United States and allied forces were at war with Iraq. Saddam Hussein and other Iraqi leaders threatened terrorist acts against the United States and its allies. Kuhn became concerned about the safety of those traveling to Arizona, especially its European employees. By mid-February, 11 of the top 50 dealers with expense-paid trips had either canceled their plans to attend or failed to sign up. Kuhn postponed the convention. The resort sued. The trial court discharged the contract under the doctrines of commercial impracticability and frustration of purpose. The resort appealed. Did commercial impracticability or frustration of purpose discharge the contract? **Argument for Scottsdale Plaza Resort:** The resort had no way of knowing that Kuhn anticipated bringing executives from Europe, and even less reason to expect that if anything interfered with their travel, the entire convention would become pointless. Most of the dealers could have attended the convention, and the resort stood ready to serve them. **Argument for Kuhn:** The parties never anticipated the threat of terrorism. Kuhn wanted this convention so that its European executives, among others, could meet top North American dealers. That is now impossible. No company would risk employee lives for a meeting. As a result, the contract has no value at all to Kuhn, and its obligations should be discharged by law.

8. Krug International, an Ohio corporation, had a contract with Iraqi Airways to build aeromedical equipment for training pilots. Krug then contracted for Power Engineering, an Iowa corporation, to build the specialized gearbox to be used in the training equipment, for $150,000. Power did not know that Krug planned to resell the gearbox to Iraqi Airways. When Power had almost completed the gearbox, the Gulf War broke out and the United Nations declared an embargo on all shipments to Iraq. Krug notified Power that it no longer wanted the gearbox. Power sued. Please rule.

9. ***ROLE REVERSAL*** Write a multiple-choice question focusing on a contractor's claim to substantial performance. The answers should contain dollar amounts that the contractor could possibly recover, from zero to the full value of the contract.

INTERNET RESEARCH PROBLEM

Using the Internet, find a contract that contains a "commercial impracticability" clause and/or a "frustration of purpose" clause. They often go together. What is the subject of the contract generally? What did the drafters of the contract hope to achieve with the clause you have located? In your opinion, will a court enforce the clause? Why or why not? If the clause is valid, will it accomplish the purpose you have described?

You can find further practice problems at www.cengagebrain.com. See the preface of this book for website access details.

17

REMEDIES

> **Ben slams his cell phone down, turns into his driveway—and notices that the back door is open. Did he leave it that way? No. The burglar did.**

Ben is the general manager of the Starz, a professional football team. Driving home in his rusty, eight-year-old truck, he is in a sour humor. Spencer, the team's best running back, under contract to play for one more year at $2.5 million, has announced he is leaving the team to act in the new sitcom *Cutback*. Ben wonders whether he can stop Spencer from leaving the team. Even if it is possible, would it be worthwhile to make a disgruntled, out-of-condition athlete carry (and fumble) the ball? If Spencer leaves, it will cost at least $5 million to hire a runner with equal speed and power.

The G.M.'s phone rings. Louise, a dealer in rare autos, has bad news in her voice.

"I hate to tell you, Ben, but the Ferrari deal has fallen through."

"What are you talking about? We both signed! That's a binding contract!" A seller in Florida had agreed in writing to sell Ben a 1955 Ferrari 375 America Speciale for $600,000.

"*I* know it's true, and *you* know it," Louise murmurs soothingly. "But the seller has decided the car is too rare to part with."

Ben slams his cell phone down, turns into his driveway—and notices that the back door is open. Did he leave it that way? No. The burglar did. Ben has lost about $100,000 worth of jewelry, clothing, and sports memorabilia. Why didn't the alarm sound? When he demands an explanation from Alarmist, the quality assurance representative assures Ben that he will receive the full compensation due under his contract—$600. Later that night, Ben will have a long talk with his lawyer about breached contracts and remedies.

BREACHING THE CONTRACT

Someone breaches a contract when he fails to perform a duty without a valid excuse. Spencer is legally committed to play for the Starz for one more year, and is clearly breaching his contract when he informs the team that in the future he will be playing for laughs. But what can the Starz do about the runner's breach? In other words, what is the team's *remedy?* **A remedy is the method a court uses to compensate an injured party.**

Should a court stop Spencer from performing in his new sitcom? Force him to carry the pigskin for the Starz? **An order forcing someone to do something, or refrain from doing something, is an injunction.** Courts frequently grant injunctions to an employer, blocking an employee from *leaving* to work elsewhere. However, courts almost never use an injunction to force an employee to *complete* a contract with his employer, because that would force two antagonistic parties to work together. In other words, Ben can probably stop Spencer from working in television, but no court will order the running back to suit up for the Starz.

Courts also award **expectation damages**, meaning the money required to put one party in the position she would have been in had the other side performed the contract. If the Starz are forced to hire another running back for double the money they expected to pay Spencer, the team will probably recover the difference between the two players' salaries.

The Ferrari seller has breached his deal with Ben. What is his remedy? Ben does not want money damages; he wants that lovely red car. In cases of rare property, courts often award **specific performance**, forcing both parties to complete the deal. Ben should get his car.

Finally, the alarm company is trying to *insist* upon a remedy—a very limited one, which will leave Ben largely uncompensated for the burglary. Alarmist is relying on a liquidated damages clause, meaning a provision in the contract that declares in advance what one party will receive if the other side breaches. Courts sometimes—but not always—enforce these clauses. As we see later, Alarmist's liquidated clause may be too harsh and unenforceable.

How to help an injured party, without unfairly harming the other person, is the focus of remedies. Courts have struggled with remedies for centuries, but we will master the subject in one chapter. The questions and issues created by Ben's Bad Day are typical remedy problems.

> **ETHICS** Though a court may have several alternative remedies available, it is important to note that most have one thing in common: the focus is on compensating the injured party, rather than punishing the party in breach. A court must decide whether to prevent Spencer from leaving the gridiron for the television studio, but it will not consider sending fining or jailing him.
>
> Critics argue that someone who willfully breaches a contract should pay a penalty. The Ferrari seller knows he is obligated to part with his car, but tries to keep it anyway. Spencer blithely ignores his obligations to the team. Should a remedy reflect morality? In this chapter we will see very few instances in which a court punishes unethical conduct. From the Chapter 2 ethics checklist: Does this approach violate important values? ◆

IDENTIFYING THE "INTEREST" TO BE PROTECTED

The first step that a court takes in choosing a remedy is to decide what interest it is trying to protect. An **interest** is a legal right in something. Someone can have an interest in property, for example, by owning it, or renting it to a tenant, or lending money so someone else may buy it. He can have an interest in a *contract* if the agreement gives him some benefit. There are four principal contract interests that a court may seek to protect:

(Damages may be subjective or objective)

Injunction
A court order that requires someone to do something or refrain from doing something.
(2 kinds of injunctions)

Expectation damages
The money required to put one party in the position she would have been in had the other side performed the contract.

Specific performance
Forces both parties to complete the deal.

Interest
A legal right in something.

- *Expectation Interest.* This refers to what the injured party reasonably thought she would get from the contract. The goal is to put her in the position she would have been in if both parties had fully performed their obligations.

- *Reliance Interest.* The injured party may be unable to demonstrate expectation damages, perhaps because it is unclear he would have profited. But he may still prove that he *expended money* in reliance on the agreement and that in fairness he should receive compensation.

- *Restitution Interest.* The injured party may be unable to show an expectation interest or reliance. But perhaps she has conferred a *benefit* on the other party. Here, the objective is to restore to the injured party the benefit she has provided.

- *Equitable Interest.* In some cases, money damages will not suffice to help the injured party. Something more is needed, such as an order to transfer property to the injured party (specific performance) or an order forcing one party to stop doing something (an injunction).

In this chapter, we look at all four interests.

EXPECTATION INTEREST

This is the most common remedy that the law provides for a party injured by a breach of contract. **The expectation interest is designed to put the injured party in the position she would have been in had both sides fully performed their obligations.** A court tries to give the injured party the money she would have made from the contract. If accurately computed, this should take into account all the gains she reasonably expected and all the expenses and losses she would have incurred. The injured party should not end up better off than she would have been under the agreement, nor should she suffer serious loss.

William Colby was a former director of the CIA. He wanted to write a book about his 15 years in Vietnam. He paid James McCarger $5,000 for help in writing an early draft and promised McCarger another $5,000 if the book was published. Then he hired Alexander Burnham to co-write the book. Colby's agent secured a contract with Contemporary Books, which included a $100,000 advance. But Burnham was hopelessly late with the manuscript and Colby missed his publication date. Colby fired Burnham and finished the book without him. Contemporary published *Lost Victory* several years late, and the book flopped, earning no significant revenue. Because the book was so late, Contemporary paid Colby a total of only $17,000. Colby sued Burnham for his lost expectation interest. The court awarded him $23,000, calculated as follows:

	$100,000	advance, the only money Colby was promised
	−10,000	agent's fee
	= 90,000	Fee for the two authors, combined
divided by 2	= 45,000	Colby's fee
	− 5,000	owed to McCarger under the earlier agreement
	= 40,000	Colby's expectation interest
	− 17,000	Fee Colby received from Contemporary
	= 23,000	Colby's expectation damages, that is, the amount he would have received had Burnham finished on time

The *Colby* case[1] presented an easy calculation of damages. Other contracts are complex. Courts typically divide the expectation damages into three parts: (1) compensatory (or "direct") damages, which represent harm that flowed directly from the contract's breach; (2) consequential (or "special") damages, which represent harm caused by the injured party's unique situation; and (3) incidental damages, which are minor costs such as storing or returning defective goods, advertising for alternative goods, and so forth. The first two, compensatory and consequential, are the important ones.

COMPENSATORY DAMAGES

Compensatory damages are the most common monetary awards for the expectation interest. Courts also refer to these as "direct damages." **Compensatory damages are those that flow directly from the contract.** In other words, these are the damages that inevitably result from the breach. Suppose Ace Productions hires Reina to star in its new movie, *Inside Straight*. Ace promises Reina $3 million, providing she shows up June 1 and works until the film is finished. But in late May, Joker Entertainment offers Reina $6 million to star in its new feature, and on June 1 Reina informs Ace that she will not appear. Reina has breached her contract, and Ace should recover compensatory damages.

What are the damages that flow directly from the contract? Ace obviously has to replace Reina. If Ace hires Kween as its star and pays her a fee of $4 million, Ace is entitled to the difference between what it expected to pay ($3 million) and what the breach forced it to pay ($4 million), or $1 million in compensatory damages. Suppose the rest of the cast and crew are idle for two weeks because of the delay in hiring a substitute, and the lost time costs the producers an extra $2.5 million. Reina is also liable for those expenses. Both the new actress and the delay are inevitable.

Compensatory damages
Damages that flow directly from the contract.

Reasonable Certainty

The injured party must prove the breach of contract caused damages that can be quantified with reasonable certainty. What if *Inside Straight*, now starring Kween, bombs at the box office. Ace proves that each of Reina's last three movies grossed over $60 million, but *Inside Straight* grossed only $28 million. Is Reina liable for the lost profits? No. Ace cannot prove that it was Reina's absence that caused the film to fare poorly. The script may have been mediocre, or Kween's co-stars dull, or the publicity efforts inadequate. Ace *hoped* to gross over $60 million, but mere hopes create "speculative damages," worth zero. Because Ace cannot demonstrate a quantifiable box office loss directly attributable to Reina, it will get nothing for the disappointing ticket sales.

CONSEQUENTIAL DAMAGES

In addition to compensatory damages, the injured party may seek consequential damages or, as they are also known, "special damages." **Consequential damages** are those resulting from the unique circumstances of *this injured party*. The rule concerning this remedy comes from a famous 1854 case, *Hadley v. Baxendale*, which all American law students read. Now it is your turn.

Consequential damages
Foreseeable losses that are not directly related to the subject matter of a contract.

---

[1]*Colby v. Burnham*, 31 Conn. App. 707, 627 A.2d 457, 1993 Conn. App LEXIS 299 (Conn. App. Ct. 1993).

HADLEY V. BAXENDALE

9 EX. 341, 156 ENG. REP. 145
COURT OF EXCHEQUER, 1854

CASE SUMMARY

Facts: The Hadleys operated a flour mill in Gloucester. The crankshaft broke, causing the mill to grind to a halt. The Hadleys employed Baxendale to cart the damaged part to a foundry in Greenwich, where a new one could be manufactured. Baxendale promised to make the delivery in one day, but he was late transporting the shaft, and as a result, the Hadleys' mill was shut for five extra days. They sued, and the jury awarded damages based in part on their lost profits. Baxendale appealed.

Issue: *Should the defendant be liable for profits lost because of his delay in delivering the shaft?*

Decision: Reversed. The defendant is not liable for lost profits.

Reasoning: When one side breaches a contract, the other party's damages should be those that arise inevitably from the breach or those that both parties reasonably anticipated when they made the agreement. If the contract involves special circumstances and the plaintiff tells the defendant about them when they make the deal, then the defendant is liable for all injuries. On the other hand, if the plaintiff never informed the defendant about the unique situation, then the defendant should be liable only for harm that might occur in the normal course of events.

The Hadleys told Baxendale only that the article to be carried was a broken shaft from their mill. How could Baxendale have realized that a delay in delivery would prevent the mill from operating? He might have assumed, very reasonably, that the Hadleys owned a second shaft and were sending this one for repairs while the mill ground on. It would be unfair to presume that Baxendale realized that delay would halt the mill. The case should be retried, and the jury may not consider the Hadleys' lost profits.

The rule from *Hadley v. Baxendale* has been unchanged ever since: **the injured party may recover consequential damages only if the breaching party should have foreseen them when the two sides formed the contract**.

Let us return briefly to *Inside Straight*. Suppose that, long before shooting began, Ace had sold the film's soundtrack rights to Spinem Sound for $2 million. Spinem believed it would make a profit only if Reina appeared in the film, so it demanded the right to discharge the agreement if Reina dropped out. When Reina quit, Spinem terminated the contract. Now, when Ace sues Reina, it will also seek $2 million in consequential damages for the lost music revenue. If Reina knew about Ace's contract with Spinem when she signed to do the film, she is liable for $2 million. If she never realized she was an essential part of the music contract, she owes nothing for the lost profits.

Injured plaintiffs often try to recover lost profits, which courts generally award if they can be quantified. The plaintiff need not prove his damages with mathematical precision, but must provide enough information so that the fact finder can reasonably estimate a fair sum for damages. In the following case, the plaintiffs lost not only profits—but their entire business. Can they recover for harm that is so extensive? You decide.

YOU *be the* JUDGE

BI-ECONOMY MARKET, INC. V.
HARLEYSVILLE INS. CO. OF NEW YORK
2008 WL 423451
New York Court of Appeals, 2008

Facts: Bi-Economy Market was a family-owned meat market in Rochester, NY. The company was insured by Harleysville Insurance. The "Deluxe Business Owner's" policy provided replacement cost for damage to buildings and inventory. Coverage also included "business interruption insurance" for one year, meaning the loss of pretax profit plus normal operating expenses, including payroll.

The company suffered a disastrous fire, which destroyed its building and all inventory. Bi-Economy immediately filed a claim with Harleysville but the insurer responded slowly. Harleysville eventually offered a settlement of $163,000. A year later, an arbitrator awarded the Market $407,000. During that year, Harleysville paid for seven months of lost income, but declined to pay more. The company never recovered or reopened.

Bi-Economy sued, claiming that Harleysville's slow, inadequate payments destroyed the company. The company also sought consequential damages for the permanent destruction of its business. Harleysville claimed that it was only responsible for damages specified in the contract: the building, inventory, and lost income. The trial court granted summary judgment for Harleysville. The appellate court affirmed, claiming that when they entered into the contract, the parties did not contemplate damages for termination of the business. Bi-Economy appealed to the state's highest court.

You Be the Judge: Is Bi-Economy entitled to consequential damages for the destruction of its business?

Argument for Bi-Economy: Bi-Economy is a small, family business. We paid for business interruption insurance for an obvious reason: in the event of a disaster, we lacked the resources to keep going while buildings were constructed and inventory purchased. We knew that in such a calamity, we would need prompt reimbursement—compensation covering the immediate damage and our on-going lost income. Why else would we pay the premiums?

At the time we entered into the contract, Harleysville could easily foresee that if it responded slowly, with insufficient payments, we could not survive. They knew that is what we wanted to avoid—and it is just what happened. The insurer's bad faith offer of a low figure, and its payment of only seven months' lost income, ruined a fine family business. When the insurance company agreed to business interruption coverage, it was declaring that it would act fast and fairly to sustain a small firm in crisis. The insurer should now pay for the full harm it has wrought.

Argument for Harleysville: We contracted to insure the Market for three losses: its building, inventory, and lost income. After the fire, we performed a reasonable, careful evaluation and made an offer we considered fair. An arbitrator later awarded Bi-Market additional money, which we paid. However it is absurd to suggest that in addition to that, we are liable for an open-ended commitment for permanent destruction of the business.

Consequential damages are appropriate in cases where a plaintiff suffers a loss that was not covered in the contract. In this case, though, the parties bargained over exactly what Harleysville would pay in the event of a major fire. If the insurer has underpaid for lost income, let the court award a fair sum. However, the parties never contemplated an additional, enormous payment for cessation of the business. There is almost no limit as to what that obligation could be. If Bi-Market was concerned that a fire might put the company permanently out of business, it should have said so at the time of negotiating for insurance. The premium would have been dramatically higher.

Neither Bi-Market nor Harleysville ever imagined such an open-ended insurance obligation, and the insurer should not pay an extra cent.

INCIDENTAL DAMAGES

Incidental damages

Relatively minor costs that the injured party suffers when responding to the breach.

Incidental damages are the relatively minor costs that the injured party suffers when responding to the breach. When Reina, the actress, breaches the film contract, the producers may have to leave the set and fly back to Los Angeles to hire a new actress. The travel cost is an incidental damage. In another setting, suppose that Maud, a manufacturer, has produced 5,000 pairs of running shoes for Foot The Bill, a retail chain, but Foot The Bill breaches the agreement and refuses to accept the goods. Maud will have to store the shoes and advertise for alternate buyers. The storage and advertising costs are incidental expenses, and Maud will recover them.

SALE OF GOODS

Under the Uniform Commercial Code (UCC), remedies for breach of contract in the sale of goods are similar to the general rules discussed throughout this chapter. UCC Sections 2-703 through 2-715 govern the remedies available to buyers and sellers.[2]

Seller's Remedies

If a buyer breaches a sale of goods contract, the seller generally has at least two remedies. She may resell the goods elsewhere. If she acts in good faith, she will be awarded **the difference between the original contract price and the price she was able to obtain in the open market**. Assume that Maud, the manufacturer, had a contract to sell her shoes to Foot The Bill for $55 per pair and Foot The Bill's breach forces her to sell them on the open market, where she gets only $48 per pair. Maud will win $7 per pair times 5,000 pairs, or $35,000, from Foot The Bill.

Alternatively, the buyer may choose not to resell and settle for the difference between the contract price and the market value of the goods. Maud, in other words, may choose to keep the shoes. If she can prove that their market value is $48 per pair, for example, by showing what other retailers would have paid her for them, she will still get her $7 each, representing the difference between what the contract promised her and what the market would support. In either case, the money represents compensatory damages. Maud is also entitled to incidental damages, such as the storage and advertising expenses described above. But there is one significant difference under the UCC: **Most courts hold that the seller of goods is *not* entitled to consequential damages**. Suppose Maud hired two extra workers to inspect, pack, and ship the shoes for Foot The Bill. Those are consequential damages, but Maud will not recover them because she is the seller and the contract is for the sale of goods.

Buyer's Remedies

The buyer's remedies under the Code are similar to those we have already considered. She typically has two options. First, the buyer can "cover" by purchasing substitute goods. To **cover** means to make a good faith purchase of goods similar to those in the contract. The buyer may then obtain **the difference between the original contract price and her cover price**. Alternatively, if the buyer chooses not to cover, she is entitled to the difference between the original contract price and the market value of the goods.

Cover

To make a good faith purchase of goods similar to those in the contract.

Suppose Mary has contracted to buy 1,000 six-foot Christmas trees at $25 per tree from Elmo. The market suddenly rises, and in the spirit of the season, Elmo breaches his deal and sells the trees elsewhere. If Mary makes a good faith effort to cover but is forced to pay $40 per tree, she may recover the difference from Elmo, meaning $15 per tree times 1,000 trees, or

---

[2]We discuss these remedies in greater detail in Chapter 21, on commercial transactions.

$15,000. Similarly, if she chooses not to cover but can prove that $40 is now the market value of the trees, she is entitled to her $15 per tree.

Under the UCC, **the buyer *is* entitled to consequential damages provided that the seller could reasonably have foreseen them.** If Mary tells Elmo, when they sign their deal, that she has a dozen contracts to resell the trees for an average price of $50 per tree, she may recover $25 per tree, representing the difference between her contract price with Elmo and the value of the tree *to her*, based on her other contracts.[3] If she failed to inform Elmo of the other contracts, she would not receive any money based on them. The buyer is also entitled to whatever incidental damages may have accrued.

EXAM *Strategy*

Question: Chloe is a fashion designer. Her recent collection of silk-velvet evening gowns was gobbled up by high-end retailers, who clamor for more. Chloe needs 300 yards of the same fabric, by August 15. Mill House, which has supplied fabric to Chloe for many years, agrees to sell her 300 yards at $100 per yard, delivered on August 15. The market value of the fabric is $125, but Mill House gives Chloe a break because she is a major customer.

Chloe contracts with Barney's and Neiman Marcus to sell a total of 50 dresses, at an *additional* profit to Chloe of $800 per dress. On August 15, Mill House delivers defective fabric. Chloe cannot make her dresses in time, and the retailers cancel their orders. Chloe sues Mill House and wins—but what are her damages?

Strategy: To determine damages, first ask whether the contract is governed by the common law or the UCC. This agreement concerns goods, so the Code applies. The UCC permits a buyer to recover damages for the difference between the contract price and the market value of the goods. The Code also allows consequential damages if the seller could have foreseen them. Apply those standards.

Result: Because Chloe's contract enabled her to save $25 per yard for 300 yards, she is entitled to $7,500. Chloe has also lost profits of $40,000. Mill House could easily have foreseen those losses, because the supplier knew that Chloe was a designer who fabricated and sold dresses. Chloe is entitled to $47,500.

We turn now to cases where the injured party cannot prove expectation damages.

RELIANCE INTEREST

George plans to manufacture and sell silk scarves during the holiday season. In the summer, he contracts with Cecily, the owner of a shopping mall, to rent a high-visibility stall for $100 per day. George then buys hundreds of yards of costly silk and gets to work cutting and sewing. But in September, Cecily refuses to honor the contract. George sues and easily proves Cecily breached a valid contract. But what is his remedy?

---

[3]As we discuss in the section on mitigation, later in the chapter, Mary will get only her consequential damages if she attempts to cover.

George cannot establish an expectation interest in his scarf business. He *hoped* to sell each scarf for a $40 gross profit. He *planned* on making $2,000 per day. But how much would he actually have earned? Enough to retire on? Enough to buy a salami sandwich for lunch? He has no way of proving his profits, and a court cannot give him his expectation interest. Instead, George will ask for *reliance damages*. The **reliance interest** is designed to put the injured party in the position he would have been in had the parties never entered into a contract. This remedy focuses on the time and money the injured party spent performing his part of the agreement.

George should be able to recover reliance damages from Cecily. Assuming he is unable to sell the scarves to a retail store, which is probable since retailers will have made purchases long ago, George should be able to recover the cost of the silk fabric he bought and perhaps something for the hours of labor he spent cutting and sewing. But reliance damages can be difficult to win because *they are harder to quantify*. Courts prefer to compute damages using the numbers provided in a contract. If a contract states a price of $25 per Christmas tree and one party breaches, the arithmetic is easy. Judges become uncomfortable when asked to base damages on vague calculations. How much was George's time worth in making the scarves? How good was his work? How likely were the scarves to sell? If George has a track record in the industry, he will be able to show a market price for his services. Without such a record, his reliance claim becomes a tough battle.

Reliance interest

Puts the injured party in the position he would have been in had the parties never entered into a contract.

RELIANCE DAMAGES AND PROMISSORY ESTOPPEL

In several earlier chapters of this unit, we have seen that a plaintiff may sometimes recover damages based on promissory estoppel even when there is no valid contract. The plaintiff must show that the defendant made a promise knowing that the plaintiff would likely rely on it, that the plaintiff did rely, and that the only way to avoid injustice is to enforce the promise. **In promissory estoppel cases, a court will generally award only** *reliance damages.* It would be unfair to give expectation damages for the full benefit of the bargain when, legally, there has been no bargain.

In the following case, the victorious plaintiff demonstrates how unreliable reliance damages are, and how winning can be hard to distinguish from losing.

TOSCANO V. GREENE MUSIC

124 CA. APP. 4TH 685, 21 CA.RPTR.3d 732
COURT OF APPEAL OF CALIFORNIA, 2004

CASE SUMMARY

Facts: Joseph Toscano was the general manager of Fields Pianos (Fields) in Santa Ana, California. He was unhappy with his job and decided to seek other employment. Toscano contacted Michael Greene, who owned similar stores. In July, Greene offered Toscano a sales management job, starting September 1. Relying on that offer, Toscano resigned from Fields on August 1. However, in mid-August, Greene withdrew his employment offer. Toscano later found lower-paying jobs in other cities.

Toscano sued Greene for breach of contract and promissory estoppel. Greene argued that Toscano was not entitled to any expectation damages because his employment with Greene would have been at will, meaning he could lose the job at any time. Greene also urged that because Toscano was an at-will employee at Fields, he could recover at most one month's lost wage.

The trial court ruled that Toscano was entitled to reliance damages for all lost wages at Fields, starting from the day he resigned, going forward until his anticipated retirement in 2017. Toscano's expert accountant calculated his past losses (until the time of trial) at $119,061, and his future lost earnings at $417,772. The trial court awarded Toscano $536,833, and Greene appealed.

Issue: *Was Toscano entitled to reliance damages?*

Decision: Yes, Toscano was entitled to reliance damages, but only as recalculated after a new trial.

Reasoning: Toscano gave up his job with Fields, relying on Greene's promise of employment, but was then denied his new position. Toscano makes a claim of promissory estoppel. Because this is an equitable doctrine, a court applying it must make a particular effort to do what is right and just.

A plaintiff such as Toscano, lured away by a job promise that goes unfulfilled, should be allowed to recover the wages he lost at his former employment. That is basic fairness. Further, Toscano should not be denied compensation merely because he was an at-will employee at his former job. Any other holding contradicts the basic equitable principles mentioned. However, when the lower court awarded Toscano lost *future* earnings from the time of trial to his retirement, it went too far.

Toscano's expert on damages was Roberta Spoon. In calculating Toscano's lost future wages, she assumed that without the job offer from Greene, he would have remained with Fields until he retired. She made this assumption based on the fact that, in the past, Toscano had never changed jobs for any reason except an increase in pay. Her assumption, however, misses the basic point of at-will employment. Whether Toscano intended to remain with Fields until retirement is irrelevant. What counts is whether the Fields company itself wanted Toscano to remain. Because he was an at-will employee, Fields could have terminated him any time it wanted, for virtually any reason.

For an expert witness to assume that Toscano would remain at the same job for nearly a decade and a half was sheer speculation. Toscano should have presented testimony from Jerry Goldman, Toscano's boss at Fields, or some other evidence indicating that he would have been permitted to remain at the company until he retired.

The lower court award of past losses, until the time of trial, is affirmed. The award of lost future earnings is vacated, and the case is remanded for a new trial on those damages only. The judgment is otherwise affirmed.

Notice that the court never even mentions that Toscano acted in good faith, relying on Greene's promise, while the latter offered no excuse for suddenly withdrawing his offer. Is it fair to permit Greene to escape all liability? This court, like most, simply will not award significant damages where there is no contract permitting a clear calculation of losses.

The judges, though, have not entirely closed the door on Toscano. What is the purpose of the remand? What might Toscano demonstrate on remand? What practical difficulties will he encounter?

LAW AND EQUITY

Expectation and reliance interests are generally considered **legal remedies**.[4] The other interests we will examine are equitable remedies. The difference is largely historical but still may affect a plaintiff's ability to obtain help from a court. As we saw in the textbook's introductory chapter, the common law developed in England, very gradually, over many centuries. English *law* courts gave money damages to the plaintiff, so money damages became known as "legal remedies."

---

[4]As the *Toscano* case demonstrates, the terminology is flexible. In a promissory estoppel case, most courts would call reliance damages an equitable remedy.

In some cases, an English law court might refuse to hear a case, claiming that it lacked jurisdiction. Or the injured plaintiff might want more than mere money damages. For example, a plaintiff who had a contract to buy land might want the property itself, not money damages. When a law court would not or could not help, a plaintiff often took his case to the Chancellor in London. There was no jury in a Chancery case, but the Chancellor did have broader, more flexible powers than the law judges. The Chancellor's powers came to be known as **equitable remedies**. In the United States today, trial courts of general jurisdiction have the power to grant legal and equitable remedies. We now turn to an equitable remedy called restitution.

RESTITUTION INTEREST

> He did move onto the land and did receive $76,000 from the government for a year's worth of inactivity. (Nice work if you can get it.)

Restitution interest
Is designed to return to the injured party a benefit he has conferred on the other party.

Lillian and Harold Toews signed a contract to sell 1,500 acres of Idaho farmland to Elmer Funk. He was to take possession immediately, but would not receive the deed until he finished paying for the property, in 10 years. This arrangement enabled him to enroll in a government program that would pay him "set-asides" for *not* farming. Funk kept most aspects of his agreement. He did move onto the land and did receive $76,000 from the government for a year's worth of inactivity. (Nice work if you can get it.) The only part of the bargain Funk did not keep was his promise to pay. The Toewses sued. Funk had clearly breached the deal. But what remedy?

The Toewses still owned the land, so they did not need it reconveyed. Funk had no money to pay for the farm, so the Toewses would never get their expectation interest. And the Toewses had expended almost no money based on the deal, so they had no reliance interest. What they had done, though, was to *confer a benefit* on Funk. They had enabled him to obtain $76,000 in government money. The Toewses wanted a return of the benefit they had conferred on Funk, a remedy called restitution. The **restitution interest** is designed to return to the injured party a benefit that he has conferred on the other party, which it would be unjust to leave with that person. The Toewses argued that they had bestowed a $76,000 benefit on Funk and that it made absolutely no sense for him to keep it. The Idaho Court of Appeals agreed. It ruled that the Toewses had a restitutionary interest in the government set-aside money and ordered Funk to pay the money to the Toewses.[5]

Restitution is awarded in two types of cases. First, the law allows restitution when the parties have reached a contract and one of them breaches, as Funk did. In such cases, a court may choose restitution because no other remedy is available or because no other remedy would be as fair. Second, courts may award restitution in cases of quasi-contract, which we examined in earlier chapters. In quasi-contract cases, the parties never made a contract but one side did benefit the other. We consider each kind of restitution interest in turn.

RESTITUTION IN CASES OF A VALID CONTRACT

Rescission
To "undo" a contract and put the parties where they were before they made the agreement.

Restitution is a common remedy in contracts involving fraud, misrepresentation, mistake, and duress. In these cases, restitution often goes hand-in-hand with **rescission**, which means to "undo" a contract and put the parties where they were before they made the agreement.

---

[5]*Toews v. Funk*, 129 Idaho 316, 924 P.2d 217, 1994 Idaho App. LEXIS 75 (Idaho Ct. App. 1994).

Courtney sells her favorite sculpture to Adam for $95,000, both parties believing the work to be a valuable original by Barbara Hepworth. Two months later, Adam learns that the sculpture is a mere copy, worth very little. A court will permit Adam to rescind the contract on the ground of mutual mistake. At the same time, Adam is entitled to restitution of the purchase price. Courtney gets the worthless carving and Adam receives his money back.

The following case involved fraud in the sale of a valuable property.

PUTNAM CONSTRUCTION & REALTY CO. v. BYRD

632 So.2d 961, 1992 ALA. LEXIS 1289
SUPREME COURT OF ALABAMA, 1992

CASE SUMMARY

Facts: Putnam Construction & Realty Co. owned the University Square Business Center (USBC), an office complex with several major tenants, including McDonnell-Douglas, TRW, and the Army Corps of Engineers. William Byrd and some partners (the "buyers") entered into a contract to buy USBC for slightly over $17 million. They financed the purchase with a $16.2 million loan from Northwestern Mutual Life. Northwestern's loan was secured with a mortgage on the USBC, meaning that if the borrowers failed to repay the loan, Northwestern would own the property. Shortly after the sale closed, Byrd learned that several of the major tenants were leaving. The buyers sued Putnam, seeking rescission of the contract and restitution of their money. The trial court found that Putnam (the "sellers") had committed fraud. It rescinded the sales contract, returning the property to the sellers. It ordered the sellers to assume full liability for the mortgage. The trial court did not, however, order restitution of the buyers' expenses, such as the closing costs. The sellers appealed—which proved to be a big mistake.

Issue: *Were the buyers entitled to rescission and/or restitution?*

Decision: The buyers were entitled to both rescission and restitution.

Reasoning: The sellers knew that the Corps of Engineers planned to build its own facility and vacate the USBC, yet they told the buyers that the Corps would be staying. They also knew that McDonnell-Douglas was leaving but failed to inform the buyers. The sellers clearly committed fraud.

Money damages would be speculative and would leave the buyers saddled with a property that operates at a steadily increasing loss. The fairest way to compensate them is by rescinding the contract, and the trial court's ruling on that issue is affirmed. However, the buyers also incurred substantial out-of-pocket expenses because of the sellers' fraud. To compensate them for these losses, they are entitled to receive restitution damages of $483,006.75 in closing costs, $121,000 in mortgage interest payments, and $500,000 in nonrefundable fees paid to Northwestern to obtain the loan. The case is remanded for the trial court to impose all of these remedies.

ETHICS   Imagine that you are the officer from Putnam in charge of negotiating the sale of USBC to the buyers. You learn that several major tenants are soon to depart and realize that if the buyers learn this they will lower their offer or reject the deal altogether. Your boss insists you tell the buyers that all tenants will be staying. From the Chapter 2 ethics checklist: Who are the stakeholders? Is the conduct that he is urging legal? What are the consequences? What will you do? ◆

Limitations on damages
- *Forseeable*
- *Arithmitic Certainty*
- *Mitigation*

RESTITUTION IN CASES OF A QUASI-CONTRACT

George Anderson owned a valuable 1936 Plymouth. He took it to Ronald Schwegel's repair shop, and the two orally agreed that Schwegel would restore the car for $6,000. Unfortunately, they never agreed on the word "restore." Anderson thought the term meant complete restoration, including body work and engine repairs, whereas Schwegel intended body work but no engine repairs. After doing some of the work, Schwegel told Anderson that the car needed substantial engine work, and asked for Anderson's permission to allow an engine shop to do it. Anderson agreed, believing the cost was included in the original estimate. When the car was finished and running smoothly, Schwegel demanded $9,800. Anderson refused to pay more than the $6,000 agreed price, and Schwegel sued.

The court held that there was no valid contract between the parties. A contract requires a meeting of the minds. Here, said the court, there was no meeting of the minds on what "restore" included, and hence Schwegel could not recover either his expectation or his reliance interest, since both require an enforceable agreement. Schwegel therefore argued "quasi-contract." In other words, he claimed that even if there had been no valid agreement, he had performed a service for Anderson and that it would be unjust for Anderson to keep it without paying. **A court may award restitution, even in the absence of a contract, where one party has conferred a benefit on another and it would be unjust for the other party to retain the benefit.** The court ruled that Schwegel was entitled to the full $3,800 above and beyond the agreed price because that was the fair market value of the additional work. Anderson had asked for the repairs and now had an auto that was substantially improved. It would be unjust, ruled the court, to permit him to keep that benefit for free.[6]

OTHER EQUITABLE INTERESTS

In addition to restitution, the other three equitable powers that concern us are specific performance, injunction, and reformation.

SPECIFIC PERFORMANCE

Leona Claussen owned Iowa farmland. She sold some of it to her sister-in-law, Evelyn Claussen, and, along with the land, granted Evelyn an option to buy additional property at $800 per acre. Evelyn could exercise her option anytime during Leona's lifetime or within six months of Leona's death. When Leona died, Evelyn informed the estate's executor that she was exercising her option. But other relatives wanted the property and the executor refused to sell. Evelyn sued and asked for *specific performance*. She did not want an award of damages; she wanted the land itself. The remedy of specific performance forces the two parties to perform their contract.

A court will award specific performance, ordering the parties to perform the contract, only in cases involving the sale of land or some other asset that is unique. Courts use this equitable remedy when money damages would be inadequate to compensate the injured party. If the subject is unique and irreplaceable, money damages will not put the injured party in the same position she would have been in had the agreement been kept. So a court will order the seller to convey the rare object and the buyer to pay for it.

---

[6]*Anderson v. Schwegel*, 118 Idaho 362, 796 P.2d 1035, 1990 Idaho App. LEXIS 150 (Idaho Ct. App. 1990).

Historically, every parcel of land has been regarded as unique, and therefore specific performance is always available in real estate contracts. Evelyn Claussen won specific performance. The Iowa Supreme Court ordered Leona's estate to convey the land to Evelyn, for $800 per acre.[7] Generally speaking, either the seller or the buyer may be granted specific performance. One limitation in land sales is that a buyer may obtain specific performance only if she was ready, willing, and able to purchase the property on time. If Evelyn had lacked the money to buy Leona's property for $800 per acre within the six months' time limit, the court would have declined to order the sale.

EXAM *Strategy*

Question: The Monroes, a retired couple who live in Illinois, want to move to Arizona, to escape the northern winter. In May, the Monroes contract in writing to sell their house to the Temples for $450,000. Closing is to take place June 30. The Temples pay a deposit of $90,000. However, in early June, the Monroes travel through Arizona and discover it is too hot for them. They promptly notify the Temples they are no longer willing to sell and return the $90,000, with interest. The Temples sue, seeking the house. In response, the Monroes offer evidence that the value of the house has dropped from about $450,000 to about $400,000. They claim that the Temples have suffered no loss. Who will win?

Strategy: Most contract lawsuits are for money damages, but not this one. The Temples want the house. Because they want the house itself, and not money damages, the drop in value is irrelevant. What legal remedy are the Temples seeking? They are suing for specific performance. When will a court grant specific performance? Should it do so here?

Result: In cases involving the sale of land or some other unique asset, a court will grant specific performance, ordering the parties to perform the agreement. All houses are regarded as unique. The court will force the Monroes to sell their house, provided the Temples have sufficient money to pay for it.

Other unique items, for which a court will order specific performance, include such things as rare works of art, secret formulas, patents, and shares in a closely held corporation. Money damages would be inadequate for all these things since the injured party, even if she got the cash, could not go out and buy a substitute item. By contrast, a contract for a new Cadillac Escalade is not enforceable by specific performance. If the seller breaches, the buyer is entitled to the difference between the contract price and the market value of the car. The buyer can take his money elsewhere and purchase a virtually identical auto.

INJUNCTION

You move into your new suburban house on two acres of land, and the fresh air is exhilarating. But the wind shifts to the west, and you find yourself thinking of farm animals, especially pigs. It turns out that your next-door neighbor just started an organic bacon ranch, and the first 15 porkers have checked in. You check out the town's zoning code, discover that it is illegal to raise livestock in the neighborhood, and sue. But money damages will not suffice, because you

---

[7]*In re Estate of Claussen*, 482 N.W.2d 381, 1992 Iowa Sup. LEXIS 52 (Iowa 1992).

want the bouquet to disappear. You seek the equitable remedy of injunction. An **injunction** is a court order that requires someone to do something or refrain from doing something.

The court will order your neighbor immediately to cease and desist raising any pigs or other farm animals on his land. "Cease" means to stop, and "desist" means to refrain from doing it in the future. The injunction will not get you any money, but it will move the pigs out of town, and that was your goal.

Injunctions are usually stated in the negative. Look, for example, at noncompetition agreements, where the seller of a business might promise the buyer that he will not open a competing activity in a specified area. If the seller breaches the agreement by opening an identical enterprise across the street, the court will order him *not* to compete within the specified area.

In the increasingly litigious world of professional sports, injunctions are commonplace. In the following basketball case, the trial court issued a **preliminary injunction**, that is, an order issued early in a lawsuit prohibiting a party from doing something *during the course of the lawsuit.* The court attempts to protect the interests of the plaintiff immediately. If, after trial, it appears that the plaintiff has been injured and is entitled to an injunction, the trial court will make its order a **permanent injunction**. If it appears that the preliminary injunction should never have been issued, the court will terminate the order.

MILICIC V. BASKETBALL MARKETING COMPANY, INC.

2004 Pa.Super. 333, 857 A.2d 689
SUPERIOR COURT OF PENNSYLVANIA, 2004

CASE SUMMARY

Facts: The Basketball Marketing Company (BMC) markets, distributes, and sells basketball apparel and related products. BMC signed a long-term endorsement contract with a 16-year-old Serbian player, Darko Milicic, who was virtually unknown in the United States. Two years later, Milicic became the second pick in the National Basketball Association's draft, making him an immensely marketable young man.

Four days after his 18th birthday, Milicic made a buy-out offer to BMC, seeking release from his contract so that he could arrange a more lucrative one elsewhere. BMC refused to release him. A week later, Milicic notified BMC in writing that he was disaffirming the contract, and he returned all money and goods he had received from the company. BMC again refused to release Milicic.

Believing that Milicic was negotiating an endorsement deal with either Reebok or Adidas, BMC sent both companies letters informing them it had an enforceable endorsement deal with Milicic that was valid for several more years. Because of BMC's letter, Adidas ceased negotiating with Milicic just short of signing a contract. Milicic sued BMC,

seeking a preliminary injunction that would prohibit BMC from sending such letters to competitors. The trial court granted the preliminary injunction and BMC appealed.

Issue: *Is Milicic entitled to a preliminary injunction?*

Decision: Yes, Milicic is entitled to a preliminary injunction. Affirmed.

Reasoning: Like any plaintiff seeking a preliminary injunction, Milicic must prove four elements.

First, Milicic had a strong likelihood of success on the merits. Under Pennsylvania law, a minor may void a contract by disaffirming it within a reasonable time of turning 18 years old. Milicic sent BMC a letter only 11 days after his 18th birthday, unequivocally stating that he disavowed the agreement made when he was a minor. In all likelihood, Milicic will succeed in nullifying the contract with BMC.

Second, injunctive relief was necessary to prevent immediate and irreparable harm for which money damages would not adequately compensate Milicic. Top NBA picks negotiate and secure endorsements quickly, to take advantage of the excitement and publicity generated by the draft. BMC blocked Milicic's efforts to conclude an agreement with Adidas. Continued obstruction would cause Milicic irreparable harm.

Third, denying the injunction would cause greater injury than granting it. BMC violates important public policy by refusing to acknowledge a minor's power to disaffirm. The law presumes that a minor lacks the maturity to negotiate such an important agreement. When a company wants to conclude a contract with a minor, it is well-established practice to ask that a court appoint a guardian for the minor. It is astonishing that BMC, a company whose business is based entirely on contract law, failed to protect Milicic's interest—and its own—by requesting a guardian.

Finally, a preliminary injunction will restore the parties to the status quo that existed when Milicic turned 18, by preventing BMC from further interfering with Milicic's negotiations. The lower court properly granted injunctive relief.

REFORMATION

The final remedy, and perhaps the least common, is **reformation**, a process in which a court will partially "rewrite" a contract. Courts seldom do this, because the whole point of a contract is to enable the parties to control their own futures. But a court may reform a contract if it believes a written agreement includes a simple mistake. Suppose that Roger orally agrees to sell 35 acres to Hannah for $600,000. The parties then draw up a written agreement, accidentally describing the land as including 50 additional acres that neither party considered part of the deal. Roger refuses to sell. Hannah sues for specific performance, but asks the court to *reform* the written contract to reflect the true agreement. Most but not all courts would reform the agreement and enforce it.

A court may also reform a contract to save it. If Natasha sells her advertising business to Joseph and agrees not to open a competing agency in the same city anytime in the next 10 years, a court may decide that it is unfair to force her to wait a decade. It could reform the agreement and permit Natasha to compete, say, three years after the sale. But some courts are reluctant to reform contracts and would throw out the entire noncompetition agreement rather than reform it. Parties should never settle for a contract that is sloppy or overbroad, assuming that a court will later reform errors. They may find themselves stuck with a bargain they dislike or with no contract at all.

Reformation
A process in which a court will partially rewrite a contract.

SPECIAL ISSUES OF DAMAGES

Finally, we consider some special issues of damages, beginning with a party's obligation to minimize its losses.

MITIGATION OF DAMAGES

A party injured by a breach of contract may not recover for damages that he could have avoided with reasonable efforts. In other words, when one party perceives that the other has breached or will breach the contract, the injured party must try to prevent unnecessary loss. A party is expected to **mitigate** his damages, that is, to keep damages as low as he reasonably can.

Malcolm agrees to rent space in his mall to Zena, for a major department store. As part of the lease, Malcolm agrees to redesign the interior to meet her specifications. After Malcolm

Mitigate
To keep damages as low as is reasonably possible.

has spent $20,000 in architect and design fees, Zena informs Malcolm that she is renting other space and will not occupy his mall. Malcolm nonetheless continues the renovation work, spending an additional $50,000 on materials and labor. Malcolm will recover the lost rental payments and the $20,000 expended in reliance on the deal. He will *not* recover the extra $50,000. He should have stopped work when he learned of Zena's breach.

Mitigation and the Sale of Goods

The UCC emphasizes the importance of mitigation. As mentioned earlier in the chapter, when a seller breaches, a buyer has the option of obtaining cover. If the buyer fails to cover, she will generally be *denied* consequential damages. Mary has a contract to buy 1,000 Christmas trees from Elmo for $25 each. The market value is $40 per tree, but Mary has arranged various contracts to resell the trees at $50 each. If Elmo breaches, Mary should try to cover. If she makes no effort to cover, the court will award her $15 per tree, representing the difference between the contract price and market value, but will not award her the consequential damages based on her own expectation of $50 per tree.

NOMINAL DAMAGES

Nominal damages are a token sum, such as one dollar, given to a plaintiff who demonstrates that the defendant breached the contract but cannot prove serious injury. A school board unfairly fires Gemma, a teacher. If she obtains a teaching job at a better school for identical pay the very next day, she probably can show no damages at all. Nonetheless, the school wrongfully terminated her, and a court may award nominal damages.

Nominal damages
A token sum, such as one dollar, given to a plaintiff who demonstrates a breach but no serious injury.

LIQUIDATED DAMAGES

Liquidated damages clause
A provision in a contract that declares in advance what one party will receive if the other side breaches.

It can be difficult or even impossible to prove how much damage the injured party has suffered. So lawyers and executives negotiating a deal may include in the contract a **liquidated damages clause**, a provision stating in advance how much a party must pay if it breaches. Assume that Laurie has hired Bruce to build a five-unit apartment building for $800,000. Bruce promises to complete construction by May 15. Laurie insists on a liquidated damages clause providing that if Bruce finishes late, Laurie's final price is reduced by $3,000 for each week of delay. Bruce finishes the apartment building June 30, and Laurie reduces her payment by $18,000. Is that fair? The answer depends on two factors: **A court will generally enforce a liquidated damages clause if (1) at the time of creating the contract it was very difficult to estimate actual damages, and (2) the liquidated amount is reasonable.** In any other case, the liquidated damage will be considered a **penalty** and will prove unenforceable.

We will apply the two factors to Laurie's case. When the parties made their agreement, would it have been difficult to estimate actual damages caused by delay? Yes. Laurie could not prove that all five units would have been occupied or how much rent the tenants would have agreed to pay. Was the $3,000 per week reasonable? Probably. To finance an $800,000 building, Laurie will have to pay at least $6,000 interest per month. She must also pay taxes on the land and may have other expenses. Laurie does not have to prove that every penny of the liquidated damages clause is justified, but only that the figure is reasonable. A court will probably enforce her liquidated damages clause.

On the other hand, suppose Laurie's clause demanded $3,000 per day. There is no basis for such a figure, and a court will declare it a *penalty clause*, and refuse to enforce it. Laurie will be back to square one, forced to prove in court any damages she claims to have suffered from Bruce's delay.

IF its a penalty, the courts will "sever" the liquidated damages clause only BUT it still leaves the parties the right to sue each other for normal damages

In the chapter's opening scenario, the alarm company tries to invoke a liquidated damage clause that would leave Ben largely uncompensated. Depending on what the parties knew when they made the agreement, a court may well find the clause too harsh, and permit Ben to sue for his actual losses.

EXAM *Strategy*

Question: In March, James was accepted into the September ninth-grade class at the Brookstone Academy, a highly competitive private school. To reserve his spot, James's father, Rex, sent in a deposit of $2,000 and agreed in writing to pay the balance due, $19,000. If James withdrew in writing from the school by August 1, Rex owed nothing more to Brookstone. However, once that date passed, Rex was obliged to pay the full $19,000, whether or not James attended. On August 5, Rex hand-delivered to Brookstone a letter stating that James would not attend. Brookstone demanded the full tuition and, when Rex refused to pay, sued for $19,000. Analyze the case.

Strategy: When one party seeks contract damages that are specified in the agreement, it is relying on a liquidated damages clause. A court will generally enforce a liquidated damages clause provided the plaintiff can prove two things. What are those two things? Can this plaintiff meet that standard?

Result: Brookstone must prove that at the time of creating the contract, it was difficult to estimate actual damages, and that the liquidated amount is reasonable. Rex will probably argue that the liquidated amount is unreasonable, contending that a competitive school can quickly fill a vacancy with another eager applicant. Brookstone will counter that budgeting, which begins in January, is difficult and imprecise. Tuition money goes toward staff salaries, maintenance, utilities, and many other expenses. If the school cannot not rely in January on a certain income, the calculus becomes impossible. Rex had four months to make up his mind, and by August 1, the school was firmly committed to its class size and budget. In a similar case, the court awarded the full tuition to the school, concluding that the sum was a reasonable estimate of the damages.

PUNITIVE DAMAGES

We have seen that courts devote little time to morality when granting remedies for breach of contract. In most cases, a party that deliberately breaks its promise is treated the same as one that attempts but fails to honor its bargain. Occasionally, though, a court will take into account the question of what is morally right and order a breaching party to pay extra money damages because its conduct was socially intolerable.

Punitive damages are designed not to compensate the injured party but to punish the breaching party. The courts grant punitive damages in addition to the usual expectation, reliance, or restitution monies. The goal is to prevent the unethical party from repeating its offense and to deter others in society from similar behavior. Bear in mind that these are exceptional cases. In a contract case, courts will consider a punitive damages claim only when the breach of contract involves conduct such as fraud or bad faith.

Although a jury has wide discretion in awarding punitive damages, the Supreme Court has ruled that a verdict must be reasonable. In awarding punitive damages, a court must consider three "guideposts":

Malicious and
Intentional

- The reprehensibility of the defendant's conduct.

- The ratio between the harm suffered and the award.

- The difference between the punitive award and any civil penalties used in similar cases.

The Court has refused to provide a definitive ratio between compensatory and punitive damages, but has given additional guidance to lower courts:

- A trial court generally should not permit a punitive award more than nine times higher than the compensatory damages.

- The trial court may not use the defendant's wealth as an excuse to award an unreasonably high award.

When an insurance company intentionally deceived a vulnerable married couple, a Utah jury was so outraged it awarded $1 million compensatory and $145 million punitive damages. The Supreme Court reversed, ruling that the pair had suffered only economic harm and that the 145:1 ratio was irrational and intolerable.[8]

A large punitive damages award generally indicates an angry jury, as defense counsel in the following case acknowledged in homespun fashion.

ORKIN EXTERMINATING COMPANY, INC. v. JETER

2001 W.L. 1391443 832 So.2d 25
ALABAMA SUPREME COURT, 2001

CASE SUMMARY

Facts: In 1977, Artie Mae Jeter contracted with the Orkin Exterminating Company for a "subterranean-termite-treatment," which included immediate treatment for a minor infestation problem, annual inspections and reports, and a lifetime guarantee against any damage, backed up by a $100,000 bond for any necessary repairs. Beginning in 1984, Orkin inspectors found heavy termite damage to the house but continued to report to Jeter that her home was fine. When structural repairs were needed, Orkin told Jeter the damage was caused by water and charged her to install expensive floor supports.

In 1988 Jeter herself discovered swarming termites. Orkin acknowledged some termite damage, but rejected repair estimates because they were too expensive. For another 10 years the company resisted making necessary repairs. A company inspector wrote an internal memo, which included these revelations:

> I used a small hammer and could bury it in every sill plate in the home.… To my knowledge, no one has really told [her] the true extent to which her house is infested.… We took her money and never really told her the truth about the serious termite problem. … Ms. Jeter is 78 years old, black, in poor health, no money, we do not have a graph, her house was improperly treated, we sold her twice with no documentation of existing conditions, home is badly eaten up by termites to the point of breaking apart.

More years went by with no repairs. Finally, in 1999, Jeter sued. At trial, the company's lawyer said during closing arguments:

---

[8]The three guideposts were issued in *BMW of North America, Inc. v. Gore*, 517 U.S. 559, 116 S.Ct. 1589 (1996). The 9:1 ratio comes from *State Farm Mutual Automobile Insurance Co. v. Campbell*, 538 U.S. 408, 123 S.Ct. 1513 (2003).

I know my county. Y'all ain't going to return no defense verdict. This is going to be a plaintiff verdict. But, again, I speak of atonement versus crucifixion. Now ain't nobody all right; ain't nobody all wrong. Orkin has got some problems. Defense case has got some problems....

He got that last part right. The jury returned a verdict of $800,000 in compensatory damages for Jeter's emotional suffering, and a punitive damages award of $80 million. The trial court remitted the award to $400,000 and $4 million, respectively. Both sides appealed.

Issue: *Was a large punitive damages award appropriate?*

Decision: The court affirmed an award of damages that was lower but still substantial.

Reasoning: Orkin's termite inspectors and managers (branch, district, and regional) all deceived Mrs. Jeter for years.

Testimony indicated that she felt betrayed by the company and lost her "fighting spirit." She worried that she would not live long enough to see justice. At times, she refused to eat or see people. Mrs. Jeter chose not to have the family visit for what turned out to be her last Thanksgiving, fearing the floorboards would collapse under them.

Mental anguish and emotional distress cannot be precisely calibrated. We conclude that an award of $300,000 in compensatory damages is adequate to recompense the estate for her suffering, and that $2 million in punitive damages will deter the company from similar conduct in the future. The judgment of the trial court is affirmed on the condition that Mrs. Jeter's estate agree to this reduction; otherwise, the case is reversed and remanded for a new trial.

CHAPTER CONCLUSION

The powers of a court are broad and flexible and may suffice to give an injured party what it deserves. But problems of proof and the uncertainty of remedies demonstrate that the best solution is a carefully drafted contract and socially responsible behavior.

EXAM REVIEW

1. **BREACH** Someone breaches a contract when he fails to perform a duty, without a valid excuse. (p. 397)

2. **REMEDY** A remedy is the method a court uses to compensate an injured party. (p. 397)

3. **INTERESTS** An interest is a legal right in something, such as a contract. The first step that a court takes in choosing a remedy is to decide what interest it is protecting. (p. 397)

4. **EXPECTATION** The expectation interest puts the injured party in the position she would have been in had both sides fully performed. It has three components:

(a) Compensatory damages, which flow directly from the contract.
(b) Consequential damages, which result from the unique circumstances of the particular injured party. The injured party may recover consequential damages only if the breaching party should have foreseen them.
(c) Incidental damages, which are the minor costs an injured party incurs responding to a breach. (p. 398)

EXAM Strategy

Question: Mr. and Ms. Beard contracted for Builder to construct a house on property he owned, and sell it to the Beards for $785,000. The house was to be completed by a certain date, and Builder knew that the Beards were selling their own home in reliance on the completion date. Builder was late with construction, forcing the Beards to spend $32,000 in rent. Ultimately, Builder never finished the house, and the Beards moved elsewhere. They sued. At trial, expert testimony indicated the market value of the house as promised would have been $885,000. How much money are the Beards entitled to, and why?

Strategy: Normally, in cases of property, an injured plaintiff may use specific performance to obtain the land or house. However, there *is* no house, so there will be no specific performance. The Beards will seek their expectation interest. Under the contract, what did they reasonably expect? They anticipated a finished house, on a particular date, worth $885,000. They did not expect to pay rent while waiting. Calculate their losses. (See the "Result" at the end of this section.)

---

5. **RELIANCE** The reliance interest puts the injured party in the position he would have been in had the parties never entered into a contract. It focuses on the time and money that the injured party spent performing his part of the agreement. If there was no valid contract, a court might still award reliance damages under a theory of promissory estoppel. (p. 403)

EXAM Strategy

Question: Bingo is emerging as a rock star. His last five concerts have all sold out. Lucia signs a deal with Bingo to perform two concerts in one evening in Big City, for a fee of $50,000 for both shows. Lucia then rents the Auditorium for that evening, guaranteeing to pay $50,000. Bingo promptly breaks the deal before any tickets are sold. Lucia sues, pointing out that the Auditorium seats 3,000 and she anticipated selling all tickets for an average of $40 each, for a total gross of $120,000. How much will Lucia recover, if anything?

Strategy: The parties created a valid contract, and Lucia relied on it. She claims two losses: the payment to rent the hall, and her lost profits. A court may award reliance damages if the plaintiff can quantify them, and provided the damages are not speculative. Can Lucia quantify either of those losses? Both of them? Were they speculative? (See the "Result" at the end of this section.)

6. **RESTITUTION** The restitution interest returns to the injured party a benefit that she has conferred on the other party, which it would be unjust to leave with that person. Restitution can be awarded in the case of a contract created, for example, by fraud, or in a case of quasi-contract, where the parties never created a binding agreement. (p. 406)

7. **SPECIFIC PERFORMANCE** Specific performance, ordered only in cases of land or a unique asset, requires both parties to perform the contract. (p. 408)

8. **INJUNCTION** An injunction is a court order that requires someone to do something or refrain from doing something. (p. 409)

9. **REFORMATION** Reformation is the process by which a court will—occasionally—rewrite a contract to ensure that it accurately reflects the parties' agreement and/or to maintain the contract's viability. (p. 411)

10. **MITIGATION** The duty to mitigate means that a party injured by a breach of contract may not recover for damages that he could have avoided with reasonable efforts. (p. 411)

EXAM Strategy

Question: Ambrose hires Bierce for $25,000 to supervise the production of Ambrose's crop, but then breaks the contract by firing Bierce at the beginning of the season. A nearby grower offers Bierce $23,000 for the same growing season, but Bierce refuses to take such a pay cut. He stays home and sues Ambrose. How much money, if any, will Bierce recover from Ambrose, and why?

Strategy: Ambrose has certainly breached the contract. The injured party normally receives the difference between his expectation interest and what he actually received. Bierce expected $25,000 and received nothing. However, Bierce made no effort to minimize his losses. How much would Bierce have lost had he mitigated? (See the "Result" at the end of this section.)

11. **NOMINAL DAMAGES** Nominal damages are a token sum, such as one dollar, given to an injured plaintiff who cannot prove damages. (p. 412)

12. **LIQUIDATED DAMAGES CLAUSE** A liquidated damages clause will be enforced if and only if, at the time of creating the contract, it was very difficult to estimate actual damages and the liquidated amount is reasonable. (p. 412)

13. **PUNITIVE DAMAGES** Punitive damages are designed not to compensate the injured party but to punish the breaching party. (p. 413)

---

4. Result: The Beards' compensatory damages represent the difference between the market value of the house and the contract price. They expected a house worth $100,000 more than their contract price, and they are entitled to that sum. They also suffered consequential damages. The Builder knew they needed the house as of the contract date, and he could foresee that his breach would force them to pay rent. He is liable for a total of $132,000.

5. Result: Lucia can easily demonstrate that Bingo's breach cost her $50,000—the cost of the hall. However, it is uncertain how many tickets she would have sold. Unless Lucia has a strong track record selling tickets to concerts featuring Bingo, a court is likely to conclude that her anticipated profits were speculative. She will probably receive nothing for that claim.

10. Result: Even if he had mitigated, Bierce would have lost $2,000. He is entitled to that sum. However, he cannot recover the remaining $23,000. After Ambrose breached, Bierce had identical work available to him but failed to take it. His failure to mitigate is fatal.

ADDITIONAL QUESTIONS

1. Lewis signed a contract for the rights to all timber located on Nine Mile Mine. He agreed to pay $70 per thousand board feet ($70/mbf). As he began work, Nine Mile became convinced that Lewis lacked sufficient equipment to do the job well and forbade him to enter the land. Lewis sued. Nine Mile moved for summary judgment. The mine offered proof that the market value of the timber was exactly $70/mbf, and Lewis had no evidence to contradict Nine Mile. The evidence about market value proved decisive. Why? Please rule on the summary judgment motion.

2. Twin Creeks Entertainment signed a deal with U.S. JVC Corp. in which JVC would buy 60,000 feature film videocassettes from Twin Creeks over a three-year period. JVC intended to distribute the cassettes nationwide. Relying on its deal with JVC, Twin Creeks signed an agreement with Paramount Pictures, agreeing to purchase a minimum of $600,000 worth of Paramount cassettes over a two-year period. JVC breached its deal with Twin Creeks and refused to accept the cassettes it had agreed upon. Twin Creeks sued and claimed, among other damages, the money it owed to Paramount. JVC moved to dismiss the claim based on the Paramount contract, on the ground that Twin Creeks, the seller of goods, was not entitled to such damages. What kind of damages is Twin Creeks seeking? Please rule on the motion to dismiss.

3. Racicky was in the process of buying 320 acres of ranch land. While that sale was being negotiated, Racicky signed a contract to sell the land to Simon. Simon paid $144,000, the full price of the land. But Racicky then went bankrupt, before he could complete the *purchase* of the land, let alone its sale. Which of these remedies should Simon seek: expectation, restitution, specific performance, or reformation?

4. Parkinson was injured in an auto accident by a driver who had no insurance. Parkinson filed a claim with her insurer, Liberty Mutual, for $2,000 under her "uninsured motorist" coverage. Liberty Mutual told her that if she sought that money, her premiums would go "sky high," so Parkinson dropped the claim. Later, after she had spoken with an attorney, Parkinson sued. What additional claim was her attorney likely to make?

5. **CPA QUESTION** Master Mfg., Inc., contracted with Accur Computer Repair Corp. to maintain Master's computer system. Master's manufacturing process depends on its computer system operating properly at all times. A liquidated damages clause in the contract provided that Accur would pay $1,000 to Master for each day that Accur was late responding to a service request. On January 12, Accur was notified that Master's computer system had failed. Accur did not respond to Master's service request until January 15. If Master sues Accur under the liquidated damage provision of the contract, Master will:

   (a) Win, unless the liquidated damages provision is determined to be a penalty

   (b) Win, because under all circumstances liquidated damage provisions are enforceable

   (c) Lose, because Accur's breach was not material

   (d) Lose, because liquidated damage provisions violate public policy

6. **CPA QUESTION** Kaye contracted to sell Hodges a building for $310,000. The contract required Hodges to pay the entire amount at closing. Kaye refused to close the sale of the building. Hodges sued Kaye. To what relief is Hodges entitled?

   (a) Punitive damages and compensatory damages

   (b) Specific performance and compensatory damages

   (c) Consequential damages or punitive damages

   (d) Compensatory damages or specific performance

7. **YOU BE THE JUDGE** WRITING PROBLEM John and Susan Verba sold a Vermont lakeshore lot to Shane and Deborah Rancourt for $115,000. The Rancourts intended to build a house on the property, but after preparing the land for construction, they learned that a wetland protection law prevented building near the lake. They sued, seeking rescission of the contract. The trial court concluded that the parties had reached their agreement under a "mutual, but innocent, misunderstanding." The trial judge gave the Verbas a choice: They could rescind the contract and refund the purchase price, or they could give the Rancourts $55,000, the difference between the sales price and the actual market value of the land. The Rancourts appealed. Were the Rancourts entitled to rescission of the contract? **Argument for the Rancourts:** When the parties have made a mutual mistake about an important factual issue, either party is entitled to rescind the contract. The land is of no use to us and we want our money back. **Argument for the Verbas:** Both sides were acting in good faith and both sides made an honest mistake. We are willing to acknowledge that the land is worth somewhat less than we all thought, and we are willing to refund $55,000. The buyers shouldn't complain—they are getting the property at about half the original price, and the error was as much their fault as ours.

8. **ETHICS** The National Football League owns the copyright to the broadcasts of its games. It licenses local television stations to telecast certain games and maintains a "blackout rule," which prohibits stations from broadcasting home games that are not sold out 72 hours before the game starts. Certain home games of the Cleveland Browns team were not sold out, and the NFL blocked local broadcast. But several bars in the Cleveland area were able to pick up the game's signal by using special antennas. The NFL wanted the bars to stop showing the games. What did it do? Was it unethical of the

bars to broadcast the games that they were able to pick up? Apart from the NFL's legal rights, do you think it had the moral right to stop the bars from broadcasting the games?

9. ***ROLE REVERSAL*** Write a multiple-choice question involving a contract for the sale of goods. The seller breaches and the buyer definitely has compensatory damages. The test-taker must decide whether there are also consequential damages, and the total amount of damages to which the buyer is entitled.

INTERNET RESEARCH PROBLEM

You represent a group of neighborhood residents in a large city who are protesting construction of a skyscraper that will violate building height limitations. Draft a complaint, requesting an appropriate injunction. For guidance, search online for a complaint with a request for an injunction.

You can find further practice problems at www.cengagebrain.com. See the preface of this book for website access details.

COMMERCIAL TRANSACTIONS

He Sued, She Sued. Harold and Maude made a great couple because both were compulsive entrepreneurs. One evening they sat on their penthouse roofdeck, overlooking the twinkling Chicago skyline. Harold sipped a decaf coffee while negotiating, over the phone, with a real estate developer in San Antonio. Maude puffed a cigar as she bargained on a different line with a toy manufacturer in Cleveland. They hung up at the same time. "I did it!" shrieked Maude, "I made an incredible deal for the robots—five bucks each!" "No, I did it!" triumphed Harold, "I sold the 50 acres in Texas for $300,000 more than it's worth." They dashed indoors.

> **Confirming our deal—100,000 Psychopath Robots—you deliver Chicago—end of summer.**

Maude quickly scrawled a handwritten memo, which said, "Confirming our deal—100,000 Psychopath Robots—you deliver Chicago—end of summer." She didn't mention a price, or an exact delivery date, or when payment would be made. She signed her memo and faxed it to the toy manufacturer. Harold took more time. He typed a thorough contract, describing precisely the land he was selling, the $2.3 million price, how and when each payment would be made and the deed conveyed. He signed the contract and faxed it, along with a plot plan showing the surveyed land. Then the happy couple grabbed a bottle of champagne, returned to the deck—and placed a side bet on whose contract would prove more profitable. The loser would have to cook and serve dinner for six months.

Neither Harold nor Maude ever heard again from the other parties. The toy manufacturer sold the Psychopath Robots to another retailer at a higher price. Maude was forced to buy comparable toys elsewhere for $9 each.

She sued. And the Texas property buyer changed his mind, deciding to develop a Club Med in Greenland and refusing to pay Harold for his land. He sued. Only one of the two plaintiffs succeeded. Which one?

The adventures of Harold and Maude illustrate the Uniform Commercial Code (UCC) in action. The Code is the single most important source of law for people engaged in commerce and controls the vast majority of contracts made every day in every state. The Code is ancient in origin, contemporary in usage, admirable in purpose, and flawed in application. "Yeah, yeah, that's fascinating," snaps Harold, "but who wins the bet?" Relax, Harold, we'll tell you in a minute.

DEVELOPMENT OF COMMERCIAL LAW

During the fifteenth and sixteenth centuries, merchants in England and throughout Europe found the law of their respective nations cumbersome and inadequate for the settlement of commercial disputes. For example, in England, property had historically been the most important asset, and civil law revolved around the rights to land. Decisions in property disputes came slowly, and courts seldom thought in terms of a "contract." Even by the seventeenth century, English judges were only beginning to acknowledge that an exchange of mere promises, with no money or property changing hands, might lead to an enforceable agreement. But merchants dealt in the sale of goods, not real estate. Their livelihood depended upon promises, on the rapid movement of their wares, and on their ability to enforce bargains. Dissatisfied with the few remedies that courts offered, businessmen throughout England and the Continent began to treat their own customs as law and to settle disputes in trade organizations rather than civil courts. The body of rules they relied on became known as the *lex mercatoria*, or **law merchant**. The law merchant was thus a "custom made" law, created by the merchants who used it. The new doctrine focused on promises, the sale and exchange of goods, and payment.

Law merchant
Rules and customs developed by traders throughout Europe from the fifteenth to the eighteenth century.

Lord Mansfield (1705–1793), a justly famous English judge, began to use some of these commercial rules in his influential decisions, beginning the slow process of incorporating them into the common law of contract. Over the next two centuries, common law judges employed more and more of the law merchant and at the same time began to develop specialized areas within commercial law. Courts began to distinguish the law for the sale of goods from the law governing, for example, payments by check or other negotiable instruments. Similar changes took place in the United States.

Throughout the first half of the twentieth century, commercial transactions changed dramatically in this country, as advances in transportation and communication revolutionized negotiation and trade. But the law lagged behind, evolving more slowly than commercial practices, hampered by common law differences between the states. The nation needed a modernized business law to give nationwide uniformity and predictability in a new and faster world. In 1942, two groups of scholars, the American Law Institute (ALI) and the National Conference of Commissioners on Uniform State Laws (NCCUSL), began the effort to draft a modern, national law of commerce. Led by Professor Karl N. Llewellyn, the scholars debated and formulated for nearly a decade. Finally, in 1952, Llewellyn and colleagues published their work—the Uniform Commercial Code. The entire Code is available online at **http://www.law.cornell.edu**.

Article 1: *General Provisions*	The purpose of the code, general guidance in applying it, and definitions.
Article 2: *Sale of Goods*	The sale of *goods*, such as a new car, 20,000 pairs of gloves, or 101 Dalmatians. This is one of the two most important articles in the UCC.
Article 2A: *Leases*	A temporary exchange of goods for money, such as renting a car.
Article 3: *Negotiable Instruments*	The use of checks, promissory notes, and other negotiable instruments.
Article 4: *Bank Deposits and Collections*	The rights and obligations of banks and their customers.
Article 4A: *Funds Transfers*	An instruction, given by a bank customer, to credit a sum of money to another's account.
Article 5: *Letters of Credit*	The use of credit, extended by two or more banks, to facilitate a contract between two parties who do not know each other and require guarantees by banks they trust.
Article 6: *Bulk Transfers*	The sale of a major part of a company's inventory or equipment. This article has been repealed in all but a few states.
Article 7: *Warehouse Receipts, Bills of Lading, and Other Documents of Title*	Documents proving ownership of goods that are being transported or stored. This article is being revised as we go to press.
Article 8: *Investment Securities*	Rights and liabilities concerning shares of stock or other ownership of an enterprise.
Article 9: *Secured Transactions*	A sale of goods in which the seller keeps a financial stake in the goods he has sold, such as a car dealer who may repossess the car if the buyer fails to make payments. This is one of the two most important articles in the Code.

THE CODE TODAY

The ALI and the NCCUSL revised the Code in 1957 and once again during the 1970s. Then, beginning in the mid-1980s, the two groups began their most ambitious overhaul, seeking to make substantial changes to almost all of the articles and to add new ones as well. The goals were to acknowledge lessons learned from the Code's first half-century; to accommodate new technology, such as sales made over the Internet; and to serve a business world that had shifted much of its focus from traditional manufacturing to services and information.

The ALI and the NCCUSL have revised the Code several times since then, with important changes coming as recently as 2003. Remember, though, that the UCC is the creation of scholars. No section of the Code has any legal effect until a state legislature adopts it. In fact, all 50 states and the District of Columbia have adopted the UCC, but not all have used identical versions.

This book discusses and applies provisions of the Code that have been widely adopted. Article 9, on secured transactions, is one of the two most important in the Code. The commissioners completely rewrote Article 9 at the turn of the millennium, and this text reflects those changes because every state has adopted them. The commissioners have also revised Article 1, which provides definitions and general guidance, and Article 2, on sales. However, as this book goes to press, very few states have adopted revised Article 1, and none have adopted revised Article 2. We focus on existing law, not the proposed changes to Articles 1 and 2. Finally, Article 6, on bulk transfers, has been repealed in most states, and we will discuss it only briefly, in Chapter 18.

The next four chapters highlight elements of the Code *that have changed the common law rules of contract*.

Harold and Maude, Revisited

Harold and Maude each negotiated what they believed was an enforceable agreement, and both filed suit: Harold for the sale of his land, Maude for the purchase of toy robots. Only one prevailed. The difference in outcome demonstrates one of the changes that the UCC has wrought in the law of commercial contracts and illustrates why everyone in business needs a working knowledge of the Code. As we revisit the happy couple, Harold is clearing the dinner dishes. Maude sits back in her chair, lights a cigar, and compliments her husband on the apple tart. Harold, scowling and spilling coffee, wonders what went wrong.

Harold's contract was for the sale of land and governed by the common law of contracts. The common law statute of frauds requires any agreement for the sale of land to be in writing and *signed by the defendant*, in this case the buyer in Texas. Harold signed it, but the buyer never did, so Harold's meticulously detailed document was worth less than a five-cent cigar.

Maude's quickly scribbled memorandum, concerning psychotic robot toys, was for the sale of goods and was governed by Article 2 of the UCC. The Code requires less detail and formality in a writing. Because Maude and the seller were both merchants, the document she scribbled could be enforced *even against the defendant*, who had never signed anything. The fact that Maude left out the price and other significant terms was not fatal to a contract under the UCC, though under the common law such omissions would have made the bargain unenforceable. We will look in greater detail at these UCC changes. For now it is enough to see that the Code has carved major changes into the common law of contracts, alterations that Harold is beginning to appreciate.

This Unit of the Text

This unit covers three principal subjects, all relating to commercial transactions that the Code governs. The first chapters concern the sale of goods and focus primarily on Article 2. In the present chapter we emphasize how Code provisions work together to change the common law. In the following chapters we examine title to goods (Chapter 19), then warranties and product liability (Chapter 20), and, finally, performance and remedies (Chapter 21).

The next group of three chapters (Chapters 22–24) surveys the law of negotiable instruments. Checks are the most common kind of negotiable instrument, but we will see that there are many other varieties and that each creates different rights and obligations. We conclude the unit with a chapter devoted to secured transactions (Chapter 25), that is, a sale of goods in which the seller keeps a financial stake in the goods he has sold, and a chapter that analyzes bankruptcy law (Chapter 26).

UCC BASICS

CODE'S PURPOSE

The Uniform Commercial Code proclaims its purposes clearly:

UCC Section 1-102(2): Underlying purposes and policies of this Act are

(a) to simplify, clarify and modernize the law governing commercial transactions;

(b) to permit the continued expansion of commercial practices through custom, usage and agreement of the parties;

(c) to make uniform the law among the various jurisdictions.

This is not mere boilerplate. To "modernize," in (a), requires a focus on the needs of contemporary businesspeople, not on rules developed when judges rode horseback. Suppose a court must decide whether a writing is detailed enough to satisfy the Code's statute of frauds. The judge may rely on Section 1-102 to decide that because modern commerce is so fast, even the skimpiest of writings is good enough to demonstrate that the parties had reached a bargain. In doing so, the judge would deliberately be turning away from legal history to accommodate business practices in an electronic age.

Look at (c), which urges uniformity. Assume that a state supreme court must decide whether a merchant acted in good faith when trying to modify an unprofitable contract. The court may look to the high courts of other states for guidance, not because they are binding (which they are not) or even persuasive (which they may not be) but because uniformity is a valuable goal in itself.

Section 1-102 also states that "[t]his Act shall be liberally construed and applied to promote its underlying purposes," meaning that when in doubt, courts should focus on the goals described. The Code emphasizes *getting the right results*, rather than following rigid rules of contract law.

SCOPE OF ARTICLE 2

Because the UCC changes the common law, it is essential to know whether the Code applies in a given case. Negotiations may lead to an enforceable agreement when the UCC applies, even though the same bargaining would create no contract under the common law.

Goods

Objects that are movable, other than money and investment securities.

UCC Section 2-102: Article 2 applies to the sale of goods.[1] Goods are things that are movable, other than money and investment securities. Hats are goods, and so are railroad cars, lumber, books, and bottles of wine. Land is not a good, nor is a house. So an agreement for the delivery of 10,000 board feet of white pine is a contract for the sale of goods, and Article 2 governs it. But the article does not apply to a contract for the sale of an office building. A skyscraper is not movable (although an entire city *may* be [2]).

---

[1] Officially, Article 2 tells us that it applies to *transactions* in goods, which is a slightly broader category than sale of goods. But most sections of Article 2, and most court decisions, focus exclusively on sales, and so shall we.

[2] "If you are lucky enough to have lived in Paris as a young man, then wherever you go for the rest of your life, it stays with you, for Paris is a moveable feast." Ernest Hemingway, 1950.

Article 2 regulates **sales**, which means that one party transfers title to the other in exchange for money. If you sell your motorcycle to a friend, that is a sale of goods. If you lend the bike to your friend for the weekend, that is not a sale and Article 2 does not apply. Article 2 also does not apply to the leasing of goods, for example, when you rent a car. A sale involves a permanent change in ownership, whereas a lease concerns a temporary change in possession.

Leasing goods is an enormous part of business these days. Virtually every kind of commercial and industrial equipment, from computers to tractors to coffee pots, is leased every day around the country. For example, when you fly home, the aircraft you sit in is quite likely leased to the airline from which you bought your ticket. Over 20 percent of all capital investment in the United States is directly related to equipment leasing. Because leasing is so important, the drafters of the Code added an article to cover the subject.

Article 2A governs the leasing of goods. Most of the states have adopted Article 2A, though unfortunately not all have adopted the same version. The law of leasing is therefore less uniform than that of sales. How does Article 2A compare to Article 2? Overall, it is similar, and many sections are almost identical. But there are some important differences, and anyone engaging in a significant amount of commercial leasing must become familiar with Article 2A. For our purposes, leasing law is a variation on the theme of Article 2, and we will concentrate on the principal melody of sales.

Mixed Contracts

Sophocles University hires ClickOn Computer to design software for the university's computerized grading system, which must be capable of recording and storing all grades, making the grades available to the students online, computing averages, and printing transcripts. ClickOn agrees to design the software, install it, and train the staff in its use. But things go badly from day one. Sophocles gives ClickOn an "F" for effort and refuses to pay a nickel. Did the parties have an enforceable contract? Most of the bargaining was oral, and the only writings were a few short letters. If the common law governs the deal, it will be difficult or impossible to show an offer and acceptance with definite terms. But if the UCC controls, the writings may suffice to show a binding agreement.

To determine whether the UCC governs, we need to know what kind of an agreement the parties made. Was it one for the sale of goods (UCC) or one for services (common law)? In fact the agreement combined both goods and services and was therefore a *mixed contract*. **In a mixed contract involving sales and services, the UCC will govern if the** *predominant purpose* **is the sale of goods, but the common law will control if the predominant purpose is services.**

If ClickOn sues, the court must determine whether the predominant purpose was the design of the software and the training of staff, which are service work, or the sale of the software, which is a transaction in goods. In this case, the sale of the software predominated. ClickOn did its design work in order to sell an expensive software package to a customer. It was the software that generated the contract, not ClickOn's work in preparing it. So the UCC does govern, and ClickOn may have a valid contract. We return to this issue of mixed contracts later in the chapter, as we see how Section 2-102 interacts with other Code provisions.

Merchants

The UCC, we know, evolved indirectly from the law merchant, the commercial law developed by business people themselves. And the Code still attempts to meet the unique needs of the business world. But while the UCC offers a contract law that is more flexible than the common law, it also requires a higher level of responsibility from the merchants it serves.

Those who make a living by crafting agreements are expected to understand the legal consequences of their words and deeds. Thus many sections of the Code offer two rules: one for "merchants" and one for everybody else.

UCC Section 2-104: A **merchant** is someone who routinely deals in the particular goods involved, *or* who appears to have special knowledge or skill in those goods, *or* who uses agents with special knowledge or skill in those goods. A used car dealer is a "merchant" when it comes to selling autos, because he routinely deals in them. He is not a merchant when he goes to a furniture store and purchases a new sofa. The salesman who sells new sofas is a merchant for that purpose.

The UCC frequently holds a merchant to a higher standard of conduct than a non-merchant. For example, a merchant may be held to an oral contract if she received written confirmation of it, even though the merchant herself never signed the confirmation. That same confirmation memo, arriving at the house of a non-merchant, would *not* create a binding deal. We will see many instances of this dual level of responsibility, one for a merchant and the other for a non-merchant. More often than not, it is apparent whether the parties are merchants. If a manufacturer of toy balloons agrees to sell 10,000 boxes of balloons to a toy retailer, both parties obviously are merchants. Other cases are less clear. Is a farmer a merchant? Farmers work long, hard hours in the field, yet today they may also be sophisticated commodities traders. Some courts have concluded they are merchants, but almost as many have decided they are not.

Merchant

Generally, someone who routinely deals in the particular goods involved.

GOOD FAITH AND UNCONSCIONABILITY

Good Faith

The UCC imposes a duty of good faith in the performance of all contracts. Here is a $900,000 example.

The Kansas Municipal Gas Agency (KMGA) purchased natural gas for cities and towns in Kansas. KMGA requested proposals for a long-term gas contract from suppliers, stressing its need for a guaranteed supply. Vesta Energy Co. responded, and the two sides agreed on essential terms, including price. Vesta began supplying natural gas while they worked out the last details of a long-term contract.

Suddenly, Vesta asked for a *force majeure* clause, which permits either party to cancel a contract in the event of specified disasters, such as tornadoes or other acts of God. Such clauses are common in the gas industry. But Vesta asked that the clause also permit it to end the arrangement in case of "failure of supply," meaning that Vesta could cancel the deal if it was unable to find affordable supplies. KMGA rejected the proposal, and Vesta stopped supplying gas. KMGA sued, claiming that Vesta had made its *force majeure* proposal in bad faith.

For *non-merchants*, good faith means honesty in fact. For a *merchant*, good faith means honesty in fact *plus* the exercise of reasonable commercial standards of fair dealing.[3] Thus, when parties perform a contract, or in certain cases when they negotiate, neither side may lie or mislead. Further, a party who is a merchant must act as fairly as the business community routinely expects.

The court found that Vesta had acted in bad faith. The parties already had a working agreement, and Vesta had sabotaged it because the price of natural gas had unexpectedly shot up 75 percent. To escape the unprofitable deal, Vesta proposed an outrageous *force majeure*

---

[3] UCC Sections 1-201(19), 1-203, and 2-103.

clause, knowing that KMGA would reject it. Based on Vesta's bad faith negotiating, the court awarded KMGA $904,000, the amount the company lost by purchasing gas elsewhere.[4]

Unconscionability

The UCC employs a second principle to encourage fair play and just results: the doctrine of unconscionability. UCC Section 2-302: A contract may be **unconscionable** if it is shockingly one-sided and fundamentally unfair. If a court concludes that some part of a contract is unconscionable, it will refuse to enforce that provision. Courts seldom find a contract unconscionable if the two parties are businesses, but they are quicker to apply the doctrine when one party is a consumer.

Suppose Bill's Builderia sells building equipment. For every sales contract, Bill uses a pre-printed form that says, among other things, that the buyer takes the item "as is" and that Bill is not liable for repairs or for compensatory or consequential damages. If Bill sells a $3,000 power mower to a landscape contractor and the machine falls to pieces, a court will probably enforce the limitation on liability. The law assumes that a professional contractor will have the sophistication to read and understand the contract and can bargain for different terms if he is unhappy. But if the buyer is a consumer, such as a homeowner intent on mowing his own lawn, a court will probably declare the clause *unconscionable*. Bill is in the business of selling the equipment and knows the risks. He has drafted the pre-printed contract. The homeowner is unlikely even to read the entire agreement, let alone understand phrases like "consequential damages." It would be unfair to enforce the clause against the consumer. We will look at this issue in more detail in Chapter 20, on warranties and products liability.

Good Faith and Unconscionability Distinguished.   The doctrine of good faith focuses on a party's behavior as it performs an agreement: Was it attempting to carry out its obligations in a reasonable manner and do what both sides expected when they made the deal? Unconscionability looks primarily at the contract itself. Are any terms so grossly unfair that a court should reform or ignore them?

Next we examine how the basic ideas of scope, merchant status, and good faith interact with other UCC provisions in the creation of a contract.

> **Unconscionable**
> Shockingly one-sided and fundamentally unfair.

CONTRACT FORMATION

The common law expected the parties to form a contract in a fairly predictable and traditional way: the offeror made a clear offer that included all important terms, and the offeree agreed to all terms. Nothing was left open. The drafters of the UCC recognized that business people frequently do not think or work that way and that the law should reflect business reality.

FORMATION BASICS: SECTION 2-204

UCC Section 2-204 provides three important rules that enable parties to make a contract quickly and informally:

1. *Any Manner That Shows Agreement.* The parties may make a contract in any manner sufficient to show that they reached an agreement. They may show the agreement with words, writings, or

---

[4] *Kansas Municipal Gas Agency v. Vesta Energy Co.*, 843 F.Supp. 1401, 1994 U.S. Dist. LEXIS 2240 (D. Kan. 1994).

even their conduct. Lisa negotiates with Ed to buy 300 barbecue grills. The parties agree on a price, but other business prevents them from finishing the deal. Then six months later Lisa writes, "Remember our deal for 300 grills? I still want to do it if you do." Ed doesn't respond, but a week later a truck shows up at Lisa's store with the 300 grills, and Lisa accepts them. The combination of their original discussion, Lisa's subsequent letter, Ed's delivery, and her acceptance all adds up to show that they reached an agreement. The court will enforce their deal, and Lisa must pay the agreed-upon price.

2. *Moment of Making Is Not Critical.* The UCC will enforce a deal even though it is difficult, in common law terms, to say exactly when it was formed. Was Lisa's deal formed when they orally agreed? When he delivered? She accepted? The Code's answer: It does not matter. The contract is enforceable.

3. *One or More Terms May Be Left Open.* The common law insisted that the parties clearly agree on all important terms. If they did not, there was no meeting of minds and no enforceable deal. The Code changes that. **Under the UCC, a court may enforce a bargain even though one or more terms were left open.** Lisa's letter never said when she required delivery of the barbecues or when she would pay. Under the UCC, the omission is not fatal. As long as there is some certain basis for giving damages to the injured party, the court will do just that. Suppose Lisa refused to pay, claiming that the agreement included no date for her payment. A court would rule that the parties assumed she would pay within a commercially reasonable time, such as 30 days.

In the following case, we can almost see the roller coasters, smell the cotton candy—and hear the carnival owners arguing. Because the cases in this chapter involve more than one Code section, we will outline the relevant provisions at the outset.

CODE PROVISIONS DISCUSSED IN THIS CASE

Issue	Relevant Code Section
1. What law governs?	UCC Section 2-102: Article 2 applies to the sale of goods.
2. Did the parties form a contract?	UCC Section 2-204: The parties may make a contract in any manner sufficient to show agreement.

JANNUSCH V. NAFFZIGER

2008 WL 540877
ILLINOIS COURT OF APPEALS, 2008

CASE SUMMARY

Facts: Festival Foods prepares and sells concessions at carnivals in the Midwest. Owners Gene and Martha Jannusch made a verbal agreement to sell the business to the Naffzigers for $150,000. They paid $10,000 and took possession of the Festival Foods truck and trailer. They paid taxes and employees, bought supplies, and sold food at six events.

Because they had earned less at the carnivals than they had expected, the Naffzigers returned the truck and trailer and refused to pay the remaining $140,000. At trial, they argued that no definite agreement had been reached.

The common law requires a meeting of the minds for a contract to be created. Under the UCC, parties may form a contract in "any manner sufficient to show agreement."

The Naffzigers argued that the UCC did not apply to their agreement. The trial court agreed and ruled that a contract did not exist because there had never been a meeting of the minds. The Jannnuschs appealed.

Issues: *Does the common law govern or the UCC? Did the parties form a contract?*

Decision: The UCC applies to the contract. Under the UCC, an enforceable agreement existed. Reversed and remanded.

Reasoning: Defendants argue that the purchase of a business is not a sale of goods. However, Article 2 of the UCC applies to an agreement so long as the *predominant purpose* of the deal is a sale of goods. The truck and trailer were valuable assets, and those goods were the centerpiece of the contract. Thus, the UCC does apply.

Therefore, we must next ask whether the parties had shown agreement. They set the price at $150,000. They discussed which items were to be included. The defendants took and used the items at six different carnivals. Under the UCC, these exchanges are enough to create an enforceable contract. The Naffzigers breached the contract when they returned the truck and trailer.

Based on the UCC, the Jannuschs won a case they would have lost under the common law. Next we look at changes the Code has made in the centuries-old requirement of a writing.

STATUTE OF FRAUDS

UCC Section 2-201 requires a writing for any sale of goods worth $500 or more. However, under the UCC, the writing need not completely summarize the agreement, and it need not even be entirely accurate. Once again, the Code is modifying the common law rule, permitting parties to enforce deals with less formality. In some cases, the court grants an exception and enforces an agreement with no writing at all. Here are the rules.

CONTRACTS FOR GOODS WORTH $500 OR MORE

Section 2-201 demands a writing for any contract of goods over this limit, meaning that virtually every significant sale of goods has some writing requirement. Remember that a contract for goods costing less than $500 is still covered by the UCC, but it may be oral.

Writing Sufficient to Indicate a Contract

The Code only requires a writing *sufficient to indicate* that the parties made a contract. In other words, the writing need not *be* a contract. A simple memo is enough, or a letter or informal note, mentioning that the two sides reached an agreement, is enough. **In general, the writing must be signed by the defendant,** that is, whichever party is claiming there was no deal. Dick signs and sends to Shirley a letter saying, "This is to acknowledge your agreement to buy all 650 books in my rare book collection for $188,000." Shirley signs nothing. A day later, Louis offers Dick $250,000. Is Dick free to sell? No. He signed the memo, it indicates a contract, and Shirley can enforce it against him.

Now reverse the problem. Suppose that after Shirley receives Dick's letter, she decides against rare books in favor of original scripts from the *South Park* television show. Dick sues. Shirley wins because *she* signed nothing.

Incorrect or Omitted Terms

If the writing demonstrates the two sides reached an agreement, it satisfies Section 2-201 even if it omits important terms or states them incorrectly. Suppose Dick writes "$1888,000," indicating almost $2 million, when he meant to write "$188,000." The letter still shows that the parties made a deal, and the court will enforce it, relying on oral testimony to determine the correct price.

Enforceable Only to Quantity Stated

Since the writing only has to indicate that the parties agreed, it need not state every term of their deal. But one term is essential: quantity. **The Code will enforce the contract only up to the quantity of goods stated in the writing.** This is logical, since a court can surmise other terms, such as price, based on market conditions. Buyer agrees to purchase pencils from Seller. The market value of the pencils is easy to determine, but a court would have no way of knowing whether Buyer meant to purchase 1,000 pencils or 100,000; the quantity must be stated.

Merchant Exception

This is a major change from the common law. **When two merchants make an oral contract, and one sends a confirming memo to the other within a reasonable time, and the memo is sufficiently definite that it could be enforced against the sender herself, then the memo is also valid against the merchant who receives it, unless he objects within 10 days.** Laura, a tire wholesaler, signs and sends a memo to Scott, a retailer, saying, "Confm yr order today—500 tires cat #886—cat price." Scott realizes he can get the tires cheaper elsewhere and ignores the memo. Big mistake. Both parties are merchants, and Laura's memo is sufficient to bind her. So it also satisfies the statute of frauds *against Scott*, unless he objects within 10 days.

The following case illustrates the merchant exception in action.

CODE PROVISIONS DISCUSSED IN THIS CASE

Issue	Relevant Code Section
1. Was there a writing sufficient to indicate a contract?	UCC Section 2-201 requires a writing for any sale of goods worth $500 or more.
2. Did the purchase orders satisfy the merchant exception?	UCC Section 2-201(2), the "merchant exception." When two merchants make an oral contract, and one sends a confirming memo to the other within a reasonable time, and the memo is sufficiently definite that it could be enforced against the sender herself, then the memo is also valid against the merchant who receives it, unless he objects within 10 days.

RAPOCA ENERGY COMPANY, L.P. V. AMCI EXPORT CORPORATION

2001 WL 401424
UNITED STATES DISTRICT COURT FOR THE WESTERN DIVISION OF VIRGINIA, 2001

CASE SUMMARY

Facts: Robert Moir, an AMCI executive, met with Rapoca's officer, Gary Chilcot, at O'Charley's Restaurant, and discussed buying a large quantity of coal from Rapoca. According to AMCI, the two agreed that Rapoca would sell 140,000 tons of coal. AMCI confirmed this in two purchase orders (P.O.s), which it sent to Rapoca. Rapoca's version was very different. Chilcot stated that the parties never reached an oral agreement, that the P.O.s were inconsistent as to the quantity of coal, and that the price was too low for a reasonable seller to have agreed. What is clear is that Rapoca did not respond in writing to the P.O.s for several months.

Rapoca filed suit, seeking a declaration from the court that it had no contractual obligation to AMCI. The company argued that there had been no agreement, and that even if the parties had orally agreed, the P.O.s did not satisfy the statute of frauds. AMCI counterclaimed, seeking damages for its costs in buying coal elsewhere. The judge first ruled that the parties had in fact reached an oral agreement. That left one important issue remaining.

Issue: *Did the Purchase Orders (P.O.s) satisfy the statute of frauds?*

Decision: Yes, the Purchase Orders (P.O.s) satisfied the statute of frauds.

Reasoning: There was no signed contract in this case, and that creates a statute of frauds problem. AMCI argues that the P.O.s satisfied the merchant exception.

Rapoca received the P.O.s within a reasonable time after the parties met and bargained. The company did not object to the orders within 10 days. One question remains: Were the two documents confirmation of a contract?

The P.O.s contain this statement: "This order must be acknowledged by the return of the signed second copy."

The P.O.s then include a space, labeled "Accepted and Agreed," for the recipient's signature. This demonstrates, Rapoca argues, that the P.O.s were merely offers, not confirmations of an agreement, and created a binding agreement only when the recipient signed its acceptance.

Rapoca also contends that neither document refers to any specific oral contract, suggesting that none was formed. Further, both documents state that delivery of coal after the date of purchase constitutes acceptance of the order. These facts strengthen the argument that no contract had been formed when the P.O.s were sent.

However, the more important evidence is that the industry routinely used such P.O.s to confirm oral agreements. Gary Chilcot, Rapoca's officer, testified as follows:

THE COURT: And why do you think you get a purchase order? What's the...reason for that?
WITNESS: Well, it's, it's a reconfirmation of what was verbally agreed to.
THE COURT: So that in your experience there normally is an agreement as to the sale which is typically oral?
WITNESS: Typically.
THE COURT: And that...is followed by the purchaser sending you or your company a purchase order which confirms the terms?
WITNESS: Correct.

P.O.s were simply not used as offer sheets. They were rarely signed and returned. The practice was to use them as confirmation of prior oral agreements, despite the "acceptance" language.

The P.O.s were writings in confirmation of a contract and satisfied the merchant exception to the statute of frauds. The contract is valid and enforceable.

EXAM *Strategy*

Question: Marko, a sporting goods retailer, speaks on the phone with Wholesaler about buying 500 footballs. After the conversation, Marko hand writes this message: "Confirming our discussion—you will deliver to us 'Pro Bowl' model footballs—$45 per unit—arrival our store no later than July 20 this year." Marko signs and faxes the note to Wholesaler. Wholesaler reads the fax but then gets an order from Lana for the same model football at $51 per unit. Wholesaler never responds to Marko's fax and sells his entire supply to Lana. Two weeks later, Marko is forced to pay more from another seller, and sues Wholesaler. Marko argues that under merchant exception, his fax was sufficient to satisfy the statute of frauds. Is he right?

Strategy: The merchant exception to the statute of frauds only applies to . . . merchants. Are these two parties merchants? Yes, they are, and the exception potentially applies. Under this exception, a memo that could be enforced against the sender himself may bind the merchant who receives it. Could this memo be enforced against Marko? Make sure that you know what terms must be included to make a writing binding.

Result: The writing must indicate that the two parties reached an agreement. Marko's memo does so, because he says he is confirming their discussion. Even if some terms are omitted, the writing may still suffice. However, the memo will only be enforced to the quantity of goods stated. Marko stated no quantity—a fatal error. His writing fails to satisfy the statute of frauds, and he will lose the suit.

Special Circumstances

Finally, an oral contract *may* be enforceable, even without a written memorandum, if (1) the seller is specially manufacturing the goods for the buyer, or (2) the defendant admits in court proceedings that there was a contract, or (3) the goods have been delivered or they have been paid for. We discuss these exceptions in detail in Chapter 14, on written contracts.

ADDED TERMS: SECTION 2-207

Under the common law's mirror image rule, when one party makes an offer, the offeree must accept those exact terms. If the offeree adds or alters any terms, the acceptance is ineffective and the offeree's response becomes a counteroffer. In one of its most significant modifications of contract law, the UCC changes that result. **Under Section 2-207, an acceptance that adds or alters terms will often create a contract.** The Code has made this change in response to *battles of the form*. Every day, corporations buy and sell millions of dollars of goods using pre-printed forms. The vast majority of all contracts involve such documents. Typically, the buyer places an order using a pre-printed form, and the seller acknowledges with its own pre-printed acceptance form. Because each form contains language favorable to the party sending it, the two documents rarely agree. The Code's drafters concluded that the law must cope with real practices.

We discuss Section 2-207 in detail in Chapter 10 and summarize it here only to emphasize how it works with other UCC provisions. The section is confusing, and a diagram helps. **For a schematic look at UCC Section 2-207, see the illustration on page 258.**

Intention

The parties must still *intend* to create a contract. Section 2-207 is full of exceptions, but there is no change in this basic requirement of contract law. If the differing forms indicate that the parties never reached agreement, there is no contract.

Additional or Different Terms

An offeree may include a new term in his acceptance and still create a binding deal. Suppose Breeder writes to Pet Shop, offering to sell 100 guinea pigs at $2 each. Pet Shop faxes a memo saying, "We agree to buy 100 g.p. We get credit for any unhealthy pig." Pet Shop has added a new term, concerning unhealthy pigs, but the parties *have* created a binding contract because the writings show they intended an agreement. Now the court must decide what the terms of the contract are, since there is some discrepancy. The first step is to decide whether the new language is an *additional term* or a *different term*.

Additional Terms.   **Additional terms** are those that raise issues not covered in the offer. The "unhealthy pig" issue is an additional term because the offer said nothing about it. **When both parties are *merchants*, additional terms generally become part of the bargain.** Pet Shop's insistence on credit for sick guinea pigs is binding on Breeder. In three circumstances, however, additional terms *do not* bind the parties:

- If the original offer *insisted on its own terms*. If Breeder offered the pets for sale "on these and no other terms," Pet Shop's additional language would not become part of their deal.

- If the additional terms *materially alter* the offer. Pet Shop's new language about credit for unhealthy animals is fairly uncontroversial. But suppose Pet Shop wrote back, "Breeder is liable for any illness of any animal in Pet Shop within 90 days of shipment of guinea pigs." Breeder would potentially have to pay for a $500 iguana with pneumonia or a $6,000 parrot with gout. This is a material alteration of the bargain and is not part of the contract.

- If the offeror *promptly objects* to the new terms. If Breeder received Pet Shop's fax and immediately called up to say, "no credit for unhealthy pigs," then Pet Shop's additional term is not part of their deal.

In all other circumstances, additional terms do become part of an agreement between merchants.

Different Terms.   These are terms that contradict those in the offer. Suppose Brilliant Corp. orders 1,500 cellular phones from Makem Co., for use by Brilliant's sales force. Brilliant places the order using a pre-printed form stating that the product is fully warranted for normal use and that seller is liable for compensatory *and consequential* damages. This means, for example, that Makem could be liable for lost profits if a salesman's phone fails during a lucrative sales pitch. Makem responds with its own memo stating that in the event of defective phones, Makem is liable only to repair or replace, and *is not liable for consequential damages, lost profits, or any other damages*.

Makem's acceptance has included a *different* term because its language contradicts the offer. Almost all courts would agree that the parties intended to reach an agreement and therefore the contract is enforceable. The question is, what are its terms? Is the full warranty of the offer included, or the very limited warranty of the acceptance? The majority of states hold that **different terms cancel each other out**. Neither party's language goes into the contract. But what then *are* the terms of the deal?

If the evidence indicates that the parties had orally agreed on the issue disputed in the forms, then the courts will ignore the contradictory writings and enforce the oral contract. **If there is no clear oral agreement, the Code supplies its own terms, called gap-fillers,** which cover prices, delivery dates and places, warranties, and other subjects. In the cellular phone case, the contradicting warranty provisions cancel each other out. The parties had not orally agreed on a warranty, so a court would enforce the Code's gap-filler warranty, which does permit recovery of compensatory and consequential damages. Therefore, Makem *would* be liable for lost profits. We outline most of the gap-filler terms in Chapter 10. Warranty provisions are analyzed in greater detail in Chapter 20.

In the following case, the Rhode Island Supreme Court seeks the fairest method of sorting out conflicting terms.

CODE PROVISIONS DISCUSSED IN THIS CASE

Issue	Relevant Code Section
1. Which are the terms of this agreement?	UCC Section 2-207: *Additional* terms generally but not always become part of the bargain. *Different* terms generally cancel each other out.
2. What is the Code's gap-filler provision concerning delivery?	UCC Section 2-309: The time for shipment or delivery if not agreed upon is a reasonable time.
3. What is a "reasonable" delivery time?	UCC Section 1-204: A "reasonable" time depends on the nature, purpose, and circumstances of the action.

SUPERIOR BOILER WORKS, INC. v. R. J. SANDERS, INC.

711 A.2d 628
SUPREME COURT OF RHODE ISLAND, 1998

CASE SUMMARY

Facts: R. J. Sanders, Inc., had a contract with the federal government to install the heating system at a federal prison camp. The company negotiated with Superior Boiler Works to purchase three large commercial units. On March 27, Superior sent a proposal to Sanders, offering to sell three boilers for a total of $156,000 and estimating time of delivery at four weeks. The parties exchanged further documents and held various discussions. Finally, on July 20, Sanders sent a "purchase order" for three boilers, agreeing to pay $145,827 and stating "Date required: 4 Weeks," that is, August 20. On August 6, Superior sent a "sales order," agreeing to sell the three boilers at that price, but providing a shipping date of October 1. This later delivery date forced Sanders to rent temporary boilers at a cost of $45,315. On October 1, Superior shipped the boilers, which arrived on October 5. Sanders sent a check in the amount of $100,000, claiming that Superior had delivered the boilers late and deducting the cost of its

rental equipment. Superior sued for the additional $45,000 and moved for summary judgment, which the trial court granted. Sanders appealed, claiming that the contract had required Superior to deliver the boilers within four weeks.

Issue: *Did Superior's October delivery breach the contract?*

Decision: Superior did not breach the contract. Affirmed.

Reasoning: Sanders's amended purchase order of July 20 and Superior's August 6 response agree on the specifications and price of the boilers. Although the documents disagree on time of delivery, they still create a contract because both parties *intended* to be bound. The time of delivery should be settled under UCC Section 2-207 (2).

Courts in other states rule in a variety of ways when faced with terms that differ. Rhode Island adopts the "knock-out" rule: Conflicting contract terms knock each other out, leaving a hole to be filled by the Code's gap-filler provision. It is true that this may result in a contract provision that neither party wants; however, each side may protect against this by insisting that agreement be made on its own terms.

Section 2-309 states that if the parties do not agree on the time for delivery, it should be a *reasonable* time. Normally, it is for the fact finder to determine reasonableness from all of the circumstances surrounding the transaction, including the parties' earlier deals, standard trade usage, and so on. See UCC Section 1-204 (2). In this case, though, all of the evidence demonstrates that, measured by industry standards, Superior's performance was reasonable.

EXAM *Strategy*

Question: Martin, a diamond wholesaler, writes Serge, a jewelry retailer, offering to sell 75 specified diamonds for $2 million. Martin's offer sheet specifies the price, quantity, date of delivery and other key terms. The sheet also states, "Offer is made on these terms and no other." Serge sends Martin his own purchase order, naming the diamonds, price and so forth, but adding a clause requiring any disputes to be settled by a diamond-industry arbitrator. In the diamond industry, arbitration by such a person is standard. Martin does not object to the arbitration clause. Martin delivers the gems but Serge refuses to pay the full price, claiming that many of the stones are of inferior quality. Martin sues for the balance due, but Serge insists that any dispute must be settled by arbitration. May Martin litigate or must he arbitrate the case?

Strategy: Under the common law, there might not be a contract between these parties, because Serge added a new term. However, this agreement concerns the sale of goods, meaning that the UCC governs. Under UCC Section 2-207, when both parties are merchants (as they are here), additional terms become part of the contract except in three instances. Review those three instances, and apply them here.

Result: Additional terms become part of the agreement unless the original offeror insisted on its own terms, the new term materially alters the offer, or the offeror promptly rejects the new term. Martin's offer insisted on its own terms and Serge's arbitration clause does not become part of the agreement. Martin may litigate his dispute.

OPEN TERMS: SECTIONS 2-305 AND 2-306
Open Prices

If the contract permits the buyer or seller to determine the price during contract performance, Section 2-305 requires that she do so in good faith.

Under Section 2-305, the parties may conclude a contract even though they have not settled the price. Again, this is a change from the common law, which required certainty of such an important contract term. Under the Code, if the parties have not stated one, **the price is a reasonable price at the time of delivery.** A court will use market value and other comparable sales to determine what a reasonable price would have been. If the contract permits the buyer or seller to *determine* the price during contract performance, Section 2-305 requires that she do so in good faith, as the following case demonstrates.

CODE PROVISIONS DISCUSSED IN THIS CASE

Issue	Relevant Code Sections
1. May the parties form a binding agreement without specifying the price?	UCC Section 2-305(1): The parties may conclude a contract even though they have not settled the price.
2. May a contract permit one party to settle the price?	UCC Section 2-305(2): "A price to be fixed by the seller or by the buyer" requires that it be fixed in good faith.
3. What does *good faith* mean?	UCC Sections 1-201(19), 1-203 and 2-103: For *non-merchants*, good faith means honesty in fact. For a *merchant*, good faith means honesty in fact *plus* the exercise of reasonable commercial standards of fair dealing.

MATHIS V. EXXON CORPORATION

302 F.3d 448
FIFTH CIRCUIT COURT OF APPEALS, 2002

CASE SUMMARY

Facts: Exxon marketed gasoline to retailers in three ways. *Franchisees* (who owned local gas stations) were required to purchase a minimum number of gallons per month. Exxon set the price each month, known as the dealer tank wagon price (DTW). *Jobbers* (distributors who could resell to dealers) paid the "rack price," which was generally lower than the DTW. *Company-operated retail stores* (CORS) paid nothing because Exxon owned them.

A group of 54 Texas franchisees sued, claiming that Exxon set their gasoline prices artificially high. The plaintiffs alleged that Exxon wanted to drive them out of business and replace their franchises with more profitable CORS. The evidence indicated that the franchisees' DTW was consistently higher than the rack price paid by jobbers. Many plaintiffs testified that their franchises had become unprofitable. One study showed that 62 percent of franchisees in Corpus Christi, Texas, were selling gas below the price they paid for it. Plaintiffs' expert testified that 75 percent of their competitors could buy gasoline at a lower price.

The plaintiffs argued that this evidence demonstrated that Exxon set the prices in bad faith. The jury agreed, awarding the plaintiffs $5.7 million, plus $2.3 million in attorney's fees. Exxon appealed.

Issue: *Did Exxon set the prices in bad faith?*

Decision: Yes, Exxon set the prices in bad faith. Affirmed.

Reasoning: The UCC rejects the notion that a seller may fix any price it wants. When a contract permits a seller to set the price, it must do so in good faith. These franchisees allege bad faith. Lawsuits like this are rare because a mere allegation of bad faith is unpersuasive. Here, though, the plaintiffs offered considerable evidence of Exxon's bad faith.

There was testimony and documentation indicating that Exxon planned to replace many of its franchises with CORS. The plaintiffs also showed that the DTW price was higher than the rack price, and that Exxon prevented franchisees from purchasing gas from jobbers. Because of the unnaturally high price that franchisees were forced to pay for their gas, many of their dealerships were unprofitable and uncompetitive.

An Exxon document stated the company's "marketing strategy is to reduce Dealer stores." Another company paper indicated that Exxon wanted to reduce dealer stores in Houston from 95 to 45. Exxon's regional director acknowledged that the company made greater profits from CORS than from franchises. CORS with convenience stores were the most profitable and were considered the wave of the future. The number of dealer stations declined steadily. Even though Exxon was moving to replace independent dealers with CORS, it never made that position clear to its franchisees.

There was more than enough evidence to support the jury's conclusion that Exxon set its prices in bad faith.

EXAM *Strategy*

Question: Coffee Retailer sends a form to Cupper, ordering 100 cartons of specified coffee cups to be delivered the first of each month for six months. The order form says nothing about price. For three months, Cupper delivers on time and sends an invoice, which Retailer pays. On the fourth month, Cupper's invoice is 8% higher than before. Retailer refuses to pay the increase and informs Cupper that it will accept no more deliveries. Cupper sues. Retailer claims there was no enforceable contract. Cupper says there was a bargain and that it has the right to determine the price. Who is right?

Strategy: Retailer's offer included no price. Under the common law, the absence of such an essential term would mean there was no contract. However, these are goods, and under the UCC the parties can make an enforceable deal without specifying the price. This is a valid contract. The companies may, if they choose, permit one party to determine the price. Did they do so here? If so, is Cupper's conduct reasonable? If the parties did not allow one side to set the price, how would a court do so?

Result: This contract neither stated a price nor allowed one party to determine it. That means that the price is a reasonable one at the time of delivery. A court will use market value, and any comparable sales, to determine the price.

Output and Requirements Contracts

Under Section 2-306, an output contract obligates the seller to sell all of his output to the buyer, who agrees to accept it. Suppose Joel has a small plant in which he manufactures large plants, that is, handcrafted artificial flowers and trees, made of silk and other expensive materials. Joel isn't sure how many he can produce in a year, but wants a guaranteed market. He makes an output contract with Yolanda, in which he promises to sell the entire output of his plant and she agrees to buy it all.

A requirements contract is the reverse, obligating a buyer to purchase all of his needed goods from the seller. Joel might sign a requirements contract with Worm Express, agreeing to buy from Worm all of the silk he needs. Both output and requirements contracts are valid under the Code, although they create certain problems. By definition, the exact quantity of goods is not specified. But then how much may one party demand? Is there any upper or lower limit?

The UCC requires that the parties in an output or requirements contract make their demands in good faith. For example, in a requirements contract, a buyer may not suddenly increase her demand far beyond what the parties expected merely because there has been a market change. Suppose the price of silk skyrockets. Joel's requirements contract obligates Worm Express to sell him all the silk he needs. Could Joel demand 10 times the silk he had anticipated, knowing he could resell it at a big profit to other manufacturers? No. That would be bad faith. Come on, Joel, play by the rules.

May the buyer *reduce* his demand far below what the parties anticipated? Yes, so long as he makes the reduction in good faith.

MODIFICATION

Terry, a business consultant, agrees to work for Awkward Co. to create a corporate reorganization plan and oversee its implementation. He promises to finish the job by October 15. By September, Terry is far behind schedule and asks Awkward for an extra three months and for 30 percent extra pay. Terry hints broadly that if the company refuses, he will walk off the job. Awkward agrees in writing to the extra time and money, and Terry finally finishes. Awkward then sues, based on Terry's late completion and overcharge. Who wins? Awkward. This was a services contract. Under the common law, a modification is invalid unless supported by additional consideration, which Terry never gave. Had the contract been one for the sale of goods, however, the outcome would have been different.

UCC Section 2-209: An agreement modifying a contract needs no consideration to be binding. Suppose Jeanette makes a deal to buy a used Mercedes "in good running order" from her sister, Valerie, for $29,000. Valerie writes to Jeanette confirming the agreement and promising to bring the car the following week. But before Valerie can deliver the car, a major transmission problem makes it inoperable. Valerie pays $1,200 to repair it. She telephones Jeanette and explains the extra cost. Jeanette faxes a note, promising to split the cost of the repair. Is Jeanette's promise enforceable? Valerie was already obligated to deliver a car in good running order. But under the UCC, contract modifications need no additional consideration to be valid. The UCC also permits the parties to modify some contracts orally. Regrettably, the Code is not crystal clear about which changes may be oral and which must be written. The wise executive will insist that all parties sign any proposed modifications. For better or worse, though, Section 2-209 clearly implies that some alterations may be enforceable even with nothing in writing, so never orally agree to a contract change unless you are prepared to live with it.[5]

Parties make a contract attempting to control their futures. But one party's certainty can be undercut by the ease with which the other party may obtain a modification. Section 2-209 acknowledges this tension by enabling the parties to limit changes. **The parties may agree to prohibit oral modifications and insist that all modifications be in writing and signed. Between merchants, such a clause is valid. But if either party is *not* a merchant, such a clause is valid only if the non-merchant *separately* signs it.**

Once again the Code gives greater protection to non-merchants than to merchants. Two merchants may agree, as part of their bargain, that any future modifications will be valid only if written and signed. But this limitation on modifications is not valid against a non-merchant unless she separately signs the limiting clause itself. Suppose a furniture retailer orders 200 beds from a manufacturer. The retailer's order form requires any modifications to be in writing. The manufacturer initials the retailer's form at the bottom. The parties have a valid agreement and no oral modifications will be enforced. But suppose the retailer sells a bed to a customer. The sales form also bars oral modifications. That prohibition is void unless the customer separately signs it.

The following case looks at an oral modification.

---

[5] The confusion stems from the ambiguous language of Section 2-209(3), which requires a writing if "the contract as modified" is covered by Section 2-201, the statute of frauds provision. Some courts have interpreted this to mean that once a contract is covered by Section 2-201 and needs a writing to be enforceable, any modifications must also be in writing. But others have suggested that a writing is obligatory only if the modification brings the contract within Section 2-201 *for the first time*, or if the *modification itself* falls within Section 2-201, or if the modification *changes the quantity* terms of the original contract. There is no definitive answer to this problem, as the court noted in *Flowers Ginning Co. v. Arma, Inc.*, 1997 U.S. App. LEXIS 1054 (4th Cir. 1997). Actually there is: Get it write.

CODE PROVISIONS DISCUSSED IN THIS CASE

Issue	Relevant Code Sections
1. May the parties prohibit oral modifications of the contract?	UCC Section 2-209(2): A signed agreement that excludes modification or rescission except by a signed writing cannot be otherwise modified or rescinded.
2. Did Marley's conduct waive the prohibition on modification?	UCC Section 2-209(4): Although an attempt at modification or rescission does not satisfy the requirements of subsection (2), it can operate as a waiver.

YOU *be the* JUDGE

THE MARLEY COOLING TOWER COMPANY V. CALDWELL ENERGY & ENVIRONMENTAL, INC.

280 F. Supp. 2d 651 United States District Court for the Western District of Kentucky, 2003

Facts: Caldwell manufactured and installed cooling systems for power plants. Caldwell agreed with Duke/Fluor Daniel (D/FD) to install such a system in Aiken, South Carolina. The contract stated that Caldwell would pay liquidated damages of $5,000 per day if the system was late.

Marley agreed to ship to Caldwell all of the material and equipment needed to build the cooling system, and to deliver it no later than April 1. The Marley-Caldwell contract stated that "Neither Marley or the Purchaser shall be responsible or held liable for any special, indirect, consequential, liquidated and/or punitive damages." The agreement also provided that there could be no contract changes without a signed, written modification.

Marley delivered its material almost two months behind schedule, making Caldwell late in fulfilling its obligations to build the cooling system. D/FD assessed Caldwell liquidated damages of $135,000. Caldwell attempted to pass this cost, which it called "backcharges," on to Marley by paying $135,000 less than Marley's invoice demanded.

Marley sent Caldwell a letter, stating "We would like to work with you to resolve this issue. However, before we can agree to these backcharges, we must have [certain specified] documents." Caldwell supplied the documents, and also sent a change order, indicating that Marley accepted the backcharges. The change order stated that it would not be valid until signed by both Caldwell and Marley. A Marley executive agreed on the telephone to accept the backcharges, but Marley never signed or returned the change order. Marley later rejected the charges. When Caldwell refused to pay the full contract price, Marley sued. Both sides moved for summary judgment.

You Be the Judge: Is Marley obligated to pay the backcharges?

Argument for Marley: There are two contracts here, and both are clear. First, Caldwell consented to a large liquidated damage clause with D/FD, and now regrets its contract. Too late. Next time the company agrees to such a clause, it should either obtain insurance or insist on a parallel agreement from *its* suppliers. Caldwell's failure to protect itself entitles the company to sympathy—but no money. Second, Caldwell agreed that Marley would not be liable for any liquidated or consequential damages. The Caldwell-Marley contract also prohibited oral modification. This agreement was made by qualified lawyers representing experienced merchants.

The fact that a Marley executive acknowledged, by phone, the company's ambivalence does not change the contract or the law. UCC Section 2-209 was written for cases like this. Companies in the midst of a dispute should discuss the matter freely, without worrying that a spontaneous comment will prove costly. Marley openly considered its options knowing that only a signed

continued

modification would create liability. Caldwell asked for such a written modification, but Marley signed nothing. End of case.

Argument for Caldwell: Let us start with what is obvious, undisputed, and most important: Marley caused the problem. Marley delivered its material late, without excuse. In fairness, that should make the outcome clear: A company that causes the harm pays for it.

That of course is why a Marley executive acknowledged the justice of the backcharges. The same executive asked for certain verifying documents. Was that request made in bad faith, or as a joke? No. Marley had agreed in principle to cover the backcharges and wanted assurance that the costs were real. Caldwell promptly supplied the documents, proving that the costs were only too real.

Marley's actions in requesting documents, and then agreeing to pay the backcharges, were a clear waiver of the "no-oral-modification" rule. A signed modification is a silly formality. The Code is designed to cut through legal technicalities and enable experienced merchants to conduct business as usual. Telephone calls, and oral modifications, qualify as routine business. UCC Section 2-209(4) allows a waiver by words-and-action because that is how companies do business. Let Marley pay for the damage it caused *and explicitly acknowledged.*

The following table concludes this chapter with an illustration of the Code's impact on the common law.

SELECTED CODE PROVISIONS THAT CHANGE THE COMMON LAW

Issue	Common Law Rule	UCC Sec.	UCC Rule	Example
Contract formation	Offer must be followed by acceptance that shows meeting of the minds on all important terms.	Section 2-204 and Section 2-305	Contract can be made in any manner sufficient to show agreement; moment of making not critical; one or more terms, including the price, may be left open.	Tilly writes Meg, "I need a new van for my delivery company." Meg delivers a van and Tilly starts to use it. Under the common law, there is no contract, because no price was ever mentioned; under the UCC, the writing plus the conduct show an intention to contract (2-204). The price is a *reasonable* one (2-305).
Writing requirement	All essential terms must be in writing.	Section 2-201	Any writing is sufficient if it indicates a contract; terms may be omitted or misstated; "merchant" exception can create a contract enforceable against a party who receives the writing and does nothing within 10 days.	Douglas, a car dealer, signs and sends to Michael, another dealer, a memo saying, "Confirming our deal for your blue Rolls." Michael reads it but ignores it; 10 days later Douglas has satisfied the statute of frauds under the UCC's merchant exception.
Added terms in acceptance	An acceptance that adds or changes any term is a counteroffer.	Section 2-207	Additional or different terms are not necessarily counteroffers; their presence does not prevent a contract from being formed, and in some cases the new terms will become a part of the bargain.	Roberts sends a pre-printed form to Julia, offering to buy 25 computers and stating a price; Julia responds with her own pre-printed form, accepting the offer but adding a term that balances unpaid after 30 days incur a finance charge. The additional term is not a counteroffer; there is a valid contract; and the finance charge is part of the bargain.

Issue	Common Law Rule	UCC Sec.	UCC Rule	Example
Modification	A modification is valid only if supported by new consideration.	Section 2-209	A modification needs no consideration to be binding.	Martin, a computer manufacturer, agrees to sell Steve, a retailer, 500 computers at a specified price, including delivery. The next day Martin learns that his delivery costs have gone up 20%; he calls Steve, who faxes a note agreeing to pay 15% extra. Under the common law, the modification would be void; under the Code, it is enforceable.

CHAPTER CONCLUSION

The Uniform Commercial Code enables parties to create a contract quickly. While this can be helpful in a fast-paced business world, it also places responsibility on executives. Informal conversations may cause at least one party to conclude that it has a binding agreement—and the law may agree.

EXAM REVIEW

1. **UNIFORM COMMERCIAL CODE** The Code is designed to modernize commercial law and make it uniform throughout the country. (p. 426)

2. **SALE OF GOODS** Article 2 applies to the sale of goods, which are movable things other than money and investment securities. (p. 426)

3. **LEASING** Article 2A governs the leasing of goods. (p. 427)

4. **MIXED CONTRACTS** In a mixed contract involving goods and services, the UCC applies if the predominant purpose is the sale of goods. (p. 427)

5. **MERCHANTS** A merchant is someone who routinely deals in the particular goods involved, or who appears to have special knowledge or skill in those goods, or who uses agents with special knowledge or skill. The UCC frequently holds a merchant to a higher standard of conduct than a non-merchant. (p. 428)

6. **GOOD FAITH** The UCC imposes a duty of good faith in the performance of all contracts. (p. 428)

7. **UNCONSCIONABILITY** A contract is unconscionable if it is shockingly one-sided and fundamentally unfair. A court is much likelier to use unconscionability to protect a consumer than a corporation. (p. 429)

EXAM Strategy

Question: Jim Dan, Inc. owned a golf course that had trouble with crab grass. Jim Dan bought 20 bags of Scotts Pro Turf Goosegrass/Crabgrass Control for $835 and applied it to the greens. The Pro Turf harmed the greens, causing over $36,000 in damage. Jim Dan sued Scotts. Scotts defended by claiming that it sold the Pro Turf with a clearly written, easy-to-read disclaimer that stated that in the event of damage, the buyer's only remedy would be a refund of the purchase price. Jim Dan, Inc. argued that the clause was unconscionable. Please rule.

Strategy: There are two steps to deciding an issue of unconscionability. First, does the contract involve a consumer, or is this an agreement between two businesses? Second, is the agreement shockingly one-sided? (See the "Result" at the end of this section.)

8. **FORMATION** UCC Section 2-204 permits the parties to form a contract in any manner that shows agreement. (p. 429)

9. **WRITING** For the sale of goods worth $500 or more, UCC Section 2-201 requires some writing that indicates an agreement. Terms may be omitted or misstated, but the contract will be enforced only to the extent of the quantity stated. (p. 431)

EXAM Strategy

Question: To satisfy the UCC statute of frauds regarding the sale of goods, which of the following must generally be in writing?

(a) Designation of the parties as buyer and seller

(b) Delivery terms

(c) Quantity of the goods

(d) Warranties to be made

Strategy: Okay, this may be overkill. But the question illustrates two basic points of UCC law: First, the Code allows a great deal of flexibility in the formation of contracts. Second, there is one term for which no flexibility is allowed. Make sure you know which it is. (See the "Result" at the end of this section.)

10. **MERCHANT'S EXCEPTION** When two merchants make an oral contract, and one sends a confirming memo to the other within a reasonable time, and the memo is sufficiently definite that it could be enforced against the sender herself, then the merchant who receives it will also be bound unless he objects within 10 days. (p. 432)

11. **ADDITIONAL TERMS** UCC Section 2-207 governs an acceptance that does not "mirror" the offer. *Additional terms* usually, but not always, become part of the contract. *Different terms* contradict a term in the offer. When that happens, most courts reject both parties' proposals and rely on gap-filler terms. (p. 435)

EXAM Strategy

Question: Cookie Co. offered to sell Distrib Markets 20,000 pounds of cookies at $1.00 per pound, subject to certain specified terms for delivery. Distrib replied in writing as follows: "We accept your offer for 20,000 pounds of cookies at $1.00 per pound, weighing scale to have valid city certificate." Under the UCC:

(a) A contract was formed between the parties

(b) A contract will be formed only if Cookie agrees to the weighing scale requirement

(c) No contract was formed because Distrib included the weighing scale requirement in its reply

(d) No contract was formed because Distrib's reply was a counteroffer

Strategy: Distrib's reply included a new term. That means it is governed by UCC 2-207. Is the new term an additional term or a different term? An additional term goes beyond what the offeror stated. Additional terms become a part of the contract except in three specified instances. A different term contradicts one made by the offeror. Different terms generally cancel each other out. (See the "Result" at the end of this section.)

12. **PRICE** Under UCC Section 2-305 a contract is enforceable even if the price is not stated. In such cases the price must be reasonable. (p. 437)

13. **MODIFICATION** UCC Section 2-209 permits contracts to be modified even if there is no consideration. The parties may prohibit oral modifications, but such a clause is ineffective against a non-merchant unless she signed it. (p. 440)

7. Result: This is a bargain between two businesses, and courts rarely find clauses in such agreements unconscionable. The assumption is that sophisticated business people understand what they are getting into and are able to protect themselves. If Jim Dan could run a golf course, the company was sophisticated enough to understand the simple disclaimer in this contract. Scotts wins.

9. Result: (D). The contract will be enforced only to the extend of the quantity stated.

11. Result: The "valid city certificate" phrase raises a new issue; it does not contradict anything in Cookie's offer. That means it is an additional term, and becomes part of the deal unless Cookie insisted on its own terms, the additional term materially alters the offer, or Cookie promptly rejects it. Cookie did not insist on its terms, this is a minor addition, and Cookie never rejected it. The new term is part of a valid contract and the answer is "a."

ADDITIONAL QUESTIONS

1. ***CPA QUESTION*** With regard to a contract governed by the UCC sales article, which one of the following statements is correct?

    (a) Merchants and non-merchants are treated alike.

    (b) The contract may involve the sale of any type of personal property.

    (c) The obligations of the parties to the contract must be performed in good faith.

    (d) The contract must involve the sale of goods for a price $500 or more.

2. ***ETHICS*** Systems Design designed and installed a software system for the savings accounts of the Kansas City Post Office Employees Credit Union. The software caused many problems and, ultimately, a lawsuit. The court had to decide whether the UCC governed. In similar cases, courts from other states had found that such a contract was *predominantly for the sale of goods*. Based on that, and on the doctrine of *uniformity*, the court ruled that the UCC governed. What does "predominantly for the sale of goods" have to do with the decision? Why is "uniformity" a factor? A word about the ethics of uniformity. From the perspective of two parties in a business dispute, what is potentially *threatening* about the idea of uniformity? Why is the doctrine potentially *attractive* to two business executives attempting to negotiate a contract?

3. Mail Code, Inc. manufactured bar code machines for reading addresses on envelopes. Its offices were in Indiana. John Grauberger, who lived in Kansas, applied to become a dealer for the Mail Code machine in the Kansas area. He signed a dealer application form, agreeing to abide by the terms printed on it. Mail Code informed Grauberger that it accepted him as a dealer and showed him a dealer agreement outlining his duties. The agreement contained a "forum selection" clause, stating that any disputes would be settled in a court in Indiana. Grauberger made no objection. He purchased a bar code machine for $31,000, but it did not work. Grauberger sued in Kansas, but Mail Code attempted to have the case dismissed because it had not been brought in Indiana. Did the parties have a valid agreement? Was the forum selection clause part of the agreement?

4. The Massachusetts Bay Transit Authority (MBTA) awarded the Perini Corp. a large contract to rehabilitate a section of railroad tracks. The work involved undercutting the existing track, removing the ballast and foundation, rebuilding the track, and disposing of the old material. Perini solicited an offer from Atlantic Track & Turnout Co. for Atlantic to buy whatever salvageable material Perini removed. Perini estimated the quantity of salvageable material that would be available.

Atlantic offered to purchase "all available" material over the course of Perini's deal with the MBTA, and Perini accepted. But three months into the project, the MBTA ran short of money and told Perini to stop the undercutting part of the project. That was the work that made Perini its profit, so Perini requested that the MBTA terminate the agreement, which the agency did. By that point Perini had delivered to Atlantic only about 15 percent of the salvageable material that it had estimated. Atlantic sued. What kind of contract do the parties have? Who should win and why?

5. Nina owns a used car lot. She signs and sends a fax to Seth, a used car wholesaler who has a huge lot of cars in the same city. The fax says, "Confirming our agrmt—I pick any 15 cars fr yr lot—30% below blue book." Seth reads the fax, laughs, and throws it away. Two weeks later, Nina arrives and demands to purchase 15 of Seth's cars. Is he obligated to sell?

6. The Brugger Corp. owned a farm, operated by Jason Weimer, who acted as the company's business agent. Tri-Circle, Inc. was a farm equipment company. On behalf of Brugger, Weimer offered to buy from Tri-Circle certain equipment for use on the farm. Tri-Circle accepted the offer, using a pre-printed form. The form included a finance charge for late payment. Weimer's offer had said nothing about finance charges, but he made no objection to the new term. Tri-Circle supplied the farm equipment but later alleged that Brugger had refused to pay for $12,000 worth of the supplies. Tri-Circle sued. In deciding whether Tri-Circle was entitled to finance charges, the court first inquired whether Brugger, Weimer, and Tri-Circle were merchants. Why did it look into that issue? *Were* they merchants?

7. Which one of the following transactions is not governed by Article 2 of the UCC?

   (a) Purchasing an automobile for $35,000

   (b) Leasing an automobile worth $35,000

   (c) Purchasing a radio worth $449

8. Are you the typical student who just cannot get enough questions and quizzes about the UCC? See the "Construction Law Survival Manual" section of www.fullertonlaw. com. The Web site has a long discussion of the UCC, interspersed with contract hypotheticals and questions.

9. ***YOU BE THE JUDGE*** WRITING PROBLEM Brewster manufactured plastic bottles. Dial made personal care products at many plants around the country, including one in Salem, Virginia. The companies agreed that Dial would purchase from Brewster all of the plastic bottles it needed for its Salem factory. Dial estimated its requirements for one year at 7,850,000 bottles, but added a clause stating that "quantities are estimated only and do not bind Dial to purchase any minimum quantity." A few months later, Dial concluded that its Salem plant was unprofitable. The company closed the factory and notified Brewster that it would buy no bottles at all. Brewster sued. Did Dial have the right to reduce its orders to zero? **Argument for Brewster:** The parties had a clear contract for a massive number of bottles. Dial knew that this contract was extremely important to Brewster. Although Dial had some right to adjust its orders, it had no right to reduce them to zero. **Argument for Dial:** The issue is whether Dial acted in good faith. It did.

The company had a legitimate reason for closing the factory—it was losing money—and with no factory it certainly did not need any bottles.

10. **ROLE REVERSAL** Write a multiple-choice question that contrasts the common law rules of contract formation with those of UCC Section 2-204.

INTERNET RESEARCH PROBLEM

Online, find a current dispute involving either *additional* or *different* contract terms. Analyze the case, using UCC 2-207, and predict the outcome.

You can find further practice problems at www.cengagebrain.com. See the preface of this book for website access details.

OWNERSHIP AND RISK

He drove his truck fast along the rough country road, hurrying through the shadows of the Cascade Mountains, passing close to the Rogue River. The door panel, freshly painted, read "Ernest Jenkins, Cattle Buyer." Spinning the wheel hard left he drove through an impressive gate, under a wooden sign proclaiming "Double Q Ranch." He knew the ranch by reputation and quickly saw that it was prosperous—a good place for a man like him to do business.

He introduced himself to Kate Vandermeer, the Double Q's business manager, and expressed an interest in buying 300 head of cattle. Vandermeer and the man mounted horses and rode out to inspect the herd. Vandermeer noticed that his boots were brand new and that he rode awkwardly.

> Vandermeer noticed that his boots were brand new and that he rode awkwardly.

He was satisfied with the cattle, so the two bargained, sitting on horseback and looking into the sunset. Vandermeer started at $310,000 and was surprised at how quickly they reached an agreement, at $285,000, a price she considered excellent. They agreed that Vandermeer would deliver the cattle by truck, in one week, in a nearby town. He would pay with a cashier's check and take possession of the cattle and all ownership documents, such as brand inspection certificates and veterinarian's certificates. Back at the ranch, Vandermeer offered him a drink, but he had to hurry to another appointment.

The next week, right on schedule, he arrived on Thursday and presented his cashier's check for the full amount. When they had transferred the livestock, Vandermeer suggested they talk over some future business, but he was again in a rush. They shook hands and parted, the man heading due east, fast.

The Double Q's bank sent the cashier's check for collection, but learned early the following week that it was forged. Vandermeer called the State Police, who traced the man's movements to the state line. Three weeks later and 1,600 miles east, the FBI located the cattle, with the prominent "QQ" brand, in stockyards in Omaha. Ned Munson had purchased the cattle from the man for $225,000, which he considered a bargain. He had paid with a cashier's check. Ernest Jenkins, of course, had disappeared—literally. The truck's freshly painted door now read, "Ted J. Pringle, Grain Merchant," and it was parked a long, long way from Omaha.

LEGAL INTEREST

Who owns the cows? The Double Q wanted its cattle back or $285,000. If Munson was dumb enough to pay money to a thief, that wasn't the ranch's problem. But Ned Munson claimed the cows were his. He had paid a fair price to a man who appeared to own them. If Vandermeer was so foolish as to give up the cattle to a con artist, let the ranch suffer the consequences. The Double Q sued. Both parties to this lawsuit are unhappy, but happily they have illustrated the theme for our chapter: When two parties claim a conflicting legal interest in particular goods, *who loses?* Who obtains the law's protection? These are disputes over *conflicting interests in goods*.

An interest is a legal right in something. More than one party can have an interest in particular goods. Suppose you lease a new car from a dealer, agreeing to pay $300 per month for three years. Several parties will have legal interests in the car. The dealer still *owns* the car—interest number one. At the end of three years, the dealer gets it back. For three years, you have the use of the car—interest number two. You may use the car for all normal purposes but are obligated to make monthly payments. Your payments go to a finance agency, which has made an arrangement with the dealer, to obtain the right to your $300 monthly payment. The finance agency has a *security interest* in the car—interest number three. If you fail to pay on time, the finance company has the right to repossess your car. If you take the car to a garage for maintenance, the garage has *temporary possession* of the car—interest number four. The garage has the right to keep the car locked up over night, to work on it, and to test drive it. Sometimes legal interests can clash, and it is those conflicts we look at here.

Often the parties will claim ownership, each arguing that his interest is stronger than the other's. But in this chapter we also consider cases where each party argues that the *other* one owns the goods. Suppose a seller manufactures products for a buyer, but while the goods are being shipped, they are destroyed in a fire. Seller may argue that it no longer owned the goods, but buyer will claim it had not yet acquired them. In other cases, a *third party* will be involved. You pay $30,000 cash to buy a new car and expect to pick it up in three days. But the day before you arrive, the dealer's bank seizes all of the cars on the lot, claiming the dealer has defaulted on loans. Now the fight over legal interest is between you and the bank, with the dealer a relatively passive observer.

In the cattle case, three parties had a legal interest in the goods. The Double Q ranch originally had valid **title** to the cattle, **meaning the normal rights of ownership**. Ernest Jenkins, the scam artist, acquired a lesser interest. His contract with Double Q was fraudulent because Jenkins intended to cheat the ranch. Nonetheless, he did have an agreement. He obtained **voidable title**, meaning limited rights in the goods, inferior to those of the owner.[1] Finally, Ned Munson makes a claim to the cattle based on his payment and his possession of the cows and all documents.

Voidable title

Limited rights in goods, inferior to those of the owner.

The court will use various sections of the UCC to determine who keeps the cows and who bears the loss. Ned Munson should win the cattle. He was probably acting in good faith and a commercially reasonable manner when he bought the cows from a man who appeared to be a lawful cattle buyer. The Double Q must bear the loss. If, however, the Double Q can convince a court that Munson acted irresponsibly because he had grounds for suspecting Jenkins, the court might order Munson to pay for the cattle.[2]

ETHICS As we look at this issue and others like it, ask yourself whether the UCC rules and the court decisions accomplish two sensible goals: (1) to be fair to innocent parties and (2) to encourage reasonable business practices nationwide. Both Munson and the Double Q were innocent parties. Jenkins was the bad guy. Why let Munson keep the livestock? Because he probably did all that a reasonable businessperson should do in buying cattle. He paid a fair (though low) price to a man who had all the normal ownership documents. The Code *could* place a greater burden on Munson and require, for example, that he investigate Jenkins's background. The law *could* force Munson to check the history of the cattle and find out how Jenkins acquired them. But such rules would hogtie the cattle industry. Most sales are legitimate; cattle ranchers and buyers must be able to buy and sell quickly, responding to market conditions and opportunities for profit.

Notice that in this case and most others, the Code focuses on basic fairness and sensible business practices. Munson wins because he acted reasonably and in good faith, *not* because he happens to hold certain certificates to the animals. The Code's authors have labored to get away from legal formalities and give results that make sense, as we see in the next section. As you encounter the various commercial problems, bear in mind these issues from the Chapter 2 ethics checklist: Who are the stakeholders? What are the alternatives? Has the process been fair? ◆

IDENTIFICATION, TITLE, AND INSURABLE INTEREST

Historically, courts settled disputes about legal interest by looking at one thing: title. The drafters of the UCC concluded that "title" was too abstract an answer for the assorted practical questions that arose. It could be hard to prove exactly who did have title, and it made no sense to settle a wide variety of business problems with one legal idea. Today, title is only one of several issues that a court will use to resolve conflicting interests in goods. *Identification* and *insurable interest* have become more important as title has diminished in significance. We can begin to understand all three doctrines if we examine how title passes from seller to buyer.

---

[1] We discuss voidability in detail in Chapter 13, on capacity and consent.
[2] For a cattle case that raises these and other issues, see *Rudiger Charolais Ranches v. Van De Graaf Ranches*, 994 F.2d 670, 1993 U.S. App. LEXIS 12412 (9th Cir. 1993).

EXISTENCE AND IDENTIFICATION

Title in goods can pass from one person to another only if the goods exist and have been identified to the contract.

Existence

Goods must exist before title can pass.[3] Although most goods do exist when people buy and sell them, some have not yet come into being, such as crops to be grown later. A farmer may contract to sell corn even before it is planted, but title to the corn cannot pass until the corn exists.

Identification

Goods must be identified to the contract before title can pass.[4] This means that the parties must have designated the specific goods being sold. Identification is an important concept that applies in other areas besides the passing of title. Often identification is obvious. If Dealer agrees to sell to Buyer a 60-foot motor yacht with identification number AKX472, the parties have identified the goods. But suppose Paintco agrees to sell Brushworks 1,000 gallons of white base paint at a specified price. Paintco has 25,000 gallons in its warehouse. Title cannot pass until Paintco identifies the specific gallons that will go to Brushworks.

The parties may agree in their contract how and when they will identify the goods.[5] They are free to identify them to the contract any way they want. Paintco and Brushworks might agree, for example, that within one week of signing the sales agreement, Paintco will mark appropriate gallons. If the gallons are stored 50 to a crate, then Paintco will have a worker stick a "Brushworks" label on 20 crates. Once the label is on, the goods are identified to the contract.

If the parties do not specify, identification will occur according to these rules:[6]

- Identification occurs when the parties enter into a contract if the agreement describes specific goods that already exist. If the Dealer agrees to sell a yacht and the parties include the ID number in their contract, the goods are identified (even though the parties never use the term "identify").

- For unborn animals, identification generally takes place when they are conceived; for crops, identification normally happens when they are planted.

- For other goods, identification occurs when the seller marks, ships, or in some other way indicates the exact goods that are going to the buyer.

▰▰ EXAM *Strategy*

Question: Arielle, an artist, has 25 hand-painted room screens in her studio. She contracts to sell five of them to Retailer for $5,000 each. The contract allows Arielle to choose which five she will sell. Arielle moves five screens from her studio to a warehouse, but a week later

---

[3] UCC Section 2-105(2).
[4] UCC Section 2-401(1).
[5] UCC Section 2-501(1).
[6] UCC Section 2-501.

a fire destroys the building and its contents. Two insurance companies dispute whether title to the screens has passed to Retailer. The warehouse insurer claims the goods were identified and title passed; Retailer's insurer says the goods were not identified and title never passed. The contract says nothing about identification. Have the goods been identified?

Strategy: Title cannot pass until the goods have been identified to the contract. Identification can occur in three ways: the parties describe specific goods that already exist; animals are conceived or crops planted; or the seller marks, ships or otherwise indicates which are going to the buyer. Did any of those things happen?

Result: The parties never described the goods. The goods are neither animals nor crops. However, when Arielle moved five of the screens to the warehouse, she "indicated which goods were going to the buyer." The goods were identified.

PASSING OF TITLE

Once goods exist and are identified to the contract, title can pass from one person to another. **Title may pass in any manner on which the parties agree (UCC Section 2-401).** Once again, the Code allows the parties to control their affairs with commonsense decisions. The parties can agree, for example, that title passes when the goods leave the manufacturer's factory, or when they reach the shipper who will transport them, or at any other time and place. If the parties do not agree on passing title, Section 2-401 decides. There are two possibilities:

- *When the goods are being moved,* title passes to the buyer when the seller completes whatever transportation it is obligated to do. Suppose the Seller is in Milwaukee and the Buyer is in Honolulu. The contract requires the Seller to deliver the goods to a ship in San Francisco. Title passes when the goods reach the ship.

- *When the goods are not being moved,* title passes when the seller delivers ownership documents to the buyer. Suppose Seller, located in Louisville, has already manufactured 5,000 baseball bats, which are stored in a warehouse in San Diego. Under the terms of their contract, Buyer will take possession of the bats at the warehouse. When Seller gives Buyer ownership documents, title passes. If the contract does not require Seller to give such documents, title passes when the parties form the contract. For example, if the Buyer owns the warehouse where the bats are stored, Buyer needs no documents to take possession; title passes when the parties reach agreement.

The following case raises issues of identification and title.

CODE PROVISIONS DISCUSSED IN THIS CASE	
Issue	**Relevant Code Section**
1. In which state were goods identified to the contracts?	UCC Section 2-501(1): The parties may agree in their contract how and when they will identify the goods; otherwise, they are identified as specified in Section 2-501 (a),(b) or (c).
2. In which state did title pass?	UCC Section 2-402: Title may pass in any manner on which the parties agree; otherwise, it passes as specified in Section 2-401.

CIRCUIT CITY STORES, INC. v. COMMISSIONER OF REVENUE

439 MASS. 629, 790 N.E.2d 636
SUPREME JUDICIAL COURT OF MASSACHUSETTS, 2003

CASE SUMMARY

Facts: Circuit City, which sold electronic goods, permitted customers to pay for goods at one store but pick them up at another. Because Massachusetts imposed a 5 percent sales tax on all goods sold in the state, but neighboring New Hampshire had no sales tax, many Massachusetts customers chose to save the 5 percent by collecting their goods at a New Hampshire store.

For these "alternative location" sales, the customer receipt indicated where the item had been bought and where it would be picked up. The receipt also said, "reserved," meaning simply that in the collection store, one less item was available to other customers. Until the merchandise was picked up, the customer could demand a refund or request to collect the item in the store where she had paid for it.

The Massachusetts Commissioner of Revenue demanded sales tax on the "alternative location" sales, claiming that it was a sale in Massachusetts because that is where title passed. Circuit City claimed that it owed no sales tax, because (1) the goods were not identified to the contract until a customer picked them up in New Hampshire, and (2) title passed in New Hampshire. The case reached the highest court in Massachusetts.

Issue: *Where were the goods identified to the contract? Where did title to the goods pass?*

Decision: Title passed in Massachusetts. The goods were identified.

Reasoning: Circuit City claims that it does not credit the sale, or consider that it occurred, until the customer picks up the merchandise. Seller and buyer have agreed, the company asserts, that the transaction in Massachusetts is merely an order for goods, not a concluded sale. The facts suggest otherwise.

The sales receipt contains a description of the item purchased and the time and date of sale. The warranty takes effect at that moment. The sales receipt also gives the customer the right to pick up the merchandise without further payment. What is more, Circuit City credits the sale to its Massachusetts store; the commission goes to the Massachusetts sales associate. Finally, Circuit City considers itself to have fully performed its part of the bargain by noting the alternative location for pickup; from that point on, it is the customer who is obligated to collect the goods. All of this evidence suggests a completed sale made in Massachusetts.

Circuit City correctly notes that under the UCC, no title can pass until goods have been identified to the contract. The company argues that this does not occur until a customer picks up the merchandise and the serial number of a particular unit is scanned into the computer. In fact, though, the customer's sales receipt includes a reserve notation, which indicates that merchandise must be set aside for that particular transaction. That is identification. It is true that at that point, an item has not been specified by serial number, but that is unnecessary for identification. Customers choose their goods only by make and model. Identification by serial number is unnecessary to pass title.

Affirmed.

INSURABLE INTEREST

Closely related to identification and title is the idea of insurable interest. Anyone buying or selling expensive goods should make certain that the goods are insured. There are some limits, though, on who may insure goods, and when. As we saw in Chapter 12, a party may insure something—property, a human life—only when she has a legitimate interest in it. If the person buying the policy lacks a real interest in the thing insured, the law regards the policy as a gambling contract and considers it void.

When does someone have an insurable interest in goods? The Code gives one answer for buyers and one for sellers. **A buyer obtains an insurable interest when the goods are identified to the contract (UCC Section 2-501).** Suppose, in January, Grain Broker contracts with Farmer to buy his entire wheat crop. Neither party mentions "identification." In January, the crop is not identified, and Broker has no insurable interest. In May, after weeks of breaking the soil, Farmer plants his wheat crop. Once he has planted it, the goods are identified. The Broker, who now has an insurable interest, purchases insurance. In July, a drought destroys the crop, and the Broker never gets one grain of wheat. The Broker need not worry: he is insured.

The seller's insurable interest is different. **The seller retains an insurable interest in goods so long as she has either title to the goods or a security interest in them (UCC Section 2-501).** "Security interest" refers to cases in which the buyer still owes the seller some money for the goods. Suppose Flyola Manufacturing sells a small aircraft to WingIt, a dealer, for $300,000. WingIt pays $30,000 cash and agrees to pay interest on the balance until it sells the plane. Flyola has an insurable interest even while the aircraft is in WingIt's showroom and may purchase insurance anytime until WingIt pays off the last dime.

What this means is that a seller and buyer can have an insurable interest in the same goods simultaneously. Suppose the heavy metal band Gentle Bunnies hires Inkem Corp., in Minneapolis, to make 25,000 T-shirts with the Gentle Bunnies logo, for sale at rock concerts. The parties agree that the T-shirts are identified as soon as the logo is printed, and that title will pass when Inkem delivers the T-shirts to the office of the Bunnies' manager in Kansas City. Inkem obviously has an insurable interest while the company is making the T-shirts and continues to have an interest until it delivers the T-shirts in Kansas City. But the Gentle Bunnies' insurable interest arises the moment their logo is stamped on each shirt, so the Bunnies could insure the goods while they are still stored in Inkem's factory. Why would the Bunnies spend hard earned cash to insure goods they do not have? They may be uncertain that Inkem has obtained proper insurance.

In the following case, a car accident leads several insurance companies to dispute who owned the damaged auto. Each company wants to claim that the car belonged to—someone *else*.

CODE PROVISIONS DISCUSSED IN THIS CASE

Issue	Relevant Code Section
1. Which party had title to the car?	UCC Section 2-401: Title to goods may pass in any manner on which the parties agree.
2. Did the seller have an insurable interest in the car?	UCC Section 2-501: The seller retains an insurable interest in the goods as long as it holds title to or a security interest in them.

VALLEY FORGE INSURANCE CO. V. GREAT AMERICAN INSURANCE CO.

1995 OHIO APP. LEXIS 3939
OHIO COURT OF APPEALS, 1995

CASE SUMMARY

Facts: On a Friday afternoon, Karl and Linda Kennedy went to John Nolan Ford to buy a new Ford Mustang. The parties signed all necessary documents, including a New Vehicle Buyer's Order, an Agreement to Provide Insurance, and credit applications. The Kennedys made a down payment but could not arrange financing before the dealership closed. John Nolan Ford determined that the Kennedys were creditworthy and allowed them to take the car home for the weekend. That evening, Karl Kennedy permitted his brother-in-law, Cella, to take the car for a drive, along with a passenger named Campbell. Cella wrecked the car, injuring his passenger. Campbell sued, and the question was which insurance company was liable for all of the harm: John Nolan Ford's insurer (Milwaukee Mutual), Cella's insurer (Valley Forge), or Kennedy's insurer (Great American). The trial court ruled that title had never passed to Kennedy and found Milwaukee Mutual liable. The company appealed.

Issue: *Had title passed to Kennedy at the time of the accident?*

Decision: Affirmed. Title had not yet passed to Kennedy.

Reasoning: Milwaukee Mutual asserts that the risk of loss passed to the Kennedys when the car was delivered to them. However, the signed contract states that the buyer acquires "no right, title, or interest" in the automobile until it is delivered and either the full purchase price is paid in cash or satisfactory financing is arranged. At the time of the accident, the Kennedys had neither paid cash nor signed a financing agreement. Title never passed.

Milwaukee also argues that the Kennedys agreed to insure the automobile. The contract, though, does not state when the Kennedys were obligated to obtain insurance. It would be logical for them to do so after they had obtained title. Because the contract is ambiguous on this point, the agreement must be interpreted against the party who wrote it—namely, the automobile dealer. John Nolan Ford still had the risk of loss when the accident occurred.

WHEN THE SELLER HAS IMPERFECT TITLE

BONA FIDE PURCHASER

Some people are sleazy, and sales law must accommodate that reality. In the chapter opener, we saw a scam artist purchase cattle fraudulently from a respectable ranch and sell them to an honest dealer. The bad guy skipped town, leaving a dispute between two innocent companies. Either the original owner (the ranch) or the buyer (the cattle dealer) must bear the loss. Who loses?

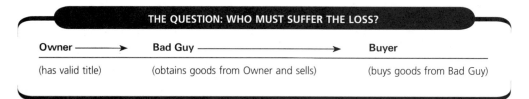

THE QUESTION: WHO MUST SUFFER THE LOSS?

Owner ⟶ Bad Guy ⟶ Buyer

(has valid title)   (obtains goods from Owner and sells)   (buys goods from Bad Guy)

First we need to know what kind of title Bad Guy obtains: Is it void or voidable? If Bad Guy *steals* the goods from Owner, Bad Guy obtains **void title, which is no title at all**. When Bad Guy sells the goods to Buyer, she also gets *no title at all*. Abe steals Marvin's BMW and promptly sells it to Elaine for $35,000 cash. Two weeks later, the police locate the car. When Abe stole it, he obtained void title. He had no title to convey to Elaine and that is what she received—none. Elaine must return the car to Marvin and suffer the $35,000 loss for Abe's theft. This policy makes sense because Marvin has done nothing wrong. If the law permitted Elaine to get valid title, it would encourage theft.

If Bad Guy *purchases* the goods from Owner, using fraud or deception, he obtains **voidable** title, meaning limited rights in the goods, inferior to those of the owner. The owner should be able to recover the goods from the Bad Guy, but not from anyone else who ends up with them. Suppose Emily agrees to buy Marvin's *other* car, a Jeep. She gives him a check for $20,000 and he signs the vehicle over to her. Emily knows her check will bounce; she has used fraud to obtain the car. As a result, Emily obtains only voidable title. If Marvin learns of the deception before Emily sells the car to someone else, he will get his Jeep back.

Unfortunately, Emily is slippery, not stupid. She quickly sells the Jeep to Seth for cash. By the time Emily's check bounces, Emily is gone and Seth has the car. Who keeps the Jeep? Seth wins the car if he is a bona fide purchaser. **A person with voidable title has power to transfer valid title for value to a good faith purchaser, generally called a** *bona fide purchaser* **or** *BFP*.[7]

Seth can prove that he is a bona fide purchaser by showing two things:

- That he gave value for the goods, *and*

- That he acted in good faith.

It is generally easy for purchasers to show that they gave value. The buyer could give cash or a check or could agree to extinguish a debt, that is, to forgive some money that Bad Guy owed. The real issue becomes whether the buyer acted in good faith. If Seth paid a reasonable purchase price and Emily showed him convincing identification and signed over to him all purchase documents, Seth acted in good faith. He keeps the Jeep and Marvin loses.

On the other hand, suppose Seth knows the brand new Jeep is worth more than $28,000. Emily seems in a frantic hurry to sell the car. She cannot produce the car's registration but promises to send it within three days. Emily's conduct, together with the $8,000 discount, would make a reasonable person suspicious. Seth is not acting in good faith and therefore is not a bona fide purchaser. Marvin receives the car back, and Seth pays dearly for his automotive lust.

THE ANSWER: WHO LOSES?

Owner ⟶	Bad Guy ⟶	Buyer
The Owner has good title.	(1) Bad Guy STEALS the goods, obtaining *void* title (no title) and sells to the Buyer.	Buyer receives no title.
	(2) Bad Guy PURCHASES the goods, obtaining *voidable* title, and sells to the Buyer.	(a) If the Buyer gives value for the goods and acts in good faith, he is a BFP and receives good title. (b) If the Buyer is not a BFP, he receives no title.

In the following case we definitely have a bad guy. Did he obtain voidable title? Could he pass on good title to someone else?

---

[7] UCC Section 2-403(1).

PEOPLE V. SIMMONS

2003 WL 21350737
CALIFORNIA COURT OF APPEALS, 2003

CASE SUMMARY

Facts: Scott Simmons evidently had a sentimental streak, which is why he paid $70,000 for a 15-carat, heart-shaped diamond ring from Archer Estate Jewelers. He had a different streak, as well, which is why he used a fraudulent check to make the purchase.

Simmons took the diamond, and the accompanying gemological certificate, to a jewelry store/pawnshop operated by Glenn Verdult. Verdult bought the ring from Simmons, paying with a $40,000 cashier's check. Simmons was arrested for passing a bad check, and the police seized the rock.

The trial court awarded the ring to Archer and Verdult appealed.

Issue: *Who was entitled to the diamond ring?*

Decision: Reversed and remanded to determine whether Verdult was a good faith purchaser.

Reasoning: A thief obtains only void title to the stolen property and therefore cannot convey valid title in those goods. However, the rules are different when a criminal acquires the property by purchase. The Code defines "purchase" as taking by sale, gift, or any other *voluntary* transaction. A swindler who fraudulently induces a victim to deliver goods voluntarily is a purchaser, not a thief.

Because the transfer is voluntary, the criminal obtains voidable title. He may transfer valid title to a good faith purchaser for value.

Archer voluntarily delivered the diamond to Simmons in exchange for a personal check in the amount of $70,000. Although the bargain was fraudulent on Simmons's part, it was voluntary on Archer's. Simmons acquired voidable title and had the power to convey good title to a good faith purchaser.

Whether someone qualifies as a good faith purchaser depends upon the reasonable person standard. If the goods are offered at an unusually low price, a reasonable buyer would suspect theft and reject the bargain. The fact finder must determine whether a purchaser acted reasonably.

Simmons offered Verdult not only the diamond, which he had recently purchased, but also the gemological certificate. Verdult bought the ring for $40,000. The trial court did not determine whether Verdult acted in good faith because it ruled that Archer owned the ring. That was in error. The trial court must determine whether Verdult acted in good faith. If he did, he obtains good title; if not, he gets nothing.

Reversed and remanded to determine whether Verdult acted in good faith.

EXAM *Strategy*

Question: In this chapter's introduction, a con artist uses a forged check to buy cattle. The issue raised is who must bear the loss—the original owner, or the buyer. Add facts to the story such that Vandermeer, the original owner, *wins* the case.

Strategy: If the con artist had *stolen* the cattle, he could convey no title, and Vandermeer would win. However, the bad guy in fact used a forged check, so he obtained *voidable* title. A buyer is a BFP, and receives good title from such a seller, if the buyer gives value and acts in good faith. We know that Munson gave value. Focus on the issue of good faith.

Result: Facts such as these would disqualify Munson as a BFP: "Munson knew that the market value of the cattle was about $275,000. The 'merchant' wanted to sell him the cows instantly, and was willing to give an enormous discount, down to $225,000. In a liquid market, with plenty of buyers, there was no legitimate business reason for such a discount." Under those facts, Munson should have been suspicious, and is not a BFP.

....

ENTRUSTMENT

Your old Steinway grand piano needs a complete rebuilding. You hire Fred Showpan, Inc., a company that repairs and sells instruments. Showpan hauls your piano away and promises to return it in perfect shape. Two months later, you are horrified to spot Showpan's showroom boarded up and pasted with bankruptcy notices. Worse still, you learn that Fred sold your beloved instrument to a customer, Frankie List. When you track down List, he gives you nothing but a sonatina, claiming he paid $18,000 for the piano and likes it just fine. Is he entitled to keep it?

Quite likely he is. Section 2-403(1), the BFP provision we just discussed, would not apply because Showpan did not *purchase* the piano from you. But Section 2-403(2) does apply. This is the "entrustment" section, and it covers cases in which the owner of goods voluntarily leaves them with a merchant, who then sells the goods without permission. According to **UCC Section 2-403(2), any entrusting to a merchant who deals in goods of that kind gives him power to transfer all rights of the entruster to a** buyer in the ordinary course of business **(BIOC).** There are several important ideas in this section:

Entrusting means delivering goods to a merchant or permitting the merchant to retain them.[8] In the piano example, you clearly entrusted goods to a merchant. If you buy a used car from Fast Eddie's Fast Wheels and then leave it there for a week, while you obtain insurance, you have entrusted it to Eddie.

Buyer in the ordinary course of business (BIOC)
One who acts in good faith, without knowing that the sale violates the owner's rights.

Deals in Goods of That Kind

The purpose of the section is to protect innocent buyers who enter a store, see the goods they expect to find, and purchase something, having no idea that the storekeeper is illegally selling the property of others. Buyers should not have to demand proof of title to everything in the store. Further, if someone has to bear the risk, let it be the person who has entrusted her goods; she is in the best position to investigate the merchant's integrity. But this protection does not extend to a buyer who arrives at a vacuum cleaner store and buys an $80,000 mobile home parked in the lot.

In the Ordinary Course of Business

A **buyer in the ordinary course of business (BIOC)** is one who acts in good faith, without knowing that the sale violates the owner's rights. If Frank List buys your piano assuming that Showpan owns it, he has acted in good faith. If Frank was your neighbor and recognized your instrument, he is not buying in the ordinary course of business and must hand over the piano.

Of course, a merchant who violates the owner's rights is liable to that owner. If Showpan were still in business when you discovered your loss, you could sue and recover the value of the piano. The problems arise when the merchant is unable to reimburse the owner.

---

[8] For a discussion of who is and who is not a merchant, see Chapter 18.

EXAM *Strategy*

Question: Pamela went to University Used Auto and asked if the company had a Lincoln Navigator. University had no such car, but a sales representative told Pamela that he would find her one. The representative contacted Royal auto dealership, which sold new and used cars. Royal agreed to supply University with a car, on the understanding that an interested buyer would pay *Royal*, which in turn would give a finder's fee to University. The companies had worked this way in the past. Royal delivered a Navigator as requested. But when the used car company sold the vehicle to Pamela, the company instructed her to pay University directly, which she did. Royal sued Pamela, seeking the car, and the court had to determine whether there had been an entrustment. Royal argued that it never entrusted the Navigator to University, because the parties agreed to require payment to Royal.

Strategy: Entrustment means delivering goods to a merchant who routinely deals in such articles.

Result: Royal delivered a used car to a used car dealer. That is entrustment. It is true that both dealers understood that Pamela was to pay Royal—but she did not know that. Entrustment protects good faith buyers, and Pamela wins.

In the following case, we definitely have an entrustment. Do we have a BIOC?

LINDHOLM v. BRANT

283 CONN. 65, 925 A.2d 1048
SUPREME COURT OF CONNECTICUT, 2007

CASE SUMMARY

Facts: Kerstin Lindholm and her husband, Magnus, were art collectors. For over 30 years, an art dealer named Anders Malmberg sold paintings for the couple and bought others for them, including an Andy Warhol picture called *Red Elvis*. In 1989, Malmberg arranged for Kerstin Lindholm to loan *Red Elvis* to the Museum of Modern Art in New York, as part of a major exhibition on Warhol. The exhibit also included paintings owned by Peter Brant. Brant saw *Red Elvis* at the show, was interested in the painting, and learned that Kerstin was the owner, represented by Malmberg.

A decade later, another dealer, Stellan Holm, told Brant that Malmberg had purchased *Red Elvis* and might sell it. In fact, the Lindholms still owned the picture.

Brant orally agreed to pay Malmberg $2.9 million for *Red Elvis*. With nothing in writing, he made a $900,000 deposit. Then Brant learned that the Lindholms were involved in a bitter divorce. Concerned that Magnus Lindholm might

make claims to the picture, he hired a lawyer to investigate. The lawyer reported finding no liens or art-loss claims, but told Brant that this did not prove that Malmberg owned the painting.

Brant asked Malmberg for documents proving that Kerstin had sold him the picture, but Malmberg refused, pointing out that confidentiality was the norm in the art world. Eventually, after Malmberg arranged loans of *Red Elvis* to the Guggenheim Museum and yet another exhibition, in Denmark, Brant paid the remaining $2 million and received the picture. Meanwhile Kirsten, assuming she owned *Red Elvis*, arranged to sell to a Japanese buyer for $4.6 million, only to learn that Brant now claimed to own it.

Kerstin sued. The trial court ruled that Brant was a BIOC, entitled to keep the painting. Kerstin appealed, and the case reached Connecticut's highest court.

Issue: *Was Brant a BIOC?*

Decision: Yes, Brandt was a buyer in the ordinary course of business. Affirmed.

Reasoning: Handshake agreements are common in the art world. Wealthy buyers rarely ask for an invoice or proof of ownership. Although Brandt had no absolute, documentary proof that Malmberg owned *Red Elvis*, he did have reasonable evidence that he was dealing with the painting's true owner.

First, he had the word of two reputable art dealers. Second, Brandt's lawyer investigated and found no liens or unresolved claims to the painting. Third, the Guggenheim released the painting to a warehouse in Denmark at Malmberg's order, and the museum releases art only to an owner or an owner's authorized agent.

Brandt acted in good faith. He qualifies as a BIOC and is entitled to keep the painting.

Creditor's Rights

In the entrustment section, we considered the rights of the *owner* of goods and how her interests might conflict with those of a merchant and a buyer. A related issue concerns a *creditor*, that is, someone with a financial stake in the goods that the merchant is selling. Suppose a merchant borrows money from a finance company to buy fish tanks with built-in televisions, to entertain bored guppies. The finance company is now the merchant's creditor. The merchant agrees that when she sells any of the TV Tanks, she will pay a percentage of the proceeds to the finance company. But if she sells tanks to a buyer without giving one cent to her creditor, does the buyer get to keep the fish tanks? To determine an answer, we need to know whether the sale was made in the ordinary course of business.

Ordinary Sales

Article 9 of the Code controls the rights of secured parties. We look closely at it in Chapter 25. Briefly, UCC Section 9-320 governs the rights of a creditor, a merchant, and a buyer in the ordinary course of business. Suppose the Nickel & Dime Bank loans Yoyo's Yacht Sales $100,000 to purchase two yachts wholesale. The yachts arrive at Yoyo's and remain in the showroom, but Nickel & Dime retains a security interest in both. If Yoyo fails to repay its loan, the bank is entitled to seize the yachts. Further, Yoyo is obligated to notify the bank immediately of a sale and hold the money until the bank gets its share. Unaware of Nickel & Dime's security interest, Liz pays $80,000 for one of the yachts. Yoyo grabs the money and sails into the horizon, leaving the bank in his wake. May Nickel & Dime take Liz's new yacht? No. **UCC Section 9-320 generally permits a buyer in the ordinary course of business to take the goods free and clear of the security interest.**

> Yoyo grabs the money and sails into the horizon, leaving the bank in his wake.

Naturally, there are exceptions, and you will *not* want to miss the full story in the secured transactions chapter. But for present purposes, the ordinary customer who purchases goods from a store will keep them regardless of any problems the store has with its creditors. The policy behind the law is obvious: to enable consumers to buy and merchants to sell. If you had to trace the chain of title before you bought a pair of sneakers at Discount City, commerce would grind to a halt and many of us would be barefoot. Section 9-320 keeps things flowing along.

BULK SALES

Beryl, a rich college student who likes fast cars, strolls into Pearl's High Performance Cars and buys a silver Jaguar. "I think," she says, blithely surveying the showroom and pointing at a yellow Lamborghini, "I'll have that lovely one as well." Before she is done, Beryl buys three Ferraris, an Aston Martin, and four Porsches, along with Pearl's desks, chairs, water cooler, and filing cabinet—everything in the store. Pearl has made a bulk sale. **A bulk sale is one that includes most or all of the inventory in a store.** Historically, these transactions were considered troublesome because a retailer could purchase his entire inventory on credit, sell it all to one buyer, and flee without paying his creditors. To prevent such fraud, **UCC Article 6 places special obligations on both parties in a bulk transaction,** requiring sellers and buyers to make sure that creditors are notified *before* the sale takes place, so that the creditors can protect their interests.

Today, though, the danger of bulk sale fraud has largely disappeared. Article 9 of the UCC makes it easy and inexpensive for creditors to protect their security interests (see Chapter 25). As a result, **most but not all states have repealed Article 6**. A bulk sale is generally treated like any other.

RETURNABLE GOODS

Sometimes the seller will allow the buyer to return goods even when he has no complaints about their quality. This, too, can create a problem for creditors. A bank may extend a loan to a business based on the inventory. The bank is willing to lend money because it can seize the goods if the merchant fails to pay on time. But what if the merchant *does not own* some of the goods, because he intends to return them to the original owner? If the merchant fails to pay his loan, who gets the goods—the creditor (bank) or the owner of the goods? The Code considers two types of contract that permit a buyer to return goods.

Sale on Approval

Sale on approval

Occurs when a buyer takes goods intending to use them herself but has the right to return them.

If a buyer takes goods intending to use them herself, but has the right to return the goods to the seller, it is a "**sale on approval**." Max manufactures bar code readers, the machines that scan magnetic bar codes on merchandise. He wants to sell half a dozen to Pinky's Superette, but Pinky isn't sure the machines are worth the price. To encourage Pinky, Max allows her to take the machines and try them out. At the end of 60 days she may return them or pay full price. There really is no *sale* until Pinky has formally accepted the goods.

Under UCC Section 2-326(2), in a sale on approval, the goods *are not* subject to the buyer's creditors until the buyer accepts them. Suppose Pinky has borrowed $200,000 from the bank and has given a security interest "in all goods in the store now or in the future." The bar code machines are "goods in the store," and if Pinky fails to pay her loans, the bank will try to seize the equipment. But this is a sale on approval, and the bank has no right to Max's machines.

A finance company will often extend credit based on a merchant's inventory. A creditor considering such a loan must determine what goods, if any, are "sale on approval," since those goods give the creditor no security.

Sale or Return

Sale or return

Occurs when a buyer takes goods intending to *resell* them but has the right to return them to the seller.

If a buyer takes goods intending to *resell* them, but has the right to return the goods to the seller, it is a "**sale or return**." This is generally the same as a *consignment*. The owner is called the *consignor* and the buyer is the *consignee*. Yvonne runs a used car lot. Trent offers to sell Yvonne his used Mustang auto for $937, but it is in such poor shape Yvonne doubts there's a teenager in the county dumb enough to buy it. "My brother's real dumb," Trent suggests hopefully. But Yvonne offers instead to place the car on her lot and try to sell it. She will pay Trent nothing for the car but will keep 20 percent of the price if she can sell it. The name "sale or return" is misleading, since Trent has sold nothing so far and Yvonne will never be a true buyer.

Under **UCC Section 2-326, in a sale or return, the goods are subject to the claims of the buyer's creditors**. Suppose Yvonne fails to pay back some loans. Her creditors will instantly round up the Mustang, and Trent will never get a dime for his car.[9]

The issues we have looked at thus far involve someone doing something wrong, often a scoundrel selling goods that he never owned. Now we turn to cases where there may be no wrongdoer.

RISK OF LOSS

Accidents hurt businesses. When goods are damaged, the law may again need to decide whether it is the seller or buyer who must suffer the loss. In the cases we have seen thus far, the parties were arguing, "It's mine!"—"Like heck, it's *mine!*" In risk of loss cases, the parties are generally shouting, "It was yours!"—"No way, chump, it was *yours!* "

Athena, a seafood wholesaler, is gearing up for the Super Bowl, which will bring 110,000 hungry visitors to her city for a week of eating and gabbing. Athena orders 25,000 lobsters from Poseidon's Fishfoods, 500 miles distant, and simultaneously contracts with a dozen local restaurants to resell them. Poseidon loads the lobsters, still kicking, into refrigerated railcars owned by Demeter Trucking. But halfway to the city, the train collides with a prison van. None of the convicts escape, but the lobsters do, hurtling into the swamps from which they are never recaptured. Athena loses all of her profits and sues. As luck would have it, Demeter Trucking had foolishly economized by letting its insurance lapse. Poseidon claims the goods were out of its hands. Who loses?

The common law answered this problem by looking at which party had title to the goods at the time of loss. But the Code again rejects this abstract concept, striving once more for a practical solution. The UCC permits the parties to agree on who bears the risk of loss. **UCC Section 2-509(4) states that the parties may allocate the risk of loss any way they wish.**

Often the parties will do just that, avoiding arguments and litigation in the event of an accident. As part of her agreement with Poseidon, Athena should have included a one-sentence clause, such as "Seller bears all risk of loss until the lobsters are delivered to Athena's warehouse." So long as the parties make their risk allocation clear, the Code will enforce it.

SHIPPING TERMS

The parties can quickly and easily allocate the risk of loss by using common shipping terms that the Code defines. FOB means free on board; FAS indicates free alongside a ship; and CIF stands for cost, insurance, and freight. By combining these designations with other terms, the parties can specify risk in a few words:

---

[9] **UCC Article 2 Alert.** Section 2-326 previously permitted a consignor to protect her goods from a creditor by taking any of three specified steps. Those three protective steps *have been deleted* (the changes are not mere proposals), so that this section conforms to Article 9 revisions. Anyone considering consignment should be aware of the risk of losing goods to a creditor, and should take appropriate steps to protect them pursuant to Article 9.

- *FOB place of shipment.* The seller is obligated to put the goods into the possession of the carrier at the place named. The seller bears the expense and risk until they are in the carrier's possession. From that moment onward, the buyer bears the risk.

- *FOB place of destination.* The seller must deliver the goods at the place named and bears the expense *and risk* of shipping.

- *FAS a named vessel.* The seller at his expense *and risk* must deliver the goods alongside the named vessel and obtain proper receipts.

- *CIF.* The price includes in a lump sum the cost of the goods and the insurance and freight to the named destination.

- *C & F.* The price includes in a lump sum the cost of the goods and freight, but *not* insurance.

Thus, if Athena had put a clause in her contract saying, "FOB Athena's warehouse," Poseidon would have born the risk of any loss up to the time the lobsters were unloaded in Athena's possession. Poseidon would then have known that it must insure the lobsters during transit. For an example of all shipping terms, as they actually appear in the statutes of one state (Maine), see **http://janus.state.me.us.**

When the Parties Fail to Allocate the Risk

If the parties fail to specify when the risk passes from seller to buyer, the Code provides the answer. When neither party breached the contract, Section 2-509 determines the risk; when a party has breached the contract, Section 2-510 governs. The full analysis of risk is somewhat intricate, so we first supply you with a short version: **When neither party has breached, the risk of loss generally passes from seller to buyer when the seller has transported the goods as far as he is obligated to. When a party has breached, the risk of loss generally lies with that party.**

And now, for the courageous, the full version of how the Code allocates the risk of loss when the parties failed to specify it.

When Neither Party Breaches

In the example of Athena and Poseidon, both parties did what they were supposed to do, so there was no breach of contract. To settle these cases, we need to know whether the contract obligated the seller to ship the goods or whether the goods were handled in some other way. There are three possibilities: (1) the contract required the seller to ship the goods, or (2) the contract involved a bailment, or (3) other cases.

If the Seller Must Ship the Goods. Most contracts require the seller to arrange shipment of the goods. In a *shipment contract*, the seller must deliver the goods *to a carrier*, which will then transport the goods to the buyer. The carrier might be a trucking company, railroad, airline, or ship, and is generally located near the seller's place of business. **In a shipment contract, the risk passes to the buyer when the seller delivers the goods to the carrier.** Suppose Old Wood, in North Carolina, agrees to sell $100,000 worth of furniture to Pioneer Company, in Anchorage. The contract requires Old Wood to deliver the goods to Great Northern Railroad lines in Chicago. From North Carolina to Chicago, Old Wood bears the risk of loss. Once the furniture is on board the train in Chicago, the risk of loss passes to Pioneer. If the train derails in Montana and every desk and chair is squashed, Pioneer owes the full $100,000 to Old Wood.

In a *destination contract*, the seller is responsible for delivering the goods *to the buyer*. In a destination contract, risk passes to the buyer when the goods reach the destination. If the contract required Old Wood to deliver the furniture to Pioneer's warehouse in Anchorage, then Old Wood bears the loss for the entire trip. If the train travels 3,000 miles and then plunges off a bridge in Alaska, 45 feet from its destination, Old Wood picks up the tab.

If There Is a Bailment.   Freezem Corp. produces 500 room air conditioners and stores them in Every-Ware's Warehouse. This is a **bailment, meaning that one person or company is legally holding goods for the benefit of another.** Freezem is the **bailor,** the one who owns the goods, and Every-Ware is the **bailee,** the one with temporary possession. Suppose Freezem agrees to sell 300 of its air conditioners to KeepKool Appliances. KeepKool does not need the machines in its store for six months, so it plans to keep them at Every-Ware's until then. But two weeks after Freezem and KeepKool make their deal, Every-Ware burns to the ground. Who bears the loss of the 300 air conditioners? **If the contract requires a bailee to hold the goods for the buyer, the risk passes when the buyer obtains documents entitling her to possession, or when the bailee acknowledges her right to the goods.** If fire broke out in Every-Ware's before KeepKool received any documents enabling it to take the air conditioners away, then the loss would fall on Freezem.

Bailor
The one who owns goods legally held by another.

Bailee
The one with temporary possession of another's goods.

Other Cases.   The great majority of contracts involve either shipment by the seller or a bailment. In the remaining cases, if the seller is a *merchant*, risk passes to the buyer on receipt. This means that a merchant is only off the hook if the buyer actually accepts the goods. If the seller is *not a merchant*, risk passes when the seller tenders the goods, meaning that she makes them available to the buyer. The Code is giving more protection to buyers when they deal with a merchant. But if the buyer is purchasing from a non-merchant, the Code assumes they are on equal footing, and the seller is relieved of liability when she merely tenders the goods.

When One Party Breaches

Still there? Excellent. We now look at how the Code allocates risk when one of the parties does breach. Again there are three possibilities: (1) seller breaches and buyer rejects; (2) seller breaches, buyer accepts, but then revokes; or (3) buyer breaches.

Seller Breaches and Buyer Rejects.   PlayStore, a sporting goods store, orders 75 canoes from Floataway. PlayStore specifies that the canoes must be 12 feet long, lightweight metal, dark green. Floataway delivers 75 canoes to Truckit, a trucking company. When Truckit's trucks arrive, PlayStore finds that the canoes are the right material and color, but 18 feet long. PlayStore rejects the craft, and Truckit heads back to Floataway. But one of the trucks is hijacked and the 25 canoes it carries are never recovered. Floataway demands its money for the 25 lost canoes. Who loses?

Floataway had delivered **nonconforming goods,** that is, merchandise which differs from that specified in the contract. A buyer has a right to reject nonconforming goods. **When the buyer rejects nonconforming goods, the risk of loss remains with the seller until he cures the defect or the buyer decides to accept the goods.** In our example, Floataway must suffer the loss for the stolen canoes. If PlayStore had decided to accept the canoes, even though they were the wrong size, then the risk would have passed to the sports store.

Nonconforming goods
Merchandise that differs from that specified in the contract.

Seller Breaches, Buyer Accepts, but Then Revokes.   PlayStore orders 200 tennis rackets from High Strung. When the rackets arrive, they seem fine, so the store accepts them. But then a salesperson notices that the grips are loose. Every racket has the same problem. PlayStore returns the rackets to High Strung, but they are destroyed when a blimp crashes into the delivery truck. **When a buyer accepts goods but then rightfully revokes acceptance, the risk remains with the seller to the extent the buyer's insurance will not cover the loss.** If PlayStore's insurance covers the damaged rackets, there is no problem. If PlayStore's insurance does not cover the loss of goods in transit, High Strung must pay.

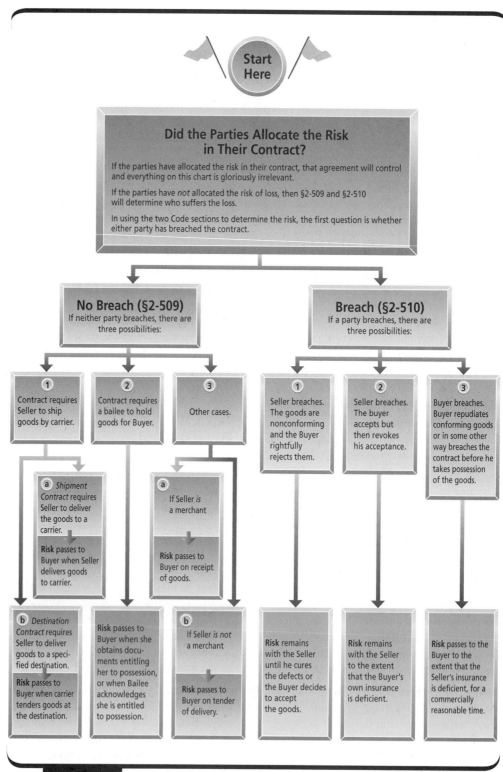

Start Here

Did the Parties Allocate the Risk in Their Contract?

If the parties have allocated the risk in their contract, that agreement will control and everything on this chart is gloriously irrelevant.

If the parties have *not* allocated the risk of loss, then §2-509 and §2-510 will determine who suffers the loss.

In using the two Code sections to determine the risk, the first question is whether either party has breached the contract.

No Breach (§2-509)
If neither party breaches, there are three possibilities:

Breach (§2-510)
If a party breaches, there are three possibilities:

1. Contract requires Seller to ship goods by carrier.

2. Contract requires a bailee to hold goods for Buyer.

3. Other cases.

1. Seller breaches. The goods are nonconforming and the Buyer rightfully rejects them.

2. Seller breaches. The buyer accepts but then revokes his acceptance.

3. Buyer breaches. Buyer repudiates conforming goods or in some other way breaches the contract before he takes possession of the goods.

a *Shipment Contract* requires Seller to deliver the goods to a carrier.

Risk passes to Buyer when Seller delivers goods to carrier.

a If Seller *is* a merchant

Risk passes to Buyer on receipt of goods.

b *Destination Contract* requires Seller to deliver goods to a specified destination.

Risk passes to Buyer when carrier tenders goods at the destination.

Risk passes to Buyer when she obtains documents entitling her to possession, or when Bailee acknowledges she is entitled to possession.

b If Seller *is not* a merchant

Risk passes to Buyer on tender of delivery.

Risk remains with the Seller until he cures the defects or the Buyer decides to accept the goods.

Risk remains with the Seller to the extent that the Buyer's own insurance is deficient.

Risk passes to the Buyer to the extent that the Seller's insurance is deficient, for a commercially reasonable time.

Exhibit 19.1

Buyer Breaches.   One last time. PlayStore orders 60 tents from ExploreMore. About the time the tents leave the factory, PlayStore decides to drop its line of camping goods and specialize in team sports. PlayStore notifies ExploreMore it wants to explore less, and will not pay. The tents are destroyed in a collision involving a prison van and a train carrying lobsters. This time, PlayStore is liable. **When a buyer breaches the contract before taking possession, it assumes the risk of loss to the extent the seller's insurance is deficient.**

Exhibit 19.1 should clarify.

In the following case, neither party breached, so Section 2-509 governs.

CODE PROVISIONS DISCUSSED IN THIS CASE

Issue	Relevant Code Section
1. Did the parties create a bailment?	In a bailment, one person legally holds goods for the benefit of another.
2. Which party bore the risk of the horse's death?	UCC Section 2-509(2): If the contract requires a bailee to hold the goods for the buyer, the risk passes when the buyer obtains documents entitling her to possession, or when the bailee acknowledges her right to the goods.

HARMON V. DUNN

1997 TENN. APP. LEXIS 217
TENNESSEE COURT OF APPEALS, 1997

CASE SUMMARY

Facts: Bess Harmon owned a two-year-old Tennessee Walking Horse named Phantom Recall. Harmon, who lived in Tennessee, boarded her horse with Steve Dunn, at his stables in Florence, Alabama. Dunn cared for Phantom Recall and showed him at equestrian events. Harmon instructed Dunn to sell the horse for $25,000, and Dunn arranged for his friend Scarbrough to buy the colt. On June 30, Dunn delivered Scarbrough's $25,000 check to Harmon, who handed over the horse's certificate of registration and a "transfer of ownership" document. That night at a horse show, Dunn told Scarbrough that he had delivered the check and had the ownership papers in his car. Dunn did not actually give the documents to his friend. Scarbrough knew that Phantom Recall was at Dunn's stable, where Scarbrough had boarded other horses. Sadly, the colt developed colitis and died suddenly, on July 4. Scarbrough stopped payment on his check, and Harmon sued for her money. The trial court found for Harmon, and Scarbrough appealed.

Issue: *Which party bore the risk of Phantom Recall's death?*

Decision: Scarbrough must suffer the loss. Affirmed.

Reasoning: UCC Section 2-509(2) governs those cases where there is no breach of contract and the goods are held by a bailee to be delivered without being moved. Dunn was certainly Harmon's bailee. He worked for Harmon, trained Phantom Recall, and transported the horse to various shows. Because the agreement between Scarbrough and Harmon did not require Phantom Recall to be moved anywhere for delivery, this section of the Code applies. Under UCC Section 2-509(2), the risk of loss passes to the buyer:

(a) On his receipt of a negotiable document of title covering the goods, or

(b) On acknowledgment by the bailee of the buyer's right to possession of the goods.

Scarbrough obtained control of the horse no later than July 1. He did not receive the ownership documents then, but the papers were already in Dunn's hands, and all parties knew it. Nothing prevented Scarbrough from exercising complete ownership of Phantom Recall as of that date, and he also acquired the risk of loss. Judgment for Harmon.

CHAPTER CONCLUSION

The Code enables the parties in most commercial transactions to control their own destiny. It reduces the importance of abstract terms like "title," and allows buyer and seller to specify when goods are identified and when risk shifts. Owners and creditors can anticipate problems and protect themselves. But the provisions only work if business people understand the rules and apply them.

EXAM REVIEW

1. **INTEREST AND TITLE** An *interest* is a legal right in something. *Title* means the normal rights of ownership. (p. 450)

2. **IDENTIFICATION** Goods must *exist* and be *identified* to the contract before title can pass. The parties may agree in their contract how and when they will identify goods; if they do not specify, the Code stipulates when it happens. The parties may also state when title passes, and once again, if they do not, the Code provides rules. (p. 452)

EXAM Strategy

CPA Question: On September 10, Bell Corp. entered into a contract to purchase 50 lamps from Glow Manufacturing. Bell prepaid 40 percent of the purchase price. Glow became insolvent on September 19 before segregating, in its inventory, the lamps to be delivered to Bell. Bell will not be able to recover the lamps because:

(a) Bell is regarded as a merchant

(b) The lamps were not identified to the contract

(c) Glow became insolvent fewer than 10 days after receipt of Bell's prepayment

(d) Bell did not pay the full price at the time of purchase

Strategy: In analyzing issues about ownership, remember that title can never change hands until the goods have been identified to the contract. Identification can occur in three ways: the parties describe specific goods that already exist; animals are conceived or crops planted; or the seller marks, ships or otherwise indicates which are going to the buyer. (See the "Result" at the end of this section.)

---

3. **INSURABLE INTEREST** A buyer obtains an *insurable interest* when the goods are identified to the contract. A seller retains an insurable interest in goods as long as she has either title or a security interest in them. (p. 454)

---

4. **VOID AND VOIDABLE TITLE** *Void title* is no title at all. *Voidable title* means limited rights in the goods, inferior to those of the owner. A person with voidable title has power

to transfer good title to a *bona fide purchaser (BFP)*, that is, someone who purchases in good faith, for value. (p. 457)

---

5. **ENTRUSTING** Any *entrusting* of goods to a merchant who deals in goods of that kind gives him the power to transfer all rights of the entruster to a buyer in the ordinary course of business. (p. 459)

---

6. **BIOC** A buyer in the ordinary course of business generally takes goods free and clear of any security interest. (p. 459)

EXAM Strategy

Question: Fay Witcher owned a Ford Bronco. Steve Risher operated a used car lot. Witcher delivered his automobile to Risher, asking him to resell it if he could. Witcher specified that he wanted all cash for his car, not cash plus a trade-in. Risher sold the car to Richard Parker for $12,800, but took a trade-in as part payment. Risher promised to deliver the Bronco's certificate of title to Parker within a few days, but never did. He was also obligated to deliver proceeds of the sale to Witcher, and of course failed to do that. Parker claimed that the car was rightfully his. Witcher argued that Parker owned nothing because he never got the title and because Witcher never got his money. Who loses?

Strategy: Any *entrusting* of goods to a merchant who deals in goods of that kind gives him the power to transfer all rights of the entruster to a buyer in the ordinary course of business. A buyer in the ordinary course of business generally takes goods free and clear of any security interest. Did Witcher entrust the auto? Was Parker a BIOC? Why or why not? (See the "Result" at the end of this section.)

---

7. **SALES ON APPROVAL** In a sale on approval, the goods *are not* subject to the buyer's creditors until the buyer accepts them; in a sale or return, the goods *are* subject to the buyer's creditors. (p. 462)

---

8. **RISK OF LOSS** In their contract, the parties may allocate the *risk of loss* any way they wish. If they fail to do so, the Code provides several steps to determine who pays for any damage. When neither party has breached, the risk of loss generally passes from seller to buyer when the seller has transported the goods as far as he is obligated to. When a party has breached, the risk of loss generally lies with the party that has breached. (p. 463)

EXAM Strategy

Question: Bradkeyne International, Ltd., an English company, bought a large quantity of batteries from Duracell, Inc. The contract specified delivery "FOB cargo ship, Jacksonville, Florida." Duracell supervised the loading of the batteries onto a ship in Jacksonville in early July, and they arrived in England in August. When loaded onto the ship, the batteries were conforming goods that could be used for normal purposes. But on board the ship, excessive heat damaged them. By the time they reached England, they were worth only a fraction of the original price. Bradkeyne sued Duracell. Who loses?

Strategy: The advantage of standard shipping terms is that they make business predictable and exam questions easy. If you know what "FOB cargo ship, Jacksonville, Florida" means, you know the answer. (See the "Result" at the end of this section.)

2. Result: The contract was silent about which goods were involved; neither animals nor plants were involved; and Glow never segregated the lamps. The lamps were never identified to the contract, and the correct answer is (b).

6. Result: Risher was a merchant dealing in automobiles, meaning that Witcher did entrust the car to him. Parker was a BIOC: He acted in good faith, without knowing that the sale violated the agreement between Witcher and Risher. Parker wins, and keeps the car.

8. Result: "FOB cargo ship, Jacksonville, Florida" means that the seller bears all risks until the goods are placed in the carrier's possession. From that moment onward, the buyer bears the risk. The batteries were fine when delivered, so Duracell was off the hook once they were on board. Bradkeyne bears the loss.

ADDITIONAL QUESTIONS

1. **CPA QUESTION** On Monday, Wolfe paid Aston Co., a furniture retailer, $500 for a table. On Thursday, Aston notified Wolfe that the table was ready to be picked up. On Saturday, while Aston was still in possession of the table, it was destroyed in a fire. Who bears the loss of the table?

   (a) Wolfe, because Wolfe had title to the table at the time of loss

   (b) Aston, unless Wolfe is a merchant

   (c) Wolfe, unless Aston breached the contract

   (d) Aston, because Wolfe had not yet taken possession of the table

2. **CPA QUESTION** Under UCC Article 9 on secured transactions, which of the following statements is correct concerning the disposition of goods by a secured creditor after a debtor defaults on a loan?

   (a) A good faith purchaser of the goods for value and without knowledge of any defects in the sale takes free of any security interest.

   (b) The debtor may not redeem the goods after the default.

(c) Secured creditors retain the right to redeem the goods after they are sold to a third party.

(d) The goods may be disposed of only at a public sale.

3. Franklin Miller operated Miller Seed Co. in Pea Ridge, Arkansas. He bought, processed, and sold fescue seed, which is used for growing pasture and fodder grass. Farmers brought seed to Miller who would normally clean, bag, and store it. In some cases the farmers authorized Miller to sell the seed, in some cases not. Miller mixed together the seed that was for sale with the seed in storage so that a customer could not see any difference between them. Miller defaulted on a $380,000 loan from the First State Bank of Purdy. First State attempted to seize all of the seed in the store. Tony Havelka, a farmer, protested that his 490,000 pounds of seed was merely in storage and not subject to First State's claim. Who is entitled to the seed?

4. **ETHICS** Myrna and James Brown ordered a $35,000 motor home from R.V. Kingdom, Inc. The manufacturer delivered the vehicle to R.V. Kingdom, with title in the dealer's name. The Browns agreed to accept the motor home, but they soon regretted spending the money and asked R.V. Kingdom to resell it. The motor home stayed on R.V. Kingdom's lot for quite a few months, but when the Browns decided to come get it, they learned that R.V. Kingdom had illegally used the vehicle as collateral for a loan and that a bank had repossessed it. The Browns filed a claim with their insurance company, State Farm. The insurer agreed that the vehicle had been stolen and agreed that the Browns' policy covered newly acquired vehicles. But the company refused to pay, claiming that the Browns had not taken title or possession to the goods and therefore had no insurable interest. The Browns sued. Please rule on their case. Let us also look at the ethics of the case by creating a contrasting hypothetical. Suppose that among the insurance company's thousands of customers was Arvee, a recreational vehicle dealership similar to the one in the real case. Imagine that Arvee had taken in an automobile for resale from a customer named Parker, and kept the vehicle on its lot. If Parker's auto were stolen, what argument would the insurance company be making? How would the company define insurable interest in *that* case?

5. John C. Clark, using an alias, rented a Lexus from Alamo Rent-A-Car in San Diego, California. Clark never returned the car to Alamo and obtained a California "quick title" using forged signatures. He then advertised in the *Las Vegas Review Journal* newspaper and sold the car to Terry and Vyonne Mendenhall for $34,000 in cash. The Mendenhalls made improvements to the car, had it insured, smog and safety tested, registered, licensed, and titled in the state of Utah. When Alamo reported the car stolen, the Nevada Department of Motor Vehicles seized the auto and returned it to Alamo. The Mendenhalls sued Alamo. The trial court concluded that the Mendenhalls had purchased the car for value and without notice that it was stolen, and were bona fide purchasers entitled to the Lexus. Alamo appealed. Please rule.

6. Universal Consolidated Cos. contracted with China Metallurgical Import and Export Corp. (CMIEC) to provide CMIEC with new and used equipment for a cold rolling steel mill. Universal then contracted with Pittsburgh Industrial Furnace Co. (Pifcom) to engineer and build much of the equipment. The contract required Pifcom to deliver the finished equipment to a trucking company, which would then transport it to Universal. Pifcom delivered the goods to the trucking company as scheduled. But before all of the goods reached Universal, CMIEC notified Universal it was canceling

the deal. Universal, in turn, notified Pifcom to stop work, but all goods had been delivered to the shipper and ultimately reached Universal. Pifcom claimed that it retained title to the goods, but Universal claimed that title had passed to it. Who is right?

7. **YOU BE THE JUDGE** WRITING PROBLEM Construction Helicopters paid Heli-Dyne Systems $315,000 for three helicopters that were in Argentina. Two were ready to fly and one was disassembled for routine maintenance. The contract said nothing about risk of loss (the parties could have saved a lot of money by reading this chapter). Heli-Dyne arranged for an Argentine company to oversee their loading on board the freight ship *Lynx*. The two helicopters and 25 crates containing the disassembled craft were properly loaded, but when the ship arrived in Miami, only 7 of the crates appeared. Heli-Dyne refused to supply more parts and Construction sued. Who bears the loss? **Argument for Construction:** Construction had no control over the goods until they reached Miami. Although we do not know exactly what happened to the crates, we know the one party that had *nothing* to do with the loss: Construction. The company should not pay for damage it never caused. **Argument for Heli-Dyne:** Because the contract failed to specify risk of loss, it is a shipment contract. In such an agreement, risk of loss passes to the buyer when the seller delivers the goods to a carrier. Heli-Dyne delivered the goods and has no further responsibility.

8. **CPA QUESTION** Quick Corp. agreed to purchase 200 typewriters from Union Suppliers, Inc. Union is a wholesaler of appliances and Quick is an appliance retailer. The contract required Union to ship the typewriters to Quick by common carrier, "FOB Union Suppliers, Inc. Loading Dock." Which of the parties bears the risk of loss during shipment?

   (a) Union, because the risk of loss passes only when Quick receives the typewriters

   (b) Union, because both parties are merchants

   (c) Quick, because title to the typewriters passed to Quick at the time of shipment

   (d) Quick, because the risk of loss passes when the typewriters are delivered to the carrier

9. **ROLE REVERSAL** Write a multiple-choice question concerning either insurable interest, bona fide purchaser, or entrustment.

INTERNET RESEARCH PROBLEM

You own two powerful Clydesdale draft horses. A friend asks to borrow the horses for three months to give hayrides. You agree, provided your friend takes proper care of these valuable animals, providing good feed, adequate rest, and veterinary treatment. Find a bailment contract online, and draft a simple agreement protecting your horses.

You can find further practice problems at www.cengagebrain.com. See the preface of this book for website access details.

WARRANTIES AND PRODUCT LIABILITY

You are sitting in a fast-food restaurant in Washington, D.C. Your friend Harley, who works for a congressman, is eating with one hand and gesturing with the other. "We want product liability reform and we want it now," he proclaims, stabbing the air with his free hand. "It's absurd, these multimillion dollar verdicts, just because something has a *slight defect*." He waves angrily at the absurdity, takes a ferocious bite from his burger— and with a loud CRACK breaks a tooth. Harley howls in pain and throws down the bun, revealing a large piece of bone in the meat. As he tips back in misery, his defective chair collapses, and Harley slams into the tile, knocking himself unconscious. Hours later, when he revives in the hospital, he refuses to speak to you until he puts in a call to his lawyer.

> He waves angrily at the absurdity, takes a ferocious bite from his burger—and with a loud CRACK breaks a tooth.

PRODUCT LIABILITY

Harley and his lawyer will be chatting about **product liability**, which refers to goods that have caused an injury. The harm may be physical, as it was in Harley's case. Or it can be purely economic, as when a corporation buys a computer so defective it must be replaced, costing the buyer lost time and profits. The injured party may have a choice of possible remedies, including:

- *Warranty,* which is an assurance provided in a sales contract

- *Negligence,* which refers to unreasonable conduct by the defendant, and

- *Strict liability,* which prohibits defective products whether the defendant acted reasonably or not.

We discuss each of these remedies in this chapter. What all product liability cases have in common is that a person or business has been hurt by goods. We focus primarily on cases where the *sale* of goods leads to the injury, but we also examine product liability issues where there has been no sale. We begin with warranties.

A **warranty** is a contractual assurance that goods will meet certain standards. It is normally a manufacturer or a seller who gives a warranty, and a buyer who relies on it. A warranty might be explicit and written: "The manufacturer warrants that the light bulbs in this package will provide 100 watts of power for 2,000 hours." Or a warranty could be oral: "Don't worry, this machine can harvest any size of wheat crop ever planted in the state." The manufacturer may offer a warranty as a means of attracting buyers: "We provide the finest, bumper-to-bumper warranty in the automobile industry." Or *the law itself* may impose a warranty on goods, requiring the manufacturer to meet certain standards whether it intends to or not. Here we consider two broad categories: express warranties and implied warranties.

Warranty
A contractual assurance that goods will meet certain standards.

EXPRESS WARRANTIES

An **express warranty** is one that the seller creates with his words or actions.[1] Whenever a seller *clearly indicates* to a buyer that the goods being sold will meet certain standards, she has created an express warranty. For example, if the sales clerk for a paint store tells a professional house painter that "this exterior paint will not fade for three years, even in direct sunlight," that is an express warranty and the store is bound by it. Or, if the clerk gives the painter a brochure that makes the same promise, the store is again bound by its express warranty. On the other hand, if the sales person merely says, "I know you're going to be happy with this product," there is no warranty, because the promise is too vague. The UCC establishes that the seller may create an express warranty in three ways: (1) with an affirmation of fact or a promise; (2) with a description of the goods; or (3) with a sample or model. In addition, the buyer must demonstrate that what the seller said or did was the *basis of the bargain.*

Express warranty
One that the seller creates with his words or actions.

AFFIRMATION OF FACT OR PROMISE

Any affirmation of fact—or any promise—can create an express warranty.[2] An affirmation of fact is simply a statement about the nature or quality of the goods, such as "This scaffolding is

---

[1] UCC Section 2-313.
[2] UCC Section 2-313(1)(a).

made from the highest grade of steel available at any price," or "This car will accelerate from 0 to 60 in 8.3 seconds." A promise includes phrases such as "We guarantee you that this air conditioning system will cool your building to 72 degrees, regardless of the outdoor temperature."

A common problem in cases of express warranty is to separate true affirmations of fact from mere sales puffery or seller's opinion, which creates no express warranty. "You meet the nicest people on a Honda" is mere puffery. If you purchase a Honda and meet only deadbeats, the manufacturer owes you nothing.

A statement is more likely to be an affirmation of fact if:

- **It is specific and can be proven true or false.** Suppose the brochures of a home builder promise to meet "the strictest building codes." Since there is a code on file, the builder's work can be compared to it, and his promise is binding.

- **It is written.** An oral promise *can* create an express warranty. But promises in brochures are more likely to be taken seriously. Statements in a *written contract* are the likeliest of all to create a binding warranty.

- **Defects are not obvious.** If a used car salesman tells you that a car is rust free, when the driver's door is pockmarked with rust, you should not take the statement seriously—since a court will not, either.

- **Seller has greater expertise.** If the seller knows more than the buyer, his statements will be more influential with buyer and court alike. If your architect assures you that the new porch will be warm in winter, the law recognizes that you will naturally rely on her expertise.

DESCRIPTION OF GOODS

Any description of the goods can create an express warranty.[3] The phrase could be oral or written. A description might be a label on a bag of seed, referring to the seed as a particular variety of tomato; it could be a tag on airplane parts, assuring the buyer that the goods have met safety tests. Wherever the words appear, if they describe the goods as having particular characteristics or qualities, the seller has probably created an express warranty.

SAMPLE OR MODEL

Any sample or model can create an express warranty.[4] A sample can be a very effective way of demonstrating the quality of goods to a customer. However, a seller who uses a sample is generally warranting that the merchandise sold will be just as good.

BASIS OF BARGAIN

The seller's conduct must have been part of the basis of the bargain. To prove an express warranty, a buyer must demonstrate that the two parties *included the statements or acts in their bargain*. Some courts have interpreted this to mean that the buyer must have *relied* on the seller's statements. There is logic to this position. For example, suppose a sales brochure makes certain assurances about the quality of goods, but the buyer never sees the brochure

---

[3] UCC Section 2-313(1)(b).
[4] UCC Section 2-313(1)(c).

until she files suit. Should the seller be held to an express warranty? Some courts would rule that the seller is not liable for breach of warranty.

Other courts, however, have ruled that a seller's statement can be part of the basis of the bargain even when the buyer has not clearly relied on it. These courts are declaring that a seller who chooses to make statements about his goods will be held to them, *unless the seller can convince a court that he should not be liable*. This is a policy decision, taken by many courts, to give the buyer the benefit of the doubt, since the seller is in the best position to control what he says. The issue arises in the following case.

RITE AID CORP. v. LEVY-GRAY

391 MD. 698, 894 A.2d 563
COURT OF APPEALS OF MARYLAND, 2006

CASE SUMMARY

Facts: Dr. Ronald Geckler diagnosed Ellen Levy-Gray with Lyme disease, and prescribed doxycycline. Geckler told Levy-Gray that while taking the drug she must stop nursing her son, but he provided her with no other information. Levy-Gray had the prescription filled at a Rite-Aid pharmacy she knew and trusted. With the medication, the pharmacy included its own pamphlet, called "Rite Advice." The cover page said, "Inside is everything you need to know about your prescription. It covers everything in writing from dosage to side effects." The inside of the pamphlet stated, in part:

IMPORTANT NOTE: THE FOLLOWING INFORMATION IS INTENDED TO SUPPLEMENT, NOT SUBSTITUTE FOR, THE EXPERTISE AND JUDGMENT OF YOUR PHYSICIAN, PHARMACIST OR OTHER HEALTHCARE PROFESSIONAL.

HOW TO TAKE THIS MEDICATION: Take each dose with a full glass of water (4 oz. or 120 ml) or more. Take with food or milk if stomach upset occurs unless your doctor directs you otherwise.

Doxycyline immediately upset Levy-Gray's stomach, so she began to take the medicine with milk. In order to maintain her breast milk, so that she could resume nursing when the treatment ended, Levy-Gray also consumed eight glasses of milk per day, grilled cheese sandwiches, ice cream, and so forth. Because her Lyme disease did not improve, her brother, a doctor in another specialty, recommended that she stop using dairy products. Her symptoms briefly improved

but ultimately she was diagnosed with post-Lyme syndrome, a chronic autoimmune response.

Levy-Gray sued Rite-Aid for breach of an express warranty. She claimed that the instructions to take Doxycyline with milk rendered the drug ineffective and caused her chronic condition. At trial, her expert witness testified that taking dairy products with the drug prevented the drug from being absorbed into the body. Rite-Aid's expert stated any loss of absorption was modest and had no effect on her treatment. The company also claimed that the pamphlet could not have been part of the basis of the bargain because Levy-Gray never saw it until after she bought the medication.

The jury found that Rite-Aid had breached a warranty, and awarded Levy-Gray $250,000. Rite-Aid appealed; the intermediate appeals court affirmed, and the state's highest court took the case.

Issue: *Did Rite-Aid breach an express warranty?*

Decision: Yes, it breached an express warranty. Affirmed.

Reasoning: Rite Aid contends that the advice given in the pamphlet was not an express warranty. It was not part of any negotiation with Levy-Gray, and she did not read it until after she paid for her medication. But timing is not key. The essential issue is whether the advice can reasonably be considered part of the contract.

Some sellers do not deliver warranties until long after goods are sold, but courts may still find them to be part of the "basis of the bargain."

Rite Aid's pamphlet stated, "Inside is everything you need to know about your prescription." The jury acted reasonably when it determined the later statement, "Take with food or milk if upset stomach occurs," *warranted* that milk would not lessen the effectiveness of doxycycline.

DEVIL'S ADVOCATE   How can a statement be the basis of the bargain if one party never heard or read it until after she purchased the product? Obviously the pamphlet had no influence on the consumer's decision to form the contract. And even if the unread notice was somehow part of the bargain, it never urged users to consume eight glasses of milk per day while eating grilled cheese sandwiches and ice cream. The right step for any patient, before adopting such an extreme course, is to check with her doctor. Common sense should be part of good legal doctrine. ◆

EXAM *Strategy*

Question: Melinda, a rock singer, goes to Stereo Shop to buy equipment for her home recording studio. She likes a $15,000 unit on display, and the sales clerk shows her how to record, edit and burn CDs. "It's a terrific unit," he says. "Record a song, see if you like it." She records a song in the store, and the CD is flawless. Impressed, Melinda buys the equipment. However, when the equipment is set up in her home, Melinda's recordings frequently have static in them, forcing her to rerecord. When Stereo Shop is unable to remedy the problem, Melinda sues for breach of warranty. Did Stereo Shop create a warranty? Who is likely to win?

Strategy: Begin by recalling how a seller creates a warranty. One way that this can happen is with an affirmation of fact. These claims are generally strongest if the statement was in writing and specific. A description of the goods may also lead to a warranty, as may use of a sample or model.

Result: The clerk's statement that "It's a terrific unit" is oral and general. Courts will consider it nothing more than puffery. The clerk made no additional description of the goods. However, the clerk used a model, knowing that Melinda would rely on the demonstration, which she did. A seller who takes advantage of a model warrants that the merchandise sold will be just as good. Melinda will win her claim for breach of an express warranty, unless Stereo Shop can show that the static is caused by Melinda's improper use of the equipment.

IMPLIED WARRANTIES

Sean decides to plow driveways during the winter. Emily sells him a snowplow and installs it on his truck, but she makes no promises about its performance. When winter arrives, Sean has plenty of business, but finds that the plow cannot be raised or lowered whenever the temperature falls below 40 degrees. He demands a refund from Emily, but she declines, saying, "I never said that thing would work in the winter. No express warranties, no luck." Scandalous! Is she off the hook? No. It is true she made no express warranties. But many sales are covered by implied warranties.

Implied warranties are those created by the Code itself, not by any act or statement of the seller. The Code's drafters concluded that goods should generally meet certain standards of quality, regardless of what the seller did or did not say. So the Code creates an implied warranty of merchantability and an implied warranty of fitness.

IMPLIED WARRANTY OF MERCHANTABILITY

This is the most important warranty in the Code. Buyers, whether individual consumers or billion dollar corporations, are likelier to rely on this than any other section, and sellers must understand it thoroughly when they market goods. **Unless excluded or modified, a warranty that the goods shall be merchantable is implied in a contract for their sale, if the seller is a merchant with respect to goods of that kind.** Merchantable means that the goods are fit for the ordinary purposes for which they are used.[5] This rule contains several important principles:

> **Merchantable**
>
> Means that the goods are fit for the ordinary purposes for which they are used.

- *Unless excluded or modified* means that the seller does have a chance to escape this warranty. We later discuss what steps a seller may take if she wants to sell goods that are *not* merchantable.

- *Merchantability* requires that goods be fit for their normal purposes. A ladder, to be merchantable, must be able to rest securely against a building and support someone who is climbing it. The ladder need not be serviceable as a boat ramp.

- *Implied* means that the law itself imposes this liability on the seller.

- A *merchant with respect to goods of that kind* means that the seller is someone who routinely deals in these goods or holds himself out as having special knowledge about these goods.

Dacor Corp. manufactured and sold scuba diving equipment. Dacor ordered air hoses from Sierra Precision, specifying the exact size and couplings so that the hose would fit tightly and safely into Dacor's oxygen units. Within about one year, customers returned a dozen Dacor units, complaining that the hose connections had cracked or sheared and were unusable. Dacor recalled 16,000 units and refit them with safe hoses, at a cost of more than $136,000. Dacor sued Sierra, claiming a breach of the implied warranty of merchantability. The Illinois court first ruled that Sierra was a merchant with respect to scuba hoses because it routinely manufactured and sold them. The court then ruled:

> There is no evidence suggesting that these hose assemblies were subjected to anything other than normal use. Since the kind of failure experienced in connection with the returned hose assemblies would be life-threatening if it occurred under water, the hose assemblies were not fit for the purpose for which they were used within the meaning of section 2-314.

The court ordered Sierra to pay $136,721.[6]

The scuba equipment was not merchantable, because a properly made scuba hose should never crack under normal use. But what if the product being sold is food, and the food contains something that is harmful—yet quite normal?

---

[5] UCC Section 2-314(1).
[6] *Dacor Corp. v. Sierra Precision*, 1993 U.S. Dist. LEXIS 8009 (N.D. Ill. 1993).

GOODMAN V. WENCO FOODS, INC.

333 N.C. 1, 423 S.E.2d 444, 1992 N.C. LEXIS 671
SUPREME COURT OF NORTH CAROLINA, 1992

CASE SUMMARY

Facts: Fred Goodman and a friend stopped for lunch at a Wendy's restaurant in Hillsborough, North Carolina. Goodman had eaten about half of his double hamburger when he bit down and felt immediate pain in his lower jaw. He took from his mouth a triangular piece of cow bone, about one-sixteenth to one-quarter inch thick and one-half inch long, along with several pieces of his teeth. Goodman's pain was intense, and his dental repairs took months.

The restaurant purchased all of its meat from Greensboro Meat Supply Company (GMSC). Wendy's required its meat to be chopped and "free from bone or cartilage in excess of 1/8 inch in any dimension." GMSC beef was inspected continuously by state regulators and was certified by the United States Department of Agriculture (USDA). The USDA considered any bone fragment less than three-quarters of an inch long to be "insignificant."

Goodman sued, claiming a breach of the implied warranty of merchantability. The trial court dismissed the claim, ruling that the bone was natural to the food and that the hamburger was therefore fit for its ordinary purpose. The appeals court reversed this, holding that a hamburger could be unfit even if the bone occurred naturally. Wendy's appealed to the state's highest court.

Issue: *Was the hamburger unfit for its ordinary purpose because it contained a harmful but natural bone?*

Decision: Affirmed. Even if the harmful bone occurred naturally, the hamburger could be unfit for its ordinary purpose.

Reasoning: When an object in food harms a consumer, the injured person may recover even if the substance occurred naturally, provided that a reasonable consumer would not expect to encounter it. A triangular, one-half-inch bone shaving may be inherent to a cut of beef, but whether a reasonable consumer would anticipate it is normally a question for the jury.

Wendy's hamburgers need not be perfect, but they must be fit for their intended purpose. It is difficult to imagine how a consumer could guard against bone particles, short of removing the hamburger from its bun, breaking it apart, and inspecting its small components.

Wendy's argues that because its meat complied with federal and state standards, the hamburgers were merchantable as a matter of law. However, while compliance with legal standards is evidence for the juries to consider, it does not ensure merchantability. A jury could still conclude that a bone this size in hamburger meat was reasonably unforeseeable and that an injured consumer was entitled to compensation.

IMPLIED WARRANTY OF FITNESS FOR A PARTICULAR PURPOSE

The other warranty that the law imposes on sellers is the implied warranty of fitness for a particular purpose. This cumbersome name is often shortened to the *warranty of fitness*. **Where the seller at the time of contracting knows about a particular purpose for which the buyer wants the goods, and knows that the buyer is relying on the seller's skill or judgment, there is (unless excluded or modified) an implied warranty that the goods shall be fit for the purpose.**[7] Here are the key points:

- *Particular Purpose.* The seller must know about some special use that the buyer plans for the goods. For example, if a lumber salesman knows that a builder is purchasing lumber to construct houses in swampland, the Code implies a warranty that the lumber will withstand water.

[7] UCC Section 2-315.

- *Seller's Skill.* The buyer must be depending upon the seller's skill or judgment in selecting the product, and the seller must know it. Suppose the builder says to the lumber salesman, "I need four-by-eights that I will be using to build a house in the swamp. What do you have that will do the job?" The builder's reliance is obvious and the warranty is established. By contrast, suppose that an experienced Alaskan sled-driver offers to buy your three huskies, telling you she plans to use them to pull sleds. She has the experience and you do not, and if the dogs refuse to pull more than a one-pound can of dog food, you have probably breached no implied warranty.

- *Exclusion or Modification.* Once again, the seller is allowed to modify or exclude any warranty of fitness, as we see below.

WARRANTIES COMPARED

Express Warranty	Implied Warranty of Merchantability	Implied Warranty of Fitness for a Particular Purpose
The Rule: Seller can create an express warranty with any affirmation or promise, with any description of the goods, or with any sample or model, provided the words or sample are part of the basis of the bargain.	*The Rule:* With certain exceptions, the Code implies a warranty that the goods will be fit for their ordinary purpose.	*The Rule:* With some exceptions, the Code implies a warranty that the goods are fit for the buyer's special purpose, provided that the seller knows of that purpose when the contract is made and knows of the buyer's reliance.
Example: Manufacturer sends Retailer a brochure describing its brand of children's bicycle. The brochure states that "these bikes will last for a minimum of eight years of normal use." If the handlebars snap off after six months, Manufacturer has breached its express warranty.	*Example:* Manufacturer sells Retailer 300 "children's bicycles." There is no brochure and no promise made by Manufacturer about the bikes' quality. The UCC implies a warranty that the bikes will be fit for ordinary riding by children. But the cycles might not be strong enough to withstand mountain racing, and there is no warranty to that effect.	*Example:* Retailer orders from Manufacturer "300 mountain bikes, for racing," and Manufacturer agrees. The UCC implies a warranty that the bikes will withstand the added stress of mountain racing.

Two Last Warranties: Title and Infringement

Strapped for cash, Maggie steals her boyfriend's rusty Chevy and sells it to Paul for $2,500. As we saw in Chapter 19, Maggie gets no valid title by her theft, and therefore Paul receives no title either. When the boyfriend finds his car parked at a nightclub, he notifies the police and gets his wheels back. Poor Paul is out of pocket $2,500 and has no car to show for it. That clearly is unjust, and the UCC provides Paul with a remedy: **the seller of goods warrants that her title is valid and that the goods are free of any security interest that the buyer knows nothing about, unless the seller has clearly excluded or modified this warranty.**[8] Once again, the Code is imposing a warranty on any seller except those who explicitly exclude or modify it. When Maggie sells the car to Paul, she warrants her valid title to the car and simultaneously breaches that warranty, since she obviously has no title. Paul will win a lawsuit against Maggie for $2,500.

The same Code section imposes a warranty against claims of infringement by third parties. **Unless otherwise agreed, a seller who is a merchant warrants that the goods are free of any rightful claim of copyright, patent, or trademark infringement.**[9] Wesley sells to Komputer

---

[8] UCC Section 2-312(1).
[9] UCC Section 2-313(3).

Corp. a device that automatically blasts purple smoke out of a computer screen anytime a student's paper is really dreadful. Unless Komputer Corp. agrees otherwise, Wesley is automatically giving the buyer a warranty that no one else invented the device or has any copyright, patent, or trademark in it.

DISCLAIMERS AND DEFENSES

There are several limitations on warranties. A seller may disclaim *warranties*, meaning that he eliminates express or implied warranties covering the goods. Or the seller may limit the buyer's *remedy*, which means that even if there is a breach of warranty, the buyer still may have only a very limited chance to recover against the seller.

DISCLAIMERS

A **disclaimer** is a statement that a particular warranty *does not* apply. The Code permits the seller to disclaim most warranties.

Disclaimer
A statement that a particular warranty does not apply.

Oral Express Warranties

Under the Code, a seller may disclaim an oral express warranty. Suppose Traffic Co. wants to buy a helicopter from HeliCorp for use in reporting commuter traffic. HeliCorp's salesman tells Traffic Co., "Don't worry, you can fly this bird day and night for six months with nothing more than a fuel stop." HeliCorp's contract may disclaim the oral warranty. The contract could say, "HeliCorp's entire warranty is printed below. Any statements made by any agent or salesperson are disclaimed and form no part of this contract." That disclaimer is valid. If the helicopter requires routine servicing between flights, HeliCorp has not breached an oral warranty.

Written Express Warranties

This is the one type of warranty that is difficult or impossible to disclaim. If a seller includes an express warranty in the *sales contract*, any disclaimer is invalid. Suppose HeliCorp sells an industrial helicopter for use in hauling building equipment. The sales contract describes the aircraft as "operable to 14,000 feet." Later, in the contract, a limited warranty disclaims "any other warranties or statements that appear in this document or in any other document." That disclaimer is invalid. The Code will not permit a seller to take contradictory positions in one document. The goal is simply to be fair, and the Code assumes that it is confusing and unjust for the seller to say one thing to help close a deal and the opposite to limit its losses.[10]

What if the express written statement is in a different document, such as a sales brochure? The disclaimer is void if it would *unfairly surprise* the buyer. Assume, again, that HeliCorp promises a helicopter that requires no routine maintenance for six months, but this time the promise appears in a sales brochure that Traffic Co. reads and relies on. If HeliCorp attempts to disclaim the written warranty, it will probably fail. Most people take written information seriously.

Implied Warranties

A seller may disclaim the implied warranty of merchantability provided he *actually mentions the word "merchantability"* and makes the disclaimer conspicuous. Courts demand to see the word

---

[10] UCC Section 2-316(1).

"merchantability" in the disclaimer to be sure the buyer realized she was giving up this fundamental protection. If the word is there and the disclaimer is conspicuous enough that the buyer should have seen it, she has forfeited the warranty. A seller may disclaim the implied warranty of fitness with any language that is clear and conspicuous.

General Disclaimers

To make life easier, the Code permits a seller to disclaim all implied warranties by conspicuously stating that the goods are sold "as is" or "with all faults." Notice the tension between this provision and the discussion about disclaiming a warranty of merchantability. A seller who wants to disclaim *only* the warranty of merchantability must explicitly mention that term; but a seller wishing to exclude *all* implied warranties may do so with a short expression, such as "sold as is."

Consumer Sales

As we have seen many times in the Code, protection is often stronger for consumers than for businesses. *Many states prohibit a seller from disclaiming implied warranties in the sale of consumer goods.* In these states, if a home furnishings store sells a bunk bed to a consumer, and the top bunk tips out the window on the first night, the seller is liable. If the sales contract clearly stated "no warranties of merchantability or fitness," the court would reject the clause and find that the seller breached the implied warranty of merchantability.

EXAM *Strategy*

Question: Marcos's backyard pool, which measured 35 by 18 feet, needed a new filter. A sales brochure stated, "This filter will keep any normal backyard pool, up to 50 feet by 25, clean and healthy all summer for a minimum of 5 years." Marcos signed a sales contract, which included this disclaimer: "The filter will work to normal industry standards. This is the only warranty. No other statements, written or oral, apply. Pools vary widely, and the Seller cannot guarantee any specific level of performance or cleanliness. Buyer agrees to this disclaimer." The filter failed to keep Marcos's pool clean, and he sued for breach of warranty. Who should win?

Strategy: Sellers are often able to disclaim oral warranties, but written warranties are difficult to disclaim. Here, the initial promise and the disclaimer were in different documents. Does that change the outcome? Finally, Marcos was a consumer. Courts treat consumers differently from corporate buyers.

Result: It is difficult or impossible for sellers to disclaim written warranties, even if the promise and disclaimer are in different documents. A disclaimer that would unfairly surprise the buyer is probably void. Marcos relied on the sales brochure—as the company intended—and the seller will probably lose. Furthermore, most states give extra protection to consumers, knowing that they are less sophisticated buyers. A court is likely to find in favor of Marcos based on the seller's express warranty as well as the implied warranties of merchantability and fitness.

REMEDY LIMITATIONS

Simon Aerials, Inc., manufactured boomlifts, the huge cranes used to construct multistoried buildings. Simon agreed to design and build eight unusually large machines for Logan Equipment Corp. Simon delivered the boomlifts late, and they functioned poorly. Logan requested dozens of repairs and modifications, which Simon attempted to accomplish over many months, but the equipment never worked well. Logan gave up and sued for $7.5 million, representing the profits it expected to make from renting the machines and the damage to its reputation. Logan clearly had suffered major losses, and it recovered—nothing. How could that be?

Simon had negotiated a **limitation of remedy** clause, by which **the parties may limit or exclude the normal remedies permitted under the Code**.[11] These important rights are entirely distinct from disclaimers. A disclaimer limits the seller's warranties and thus affects whether the seller has breached her contract. A remedy limitation, by contrast, states that if a party does breach its warranty, the injured party will not get all of the damages the Code normally allows.

In its contract, Simon had agreed to repair or replace any defective boomlifts, but that was all. The agreement said that if a boomlift was defective, and Logan lost business, profits, and reputation, Simon was not liable. The court upheld the remedy limitation. Since Simon had repeatedly attempted to repair and redesign the defective machines, it had done everything it promised to do. Logan got nothing.[12]

We compare disclaimers and remedy limitations in the table below.

COMPARISON OF DISCLAIMERS AND REMEDY LIMITATIONS

Code Section	Purpose	Setting	Contract Language	Result
Disclaimers: UCC Section 2-316	Limits warranties, whether express or implied. This section will determine *whether there has been a breach*.	Seller sells Buyer a used "tire shredding machine." UCC Section 2-314 implies a warranty of merchantability, meaning that the machine will be good for its ordinary purpose, which is shredding tires in a commercial recycling business.	Seller includes in the contract a clause stating that the tire shredder is sold "as is." Under Section 2-316, this phrase excludes all implied warranties, meaning that the implied warranty of merchantability will NOT apply here.	One tire goes through the machine, the tire emerges completely intact, and the machine falls to pieces. *Result:* Seller has NOT breached the contract, and Buyer gets no damages.
Remedy limitations: UCC Section 2-719	Limits the remedies available *when one party has breached* the contract.	Seller sells Buyer 10,000 computer circuit boards at $200 each, which Buyer uses in its laptops.	Seller requires a clause limiting Buyer's remedies to "replace or repair." If the boards fail, Seller will replace or repair them for free. But Buyer is permitted NO OTHER REMEDY. Buyer may not seek consequential damages, which would include lost profits and injured reputation.	All of the boards malfunction, and Buyer's customers are angry *at Buyer*. Buyer must take the computers back, losing all of its expected profits and also suffering a serious loss of reputation in the high-tech world. Seller IS in breach of the contract and must repair or replace all circuit oards at its expense. But Seller owes NOTHING for Buyer's lost profits or injured reputation.

Consequential Damages

Simon's contract clause was a typical one. Sellers frequently use a remedy limitation to avoid liability for consequential damages, which can be vast. Recall that a party injured by breach of contract normally gets *compensatory* damages.[13] In the sale of goods that means the difference

---

[11] UCC Section 2-719. A few states prohibit remedy limitations, but most permit them.
[12] *Logan Equipment Corp. v. Simon Aerials, Inc.*, 736 F. Supp. 1188, 1990 U.S. Dist. LEXIS 5720 (D. Mass. 1990).
[13] Compensatory, consequential, and incidental damages are discussed in Chapter 17, on remedies.

between the value of the goods promised and those actually delivered. A seller can anticipate and probably tolerate such damages, since the seller understands exactly how much it costs to repair or replace the goods it has sold. **Consequential damages**, however, are different. They are losses stemming from the particular requirements of the buyer. The buyer might have entered into dozens of contracts in reliance on the goods it expects from the seller. The seller will have no way of knowing how great the consequential damages could be. Logan Equipment claimed that it would have earned profits in the millions, and it was just such a claim that Simon had determined to avoid.

Notice that there is one major limitation on these clauses: **an exclusion of consequential damages is void if it is unconscionable.** "Unconscionable" means that a remedy restriction is shockingly one-sided and fundamentally unfair.[14] If the buyer is a consumer, a court will be likelier to consider such an exclusion unfair, since the typical consumer will not understand the terms and may never even notice them. If the buyer is a consumer who suffers a *personal injury*, a court is nearly certain to reject the exclusion. It is unfair for a corporation to market defective goods and escape liability because an unsuspecting consumer failed to understand contract language. Suppose Byron buys a hot-air popper that comes with a label excluding consequential damages. Byron is seriously burned when the popper ignites. Virtually all courts will ignore the consequential damages exclusion and apply a warranty of merchantability to the popper, permitting Byron to recover his full damages. His compensatory damages are insignificant: the cost of a new popper. His consequential damages are enormous: medical expenses, pain and suffering, and lost income.

However, when the buyer is a corporation, courts assume it had adequate legal advice and an opportunity to reject unacceptable terms. When two companies agree to a remedy limitation, they are allocating the risk of loss as one part of their bargain. A court will seldom substitute its judgment for that of the contracting companies. In the *Logan Equipment* case, both parties were corporations, and sophisticated executives negotiated the boomlift sale. The court found nothing unconscionable in the bargain and enforced the limitation that the parties had agreed to.[15]

PRIVITY

When two parties contract, they are *in privity*. If Lance buys a chainsaw from the local hardware store, he is in privity with the store. But Lance has no privity with Kwiksaw, the manufacturer of the chain saw. Under traditional contract law, a plaintiff injured by a breach of contract could only sue a defendant with whom he had privity. So, a hundred years ago, if Lance's chainsaw had been seriously defective, he could have sued only the store. Kwiksaw would have defended successfully, claiming "lack of privity." This hurt consumers because the local retailer might have lacked assets to compensate for serious injuries. Today, privity is gradually disappearing as a defense. The various states are approaching the issue in different ways, so there is no one rule. We can, however, highlight the trends.

Personal Injury

Where a product causes a personal injury, most states permit a warranty suit even without privity. If the chain on Lance's power saw flies off and slashes his arm, he has suffered a personal injury. Of course, he may sue the store, with which he has privity. But he wants to sue

---

[14] UCC Section 2-719. We discuss unconscionability under the Code in Chapter 18.
[15] *Logan Equipment*, 736 F.Supp. at 1195.

the manufacturer, which has more money. In the majority of states, he will be able to sue the manufacturer for breach of warranty even though he had no privity with it.[16] (Note that Lance is sure to make other claims against the manufacturer, including *negligence* and *strict liability*, both discussed below.)

Economic Loss

If the buyer suffers only economic loss, privity *may* still be required to bring a suit for breach of warranty. If the buyer is a business, the majority of states require privity. Fab-Rik makes fabric for furniture and drapes, which it sells to various wholesalers. Siddown makes sofas. Siddown buys Fab-Rik fabric from a wholesaler and, after installing it on 200 sofas, finds the material defective. Siddown may sue the wholesaler but, in most states, will be unable to sue Fab-Rik for breach of any warranties. There was no privity.

By contrast, when the buyer is a consumer, more states will permit a suit against the manufacturer, even without privity. Lance, the consumer, buys his power saw to landscape his property. This time the saw malfunctions without injuring him, but Lance must buy a replacement saw for considerably more money. Many states—but not all—will permit him to recover his losses from Kwiksaw, the manufacturer, on the theory that Kwiksaw intends its product to reach consumers and is in the best position to control losses.

In the following case, a jailhouse tragedy prompts a product liability suit.

REED V. CITY OF CHICAGO

263 F.SUPP.2d 1123
UNITED STATES DISTRICT COURT FOR THE NORTHERN DISTRICT OF ILLINOIS, 2003

CASE SUMMARY

Facts: J.C. Reed was arrested and brought to Chicago's Fifth District Police Station. Police were allegedly aware that he was suicidal, having seen him slash his wrists earlier. They removed his clothing and dressed him in a paper isolation gown. Sadly, Reed used the gown to hang himself.

Reed's mother, on his behalf, sued the police (for failing to monitor a suicidal inmate) and also Cypress Medical Products, the manufacturer of the isolation gown. The claim was that the gown should have been made of material that would tear if someone attempted to hang himself with it.

---

[16] The Code offers three alternative versions of its rule concerning privity: UCC Section 2-318, Alternatives A, B, and C, with each state free to adopt whichever version the legislature prefers. Alternative A, the most restrictive, extends a warranty in the cases of personal injury to the buyer and members of his household. But the comments of this section indicate that this extension to household members does not *preclude* claims brought by non-household members. The drafters have left it up to the states to decide whether additional injured parties could sue. Several states that have adopted this version of the privity rule have permitted warranty claims by injured parties who were not household members. Dahlia buys a weed cutter manufactured by Thorn and sold by Hardware, and loans it to Rose, who is cut when it malfunctions. Many, but not all, states that have adopted Alternative A would allow Rose to sue Thorn. Alternative B is more expansive, explicitly permitting a warranty suit by any injured natural person (non-corporation) who could reasonably be affected by the product. In states that have adopted this section, Rose would certainly be permitted to sue Thorn. Alternative C, the most expansive, permits recovery by natural persons and corporations and allows suits for economic loss as well as personal injury. What does all this mean? The privity requirement is disappearing in personal injury cases and diminishing in cases of economic loss.

Cypress moved to dismiss the suit, claiming that Reed had no privity with the company.

Issue: *Could Reed maintain a lawsuit against Cypress despite lack of privity?*

Decision: Privity is not required. Reed may sue Cypress.

Reasoning: Historically, a plaintiff lost a breach of warranty suit if he lacked privity with the defendant. However, UCC Section 2-318 now extends an express or implied warranty to any injured person who is in the family or household of the buyer, or who is a guest in the home, if it is reasonable to expect that he might use the goods or be affected by a breach of warranty. What is more, Illinois decisions have expanded the class of potential plaintiffs beyond those mentioned in Section 2-318.

Most of the successful suits have arisen in employment cases. For example, a plaintiff was injured using a bandsaw that his employer had purchased. The court held that the worker was a third party beneficiary of the sales contract and that his safety was part of the basis of the bargain made by the employer. The employee could sue the manufacturer. By contrast, in a case not related to employment, a court refused to allow a warranty claim by a university football player injured because of a defective helmet that the school had purchased.

The facts of this case indicate that the class of plaintiffs who can sue for breach of warranty must be expanded to include injured parties such as Reed. The only users of the gowns that Cypress manufactures will be potentially suicidal detainees. Their safety was necessarily part of the bargain between seller and buyer, whether expressed or implied. If such a detainee is not covered by the warranty, no one will be. A detainee covered by the warranty must be able to enforce it.

Cypress's motion to dismiss is denied.

Buyer's Misconduct

Misuse by the buyer will generally preclude a warranty claim.[17] Common sense tells us that the seller only warrants its goods if they are properly used. Lord & Taylor warranted that its false eyelashes would function well and cause no harm. But when Ms. Caldwell applied them, they severely irritated one eye. She sued but the store prevailed. Why? Caldwell applied the eyelashes improperly, getting the glue into one eye. On her other eye she used the product correctly and suffered no harm. Her misuse proved painful to her eye—and fatal to her lawsuit.[18]

Statute of Limitations and Notice of Breach

It is right that a seller be responsible for the goods it places in the market. On the other hand, a seller should not face potential liability *forever*. A company cannot be a perpetual insurer for goods that it sold decades earlier. And so the UCC imposes two important time limits on a buyer's claim of breach.

The Code prescribes a four-year statute of limitations. This means that the buyer must bring any lawsuit for breach of a warranty no later than four years after the goods were delivered. When the parties contract, they may shorten that period to no less than one year, but they may not extend it. Suppose PlaneJane, an airline, buys 10 new aircraft from Flyem, a manufacturer, taking delivery on June 1, 2004. In the fall of 2007, PlaneJane begins to discover structural weaknesses in the wings, which Flyem repeatedly repairs over the next few months. PlaneJane must decide whether to file a lawsuit. If the airline believes all problems are corrected, fine. But if it has any doubts about the aircraft fitness, PlaneJane

---

[17] Some courts characterize the misuse as "comparative negligence" or "contibutory negligence" or "failure of proximate cause." These tort terms are discussed in Chapter 6 dealing with negligence and strict liability. For our purposes here, it is enough to understand that misuse generally precludes a warranty claim.

[18] *Caldwell v. Lord & Taylor, Inc.*, 142 Ga. App. 137, 235 S.E.2d 546 (Ga. Ct. App. 1977).

must sue promptly. On June 2, 2008, any lawsuit for breach of warranty is barred by the statute of limitations.

The Code puts an additional burden on a buyer asserting a breach of warranty. **The UCC requires that a buyer notify the seller of defects within a reasonable time.**[19] The purpose here is to enable the seller to cure, by repairing or replacing, any problems with the goods. Ideally, a seller that receives notice of a potential breach will fix the problem and there will *be* no lawsuit.

The circumstances will determine what is a "reasonable" amount of time. An inexperienced consumer could reasonably take many months to figure out that a new laptop computer had a serious operating defect. Further, a delay of six or eight months would not harm a large computer manufacturer. On the other hand, a corporate buyer of perishable food products must act very fast if it claims the goods are defective.

NEGLIGENCE

A buyer of goods may have remedies other than warranty claims. One is negligence, which we discuss in detail in Chapter 6. Here we focus on how this law applies to the sale of goods. Negligence, as you will recall, is notably different from contract law. In a contract case, the two parties have reached an agreement, and the terms of their bargain will usually determine how to settle any dispute. If the parties agreed that the seller disclaimed all warranties, then the buyer may be out of luck. But in a negligence case, there has been no bargaining between the parties, who may never have met. A consumer injured by an exploding cola bottle is unlikely to have bargained for her beverage with the CEO of the cola company. Instead, the law *imposes* a standard of conduct on everyone in society, corporation and individual alike. The two key elements of this standard, for present purposes, are *duty* and *breach*. A plaintiff injured by goods she bought must show that the defendant, usually a manufacturer or seller of a product, had a duty to her and breached that duty.[20] A defendant has a duty of due care to anyone who could foreseeably be injured by its misconduct. Generally, it is the duty to act as *a reasonable person* would in like circumstances; a defendant who acts unreasonably has breached its duty.

> A consumer injured by an exploding cola bottle is unlikely to have bargained for her beverage with the CEO of the cola company.

In negligence cases concerning the sale of goods, plaintiffs most often raise one or more of these claims:

- *Negligent Design.* The buyer claims that the product injured her because the manufacturer designed it poorly. Negligence law requires a manufacturer to design a product free of *unreasonable* risks. The product does not have to be absolutely safe. An automobile that guaranteed a driver's safety could be made but would be prohibitively expensive. Reasonable safety features must be built in, if they can be included at a tolerable cost.

---

[19] UCC Section 2-607.

[20] A plaintiff in a negligence case must also prove three other elements: factual causation, foreseeable type of harm, and injury. For a discussion of those elements, see Chapter 6. We focus in this chapter on duty and breach because those two elements take on special importance in product liability cases.

- *Negligent Manufacture.* The buyer claims that the design was adequate but that failure to inspect or some other sloppy conduct caused a dangerous product to leave the plant.

- *Failure to Warn.* A manufacturer is liable for failing to warn the purchaser or users about the dangers of normal use and also foreseeable misuse. However, there is no duty to warn about obvious dangers, a point evidently lost on some manufacturers. A Batman costume came with this statement: "For play only: Mask and chest plate are not protective; cape does not enable user to fly."

In the following case, the plaintiffs raise issues of negligent design and failure to warn, concerning a disposable lighter. You decide.

YOU *be the* JUDGE

BOUMELHEM V. BIC CORP.

211 Mich.App. 175, 535 N.W.2d 574, Mich. App. LEXIS 228
Michigan Court of Appeals, 1995

Facts: Ibrahim Boumelhem, aged four, began playing with a Bic disposable lighter that his parents had bought. He started a fire that burned his legs and severely burned his six-month-old brother over 85 percent of his body. Ibrahim's father sued Bic, claiming that the lighter was negligently designed because it could have been child-proof. He also claimed failure to warn because the lighter did not clearly warn of the danger to children.

The *Boumelhem* court considered evidence and analyses from several other cases against Bic. The court noted that consumers use over 500 million disposable lighters annually in the United States. Each lighter provides 1,000 to 2,000 lights. During one three-year period, children playing with disposable lighters started 8,100 fires annually, causing an average of 180 people to die every year, of whom 140 were children under five. Another 990 people were injured. The average annual cost of deaths, injuries, and property damage from child-play fires was estimated at $310 to $375 million, or 60 to 75 cents per lighter sold. Bic had acknowledged in earlier litigation that it was foreseeable lighters would get into children's hands and injure them. Bic had also agreed that it was feasible to make a more child-resistant lighter.

The trial court relied on a Michigan case. In *Adams v. Perry Furniture Co.*, [21] four minor children had died in a fire started when one of them was playing with a Bic lighter. The Adams court had found no negligent design and no failure to warn, and dismissed all claims. The trial court in the present case followed Adams and dismissed Boumelhem's claims. He appealed.

You Be the Judge: Did Bic negligently design its disposable lighter? Did Bic negligently fail to warn of the lighter's dangers?

Argument for Boumelhem: Your honors, the *Adams* court decided the issues wrongly. There is a reason that new plaintiffs are back in this court, the year after *Adams*, raising related issues against Bic: the company is killing hundreds of children every year. In its efforts to maximize corporate profits, it is literally burning these children to death and injuring hundreds more. That's wrong.

Bic has acknowledged that its disposable lighters can and will get into the hands of children. Bic knows full well that its product will injure or kill a certain percentage of these children—very young children. Bic has admitted that it could design a child-proof lighter, and it knows perfectly well how to include effective warnings on its lighters. But rather than improve product design and give effective warnings, Bic prefers to do business as usual and litigate liability for injured and murdered children.

We ask this court to rule that Bic breached its duty to design and manufacture a lighter that will keep our kids safe, and breached its duty to warn.

Argument for Bic: Your honors, the Bic Corp. is as horrified as anyone over the injuries to these children and the deaths of other kids. But Bic is not responsible. The children's parents

---

[21] 198 Mich. App. 1, 497 N.W.2d 514, 1993 Mich. App. LEXIS 33 (Mich. Ct. App. 1993).

continued

are responsible. We sympathize with their grief but not with their attempt to pass parental responsibility onto the shoulders of a corporation. There are several reasons Bic is not liable in this case.

First, the *Adams* court decided the matter, and that precedent is binding.

Second, Bic has no duty to design a different lighter. The test in design defect cases is whether the risks are unreasonable in light of the foreseeable injuries. Young children can hurt themselves in countless ways, from falls to poisonings to automobile injuries. There is one answer to these dangers, and it is called good parenting. The parents who bought this lighter purchased it

because it could start a fire. The moment they purchased it, they assumed the obligation to keep it away from their children. These are useful products, which is why Bic sells hundreds of millions per year. Other consumers should not be forced to pay an outrageously high price for a simple tool, just because some parents fail to do their job.

The failure to warn argument is even weaker. The law imposes no failure to warn when the danger is obvious. Every adult knows that lighters are *potentially* dangerous, if misused, or if passed on to children. Does the court really think anyone would be helped by a warning that said, "This lighter starts fires. Don't give it to children."

STRICT LIABILITY

The other tort claim that an injured person can bring against the manufacturer or seller of a product is strict liability. Like negligence, strict liability is a burden created by the law rather than by the parties. And, as with all torts, strict liability concerns claims of physical harm. But there is a key distinction between negligence and strict liability: in a negligence case, the injured buyer must demonstrate that the seller's conduct was unreasonable. Not so in strict liability.

In strict liability, the injured person need not prove that the defendant's conduct was unreasonable. The injured person must show only that the defendant manufactured or sold a product that was defective and that the defect caused harm. Almost all states permit such lawsuits, and most of them have adopted the summary of strict liability provided by the Restatement (Second) of Torts **Section 402A**. Because Section 402A is the most frequently cited section in all of tort law, we quote it in full:

(1) One who sells any product in a defective condition unreasonably dangerous to the user or consumer or to his property is subject to liability for physical harm thereby caused to the ultimate user or consumer, or to his property, if

  (a) the seller is engaged in the business of selling such a product, and

  (b) it is expected to and does reach the user or consumer without substantial change in the condition in which it is sold.

(2) The rule stated in Subsection (1) applies although

  (a) the seller has exercised all possible care in the preparation and sale of his product, and

  (b) the user or consumer has not bought the product from or entered into any contractual relation with the seller.

These are the key terms in subsection (1):

- *Defective condition unreasonably dangerous to the user.* The defendant is liable only if the product is defective when it leaves his hands. There must be something wrong with the goods. If they are reasonably safe and the buyer's mishandling of the goods causes the harm, there is no strict liability. If you attempt to open a soda bottle by knocking the cap against a counter, and the glass shatters and cuts you, the manufacturer owes nothing. A carving knife can produce a lethal wound, but everyone knows that, and a sharp knife is not unreasonably dangerous. On the other hand, prescription drugs may harm in ways that neither a layperson nor a doctor would anticipate. The manufacturer *must provide adequate warnings* of any dangers that are not apparent.

- *In the business of selling.* The seller is liable only if she normally sells this kind of product. Suppose your roommate makes you a peanut butter sandwich and, while eating it, you cut your mouth on a sliver of glass that was in the jar. The peanut butter manufacturer faces strict liability as does the grocery store where your roommate bought the goods. But your roommate is not strictly liable because he does not serve sandwiches as a business.

- *Reaches the user without substantial change.* Obviously, if your roommate put the glass in the peanut butter thinking it was funny, neither the manufacturer nor the store is liable.

  And here are the important phrases in subsection (2).

- *Has exercised all possible care.* This is the heart of strict liability, which makes it a potent claim for consumers. *It is no defense that the seller used reasonable care.* If the product is dangerously defective and injures the user, the seller is liable even if it took every precaution to design and manufacture the product safely. Suppose the peanut butter jar did in fact contain a glass sliver when it left the factory. The manufacturer proves that it uses extraordinary care in keeping foreign particles out of the jars and thoroughly inspects each container before it is shipped. The evidence is irrelevant. The manufacturer has shown that it was not *negligent* in packaging the food, but reasonable care is irrelevant in strict liability.

- *No contractual relation.* Remember "privity," from the warranty discussion? Privity only exists between the user and the person from whom she actually bought the goods. This sentence in Section 402A means that *privity is not required.* Suppose the manufacturer that made the peanut butter sold it to a distributor, which sold it to a wholesaler, which sold it to a grocery store, which sold it to your roommate. You may sue the manufacturer, distributor, wholesaler, and store, even though you had no privity with any of them.

Restatement (Third) and Contemporary Trends

We saw that under traditional negligence law, a company could be found liable based on design, manufacture, or failure to warn. The same three activities can give rise to a claim of strict liability. It will normally be easier for a plaintiff to win a claim of strict liability, because she does not need to demonstrate that the manufacturer's conduct was unreasonable.

If the steering wheel on a brand new car falls off, and the driver is injured, that is a clear case of defective manufacturing, and the company will be strictly liable. Those are the easy cases. As courts have applied Section 402A, defective design cases have been more contentious. Suppose a vaccine that prevents serious childhood illnesses inevitably causes brain damage in a very small number of children, because of the nature of the drug. Is the manufacturer liable? What if a racing sailboat, designed only for speed, is dangerously unstable in the hands of a less experienced sailor? Is the boat's maker responsible for fatalities? Suppose an automobile made of lightweight metal uses less fuel but exposes its occupants to more serious injuries in an accident. How is a court to decide whether the design was defective? Often, these design cases also involve issues of warnings: Did drug designer diligently detail dangers to doctors? Should sailboat seller sell speedy sailboat solely to seasoned sailors?

Over the years, most courts have adopted one of two tests for design and warning cases. The first is *consumer expectation.* Here, a court finds the manufacturer liable for defective design if the product is less safe than a reasonable consumer would expect. If a smoke detector has a 3 percent failure rate, and the average consumer has no way of anticipating that danger, effective cautions must be included, though the design may be defective anyway. Many states have moved away from that test, and now use a *risk-utility test*. Here, a court must weigh the benefits for society against the dangers that the product poses. Principal factors in the risk-utility test include:

- The *value* of the product,
- The *gravity* of the danger (how bad will the harm be),
- The *likelihood* that such danger will occur (the odds),
- The mechanical feasibility of a *safer alternative* design, and
- The *adverse consequences* of an alternative design (greater cost, different risks created).

Because of the conflicting court decisions, the American Law Institute drafted the Restatement (Third) of Torts: Product Liability, in an attempt to harmonize judicial opinions about product liability generally and design defects in particular. The new Restatement treats manufacturing cases differently from those involving design defects and failure to warn.

- In manufacturing cases, a product is defective whenever it departs from its intended design, regardless of how much care was taken. This is the traditional standard.
- In design and warnings cases, a product is defective only when the *foreseeable risks* of harm could have been reduced by using a reasonable alternative design or warning. So-called "strict" liability in these cases is beginning to resemble plain old negligence. If courts adopt this new approach, it will become more difficult for plaintiffs to win a design or warning case, because they will need to prove that the manufacturer should have foreseen the danger and could have done something about it.

There is no strong trend in how judges examine these cases: courts tend to pick and choose the analytic tools they use. Most still regard Section 402A as the basic law for all strict liability lawsuits. In design cases, many courts use the risk-utility test, quite a few still examine consumer expectation, and some permit both analyses. Most states consider the availability of alternative designs to be important, and some consider it essential. And finally, as the following case indicates, some courts employ elements of the Restatement Third—with plenty of disagreement.

UNIROYAL GOODRICH TIRE COMPANY V. MARTINEZ

977 S.W.2d 328
TEXAS SUPREME COURT, 1998

CASE SUMMARY

Facts: When Roberto Martinez, a mechanic, attempted to mount a 16-inch tire on a 16.5-inch rim (wheel), the tire exploded, causing him serious, permanent injuries. He sued Goodrich, the tire manufacturer; the Budd Company, which made the rim; and Ford Motor Company, which designed it. Budd and Ford settled out of court, and the case proceeded against Goodrich.

The tire had a conspicuous label, advising users never to mount a 16-inch tire on a 16.5-inch rim, warning of the danger of severe injury or death, and including a picture of a worker thrown into the air by an explosion. The label also urged the user never to lean or reach over the assembly while working. Martinez ignored the warnings.

Martinez admitted that the warnings were adequate, but claimed that Goodrich was strictly liable for failing to use a safer "bead" design. The bead, a rubber-encased steel wire, encircles the tire and holds it to the rim. Martinez's expert testified that an alternate design, used by other tire manufacturers, would have prevented his injury. The trial court gave judgment for Martinez in the amount of $10,308,792.45, the Court of Appeals affirmed, and Goodrich appealed to the state's highest court.

Issue: *When warnings are adequate, is a manufacturer still obligated to use a safer alternative design?*

Decision: The manufacturer was obligated to use a safer design. Affirmed.

Reasoning: The Restatement (Second) declared that a product was not defectively designed if it included adequate warnings. However, the Restatement (Third) has rejected this view. Under the new Restatement, the key question remains whether a safer alternative existed. To decide the issue, a court should look at a broad range of factors: the probability and magnitude of potential harm, instructions and warnings included, consumer expectations, cost of alternative design, and product longevity.

Goodrich urges this court to follow the old rule, from the Restatement (Second). We decline. People often ignore warnings. A redesigned tire would have prevented this accident. The company's competitors incorporated the safer bead design almost a decade before this accident occurred, and Goodrich itself followed suit a year after Martinez was hurt. A Goodrich expert acknowledged that if one of his loved ones were inflating a tire, he would prefer the tire to have a single bead design.

Dissent's Reasoning: Goodrich put a prominent, pictographic warning on the tire. Martinez saw it and ignored it. Thousands of these tires were sold, but only one other person ever claimed this type of injury. When the probability of harm is so low and the warnings adequate, the company has done all that should be required.

ECONOMICS AND THE LAW   Smoking is expensive. In fact, virtually all state governments concluded that tobacco use causes lung cancer, emphysema, heart disease, and other illnesses, and that these ailments are very expensive to treat. The states filed suit against the tobacco industry, which settled most of the cases for a total of about $206 *billion*, to be paid gradually between the years 2000 and 2025. That is a lot of money, even for a profitable industry.

Ironically, one economist claims that the settlements make little money sense, because cigarettes are self-financing. This expert concedes that tobacco use causes expensive illnesses, yet argues that the increased costs are offset by savings due to earlier mortality! Because smokers die younger than others, states pay less money for nursing homes and pensions. These savings more than offset the increased medical costs of smoking.

If that is correct, then why would the tobacco industry agree to the pricey settlements? This economist suggests that a tobacco industry defense based on earlier mortality would be very risky to make in court. Jurors might find the argument so offensive that they would impose even higher punitive damages.[22] ◆

TORT REFORM

Some people believe that jury awards are excessive and need statutory reform. About one-half of the states have passed limits on tort awards. The laws vary, but many work this way. A jury is

---

[22] W. Kip Viscusi, "The Governmental Composition of the Insurance Costs of Smoking," *Journal of Law and Economics*, 1999, vol. 42, p. 575.

permitted to award whatever it considers fair for *economic* damages, meaning lost wages and medical expenses. However, *non-economic* damages (pain and suffering), together with any punitive award, may not exceed a prescribed limit, such as three times the economic damages, or sometimes a flat cap, such as $250,000 total. These restrictions can drastically lower the total verdict.

Other states have created special rules for particular kinds of product liability. *Unavoidably unsafe* prescription drugs are an example. Suppose that a plaintiff proves that a prescription medicine caused her grievous, permanent harm, and that one percent of all users will suffer similar damage. If the pharmaceutical company can demonstrate that it is impossible to manufacture the drug to eliminate all danger, many states will deny the plaintiff any damages. These states have essentially decided that the benefits of that prescription medicine outweigh its risks. If the medicine is unavoidably unsafe, that is, it cannot be made safer, the company should not be held liable; large verdicts might drive pharmaceutical firms out of a business that has great social value.

Opponents consider tort reform misleading and dangerous to society. They state that the real goal of the so-called "reform" is to free irresponsible corporations from any potential liability, enabling them to save money while injuring innocent people. Opponents argue that there is no evidence linking product liability cases to higher insurance costs. Jury verdicts nationwide have been declining. They insist that giving 12 average members of society a say in product safety benefits everyone.

EXAM *Strategy*

Question: Warm, Inc. sells large, portable space heaters for industrial use. Warm sells Little Factory a unit and installs it. The sales contract states, "This heating unit is sold as is. There are no warranties, express or implied." On the third night the unit is used, it causes a fire and burns down the factory. Little sues Warm. At trial, the evidence indicates that a defect in the unit caused the fire, but also that this was unprecedented at Warm. The company employed more than the usual number of quality inspectors, and its safety record was the best in the entire industry. Discuss the effect of the sales contract and Warm's safety record. Predict who will win.

Strategy: The question raises three separate issues: warranty (the disclaimer), negligence (the safety record), and strict liability (the defect). What language most effectively disclaims warranties? What must a plaintiff prove to win a negligence case? To prove a strict liability case?

Result: A company may disclaim all warranties by stating the product is sold "as is," especially when selling to a corporate buyer. Warm's disclaimer is effective. The company's safety record is so good that there seems to be no case for negligence. However, Little Factory still wins its lawsuit. The product was unreasonably dangerous to the user. Warm was in the business of selling such heaters, and installed the heater itself. In a strict liability case, Warm's safety efforts will not save it.

TIME LIMITS: TORT VERSUS CONTRACT

Statutes of Limitations in Tort

We have seen that for *warranty* cases, the UCC imposes a four-year statute of limitation. By contrast, most states have a different statute of limitations for tort claims. Many states set a three-year limit, though some are shorter and others longer. But the key element is this: in a tort case, the statute of limitations runs *from the time the defect was discovered*. Even though the three-year period is shorter, the time for filing a suit may be much longer because a defect may not appear for many years.

Many product liability cases involve both warranty and tort claims. Should a court apply the statute of limitations from the Code or from tort law? The analysis begins with the **economic loss doctrine**: when an injury is purely economic, and arises from a contract made by two businesses, the injured party may only sue under the UCC. This rule is primarily for contracts between two businesses; if the buyer is a consumer, most courts will not apply it. The economic loss doctrine has two important consequences for corporate buyers.

First, **the four-year statute of limitations will apply in all cases of economic loss**. Suppose a corporation discovers that a product it purchased six years ago is defective and has caused major losses. The company probably has no remedy. Neibarger purchased an automated milking system for his dairy from Universal Cooperatives. Over the next few years, many of his cows became sick with mastitis; some died, and others had to be sold for beef. Seven years after he bought the equipment, Neibarger learned that Universal had improperly designed and installed the vacuum system that is an essential part of the machine. He sued, claiming massive damage to his farming operation, but the Michigan Supreme Court applied the economic loss doctrine. Neibarger's loss was commercial, resulting from a contract that two corporations had negotiated. His only possible remedy was under the UCC, but the Code's statute of limitations had expired. In the end he had no remedy.[23]

Second, **where the sales contract includes proper disclaimers or remedy limitations, a buyer barred from a negligence case may have no remedy at all**. The economic loss doctrine prohibits a corporation from suing in negligence when its loss is purely commercial. That leaves a lawsuit under the UCC. But if the seller has disclaimed all warranties and/or prohibited certain remedies (such as consequential damages), the buyer may be left with no basis for a lawsuit.

A Final Issue: Statutes of Repose

In tort cases, the passage of time provides a seller with two possible defenses. We have seen that the statute of limitations requires that a lawsuit be brought within a specified period, such as three years, beginning when the defect is discovered or should have been discovered. **A statute of repose places an absolute limit on when a lawsuit may be filed, regardless of when the defect is discovered.** Jeffrey Oats was riding in the back seat of a Nissan sports car when it was involved in an accident. Tragically, Oats suffered spinal cord injuries that left him a quadriplegic. Oats sued Nissan, based on defective design, claiming that the rear seat lacked adequate head and leg room and that the car's body panels lacked sufficient strength. He argued that these defects only became apparent in an accident. But the Idaho Supreme Court dismissed his claims because the car was 11 years old at the time of the accident. The Idaho statute of repose prohibits most product liability suits filed more than 10 years after the goods were sold, regardless of when the defects were discoverable.[24]

---

[23] *Neibarger v. Universal Cooperatives, Inc.*, 439 Mich. 512, 486 N.W.2d 612, 1992 Mich. LEXIS 1502 (1992).
[24] *Oats v. Nissan Motor Corp.*, 126 Idaho 162, 879 P.2d 1095, 1994 Ida. LEXIS 116 (1994).

Economic loss doctrine

When an injury is purely economic, and arises from a contract made by two businesses, the injured party may only sue under the UCC.

OTHER LEGISLATION

LEMON LAWS

It is intensely frustrating—and expensive—for consumers when a new car is defective and spends more time in the repair shop than on the road. So, many states have passed lemon laws, which entitle the buyer to receive a refund if the car has defects that substantially impair its value and safety. This right may prove more valuable than a limited warranty, which might only entitle the buyer to repeated attempts at servicing.

CONSUMER PROTECTION LAWS

Virtually all states also have consumer protection laws, which focus on a merchant's bad faith or deceit. Consumers can use these statutes to recover for defective goods or inadequate service.

MAGNUSON-MOSS WARRANTY ACT

This statute protects consumers who purchase household goods by ensuring basic fairness in the seller's warranty. The statute does not *require* any warranties at all, but covers cases in which a seller chooses to give one. Most sellers of consumer goods do provide some form of express warranty to attract buyers. Magnuson-Moss requires the seller to indicate whether a warranty is full or limited, and to describe clearly what is and is not warranted. The Act also sets certain minimum standards for an express warranty, requiring, for example, that at the very least a seller agree to repair or replace a defective item. Finally, the Act generally forbids a seller who has chosen to give an express warranty to disclaim implied warranties such as the Code's warranties of merchantability and fitness. For a detailed look at Magnuson-Moss, visit **http://www.ftc.gov**.

CHAPTER CONCLUSION

Both sellers and buyers of goods must understand the basic principles of product liability law. A seller must understand warranty, negligence, and strict liability law and consider all of those principles when designing, manufacturing, and marketing goods. A buyer, on the other hand, should be aware that each theory provides a possible basis for compensation and that consumers receive particularly strong protection.

EXAM REVIEW

Products can injure. The harm may be economic or physical. The plaintiff might have a remedy in *warranty*, which is found in the UCC, or one in *tort*, either for negligence or strict liability. The economic loss doctrine states that, when the injured party is a corporation and the harm is purely economic, the only remedies available are the warranty provisions of the Code. If a corporation suffers physical injury, it will probably be able to sue in tort. A consumer who suffers a physical injury can definitely sue in both tort and warranty, and a consumer who suffers an economic injury can generally, but not always, sue in both.

The Code prescribes a four-year statue of limitation for breaches of warranty. In tort cases, the statute of limitations runs from whenever the plaintiff should have discovered the defect. For ease of review, the following chart summarizes the different warranty and tort remedies.

	Contract or Tort	Source of Law	Summary of the Rule	Example	Potential Issue
Express Warranty	Contract	UCC Section 2-313	May be created by an affirmation of fact, a promise, a description of goods, or a sample, but it must have been the basis of the bargain.	Salesman says, "This helicopter will operate perfectly at 16,000 feet."	Written contract may disclaim any and all *oral* warranties.
Implied Warranty of Merchantability	Contract	UCC Section 2-314	The Code implies that the goods are fit for their ordinary use.	Buyer purchases a deep freezer. The Code implies a warranty that it will keep food frozen.	Seller may disclaim this warranty only if a conspicuous disclaimer includes the word "merchantability."
Implied Warranty of Fitness	Contract	UCC Section 2-315	The Code implies that the goods are fit for buyer's special purpose that seller knows about.	Where seller knows (1) buyer wants pine trees to plant in sandy soil, and (2) buyer is relying on seller's judgment, the trees carry an implied warranty that they will grow in that soil.	Seller may disclaim this warranty with conspicuous writing, but note that some states will disregard a disclaimer of *any* implied warranty in a consumer sale.
Implied Warranty of Title	Contract	UCC Section 2-312	The Code implies that seller has good title, free of any security interests and claims of patent, copyright, or trademark.	Seller sells a stolen car to buyer, who must later return it to the rightful owner. Seller has breached his warranty of good title and owes buyer her full damages.	Buyer is not protected against any security interests that she knows about.
Negligence	Tort	Common law	Seller is liable if she fails to show level of conduct that a *reasonable person* would use.	Manufacturer sells bathing suit made of miracle fabric; buyer swims in ocean where saltwater makes garment transparent; seller's failure to test the suit in saltwater was unreasonable and leaves seller liable. If seller had thoroughly tested and this was a freak occurrence, there would probably be no negligence.	No duty to warn if the danger is obvious. (In the bathing suit example, the danger is *not* obvious and there was a duty to warn.)
Strict Liability	Tort	Reinstatement Section 402A (subject to new revisions) and common law	Seller liable if the product leaves in a dangerously defective condition.	Can of barbecue lighter fluid explodes in the user's hand because the can's metal was defective; manufacturer took every reasonable precaution to test and inspect every can leaving factory; that reasonable care is *irrelevant* and seller is liable.	Injured buyer need not prove negligence but must prove that the product was defective.

ADDITIONAL QUESTIONS

1. **CPA QUESTION** Vick bought a used boat from Ocean Marina that disclaimed "any and all warranties." Ocean was unaware the boat had been stolen from Kidd. Vick surrendered it to Kidd when confronted with proof of the theft. Vick sued Ocean. Who prevails?

    (a) Vick, because the implied warranty of title has been breached
    (b) Vick, because a merchant cannot disclaim implied warranties
    (c) Ocean, because of the disclaimer of warranties
    (d) Ocean, because Vick surrendered the boat to Kidd

2. **CPA QUESTION** To establish a cause of action based on strict liability in tort for personal injuries resulting from using a defective product, one of the elements the plaintiff must prove is that the seller (defendant):

    (a) Failed to exercise due care
    (b) Was in privity of contract with the plaintiff
    (c) Defectively designed the product
    (d) Was engaged in the business of selling the product

3. Leighton Industries needed steel pipe to build furnaces for a customer. Leighton sent Callier Steel an order for a certain quantity of "A 106 Grade B" steel. Callier confirmed the order and created a contract by sending an invoice to Leighton, stating that it would send "A 106 Grade B" steel, as ordered. Callier delivered the steel and Leighton built the furnaces, but they leaked badly and required rebuilding. Tests demonstrated that the steel was not, in fact, "A 106 Grade B," but an inferior steel. Leighton sued. Who wins?

4. **YOU BE THE JUDGE** WRITING PROBLEM United Technologies advertised a used Beechcraft Baron airplane for sale in an aviation journal. Attorney Thompson Comerford was interested and spoke with a United agent who described the plane as "excellently maintained" and said it had been operated "under Section 135 flight regulations," meaning the plane had been subject to airworthiness inspections every 100 hours. Comerford arrived at a Dallas airport to pick up the plane, where he paid $80,000 for it. He signed a sales agreement stating that the plane was sold "as is" and that there were "no representations or warranties, express or implied, including the condition of the aircraft, its merchantability or its fitness for any particular purpose." Comerford attempted to fly the plane home, but immediately experienced problems with its brakes, steering, ability to climb, and performance while cruising. (Otherwise it was fine.) He sued, claiming breach of express and implied warranties. Did United Technologies breach express or implied warranties? **Argument for Comerford:** United described the airplane as "excellently maintained," knowing that Mr. Comerford would rely on that information. United bragged about Section 135 servicing, when that was obviously a lie. The company should not be allowed to say one thing and put the opposite in writing. **Argument for United Technologies:** Comerford is a lawyer, and we assume he can read. The contract could not have been clearer. The plane was sold as is. There were no warranties. If Comerford disliked the terms, he should have bargained for a different contract—or walked away. He knew he was buying a risky plane, and it is his to keep.

5. Round Tire Co. sells 1,000 tires to Green Rent-a-Car for use on Green's fleet. The same day it sells one new tire to Betty Blue for use on her car. For both sales, Round uses a sales agreement that includes: "LIMITATION OF REMEDIES. Round agrees

to repair or replace any tire which Round determines was defective, within 12 months or 25,000, whichever comes first. Buyer agrees that this is Buyer's SOLE REMEDY; Buyer is not entitled to consequential or incidental damages or any other remedy of any kind." All of Round's tires prove defective. Green is so disgusted it immediately purchases substitute tires from another manufacturer. Green loses $12,000 in extra tire costs and $75,000 in lost rental payments because many of its cars must be off the road waiting for tires. Betty Blue's new tire blows out as she is driving to church, and Betty suffers broken bones. Green and Blue both sue. Predict the outcomes.

6. **ETHICS** Texaco, Inc., and other oil companies sold mineral spirits in bulk to distributors, which then resold to retailers. Mineral spirits are used for cleaning. Texaco allegedly knew that the retailers, such as hardware stores, frequently packaged the mineral spirits (illegally) in used half-gallon milk containers and sold them to consumers, often with no warnings on the packages. Mineral spirits are harmful or fatal if swallowed. David Hunnings, aged 21 months, found a milk container in his home, swallowed the mineral spirits, and died. The Hunnings sued Texaco in negligence. The trial court dismissed the complaint and the Hunnings appealed. What is the legal standard in a negligence case? Have the plaintiffs made out a valid case of negligence? Remember that at this stage a court is not deciding who wins, but what standard a plaintiff must meet in order to take its case to a jury. Assume that Texaco knew about the repackaging and the grave risk, but continued to sell in bulk because doing so was profitable. (If the plaintiffs cannot prove those facts, they will lose even if they *do* get to a jury.) Would that make you angry? Does that mean such a case should go to a jury? Or would you conclude that the fault still lies with the retailer and/or the parents? In that case, the court should dismiss the suit against Texaco.

7. Boboli Co. wanted to promote its "California style" pizza, which it sold in supermarkets. The company contracted with Highland Group, Inc., to produce 2 million recipe brochures, which would be inserted in the carton when the freshly baked pizza was still very hot. Highland contracted with Comark Merchandising to print the brochures. But when Comark asked for details concerning the pizza, the carton, and so forth, Highland refused to supply the information. Comark printed the first lot of 72,000 brochures, which Highland delivered to Boboli. Unfortunately, the hot bread caused the ink to run, and customers opening the carton often found red or blue splotches on their pizzas. Highland refused to accept additional brochures, and Comark sued for breach of contract. Highland defended by claiming that Comark had breached its warranty of merchantability. Please comment.

8. **CPA QUESTION** Which of the following conditions must be met for an implied warranty of fitness for a particular purpose to arise?: I. The warranty must be in writing. II. The seller must know that the buyer was relying on the seller in selecting the goods.

    (a) I only
    (b) II only
    (c) Both I and II
    (d) Neither I nor II

9. **CPA QUESTION** Under the UCC sales article, an action for breach of the implied warranty of merchantability by a party who sustains personal injuries may be successful against the seller of the product only when:

(a) The seller is a merchant of the product involved

(b) An action based on negligence can also be successfully maintained

(c) The injured party is in privity of contract with the seller

(d) An action based on strict liability in tort can also be successfully maintained

10. **CPA QUESTION** Which of the following factors is least important in determining whether a manufacturer is strictly liable in tort for a defective product?

(a) The negligence of the manufacturer

(b) The contributory negligence of the plaintiff

(c) Modifications to the product by the wholesaler

(d) Whether the product caused injuries

11. **ROLE REVERSAL** Write an essay question concerning a household product that injures a buyer. The buyer sues under theories of warranty and strict liability. The buyer should have a strong claim based on one theory but no reasonable claim based on the other.

INTERNET RESEARCH PROBLEM

Find crash test results for various automobiles. Which cars are safer than average? Less safe? How important is auto safety to you? Are you willing to pay more for a safe car? Who should be the final judge of auto safety; auto companies, insurance companies, juries, government regulators, or consumers?

You can find further practice problems at www.cengagebrain.com. See the preface of this book for website access details.

21 PERFORMANCE AND REMEDIES

Was it a 1930s roadster? A drag racing car from the 1950s? Both. Neither. *Untouchable.* When the Plymouth Prowler first hit the road, with its motorcycle-styled front fenders and low-slung hot rod body, it was nearly impossible to get your hands on one. Dealers were swamped with orders, but they did not know if they would receive a single car from the manufacturer. Donald Hessler was one of those who wanted a Prowler—and he was a determined man.

> **Donald Hessler was one of those who wanted a Prowler—and he was a determined man.**

Hessler went to Crystal Lake Chrysler-Plymouth, met with its owner, Gary Rosenberg, and signed an agreement to buy a Prowler anytime during the next year for $5,000 over the manufacturer's list price. Three months later Rosenberg revealed that the list price would be $39,000. However, the car dealer also entered into a contract to sell a Prowler to another customer for $50,000.

The next time they spoke, Rosenberg told Hessler that Crystal Lake would not be allotted any Prowlers. The eager buyer, though, responded that a Chrysler representative had told him Crystal Lake would receive at least one car. Rosenberg was furious with a customer who had "gone behind his back" to contact Chrysler, and he said he would not sell Hessler a car, even if he did receive one.

Hessler telephoned 38 Chrysler dealers, but none would promise him a car. One month later, at a promotional event for the car, he saw a new Prowler—with Crystal Lake's name on it! He located Rosenberg, offered to buy the car on the spot—and was again rebuffed. Frustrated and angry, but still determined, Hessler somehow found a Prowler later the same day from another dealer, and bought it—for $77,706.

Ecstatic with his new car, Hessler drove straight to court, where he sued Crystal Lake.

Was Rosenberg within his rights, refusing to sell a car to Hessler? Was the customer entitled to any compensation for spending so much more on the coveted auto? These are typical issues of *contract performance* under the Code, which we look at in this chapter, along with principles of *remedy*. Technically, when Hessler bought a car elsewhere, he was *covering*. Did he act reasonably in spending $30,000 above the price set by Crystal Lake, and almost $40,000 above list price? You will have to wait a few pages to find out, but we promise to give you the answer before anyone else gets it.

Surely it is a good idea to begin this final chapter on sale of goods issues in good faith.

GOOD FAITH

The R. G. Ray Corp. needed T-bolts to use in certain automobile parts it was manufacturing for the Garrett Co. Ray contracted for Maynard Manufacturing to deliver 57,000 T-bolts and provided Maynard with detailed specifications. The contract stated that Ray would be the "final judge" of whether the T-bolts conformed to its specifications and that Ray had the right to return any or all non-conforming bolts. **Conforming goods satisfy the contract terms. Non-conforming goods do not.**[1]

Unfortunately, Ray rejected the 57,000 bolts and sued, demanding every penny it had paid as well as additional damages for its lost business with Garrett. Ray moved for summary judgment, pointing out that the contract explicitly allowed it to judge the bolts, to reject any it found unsatisfactory, and to cancel the contract. The court acknowledged that the contract did give Ray these one-sided powers, yet it denied summary judgment. There was still an issue of *good faith*.

The Code requires *good faith* in the performance and enforcement of every contract. Good faith means honesty in fact. Between merchants, it also means the use of reasonable commercial standards of fair dealing.[2] So Ray's right to reject the T-bolts was not absolute. There was some evidence that Ray had lost its contract with Garrett for reasons having nothing to do with Maynard's T-bolts. If that was true, and Ray had rejected the T-bolts simply because it no longer needed them, then Ray acted in bad faith and would be fully liable on the contract. The court ruled that Maynard should have its day in court to prove bad faith.[3]

With this good faith requirement in mind, we look first at the seller's obligations, and then at those of the buyer.

---

[1] UCC Section 2-106(2).
[2] UCC Sections 1-203, 2-103(1)(b).
[3] *R. G. Ray Corp. v. Maynard Manufacturing Co.*, 1993 U.S. Dist. LEXIS 15754 (N.D. Ill. 1993).

SELLER'S OBLIGATIONS (AND A FEW RIGHTS)

The seller's primary obligation is to deliver conforming goods to the buyer.[4] But because a buyer might not be willing or able to accept delivery, the UCC demands only that the seller make a reasonable *attempt* at delivery. **The seller must *tender* the goods, which means to make conforming goods available to the buyer.**[5] Normally, the contract will state where and when the seller is obligated to tender delivery. For example, the parties may agree that Manufacturer is to tender 1,000 computer printers at a certain warehouse on July 3. If Manufacturer makes the printers available on that date, Buyer is obligated to pick them up then and there, and is in breach if it fails to do so.

Although a seller must always tender delivery, that does not mean a seller always transports the goods. Sometimes the contract will require the buyer to collect the goods. Regardless of where delivery is being made, however, the seller must (1) make the goods available at a reasonable time, (2) keep the goods available for a reasonable period, and (3) deliver to the buyer any documents that it needs to take possession. And as we have said, the seller is expected to deliver *conforming* goods, which brings us to the next rule.

PERFECT TENDER RULE

Under the perfect tender rule, the buyer may reject the goods if they fail *in any respect* to conform to the contract.[6] Under the common law, before the Code was drafted, the perfect tender rule required that the seller deliver goods that conformed absolutely to the contract specifications. The buyer had the right to reject goods with even minor deviations. Although commentators had criticized the rule for decades and courts had carved many exceptions into the rule, the drafters of the UCC retained it.

Stanley and Joan Jakowski agreed to buy a new Camaro automobile from Carole Chevrolet. The contract stated that Carole would apply a polymer undercoating. The Jakowskis paid in full for the car but the next day informed Carole that the car lacked the undercoating. Carole acknowledged the defect and promised to apply the undercoating, but before it could do so, a thief stole the car. The Jakowskis demanded their money back, but Carole refused, saying that the risk of loss had passed to the Jakowskis when Carole tendered delivery. The Jakowskis sued, claiming that they had rejected the Camaro as non-conforming. Carole responded that this was absurd: the car was perfect in every respect except for the very minor undercoating, which Carole had promised to fix promptly. Carole Chevrolet was correct in its description of the car, but lost the case because of the perfect tender rule.

The New Jersey court found that the defect was minor, but said that, "despite seller's assertion to the contrary, the degree of their nonconformity is irrelevant in assessing the buyer's concomitant right to reject them.... [N]o particular quantum of nonconformity is required." The Jakowskis had lawfully rejected non-conforming goods, and Carole Chevrolet was forced to pay them the full value of the missing car.[7]

---

[4] UCC Section 2-301.
[5] UCC Section 2-503.
[6] UCC Section 2-601.
[7] *Jakowski v. Carole Chevrolet, Inc.*, 180 N.J. Super. 122, 433 A.2d 841, 1981 N.J. Super. LEXIS 635 (N.J. Super. Ct. 1981).

RESTRICTIONS ON THE PERFECT TENDER RULE

The Code includes sections that limit the perfect tender rule's effect. Indeed, courts often apply the limitations more enthusiastically than the rule itself, and so while perfect tender is the law, it must be understood in the context of other provisions. We will look at the most common ways that the law—or the parties themselves—undercut the perfect tender rule. In doing so, we will see the typically flexible approach that the Code takes to a business transaction, in contrast to the inflexible and potentially harsh results of the perfect tender rule.

Usage of Trade, Course of Dealing, and Course of Performance

The Code takes the commonsense view that a contract for the sale of goods does not exist in a vacuum. **"Usage of trade" means any practice that members of an industry *expect* to be part of their dealings.**[8] The Code requires that courts consider trade usage when they interpret contracts, which means that the perfect tender rule may not permit a buyer to reject goods with minor flaws. For example, the textile industry interprets the phrase "first quality fabric" to permit a limited number of flaws in most materials. If a seller delivers 1,000 bolts of fabric and 5 of them have minor defects, the seller *has not* violated the perfect tender rule; in the textile industry, such a minor non-conformity *is* perfect tender.

The course of dealing between the two parties may also limit the rule. **"Course of dealing" refers to previous commercial transactions between the same parties.**[9] The Code requires that the current contract be interpreted in the light of any past dealings that have created reasonable expectations. Suppose a buyer orders 20,000 board feet of "highest grade pine" from a lumber company, just as it has in each of the three previous years. In the earlier deliveries, the buyer accepted the lumber even though 1 or 2 percent was not the highest grade. That course of dealing will probably control the present contract, and the buyer will not be permitted suddenly to reject an entire shipment because 1 percent is a lower grade of pine.

The course of performance has the same effect on contract interpretation. **"Course of performance" refers to the history of dealings between the parties *in this one contract*, and thus assumes that it is the kind of contract demanding an ongoing relationship.**[10] Suppose a newspaper company signs a deal to purchase five tons of newsprint from a paper company every week for a year, and the contract also specifies the grade of paper to be delivered. If, during the first three months, the newspaper company routinely accepts paper containing a small number of flaws, that course of performance will control the contract. During the final month, the newspaper may not suddenly reject the type of paper it had earlier accepted.

Parties' Agreement

The parties may limit the effect of the perfect tender rule by drafting a contract that permits imperfection in the goods. In some industries this is routine practice. For example, contracts requiring the seller to design or engineer goods specially for the buyer will generally state a level of performance that the equipment must meet. If the goods meet the level described, the buyer has no right to reject, even if the product has some flaws.

Cure

A basic goal of the UCC is a fully performed contract that leaves both parties satisfied. The seller's right to *cure* helps achieve this goal. **When the buyer rejects non-conforming goods, the seller has**

---

[8] UCC Section 1-205(2).
[9] UCC Section 1-205(1).
[10] UCC Section 2-208(1).

the right to cure, by delivering conforming goods before the contract deadline.[11] LightCo is obligated to deliver 10,000 specially manufactured bulbs to Burnout Corp. by September 15. LightCo delivers the bulbs on August 20, and on August 25 Burnout notifies the seller that the bulbs do not meet contract specifications. If LightCo promptly notifies Burnout that it intends to cure and then delivers conforming light bulbs on September 15, it has fulfilled its contract obligations, and Burnout must accept the goods. A contract should not fail when a seller shows every willingness to cure the problem.

The seller may even cure *after the contract deadline* if the seller (1) reasonably believed the original goods were acceptable and (2) promptly notified the buyer of his intent to cure within a reasonable time. This gives the seller a second chance to replace defective goods. Suppose Chip Co. delivers 25,000 computer chips to Assembler one day before the contract deadline, and two days later Assembler notifies Chip that the goods are defective. If Chip had thoroughly tested the chips before they left its factory and reasonably believed they met contract specifications, then Chip may cure by promptly notifying Assembler that it will supply conforming goods within a reasonable period. Thus, even if the conforming chips arrive two weeks after the contract deadline, Chip will have cured unless Assembler can show that the delay caused it serious harm.

In the case that follows, the choir can sing much better than the appellate judges—but how do their *robes* compare?

ZION TEMPLE FIRST PENTECOSTAL CHURCH OF CINCINNATI, OHIO, INC. v. BRIGHTER DAY BOOKSTORE & GIFTS

2004 WL 23150323
COURT OF APPEALS OF OHIO, 2004

CASE SUMMARY

Facts: Zion Temple First Pentecostal Church needed new choir robes. Brighter Day Bookstore was a retailer that sold robes manufactured by Murphy Cap & Gown. Rosalind Bush of Brighter Day showed Glenda Evans of Zion a robe and a sample board of Murphy products. The board showed various fabrics in diverse colors. A disclaimer on the board said, "all shades subject to dye lot variations." Evans ordered choir robes and overlays in colors and fabrics that she selected.

Murphy then sent sample swatches to Brighter Day, stating they were cut from the actual cloth that would be used for the Zion Temple robes. Bush called Evans to see if she wished to see the swatches, but Evans declined, saying she trusted Bush's judgment. Bush told Murphy to proceed with the order.

When Brighter Day delivered the robes to the Zion Temple, Evans and other church members found many faults. They did not like the color or material, which they considered

very different from the board sample. The sleeves had been attached facing the wrong way. And on the overlays, the Velcro and tags were visible.

Zion complained to Murphy. The manufacturer offered to repair the sleeves, but Zion declined the offer because of the other problems. Zion returned the robes, and when it failed to get its money back, filed suit.

Zion claimed Murphy breached its warranty by delivering goods that differed from the sample board, and had the sleeve and overlay problems. The trial court gave summary judgment for the defendants, and Zion Temple appealed.

Issues: *Did Murphy breach its warranty? Did Zion Temple afford Murphy a chance to cure?*

Decision: Murphy breached its warranty. It is unclear whether Murphy offered to cure all the problems and whether Zion

[11] UCC Section 2-508.

afforded the company an adequate chance to remedy them. Remanded.

Reasoning: Before delivering the robes, Murphy sent a sample robe to Zion, as well as fabric swatches. These all became part of the contract, creating express warranties. As to the color and feel of the fabric, the robes that Murphy delivered in fact conformed to the contract samples the company had sent. Zion had no right to reject the robes based on either of those qualities.

However, there were other problems with the garments. The sleeves clearly did not match the pictures in the catalog. Zion also claimed that Velcro was visible on the reversible overlays, and that tags could be seen when the overlays were reversed. The sample robe had no such problems. The one acknowledged defect (sleeves) and two alleged problems (tags and Velcro) gave Zion the right to reject the goods, and the church promptly did so.

At that point, Murphy had a right to cure within a reasonable time. The company indicated its willingness to remedy the defective sleeves, but it said nothing about curing the problems concerning tags and Velcro. There are material fact disputes as to whether the alleged defects violated the express warranty, whether they rendered the robes nonconforming, and whether Zion gave Murphy sufficient time to cure.

Summary judgment for Murphy is reversed. The case is remanded to determine whether the goods failed to conform to the sample robe and whether Murphy had a fair chance to cure.

EXAM *Strategy*

Question: Xuberant Inc. orders 2000 wrist watches from Timely Co. The watches, with Xuberant's logo on the face, are to be delivered by September 15, so that Xuberant can give them away at its September 25 sales convention. Timely tests the watches and is satisfied they work. But when Xuberant receives them, on September 15, the company rejects them because its name is misspelled. Timely offers to correct the error and deliver the new watches by September 22, but Xuberant refuses and sues. Likely outcome?

Strategy: Timely has delivered nonconforming goods, and Xuberant is entitled to reject them. However, the seller has the right to cure by delivering conforming goods before the contract deadline. Timely is offering to deliver shortly after the deadline. Is it entitled to do so?

Result: If the seller reasonably believed the goods were conforming, it may cure within a reasonable time after the deadline. If the court believes that Timely's spelling error was unreasonable, the company has no right to cure. However, a basic goal of the code is a fully performed contract. A court is likely to declare that the error was excusable and the new delivery date adequate for Xuberant's purpose. Timely will probably win.

Substantial Impairment
In two cases the Code permits a buyer to refuse goods only if their non-conformity *substantially impairs their value*. This is a higher standard for the buyer to meet. **A buyer who claims goods are non-conforming must show that the defects *substantially impair* their value (1) if the buyer is revoking acceptance of goods or (2) if the buyer is rejecting an installment.** So a buyer who accepts a dozen cement mixers, but later discovers problems with their engines, may revoke his acceptance only by showing that the defects have caused him serious problems. Similarly, if a contract requires a buyer to accept one shipment of diesel fuel each month for two years, the buyer may reject one monthly installment only if the problem with the fuel substantially lowers its value. We consider this issue from the buyer's perspective later in the chapter.

Destruction of the Goods

A farmer contracts to sell 250,000 pounds of sunflowers to a broker. The contract describes the 250 acres that the farmer will plant to grow the flowers. He plants his crop on time but a drought destroys most of the plants, and he is able to deliver only 75,000 pounds. Is the farmer liable for the flowers he could not deliver? No. Is the broker required to accept the smaller crop? No. **If identified goods are totally destroyed before risk passes to the buyer, the contract is void. If identified goods are partially destroyed, the buyer may choose whether to accept the goods at a reduced price or void the contract.**[12]

The crop of sunflowers was identified to the contract when the farmer planted it. When a drought destroyed most of the crop, the contract became voidable. The buyer had the right to accept the smaller crop, at a reduced price, or to reject the crop entirely. The farmer is not liable for the shortfall, because the destruction was not his fault.[13]

Commercial Impracticability

Commercial impracticability means that a supervening event excuses performance of a contract, if the event was not within the parties' contemplation when they made the agreement.[14] An event is "supervening" if it interrupts the normal course of business and dominates performance of the contract. But a supervening event will excuse performance only if neither party had thought there was any serious chance it would happen.

Harris RF Systems was an American company that manufactured radio equipment. Svenska, a Swedish corporation, bought Harris radio systems and sold them in many countries, including Iran. One contract required Harris to ship a large quantity of spare radio parts, which Svenska would pay $600,000 for and then resell in Iran. Harris attempted to ship the parts to Svenska but U.S. Customs seized the goods, and the U.S. Department of Defense then notified Harris that it feared the parts would be of military value to Iran. Harris executives met several times with Defense Department officials and officers of Svenska, attempting to work out a compromise.

The Defense Department acknowledged that technically Harris was licensed to ship the goods but made two things clear: first, that it would litigate rather than permit the goods to reach Iran, and second, that if Harris attempted to complete the sale in Iran, the department would place all of Harris's future radio shipments on a Munitions List, making it difficult to ship them anywhere in the world. Svenska, on the other hand, pointed out that it had binding contracts to deliver the radio parts to various customers in Iran. If the parts were not forthcoming, Svenska would hold Harris liable for all of its losses. Harris attempted to reach a satisfactory compromise with all parties but failed and eventually agreed not to ship the parts overseas.

Svenska sued. Harris defended, relying on commercial impracticability. Harris persuaded the court that neither party had foreseen the government's intervention and that both parties realized it would be virtually impossible to export goods the Defense Department was determined to block. The court dismissed Svenska's suit.[15]

Sellers offer many excuses to avoid contracts. A merchant may plead that her own supply of goods failed. Courts generally assume that the parties did contemplate failure of supply, and

[12] UCC Section 2-613. Identification of goods is discussed in Chapter 19, on ownership and risk.
[13] Based on *Red River Commodities, Inc. v. Eidsness*, 459 N.W.2d 805, 1990 N.D. LEXIS 159 (N.D. 1990).
[14] UCC Section 2-615.
[15] *Harriscom Svenska AB v. Harris Corp.*, 1990 U.S. Dist. LEXIS 20006 (W.D.N.Y. 1990).

therefore reject the excuse, holding the seller liable. On the other hand, natural disasters, such as hurricanes or tornadoes, may relieve a party from performing.

In the following case, you decide whether the seller's unexpected problem created true impossibility.

YOU *be the* JUDGE

SPECIALTY TIRES OF AMERICA, INC. V. THE CIT GROUP/EQUIPMENT FINANCING, INC.

82 F. Supp. 2d 434
United States District Court for the Western
District of Pennsylvania, 2000

Facts: CIT Group, a major equipment leasing company, leased 11 tire press machines to Condere Corporation, in Natchez, Mississippi, maintaining the right to repossess the goods if Condere defaulted on its payments. After making some payments, Condere (did you guess?) stopped making payments and filed for bankruptcy in the Southern District of Mississippi. Specialty Tires wanted to expand production in that area and was interested in purchasing the machines. CIT and Specialty executives toured the Condere factory to examine the tire presses and discuss the logistics of their removal. Condere officials cooperated fully, acknowledging that CIT had the right to immediate possession and assisting in the transportation plans. CIT then agreed to sell the goods to Specialty for $250,000.

When CIT attempted to ship the presses to Specialty, Condere surprised everyone by refusing access to the equipment. Instead, Condere (without the necessary permission of the bankruptcy court) offered CIT a check to cover its lease payments. CIT refused the payment and filed a complaint in the bankruptcy case, asking the court in Mississippi to award it the goods. Meanwhile, Specialty filed suit against CIT, in Pennsylvania, for breach of contract. In the Pennsylvania court, CIT moved for summary judgment, claiming commercial impracticability.

You Be the Judge: Should CIT be discharged based on commercial impracticability?

Argument for CIT: Your honor, CIT cannot deliver goods that it cannot even get its hands on. Specialty bargained for these 11 tire presses, not for just any machines. The parties toured Condere's factory, identified all the equipment, and negotiated terms based on delivery of these goods. Con-

dere assured everyone that the presses would be ready for delivery. CIT could not have foreseen Condere's bizarre turnabout or made provisions to protect itself. This is not a case where a seller, unable to deliver 1,000 bushels of apples, can supply identical goods from another source. There was nothing CIT could do to remedy the situation but direct Specialty to the bankruptcy court, and Specialty has refused to enter into those proceedings. While we are sympathetic to Specialty's frustration, the fault lies entirely with Condere. It is impossible to move these goods without an order from the bankruptcy court, and neither CIT nor any other company should suffer a large loss for failing to do something that it cannot physically, theoretically, or legally accomplish.

Argument for Specialty: Your honor, companies enter into contracts to control future events and protect against risks. When CIT agreed to this contract, the company was promising either to deliver the goods or suffer the consequences. We realize it is Condere's irresponsible behavior that has induced this logjam. The question, though, is not who caused the snafu, but who must suffer the consequences. Specialty planned a major expansion in the area using these tire presses, and now is losing money based on factory space rented, other overhead incurred, and lost profits. Specialty has done nothing wrong at all, and should not endure those losses. CIT chose to lease the goods to Condere, and chose to promise our client that the presses would be delivered on time. Perhaps CIT should select its business partners more scrupulously, or buy additional insurance. Those are risk/benefit decisions for CIT to make in the future. Right now it is time for CIT to pay up.

The accompanying chart outlines the seller's obligations.

Basic Obligation: The sellers basic obligation is to deliver conforming goods. **The perfect tender rule permits the buyer to reject the goods if they are in any way non-conforming.** But many Code provisions limit the harshness of the perfect tender rule.

Limitation on Seller's Obligation	Code Provision	Effect on Seller's Obligations
Good faith	Section 1-201(19) and Section 2-103(1)(b)	Prohibits the buyer from using the perfect tender rule as a way out of a contract that has become unprofitable.
Course of dealing, usage of trade, and course of performance	Section 1-205(1), Section 1-205(2), and Section 2-208	If applicable, will limit the buyer's right to reject for relatively routine defects.
The parties' agreement	Section 2-106	May describe tolerances for imperfections in the goods.
Cure	Section 2-508	Allows the seller to replace defective goods with conforming goods, if time permits.
Revocation of acceptance	Section 2-608	A buyer who has accepted goods may later revoke them only if she can show that the defects *substantially impair* its value.
Installment contracts	Section 2-612	A buyer may reject an installment only if the defects *substantially impair* its value.
Destruction of goods	Section 2-613	If goods identified to the contract are destroyed, the contract is void.
Commercial impracticability	Section 2-615	A supervening event excuses performance of a contract, if the event was not within the parties' contemplation when they made the agreement.

BUYER'S OBLIGATIONS (AND A FEW RIGHTS)

The buyer's primary obligation is to accept conforming goods and pay for them.[16] The buyer must also **provide adequate facilities to receive the goods.**[17] For example, if the contract requires the seller to deliver to the buyer's warehouse, and the parties anticipate that delivery will be by rail, then the buyer must have facilities for unloading railcars at its warehouse.

[16] UCC Section 2-301.
[17] UCC Section 2-503(1)(b).

INSPECTION AND ACCEPTANCE

The buyer generally has the right to inspect the goods before paying or accepting.[18] If the contract is silent on this issue, the buyer may inspect. Typically, a buyer will insist on this right. An exception is contracts in which the parties agree there is *no* right to inspect—for example, a contract allowing shipment *C.O.D.*, which means "cash on delivery." In that case, the buyer must pay upon receipt and do her inspecting later.

Along with the right of inspection comes the obligation to do it within a reasonable time and to notify the seller promptly if the buyer intends to reject the goods. **The buyer accepts goods** if (1) after a reasonable opportunity to inspect, she indicates to the seller that the goods are conforming or that she will accept them in spite of non-conformity; or (2) she has had a reasonable opportunity to inspect the goods and has *not rejected them;* or (3) she performs some act indicating that she now owns the goods, such as altering or reselling them.[19]

Partial Acceptance

A buyer has the right to accept some goods while rejecting others if the goods can be divided into *commercial units*. Such a unit is any grouping of goods that the industry normally treats as a whole. For example, one truckload of gravel would be a commercial unit. If the contract called for 100 truckloads of gravel, a buyer could accept the 10 that conformed to contract specifications while rejecting the 90 that did not.

Revocation

As we mentioned earlier, a buyer has a limited right to revoke acceptance of goods. **A buyer may revoke acceptance but only if the non-conformity *substantially impairs* the value of the goods and only if she had a legitimate reason for the initial acceptance.**[20] This means the perfect tender rule does *not* apply: a buyer in this situation may not revoke because of minor defects. Further, the buyer must show that she had a good reason for accepting the goods originally. Acceptable reasons would include defects that were not visible on inspection or defects that the seller promised but failed to cure.

The following case deals with three related concepts: rejection, cover, and revocation. Have a peek inside the trailer, but mind the slippery puddles.

LILE V. KIESEL

871 N.E.2d 995
INDIANA COURT OF APPEALS, 2007

CASE SUMMARY

Facts: Edward and Kelly Kiesel bought a new pull-behind trailer from James Lile, the owner of Lile's Trailer Sales. That same day, the couple took their new trailer on its first outing. Because this was a camping trip, it rained all night, and in the morning, the Kiesels noticed water inside the trailer, near the door. The next time it rained, Edward noticed more water pooling in various parts of the trailer. A week later, Edward brought the trailer in for repairs.

---

[18] UCC Section 2-513.
[19] UCC Section 2-606.
[20] UCC Sections 2-607, 608.

Lile repaired the roof, using new silicone. However, a week later the trailer again leaked, and Kelly reported this to Lile, demanding a full refund. Lile refused a refund but offered to seal any leaks, replace interior walls, and sand and paint the exterior. The Kiesels instead took the trailer to a different auto body shop, where the owner said that extensive interior rust indicated the trailer had leaked longer than the Kiesels owned it. The Kiesels sued. Lile claimed that the Kiesels had accepted the vehicle and unfairly refused repairs. The trial court awarded the Kiesels the full price of the trailer, and Lile appealed.

Issue: *Were the Kiesels entitled to the trailer's purchase price?*

Decision: Yes, they were entitled to the full purchase price. Affirmed.

Reasoning: The Kiesels lost their right to *reject* the trailer when they accepted it. But under the UCC, a buyer may *revoke* an acceptance if non-conforming goods have a substantial problem that cannot easily be discovered.

The leaks and subsequent water damage substantially reduced the value of the trailer. The plaintiffs could not have discovered them by making a reasonable inspection prior to the sale.

Lile argues that the Kiesels acted in bad faith when they declined his offer to make repairs. But the UCC only gives sellers a right to cure defects when buyers reject goods. The Kiesels accepted the trailer. *They did not reject it—they revoked their acceptance.* Lile therefore has no right to cure.

The Kiesels are entitled to a refund of the trailer's price.

Rejection

The buyer may reject non-conforming goods by notifying the seller within a reasonable time.[21] Huntsville Hospital purchased electrocardiogram equipment from Mortara Instrument for $155,000. The equipment failed to work properly and caused continual problems for the hospital, which notified Mortara within a reasonable time that it was rejecting. The hospital asked Mortara to pick up the equipment and refund the full purchase price, but Mortara did neither. When the hospital sued, Mortara claimed that the hospital should have returned the equipment to Mortara and that its failure left it liable for the full cost. The court of appeals was unpersuaded and gave judgment for the hospital, declaring that the hospital's only obligation was to notify the seller of a rejection and hold the goods for the seller to collect.[22]

Installment Contracts

An **installment contract** is one that requires goods to be delivered in separate lots. If Bus Co. contracts for Oil Co. to deliver 5,000 gallons of gasoline every week for one year, that is an installment contract. **A buyer may reject a non-conforming installment but only if it** *substantially impairs* **the value of that installment and cannot be cured.**[23] The perfect tender rule does not apply. Bus Co. has no right to reject an installment containing 4,900 gallons of gasoline, because the minor shortfall does not impair the shipment's substantial value. On the other hand, if Oil Co. delivered gasoline with lead in it, Bus Co. could reject it, since Bus Co. is legally prohibited from using the gas. (Remember, though, that Oil Co., like all sellers, has the right to cure.)

---

[21] UCC Sections 2-601, 602.
[22] *Huntsville Hospital v. Mortara Instrument*, 57 F.3d 1043, 1995 U.S. App. LEXIS 16925 (11th Cir. 1995).
[23] UCC Section 2-612.

REMEDIES: ASSURANCE AND REPUDIATION

We have looked at the rights and obligations of the two parties. Now we turn our attention to the remedies they may employ. The first, assurance and repudiation, is available to both buyer and seller.

ASSURANCE

One party to a contract may begin to fear that the other is not going to perform its obligations. **When there are reasonable grounds for insecurity, a party may demand written assurance of performance from the other party, and until he receives it, generally may suspend his own performance.**[24] Suppose Auto Co. plans to give away 50,000 DVDs as a promotion for its new car, to be introduced October 1. VidKids has promised to copy, package, and deliver the discs no later than September 20. On September 1, Auto learns that VidKids has not yet begun to package the goods. Auto may demand written assurance that VidKids will meet the deadline. VidKids is obligated to respond promptly and assure Auto that it will perform.

REPUDIATION

A party repudiates a contract by indicating that it will not perform. A party may repudiate by notifying the other party that it will not perform, by making it clear from its conduct, or by failing to answer a demand for assurance. Suppose VidKids' president calls Auto and admits, "We're having a lot of staff problems. The earliest we're going to get you the DVDs is mid- or late October." VidKids has repudiated the contract. Similarly, if VidKids fails to respond to Auto's demand for assurance, Auto may consider that a repudiation.

> We're having a lot of staff problems. The earliest we're going to get you the DVDs is mid- or late October.

When one party repudiates the contract, the other party may (1) for a reasonable time await performance or (2) resort to any remedy for breach of contract. In *either* case it may suspend its own performance.[25] In the VidKids case, it would be unreasonable for Auto to wait, because time is of the essence. So once VidKids has repudiated, Auto should protect itself by pursuing a remedy for breach, such as arranging for another company to produce the goods. (We discuss the buyer's remedies for breach later in this chapter.)

We turn now to remedies intended exclusively for the seller.

SELLER'S REMEDIES

When a buyer breaches a contract, the Code provides the seller with a variety of potential remedies. Exactly which ones are available depends upon who has the goods (buyer or seller) and what steps the seller took after the buyer breached. The seller can always **cancel the contract**. She may also be able to:

---

[24] UCC Section 2-609.
[25] UCC Section 2-610.

- Stop delivery of the goods

- Identify goods to the contract

- Resell and recover damages

- Obtain damages for non-acceptance, or

- Obtain the contract price.

Stop Delivery

Sometimes a buyer breaches before the seller has delivered the goods, for example, by failing to make a payment due under the contract or perhaps by repudiating the contract. If that happens, **the seller may refuse to deliver the goods.**[26] If, when the buyer breaches, the seller has already placed the goods in the hands of a carrier, the seller may instruct the carrier not to deliver the goods provided the shipment is at least a carload or larger.

Identify Goods to the Contract

If the seller has not yet identified goods to the contract when the buyer breaches, he may do so as soon as he learns of the breach.[27] Suppose an electronics manufacturer, with 5,000 compact disc players in its warehouse, learns that a retailer refuses to pay for the 800 units it contracted to buy. The manufacturer may now attach a label to 800 units in its warehouse, identifying them to the contract. This will help it recover damages when it resells the identified goods or uses one of the other remedies described below.

Resale

A seller may resell goods that the buyer has refused to accept, provided she does it reasonably. **If the resale is commercially reasonable, the seller may recover the difference between the resale price and contract price, plus incidental damages, minus expenses saved.**[28] Incidental damages are expenses the seller incurs in holding the goods and reselling them, costs such as storage, shipping, and advertising for resale. The seller must deduct expenses saved by the breach. For example, if the contract required the seller to ship heavy machinery from Detroit to San Diego, and the buyer's breach enables the seller to sell its goods in Detroit, the seller must deduct from its claimed losses the transportation costs that it saved.

A seller who acts in a commercially reasonable manner is entitled to the following damages:

> Contract price (the price Seller expected from the original contract)
> -   the resale price (the money Seller got at resale)
> +   incidental damages (storage, advertising, etc.)
> -   <u>expenses saved</u>
> =   Seller's damages

A seller is also permitted to resell goods privately, that is, by simply negotiating a deal with another party. But if the seller does so, she must first give the buyer reasonable notice of the private resale.

---

[26] UCC Section 2-705.
[27] UCC Section 2-704.
[28] UCC Section 2-706.

EXAM *Strategy*

Question: Fork manufactures forklift trucks. Fork agrees to sell 10 trucks, for $30,000 each, to McKnife. Fork will store the trucks in a warehouse near McKnife for 3 months, when the buyer will collect them. Storage will cost Fork $2,000 per month. A week after signing the deal, before Fork has moved the trucks to the warehouse, McKnife notifies Fork it cannot pay for the trucks. Fork spends $2,000 advertising the machines, and sells them for $25,000 each in a commercially reasonable manner. Fork then sues McKnife. Fork will win—but how much?

Strategy: Apply the formula outlined above.

Result: Fork is entitled to

	The contract price	$300,000
−	the resale price	250,000
+	incidental damages	2,000
−	expenses saved	6,000
=	Fork's damages	46,000

DAMAGES FOR NON-ACCEPTANCE

A seller who does not resell, or who resells unreasonably, may recover the difference between the original contract price and the market value of the goods at the time of delivery.[29] Oilko agrees to sell Retailer 100,000 barrels of a certain grade of gasoline for $60 per barrel, to be delivered in Long Beach, California, on November 1. Oilko tenders the gasoline on November 1, but Retailer refuses to accept it. On February 20, Oilko resells the gasoline to another purchaser for $52 per barrel and sues Retailer for $800,000 (the difference between its contract price and what it finally obtained), plus the cost of storage. Will Oilko win? No. Oilko's resale was unreasonable. Because there is a ready market for gasoline, Oilko should have resold immediately. Because Oilko acted unreasonably, it will not obtain damages under the Code's resale provision. Oilko will be forced to base its damages on market value.

Often this remedy will be less valuable to the seller than resale damages. Suppose that on November 1 the market value of Oilko's gasoline was $59 per barrel. Oilko's contract with Retailer was actually worth only $1 per barrel to Oilko, the amount by which its contract price exceeded the market value. That is all that Oilko will get in court.[30] A seller with a chance to resell should be certain to do it reasonably. If Oilko had resold promptly and for some reason obtained only $52 per barrel, it probably would have recovered its entire $800,000 loss. The following chart compares resale and non-acceptance damages:

---

[29] UCC Section 2-708.
[30] Based on *Baii Banking Corp. v. Atlantic Richfield Co.*, 1993 U.S. Dist. LEXIS 14107 (S.D.N.Y. 1993).

Resale Damages Section 2-706		Non-Acceptance Damages Section 2-708	
Contract price	$6,000,000	Contract price	$6,000,000
Resale price	−5,200,000	Market value of goods	−5,900,000
	$ 800,000		$ 100,000

ACTION FOR THE PRICE

The seller may recover the contract price if (1) the buyer has accepted the goods *or* (2) the seller's goods are conforming and the seller is unable to resell after a reasonable effort.[31] Royal Jones was a company that constructed rendering plants, that is, factories that use sophisticated equipment to extract valuable minerals from otherwise useless material. Royal Jones contracted for First Thermal to construct three rendering tanks, at a cost of $64,350. First Thermal built the tanks to Royal Jones's specifications but Royal Jones never accepted or paid for them, and First Thermal sued. Royal Jones argued that First Thermal deserved no money because it had not attempted to resell the goods, but the court awarded the full contract price, stating:

> First Thermal proved that any effort at resale would have been unavailing because these were the only rendering tanks First Thermal ever made, the tanks were manufactured according to Royal Jones's specifications, First Thermal had no other customers to which it could resell the tanks, and it was unaware how the tanks could have been marketed for resale.[32]

Resale is normally the safest route for an injured seller to recover the maximum amount, but when it is unrealistic, as in the *First Thermal* case, a lawsuit for the full price is appropriate. All of the seller's remedies are summarized in the chapter review at the end of the chapter. We now move on to the buyer's remedies.

BUYER'S REMEDIES

The buyer, too, has a variety of potential remedies. If a seller fails to deliver goods or if the buyer rightfully rejects the goods, the buyer is entitled to **cancel the contract**. She may also **recover money paid** to the seller, assuming she has not received the goods. In addition, she may be able to:

- Cover

- Obtain damages for non-delivery

- Obtain incidental *and consequential* damages

- Recover the goods themselves by an order for specific performance, or

- Recover liquidated damages.

---

[31] UCC Section 2-709.

[32] *Royal Jones & Associates, Inc. v. First Thermal Systems, Inc.*, 566 So.2d 853, 1990 Fla. App. LEXIS 6596 (Fla. Ct. App. 1990).

COVER

If the seller breaches, the buyer may "cover" by reasonably obtaining substitute goods; it may then obtain the difference between the contract price and its cover price, plus incidental and consequential damages, minus expenses saved.[33] Casein, a protein derived from milk, is used to make cheese and to process many other foods. Erie Casein Co. contracted with Anric Corp. to supply several hundred thousand pounds of casein for about $1 per pound. Half was to be delivered in March of the first year and the other half in March of the second year. By May of the first year, Anric had not finished its first delivery because it was having difficulty obtaining the casein, but Erie told Anric to keep trying. Anric delivered some of the casein later the same year, but by March of the second year was forced to admit it could not meet the second delivery. Anric suggested that it might be able to obtain more casein in the autumn of that second year.

Erie waited until August of the second year, but finally obtained its casein elsewhere at a price of $1.45 per pound. Erie sued Anric for the extra money it had paid, about $66,000. Anric argued that Erie had no right to the difference, because Erie had waited until the price of casein was sky-high before obtaining substitute goods.

The court found for Erie. Even though the company might have covered a year earlier, when the price was much lower, it was reasonable for the buyer to wait because Anric indicated it might be able to supply the goods later. Erie had acted in good faith, and when it ultimately covered, it did so at the best price it could find. An injured buyer does not have to do a perfect job of covering, only a reasonable job, and Erie got its full $66,000.[34]

Note that an injured buyer may also be awarded consequential damages, which we discuss below. Finally, if covering saves expense, the savings are deducted from any damages.

We hope that you recall Donald Hessler, whom we met in the chapter opener. We last saw him circling the courthouse in his Plymouth Prowler, anxiously awaiting the outcome of his suit against the dealership that promised him the same car for a lot less money. It has been a long wait; you and Donald deserve an answer.

HESSLER V. CRYSTAL LAKE CHRYSLER-PLYMOUTH, INC.

338 Ill.App.3d 1010, 788 N.E.2d 405, 273 Ill.Dec. 96
APPELLATE COURT OF ILLINOIS, 2003

CASE SUMMARY

Facts: The facts are provided in the chapter opening. The trial court awarded Hessler $29,853, representing the difference between his contract with Crystal Lake and the sum he ultimately spent purchasing a new Prowler. Crystal Lake appealed, arguing that Hessler covered unreasonably.

Issue: *Did Hessler cover reasonably?*

Decision: Yes, Hessler covered reasonably. Affirmed.

Reasoning: Crystal Lake contracted to deliver a Prowler to Hessler as quickly as possible. But shortly thereafter, the company told Hessler—repeatedly— that it would not in fact sell him a car. In doing so, Crystal Lake breached the contract.

The dealer argues that the trial court damages were excessive, claiming that Hessler covered unreasonably. The company contends that, after it refused to sell Hessler a car,

---

[33] UCC Section 2-712.
[34] *Erie Casein Co. v. Anric Corp.*, 217 Ill. App. 3d 602, 577 N.E.2d 892, 1991 Ill. App. LEXIS 1429 (Ill. App. Ct. 1991).

the buyer should have re-contacted the 38 dealers that he had called in September.

Instead, the same day that Hessler learned he would not obtain a car from Crystal Lake, he visited another dealer and bought a Prowler for about $40,000 above list price.

Comment 2 to Section 2-712 of the UCC provides, in relevant part:

"The test of proper cover is whether at the time and place the buyer acted in good faith and in a reasonable manner, and it is immaterial that hindsight may later prove that the method of cover used was not the cheapest and most effective."

The lower court heard testimony from both parties about the Prowler's limited supply. It also heard the plaintiff's testimony about his unsuccessful efforts to obtain a car one month earlier. The court concluded that Hessler ultimately paid the "best price" available and had covered reasonably. The evidence supports that finding, and the judgment is affirmed.

DEVIL'S ADVOCATE   It is fine for a buyer to cover, but Hessler's conduct is absurd. He bought a car for nearly *double* the contract price. A buyer's behavior must be reasonable, and no court should reward conduct that is clearly obsessive. This purchase was not required by business or financial pressures. We have here a man who believes he is entitled to whatever he wants. If Hessler decides he must have a Prowler *at any price,* then in fairness he should be the one to *pay* that price. ◆

NON-DELIVERY

In some cases, the buyer does not cover, or fails to cover *reasonably*, leaving it with damages for non-delivery. **The measure of damages for non-delivery is the difference between the market price at the time the buyer learns of the breach and the contract price, plus incidental and consequential damages, minus expenses saved.**[35] Suppose that, in the case described above, Erie had not covered but simply filed suit against Anric. Instead of its $66,000, Erie would have obtained the difference between its contract price with Anric and the market value on the date of breach. That market price was probably only a few pennies higher than the contract price, and Erie would have obtained less than $10,000.

ACCEPTANCE OF NON-CONFORMING GOODS

A buyer will sometimes accept non-conforming goods from the seller, either because no alternative is available or because the buyer expects to obtain some compensation for the defects. **Where the buyer has accepted goods but notified the seller that they are non-conforming, he may recover damages for the difference between the goods as promised and as delivered, plus incidental and consequential damages.**[36]

INCIDENTAL AND CONSEQUENTIAL DAMAGES

An injured buyer is generally entitled to incidental and consequential damages. Incidental damages cover such costs as advertising for replacements, sending buyers to obtain new goods, and shipping the replacement goods. Consequential damages can be much more extensive and may include lost profits. A buyer expecting to resell goods may obtain the loss of profit caused by the seller's failure to deliver.

---

[35] UCC Section 2-713.
[36] UCC Section 2-714.

A buyer, however, only gets consequential damages for harm that was unavoidable. Suppose Wholesaler has a contract to sell 10,000 rosebushes at $10 per bush to Flora-Mora. Wholesaler contracts to buy 10,000 rosebushes from Growem at $6 per bush, but Growem fails to deliver. Wholesaler in fact could obtain comparable roses at $8 per bush, but fails to do so and loses the chance to sell to FloraMora. Wholesaler sues Growem, seeking the $4 per bush profit it would have made on the FloraMora deal. The company will receive only $2 per bush, representing the difference between its contract price and the market value of the plants. Wholesaler will be denied the additional $2 per bush because it failed to cover.

In the following case, the court decides whether *future* profits may be too speculative to award as consequential damages.

SMITH v. PENBRIDGE ASSOCIATES, INC.

440 Pa. Super. 410, 655 A.2d 1015, 1995 Pa. Super. LEXIS 574
SUPERIOR COURT OF PENNSYLVANIA, 1995

CASE SUMMARY

Facts: Donna and Alan Smith wanted to raise emus, which are flightless Australian birds that look like ostriches. The creatures produce rapidly in almost any terrain and are sold for their meat, which is high in protein and low in fat, and for their oil, leather, and feathers. The Smiths paid Tomie Clark, the manager of Penbridge Farms, $4,000 as a down payment for "Andrew" and "Rachel," which the farm called a "proven breeder pair." Since it is impossible to discern an emu's gender by looking, the Smiths asked Clark several times if the two birds were male and female, and he assured them that the pair had successfully produced chicks the previous breeding season.

The Smiths placed the prospective lovebirds in the same pen, but the breeding season passed without a hint of romance. Donna Smith noticed that both birds were grunting, something that only male emus do. She phoned Penbridge Farms, which advised her to "vent sex" the animals, a manual procedure used to determine gender. Donna performed this agreeable task and learned that Andrew and Rachel were both gentlemen. The would-be breeders asked for their money back, but Penbridge refused, so the Smiths flew into court. The trial judge awarded the couple $105,215, representing lost profits from their anticipated chicks. Penbridge appealed,

arguing that a buyer cannot count her chicks before they have hatched.

Issue: *Did the trial court err by awarding lost profits?*

Decision: Affirmed. The Smiths were entitled to lost profits.

Reasoning: Penbridge argued that the evidence was too speculative to award consequential damages for lost profits. The company claimed that since breeding emus is a new business, there are no reliable data from which to project profits. However, Section 2-715(2) of the UCC permits consequential damages for any loss resulting from requirements that the seller knew about at the time of contracting, if the loss could not be prevented by cover.

The "proven breeder pair" had supposedly produced 16 chicks the previous season. The trial court found that the value of a 3-month-old emu chick produced that year was $5,000. The court then calculated incidental and consequential damages at $90,000, based on conservative estimations of chick production. This was a reasonable approach. Although the amount is not absolutely certain, the breaching party should not escape liability merely because damages cannot be calculated with perfect accuracy.

SPECIFIC PERFORMANCE

If the contract goods are unique, or the buyer is unable to obtain cover, the buyer may be allowed *specific performance,* which means a court order requiring the seller to deliver those particular goods.[37] This remedy is most common when the goods are one-of-a-kind. Suppose Gallery agreed to sell to Trisha an original Corot painting for $120,000 but then refused to perform (because another buyer offered more money). Trisha can obtain specific performance because the painting cannot be replaced: the court will order Gallery to deliver the work. By contrast, a car rental company stymied by a dealer's refusal to sell 500 new Ford Mustangs will not obtain specific performance, since the rental company can simply buy the same cars from another dealer (cover) and sue for the difference.

LIQUIDATED DAMAGES

Liquidated damages are those that the parties agree, at the time of contracting, will compensate the injured party. **They are enforceable, but only in an amount that is reasonable in light of the harm, the difficulties of proving actual loss, and the absence of other remedies.**[38] A clause that establishes unreasonably large or unreasonably small liquidated damages is void. Courts only enforce a liquidated damages clause if it would have been difficult to estimate actual damages when the parties reached the agreement.

Cessna Aircraft agreed to build a "Citation V" business jet and sell it to Aero Consulting for $3,995,000. Cessna's contract required Aero to pay an initial deposit of $125,000, a second deposit of $300,000 six months prior to delivery, and the balance upon delivery. The contract also stated that if Aero failed to pay the balance due, Cessna would keep all deposited monies by way of liquidated damages.

Aero made both deposits and Cessna built the plane and tendered it to Aero, but Aero refused to pay the full balance due. Cessna notified Aero that it would keep the $425,000 deposited. When Aero sued, seeking a return of the deposits, the issue was whether this liquidated damage was fair. The court concluded that it was. At the time Cessna entered into the deal, it was difficult to estimate actual damages in the event of Aero's breach. The long period required to build a jet aircraft and the uncertainties about supply and demand in the marketplace meant that neither party could say for sure how much Cessna would lose should Aero breach. Further, the liquidated damage here was about 10 percent of the total cost, not an unreasonably high figure. Cessna kept the money (and the plane).[39]

EXAM *Strategy*

Question: You have a gray-market problem. Your California vineyard has strong sales throughout the United States, and it is time to expand into Europe. To penetrate foreign markets, you offer your product at steep discounts to a Swiss importer. Your intent is that the importer will sell your wine inexpensively to retailers, so that low prices will entice consumers. The danger, though, is that the importer will return the wine to the United States and undersell your own product in an established market, taking advantage of your advertising and

---

[37] UCC Section 2-716.

[38] UCC Section 2-718.

[39] *Aero Consulting Corp. v. Cessna Aircraft Co.,* 867 F. Supp. 1480, 1994 U.S. Dist. LEXIS 16668 (D. Kan. 1994).

infuriating established dealers. Such a resale could occur before your wine ever left the country. What can you do to keep this problem from fermenting?

Strategy: A liquidated damages clause can put teeth into your plan to sell the wine to overseas consumers. You might specify substantial compensation if any of your exported wine finds its way back home. However, an overly aggressive clause will be declared a penalty—and void. How can you avoid such a disaster?

Result: Liquidated damages are enforceable in an amount that is reasonable in light of the harm and the difficulties of proving actual loss. Your clause may certainly compensate you for lost goodwill among domestic retailers, and for harm to your efforts at establishing the brand in Europe. Make *good faith* estimates of those losses—if the clause gives you too much compensation, a court may void it altogether. Lost profits per case sold in the United States are probably easy to calculate, and should *not* be part of the liquidated damages clause.

Damage Limitations and Exclusions

The Code allows parties to draft a contract that limits or excludes the normal remedies discussed in this chapter. For example, parties can agree that if the seller delivers non-conforming goods, the buyer's only remedy is to demand repair or replacement. We discussed these limits in the preceding chapter and will not repeat the information here. By way of a quick summary, we can say that while the parties may exclude most remedies, there are two important restrictions:

- **A court generally will not enforce a limitation that leaves the injured party with no remedy at all.** Suppose a remedy limitation states that a buyer of software is only entitled to repair, but the software is so badly designed that no amount of repairing solves the problem. A court will ignore the limitation, and the buyer will be entitled to the full range of remedies we have discussed.

- **A court will not enforce an unconscionable exclusion of consequential damages.** If the buyer is a consumer, a court is likely to ignore any exclusion of consequential damages. So, if a consumer purchases a used car from a dealer who excludes such damages, and the consumer is injured when the radiator explodes, the contract limitation will do the seller no good.

CHAPTER CONCLUSION

The drafters of the Code intended the law to reflect contemporary commercial practices, but also to require a satisfactory level of sensible, ethical behavior. For example, the Code allows numerous exceptions to the perfect tender rule so that a buyer may not pounce on minor defects in goods to avoid a contract that has become financially burdensome. Similarly, a seller forced to resell his goods must do so in a commercially reasonable manner. Good faith and common sense are the hallmarks of contract performance and remedies.

EXAM REVIEW

1. **GOOD FAITH** The Code requires good faith in the performance and enforcement of every contract. (p. 501)

2. **CONFORMING GOODS** Conforming goods are those that satisfy the contract terms; non-conforming goods fail to do so. (p. 502)

3. **TENDER** The seller must tender the goods, which means make conforming goods available to the buyer. The perfect tender rule permits a buyer to reject goods that are non-conforming in any respect, although there are numerous exceptions. (p. 502)

4. **USAGE OF TRADE** Usage of trade, course of dealing, and course of performance may enable a seller to satisfy the perfect tender rule even though there are some defects in the goods. (p. 503)

5. **CURE** When the buyer rejects non-conforming goods, the seller has the right to cure by delivering conforming goods before the contract deadline. (p. 503)

EXAM Strategy

Question: Allied Semi-Conductors International agreed to buy 50,000 computer chips from Pulsar, for a total price of $365,750. Pulsar delivered the chips, which Allied then sold to Apple Computer. But at least 35,000 of the chips proved defective so Apple returned them to Allied, which sent them back to Pulsar. Pulsar agreed to replace any defective chips, but only after Allied, at its expense, tested each chip and established the defect. Allied rejected this procedure and sued. Who wins?

Strategy: The chips were non-conforming goods, and Allied was entitled to reject them. Pulsar, in turn, had a right to cure the defects, that is, to solve the problem that it created. Did Pulsar offer to cure? (See the "Result" at the end of this section.)

---

6. **DESTRUCTION OF THE GOODS** If identified goods are destroyed before risk passes to the buyer, the contract is void. (p. 506)

EXAM Strategy

CPA Question: Under a contract governed by the UCC sales article, which of the following statements is correct?

(a) Unless both the seller and the buyer are merchants, neither party is obligated to perform the contract in good faith.

(b) The contract will not be enforceable if it fails to expressly specify a time and a place for delivery of the goods.

(c) The seller may be excused from performance if the goods are accidentally destroyed before the risk of loss passes to the buyer.

(d) If the price of the goods is less than $500, the goods need not be identified to the contract for title to pass to the buyer.

Strategy: (a) Sounds unlikely. Remind yourself which contracts must be performed in good faith. (b) As we learned in Chapter 18, the Code permits open terms. What are they? (c) Review the rules on destruction of the goods (d) Goods must be identified to the contract before title can pass. Is there an exception for goods under $500? See Chapter 18. (See the "Result" at the end of this section.)

7. **COMMERCIAL IMPRACTICABILITY** Under commercial impracticability, a supervening event excuses performance if it was not within the parties' contemplation when they made the contract. (p. 506)

8. **INSPECTION** The buyer generally has the right to inspect goods before paying or accepting. If the buyer does not reject goods within a reasonable time after inspecting them, she may be deemed to have accepted them. (p. 509)

EXAM Strategy

CPA Question: Smith contracted in writing to sell Peters a used personal computer for $600. The contract did not specifically address the time for payment, place of delivery, or Peters's right to inspect the computer. Which of the following statements is correct?

(a) Smith is obligated to deliver the computer to Peters's home.

(b) Peters is entitled to inspect the computer before paying for it.

(c) Peters may not pay for the computer using a personal check unless Smith agrees.

(d) Smith is not entitled to payment until 30 days after Peters receives the computer.

Strategy: This question should be no problem. Three of the four possible answers offer rules that appear *nowhere* in the Code. (a) There is no reference in the Code to "home delivery" of goods. (b) The buyer has the right to inspect goods before paying or accepting, unless the contract specifies otherwise. (c) Nowhere does the UCC prohibit payment by check. (d) You have never read in the Code any presumption of a 30 day delay in payment—so do not imagine one. (See the "Result" at the end of this section.)

9. **REVOCATION** A buyer may revoke his acceptance of non-conforming goods, but only if the defects substantially impair the value of the goods. (p. 509)

10. **REJECTION** A buyer may reject non-conforming goods by notifying the seller within a reasonable time. (p. 510)

The following chart summarizes the contrasting remedies available to the two parties:

Seller's Remedies	Issue	Buyer's Remedies
Section 2-705: The seller generally may stop delivery, whether it was to be done by the seller herself or a carrier.	DELIVERY	Section 2-716: Specific performance: Buyer may obtain specific performance only if the goods are unique.
Section 2-706: Resale: If the resale is made in good faith and a commercially reasonable manner, the seller may recover the difference between the resale price and the contract price, plus incidental costs, minus savings.	WHEN THE INJURED PARTY MAKES AN ALTERNATE CONTRACT	Section 2-712: Cover: The buyer may purchase alternate goods and obtain the difference in price, plus incidental and consequential damages, minus expenses saved.
Section 2-708: Non-acceptance: The measure of damages for non-acceptance is the difference between the market price at time the time and place of tender and the contract price (plus incidental damages minus expenses saved).	WHEN THE GOODS HAVE NOT CHANGED HANDS	Section 2-713: Non-delivery: If the seller fails to deliver, the buyer's damages are the difference between the market price at the time he learned of the breach and the contract price (plus incidental and consequential damages, minus expenses saved).
Section 2-709: The seller may sue for the price.	WHEN THE BUYER HAS ACCEPTED THE GOODS	Section 2-714: A buyer who has accepted non-conforming goods and notified the seller may recover damages for resulting losses.
Sections 2-706, 2-708, 2-709, 2-710: The seller is entitled to incidental damages but not consequential damages.	INCIDENTAL AND CONSEQUENTIAL DAMAGES	Section 2-715: The buyer is entitled to incidental and consequential damages.

LIQUIDATED DAMAGES
Section 2-718: Either party may obtain liquidated damages but only in an amount that is reasonable at the time of the contract.

REMEDY LIMITATION
Section 2-719: The parties may add or exclude remedies, but no remedy limitation will be allowed if it results in the injured party obtaining no relief at all; consequential damages may not be limited in cases where doing so would be unconscionable.

5. Result: Pulsar never offered a true cure. When the seller delivers defective goods and wishes to cure, it must take all steps—at its expense—to fix the problem. Pulsar could cure only by delivering, at its expense and in a timely manner, 50,000 conforming chips. Pulsar failed to cure, and Allied recovers the entire purchase price.

6. Result: (a) is wrong because all contracts must be performed in good faith. (b) is wrong because a contract with open terms is enforceable. (c) is the right answer because it correctly states the rule on destruction of goods. (d) is wrong because title never passes unless the goods were identified to the contract.

8. Result: (b) is the correct answer. Peters is entitled to inspect the computer unless the contract states otherwise, which it did not.

ADDITIONAL QUESTIONS

1. **CPA QUESTION** Cara Fabricating Co. and Taso Corp. agreed orally that Taso would custom manufacture a compressor for Cara at a price of $120,000. After Taso completed the work at a cost of $90,000, Cara notified Taso that the compressor was no longer needed. Taso is holding the compressor and has requested payment from Cara. Taso has been unable to resell the compressor for any price. Taso incurred storage fees of $2,000. If Cara refuses to pay Taso and Taso sues Cara, the most Taso will be entitled to recover is:

   (a) $92,000
   (b) $105,000
   (c) $120,000
   (d) $122,000

2. Jewell-Rung was a Canadian corporation that imported and sold men's clothing at wholesale. Haddad was a New York corporation that manufactured and sold men's clothing under the "Lakeland" label. The companies agreed that Haddad would sell 2,325 Lakeland garments to Jewell-Rung, for $250,000. Jewell-Rung began to take orders for the garments from its Canadian customers. Jewell-Rung had orders for about 372 garments when it learned that Haddad planned to allow another company, Olympic, the exclusive Canadian right to manufacture and sell Lakeland garments. Jewell-Rung sued Haddad for its lost profits. Haddad moved for summary judgment, claiming that Jewell-Rung could not recover lost profits because it had not "covered." Is Haddad right? Why might Jewell-Rung not have covered?

3. **ETHICS** Laura and Bruce Trethewey hired Basement Waterproofing Nationwide, Inc., to waterproof the walls in their basement for a fee of $2,500. BWNI's contract stated: "BWNI will service any seepage in the areas waterproofed at no additional cost to the customer. All labor and materials will be at the company's expense. Liability for any damage shall be limited to the total price paid for this contract." The material that BWNI used to waterproof the Tretheweys' walls swelled and caused large cracks to open in the walls. Water poured into the basement, and the Tretheweys ultimately spent $38,000 to repair the damage. They sued, claiming negligence and breach of warranty, but BWNI claimed its liability was limited to $2,500. Please rule. Apart from the legal ruling, comment on ethics. BWNI wanted to protect itself against unlimited damage claims. Is this a legitimate way to do it? Is this how BWNI would wish to be treated itself? If you think BWNI *did* behave ethically, what advice would you have for consumers who hire home improvement companies? If you believe the company did *not* behave ethically, imagine that you are a BWNI executive, charged with drafting a standard contract for customers. How would you protect your company's interests while still acting in a way you consider moral?

4. Cargill, Inc., sold cottonseed, which is used in feed for dairy cattle. Bill Storms, a dairy farmer, agreed to buy 17 truckloads of cottonseed from Cargill for $176 per ton, to be delivered at Storms's farm. Storms had the option of accepting the seed at any time during the next nine months. Over the first two months, Storms ordered three truckloads of seed and paid Cargill, but Storms then informed Cargill that he would accept no more cottonseed. What rights does Cargill have?

5. Mastercraft Boat manufactured boats and often used instrument panels and electrical systems assembled and/or manufactured by Ace Industries. Typically, Ace would order electrical instruments and other parts and assemble them to specifications that Mastercraft provided. Mastercraft decided to work with a different assembler, M & G Electronics, so it terminated its relationship with Ace. Mastercraft then requested that Ace deliver all of the remaining instruments and other parts that it had purchased for use in Mastercraft boats. Ace delivered the inventory to Mastercraft, which inspected it and kept some of the items, but returned others to Ace, stating that the shipment had been unauthorized. Later, Mastercraft requested that Ace deliver the remaining parts (which Mastercraft had sent back to Ace) to M & G, which Ace did. Mastercraft then refused to pay for these parts, claiming that they were non-conforming. Is Ace entitled to its money for the parts?

6. Lewis River Golf, Inc., grew and sold sod. It bought seed from defendant, O. M. Scott & Sons, under an express warranty. But the sod grown from the Scott seeds developed weeds, a breach of Scott's warranty. Several of Lewis River's customers sued, unhappy with the weeds in their grass. Lewis River lost most of its customers, cut back its production from 275 acres to 45 acres, and destroyed all remaining sod grown from Scott's seeds. Eventually, Lewis River sold its business at a large loss. A jury awarded Lewis River $1,026,800, largely for lost profits and loss of goodwill. Scott appealed, claiming that a plaintiff may not recover for lost profits and goodwill. Comment.

7. **CPA QUESTION** On February 15, Mazur Corp. contracted to sell 1,000 bushels of wheat to Good Bread, Inc., at $6 per bushel with delivery to be made on June 23. On June 1, Good advised Mazur that it would not accept or pay for the wheat. On June 2, Mazur sold the wheat to another customer at the market price of $5 per bushel. Mazur had advised Good that it intended to resell the wheat. Which of the following statements is correct?

   (a) Mazur can successfully sue Good for the difference between the resale price and the contract price.
   (b) Mazur can resell the wheat only after June 23.
   (c) Good can retract its anticipatory breach at any time before June 23.
   (d) Good can successfully sue Mazur for specific performance.

8. The AM/PM Franchise association was a group of 150 owners of ARCO Mini-Market franchises in Pennsylvania and New York. Each owner had an agreement to operate a gas station and mini-market, obtaining all gasoline, food, and other products, from ARCO. The Association sued, claiming that ARCO had experimented with its formula for unleaded gasoline, using oxinol, and that the poor-quality gas had caused serious engine problems and a steep drop in customers. The Association demanded (1) lost profits for gasoline sales, (2) lost profits for food and other items, and (3) loss of goodwill. The trial court dismissed the case, ruling that the plaintiff's claims were too speculative, and the Association appealed. Please rule.

9. ***YOU BE THE JUDGE*** WRITING PROBLEM Clark Oil agreed to sell Amerada Hess several hundred thousand barrels of oil at $24 each by January 31, with the sulfur content not to exceed 1 percent. On January 26, Clark tendered oil from various ships. Most of the oil met specifications, but a small amount contained excess sulfur. Hess rejected all of the oil. Clark recirculated the oil, meaning that it blended the high-sulfur oil with the rest, and notified Amerada that it could deliver 100 percent of the oil, as specified, by January 31. Hess did not respond. On January 30, Clark offered to replace the oil with an entirely new shipment, due to arrive February 1. Hess rejected the offer. On February 6, Clark retendered the original oil, all of which met contract terms, and Hess rejected it. Clark sold the oil elsewhere for $17.75 per barrel and filed suit. Is Clark entitled to damages? **Argument for Clark:** A seller is entitled to cure any defects. Clark did so in good faith and offered all of the oil by the contract deadline. Clark went even further, offering an entirely new shipment of oil. Hess acted in bad faith, seeking to obtain cheaper oil. Clark is entitled to the difference between the contract price and its resale price. **Argument for Hess:** Hess was entitled to conforming goods, and Clark failed to deliver. Under the perfect tender rule, that is the end of the discussion. Hess had the right to reject non-conforming goods, and it promptly did so. Hess chose not to deal further with Clark because it had lost confidence in Clark's ability to perform.

10. ***ROLE REVERSAL*** Write a multiple-choice question that involves a buyer's rejection of goods, the perfect tender rule, and one of the following: usage of trade, course of dealing, or course of performance.

INTERNET RESEARCH PROBLEM

Online, find a case focusing on UCC Section 2-615. How would you draft a contract to avoid the problem that arose?

You can find further practice problems at www.cengagebrain.com. See the preface of this book for website access details.

22

CREATING A NEGOTIABLE INSTRUMENT

The figure lay on the couch by the fireplace. No signs of violence were visible, and a casual observer would have thought the man was napping. But Detective Waterston's trained eye immediately recognized the unnatural stiffness and pallor of a corpse. Walking behind the body, she saw matted blood against black hair and a heavy brass fireplace iron on the floor. She also noticed the crumpled document clutched in the victim's hand.

> **In his rage and frustration, Jenkins picked up the first thing that came to hand and struck Haverstock with the brass iron.**

As the coroner was removing the body, Waterston slipped the crumpled paper out of the corpse's grasp. Sergeant Malloy asked whether she was ready to interview witnesses. "No," she said thoughtfully, looking at the document, "I believe I have everything I need right here." An hour later, the police arrested Tony Jenkins, the dead man's business partner. Jenkins immediately confessed.

"How did you know?" Malloy demanded.

"Simple," Waterston responded, "The answer is right here on this promissory note." She spread the crumpled page on the table. "On the front, it's a straightforward note for $1 million, payable by Tony Jenkins, the accused, to Letitia Lamour on August 1. You remember—she was recently arrested for selling fraudulent securities. Jenkins must have invested in one of her enterprises.

"It gets even more interesting on the back, though," she said, turning the paper over. "Lamour held on to the note for some time. But you see, on August 15th, she wrote on the back 'Pay to the order of Sebastian Haverstock.'"

"The dead man," Malloy whistled through his teeth.

"Precisely. Haverstock and Jenkins were planning to take their computer software company public in a month or two. The sale would have made them both wealthy men. But Haverstock called Jenkins to demand payment on the note. Jenkins did not have a million dollars; he had lost everything in a series of unfortunate investments. Haverstock demanded that Jenkins turn over his shares in the company as payment for the note. In his rage and frustration, Jenkins picked up the first thing that came to hand and struck Haverstock with the brass iron. An antique instrument and very heavy.

"It's a shame, really," Detective Waterston continued. "If Jenkins had understood Article 3 of the Uniform Commercial Code, he would not have been tempted to murder. In fact, he owed Haverstock nothing. You see, the note was overdue—it should have been paid on August 1st, but today is the 31st. You can't be a holder in due course on an overdue note. Since Haverstock was not a holder in due course, Jenkins could have used the fraud claim he had against Lamour as a defense to Haverstock's demand for payment. In any event, Haverstock was well aware that Lamour had committed fraud—he was the one who set her up in business in the first place. Jenkins could have used Haverstock's knowledge of the fraud as another weapon against any demands for payment. That legal weapon would have been a better choice than a fireplace iron," Waterston concluded wryly.

COMMERCIAL PAPER

Commercial paper plays an important role in your life if you write checks or borrow money. Historically speaking, however, commercial paper is a relatively new development. In early human history, people lived on whatever they could hunt, grow, or make for themselves. Imagine what your life would be like if you had to subsist only on what you could make yourself. Over time, people improved their standard of living by bartering for goods and services they could not make themselves. But traders needed a method for keeping account of who owed how much to whom. That was the role of currency. Many items have been used for currency over the years, including silver, gold, copper, and cowrie shells. Even cigarettes were used briefly in Greece at the end of World War II after Hitler's troops left. These currencies have two disadvantages—they are easy to steal and cumbersome to carry.

Sweden had traditionally used copper as currency. These ingots were very large and heavy (heavier even than gold), so it was not surprising when, in 1661, Sweden became the first country in Europe to try paper currency. This effort was not a success because too much paper money was printed, and so the president of the bank went to prison.

Ultimately paper currency did catch on, but it created new problems—it was even easier to steal than gold. As a result, money had to be kept in a safe place, and banks developed to meet that need. However, money in a vault is not very useful unless it can be readily spent. Society needed a system for transferring paper funds easily. Commercial paper is that system.

Commercial paper is a contract to pay money. It is used as:

- *A Substitute for Money.* When Darla stops at Drive-In-Convenience to buy food for dinner, she has only 32¢ in her wallet. Not a problem, she can pay by check. Darla's check is a promise that she has money in the bank. It is also an order to the bank to transfer funds to Drive-In-Convenience. Darla is going to eat immediately (in the car on the way home), and the store would also like to be paid quickly. For commercial paper to be a substitute for money, it must be payable on demand.

Promissory note

A written promise to pay money.

- *A Loan of Money.* This type of commercial paper is a contract to pay what is owed sometime in the future. Darla buys a beautiful concert grand piano that costs more than her parents paid for their first house. She does not have enough money in the bank to write a check for the full amount, so she signs a **promissory note**, that is, an assurance that she will pay for the piano in five years. The manager at the Angel House of Music does not expect to take the note to Darla's bank and be paid right away; he understands that he will have to wait.

The four previous chapters covered the Uniform Commercial Code (UCC) and the sale of goods. This chapter and the following two focus on Articles 3 and 4 of the UCC as they regulate commercial paper.[1] The purpose of the UCC articles on negotiable instruments is to facilitate commerce. When the U.S. Treasury issues money, it is consistent—all dollar bills look alike. But when practically the entire population of the United States issues commercial paper, creativity takes over and consistency disappears. The purpose of Articles 3 and 4 is to transform these pieces of paper into something almost as easily transferable and reliable as currency.

The fundamental "rule" of commercial paper can be stated this way:

The possessor of a piece of commercial paper has an unconditional right to be paid, so long as (1) the paper is *negotiable*; (2) it has been *negotiated* to the possessor; (3) the possessor is a *holder in due course*; and (4) the issuer cannot claim any of a limited number of "real" *defenses*.

This rule is the backbone of the chapter, and in the following sections, we define and explain its terms: "negotiable," "negotiated," "holder in due course," and "defenses." You will want to keep this rule in mind throughout the chapter.

TYPES OF NEGOTIABLE INSTRUMENTS

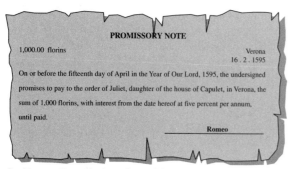

PROMISSORY NOTE

1,000.00 florins   Verona
                                                                16 . 2 . 1595

On or before the fifteenth day of April in the Year of Our Lord, 1595, the undersigned promises to pay to the order of Juliet, daughter of the house of Capulet, in Verona, the sum of 1,000 florins, with interest from the date hereof at five percent per annum, until paid.

                                                                Romeo

In this note, Romeo is the maker and Juliet is the payee.

There are two kinds of commercial paper: negotiable and non-negotiable instruments. Article 3 of the Code covers only negotiable instruments; non-negotiable instruments are governed by ordinary contract law. There are also two categories of negotiable instruments: notes and drafts. The essential difference between the two is that a note is a promise to do something while a draft is an *order* to someone else to do it. This is an overview; now for the details

A **note** (also called a **promissory note**) is your promise that you will pay money. A promissory note is used in virtually every loan transaction, whether the borrower is buying a multimillion dollar company, a house, or a TV set. For example, the National

---

[1] In 2002, the Uniform Law Commissioners approved a revision of Articles 3 and 4 that deals with changing technology for checks and other paper instruments. So far, only ten states have passed this new version. Therefore, this chapter is based on the older version.

Basketball Association permits players to borrow money from their team. If LeBron James borrows $5 million from the Miami Heat, he must sign a note promising to repay the money. James is the **maker** because he is the one who has made the promise. His team is called the **payee** because it expects to be paid. Remember that only *two* parties are involved in a note: the maker and the payee. Some notes are due at a definite date in the future. Others are **payable on demand**, which means that the maker must pay whenever he is asked. Thus, James's note could be payable, say, in three years when his contract expires, or it could be payable on demand (which means that, if his team is ever annoyed at him, it could insist on immediate payment).

If the note is made by a bank, it is called a **certificate of deposit** (also known as a CD). When investors loan money to a bank, the bank gives them a note promising to repay the loan at a specific date in the future. The bank is the maker and the investor is the payee. The bank pays a higher rate of interest on CDs than it does on regular savings accounts because the investor cannot demand payment on the CD until its due date. In return for the lower rate on a savings account, the depositor can withdraw that money anytime.

A **draft** is an order directing someone else to pay money for you. A **check** is the most common form of a draft—it is an order telling a bank to pay money. In a draft three people are involved: the **drawer** orders the **drawee** to pay money to the **payee**. Now before you slam the book shut in despair, let us sort out the players. Suppose that Maria Sharapova wins a tennis tournament. The WTA Tour writes her a check for $1 million. This check is an order by the WTA Tour (the drawer) to its bank (the drawee) to pay money to Sharapova (the payee). The terms make sense if you remember that, when you take money out of your account, you *draw* it out. Therefore, when you write a check, you are the draw*er* and the bank is the draw*ee*. The person to whom you make out the check is being paid, so he is called the pay*ee*.

The following table illustrates the difference between notes and drafts. Even courts sometimes confuse the terms *drawer* (the person who signs a check) and *maker* (someone who signs a promissory note). But the UCC is a very precise set of rules, so it is important to get the details right. **Issuer** is an all-purpose term that means both maker and drawer.

	Who Pays	Who Plays
Note	You make a promise that you will pay.	Two people are involved: maker and payee.
Draft	You order someone else to pay.	Three people are involved: drawer, drawee, and payee.

Sharapova presumably feels confident that the WTA Tour has enough money in its account to cover the check. When Stewart Student goes to the MegaLoud store to buy a $10,000 sound system, MegaLoud has no way of knowing if his check is good. Even if MegaLoud calls the bank to confirm Stewart's balance, he could withdraw it all by the time the check is deposited that evening. To protect itself, MegaLoud insists upon a cashier's check. A **cashier's check** is drawn by a bank on itself. When Stewart asks for a cashier's check, the bank takes the money out of his account on the spot and then issues a check itself, payable out of its own funds. When MegaLoud gets the cashier's check from Stewart, it knows that the check is good so long as the bank itself is solvent.

Maker
The issuer of a promissory note.

Payee
Someone who is owed money under the terms of an instrument.

Payable on demand
The maker must pay whenever he is asked.

Certificate of deposit
A note that is made by a bank. (Also known as a CD.)

Draft
The drawer of this instrument orders someone else to pay money.

Check
The most common form of a draft, it is an order telling a bank to pay money.

Drawer
The person who issues a draft.

Drawee
The one ordered by the drawer to pay money to the payee.

Issuer
The maker of a promissory note or the drawer of a draft.

Cashier's check
A check that is drawn by a bank on itself.

Accepts
Signs.

Trade acceptance
A draft drawn by a seller of goods on the buyer and payable to the seller or some third party.

Sight draft
Payable on demand.

Time draft
Payable in the future.

All checks are drafts, but not all drafts are checks. A draft is a check only if it is drawn on a bank. Sometimes drafts are drawn on individuals or companies. Suppose that in September, Sasha's Saddlery sells 16 saddles to the Circle S Stable. The stable expects that, in December, it will receive its first deposits from tourists making reservations for the following summer. The stable promises to pay Sasha $8,000 in January. Sasha is happy to make the sale, but she needs the funds now. So she prepares a draft ordering Circle S to pay $8,000 to Citizen's Bank in January. After Circle S signs (**accepts**) the draft, Sasha takes it to Citizen's, which investigates Circle S's credit reputation. Satisfied, it agrees to buy the draft for $7,000. (It pays less than the full amount because it has to wait for the money and because there is always a chance Circle S will not pay.) Sasha is the drawer, Circle S the drawee, and Citizen's Bank the payee. So Sasha's Saddlery receives $7,000 from Citizen's in September. In January, Circle S pays Citizen's the full $8,000.

The draft on Circle S is a **trade acceptance**, which is a draft drawn by a seller of goods on the buyer and payable to the seller or some third party. In our case, Sasha is the seller, Circle S the buyer, and Citizen's the third party that will be paid. To be valid, the draft must be accepted (that is, signed) by the buyer. A **sight draft** is payable on demand; a **time draft** is payable in the future. Circle S's draft is a time draft because it is not payable until January.

Sasha books a trip to England to find a new supplier of saddles. Concerned about carrying too much cash, she decides to buy $5,000 of traveler's checks. To purchase the checks, Sasha goes to a bank (such as Citizen's) or a company (such as American Express) and pays $1,000 plus a handling fee of about 1 percent. Before she leaves the building, she signs the front of the checks. When she needs to make a purchase in England, she signs the front of the check again. The payee then compares the two signatures to make sure they are the same, indicating that the checks are valid. Once the payee has accepted the checks, only Citizen's is liable. The payee's bank presents the checks to Citizen's for payment. Note that Citizen's is both the drawer and the drawee because it issues the checks in its own name (as drawer) and it pays the checks when presented (as drawee). If the checks are drawn on American Express, they are technically drafts, not checks, because American Express is not a bank. Traveler's checks have two advantages: (1) the English merchant accepts a check from Sasha, whom he does not know, because he trusts Citizen's (or American Express); and (2) if Sasha loses the checks, Citizen's (or American Express) will replace them for free.

NEGOTIABILITY

To work as a substitute for money, commercial paper must be freely transferable in the marketplace. In other words, it must be *negotiable*. Suppose that Krystal buys a used car from the Trustie Car Lot for her business, Krystal Rocks. She cannot afford to pay the full $15,000 right now, but she is willing to sign a note promising to pay later. As long as Trustie keeps the note, Krystal's obligation to pay is contingent upon the validity of the underlying contract. If, for instance, the car is defective, then Krystal might not be liable to Trustie for the full amount of the note. Trustie, however, does not want to keep the note. He needs the cash *now* so that he can buy more cars to sell to other customers. Reggie's Finance Co. is happy to buy Krystal's promissory note from Trustie, but the price Reggie is willing to pay depends upon whether her note is negotiable.

The possessor of *non*-negotiable commercial paper has the same rights—no more, no less—as the person who made the original contract. With non-negotiable commercial paper, the transferee's rights are *conditional* because they depend upon the rights of the original party to the contract. If, for some reason, the original party loses his right to be paid, so does the transferee. The value of non-negotiable commercial paper is greatly reduced because the transferee cannot be absolutely sure what his rights are or whether he will be paid at all.

If Krystal's promissory note is non-negotiable, Reggie gets exactly the same rights that Trustie had. As the saying goes, he steps into Trustie's shoes. Other people's shoes may not be a good fit. Suppose that Trustie tampered with the odometer and, as a result, Krystal's car is worth only $12,000 instead of the $15,000 she paid for it. If, under contract law, she owes Trustie only $12,000, then that is all she has to pay Reggie, even though the note *says* $15,000.

The possessor of *negotiable* commercial paper has *more* rights than the person who made the original contract. With negotiable commercial paper, the transferee's rights are *unconditional* and generally do not depend upon the rights of the original party to the contract. As long as the transferee is a *holder in due course* (discussed later in this chapter), he is entitled to be paid the full amount of the note, regardless of the relationship between the original parties (with a few limited exceptions). If Krystal's promissory note is a negotiable instrument, she must pay the full amount to whoever has possession of it, no matter what complaints she might have against Trustie. Even if the car explodes within the month, Krystal must still pay Reggie the full $15,000. If, however, Trustie keeps the note, Krystal can subtract from what she owes *him* any claims she has against him for breach of contract because, as the original party to the note, Trustie cannot be a holder in due course. Therefore, Reggie (and any subsequent holder in due course) is in a better position than Trustie.

Exhibit 22.1 illustrates the difference between negotiable and non-negotiable commercial paper.

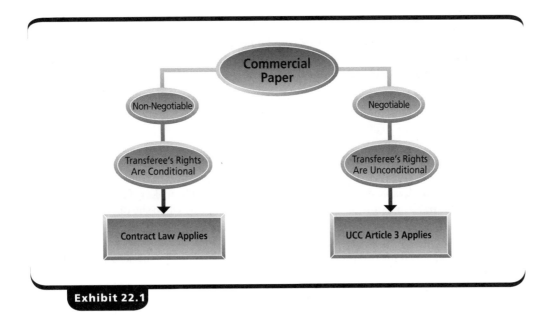

Exhibit 22.1

REQUIREMENTS FOR NEGOTIABILITY

Because negotiable instruments are more valuable than non-negotiable ones, it is important for buyers and sellers to be able to tell, easily and accurately, if an instrument is indeed negotiable. An instrument is negotiable if it meets the six standards set out in UCC Section 3-104(a).[2]

1. *The Instrument Must Be in* **Writing.** Trustie cannot negotiate Krystal's *oral* promise to pay $15,000. However, the writing need not be on any official form or even on paper. To protest a speeding ticket, Barry Lee Brown of Missoula, Montana, wrote a check for the $35 fine on a pair of old (but clean!) underpants. The bank cashed it.

2. *The Instrument Must Be* **Signed** *by the Maker or Drawer.* Any signature counts—initials, an "X," a stamp—as long as the issuer intends to indicate her signature. If Krystal normally signs her documents with an interlocking heart logo, that symbol counts as a signature.

3. *The Instrument Must Contain an* **Unconditional Promise** *or* **Order** *to Pay.* The whole point of a negotiable instrument is that the holder can sleep soundly at night confident that he will be paid *without conditions*. If Krystal's promissory note says, "I will pay $15,000 as long as the car is still in working order," it is not negotiable. If, however, the note says, "I will pay $15,000 for the yellow car," it is negotiable because this statement is not a *condition*, it is simply describing the transaction.

   The instrument must also contain a promise or order to pay. It is not enough simply to say, "Krystal owes Trustie $15,000." She has to indicate that she owes the money and also that she intends to pay it. "Krystal promises to pay Trustie $15,000," would work.

4. *The Instrument Must State a* **Definite Amount** *of Money.* It is not easy to sell an instrument if the buyer cannot tell how much it is worth; to be negotiable, therefore, the document must clearly state "within its four corners" how much money is owed. If the document is a note, with interest due, matters become more complicated. The holder may not be able to tell how much interest is owing simply by looking at the note. If Krystal's note says, "$15,000 with annual interest of 10 percent," Reggie can easily calculate the interest. If, on the other hand, the note says, "with interest at 1 percent above prime rate," Reggie cannot tell the total amount owed unless he checks the prime rate online. No matter: under Section 3-112, an instrument with a variable interest rate is considered to be negotiable, even though the holder must look elsewhere to calculate the amount owing. Suppose that Krystal's note says, "I promise to pay $15,000 worth of diamonds." This note is not negotiable because it does not state a definite amount of *money*.

5. *The Instrument Must Be Payable on* **Demand** *or at a* **Definite Time.** To determine what an instrument is worth, the holder must know when he will be paid. Ten thousand dollars today is worth more than $10,000 the day the earth stands still.

   A demand instrument must be paid whenever the holder requests payment. If an instrument is undated, it is treated as a demand instrument and is negotiable. There is one exception to this rule. If an undated promissory note says, "payable in 90 days," the instrument is not payable on demand and is non-negotiable. The maker of the note clearly did not intend to pay it on demand, but there is no way of knowing when she did intend to pay it.

   An instrument can be negotiable even if it will not be paid until some time in the future, provided that the payment date can be determined *when the document is made*. A graduate of a well-known prep school wrote a generous check to his alma mater, but for

---

[2] Section 3-104(a) sets out all the requirements of negotiability. Sections 3-105 to 3-119 then describe the requirements in more detail.

payment date he put, "The day the headmaster is fired." This check is not negotiable because it is neither payable on demand nor at a definite time. When the check was written, no one knew when (or whether) the headmaster would be fired. If the headmaster is finally fired, the check does not suddenly become negotiable.

Suppose that Krystal simply signs her note without specifying the due date. Reggie can demand payment anytime. By contrast, if the due date on the note is Easter 2015, Reggie may have to check his calendar to figure out when that is (since the date of Easter changes every year), but the note is nonetheless negotiable. If, however, the due date on the note is "three months after Krystal receives her MBA degree," the note is non-negotiable because the date of Krystal's graduation is uncertain.

6. ***The Instrument Must Be Payable to* Order *or to* Bearer.** To be negotiable, an instrument must be either order paper or bearer paper. **Order paper** must include the words "Pay to the order of" Trustie (or an equivalent, such as "Pay to Trustie, or order"). If the note simply says "Pay to Trustie," it is not negotiable. By including the word "order," the maker is indicating that the instrument is not limited to only one person. "Pay to the order of Trustie Car Lot" means that the money will be paid to Trustie *or to anyone Trustie designates.*

> **Order paper**
> An instrument that includes the words "pay to the order of" or their equivalent.

If the note is made out "To bearer," it is **bearer paper** and can be redeemed by any holder in due course. The good news is that bearer paper is easily and freely transferable, but the bad news is that it may be too easily redeemed. Suppose that Krystal's note is payable to bearer, and Reggie mails it to his sweetheart Sue as a birthday present. If dastardly Dan steals the note from Sue's mailbox and sells it to unknowing Neal, Krystal will have to pay Neal when he presents the note.

> **Bearer paper**
> A note is bearer paper if it is made out to "bearer" or it is not made out to any specific person. It can be redeemed by any holder in due course.

A note is bearer paper if it is made out to "bearer" or it is *not* made out to any specific person. If Krystal's note says, "Pay to the order of cash," or "Pay to the order of a Happy Birthday," it is bearer paper. If Krystal signs a note but leaves blank the space after "Pay to the order of," that note is bearer paper, and any holder in due course can redeem it.

The rules for checks are different from other negotiable instruments. If filled out properly, checks are negotiable. And sometimes they are negotiable even if not filled out correctly. Most checks are pre-printed with the words, "Pay to the order of," but sometimes people inadvertently cross out "order of." Even so, the check is still negotiable. Checks are frequently received by consumers who, sadly, have not completed a course on business law. The drafters of the UCC did not think it fair to penalize them when the drawer of the check was the one who made the mistake. If a check is made out to "Reggie *and* Sue," both payees must sign it before it can be transferred. If the check is made out to "Reggie *or* Sue," the signature of either is sufficient.

EXAM *Strategy*

Question: Sam had a checking account at Piggy Bank. Piggy sent him special checks that he could use to draw down a line of credit. When he used these checks, Piggy did not take money out of his account; instead it treated the checks as loans and charged him interest. Piggy then sold these used checks to Wolfe. Were the checks negotiable instruments?

Strategy: When faced with a question about negotiability, begin by looking at the list of six requirements. In this case, there is no reason to doubt that the checks are in writing, signed by the issuer, with an unconditional promise to pay to order at a definite time. But do the checks state a definite amount of money? Can the holder "look at the four corners of the check" and determine how much Sam owes?

Result: Sam was required to pay back the face amount of the check *plus* interest. Wolfe does not know the amount of the interest unless he reads the loan agreement. Therefore, the checks are not negotiable.

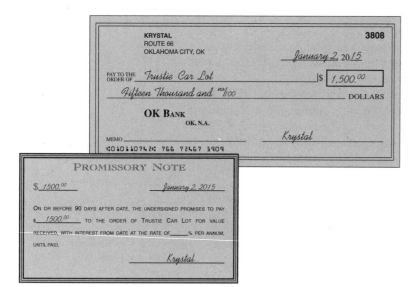

INTERPRETATION OF AMBIGUITIES

Perhaps you have noticed that people sometimes make mistakes. Although the UCC establishes simple and precise rules for creating negotiable instruments, people do not always follow these rules to the letter. It might be tempting simply to invalidate defective documents (after all, money is at stake here). But, instead, the UCC favors negotiability and has rules to resolve uncertainty and supply missing terms.

Notice anything odd about the check pictured here? Is it for $1,500 or $15,000? When the terms in a negotiable instrument contradict each other, three rules apply:

- Words take precedence over numbers.

- Handwritten terms prevail over typed and printed terms.

- Typed terms win over printed terms.

According to these rules, Krystal's check is for $15,000 because, in a conflict between words and numbers, words win.

What is wrong with the promissory note shown here? The interest rate is left blank. When this happens, UCC Section 3-112 directs that the judgment rate applies. The **judgment rate** is simply the rate that courts use on court-ordered judgments.

In the following case, the amount of the check was not completely clear. Was it a negotiable instrument?

Judgment rate

The interest rate that courts use on court-ordered judgments.

YOU *be the* JUDGE

BLASCO V. MONEY SERVICES CENTER

2006 BANKR. LEXIS 2899
United States Bankruptcy Court
for the Northern District of Alabama, 2006

Facts: Christina Blasco ran out of money. She went to the Money Services Center (MSC) and borrowed $500. To repay the loan, she gave MSC a check for $587.50, which it promised not to cash for two weeks. This kind of transaction is called a "payday loan" because it is made to someone who needs money to tide over until the next paycheck. (Note that in this case, Blasco was paying 17.5 percent interest for a two-week loan, which is an annual compounded interest rate of 6500 percent. This is the dark side of payday loans—interest rates are often exorbitant.)

Before MSC could cash the check, Blasco filed for bankruptcy protection. Although MSC knew about Blasco's filing, it deposited the check. It is illegal for creditors to collect debts after a bankruptcy filing, except that creditors *are* entitled to payment on negotiable instruments.

Ordinarily, checks are negotiable instruments, but only if they are for a definite amount. This check had a wrinkle: the numerical amount of the check was $587.50 but the amount in words was written as "five eighty-seven and 50/100 dollars." Did the words mean "five *hundred*

continued

eighty-seven" or "five *thousand* eighty-seven" or perhaps "five *million* eighty-seven"? Was the check negotiable despite this ambiguity?

You Be the Judge: Was this check a negotiable instrument? Was it for a definite amount?

Argument for Blasco: For a check to be negotiable, two rules apply:
1. The check must state a definite amount of money, which is clear within its four corners.

2. If there is a contradiction between the words and numbers, words take precedence over numbers.

Words prevail over numbers, which means that the check is for "five eighty-seven and 50/100 dollars." This

amount is not definite. A holder cannot be sure of the precise amount of the check simply by looking within its four corners. Therefore the check is not a negotiable instrument and MSC had no right to submit it for payment.

Argument for MSC: Blasco is right about the two rules. However, she is wrong in their interpretation. If there is a *contradiction* between the words and numbers, words take precedence over numbers. In this case, there was no contradiction. The words were ambiguous, but they did not contradict the numbers. If the words had said "five *thousand* eighty-seven," that would have been a contradiction. Instead, the numbers simply clarified the words. Even someone who was a stranger to this transaction could safely figure out the amount of the check. Therefore, it is negotiable.

NEGOTIATION

Remember the fundamental rule that underlies this chapter: the possessor of a piece of commercial paper has an unconditional right to be paid, as long as (1) the paper is negotiable, (2) it has been negotiated to the possessor, (3) the possessor is a holder in due course, and (4) the issuer cannot claim any of a limited number of "real" defenses.

Negotiation means that an instrument has been transferred to the holder by someone *other than the issuer.* If the issuer has transferred the instrument to the holder, then it has not been negotiated and the issuer can refuse to pay the holder if there was some flaw in the underlying contract. Thus, if Jake gives Madison a promissory note for $2,000 in payment for a new computer, but the computer crashes and burns the first week, Jake has the right to refuse to pay the note. Jake was the issuer, and the note was not negotiated. But if, before the computer self-destructs, Madison indorses and transfers the note to Kayla, then Jake is liable to Kayla for the full amount of the note, regardless of his claims against Madison.

To be negotiable, an instrument must be order paper (payable to the order of someone) or bearer paper (payable to anyone in possession). Note that a check made out to "cash" is bearer paper. These two types of instrument have different rules for negotiation: **to be negotiated, order paper must first be** *indorsed* **and then** *delivered* **to the transferee. Bearer paper must simply be** *delivered* **to the transferee; no indorsement is required.**[3]

In its simplest form, an **indorsement** is the signature of the payee. Tess writes a rent check for $475 to her landlord, Larnell. He would like to use this money to pay Patty for painting the building. If Larnell signs the back of the check and delivers it to Patty, he has met the two requirements for negotiating order paper: indorsement and delivery. If Larnell delivers the check to Patty but forgets to sign it, the check has not been indorsed and therefore cannot be negotiated—it has no value to Patty. Similarly, the check is no use to Patty if Larnell signs it

Indorsement
The signature of a payee.

[3] Section 3-201. The UCC spells the word "indorsed." Outside the UCC, the word is more commonly spelled "endorsed."

but never gives it to her. If someone forges Larnell's name, the indorsement is invalid and no subsequent transfer counts as a negotiation.

There are three different types of indorsements:

- *Blank Indorsement.* A blank indorsement occurs when Larnell simply signs the check on the back without designating any particular payee. A blank indorsement turns the check into bearer paper. Larnell can give the check to Patty the painter or Ellen the electrician. In either case, he has properly negotiated the check.

- *Special Indorsement.* A special indorsement limits an instrument to one particular person. If Larnell writes on the back of the check, "Pay Ellen Wilson" or "Pay to the order of Ellen Wilson," then only Ellen can cash the check.

- *Restrictive Indorsement.* A restrictive indorsement limits the check to one particular use. When Ellen receives the check from Larnell, she writes on the back, "For deposit only," and then signs her name. The check can only be deposited in Ellen's account. If Conrad finds the check, he cannot cash it or deposit it in his own account. This type of indorsement is the safest.

EXAM *Strategy*

Question: Tess makes a check out to cash and delivers it to Larnell. He writes on the back, "Pay to the order of Patty." She signs her name. Is this check bearer paper or order paper? Has it been negotiated?

Strategy: Whenever a negotiable instrument is transferred, it is important to ask if the instrument has been properly negotiated. To be negotiated, order paper must be indorsed and delivered; bearer paper need only be delivered, but in both cases by someone other than the issuer.

Result: This check changes back and forth between order and bearer paper, depending on what the indorsement says. When Tess makes out a check to cash, it is bearer paper. When she gives it to Larnell, it is not negotiated because she is the issuer. When he writes on the back "Pay to the order of Patty," it becomes order paper. When he gives it to Patty, it is properly negotiated because he is not the issuer and he has both indorsed the check and transferred it to Patty. When she signs it, the check becomes bearer paper. And so on it could go forever.[4]

HOLDER IN DUE COURSE

Holder in due course
Someone who has given value for an instrument, in good faith, without notice of outstanding claims or other defenses.

A **holder in due course** has an automatic right to receive payment for a negotiable instrument (unless the issuer can claim a limited number of "real" defenses). If the possessor of an instrument is not a holder in due course, then his right to payment depends upon the

---

[4] Even when all the space on the back of the check is filled, the holder can attach a separate paper for indorsements, called an **allonge**.

relationship between the issuer and payee. He inherits whatever claims and defenses arise out of that contract. Clearly, then, holder in due course status dramatically increases the value of an instrument because it enhances the probability of being paid.

REQUIREMENTS FOR BEING A HOLDER IN DUE COURSE

Under Section 3-302 of the UCC, a holder in due course is a *holder* **who has given** *value* **for the instrument, in** *good faith, without notice* **of outstanding claims or other defects.**

> … holder in due course status dramatically increases the value of an instrument because it enhances the probability of being paid.

Holder

A holder in due course must, first of all, be a holder. For order paper, a **holder** is anyone in possession of the instrument if it is payable to or indorsed to her. For bearer paper, a **holder** is anyone in possession. When Felix borrows money from his mother, she insists that he sign a promissory note for the loan. He promptly writes, "I hereby promise to pay to the order of Imogene $5,000." He signs his name and gives the note to her. She is a holder because she has possession of the instrument and it is payable to her. She would like to give the note to her lawyer, Lance, to pay the legal bill she incurred when Felix smashed up a nightclub. If she simply hands the note to Lance, he is not a holder because the note is not payable to him. If she writes on the back of the note, "Pay to the order of Lance," but does not give it to him, he is not a holder either.

Holder
For order paper, anyone in possession of the instrument if it is payable to or indorsed to her. For bearer paper, anyone in possession.

Value

A holder in due course must give value for an instrument. **Value** means that the holder has *already* done something in exchange for the instrument. Lance has already represented Felix, so he has given value. Once Imogene indorses and delivers the note to Lance, he is a holder in due course.

Although a promise to do something in the future is *consideration* under contract law, such a promise does not count as *value* under Article 3. If the holder receives an instrument in return for a promise, he does not deserve to be paid unless he performs the promise. But if he were a holder in due course, he would be entitled to payment whether he performed or not. For example, suppose that Imogene gave Lance the promissory note in exchange for his promise to represent Felix in an upcoming arson trial. Lance would not be a holder in due course because he has not yet performed the service. It would be unfair for him to be a holder in due course, with an unconditional right to be paid, if he, in fact, does not represent Felix.

Someone who receives a negotiable instrument as a gift is not a holder in due course because he has not given value. If Imogene gives Felix's note to her daughter, Joy, as a birthday present, Joy is not a holder in due course.

Value
The holder has *already* done something in exchange for the instrument.

Good Faith

There are two tests to determine if a holder acquired an instrument in good faith. The holder must meet both of these tests:

- *Subjective Test.* Did the holder *believe* the transaction was honest in fact?

- *Objective Test.* Did the transaction *appear* to be commercially reasonable?

Felix persuades his elderly neighbor, Hope, that he has invented a fabulous beauty cream guaranteed to remove wrinkles. She gives him a $10,000 promissory note, payable in

90 days, in return for exclusive sales rights in Pittsburgh. Felix sells the note to his old friend Dick for $2,000. Felix never delivers the sales samples to Hope. When Dick presents the note to Hope, she refuses to pay on the grounds that Dick is not a holder in due course. She contends that he did not buy the note in good faith.

Dick fails both tests. Any friend of Felix knows he is not trustworthy, especially when presenting a promissory note signed by an elderly neighbor. Dick did not believe the transaction was honest in fact. Also, $10,000 notes are not usually discounted to $2,000; $9,000 would be more normal. This transaction is not commercially reasonable, and Dick should have realized immediately that Felix was up to no good.

In the following case, the plaintiff also failed two tests: he neither gave value nor acted in good faith.

ROSENBAUM V. BULOW

1997 BANKR. LEXIS 555
UNITED STATES BANKRUPTCY COURT FOR THE EASTERN DISTRICT OF NORTH CAROLINA, 1997

CASE SUMMARY

Facts: Maude Knox Rosenbaum was convicted of "obtaining property by false pretenses" (that is, "fraud"). Pending the outcome of her appeal, she was sent to Women's Prison in Raleigh, North Carolina. Prison was not to her liking, but she could not raise bail of $50,000. Nor could she find a bondsman willing to post bail for her.[5]

Rosenbaum turned to her sister, Louise Knox, for help. Knox asked for money from a number of friends and acquaintances, who evidently felt Rosenbaum was just fine where she was. Finally, Harvey Bowen, a local used-car dealer, agreed to post the $7,500 bond in exchange for a $7,500 promissory note secured by Rosenbaum's house. In other words, Bowen asked to be paid $7,500 even though he was entitled to a refund of his entire bond if Rosenbaum returned to prison as required. There was only one problem with this arrangement: Bowen was not a licensed bondsman. Thus, under state law, Rosenbaum had no obligation to pay him for posting bail. Shortly after obtaining the note from Rosenbaum, Bowen attempted to solve this problem by asking her to sign a second note that was identical to the first, except this time W. F. Bulow was the payee. (Bulow was married to

Bowen's niece, but he was not a licensed bondsman either.) When Bulow tried to collect on the note, Rosenbaum argued that he was not entitled to be paid because he neither gave value nor acted in good faith.

Issues: *Did Bulow give value for the promissory note? Did he act in good faith?*

Decision: Bulow did not give value for the promissory note, nor did he act in good faith. The note is void and unenforceable.

Reasoning: Bowen gave value to Rosenbaum for the note, but Bulow did not give value either to Bowen or Rosenbaum. Bulow was simply part of a scheme by Bowen to mask his own illegal activity.

Nor was Bulow acting in good faith. He did not know Rosenbaum before receiving the note, and he gave her nothing of value in return. Even if Bulow did not know about Bowen's unsavory activity, he had an obligation to ask questions before accepting a $7,500 note and a mortgage from a perfect stranger.

---

[5] Typically, a prisoner will be released if a licensed bail bondsman is willing to post a cash bond equal to 15 percent of bail (in this case $7,500). The prisoner pays the bondsman a fee equal to 10 percent of the bond (here it would be $750). If the prisoner fails to return to prison when ordered by the court, the bondsman must pay the balance owing (that is, $42,500). Naturally, a licensed bondsman will post bail only if he is quite sure the defendant will return as promised. When the defendant does return, the bondsman gets back the bond of $7,500 and keeps the $750 fee as well.

ETHICS   In Chapter 2 on ethics, we talked about Right v. Right. This case is, in some sense, about Wrong v. Wrong. Harvey Bowen serves as a bondsman, although he is not licensed. Maude Rosenbaum refuses to pay $7,500, although she has signed a promissory note. Why did the court view her act as less wrong than his? ◆

Notice of Outstanding Claims or Other Defects

In certain circumstances, a holder is on notice that an instrument has an outstanding claim or other defect.

1. *The Instrument Is Overdue.* An instrument is overdue the day after its due date. At that point, the recipient is on notice that it may have a defect. He ought to wonder why no one has bothered to collect the money owed. However, an instrument is not overdue simply because the interest is unpaid. If, on July 25, Dick buys Harriet's note that was due on July 24, Dick is not a holder in due course because the note is overdue. But if he buys the note on July 23, knowing that Harriet has not paid all the interest owing, he can still be a holder in due course.

   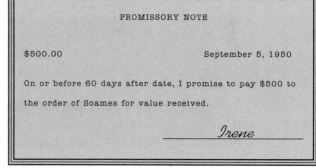

   The holder of this note should realize that there may be a problem.

   A check is overdue 90 days after its date. Any other *demand* instrument is overdue (1) the day after a request for payment is made or (2) a reasonable time after the instrument was issued. Suppose that Felix tries to sell Tom a demand note from Hope. If Felix happens to mention, "I asked the old lady for the money yesterday, but so far, no luck," then Tom is not a holder in due course because he knows the note is overdue.

2. *The Instrument Is Dishonored.* To dishonor an instrument is to refuse to pay it. If Tom knows that Hope has refused to pay her note, then Tom cannot be a holder in due course. Likewise, once a check has been stamped "Insufficient Funds" by the bank, it has been dishonored, and no one who obtains it afterward can be a holder in due course.

3. *The Instrument Is Altered, Forged, or Incomplete.* Anyone who knows that an instrument has been altered or forged cannot be a holder in due course. Suppose Joe wrote a check to Tony for $200. While showing the check to Liza, Tony cackles to himself and says, "Can you believe what that goof did? Look, he left the line blank after the words 'two hundred.'" Taking his pen out with a flourish, Tony changes the zeroes to nines and adds the words, "ninety-nine." He then indorses the check over to Liza, who is definitely not a holder in due course. However, if, instead of giving the check to Liza, Tony sells it to Kate, she is a holder in due course because she had no idea the check had been altered.

   Likewise, if Joe filled out the check, but failed to sign it, Liza cannot be a holder in due course after she watches Tony fill in Joe's signature. And even if Liza did not see the forgery, she might be on notice if Tony has misspelled Joe's name as "Jo."

   Sometimes people (foolishly) sign blank promissory notes or checks. These issuers are liable for any amount subsequently filled in. However, anyone who is aware that a material term was added later is not a holder in due course. Suppose that Joe gives Tony a signed, blank check. If Tony fills in the amount in front of Liza, then naturally she is not a holder in due course. But if Tony fills in the check *before* he gives it to Liza, she is a holder in due course.

4. *The Holder Has Notice of Certain Claims or Disputes.* No one can qualify as a holder in due course if she is on notice that (1) someone else has a claim to the instrument or (2) there is a dispute between the original parties to the instrument. Matt hires Sheila to put aluminum siding

on his house. In payment, he gives her a $15,000 promissory note with the due date left blank. They agree that the note will not be due until 60 days after completion of the work. Despite the agreement, Sheila fills in the date immediately and sells the note to Rupert at American Finance Corp., who has bought many similar notes from Sheila. Rupert knows that the note is not supposed to be due until after the work is finished. Usually, before he buys a note from her, he demands a signed document from the homeowner certifying that the work is complete. Also, he lives near Matt and can see that Matt's house is only half finished. Rupert is not a holder in due course because he has reason to suspect there is a dispute between Sheila and Matt.

Holder in due course status is determined *when the holder receives the instrument.* If, at the very moment when he takes possession, the holder has no notice of outstanding claims or other defects, then he is a holder in due course, no matter what else happens afterward. If Rupert knows nothing of Sheila's sneaky ways when he buys Matt's note, then he is a holder in due course even if Matt calls him 10 minutes later to report that Sheila has violated their contract.

In the following case, Avon thought that American Express should have realized something fishy was going on.

HARTFORD ACCIDENT & INDEMNITY CO. v. AMERICAN EXPRESS, CO.

74 N.Y.2d 153, 542 N.E.2d 1090, 1989 N.Y. LEXIS 881
NEW YORK COURT OF APPEALS, 1989

CASE SUMMARY

Facts: As manager of the import/export department at Avon Products, Stratford Skalkos had authority to requisition checks up to $25,000 on his signature alone. For nearly three years, Skalkos used that authority to steal $162,538.65 from Avon. Skalkos followed a simple pattern: he altered the names of the payees so that, although they *sounded* like company suppliers, they were actually businesses to whom he owed money personally. For example, he used Avon checks made out to "Amerex Corp." to pay his American Express bill and checks to "Metropolitan Opng. Co." to pay the Metropolitan Opera Association, Inc. for opera tickets. By the movement of one letter, E. J. Audi, Inc. (a furniture store) became "E. Jaudi, Inc."

Avon sued the recipients of the checks, demanding that the funds be returned. The trial court ruled that the defendants were entitled to keep the money because they were holders in due course and thus took the checks free of any claims or defenses. Avon appealed.

Issue: *Were the defendants holders in due course?*

Decision: Yes, the defendants were holders in due course and may keep the funds they received from Skalkos.

Reasoning: According to UCC Section 3-304(1)(a), defendants must repay Avon if the checks were "so irregular as to call into question [their] validity." Avon argued that the misspelled names on the checks should have alerted the defendants that something was wrong. However, these misspellings were so minor that a recipient would not necessarily know the checks had been wrongly issued. Nor should a furniture store or an opera company be surprised to receive corporate checks. Businesses often pay their employees' personal expenses—to maintain a residence in a high-rent district, to entertain customers, to travel, and so on.

Of all the parties involved in this case, Avon was clearly most at fault. Its misplaced trust or inattention permitted an employee to steal money for several years. Avon was in the best position to prevent the losses or to protect itself with insurance.

SHELTER RULE ~~No Q's~~

Under the shelter rule, the transferor of an instrument passes on all of his rights. When a holder in due course transfers an instrument, the recipient acquires all the same rights *even if she is not a holder in due course herself*.[6]

Cigna Insurance Company sent James Mills a check for $484.12 in payment for his insurance claim. Dishonest fellow that he was, Mills told Cigna that he had never received the check because it had been sent to the wrong address. Cigna stopped payment and issued a new check. Mills took the old check to Sun's Market and used it to buy goods there. When Sun deposited the check at its bank, the bank refused to pay and stamped the check "Stop Payment." At this point, Sun was a holder in due course and was entitled to payment from Cigna. Instead of presenting the check itself, Sun sold it to Robert Triffin, who was in the business of buying dishonored instruments. Triffin then sued Cigna for payment. Triffin acknowledged that he was not a holder in due course because he knew the check had been dishonored. However, under the shelter rule, he acquired Sun's rights as a holder in due course, and he was entitled to payment.[7]

The point of the shelter rule is not to benefit Mills or Triffin; it is to protect Sun. It would not do Sun much good to be a holder in due course if it were unable to sell the instrument to anyone.

There is one small exception to the shelter rule. If a holder in due course transfers the instrument back to a prior holder who was a party to fraud involving the instrument, that prior holder does not acquire the rights of a holder in due course. Thus, if Triffin transferred the check back to Mills, then Mills would not be entitled to payment from Cigna (even if he had the nerve to ask).

DEFENSES AGAINST A HOLDER IN DUE COURSE

Negotiable instruments are meant to be a close substitute for money, and, as a general rule, holders expect to be paid. However, an issuer may legitimately refuse to pay an instrument under certain circumstances. Section 3-305 of the UCC lists so-called *real* defenses that an issuer may legitimately use even against a holder in due course. If the holder is not in due course but is simply a plain ordinary holder, the issuer may use both real defenses and *personal* defenses. **Real and personal defenses are valid against an ordinary holder; only real defenses can be used against a holder in due course.**

Real Defenses

The following real defenses are valid against both a holder and a holder in due course:

Forgery.   If Sharon forges Jared's name to a promissory note and sells it to Jennifer, Jared does not have to pay Jennifer, even if she is a holder in due course.

Bankruptcy.   If Jared's debts are discharged in a bankruptcy proceeding after he has signed a promissory note, he does not have to pay the note, even to a holder in due course.

Minority.   If a minor has the right to void a contract under state law, then he also has the right not to pay a negotiable instrument, even to a holder in due course.

---

[6] Section 3-203(b).

[7] *Triffin v. Cigna*, 297 N.J. Super. 199; 687 A.2d 1045; 1997 N.J. Super. LEXIS 50 (Sup. Ct. N.J., App. Div., 1997).

Alteration.   If the amount of an instrument is wrongfully changed, the holder in due course can collect only the original (correct) amount. If the instrument was incomplete, the holder in due course can collect the full face amount, even if the instrument was incorrectly filled in. Suppose that Jared gives a $2,000 promissory note to Rose. As soon as he leaves, she whips out her pen and adds a zero to the note. She then takes it to the auto showroom to pay for her new car. If the showroom is a holder in due course, it is entitled to be paid the original amount of the note ($2,000), not the altered amount ($20,000). But, if Jared had accidentally forgotten to fill out the amount of the note, and Rose wrote in $20,000, the showroom could recover the full $20,000. Although the two notes *look* the same, they have a different result. In the case where Rose changed the amount, Jared was not to blame; but he *was* at fault for signing a blank note.

Duress, Mental Incapacity, or Illegality.   These are customary contract defenses that you remember well from your study of contracts. They are a defense against a holder in due course if they are severe enough to make the underlying transaction void (not simply voidable) under state law. An instrument is not valid even in the hands of a holder in due course if, for example, Rose holds a gun to Jared's head to force him to sign it; or Jared has been declared mentally incompetent at the time he signs it; or Jared is using the instrument to pay for something illegal (cocaine, say).

Fraud in the Execution.   In cases of fraud in the execution, the issuer has been tricked into signing without knowing what the instrument is and without any reasonable way to find out. In such instances, even a holder in due course cannot recover. Jared cannot read English. Helen, his boss, tells him that he must sign a document required by the company's health insurance plan. In fact, the document is a promissory note, payable to Helen. Jared does not have to pay the note, even to a holder in due course, because of fraud in the execution.

Personal Defenses

Personal defenses are valid against a holder, but *not* against a holder in due course. Typically, personal defenses have some connection to the initial transaction in which the instrument was issued.

Breach of Contract.   Ross signs a contract to sell a new airplane to Paige in return for a $1 million promissory note. If Paige discovers that the plane is defective and that Ross has breached the contract, she can refuse to pay him because he is a mere holder. If, however, Ross sells the note to Helga, a holder in due course, Paige must pay her.

Lack of Consideration.   Ross gives his mother, Gertrude, a $1,000 check for her birthday. Then they have a disagreement over where to spend Thanksgiving, so Ross stops payment on Gertrude's check. Gertrude has no right to the $1,000 because she is a mere holder who did not give value for the check. But if Gertrude has already cashed the check at her bank, Ross must pay the bank because it is a holder in due course. Even though the check was a gift, and therefore lacking in value, the bank is a holder in due course because it has given value for the check, even if Gertrude has not.

Prior Payment.   Two years before, Gertrude had loaned Ross money to start his airplane business. When he paid off the note to Gertrude, he forgot to retrieve the original from her. Angry at him over the check, she sells the note to Carla. Of course, Ross would not have to pay Gertrude *again*, but he cannot refuse to pay Carla, who is a holder in due course. The moral is: when you pay off a note, be sure to retrieve it or mark it canceled.

Unauthorized Completion.   Ross writes a check to Carla to pay the note. He forgets to fill in the amount of the check, but Carla very helpfully does, for $5,000 more than he actually owes. If she uses that check to pay her debt at the bank, the bank is a holder in due course, and Ross must honor the check. Remember, however, that if the bank knew Carla had filled in the amount, it would not be a holder in due course and could not recover on the check.

Fraud in the Inducement.   Suppose that Carla gives Sean a promissory note to buy stock in his company. It turns out that the company is a fraud. Carla would not have to pay Sean (a holder), but, if Sean transfers the note to Peter, a holder in due course, Carla must pay Peter even though the underlying contract was fraudulent. Note that *fraud in the execution* (real defense) has a different result from *fraud in the inducement* (personal defense).

Non-Delivery.   The note that Carla issued to Sean was bearer paper. When Oliver steals it and sells it to a holder in due course, Carla must pay the note even though neither she nor Sean had ever delivered it to the holder. Carla would not have to pay Oliver because he is a mere holder and she did not deliver it to him.

The following table lists, for quick reference, real and personal defenses.

Real Defenses	Personal Defenses
Forgery	Breach of contract
Bankruptcy	Lack of consideration
Minority	Prior payment
Alteration	Unauthorized completion
Duress	Fraud in the inducement
Mental incapacity	Non-delivery
Illegality	
Fraud in the execution	

Claims in Recoupment

A **claim in recoupment** is not the same as a defense, but it has a similar impact. It means that the issuer subtracts (i.e., "sets off") any other claims he has against the initial payee from the amount he owes on the instrument. The distinction is subtle, but a *claim in recoupment* means, "I'm not going to pay the full amount of the instrument because she owes me money for something else" whereas a *defense* means, "I'm not going to pay the full amount of the instrument because there is some problem with the instrument itself or the underlying deal on which the instrument is based."

A claim in recoupment is valid against a holder but not against a holder in due course. Carla gives Sean a promissory note to pay for stock that turns out to be fraudulent. Therefore, Carla has a defense against Sean when he requests that she pay her note. Suppose, however, that the stock is perfectly legitimate, but Sean has never paid Carla $18,000 for the used car he bought from her. When Sean presents the note on the stock deal for payment, Carla makes a claim for recoupment and subtracts $18,000 from the amount owing on the note. If, however, Sean had already sold the note to Olaf, a holder in due course, Carla would have to pay the full amount of the note and then sue Sean for the $18,000.

Claim in recoupment
The issuer subtracts (i.e., "sets off") any other claims he has against the initial payee from the amount he owes on the instrument.

EXAM *Strategy*

Question: Jack agreed to loan Tim money. Although Tim signed a promissory note, Jack never actually gave Tim the money. Jack sold the note to Leslie. Can Leslie collect from Tim? Would it matter if Leslie knew that Tim never received the money?

Strategy: Whenever a question asks if someone will be paid on a negotiable instrument, the first step is to determine if she is a holder in due course. The second step is to ask if there are any applicable defenses.

Result: If Leslie *knew* that Jack had never paid Tim, then she is a mere holder, not a holder in due course. Tim can use any personal defenses (such as lack of consideration) against a holder. In that case, Tim does not have to pay Leslie. But, if Leslie did not know of the dispute, she is a holder in due course and can collect from Tim, despite the fact that Tim never received payment from Jack.

CONSUMER EXCEPTION

In the eighteenth and nineteenth centuries, negotiable instruments often circulated through several hands. The business community treated them as money. The concept of holder in due course was essential because the instruments had little use if they could not be transferred for value. In the modern banking system, however, instruments are much less likely to circulate. Currently, the most common use for negotiable instruments is in consumer transactions. A consumer pays for a refrigerator by giving the store a promissory note. The store promptly sells the note to a finance company. Even if the refrigerator is defective, under Article 3 the consumer must pay full value on the note because the finance company is a holder in due course.

Some commentators have argued that the concept of holder in due course no longer serves a useful purpose and that it should be eliminated once and for all (and with it Article 3 of the UCC). No state has yet taken such a dramatic step. Instead, some states require promissory notes given by a consumer to carry the words "consumer paper." Notes with this legend are non-negotiable.

> **Consumer credit contract**
> A contract in which a consumer borrows money from a lender to purchase goods and services from a seller who is affiliated with the lender.

Meanwhile, the Federal Trade Commission (FTC) has special rules for consumer credit contracts. A **consumer credit contract** is one in which a consumer borrows money from a lender to purchase goods and services from a seller who is affiliated with the lender. If Sears loans money to Gerald to buy a high definition TV at Sears, that is a consumer credit contract. It is not a consumer credit contract if Gerald borrows money from his cousin Vinnie to buy the TV from Sears. The FTC requires all promissory notes in consumer credit contracts to contain the following language:

NOTICE
ANY HOLDER OF THIS CONSUMER CREDIT CONTRACT IS SUBJECT TO ALL CLAIMS AND DEFENSES WHICH THE DEBTOR COULD ASSERT AGAINST THE SELLER OF GOODS OR SERVICES OBTAINED WITH THE PROCEEDS HEREOF.

Under Section 3-106(d) of the UCC, no one can be a holder in due course of an instrument with this language. If the language is omitted from a consumer note, it is possible to be a holder in due course, but the seller is subject to a fine.

In the following case, the plaintiff borrowed money from Sterling to pay Mayflower. The FTC rule applied because the two companies were "affiliated."

SCOTT V. MAYFLOWER HOME IMPROVEMENT CORP.

363 N.J. SUPER. 145; 831 A.2d 564; 2001 N.J. SUPER. LEXIS 524
SUPERIOR COURT OF NEW JERSEY, 2001

CASE SUMMARY

Facts: Mary Johnson signed a contract with Mayflower Home Improvement Corporation for repair work on her home. The contract specified a fee of $25,900. Later, Mayflower arranged for Johnson to pay for this work by borrowing money from Sterling Resources. In the note she signed with Sterling, the price was unconscionably high—$50,108.60—and so was the interest rate—17.98 percent.

Johnson alleges that Mayflower was running a scam. It hired unlicensed salespeople who targeted minority neighborhoods. The contracts prepared by the salespeople specified the work in general terms but omitted the name, make, quality, and model of the products and materials to be used. The contracts did not specify the interest rate or the total cost. The contractor's work was done in a shoddy or incomplete manner, often using poor-quality materials.

Sterling routinely loaned money to Mayflower customers. The interest rates on these loans were between 15 percent and 19 percent. Sterling then sold the loans to banks and other financial institutions (the Lender).

When Johnson failed to make the payments due on the note, the Lender sued her. It moved for summary judgment against Johnson on the grounds that, as a holder in due course, it was entitled to enforce the note regardless of her claims against Mayflower or Sterling. Johnson responded that, under the FTC Consumer Holder Rule, the Lender was not a holder in due course. Therefore, the Lender was subject to whatever defenses she had against Sterling or Mayflower.

Issues: *Was the Lender a holder in due course? Can it enforce the note against Johnson?*

Decision: No, the Lender was not a holder in due course. It cannot enforce the note against Johnson. Summary judgment is granted to Johnson.

Reasoning: Before the FTC adopted its Consumer Holder Rule, unethical merchants used the "Holder in Due Course" doctrine to victimize thousands of innocent consumers. They sold shoddy furniture, defective aluminum siding, and cars that were lemons. The defrauded consumer paid with a note that the merchants immediately sold. Even after discovering the fraud, the consumer still had to pay the note when a holder in due course presented it. But under the Consumer Holder Rule, the holder of a consumer note must step into the shoes of the seller. If the seller has no right to be paid, then neither does any subsequent holder. Any lender who is offered a consumer note with the FTC Consumer Holder notice should either refuse to buy it or should purchase insurance against any losses if the note turns out to be unenforceable.

In this case, the FTC Consumer Holder notice was conspicuously printed on Mary Johnson's note. As a result, all holders knew that the FTC Consumer Holder Rule applied.

CHAPTER CONCLUSION

Whenever someone acquires commercial paper, the first question he ought to ask is "How certain is it that I will be paid the face value of this document?" Article 3 of the UCC contains the answer to this question: if a negotiable instrument is negotiated to a holder in due course, then that holder knows he has an unconditional right (subject only to a few real defenses) to be paid the value of the note. In some ways, Article 3 is like a marine drill instructor: rigid, but predictable if you follow the rules.

EXAM REVIEW

1. **COMMERCIAL PAPER** Commercial paper is a contract to pay money. It can be used either as a substitute for money or as a loan of money. (p. 528)

2. **THE FUNDAMENTAL RULE OF COMMERCIAL PAPER** The possessor of a piece of commercial paper has an unconditional right to be paid, so long as:

   - The paper is negotiable,
   - It has been negotiated to the possessor,
   - The possessor is a holder in due course, and
   - The issuer cannot claim any of the few "real" defenses. (p. 528)

3. **NEGOTIABILITY** The possessor of non-negotiable commercial paper has the same rights—no more, no less—as the person who made the original contract. The possessor of negotiable commercial paper has more rights than the person who made the original contract. (pp. 530–531)

4. **REQUIREMENTS FOR NEGOTIABILITY** To be negotiable, an instrument must:

   - Be in writing,
   - Be signed by the maker or drawer,
   - Contain an unconditional promise or order to pay,
   - State a definite amount of money,
   - Be payable on demand or at a definite time, and
   - Be payable to order or to bearer. (pp. 532–533)

5. **AMBIGUITY** When the terms in a negotiable instrument contradict each other, three rules apply:

   - Words take precedence over numbers.
   - Handwritten terms prevail over typed and printed terms.
   - Typed terms win over printed terms. (p. 534)

6. **NEGOTIATION** To be negotiated, order paper must first be indorsed and then delivered to the transferee. Bearer paper must simply be delivered to the transferee; no indorsement is required. (p. 535)

7. **HOLDER IN DUE COURSE** A holder in due course is a holder who has given value for the instrument, in good faith, without notice of outstanding claims or other defects. (p. 536)

EXAM Strategy

Question: After Irene Nusor fell behind on her mortgage payments, she answered an advertisement from Best Financial Consultants offering attractive refinancing opportunities. During a meeting at a McDonald's restaurant, a Best representative told her that the company would arrange for a complete refinancing of her home, pay off two of her creditors, and give her an additional $5,000 in spending money. Nusor would have to pay Best only $4,000. Nusor signed a blank promissory note that was filled in later by Best representatives for $14,986.61. Best did not fulfill its promises to Nusor, but within two weeks, it sold the note to Robin Parkhill for just under $14,000. Nusor refused to pay the note, alleging that Parkhill was not a holder in due course. Is Nusor liable to Parkhill?

Strategy: Whenever a question asks if someone is a holder in due course, begin by reviewing the requirements for being a holder in due course. Is this person a *holder* who has given *value* for the instrument, in *good faith*, *without notice* of outstanding claims or other defects? (See the "Result" at the end of this section.)

8. **REAL DEFENSES** These real defenses are valid against both a holder and a holder in due course:

- Forgery
- Bankruptcy
- Minority
- Alteration
- Duress, mental incapacity, or illegality
- Fraud in the execution (pp. 541–542)

9. **PERSONAL DEFENSES** These personal defenses are valid against any holder except a holder in due course:

- Breach of contract
- Lack of consideration
- Prior payment
- Unauthorized completion
- Fraud in the inducement
- Non-delivery (pp. 542–543)

EXAM Strategy

Question: Gary Culver, a farmer in Missouri, was having financial problems. He agreed to let Nasib Ed Kalliel assume control of the farm's finances. After a few months, Culver begged Kalliel for money. One week later, $30,000 was wire-transferred to Culver from the Rexford State Bank. Culver thought that Kalliel would be responsible for repaying this sum. A man who worked for Kalliel stopped Culver on the street and asked him to sign a receipt for the $30,000. Culver signed without intending to commit himself to repaying the money. In fact, the document Culver signed was a blank promissory note, payable to Rexford. Someone later filled in the blanks, putting in $50,000 instead of $30,000. Kalliel had received $50,000 before transferring $30,000 to Culver. When Rexford sued Culver to enforce the note, Culver asserted the defense of fraud. Is Culver liable on the note?

Strategy: Whenever someone alleges a defense, the first step is to determine if the defense is real or personal. Personal defenses are not valid against a holder in due course. (See the "Result" at the end of this section.)

10. **A CLAIM IN RECOUPMENT** A claim in recoupment cannot be used against a holder in due course. (p. 543)

11. **CONSUMER CREDIT CONTRACTS** The Federal Trade Commission requires all promissory notes in consumer credit contracts to contain language preventing any subsequent holder from being a holder in due course. (p. 544)

EXAM Strategy

Question: Gina and Douglas Felde purchased a Chrysler car with a 70,000-mile warranty. They signed a loan contract with the dealer to pay for the car in monthly installments. The dealer sold the contract to the Chrysler Credit Corp. Soon, the car developed a tendency to accelerate abruptly and without warning. Two Chrysler dealers were unable to correct the problem. The Feldes filed suit against Chrysler Credit Corp., but the company refused to rescind the loan contract. The company argued that, as a holder in due course on the note, it was entitled to be paid regardless of any defects in the car. How would you decide this case if you were the judge?

Strategy: Whenever consumers are involved, consider the possibility that there is a consumer credit contract. The plaintiffs in this case are consumers who have borrowed money from a lender to purchase goods from a seller who is affiliated with the lender (both seller and lender are owned by Chrysler). Thus the contract is a consumer credit contract. (See the "Result" at the end of this section.)

---

7. Result: In this case, Parkhill is a holder who has given value. Did she act in good faith? We don't know if she actually *believed* the transaction was honest, but the court held that the transaction did not *appear* to be commercially reasonable because Parkhill's profit was so high. Thus Parkhill was not a holder in due course, and Nusor was not liable to her.

9. Result: Fraud in the execution is a real defense; fraud in the inducement is personal. In this case, there was no fraud in the execution. Culver could have read the note he signed, but did not bother. Kalliel committed fraud in the inducement, but that is not a valid defense because the Bank is a holder in due course.

11. Result: Chrysler Credit was not a holder in due course. Therefore, it is subject to any defenses that the Feldes might have against the dealer, including that the car was defective.

ADDITIONAL QUESTIONS

1. Sam Kay signed a promissory note for $220,000 that was payable to Investments, S.A., Inc., a company of which he was the principal stockholder. The company then indorsed the note over to its lawyers to pay past and future legal fees. Kay claimed the company owed $3,557.53 in fees; the lawyers testified they had performed "more than $20,000" worth of work on the date they received the note. Were the lawyers holders in due course?

2. **CPA QUESTION** In order to negotiate bearer paper, one must:

   (a) Indorse the paper

   (b) Indorse and deliver the paper with consideration

   (c) Deliver the paper

   (d) Deliver and indorse the paper

3. **CPA QUESTION** Bond fraudulently induced Teal to make a note payable to Wilk, to whom Bond was indebted. Bond delivered the note to Wilk. Wilk negotiated the instrument to Monk, who purchased it with knowledge of the fraud and after it was overdue. If Wilk qualifies as a holder in due course, which of the following statements is correct?

   (a) Monk has the standing of a holder in due course through Wilk.

   (b) Teal can successfully assert the defense of fraud in the inducement against Monk.

   (c) Monk personally qualifies as a holder in due course.

   (d) Teal can successfully assert the defense of fraud in the inducement against Wilk

4. Shelby wrote the following check to Dana. When is it payable and for how much?

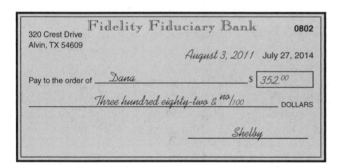

5. How would you advise this troubled newspaper reader?

   Q: I have paid off a loan and have a receipt from the lender for payment, but the lender will not give me the original promissory note. Do I need the original promissory note?

6. On June 30, John N. Willis signed a demand promissory note for $1,620 to the Camelot Country Club in Carrollton, Texas. The note stated that it was being given in payment for a membership in the country club, but, in fact, the club was insolvent, its memberships had no value, and Willis was already a member. He was also the club's golf pro. Willis signed the note at the request of the club's manager to enable the club to borrow money from the Commonwealth National Bank to meet its payroll. The Bank of Dallas purchased the note on July 14 and immediately made demand. Willis alleged the note was overdue and therefore the bank could not be a holder in due course. Do you agree?

7. **YOU BE THE JUDGE** WRITING PROBLEM A columnist for the *Arizona Republic/ Phoenix Gazette* received the following problem from a reader. How would you answer it?

   A check cashing company was suing a local businessman. The check cashing company said they accepted a check this businessman had given an ex-employee and later found out he had stopped payment. "We cannot locate the ex-employee, so we opted to sue the issuing company," they said. The businessman said that he found out after he had given this ex-employee a check that he had made a mistake. He had the bank issue a stop payment. "I have a right to tell our bank not to pay a check. The check is null and void," the businessman said. "It is a worthless piece of paper. Go after the person who gave you the check." The check company argued that a check is a negotiable instrument. Placed in interstate commerce, the check is a promise to pay the holder in due course. The stop payment only stopped the bank from paying the check. The company that issued the check placed it in interstate commerce and is legally bound to pay the face amount of the check, the check company argued. "We are the holder and have a right to be paid." Who is right?[8]

8. Catherine Wagner suffered serious physical injuries in an automobile accident and became acutely depressed as a result. One morning, she received a check for $17,400 in settlement of her claims arising out of the accident. She indorsed the check and placed it on the kitchen table. She then called Robert Scherer, her longtime roommate, to tell him the check had arrived. That afternoon, she jumped from the roof of her apartment building, killing herself. The police found the check and a note from her, stating that she was giving it to Scherer. Had Wagner negotiated the check to Scherer?

9. **ETHICS** S. J. Littlegreen owned the Lookout Mountain Hotel. In financial trouble, he put the hotel on the market at a price of $850,000. C. Abbott Gardner was his real estate agent. To obtain more time to sell, Littlegreen decided to refinance his debt. Mr. Rupe agreed to lend Littlegreen $300,000. When this loan was ready for closing, Gardner informed Littlegreen that he expected a commission of 5 percent of the amount of the loan, or $15,000. Gardner threatened to block the loan if his demands were not met. Littlegreen needed the proceeds of the loan badly, so he agreed to give Gardner $4,000 in cash and a promissory note for $11,000. On what grounds might Littlegreen claim that the note is invalid? Would this be a valid defense? Even if Gardner was in the right legally, was he in the right ethically? Would he like everyone in town to know that he had squeezed Littlegreen in this way? How would he have felt if he had been in Littlegreen's position? Does might make right?

10. **ROLE REVERSAL** Write a multiple-choice question that concerns a holder in due course.

INTERNET RESEARCH PROBLEM

Go to **https://www.legaldocs.com** (or an equivalent site) and fill in the blanks of a promissory note. Who is the maker, and who is the payee of your note? Did you create a demand note?

You can find further practice problems at www.cengagebrain.com. See the preface of this book for website access details.

---

[8] Quentin v. Tolby, "Stopping Payment Not Always Enough," *Arizona Republic/Phoenix Gazette*, July 4, July 4, 1995, p. 3. Reprinted with permission of the author.

LIABILITY FOR NEGOTIABLE INSTRUMENTS

Willie groaned under his breath. How had he ever gotten into this mess? Producing a rock video for the Hot Tamales had seemed a golden opportunity. He loved the music, and he didn't even mind living in a trailer on location, but the business end was driving him to despair. That morning, he had glanced out his trailer window and seen Vidalia slinking across the set. How could he have been so stupid as to let her finance the video? "Willie, darling," she had purred, as a circle of smoke from her cigarette caught in his throat, "I know that your promissory note for $50,000 isn't due 'til next month, but I simply do *not* like the music in this video, and I *cannot* support what I do not like. It would be so bad for my karma. But, take your time, dearest one, my driver will be back this afternoon to collect what you owe me."

> I *cannot* support what I do not like. It would be so bad for my karma.

Sitting in his trailer holding his head in his hands, Willie heard a timid knock. Opening the door, he saw a teenage girl smiling at him. "Hi, Mister Willie," she beamed. "I'm Vera Brown. My mom sent me over to collect the rent check for the trailer. And could I please, please have your autograph? Your work is so awesome."

Willie smiled. "Sure, kiddo, here's my autograph and here's the rent check."

Seeing a helpful, enthusiastic kid like Vera helped brighten an otherwise dark day. But his spirits took a blow later that afternoon when the landlady came by for her check and Willie discovered she had no daughter. He immediately called his bank to stop payment on the check, only to discover that his balance was zero dollars and zero cents. Vera had used her computer to create a second check drawn on Willie's account. She had then forged his signature and cashed both checks before skipping town.

To understand the full impact of the day's catastrophes, Willie needs a crash course on liability for negotiable instruments:

- **The Promissory Note to Vidalia.** When Willie gave a promissory note in payment for the debt, the debt was *suspended* until the note comes due. *Verdict:* Vidalia cannot collect her money until next month, when the note is due.

- **The Rent Check to the Landlady.** Vera was not Mrs. Brown's lovely daughter; she was an impostor. Banks are not liable on checks that the issuer voluntarily gives to an impostor.[1] *Verdict:* The bank will not reimburse Willie for the rent check. Of course, Willie must still pay the landlady.

- **The Check That Vera Forged.** A bank is liable if it pays a check on which the issuer's name is forged. *Verdict:* The bank must reimburse Willie for the second check.

INTRODUCTION

In Chapter 22, you learned that the issuer of a negotiable instrument is liable to a holder in due course, unless the issuer can assert one of a limited number of real defenses. Against a mere holder, an issuer can assert both personal and real defenses. The life of a negotiable instrument, however, is more complicated than these simple statements indicate. Not everyone who signs a negotiable instrument is an issuer, and not everyone who presents an instrument for payment is a holder in due course or even a holder. This chapter focuses on the liability of these extra players: non-issuers who sign an instrument and non-holders who receive payment. The liability of someone who has signed an instrument is called **signature liability**. The liability of someone who receives payment on an instrument is called **warranty liability**

WARNING: The material in this chapter is complex. Please do not proceed further until you understand the prior paragraph.

THE CONTRACT VERSUS THE INSTRUMENT

People generally do not hand out promissory notes or checks to random strangers. Negotiable instruments are issued to fulfill a contract. The instruments create a *second* contract to pay the debt created by the *first* agreement. When Beverly agrees to buy a house from John, that is Contract No. 1. When she gives him a promissory note in payment, that is Contract No. 2. When Jodie buys lunch with a Visa card, her promise to repay Visa by check at the end of the month is Contract No. 1. The check she mails to Visa is Contract No. 2.

Once an instrument has been accepted in payment for a debt, the debt is *suspended* until the instrument is paid or dishonored. When Beverly buys a house from John, she pays with a promissory note that is not due for five years. Until she defaults on the note, he cannot sue her for payment even if, after a year, he decides he wants all the money right away. When Visa receives Jodie's check, her debt is suspended until the company tries to cash the check. If the check is returned for insufficient funds, the obligation is revived and Visa can pursue Jodie until she pays it for real.

Signature liability
The liability of someone who signs an instrument.

Warranty liability
The liability of someone who receives payment on an instrument.

---

[1] You remember from Chapter 22 that *issuer* means the *drawer* of a check or the *maker* of a note.

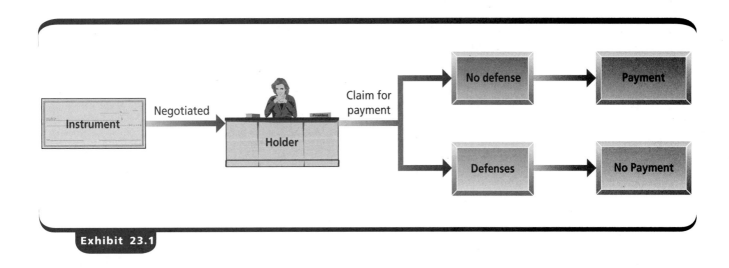

Exhibit 23.1

ENFORCING AN INSTRUMENT

The signature liability rules determine who is liable on an instrument. But *to whom* are they liable? Who has the right to demand payment? Uniform Commercial Code (UCC) Section 3-301 provides this list:

- A holder of the instrument

- Anyone to whom the **shelter rule** applies (that is, any non-holder with the rights of a holder; review the shelter rule discussion in Chapter 22 if this explanation makes no sense to you)

- A holder who has lost the instrument[2]

Recall that a holder is someone in possession of an instrument that has been validly negotiated.[3] Keep in mind, however, that the real and personal defenses discussed in Chapter 22 can be used against a holder. Therefore, in practice, the answer to the question "Who has the right to demand payment on an instrument?" is "A holder against whom no defenses can be used." Exhibit 23.1 illustrates this concept.

PRIMARY VERSUS SECONDARY LIABILITY

A number of different people may be liable on the same negotiable instrument, but some are *primarily* liable, others are only *secondarily* liable. Someone with **primary liability** is unconditionally liable—he must pay unless he has a valid defense. Those with **secondary liability** pay only if the person with primary liability does not. The holder of an instrument must first ask for payment from those who are primarily liable before making demand against anyone who is only secondarily liable.

---

[2] Although technically some non-holders (such as a holder who has lost the instrument) can demand payment, in this chapter we use the term "holder" as shorthand to include anyone entitled to enforce an instrument.

[3] Negotiation is discussed in Chapter 22.

THE PAYMENT PROCESS

The payment process comprises as many as three steps:

Presentment

A holder of an instrument makes a demand for payment.

Dishonor

An obligor refuses to pay an instrument that is due.

- *Presentment.* Presentment means that the holder of the instrument demands payment from someone who is obligated to pay it (such as the maker or drawee).[4] To present, the holder must (1) exhibit the instrument, (2) show identification, and (3) surrender the instrument (if paid in full) or give a receipt (if only partially paid).

- *Dishonor.* The instrument is due, but the maker (of a note) or the drawee (of a draft) refuses to pay.[5]

- *Notice of Dishonor.* The holder of the instrument notifies those who are secondarily liable that the instrument has been dishonored.[6] This notice can be given by any reasonable means, including oral, written, or electronic communication. It must, however, be given within 30 days of the dishonor (except in the case of banks, which must give notice by midnight of the next banking day). The notice must simply identify the instrument and indicate that it has been dishonored. Anyone who has ever bounced a check has received a notice of dishonor—a check stamped "Insufficient Funds."

In the following case, the holder of a check presented it for payment to a bank. But then the holder gave a thumbs-down to the bank's request for identification. Was the bank's requirement a reasonable effort to prevent check fraud or an illegitimate encroachment on privacy? You be the judge.

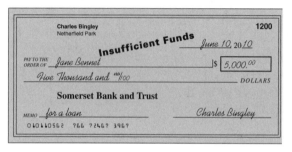

This check has been dishonored.

YOU *be the* JUDGE

MESSING v. BANK OF AMERICA
373 Md. 672, 2003 Md. LEXIS 155
Court of Appeals of Maryland, 2003

Facts: Jeff Messing attempted to cash a check for $976 at a Bank of America branch office in Baltimore. The check was made out to Messing and drawn on the Bank of America. When the teller requested identification, Messing presented his driver's license and a major credit card.

Bank of America policy required a thumbprint signature from anyone wishing to cash a check who did not have an account at the bank. A thumbprint signature is created by applying one's right thumb to an inkless fingerprinting device that leaves no ink stain or residue. The thumbprint is then placed on the face of the check. This process is neither messy nor time consuming.

Because Messing did not have an account at the Bank of America, the teller asked him to give his thumbprint. When Messing declined, the teller refused to cash the check.

You Be the Judge: Was the bank's thumbprint policy permissible under the UCC? Had Messing provided reasonable identification?

Argument for Messing: The UCC provides that anyone wishing to cash a check must provide "reasonable identifica-

---

[4] UCC Section 3-501.
[5] UCC Section 3-502.
[6] UCC Section 3-503.

continued

tion." Messing provided a driver's license and credit card—which are standard methods of identification, acceptable everywhere. The bank is trying to expand the scope of the UCC.

To require a thumbprint is an invasion of privacy that smacks of Big Brother. The bank might, for example, turn the thumbprint over to the police without Messing's permission. Moreover, it is difficult to see how a thumbprint would prevent check fraud since the teller did not have Messing's prints on file. Therefore, she could not tell if he was really Jeff Messing or not.

Argument for the Bank: The official comment to the UCC provides that "Authentication may be printed, stamped or written; it may be by initials or by thumbprint." So the UCC certainly contemplates that thumbprints can be used for identification. Moreover, the process of giving a thumbprint signature is not inconvenient—it requires only one finger and no ink.

The bank's objective is not to invade Messing's privacy, but to prevent check fraud. These losses have been growing at an average rate of 17.5% per year. The American Bankers Association and more than 30 state bankers associations have endorsed thumbprint programs.

Although Messing is correct that a thumbprint cannot be used, in most instances, to confirm the identity of the person cashing the check, it does assist in the identification of the checkholder should the check later prove to be bad. It therefore serves as a powerful deterrent to those who might otherwise attempt to pass a bad check.

SIGNATURE LIABILITY

Virtually everyone who signs an instrument is potentially liable for it, but the liability depends upon the capacity in which it was signed. The maker of a note, for example, has different liability from an indorser. Capacity can sometimes be difficult to determine if the signature is not labeled—"maker," "indorser," "guarantor," "acceptor," etc. (All of these terms will be defined below.) In the absence of a label, courts generally look at the location of the signature. Someone who signs a check or a note in the lower right-hand corner is presumed to be an issuer. If a drawee bank signs on the face of a check, it is an acceptor. Someone who signs on the back of an instrument is considered to be an indorser.

MAKER

As you remember from Chapter 22, the issuer of a note is called the **maker**. **The maker is** *primarily* **liable.**[7] He has promised to pay, and pay he must, unless he has a valid defense.[8] If two makers sign a note, they are both **jointly and severally** liable. The holder can demand full payment from either or partial payment from both. Suppose that Shane offers to buy Marilyn's bookstore in return for a $20,000 promissory note. Because Shane has no assets, Marilyn insists that his supplier, Alexis, also sign the note as co-maker. Once Alexis signs the note, Marilyn has the right to demand full payment from either her or Shane. Of course, if Alexis pays the note, she can demand that Shane reimburse her. If Shane refuses, it is Alexis's problem, not Marilyn's.

DRAWER

A check is the most common form of a draft—it is an order telling a bank to pay money. Throughout this chapter, we will use checks as an example because they are the most familiar

---

[7] UCC Section 3-412.
[8] For example, if the maker goes bankrupt, he does not have to pay the note because bankruptcy is a defense even against a holder in due course.

form of draft, but these same rules apply to all drafts. The drawer is the person who writes the check.

The drawer of a check has *secondary* liability. He is not liable until he has received notice that the bank has dishonored the check. [9] Although the bank pays the check with the drawer's funds, the drawer is secondarily liable in the sense that he does not have to write a new check or give cash to the holder unless the bank dishonors the original check. Suppose that Shane writes a $10,000 check to pay Casey for new inventory. Casey is nervous and, before he can get to the bank to deposit the check, he calls Shane seven times to ask whether the check is good. He even asks Shane for payment in cash instead of by check. Shane finally snarls at Casey, "Just go cash the check and get off my back, will you?" At this point, Casey has no recourse against Shane because Shane is only secondarily liable.

Sadly, however, Casey's fears are realized. When he presents the check to the bank teller, she informs him that Shane's account is overdrawn. Casey snatches the check off the counter and hurries over to Shane's shop. It makes no difference that Casey forgot to let the teller stamp "Insufficient Funds" on the check—notice of dishonor can be made orally. Once the bank has refused to pay, the check has been dishonored. Casey has informed Shane, who must now pay the $10,000.

Anne Elliot is only secondarily liable, but no one is primarily liable until the bank accepts the check.

DRAWEE

Drawee

The bank on which a check is drawn.

The **drawee** is the bank on which a check is drawn. Since the draw*er* of a check is only secondarily liable, logically you might expect the drawee bank to be primarily liable. That is not the case, however. When a drawer signs a check, the instrument enters a kind of limbo. **The bank is not liable to the holder and owes no damages to the holder for refusing to pay the check.** [10] The bank may be liable to the *drawer* for violating their checking account agreement, but this contract does not extend to the holder of the check.

When a holder presents a check, the bank can do one of the following:

• Pay the check. In this case, the holder has no complaints.

• Dishonor the check. In this case, the holder must pursue remedies against the drawer.

What if Casey is afraid to take a check from Shane? After all, even if Shane has enough money in his account at the moment, it may be gone by the time Casey deposits the check and his bank presents it for payment. To protect himself, Casey can insist that Shane give him a certified check. A **certified** or **accepted** check is one that the drawee bank has signed. [11] This signature is a promise that the bank will pay the check out of its own funds. The bank then becomes *primarily* liable, and Casey is sure to be paid as long as the bank stays solvent. To protect itself once it certifies the check, Shane's bank will immediately remove that money from his account.

In the following case, the real estate lawyer relied on written and oral promises, but not on a certified check. As the court pointed out, he was "bamboozled."

[9] UCC Section 3-414.
[10] UCC Section 3-408.
[11] UCC Section 3-409.

HARRINGTON V. MACNAB

163 F.Supp.2d 583; 2001 U.S. Dist. LEXIS 15314
UNITED STATES DISTRICT COURT FOR THE DISTRICT OF MARYLAND, 2001

CASE SUMMARY

Facts: The MacNabs purchased a piece of property from Richard Harrington's client. Although Harrington was an experienced attorney, he made a bad mistake. The MacNabs came to the closing with a personal check drawn on their Merrill Lynch cash management account for $150,128.70. The check had not been certified. Harrington should have refused to close, but instead called Merrill Lynch and spoke with a Ms. Ruark. She told him there were sufficient funds in the MacNabs' account to cover the check and that she would put a hold on the account in the amount of the check. When asked to confirm this promise in writing, Ruark sent the following fax to Harrington: "This letter is to verify that the funds are available in the Merrill Lynch account. There is a pend on the funds for the check that was given you."

In fact, the MacNabs' account did not contain sufficient *cleared* funds to cover the check, which bounced. The MacNabs repeatedly promised to make the check good, but never did. Harrington paid his clients the amount owing and then sued the MacNabs. Although he eventually obtained a judgment against them, they did not pay him the full amount. He also sought recovery from Merrill Lynch.

Issue: *Is Merrill Lynch liable to Harrington as the drawee of the check?*

Decision: Merrill Lynch is not liable. Its motion for summary judgment is granted.

Reasoning: Under the UCC, a payee can recover from a drawee bank on a bad check only if:

1. The payee has a special contract with the drawee bank. In this case, there was no special relationship between Merrill Lynch and Harrington's clients. Simply inquiring about the funds in the payor's account does not create a special contract. Or,

2. The drawee bank has accepted the check. Acceptance does not occur until the drawee bank signs the check. To permit the oral certification of the check in this case would be a clear violation of the policies of the UCC and hundreds of years of commercial law.

INDORSER

An **indorser** is anyone, other than an issuer or acceptor, who signs an instrument. Shane gives Hannah a check to pay her for installing new shelves in his bookstore. On the back of Shane's check, Hannah writes, "Pay to Christian," signs her name, and then gives the check to Christian in payment for back rent. Underneath Hannah's name, Christian signs his own name and gives the check to Trustie Car Lot as a deposit on his new Prius. Hannah and Christian are both indorsers. This is the chain of ownership:

Indorser
Anyone, other than an issuer or acceptor, who signs an instrument.

Shane (issuer) → Hannah (indorser) → Christian (indorser) → Trustie (holder)

Indorsers are *secondarily* liable; they must pay if the issuer or drawee does not. But indorsers are liable only to those who come *after* them in the chain of ownership, not to those who held the instrument beforehand.[12] If Shane refuses to pay Trustie, the auto dealership can demand payment from Christian or Hannah. If Christian pays Trustie, Christian can then demand payment from Hannah. If, however, Hannah pays Trustie, she has no right to go after Christian because he is not liable to a previous indorser.

There are some exceptions to this rule. **Indorsers are not liable if:**

1. they write the words "without recourse" next to their signature on the instrument,

2. a bank certifies the check, ~makes the bank primary and everyone else is off the hook~

3. the check is presented for payment more than 30 days after the indorsement, or

4. the check is dishonored and the indorser is not notified within 30 days.[13]

Christian has doubts about the creditworthiness of Hannah and Shane, so he writes the words "without recourse" when he indorses the check to Trustie. This sounds like a good idea and perhaps every indorser should try it. However, if the manager of Trustie Car Lot is familiar with the UCC, he will not accept an instrument that has been indorsed without recourse because he wants to make sure that Christian is also liable, not just Shane and Hannah. After all, Christian is the person he knows.

ACCOMMODATION PARTY

An **accommodation party** is someone—other than an issuer, acceptor, or indorser—who adds her signature to an instrument for the purpose of being liable on it.[14] The accommodation party typically receives no direct benefit from the instrument but is acting for the benefit of the **accommodated party**. Shane wants to buy a truck from the Trustie Car Lot. Trustie, however, will not accept a promissory note from Shane unless his father, Walter, also signs it. Shane has no assets, but Walter is wealthy. When Walter signs, he becomes an accommodation party to Shane, who is the accommodated party. The accommodation party can sign for an issuer, acceptor, or indorser. Anyone who signs an instrument is deemed to be an accommodation party unless it is clear that he is an issuer, acceptor, or indorser.

An accommodation party has the same liability to the holder as the person for whom he signed. The holder can make a claim directly against the accommodation party without first demanding payment from the accommodated party. Walter is liable to Trustie, whether or not Trustie first demands payment from Shane. If forced to pay Trustie, Walter can try to recover from Shane.

An accommodation party sounds like what non-lawyers would call a "guarantor," but under the UCC, these terms sometimes have a different meaning. Someone who writes "I guarantee this *instrument*" is an accommodation party. But someone who writes "I guarantee *collection*" is not liable until the accommodated party fails to pay. If Walter had written "to guarantee collection" before signing his name, Trustie could not have collected from him until Shane refused to pay the note.

In an earlier example, Shane's supplier, Alexis, had signed a note as co-maker. What is the difference between a co-maker and an accommodation party? The co-maker is liable both to the holder and to the other co-maker. The accommodation party is liable only to the holder, not to the other maker. If Shane pays the note on which Alexis is co-maker, then Alexis is liable

---

[13] UCC Section 3-415.
[14] UCC Section 3-419.

In Re Couchot

169 B.R. 40, 1994 Bankr. LEXIS 899
United States Bankruptcy Court, Southern District of Ohio, 1994

CASE SUMMARY

Facts: Kathy J. Couchot and her mother-in-law, Jean Couchot, borrowed $6,317.48 from Star Bank to pay the funeral expenses of Kathy's husband. Jean executed a note to the bank, and Kathy signed as an accommodation party. To disburse the proceeds of the loan, Star Bank issued a check payable to "Kathy *and* Jean Couchot." Somehow this check was altered to read "Kathy *or* Jean Couchot." Jean cashed the check and used the loan proceeds to pay her son's funeral expenses and some of Kathy's back taxes and insurance premiums. Jean did not repay the loan to the bank; Kathy made six payments before defaulting.

Issues: *Is an accommodation party liable for the full amount of a note when she received only a small portion of the proceeds? Is an accommodation party liable even though the check was altered?*

Decision: Kathy Couchot is liable for the full amount of the note. It makes no difference that the check was altered.

Reasoning: Accommodation parties often say "I'm not liable because I did not receive any consideration for the loan." This is a losing argument. The accommodation party is liable whether or not she obtained *any* of the proceeds. Her consideration is whatever the original debtor received. Although Kathy Couchot got only a small part of the proceeds of the loan, she is liable for the full amount and would be even if she had received nothing. Her consideration is whatever her mother-in-law obtained.

The fact that the check was altered makes no difference either. The proceeds of the check were used exactly as Kathy and Jean had intended. There was no fraud here, and Kathy is liable.

to him for half the payment. But if Shane pays the note on which Walter is the accommodation party, Walter has no liability to Shane.

In the following case, an accommodation party argued that she was not liable because she did not receive the proceeds from the loan. Was she correct in her interpretation of the UCC?

AGENT

Many business transactions are conducted by agents acting on behalf of a principal. A corporation, for example, cannot sign an instrument itself; all of its transactions must be conducted by company employees. When signing for a principal, the agent must be careful to ensure that only the principal is liable.

To avoid personal liability when signing an instrument, an agent must (1) indicate that she is signing as an agent and (2) give the name of the principal.[15] An agent who fails to follow these two simple steps will be *personally* liable on the instrument to any holder in due course who did not know that the agent was acting for someone else. The agent will not be liable to holders who are not in due course if she can prove that the original parties did not intend for her to be liable. An agent who signs her name, "Harley Calhoun, as agent for Slippery Corp."

---

[15] UCC Section 3-402.

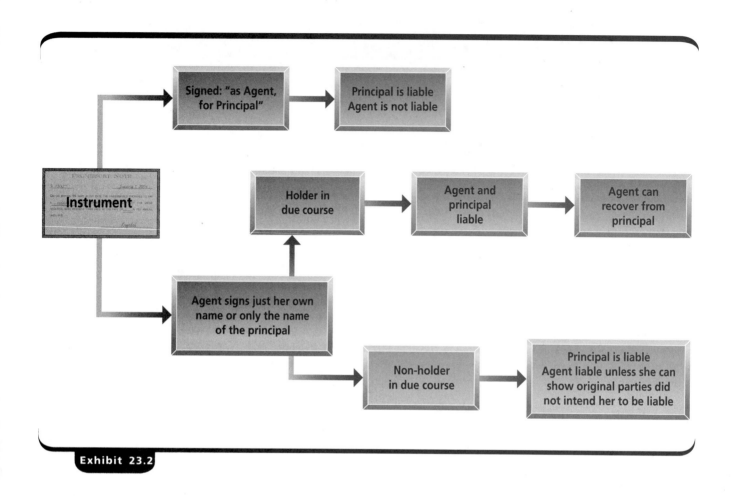

Exhibit 23.2

is safe; she is not liable on the instrument. But if Harley simply signs the note, "Harley Calhoun, Agent," then she will be personally liable to Ralph, a holder in due course, unless she can prove that Ralph knew she was acting for someone else when he acquired the note. (That is a great deal of trouble easily avoided by simply including the name of the principal.) Even if Ralph is not a holder in due course, Harley will be liable unless she can prove that the original parties never intended her to be.

The principal is liable if the agent signs correctly, the agent signs just her own name, or the agent signs only the name of the principal. Thus, if Harley signs the note, "Harley Calhoun" or "Slippery Corp.," the corporation is liable to Ralph (and so is Harley). He can sue either. If Ralph recovers from Harley, she can try to recover from Slippery; but if the company goes out of business, Harley will find herself in a sticky situation. Exhibit 23.2 illustrates the liability of agents and principals.

Checks are an exception to this general rule on agent liability. If an agent is authorized to sign a check on the principal's bank account, the agent is not personally liable even if she forgets to indicate that she is simply an agent. Because the check is probably printed with the principal's name anyway, no one is likely to think that the check is coming out of the agent's personal funds.

EXAM *Strategy*

Question: Harold wants to buy a power catamaran for the low, low price of $175,000. He offers to give the dealer a promissory note, but the dealer will not make the sale unless Harold's significant other, Maude, also signs the note. She writes her name across the top front. When and to whom is Maude liable?

Strategy: Whenever a case involves the liability of someone who has signed an instrument, you must start by reviewing the rules on signature liability. Ask first what kind of signer Maude is. Then determine the liability for someone who signs in that capacity.

Result: If Maude had signed the note in the lower right-hand corner, she would be a co-maker. An indorser signs on the back. An acceptor is a drawee bank. Maude is none of these things. But we know that unless a signer is clearly a co-maker, acceptor, or indorser, she is deemed to be an accommodation party. So that is what Maude is. The dealer can seek payment from her without first demanding payment from Harold but she is not liable to Harold.

WARRANTY LIABILITY

Warranty liability rules apply when someone receives payment on an instrument that is invalid because it has been forged, altered, or stolen.

BASIC RULES OF WARRANTY LIABILITY

1. **The culprit is always liable.** If a forger signs someone else's name to an instrument, that signature counts as the forger's, not as that of the person whose name she signed. The forger is liable for the value of the instrument plus any other expenses or lost interest that subsequent parties may experience because of the forgery. If Hope signs David's name on one of his checks, Hope is liable, but not David. Although this is a sensible rule, the problem is that forgers are difficult to catch and, even when found, often do not have the money to pay what they owe.

2. **The drawee bank is liable if it pays a check on which the *drawer's* name is forged. The bank can recover from the payee only if the payee had reason to suspect the forgery.**[16] If a bank cashes David's forged check, it must reimburse him whether or not it ever recovers from Hope. Suppose that Hope forged the check to pay for a new tattoo. If Gus, the owner of the tattoo parlor, deposits the check and the bank pays it, the bank cannot recover from Gus unless he had reason to suspect the forgery. Perhaps Gus did suspect because the mystery customer asked to have "Hope" tattooed on her biceps, not "David." She did not look much like a "David" either.

   Why hold the bank liable for something that is not its fault? In theory, the bank has David's signature on file and can determine that Hope's version does not match. As the saying goes, the drawee must know the drawer's signature as a mother knows her own child. Such a rule may have been appropriate in an era when people went to their neighborhood bank to cash checks and a teller would indeed recognize dear Miss Plotkin's signature. In this day and age, most checks—especially those for small amounts—are handled by machine, so perhaps this rule makes less sense. Nonetheless, the rule stands, for good reason or bad. Banks have two choices: (1) examine the signature on each presented check or (2) purchase forgery insurance.

[16] UCC Section 3-418.

3. **In any other case of wrongdoing, a person who first acquires an instrument from a culprit is ultimately liable to anyone else who pays value for it.** These rules are based on the provisions in Article 3 of the UCC that establish transfer and presentment warranties.

TRANSFER WARRANTIES

When someone transfers an instrument, she warrants that:

- She is a holder of the instrument

- All signatures are authentic and authorized

- The instrument has not been altered

- No defense can be asserted against her, and

- As far as she knows the issuer is solvent.[17]

When someone transfers an instrument, she promises that it is valid. The culprit—the person who created the defective instrument in the first place—is always liable, but if he does not pay what he owes, the person who took it from him is liable in his place. She may not be that much at fault, but she is more at fault than any of the other innocent people who paid good value for the instrument.

Suppose that Annie writes a check for $100 to pay for a fancy dinner at Barbara's Bistro. Cecelia steals the check from Barbara's cash register, indorses Barbara's name, and uses the check to buy a leather jacket from Deirdre. In her turn, Deirdre takes the check home and indorses it over to her condominium association to pay her monthly service fee. Barbara notices the check is gone and asks Annie to stop payment on it. Once payment is stopped, the condominium association cannot cash the check. Who is liable to whom? The chain of ownership looks like this:

| Annie | Barbara | Cecelia (the culprit) | Deirdre | Condominium Association |

Cecelia is the culprit and, of course, she is liable. Unfortunately, she is currently studying at the University of the Azores and refuses to return to the United States. The condominium association makes a claim against Deirdre. When she transferred the check, she warranted that all the signatures were authentic and authorized, but that was not true because Barbara's signature was forged. (Deirdre should have asked Cecelia for identification.) Deirdre cannot make a claim against Annie or Barbara because neither of them violated their transfer warranties—all the signatures at that point were authentic and authorized.

There are a few additional wrinkles to the transfer warranty rules:

- When someone violates the transfer warranties, she is liable for the value of the instrument, plus expenses and interest. If the condominium association is charged a fee by the bank for the returned check, Deirdre must pay it.

---

[17] UCC Section 3-416.

- Transfer warranties flow to all subsequent holders in good faith who have indorsed the instrument. If the condominium association indorses the check over to its maintenance company, Deirdre is liable to the condo association when the maintenance company makes a claim against it.

- If the instrument is *bearer* paper, the transfer warranties extend only to the first transferee. If Annie had made her check out to cash, it would have been bearer paper, and her transfer warranties would have extended only to Barbara. If Barbara transfers the check to Hannah, Barbara's transfer warranties extend to Hannah; Annie's do not.

- If a warranty claim is not made within 30 days of discovering the breach, damages are reduced by the amount of harm that the delay caused. Suppose that the condominium association waits two months to tell Deirdre the check is invalid. Cecelia has been into Deirdre's store several times to try on matching leather pants. By the time Deirdre finds out the check is bad, Cecelia has again left town. Deirdre may not be liable on the check at all because the delay has prevented her from making a claim against Cecelia.

- Transfer warranties apply only if the instrument has been transferred for consideration. Suppose Deirdre gives the check to an employee, Emily, as a birthday present. When the check turns out to be worthless, Emily has no claim against Deirdre.

COMPARISON OF SIGNATURE LIABILITY AND TRANSFER WARRANTIES

Transfer warranties fill in holes left by the signature liability rules:

- A forged signature is invalid and therefore creates no signature liability on the part of the person whose name was signed. However, someone who receives a forged instrument may recover under transfer warranty rules, which provide that anyone who transfers a forged instrument is liable for it.

- The signature liability rules do not apply to the transfer of bearer paper. Bearer paper can be negotiated simply by delivery; no indorsement is required. No signature means no signature liability (for anyone other than the issuer—who is the only person actually signing the instrument). Transfer warranties apply to each transfer of bearer paper (although the transferor of bearer paper is liable only to the person to whom he gives the instrument, not to any transferees further down the line).

- Under the signature liability rules, the holder of an instrument cannot make a claim until the indorser or drawer has been notified that the instrument was presented and dishonored.[18] Under the transfer warranty rules, the holder need not wait for presentment or dishonor before making a claim against the transferor.

PRESENTMENT WARRANTIES

Transfer warranties impose liability on anyone who sells a negotiable instrument, such as Deirdre. **Presentment warranties** apply to someone who demands payment for an instrument from the maker, drawee, or anyone else liable on it. Thus, if the condominium association cashes Annie's check, it is subject to presentment warranties because it is demanding payment from her bank, the drawee. In a sense, transfer warranties apply to all transfers *away* from the issuer; presentment warranties apply when the instrument *returns* to the maker or drawee for payment. As a general rule, payment on an instrument is final, and the payer has no right to a refund, unless the presentment warranties are violated.

---

[18] UCC Section 3-503(a).

Anyone who presents a *check* for payment warrants that:

- She is a holder

- The check has not been altered, and

- She has no reason to believe the drawer's signature is forged.[19]

If any of these promises is untrue, the bank has a right to demand a refund from the presenter. Suppose that Adam writes a $500 check to pay Bruce for repairing his motorcycle. Bruce changes the amount of the check to $1,500 and indorses it over to Chip as payment for an oil bill. When Chip deposits the check, the bank credits his account for $1,500 and deducts the same amount from Adam's account. When Adam discovers the alteration, the bank is forced (for reasons discussed in Chapter 24) to credit his account for $1,000. Chip violated his *presentment* warranties when he deposited an altered check (even though he did not *know* it was altered). Although Chip was not at fault, he must still reimburse the bank for $1,000. But Chip is not without recourse—Bruce violated his *transfer* warranties to Chip (by transferring an altered check). Bruce must repay the $1,000. Chip loses out only if he cannot make Bruce pay. In the following case, which bank is liable for a check gone bad?

WACHOVIA BANK V. FOSTER BANCSHARES

2005 U.S. DIST. LEXIS 16356
UNITED STATES DISTRICT COURT FOR THE NORTHERN DISTRICT OF ILLINOIS, 2005

CASE SUMMARY

Facts: MediaEdge wrote a check on its account at Wachovia for $133,026 payable to CMP Media. Before CMP received the check, someone changed the payee to Sunjin Choi Choi and then deposited the altered check into Choi's account at Foster Bancshares. Foster presented the check to Wachovia for payment. Wachovia paid Foster from MediaEdge's account. The diagram on the right traces the route of the check.

When MediaEdge learned that CMP had never received the check, it sued Wachovia for reimbursement. Wachovia, in turn, filed suit against Foster.

Issue: *Who is liable for paying the stolen check? Wachovia or Foster?*

Decision: Foster is liable for the bad check.

Reasoning: Anyone who presents a check for payment warrants that it has not been altered. But the check that Foster presented to Wachovia *had* been altered. The payee had been changed from CMP Media to Choi.

Someone will be liable for the missing money. The UCC allocates that loss to Foster because it violated its presentment warranties.

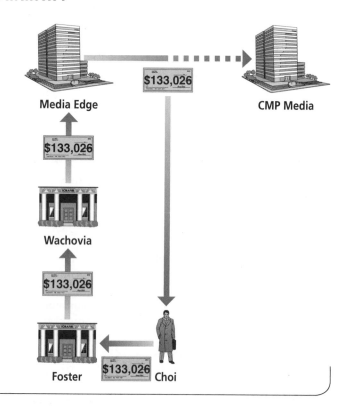

The presentment warranty rules for a promissory note are different from those for a check. **Anyone who presents a *promissory note* for payment makes only one warranty—that he is a holder of the instrument.** Someone presenting a note does not need to warrant that the note is unaltered or the maker's signature is authentic because a note is presented for payment to the issuer himself. The issuer presumably remembers the amount of the note and whether he signed it. Suppose Adam gives a promissory note to Bruce to pay for a new motorcycle. If Bruce increases the note from $5,000 to $10,000 before he presents it for payment in six months' time, Adam will almost certainly realize the note has been changed and refuse to pay it.

The presenter of a note warrants that he is a holder. A forged signature prevents subsequent owners from being a holder, so anyone who presents a note with a forged signature is violating the presentment warranties. Suppose that Bruce is totally honest and does not alter the note, but Chip steals it and forges Bruce's indorsement before passing the note on to Donald, who presents it to Adam for payment. Donald has violated his *presentment* warranties because he is not a holder. Adam can refuse to pay him. For his part, Donald can claim repayment from Chip who violated his *transfer* warranties by passing on a note with a forged signature.

EXAM *Strategy*

Question: Hillary owed Evan $500. She gave Evan's roommate John a check made out to Evan. John indorsed the check to Mike and signed Evan's name. Mike deposited the check in his account at the Amstel Bank. Amstel removed $500 from Hillary's account. Are Evan and Mike liable on this check?

Strategy: Whenever an instrument goes astray, begin by asking which warranties have been violated and by whom.

Result: Transfer warranties apply to all transfers *away* from the issuer; presentment warranties apply when the instrument *returns* to the maker or drawee for payment. John violated transfer warranties because Evan's signature is neither authentic nor authorized. When Mike deposited the check, he violated presentment warranties because he is not a holder. Remember from Chapter 22 that a holder is anyone in possession of an instrument if it is payable to or indorsed to him. This check was not properly indorsed to Mike because Evan has not signed it. In the next section, we will see that Amstel is also liable.

OTHER LIABILITY RULES

This section contains other UCC rules that establish liability for wrong doing on instruments.

CONVERSION LIABILITY

Conversion means that (1) someone has stolen an instrument or (2) a bank has paid a check that has a forged indorsement.[20] The rightful owner of the instrument can recover from either the thief or the bank.

For example, Glenn Altman was a lawyer representing Barbara Kirchoff. He settled her case for $12,000, but when he received the check, he forged her indorsement and deposited

...he forged her indorsement and deposited the check in his own account without telling her.

Conversion
(1) Someone has stolen an instrument or
(2) A bank has paid a check that has a forged indorsement.

[20] UCC Section 3-420.

the check in his own account without telling her. He gave her the money four months later, but by then she had discovered his dishonesty. What claims do the various parties have?

Kirchoff has a claim against the bank because it paid a check with a forged indorsement. If the bank pays Kirchoff, then it can recover from Altman because he violated his presentment warranties. Note, however, that Kirchoff could not sue Altman for violating presentment warranties because he had not presented the check to her for payment. Nor could she sue him for violating transfer warranties because he had not transferred the check *to* her. To the contrary, he had transferred the check *away* from her.

Kirchoff also has a claim against Altman for conversion because he stole the check from her.[21] What about the issuer of the check—can it also sue Altman for conversion? No, an action for conversion cannot be brought by an issuer because the check technically belongs to the payee (Kirchoff). The issuer can bring a claim only against the bank that pays the forged check.

IMPOSTOR RULE

If someone issues an instrument to an impostor, then any indorsement in the name of the payee is valid so long as the person (a bank, say) who pays the instrument does not know of the fraud.[22] A teenager knocks on your door one afternoon. He tells you he is selling magazine subscriptions to pay for a school trip to Washington, D.C. After signing up for *Career* and *Popular Accounting*, you make out a check to "Family Magazine Subscriptions." Unfortunately, the boy does not represent Family Magazine at all. He does cash the check, however, by forging an indorsement for the magazine company. Is the bank liable for cashing the fraudulent check?

No. The teenager was an impostor—he said he represented the magazine company, but he did not. If anyone indorses the check in the name of the payee (Family Magazine Subscriptions), you must pay the check and the bank is not liable. Does this rule seem harsh? Maybe, but you were in the best position to determine if the teenager really worked for the magazine company. You were more at fault than the bank, and you must pay. Of course, the teenager would be liable to you, if you could ever find him.

FICTITIOUS PAYEE RULE

If someone issues an instrument to a person who does not exist, then any indorsement in the name of the payee is valid as long as the person (a bank, say) who pays the instrument does not know of the fraud.[23] The *impostor* rule applies if you give a check with a real name to the wrong person. The *fictitious payee* rule applies if you write a check to someone who does not exist. This type of fraud can be very difficult to prevent. Even a large law firm was stung. Dennis Masellis, the manager of payroll for Baker & McKenzie's New York office, stole more than $7 million from the firm by creating fictitious employees and then depositing their salaries in his own account.

EMPLOYEE INDORSEMENT RULE

If an employee with responsibility for issuing instruments forges a check or other instrument, then any indorsement in the name of the payee, or a similar name, is valid so long as the person

---

[21] A payee (i.e., Kirchoff) cannot bring a claim for conversion unless she actually *receives* the check. In this case, Altman was Kirchoff's agent and he received the check for her so she could bring a conversion action against him.

[22] UCC Section 3-404(a).

[23] UCC Section 3-404(b).

(a bank, say) who pays the instrument does not know of the fraud.[24] A dishonest employee, especially one with the authority to issue checks, has the opportunity to steal a great deal of money. The employer cannot shift blame (and liability) onto the bank that unknowingly cashes the forged checks because the employer was more to blame—it not only hired the thief, it failed to supervise him carefully.

Dennis M. Hartotunian had a major gambling problem—he owed nearly $10 million. Unfortunately, he was also the controller and accountant for the Aesar Group, a precious metals company. Over the course of three years, he wrote himself 154 checks worth $9.24 million. Any check for more than $500 required the signature of Aesar's general manager, but Hartotunian forged it. After an internal audit revealed that millions were missing, company officers asked to talk with Hartotunian. When he heard they were coming, he walked out and never came back.

It is always a bad sign when the company controller disappears. If an employee is generally authorized to prepare or sign checks, then the bank is not liable on checks that the employee forges. Hartotunian was clearly covered by this rule because he was the company controller. If he had been a mailroom employee without authority to sign checks, the bank would have been liable. The employee indorsement rule applies to both single and double forgeries. In a *single forgery*, the employee writes a check to himself, signs his employer's name, and cashes the check. In a *double forgery*, the employee writes a check to someone else, forges his employer's name, and also forges the name of the payee.

NEGLIGENCE

Regardless of the impostor rule, the fictitious payee rule, and the employee indorsement rule (the "three rules"), **anyone who behaves negligently in creating or paying an unauthorized instrument is liable to an innocent third party**. If two people are negligent, they share the loss according to their negligence. Here are two examples:

- Anyone who is careless in paying an unauthorized instrument is liable, despite the three rules.[25] Suppose that the boy selling bogus magazine subscriptions goes into the bank and indorses the check: "Family Magazine Subscriptions, by Butch McGraw." The teller peers over her counter and sees a 13-year-old boy standing there with torn jeans and a baseball cap on backwards. She may be negligent if she cashes the check without asking for further identification.

- **Anyone who is careless in allowing a forged or altered instrument to be created is also liable, whether or not he has violated one of the three rules.** The classic case establishing this rule was *Young v. Grote*, an 1827 English case. A businessman who was going abroad signed five checks and gave them to his wife with instructions that they were to be used for business expenses. A clerk in the company helpfully showed the missus how to fill out the checks, carefully instructing her to leave a blank space in front of the number. The clerk used this space to add a "3" in front of a "50" and then cashed the £350 check. The court held that the drawee bank was not liable because, "If Young, instead of leaving the check with a female, had left it with a man of business, he would have guarded against fraud in the mode of filling it up."[26] Today, we hiss at the sexist sentiment, but it illustrates the point. Anyone who

---

[24] UCC Section 3-405.

[25] UCC Sections 3-404(d), 3-405(b).

[26] *Young v. Grote*, 4 Bing. 253 (Common Pleas), quoted in Douglas J. Whaley, *Problems and Materials on Payment Law* (Boston: Little, Brown & Co., 1995), at 253.

carelessly creates a situation that facilitates the forgery or alteration of an instrument cannot recover against a party who pays the instrument in good faith.

In the following case, the Professional Golf Association had a bad lie. Who must take penalty strokes—the PGA or its bank?

YOU *be the* JUDGE

GULF STATES SECTION, PGA, INC. V. WHITNEY NATIONAL BANK OF NEW ORLEANS

689 SO.2d 638, 1997 La. App. LEXIS 167 Court of Appeal of Louisiana, Fourth Circuit, 1997

Facts: Robert Brown was the executive director of the Gulf States Section of the Professional Golf Association (PGA). He was responsible for paying bills and handling the bank account. Brown used Quicken, a software program, to write checks. These checks were kept in a box beneath the printer stand in his office.

Adrenetti Collins was a secretary who worked in the PGA office with Brown. During a four-month period, she forged 18 PGA checks totaling $22,699.81. To avoid detection, she intercepted two of the bank statements sent by Whitney National Bank and replaced them with forged statements that left out the numbers of the checks she had stolen. The usual Whitney statement was printed on vanilla-colored paper measuring a non-standard 6¾ × 11 inches. The forged statements were on standard 8½ × 11 inch white paper. They were not dated but they did contain the Whitney logo. Brown received two forged statements and then no statements at all for two months. Shortly thereafter, Collins asked for a leave of absence.

Whitney's policy was to verify signatures on checks equal to or greater than $5,000. One of the forged checks was in the amount of $5,000, but Whitney did not verify Brown's signature before paying it. Brown's signature was a semilegible letter or two and a long loop. The forged signature on the check looked very similar to the real one.

You Be the Judge: Is Whitney liable to the PGA for the forged checks it paid?

Argument for the PGA: The general rule is that a person is not liable on an instrument unless his signature appears on it. Brown's signature did not appear on these checks, so only the bank is liable on them.

As for the PGA's alleged negligence, Brown traveled extensively and was not available to supervise the office staff carefully. If this is negligence, then half the companies in America are negligent, too. Do not forget that Brown stored the checks in his private office. Whitney admits that it did not verify the signatures on any of the checks, even the one for $5,000. This is in direct violation of its own policies. If Whitney had simply followed its policies, the forgeries would have been detected months earlier.

Argument for Whitney: Generally, a bank is liable for forged checks unless it can show that (1) the customer was negligent; (2) the negligence substantially contributed to the forgery; and (3) the bank paid the forged instruments in accordance with reasonable commercial banking industry standards.

The PGA was clearly negligent in this case. The checks should have been locked up, not sitting under the printer in an open box. Brown should have realized that checks were missing, and he should have noticed that the bank statements were forged. Without his negligence, Collins could never have committed the forgeries. In any event, she would have been caught much earlier—when the first bank statement was received, not four months later.

As for the bank's failure to verify Brown's signature, the forgery was close enough to his sloppy writing that no one could have realized the signature was a fake.

EXAM *Strategy*

Question: Jonathan is the head of payroll at Yearbook. He issues checks to his sister, Elizabeth, who happens *not* to work for Yearbook. She does, however, deposit the checks into her bank account. A teller at the bank knows that Elizabeth does not work for Yearbook but he deposits the checks for her without raising any questions. Is the bank liable for the fraudulent checks?

Strategy: Whenever fraudulent checks are signed by an authorized employee, you will naturally think first of the Employee Indorsement Rule. However, it is important to remember that the bank's negligence overrides the Employee Indorsement Rule.

Result: If the bank were not negligent, then under the Employee Indorsement Rule, it would not be liable because Jonathan was authorized to sign checks. However, because the bank was negligent in paying the checks, it must share the loss with Yearbook. The amount each would have to pay depends upon their share of the blame.

CRIMES

It is beyond the scope of this chapter to catalog all of the crimes that can be committed with negotiable instruments, but students should be aware of these.

Bouncing a Check

It is illegal to write a check on an account that has insufficient funds. Generally, no serious penalties are imposed if sufficient funds are immediately deposited. (This is a good thing, considering that more than 450 *million* checks bounce each year.) However, both banks and merchants impose substantial fees for their trouble. People who make a career of bouncing checks may find they have plenty of time to bone up on UCC Article 3 in the prison library.

Check Kiting

It is illegal to kite checks. E. F. Hutton was a thriving brokerage firm until ambitious branch managers began boosting profits with a check-kiting scheme. A Hutton manager would overdraw an account in Bank A and deposit that check in Bank B. Bank B would begin paying interest on the funds before the check had cleared. The manager would then write a check on Bank B to cover the deficit in Bank A, in the process overdrawing Bank B. One Hutton account in a Virginia bank was overdrawn by an average of $9 million a day. Interest earned on these overdrafts accounted for as much as 70 percent of the Washington office's gross income. In 20 months, Hutton made at least $8 million, but the resulting scandal drove the firm out of business.

Forgery

It is illegal to forge an instrument or to pass on (**utter**) an instrument that one knows to be forged. In the United States each year, more than 500 million checks are forged, with a total value of more than $20 billion.

Utter

To pass on an instrument that one knows to be forged.

DISCHARGE

DISCHARGE OF THE OBLIGOR

Discharge

Liability on an instrument terminates.

Discharge means that liability on an instrument terminates. Article 3 establishes five different ways to discharge an instrument:[27]

- *By Payment.* Payment discharges an instrument, as long as the payment is *from* someone obliged to pay and goes *to* the holder. If you mail a check to the wrong bank when paying off a promissory note, you obviously have not discharged the note. Or if you ask an employee to take money to the bank to pay off the note, but she goes to Hawaii instead, no discharge has occurred. Similarly, payment does not discharge an instrument if the payor knows that the instrument is stolen. Suppose you have given a promissory note to Lou. He complains to you that his employee Stephanie stole it. If you pay Stephanie when she presents the note, you have not discharged it.

- *By Agreement.* The parties to the instrument can agree to a discharge, even if the instrument is not paid. The discharge, however, must be in writing; it cannot be oral. You give a promissory note to your company to pay for company stock. The company president tells you that the company will forgive the loan and discharge the note as a reward for your fabulous performance. A few months later the president is ousted. Your agreement was not in writing and you are liable on the note. (You may have a contract claim against the company, but the note itself is still valid.)

- *By Cancellation.* Cancellation means the intentional, voluntary surrender, destruction, or disfigurement of an instrument. If Ted accidentally forgets to take a check out of his pocket before throwing his shirt in the wash, he has not canceled the check (even though it was destroyed) because the destruction was unintentional. If, while arguing with his business partner, he takes her promissory note and tears it into a thousand pieces while screaming, "This is what I think of you and your business skills," he has canceled the note. He could achieve the same result less dramatically by simply writing "canceled" on it or by giving it back to her.

- *By Certification.* When a bank certifies or accepts a check, the drawer and all indorsers of the check are discharged, and only the bank is liable.

- *By Alteration.* An instrument is discharged if its terms are intentionally changed. Laura gives Todd a promissory note. Thinking he is being very clever, Todd changes the amount of her note from $200 to $2,000. He has actually done Laura a favor because he has discharged the note.

    Keep in mind, however, that no discharge is effective against a holder in due course who acquires the instrument without knowledge of the discharge. If Todd sells Laura's note to Max, who does not know of the discharge, Max can enforce the instrument against Laura, but only for the original amount of $200.

DISCHARGE OF AN INDORSER OR ACCOMMODATION PARTY

Article 3 provides that virtually any change in an instrument that harms an indorser or accommodation party also discharges them unless they consent to the change. These fatal changes include an extension of the due date on the instrument, a material modification of the

---

[27] UCC Article 3, Part 6.

instrument, or any impairment of the collateral that secures the instrument. When Chelsea borrows money from Jordan, she signs a promissory note due on December 24. Helena guarantees the note. Chelsea cannot pay, but Jordan does not have the stomach for declaring Chelsea in default on Christmas Eve. He generously extends the due date for another week. Helena is no longer liable, even secondarily, because Jordan has granted an extension of the due date.

CHAPTER CONCLUSION

It is never wise to play an important game without understanding the rules. Virtually everyone uses negotiable instruments regularly to pay bills or borrow money. Although the rules sometimes seem complex, it is important to know them well.

EXAM REVIEW

1. **PRIMARY V. SECONDARY LIABILITY** Someone who is primarily liable on a negotiable instrument must pay unless he has a valid defense. Those with secondary liability only pay if the person with primary liability does not. (p. 553)

2. **PAYMENT PROCESS** The payment process for a negotiable instrument comprises as many as three steps:
   - *Presentment.* The holder makes a demand for payment to the issuer.
   - *Dishonor.* The instrument is due, but the issuer does not pay.
   - *Notice of Dishonor.* The holder of the instrument notifies those who are secondarily liable that the instrument has been dishonored. (p. 554)

3. **PRIMARY SIGNATURE LIABILITY** The maker of a note is primarily liable. (p. 555)

4. **SECONDARY SIGNATURE LIABILITY**
   (a) The drawer of a check has secondary liability: he is not liable until he has received notice that the bank has dishonored the check.
   (b) Indorsers are secondarily liable; they must pay if the issuer does not. But an indorser is only liable to those who come after him in the chain of ownership, not to those who held the instrument before he did. (p. 556)

EXAM Strategy

Question: Sidney Knopf entered into a contract for $35,000 with MacDonald Roofing Co., Inc., to reroof Knopf's building. Knopf made his initial payment by writing a check for $17,500 payable to "MacDonald Roofing Company, Inc., and D-FW Supply Company." MacDonald took the check to D-FW and requested an indorsement. MacDonald Roofing was a customer of D-FW, so D-FW indorsed the check. When MacDonald failed to complete the roofing work, Knopf filed suit for damages against D-FW. Knopf argues that D-FW was liable as an indorser. Do you agree?

Strategy: Whenever you are faced with an issue of indorser liability, remember that indorsers are only liable to those who come after them in the chain of ownership. (See the "Result" at the end of this section.)

5. **SIGNATURE LIABILITY FOR AN ACCOMMODATION PARTY** The accommodation party signs an instrument to benefit the accommodated party. By signing the instrument, an accommodation party agrees to be liable on it, whether or not she directly benefits from it. (p. 558)

6. **SIGNATURE LIABILITY OF AN AGENT** To avoid personal liability when signing an instrument, an agent must indicate that he is signing as an agent and must give the name of the principal. (p. 559)

7. **WARRANTY LIABILITY** The basic rules of warranty liability are as follows:
   - The culprit is always liable.
   - The drawee bank is responsible if it pays a check on which the drawer's name is forged.
   - In any other case of wrongdoing, a person who initially acquires an instrument from a culprit is ultimately liable to anyone else who pays value for it. (p. 561)

8. **TRANSFER WARRANTIES** When someone transfers an instrument, she warrants that:
   - She is a holder of the instrument
   - All signatures are authentic and authorized
   - The instrument has not been altered
   - No defense can be asserted against her, and
   - As far as she knows the issuer is solvent. (p. 562)

9. **PRESENTMENT WARRANTIES FOR A CHECK** Anyone who presents a check for payment warrants that:
   - She is a holder
   - The check has not been altered, and
   - She has no reason to believe the drawer's signature is forged. (p. 563)

10. **PRESENTMENT WARRANTIES FOR A NOTE** The presenter of a note only warrants that he is a holder. (p. 564)

11. **CONVERSION** Conversion means that (1) someone has stolen an instrument or (2) a bank has paid a check that has a forged indorsement. (p. 565)

EXAM Strategy

Question: Marie Kless hired an attorney, James R. Gunderman, to collect money owed her on a mortgage. When he received the check payable to Kless for $26,676.16, he forged her indorsement and deposited the check in his own account at Manufacturers Hanover Trust Co. He later withdrew the entire amount. Is the bank liable to Kless?

Strategy: Checks go astray in two ways: either someone transfers the check on purpose (to the wrong person or for the wrong reason, but nonetheless, on purpose) or someone steals the check. Whenever the check is stolen, it is conversion. In the case of conversion, the rightful owner can recover from either the bank that pays the check or the thief. (See the "Result" at the end of this section.)

12. **IMPOSTOR RULE** If someone issues an instrument to an impostor, then any indorsement in the name of the payee is valid as long as the person who pays the instrument is ignorant of the fraud. (p. 566)

13. **FICTITIOUS PAYEE RULE** If someone issues an instrument to a person who does not exist, then any indorsement in the name of the payee is valid as long as the person who pays the instrument does not know of the fraud. (p. 566)

14. **EMPLOYEE INDORSEMENT RULE** If an employee with responsibility for issuing instruments forges a check or other instrument, then any indorsement in the name of the payee is valid as long as the person who pays the instrument is ignorant of the fraud. (p. 566)

15. **LIABILITY FOR NEGLIGENCE** Anyone who behaves negligently in creating or paying an unauthorized instrument is liable to an innocent third party. (p. 567)

16. **DISCHARGE** Discharge means that liability on an instrument terminates. An instrument may be discharged by payment, agreement, cancellation, certification, or alteration. (p. 570)

EXAM Strategy

***CPA Question*:** Vex Corp. executed a negotiable promissory note payable to Tamp, Inc. The note was collaterized by some of Vex's business assets. Tamp negotiated the note to Miller for value. Miller indorsed the note in blank and negotiated it to Bilco for value. Before the note became due, Bilco agreed to release Vex's collateral. Vex refused to pay Bilco when the note became due. Bilco promptly notified Miller and Tamp of Vex's default. Which of the following statements is correct?

(a) Bilco will be unable to collect from Miller because Miller's indorsement was in blank.
(b) Bilco will be able to collect from either Tamp or Miller because Bilco was a holder in due course.
(c) Bilco will be unable to collect from either Tamp or Miller because of Bilco's release of the collateral.
(d) Bilco will be able to collect from Tamp because Tamp was the original payee.

Strategy: For this question, you can save time by quickly identifying the one right answer and not agonizing over each possibility. You know that if an indorser is in any way harmed by the acts of a subsequent holder, the indorser is discharged. (See the "Result" at the end of this section.)

4. Result: In this case, Knopf issued the check and came before D-FW in the chain of ownership. D-FW is not liable.

11. Result: Kless can recover from Manufacturers Hanover.

16. Result: In this case, Bilco has released Vex's collateral, thereby harming the two indorsers because now there are fewer assets that can be used to pay the note. The correct answer is c.

ADDITIONAL QUESTIONS

1. ***CPA QUESTION*** A check has the following indorsements on the back:

Paul Frank

without recourse

George Hopkins

payment guaranteed

Ann Quarry

Collection guaranteed

Rachel Ott

Which of the following conditions occurring subsequent to the indorsements would discharge all of the indorsers?

(a) Lack of notice of dishonor

(b) Late presentment

(c) Insolvency of maker

(d) Certification of check

2. **CPA QUESTION** Which of the following actions does not discharge a prior party to a commercial instrument?

   (a) Good faith payment or satisfaction of the instrument

   (b) Cancellation of that prior party's indorsement

   (c) The holder's oral renunciation of that prior party's liability

   (d) The holder's intentional destruction of the instrument

3. Phariss operated a business known as Railroad Salvage Co. He filed a claim in bankruptcy court against the Chicago, Rock Island and Pacific Railroad. Phariss then left Iowa and closed his bank account with the Security State Bank in Independence. Somehow, Carl Eddy obtained possession of the check that the railroad issued in payment of Phariss's claim. Eddy indorsed the check "Railroad Salvage Co. Carl Eddy" and deposited it in his own account at Security State Bank. After Eddy filed for bankruptcy, Phariss sued the bank, alleging that it was liable to him for having paid the check over an unauthorized indorsement. Is Security State Bank liable to Phariss? On what theory?

4. **YOU BE THE JUDGE** WRITING PROBLEM Melco, Inc., issued a promissory note for $12,000, payable to the order of Marjorie Irene Floor. On the back of the note, Charles Melvin had signed the following statement: "For and in consideration of funds advanced herein to Melco, Inc., we irrevocably guarantee Marjorie Irene Floor against loss by reason of non-payment of this note." Floor sued Melvin to enforce the note before demanding payment from the issuer. Is Melvin liable on the note before demand is made on the issuer? **Argument for Floor:** Melvin was an accommodation party and, as such, was liable on the instrument even if no demand had been made on the issuer. **Argument for Melvin:** If the accommodation party writes, "I guarantee collection," he is not liable until the issuer fails to pay. In this case, the words Melvin wrote are the equivalent of "I guarantee collection." **Floor's response:** To avoid liability in this case, Melvin had to comply with the exact requirements of the statute. How was she to know that he thought he was writing the equivalent of "I guarantee collection"?

5. Using the company's check-signing machine, Doris Britton forged $148,171.30 of checks on the account of her employer, Winkie, Inc. One of Britton's jobs at the company was to prepare checks for the company president, W. J. Winkie, Jr., to sign. He did not (1) look at the sequence of check numbers; (2) examine the monthly account statements; or (3) reconcile company records with bank statements. Winkie's bank, as a matter of policy, did not check indorsements on checks with a face value of less than $1,000. By accident, it paid a forged check that had not even been indorsed. Is the bank liable to Winkie, Inc., for the forged checks?

6. **ETHICS** Steven was killed in an automobile accident. His wife, Debra, was the beneficiary of a life insurance policy for $60,000. She decided to move from Bunkie to Sulphur, Louisiana. Before she could leave, however, arrangements had to be made to settle

outstanding debts. Debra executed a document authorizing her mother-in-law, Helen, to sign checks on Debra's account at the bank. Debra also signed several blank checks and gave them to Helen with instructions to use them to pay off the remaining debt on Debra's trailer. When Helen received the life insurance checks, she deposited them in Debra's account. So far so good. But then she immediately withdrew $50,000 from the account by using one of the blank checks Debra had left her. She did not use these funds to pay off the trailer debt. When Debra discovered the theft, she sued the bank for having paid an unauthorized check. How would you rule in this case? Debra has suffered a grievous loss—her husband died tragically in an automobile accident. She trusted her mother-in-law and counted on her help. Should the bank show compassion? If the bank made good on the forged checks, how great would be the injury to the bank's shareholders compared with the harm to Debra if she loses this entire sum?

7. James A. Arnold and Marvin D. Smith signed two promissory notes for a total of $25,000 payable to the Bostwick Banking Co. The defendants argued that they were not liable on the notes because they had signed as agents for Sunshine Sales Corp. The notes made no reference to Sunshine, but the defendants alleged that an officer at Bostwick had promised to type "Sunshine Sales Corporation" above their signatures on the notes. Are the defendants liable on the notes?

8. Merlyn Yagow borrowed money from P.C.A. to finance his farming expenses. Fearing that Yagow would not be able to pay his debt, P.C.A. required him to accept payment for his crops with checks that named him and P.C.A. as co-payees. This way, Yagow could not cash the checks without P.C.A.'s indorsement. Yagow sold corn to Farmer's Co-op Elevator, which paid $5,698.71 by check made out to "Merlyn Yagow, Alvin Yagow, P.C.A." When Yagow deposited this check, the comma between Alvin Yagow and P.C.A. appeared as "or." The check was indorsed by Merlin Yagow alone, not by P.C.A. When P.C.A. sued the bank for having paid this check, the bank in turn, filed suit against Yagow demanding indemnification for the P.C.A. claims. What claim did the bank make against Yagow?

9. *ROLE REVERSAL* Write a short-answer question that tests the reader's knowledge of at least one of the transfer warranties.

INTERNET RESEARCH PROBLEM

The United States Secret Service offers advice on how to avoid check fraud. To find it, Google "secret service how to avoid check fraud pdf" and click on "Check Fraud." Have you ever violated this advice and left yourself vulnerable to fraud?

You can find further practice problems at www.cengagebrain.com. See the preface of this book for website access details.

Arriving in New York from his native Bangladesh, Abdul Matin worked as a waiter in a restaurant in lower Manhattan. Through grueling effort and remarkable thrift, he managed to save $70,000, which he deposited in an account at the Chase Manhattan Bank. Then word came from home that his father was ill. Matin left in a hurry, expecting to return promptly. In the end, though, it was two years before he arrived back in New York. Imagine his horror and panic when he discovered upon his return that his bank account had no money left. Someone had used forged checks to empty the account. Matin told bank employees what had happened and begged for his money back. But Chase refused to make good on the missing funds because Matin had not reported the forgeries within one year, as the Uniform Commercial Code (UCC) requires.

Is Matin simply out of luck? Does he have to start all over again, working and saving, saving and working? To find out, read on.

> Imagine his horror and panic when he discovered upon his return that his bank account had no money left. Someone had used forged checks to empty the account.

INTRODUCTION

Americans write about 30 billion checks each year. They also execute 11 billion transactions at more than 383,000 automatic teller machines (ATMs) found every place from banks, grocery stores, and airports to the Grand Canyon. (ATMs are also in Antarctica and Buckingham Palace.) This chapter is about the laws that govern the relationship between banks and their customers for checks and credit and debit cards, as well as electronic fund transfers at ATMs. Parts of this chapter will seem familiar to you from reading Chapter 23. Because checks are a form of draft, they are covered by Article 3 of the UCC. Article 4 governs bank deposits and collections. Some of the provisions in Article 4 are very similar to those in Article 3. When the two conflict, Article 4 controls.

WHO'S WHO

UCC Section 4–105 defines the different roles of banks:

- *Depositary Bank.* The first bank to *take* a check is called the depositary bank. (A bank that *cashes* a check is not a depositary bank.) Suppose that the New York Yankees, Inc., writes a check on its account at Citibank to pay star player Alex Rodriguez. If he deposits the check in his account at Bank of America, then Bank of America is the depositary bank.

- *Payor Bank.* A bank that is called a *drawee* bank in Article 3 is termed a *payor* bank in Article 4 because it pays the issuer's check. The New York Yankees, Inc., is the issuer of the check, and Citibank is the payor bank.

- *Intermediary Bank.* An intermediary bank is any bank that handles a check during the collection process, *except* the depositary or payor bank. Instead of presenting the check directly to Citibank for payment, Bank of America may send it to the Federal Reserve Bank, which serves as a central clearinghouse for checks. The Federal Reserve then sends the check to Citibank for payment. The Federal Reserve is an intermediary bank.

- *Collecting Bank.* A collecting bank is any bank that handles a check during the collection process, except the payor bank. Both Bank of America and the Federal Reserve are collecting banks.

- *Presenting Bank.* A presenting bank is a bank that submits a check to the payor bank. The Federal Reserve is the presenting bank.

As you can see, the same bank may carry several different labels. Exhibit 24.1 sets out the roles that the various banks play in the transaction between the Yankees and Alex Rodriguez.

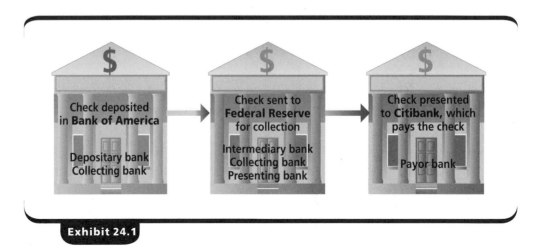

Exhibit 24.1

CHECKING ACCOUNTS

When a customer deposits money in a checking account, the bank becomes a debtor to the customer—the bank owes the customer money. At the same time, the bank serves as an agent for the customer. The legal relationship between the customer and the bank is based on both the checking account agreement and Article 4. The checking account agreement is simply a contract between the bank and the customer. Article 4 is, in essence, a default option; it applies unless the bank and customer agree to different terms. No matter what the agreement says, however, a bank cannot avoid liability for careless or bad faith actions.

THE BANK'S DUTY TO PROVIDE INFORMATION

The UCC does not require banks to provide customers with a monthly statement that lists transactions. Virtually every bank does so, however, because customers expect it. If a bank provides a statement, it must either include copies of canceled checks or a list of check numbers, amounts, and dates of payment.[1] Returning copies of canceled checks is an expensive habit that many banks would like to break.[2] Nonetheless, most banks still do return these copies because customers like to have them. People find that a copy of a canceled check is the best proof that a bill has been paid. If a bank does not return copies of canceled checks, it must keep legible copies on hand for seven years and provide copies to customers within a reasonable time.

The Truth in Savings Act[3] requires banks that send statements to include:

- The interest rate paid on the account

- The amount of interest the account has earned

- Any fees imposed by the bank

- The number of days covered by the statement

Before customers open an account (and in advertisements), a bank must disclose:

- The interest rate paid on the account

- How long this interest rate will be in effect

- Any requirements (such as minimum account balance or initial deposit) that the customer must meet to earn the advertised rate

- Any fees or penalties imposed by the bank

THE BANK'S DUTY TO PAY

A bank must pay a check if the check is authorized by the customer and complies with the terms of the checking account agreement.[4] A bank may, however, choose the order in which it pays

---

[1] UCC Section 4–406.

[2] Originally, banks returned checks because they did not want the expense of storing all that paper. With advances in technology and increases in postal rates, it is now cheaper simply to store microcopies.

[3] 12 U.S.C. Sections 4301–4313.

[4] UCC Section 4–401(a), 4–402(a).

authorized checks. Suppose that Elizabeth writes a check to each of her four sisters: Jane ($100), Mary ($50), Lydia ($40), and Kitty ($10). When the sisters appear at the bank the next morning to cash the checks, they discover Elizabeth has only $100 in her account. The bank is free to choose which sisters it pays. It is not forced to pay the sister who appears first nor must it pay Mary, Lydia, and Kitty together, instead of Jane by herself.

A bank does not have to bounce checks; it can, if it chooses, pay a check even if that causes an overdraft. Once an account has an overdraft, the bank may either repay itself out of the customer's next deposit or try to collect the amount directly from the customer. For example, a bookie demanded that a gambler repay his debts *immediately*. The gambler did not want to pay, but he also did not want his legs broken. It was midnight and no banks were open. He wrote a check, knowing that his account was virtually on empty. It is not clear what he thought the bookie would do when the check bounced, but at that particular midnight, he was more concerned with the present than the future. His plan was upset, however, when the bank honored his check, despite the overdraft, and then demanded payment from him. Though highly indignant, he nonetheless had to pay. There is a moral to this story about both overdrafts and gambling.

WRONGFUL DISHONOR

If a bank violates its duty and wrongfully dishonors an authorized check, it is liable to the customer for all *actual* **and** *consequential* **damages.** Bouncing a check is not only embarrassing, it can cost real money—a retailer may charge for a returned check, the customer's credit rating may suffer, or the customer may even be arrested. When it has wrongfully dishonored a check, the bank is liable for these damages. The following case illustrates how devastating the wrongful dishonor of checks can be.

GOLDSMITH MOTORS CORP. V. CHEMICAL BANK

41 A.D.3d 648; 838 N.Y.S.2d 631; 2007 N.Y. APP. DIV. LEXIS 7724
SUPREME COURT OF NEW YORK, APPELLATE DIVISION, 2007

CASE SUMMARY

Facts: Goldsmith Motors was a car dealership in New York. Chemical Bank admitted that it wrongfully dishonored some of the dealership's checks. Goldsmith's president testified that the wrongful dishonor caused a series of ill effects: employee morale suffered; good salespeople quit; parts suppliers required cash on delivery; one auto body shop refused to release its customers' vehicles unless it was paid by Goldsmith in advance; and the body shop's owner told other businesses not to deal with Goldsmith. Moreover, the bank that financed Goldsmith's operations began conducting more frequent, disruptive floor plan checks, raised its interest rates, and refused to allow the dealership to purchase cars at auctions, thereby adding to its financial difficulties. Business at Goldsmith declined, its income decreased, its expenses increased, and it began

to lose money. Goldsmith's president claimed that the wrongful dishonoring of the checks led to the ruination of his dealership, which eventually closed its doors. An expert witness testified at trial that having checks returned for insufficient funds has a "horrible effect" on a dealership's business and that, in this case, it appeared to have caused Goldsmith's failure.

The trial court refused to permit the dealership to ask for punitive damages. The jury awarded Goldsmith damages of $2.31 million for injury to its reputation and business and $660,000 for lost profits, but the trial court set aside the verdict. Goldsmith appealed.

Issue: *What damages must a bank pay when it wrongfully dishonors a customer's checks?*

Decision: The bank is liable for damages caused by its wrongful dishonor. But it is liable for punitive damages only if it acted maliciously or recklessly.

Reasoning: Under the UCC, a bank is liable for damages caused by its wrongful dishonor of checks. To recover from the bank, Goldsmith had to show that the bank's wrongful dishonor of the checks was a substantial factor in the disasters that befell the dealership. It is for the jury to determine whether the bank caused Goldsmith's problems and how much the damages were. Given the evidence in this case, the jury made a rational decision. The trial court was wrong in setting aside the jury's verdict.

The bank is liable for punitive damages only if it acted maliciously or recklessly. There was no evidence of such behavior, so the trial court was correct when it refused to let Goldsmith request punitive damages.

The Death of a Customer

If a customer dies, the bank may continue to pay checks *for 10 days* after it learns of the death, unless it receives a stop payment order from someone claiming an interest in the account.[5] After all, the customer was alive when he wrote the checks. Refusing to pay may cause hardship for innocent merchants who accepted checks in return for goods. A refusal to pay may also complicate matters for his family when they sort out his financial affairs. Certainly, the last thing his widow wants is for all his checks to bounce.

In reality, however, banks typically do freeze an account after the holder dies. First, a bank must stop payment on checks if someone else makes a claim to the funds in the account, no matter how weak that claim is. If Mildred, a seventh cousin twice removed, makes a claim, the bank must stop payment. Second, although Article 4 permits banks to pay checks even after the customer has died, most states require banks to freeze enough money to cover the decedent's taxes. Because the bank does not know what the decedent will ultimately owe, it typically freezes the entire account.

Incompetent Customers

Once a bank is notified that a court has found a customer to be incompetent, it is liable if it pays the customer's checks. The bank is under no obligation to determine competence itself. It may continue to pay checks until it has received notice that a court has determined the customer is incompetent.

Forgery

If a bank pays a check on which the issuer's name is forged, it must recredit the issuer's account. When a bank pays a forged check, either the bank or the customer will lose money, except in the unlikely event that the forger repays what he has stolen. As a matter of policy, the drafters of the UCC decided that the payor bank should bear the risk of forgery, rather than the customer. Most banks take two steps to guard against losses: they examine the signatures on all checks above a certain dollar amount, and they carry forgery insurance.

Alteration

If a bank pays a check that has been altered, the customer is liable only for the original terms of the check, and the bank is liable for the balance.[6] There is one exception to this rule: if the

[5] UCC Section 4–405.
[6] UCC Section 4–401(d).

| Exhibit 24.2 | If the bank pays this check, it is liable for the full amount because the check has obviously been altered. | Anna Karenina originally wrote this check for $9.60. Because the check looks unaltered, she is liable for $9.60, and the bank is liable for the balance. |

alteration is obvious, the bank is liable for the full amount of the check because it should have known better than to pay it in the first place. Exhibit 24.2 illustrates this rule.

Completion

If an incomplete check is later filled in by someone other than the original issuer, the bank is not liable unless it was on notice that the completion was improper.[7] Joey and Lisa want to buy, renovate, and resell a two-family house. They think they have located the perfect choice, but negotiations are still incomplete when Joey leaves town on business for a few days. He signs a blank check and leaves it with Lisa to pay his half of the deposit, if their offer is accepted. Lisa absentmindedly uses the check as a bookmark and forgets to remove it before she returns the book to the library. Marian the librarian finds the check and, glorying in the thought of hundreds of new books, fills in the library's name and the amount of $10,000. If Lisa realizes the check is missing and notifies the bank, then the bank is liable to Joey if it later pays the check. Otherwise, the bank owes Joey nothing.

EXAM *Strategy*

Question: For three weeks in a row, Peyton wrote a check to his yoga instructor, Eli. Unfortunately, each week Eli changed the amount of the check from $50 to $150 before depositing it. Because of these alterations, Peyton's checking account was overdrawn, but the bank kept honoring Eli's checks anyway. The overdraft caused Peyton's check to the neighborhood dry cleaners to bounce, so he was banned from taking his clothes there. He then had to pay more to have his clothes cleaned at a different cleaners. What is the bank's liability?

Strategy: When faced with an issue of the bank's liability, review the rules that govern its relationship with its customers. Here, three rules are involved: the bank's duty to pay, its liability for altered checks, and wrongful dishonor.

---

[7] UCC Section 4–401(d).

Result: The bank has the right to pay checks, even if the payment causes an overdraft. So it would have no liability to Peyton for failing to bounce the checks to Eli, if those checks had really been for $150. The bank is, however, liable for $100 on each check—the difference between the amount Peyton wrote and the amount Eli received. As for the checks to the dry cleaners, the bank wrongfully dishonored them because technically, Peyton had enough money in his account to cover them. Therefore, the bank is responsible for his more expensive dry cleaning.

Comparative Negligence and Bank Statements

Customers must use reasonable care in examining their bank statements to look for forged or altered checks. If a customer is careless, the bank is not liable for the faulty checks. Moreover, if a customer fails to notify the bank of a forgery or alteration within 30 days of receiving a statement, then the bank is not liable for any subsequent bad checks by the same wrongdoer. However, if both the customer and the bank are careless, a comparative negligence standard is used, and the bank's liability is reduced by the amount of the customer's negligence.[8] In any case, a customer cannot recover for a forgery or alteration if it is reported more than one year after receiving the statement that first revealed the problem.

In the following case, Abdul Matin failed to report forgeries on his account within the one-year period. Is the bank liable? You be the judge.

YOU *be the* JUDGE

MATIN V. CHASE MANHATTAN BANK
10 A.D.3d 447; 781 N.Y.S.2d 158; 2004 N.Y.
App. Div. LEXIS 10387
Supreme Court of New York, 2004

Facts: Abdul Matin returned home from a lengthy trip abroad only to discover that some unknown person had used forged checks to empty his account at the Chase Manhattan Bank. The culprit also forged a change of address card so that the bank sent the monthly statements to a different address. When Matin asked for a refund, the bank refused on the grounds that Matin had not reported the forgeries within one year as required by the UCC. After Matin filed suit, the court granted Chase's motion for summary judgment.

You Be the Judge: Is the bank liable for forged checks that were not reported within one year?

Argument for Matin: Under the UCC, a bank is liable for any forged checks that it pays so long as the customer reports the forgeries within one year after the bank makes the statement *available to him*. In this case, Matin never received the bank statements because they were sent to the wrong address. He did report the loss within minutes after he realized what had happened. He complied with the UCC and the bank is liable to him.

Argument for Chase Manhattan: Matin was away for two years. Even if the bank had mailed the statements to his correct address in the United States, he would never have received them and would never have noticed the forgeries. If he had a friend or family member checking his mail, then that person should have notified the bank when no statements arrived. In that case, the bank could have prevented further forgeries.

Under the UCC one-year rule, bank customers need to check periodically to make sure that nothing is wrong with their accounts. Matin failed to do this.

---

[8] UCC Section 4–406.

Stale Checks

A bank is not *required* to pay checks that are presented more than six months after their date, but it is not liable if it does pay. [9] In 1962, John Glenn became the first person to orbit the earth. Many people were so eager to have his autograph that they did not cash checks he gave them. In 1974, Glenn was elected senator from Ohio. Suppose that one of his admirers became so disgusted with his political views that she no longer treasured his autograph and tried, in 1974, to cash a check from 1962. Would she be successful? Although Glenn's bank, as a matter of policy, would probably reject the 12-year-old check, it would not be liable to Glenn if it paid.

Post-Dated Checks

A post-dated check is one that is presented for payment before its date. **A bank is not liable for paying a post-dated check unless the customer has notified the bank in advance that a post-dated check is coming.** [10] Under the old version of Article 4, banks were not supposed to cash checks until their due date. So, for example, customers could mail off a set of post-dated checks to pay all their bills while on vacation, knowing that the bank would not pay the checks until their due dates. When Article 4 was revised, however, banks argued that this rule was impractical at a time when most banks use machines to process checks. The extra expense of manually reviewing each check is not worth the limited benefit to a few customers.

Stop Payment Orders

Even if a check is authorized when issued, the customer has the right to stop payment later. **As a general rule, if a bank pays a check over a stop payment order, it is liable to the customer for any loss he suffers.** [11] However, a bank customer must be aware of these additional rules:

- Any account holder has the right to stop payment, even someone who did not sign the check.

- A stop payment order is valid only if it describes the check with reasonable certainty and the bank receives the order before paying, or certifying, the check.

- An oral stop payment order is valid for only 14 days; a written order expires in six months. This is an important point. Many people think that, once they have stopped payment on a check, they can relax and forget about it. Not true. One woman, for example, wrote a $1,000 check to a contractor. When he told her he had lost the check, she stopped payment and gave him a new one, which he promptly cashed. Ten months later, he cashed the old check, too. The customer could have continued to renew the stop payment order every six months, but that would have been a hassle. The only surefire method for stopping a check permanently is to close the old account and open a new one.

> Many people think that, once they have stopped payment on a check, they can relax and forget about it. Not true.

Typically, a customer issues a stop payment order because she is having a disagreement over a contract. The customer may or may not be in the right. If a bank accidentally pays a check in violation of a stop payment order, it retains the right to recover from whichever party to the contract was wrong. The "bank is **subrogated to** " the rights of the parties, which means that the bank can substitute for, or take the place of, either party. Section 4–407

Subrogated to
The bank can substitute for, or take the place, of, a party.

---

[9] UCC Section 4–404.
[10] UCC Section 4–401(c).
[11] UCC Section 4–403.

provides: **If a bank pays a check despite a valid stop payment order, it inherits the rights of the customer against the payee and of the payee against the customer.** In the following case, the plaintiff gambled and lost—twice: once in a casino and once in court.

SEIGEL V. MERRILL LYNCH, PIERCE, FENNER & SMITH, INC.

745 A.2d 301; 2000 D.C. APP. LEXIS 21
DISTRICT OF COLUMBIA COURT OF APPEALS, 2000

CASE SUMMARY

Facts: During a two-month period, Walter Seigel gambled—a lot—at casinos in Atlantic City, New Jersey. To buy gambling chips, he wrote checks to the various casinos. These checks were drawn on his cash management account at Merrill Lynch.[12] Once the spree was over, and Seigel had lost all of his chips (if not his marbles), he called his broker to ask if there was any way he could avoid paying his gambling debts. At the broker's suggestion, Seigel placed a stop payment order on the checks. Merrill Lynch did dishonor many of the checks but accidentally paid checks totaling $143,000. (This number provides some evidence of the extent of Seigel's problem.)

Seigel sued Merrill Lynch, demanding a return of the $143,000 plus interest. The trial court granted Merrill Lynch's motion for summary judgment.

Issue: *Did Seigel suffer a loss when Merrill Lynch paid a check over his stop payment order?*

Decision: Affirmed. Seigel did not suffer a loss and cannot recover from Merrill Lynch.

Reasoning: Under the UCC, a bank is liable when it pays a check in violation of a stop payment order only if the customer actually suffers a loss from the payment. In this case, Seigel was not harmed because he was liable to the casinos for the full amount of the check whether or not Merrill Lynch paid it.

Seigel alleges that he would not have been liable to the casinos for two reasons: illegality and duress. He argues that because he was a compulsive gambler, the casinos had violated New Jersey law by accepting his check. However, the casinos would be in violation of the law only if the Casino Control Commission had issued a specific order prohibiting them from accepting Seigel's check. No such order was ever issued.

As for the duress argument, compulsive gambling, in and of itself, is not a defense to a contract action in New Jersey. Seigel did not produce any evidence that his gambling problem constituted unconscionable duress.

Because this check was enforceable whether or not Merrill Lynch stopped payment, Seigel suffered no loss when the check was paid. Therefore, Merrill Lynch is not liable to Seigel.

DEVIL'S ADVOCATE If Merrill Lynch had dishonored all the checks, it is possible that Seigel might not have had to pay in the end—the casinos might not have bothered to sue him. He lived in Maryland, not New Jersey, and the expense and effort of filing suit in another jurisdiction might not have been worth the effort. Also, he was a good customer at the casinos and had already paid them substantial sums. They might not have wanted to alienate him. In any event, a lawsuit would have taken some years and delayed the day on which Seigel actually had to pay. He would have been better off if Merrill Lynch had done as it promised and dishonored the checks.

---

[12] Article 4 of the UCC technically applies only to banks. However, the parties to this case agreed that the negotiable instruments drawn by Seigel were checks. Furthermore, the official comment to UCC Section 4–403 notes that "by analogy the rule extends to drawers other than banks." Therefore, the court treated Merill Lynch as a bank.

Substitute Checks

Suppose that you own a cottage on the coast in Florida which you rent to Ella from Seattle. As soon as her rent check arrives, you deposit it into your account. The next day, you want to write a check against those funds to pay your credit card bill. No chance the bank will let you do that. Ella's check has a long route to travel before your bank can tell if it is good or not. Your Miami bank will send the check to the Federal Reserve Bank in Atlanta, which will send the check to the Federal Reserve Bank in San Francisco, which will present the check for payment at Ella's bank in Seattle. Like a game of hot potato, each bank in the collection process must pass a check along before midnight of the next banking day after it receives the check (the so-called **midnight deadline**).

If the check is good, the Seattle bank simply lets the midnight deadline expire in silence. If the Seattle bank dishonors the check, it can either return the item along the same route that the check originally traveled, or the bank can return the check directly to Miami.

Checks are physically transported by airplane or ground transportation—so that even with the midnight deadline, the process is slow and expensive. This problem was compounded after September 11, 2001, when air traffic was shut down for days. Checks piled up at banks across the country.

In an effort to bring the banking system into the twenty-first century, Congress passed the Check 21 Act. This statute creates a new negotiable instrument called a **substitute check**. Any bank that receives a paper check has the right to encode both the front and back electronically and then destroy the original. It can then send that check electronically to the other banks in the check-clearing process. However, if a bank prefers not to accept an electronic check, it has the right to receive a substitute check instead. This substitute is simply a paper printout of the electronic version. **The substitute check is legally the same as the original check.** (Exhibit 24.3 is a picture of a substitute check.) Note that Check 21 does not require a bank to create substitute checks or to accept electronic checks; it simply requires banks to accept paper substitute checks. The hope is that, as banks gradually switch to electronic transmissions, checks will travel faster and depositors will have access to their funds sooner. Imagine how much faster Ella's check could travel electronically than on planes and trains.

In the previous chapter, we learned about warranty liability. Under Check 21, **a bank that transfers or presents an electronic or a substitute check gives a** *warranty of legal equivalency*. The bank is warranting to the drawer, the payee, the depositor, any indorser, and any bank that receives the check that:

- The substitute check is an accurate image of the original check

- No bank, issuer, or indorser will be asked to pay a check that he has already paid.

This warranty protects recipients of substitute checks from any losses caused by the substitution process. For example, if someone does end up paying a check twice, then the bank that created the substitute check is liable for not destroying the original check.

What does Check 21 mean to you? Funds may clear faster, which means that you need to be sure you have enough money in your account to cover checks that you write. It also means that you may receive some substitute checks with your bank statement each month. If you request a copy of a check from your bank, it may give you the original check, a substitute check, or a copy of the original check.

Midnight deadline

A rule that each bank in the collection process must pass a check along before midnight of the next banking day after it receives the check.

Substitute check

A paper printout of the electronic version of a check, which is legally the same as the original.

EXAM *Strategy*

Question: Robert Triffin bought two checks that had been dishonored by Commerce Bank for insufficient funds. His plan was to try to recover against the issuer of the checks. The checks he purchased were substitute checks, not the originals. Triffin alleged that some of the words that had been written on the original checks were missing from the substitute checks. He sued Commerce Bank for violating the Check 21 Act. Is Commerce liable to Triffin?

Strategy: Any question about substitute checks requires you to review the warranties under the Check 21 statute. A bank that transfers a substitute check gives a warranty that the substitute check is an accurate representation of the original. This warranty protects against any loss because of the substitution process.

Result: Commerce Bank was not liable. While Triffin claimed that the check was not an accurate copy of the original, he did not allege that he had suffered any harm as a result. No harm to the holder of the check means no liability to the bank.

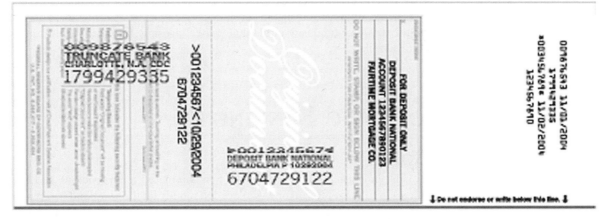

Exhibit 24.3   A substitute check.

Item Deposited	When Funds May be Withdrawn by Check
Cash Cashiers Check Certified Check U.S. Government Check Check Drawn on same bank Wire Transfer	• Next business day, if deposited with a teller • Second business day, if deposited in an ATM
Local Check (both the depositary bank and the payor bank are in the same region)	• Next business day, for the first $100 • Second business day, for the balance up to $5,000 • Ninth business day, for the balance over $5,000
Nonlocal Check	• Next business day, for the first $100 • Fifth business day, for the balance up to $5,000 • Ninth business day, for the balance over $5,000

Exhibit 24.4

Expedited Funds Availability Act

Although, in theory, Check 21 will permit banks to process checks more quickly and put money in a customer's bank account faster, this statute does not regulate how soon funds must be available for withdrawal. That is left to the Expedited Funds Availability Act (EFAA), [13] which specifies the maximum time a bank may hold funds before allowing a customer to withdraw them. (A bank can always pay earlier if it wants.) Exhibit 24.4 lists rules that establish how quickly you can write a check against funds in your account.

Customers must, however, wait longer to withdraw cash than they do to write a check. [14] Banks are at greater risk when customers withdraw cash than when they write a check: the bank still has a number of days before a check must be paid; the cash is gone immediately. Thus, under the EFAA, a customer can withdraw only the first $100 in cash on the next business day after depositing a check. He can withdraw $400 more in cash by 5:00 p.m. on the same day that the funds are available for check writing. The rest of the deposit can be withdrawn the day after funds are available for check writing. Exhibit 24.5 illustrates these rules on funds availability.

Electronic Banking

Back to the Future

In 1968, a bank in Philadelphia installed the first automated teller machine (ATM) in the United States. Until that time, anyone who needed money for the weekend had two choices: cash a check at the bank before it closed (at 3:00 p.m. on Friday, 1:00 p.m. on Saturday) or find a

---

[13] 12 U.S.C. Sections 4001–4010.

[14] These hold periods do not apply to new accounts, accounts with repeated overdrafts, and any other situation in which a bank has reasonable cause to believe the check is uncollectible.

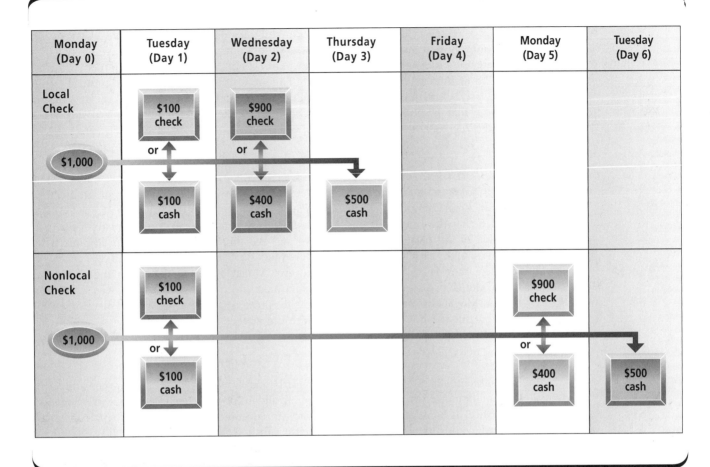

	Monday (Day 0)	Tuesday (Day 1)	Wednesday (Day 2)	Thursday (Day 3)	Friday (Day 4)	Monday (Day 5)	Tuesday (Day 6)
Local Check	$1,000	$100 check or $100 cash	$900 check or $400 cash	$500 cash			
Nonlocal Check	$1,000	$100 check or $100 cash				$900 check or $400 cash	$500 cash

Exhibit 24.5   When cash may be withdrawn.[15]

local merchant who would cash a small check after hours. The same person had two options for paying a bill: cash or check. Today, thanks to advances in electronic fund transfers, we have options that were barely imagined a generation ago, such as debit cards and online payment of bills. In 2003, for the first time, consumers used debit and credit cards in stores more often than checks or cash. Now debit cards are used more often than credit cards.

Consumers can obtain cash day or night and pay their bills with a few clicks of the mouse. And banks save money—electronic transmission is less expensive than shipping billions of checks around the globe. But the advances in technology are so new that this area of the law is changing rapidly and will undoubtedly continue to do so for some time.

ELECTRONIC FUND TRANSFER ACT

Moneys that are moved between accounts by means of a computer, an ATM, or a wire transfer are called **electronic funds**. In the beginning, electronic fund transfers were governed by

Electronic funds
Moneys that are moved between accounts by means of a computer, an ATM, or a wire transfer.

[15] Adapted from a chart prepared by the Federal Reserve Board. Reprinted in Douglas J. Whaley, *Problems and Materials on Payment Law* (Boston: Little, Brown & Co., 1995), p. 218.

contract between a bank and its customers, not by state or national statutes. Some banks treated their customers better than others. For example, roughly one-third of banks refused to recredit a customer for unauthorized transfers. Thus, if Biff stole Marty's ATM card and emptied his account, Marty was simply out of luck. Gradually, states began to regulate electronic transfers. This was better than nothing, but it did not solve the problem of interstate transfers. In 1978, Congress passed the Electronic Fund Transfer Act (EFTA)[16] to protect **consumers**. The statute defines a consumer as "any natural person," that is, not a corporation or business. Following are the major provisions of the EFTA.

Consumer

Any natural person, that is, not a corporation or business.

Required Electronic Fund Transfers

An employer may require its employees to receive paychecks via an electronic fund transfer but it cannot specify the particular bank. Suppose the CEO of MegaCorp. has decided that the company must cut costs to stay competitive in its industry. Her chief financial officer tells her the company can save thousands of dollars in administrative expenses if it pays employees via electronic fund transfers instead of by check. In addition, the Dawes Bank will agree to give MegaCorp. favorable financing on a major loan if the company pays all employees by electronic fund transfer to Dawes. Under the EFTA, MegaCorp. can require all employees to receive their pay via an electronic fund transfer, but the company cannot require employees to be paid at Dawes.

Cards

If a bank sends an electronic fund transfer card (for example, an ATM card) to a consumer who has not requested it, the card must be invalid until the consumer requests validation. Otherwise, if banks sent valid ATM cards to consumers who were not expecting them, the cards could be stolen and used without the consumer ever knowing. To validate a card, the bank typically assigns the consumer a PIN (personal identification number). The card does not work unless the PIN is entered with each transaction.

Documentation

A bank must provide consumers with (1) a transaction statement each time an electronic fund transfer is made at an ATM and (2) a monthly (or, in the case of infrequent transactions, quarterly) statement reporting all electronic fund transfers for the period.

Preauthorized Transfers

Consumers sometimes ask banks to wire funds on a regular basis—to pay the monthly mortgage, say. A bank may not make preauthorized transfers without written instructions from the consumer. The consumer can stop payment of the transfer by oral or written notice up to three business days before the scheduled date. In the following case, a customer sued her bank for making a preauthorized transfer that she thought she had stopped.

---

[16] 15 U.S.C. Section 1693.

BROXTON-KING V. LaSALLE BANK, N.A.

2001 U.S. Dist. LEXIS 14653
UNITED STATES DISTRICT COURT FOR THE NORTHERN DISTRICT OF ILLINOIS, 2001

CASE SUMMARY

Facts: Eunice Broxton-King paid $28 a month to belong to the YMCA. On the first day of each month, this sum was transferred automatically from her account at the LaSalle Bank to the YMCA. On August 31, Broxton-King went to the bank, paid an overdraft on her account, and then closed it. However, on September 1, the bank transferred $28 to the YMCA. Because there was no money in her account, the bank charged an overdraft fee of $22 and a service charge of $3. The overdraft totaled $53. On September 7, the bank sent Broxton-King a notice of this overdraft. She told the bank that her account had been closed on August 31, that the debit to the YMCA should be stopped, and the fees refunded. But on October 1, the bank again debited plaintiff's checking account for the $28 YMCA fee and added an additional $27 in overdraft and service fees.

Alleging that the bank had violated the EFTA, Broxton-King filed a *pro se*[17] lawsuit. The bank filed a motion to dismiss.

Issue: *Did the bank violate the EFTA?*

Decision: The bank's transfer on September 1 did not violate the EFTA, but its transfer on October 1 did. The defendant's motion to dismiss is granted in part and denied in part.

Reasoning: Under Section 1693e of the EFTA, a consumer may stop payment of an electronic fund transfer by notifying the bank orally or in writing up to three business days before the scheduled date of the transfer. Because Broxton-King did not close out her account until the day before the September 1 transfer, the bank's action on that date did not violate the EFTA.

The bank argues that because Broxton-King did not pay off the September 1 overdraft, her account was still open on October 1 and thus the October transfer was valid. The EFTA does not require that an account be closed for a stop transfer order to be valid. Therefore, the bank's transfer on October 1 violated the EFTA. The bank's motion to dismiss is granted as to the September 1 transaction but denied as to the October 1 transfer.

ERRORS

If, within 60 days of receiving a bank statement, a consumer tells the bank (either orally or in writing) that the account is in error, the bank must investigate and report the result of its investigation to the consumer within 10 business days. If the bank discovers an error, it must recredit the consumer's account (including interest) within one business day. If the bank cannot complete its investigation within 10 business days, it must provisionally recredit the consumer's account (including interest) pending the termination of its investigation, which must be completed within 45 calendar days. If the bank finds there was no error, it must give the consumer a full explanation in writing within three business days of so finding. When a bank violates this provision, it must pay the consumer treble damages (three times the amount in dispute). Exhibit 24.6 illustrates these rules.

The EFTA addresses the following kinds of errors:

- *Unauthorized Transfer.* Someone withdraws money from an account without permission.

- *Disbursement Error.* The consumer receives $80 from the ATM, but $100 is deducted from her account.

---

[17] Instead of hiring a lawyer, she represented herself.

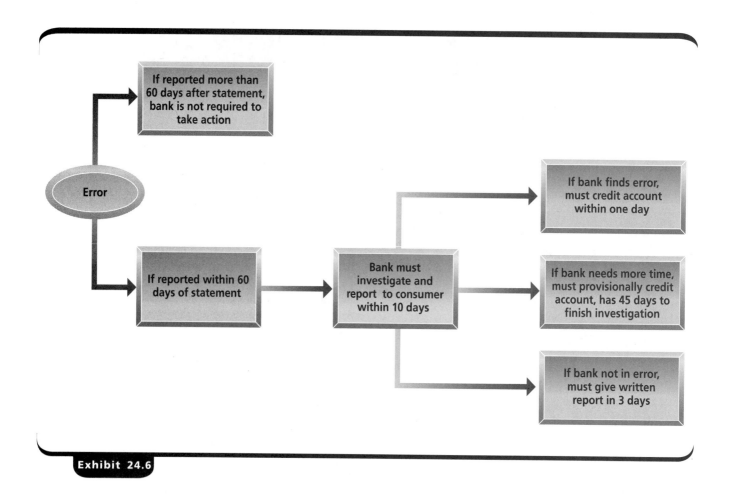

Exhibit 24.6

- *Omitted Transfer.* A transfer is never applied to an account. (For some reason, omitted deposits are reported more often than omitted withdrawals.)

- *Computational Error.* The bank makes a mathematical miscalculation.

CONSUMER LIABILITY FOR UNAUTHORIZED TRANSACTIONS

When a thief steals an ATM or debit card, it is important for the consumer to report the theft to the bank as quickly as possible.[18] If she reports the loss within two days of discovering it, she is liable only for the first $50 stolen. If she reports the loss after two days, but within 60 days of receiving her bank statement that shows the unauthorized withdrawal, she is liable for a maximum of $500. After 60 days, she is liable for the full amount.

If an unauthorized transfer takes place without the use of a stolen card, then the consumer is not liable at all so long as she reports the loss within 60 days of receiving a bank statement

---

[18] The Federal Trade Commission offers advice about what to do if you lose a credit card. To find the advice on the FTC's website, Google "what to do if credit card is lost or stolen."

that shows the loss. After 60 days, however, she is liable for the full amount. If the bank fails to give a consumer either a PIN or some other device to make unauthorized withdrawals difficult, the consumer is not liable for any amount. You remember that, if a customer's negligence contributes to a check forgery, the bank may not be liable. That is not true for electronic funds: the bank is liable even if the customer was negligent. Suppose Marty writes his PIN on his ATM card and then accidentally leaves the card at the ATM. When Biff uses the card to withdraw funds, the bank is still liable for any withdrawal in excess of $50 (which is why many banks limit daily withdrawals to, say, $500).

EXAM *Strategy*

Question: When a man robbed a convenience store, he locked the clerk in the bathroom and took her purse. Forty minutes later, he used her ATM card to withdraw $500 from a bank and her checkbook to write a check on her account. He forged her signature on the check. Who is liable for the money removed from the clerk's account?

Strategy: Remember that the rules for ATM cards and checks are different. The bank is liable for the full amount of a forged check, but it is liable only for unauthorized electronic fund transfers that exceed $50.

Result: If the clerk notifies the bank within two days of the theft, she will lose only $50.

BANK'S LIABILITY

As we have seen, the bank's liability for *unauthorized* transfers depends upon how soon the consumer reports the loss. In addition, a bank is liable to a consumer for any damages caused by the bank's failure to make an *authorized* electronic fund transfer. Bert asks the Tomes Bank to transfer funds every month to pay his mortgage. He goes off hiking in Alaska for the summer, secure in the knowledge that his mortgage will be paid while he is gone. When he returns to find his house in foreclosure proceedings because the bank did not make the payments, he can recover damages from the bank.

SYSTEM MALFUNCTION

If a system malfunction prevents an electronic fund transfer, the consumer's obligation to make the payment is suspended until the malfunction is repaired or until the intended recipient has, in writing, requested nonelectronic payment. If Bert's mortgage payment is not made because of a system malfunction, the mortgage company cannot charge him a penalty or foreclose on his house during the time the system is down. In fact, he has no obligation to make the payment until the system is working again or until the mortgage company, in writing, requests payment by check.

DISCLOSURE

All of these rules must be disclosed to the consumer (in readily understandable language!) before she opens an account that has electronic fund transfer capability. In addition, banks are required to notify customers of all ATM fees. This notice must appear on or near the machine and also on the screen at a point during the transaction where the customer still has an opportunity to back out without paying a fee.[19]

---

[19] ATM Fee Reform Act of 1999, 15 U.S.C. 1693b(d).

The goal of the EFTA is to protect consumers. As the following case illustrates, however, that protection goes only so far. It is important for consumers to pay careful attention to the EFTA time limits.

KRUSER V. BANK OF AMERICA

230 CAL.APP.3d 741, 1991 CAL. APP. LEXIS 523, 281 CAL. RPTR. 463
COURT OF APPEAL OF CALIFORNIA, 1991

CASE SUMMARY

Facts: Mr. and Mrs. Kruser each had an ATM card for their joint account at the Bank of America (Bank). The Bank referred to this as a "Versatel" card. Mr. Kruser believed his card was destroyed in September 1986. It turned out, however, that someone used it to make an unauthorized withdrawal of $20 from the account in December 1986. That same month, Mrs. Kruser underwent surgery and was hospitalized for 11 days. She then spent six or seven months recuperating at home. Her recovery underwent a nasty setback, however, when she discovered in September 1987 that someone had illegally withdrawn $9,020 from the account during July and August 1987. The Bank refused to refund the money. The Krusers sued, but the trial court granted the Bank's motion for summary judgment. The Krusers appealed.

Issue: *Did the Krusers' failure to report the unauthorized withdrawal in December prevent them from recovering the much larger amount stolen in July and August?*

Decision: Affirmed. The bank is not liable to the Krusers for the money stolen out of their account.

Reasoning: The Krusers argued that the initial theft of $20 was so small and happened so long before the much larger theft that they did not have sufficient warning that someone was illegally using their ATM card. They further argued that the purpose of the EFTA is to protect consumers, and, therefore, the bank should pay.

If the Krusers had reported the initial theft of $20, the bank would have canceled their ATM card, and the larger sum would not have been stolen. Mrs. Kruser's illness is no excuse because, during her recuperation, she did review bank statements. Moreover, if she was too ill to look at the statements, Mr. Kruser could have done so.

ETHICS Someone uses Mr. Kruser's ATM card to withdraw $20. Mrs. Kruser undergoes major surgery and fails to notice the unauthorized withdrawal. (How many *healthy* people would notice one unauthorized $20 withdrawal?) Six months later, someone steals more than $9,000 from the Krusers' account and the Bank refuses to pay. It litigates the case to the appeals court, undoubtedly incurring well more than $9,000 in legal fees. Why did the Bank do this? Was it the right thing to do? What are the consequences of the Bank's decision? ◆

WIRE TRANSFERS

Electronic fund transfers are important to consumers, but the amount of money they transfer pales in comparison with wholesale wire transfers among banks and their commercial customers. Within the United States, the Federal Reserve system maintains a wire transfer system called "Fedwire." More than $2.1 trillion is sent each day via Fedwire; the average amount per transaction is $3.6 million. International wire transfers are handled by Clearing-house Interbank Payments System (CHIPS), based in New York. About $1.4 trillion is sent through CHIPS each day; the average wire is over $5 million.

UCC Article 4A regulates *nonconsumer* wire transfers, which are a type of **payment order.** Article 3 deals with checks.[20] The difference between a check and a payment order has sometimes been described as push-pull. A check permits the payee to *pull* money out of the issuer's account while a payment order *pushes* money out of the issuer's account into the payee's.

Payment order

Transfers money from the issuer's account into the payee's.

Suppose that Cooper, Inc., plans to buy Maxine, Inc.'s water ride park in Columbia, South Carolina. Cooper could write a check for $1 million to Maxine on Cooper's CoopBank. When Maxine presents that check for payment, CoopBank will pull $1 million out of Cooper's account. If, however, Cooper sends a wire to Maxine for the same amount, CoopBank takes the money out of the account and then uses a wire to push that money to the local Federal Reserve Bank. The Federal Reserve Bank debits CoopBank's account there and pushes the funds to Maxine's bank, MaxBank. The Federal Reserve notifies MaxBank that it has received $1 million for Maxine. MaxBank pushes the money into Maxine's account. Exhibit 24.7 illustrates the difference between checks and payment orders.

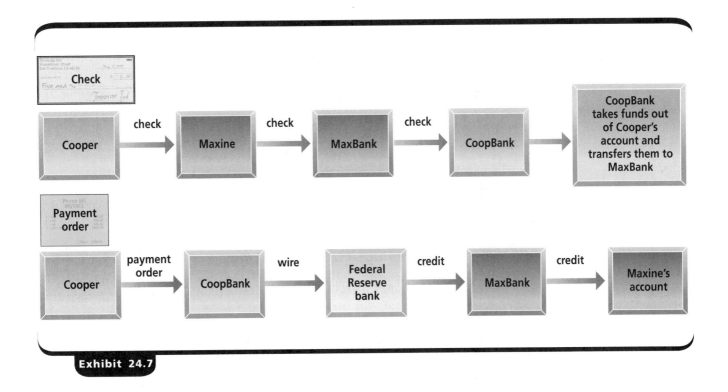

Exhibit 24.7

---

[20] You remember that the Electronic Fund Transfer Act regulates wire transfers involving consumers.

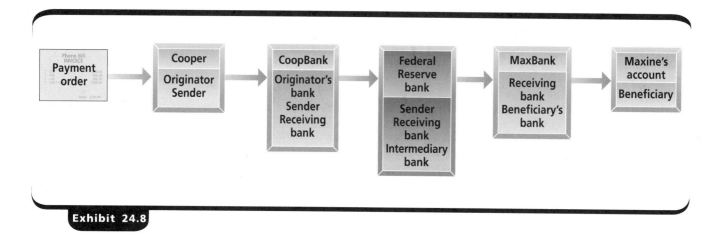

Exhibit 24.8

Article 4A uses the following terminology to describe the various participants in a wire transfer:

- *Originator.* The person who sends the first payment order in a transaction (Cooper)

- *Originator's Bank.* The bank that issues the originator's payment order (CoopBank)

- *Sender.* Anyone who gives instructions to a receiving bank (Cooper, CoopBank, and Federal Reserve Bank)

- *Beneficiary.* The person who receives the payment order (Maxine)

- *Receiving Bank.* Any bank to which the sender's instructions are sent (CoopBank, Federal Reserve Bank, and MaxBank)

- *Intermediary Bank.* Any receiving bank other than the originator's bank or the beneficiary's bank (Federal Reserve Bank)

- *Beneficiary's Bank.* The bank identified in the payment order, which has an account in the beneficiary's name (MaxBank)

Exhibit 24.8 illustrates the terminology used to describe the participants in Cooper's wire transfer to Maxine.

Wire transfers often involve very large sums of money. What happens when mistakes occur, as mistakes inevitably will?

Bank Sends the Wrong Amount of Money

If a bank sends more money than the payment order specified, it is liable for the extra amount. Its recourse is to recover the excess from the beneficiary. If the bank sends too little money, the originator must pay only the amount sent, not the amount of the order.[21]

Bank Sends Money to the Wrong Person

If any bank issues a payment order to the wrong person, the bank is liable for the full amount of the payment. It can try to recover from the unintended recipient. The originator and any prior bank are not liable.[22]

---

[21] UCC Section 4A-303(a), (b).
[22] UCC Section 4A-303(c).

Sometimes, a beneficiary's bank receives a payment order with an account name and number that do not match. If the bank notices the mismatch, it should not pay any account. If the bank does not notice and pays the account specified by the number, it is not liable even if that turns out to be the wrong account. The originator is liable. If the beneficiary's bank relies on the name instead of the number, it is liable and must reimburse the originator. As you can imagine, banks have a tendency to look only at the account number, not at the name. There is, however, one major exception to this rule. If a nonbank originator gives the wrong number and the right name, he is not liable when the payment is made to the wrong person unless his bank warned him that the beneficiary's bank would make payment based on the number, not the name.[23]

PRIVACY

Think about how much information your bank knows about you. Add to that what your insurance company, stock brokerage, and credit card companies know. Imagine that they can sell that information to anyone they wish, without telling you. Are you nervous yet?

This is the problem that the Gramm-Leach-Bliley Act of 1999 (GLB) sought to solve.[24] **Under this statute, banks and other financial institutions must disclose to consumers any non-public information they wish to reveal to third parties. A financial institution cannot disclose this private information if the consumer opts out (that is, denies permission).** Note that GLB permits financial institutions to provide information to third parties unless the consumer affirmatively requests privacy.

After this statute passed, consumers were inundated with a blizzard of notification forms. Thinking that these notices were junk mail, many customers never even bothered to open them. Consumer advocates complained that in many cases opting out was made deliberately difficult—the instructions were unclear and opting out generally had to be done by snail mail instead of online. Also, many companies failed to send out the required notices.

A small number of states have established rules that go further than the GLB. These states require an "opt-in" standard, which means that a financial institution cannot divulge private data unless the consumer affirmatively grants permission. The distinction between opt in and opt out is important—typically 30 percent of consumers opt out, while only 1 percent of consumers opt in.

CHAPTER CONCLUSION

This area of law merits careful study for two reasons. First, it is important to everyone who has ever written a check or used an ATM, which is to say, virtually everyone. Second, the law is changing rapidly. A generation ago, no one would have asked "How much do I owe if my ATM card is stolen?" because ATMs did not exist. In some cases, the questions are still the same—"When can a bank pay a post-dated check?"—but now the answer is different.

---

[23] UCC Section 4A-207.
[24] 15 U.S.C. Section 6801.

EXAM REVIEW

1. **WRONGFUL DISHONOR** If a bank wrongfully dishonors an authorized check, it is liable to the customer for all actual and consequential damages. (p. 580)

2. **DEATH OR INCOMPETENCE** A bank is not liable for paying the checks of an incompetent customer until it knows that the customer has been adjudicated incompetent. If a customer dies, the bank may continue to pay checks for 10 days after it learns of the death, unless it receives a stop payment order from someone claiming an interest in the account. (p. 581)

3. **FORGERY** If a bank pays a check on which the issuer's name is forged, it must recredit the issuer's account. (p. 581)

4. **ALTERATION** If a bank pays a check that has been altered, the customer is liable only for the original terms of the check, and the bank is liable for the balance. (p. 581)

5. **COMPLETION** If a bank pays an incomplete check that was filled in by someone other than the original issuer, the bank is not liable unless it was on notice that the completion was improper. (p. 582)

6. **STALE CHECKS** A bank is not required to pay checks that are presented more than six months after their date, but it is not liable if it does pay. (p. 584)

EXAM Strategy

Question: An employee lost her paycheck and did not find it for 19 years (okay, her house was a tad untidy). Nothing on the check said that it must be cashed within a certain amount of time. Is this check valid?

Strategy: Most of the rules on checks are straightforward, but this is one case when the bank has choices. The right answer is simply to describe these choices. (See the "Result" at the end of this section.)

7. **POST-DATED CHECKS** A bank has no liability for paying a check before its date unless the customer notifies the bank in advance that the check is coming. (p. 584)

8. **STOP PAYMENT ORDERS** If a bank pays a check over a stop payment order, it is liable to the customer for any loss he suffers as a result. The bank is subrogated to the rights of both the customer and the payee. (p. 584)

EXAM Strategy

Question: Begg & Daigle, Inc., wrote a check for $31,989.80 to Newwall Interior Partitions, Inc. Begg then asked Chemical Bank to stop payment on the check. In November, the bank accidentally paid the check. This payment was reflected in Begg's November statement, but Begg did not discover the mistaken payment until the following February. In the meantime, Begg sent a second check to Newwall in payment of the full amount. Begg demanded that the bank recredit its account for the amount of the stopped check. Is the bank liable for paying this check over the stop payment order?

Strategy: There are two competing mistakes here—the bank paid a check on which there was a stop payment order; and the customer waited three months to tell the bank about its mistake. In such a case, banks are generally held to a higher standard than consumers. Also, as a general rule, if the customer can prove a loss, the bank is liable on a stop payment order, period. (See the "Result" at the end of this section.)

---

9. **SUBSTITUTE CHECKS** A substitute check is legally the same as an original check. A bank that transfers or presents an electronic or a substitute check gives a *warranty of legal equivalency*. The bank is warranting to the drawer, the payee, the depositor, any indorser, and any bank that receives the check that the substitute check is an accurate image of the original check. (p. 586)

---

10. **VALIDATION OF ATM CARDS** If a bank sends an electronic fund transfer card (for example, an ATM card) to a consumer who has not requested it, the card must be invalid until the consumer requests validation. (p. 590)

---

11. **ERRORS IN BANK STATEMENTS** If, within 60 days of receiving a bank statement, a consumer tells the bank (either orally or in writing) that the account is in error, the bank must investigate and report the result of its investigation to the consumer within 10 business days. (p. 591)

---

12. **UNAUTHORIZED TRANSFERS** When a thief uses a stolen ATM or debit card to withdraw money from a bank account, the consumer is not liable for more than $50, provided she notifies the bank within two business days that the card has been stolen. (p. 592)

---

13. **PAYMENT ORDERS** If a bank issues a payment order to the wrong person, the bank is liable for the full amount of the payment. (p. 595)

EXAM Strategy

Question: Shawmut Bank in Massachusetts transferred $10,000 from the account of American Optical Corp. via Fedwire to the account of Fernando Degan at the First American Bank in West Palm Beach, Florida. Although the money was intended for Degan and the payment order had his name alone, Shawmut listed an account number at First American that was jointly held by Degan and Joseph Merle, rather than the account that was held solely by Degan. Once the money was transferred into the joint account, Merle withdrew it. Shawmut sued First American, alleging that First American was liable for the mistaken transfer because it had placed the funds in a joint account, not in Degan's sole account as the payment order had indicated. Is First American liable to Shawmut?

Strategy: This is one of those cases where the rules on banks are straightforward: in executing a payment order, a bank may rely on the account number, instead of the name. (See the "Result" at the end of this section.)

---

14. **GRAMM-LEACH-BLILEY ACT** Banks and other financial institutions must disclose to consumers any non-public information they wish to reveal to third parties. A financial institution cannot disclose this private information if the consumer *opts out* (that is, denies permission). (p. 597)

---

6. Result: The bank is not required to cash the check, but it can if it wants (or if it fails to notice the date).

8. Result: The bank is liable for the full amount of the check.

13. Result: First American had placed the money in the account that matched the number on the wire, so it was not liable even though the names did not match.

ADDITIONAL QUESTIONS

1. Woodhaven Knitting Mills wrote a check to Ava Industries for $19,500, drawn on Manufacturers Hanover Trust Co. Woodhaven asked Manufacturers Hanover to stop payment on the check, but the bank paid the check accidentally. The bank was subrogated to Woodhaven's interest against Ava, and Ava paid the bank $5,000. As a result, the bank's loss was reduced from $19,500 to $14,500. The bank filed suit against Woodhaven for $14,500, alleging that Woodhaven owed that sum to Ava. Does the bank have a valid claim against Woodhaven?

2. Hassan Qassemzadeh had an account at the IBM Poughkeepsie Employees Federal Credit Union. On December 1, he wrote a check for $9.60, which was altered and subsequently cashed for $9,000.60. In January, the Credit Union mailed his statement to his niece, as he had directed. This statement indicated that the check had been paid on January 6 for $9,000.60. Qassemzadeh notified the Credit Union

of the alteration the following January. Is the Credit Union liable to Qassemzadeh for the amount of the altered check?

3. Barry Minkow founded ZZZZ Best, a publicly traded carpet cleaning company. The company had a $5 million line of credit from Prudential Bache. Sheri Elowsky was the vice president at Prudential in charge of the ZZZZ Best account. After Minkow flew her to Los Angeles and wined and dined her for the weekend, she approved a $225,000 extension on the company's line of credit. Minkow gave her a post-dated $2 million check to pay down the loan. Two days later, ZZZZ Best's stock price dropped steeply. Minkow would not return Elowsky's phone calls. She then discovered that Minkow had resigned from the board and the $2 million check would not be honored. Is there anything Elowsky could have done to reduce Prudential Bache's losses?

4. **CPA QUESTION** In general, which of the following statements is correct concerning the priority among checks drawn on a particular account and presented to the drawee bank on a particular day?

   (a) The checks may be charged to the account in any order convenient to the bank.

   (b) The checks may be charged to the account in any order, provided no charge creates an overdraft.

   (c) The checks must be charged to the account in the order in which the checks were dated.

   (d) The checks must be charged to the account in the order of lowest amount to highest amount to minimize the number of dishonored checks.

5. Rev. Janet Hooper Ritchie knew that the shoe store at Buckland Hills mall in Manchester, Connecticut, would not accept a Discover credit card, so she stopped at an ATM for a $100 cash advance. Ritchie, a Congregational minister, inserted her card only to have it returned with a slip that said her withdrawal had been rejected. Ritchie thought that it was odd the slip did not bear the name of a bank. A few days later, she learned she was one of more than 100 customers bilked of confidential code information through the phony ATM. The crooks made off with a total of $100,000 after using the code information obtained by the ATM to make counterfeit bank cards. They used these fake cards to hit ATMs up and down the East Coast and pillage customer accounts. Who is liable for these losses—the banks or the customers whose accounts were looted?

6. **ETHICS** Sandra Bisbey authorized her bank to make monthly electronic fund transfers to her life insurance company. In September, Bisbey's account did not have enough funds to cover this payment, so no transfer was made. In October, Bisbey's account still lacked sufficient funds, but the bank made payments for both months anyway and sent two overdraft notices to her (but did not charge an overdraft fee). Bisbey, having forgotten her nonpayment in September, believed that the bank had erroneously made two payments in October. She called the bank to report this alleged error. Ten days later, an official of the bank telephoned her and explained that both payments had been proper. Bisbey filed suit under the EFTA, alleging that the bank unlawfully failed to inform her of the result of its investigation. Did the bank violate the EFTA? Is it liable even if its violation caused no harm to the plaintiff? The bank's actions actually benefited Bisbey: she

received insurance coverage without paying an overdraft fee. Was it right for her to file suit under these circumstances? What guidance can you obtain from the ethics checklist in Chapter 2?

7. Harriet goes to the teller window and deposits a $1,000 tax refund check from the United States Treasury into her checking account. Two business days later, she sees the apartment of her dreams and wants to withdraw the entire $1,000 in cash to put down a security deposit and first month's rent on the apartment before anyone else sees it. She:

    (a) Can withdraw only $400

    (b) Can withdraw the whole amount

    (c) Cannot withdraw anything

8. **YOU BE THE JUDGE** WRITING PROBLEM Roger Duchow (owner of Duchow's Marine, Inc.) borrowed money from General Electric Capital Corp. (GECC) to buy boats for his business. He agreed that when he sold a boat, he would deposit the funds in a blocked account at Central Bank. Funds could be withdrawn from this blocked account only with GECC's signature. Duchow also had a separate, unrestricted account at Central. Duchow sold a yacht and, in an effort to defraud GECC, told the buyer to wire the $215,000 purchase price to the unrestricted account. The buyer's bank sent the wire transfer to an intermediary bank, Banker's Bank. But Banker's instructions to Central included only Duchow's name, omitting his account number. As luck would have it, the money was put in the blocked account. Duchow immediately ordered Central to transfer the funds to his unrestricted account, which Central did. Duchow quickly spent the money and had no other assets. Is Central liable to GECC?

    Argument for Central: The Bank simply followed instructions that Banker's had originally issued and that had been accidentally left off the payment order. Central was not to blame for Duchow's fraud.

    Argument for GECC: Central had an obligation to follow the wire instructions. But once the funds landed in the blocked account, Central had to make a nonclerical decision—to move or not to move. No law required it to transfer the funds, especially since the account clearly had GECC's name on it.

9. When Heidi submits a claim to her health insurance company, it refuses to reimburse her unless she also provides a copy of the check that she used to pay the doctor. The company wants proof that she has indeed paid. When she requests the cancelled check from her bank, it sends her a substitute check. Her health insurance company refuses to accept this check—it demands a copy of the original. How can Heidi provide proof to the insurance company?

10. **ROLE REVERSAL** Write a multiple-choice question that involves consumer liability for unauthorized transactions.

INTERNET RESEARCH PROBLEM

Go to the websites of the financial institutions at which you have accounts. See if there is any way you can opt out online (for purposes of the GLB). Do the websites disclose what you must do to opt out?

You can find further practice problems at www.cengagebrain.com. See the preface of this book for website access details.

25 | SECURED TRANSACTIONS

Dear Help-For-All:

Look, somebody out there is crazy. When I got out of school, I paid $18,000 for a used Jeep. I made every payment—*every one*—for over two years. I shelled out over 9,000 bucks for that car. Then I got laid off through no fault of my own, which even my boss admits. I missed a few payments and the bank repossessed the car. OK, fair enough, I can see that. They auction off the Jeep. Now the bank's lawyer phones and says I'm still liable for over $5,000. What is this, a joke? I owe money for a car I can't even drive anymore? Come on, admit something is out of whack here.

> Signed,
> Still Sane, I Hope

I owe money for a car I can't even drive anymore?

Dear Still Sane,

I am sympathetic with your story, but unfortunately, the bank is entitled to its money. Here is how the law sees your plight. When you bought the car, you signed two documents: a note, in which you promised to pay the full balance owed, and a security agreement, which said that if you stopped making payments, the bank could repossess the vehicle and sell it.

There are two problems. First, even after two years of writing checks, you might still have owed about $10,000 (because of interest). Second, cars depreciate quickly. Your $18,000 vehicle probably had a market value of about $8,000 thirty months later. The security agreement allowed the bank to sell the Jeep at auction, where prices are still lower. Your car evidently fetched about $5,000. That leaves a deficiency of $5,000—for which you are legally responsible, regardless of who is driving the car.

Hoping the busses are on time,

Help-for-Almost-All

REVISED ARTICLE 9: TERMS AND SCOPE[1]

We can sympathize with "Still Sane," but the bank is entitled to its money. The buyer and the bank had entered into a secured transaction, meaning that one party gave credit to another, demanding in return an assurance of repayment. Whether a used car lot sells a car on credit for $18,000, or a bank takes collateral for a $600 million corporate loan, the parties have created a secured transaction.

Article 9 of the UCC governs secured transactions in personal property. It is essential to understand the basics of this law because we live and work in a world economy based solidly—or shakily—on credit. Gravity may cause the earth to spin, but secured transactions keep the commercial world going 'round. The quantity of disputes tells us how important this law is: about *one-half of all UCC lawsuits* involve Article 9. This part of the Code employs terms not used elsewhere, so we must lead off with some definitions:

- **Fixtures** are goods that have become attached to real estate. For example, heating ducts are *goods* when a company manufactures them and also when it sells them to a retailer. But when a contractor installs the ducts in a new house, they become *fixtures*.

- **Security interest** means an interest in personal property or fixtures that secures the performance of some *obligation*. If an automobile dealer sells you a new car on credit and retains a security interest in the car, it means she is keeping legal rights *in your car*, including the right to drive it away if you fall behind in your payments. Usually, the obligation is to pay money, such as the money due on the new car. Occasionally, the obligation is to perform some other action, but in this chapter, we concentrate on the payment of money because that is what security interests are generally designed to ensure.

- **Secured party** is the person or company that holds the security interest. The automobile dealer who sells you a car on credit is the secured party.

- **Collateral** is the property subject to a security interest. When a dealer sells you a new car and keeps a security interest, the vehicle is the collateral.

- **Debtor and Obligor.** For our purposes, **debtor** refers to a person who has some original ownership interest in the collateral. (Having a security interest in the collateral does not make one a debtor.) If Alice borrows money from a bank and uses her Mercedes as collateral, she is the debtor because she owns the car. **Obligor** means a person who must repay money, or perform some other task.

Fixtures
Goods that have become attached to real estate.

Security interest
An interest in personal property or fixtures that secures the performance of an obligation.

Secured party
A person or company that holds a security interest.

Collateral
Property that is subject to a security interest.

Debtor
A person who has original ownership interest in the collateral.

Obligor
A person who must repay money or perform some other task to satisfy a debt.

---

[1] In this chapter, we use more footnotes than usual, for two reasons. First, Article 9 is a challenging series of interlocking provisions, and many readers will want to peruse the actual Code (in the appendix) to reinforce the myriad concepts. Second, the revised Article 9 is substantially rewritten and entirely renumbered; experienced practitioners may appreciate guidelines as they encounter new rules and discover familiar concepts in unexpected places.

Throughout this chapter, the obligor and debtor will generally be the same person, but not always. When Alice borrows money from a bank and uses her Mercedes as collateral, she is the obligor, because she must repay the loan; as we know, Alice is also the debtor. However, suppose that Toby borrows money from a bank and provides no collateral; Jake co-signs the loan as a favor to Toby, using his Steinway piano as collateral. *Jake* is the only debtor, because he owns the piano. *Both parties* are obligors, because both have agreed to repay the loan.

Security agreement

A contract in which the debtor gives a security interest to the secured party.

Default

The failure of a debtor to pay money due on a loan or credit purchase.

Repossession

Occurs when the secured party takes back collateral because the debtor has defaulted.

Perfection

A series of steps that the secured party must take to protect its rights in the collateral against people other than the debtor.

Financing statement

A document that the secured party files to give the general public notice that it has a secured interest in the collateral.

Record

Information written on paper or stored in an electronic or other medium.

- **Security agreement** is the contract in which the debtor gives a security interest to the secured party. This agreement protects the secured party's rights in the collateral.

- **Default** occurs when the debtor fails to pay money that is due, for example, on a loan or for a purchase made on credit. Default also includes other failures by the debtor, such as failing to keep the collateral insured.

- **Repossession** occurs when the secured party takes back collateral because the debtor has defaulted. Typically, the secured party will demand that the debtor deliver the collateral; if the debtor fails to do so, the secured party may find the collateral and take it.

- **Perfection** is a series of steps the secured party must take to protect its rights in the collateral against people other than the debtor. This is important because if the debtor cannot pay his debts, several creditors may attempt to seize the collateral, but only one may obtain it. To perfect its rights in the collateral, the secured party will typically file certain papers with a state agency.

- **Financing statement** is a document that the secured party files to give the general public notice that it has a secured interest in the collateral.

- **Record** refers to information written on paper *or* stored in an electronic or other medium.

- **Authenticate** means to sign a document *or* to use any symbol or encryption method that identifies the person and clearly indicates she is adopting the record as her own. You authenticate a security agreement when you sign the papers at an auto dealership. A corporation electronically authenticates a loan agreement by using the Internet to transmit an encrypted signature.

Here is an example using the terms just discussed. A medical equipment company manufactures a CAT scan machine and sells it to a clinic for $2 million, taking $500,000 cash and the clinic's promise to pay the rest over five years. The clinic simultaneously authenticates a security agreement, giving the manufacturer a security interest in the CAT scan. If the clinic fails to make its payments, the manufacturer can repossess the machine. The manufacturer then electronically files a financing statement in an appropriate state agency. This *perfects* the manufacturer's rights, meaning that its security interest in the CAT scanner is now valid against all the world. Exhibit 25.1 illustrates this transaction.

If the clinic goes bankrupt and many creditors try to seize its assets, the manufacturer has first claim to the CAT scan machine. The clinic's bankruptcy is of great importance. When a debtor has money to pay all of its debts, there are no concerns about security interests. A creditor insists on a security interest to protect itself in the event the debtor *cannot* pay all of its debts. The secured party intends (1) to give itself a legal interest in specific property of the debtor and (2) to establish a priority claim in that property, ahead of other creditors. In this chapter, we look at a variety of issues that arise in secured transactions.

Article 9 Revisions

Throughout the 1990s, the American Law Institute and the National Conference of Commissioners on Uniform State Laws worked on significant revisions of Article 9. The drafters made

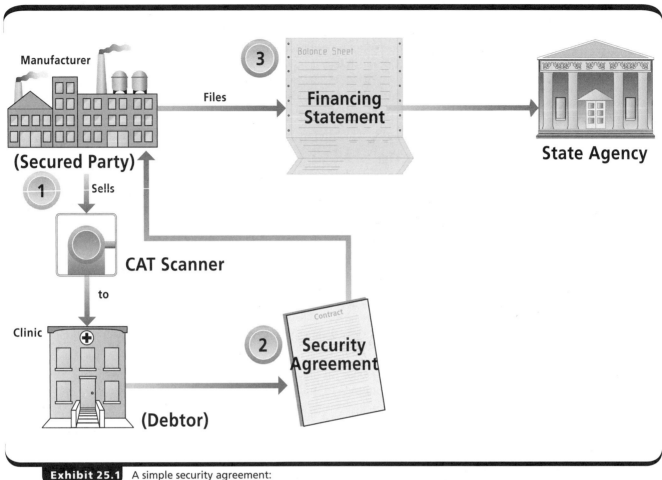

Exhibit 25.1 A simple security agreement:
(1) The manufacturer sells a CAT scan machine to a clinic, taking $500,000 and the clinic's promise to pay the balance over five years.
(2) The clinic simultaneously authenticates a security agreement.
(3) The manufacturer perfects by electronically filing a financing statement.

their final recommendations in 2000, and the proposed revisions are now the law in all states. The revisions have expanded the number of transactions that Article 9 covers, and clarified the rules for creating, perfecting, and enforcing security interests. In a bow to e-commerce, Article 9 is now **medium-neutral,** meaning that it permits security interests to be created and filed electronically or in any other form (as well as on paper). The revisions also strengthen some provisions concerning consumer transactions.

All citations in this chapter are to the 2000 Revision of Article 9. The UCC is available online at **http://www.law.cornell.edu.**[2] For the actual statutory versions of Article 9 that have been adopted state-by-state, go to **http://www.law.cornell.edu.**

---

[2] When researching any article of the Code online, be certain that you are reading the most recent revision.

SCOPE OF REVISED ARTICLE 9

Article 9 applies to any transaction intended to create a security interest in personal property or fixtures. The personal property used as collateral may be goods, such as cars or hats, but it may also be a variety of other things:

- **Instruments.** Drafts, checks, certificates of deposit, and notes may all be used as collateral, as may stocks, bonds, and other securities.

- **Investment Property**, which refers primarily to securities and related rights.

- **Documents of Title.** These are papers used by an owner of goods who ships or stores them. The documents are the owner's proof that he owns goods no longer in his possession. For example, an owner sending goods by truck will obtain a *bill of lading*, a receipt indicating where the goods will be shipped and who gets them when they arrive. Similarly, a *warehouse receipt* is the owner's receipt for goods stored at a warehouse. The owner may use these and other similar documents of title as collateral.

- **Account** means a right to receive payment for goods sold or leased. This includes, for example, accounts receivable, indicating that various buyers owe a merchant money for goods they have already received. The category now includes health-care-insurance receivables.

- **Deposit Accounts.** Article 9 now covers security interests in deposit accounts (money placed in banks).

- **Commercial Tort Claims.** An organization that has filed a tort suit may use its claim as collateral. Personal injuries to individuals are not covered by this article.

- **General Intangibles.** This is a residual category, designed to include many kinds of collateral that do not appear elsewhere on the list, such as copyrights, patents, trademarks, goodwill, and the right to payment of some loans.

- **Chattel Paper.** This is a record that indicates two things: (1) an obligor owes money and (2) a secured party has a security interest in specific goods. Chattel paper most commonly occurs in a consumer sale on credit. If a dealer sells an air conditioner to a customer, who agrees in writing to make monthly payments and also agrees that the dealer has a security interest in the air conditioner, that agreement is chattel paper. The confusing point is that the same chattel paper may be collateral for a second security interest. The dealer who sells the air conditioner could use the chattel paper to obtain a loan. If the dealer gives the chattel paper to a bank as collateral for the loan, the bank has a security interest *in the chattel paper*, while the dealer continues to have a security interest *in the air conditioner*. **Electronic chattel paper** is the same thing except that it is an electronic record rather than a written one.

- **Goods** means movable things, including fixtures, crops, and manufactured homes. For purposes of secured transactions, the Code divides goods into additional categories. In some cases, the rights of the parties will depend upon what category the goods fall into. These are the key categories:

  - *Consumer goods* are those used primarily for personal, family, or household purposes.

  - *Farm products* are crops, livestock, or supplies used directly in farming operations (as opposed to the business aspects of farming).

- *Inventory* consists of goods held by someone for sale or lease, such as all of the beds and chairs in a furniture store.

- *Equipment* refers to things used in running a business, such as the desks, telephones, and computers needed to operate a retail store.

Software

Article 9 takes into account the increasingly important role that computer software plays in all business. The Code distinguishes *software* from *goods*, and this becomes important when competing creditors are fighting over both a computer system and the software inside it. A program embedded in a computer is goods *if* it is customarily considered part of those goods *or if* by purchasing the goods the owner acquires the right to use the program. A program that does *not* meet those criteria is termed *software*, and will be treated differently for some purposes.

In sum, Article 9 applies anytime the parties intended to create a security interest in any of the items listed above.

ATTACHMENT OF A SECURITY INTEREST

Attachment is a vital step in a secured transaction. This means that the secured party has taken three steps to create an enforceable security interest:

- The two parties made a security agreement, *and either* the debtor has *authenticated a security agreement* describing the collateral *or* the secured party has obtained *possession* or *control;*

- The secured party has given value to obtain the security agreement; and

- The debtor has rights in the collateral.[3]

Attachment
A three-step process that creates an enforceable security interest.

AGREEMENT

Without an agreement, there can be no security interest. Generally, the agreement will be in writing and signed by the debtor, or electronically recorded and authenticated by the debtor. The agreement must reasonably identify the collateral. A description of collateral by *type* is often acceptable. For example, a security agreement may properly describe the collateral as "all equipment in the store at 123 Periwinkle Street."[4] In a security agreement for consumer goods, however, a description by type is *not* sufficient, and more specificity is required.

A security agreement at a minimum might:

- State that Happy Homes, Inc., and Martha agree that Martha is buying an Arctic Co. refrigerator and identify the exact unit by its serial number;

- Give the price, the down payment, the monthly payments, and interest rate;

---

[3] UCC Section 9-203.

[4] A security agreement may not use a **super-generic term** such as "all of Smith's personal property." We will see later that, by contrast, such a super-generic description is legally adequate in a *financing statement.*

- State that because Happy Homes is selling Martha the refrigerator on credit, it has a security interest in the refrigerator; and

- Provide that if Martha defaults on her payments, Happy Homes is entitled to repossess the refrigerator.

An actual security agreement will add many details, such as Martha's obligation to keep the refrigerator in good condition and to deliver it to the store if she defaults; a precise definition of "default"; and how Happy Homes may go about repossessing the goods if Martha defaults.

CONTROL AND POSSESSION

In many cases, the security agreement need not be in writing if the parties have an oral agreement and the secured party has either **control** or **possession**. For many kinds of collateral, it is safer for the secured party actually to take the item than to rely upon a security agreement. The rules follow.

Control

For deposit accounts, electronic chattel paper and certain other collateral, the security interest attaches if the secured party has *control*. The Code specifies exactly what the secured party must do to obtain control for each type of collateral. In a general sense, *control means that the secured party has certain exclusive rights to dispose of the collateral.*

- Deposit account (in a bank). The secured party has control if it is itself the bank holding the deposit or if the debtor has authorized the bank to dispose of funds according to the secured party's instructions.

- Electronic chattel paper. A secured party has control of electronic chattel paper when it possesses the only authoritative copy of it, and the record(s) designate the secured party as the assignee. This means that the parties have agreed on an electronic method to verify the uniqueness of the record, so that any copies of the electronic original are clearly recognizable as reproductions.

- Investment property and letter-of-credit rights. The Code specifies analogous methods of controlling investment properties and letter-of-credit rights.[5]

Possession

For most other forms of collateral, including goods, securities, and most other items, a security interest attaches if the secured party has *possession*. For example, if you loan your neighbor $175,000 and he gives you a Winslow Homer watercolor as collateral, you have an attached security interest in the painting once it is in your possession. It would still be wise to put the agreement in writing, to be certain both parties understand all terms and can prove them if necessary, but the writing is not legally required.

The following case is typical of Article 9 disputes in that it was fought out in bankruptcy court. A debtor claimed to have a security interest in property owned by a bankrupt company. Had the parties made a security agreement? The court decided the case based on former Article 9, but the outcome would be the same under the revised Code.

---

[5] *Control* is described in the following Sections: 9-104 (deposit accounts), 9-105 (electronic chattel paper), 9-106 (investment property), and 9-107 (letter-of-credit rights).

In Re CFLC, Inc.

209 B.R. 508, 1997 Bankr. LEXIS 821
United States Bankruptcy Appellate Panel of the Ninth Circuit, 1997

CASE SUMMARY

Facts: Expeditors was a freight company that supervised importing and exporting for Everex Systems, Inc. Expeditors negotiated rates and services for its client and frequently had possession of Everex's goods. During a 17-month period, Expeditors sent over 300 invoices to Everex. Each invoice stated that the customer either had to accept all of the invoice's terms or to pay cash, receiving no work on credit. One of those terms gave Expeditors a general lien on all of the customer's property in its possession. In other words, if the customer failed to pay a bill, Expeditors claimed the right to retain the goods, auction them, and keep enough of the proceeds to pay its overdue bills.

Everex filed for bankruptcy. Expeditors expedited its way into the court proceedings, claiming the right to sell Everex's goods, worth about $81,000. The trial judge rejected the claim, ruling that Expeditors lacked a valid security interest. Expeditors appealed.

Issue: *Did Expeditors have a security interest in Everex's goods?*

Decision: Affirmed. Expeditors had no security interest in the goods.

Reasoning: Expeditors and Everex never explicitly agreed to create a security interest. Expeditors did send many invoices with terms that the company wished to be part of a general agreement. However, repetitively mailing such documents does not make a security agreement. Everex said nothing about the invoice terms and did nothing to indicate that it agreed to a lien on its goods. All Everex did was pay the invoices.

If the parties had reached an initial agreement, then the invoices might be evidence of a continuing security interest. Without such a clear agreement, though, there is no security interest.

EXAM *Strategy*

Question: Hector needs money to keep his business afloat. He asks his uncle for a $1 million loan. The uncle agrees, but he insists that his nephew grant him a security interest in Hector's splendid gold clarinet, worth over $2 million. Hector agrees. The uncle prepares a handwritten document summarizing the agreement and asks his nephew to sign it. Hector hands the clarinet to his uncle and receives his money, but he forgets to sign the document. Has a security agreement attached?

Strategy: Attachment occurs if the parties made a security agreement and there was authentication or possession; the secured party has given value; and the debtor had rights in the collateral.

Result: Hector agreed to give his uncle a security interest in the instrument. He never authenticated (signed) the agreement, but the uncle did take possession of the clarinet. The uncle gave Hector $1 million, and Hector owned the instrument. Yes, the security interest attached.

VALUE

For the security interest to attach, the secured party must give value. Usually, the value will be apparent. If a bank loans $400 million to an airline, that money is the value, and the bank, therefore, may obtain a security interest in the planes that the airline is buying. If a store sells a living room set to a customer for a small down payment and two years of monthly payments, the value given is the furniture.

Future Value

The parties may also agree that some of the value will be given in the future. For example, a finance company might extend a $5 million line of credit to a retail store, even though the store initially takes only $1 million of the money. The remaining credit is available whenever the store needs it to purchase inventory. The Code considers the entire $5 million line of credit to be value.[6]

DEBTOR RIGHTS IN THE COLLATERAL

The debtor can grant a security interest in goods only if he has some legal right to those goods himself. Typically, the debtor owns the goods. But a debtor may also give a security interest if he is leasing the goods or even if he is a bailee, meaning that he is lawfully holding them for someone else. Suppose Importer receives a shipment of scallops on behalf of Seafood Wholesaler. Wholesaler asks Importer to hold the scallops for three days as a favor, and to keep a customer happy, Importer agrees. Importer then arranges a $150,000 loan from a bank, using the scallops as collateral. Although Importer has acted unethically, it does have *some right* in the collateral—the right to hold them for three days. That is enough to satisfy this rule.

By contrast, suppose Railroad is transporting 10 carloads of cattle on behalf of Walter, the owner. A devious Meat Dealer uses forged documents to trick Railroad into believing that Meat Dealer is entitled to the animals. Meat Dealer trucks the cattle away and uses them to obtain a bank loan, giving the bank a security interest in the animals. That "security interest" has never attached and is invalid, because Dealer had *no* legal interest in the cattle. When Walter, the rightful owner, locates his cattle, he may take them back. The bank can only hope to find the deceitful Dealer, who in fact has probably disappeared.

Result

Once the security interest has attached to the collateral, the secured party is protected against the debtor. If the debtor fails to pay, the secured party may repossess the collateral.

ATTACHMENT TO FUTURE PROPERTY

The security agreement may specify that the security interest attaches to personal property that the debtor does not yet possess but might obtain in the future.

After-acquired property
Items that the debtor obtains after the parties have made their security agreement.

After-Acquired Property

After-acquired property refers to items that the debtor obtains after the parties have made their security agreement. **The parties may agree that the security interest attaches to after-acquired**

---

[6] UCC Section 9-204(c).

property.[7] Basil is starting a catering business, but owns only a beat-up car. He borrows $55,000 from the Pesto Bank, which takes a security interest in the car. But Pesto also insists on an after-acquired clause. When Basil purchases a commercial stove, cooking equipment, and freezer, Pesto's security interest attaches to each item as Basil acquires it.

Proceeds

Proceeds are whatever is obtained by a debtor who sells the collateral or otherwise disposes of it. **The secured party automatically obtains a security interest in the proceeds of the collateral, unless the security agreement states otherwise.**[8] Suppose the Pesto Bank obtains a security interest in Basil's $4,000 freezer. Basil then decides he needs a larger model and sells the original freezer to his neighbor for $3,000. The $3,000 cash is proceeds, in which Pesto automatically obtains a security interest. If for some reason the parties do not want the security interest to extend to proceeds (which would be very unusual), they must make that clear in the security agreement.

PERFECTION

NOTHING LESS THAN PERFECTION

Once the security interest has attached to the collateral, the secured party is protected *against the debtor*. Pesto Bank loaned money to Basil and has a security interest in all of his property. If Basil defaults on his loan, Pesto may insist he deliver the goods to the bank. If he fails to do that, the bank can seize the collateral. But Pesto's security interest is valid only against Basil; if a third person claims some interest in the goods, the bank may never get them. For example, Basil might have taken out *another* loan, from his friend Olive, and used the same property as collateral. Olive knew nothing about the bank's original loan. To protect itself against Olive, and all other parties, the bank must *perfect* its interest.

There are several kinds of perfection:

- Perfection by filing

- Perfection by possession

- Perfection of consumer goods

- Perfection of movable collateral and fixtures

In some cases, the secured party will have a choice of which method to use; in other cases, only one method works.

PERFECTION BY FILING

The most common way to perfect is by filing a financing statement with one or more state agencies. A **financing statement** gives the names of all parties, describes the collateral, and outlines the security interest, enabling any interested person to learn about it. Suppose the

---

[7] UCC Section 9-204(a).
[8] UCC Section 9-203(f).

Pesto Bank obtains a security interest in Basil's catering equipment and then perfects by filing with the Secretary of State in the state capital. When Basil asks his friend Olive for a loan, she will check the records to see if anyone has a security interest in the catering equipment. Olive's search uncovers Basil's previous security agreement, and she realizes it would be unwise to make the loan. If Basil were to default, the collateral would go straight to Pesto Bank, leaving Olive empty-handed. See Exhibit 25.2

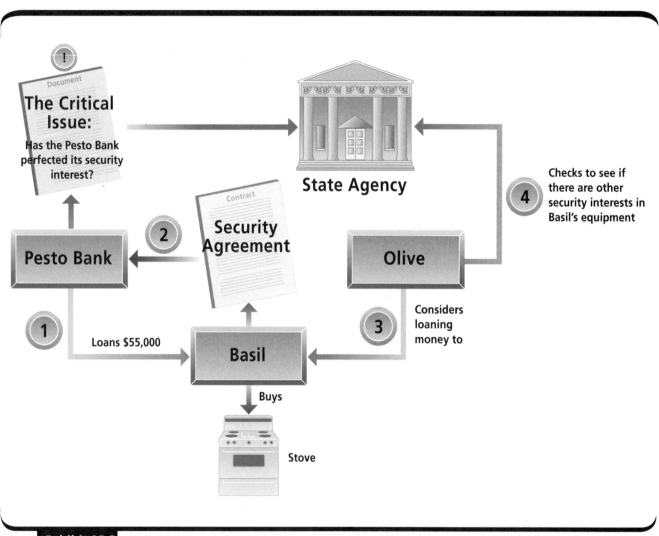

Exhibit 25.2 The Pesto Bank:
(1) Loans money to Basil and
(2) Takes a security interest in his equipment.

Later, when Olive:
(3) Considers loaning Basil money, she will
(4) Check to see if any other creditors already have a security interest in his goods.

Article 9 prescribes one form, to be used nationwide for financing statements.[9] The financing form is available online at many websites. Remember that the filing may be done on paper or electronically.

If the collateral is either *accounts* or *general intangibles*, filing is the only way to perfect. Suppose Nester uses his copyright in a screenplay as collateral for a loan. The bank that gives him the loan may perfect *only* by filing.

The most common problems that arise in filing cases are (1) whether the financing statement contained enough information to put other people on notice of the security interest and (2) whether the secured party filed the papers in the right place.

Contents of the Financial Statement

A financing statement is sufficient if it provides the name of the debtor, the name of the secured party, and an indication of the collateral.[10]

The name of the debtor is critical because that is what an interested person will use to search among the millions of other financing statements on file. Faulty descriptions of the debtor's name have led to thousands of disputes and untold years of litigation, as subsequent creditors have failed to locate any record of an earlier claim on the debtor's property. In response, the Code is now very precise about what name must be used. If the debtor is a "registered organization," such as a corporation, limited partnership, or limited liability company, the official, registered name of the company is the only one acceptable. If the debtor is a person, or an unregistered organization (such as a club), then the *correct* name is required. Trade names are not sufficient. Because misnamed debtors have created so much conflict, the Code now offers a straightforward test: A financing statement is effective if a computer search run under the debtor's correct name produces it. That is true even if the financing statement used the *incorrect* name. If the search does not reveal the document, then the financing statement is ineffective as a matter of law. The burden is on the secured party to file accurately, not on the searcher to seek out erroneous filings.[11]

The collateral must be described reasonably so that another party contemplating a loan to the debtor will understand which property is already secured. A financing statement could properly state that it applies to "all inventory in the debtor's Houston warehouse." If the debtor has given a security interest in everything he owns, then it is sufficient to state simply that the financing statement covers "all assets" or "all personal property."

The filing must be done by the debtor's last name. But which name is the last? Conflicting cultural traditions create ambiguity, as the following case indicates. Did the court get it right?

CORONA FRUITS & VEGGIES, INC. V. FROZSUN FOODS, INC.

143 CAL. APP. 4TH 319, 48 CAL. RPTR. 3d 868
CALIFORNIA COURT OF APPEALS, 2006

CASE SUMMARY

Facts: Corona Fruits & Veggies (Corona) leased farmland to a strawberry farmer named Armando Munoz Juarez. He signed the lease, "Armando Munoz." Corona advanced money for payroll and farm production expenses. The company filed a UCC-1 financing statement, claiming a security interest in the strawberry crop. The financing statement listed the debtor's

---

[9] UCC Section 9-521.
[10] UCC Section 9-502(a).
[11] UCC Section 9-506(c).

name as "Armando Munoz." Six months later, Armando Munoz Juarez contracted with Frozsun Foods, Inc., to sell processed strawberries. Frozsun advanced money and filed a financing statement listing the debtor's name as "Armando Juarez."

By the next year, our good farmer owed Corona $230,000 and Frozsun $19,600. When the farmer was unable to make payments on Corona's loan, the company repossessed the farmland and harvested the strawberry crop. Both Corona and Frozsun claimed the proceeds of the crop. The trial court awarded the money to Frozsun, finding that Corona had filed its financing statement under the wrong last name and therefore had failed to perfect its security interest in the strawberry crop. Corona appealed.

Issue: *Did Corona correctly file its financing statement?*

Decision: No, Corona did not correctly file. Affirmed.

Reasoning: Because UCC-1 financing statements are indexed by last name, it is essential that a creditor use the correct surname. This debtor's true last name was "Juarez," not "Munoz." Corona's own business records, receipts, and checks all refer to him as "Juarez," as do his green card and photo ID.

The record indicates that Frozsun's agent conducted a "Juarez" debtor name search and did not discover appellants' UCC-1 financing statement. The secured party, not the debtor or uninvolved third parties, has the duty of ensuring proper filing and indexing of the notice.

Corona contends that since the debtor is from Mexico, we should follow the traditions of that country, where the surname is formed by listing the father's name, then the mother's. But the strawberries were planted in California, not Mexico. This is where the debt arose and the UCC-1 was filed. The state cannot organize a filing system that will accommodate naming practices in all foreign countries.

Corona failed to file properly, and its security interest never perfected.

Debtor's Signature. Notice one important item that is *not* required on a financing statement: the debtor's signature. The drafters have greatly facilitated electronic filing by eliminating the old requirement that a debtor sign. Does this allow a secured party to create any financing statement it wishes? No. The debtor must have entered into a valid security agreement before the secured party is entitled to file any financing statement. Of course, there is the possibility of a fraudulent filing, but the drafters reasoned that the efficiency achieved far outweighs the dangers.

Place of Filing

This is a big country, and potential creditors do not want to stagger from one end of it to the other to learn whether particular collateral is already secured elsewhere. Article 9 specifies *where* a secured party must file. These provisions may vary from state to state, so it is essential to check local law, because a misfiled record accomplishes nothing. The general rules are as follows.

A secured party must file **in the state of the debtor's location.** An *individual* is located at his principal residence. If Luigi, the debtor, lives in Baltimore, works in Virginia, and has a vacation home in Key West, a secured party must file in Maryland. An organization that has only one place of business is located in that state. If the organization has more than one place of business, it is located at its chief executive office.[12]

Article 9 prescribes central filing within the state for most types of collateral. For *goods*, the central location will typically be the Secretary of State's office, although a state may designate some other office if it wishes. For *fixtures*, the secured party generally has a choice

---

[12] UCC Section 9-307.

between filing in the same central office that is used for goods, or filing in the local county office that would be used to file real estate mortgages.[13]

Duration of Filing

Once a financing statement has been filed, it is effective for five years (except for a manufactured home, where it lasts 30 years). After five years the statement will expire and leave the secured party unprotected, unless she files a continuation statement within six months prior to expiration. The continuation statement is valid for an additional five years and a secured party may file one periodically, forever.[14]

PERFECTION BY POSSESSION OR CONTROL

For most types of collateral, in addition to filing, a secured party generally may perfect by possession or control. So if the collateral is a diamond brooch or 1,000 shares of stock, a bank may perfect its security interest by holding the items until the loan is paid off. When the debtor gives collateral to the secured party, it is often called a **pledge**: the debtor pledges her goods to secure her performance, and the secured party (sometimes called the pledgee) takes the goods to perfect its interest.

Pledge
A secured transaction in which a debtor gives collateral to the secured party.

Possession

When may a party use possession? Whenever the collateral is **goods, negotiable documents, instruments, money, chattel paper that is tangible (as opposed to electronic), or most securities.**[15]

Perfection by possession has some advantages. First, notice to other parties is very effective. No reasonable finance company assumes that it can obtain a security interest in a Super Bowl championship ring when *another creditor* already holds the ring. Second, possession enables the creditor to ensure that the collateral will not be damaged during the life of the security interest. A bank that loans money based on a rare painting may worry about the painting's condition, but it knows the painting is safe if it is locked up in the bank's vault. Third, if the debtor defaults, a secured party obviously has no difficulties repossessing goods that it already holds.

Of course, for some collateral, possession is impractical. If a consumer buys a new yacht on credit, the seller can hardly expect to perfect its security interest by possession. The buyer would become edgy sailing the boat around the dealer's parking lot. In such a case, the secured party must perfect by filing.

Mandatory Possession

A party *must* perfect a security interest in money by taking possession.[16] Money is easy to transfer and impossible to distinguish from other cash. So a party with a security interest

---

[13] UCC Section 9-501.
[14] UCC Section 9-515.
[15] UCC Section 9-313.
[16] UCC Section 9-312(b)(3). Note that this section is an important change from the former article, which required possession for money *and* instruments. The revised article permits perfection of instruments by filing, which will be useful when a debtor has a continuous stream of notes arriving from the makers of the notes (borrowers).

in money must take possession to perfect. Suppose Ed's Real Estate claims that Jennifer, a former employee, has opened her own realty business in violation of their noncompetition agreement. Jennifer promises to move her business to another city within 90 days, and Ed agrees not to sue. To secure Jennifer's promise to move, Ed takes a security interest in $50,000 cash. If she fails to move on time, he is entitled to the money. To perfect that interest, Ed must take possession of the money and hold it until Jennifer is out of town.

Control

A security interest in investment property, deposit accounts, letter-of-credit rights, and electronic chattel paper may be perfected by control.[17] We have described control above, in the section on attachment. In general, *control means that the secured party has certain exclusive rights to dispose of the collateral.* Recall, for example, that a secured party which is a bank has control of any deposit account located in that bank.

Mandatory Control. Security interests in deposit accounts and letter-of-credit rights may be perfected *only* by control.[18] Once again, filing would be ineffectual with forms of collateral so easily moved, and the Code will grant perfection only to a secured party that has control.

Care of the Collateral

Possession and control give several advantages to the secured party, but also one important duty: **a secured party must use reasonable care in the custody and preservation of collateral in her possession or control.**[19] If the collateral is something tangible, such as a painting, the secured party must take reasonable steps to ensure that it is safe from harm. What does "reasonable care" mean when the collateral is something as volatile as shares of stock? The following case is an early response under the revised article.

LAYNE V. BANK ONE

395 F.3d 271
UNITED STATES COURT OF APPEALS FOR THE SIXTH CIRCUIT, 2005

CASE SUMMARY

Facts: Charles E. Johnson was the founder and CEO of PurchasePro.com, Inc., and Geoff Layne was its marketing director. When their Internet stock went public, both officers suddenly owned shares worth millions of dollars. To increase his liquidity, Johnson took out a loan for $2.8 million from Bank One, and Layne borrowed $3.25 million. Each secured the loan with shares of PurchasePro stock.

The loan agreement required a loan-to-value (LTV) ratio of 50 percent, meaning that the value of the shares had to be at least double the outstanding loan balance. If the value of the shares sank below the required level, the two men could either pay off some of the loan or offer additional security. If the two borrowers failed to remedy the problem, the Bank was entitled (but not obligated) to sell the shares. Johnson secured his loan with $6.9 million worth of PurchasePro stock.

In February, Internet stocks suddenly plummeted, and both loans immediately exceeded their LTV ratio. Johnson and Layne spoke with the Bank several times, stating that they would offer additional collateral. During March and April, more calls went back and forth, with the debtors

---

[17] UCC Section 9-314(a).
[18] UCC Section 9-312(b)(1).
[19] UCC Section 9-207.

occasionally suggesting that the collateral be sold, while at other times agreeing to provide more security. Finally, in July, over a four-day period, the Bank sold Johnson's PurchasePro shares for $524,757, less than 10 percent of its original worth.

Johnson and Layne both filed suit against the Bank, claiming that it failed to exercise reasonable care of the collateral. The trial court gave judgment for the Bank, and the plaintiffs appealed.

Issue: *Did the Bank exercise reasonable care of the shares?*

Decision: Yes, the Bank exercised reasonable care. Affirmed.

Reasoning: A secured party must take reasonable care to preserve the value of collateral such as stock. However, the comment to Section 9-207 states that the secured party is not liable for a drop in the value of pledged instruments, including shares, even if timely action might have prevented the decline. It is the borrower who decides to buy stock, not the lender. A secured party merely accepts the shares as collateral, and it does not itself invest in the issuing firm. The stock market is notoriously volatile. Requiring a secured party to sell shares held as collateral to avoid losses would shift the investment risk from borrower to lender.

If the borrower is concerned with the decline in share value, it is his responsibility to act, using other assets to reduce the outstanding loan, substituting different collateral for the stock, or selling the pledged shares himself and paying off the loan.

PERFECTION OF CONSUMER GOODS

The Code gives special treatment to security interests in most consumer goods. Merchants sell a vast amount of consumer goods on credit. They cannot file a financing statement for every bed, television, and stereo for which a consumer owes money. Yet perfecting by possession is also impossible, since the consumer will take the goods home. To understand the UCC's treatment of these transactions, we need to know two terms. The first is *consumer goods*, which as we saw earlier means goods used primarily for personal, family, or household purposes. The second term is *purchase money security interest.*

A **purchase money security interest (PMSI)** is one taken by the person who sells the collateral or by the person who advances money so the debtor can buy the collateral.[20] Assume the Gobroke Home Center sells Marion a $5,000 stereo system. The sales document requires a payment of $500 down and $50 per month for the next three centuries, and gives Gobroke a security interest in the system. Because the security interest was "taken by the seller," the document is a PMSI. It would also be a PMSI if a bank had loaned Marion the money to buy the system and the document gave the bank a security interest.

But aren't all security interests PMSIs? No, many are not. Suppose a bank loans a retail company $800,000 and takes a security interest in the store's present inventory. That is not a PMSI since the store did not use the money to purchase the collateral.

Purchase money security interest (PMSI)

An interest taken by the person who sells the collateral or advances money so the debtor can buy it.

---

[20] UCC Section 9-103. This is a complete rewrite of the former PMSI section. The most important substantive changes concern *non-consumer* PMSIs, and are only of passing interest to us. One noteworthy point is that in non-consumer cases, the section explicitly permits collateral to have *dual status*, meaning that goods can be subject simultaneously to a PMSI and an ordinary security interest. Suppose a bank loans $100,000 to a restaurant to purchase furniture, taking a PMSI in the goods. Two years later, the restaurant refinances, agreeing to borrow an additional $25,000, and using the furniture as collateral for the entire $125,000. The bank has a PMSI *only* for $100,000; as to the remaining $25,000, the bank has an ordinary security interest. The difference may be crucial if competing creditors seek to repossess the same tables and chairs. The bank should obtain priority for its PMSI, but may not fare as well for the remaining security interest.

What must Gobroke Home Center do to perfect its security interest? Nothing. **A PMSI in consumer goods perfects automatically, without filing.**[21] Marion's new stereo is clearly consumer goods, because she will use it only in her home. Gobroke's security interest is a PMSI, so the interest has perfected automatically. (See Exhibit 25.3)

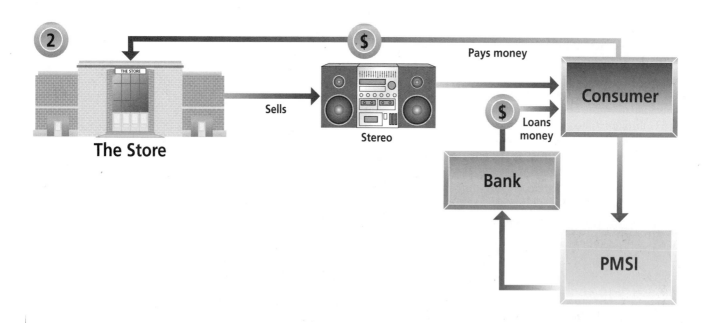

Exhibit 25.3 A purchase money security interest can arise in either of two ways. In the first example, a store sells a stereo to a consumer on credit; the consumer in turn signs a PMSI, giving the store a security interest in the stereo. In the second example, the consumer buys the stereo with money loaned from a bank; the consumer signs a PMSI giving the *bank* a security interest in the stereo.

---

[21] UCC Section 9-309(1).

EXAM *Strategy*

Question: Winona owns a tropical fish store. To buy a spectacular new tank, she borrows $25,000 from her sister, Pauline, and signs an agreement giving Pauline a security interest in the tank. Pauline never files the security agreement. Winona's business goes belly up, and both Pauline and other creditors angle to repossess the tank. Does Pauline have a perfected interest in the tank?

Strategy: Generally, a creditor obtains a perfected security interest by filing or possession. However, a PMSI in consumer goods perfects automatically, without filing. Was Pauline's security agreement a PMSI? Was the fish tank a consumer good?

Result: A PMSI is one taken by the person who sells the collateral or advances money for its purchase. Pauline advanced the money for Winona to buy the tank, so Pauline does have a PMSI. Consumer goods are those used primarily for personal, family, or household purposes. Winona does not sleep with the fish—we hope—so this was not a consumer purchase. Pauline failed to perfect and is unprotected against other creditors.

PERFECTION OF MOVABLE COLLATERAL AND FIXTURES

The rules for perfection are slightly different for security interests in movable goods, such as cars and boats, and in fixtures. We look briefly at each.

Movable Goods Generally

Goods that are easily moved create problems for creditors. Suppose a bank in Colorado loans Dorothy money, takes a security interest in her Degas sculpture, and perfects its interest in the proper state offices in Colorado. But then Dorothy moves to Ohio and uses the same collateral for another loan. A lender in Ohio will never discover the security interest perfected in Colorado. If Dorothy defaults, who gets the sculpture?

For most collateral, when the *debtor moves* to a new state, a security interest from the old state remains perfected for four months; when the *collateral is transferred* to a new state, the security interest remains perfected for one year.[22] If the secured party re-perfects in the new state within the time limits mentioned, the security interest remains valid until it would normally expire. If the secured party fails to re-perfect in the new state, the security interest lapses. Suppose Dorothy takes her Degas into Ohio on February 10 and on March 5 uses it as collateral for a new loan. The original Colorado bank still has a valid security interest in the sculpture and may seize the art if Dorothy defaults. But if Dorothy applies for her new loan on October 10, and the Colorado bank has failed to re-perfect, the Colorado bank has lost its protection.

Motor Vehicles and the Like

The Code provisions about perfecting generally do not apply to motor vehicles, trailers, mobile homes, boats, or farm tractors.[23] Because all of these are so numerous and so mobile, filing may be ineffective and possession is impossible. As a result, almost all states have created special laws to deal with this problem. Anyone offering or taking a security interest in any of these goods must consult local law.

---

[22] UCC Section 9-316(a).
[23] UCC Section 9-311(a)(2).

State title laws generally require that a security interest in an automobile be noted directly on the vehicle's certificate of title. A driver needs a certificate of title to obtain registration plates, so the law presumes that the certificate will stay with the car. By requiring that the security interest be noted on the certificate, the law gives the best possible notice to anyone thinking of buying the car or accepting it as collateral. Generally, if a buyer or lender examines the certificate and finds no security interest, he may accept the vehicle for sale, or as collateral, and take it free of any interest. In most states, the same requirement applies to boats.

Fixtures

Fixtures, you recall, are goods that have become attached to real estate. A security interest may be created in goods that *are* fixtures and may continue in goods that *become* fixtures; however, the Code does not permit a security interest in ordinary building materials, such as lumber and concrete, once they become part of a construction project.

The primary disputes in these cases are between a creditor holding a security interest in a fixture, such as a furnace, and another creditor with rights in the real estate, such as a bank holding a mortgage on the house. The issues are complex, involving local real property law, and we cannot undertake here a thorough explanation of them. However, we can highlight the issues that arise so that you can anticipate the potential problems. Common disputes concern:

- The status of the personal property when the security interest was created (was it still goods or already a fixture?);

- The status of the real estate (does the debtor *also* have a legal interest in the *real property?*);

- The type of perfection (which was recorded first, the security interest in the fixture or the real estate? does the secured party hold a PMSI?); and

- The physical status of the fixture (can it be removed without harming the real estate?).[24]

Any creditor who considers accepting collateral that might become a fixture must anticipate these problems and clarify with the debtor exactly what she plans to do with the goods. Armed with that information, the creditor should consult local law on fixtures and make an appropriate security agreement (or refuse to accept the fixture as collateral).

PROTECTION OF BUYERS

Generally, once a security interest is perfected, it remains effective regardless of whether the collateral is sold, exchanged, or transferred in some other way. Bubba's Bus Co. needs money to meet its payroll, so it borrows $150,000 from Francine's Finance Co., which takes a security interest in Bubba's 180 buses and perfects its interest. Bubba, still short of cash, sells 30 of his buses to Antelope Transit. But even that money is not enough to keep Bubba solvent: he defaults on his loan to Francine and goes into bankruptcy. Francine pounces on Bubba's buses. May she repossess the 30 that Antelope now operates? Yes. The security interest continued in the buses even after Antelope purchased them, and Francine can whisk them away. (Antelope has a valid claim against Bubba for the value of the buses, but the claim may prove fruitless, since Bubba is bankrupt.)

There are some exceptions to this rule. The Code gives a few buyers special protection.

---

[24] UCC Section 9-334.

Buyers in Ordinary Course of Business

A **buyer in ordinary course of business (BIOC)** is someone who buys goods in good faith from a seller who routinely deals in such goods.[25] For example, Plato's Garden Supply purchases 500 hemlocks from Socrates' Farm, a grower. Plato is a BIOC: he is buying in good faith, and Socrates routinely deals in hemlocks. This is an important status, because a BIOC is generally not affected by security interests in the goods. However, if Plato realized that the sale violated another party's rights in the goods, there would be no good faith. If Plato knew that Socrates was bankrupt and had agreed with a creditor not to sell any of his inventory, Plato would not achieve BIOC status.

A buyer in ordinary course of business takes the goods free of a security interest created by his seller even though the security interest is perfected.[26] Suppose that, a month before Plato made his purchase, Socrates borrowed $200,000 from the Athenian Bank. Athenian took a security interest in all of Socrates' trees and perfected by filing. Then Plato purchased his 500 hemlocks. If Socrates defaults on the loan, Athenian will have *no right* to repossess the 500 trees that are now at the Garden Supply. Plato took them free and clear. (Of course, Athenian can still attempt to repossess other trees from Socrates.)

The BIOC exception is designed to encourage ordinary commerce. A buyer making routine purchases should not be forced to perform a financing check before buying. But the rule creates its own problems. A creditor may extend a large sum of money to a merchant based on collateral, such as inventory, only to discover that by the time the merchant defaults the collateral has been sold.

Buyer in ordinary course of business (BIOC)
Someone who buys goods in good faith from a seller who routinely deals in such goods.

EXAM *Strategy*

Question: Troy owns an art gallery specializing in Greek artifacts. To modernize the gallery, Troy borrows $150,000 from the Sparta Bank, which takes a security interest in all of his inventory. Sparta promptly perfects. A month later, Troy sells Helen an Athenian warrior's helmet for $675,000. Helen does not bother to perform a financing check, and she is unaware of Sparta's security interest. Troy soon goes bankrupt, and Sparta attempts to seize all of the inventory, including the helmet. Sparta proves that a routine financing check would have revealed its interest. Who wins the helmet?

Strategy: A creditor perfects a security interest to ensure that it is protected against all the world. However, exceptions leave the secured party unprotected in certain cases, including those of consumers. Analyze this case using that exception.

Result: A BIOC takes the goods free of a security interest created by his seller. Helen acted in good faith, buying from a dealer who routinely dealt in such goods. And it was Troy, Helen's seller, who created the security interest. Helen takes the helmet free of the bank's security interest, despite the fact that it was perfected.

---

[25] UCC Section 1-201(9).

[26] UCC Section 9-320(a). In fact, the buyer takes free of the security interest *even if the buyer knew of it.* Yet a BIOC, by definition, must be acting in good faith. Is this a contradiction? No. Plato might know that a third party has a security interest in Socrates' crops, yet not realize that his purchase violates the third party's rights. Generally, for example, a security interest will permit a retailer to sell consumer goods, the presumption being that part of the proceeds will go to the secured party. A BIOC cannot be expected to determine what a retailer plans to do with the money he is paid.

Because the BIOC exception undercuts the basic protection given to a secured party, the courts interpret it narrowly. BIOC status is available only if the *seller created the security interest*. Oftentimes, a buyer will purchase goods that have a security interest created by someone other than the seller. If that happens, the buyer is not a BIOC. However, should that rule be strictly enforced even when the results are harsh? You make the call.

YOU *be the* JUDGE

CONSECO FINANCE SERVICING CORP. v. LEE
2004 WL 1243417
Court of Appeals of Texas, 2004

Facts: Lila Williams purchased a new Roadtrek 200 motor home from New World R.V. Inc. She paid about $14,000 down and financed $63,000, giving a security interest to New World. The RV company assigned its security interest to Conseco Finance, which perfected. Two years later, Williams returned the vehicle to New World (the record does not indicate why), and New World sold the RV to Robert and Ann Lee, for $42,800. A year later, Williams defaulted on her payments to Conseco.

The Lees sued Conseco, claiming to be BIOCs and asking for a court declaration that they had sole title to the Roadtrek. Conseco counterclaimed, seeking title based on its perfected security interest. The trial court ruled that the Lees were BIOCs, with full rights to the vehicle. Conseco appealed.

You Be the Judge: Were the Lees BIOCs?

Argument for Conseco: Under UCC Section 9-319, a buyer in ordinary course takes free of a security interest *created by the buyer's seller*. The buyers were the Lees. The seller was New World. New World did not create the security interest—Lila Williams did. There is no security interest created by New World. The security interest held by Conseco was created by someone else (Williams) and is not affected by the Lees' status as BIOC. The law is clear, and Conseco is entitled to the Roadtrek.

Argument for the Lees: Conseco weaves a clever argument, but let's remove the mumbo-jumbo and look at what they are saying. Two honest buyers, acting in perfect good faith, can walk into an RV dealership, spend $42,000 for a used vehicle, and end up with—nothing. Conseco claims it is entitled to an RV that the Lees paid for because someone that the Lees have never dealt with, never even heard of, gave *to this RV seller* a security interest which the seller, years earlier, passed on to a finance company. Conseco's argument defies common sense and the goals of Article 9.

Rebuttal from Conseco: The best part of the Lees' argument is the emotional appeal; the worst part is the law. Yes, $42,000 is a lot of money. That is why a reasonable buyer is careful to do business with conscientious, ethical sellers. New World, which knew that Williams financed the RV and knew who held the security interest, never bothered to check on the status of the payments. If the Lees have suffered wrongdoing, it is at the hands of an irresponsible seller—the company they chose to work with, the company from whom they must seek relief.

Rebuttal from the Lees: The purpose of the Code is to make dealing fair and commerce work; one of its methods is to get away from obscure, technical arguments. Conseco's suggestion would demolish the used-car industry. What buyers will ever pay serious money—*any* money—for a used vehicle, knowing that thousands of dollars later, the car might be towed out of their driveway by a finance company they never heard of?

BUYERS OF CONSUMER GOODS

Another exception exists to protect buyers of consumer goods who do not realize that the item they are buying has a security interest in it. This exception tends to apply to relatively casual purchases, such as those between friends. Typically the pattern is that one purchaser buys consumer goods on credit and then resells. The original purchaser is considered a debtor-seller, since she still owes money but is now selling to a second buyer. **In the case of consumer goods purchased from a debtor-seller, a buyer takes free of a security interest if he is not aware of the security interest, he pays value for the goods, he is buying for his own family or household use, and the second party has not yet filed a financing statement.**[27]

Here is how this exception works. Charles Lau used a Sears credit card to buy a 45-inch TV, a sleeper sofa, loveseat, entertainment center, diamond ring, gold chain, and microwave. He had the items delivered to the house of his girlfriend, Teresa Rierman, because he did not want his father to know he had been using the credit card (can't imagine why). Lau later sold the items to Rierman's family and then (need we say it?) defaulted on his payments to Sears and declared bankruptcy. Sears attempted to repossess its merchandise, but the Riermans claimed they were innocent buyers. The court ruled that if the Riermans could show that they knew nothing about Sears's security interest in the goods, they could keep the goods.[28]

This rule may be confusing because earlier we discussed the automatic perfection of a security interest in consumer goods. When Sears sold the merchandise to Lau, it took a purchase money security interest in consumer goods. That interest perfected automatically (without filing) and was valid against *almost* everyone. Suppose Lau had used the furniture as collateral to obtain a bank loan. Sears would have retained its perfected security interest in the goods, and when Lau defaulted, Sears could have repossessed everything, leaving the bank with no collateral and no money.

The one person that Sears's perfect security interest could not defeat, however, was a buyer purchasing for *personal use without knowledge of the security interest*—in other words, the Riermans. Assuming the Riermans knew nothing of the security interest, they win. If Sears considers this type of loss important, it must, in the future, protect itself by filing a financing statement. Taking this extra step will leave Sears protected against everyone. Then, if a buyer defaults, Sears can pull the sofa out from under any purchaser.

BUYERS OF CHATTEL PAPER, INSTRUMENTS, AND DOCUMENTS

We have seen that debtors often use chattel paper, instruments, or documents as collateral. Because each of these is so easily transferred, the Code gives buyers special protection. **A buyer who purchases chattel paper or an instrument in the ordinary course of her business, and then takes possession, generally takes free of any security interest.**[29]

Suppose Tele-Maker sells 500 televisions to Retailer on credit, keeping a security interest in the televisions and the proceeds. The proceeds are any money or paper that Retailer earns from selling the sets. Retailer sells 300 of the sets to customers, most of whom pay on credit. The customers sign chattel paper, promising to pay for the sets over time (and giving Retailer a security interest in the sets). All of this chattel paper is proceeds, so Tele-Maker has a perfected security interest in it. The chattel paper is worth about $150,000 if all of the customers pay in full. But Retailer wants money now, so Retailer sells its chattel paper to Financer, who pays $120,000 cash for it. Next, Retailer defaults on its obligation to pay Tele-Maker for the sets. Tele-Maker cannot repossess the televisions, because each customer was a BIOC (buyer in ordinary course of business) and took the goods free of any security interest. So Tele-Maker attempts to repossess the *chattel paper*. Will it succeed? No. The buyer of chattel paper takes it free of a perfected security interest. See Exhibit 25.4.

What could Tele-Maker have done to prevent this disaster?

---

[27] UCC Section 9-320.
[28] *In re Lau*, 140 B.R. 172, 1992 Bankr. LEXIS 671 (N.D. Ohio 1992). The case was decided under the former Article 9, but the outcome would be the same under the revised version.
[29] UCC Section 9-330(a)(b)(d).

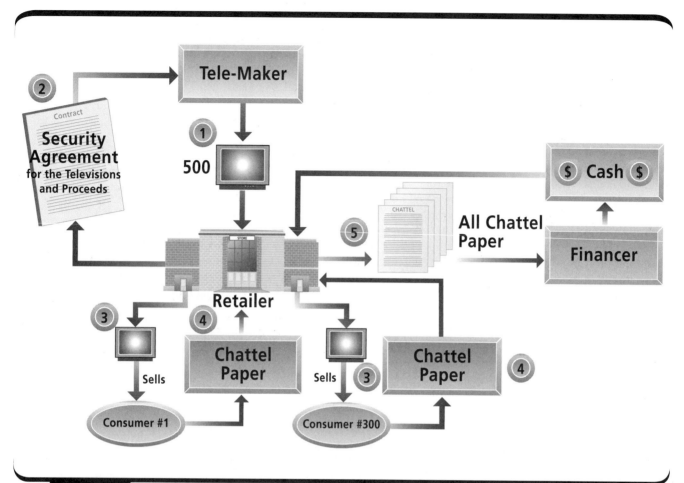

Exhibit 25.4 The buyer of chattel paper takes it free of a perfected security interest. In this case: Tele-Maker (1) sells 500 units to Retailer on credit, keeping (2) a security interest in the televisions and the proceeds. Retailer (3) sells the sets to customers who (4) sign chattel paper. Retailer (5) sells the chattel paper to Financer and then defaults on its obligations to Tele-Maker.

Other Paper

Similar rules apply for holders in due course of instruments (discussed in Chapters 22 and 23, on negotiable instruments) and for purchasers of securities and documents of title. Those parties obtain special rights, described in Articles 3, 7, and 8 of the Code. The details of those rules are beyond the scope of this chapter, but once again, the lesson for any lender is simple: a security interest is safest when the collateral is in your vault. If you do not take possession of the paper, you may lose it to an innocent buyer.[30]

LIENS

Law student Paul King got a costly lesson when his $28.09 check for an oil change bounced and the repo man snatched his prized Corvette. The bill for the car's return:

---

[30] UCC Section 9-331.

$644. King was a third-year law student, working part-time in a private firm in Houston. He had just walked in from lunch when co-workers told him his car was being towed.

"I thought they were joking," King said. They weren't. King saw a tow truck backing up to his car and hurried out to speak with the workers. They advised him that Texas law authorized them to pick up his car to satisfy a lien, for work done to the car. King hurried inside to telephone the company that had performed the oil change. Unable to make a deal on the phone, he ran back outside and found—no car.

King phoned Harris County Repossession to see about getting his car back. That's easy, they told him. But you owe some fees: $28.09 for the oil change, $20 for the returned check, $25 for the legal notice in the newspapers, $21.24 per day for storage—plus, of course, the $550 repossession fee.[31]

Is that legal? Probably. The service station had a lien on the car. A **lien** is a security interest created by law (rather than by agreement). State and federal law both allow parties to assert a lien against a debtor under prescribed conditions. For example, a state may claim a lien based on unpaid taxes; the state is giving notice to the world that it may seize the debtor's property and sell it. A company may claim a lien based on work performed by the debtor.

To understand the difference between a lien and a security interest, assume that when Paul King bought his Corvette, he made a down payment and signed a security agreement to ensure future payments. *His agreement* gave the dealer a security interest in the sports car. Later, when he paid for an oil change, his check bounced. *State law* gave the service station a lien on the auto, meaning the right to hold the car if it is in the garage and to seize the auto if it is elsewhere. Because automobile repossessions provide such a graphic view of secured transactions, we will return to the subject later in the chapter. In this case, the oil company had an **artisan's lien**, meaning a security interest in personal property created when a worker makes some improvement to the property. A car mechanic, a computer repairman, and a furniture restorer all create artisan's liens. A **mechanic's lien** is similar, created when a worker improves real property. A carpenter who puts an addition on a kitchen and a painter who paints the kitchen's interior both have a mechanic's lien on the house. The owner of an apartment may obtain a **landlord's lien** in a tenant's personal property if the tenant fails to pay the rent. These security interests vary from state to state, so an affected person must consult local law. Because liens are the creation of statutes, rather than agreements, Article 9 generally does not apply. The one aspect of liens that Article 9 does govern is priority between lienholders and other secured parties, which we examine in the following section. In Paul King's case, the repair shop certainly had a valid lien on his car, even though the amount in question was small. The company's method of *collecting* on its lien is more debatable. King admitted that the company had telephoned him and given him a chance to pay for the bounced check. Some courts would hold that the repair shop had done all it was required to do, but others might rule that it should have shown more patience and avoided running up the bill.

Lien
A security interest created by law, rather than by agreement.

Artisan's lien
A security interest in personal property.

Mechanic's lien
A security interest created when a worker improves real property.

---

[31] Rad Sallee and James T. Campbell, "Repo Men Hitch Up Big Fee to Car," *Houston Chronicle*, Oct. 15, 1991, Section A, p. 21. Copyright 1991 Houston Chronicle Publishing Company. Reproduced with permission of Houston Chronicle Publishing Company via Copyright Clearance Center.

PRIORITIES AMONG CREDITORS

What happens when two creditors have a security interest in the same collateral? The party who has **priority** in the collateral gets it. Typically, the debtor lacks assets to pay everyone, so all creditors struggle to be the first in line. After the first creditor has repossessed the collateral, sold it, and taken enough of the proceeds to pay off his debt, there may be nothing left for anyone else. (There may not even be enough to pay the first creditor all that he is due, in which case that creditor will sue for the deficiency.) Who gets priority? There are three principal rules.

The first rule is easy: **a party with a perfected security interest takes priority over a party with an unperfected interest**.[32] This, of course, is the whole point of perfecting: to ensure that your security interest gets priority over everyone else's. On August 15, Meredith's Market, an antique store, borrows $100,000 from the Happy Bank, which takes a security interest in all of Meredith's inventory. Happy Bank does not perfect. On September 15, Meredith uses the same collateral to borrow $50,000 from the Suspicion Bank, which files a financing statement the same day. On October 15, as if on cue, Meredith files for bankruptcy and stops paying both creditors. Suspicion wins because it holds a perfected interest, whereas the Happy Bank holds merely an unperfected interest.

The second rule: **if neither secured party has perfected, the first interest to attach gets priority**.[33] Suppose that Suspicion Bank and Happy Bank had both failed to perfect. In that case, Happy Bank would have the first claim to Meredith's inventory, since Happy's interest *attached* first.

And the third rule follows logically: **between perfected security interests, the first to file or perfect wins**.[34] Diminishing Perspective, a railroad, borrows $75 million from the First Bank, which takes a security interest in Diminishing's rolling stock (railroad cars) and immediately perfects by filing. Two months later, Diminishing borrows $100 million from Second Bank, which takes a security interest in the same collateral and also files. When Diminishing arrives, on schedule, in bankruptcy court, both banks will race to seize the rolling stock. First Bank gets the railcars because it perfected first.

March 1:	April 2:	May 3:	The Winner:
First Bank loans money and perfects its security interest by filing a financing statement.	Second Bank loans money and perfects its security interest by filing a financing statement.	Diminishing goes bankrupt, and both banks attempt to take the rolling stock.	First Bank, because it perfected first.

The general rules of priority are quite straightforward; however, you will not be surprised to learn that there are some exceptions.

---

[32] UCC Section 9-322(a)(2).
[33] UCC Section 9-322(a)(3).
[34] UCC Section 9-322(a)(1).

FILING VERSUS CONTROL OR POSSESSION

Recall that a secured party *may* use either filing or control to perfect its security interest in deposit accounts, investment property, and letter-of-credit rights. Which method *should* the secured party use? Control. **For these three types of collateral, a secured party who has control wins over a party who merely filed.**[35] Early Bank obtains a security interest in Lionel's investment property, and perfects by filing. Nine months later, Late Bank obtains a security interest in the same property, and perfects by taking control. Late Bank wins.

Similarly, a secured party may perfect its interest in an *instrument* either by filing or possession. Once again, possession is the better idea: **between competing secured parties, the one who possesses wins, even over one who filed earlier.**[36]

PRIORITY INVOLVING A PURCHASE MONEY SECURITY INTEREST

You may recall that a purchase money security interest (PMSI) is a security interest taken by the seller of the collateral or by a lender whose loan enables the debtor to buy the collateral. A PMSI can be created only in goods, fixtures and software. On November 1, Manufacturer sells a specially built lathe to Tool Shop for $80,000 and takes a security interest in the lathe. The parties have created a PMSI. Parties holding a PMSI often take priority over other perfected security interests in the same goods, even if the other security interest was perfected first. How can the conflict arise? Suppose that on February 1, Tool Shop had borrowed $100,000 from the Gargoyle Bank, giving Gargoyle a security interest in after-acquired property. When the lathe arrives at the Tool Shop on November 1, Gargoyle's security interest attaches to it. But Manufacturer has a PMSI in the lathe, and hence the conflict.

We need to examine PMSIs involving inventory and those involving noninventory. **Inventory** means goods that the seller is holding for sale or lease in the ordinary course of its business. The furniture in a furniture store is inventory; the store's computer, telephones, and filing cabinets are not.

Inventory
Goods that a seller is holding for sale or lease in the ordinary course of its business.

PMSI in Inventory

A PMSI in inventory takes priority over a conflicting perfected security interest (even one perfected earlier), if two conditions are met:

- Before filing its PMSI, the secured party must check for earlier security interests and, if there are any, must notify the holder of that interest concerning the new PMSI; and

- The secured party must then perfect its PMSI (normally by filing) *before* the debtor receives the inventory.[37]

If the holder of the PMSI has met both of these conditions, its PMSI takes priority over any security interests filed earlier, as illustrated in the following chart

---

[35] UCC Sections 9-327, 9-328, 9-329. If more than one creditor has control of the same collateral, the security interests rank according to the time of obtaining control.
[36] UCC Section 9-330(d).
[37] UCC Section 9-324(b)(c).

A PMSI IN INVENTORY MAY OBTAIN PRIORITY

1. February 1:	**2. March 2:**	**3. March 3:**	**4. March 4:**
Coltrane Bank loans Monk's Jazz Store $90,000, taking a security interest in all after-acquired property, including inventory.	Monk offers to buy 10 saxophones from Webster's Supply for $3,000 each.	Webster checks the financing records and learns that Coltrane Bank has a security interest in all of Monk's after-acquired property.	Webster notifies Coltrane Bank that he is selling 10 saxophones to Monk for $30,000 and is taking a PMSI in the instruments, which Webster carefully describes.
5. March 4:	**6. March 5:**	**7. September:**	**8. The Winner:**
Webster files a financing statement indicating a PMSI in the 10 saxophones.	Webster sells the 10 saxophones to Monk.	Monk goes bankrupt.	Webster. His PMSI in inventory takes priority over Coltrane's earlier interest.

PMSI in Noninventory Collateral

PMSIs are often given for noninventory goods. When Tool Shop bought the lathe, in the example above, the company gave a PMSI to the seller. The bank simultaneously obtained a security interest in the same lathe, based on its after-acquired property interest. Who wins?

A PMSI in collateral other than inventory takes priority over a conflicting security interest if the PMSI is perfected at the time the debtor receives the collateral or within 20 days after he receives it.[38] So long as Computer Co. perfects (by filing) within 20 days of delivering the computer, its PMSI takes priority over the bank's earlier security interest. Manufacturer may repossess the machine, and the bank may never get a dime back.

Again, we must note that the PMSI exception undercuts the ability of a creditor to rely on its perfected security interest. As a result, courts insist that a party asserting the PMSI exception demonstrate that it has complied with every requirement.

The following case, a conflict between a purchase money security interest and an earlier perfected interest, was decided under the former Article 9, but the outcome would be the same under the revised law.

CITIZENS BANK OF AMERICUS v. FEDERAL FINANCIAL SERVICES, INC.

509 S.E.2d 339
GEORGIA COURT OF APPEALS, 1998

CASE SUMMARY

Facts: Charles H. Logging, Inc. (Charles H.) began negotiations to buy a logging skidder from Pioneer Machinery. On December 5, Charles H. borrowed $22,520 from Citizens Bank of Americus, signing a promissory note and UCC financing statement the next day. Charles H. used the loan proceeds to satisfy debts; it did not take possession or ownership of the skidder.

On December 18, Pioneer delivered the skidder to Charles H. for demonstration purposes only, and on December 30, the logging company indicated that it wished to buy

---

[38] UCC Section 9-324(a).

the machine. Charles H. signed a contract of sale, which obligated the company to obtain adequate insurance before the deal would go through.

On February 6, Charles H. obtained the required insurance, borrowed the purchase money from Federal Financial Services, Inc., and signed a UCC financing statement listing the skidder as collateral. Federal Financial remitted the loan proceeds to Pioneer, as payment for the machine, and on February 10, filed its financing statement. When Charles H. failed to pay its debts, Citizens Bank and Federal Financial both claimed a security interest in the skidder. Federal Financial claimed that it had a purchase money security interest (PMSI), which took priority over the other bank's interest. The trial court agreed and gave judgment. Citizens Bank appealed.

Issue: *Did Federal Financial have a PMSI that took priority over a security interest that was filed earlier?*

Decision: Yes, Federal Financial's interest was a valid PMSI and took priority.

Reasoning: Generally, when perfected security interests conflict, they rank in priority by time of filing. However, under UCC Section 9-324, a PMSI in collateral other than inventory has priority over a previously perfected security interest, if the PMSI is perfected at the time the debtor receives possession of the collateral, or within 20 days thereafter.

Citizens Bank's perfected security interest does not qualify as a PMSI because the funds that it lent were not used to buy the skidder. Federal Financial's interest is a PMSI—but did it obtain priority? On December 18, Charles H. took possession. Pioneer still owned the skidder, and Charles H. was not yet a debtor. Charles H. bought the machine on February 6, paying with proceeds from the Federal Financial loan and becoming a debtor on that date. Since Charles H. already had possession, the two factors necessary to create a PMSI (a debtor with possession) converged on February 6. Federal Financial filed its PMSI on February 10, well within the 20-day limit, and its PMSI did obtain priority.

RIGHTS OF THIRD PARTIES

Article 9 now explicitly provides the rights and duties of *third parties*, meaning those who may be affected by a secured transaction even though they are neither debtor nor secured party. Significant issues raised include the rights and duties of assignees. (This textbook discusses assignment and assignees in Chapter 15, on third parties.) These issues go beyond the scope of this chapter; interested readers should consult Part Four of Article 9, Sections 9-401 through 9-408.

DEFAULT AND TERMINATION

We have reached the end of the line. Either the debtor has defaulted, or it has performed its obligations and may terminate the security agreement.

DEFAULT

The parties define "default" in their security agreement. **Generally, a debtor defaults when he fails to make payments due or enters bankruptcy proceedings.** The parties can agree that other acts will constitute default, such as the debtor's failure to maintain insurance on the collateral. When a debtor defaults, the secured party has two principal options: (1) it may take possession of the collateral, or (2) it may file suit against the debtor for the money owed. The secured party does not have to choose between these two remedies; it may try one remedy, such as repossession, and if that fails, attempt the other.[39]

---

[39] UCC Section 9-601(a)(b)(c).

Taking Possession of the Collateral

When the debtor defaults, the secured party may take possession of the collateral.[40] How does the secured party accomplish this? In either of two ways: The secured party may act on its own, without any court order, and simply take the collateral, provided this can be done *without a breach of the peace*. Otherwise, the secured party must file suit against the debtor and request that the court *order* the debtor to deliver the collateral.

Suppose a consumer bought a refrigerator on credit and defaulted. The security agreement may require the consumer to make the collateral available in a reasonable time and manner, such as by emptying the refrigerator of all food and having it ready for a carrier to take away. When the refrigerator is ready, the retailer can haul it away. What if the consumer refuses to cooperate? May the retailer break into the consumer's house to take the collateral? No. Breaking into a house is a clear breach of the peace and violates Article 9.

Secured parties often repossess automobiles without the debtor's cooperation. Typically, the security agreement will state that, in the event of default, the secured party has a right to take possession of the car and drive it away. As we saw earlier, the secured party could be the seller, or it could be a mechanic with an artisan's lien on the car.

Disposition of the Collateral

Once the secured party has obtained possession of the collateral, it has two choices. The secured party may (1) dispose of the collateral or (2) retain the collateral as full satisfaction of the debt.

Disposal of the Collateral.   **A secured party may sell, lease, or otherwise dispose of the collateral in any commercially reasonable manner.**[41] Typically, the secured party will sell the collateral in either a private or a public sale. First, however, the debtor must receive *reasonable notice* of the time and place of the sale so that she may bid on the collateral. The higher the price that the secured party gets for the collateral, the lower the balance still owed by the debtor. Giving the debtor notice of the sale, and a chance to bid, ensures that the collateral will not be sold for an unreasonably low price.

Suppose Bank loans $65,000 to Farmer to purchase a tractor. While still owing $40,000, Farmer defaults. Bank takes possession of the tractor and then notifies Farmer that it intends to sell the tractor at an auction. Farmer has the right to attend and bid on the tractor.

When the secured party has sold the collateral, it applies the proceeds of the sale: first, to its expenses in repossessing and selling the collateral, and second, to the debt.[42] Assume Bank sold the tractor for $35,000 and that the process of repossessing and selling the tractor cost $5,000. Bank applies the remaining $30,000 to the debt.

Deficiency or Surplus.   The sale of the tractor yielded $30,000 to be applied to the debt, which was $40,000. The disposition has left a **deficiency**, that is, insufficient funds to pay off the debt. **The debtor is liable for any deficiency.** So the bank will sue the farmer for the remaining $10,000. On the other hand, sometimes the sale of the collateral yields a **surplus**, that is, a sum greater than the debt. In that case, the secured party must pay the surplus to the debtor.[43]

Deficiency
Having insufficient funds to pay off a debt.

Surplus
A sum of money greater than the debt incurred.

[40] UCC Section 9-609.
[41] UCC Section 9-610.
[42] UCC Section 9-615(a).
[43] UCC Section 9-615(d).

When a secured party disposes of collateral in a *commercially unreasonable* manner, then a deficiency or surplus claim may be adjusted based on the sum that *should* have been obtained.[44] Suppose that Seller, who is owed $300,000, repossesses 500 bedroom sets from a hotel and, without giving proper notice, quickly sells them for a net amount of $200,000. Seller sues for the $100,000 deficiency. If a court determines that a properly announced sale would have netted $250,000, Seller is only entitled to a deficiency judgment of $50,000. Similarly, if the collateral is sold *to the secured party* or someone related, and the price obtained is significantly below what would be expected, then any deficiency or surplus must be calculated on what the sale would normally have brought. This protects the debtor from a sale in which the secured party has followed all formalities but ended up owning the goods for a suspiciously low price.[45]

Acceptance of Collateral.   In many cases, the secured party has the option to satisfy the debt simply by keeping the collateral. **Acceptance** refers to a secured party's retention of the collateral as full or partial satisfaction of the debt. *Partial satisfaction* means that the debtor will still owe some deficiency to the secured party. This is how the system works.[46]

A secured party who wishes to accept the collateral must notify the debtor. If the debtor agrees in an authenticated record, then the secured party may keep the collateral as full *or* partial satisfaction of the debt. If the debtor does not respond within 20 days, the secured party may still accept the collateral as *full* satisfaction but *not* as partial satisfaction. In other words, the debtor's silence does not give the secured party the right to keep the goods and still sue for more money.

Suppose the buyer of a $13 million yacht, *Icarus,* has defaulted, and the retailer has repossessed the boat. The firm may decide the boat is worth more than the debt, so it notifies the buyer that it plans to keep *Icarus.* If the buyer does not object, the retailer automatically owns the boat after 20 days.

If the buyer promptly objects to acceptance, the retailer must then dispose of *Icarus* as described above, typically by sale. Why would a debtor object? Because she believes the boat is worth more than the debt. The debtor anticipates that a sale will create a surplus.

Consumers receive additional protection. A secured party may not accept collateral that is consumer goods if the debtor has possession of the goods *or* if the debtor has paid 60 percent of the purchase price. If Maud has defaulted on an oven that is in her kitchen, the Gobroke retail store may be entitled to repossess the oven, but the company must then dispose of the goods (sell the oven) and apply the proceeds to Maud's debt. Similarly, if Ernest is paying for his $10,000 television set in a "layaway" plan, with Gobroke warehousing the goods until the full price is paid, the store may not accept the television once Ernest has paid $6,000. Finally, a secured party is never permitted to accept consumer goods in partial satisfaction.[47]

Right of Redemption.   Up to the time the secured party disposes of the collateral, the debtor has the right to **redeem** it, that is, to pay the full value of the debt. If the debtor redeems, she obtains the collateral back. Sylvia borrows $25,000 from the bank and pledges a ruby necklace as collateral. She defaults, still owing $9,000, and the bank notifies her that it will sell the necklace. If Sylvia pays the full $9,000 before the sale occurs, plus any expenses the bank has incurred in arranging the sale, she receives her necklace back.[48]

---

[44] UCC Section 9-626(a)(3).
[45] UCC Sections 9-615(f), 9-626(a)(5).
[46] UCC Section 9-620.
[47] UCC Section 9-620(a)(3), (e), (g).
[48] UCC Section 9-623.

Acceptance
Retention of the collateral by a secured party as full or partial satisfaction of a debt.

Redeem
To pay the full value of a debt to get the collateral back.

Proceeding to Judgment

Occasionally, the secured party will prefer to ignore its rights in the collateral and simply sue the debtor. **A secured party may sue the debtor for the full debt.**[49] Why would a creditor, having gone to so much effort to perfect its security interest, ignore that interest and simply file a lawsuit? The collateral may have decreased in value and be insufficient to cover the debt. Suppose a bank loaned $300,000 to a debtor to buy a rare baseball cap. The debtor defaults, owing $190,000. The bank discovers that the cap is now worth only $110,000. It is true that the bank could sell the cap and sue for the deficiency. But the sale will take time, and the outcome is uncertain. Suppose the bank knows that the debtor has recently paid cash for a $2 million house. The bank may promptly file suit for the full $190,000. The bank will ask the court to freeze the debtor's bank account and legally hold the house until the suit is resolved. The bank expects to prove the debt quickly—the loan documents are clear, and the amount of debt is easily calculated. It will obtain its $190,000 without ever donning the cap. Of course, the bank has the option of doing both things simultaneously: It may slap on the cap and a lawsuit all at once.

TERMINATION

Termination statement

A document indicating that a secured party no longer claims a security interest in the collateral.

Finally, we need to look at what happens when a debtor *does not* default, but pays the full debt. (You are forgiven if you lost track of the fact that things sometimes work out smoothly.) Once that happens, the secured party must complete a **termination statement**, a document indicating that it no longer claims a security interest in the collateral.[50]

For a consumer debt, the secured party must file the termination statement in every place that it filed a financing statement. The secured party must do this within one month from the date the debt is fully paid, or within 20 days of a demand from the consumer, whichever comes first. For other transactions, the secured party must within 20 days either file the termination statement or send it to the secured party so that he may file it himself. In both cases, the goal is the same: to notify all interested parties that the debt is extinguished.

CHAPTER CONCLUSION

Secured transactions are essential to modern commerce. Billions of dollars' worth of goods are sold on credit annually, and creditors normally demand an assurance of payment. A secured party that understands Article 9 and follows its provisions to the letter should be well protected. A company that operates in ignorance of Article 9 invites disaster, because others may obtain superior rights in the goods, leaving the "secured" party with no money, no security—and no sympathy from the courts.

EXAM REVIEW

1. **ARTICLE 9** Article 9 applies to any transaction intended to create a security interest in personal property or fixtures. (p. 605)

---

[49] UCC Section 9-601(a).
[50] UCC Section 9-513.

2. **ATTACHMENT** Attachment means that (1) the two parties made a security agreement, *and* either the debtor has *authenticated a security agreement* describing the collateral *or* the secured party has obtained *possession* or *control;* and (2) the secured party gave value in order to get the security agreement; and (3) the debtor has rights in the collateral. (p. 609)

3. **AFTER-ACQUIRED PROPERTY** A security interest may attach to after-acquired property. (p. 612)

4. **PERFECTION** Attachment protects against the debtor. Perfection of a security interest protects the secured party against parties other than the debtor. (p. 613)

5. **FILING** Filing is the most common way to perfect. For many forms of collateral, the secured party may also perfect by obtaining either possession or control. (p. 613)

6. **PMSI** A purchase money security interest (PMSI) is one taken by the person who sells the collateral or advances money so the debtor can buy the collateral. (p. 619)

7. **PMSI PERFECTION** A PMSI in consumer goods perfects automatically, without filing. (p. 620)

EXAM Strategy

Question: John and Clara Lockovich bought a 22-foot Chaparrel Villian II boat from Greene County Yacht Club for $32,500. They paid $6,000 cash and borrowed the rest of the purchase price from Gallatin National Bank, which took a security interest in the boat. Gallatin filed a financing statement in Greene County, Pennsylvania, where the bank was located. But Pennsylvania law requires financing statements to be filed in the county of the debtor's residence, and the Lockoviches lived in Allegheny County. The Lockoviches soon washed up in bankruptcy court. Other creditors demanded that the boat be sold, claiming that Gallatin's security interest had been filed in the wrong place. Who wins? (Please be advised: this is a trick question.)

Strategy: Gallatin National Bank obtained a special kind of security interest in the boat. Identify that type of interest. What special rights does this give to the bank? (See the "Result" at the end of this section.)

8. **BIOC** A buyer in ordinary course of business (BIOC) takes the goods free of a security interest created by his seller even though the security interest is perfected. (p. 623)

9. **CHATTEL PAPER** A buyer who purchases chattel paper or an instrument in good faith in the ordinary course of his business, and then obtains possession or control, generally takes free of any security interest. (p. 625)

10. **PRIORITY** Priority among secured parties is generally as follows:
    (a) A party with a perfected security interest takes priority over a party with an unperfected interest.
    (b) If neither secured party has perfected, the first interest to attach gets priority.
    (c) Between perfected security interests, the first to file or perfect wins. (p. 628)

Question: Barwell, Inc., sold McMann Golf Ball Co. a "preformer," a machine that makes golf balls, for $55,000. Barwell delivered the machine on February 20. McMann paid $3,000 down, the remainder to be paid over several years, and signed an agreement giving Barwell a security interest in the preformer. Barwell did not perfect its interest. On March 1, McMann borrowed $350,000 from First of America Bank, giving the bank a security interest in McMann's present and after-acquired property. First of America perfected by filing on March 2. McMann, of course, became insolvent, and both Barwell and the bank attempted to repossess the preformer. Who gets it?

Strategy: Two parties have a valid security interest in this machine. When that happens, there is a three-step process to determine which party gets priority. Apply it. (See the "Result" at the end of this section.)

11. **PMSIS AND PRIORITY** A PMSI may take priority over a conflicting perfected security interest (even one perfected earlier) if the holder of the PMSI meets certain conditions. (p. 628)

12. **CONTROL OR POSSESSION** For deposit accounts, investment property, letter-of-credit rights, and instruments, a secured party who obtains control or possession takes priority over one who merely filed. (p. 629)

13. **DEFAULT** When the debtor defaults, the secured party may take possession of the collateral on its own, without a court order, if it can do so without a breach of the peace. (p. 631)

14. **DISPOSAL OF COLLATERAL** A secured party may sell, lease, or otherwise dispose of the collateral in any commercially reasonable way; in many cases it may accept the collateral in full or partial satisfaction of the debt. The secured party may also ignore the collateral and sue the debtor for the full debt. (p. 632)

EXAM Strategy

Question: Jerry Payne owed the First State Bank of Pflugerville $342,000. The loan was secured by a 9.25-carat diamond ring. The bank claimed a default on the loan and, without notifying Payne, sold the ring. But the proceeds did not pay off the full debt, and the bank sued Payne for the deficiency. Is Payne liable for the deficiency?

Strategy: A secured party may dispose of the collateral in any commercially reasonable way. What must the secured party do to ensure commercial reasonableness? (See the "Result" at the end of this section.)

15. **TERMINATION** When the debtor pays the full debt, the secured party must complete a termination statement, notifying the public that it no longer claims a security interest in the collateral. (p. 634)

7. Result: Gallatin advanced the money that the Lockoviches used to buy the boat, meaning the bank obtained a PMSI. A PMSI in consumer goods perfects automatically, without filing. The boat was a consumer good. Gallatin's security interest perfected without any filing at all, and so the bank wins.

10. Result: This question is resolved by the first of those three steps. A party with a perfected security interest takes priority over a party with an unperfected interest. The bank wins because its perfected security interest takes priority over Barwell's unperfected interest.

14. Result: The secured party must give the debtor notice of the time and place of the sale. This ensures that the debtor may bid on the collateral, preventing an unreasonably low sales price. The bank failed to give such notice, and so it lost its right to the deficiency.

ADDITIONAL QUESTIONS

Note to the student: The following cases and problems were decided under the former Article 9. In each instance the outcome would be the same under the revised code, although the relevant sections of Article 9 have been renumbered and probably rewritten.

1. *CPA QUESTION* Under the UCC Secured Transactions Article, which of the following actions will best perfect a security interest in a negotiable instrument against any other party?

    (a) Filing a security agreement

    (b) Taking possession of the instrument

    (c) Perfecting by attachment

    (d) Obtaining a duly executed financing statement

2. **CPA QUESTION** Under the UCC Secured Transactions Article, perfection of a security interest by a creditor provides added protection against other parties in the event the debtor does not pay its debts. Which of the following parties is not affected by perfection of a security interest?

   (a) Other prospective creditors of the debtor

   (b) The trustee in a bankruptcy case

   (c) A buyer in ordinary course of business

   (d) A subsequent personal injury judgment creditor

3. Eugene Ables ran an excavation company. He borrowed $500,000 from the Highland Park State Bank. Ables signed a note promising to repay the money and an agreement giving Highland a security interest in all of his equipment, including after-acquired equipment. Several years later, Ables agreed with Patricia Myers to purchase a Bantam Backhoe from her for $16,000, which he would repay at the rate of $100 per month, while he used the machine. Ables later defaulted on his note to Highland, and the bank attempted to take the backhoe. Myers and Ables contended that the bank had no right to take the backhoe. Was the backhoe covered by Highland's security interest? Did Ables have sufficient rights in the backhoe for the bank's security interest to attach?

4. The Copper King Inn, Inc., had money problems. It borrowed $62,500 from two of its officers, Noonan and Patterson, but that did not suffice to keep the inn going. So Noonan, on behalf of Copper King, arranged for the inn to borrow $100,000 from Northwest Capital, an investment company that worked closely with Noonan in other ventures. Copper King signed an agreement giving Patterson, Noonan, and Northwest a security interest in the inn's furniture and equipment. But the financing statement that the parties filed made no mention of Northwest. Copper King went bankrupt. Northwest attempted to seize assets, but other creditors objected. Is Northwest entitled to Copper King's furniture and equipment?

5. Sears sold a lawn tractor to Cosmo Fiscante for $1,481. Fiscante paid with his personal credit card. Sears kept a valid security interest in the lawnmower but did not perfect. Fiscante had the machine delivered to his business, Trackers Raceway Park, the only place he ever used the machine. When Fiscante was unable to meet his obligations, various creditors attempted to seize the lawnmower. Sears argued that because it had a purchase money security interest (PMSI) in the lawnmower, its interest had perfected automatically. Is Sears correct?

6. The state of Kentucky filed a tax lien against Panbowl Energy, claiming unpaid taxes. Six months later, Panbowl bought a powerful drill from Whayne Supply, making a down payment of $11,500 and signing a security agreement for the remaining debt of $220,000. Whayne perfected the next day. Panbowl defaulted. Whayne sold the drill for $58,000, leaving a deficiency of just over $100,000. The state filed suit, seeking the $58,000 proceeds. The trial court gave summary judgment to the state and Whayne appealed. Who gets the $58,000?

7. **CPA QUESTION** Mars, Inc., manufactures and sells VCRs on credit directly to wholesalers, retailers, and consumers. Mars can perfect its security interest in the VCRs

it sells without having to file a financing statement or take possession of the VCRs if the sale is made to which of the following:

(a) Retailers

(b) Wholesalers that sell to distributors for resale

(c) Consumers

(d) Wholesalers that sell to buyers in ordinary course of business

8. **ETHICS** The Dannemans bought a Kodak copier worth over $40,000. Kodak arranged financing by GECC and assigned its rights to that company. Although the Dannemans thought they had purchased the copier on credit, the papers described the deal as a lease. The Dannemans had constant problems with the machine and stopped making payments. GECC repossessed the machine and, without notifying the Dannemans, sold it back to Kodak for $12,500, leaving a deficiency of $39,927. GECC sued the Dannemans for that amount. The Dannemans argued that the deal was not a lease but a sale on credit. Why does it matter whether the parties had a sale or a lease? Is GECC entitled to its money? Finally, comment on the ethics. Why did the Dannemans not understand the papers they had signed? Who is responsible for that? Are you satisfied with the ethical conduct of the Dannemans? Kodak? GECC?

9. **YOU BE THE JUDGE** WRITING PROBLEM Dupont Feed bought and sold agricultural products. Dupont borrowed $300,000 from Wells Fargo Bank and gave Wells Fargo a security interest in all inventory, including after-acquired inventory. Wells Fargo perfected its interest by filing on June 17, 1982. Later, Dupont borrowed $150,000 from the Rushville National Bank and used the money to buy fertilizer. Dupont gave a PMSI to Rushville in the amount of $150,000. Rushville filed its financing statement in February 1984 at the County Recorder's office—the wrong place to file a financing statement for inventory. Then Dupont took possession of the fertilizer, and finally, in December 1984, Rushville filed correctly, with the Indiana Secretary of State. Dupont defaulted on both loans. Rushville seized the fertilizer, and Wells Fargo sued, claiming that it had perfected first. Rushville asserted that it had a PMSI, which took priority over an earlier-filed security interest. Does Rushville's PMSI take priority over Wells Fargo? (Go slowly, the rules are very technical.) **Argument for Rushville:** It is black letter law that PMSIs take priority over virtually everything, including interests perfected earlier. We are not fools at Rushville: we would not loan $150,000 to buy inventory if our security interest in that inventory was instantly inferior to someone else's. **Argument for Wells Fargo:** A PMSI in inventory gets priority only if the secured party perfects before the debtor receives the collateral. When Dupont obtained the fertilizer, Rushville had not perfected, because it had filed in the wrong office. It only perfected long after Dupont bought the inventory; thus, Rushville's PMSI does not get priority.

10. **ROLE REVERSAL** Write a multiple-choice question with a conflict between a secured party and a buyer in ordinary course of business.

INTERNET RESEARCH PROBLEM

Draft a security agreement in which your friend gives you a security interest in her $20,000 home entertainment system, in exchange for a loan of $12,000. Because the collateral is something that she uses daily, what special concerns do you have? How will you protect yourself? Next, find the UCC1 financing form online. Print the form, then complete it. In what office of your state should you file in order to perfect?

You can find further practice problems at www.cengagebrain.com. See the preface of this book for website access details.

BANKRUPTCY

George Bryan Brummell, known as Beau Brummell, was a celebrity in nineteenth-century England. Known for his impeccable sense of style, he was the leading arbiter of taste and fashion for more than 20 years. This role was demanding—he routinely spent five hours a day simply getting dressed. After bathing in eau de cologne and water, he would spend an hour with his hairdresser and another two hours tying his cravat. Although he had inherited modest wealth, his extravagant lifestyle brought him to ruin. He fled to France to escape his creditors, taking his lavish tastes with him. After 14 years in France, he was thrown in debtors' prison.

For actor Kim Basinger, a modern celebrity, bankruptcy had a different outcome. A Los Angeles jury ordered her to pay $8.1 million to Main Line Pictures, Inc., because she broke her promise to appear in *Boxing Helena*, a film about a doctor who cuts off his lover's arms and legs. Five days after the verdict, she filed for bankruptcy protection, claiming $5 million in assets and $11 million in liabilities.

Despite filing for bankruptcy, Basinger spent $43,000 per month, including $6,100 for clothes; $4,000 for recreation, clubs, and entertainment; $7,000 for pet care and other personal expenses; as well as $9,000 in alimony to her ex-husband.

> **Despite filing for bankruptcy, Basinger spent $43,000 per month, including $6,100 for clothes; $4,000 for recreation, clubs, and entertainment; $7,000 for pet care and other personal expenses; as well as $9,000 in alimony to her ex-husband.**

She also reported owning $592,000 in furniture and clothing and $192,000 in jewelry. In the meantime, she made no payments to creditors—those who had arranged her travel, repaired her home, or cut her grass.[1]

Traditionally, the goal of English bankruptcy law was to protect creditors and punish debtors. Creditors had the right to seize a bankrupt's assets and have him incarcerated in a squalid debtors' prison. Once in jail, the debtor had no way to earn money to pay his debts and, indeed, was required to pay the cost of his upkeep in jail. He was effectively sentenced to life in prison unless family and friends paid his debts. Many of America's first settlers fled England to escape debtors' prison. As if to compensate for England's harsh regime, American bankruptcy laws were traditionally more lenient toward debtors. Do our bankruptcy laws strike the right balance? Think about that as you read this chapter.

OVERVIEW OF THE BANKRUPTCY CODE

The federal Bankruptcy Code (Code) is divided into eight chapters. All chapters except one have odd numbers. Chapters 1, 3, and 5 are administrative rules that generally apply to all types of bankruptcy proceedings. These chapters, for example, define terms and establish the rules of the bankruptcy court. Chapters 7, 9, 11, 12, and 13 are substantive rules for different types of bankruptcies. All of these substantive chapters have one of two objectives—rehabilitation or liquidation.

REHABILITATION
The objective of Chapters 11 and 13 is to rehabilitate the debtor. Many debtors can return to financial health provided they have the time and breathing space to work out their problems. These chapters hold creditors at bay while the debtor develops a payment plan. In return for retaining some of their assets, debtors typically promise to pay creditors a portion of their future earnings.

LIQUIDATION

Straight bankruptcy
Also known as liquidation, this form of bankruptcy mandates that the bankrupt's assets be sold to pay creditors but the creditor has no obligation to share future earnings.

When debtors are unable to develop a feasible plan for rehabilitation under Chapter 11 or 13, Chapter 7 provides for liquidation (also known as a **straight bankruptcy**). Most of the debtor's assets are distributed to creditors, but the debtor has no obligation to share future earnings.

---

[1] Carol Marie Cropper, "The Basinger Bankruptcy Bomb," *New York Times*, Jan. 1, 1995, Section 3, p. 1. Copyright © 1995 by The New York Times Co. A California appeals court overturned the judgment against Basinger in the Main Line suit and ordered a new trial. On the eve of retrial, Basinger settled for $3.8 million.

CHAPTER DESCRIPTION

The following options are available under the Bankruptcy Code:

Number	Topic	Description
Chapter 7	Liquidation	The bankrupt's assets are sold to pay creditors. If the debtor owns a business, it terminates. The creditors have no right to the debtor's future earnings.
Chapter 9	Municipal bankruptcies	This chapter is not covered in this book.
Chapter 11	Reorganization	This chapter is designed for businesses and wealthy individuals. Businesses continue in operation, and creditors receive a portion of the debtor's current assets and future earnings.
Chapter 12	Family farmers	This chapter is not covered in this book.
Chapter 13	Consumer reorganizations	Chapter 13 offers reorganization for the typical consumer. Creditors usually receive a portion of the individual's current assets and future earnings.

Debtors are sometimes eligible to file under more than one chapter. No choice is irrevocable because both debtors and creditors have the right to ask the court to convert a case from one chapter to another at any time during the proceedings. For example, if creditors have asked for liquidation under Chapter 7, a bankrupt consumer may request rehabilitation under Chapter 13.

GOALS

The Bankruptcy Code has three primary goals:

- *To preserve as much of the debtor's property as possible.* In keeping with this goal, the Code requires debtors to disclose all of their assets and prohibits them from transferring assets immediately before a bankruptcy filing.

- *To divide the debtor's assets fairly between the debtor and creditors.* On the one hand, creditors are entitled to payment. On the other hand, debtors are often so deeply in debt that full payment is virtually impossible in any reasonable period of time. The Code tries to balance the creditors' desire to be paid with the debtors' right to get on with their lives unburdened by prior debts.

- *To divide the debtor's assets fairly among creditors.* Creditors rarely receive all they are owed, but at least they are treated fairly, according to established rules. Creditors do not benefit from simply being the first to file or from any other gamesmanship.

CHAPTER 7 LIQUIDATION

All bankruptcy cases proceed in a roughly similar pattern, regardless of chapter. We use Chapter 7 as a template to illustrate common features of all bankruptcy cases. Later on, the discussions of the other chapters will indicate how they differ from Chapter 7.

Filing a Petition

Any individual, partnership, corporation, or other business organization that lives, conducts business, or owns property in the United States can file under the Code. (Chapter 13, however, is available only to individuals.) The traditional term for someone who could not pay his debts was "**bankrupt**," but the Code uses the term "**debtor**" instead. We use both terms interchangeably.

A case begins with the filing of a bankruptcy petition in federal district court. The district court typically refers bankruptcy cases to a specialized bankruptcy judge. Either party can appeal the decision of the bankruptcy judge back to the district court and, from there, to the federal appeals court.

Debtors may go willingly into the bankruptcy process by filing a **voluntary petition** or they may be dragged into court by creditors who file an **involuntary petition**. Originally, when the goal of bankruptcy laws was to protect creditors, voluntary petitions did not exist; all petitions were involuntary. Because the bankruptcy process is now viewed as being favorable to debtors, the vast majority of bankruptcy filings in this country are voluntary petitions.

Voluntary Petition

Any debtor (whether a business or an individual) has the right to file for bankruptcy. It is not necessary that the debtor's liabilities exceed assets. Debtors sometimes file a bankruptcy petition because cash flow is so tight they cannot pay their debts, even though they are not technically insolvent. However, *individuals* must meet two requirements before filing:

- Within 180 days before the filing, an individual debtor must undergo credit counseling with an approved agency.

- Individual debtors may only file under Chapter 7 if they earn less than the median income in their state *or* they cannot afford to pay back at least $7,025 over five years.[2] Generally, all other debtors must file under Chapter 11 or Chapter 13. (These Chapters require the bankrupt to repay some debt.)

The voluntary petition must include the following documents:

Document	Description
Petition	Begins the case. Easy to fill out, it requires checking a few boxes and typing in little more than name, address, and Social Security number.
List of Creditors	The names and addresses of all creditors.
Schedule of Assets and Liabilities	A list of the debtor's assets and debts.
Claim of Exemptions	A list of all assets that the debtor is entitled to keep.
Schedule of Income and Expenditures	The debtor's job, income, and expenses.
Statement of Financial Affairs	A summary of the debtor's financial history and current financial condition. In particular, the debtor must list any recent payments to creditors and any other property held by someone else for the debtor.

---

[2] In some circumstances, debtors with income higher than $7,025 may still be eligible to file under Chapter 7, but the formula is highly complex and more than most readers want to know. The formula is available at 11 USC Section 707(b)(2)(A). Also, you can Google "bapcpa means test" and then browse to the Department of Justice website (**http://www.usdoj.gov).**

Bankrupt

Another term for debtor.

Debtor

Someone who cannot pay his debts and files for protection under the Bankruptcy Code.

Involuntary Petition

Creditors may force a debtor into bankruptcy by filing an involuntary petition. The creditors' goal is to preserve as much of the debtor's assets as possible and to ensure that all creditors receive a fair share. Naturally, the Code sets strict limits—debtors cannot be forced into bankruptcy every time they miss a credit card payment. **An involuntary petition must meet all of the following requirements:**

- The debtor must owe at least $14,425 in unsecured claims to the creditors who file.[3]

- If the debtor has at least 12 creditors, 3 or more must sign the petition. If the debtor has fewer than 12 creditors, any one of them can file a petition.

- The creditors must allege either that a custodian for the debtor's property has been appointed in the prior 120 days or that the debtor has generally not been paying debts that are due.

What does "a custodian for the debtor's property" mean? *State* laws sometimes permit the appointment of a custodian to protect a debtor's assets. The Code allows creditors to pull a case out from under state law and into federal bankruptcy court by filing an involuntary petition. In the event that a debtor objects to an involuntary petition, the bankruptcy court must hold a trial to determine whether the creditors have met the Code's requirements.

Once a voluntary petition is filed or an involuntary petition approved, the bankruptcy court issues an **order for relief**. This order is an official acknowledgment that the debtor is under the jurisdiction of the court, and it is, in a sense, the start of the whole bankruptcy process. An involuntary debtor must now make all the filings that accompany a voluntary petition.

Order for relief
An official acknowledgment that a debtor is under the jurisdiction of the bankruptcy court.

TRUSTEE

The trustee is responsible for gathering the bankrupt's assets and dividing them among creditors. This is a critical role in a bankruptcy case. Trustees are typically lawyers or CPAs, but any generally competent person can serve. Creditors have the right to elect the trustee, but often they do not bother. If the creditors do not elect a trustee, then the **U.S. Trustee** appoints one. Each region of the country has a U.S. Trustee selected by the U.S. attorney general. Besides appointing trustees as necessary, this U.S. Trustee oversees the administration of bankruptcy law in the region.

The U.S. Trustee
Oversees the administration of bankruptcy law in a region.

CREDITORS

After the court issues an order for relief, the U.S. Trustee calls a meeting of creditors. At the meeting, the bankrupt must answer (under oath) any question the creditors pose about his financial situation. If the creditors want to elect a trustee, they do so at this meeting.

---

[3] In Chapter 25, on secured transactions, we discuss the difference between secured and unsecured claims at some length. A secured claim is one in which the creditor has the right to foreclose on a specific piece of the debtor's property (known as **collateral**) if the debtor fails to pay the debt when due. For example, if Lee borrows money from GMAC Finance to buy a car, the company has the right to repossess the car if Lee fails to repay the loan. GMAC's loan is **secured**. An **unsecured** loan has no collateral. If the debtor fails to repay, the creditor can make a general claim against the debtor but has no right to foreclose on a particular item of the debtor's property.

Proof of claim

A form stating the name of an unsecured creditor and the amount of the claim against the debtor.

After the meeting of creditors, unsecured creditors must submit a ***proof of claim***. This document is a simple form stating the name of the creditor and the amount of the claim. The trustee and the debtor also have the right to file on behalf of a creditor. But if a claim is not filed, the creditor loses any right to be paid. The trustee, debtor, or any creditor can object to a claim on the grounds that the debtor does not really owe that money. The court then holds a hearing to determine the validity of the claim.

Secured creditors do not file proofs of claim unless the claim exceeds the value of their collateral. In this case, they are unsecured creditors for the excess amount and must file a proof of claim for it. Suppose that Deborah borrows $750,000 from Morton in return for a mortgage on her house. If she does not repay the debt, he can foreclose. Unfortunately, property values plummet, and by the time Deborah files a voluntary petition in bankruptcy, the house is worth only $500,000. Morton is a secured creditor for $500,000 and need file no proof of claim for that amount. But he is an unsecured creditor for $250,000 and will lose his right to this excess amount unless he files a proof of claim for it.

AUTOMATIC STAY

Automatic stay

Prohibits creditors from collecting debts that the bankrupt incurred before the petition was filed.

A fox chased by hounds has no time to make rational long-term decisions. What that fox needs is a safe burrow. Similarly, it is difficult for debtors to make sound financial decisions when hounded night and day by creditors shouting, "Pay me! Pay me!" The Code is designed to give debtors enough breathing space to sort out their affairs sensibly. An automatic stay is a safe burrow for the bankrupt. It goes into effect as soon as the petition is filed. An **automatic stay** prohibits creditors from collecting debts that the bankrupt incurred before the petition was filed. Creditors may not sue a bankrupt to obtain payment nor may they take other steps, outside of court, to pressure the debtor for payment. The following case illustrates how persistent creditors can be.

JACKSON V. HOLIDAY FURNITURE

309 B.R. 33, 2004 BANKR. LEXIS 548
UNITED STATES BANKRUPTCY COURT FOR THE WESTERN DISTRICT OF MISSOURI, 2004

CASE SUMMARY

Facts: In April, Cora and Frank Jackson purchased a recliner chair on credit from Dan Holiday Furniture. They made payments until November. That month, they filed for protection under the Bankruptcy Code. Dan Holiday received a notice of the bankruptcy. This notice stated that the store must stop all efforts to collect on the Jacksons' debt.

Despite this notice, a Dan Holiday collector telephoned the Jacksons' house 10 times between November 15 and December 1 and left a card in their door threatening repossession of the chair. On December 1, Frank—without Cora's knowledge—went to Dan Holiday to pay the $230 owed for November and December. He told the store owner about the

bankruptcy filing, but allegedly added that he and his wife wanted to continue making payments directly to Dan Holiday.

In early January, employees at Dan Holiday learned that Frank had died the month before. Nevertheless, after Cora failed to make the payment for the month of January, a collector telephoned her house twenty-six times between January 14 and February 19. The store owner's sister left the following message on Cora's answering machine:

Hello. This is Judy over at Dan Holiday Furniture. And this is the last time I am going to call you. If you do not call me, I will be at your house. And I expect you to call me today. If there is a problem, I need to speak to you about it. You need to call me. We need to get this thing going. You are a January and February

Chapter 26 *Bankruptcy* **647**

payment behind. And if you think you are going to get away with it, you've got another thing coming.

When Cora returned home on February 18, she found seven bright yellow slips of paper in her door jamb stating that a Dan Holiday truck had stopped by to repossess her furniture. The cards read:

"OUR TRUCK was here to **REPOSSESS** Your furniture (sic). 241–6933 Dan Holiday Furn. & Appl. Co."

The threat to send a truck was merely a ruse designed to frighten Cora. In truth, Dan Holiday did not really want the recliner back. The owner just wanted to talk directly with Cora about making payments.

Also on February 18, Dan Holiday sent Cora a letter stating that she had 24 hours to bring her account current or else **"Repossession** Will Be Made and **Legal Action Will Be Taken."** That same day, Cora's bankruptcy attorney contacted Dan Holiday. Thereafter all collection activity ceased.

Issues: *Did Dan Holiday violate the automatic stay provisions of the Bankruptcy Code? What is the penalty for a violation?*

Decision: Dan Holiday was in violation of the Bankruptcy Code. The court awarded the Jacksons their actual damages, attorneys' fees, court costs, and punitive damages.

Reasoning: Anyone injured by a creditor who violates the automatic stay provisions is entitled to recover both actual damages (including court costs and attorneys' fees) as well as punitive damages where appropriate. In this case, the court awarded actual damages of $230, because that is how much Dan Holiday coerced from Frank Jackson on December 1. The Court also awarded the Jacksons their attorneys' fees and court costs in the amount of $1,142.42.

In addition, the Jacksons were entitled to punitive damages because Dan Holiday intentionally and flagrantly violated the automatic stay provision. Dan Holiday's conduct was remarkably bad—employees called the Jackson household no less than twenty-six times in January and February.

It was not clear how much the punitive damages should be because there was no evidence presented at trial about how much Dan Holiday could afford. The court was only aware that Dan Holiday was a family-owned business that had been in existence for fifty-two years. It seemed likely that it was a relatively small business. Therefore, the Court assessed a penalty of $100 for each illegal contact with the Jacksons after December 1, when it was crystal clear that Dan Holiday knew about the Jacksons' bankruptcy filing. Under this calculation, punitive damages totaled $2,800. The Court believed that this penalty would be enough to sting the pocketbook of Dan Holiday and impress upon the company, its owners, and employees the importance of complying with the provisions of the Bankruptcy Code.

BANKRUPTCY ESTATE

The filing of the bankruptcy petition creates a new legal entity separate from the debtor—the **bankruptcy estate** All of the bankrupt's assets pass to the estate, except exempt property and new property that the debtor acquires after the petition is filed.

Bankruptcy estate
The new legal entity created when a debtor files a bankruptcy petition. All of the debtor's existing assets pass into the estate.

Exempt Property

Unpaid creditors may be angry, but generally they do not want the debtor to starve to death. **The Code permits *individual* debtors (but not organizations) to keep some property for themselves.** This exempt property saves the debtor from destitution during the bankruptcy process and provides the foundation for a new life once the process is over.

In this one area of bankruptcy law, the Code defers to state law. Although the Code lists various types of exempt property, it permits states to opt out of the federal system and define a different set of exemptions. A majority of states have indeed opted out of the Code, and for their residents the Code exemptions are irrelevant. Alternatively, some states allow the debtor to choose between state or federal exemptions.

Under the *federal* Code, a debtor is allowed to exempt only $21,625 of the value of her home. If the house is worth more than that, the trustee sells it and returns $21,625 of the proceeds to the debtor. Most *states* exempt items such as the debtor's home, household goods, cars, work tools, disability and pension benefits, alimony, and health aids. Indeed, some states set no limit on the value of exempt property. Both Florida and Texas, for example, permit debtors to keep homes of unlimited value and a certain amount of land. (Texas also allows debtors to hang on to two firearms; athletic and sporting equipment; two horses, mules, or donkeys and a saddle, blanket, and bridle for each.) Not surprisingly, these generous exemptions sometimes lead to abuses. Therefore, the Code provides that debtors can take advantage of state exemptions only if they have lived in that state for two years prior to the bankruptcy. And they can exempt only $146,450 of any house that was acquired during the 40 months before the bankruptcy.

Voidable Preferences

Preference
When a debtor unfairly pays creditors immediately before filing a bankruptcy petition.

A major goal of the bankruptcy system is to divide the debtor's assets fairly among creditors. It would not be fair, or in keeping with this goal, if debtors were permitted to pay off some of their creditors immediately before filing a bankruptcy petition. These transfers are called **preferences** because they give unfair preferential treatment to some creditors. The trustee has the right to void such preferences.

Preferences can take two forms: payments and liens. A payment simply means that the debtor gives a creditor cash that would otherwise end up in the bankruptcy estate. A lien means a security interest in the debtor's property. In bankruptcy proceedings, secured creditors are more likely to be paid than unsecured creditors. If the debtor grants a security interest in specific property, he vaults that creditor out of the great unwashed mass of unsecured creditors and into the elite company of secured creditors. If it happens immediately before the petition is filed, it is unfair to other unsecured creditors.

The trustee can void any transfer (whether payment or lien) that meets all of the following requirements:

- The transfer was to a creditor of the bankrupt.

- It was to pay an existing debt.

- The creditor received more from the transfer than she would have received during the bankruptcy process.

- The debtor's liabilities exceeded assets at the time of the transfer.

- The transfer took place in the 90-day period before the filing of the petition.

Insider
Family members of an individual debtor, officers and directors of a corporation, or partners of a partnership.

In addition, the trustee can void a transfer to an insider that occurs in the *year* preceding the filing of the petition. **Insiders** are family members of an individual debtor, officers and directors of a corporation, or partners of a partnership.

Fraudulent Transfers

Suppose that a debtor sees bankruptcy inexorably approaching across the horizon like a tornado. He knows that, once the storm hits and he files a petition, everything he owns except a few items of exempt property will become part of the bankruptcy estate. Before that happens, he may be tempted to give some of his property to friends or family to shelter it from the tornado. If he succumbs to temptation, however, he is committing a fraudulent transfer.

A transfer is fraudulent if it is made within the year before a petition is filed and its purpose is to hinder, delay, or defraud creditors. The trustee can void any fraudulent transfer. The debtor has committed a crime and may be prosecuted.

Not all payments by a debtor prior to filing are considered voidable preferences or fraudulent transfers. **A trustee cannot void pre-petition payments made *in the ordinary course.*** In a business context, that means a trustee cannot void payments from, say, a grocery store to its regular cookie supplier. For consumers, the trustee cannot void payments below $600 or other routine payments, say, to the electric or water company. In these situations, the bankrupt is clearly not trying to cheat creditors. Even the insolvent are allowed to shower with the light on.

> Even the insolvent are allowed to shower with the lights on.

Payment of Claims

Imagine a crowded delicatessen on Saturday evening. People are pushing and shoving because they know there is not enough food for everyone; some customers will go home hungry. The delicatessen could simply serve whoever pushes to the front of the line, or it could establish a number system to ensure that the most deserving customers are served first—long-time patrons or those who called ahead. The Code has, in essence, adopted a number system to prevent a free-for-all fight over the bankrupt's assets. Indeed, one of the Code's primary goals is to ensure that creditors are paid in the proper order, not according to who pushes to the front of the line.

All claims are placed in one of three classes: (1) secured claims, (2) priority claims, and (3) unsecured claims. The second class—priority claims—has seven subcategories; the third class—unsecured claims—has three. **The trustee pays the bankruptcy estate to the various classes of claims in order of rank.** A higher class is paid in full before the next class receives any payment at all. In the case of *priority* claims, each *subcategory* is paid in order, with the higher subcategory receiving full payment before the next subcategory receives anything. If there are not enough funds to pay an entire subcategory, all claimants in that group receive a pro rata share. The rule is different for unsecured claims. All categories of *unsecured* claims are treated the same, and if there are not enough funds to pay the *entire* class, everyone in the class shares pro rata. If, for example, there is only enough money to pay 10 percent of the claims owing to unsecured creditors, then each creditor receives 10 percent of her claim. In bankruptcy parlance, this is referred to as "getting 10 cents on the dollar." The debtor is entitled to any funds remaining after all claims have been paid. The payment order is shown in Exhibit 26.1.

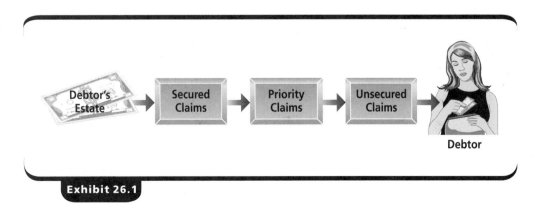

Exhibit 26.1

Secured Claims

Creditors whose loans are secured by specific collateral are paid first. Secured claims are fundamentally different from all other claims because they are paid by selling a specific asset, not out of the general funds of the estate. Sometimes, however, collateral is not valuable enough to pay off the entire secured debt. In this case, the creditor must wait in line with the unsecured creditors for the balance. Deborah (whom we met earlier in the section entitled "Creditors") borrowed $750,000 from Morton, secured by a mortgage on her house. By the time she files a voluntary petition, the house is worth only $500,000. Morton is a secured creditor for $500,000 and is paid that amount as soon as the trustee sells the house. But Morton is an unsecured creditor for $250,000 and will only receive this amount if the estate has enough funds to pay the unsecured creditors.

Priority Claims

There are seven subcategories of priority claims. Each category is paid in order, with the first group receiving full payment before the next group receives anything.

- *Alimony and Child Support.* The trustee must first pay any claims for alimony and child support. However, if the trustee is administering assets that could pay these support claims, then the trustee's fees are paid first.

- *Administrative Expenses.* These include fees to the trustee, lawyers, and accountants.

- *Gap Expenses.* If creditors file an involuntary petition, the debtor will continue to operate her business until the order for relief. Any expenses she incurs in the ordinary course of her business during this so-called **gap period** are paid now.

- *Payments to Employees.* The trustee now pays back wages to the debtor's employees for work performed during the 180 days prior to the date of the petition. The trustee, however, can pay no more than $11,725 to each employee. Any other wages become unsecured claims.

- *Employee Benefit Plans.* The trustee pays what the debtor owes to employee pension, health, or life insurance plans for work performed during the 180 days prior to the date of the petition. The total payment for wages and benefits under this and the prior paragraph cannot exceed $11,725 times the number of employees.

- *Consumer Deposits.* Any individual who has put down a deposit with the bankrupt for consumer goods is entitled to a refund of up to $2,600. If Stewart puts down a $3,000 deposit on a Miata sports car, he is entitled to a refund of $2,600 when the Trustie Car Lot goes bankrupt.

- *Taxes.* The trustee pays the debtor's income taxes for the three years prior to filing and property taxes for one prior year.

- *Drunken Injuries.* The trustee next pays the claims of anyone injured by a bankrupt who was driving a vehicle while drunk or on drugs.

Gap period

The period between the time that creditors file an involuntary petition and the court issues the order for relief.

Unsecured Claims

Last, and frequently very much least, the trustee pays unsecured claims. All three of these unsecured subcategories have an equal claim and must be paid together.

- *Secured Claims That Exceed the Value of the Available Collateral.* If funds permit, the trustee pays Morton the $250,000 that his collateral did not cover.

- *Priority Claims That Exceed the Priority Limits.* The trustee now pays employees, Stewart, and the tax authorities who were not paid in full the first time around because their claims exceeded the priority limits.

- *All Other Unsecured Claims.* Unsecured creditors have now reached the delicatessen counter. They can only hope that some food remains.

DISCHARGE

Filing a bankruptcy petition is embarrassing, time-consuming, and disruptive. It can affect the debtor's credit rating for years, making the simplest car loan a challenge. To encourage debtors to file for bankruptcy despite the pain involved, the Code offers a powerful incentive: the **fresh start**. Once a bankruptcy estate has been distributed to creditors, they cannot make a claim against the debtor for money owed before the filing, *whether or not they actually received any payment*. These pre-petition debts are **discharged**. All is forgiven, if not forgotten.

Discharge is an essential part of bankruptcy law. Without it, debtors would have little incentive to take part. To avoid abuses, however, the Code limits both the type of debts that can be discharged and the circumstances under which discharge can take place. In addition, a debtor must complete an approved course on financial management before receiving a discharge.

Debts That Cannot Be Discharged

The following debts are *never* discharged, and the debtor remains liable in full until they are paid:

- Income taxes for the three years prior to filing and property taxes for the prior year.

- Money obtained fraudulently. Kenneth Smith ran a home repair business that fleeced senior citizens by making unnecessary repairs. Three months after he was found liable for fraud, he filed a voluntary petition in bankruptcy. The court held that his liability on the fraud claim could not be discharged.[4]

- Any loan of more than $600 that a consumer uses to purchase luxury goods within 90 days before the order for relief is granted.

- Cash advances on a credit card totaling more than $875 that an individual debtor takes out within 70 days before the order for relief.

- Debts omitted from the Schedule of Assets and Liabilities that the debtor filed with the petition, if the creditor did not know about the bankruptcy and therefore did not file a proof of claim.

- Money that the debtor stole or obtained through a violation of fiduciary duty.

- Money owed for alimony or child support.

- Debts stemming from intentional and malicious injury.

- Fines and penalties owed to the government.

Fresh start

After the termination of a bankruptcy case, creditors cannot make a claim against the debtor for money owed before the initial bankruptcy petition was filed.

Discharge

The debtor no longer has an obligation to pay a debt.

---

[4] *In re Smith*, 848 F.2d 813, 1988 U.S. App. LEXIS 8037 (7th Cir. 1988).

- Liability for injuries caused by the debtor while operating a vehicle under the influence of drugs or alcohol. Yet another reason why friends don't let friends drive drunk.

- Liability for breach of duty to a bank. During the 1980s, a record number of savings and loans failed because their officers had made too many risky loans (in some cases to friends and family). This provision, added to the Code in 1990, was designed to prevent these officers from declaring bankruptcy to avoid their liability to bank shareholders.

- Debts stemming from a violation of securities laws.

- Student loans can be discharged only if repayment would cause undue hardship. As the following case illustrates, proving undue hardship is difficult.

In Re Stern

288 B.R. 36; 2002 Bankr. LEXIS 1609
United States Bankruptcy Court for the Northern District of New York, 2002

CASE SUMMARY

Facts: James Stern took out student loans to attend Bates College and Syracuse College of Law. Afterwards, he had difficulty finding a job as a lawyer, so he opened his own practice. His annual income averaged $17,000, while his wife's earnings averaged $18,000.

Stern was sued for malpractice. Although he won the case, his malpractice premiums increased so much that he could no longer afford the insurance. Believing that his debt and default on his student loans made him unemployable as a lawyer, he moved with his wife to her native country, France. Unfortunately, he did not speak French and, therefore, could not obtain a job, even as a street sweeper. His wife's total income over six months in France was $2,200. Even more unfortunately, their expenses in France were higher than in the United States.

After paying back $27,000, Stern still owed $147,000 in student loans: $56,000 in principal and $91,000 in interest. Stern calculated that paying his debt would cost $1,167 per month over 30 years. He asked the court to discharge these student loans on grounds of undue hardship. As he put it, "I'm never going to be able to get a house, I'm never going to be able to have a car, and I won't—you know, I want to have kids. I want to be responsible, and I can't—I can't possibly pay this amount and have a life, not with what I expect I'll be able to earn."

Issue: *Is Stern entitled to a discharge of his student loans?*

Decision: The court did not allow the discharge of these loans.

Reasoning: Educational loans are different from most business loans because they are made without security or co-signers. The lender must rely for repayment solely on the debtor's income (which presumably will increase as a result of the education). These loans are, in a sense, a mortgage on the student's future.

Although Stern has a J.D., he is not required to practice law. However, he must use his education to earn an income that will permit repayment of his loans.

Stern has not only failed to maximize his income, he has also failed to minimize his expenses. He moved to France where his expenses are higher, but he cannot even get a job as a street sweeper because he does not speak French.

Instead of repaying his loans, Stern would like to be able to buy a house or raise children. These desires, while understandable, do not constitute an undue hardship that warrants even a partial discharge. To obtain a discharge, Stern must prove more than his present inability to pay his student loans. He must also show that his current financial hardship is likely to be long term.

While Stern and his wife have experienced some bumps in the road, their future is under their control. They are young and healthy and have a good education. Indeed, the student loans permitted Stern to obtain an education that opens job opportunities not available to others who could not afford such an education.

Circumstances That Prevent Debts from Being Discharged

Apart from identifying the *kinds* of debts that cannot be discharged, the Code also prohibits the discharge of debts under the following *circumstances:*

- *Business Organizations.* Under Chapter 7 (but *not* the other chapters), only the debts of individuals can be discharged, not those of business organizations. Once its assets have been distributed, the organization must cease operation. If it continues in business, it is responsible for all pre-petition debts. Shortly after E. G. Sprinkler Corp. entered into an agreement with its union employees, it filed for bankruptcy under Chapter 7. Its debts were discharged, and the company began operation again. A court ordered it to pay its obligations to the employees because, once the company resumed business, it was responsible for all of its pre-filing debts.[5]

- *Revocation.* A court can revoke a discharge within one year if it discovers the debtor engaged in fraud or concealment.

- *Dishonesty or Bad Faith Behavior.* The court may deny discharge altogether if the debtor has, for example, made fraudulent transfers, hidden assets, falsified records, disobeyed court orders, refused to testify, or otherwise acted in bad faith. For instance, a court denied discharge under Chapter 7 to a couple who failed to list 15 pounds of marijuana on their Schedule of Assets and Liabilities. The court was unsympathetic to their arguments that a listing of this asset might have caused larger problems than merely being in debt.[6]

- *Repeated Filings for Bankruptcy.* Congress feared that some debtors, attracted by the lure of a fresh start, would make a habit of bankruptcy. Therefore, a debtor who has received a discharge under Chapter 7 or 11 cannot receive another discharge under Chapter 7 for at least eight years after the prior filing.

ETHICS   Banks and credit card companies lobbied Congress hard for this prohibition against repeated bankruptcy filings. They argued that irresponsible consumers run up debt and then blithely walk away. You might think that, if this were true, lenders would avoid customers with a history of bankruptcy. New research indicates, though, that lenders actually *target* those consumers, repeatedly sending them offers to borrow money. The reason is simple: These consumers are much more likely to take cash advances, which carry very high interest rates. And this is one audience that *must* repay its loans for the simple reason that these borrowers cannot declare bankruptcy again.[7] Is this strategy ethical? ◆

Reaffirmation

Sometimes debtors are willing to **reaffirm** a debt, meaning they promise to pay even after discharge. They may want to reaffirm a secured debt to avoid losing the collateral. For example, a debtor who has taken out a loan secured by a car may reaffirm that debt so that the finance company will agree not to repossess it. Sometimes debtors reaffirm because they feel guilty, or they want to maintain a good relationship with the creditor. They may have borrowed from a family member or an important supplier. Because discharge is a fundamental pillar of the bankruptcy

Reaffirm
To promise to pay a debt even after it is discharged.

---

[5] *In re Goodman*, 873 F.2d 598, 1989 U.S. App. LEXIS 5472 (2d Cir. 1989).
[6] *In re Tripp*, 224 B.R. 95, 1998 Bankr. LEXIS 1108 (1998).
[7] See Porter, Katherine M., "Bankrupt Profits: The Credit Industry's Business Model for Postbankruptcy Lending" University of Iowa Legal Studies Research Paper No. 07–26. Available by Googling "ssrn katherine porter bankrupt profits."

process, courts look closely at each reaffirmation to ensure that the creditor has not unfairly pressured the bankrupt. To be valid, the reaffirmation must meet the following requirements:

- It must not violate common law standards for fraud, duress, or unconscionability. If creditors force a bankrupt into reaffirming a debt, the reaffirmation is invalid.

- It must have been filed in court before the discharge is granted.

- It must include the detailed disclosure statement required by the statute (Section 524).

- It must clearly disclose that the debtor has the right to rescind at any time up to the date of the discharge or 60 days after the agreement is filed in court, whichever is later.

- Either the court must determine that the agreement is in the debtor's best interest and does not impose undue hardship, or the attorney representing the debtor must file an affidavit in court stating that the debtor's consent was informed and voluntary and the agreement does not create a hardship.

- In the case of an individual debtor, the court must explain both the terms of the agreement and the fact that it is not required by law.

Money has never been known to simplify family relationships. In the following case, the debtors' finances were complicated by the fact that they had borrowed from her mother and were living with his parents. The court stepped in to protect the (adult) children from reaffirming a debt.

In Re John & Julie Hoffman

358 B.R. 839; 2006 Bankr. LEXIS 3841
United States Bankruptcy Court for the Western District of Virginia, 2006

CASE SUMMARY

Facts: The Hoffmans filed for relief under Chapter 7. Among their debts was a loan for $11,500, secured by their 1999 Dodge Caravan. The car was worth less than half the amount of the loan. Paying back twice the value of the car made no economic sense, so ordinarily they would have defaulted on the loan. The problem was that Mrs. Hoffman's mother was a co-signer. If the Hoffmans defaulted, she would have to pay. To protect her, the Hoffmans signed a reaffirmation agreement promising to repay the car loan at the rate of $96 a week for four years. To darken further an already unhappy picture, the Hoffmans' monthly income of $4,799.12 was $35.87 less than their expenses. Because they had lost their house, they were living with his parents and paying $600 a month in rent.

The Hoffmans' lawyer refused to approve the reaffirmation agreement because it had a negative monthly budget. They asked the Court for approval.

Issue: *Will the court approve a reaffirmation agreement that shows a negative monthly budget?*

Decision: The court did not approve the reaffirmation agreement.

Reasoning: For the court to approve a reaffirmation agreement, there must be some evidence that the debtors are able to make the required payments. The Hoffmans' income is $36 a month less than their expenses, and their financial position is likely to get even worse because Mrs. Hoffman has accepted a job that pays $2,000 a month less than she is earning now.

Although the Court appreciates the Hoffmans' desire to protect her mother, the court must base its decision on their economic best interest. They can always make voluntary payments on the car, but the court will not approve an agreement that requires them to do so.

CHAPTER 11 REORGANIZATION

For a business, the goal of a Chapter 7 bankruptcy is euthanasia—putting it out of its misery by shutting it down and distributing its assets to creditors. Chapter 11 has a much more complicated and ambitious goal—resuscitating a business so that it can ultimately emerge as a viable economic concern. Keeping a business in operation benefits virtually all company stakeholders: employees, customers, creditors, shareholders, and the community.

Both individuals and businesses can use Chapter 11. Businesses usually prefer Chapter 11 over Chapter 7 because Chapter 11 does not require them to dissolve at the end as Chapter 7 does. The threat of death creates a powerful incentive to try rehabilitation under Chapter 11. Individuals, however, tend to prefer Chapter 13 because it is specifically designed for them.

A Chapter 11 proceeding follows many of the same steps as Chapter 7: a petition (either voluntary or involuntary), order for relief, meeting of creditors, proofs of claim, and an automatic stay. There are, however, some significant differences.

DEBTOR IN POSSESSION

Chapter 11 does not require a trustee. The bankrupt is called the **debtor in possession** and, in essence, serves as trustee. The debtor in possession has two jobs: to operate the business and to develop a plan of reorganization. A trustee is chosen only if the debtor is incompetent or uncooperative. In that case, the creditors can elect the trustee, but if they do not choose to do so, the U.S. Trustee appoints one.

CREDITORS' COMMITTEE

In a Chapter 11 case, the creditors' committee plays a particularly important role because typically there is no neutral trustee to watch over their interests. The committee has the right to help develop the plan of reorganization and to participate in any other way necessary to protect the interests of its constituency. Moreover, the Bankruptcy Code requires the committee to communicate diligently with all creditors. The U.S. Trustee typically appoints the seven largest *un*secured creditors to the committee. However, the court may require the U.S. Trustee to appoint some small business creditors to the committee. Secured creditors do not serve because their interests require less protection. If the debtor is a corporation, the U.S. Trustee may also appoint a committee of shareholders. The Code refers to the **claims** of creditors and the **interests** of shareholders.

PLAN OF REORGANIZATION

Once the bankruptcy petition is filed, an automatic stay goes into effect to provide the debtor with temporary relief from creditors. The next stage is to develop a plan of reorganization that provides for the payment of debts and the continuation of the business. For the first 120 days (which the court can extend up to 18 months), the debtor has the exclusive right to propose a plan. If the debtor fails to file a plan, or if the court rejects it, then creditors and shareholders can develop their own plan.

CONFIRMATION OF THE PLAN

Anyone who proposes a plan of reorganization must also prepare a **disclosure statement** to be mailed out with the plan. The purpose of this statement is to provide creditors and shareholders with enough information to make an informed judgment. The statement describes the company's business, explains the plan, calculates the company's liquidation value, and assesses the likelihood that the debtor can be rehabilitated. The court must approve a disclosure statement before it is sent to creditors and shareholders.

All the creditors and shareholders have the right to vote on the plan of reorganization. In preparation for the vote, each creditor and shareholder is assigned to a class. Everyone in a class has similar claims or interests. Chapter 11 classifies claims in the same way as Chapter 7: (1) secured claims, (2) priority claims, and (3) unsecured claims. Each secured claim is usually in its own class because each one is secured by different collateral. Shareholders are also divided into classes, depending upon their interests. For example, holders of preferred stock are in a different class from common shareholders.

Creditors and shareholders receive a ballot with their disclosure statement to vote for or against the plan of reorganization. After the vote, the bankruptcy court holds a **confirmation hearing** to determine whether it should accept the plan. **The court will approve a plan if a majority** *of each class* **votes in favor of it.** Even if some classes vote against the plan, the court can still confirm it under what is called a **cramdown** (as in "the plan is crammed down the creditors' throats"). The court will not impose a cramdown unless, in its view, the plan is feasible and fair. If the court rejects the plan of reorganization, the creditors must develop a new one. In the following case, the court did impose a cramdown.

In Re Fox

2000 BANKR. LEXIS 1713
UNITED STATES BANKRUPTCY COURT, DISTRICT OF KANSAS, 2000

CASE SUMMARY

Facts: Donald Fox founded Midland Fumigant, Inc., a company in the business of fumigating stored wheat, corn, and other grain. In a prior case, a competitor, United Phosphorus, Ltd., obtained a verdict of $2 million against Midland and Fox for fraud.

Unable to pay the judgment, Fox filed a voluntary petition under Chapter 11 of the Bankruptcy Code. His plan of reorganization envisioned that he would use revenues from Midland to pay off his creditors in full over five years, with interest. To ensure that the plan of reorganization was feasible, Fox hired CPA Kirk W. Wiesner to analyze Midland's financial statements and prepare projections of its income and expenses. Wiesner also reviewed Midland's operations, business, products, and the industry. He concluded that the plan's projections were conservative and could easily be met.

Midland had six classes of creditors. All of the classes accepted the plan, except the two classes in which United was a member. The bankruptcy judge noted that United had an incentive to oppose Midland's reorganization because this business was highly competitive and, if Midland were to cease operations, United would be able to raise its prices substantially.

Issue: *Was Fox's Plan of reorganization feasible and fair? Should the court impose a cramdown?*

Decision: Fox's Plan of reorganization was feasible and fair. The court did impose a cramdown.

Reasoning: Fox proposed a Plan that paid all creditors in full, with interest. United, the only creditor to object, was to be paid in full within sixteen months.

Fox's goal under the Plan—to keep his business in operation—is consistent with the purposes of the Code. But the Code's objective is also to prevent visionary plans that promise creditors and shareholders more than the debtor can possibly achieve. United contends that Fox's Plan is not feasible because its financial projections are unrealistic. United's fears, however, are not supported by the evidence. An expert witness, Kirk Wiesner, analyzed Midland's financial statements and determined that Midland would have sufficient income and cash flow to comply with the Plan. The court finds Wiesner a reliable witness because his projections in the past have been conservative.

The Plan has a reasonable chance of success and is not likely to result in liquidation or further financial reorganization. Moreover, the U.S. Trustee has filed a statement in support of confirmation. Therefore, debtor's Plan is confirmed over the objection of United and over the dissenting votes of two classes of creditors.

DISCHARGE

A confirmed plan of reorganization is binding on the debtor, creditors, and shareholders. **The debtor now owns the assets in the bankrupt estate, free of all obligations except those listed in the plan.** Under a typical plan of reorganization, the debtor gives some current assets to creditors and also promises to pay them a portion of future earnings. In contrast, the Chapter 7 debtor typically relinquishes all assets (except exempt property) to creditors but then has no obligation to turn over future income. Exhibit 26.2 illustrates the steps in a Chapter 11 bankruptcy.

SMALL BUSINESS BANKRUPTCY

Out of concern that the lengthy procedure in Chapter 11 was harming the creditors of small businesses, in 2005 Congress included provisions designed to speed up the process for businesses with less than $2 million in debt. After the order for relief, the bankrupt has the exclusive right to file a plan for 180 days. Both a plan and a

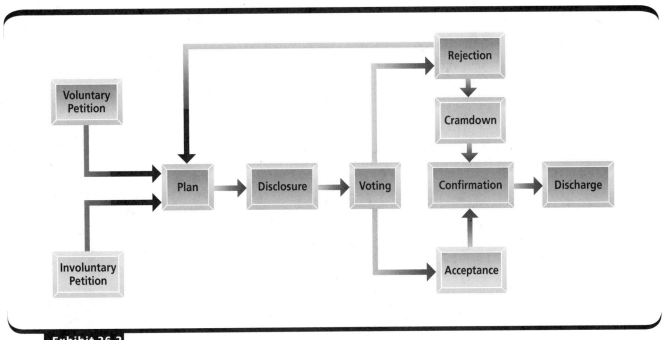

Exhibit 26.2

disclosure statement must be filed within 300 days. The court must confirm or reject the plan within 45 days after its filing. If these deadlines are not met, the case can be converted to Chapter 7 or dismissed.

CHAPTER 13 CONSUMER REORGANIZATIONS

The purpose of Chapter 13 is to rehabilitate an individual debtor. It is not available at all to businesses or to individuals with more than $360,475 in unsecured debts or $1,081,400 in secured debts. Under Chapter 13, the bankrupt consumer typically keeps most of her assets in exchange for a promise to repay some of her debts using future income. Therefore, to be eligible, the debtor must have a regular source of income. Individuals usually choose this chapter because it is easier and cheaper than Chapters 7 and 11. Consequently, more money is retained for both creditors and debtor.

As you read at the beginning of the chapter, debtors can convert from one chapter to another, as they wish. In this case, the trustees objected to a conversion. The case went all the way to the Supreme Court, which split 5–4. How would you have voted?

YOU *be the* JUDGE

MARRAMA v. CITIZENS BANK OF MASSACHUSETTS

127 S.Ct. 1105; 2007 U.S. LEXIS 2651 SUPREME COURT OF THE UNITED STATES, 2007

Facts: When Robert Marrama filed a voluntary petition under Chapter 7, he lied. Although he disclosed that he was the sole beneficiary of a trust that owned a house in Maine, he listed its value as zero. Marrama also denied that he had transferred any property during the prior year. Neither statement was true: The Maine property was valuable (how many houses are worth zero?) and he had given it for free to the trust seven months prior to filing for bankruptcy protection. Marrama also lied when he claimed that he was not entitled to a tax refund. In fact, he knew that a check for $8,700 from the Internal Revenue Service was in the mail.

Once Marrama found out that the bankruptcy trustees were going after the Maine property, he filed a notice to convert his Chapter 7 bankruptcy to Chapter 13. The trustee and creditors objected. They contended that because Marrama had acted in bad faith when he tried to conceal the Maine property from his creditors, he should not be permitted to convert. The bankruptcy court and the appeals court agreed. The Supreme Court granted *certiorari*.

You Be the Judge: Can a bankruptcy court refuse to allow a debtor to convert from Chapter 7 to Chapter 13?

Argument for Marrama: Under the Bankruptcy Code, a Chapter 7 debtor may convert a case, with only two restrictions. First, the bankrupt can convert only once. Second, the debtor must meet the conditions that would have been required for him to file under the new chapter in the first place. Nothing in the Code suggests that a bankruptcy judge has the right to prohibit a conversion because of the debtor's bad faith.

If a debtor acts in bad faith, the court has other remedies: It can convert the case back to a Chapter 7 liquidation; it can refuse to approve the plan of payment; or it can charge the debtor with perjury. That is the law, whether the Court likes it or not.

Argument for the Bankruptcy Trustee: A bankruptcy court has the unquestioned right to dismiss a Chapter 13 petition if the debtor demonstrates bad faith. There seems no logical reason why a court would have the right to dismiss a case for bad faith, but not the right to prohibit a filing under Chapter 13 to begin with. In both cases, the court is simply saying that the individual does not qualify as a debtor under Chapter 13. That individual is not a member of the class of honest but unfortunate debtors whom the bankruptcy laws were enacted to protect.

EXAM *Strategy*

Question: Why did Marrama first file under Chapter 7 and then try to switch to Chapter 13 after he was caught lying?

Strategy: This question is a good test of your understanding of the advantages and disadvantages of the different chapters. For help in answering this question, you might want to look at the chart at the end of the chapter. Remember that Chapter 7 is a liquidation provision—it takes more of the bankrupt's money upfront but then discharges his debts and gives him a fresh start for the future. Chapter 13 does not take as many assets during the bankruptcy process but may attach all the debtor's disposable income for the next five years.

Result: Marrama filed under Chapter 7 in the hope that he could hold on to his house while all his debts were discharged. Once that plan failed, he tried to switch to Chapter 13 in the hope that he could keep the house and give up his disposable income instead. This case illustrates the different emphases of Chapters 7 and 13.

A bankruptcy under Chapter 13 generally follows the same course as Chapter 11: the debtor files a petition, creditors submit proofs of claim, the court imposes an automatic stay, the debtor files a plan, and the court confirms the plan. But there are some differences.

Beginning a Chapter 13 Case

To initiate a Chapter 13 case, the debtor must file a voluntary petition. **Creditors cannot use an involuntary petition to force a debtor into Chapter 13.** In all Chapter 13 cases, the U.S. Trustee appoints a trustee to supervise the debtor, although the debtor remains in possession of the bankruptcy estate. The trustee also serves as a central clearinghouse for the debtor's payments to creditors. The debtor pays the trustee who, in turn, transmits these funds to creditors. For this service, the trustee is allowed to keep 10 percent of the payments.

Plan of Payment

The debtor must file a plan of payment within 15 days after filing the voluntary petition. Only the debtor can file a plan; the creditors have no right to file their own version. Under the plan, the debtor must (1) commit some future earnings to pay off debts, (2) promise to pay all secured and priority claims in full, and (3) treat all remaining classes equally. If the plan does not provide for the debtor to pay off creditors in full, then all of the debtor's disposable income for the next five years must go to creditors.

Within 30 days after filing the plan of payment, the debtor must begin making payments to the trustee under the plan. The trustee holds these payments until the plan is confirmed and then transmits them to creditors. The debtor continues to make payments to the trustee until the plan has been fully implemented. If the plan is rejected, the trustee returns the payments to the debtor.

Only the bankruptcy court has the authority to confirm or reject a plan of payment. Creditors have no right to vote on it. However, to confirm a plan, the court must ensure that:

- The creditors have the opportunity to voice their objections at a hearing;

- All of the unsecured creditors receive at least as much as they would have under Chapter 7;

- The plan is feasible and the bankrupt will be able to make the promised payments;

- The plan does not extend beyond three years without good reason and in no event lasts longer than five years; and

- The debtor is acting in good faith, making a reasonable effort to pay obligations.

DISCHARGE

Once confirmed, a plan is binding on all creditors, whether they like it or not. **The debtor is washed clean of all pre-petition debts except those provided for in the plan, but, unlike Chapter 7, the debts are not** *permanently* **discharged.** If the debtor violates the plan, all of the debts are revived, and the creditors have a right to recover them under Chapter 7. The debts become permanently discharged only when the bankrupt fully complies with the plan.

If the debtor's circumstances change, the debtor, the trustee, or unsecured creditors can ask the court to modify the plan. Most such requests come from debtors whose income has declined. However, if the debtor's income rises, the creditors or the trustee can ask that payments increase, too.

EXAM *Strategy*

Question: The opening scenario tells the story of movie actor Kim Basinger, who filed for bankruptcy. See if you can figure out which chapter she chose. Why would this make more sense than the others? Why might she switch chapters?

Strategy: It is important to remember the key differences among the various chapters. Look at the chart below. Chapter 13 is for consumers with relatively modest debts. Chapter 11 permits the debtor to keep more assets but requires ongoing payment. Also, the creditors must approve the plan of reorganization. If neither of these Chapters works, Chapter 7 is the default option.

Result: Basinger was not eligible to file under Chapter 13 because she had debts of $11 million. She first filed under Chapter 11, but then her creditors would not approve her plan of reorganization, so she converted to Chapter 7.

CHAPTER CONCLUSION

Whenever an individual or organization incurs more debts than it can pay in a timely fashion, everyone loses. The debtor loses control of his assets and the creditors lose money. Bankruptcy laws cannot create assets where there are none (or not enough), but they can ensure that the debtor's assets, however limited, are fairly divided between the debtor and creditors. Any bankruptcy system that accomplishes this goal must be deemed a success. Is the U.S. Bankruptcy Code fair?

EXAM REVIEW

This chart sets out the important elements of each bankruptcy chapter.

	Chapter 7	Chapter 11	Chapter 13
Objective	Liquidation	Reorganization	Consumer reorganization
Who May Use It	Individual or organization	Individual or organization	Individual
Type of Petition	Voluntary or involuntary	Voluntary or involuntary	Only voluntary
Administration of Bankruptcy Estate	Trustee	Debtor in possession (trustee selected only if debtor is unable to serve)	Trustee
Selection of Trustee	Creditors have right to elect trustee; otherwise, U.S. Trustee makes appointment	Usually no trustee	Appointed by U.S. Trustee
Participation in Formulation of Plan	No plan is filed	Both creditors and debtor can propose plans	Only debtor can propose a plan
Creditor Approval of Plan	Creditors do not vote	Creditors vote on plan, but court may approve plan without the creditors' support	Creditors do not vote on plan
Impact on Debtor's Post-petition Income	Not affected; debtor keeps all future earnings	Must contribute toward payment of pre-petition debts	Must contribute toward payment of pre-petition debts

ADDITIONAL QUESTIONS

EXAM Strategy

1. **Question:**   Mark Milbank built custom furniture in Port Chester, New York. His business was unsuccessful, and he repeatedly borrowed money from his wife and her father. He promised that the loans would enable him to spend more time with his family. Instead, he spent more time in bed with his next-door neighbor. After the divorce, his ex-wife and her father demanded repayment of the loans. Milbank filed for protection under 13. What could his ex-wife and her father do to help their chances of being repaid?

   Strategy: First ask yourself what kind of creditor they are: secured or unsecured. Then think about what creditors can do to get special treatment. (See the "Result" at the end of this section.)

EXAM Strategy

2. **Question:** James Hartley, the owner of an auto parts store, told an employee, Rickey D. Jones, to clean and paint some tires in the basement. Highly flammable gasoline fumes accumulated in the poorly ventilated space. Hartley threw a firecracker into the basement, as a joke, intending only to startle Jones. Sparks from the firecracker caused an explosion and fire that severely burned Jones. He filed a personal injury suit against Hartley for $1 million. Is this debt dischargeable under Chapter 7?

Strategy: Review the list of debts that cannot be discharged. You will see that a debtor is entitled to a discharge unless his behavior is exceptionally bad, involving theft, tax fraud, or the like. Injuries caused by a stupid accident are dischargeable, not those caused intentionally or maliciously. (See the "Result" at the end of this section.)

EXAM Strategy

3. **CPA QUESTION** A voluntary petition filed under the liquidation provisions of Chapter 7 of the federal Bankruptcy Code:

(a) Is not available to a corporation unless it has previously filed a petition under the reorganization provisions of Chapter 11 of the Code

(b) Automatically stays collection actions against the debtor **except** by secured creditors

(c) Will be dismissed unless the debtor has 12 or more unsecured creditors whose claims total at least $5,000

(d) Does **not** require the debtor to show that the debtor's liabilities exceed the fair market value of assets

Strategy: One strategy for multiple choice questions is to look down the list quickly to see if you recognize immediately that the answers are clearly right or wrong. (a) is clearly wrong. You may remember that the automatic stay applies to all creditors, so (b) is wrong, too. Instead of trying to remember the amount of debt that the unsecured creditors must have, look at the fourth answer. You might remember having read almost that exact sentence in the chapter. (See the "Result" at the end of this section.)

4. **CPA QUESTION** Decal Corp. incurred substantial operating losses for the past three years. Unable to meet its current obligations, Decal filed a petition of reorganization under Chapter 11 of the federal Bankruptcy Code. Which of the following statements is correct?

(a) A creditors' committee, if appointed, will consist of unsecured creditors.

(b) The court must appoint a trustee to manage Decal's affairs.

(c) Decal may continue in business only with the approval of a trustee.

(d) The creditors' committee must select a trustee to manage Decal's affairs.

5. After filing for bankruptcy, Yvonne Brown sought permission of the court to reaffirm a $6,000 debt to her credit union. The debt was unsecured and she was under no obligation to pay it. The credit union had published the following notice in its newsletter:

> If you are thinking about filing bankruptcy, THINK about the long-term implications. This action, filing bankruptcy, closes the door on TOMORROW. Having no credit means no ability to purchase cars, houses, credit cards. Look into the future—no loans for the education of your children.

Should the court approve Brown's reaffirmation?

6. **ETHICS** On November 5, The Fred Hawes Organization, Inc., a small subcontractor, opened an account with Basic Distribution Corp., a supplier of construction materials. Hawes promised to pay its bills within 30 days of purchase. Although Hawes purchased a substantial quantity of goods on credit from Basic, it made few payments on the accounts until the following March when it paid Basic over $21,000. On May 14, Hawes filed a voluntary petition under Chapter 7. Does the bankruptcy trustee have a right to recover this payment? Is it fair to Hawes's other creditors if Basic is allowed to keep the $21,000 payment?

7. Robert Britton was an office manager at the Academy of Cosmetic Surgery Medical Group. Mary Price made an appointment for a consultation about a lipectomy (removal of abdominal fat). Britton wore a name tag that identified him as a doctor, and was addressed as "doctor" by the nurse. Britton and the nurse then examined Price. Britton touched the area of her stomach where there was excess fat and showed her where the incision would be made. A doctor who worked for the Academy actually performed the surgical procedure on Price at the Academy's offices, with Britton present. After the procedure, Price went to a hospital suffering from severe pain. The hospital staff found that a tube had been left in her body at the site of the incision. The area of the incision became infected, and Price ultimately required corrective surgery. The jury awarded her $275,000 in damages in a fraud suit against Britton. He subsequently filed a Chapter 7 bankruptcy petition. Is this judgment dischargeable in bankruptcy court?

8. **YOU BE THE JUDGE** WRITING PROBLEM Lydia D'Ettore received a degree in computer programming at the DeVry Institute of Technology, with a grade-point average of 2.51. To finance her education, she borrowed $20,516.52 from a federal student loan program. After graduation, she could not find a job in her field, so she went to work as a clerk at an annual salary of $12,500. D'Ettore and her daughter lived with her parents free of charge. After setting aside $50 a month in savings and paying bills that included $233 for a new car (a Suzuki Samurai) and $50 for jewelry from Zales, her disposable income was $125 per month. D'Ettore asked the bankruptcy court to discharge the debts she owed DeVry for her education. Did the debts to the DeVry Institute impose an undue hardship on D'Ettore? **Argument for D'Ettore:** Lydia D'Ettore lives at home with her parents. Even so, her disposable income is a meager $125 a month. She would have to spend every single penny of her disposable income for nearly 15 years to pay back her $20,500 debt to DeVry. That would be an undue hardship. **Argument for the Creditors:** The U.S. government guaranteed D'Ettore's loan. Therefore, if the court discharges it, the American taxpayer will have to pay the bill. Why should taxpayers subsidize an irresponsible student? D'Ettore must also stop buying new cars and jewelry. And why should the government pay her debts while she saves money every month?

9. **CPA QUESTION** Unger owes a total of $50,000 to eight unsecured creditors and one fully secured creditor. Quincy is one of the unsecured creditors and is owed $6,000. Quincy has filed a petition against Unger under the liquidation provisions of Chapter 7 of the federal Bankruptcy Code. Unger has been unable to pay debts as they become due. Unger's liabilities exceed Unger's assets. Unger has filed papers opposing the bankruptcy petition. Which of the following statements regarding Quincy's petition is correct?

(a) It will be dismissed because the secured creditor failed to join in the filing of the petition.

(b) It will be dismissed because three unsecured creditors must join in the filing of the petition.

(c) It will be granted because Unger's liabilities exceed Unger's assets.

(d) It will be granted because Unger is unable to pay Unger's debts as they become due.

10. Dr. Ibrahim Khan caused an automobile accident in which a fellow physician, Dolly Yusufji, became a quadriplegic. Dr. Khan signed a contract for the lifetime support of Dr. Yusufji. When he refused to make payments under the contract, she sued him and obtained a judgment for $1,205,400. Dr. Khan filed a Chapter 11 petition. At the time of the bankruptcy hearing, five years after the accident, Dr. Khan had not paid Dr. Yusufji anything. She was dependent on a motorized wheelchair; he drove a Rolls-Royce. Is Dr. Khan's debt dischargeable under Chapter 11

11. **ROLE REVERSAL** Write a multiple-choice question that highlights the difference between Chapters 7 and 11.

1. Result: The father and the ex-wife were unsecured creditors who, as a class, come last on the priority list. The court granted their request not to discharge their loans on the grounds that Milbank had acted in bad faith.

2. Result: Hartley's behavior was foolish, but his debt to Jones was dischargeable because the injury was not intentional or malicious.

3. Result: D is the correct answer.

INTERNET RESEARCH PROBLEM

Look on the web for your state's rules on exempt property. Compared with other states and the federal government, is your state generous or stingy with exemptions? In considering a new bankruptcy statute, Congress struggled mightily over this issue. What do you think is a fair exemption?

You can find further practice problems at www.cengagebrain.com. See the preface of this book for website access details.

EMPLOYMENT, BUSINESS ORGANIZATIONS AND PROPERTY

CHAPTER

27

AGENCY

Folding shirts all day long can get pretty boring. What is a guy to do, if not bond with the other store clerks? So it was that Justin Kiser and Germania became friends while working at a Ralph Lauren Polo store in San Francisco.

> **Polo sued Kiser, alleging that he had violated his duty of loyalty. He responded that he was such a low-level employee, he had no duty to the company. Call it the "Sales clerks don't count" defense.**

She left her job, but not her taste for Ralph Lauren clothing. Luckily, Justin was a loyal friend, if not a loyal employee. He let her buy clothing using merchandise credits made out to fake people. He also let her use his employee discount. Not surprisingly, both of these activities were against store policies.

Polo sued Kiser, alleging that he had violated his duty of loyalty. He responded that he was such a low-level employee, he had no duty to the company. Call it the "Sales clerks don't count" defense. What obligation *do* workers have to their employers? Do the same rules apply to clerks and CEOs? Read on in this chapter to find out what happened to Justin Kiser in the case of *Otsuka v. Polo Ralph Lauren Corporation*.

Thus far, this book has primarily dealt with issues of individual responsibility: What happens if *you* knock someone down or *you* sign an agreement? Agency law, on the other hand, is concerned with your responsibility for the actions of others. What happens if your agent assaults someone or enters into an agreement? Agency law presents a significant trade-off: if you do everything yourself, you have control over the result. But the size and scope of your business (and your life) will be severely limited. Once you hire other people, you can accomplish a great deal more, but your risks increase immensely. Your agents may violate your instructions and still you could be liable for what they have done. Though it might be safer to do everything yourself, that is not a practical decision for most business owners (or most people). The alternative is to hire carefully and to limit the risks as much as possible by understanding the law of agency.

Vicariously liable

The driver is held liable BUT the injured party may also impute Safeway

CREATING AN AGENCY RELATIONSHIP

Principals have substantial liability for the actions of their agents.[1] Therefore, disputes about whether an agency relationship exists are not mere legal quibbles but important issues with potentially profound financial consequences.

(Must do something for someone else)

In an agency relationship, someone (the agent) agrees to perform a task for, and under the control of, someone else (the principal). **To create an agency relationship, there must be:**

- A **principal** and
- An **agent**
- Who mutually **consent** that the agent will act on behalf of the principal and
- Be subject to the principal's **control**
- Thereby creating a **fiduciary** relationship.[2]

The principal may authorize an agent to do something BUT only if to the extent that the principal can do it himself

i.e. A 17 year old may not authorize a 22 year old to buy him Jack Daniels, bic the 17 year old cant do it himself

(a relationship based on trust)
The principal is trusting the agent to fulfill his task/obligation under the principal's authorization

Principal
In an agency relationship, the person for whom an agent is acting.

Agent
In an agency relationship, the person who is acting on behalf of a principal.

CONSENT

To establish consent, the principal must ask the agent to do something, and the agent must agree. In the most straightforward example, you ask a neighbor to walk your dog and she agrees. Matters were more complicated, however, when Steven James met some friends one evening at a restaurant. During the two hours he was there, he drank four to six beers. (It is probably a bad sign that he cannot remember how many.) From then on, one misfortune piled upon another. After leaving the restaurant at about 7:00 p.m., James sped down a highway and crashed into a car that had stalled on the roadway, thereby killing the driver. James told the police at the scene that he had not seen the parked car (another bad sign). Evidently, James's lawyer was not as perceptive as the police in recognizing drunkenness. In a misguided attempt to help his client, James's lawyer took him to the local hospital for a blood test. Unfortunately, the test confirmed that James had indeed been drunk at the time of the accident.

---

[1] The word "principal" is always used when referring to a person. It is not to be confused with the word "principle," which refers to a fundamental idea.

[2] Section 1.01 of the Restatement (Third) of Agency (2006), prepared by the American Law Institute.

The attorney knew that if this evidence was admitted at trial, his client would soon be receiving free room and board from the Massachusetts Department of Corrections. So at trial, the lawyer argued that the blood test was protected by the client-attorney privilege because the hospital had been his agent and therefore a member of the defense team. The court disagreed, however, holding that the hospital employees were not agents for the lawyer because they had not consented to act in the role.

The court upheld James's conviction of murder in the first degree by reason of extreme atrocity or cruelty.[3]

CONTROL

Principals are liable for the acts of their agents because they exercise control over the agents. If principals direct their agents to commit an act, it seems fair to hold the principal liable when that act causes harm. How would you apply that rule to the following situation?

William Stanford was an employee of the Agency for International Development. While on his way home to Pakistan to spend the holidays with his family, his plane was hijacked and taken to Iran, where he was killed. Stanford had originally purchased a ticket on Northwest Airlines but had traded it for a seat on Kuwait Airways (KA). The airlines had an agreement permitting passengers to exchange tickets from one to the other. Stanford's widow sued Northwest on the theory that KA was Northwest's agent. The court found, however, that no agency relationship existed because Northwest had no control over KA.[4] Northwest did not tell KA how to fly planes or handle terrorists; therefore, it should not be liable when KA made fatal errors. An agent and principal must not only consent to an agency relationship, but the principal must also have control over the agent.

FIDUCIARY RELATIONSHIP

A fiduciary relationship is a special relationship, with high standards. The beneficiary places special confidence in the fiduciary who, in turn, is obligated to act in good faith and candor, putting his own needs second. The purpose of a fiduciary relationship is for one person to benefit another. **Agents have a fiduciary duty to their principals.**

> *Agents have a fiduciary duty to their principals, benefiting them in some way or another*

All three elements—consent, control, and a fiduciary duty—are necessary to create an agency relationship. In some relationships, for example, there might be a *fiduciary duty* but no *control*. A trustee of a trust must act for the benefit of the beneficiaries, but the beneficiaries have no right to control the trustee. Therefore, a trustee is not an agent of the beneficiaries. *Consent* is present in every contractual relationship, but that does not necessarily mean that the two parties are agent and principal. If Horace sells his car to Lily, they both expect to benefit under the contract, but neither has a *fiduciary duty* to the other and neither *controls* the other, so there is no agency relationship.

> *If the subject-matter is in writing, the agency must also be in writing*

ELEMENTS NOT REQUIRED FOR AN AGENCY RELATIONSHIP

Consent, control, and a fiduciary relationship are necessary to establish an agency relationship. The following elements are **not** required:

- *A Written Agreement.* In most cases an agency agreement does not have to be in writing. An oral understanding is valid, except in one circumstance—the **equal dignities rule.** According to this rule, if an agent is empowered to enter into a contract that must be in

> • **Equal dignities rule**
> If an agent is empowered to enter into a contract that must be in writing, then the appointment of the agent must also be written.

> *concerned w/ certain agreements that MUST be in writing to be enforceable*

---

[3] *Commonwealth v. James,* 427 Mass. 312, 693 N.E.2nd 148, 1998 Mass. LEXIS 175.
[4] *Stanford v. Kuwait Airways Corp.,* 648 F. Supp. 1158, 1986 U.S. Dist. LEXIS 18880 (S.D.N.Y. 1986).

writing, then the appointment of the agent must also be written. For example, under the statute of frauds, a contract for the sale of land is unenforceable unless in writing, so the agency agreement to sell land must also be *in writing.*

- *A Formal Agreement.* The principal and agent need not agree formally that they have an agency relationship. They do not even have to think the word "agent." So long as they act like an agent and a principal, the law will treat them as such.

- *Consideration.* An agency relationship need not meet all the standards of contract law. For example, a contract is not valid without consideration, but an agency agreement is valid *even if the agent is not paid.*

•DUTIES OF AGENTS TO PRINCIPALS (what is it that we owe the bosses)

Agents owe a fiduciary duty to their principals. There are four elements to this duty.

DUTY OF LOYALTY

An agent has a fiduciary duty to act loyally for the principal's benefit in all matters connected with the agency relationship.[5] The agent has an obligation to put the principal first, to strive to accomplish the principal's goals. Remember Justin Kiser from the beginning of the chapter. Did he violate his duty of loyalty?

OTSUKA V. POLO RALPH LAUREN CORPORATION

2007 U.S. DIST. LEXIS 86523
UNITED STATES DISTRICT COURT FOR THE NORTHERN DISTRICT OF CALIFORNIA, 2007

CASE SUMMARY

Facts: The facts were set out in the opening scenario. Kiser filed a motion to dismiss on the grounds that he was such a low-level employee that he did not owe a duty of loyalty to Polo.

Issue: *Do all employees owe a duty of loyalty to their employer?*

Decision: Yes, all employees owe a duty of loyalty.

Reasoning: The cases cited by Polo to support its claim involved higher-level employees than Kiser, who was simply a clerk in a Polo store. No matter—the Restatement (Third) of Agency clearly states that all employees are agents and owe a duty of loyalty to their employers. All employees must put their employer's interests first.

The various components of the duty of loyalty follow.

---

[5] Restatement (Third) of Agency Section 8.01.

Outside Benefits

An agent may not receive profits unless the principal knows and approves. Suppose that Hope is an employee of the agency Big Egos and Talents, Inc. (BEAT). She has been representing Will Smith in his latest movie negotiations.[6] Smith often drives her to meetings in his new Maybach. He is so thrilled that she has arranged for him to star in the new movie *Little Men* that he buys her a Maybach. Can Hope keep this generous gift? Only with BEAT's permission. She must tell BEAT about the Maybach; the company may then take the vehicle itself or allow her to keep it.

Confidential Information

The ability to keep secrets is important in any relationship, but especially a fiduciary relationship. Agents can neither disclose nor use for their own benefit any confidential information they acquire during their agency. As the following case shows, this duty continues even after the agency relationship ends.

ABKCO MUSIC, INC. V. HARRISONGS MUSIC, LTD.

722 F.2d 988, 1983 U.S. App. LEXIS 15562
UNITED STATES COURT OF APPEALS FOR THE SECOND CIRCUIT, 1983

CASE SUMMARY

Facts: Bright Tunes Music Corp. (Bright Tunes) owned the copyright to the song "He's So Fine." The company sued George Harrison, a Beatle, alleging that the Harrison composition "My Sweet Lord" copied "He's So Fine." At the time the suit was filed, Allen B. Klein handled the business affairs of the Beatles.

Klein (representing Harrison) met with the president of Bright Tunes to discuss possible settlement of the copyright lawsuit. Klein suggested that Harrison might be interested in purchasing the copyright to "He's So Fine." Shortly thereafter, Klein's management contract with the Beatles expired. Without telling Harrison, Klein began negotiating with Bright Tunes to purchase the copyright to "He's So Fine" for himself. To advance these negotiations, Klein gave Bright Tunes information about royalty income for "My Sweet Lord"—information that he had gained as Harrison's agent.

The trial judge in the copyright case ultimately found that Harrison had infringed the copyright on "He's So Fine" and assessed damages of $1,599,987. After the trial, Klein purchased the "He's So Fine" copyright from Bright Tunes

and with it, the right to recover from Harrison for the breach of copyright.

Issue: *Did Klein violate his fiduciary duty to Harrison by using confidential information after the agency relationship terminated?*

Decision: Klein did violate his fiduciary duty to Harrison.

Reasoning: While serving as Harrison's agent, Klein learned confidential information about royalty income for "My Sweet Lord." An agent has a duty not to use confidential information to compete against his principal. This duty continues even after the agency relationship ends. A former agent does have the right to compete against his principal using general business knowledge or publicly available information. However, the information that Klein passed on to Bright Tunes was not publicly available.

Although some years separated Klein's attempt to buy the copyright for Harrison and his later purchase for himself, Klein was still under a duty to Harrison. Klein's conduct did not meet the standard required of him as a former fiduciary.

---

[6] Do not be confused by the fact that Hope works as an agent for movie stars. As an employee of BEAT, her duty is to the company. She is an agent of BEAT, and BEAT works for the celebrities.

To listen to the two songs involved in this case, tune in to **http://www.copyrightwebsite. com/.**

> **ETHICS**   Klein was angry that the Beatles had failed to renew his management contract. Was it reasonable for him to think that he owed no duty to the principal who had fired him? Should his sense of ethics have told him that his behavior was wrong? Would the ethics checklist in Chapter 2 have helped Klein to make a better decision? Why would George Harrison prefer to owe money to Bright Tunes than to Klein?   ◆

Competition with the Principal

Agents are not allowed to compete with their principal in any matter within the scope of the agency business. If Allen Klein had purchased the "He's So Fine" copyright while he was George Harrison's agent, he would have committed an additional sin against the agency relationship. Owning song rights was clearly part of the agency business, so Klein could not make such purchases without Harrison's consent. Once the agency relationship ends, however, so does the rule against competition. Klein was entitled to buy the "He's So Fine" copyright after the agency relationship ended (so long as he did not use confidential information).

Conflict of Interest between Two Principals

Unless otherwise agreed, an agent may not act for two principals whose interests conflict. Suppose Travis represents both director Steven Spielberg and actor Julia Roberts. Spielberg is casting the title role in his new movie, *Nancy Drew: Girl Detective*, a role that Roberts covets. Travis cannot represent these two clients when they are negotiating with each other unless they both know about the conflict and agree to ignore it. The following example illustrates the dangers of acting for two principals at once.

EXAM *Strategy*

Question: The Sisters of Charity was an order of nuns in New Jersey. Faced with growing health care and retirement costs, they decided to sell off a piece of property. The nuns soon found, however, that the world is not always a charitable place. They agreed to sell the land to Linpro for nearly $10 million. But before the deal closed, Linpro signed a contract to resell the property to Sammis for $34 million. So, you say, the sisters made a bad deal. There is no law against that. But it turned out that the nuns' law firm also represented Linpro. Their lawyer at the firm, Peter Berkley, never told the sisters about the deal between Linpro and Sammis. Was that the charitable—or legal—thing to do?

Strategy: Always begin by asking if there is an agency relationship. Was there consent, control, and a fiduciary relationship? *Consent*: Berkley had agreed to work for the nuns. *Control*: they told him what he was to do—sell the land. The purpose of a *fiduciary relationship* is for one person to benefit another. The point of the nuns' relationship with Berkley is for him to help them. Once you know there is an agency relationship, then ask if the agent has violated his duty of loyalty.

Result: You know that an agent is not permitted to act for two principals whose interests conflict. Here, Berkley is working for the nuns, who want the highest possible price for their land, and Linpro, who wants the lowest price. Berkley has violated his duty of loyalty.

Agency coupled w/ an interest (The agent buying into a little of the action/ interest/ profit from a principal's transaction w/ another party) as long as the principal agrees

Secretly Dealing with the Principal

If a principal hires an agent to arrange a transaction, the agent may not become a party to the transaction without the principal's permission. Matt Damon became an overnight sensation after starring in the movie *Good Will Hunting*. Suppose that he hired Trang to read scripts for him. Unbeknownst to Damon, Trang had written her own script, which she thought would be ideal for him. She may not sell it to him without revealing that she wrote it herself. Damon may be perfectly happy to buy Trang's script, but he has the right, as her principal, to know that she is the person selling it.

Appropriate Behavior

An agent may not engage in inappropriate behavior that reflects badly on the principal. This rule applies even to *off-duty* conduct. For example, a coed trio of flight attendants went wild at a hotel bar in London. They kissed and caressed each other, showed off their underwear, and poured alcohol down their trousers. The airline fired two of the employees and gave a warning letter to the third.

Additional Duty- Discourse

OTHER DUTIES OF AN AGENT

Before Taylor left for a five-week trip to England, he hired Claudia to rent his vacation house. Claudia never got around to listing his house on the regional rental list used by all the area brokers, but when the Fords contacted her looking for rental housing, she did show them Taylor's place. They offered to rent it for $750 per month.

Claudia called Taylor in England to tell him. He responded that he would not accept less than $850 a month, which Claudia thought the Fords would be willing to pay. He told Claudia to call back if there was any problem. The Fords decided that they would go no higher than $800 a month. Instead of calling Taylor in England, Claudia left a message on his home answering machine. When the Fords pressed her for an answer, she said she could not get in touch with Taylor. Not until Taylor returned home did he learn that the Fords had rented another house. Did Claudia violate any of the duties that agents owe to their principals?

Duty to Obey Instructions

An agent must obey her principal's instructions unless the principal directs her to behave illegally or unethically. Taylor instructed Claudia to call him if the Fords rejected the offer. When Claudia failed to do so, she violated her duty to obey instructions. If, however, Taylor had asked her to say that the house's basement was dry, when in fact it looked like a swamp every spring, Claudia would be under no obligation to follow those illegal instructions.

Duty of Care

An agent has a duty to act with reasonable care. In other words, an agent must act as a reasonable person would, under the circumstances. A reasonable person would not have left a message on Taylor's home answering machine when she knew he was in Europe.

Under some circumstances, an agent is held to a higher—or lower—standard than usual. **An agent with special skills is held to a higher standard because she is expected to use those skills.** A trained real estate agent should know enough to use the regional rental list.

But suppose Taylor had asked his neighbor, Jed, to help him sell the house. Jed is not a trained real estate agent, and he is not being paid, which makes him a *gratuitous agent*. A gratuitous agent is held to a lower standard because he is doing his principal a favor and, as the old saying goes, you get what you pay for—up to a point. **Gratuitous agents are liable if they commit *gross* negligence, but not *ordinary* negligence.** If Jed, as a gratuitous agent, left Taylor

Duties are all the same Remember, there's no consideration (duties are all held liable whether one is getting paid or not)

an important message on his answering machine because he forgot about the trip to England, he would not be liable to him for that ordinary negligence. But if the answering machine had a message that *warned* him Taylor was away and would not be picking up messages, he would be liable for gross negligence and a violation of his duty.

Duty to Provide Information

An agent has a duty to provide the principal with all information in her possession that she has reason to believe the principal wants to know. She also has a duty to provide accurate information. Claudia knew that the Fords had counter offered for $800 a month. She had a duty to pass this information on to Taylor.

Duty to Account (account for money, sale of goods, documents)

EXAM *Strategy*

Question: Jonah tells his friend Derek that he would like to go parasailing. Derek is very enthusiastic and suggests that they try an outfit called Wind Beneath Your Wings because he has heard good things about them. Derek offers to arrange everything. He makes a reservation, puts the $600 fee on his credit card, and picks Jonah up to drive him to the Wings location. What a friend! The day does not turn out as Jonah had hoped. While up in the air over the Pacific Ocean, his sail springs a leak. He goes plummeting into the sea and breaks both legs. While recuperating in the hospital, he learns that Wings is unlicensed. He also sees an ad for Wings offering parasailing for only $350. And Derek is listed in the ad as one of the company's owners. Is Derek an agent for Jonah? Has he violated his fiduciary responsibility?

Strategy: There are three issues to consider in answering this question: (1) Was there an agency relationship? This requires consent, control, and a fiduciary relationship. (2) Is anything missing—does it matter if the agent is unpaid or the contract is not in writing? (3) Has the agent fulfilled his duties?

Result: There is an agency relationship: Derek had agreed to help Jonah; it was Jonah who set the goal for the relationship (parasailing); the purpose of this relationship is for one person to benefit another. Derek has violated his duty to exercise due care. He should not have taken Jonah to an unlicensed company. He has also violated his duty to provide information: He should have told Jonah the true cost for the lessons and also revealed that he was a principal of the company. And he violated his duty of loyalty when he worked for two principals whose interests were in conflict.

PRINCIPAL'S REMEDIES WHEN THE AGENT BREACHES A DUTY

A principal has three potential remedies when an agent breaches her duty:

Agency agreement ends (the principal may sue for damages)

- The principal can recover from the agent any **damages** the breach has caused. Thus, if Taylor can only rent his house for $600 a month instead of the $800 the Fords offered, Claudia would be liable for $2,400—$200 a month for one year.

- If an agent breaches the duty of loyalty, he must turn over to the principal any **profits** he has earned as a result of his wrongdoing. Thus, after Klein violated his duty of loyalty to Harrison, he forfeited profits he would have earned from the copyright of "He's So Fine."

(restitution)

- If the agent has violated her duty of loyalty, the principal may **rescind** the transaction. When Trang sold a script to her principal, Matt Damon, without telling him that she was the author, she violated her duty of loyalty. Damon could rescind the contract to buy the script.[7]

DUTIES OF PRINCIPALS TO AGENTS

In a typical agency relationship, the agent agrees to perform tasks for the principal, and the principal agrees to pay the agent. The range of tasks undertaken by an agent is limited only by the imagination of the principal. Because the agent's job can be so varied, the law has needed to define an agent's duties carefully. The role of the principal, on the other hand, is typically less complicated—often little more than writing a check to pay the agent. Thus the law enumerates fewer duties for the principal. Primarily, the principal must reimburse the agent for reasonable expenses and cooperate with the agent in performing agency tasks. The respective duties of agents and principals can be summarized as follows:

Duties of Agents to Principals	Duty of Principals to Agents
Duty of loyalty	Duty to reimburse the agent
Duty to obey instructions	Duty to cooperate
Duty of care	
Duty to provide information	

As a general rule, the principal must indemnify (i.e., reimburse) the agent for any expenses she has reasonably incurred. These reimbursable expenses fall into three categories:

- **A principal must indemnify an agent for any expenses or damages reasonably incurred in carrying out his agency responsibilities.** For example, Peace Baptist Church of Birmingham, Alabama, asked its pastor to buy land for a new church. He paid part of the purchase price out of his own pocket, but the church refused to reimburse him. Although the pastor lost in church, he won in court.[8]

(handwritten note in margin: • A duty to indemnify / Term / Achieving a purpose)

---

[7] A principal can rescind his contract with an agent who has violated her duty, but, as we shall see later in the chapter, the principal might not be able to rescind a contract with a third party when the agent misbehaves.

[8] *Lauderdale v. Peace Baptist Church of Birmingham*, 246 Ala. 178, 19 So.2d 538, 1944 Ala. LEXIS 508 (1944).

- **A principal must indemnify an agent for tort claims brought by a third party if the principal authorized the agent's behavior and the agent did not realize he was committing a tort.** Marisa owns all the apartment buildings on Elm Street, except one. She hires Rajiv to manage the units and tells him that, under the terms of the leases, she has the right to ask guests to leave if a party becomes too rowdy. But she forgets to tell Rajiv that she does not own one of the buildings, which happens to house a college sorority. One night, when the sorority is having a rambunctious party, Rajiv hustles over and starts ejecting the noisy guests. The sorority is furious and sues Rajiv for trespass. If the sorority wins its suit against Rajiv, Marisa would have to pay the judgment, plus Rajiv's attorney's fees, because she had told him to quell noisy parties, and he did not realize he was trespassing.

- **The principal must indemnify the agent for any liability she incurs from third parties as a result of entering into a contract on the principal's behalf, including attorney's fees and reasonable settlements.** An agent signed a contract to buy cucumbers for Vlasic Food Products Co. to use in making pickles. When the first shipment of cucumbers arrived, Vlasic inspectors found them unsuitable and directed the agent to refuse the shipment. The agent found himself in a pickle when the cucumber farmer sued. The agent notified Vlasic, but the company refused to defend him. He settled the claim himself and, in turn, sued Vlasic. The court ordered Vlasic to reimburse the agent because he had notified them of the suit and had acted reasonably and in good faith.[9]

DUTY TO COOPERATE

Principals have a duty to cooperate with their agent:

- **The principal must furnish the agent with the opportunity to work.** If Lewis agrees to serve as Ida's real estate agent, Ida must allow Lewis access to the house. It is unlikely that Lewis will be able to sell the house without taking anyone inside.

- **The principal cannot unreasonably interfere with the agent's ability to accomplish his task.** Ida allows Lewis to show the house, but she refuses to clean it and then makes disparaging comments to prospective purchasers. "I really get tired of living in such a dank, dreary house," she says. "And the neighborhood children are vicious juvenile delinquents." This behavior would constitute unreasonable interference with an agent.

- **The principal must perform her part of the contract.** Once the agent has successfully completed the task, the principal must pay him, even if the principal has changed her mind and no longer wants the agent to perform. Ida is a 78-year-old widow who has lived alone for many years in a house that she loves. Her asking price is outrageously high. But lo and behold, Lewis finds a couple happy to pay Ida's price. There is only one problem. Ida does not really want to sell. She put her house on the market because she enjoys showing it to all the folks who move to town. She rejects the offer. Now there is a second problem. The contract provided that Lewis would find a willing buyer at the asking price. Because he has done so, Ida must pay his real estate commission even if she does not want to sell her house.

---

[9] *Long v. Vlasic Food Products Co.*, 439 F.2d 229, 1971 U.S. App. LEXIS 11455 (4th Cir. 1971).

Terminating an Agency Relationship

Either the agent or the principal can terminate the agency relationship at any time. In addition, the relationship terminates automatically if the principal or agent can no longer perform their required duties or a change in circumstances renders the agency relationship pointless.

> Hiring an agent is not like buying a book. You might not care which copy of the book you buy, but you do care which agent you hire.

•Termination by Agent or Principal

The two parties—principal and agent—have five choices in terminating their relationship:

- *Term Agreement.* The principal and agent can agree in advance how long their relationship will last. Alexandra hires Boris to help her purchase exquisite enameled Easter eggs made for the Russian czars by Fabergé. If they agree that the relationship will last five years, they have a term agreement.

- *Achieving a Purpose.* The principal and agent can agree that the agency relationship will terminate when the principal's goals have been achieved. Alexandra and Boris might agree that their relationship will end when Alexandra has purchased 10 eggs.

- *Mutual Agreement.* No matter what the principal and agent agree at the start, they can always change their minds later on, as long as the change is mutual. If Boris and Alexandra originally agree to a five-year term, but after only three years Boris decides he wants to go back to business school and Alexandra runs out of money, they can decide together to terminate the agency.

- *Agency at Will.* If they make no agreement in advance about the term of the agreement, either principal or agent can terminate at any time.

- *Wrongful Termination.* An agency relationship is a personal relationship. Hiring an agent is not like buying a book. You might not care which copy of the book you buy, but you do care which agent you hire. If an agency relationship is not working out, the courts will not force the agent and principal to stay together. **Either party always has the *power* to walk out. They may not, however, have the *right*.** If one party's departure from the agency relationship violates the agreement and causes harm to the other party, the wrongful party must pay damages. He will nonetheless be permitted to leave. If Boris has agreed to work for Alexandra for five years but he wants to leave after three, he can leave, provided he pays Alexandra the cost of hiring and training a replacement.

If the agent is a **gratuitous** agent (i.e., is not being paid), he has both the power and the right to quit any time he wants, regardless of the agency agreement. If Boris is doing this job for Alexandra as a favor, he will not owe her damages when he stops work.

Principal or Agent Can No Longer Perform Required Duties

If the principal or the agent is unable to perform the duties required under the agency agreement, the agreement terminates.

- **If either the agent or the principal fails to obtain (or keep) a license necessary to perform duties under the agency agreement, the agreement ends.** Caleb hires Allegra to represent him in a lawsuit. If she is disbarred, their agency agreement terminates because the agent is no longer allowed in court. Alternatively, if Emil hires Bess to work in his gun shop, their agency relationship terminates when he loses his license to sell firearms.

- **The bankruptcy of the agent or the principal terminates an agency relationship only if it affects their ability to perform.** Bankruptcy rarely interferes with an agent's responsibilities. After all, there is generally no reason why an agent cannot continue to act for the principal whether the agent is rich or poor. If Lewis, the real estate agent, becomes bankrupt, he can continue to represent Ida or anyone else who wants to sell a house. The bankruptcy of a principal is different, however, because after filing for bankruptcy, the principal loses control of his assets. A bankrupt principal may be unable to pay the agent or honor contracts that the agent enters into on his behalf. Therefore, the bankruptcy of a principal is more likely to terminate an agency relationship.

- **An agency relationship terminates upon the death or incapacity of either the principal or the agent.** Agency is a personal relationship, and when the principal dies, the agent cannot act on behalf of a nonexistent person. Of course, a nonexistent person cannot act either, so the relationship also terminates when the agent dies. Incapacity has the same legal effect because either the principal or the agent is at least temporarily unable to act.

- **If the agent violates her duty of loyalty, the agency agreement automatically terminates.** Agents are appointed to represent the principal's interest; if they fail to do so, there is no point to the relationship. Sam is negotiating a military procurement contract on behalf of his employer, Missiles R Us, Inc. In the midst of these negotiations, he becomes very friendly with Louisa, the government negotiator. One night over drinks, he tells Louisa what Missiles' real costs are on the project and the lowest bid it could possibly make. By passing on this confidential information, Sam has violated his duty of loyalty, and his agency relationship terminates.

CHANGE IN CIRCUMSTANCES

After the agency agreement is negotiated, circumstances may change. If these changes are significant enough to undermine the purpose of the agreement, the relationship ends automatically. Andrew hires Melissa to sell his country farm for $100,000. Shortly thereafter, the largest oil reserve in North America is discovered nearby. The farm is now worth 10 times Andrew's asking price. Melissa's authority terminates automatically. Other changes in circumstance that affect an agency agreement are:

- *Change of Law.* If the agent's responsibilities become illegal, the agency agreement terminates. Oscar has hired Marta to ship him succulent avocados from California's Imperial Valley. Before she sends the shipment, Mediterranean fruit flies are discovered, and all fruits and vegetables in California are quarantined. The agency agreement terminates because it is now illegal to ship the California avocados.

- *Loss or Destruction of Subject Matter.* Andrew hired Damian to sell his Palm Beach condominium, but before Damian could even measure the living room, Andrew's creditors attached the condo. Damian is no longer authorized to sell the real estate because Andrew has "lost" the subject matter of his agency agreement with Damian.

EFFECT OF TERMINATION

Once an agency relationship ends, the agent no longer has the authority to act for the principal. If she continues to act, she is liable to the principal for any damages he incurs as a result. The

Mediterranean fruit fly quarantine ended Marta's agency. If she sends Oscar the avocados anyway and he is fined for possession of a fruit fly, Marta must pay the fine.

The agent loses her authority to act, but some of the duties of both the principal and agent continue even after the relationship ends:

- *Principal's Duty to Indemnify Agent.* Oscar must reimburse Marta for expenses she incurred before the agency ended. If Marta accumulated mileage on her car during her search for the perfect avocado, Oscar must pay her for gasoline and depreciation. But he owes her nothing for her expenses after the agency relationship ends.

- *Confidential Information.* Remember the "He's So Fine" case earlier in the chapter. George Harrison's agent used confidential information to negotiate on his own behalf the purchase of the "He's So Fine" copyright. An agent is not entitled to use confidential information even after the agency relationship terminates.

LIABILITY

Thus far, this chapter has dealt with the relationship between principals and agents. Although an agent can dramatically increase his principal's ability to accomplish her goals, an agency relationship also dramatically increases the risk of legal liability to third parties. A principal may be liable in contract for agreements that the agent signs and also liable in tort for harm the agent causes. Indeed, once a principal hires an agent, she may be liable to third parties for his acts, even if he disobeys instructions. Agents may also find themselves liable to third parties.

PRINCIPAL'S LIABILITY FOR CONTRACTS

Many agents are hired for the primary purpose of entering into contracts on behalf of their principals. Salespeople, for example, may do little other than sign on the dotted line. Most of the time, the principal is delighted to be bound by these contracts. But even if the principal is unhappy (because, say, the agent has disobeyed orders), the principal generally cannot rescind contracts entered into by the agent. After all, if someone is going to be penalized, it should be the principal who hired the disobedient agent, not the innocent third party.

The principal is bound by the acts of an agent if (1) the agent had *authority,* or (2) the principal, for reasons of fairness, is *estopped* from denying that the agent had authority, or (3) the principal *ratifies* the acts of the agent.

To say that the principal is "bound by the acts" of the agent means that the principal is as liable as if he had performed the acts himself. It also means that the principal is liable for statements the agent makes to a third party. Thus, when a lawyer lied on an application for malpractice insurance, the insurance company was allowed to void the policy for the entire law firm. It was as if the firm had lied. In addition, the principal is deemed to know any information that the agent knows or should know.

• *Authority*

A principal is bound by the acts of an agent if the agent has authority. There are three types of authority: express, implied, and apparent. Express and implied authority are categories of actual authority because the agent is truly authorized to act for the principal. In apparent authority, the principal is liable for the agent's actions even though the agent was *not* authorized.

Express Authority   The principal grants **express authority** by words or conduct that, reasonably interpreted, cause the agent to believe the principal desires her to act on the principal's account.[10] In other words, the principal asks the agent to do something and the agent does it. Craig calls his stockbroker, Alice, and asks her to buy 100 shares of Banshee Corp. for his account. She has *express authority* to carry out this transaction.

Implied Authority   Unless otherwise agreed, authority to conduct a transaction includes authority to do acts that are reasonably necessary to accomplish it.[11] David has recently inherited a house from his grandmother. He hires Nell to auction off the house and its contents. She hires an auctioneer, advertises the event, rents a tent, and generally does everything necessary to conduct a successful auction. After withholding her expenses, she sends the tidy balance to David. Totally outraged, he calls her on the phone, "How dare you hire an auctioneer and rent a tent? I never gave you permission! I absolutely *refuse* to pay these expenses!"

(anything reasonably necessary to carry out the express authority)

David is wrong. A principal almost never gives an agent absolutely complete instructions. Unless some authority is implied, David would have had to say, "Open the car door, get in, put the key in the ignition, drive to the store, buy stickers, mark an auction number on each sticker ..." and so forth. To solve this problem, the law assumes that the agent has authority to do anything that is reasonably necessary to accomplish her task.

Apparent Authority   A principal can be liable for the acts of an agent who is not, in fact, acting with authority if the principal's conduct causes a third party reasonably to believe that the agent is authorized. In the case of *express* and *implied* authority, the principal has authorized the agent to act. Apparent authority is different: the principal has *not* authorized the agent, but has done something to make an innocent third party *believe* the agent is authorized. As a result, the principal is every bit as liable to the third party as if the agent did have authority.

(The agent is NOT involved. Communication is only between the principal and 3P)

For example, Zbigniew Lambo and Scott Kennedy were brokers at Paulson Investment Co., a stock brokerage firm in Oregon. The two men violated securities laws by selling unregistered stock, which ultimately proved to be worthless. Kennedy and Lambo were liable, but they were unable to repay the money. Either Paulson or its customers would end up bearing the loss. What is the fair result? The law takes the view that the principal is liable, not the third party, because the principal, by word or deed, allowed the third party to believe that the agent was acting on the principal's behalf. The principal could have prevented the third party from losing money.

Although the two brokers did not have *actual* or *implied* authority to sell the stock (Paulson had not authorized them to break the law), the company was nonetheless liable on the grounds that the brokers had *apparent* authority. Paulson had sent letters to its customers notifying them when it hired Kennedy. The two brokers made sales presentations at Paulson's offices. The company had never told customers that the two men were not authorized to sell this worthless stock.[12] Thus the agents *appeared* to have authority, even though they did not. Of course, Paulson had the right to recover from Kennedy and Lambo if it could ever compel them to pay.

Remember that the issue in apparent authority is always what the *principal* has done to make the *third party* believe that the *agent* has authority. Suppose that Kennedy and Lambo never worked for Paulson but, on their own, printed up Paulson stationery. The company would not be liable for the stock the two men sold because it had never done or said anything that would reasonably make a third party believe that the men were its agents.

---

[10] Restatement (Third) of Agency Section 2.01.
[11] Restatement (Third) of Agency Section 2.02.
[12] *Badger v. Paulson Investment Co.*, 311 Ore. 14, 803 P.2d 1178, 1991 Ore. LEXIS 7 (S.Ct. OR 1991).

An agent has no authority or oversteps his authority BUT, the Principal still accepts it

Ratification

If a person accepts the benefit of an unauthorized transaction or fails to repudiate it, then he is as bound by the act as if he had originally authorized it. He has *ratified* **the act.**[13] Many of the cases in agency law involve instances in which one person acts *without* authority for another. To avoid liability, the alleged principal shows that he had not authorized the task at issue. But sometimes after the fact, the principal decides that he approves of what the agent has done even though it was not authorized at the time. The law would be perverse if it did not permit the principal, under those circumstances, to agree to the deal the agent has made. The law is not perverse, but it is careful. Even if an agent acts without authority, the principal can decide later to be bound by her actions so long as these requirements are met:

- The "agent" indicates to the third party that she is acting for a principal.

- The "principal" knows all the material facts of the transaction.

- The "principal" accepts the benefit of the whole transaction, not just part.

- The third party does not withdraw from the contract before ratification.

A night clerk at the St. Regis Hotel in Detroit, Michigan, was brutally murdered in the course of a robbery. A few days later, the *Detroit News* reported that the St. Regis management had offered a $1,000 reward for any information leading to the arrest and conviction of the killer. Two days after the article appeared, Robert Jackson turned in the man who was subsequently convicted of the crime. But then it was Jackson's turn to be robbed—the hotel refused to pay the reward on the grounds that the manager who had made the offer had no authority. Jackson still had one weapon left: he convinced the court that the hotel had ratified the offer. One of the hotel's owners admitted he read the *Detroit News*. The court concluded that if someone reads a newspaper, he is sure to read any articles about a business he owns; therefore, the owner must have been aware of the offer. He accepted the benefit of the reward by failing to revoke it publicly. This failure to revoke constituted a ratification, and the hotel was liable.[14]

Subagents

Many of the examples in this chapter involve a single agent acting for a principal. Real life is often more complex. Daniel, the owner of a restaurant, hires Michaela to manage it. She in turn hires chefs, waiters, and dishwashers. Daniel has never even met the restaurant help, yet they are also his agents, albeit a special category called **subagent.** Michaela is called an **intermediary agent**—someone who hires subagents for the principal.

As a general rule, an agent has no authority to delegate her tasks to another unless the principal authorizes her to do so. But when an agent is authorized to hire a subagent, the principal is as liable for the acts of the subagent as he is for the acts of a regular agent. Daniel authorizes Michaela to hire a restaurant staff. She hires Lydia to serve as produce buyer. When Lydia buys food for the restaurant, Daniel must pay the bill.

AGENT'S LIABILITY FOR CONTRACTS

The agent's liability on a contract depends upon how much the third party knows about the principal. Disclosure is the agent's best protection against liability.

---

[13] Restatement (Third) of Agency Section 4.01.
[14] *Jackson v. Goodman*, 69 Mich. App. 225, 244 N.W.2d 423, 1976 Mich. App. LEXIS 741 (Mich. Ct. App. 1976).

Fully Disclosed Principal

An agent is not liable for any contracts she makes on behalf of a *fully* disclosed principal. A principal is fully disclosed if the third party knows of his *existence* and his *identity*. Augusta acts as agent for Parker when he buys Tracey's prize-winning show horse. Augusta and Tracey both grew up in posh Grosse Pointe, Michigan, where they attended the same elite schools. Tracey does not know Parker, but she figures any friend of Augusta's must be OK. She figures wrong—Parker is a charming deadbeat. He injures Tracey's horse, fails to pay the full contract price, and promptly disappears. Tracey angrily demands that Augusta make good on Parker's debt. Unfortunately for Tracey, Parker was a fully disclosed principal—Tracey knew of his *existence* and his *identity*. Although Tracey partly relied on Augusta's good character when contracting with Parker, Augusta is not liable because Tracey knew who the principal was and could have (should have) investigated him. Augusta did not promise anything herself, and Tracey's only recourse is against the principal, Parker (wherever he may be).

To avoid liability when signing a contract on behalf of a principal, an agent must clearly state that she is an agent and must also identify the principal. Augusta should sign a contract on behalf of her principal, Parker, as follows: "Augusta, as agent for Parker" or "Parker, by Augusta, Agent."

Unidentified Principal

In the case of an *unidentified* principal, the third party can recover from either the agent or the principal. (An unidentified principal is also sometimes called a "partially disclosed principal.")[15] A principal is unidentified if the third party knew of his *existence* but not his *identity*. Suppose that, when approaching Tracey about the horse, Augusta simply says, "I have a friend who is interested in buying your champion." Any friend of Augusta's is a friend of Tracey's—or so Tracey thinks. Parker is an unidentified principal because Tracey knows only that he exists, not who he is. She cannot investigate his creditworthiness because she does not know his name. Tracey relies solely on what she is able to learn from the agent, Augusta. Both Augusta and Parker are liable to Tracey. (They are jointly and severally liable, which means that Tracey can recover from either or both of them. She cannot, however, recover more than the total that she is owed: if her damages are $100,000, she can recover that amount from either Augusta or Parker, or partial amounts from both, but in no event more than $100,000.)

Undisclosed Principal

In the case of an *undisclosed* principal, the third party can recover from either the agent or the principal. A principal is undisclosed if the third party did not know of his existence. Suppose that Augusta simply asks to buy the horse herself, without mentioning that she is purchasing it for Parker. In this case Parker is an undisclosed principal because Tracey does not know that Augusta is acting for someone else. Both Parker and Augusta are jointly and severally liable. As Exhibit 27.1 illustrates, the principal is always liable, but the agent is not unless the principal's identity is a mystery.

In some ways, the concept of an undisclosed principal violates principles of contract law. If Tracey does not even know that Parker exists, how can they have an agreement or a meeting of the minds? Is such an arrangement fair to Tracey? No matter, a contract with an undisclosed principal is binding. The following incident illustrates why.

---

[15] In the past, courts used the term "partially disclosed principal" instead of "unidentified principal." However, the Restatement (Third) of Agency now uses "unidentified principal," so we do, too. (See Section 1.04.)

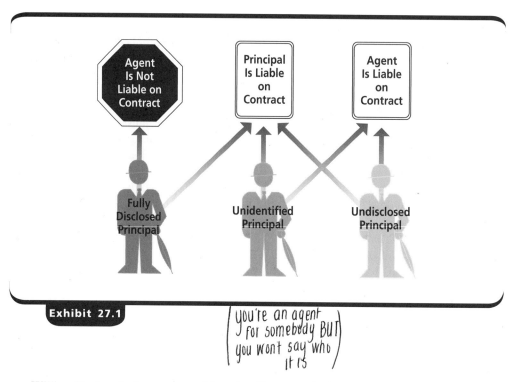

Exhibit 27.1

you're an agent for somebody BUT you won't say who it is

William Zeckendorf was a man with a plan. For years, he had been eyeing a six-block tract of land along New York's East River. It was a wasteland of slums and slaughterhouses, but he could see its potential. The meat packers had refused to sell to him, however, because they knew they would never be permitted to build slaughterhouses in Manhattan again. Finally, he got the phone call he had been waiting for. The companies were willing to sell—at $17 a square foot, when surrounding land cost less than $5. Undeterred, Zeckendorf immediately put down a $1 million deposit. But to make his investment worthwhile, he needed to buy the neighboring property—once the slaughterhouses were gone, the other land would be much more valuable. Zeckendorf was well known as a wealthy developer; he had begun his business career managing the Astor family's real estate holdings. If he personally tried to negotiate the purchase of the surrounding land, word would soon get out that he wanted to put together a large parcel. Prices would skyrocket and the project would become too costly. So he hired agents to purchase the land for him. To conceal his involvement further, he went to South America for a month. When he returned, his agents had completed 75 different purchases, and he owned 18 acres of land.

Shortly afterwards, the United Nations began seeking a site for its headquarters. President Truman favored Boston, Philadelphia, or a location in the Midwest. The UN committee suggested Greenwich or Stamford, Connecticut. But John D. Rockefeller settled the question once and for all. He purchased Zeckendorf's land for $8.5 million and donated it to the UN (netting Zeckendorf a profit of $2 million). Without the cooperation of agency law, the UN headquarters would not be in New York today.

Because of concerns about fair play, there are some exceptions to the rule on undisclosed principals. **A third party is not bound to the contract with an undisclosed principal if (1) the contract specifically provides that the third party is not bound to anyone other than the agent, or (2) the agent lies about the principal because she knows the third party would refuse to contract with him.** Suppose that a large university is buying up land in an impoverished area near its campus. An owner of a house there wants to make sure that if he sells to the university, he gets a higher price than if he sells to an individual with more limited resources. A cagey property owner, when approached by one of the university's agents, could ask for a clause in the contract providing that the agent was not representing someone else. If the agent told the truth, the owner could demand a higher price. If the agent lied, then the owner could rescind the contract when the truth emerged.

Unauthorized Agent

Thus far in this section, we have been discussing an agent's liability to a third party for a transaction that was authorized by the principal. Sometimes, however, agents act without the authority of a principal. **If the agent has no authority (express, implied, or apparent), the principal is not liable to the third party and the agent is.** Suppose that Augusta agrees to sell Parker's horse to Tracey. Unfortunately, Parker has never met Augusta and has certainly not authorized this transaction. Augusta is hoping that she can persuade him to sell, but Parker refuses. Augusta, but not Parker, is liable to Tracey for breach of contract.

PRINCIPAL'S LIABILITY FOR TORTS

An employer is liable for a tort committed by its employee acting within the scope of employment or acting with apparent authority.[16] This principle of liability is called *respondeat superior,* which is a Latin phrase that means "let the master answer." Under the theory of *respondeat superior,* the employer (that is, the principal) is liable for misbehavior by the employee (that is, the agent) whether or not the employer was at fault. Indeed, the employer is liable even if he *forbade* or tried to *prevent* the employee from misbehaving. Thus a company could be liable for the damage a worker causes while driving and talking on her cell phone, even if she is violating company policy at the time. This sounds like a harsh rule. The logic is that because the principal controls the agent, he should be able to *prevent* misbehavior. If he cannot prevent it, at least he can *insure* against the risks. Furthermore, the principal may have deeper pockets than the agent or the injured third party and thus be better able to *afford* the cost of the agent's misbehavior.

To apply the principle of *respondeat superior,* it is important to understand each part of the rule.

Employee

There are two kinds of agents: (1) *employees* and (2) *independent contractors*. **A principal *may be* liable for the torts of an employee but generally is *not* liable for the torts of an independent contractor.** Because of this rule, the distinction between an employee and an independent contractor is important.[17]

Employee or Independent Contractor?   The more control the principal has over an agent, the more likely that the agent will be considered an employee. Therefore, when determining if agents are employees or independent contractors, courts consider whether:

- The principal controls details of the work.

- The principal supplies the tools and place of work.

- The agents work full-time for the principal.

---

[16] Restatement (Third) Agency Section 7.07.

[17] In discussions of a principal's liability for an agent, the principal was traditionally referred to as a "master" and the agent as a "servant." The Restatement (Third) of Agency substitutes the terms "employer" and "employee" and so do we because these terms are more often used in the modern world. However, the Restatement adopts "nonagent service provider" instead of the traditional term "independent contractor." We do not follow the Restatement into this thicket because "independent contractor" is much more widely used than "nonagent service provider."

- The agents are paid by time, not by the job.
- The work is part of the regular business of the principal.
- The principal and agents believe they have an employer-employee relationship.
- The principal is in business.[18]

Negligent Hiring   Principals prefer agents to be considered independent contractors, not employees, because as a general rule, principals are not liable for the torts of an independent contractor. There is, however, one exception to this rule: **The principal is liable for the torts of an independent contractor *if* the principal has been negligent in hiring or supervising her.** Remember that, under *respondeat superior*, the principal is liable *without fault* for the torts of employees. The case of independent contractors is different: the principal is liable only if he was *at fault* by being careless in his hiring or supervising.

Exhibit 27.2 illustrates the difference in liability between an employee and an independent contractor.

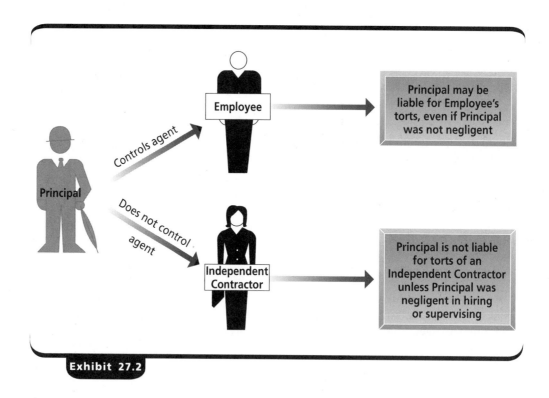

Employee

Principal may be liable for Employee's torts, even if Principal was not negligent

Controls agent

Principal

Does not control agent

Independent Contractor

Principal is not liable for torts of an Independent Contractor unless Principal was negligent in hiring or supervising

Exhibit 27.2

• *Scope of Employment*
Principals are liable only for torts that an employee commits within the *scope of employment*. If an employee leaves a pool of water on the floor of a store and a customer slips and falls, the employer is liable. But if the same employee leaves water on his own kitchen floor and a friend falls, the employer is not liable because the employee is not acting within the scope of employment. An employee is acting within the scope of employment if the act:

---

[18] Restatement (Third) of Agency Section 7.07.

- Is one that employees are generally responsible for

- Takes place during hours that the employee is generally employed

- Is part of the principal's business

- Is similar to the one the principal authorized

- Is one for which the principal supplied the tools; and

- Is not seriously criminal.

Scope of employment cases raise two major issues: authorization and abandonment.

Authorization   In authorization cases the agent is clearly working for the principal but commits an act that the principal has not authorized. Although Jane has often told the driver of her delivery van not to speed, Hank ignores her instructions and plows into Bernadette. At the time of the accident, he is working for Jane, delivering flowers for her shop, but his act is not authorized. **An act is within the scope of employment, even if expressly forbidden, if it is of the same general nature as that authorized or if it is incidental to the conduct authorized.** Hank was authorized to drive the van but not to speed. However, his speeding was of the same general nature as the authorized act, so Jane is liable to Bernadette. Was the employee in the following case acting within the scope of his employment while driving late at night on the back roads of Russia? You be the judge.

YOU *be the* JUDGE

KASHIN v. KENT

457 F.3d 1033, 2006 U.S. App. LEXIS 20496
United States Court of Appeals for
the Ninth Circuit, 2006

Facts: Douglas Kent was the Consul General of the United States in Vladivostok, Russia. One evening, he drove from his office to a gym and then home. On the way home from the gym, he was involved in an accident that left Aleksandr Kashin severely injured.

Kashin sued the United States government, claiming that Kent was within the scope of his employment at the time of the accident.

You Be the Judge: Was Kent within the scope of his employment while driving home from the gym?

Argument for Kashin: Kent was expected to, and did, work on behalf of the United States around the clock, seven days a week. He sometimes worked from home. Kent also sometimes conducted government business from his apartment or had to leave it in the middle of the night on official business. The Department of State leased and furnished Kent's apartment, which was provided to him without cost. It also reimbursed Kent for all mileage he drove in his own car.

Kent was required to pass regular and thorough medical examinations or face revocation of his medical clearance to work overseas. He had gone to the gym to work out so that he could pass this medical exam.

Argument for the United States: On the day of the accident, Kent had not been working at home. Nor was he engaged in any diplomatic activity at the time of the accident. The visit to the gym was his personal business. He had not visited the gym for purposes of taking the medical exam, nor did the State Department require him to work out at the gym. At the time of the accident, Kent was driving his own car.

Abandonment   The second major issue in a *scope of employment* case involves abandonment. **The principal is liable for the actions of the employee that occur while the employee is at work, but not for actions that occur after the employee has abandoned the principal's business.** Although the rule sounds straightforward, the difficulty lies in determining whether the employee has in fact abandoned the principal's business. The employer is liable if the employee is simply on a *detour* from company business, but the employer is not liable if the employee is off on a *frolic of his own.* Suppose that Hank, the delivery van driver, speeds during his afternoon commute home. An employee is generally not acting within the scope of his employment when he commutes to and from work, so his principal, Jane, is not liable. Or suppose that, while on the way to a delivery, he stops to view his favorite movie classic, *Dead on Arrival.* Unable to see in the darkened theater, he knocks Anna down, causing grave harm. Jane is not liable because Hank's visit to the movies is outside the scope of his employment. On the other hand, if Hank stops at the Burger Box drive-in window en route to making a delivery, Jane is liable when he crashes into Anna on the way out of the parking lot, because this time he is simply making a detour.

Negligent and Intentional Torts
The principal is liable if the employee commits a *negligent* tort that causes physical harm to a person or property. A principal is *not* liable for the *intentional* torts of the employee unless the employee intended to serve some purpose of the employer.

During an NBA basketball game, Kobe pushes Shaq into some chairs under the basket to prevent him from scoring a breakaway layup. Kobe's team is liable for his actions because he was motivated, at least in part, by a desire to help his team. But if Kobe hits Shaq in the parking lot after the playoffs are over, Kobe's team is *not* liable because he is no longer motivated by a desire to help the team. His motivation now is personal revenge or frustration.

In the following case, a priest did wrong. Was he acting within the scope of his employment? Was the Church negligent in hiring and supervising him? Was the Church liable for his criminal acts?

DOE V. LIBERATORE

478 F.SUPP.2d 742; 2007 U.S. DIST. LEXIS 19067
UNITED STATES DISTRICT COURT FOR THE MIDDLE DISTRICT OF PENNSYLVANIA, 2007

CASE SUMMARY

Facts: A number of priests wrote to James Timlin, the Bishop of Scranton, warning him that Father Albert Liberatore was engaging in a sexual relationship with one of his male students. Bishop Timlin transferred Liberatore from the school to a parish church.

Fourteen year-old John Doe was a member of Liberatore's parish. Liberatore befriended Doe, taking him on outings and giving him expensive gifts. Doe routinely slept in Liberatore's bed. A number of priests told Bishop Timlin that they feared Liberatore was sexually abusing Doe. One witness reported that she had seen Doe put his

hand down Liberatore's pants. Eventually, Doe himself told a priest that he was being sexually abused. The priest instructed Doe to forgive Liberatore and not to tell other people because it would ruin Doe's life and the lives of others.

Only after Liberatore pleaded guilty to multiple counts of sexual abuse did the Church dismiss him from the priesthood. Doe filed suit against the Church and Bishop Timlin, alleging that they were liable for the torts committed by Liberatore. The defendants filed a motion to dismiss.

Issues: *Was Liberatore acting within the scope of his employment? Were the defendants liable for his criminal acts?*

Decision: The priest's sexual misconduct was not within the scope of his employment. Nevertheless, the defendants could be liable on the grounds of negligent supervision.

Reasoning: Liberatore's sexual abuse of a child was not within the scope of his employment as a priest. In no way did it serve the purposes of the Church or Bishop Timlin.

Therefore, the Court granted summary judgment for the defendants on this issue.

However, an employer owes a duty to exercise reasonable care in hiring and supervising employees. The defendants are not negligent for *hiring* the priest at the beginning because at that point, there was no evidence he would sexually abuse children, but a jury could certainly conclude that both the Church and the Bishop had been negligent in *supervising* Liberatore.

Physical or Non-Physical Harm

In the case of *physical* torts, a principal is liable for the negligent conduct of a employee that occurs within the scope of employment. The rule for *nonphysical* torts (that is, torts that harm only reputation, feelings, or wallet) is different. **Nonphysical torts are treated more like a contract claim, and the principal is liable if the employee acted with apparent authority.**[19] For example, suppose that Dwayne buys a house insurance policy from Andy, who is an agent of the Balls of Fire Insurance Company. Andy throws away Dwayne's policy and pockets his premiums. When Dwayne's house burns down, Balls of Fire is liable because Andy was acting with apparent authority.

EXAM *Strategy*

Question: Daisy was the founder of an Internet start-up company. Mac was her driver. One day, after he had dropped her at a board meeting, he went to the car wash. There, he told an attractive woman that he worked for a money management firm. She promptly gave him money to invest. On the way out of the car wash, he was so excited that he hit another customer's expensive car. Who is liable for Mac's misdeeds?

Strategy: In determining a principal's liability, begin by figuring out whether the agent has committed a physical or non-physical tort. Remember that the principal is liable for physical torts within the scope of employment, but for nonphysical torts, she is liable only if the employee acted with apparent authority.

Result: In this case, Daisy is liable for the damage to the car because that was a physical tort within the scope of employment. But she is not liable for the investment money because Mac did not have apparent authority from her to take those funds.

AGENT'S LIABILITY FOR TORTS

The focus of this section has been on the *principal's* liability for the agent's torts. But it is important to remember that **agents are always liable for their own torts.** Agents who commit

[handwritten margin note: independent contractor (The principal is NOT held liable for tort liability) Exception: Ultra-Hazardous activity]

---

[19] Restatement (Third) Agency Section 7.08.

torts are personally responsible whether or not their principal is also liable. Even if the tort was committed to benefit the principal, the agent is still liable. So the sailor who got into a fistfight while rousting a shipmate from bed is liable even though he thought he was acting for the benefit of his principal.

This rule makes obvious sense. If the agent were not liable, he would have little incentive to be careful. Imagine Hank driving his delivery van for Jane. If he were not personally liable for his own torts, he might think, "If I drive fast enough, I can make it through that light even though it just turned red. And if I don't, what the heck, it'll be Jane's problem, not mine." Agents, as a rule, may have fewer assets than their principal, but it is important that their personal assets be at risk in the event of their negligent behavior.

If the agent and principal are *both* liable, which does the injured third party sue? The principal and the agent are *jointly and severally liable*, which means, as we have seen, that the injured third party can sue either one or both, as she chooses. If she recovers from the principal, he can sue the agent.

CHAPTER CONCLUSION

When students enroll in a business law course, they fully expect to learn about torts and contracts, corporations and partnerships. They probably do not think much about agency law; many of them have not even heard the term before. Yet it is an area of the law that affects us all because each of us has been and will continue to be both an agent and a principal many times in our lives.

EXAM REVIEW

1. **CREATING AN AGENCY RELATIONSHIP** A principal and an agent mutually consent that the agent will act on behalf of the principal and be subject to the principal's control, thereby creating a fiduciary relationship. (p. 667)

2. **ELEMENTS NOT REQUIRED** An agency relationship can exist without either a written agreement, a formal agreement, or consideration. (pp. 668–669)

3. **AN AGENT'S DUTIES TO THE PRINCIPAL** An agent owes these duties to the principal: duty of loyalty, duty to obey instructions, duty of care, and duty to provide information. (pp. 669–673)

4. **THE PRINCIPAL'S REMEDIES IN THE EVENT OF A BREACH** The principal has three potential remedies when the agent breaches her duty: recovery of damages the breach has caused, recovery of any profits earned by the agent from the breach, and rescission of any transaction with the agent. (pp. 673–674)

5. **THE PRINCIPAL'S DUTIES TO THE AGENT** The principal has two duties to the agent: to reimburse legitimate expenses, and to cooperate with the agent. (pp. 674–675)

6. **POWER AND RIGHT TO TERMINATE** Both the agent and the principal have the power to terminate an agency relationship, but they may not have the right. If the termination violates the agency agreement and causes harm to the other party, the wrongful party must pay damages. (p. 676)

7. **AUTOMATIC TERMINATION** An agency relationship automatically terminates if the principal or agent can no longer perform the required duties or if a change in circumstances renders the agency relationship pointless. (p. 676)

8. **A PRINCIPAL'S LIABILITY FOR CONTRACTS** A principal is bound by the contracts of the agent if the agent has express, implied, or apparent authority. (p. 678)

9. **EXPRESS AUTHORITY** The principal grants express authority by words or conduct that, reasonably interpreted, cause the agent to believe that the principal desires her to act on the principal's account. (pp. 678–679)

10. **IMPLIED AUTHORITY** Implied authority includes authority to do acts that are incidental to a transaction, usually accompany it, or are reasonably necessary to accomplish it. (p. 679)

11. **APPARENT AUTHORITY** Apparent authority means that a principal is liable for the acts of an agent who is not, in fact, acting with authority if the principal's conduct causes a third party reasonably to believe that the agent is authorized. (p. 679)

EXAM Strategy

Question: Dr. James Leonard wrote Dr. Edward Jacobson offering him the position of Chief of Audiology at Jefferson Medical College in Philadelphia. In the letter, Leonard stated that this appointment would have to be approved by the promotion and appointment committee. Jacobson believed that the appointment committee acted only as a "rubber stamp" affirming whatever recommendation Leonard made. Jacobson accepted Leonard's offer and proceeded to sell his house and quit his job in Colorado. You can guess what happened next. Two weeks later, Leonard sent Jacobson another letter, rescinding his offer because of opposition from the appointment committee. Does Leonard have apparent authority?

Strategy: In cases of apparent authority, begin by asking what the principal did to make the third party believe that the agent was authorized. Did the Medical College do anything? (See the "Result" at the end of this section.)

12. **AN AGENT'S LIABILITY FOR A CONTRACT** An agent is not liable for any contract she makes on behalf of a fully disclosed principal. The principal is liable. In the case of a unidentified or undisclosed principal, both the agent and the principal are liable on the contract. (p. 681)

13. **A PRINCIPAL'S LIABILITY FOR TORTS** An employer is liable for a tort committed by its employee acting within the scope of employment or acting with apparent authority. (p. 683)

EXAM Strategy

Question: While drunk, the driver of a subway car plows into the back of the car ahead of him, killing a passenger. It was against the rules for the driver to be drunk. Is the subway authority liable for the negligence of its employee?

Strategy: With a tort case, always determine first if the agents are employees or independent contractors. This worker was an employee. Then ask if the employee was acting within the scope of employment. Yes, he was driving a subway car, which is what he was hired to do. Does it matter than he had violated subway rules? No, his violation of the rules does not eliminate his principal's liability. (See the "Result" at the end of this section.)

Question: What if the subway driver had stabbed a passenger?

Strategy: In the case of an intentional tort, the principal is only liable if the agent was intending to serve some purpose of the employer. (See the "Result" at the end of this section.)

14. **INDEPENDENT CONTRACTOR** The principal is liable for the physical torts of an independent contractor only if the principal has been negligent in hiring or supervising him. (p. 684)

15. **AGENT'S LIABILITY FOR TORTS** Agents are always liable for their own torts. (p. 687)

11. Result: No. Indeed, Leonard had told Jacobson that he did not have authority. If Jacobson chose to believe otherwise, that was his problem.

13. Result: The subway authority is liable.

Result: When he stabbed a passenger, the driver was not serving the purpose of the employer so the subway authority would not be liable.

ADDITIONAL QUESTIONS

1. The German-American Vocational League was formed in New York during World War II to serve as a propaganda agency for the German Reich. Under U.S. law all foreign agents were required to register. Neither the Vocational League nor its officers registered. When they were charged with violating U.S. law, they argued that they were not agents of the German government because they had no formal agency agreement. Their one written agreement with the German Reich said nothing about being a propaganda agency. Is a formal contract necessary to establish an agency relationship?

2. **ETHICS** Radio TV Reports (RTV) was in the business of recording, transcribing, and monitoring radio and video programming for its clients. The Department of Defense (DOD) in Washington, D.C., was one of RTV's major clients. Paul Ingersoll worked for RTV until August 31. In July, the DOD solicited bids for a new contract for the following year. During this same month, Ingersoll formed his own media monitoring business, Transmedia. RTV and Transmedia were the only two bidders on the DOD contract, which was awarded to Transmedia. Did Ingersoll violate his fiduciary duty to RTV? Aside from his legal obligations, did Ingersoll behave ethically? How does his behavior look in the light of day? Was it right?

3. David and Fiona Rookard purchased tickets for a trip through Mexico from a Mexicoach office in San Diego. Mexicoach told them that the trip would be safe. It did not tell them, however, that their tickets had disclaimers written in Spanish warning that, under Mexican law, a bus company is not liable for any harm that befalls its passengers. The Rookards did not read Spanish. They were injured in a bus accident caused by gross negligence on the part of the driver. Did Mexicoach violate its duty to the Rookards?

4. Penny Wilson went to Arlington Chrysler-Plymouth-Dodge to buy an automobile. Penny told Arlington that, as a minor, she could not buy the car unless she obtained credit life insurance that would pay the balance of any loan owing if her mother died. She also disclosed that her mother had cancer. Arlington was an agent for Western Pioneer Life Insurance Co. Western Pioneer reported that a credit insurance policy would be invalid if Mrs. Wilson died within six months. In fact, the policy was invalid if Mrs. Wilson died of cancer within one year. Seven months later, Mrs. Wilson died, and Western Pioneer refused to pay. Penny Wilson sued Western Pioneer and Arlington. The trial court found Western Pioneer liable, but not Arlington. Was Western Pioneer liable for Arlington's legal expenses?

5. One Friday afternoon a custodian at the Lazear Elementary School in Oakland, California, raped an 11-year-old student in his office on the school premises. The student sued the school district on a theory of *respondeat superior*. Is the school district liable for this intentional tort by its employee?

6. One afternoon while visiting friends, tennis star Vitas Gerulaitis fell asleep in their pool house. A mechanic had improperly installed the swimming pool heater, which leaked carbon monoxide fumes into the house where he slept, killing him. His mother filed suit against the owners of the estate. On what theory would they be liable?

7. **CPA QUESTION** A principal will not be liable to a third party for a tort committed by an agent:

    a. Unless the principal instructed the agent to commit the tort

    b. Unless the tort was committed within the scope of the agency relationship

    c. If the agency agreement limits the principal's liability for the agent's tort

    d. If the tort is also regarded as a criminal act

8. A. B. Rains worked as a broker for the Joseph Denunzio Fruit Co. Raymond Crane offered to sell Rains nine carloads of emperor grapes. Rains accepted the offer on behalf of Denunzio. Later, Rains and Denunzio discovered that Crane was an agent for John Kazanjian. Who is liable on this contract?

9. Roy Watson bought vacuum cleaners from T & F Distributing Co. and then resold them door-to-door. He was an independent contractor. Before hiring Watson, the president of T & F checked with two former employers but could not remember if he called Watson's two references. Watson had an extensive criminal record, primarily under the alias Leroy Turner, but he was listed in FBI records under both Leroy Turner and Roy Watson. T & F granted Watson sales territory that included Neptune City, New Jersey. This city required that all "peddlers" such as Watson be licensed. Applicants for this license were routinely fingerprinted. T & F never insisted that Watson apply for such a license. Watson attacked Miriam Bennett after selling a vacuum cleaner to her at her home in Neptune City. Is T & F liable to Bennett?

10. **YOU BE THE JUDGE** WRITING PROBLEM Sara Kearns went to an auction at Christie's to bid on a tapestry for her employer, Nardin Fine Arts Gallery. The good news is that she purchased a Dufy tapestry for $77,000. The bad news is that it was not the one her employer had told her to buy. In the excitement of the auction, she forgot her instructions. Nardin refused to pay, and Christie's filed suit. Is Nardin liable for the unauthorized act of its agent? **Argument for Christie's:** Kearns executed a bidder form as agent for Nardin. This is a common practice for many purchasers. Christie's cannot possibly ascertain in each case the exact nature of the bidder's authority. Whether or not Kearns had actual authority, she certainly had apparent authority and Nardin is liable. **Argument for Nardin:** Kearns was not authorized to purchase the Dufy tapestry, and therefore Christie's must recover from her, not Nardin.

11. Jack and Rita Powers purchased 312 head of cattle at an auction conducted by Coffeyville Livestock Sales Co. They did not know who owned the cattle they bought. The Powers, in turn, sold 159 of this lot to Leonard Hoefling. He sued the Powers, alleging the cattle were diseased and dying in large numbers, and recovered $38,360. Are the Powers entitled to reimbursement from Coffeyville?

12. **ROLE REVERSAL** Write a multiple choice question that deals with the liability of principals for the acts of their employees.

INTERNET RESEARCH PROBLEM

Acting as an undisclosed principal, William Zeckendorf employed agents to purchase the land in New York on which the United Nations headquarters was ultimately built. Can you find any other examples on the Internet of business dealings in which agents made purchases for an undisclosed principal? Were these business arrangements ethical? What risks did the agents face?

You can find further practice problems at www.cengagebrain.com. See the preface of this book for website access details.

EMPLOYMENT LAW

"On the killing beds you were apt to be covered with blood, and it would freeze solid; if you leaned against a pillar, you would freeze to that, and if you put your hand upon the blade of your knife, you would run a chance of leaving your skin on it. The men would tie up their feet in newspapers and old sacks, and these would be soaked in blood and frozen, and then soaked again, and so on, until by nighttime a man would be walking on great lumps the size of the feet of an elephant. Now and then, when the bosses were not looking, you would see them plunging their feet and ankles into the steaming hot carcass of the steer.... The cruelest thing of all was that nearly all of them—all of those who used knives—were unable to wear gloves, and their arms would be white with frost and their hands would grow numb, and then of course there would be accidents."[1]

> ...you would see them plunging their feet and ankles into the steaming hot carcass of the steer.

---

[1] From Upton Sinclair, *The Jungle* (New York: Bantam Books, 1981), p. 80, a 1906 novel about the meat-packing industry.

INTRODUCTION

For most of history, the concept of career planning was unknown. By and large, people were born into their jobs. Whatever their parents had been—landowner, soldier, farmer, servant, merchant, or beggar—they became, too. People not only knew their place, they also understood the rights and obligations inherent in each position. The landowner had the right to receive labor from his tenants, but he also cared for them if they fell ill. Certainly, there were abuses, but at a time when people held religious convictions about their position in life and workers had few expectations that their lives would be better than their parents', the role of law was limited. The primary English law of employment simply established that, in the absence of a contract, an employee was hired for a year at a time. This rule was designed to prevent injustice in a farming society. If an employee worked through harvest time, the landowner could not fire him in the unproductive winter. Conversely, a worker could not stay the winter and then leave for greener pastures in the spring.

In the eighteenth and nineteenth centuries, the Industrial Revolution profoundly altered the employment relationship. Many workers left the farms and villages for large factories in the city. Bosses no longer knew their workers personally, so they felt little responsibility toward them. The old laws that had suited an agrarian economy with stable relationships did not fit the new employment conditions. Instead of duties and responsibilities, courts emphasized the freedom to contract. Since employees could quit their factory jobs whenever they wanted, it was only fair for employers to have the same freedom to fire a worker. That was indeed the rule adopted by the courts: unless workers had an explicit employment contract, they were employees at will. **An *employee at will* could be fired for a good reason, a bad reason, or no reason at all.** For nearly a century, this was the basic common law rule of employment. A court explained the rule this way:

> Precisely as may the employee cease labor at his whim or pleasure, and, whatever be his reason, good, bad, or indifferent, leave no one a legal right to complain; so, upon the other hand, may the employer discharge, and, whatever be his reason, good, bad, or indifferent, no one has suffered a legal wrong.[2]

However evenhanded this common law rule of employment may have sounded in theory, in practice it could lead to harsh results. The lives of factory workers were grim. It was not as if they could simply pack up and leave; conditions were no better elsewhere. For the worker, freedom to contract often meant little more than freedom to starve. Courts and legislatures gradually began to recognize that individual workers were generally unable to negotiate fair contracts with powerful employers. Since the beginning of the twentieth century, employment law has changed dramatically. Now, the employment relationship is more strictly regulated by statutes and by the common law. No longer can a boss discharge an employee for any reason whatsoever.

Note that many of the statutes discussed in this chapter were passed by Congress and therefore apply nationally. The common law, however, comes from state courts and only applies locally. We will look at a sampling of cases that illustrates national trends, even though the law may not be the same in every state.

This chapter covers four topics in employment law: (1) employment security, (2) safety and privacy in the workplace, (3) financial protection, and (4) employment discrimination.

---

[2] *Union Labor Hospital Assn. v. Vance Redwood Lumber Co.*, 112 P.886, 888, 1910 Cal. LEXIS 417 (Cal. 1910).

EMPLOYMENT SECURITY

NATIONAL LABOR RELATIONS ACT

Without unions to represent employee interests, employers could simply fire any trouble-making workers who complained about conditions in factories or mines. By joining together, workers could bargain with their employers on more equal terms. Naturally, the owners fought against the unions, firing organizers and even hiring goons to beat them up. Distressed by anti-union violence, Congress passed the **National Labor Relations Act** in 1935. Known as the **NLRA** or the **Wagner Act**, this statute:

- Created the National Labor Relations Board to enforce labor laws;

- Prohibits employers from penalizing workers who engage in union activity (for example, joining a preexisting union or forming a new one); and

- Requires employers to "bargain in good faith" with unions.

FAMILY AND MEDICAL LEAVE ACT

In 1993, Congress passed the Family and Medical Leave Act (FMLA), which guarantees both men and women up to 12 weeks of *unpaid* leave each year for childbirth, adoption, or medical emergencies for themselves or a family member. An employee who takes a leave must be allowed to return to the same or an equivalent job with the same pay and benefits. The FMLA applies only to companies with at least 50 workers and to employees who have been with the company full-time for at least a year—this is about 60 percent of all employees.

When Randy Seale's wife went into premature labor with triplets, he stayed home from his job as a truck driver with Associated Milk Producers, Inc., in Roswell, New Mexico. However, the milk of human kindness did not flow in this company's veins: it promptly fired the expectant father. Since Seale was an employee at will, the company's action would have been perfectly legal without the FMLA. But after the U.S. Department of Labor filed suit, the company agreed to pay Seale $10,000.

HEALTH INSURANCE

Companies are *not* required to provide their employees with health insurance. However, current legislation specifies that, starting in 2014, employers who have more than 50 full-time employees will have to pay a penalty if they do not provide basic health insurance. In addition, company insurance policies must cover employees' children up to the age of twenty-six.

Losing your job does not mean that you must also give up your health insurance—at least not right away. Under the Consolidated Omnibus Budget Reconciliation Act (COBRA), **former employees must be allowed to continue their health insurance for 18 months after being terminated from their job.** The catch is that employees must pay for it themselves, up to 102 percent of the cost. (The extra 2 percent covers administrative expenses.) COBRA applies to any company with 20 or more workers.

COMMON LAW PROTECTIONS

The employment at will doctrine was created by the courts. Because that rule has sometimes led to absurdly unfair results, the courts have now created a major exception to the rule—**wrongful discharge**.

Wrongful discharge
An employer may not fire a worker for a reason that violates basic social rights, duties or responsibilities.

Wrongful Discharge: Violating Public Policy

Olga Monge was a schoolteacher in her native Costa Rica. After moving to New Hampshire, she attended college in the evenings to earn U.S. teaching credentials. At night, she worked at the Beebe Rubber Co. During the day, she cared for her husband and three children. When she applied for a better job at her plant, the foreman offered to promote her if she would be "nice" and go out on a date with him. When she refused, he assigned her to a lower wage job, took away her overtime, made her clean the washrooms, and generally ridiculed her. Finally, she collapsed at work, and he fired her.[3]

Imagine that you are one of the judges who decided this case. Olga Monge has been treated abominably, but she was an employee at will and, as you well know, could be fired for any reason. But how can you let the foreman get away with this despicable behavior? The New Hampshire Supreme Court decided that even an employee at will has rights:

> We hold that a termination by the employer of a contract of employment at will which is motivated by bad faith or malice or based on retaliation is not in the best interest of the economic system or the public good and constitutes a breach of the employment contract.[4]

The *Monge* case illustrates the concept of wrongful discharge, which prohibits **an employer from firing a worker for a *bad reason.***

How do the courts define a "bad reason"? It is a reason that violates public policy. Unfortunately, this **public policy rule** is easier to name than it is to define because its definition and application vary from state to state. **In essence, the public policy rule prohibits an employer from firing a worker for a reason that violates basic social rights, duties, or responsibilities.** Almost every employee who has ever been fired feels that a horrible injustice has been done. The difficulty, from the courts' perspective, is to distinguish those cases of dismissal that are offensive enough to affront the community at large from those that outrage only the employee. The courts have primarily applied the public policy rule when an employee refuses to violate the law or insists upon exercising a legal right or performing a legal duty.

Refusing to Violate the Law   Larry Downs went to Duke Hospital for surgery on his cleft palate. When he came out of the operating room, the doctor instructed a nurse, Marie Sides, to give Downs enough anesthetic to immobilize him. Sides refused because she thought the anesthetic was wrong for this patient. The doctor angrily administered the anesthetic himself. Shortly thereafter, Downs stopped breathing. Before the doctors could resuscitate him, he suffered permanent brain damage. When Downs's family sued the hospital, Sides was called to testify. A number of Duke doctors told her that she would be "in trouble" if she testified. She did testify and, after three months of harassment, was fired. When she sued Duke University, the court held:

> It would be obnoxious to the interests of the state and contrary to public policy and sound morality to allow an employer to discharge any employee, whether the employment be for a designated or unspecified duration, on the ground that the employee declined to commit perjury, an act specifically enjoined by statute. To hold otherwise would be without reason and contrary to the spirit of the law.[5]

---

[3] *Monge v. Beebe*, 114 N.H. 130, 316 A.2d 549, 1974 N.H. LEXIS 223 (1974).
[4] *Id.* at 133.
[5] *Sides v. Duke University*, 74 N.C. App. 331, 328 S.E.2d 818, 1985 N.C. App. LEXIS 3501 (N.C. Ct. App. 1985).

As a general rule, employees may not be discharged for refusing to break the law. For example, courts have protected employees who refused to participate in an illegal price-fixing scheme, falsify pollution control records required by state law, pollute navigable waters in violation of federal law, or assist a supervisor in stealing from customers.[6]

Exercising a Legal Right **As a general rule, an employer may not discharge a worker for exercising a legal right if that right supports public policy.** Dorothy Frampton injured her arm while working at the Central Indiana Gas Co. Her employer (and its insurance company) paid her medical expenses and her salary during the four months she was unable to work. When she discovered that she also qualified for benefits under the state's workers' compensation plan, she filed a claim and received payment. One month later, the company fired her without giving a reason. In her suit against the gas company, the court held:

> The [Workers' Compensation] Act creates a duty in the employer to compensate employees for work-related injuries and a right in the employee to receive such compensation. If employers are permitted to penalize employees for filing workmen's compensation claims, a most important public policy will be undermined. Employees will not file claims for justly deserved compensation—opting, instead, to continue their employment without incident. The end result, of course, is that the employer is effectively relieved of his obligation.[7]

Performing a Legal Duty **Courts have consistently held that an employee may not be fired for serving on a jury.** Employers sometimes have difficulty replacing employees who are called up for jury duty and, therefore, prefer that their workers find some excuse for not serving. But jury duty is an important civic obligation that employers are not permitted to undermine.

What about an employee who performs a good deed that is not legally required? Kevin Gardner had just parked his armored truck in front of a bank in Spokane, Washington, when he saw a man with a knife chase the manager out of the bank. While running past the truck, the manager looked directly at Gardner and yelled, "Help me, help me." Gardner got out of his truck and locked the door. By then, the suspect had grabbed another woman, put his knife to her throat, and dragged her into the bank. Gardner followed them in, tackled the suspect, and disarmed him. The rescued woman hailed Gardner as a hero, but his employer fired him for violating a "fundamental" company rule that prohibited drivers from leaving their armored trucks unattended. However, the court held for Gardner on the grounds that, although there is no affirmative legal duty to intervene in such a situation, society values and encourages voluntary rescuers when a life is in danger.[8]

In the following case, two employees objected when their company supplied defective human tissue for transplantation into live patients. Should their behavior be protected as a matter of public policy?

---

[6] *Tameny v. Atlantic Richfield Co.*, 27 Cal. 3d 167, 610 P.2d 1330, 1980 Cal. LEXIS 171 (1980); *Trombetta v. Detroit*, T. & I. R., 81 Mich. App. 489, 265 N.W.2d 385, 1978 Mich. App. LEXIS 2153 (Mich. Ct. App. 1978); *Sabine Pilot Service, Inc. v. Hauck*, 28 Tex. Sup. J. 339, 687 S.W.2d 733, 1985 Tex. LEXIS 755 (1985); *Vermillion v. AAA Pro Moving & Storage*, 146 Ariz. 215, 704 P.2d 1360, 1985 Ariz. App. LEXIS 592 (Ariz. Ct. App. 1985).

[7] *Frampton v. Central Indiana Gas Co.*, 260 Ind. 249, 297 N.E.2d 425, 1973 Ind. LEXIS 522 (1973).

[8] *Gardner v. Loomis Armored, Inc.*, 913 P.2d 377, 1996 Wash. LEXIS 109 (1996).

KOZLOSKI V. AMERICAN TISSUE
SERVICES FOUNDATION

2006 U.S. DIST. LEXIS 95435
UNITED STATES DISTRICT COURT FOR THE DISTRICT OF MINNESOTA, 2006

CASE SUMMARY

Facts: American Tissue Services Foundation (ATSF) was in the business of supplying human tissue from cadavers for transplantation into live patients. Mike Slack, an employee of ATSF, revealed to his boss that he had falsified a donor medical record and changed the donor's blood type on the form. This falsification was not only dangerous to recipients of the tissue, it violated Food and Drug Agency (FDA) regulations. Slack was fired and the infractions were reported to the FDA, as required by law.

It turned out, however, that Slack was the foster child of the company's chairman. And, in this case, (foster) blood was thicker than water. The chairman not only hired Slack at another company as, believe it or not, a quality assurance specialist, but he fired Slack's boss and the two men who had reported the problem to the FDA. The men filed suit against ATSF for wrongful discharge, but the company filed a motion to dismiss on the grounds that the public policy doctrine in Minnesota applied only to employees who had refused to violate the law.

Issues: *Does the public policy doctrine in Minnesota apply only to employees who refuse to violate the law? Do the plaintiffs have the right to proceed with their lawsuit?*

Decision: The wrongful discharge doctrine also applies to situations in which an employee is fired for a reason that clearly violates public policy. The defendants may proceed with their lawsuit.

Reasoning: These plaintiffs were fired because they reported to their employer and the FDA their concerns that human tissue was wrongly labeled. This wrongdoing not only created grave risks for the recipients but also violated federal law. ATSF alleges that under Minnesota law, employees can bring a wrongful discharge claim only if they were fired for refusing to violate the law. This reading of the law is incorrect. Wrongful discharge also applies when the termination is for a reason that *clearly* violates public policy. This termination meets that standard. The safe use of human tissue in live patients is *clearly* a matter of public safety and, therefore, public policy.

Contract Law

Traditionally, many employers (and employees) thought that only a formal, signed document qualified as an employment contract. Increasingly, however, courts have been willing to enforce an employer's more casual promises, whether written or oral. Sometimes courts have also been willing to *imply* contract terms in the absence of an *express* agreement.

Truth in Hiring   Oral promises made during the hiring process can be enforceable, even if not approved by the company's top executives. When the Tanana Valley Medical-Surgical Group, Inc. hired James Eales as a physician's assistant, it promised him that so long as he did his job, he could stay there until retirement age. Six years later, the company fired him without cause. The Alaska Supreme Court held that the clinic's promise was enforceable.[9]

Employee Handbooks   The employee handbook at Blue Cross & Blue Shield stated that employees could be fired only for just cause and then only after warnings, notice, a hearing, and other procedures. Charles Toussaint was fired summarily five years after he

---

[9] *Eales v. Tanana Valley Medical-Surgical Group, Inc.*, 663 P.2d 958, 1983 Alas. LEXIS 430 (Alaska 1983).

joined the company. Although this decision was ultimately reviewed by the personnel department, company president, and chairman of the board of trustees, Toussaint was not given the benefit of all of the procedures in the handbook. The court held that **an employee handbook creates a contract.**[10]

Covenant of Good Faith and Fair Dealing   A covenant of good faith and fair dealing prohibits one party to a contract from interfering with the other's right to benefit under the contract. All parties are expected to behave in a fair, decent, and reasonable manner. **In some cases, courts will imply a covenant of good faith and fair dealing in an at-will employment relationship.**

When Forrest Fleming went to work for Parametric Technology Corp., the company promised him valuable stock options if he met his sales goals. He would not be able to *exercise* the options (that is, purchase the stock), however, until several years after they were granted and then only if he was still employed by the company. During his four years with Parametric, Fleming received options to purchase about 18,000 shares for a price as low as 25 cents each. The shares ultimately traded in the market for as much as $50. Although Fleming exercised some options, the company fired him three months before he became eligible to purchase an additional 1,000 shares. The jury awarded him $1.6 million in damages. Although Parametric had not violated the explicit terms of the option agreement, the jury believed it had violated the covenant of good faith and fair dealing by firing Fleming to prevent him from exercising his remaining options.[11]

Tort Law

Workers have successfully sued their employers under the following tort theories.

Defamation   **Employers may be liable for defamation when they give false and unfavorable references about a former employee.** In his job as a bartender at the Capitol Grille restaurant, Christopher Kane often flirted with customers. After he was fired from his job, his ex-boss claimed that Kane had been "fired from every job he ever had for sexual misconduct." In fact, Kane had never been fired before. He recovered $300,000 in damages for this defamation.

More than half of the states, however, recognize a qualified privilege for employers who give references about former employees. A qualified privilege means that employers are liable only for false statements that they know to be false or that are primarily motivated by ill will. After Becky Chambers left her job at American Trans Air, Inc., she discovered that her former boss was telling anyone who called for a reference that Chambers "does not work good with other people," is a "troublemaker," and "would not be a good person to rehire." Chambers was unable, however, to present compelling evidence that her boss had been primarily motivated by ill will. Neither Trans Air nor the boss was held liable for these statements because they were protected by the qualified privilege.[12]

Qualified privilege
Employers who give references are liable only for false statements that they know to be false or that are primarily motivated by ill will.

Even if the employer wins, a trial is an expensive and time-consuming undertaking. Not surprisingly, companies are leery about offering any references for former employees. The company gains little benefit from giving an honest evaluation and may suffer substantial liability. As a matter of policy, many companies instruct their managers to reveal only a person's salary and dates of employment and not to offer an opinion on job performance.

---

[10] *Toussaint v. Blue Cross & Blue Shield*, 408 Mich. 579, 292 N.W.2d 880, 1980 Mich. LEXIS 227 (1980).
[11] *Fleming v. Parametric Tech. Corp.*, 1999 U.S. App. LEXIS 14864.
[12] *Chambers v. American Trans Air, Inc.*, 577 N.E.2d 612, 1991 Ind. App. LEXIS 1413 (Ind. Ct. App. 1991).

According to one survey, only 55 percent of former employers are totally honest when they give references.

On the flip side, do employers have any obligation to warn about risky workers? **Generally, courts have held that employers do *not* have a legal obligation to disclose information about former employees.** For example, while Jeffrey St. Clair worked at the St. Joseph Nursing Home, he was disciplined 24 times for actions ranging from extreme violence to drug and alcohol use. When he applied for a job with Maintenance Management Corp. St. Joseph refused to give any information other than St. Clair's dates of employment. After he savagely murdered a security guard at his new job, the guard's family sued, but the court dismissed the case.[13]

In some recent cases, however, courts have held that, when a former worker is potentially dangerous, employers do have an obligation to disclose this information. For example, officials from two junior high schools gave Robert Gadams glowing letters of recommendation without mentioning that he had been fired for inappropriate sexual conduct with students. While an assistant principal at a new school, he molested a thirteen-year-old. Her parents sued the former employers. The court held that the writer of a letter of recommendation owes to third parties (in this case, the student) "a duty not to misrepresent the facts in describing the qualifications and character of a former employee, if making these misrepresentations would present a substantial, foreseeable risk of physical injury to the third persons."[14] As a result of cases such as this, it makes sense to disclose past violent behavior.

To assist employers who are asked for references, Lehigh economist Robert Thornton has written "The Lexicon of Intentional Ambiguous Recommendations" (LIAR). For a candidate with interpersonal problems, he suggests saying, "I am pleased to say that this person is a former colleague of mine." For a candidate with drug or alcohol problems, there are several possibilities: "She was always high in my opinion," "We remember the hours she spent working with us as happy hours," or "I would say that her real talent is getting wasted at her current job."[15]

ETHICS All joking aside, what if someone calls you to check references on a former employee who had a drinking problem? The job is driving a van for junior high school sports teams. What is the manager's ethical obligation in this situation? Many managers say that, in the case of a serious problem such as alcoholism, sexual harassment, or drug use, they will find a way to communicate that an employee is unsuitable. What if the ex-employee says she is reformed? Aren't people entitled to a second chance? Is it right to risk a defamation suit against your company to protect others from harm? What solutions does the ethics checklist in Chapter 2 suggest? Would it be just to reveal private information about a former employee? Is the process fair if you provide information that the job applicant has no opportunity to rebut because it is kept secret? ◆

Intentional Infliction of Emotional Distress **Employers who condone cruel treatment of their workers face liability under the tort of intentional infliction of emotional distress.** For example, when a 57-year-old social-work manager at Yale–New Haven Hospital

---

[13] *Moore v. St. Joseph Nursing Home, Inc.*, 184 Mich. App. 766, 459 N.W.2d 100, 1990 Mich. App. LEXIS 285 (Mich. Ct. App. 1990).

[14] *Randi W. v. Muroc Joint Unified School District*, 14 Cal. 4th 1066, 929 P.2d 582, 1997 Cal. LEXIS 10 (1997), modified, 14 Cal. 4th 1282c, 97 Cal. Daily Op. Service 1439.

[15] Robert J. Thornton, *Lexicon of Intentionally Ambiguous Recommendations*, Barnes and Noble Books, 2005.

was fired, she was forced to place her personal belongings in a plastic bag and was escorted out the door by security guards in full view of gaping co-workers. A supervisor told her that she would be arrested for trespassing if she returned. A jury awarded her $105,000.

Whistleblowing

No one likes to be accused of wrongdoing even if (or, perhaps, especially if) the accusations are true. **This is exactly what whistleblowers do: they are employees who disclose illegal behavior on the part of their employer.** Not surprisingly, many companies, when faced with such an accusation by an employee, prefer to shoot the messenger. Here is one such story.

Although FMC Corp. sold 9,000 Bradley Fighting Vehicles to the U.S. Army, there had been doubts about the Bradley from the beginning. Its purpose was to ferry soldiers across rivers during a land war in Europe, but whenever a prototype was driven into water, it leaked as badly as any car would have done. When testing supervisor Henry Boisvert refused to sign a report stating that the Bradley functioned well, FMC fired him. A jury ultimately agreed with his version of events and awarded him $171 million.

The law on whistleblowers varies across the country. As a general rule, however, whistleblowers are protected in the following situations:

- *The False Claims Act.* Boisvert recovered under the federal False Claims Act, a statute that permits anyone to bring suit against a "person" (including a company) who defrauds the government. The Act also prohibits employers from firing workers who file suit under the statute.

- *Constitutional Protection for Government Employees.* Employees of federal, state, and local governments have a right to free speech under the United States Constitution. Therefore, the government cannot retaliate against public employees who blow the whistle, as long as the employee is speaking out on a matter of public concern. For example, a New York City child welfare agency received numerous reports that six-year-old Elisa Izquierdo was being abused. After Elisa was beaten to death by her mother, ABC News broadcast an interview with a social worker from the agency. She stated on air that "The workers who are considered the best workers are the ones who seem to be able to move cases out quickly.... There are lots of fatalities the press doesn't know anything about." By giving this interview, the social worker violated New York City rules prohibiting employees from disclosing information about families supervised by city agencies. The city suspended the social worker from her job, and she sued. The court acknowledged that the government has the right to prohibit some employee speech. However, if the employee speaks on matters of public concern, the government bears the burden of justifying any retaliation. In this case, the court held for the social worker. The city reinstated her and gave her back pay.[16]

- *Statutory Protection for Federal Employees.* The Civil Service Reform Act and the Whistleblower Protection Act prevent retaliation against federal employees who report wrongdoing. They also permit the award of back pay and attorney's fees to the whistleblower. This statute was used to prevent the National Park Service from disciplining two managers who wrote a report expressing concern over development in Yellowstone National Park.

---

[16] *Harman v. City of New York*, 140 F.3d 111, 1998 U.S. App. LEXIS 5567 (2d Cir. 1998).

- *Employees of Publicly Traded Companies.* In response to a series of corporate financial scandals, Congress passed the Sarbanes-Oxley Act of 2002. Among other provisions, this act protects employees of publicly traded companies who provide evidence of fraud to investigators (whether in or outside the company). A successful plaintiff is entitled to reinstatement, back pay, and attorney's fees.

- *State Statutes.* The good news is that all 50 states have statutes that protect whistleblowers from retaliation by their employers. The bad news is that the scope of this protection varies greatly from state to state. For example, in some states, protection only extends to public employees, while in other states, all employees are covered.

- *Common Law.* Most courts will prohibit the discharge of employees who report illegal activity that relates to their own jobs. For example, a Connecticut court held a company liable when it fired a quality control director for reporting to his boss that some products had failed the quality tests.[17] Sometimes, however, courts have held that employees do not have a right to report wrongdoing if it does not relate to their own job functions. For example, Donald Smith's boss told him to ignore the fact that 73,000 pounds of caustic soda had spilled into the river next to a company warehouse. When Smith instead reported the spill to corporate headquarters, he was fired. The court held that, since Smith had no responsibility for reporting spills, the public's interest "in harmony and productivity in the workplace must prevail over the public's interest in encouraging an employee in Smith's position to express his 'informed view.'"[18]

EXAM *Strategy*

Question: When Shiloh interviewed for a sales job at a medical supply company, the interviewer promised that she could work exclusively selling medical devices and would not have to be involved in the sale of drugs. Once she began work (as an employee at will), Shiloh discovered that the sales force was organized around regions, not products, so she had to sell both devices and drugs. When she complained to her boss over lunch in the employee lunchroom, he said in a loud voice, "You are a big girl now, it's time you learned that you don't always get what you want." That afternoon, she was fired. Does she have a valid claim against the company?

Strategy: We know that Shiloh is an employee at will. We also know that she is not protected by any statute we have studied. What about the *common law*? Shiloh has had two interactions with the company—being hired and being fired. What protections does the common law provide during the hiring process? The employer's promises are enforceable. Here, the company is liable because the interviewer clearly made a promise that the company did not keep. What about the way in which Shiloh was fired? Is it intentional infliction of emotional distress? Was this treatment cruel? Probably not cruel enough to constitute intentional infliction of emotional distress.

Result: The company is liable to Shiloh for making false promises to her during the hiring process but not for the manner in which she was fired.

[17] *Sheets v. Teddy's Frosted Foods, Inc.*, 179 Conn. 471, 427 A.2d 385, 1980 Conn. LEXIS 690 (1980).
[18] *Smith v. Calgon Carbon Corp.*, 917 F.2d 1338, 1980 U.S. App. LEXIS 19193 (3rd Cir. 1980).

SAFETY AND PRIVACY IN THE WORKPLACE

WORKPLACE SAFETY

In 1970, Congress passed the Occupational Safety and Health Act (OSHA) to ensure safe working conditions. Under OSHA:

- Employers must comply with specific health and safety standards. For example, health care personnel who work with blood are not permitted to eat or drink in areas where the blood is kept and must not put their mouths on any instruments used to store blood. Protective clothing—gloves, gowns, and laboratory coats—must be impermeable to blood.

- Employers are under a general obligation to keep their workplace "free from recognized hazards that are causing or are likely to cause death or serious physical harm" to employees.

- Employers must keep records of all workplace injuries and accidents.

- The Occupational Safety and Health Administration (also known as OSHA) may inspect workplaces to ensure that they are safe. OSHA may assess fines for violations and order employers to correct unsafe conditions.

OSHA has done a lot to make the American workplace safer. In 1900, roughly 35,000 workers died and 350,000 were injured at work. One hundred years later, the workforce had grown five times larger but the number of annual deaths had fallen to 5,100.

EMPLOYEE PRIVACY

Upon opening the country's first moving assembly line in the early 1900s, Henry Ford issued a booklet, "Helpful Hints and Advice to Employees," that warned against drinking, gambling, borrowing money, taking in boarders, and practicing poor hygiene. Ford also created a department of 100 investigators for door-to-door checks on his employees' drinking habits, sexual practices, and housekeeping skills. It sounds outrageous, but in modern times employees have been fired or disciplined for such extracurricular activities as playing dangerous sports, dating co-workers, or even having high cholesterol.

The right to hire, fire, and make an honest profit is enshrined in American tradition. But so is the right to privacy. Justice Louis D. Brandeis called it the "right to be let alone—the most comprehensive of rights and the right most valued by civilized men." Employees are entitled under the common law to a **reasonable expectation of privacy**. This protection means that an employer could not, for instance, search an employee's home even if looking for items that the employee might have stolen from the company. What other protection do workers have against intrusive employers?

Off-Duty Conduct

A worker's off-duty conduct may affect her employer. For instance, a smoker may miss many days of work or have higher healthcare costs. Does a boss have the right to control employees outside of the workplace? Can a boss, say, fire a worker for smoking at home? (Someone who smokes over the weekend would still have nicotine in his blood on Monday.) Some states have passed laws that protect the right of employees to engage in any *lawful* activity when off duty, including smoking, drinking socially, having high cholesterol, being overweight, or engaging in dangerous hobbies—bungee jumping or roller blading, for instance. In the absence of such a statute, however, an employer does have the right to fire an employee for off-duty conduct.

Alcohol and Drug Testing

Government employees can be tested for drug and alcohol use only if they show signs of use or if they are in a job where this type of abuse endangers the public. Most states permit private employers to administer alcohol and drug tests, and a substantial number do.

Lie Detector Tests

Under the Employee Polygraph Protection Act of 1988, employers may not require, or even *suggest*, that an employee or job candidate submit to a lie detector test, except as part of an "ongoing investigation" into crimes that have occurred.

Electronic Monitoring of the Workplace

Technological advances in communications have raised a host of new privacy issues. Many companies monitor employee use of electronic equipment in the workplace: telephone calls, voice mail, e-mail, and Internet usage. **The Electronic Communications Privacy Act of 1986 (ECPA) permits employers to monitor workers' telephone calls and e-mail messages if (1) the employee consents, (2) the monitoring occurs in the ordinary course of business, or (3) in the case of e-mail, the employer provides the e-mail system.** However, bosses may not disclose any private information revealed by the monitoring.

Although workers may feel that their e-mail should be private, employers argue that this monitoring improves employee productivity and protects the company from lawsuits. For example, during one month, employees at IBM, Apple Computer, and AT&T logged on to *Penthouse* magazine's Web site 12,823 times, using the equivalent of more than 347 workdays. Another company discovered that some of its employees were using their company computers to buy and sell child pornography. Employers fear that even legal logging on to sexually explicit sites may give rise to sexual harassment claims.

EXAM *Strategy*

Question: To ensure that its employees did not use illegal drugs in or outside of the workplace, Rain Co. required all employees to take a lie detector test. Moreover, managers began to screen the company e-mail system for drug references. Jagger was fired for refusing to take the polygraph test. Jonathan was dismissed when a search of his e-mail revealed that he had used marijuana during the prior weekend. Has the company acted legally?

Strategy: First: As employees at will, are Jagger and Jonathan protected by a statute? The Employee Polygraph Protection Act permits employers to require a lie detector test as part of ongoing investigation into crimes that have occurred. Here, Rain has no reason to believe that a crime occurred so it cannot require a polygraph test.

Second: What about Jonathan's marijuana use? The ECPA permits Rain to monitor e-mail messages on its own system. But can the company fire Jonathan for illegal off-duty conduct? Some statutes protect employees for *legal* behavior outside the workplace, but no state protects employees for behavior that violates the law.

Result: The company is liable to Jagger for requiring him to take the lie detector test, but not to Jonathan for monitoring his e-mail or firing him for illegal drug use.

FINANCIAL PROTECTION

Congress and the states have enacted laws that provide employees with a measure of financial security. All of the laws in this section were created by statute, not by the courts.

FAIR LABOR STANDARDS ACT

Passed in 1938, the Fair Labor Standards Act (FLSA) regulates wages and limits child labor. The wage provisions do not apply to managerial, administrative, or professional staff, which means that accounting, consulting, and law firms (among others) are free to require as many hours a week as their employees can humanly perform without having to pay overtime or the minimum wage.

Minimum Wage

The federal minimum wage is $7.25 per hour, although some states have set a higher minimum. To find an interactive map reporting the minimum wage by state, Google "dol minwage america."

Overtime Pay

The FLSA does not limit the number of hours a week that an employee can work, but it does specify that workers must be paid time and a half for any hours over 40 in one week.

Child Labor

The FLSA prohibits "oppressive child labor," which means that children under 14 may work only in agriculture and entertainment. Fourteen- and fifteen-year-olds are permitted to work *limited* hours after school in nonhazardous jobs. Sixteen- and seventeen-year-olds may work *unlimited* hours in nonhazardous jobs.

WORKERS' COMPENSATION

Workers' compensation statutes ensure that employees receive payment for injuries incurred at work. Before workers' comp, injured employees could recover damages only if they sued their employer. It is the brave (or carefree) worker who is willing to risk a suit against his own boss. Lawsuits poison the atmosphere at work. Moreover, employers frequently won these suits by claiming that (1) the injured worker was contributorily negligent, (2) a fellow employee had caused the accident, or (3) the injured worker had assumed the risk of injury. As a result, seriously injured workers (or their families) often had no recourse against the employer.

Workers' comp statutes provide a fixed, certain recovery to the injured employee, no matter who was at fault for the accident. In return, employees are not permitted to sue their employers for negligence. The amounts allowed (for medical expenses and lost wages) under workers' comp statutes are often less than a worker might recover in court, but the injured employee trades the certainty of some recovery for the higher risk of rolling the dice at trial. Payments are approved by an administrative board that conducts an informal hearing into each claim.

SOCIAL SECURITY

The federal Social Security system began in 1935, during the depths of the Great Depression, to provide a basic safety net for the elderly, ill, and unemployed. **Currently, the Social Security**

system pays benefits to workers who are retired, disabled, or temporarily unemployed and to the spouses and children of disabled or deceased workers. It also provides medical insurance to the retired and disabled. The Social Security program is financed through a tax on wages that is paid by employers, employees, and the self-employed.

Although the Social Security system has done much to reduce poverty among the elderly, many worry that it cannot survive in its current form. When workers pay taxes, the proceeds do not go into a savings account for their retirement, but instead are used to pay benefits to current retirees. In 1940, there were 40 workers for each retiree; currently, there are 3.3. By 2030, when the last baby boomers retire, there will be only 2 workers to support each retiree—a prohibitive burden. No wonder baby boomers are often cautioned not to count on Social Security when making their retirement plans.

The Federal Unemployment Tax Act (FUTA) is the part of the Social Security system that provides support to the unemployed. FUTA establishes some national standards, but states are free to set their own benefit levels and payment schedules. A worker who quits voluntarily or is fired for just cause is ineligible for benefits. While receiving payments, she must make a good faith effort to look for other employment.

PENSION BENEFITS

In 1974, Congress passed the Employee Retirement Income Security Act (ERISA) to protect workers covered by private pension plans. Under ERISA, employers are not required to establish pension plans, but if they do, they must follow these federal rules. The law was aimed, in particular, at protecting benefits of retired workers if their companies subsequently go bankrupt. The statute also prohibits risky investments by pension plans. In addition, the statute sets rules on the vesting of benefits. (An employer cannot cancel *vested* benefits; *nonvested* benefits are forfeited when the employee leaves.) Before ERISA, retirement benefits at some companies did not vest until the employee retired—if he quit or was fired before retirement, even after years of service, he lost his pension. Under current law, employee benefits vest after five years of employment.

EMPLOYMENT DISCRIMINATION

In the last five decades, Congress has enacted important legislation to prevent discrimination in the workplace.

EQUAL PAY ACT OF 1963

Under the Equal Pay Act, an employee may not be paid at a lesser rate than employees of the opposite sex for equal work. "Equal work" means tasks that require equal skill, effort, and responsibility under similar working conditions. If the employee proves that she is not being paid equally, the employer will be found liable unless the pay difference is based on merit, productivity, seniority, or some factor other than sex. A "factor other than sex" includes prior wages, training, profitability, performance in an interview, and value to the company. For example, female agents sued Allstate Insurance Co. because its salary for new agents was based, in part, on prior salary. The women argued that this system was unfair because it perpetuated the historic wage differences between men and women. The court, however, held for Allstate.[19]

---

[19] *Kouba v. Allstate Insurance Co.*, 691 F.2d 873, 1982 U.S. App. LEXIS 24479 (9th Cir. 1982).

Title VII

Before 1964, it was legal to treat men and women, whites and people of color, differently in the workplace. Women, for example, could be paid less than men for the same job and could be fired if they got married or pregnant. Newspapers had different pages for men's and women's job ads. **Under Title VII of the Civil Rights Act of 1964, it is illegal for employers to discriminate on the basis of race, color, religion, sex, or national origin.** More specifically, Title VII prohibits (1) discrimination in the workplace, (2) sexual harassment, and (3) discrimination because of pregnancy. It also permits employers to develop affirmative action plans.

Proof of Discrimination

Discrimination under Title VII means firing, refusing to hire, failing to promote, or otherwise reducing a person's employment opportunities because of race, color, religion, sex, or national origin. This protection applies to every stage of the employment process from job ads to postemployment references and includes placement, wages, benefits, and working conditions.

Plaintiffs in Title VII cases can prove discrimination two different ways: disparate treatment and disparate impact.

Disparate Treatment   To prove a disparate treatment case, the plaintiff must show that she was *treated* differently because of her sex, race, color, religion, or national origin. The required steps in a disparate treatment case are:

Step 1 The plaintiff presents evidence that the defendant has discriminated against her because of a protected trait. This is called a *prima facie* **case**. The plaintiff is not required to prove discrimination; she need only create a *presumption* that discrimination occurred.

Suppose that Louisa applies for a job coaching a boys' high school ice hockey team. She was an All-American hockey star in college. Although Louisa is obviously qualified for the job, Harry, the school principal, rejects her and continues to interview other people. This is not proof of discrimination because Harry may have a perfectly good, nondiscriminatory explanation. However, his behavior *could have been* motivated by discrimination.

Step 2 The defendant must present evidence that its decision was based on *legitimate, nondiscriminatory* reasons. Harry might say, for example, that he wanted someone with prior coaching experience. Although Louisa is clearly a great player, she has never coached before.

Step 3 To win, the plaintiff must now prove that the employer discriminated. She may do so by showing that the reasons offered were simply a *pretext*. Louisa might show that Harry had recently hired a male tennis coach who had no prior coaching experience. Or Harry's assistant might testify that Harry said, "No way I'm going to put a woman on the ice with those guys." If she can present evidence such as this, Louisa wins.

In the following case, was the bartender treated differently because of her sex? You be the judge.

YOU *be the* JUDGE

JESPERSEN v. HARRAH'S

444 F.3d 1104, 2006 U.S. APP. LEXIS 9307
United States Court of Appeals for the Ninth Circuit, 2006

Facts: Darlene Jespersen was a bartender at the sports bar in Harrah's Casino in Reno, Nevada. She was an outstanding employee, frequently praised by both her supervisors and customers.

When Jespersen first went to work for Harrah's, female bartenders were encouraged, but not required, to wear makeup. Jespersen tried for a short period of time, but it made her feel sick, degraded, exposed, and violated. Moreover, wearing makeup interfered with her ability to deal with unruly, intoxicated guests because it "took away [her] credibility as an individual and as a person."

After Jespersen had been at Harrah's for almost 20 years, the casino implemented a program that required bartenders to be "well groomed, appealing to the eye." More explicitly, for men:

- Hair must not extend below top of shirt collar. Ponytails are prohibited.

- Hands and fingernails must be clean and nails neatly trimmed at all times.

- No colored polish is permitted.

- Eye and facial makeup is not permitted.

- Shoes will be solid black leather or leather type with rubber (non skid) soles.

The rules for women were:

- Hair must be teased, curled, or styled. Hair must be worn down at all times, no exceptions.

- Nail polish can be clear, white, pink, or red color only. No exotic nail art or length.

- Shoes will be solid black leather or leather type with rubber (non skid) soles.

- Makeup (foundation/ concealer and/or face powder, as well as blush and mascara) must be worn and applied neatly in complimentary colors, and lip color must be worn at all times.

An expert was brought in to show the employees (both male and female) how to dress. The workers were then photographed and told that they must look like the photographs every day at work.

When Jespersen refused to wear makeup, Harrah's fired her. She sued under Title VII. The district court granted Harrah's motion for summary judgment. Jespersen appealed.

You Be the Judge: Did Harrah's requirement that women wear makeup violate Title VII?

Argument for Jespersen: Jespersen refused to wear makeup to work because the cost—in time, money, and personal dignity—was too high.

Employers are free to adopt different appearance standards for each sex, but these standards may not impose a greater burden on one sex than the other. Men were not required to wear makeup, whereas women were. That difference meant a savings for men of hundreds of dollars and hours of time. Harrah's did not have the right to fire Jespersen for violating a rule that applies only to women, with no equivalent for men.

Argument for Harrah's: Employers are permitted to impose different appearance rules on women than on men as long as the overall burden on employees is the same. For example, it is not discriminatory to require men to wear their hair short. On balance Harrah's rules did not impose a heavier burden on women than on men.

Disparate Impact Disparate impact applies if the employer has a rule that, *on its face*, is not discriminatory, but *in practice* excludes too many people in a protected group. The steps in a disparate impact case are:

Step 1 The plaintiff must present a *prima facie* case. The plaintiff is not required to prove discrimination; he need only show a disparate impact—that the employment practice in question excludes a disproportionate number of people in a protected group (women and minorities, for instance).

Suppose that Harry will only hire teachers who are at least 5 feet 10 inches tall and weigh 170 pounds. He says he is afraid that students will literally push around anyone smaller. When Chou Ping, an Asian male, applies for a job, he cannot meet Harry's physical requirements. Chou Ping must show that Harry's rule, *in fact*, eliminates more women or minorities than white males. He might offer evidence that 50 percent of all white males can meet Harry's standard, but only 20 percent of white women and Asian males qualify.

Step 2 The defendant must offer some evidence that the employment practice was a *job-related business necessity*. Harry might produce evidence that teachers are regularly expected to wrestle students into their classroom seats. Further, he might cite studies showing his standards are essential for this task.

Step 3 To win, the plaintiff must now prove either that the employer's reason is a *pretext* or that other, *less discriminatory* rules would achieve the same results. Chou Ping might suggest that all teachers could take a self-defense course or engage in martial arts training.

Note that the mere existence of a disparate impact does not *necessarily* mean that an employment practice violates the law. When the Illinois Law Enforcement Officers Training Board created an exam to test aspiring police officers, a higher percentage of minority applicants than white candidates failed the test. Some of the unsuccessful aspirants filed suit, alleging that the exam was illegal because it had a disparate impact. In response, the board presented evidence that the exam had been very carefully prepared by a consulting company that specialized in creating such exams. The court held that the exam was legal because it was "demonstrably a reasonable measure of job performance."[20]

Color

Title VII prohibits discrimination based on both race and color. Although many people assume that they are essentially the same, that is not necessarily the case. Dwight Burch's coworkers at an Applebee's restaurant taunted him for his dark skin color. These colleagues were also African American but were lighter-skinned. Burch sued on the basis of "color discrimination."

Title VII prohibits the type of treatment that Burch allegedly suffered. While denying any wrongdoing, Applebee's settled the case by paying Burch $40,000 and agreeing to conduct antidiscrimination training.

Religion

Employers must make *reasonable accommodation* for a worker's religious beliefs unless the request would cause *undue hardship* for the business. Scott Hamby told his manager at Wal-Mart that he could never work on Sunday because that was his Sabbath. It also happened to be one of the store's busiest days. When the manager forced Hamby to quit, he sued on the grounds of religious discrimination. Lawsuits such as his are on the rise as more businesses remain open on Sundays. Wal-Mart denied wrongdoing but settled the case with a cash payment of undisclosed amount. It also established a company-wide training program on religious accommodation.

Defenses to Charges of Discrimination

Under Title VII, the defendant has three possible defenses.

Merit   A defendant is not liable if he shows that the person he favored was the most qualified. Test results, education, or productivity can all be used to demonstrate merit,

---

[20] *Bew v. Chicago*, 252 F.3d 891, 2001 U.S. App. LEXIS 9247 (7th Cir. 2001).

provided they relate to the job in question. Harry can show that he hired Bruce instead of Louisa because Bruce has a master's degree in physical education and seven years of coaching experience. On the other hand, the fact that Bruce scored higher on the National Latin Exam in the eighth grade is not a good reason to hire him over Louisa.

ECONOMICS AND THE LAW   It is easy to say that the most qualified person should be hired or promoted. But how do you measure merit? For example, in Santa Clara, California, Paul Johnson scored higher on the dispatcher exam than Diane Joyce, but the county hired Joyce, in part because no woman had ever held the job of radio dispatcher there.[21] This case ultimately reached the U.S. Supreme Court on the issue of whether a less qualified woman could be promoted over a more qualified man. (The court ruled that she could.)

So do we feel sorry for Paul Johnson? Of course, we feel sorry for anyone who does not get the job of his dreams. It turns out, however, that his score on the dispatcher exam had been 75 out of 100; hers was 73. This two-point difference is not persuasive evidence that Johnson would be a better radio dispatcher than Joyce. Indeed, employment tests are typically not very good predictors of on-the-job performance. They are at best blunt instruments. Moreover, a 2-point differential on a 100-point test is meaningless. As an affirmative action case, Johnson was unusual only in that the court actually reported the test scores. Typically, in such cases the actual difference in scores is rarely reported or discussed.

The moral of the story? Before concluding that a less qualified applicant has been promoted over a more qualified competitor, it is wise to ask about the validity of the test and the significance of the difference in scores.[22] ◆

Seniority   A legitimate seniority system is legal, even if it perpetuates past discrimination. Suppose that Harry has always chosen the most senior assistant coach to take over as head coach when a vacancy occurs. Because the majority of the senior assistant coaches are male, most of the head coaches are, too. Such a system does not violate Title VII.

Bona Fide Occupational Qualification   An employer is permitted to establish discriminatory job requirements if they are *essential* to the position in question. Such a requirement is called a **bona fide occupational quali fication (BFOQ)**. Catholic schools may, if they choose, refuse to hire non-Catholic teachers; mail order companies may refuse to hire men to model women's clothing. Generally, however, courts are not sympathetic to claims of BFOQ. They have, for example, almost always rejected BFOQ claims that are based on customer preference. Thus airlines could not refuse to hire male flight attendants even though travelers prefer female attendants.[23] The major exception to this customer preference rule is sexual privacy: an employer may refuse to hire women to work in a men's bathroom and vice versa.

Bona fide occupational qualification (BFOQ)
An employer is permitted to establish discriminatory job requirements if they are essential to the position in question.

Affirmative Action

Affirmative action has become a hot political issue: white males protest that such programs are reverse discrimination against them; political candidates campaign on anti-affirmative action platforms.

Affirmative action is not required by Title VII, nor is it prohibited. Affirmative action programs have three different sources:

---

[21] *Johnson v. Transportation Agency*, 489 U.S. 616, 1987 U.S. LEXIS 1387 (1987).
[22] Michael Selmi, "Testing for Equality: Merit, Efficiency, and the Affirmative Action Debate," *UCLA Law Review*, June 1995, vol. 42, p. 1251.
[23] *Diaz v. Pan American World Airways, Inc.*, 442 F.2d 385, 1971 U.S. App. LEXIS 10920 (5th Cir. 1971).

- *Litigation.* Courts have the power under Title VII to order affirmative action to remedy the effects of past discrimination.

- *Voluntary Action.* Employers can voluntarily introduce an affirmative action plan to remedy the effects of past practices or to achieve equitable representation of minorities and women.

- *Government Contracts.* In 1965, President Johnson signed Executive Order 11246, which prohibits discrimination by federal contractors. This order had a profound impact on the American workplace because one-third of all workers are employed by companies that do business with the federal government. If an employer found that women or minorities were underrepresented in its workplace, it was required to establish goals and timetables to correct the deficiency.

In 1995, however, the Supreme Court dramatically limited the extent to which the government can require contractors to establish affirmative action programs. The Court ruled that these programs are permissible only if they serve a "compelling national interest" and are "narrowly tailored" so that they minimize the harm to white males. The government must be able to show that (1) the programs are needed to overcome specific past discrimination, (2) they have time limits, and (3) nondiscriminatory alternatives are not available.[24] This case led to a sharp decrease in the number of federal contracts awarded to companies owned by women and minorities.

Sexual Harassment

When Professor Anita Hill accused Supreme Court nominee Clarence Thomas of sexually harassing her, people across the country were glued to their televisions, watching the Senate hearings on her charges. Thomas was ultimately confirmed to the Supreme Court, but "sexual harassment" became a household phrase. The number of cases—and the size of the damage awards—skyrocketed.

Everyone has heard of **sexual harassment**, but few people know exactly what it is. Men fear that a casual comment or glance will be met with career-ruining charges; women claim that men "just don't get it." So what is sexual harassment anyway? **Sexual harassment involves unwelcome sexual advances, requests for sexual favors, and other verbal or physical conduct of a sexual nature.** There are two major categories of sexual harassment: (1) *quid pro quo* and (2) hostile work environment.

> Everyone has heard of sexual harassment, but few people know exactly what it is.

Quid Pro Quo   From a Latin phrase that means "one thing in return for another," *quid pro quo* harassment occurs if any aspect of a job is made contingent upon sexual activity. In other words, when a banker says to an assistant, "You can be promoted to teller if you sleep with me," that is *quid pro quo* sexual harassment.

Hostile Work Environment   This is a more subtle claim and the one that managers worry about most. **An employee has a valid claim of sexual harassment if sexual talk and innuendo are so pervasive that they interfere with her (or his) ability to work.** Courts have found that offensive jokes, comments about clothes or body parts, and public displays of pornographic pictures can create a hostile environment. In the following case, the company president repeatedly insulted and demeaned his female employees.

Sexual harassment
Involves unwelcome sexual advances, requests for sexual favors, and other verbal or physical conduct of a sexual nature.

Quid pro quo
A Latin phrase that means "one thing in return for another."

---

[24] *Adarand Constructors, Inc. v. Pena,* 515 U.S. 200, 115 S.Ct. 2097, 1995 U.S. LEXIS 4037 (1995).

TERESA HARRIS V. FORKLIFT SYSTEMS, INC.

510 U.S. 17, 114 S.Ct. 367, 1993 U.S. LEXIS 7155
UNITED STATES SUPREME COURT, 1993

CASE SUMMARY

Facts: Teresa Harris was a manager at Forklift Systems; Charles Hardy was its president. Hardy frequently made inappropriate sexual comments to Harris and other women at the company. For example, he said to Harris, in the presence of others, "You're a woman, what do you know?" and "We need a man as the rental manager." He called her "a dumb ass woman" and suggested that the two of them "go to the Holiday Inn to negotiate her raise." He also asked Harris and other female employees to get coins from his front pants pocket. He insisted that Harris and other women pick up objects he had thrown on the ground. When Harris complained to Hardy, he apologized and claimed he was only joking. A month later, while Harris was arranging a deal with one of Forklift's customers, he asked her, in front of other employees, "What did you do, promise the guy some sex Saturday night?"

Harris sued Forklift, claiming that Hardy had created an abusive work environment. The federal trial court ruled against Harris on the grounds that Hardy's comments might offend a reasonable woman, but they were not severe enough to have a serious impact on Harris's psychological well-being. The appeals court confirmed, and the Supreme Court granted *certiorari*.

Issue: *To be a violation of Title VII, must sexual harassment seriously affect the employee's psychological well-being?*

Decision: No, a hostile or abusive environment violates Title VII, whether or not the plaintiff suffered psychological injury.

Reasoning: Title VII is not limited to economic or tangible discrimination. A workplace loaded with intimidation, ridicule, and insult creates an abusive environment that violates Title VII.

Merely uttering a swear word or two is not a violation because a reasonable person would not find that hostile or abusive. But Title VII does come into play before the victim has a nervous breakdown. An abusive environment that does not seriously affect employees' psychological well-being, nonetheless, may detract from their job performance and keep them from advancing in their careers. If the environment would reasonably be perceived, and is perceived, as hostile or abusive, Title VII does not require it also to be psychologically injurious.

Employees who commit sexual harassment are liable for their own misdeeds. But is their company also liable? The Supreme Court has held that:

- If the victimized employee has suffered a "tangible employment action" such as firing, demotion, or reassignment, the company is liable to her for sexual harassment by a supervisor.

- If the victimized employee has not suffered a tangible employment action, the company is not liable if it can prove that (1) it used reasonable care to prevent and correct sexually harassing behavior, and (2) the employee unreasonably failed to take advantage of the complaint procedure or other preventive opportunities provided by the company.[25]

---

[25] *Burlington Industries, Inc. v. Ellerth*, 524 U.S. 742, 118 S.Ct. 2257, 1998 U.S. LEXIS 4217 (1998); *Faragher v. Boca Raton*, 524 U.S. 775, 118 S.Ct. 2275, 1998 U.S. LEXIS 4216 (1998).

Corning Consumer Products Co. asks its employees to apply four tests in determining whether their behavior constitutes sexual harassment:

- Would you say or do this in front of your spouse or parents?

- What about in front of a colleague of the opposite sex?

- Would you like your behavior reported in your local newspaper?

- Does it need to be said or done at all?

Procedures and Remedies

Before a plaintiff in a Title VII case brings suit, she must first file a complaint with a federal agency, the Equal Employment Opportunity Commission (EEOC). The EEOC then has the right to sue on behalf of the plaintiff. This arrangement is favorable for the plaintiff because the government pays the legal bill. If the EEOC decides *not* to bring the case, or does not make a decision within six months, it issues a **right to sue letter**, and the plaintiff may proceed on her own in court. Many states also have their own version of the EEOC, but these state commissions are often understaffed.

Remedies available to the successful plaintiff include hiring, reinstatement, retroactive seniority, back pay, reasonable attorney's fees, and damages of up to $300,000. Two recent trends, however, have reduced employees' chances of taking home substantial damages. Concerned about a rise in discrimination lawsuits, employers now often require new hires to agree in advance to arbitrate, not litigate, any future employment claims. The Supreme Court has upheld the employers' right to do so.[26] Typically, employees receive worse results in the arbitrator's office than in the courtroom, largely because arbitrators tend to favor repeat customers (such as management) over one-time users (such as employees). But even if a case does go to trial, plaintiffs in job discrimination cases have a much worse track record than other types of plaintiffs. About 43 percent of all plaintiffs in federal district court win their cases; for discrimination plaintiffs, the win rate is only about 30 percent. Even if discrimination plaintiffs win at trial, they have a 44 percent probability of losing on appeal. Victorious plaintiffs in other types of cases are overturned only 33 percent of the time.

Pregnancy

Under the Pregnancy Discrimination Act of 1978, an employer may not fire, refuse to hire, or fail to promote a woman because she is pregnant. An employer must also treat pregnancy as any other temporary disability. If, for example, employees are allowed time off from work for other medical disabilities, women must also be allowed a maternity leave. The United States is one of only four countries in the world (along with Liberia, Papua New Guinea, and Swaziland) that does not require paid maternity leave.

AGE DISCRIMINATION

The Age Discrimination in Employment Act (ADEA) of 1967 prohibits age discrimination against employees or job applicants who are at least 40 years old. An employer may not fire, refuse to hire, fail to promote, or otherwise reduce a person's employment opportunities because he is 40 or older. Under this statute, an employer may not require a worker to retire at any age. (These retirement rules do not apply to police and top-level corporate executives.)

The procedure for an age-bias claim is similar to that under Title VII—plaintiffs must first file a charge with the EEOC. If the EEOC does not take action, they can file suit themselves.

---

[26] *Circuit City Stores, Inc. v. Adams*, 532 U.S. 105, 2001 U.S. LEXIS 2459 (2001).

During tight economic times, companies often feel great pressure to lower costs. They are sometimes tempted to replace older, higher paid workers with younger, less expensive employees. Courts traditionally held that replacing expensive, older workers with cheaper, younger ones was illegal discrimination under the ADEA. In some recent cases, however, courts have held that an employer is entitled to prefer *lower paid* workers even if that preference results in the company also choosing *younger* workers. As the court put it in one case, "An action based on price differentials represents the very quintessence of a legitimate business decision."[27]

As we have seen, Title VII permits employees to prove discrimination two ways: *disparate treatment* and *disparate impact*. Although the courts had always agreed that disparate treatment was a violation of the ADEA, they were divided on the illegality of disparate impact. In the following case, the plaintiffs convinced the Supreme Court that disparate impact is a violation of the law, but they still lost their case. Recall when reading this case that the opinion was written by the court's oldest member, 84-year-old Justice Stevens.

SMITH V. CITY OF JACKSON

2005 U.S. LEXIS 2931
SUPREME COURT OF THE UNITED STATES, 2005

CASE SUMMARY

Facts: The city of Jackson, Mississippi (the City), granted pay raises to everyone on its police force. One of the City's goals in granting these increases was to attract new recruits. Under this plan, officers with less than five years of service received proportionately greater raises than their more senior colleagues. Senior officers tended to be older. Some of these older officers filed suit under the ADEA claiming a disparate impact: that they were adversely affected by the plan because of their age. The District Court granted summary judgment to the City. The Court of Appeals affirmed.

Issues: *Is disparate impact a violation of the ADEA? Were these police officers adversely affected because of their age?*

Decision: Decision affirmed. Disparate impact is generally a violation of the ADEA. In this case, however, the City did not violate the ADEA because the officers were not adversely affected as a result of their age.

Reasoning: Title VII prohibits discrimination based on "race, color, religion, sex, or national origin," whereas the ADEA prohibits discrimination based on age. Unlike Title

VII, however, the ADEA has an additional provision protecting any action that is based on "reasonable factors other than age." (This clause is referred to as the RFOA provision.)

Because the ADEA and Title VII have similar language and were enacted at about the same time, it is reasonable to presume that Congress intended both statutes to mean the same thing. Therefore, because disparate impact is a violation of Title VII, it must also be a violation of the ADEA. Furthermore, both the Department of Labor, which initially drafted the ADEA, and the EEOC, which is charged with enforcing the statute, have consistently held that disparate impact also applies under the ADEA.

However, disparate-impact liability is narrower under the ADEA than under Title VII. This limitation is reasonable because age, unlike, say, race sometimes does affect a person's ability to perform a job. Therefore, some job criteria may be reasonable even though they have an adverse impact on older workers as a group.

Moreover, intentional discrimination on the basis of age has not occurred with the same frequency as the types of discrimination prohibited by Title VII. The RFOA provision reflects this historical difference.

---

[27] *Marks v. Loral Corp.*, 57 Cal. App. 4th 30, 1997 Cal. App. LEXIS 611 (Cal. Ct. App. 1997).

To win a case under the ADEA, an employee must do more than simply allege that there is a disparate impact on older workers or point to a general policy that causes this impact. The employee must identify the *specific* employment practices that cause any differences in outcome. Otherwise, employers could be liable for many innocent actions that may result in statistical imbalances.

In this case, the police officers have done little more than point out that the City's pay plan is more generous to younger workers than to older ones. They have not specified any test, requirement, or practice within the plan that has an adverse impact on older workers. Indeed, they could not do

so because the City's plan was based on reasonable factors other than age.

The plaintiffs proved two facts. First, almost two-thirds of the officers under 40 received raises of more than 10 percent, while fewer than half of those over 40 did. Second, the average percentage increase for officers with less than 5 years of experience was higher than for more senior officers. The City's goal was reasonable: It needed to raise the salaries of junior officers to make them competitive with comparable jobs in the market. The City acted reasonably to achieve this goal. There may have been other ways for the City to achieve its goals, but the one it selected was not unreasonable.

AMERICANS WITH DISABILITIES ACT

Passed in 1990, the Americans with Disabilities Act (ADA) prohibits employers from discriminating on the basis of disability. As with Title VII, a plaintiff under the ADA must first file a charge with the EEOC. If the EEOC decides not to file suit, the individual may do so himself.

A **disabled person** is someone with a physical or mental impairment that substantially limits a major life activity, or someone who is regarded as having such an impairment. Unhappy with Supreme Court cases limiting the rights of disabled plaintiffs, Congress recently amended the ADA to provide that the definition of major life activity includes the following tasks: caring for oneself, performing manual tasks, seeing, hearing, eating, sleeping, walking, standing, lifting, bending, speaking, breathing, learning, reading, concentrating, thinking, communicating, and working. Cell growth and digestive, bowel, bladder, neurological, brain, respiratory, circulatory, endocrine, reproductive, and immune system functions are also considered major life activities. And the definition protects *recovered* drug addicts or alcoholics but does not include sexual disorders, pyromania, exhibitionism, or compulsive gambling.

Suppose an employee has a disabling illness, but one that can be successfully treated. The employee is still considered to be disabled, even if the illness is well controlled. Thus someone with diabetes is disabled, even if the illness is managed so well that it does not interfere with major life activities. There is one important exception—someone whose vision is normal when wearing glasses or contact lenses is not disabled for purposes of the ADA.

An employer may not disqualify an employee or job applicant because of disability as long as she can, with *reasonable accommodation*, perform the *essential functions* of the job. An accommodation is not reasonable if it would create *undue hardship* for the employer. In one case, a court held that a welder who could perform 88 percent of a job was doing the essential functions. Reasonable accommodation includes buying necessary equipment, providing readers or interpreters, or permitting a part-time schedule. In determining undue hardship, *relative* cost, not *absolute* cost, is the issue. Even an expensive accommodation—such as hiring a full-time reader—is not considered an undue hardship unless it imposes a significant burden on the overall finances of the company.

Disabled person
Someone with a physical or mental impairment that substantially limits a major life activity, or someone who is regarded as having such an impairment.

An employer may not ask about disabilities before making a job offer. The interviewer may ask only whether an applicant can perform the work. Nor can an employer require applicants to take a medical exam unless the exam is (1) job-related and (2) required of all applicants for similar jobs. However, drug testing is permitted.

After a job offer has been made, an employer may require a medical test, but it must be related to the *essential functions* of the job. For example, an employer could not test the cholesterol of someone applying for an accounting job because high cholesterol is no impediment to good accounting.

An employer may not discriminate against someone because of his *relationship* with a disabled person. For example, an employer cannot refuse to hire an applicant because he has a disabled child or a spouse with cancer.

In 1997, the EEOC issued rules on the treatment of mental disabilities. These rules were based on an assumption of parity—that physical and mental disabilities should be treated the same. The difficulty is that physical ailments such as diabetes and deafness may be easy to diagnose, but what does a supervisor do when an employee is chronically late, rude, or impulsive? Does this mean that the worker is mentally disabled or just a lazy, irresponsible jerk? Among other accommodations, the EEOC rules indicated that employers should be willing to put up barriers to isolate people who have difficulty concentrating, provide detailed day-to-day feedback to those who need greater structure in performing their jobs, or allow workers on antidepressants to come to work later if they are groggy in the morning.

While lauding the ADA's objectives, many managers have been apprehensive about its impact on the workplace. Most acknowledge, however, that society is better off if every member has the opportunity to work. And as advocates for the disabled point out, we are all, at best, only temporarily able-bodied. Even with the ADA, only 29 percent of the disabled population who are of working age are actually employed, whereas 79 percent of able-bodied persons have jobs.

Every applicant feels slightly apprehensive before a job interview, but now the interviewer may be even more nervous—fearing that every question is a potential land mine of liability. Most interviewers (and students who have read this chapter) would know better than Delta Airlines interviewers who allegedly asked applicants about their sexual preference, birth control methods, and abortion history. The following list provides guidelines for interviewers.

Don't Even Consider Asking	Go Ahead and Ask
Can you perform this function with or without reasonable accommodation?	Would you need reasonable accommodation in this job?
How many days were you sick last year?	How many days were you absent from work last year?
What medications are you currently taking?	Are you currently using drugs illegally?
Where were you born? Are you a United States citizen?	Are you authorized to work in the United States?
How old are you?	What work experience have you had?
How tall are you? How much do you weigh?	Could you carry a 100-pound weight, as required by this job?
When did you graduate from college?	Where did you go to college?

Don't Even Consider Asking	Go Ahead and Ask
How did you learn this language?	What languages do you speak and write fluently?
Have you ever been arrested?	Have you ever been convicted of a crime that would affect the performance of this job?
Do you plan to have children? How old are your children? What method of birth control do you use?	Can you work weekends? Travel extensively? Would you be willing to relocate?
What is your corrected vision?	Do you have 20/20 corrected vision?
Are you a man or a woman? Are you single or married? What does your spouse do? What will happen if your spouse is transferred? What clubs, societies, or lodges do you belong to?	Leave well enough alone!

The most common gaffe on the part of interviewers? Asking women about their child-care arrangements. That question assumes the woman is responsible for child-care.

EXAM *Strategy*

Question: Pippa became pregnant the week she started work as an administrator at Awesome University. Her supervisor was so annoyed at her that he would not consider her for promotion to another job within the university. Under the university's maternity leave policy, Pippa was not entitled to any time off from work because she had not been an employee for at least a year by the time her baby was born. When she quit her job, the university cancelled her health insurance coverage. Has the university violated the law?

Strategy: First: Is Pippa protected by any statutes? The possibilities are: the FMLA, COBRA, and the Pregnancy Discrimination Act.

Second: How do these statutes apply? Under the Pregnancy Discrimination Act, an employer cannot deny a promotion to a woman because she is pregnant. Also, if employees are allowed time off for illness, they must also be allowed time off for pregnancy. Thus, if men who have heart attacks are permitted paid time off from work, women must also be paid while they recuperate from delivery.

Third: The FMLA guarantees at least 12 weeks of unpaid leave each year for childbirth but only for workers who have been employed for at least one year. Therefore, the university's maternity leave policy is legal. Finally, under COBRA, Pippa has the right to continue her health insurance for 18 months (provided she pays for it).

Result: The university has violated two statutes: the Pregnancy Discrimination Act and COBRA.

CHAPTER CONCLUSION

Although managers sometimes feel overwhelmed by the long list of laws that protect workers, the United States guarantees its workers fewer rights than virtually any other industrialized nation. For instance, Japan, Great Britain, France, Germany, and Canada all require employers to show just cause before terminating workers. Although American employers are no longer insulated from minimum standards of fairness, reasonable behavior, and compliance with important policies, they still have great freedom to manage their employees.

EXAM REVIEW

1. **TRADITIONAL COMMON LAW RULE** The traditional common law rule of employment provided that an employee at will could be fired for a good reason, a bad reason, or no reason at all. (p. 694)

2. **NATIONAL LABOR RELATIONS ACT** The National Labor Relations Act prohibits employers from penalizing workers for union activity. (p. 695)

3. **FAMILY AND MEDICAL LEAVE ACT** The Family and Medical Leave Act guarantees workers up to 12 weeks of unpaid leave each year for childbirth, adoption, or medical emergencies for themselves or a family member. (p. 695)

4. **WRONGFUL DISCHARGE** An employer who fires a worker for a bad reason is liable under a theory of wrongful discharge. (pp. 695–696)

5. **PUBLIC POLICY** Generally, an employee may not be fired for refusing to break the law, exercising a legal right, or performing a legal duty. (pp. 696–697)

EXAM Strategy

Question: When Theodore Staats went to his company's "Council of Honor Convention," he was accompanied by a woman who was not his wife, although he told everyone she was. The company fired him. Staats alleged that his termination violated public policy because it infringed upon his freedom of association. He also alleged that he had been fired because he was too successful—his commissions were so high, he outearned even the highest paid officer of the company. Has Staat's employer violated public policy?

Strategy: Is Staats protected by a statute? No. Is he being asked to break the law? No. Is he trying to perform a legal duty? No. Is he being denied a legal right? (See the "Result" at the end of this section.)

6. **PROMISES MADE DURING THE HIRING PROCESS** Promises made during the hiring process may be enforceable, even if not approved by the company's top executives. (p. 698)

EXAM Strategy

Question: When Phil McConkey interviewed for a job as an insurance agent with Alexander & Alexander, the company did not tell him that it was engaged in secret negotiations to merge with Aon. When the merger went through soon thereafter, Aon fired McConkey. Was Alexander liable for not telling McConkey about the possible merger?

Strategy: Was McConkey protected by a statute? No. Did the company make any promises to him during the hiring process? (See the "Result" at the end of this section.)

7. **HANDBOOKS** An employee handbook may create a contract. (p. 698)

8. **DEFAMATION** Employers may be liable for defamation if they give false and unfavorable references. (p. 699)

9. **WHISTLEBLOWERS** Whistleblowers receive some protection under both federal and state laws. (p. 701)

10. **OSHA** The goal of the Occupational Safety and Health Act is to ensure safe conditions in the workplace. (p. 703)

11. **EMPLOYEE PRIVACY** An employer may not violate a worker's reasonable expectation of privacy. However, unless a state has passed a statute to the contrary, employers may monitor many types of off-duty conduct (even legal activities such as smoking). Most states permit private employers to administer alcohol and drug tests. But employers may not require lie detector tests, except as part of an investigation into a crime. (p. 704)

12. **WORKERS' COMPENSATION** Workers' compensation statutes ensure that employees receive payment for injuries incurred at work. (p. 705)

13. **SOCIAL SECURITY** The Social Security system pays benefits to workers who are retired, disabled, or temporarily unemployed and to the spouses and children of disabled or deceased workers. (p. 705)

14. **ERISA** The Employee Retirement Income Security Act regulates private pension plans. (p. 706)

15. **EQUAL PAY ACT** Under the Equal Pay Act, an employee may not be paid at a lesser rate than employees of the opposite sex for equal work. (p. 706)

16. **TITLE VII** Title VII of the Civil Rights Act of 1964 prohibits employers from discriminating on the basis of race, color, religion, sex, or national origin. (p. 707)

EXAM Strategy

Question: The Duke Power Co. refused to transfer any employees at its generating plant to better jobs unless they had a high school diploma or could pass an intelligence test. The company was willing to pay two-thirds of the tuition for an employee's high school training. Neither a high school education nor the intelligence test was significantly related to successful job performance. Both requirements disqualified African Americans at a substantially higher rate than white applicants. Is the company in violation of Title VII?

Strategy: Was there evidence that blacks and whites were being treated differently? No, the same rules applied to both. But did the rules have a disparate impact? Yes, many more whites could pass the standard. Is race a protected category under Title VII? Yes. Were the standards essential for these jobs? Would other, less discriminatory rules have achieved the same result? (See the "Result" at the end of this section.)

17. **BONA FIDE OCCUPATIONAL QUALIFICATION** An employer is permitted to establish discriminatory job requirements if they are *essential* to the position in question. (p. 710)

18. **PREGNANCY DISCRIMINATION ACT OF 1978** Under the Pregnancy Discrimination Act, an employer may not fire, refuse to hire, or fail to promote a woman because she is pregnant. An employer must also treat pregnancy as any other temporary disability. (p. 713)

19. **AGE DISCRIMINATION IN EMPLOYMENT ACT** The Age Discrimination in Employment Act prohibits age discrimination against employees or job applicants who are age 40 or older. (p. 713)

20. **AMERICANS WITH DISABILITIES ACT** The ADA prohibits employers from discriminating on the basis of disability. (p. 715)

EXAM *Strategy*

Question: When Thomas Lussier filled out a Postal Service employment application, he did not admit that he had twice pleaded guilty to charges of disorderly conduct. Lussier suffered from Post Traumatic Stress Disorder (PTSD) acquired during military service in Vietnam. Because of this disorder, he sometimes had panic attacks that required him to leave meetings. He was also a recovered alcoholic and drug user. During his stint with the Postal Service, he had some personality conflicts with other employees. Once another employee hit him. He also had one episode of "erratic emotional behavior and verbal outburst." In the meantime, a postal employee in Ridgewood, New Jersey, killed four colleagues. The Postmaster General encouraged all supervisors to identify workers who had dangerous propensities. Lussier's boss discovered that he had lied on his employment application about the disorderly conduct charges and fired him. Is the Postal Service in violation of the law?

Strategy: Was Lussier disabled under the ADA? He had a mental impairment (PTSD) that substantially limited a major life activity. Could Lussier, with reasonable accommodation, perform his job? Yes. Was his firing illegal? (See the "Result" at the end of this section.)

5. Result: The court held that freedom of association is an important social right and should be protected. However, being fired for bringing a lover to an employer's convention is not a threat to public policy. Nor is discharge for being too successful.

6. Result: The court held that when Alexander hired him, it was making an implied promise that he would not be fired immediately. The company was liable for not having revealed the merger negotiations.

16. Result: The Supreme Court held that Duke Power Co. was in violation of Title VII because the job requirements did not measure performance at work. The Court stated that, "What Congress has commanded is that any tests used must measure the person for the job and not the person in the abstract."

20. Result: The court held that the Postal Service was in violation of the law because Lussier had been dismissed solely as a result of his disability.

ADDITIONAL QUESTIONS

1. Peter Oiler was a truck driver at the grocery chain Winn-Dixie. He was also a transvestite—he liked to dress as a woman. When his supervisor at Winn-Dixie found out about his cross-dressing, Oiler was fired. Is Winn-Dixie in violation of the law?

2. Reginald Delaney managed a Taco Time restaurant in Portland, Oregon. Some of his customers told Mr. Ledbetter, the district manager, that they would not be eating there so often because there were too many black employees. Ledbetter told Delaney to fire Ms. White, who was black. Delaney did as he was told. Ledbetter's report on the incident said: "My notes show that Delaney told me that White asked him to sleep with her and that when he would not that she started causing dissension within the

crew. She asked him to come over to her house and that he declined." Delaney refused to sign the report because it was untrue, so Ledbetter fired him. What claim might Delaney make against his former employer?

3. When Walton Weiner interviewed for a job with McGraw-Hill, Inc., he was assured that the company would not terminate an employee without "just cause." Weiner also signed a contract specifying that his employment would be subject to the provisions of McGraw-Hill's handbook. The handbook said, "[The] company will resort to dismissal for just and sufficient cause only, and only after all practical steps toward rehabilitation or salvage of the employee have been taken and failed. However, if the welfare of the company indicates that dismissal is necessary, then that decision is arrived at and is carried out forthrightly." After eight years, Weiner was fired suddenly for "lack of application." Does Weiner have a valid claim against McGraw-Hill?

4. **ETHICS** John Mundorf hired three women to work for Gus Construction Co. as traffic controllers at road construction sites in Iowa. Male members of the construction crew incessantly referred to the women as "f—king flag girls." They repeatedly asked the women if they "wanted to f—k" or engage in oral sex. One crew member held a woman up to the cab window so other men could touch her. Another male employee exposed himself to the women. Male employees also urinated in a woman's water bottle and the gas tank of her car. Mundorf, the supervisor, was present during some of these incidents. He talked to crew members about their conduct, but the abuse continued until the women quit. What claim might the women make against their co-workers? Is Gus Construction Co. liable for the acts of its employees? What procedure must the women follow to pursue their claim? Why do you think these men behaved this way? Why did they want to humiliate their co-workers? What should the supervisor have done when he observed these incidents? What would you have done if you were the supervisor? A fellow employee?

5. **CPA QUESTION** An unemployed CPA generally would receive unemployment compensation benefits if the CPA:

   a. Was fired as a result of the employer's business reversals

   b. Refused to accept a job as an accountant while receiving extended benefits

   c. Was fired for embezzling from a client

   d. Left work voluntarily without good cause

6. Debra Agis worked in a Ground Round restaurant. The manager informed the waitresses that "there was some stealing going on." Until he found out who was doing it, he intended to fire all the waitresses in alphabetical order, starting with the letter "A." Dionne then fired Agis. Does she have a valid claim against her employer?

7. The Lillie Rubin boutique in Phoenix would not permit Dick Kovacic to apply for a job as a salesperson. It only hired women to work in sales because fittings and alterations took place in the dressing room or immediately outside. The customers were buying expensive clothes and demanded a male-free dressing area. Has the Lillie Rubin store violated Title VII? What would its defense be?

8. **YOU BE THE JUDGE** WRITING PROBLEM Nationwide Insurance Co. circulated a memorandum asking all employees to lobby in favor of a bill that had been introduced in the Pennsylvania House of Representatives. By limiting the damages that an injured

motorist could recover from a person who caused an accident, this bill would have saved Nationwide significant money. Not only did John Novosel refuse to lobby, but he privately criticized the bill for harming consumers. Nationwide was definitely not on his side—it fired him. Novosel filed suit, alleging that his discharge had violated public policy by infringing his right to free speech. Did Nationwide violate public policy by firing Novosel? **Argument for Novosel:** The United States Constitution and the Pennsylvania Constitution both guarantee the right to free speech. Nationwide has violated an important public policy by firing Novosel for expressing his opinions. **Argument for Nationwide:** For all the high-flown talk about the Constitution, what we have here is an employee who refused to carry out company policy. If the employee prevails in this case, where will it all end? What if an employee for a tobacco company refuses to market cigarettes because he does not approve of smoking? How can businesses operate without loyalty from their employees?

9. During a job interview with Venetia, Jack reveals that he and his wife are expecting twins. Venetia asks him if he is planning to take a leave once the babies are born. When Jack admits that he would like to take a month off work, he can see her face fall. She ultimately decides not to hire him for that reason. Is Venetia violating the law?

10. ***ROLE REVERSAL*** Prepare a short-answer question in which an employee alleges that his discharge violated public policy, but you think a court would not agree.

INTERNET RESEARCH PROBLEM

Google "The Americans with Disabilities Act: A Primer for Small Business." Here, the EEOC offers advice to small employers on how to comply with some aspects of the Americans with Disabilities Act. Employers sometimes complain that the EEOC unfairly favors workers. What do you think of these EEOC guidelines? Are they fair and even-handed? As an employee, would you like your company to follow these guidelines? If you were in a supervisory role, would your view of these guidelines be different?

You can find further practice problems at www.cengagebrain.com. See the preface of this book for website access details.

29

STARTING A BUSINESS: LLCs AND OTHER OPTIONS

Poor Jeffrey Horning. If only he had understood business law. Horning owned a thriving construction company—but it was so successful his workload was crushing. To lighten his burden, he brought in two partners to take on more of the day-to-day responsibilities. It seemed a good idea at the time.

The business originally operated as a corporation—Horning Construction Company, Inc. He transferred it to Horning Construction, LLC and then gave one-third ownership each to two trusted employees, Klimowski and Holdsworth. But Horning did not pay enough attention to the legal formalities—the new LLC had no operating agreement.

Jeffrey Horning was stuck in purgatory, with two business partners he loathed and no way out.

Nothing worked out as he had planned. The two men did not take on extra work. Horning's relationship with them went from bad to worse, with the parties bickering over every petty detail and each man trying to sabotage the others. It got to the point that Klimowski sent Horning a letter full of curses. At his wit's end, Horning proposed that the LLC buy out his share of the business. Klimowski and Holdsworth refused. Really frustrated, Horning asked a court to dissolve the business on the grounds that Klimowski despised him, Holdsworth resented him, and neither of them trusted him. In his view, it was their goal "to make my remaining time with Horning, LLC so unbearable that I will relent and give them for a pittance the remainder of the company for which they have paid nothing to date."

Although the court was sympathetic, it refused to help. Because Horning LLC did not have an operating agreement that provided for a buyout, it had to depend upon the LLC statute, which only permitted dissolution "whenever it is not reasonably practicable to carry on the business." Unfortunately, Horning LLC was very successful, grossing over $25 million annually. Jeffrey Horning was stuck in purgatory, with two business partners he loathed and no way out.[1]

Every business, no matter how large, was at some point little more than a gleam in an entrepreneur's eye. The goal of the law is to balance the rights, obligations, and liabilities of entrepreneurs, managers, investors, and customers. Time and again in these next chapters, we will see that legal issues can have as profound an impact on the success of a company as any business decision. The law affects virtually every aspect of business. Wise (and successful) entrepreneurs know how to use the law to their advantage. Think of the grief Jeffrey Horning could have saved himself if he had understood the implications of the LLC statute.

To begin, entrepreneurs must select a form of organization. The correct choice can reduce taxes, liability, and conflict while facilitating outside investment. If entrepreneurs do not make a choice for themselves, the law will automatically select a (potentially undesirable) default option.

SOLE PROPRIETORSHIPS

Sole proprietorships are the most common form of business, so we begin there. A **sole proprietorship** is an unincorporated business owned by a single person. For example, Linda runs ExSciTe (which stands for Excellence in Science Teaching), a company that helps teachers prepare hands-on science experiments in the classroom using such basic items as vinegar, lemon juice, and red cabbage.

Sole proprietorships are easy and inexpensive to create and operate. There is no need to hire a lawyer or register with the government. The company is not even required to file a separate tax return—all profits and losses are reported on the owner's personal return. A very few states and some cities and towns require sole proprietors to obtain a business license. And states generally require sole proprietors to register their business name if it is different from their own. Linda, for example, would file a "d/b/a" or "doing business as" certificate for ExSciTe.

Sole proprietorships also have some serious disadvantages. First, the owner of the business is responsible for all of the business's debts. If ExSciTe cannot pay its suppliers or if a student is injured by an exploding cabbage, Linda is *personally* liable. She may have to sell her house and car to pay the debt. Second, the owner of a sole proprietorship has limited options for financing her business. Debt is generally her only source of working capital because she has no stock or memberships to sell. If someone else brings in capital and helps with the management of the business, then it is a partnership, not a sole proprietorship. For this reason, sole proprietorships work best for small businesses without large capital needs.

Sole proprietorship
An unincorporated business owned by one person.

---

[1] *In the Matter of Jeffrey M. Horning*, 816 N.Y.S.2d 877; 2006 N.Y. Misc. LEXIS 555.

CORPORATIONS

Corporations are the dominant form of organization for a simple reason—they have been around for a long time and, as a result, they are numerous and the law that regulates them is well developed.

The concept of a corporation is very old indeed—it began with the Greeks and spread from them through the Romans into English law. At the beginning, however, corporations were viewed with deep suspicion. What were shareholders doing that they needed limited liability? Why did they have to cower behind a corporate shield? For this reason, shareholders originally had to obtain special permission to form a corporation. In England, corporations could be created only by special charter from the monarch or, later, from Parliament. But with the advent of the Industrial Revolution, large-scale manufacturing enterprises needed huge amounts of capital from investors who were not involved in management and did not want to be personally liable for the debts of an organization that they were not managing. In 1811, New York became the first jurisdiction in the United States to permit routine incorporation.[2]

State laws regulate corporations, but federal statutes determine their tax status. Many states treat small corporations differently and even give them a different name: "close corporations." The federal tax code also provides more favorable tax treatment to some small corporations and calls them "S corporations." But the two sets of statutes are completely independent. Thus a close corporation or a regular (nonclose) corporation may or may not be an S corporation. Exhibit 29.1 illustrates the difference between state and Internal Revenue Service (IRS) regulation of corporations.

CORPORATIONS IN GENERAL

As is the case for all forms of organization, corporations have their advantages and disadvantages.

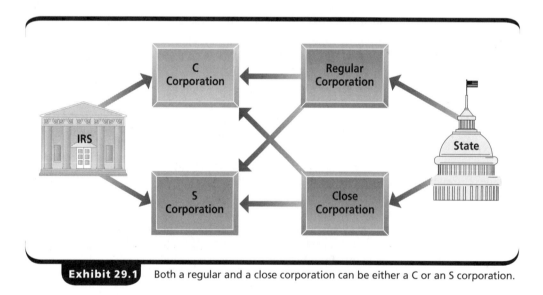

Exhibit 29.1   Both a regular and a close corporation can be either a C or an S corporation.

---

[2] An Act Relative to Incorporation for Manufacturing Purpose, 1811 N.Y. Laws, ch. 67, Section 111.

Limited Liability

If a business flops and cannot pay its bills, shareholders lose their investment in the company, but not their other assets. Likewise, if an employee is in an accident while driving a company van, the business is liable for any harm to the other driver, but its shareholders are not personally liable. Be aware, however, that limited liability does not protect against all debts. Individuals are always responsible for their *own* acts. Suppose that the careless employee who caused the accident was also a company shareholder. Both he and the company would be liable. If the company did not pay the judgment, the employee would have to, from his personal assets. A corporation protects managers and investors from personal liability for the debts of the corporation and the actions of others, but not against personal negligence (or other torts and crimes).

Transferability of Interests

Corporations provide flexibility for enterprises small (with one owner) and large (with thousands of shareholders). As we will see, partnership interests are not transferable without the permission of the other partners, whereas corporate stock can be bought and sold easily.

Duration

When a sole proprietor dies, legally so does the business. But corporations have perpetual existence: they can continue without their founders.

Logistics

Corporations require substantial expense and effort to create and operate. The cost of establishing a corporation may exceed $1,000 in legal and filing fees, not to mention the cost of the annual filings that states require. Corporations must also hold annual meetings for both shareholders and directors. Minutes of these meetings must be kept indefinitely in the company minute book.

Taxes

Because corporations are taxable entities, they must pay taxes and file returns. This is a simple sentence that requires a complex explanation. Originally, there were only three ways to do business: as a sole proprietorship, a partnership, or a corporation. The sole proprietor pays taxes on all the business's profits. A partnership is not, as we say, a taxable entity, which means it does not pay taxes itself. All income and losses are passed through to the partners and reported on their personal income tax returns. Corporations, by contrast, are taxable entities and pay income tax on their profits. Shareholders must then pay tax on dividends from the corporation. Thus a dollar is taxed only once before it ends up in a partner's bank account, but twice before it is deposited by a shareholder.

Exhibit 29.2 compares the single taxation of partnerships with the double taxation of corporations. Suppose, as shown in the exhibit, that a corporation and a partnership each receives $10,000 in additional income. The corporation pays tax at a top rate of 35 percent.[3] Thus the corporation pays $3,500 of the $10,000 in tax. The corporation pays out the remaining $6,500 as a dividend of $2,167 to each of its three shareholders. Then the shareholders are taxed at the special dividend rate of 15 percent, which means they each

---

[3] This is the federal tax rate; most states also levy a corporate tax.

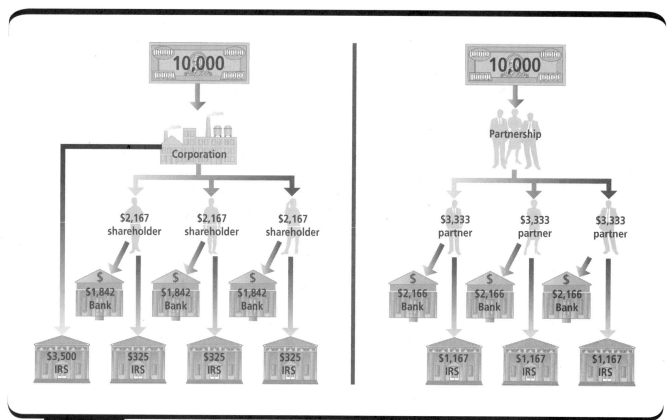

Exhibit 29.2

pay a tax of $325. They are each left with $1,842. Of the initial $10,000, almost 45 percent ($4,475) has gone to the IRS.

Compare the corporation to a partnership. The partnership itself pays no taxes, so it can pass on $3,333 to each of its partners. At a 35 percent individual rate, each partner pays an income tax of $1,167. As partners, they pocket $2,166, which is $324 more than they could keep as shareholders. Of the partnership's initial $10,000, 35 percent ($3,501) has gone to the IRS, compared with the corporation's 45 percent.

CLOSE CORPORATIONS

Close corporation

A company whose stock is not publicly traded. Also known as a closely held corporation.

Originally, the terms *close corporation* and *closely held corporation* referred simply to a company whose stock was not publicly traded (in other words, a "privately held" company). Most close corporations are small, although some privately held corporations, such as Hallmark Cards, Inc., and Mars, Inc. (maker of Mars candy bars), are huge. Beginning in New York in 1948, some states amended their corporation statutes to make special provisions for entrepreneurs. In some cases, a corporation must affirmatively elect to be treated as a close corporation; in others, any corporation can take advantage of these special provisions. Now when lawyers refer to close corporations, they usually mean not merely a privately held company, but one that has taken advantage of the close corporation provisions of its state code.

Although the provisions of close corporation statutes vary from state to state, they tend to have certain common themes:

- **Protection of Minority Shareholders.** As there is no public market for the stock of a close corporation, a minority shareholder who is being mistreated by the majority cannot simply sell his shares and depart. Therefore, close corporation statutes often provide some protection for minority shareholders. For example, the charter of a close corporation could require a unanimous vote of all shareholders to choose officers, set salaries, or pay dividends. It could grant each shareholder veto power over all important corporate decisions.

- **Transfer Restrictions.** The shareholders of a close corporation often need to work closely together in the management of the company. Therefore, statutes typically permit the corporation to require that a shareholder first offer shares to the other owners before selling them to an outsider. In that way, the remaining shareholders have some control over who their new co-owners will be.

- **Flexibility.** Close corporations can typically operate without a board of directors, a formal set of bylaws, or annual shareholder meetings.

- **Dispute Resolution.** The shareholders are allowed to agree in advance that any one of them can dissolve the corporation if some particular event occurs or, if they choose, for any reason at all. If the shareholders are in a stalemate, the problem can be solved by dissolving the corporation. Even without such an agreement, a shareholder can ask a court to dissolve a close corporation if the other owners behave "oppressively" or "unfairly."

S CORPORATIONS

Although entrepreneurs are often optimistic about the likely success of their new enterprise, in truth, the majority of new businesses lose money in their early years. Congress created S corporations (aka "S corps") to encourage entrepreneurship by offering tax breaks. The name "S corporation" comes from the provision of the Internal Revenue Code that created this form of organization.[4] **Shareholders of S corps have both the limited liability of a corporation and the tax status of a partnership.** Like a partnership, an S corp is not a taxable entity—all the company's profits and losses pass through to the shareholders, who pay tax at their individual rates. It avoids the double taxation of a regular corporation (called a "C corporation"). If, as is often the case, the startup loses money, investors can deduct these losses against their other income.

S corps do face some major restrictions:

- There can be only one class of stock (although voting rights can vary within the class).

- There can be no more than 100 shareholders.

- Shareholders must be individuals, estates, charities, pension funds, or trusts, not partnerships or corporations.

- Shareholders must be citizens or residents of the United States, not non-resident aliens.

- All shareholders must agree that the company should be an S corporation.

---

[4] 26 U.S.C. Section 1361.

Although most states follow the federal lead on S corporations, a small number treat an S corp like a regular C corporation. In these states, the companies must pay state corporate tax.

EXAM *Strategy*

Question: Consider these two entrepreneurs: Judith formed a corporation to publish a newsletter that will not generate substantial revenues. Drexel operated his construction and remodeling business as a sole proprietorship. Were these forms of organization right for these businesses?

Strategy: Prepare a list of the advantages and disadvantages of each form of organization. Sole proprietorships are best for businesses without substantial capital needs. Corporations can raise capital but are expensive to operate.

Result: Judith would be better off with a sole proprietorship—her revenues will not support the expenses of a corporation. Also, her debts are likely to be small, so she will not need the limited liability of a corporation. And no matter what her form of organization, she would be personally liable for any negligent acts she commits, so a corporation would not provide any additional protection. But for Drexel, a sole proprietorship could be disastrous because his construction company will have substantial expenses and a large number of employees. If an employee causes an injury, Drexel might be personally liable. And if his business ends up in bankruptcy, the court would liquidate his personal assets. He would be better off with a form of organization that limits his liability, such as a corporation or a limited liability company.

LIMITED LIABILITY COMPANIES

An LLC offers the limited liability of a corporation and the tax status of a partnership. Limited liability companies (LLCs) are a relatively new form of organization. Wyoming passed the first LLC statute in 1977, but most states did not follow suit until after 1991. An LLC is an extremely useful form of organization increasingly favored by entrepreneurs. It is not, however, as simple as it perhaps should be. Owing to a complex history that involves painful interaction between IRS regulations and state laws (the details of which we will spare you), the specific provisions of state laws vary greatly. An effort to remedy this confusion—the Uniform Limited Liability Company Act—has not at this point been widely accepted. Indeed, it was so heavily criticized that it was revised, but the revised statute has been adopted at this writing by only four states. Thus, we can discuss only general trends in state laws. Before forming an LLC, you should review carefully the laws in your particular state.

LIMITED LIABILITY

Members are not personally liable for the debts of the company. They risk only their investment, as if they were shareholders of a corporation. Are the members of the LLC liable in the following case? You be the judge.

YOU *be the* JUDGE

RIDGAWAY v. SILK
2004 CONN. SUPER. LEXIS 548
Superior Court of Connecticut, 2004

Facts: Norman Costello and Joseph Ruggiero were members of Silk, LLC, which owned a bar and adult entertainment nightclub in Groton, Connecticut, called Silk Stockings. Anthony Sulls went drinking there one night—and drinking heavily. Although he was obviously drunk, employees at Silk Stockings continued to serve him. Giordano and Costello were working there that night. They both greeted customers (who numbered in the hundreds), supervised employees, and performed "other PR work." When Sulls left the nightclub at 1:45 A.M. with two friends, he drove off the highway at high speed, killing himself and one of his passengers, William Ridgaway, Jr.

Ridgaway's estate sued Costello and Giordano personally. The defendants filed a motion for summary judgment seeking dismissal of the complaint.

You Be the Judge: Are Costello and Giordano personally liable to Ridgaway's estate?

Argument for Costello and Giordano: The defendants did not own Silk Stockings; they were simply members of an LLC that owned the nightclub. The whole point of an LLC is to protect members against personal liability. The assets of Silk, LLC, are at risk, but not the personal assets of Costello and Giordano.

Argument for Ridgaway's Estate: The defendants are not liable for being members of Silk, LLC; they are liable for their own misdeeds as *employees* of the LLC. They were both present at Silk Stockings on the night in question, meeting and greeting customers and supervising employees. It is possible that they might actually have served drinks to Sulls, but in any event, they did not adequately supervise and train their employees to prevent them from serving alcohol to someone who was clearly drunk. The world would be an intolerable place to live if employees were free to be as careless as they wished, knowing that they were not liable because they were members of an LLC.

TAX STATUS

As in a partnership, income flows through the company to the individual members, avoiding the double taxation of a corporation.

FORMATION

To organize an LLC, you must have a charter and you should have an operating agreement. The charter is short, containing basic information such as name and address. It must be filed with the Secretary of State in the jurisdiction in which it is being formed. An operating agreement sets out the rights and obligations of the owners, who are called "members." If an LLC does not adopt its own operating agreement, LLC statutes provide a default option. However, these standardized provisions may not be what members would choose if they thought about it. Therefore, it is often better for an LLC to prepare its own personalized operating agreement. The Horning case that began this chapter illustrates one of the many things that can go wrong when an LLC does not have an operating agreement.

On this issue, corporations have an advantage over LLCs. Corporations are so familiar that the standard documents (such as a charter, by-laws, and shareholder agreement) are well established and widely available. Lawyers can form a corporation easily and the Internet offers a host of free forms. This is not the case with LLCs. As yet, the law is so unsettled that standard forms may be dangerous, while customized forms can be expensive.

Furthermore, the law for LLCs is not well developed and varies from state to state. Unless an LLC has an operating agreement that supplements state law, members may find their rights more limited than those of corporate shareholders. For example, it is not clear if managers have a legal obligation to act in the best interest of members. Can the operating agreement simply eliminate that obligation (if it exists in the first place)? Members of an LLC reside in foggy legal territory, as the following case illustrates.

WYOMING.COM, LLC v. LIEBERMAN

2005 WY 42; 109 P.3d 883; 2005 WYO. LEXIS 48
SUPREME COURT OF WYOMING, 2005

CASE SUMMARY

Facts: Lieberman was a member of an LLC called Wyoming. com. After he withdrew, he and the other members disagreed about what his membership was worth. Wyoming.com filed a lawsuit asking the court to determine the financial rights and obligations of the parties, if any, upon the withdrawal of a member.

The Supreme Court of Wyoming reached a decision that may have sounded logical but left Lieberman in a sad twilight zone—neither in nor out of the LLC. The court ruled that Lieberman still owned part of the business despite his withdrawal as a member. So far, so good. But neither the LLC statute nor the company's operating agreement required the LLC to pay a member the value of his share. Therefore, neither party had any further rights or obligations. In other words, Lieberman was still an owner, but he was not entitled to any payment.

Not quite understanding the implications of this ruling, Lieberman filed a motion seeking financial information about the company. The original trial court denied the request on the theory that, because Lieberman had no right to a payout, the company had no obligation to give him financial data.

Issue: *Does Lieberman have a right to any financial data about Wyoming.com?*

Decision: Wyoming.com has no obligation to provide Lieberman with financial data about the company.

Reasoning: The court in the prior Lieberman case ruled that Lieberman was not entitled to any payment from Wyoming. com. Thus, there is no point in requiring the company to give him financial information. He still owns a share of the company, but he has no further rights.

One of the judges on the Court wrote a concurring opinion arguing that members of an LLC should have the same rights and responsibilites as the owners of other business organizations. But the other four judges on the court did not agree, so this part of the opinion is not binding.

FLEXIBILITY

Unlike S corporations, LLCs can have members that are corporations, partnerships, or nonresident aliens. LLCs can also have different classes of stock. Unlike corporations, LLCs are not required to hold annual meetings or maintain a minute book.

TRANSFERABILITY OF INTERESTS

Unless the operating agreement provides otherwise, the members of the LLC must obtain the unanimous permission of the remaining members before transferring their ownership rights. This is yet another reason to have an operating agreement.

DURATION

It used to be that LLCs automatically dissolved upon the withdrawal of a member (owing to, for example, death, resignation, or bankruptcy). The current trend in state laws, however, is to permit an LLC to continue in operation even after a member withdraws.

GOING PUBLIC

Once an LLC goes public, it loses its favorable tax status and is taxed as a corporation, not a partnership.[5] Thus, there is no advantage to using the LLC form of organization for a publicly traded company. And there are some disadvantages: unlike corporations, publicly traded LLCs do not enjoy a well-established set of statutory and case law that is relatively consistent across the many states. For this reason, privately held companies that begin as LLCs usually change to corporations when they go public.

It is worth noting, too, that because of securities laws, it is important for an LLC to have an operating agreement that permits managers the right, without the consent of members, to convert the LLC into a corporation at the time of a public offering.[6]

CHANGING FORMS

Some companies that are now corporations might prefer to be LLCs. However, the IRS would consider this change to be a sale of the corporate assets and would levy a tax on the value of these assets. For this reason, few corporations have made the change. However, switching from a partnership to an LLC or from an LLC to a corporation is not considered a sale and does not have the same adverse tax impact.

PIERCING THE LLC VEIL

We end with a final cautionary note. It has long been the case that, if corporate shareholders do not comply with the technicalities of the law, they may be held personally liable for the debts of the corporation (an issue that will be discussed in more depth in Chapter 30. As the following case illustrates, members of an LLC can also be held liable under the same circumstances.

BLD PRODUCTS, LTC. V. TECHNICAL PLASTICS OF OREGON, LLC

2006 U.S. DIST. LEXIS 89874
UNITED STATES DISTRICT COURT FOR THE DISTRICT OF OREGON, 2006

CASE SUMMARY

Facts: Mark Hardie was the sole member of Technical Plastics of Oregon, LLC (TPO). The company operated out of an office in Hardie's home. He regularly used TPO's accounts to pay such expenses as landscaping and house-cleaning. TPO also paid some of Hardie's personal credit card bills, loan payments on his Ford truck, the cost of constructing a deck on his house, his stepson's college bills, and the cost of family vacations to Disneyland, as well as

---

[5] 26 U.S.C. Section 7704.

[6] In this way, under Rule 144 (which is discussed in Chapter 31, on securities regulation), members can include the time during which they owned interests in the LLC when calculating their holding period for stock.

miscellaneous bills from GI Joe's, Wrestler's World, K-Mart, and Mattress World. At the same time, Hardie deposited cash advances from his personal credit cards into the TPO checking account. Hardie did not take a salary from TPO. When TPO filed for bankruptcy, it owed BLD Products approximately $120,000 for goods that it had purchased.

In some cases, a court will "pierce the veil" of a corporation and hold its shareholders personally liable for the debts of the business. BLD argued that the same doctrine should apply to LLCs and the court should hold Hardie personally liable for TPO's debts.

BLD filed for summary judgment.

Issues: *Does the doctrine of "piercing the veil" apply to LLCs? Is Hardie personally liable for TPO's debts?*

Decision: Yes, an LLC's veil can be pierced. Hardie is personally liable for TPO's debts.

Reasoning: An LLC's veil can be pierced if the following three tests are met:

1. The member (that is, Hardie) controlled the LLC;

2. The member engaged in improper conduct; and

3. As a result of that improper conduct, the plaintiff was unable to collect on a debt against the insolvent LLC.

Hardie, as the sole member and manager of TPO, clearly controlled the company. In addition, he engaged in improper conduct when he paid his personal expenses from the TPO business account. These amounts were more than occasional dips into petty cash—they indicated a disregard of TPO's separate LLC identity. Moreover, he did not keep records of these personal payments.

It is not clear whether Hardie's improper conduct prevented BLD from collecting its entire $120,000 debt. A jury will have to determine the amount that Hardie owes BLD.

CHOICES: LLC V. CORPORATION

When starting a business, which form makes the most sense—LLC or corporation? The tax status of an LLC is a major advantage over a corporation. Although an S corporation has the same tax status as an LLC, it also has all the annoying rules about classes of stock and number of shareholders. Once an LLC is established, it does not have as many housekeeping rules as corporations—it does not, for example, have to make annual filings or hold annual meetings. However, the LLC is not right for everyone. If done properly, an LLC is more expensive to set up than a corporation because it needs to have a thoughtfully crafted operating agreement. Also, venture capitalists almost always refuse to invest in LLCs, preferring C corporations instead. There are two reasons for this preference: (1) arcane tax issues and (2) C corporations are easier to merge, sell, or take public.

EXAM Strategy

Question: Hortense and Gus are each starting a business. Hortense's business is an Internet startup. Gus will be opening a yarn store. Hortense needs millions of dollars in venture capital and expects to go public soon. Gus has borrowed $10,000 from his girlfriend, which he hopes to pay back soon. Should either of these businesses organize as an LLC?

Strategy: Sole proprietorships may be best for businesses without substantial capital needs and without significant liability issues. Corporations are best for businesses that will need substantial outside capital and expect to go public shortly.

Result: An LLC is not the best choice for either of these businesses. Venture capitalists will insist that Hortense's business be a corporation, especially if it is going public soon. A yarn store has few liability issues and Gus does not expect to have any outside investors. Hence a sole proprietorship would be more appropriate for Gus's business.

GENERAL PARTNERSHIPS

A **partnership** is an unincorporated association of two or more co-owners who carry on a business for profit.[7] Each co-owner is called a *general partner*.

Traditionally, partnerships were regulated by common law, but a lack of consistency among the states became troublesome as interstate commerce grew. To solve this problem, the National Conference of Commissioners on Uniform State Laws proposed the Uniform Partnership Act (UPA) in 1914. Since then there have been several revisions, the most recent in 1997. A majority of states have now passed the latest revision, so we include them in our discussion of partnership law.

Partnership
An unincorporated association of two or more co-owners who operate a business for profit.

TAXES
As we have seen above, partnerships are not a taxable entity.

LIABILITY
Each partner is personally liable for the debts of the enterprise whether or not she caused them. Thus a partner is liable for any injury that another partner or an employee causes while on partnership business as well as for any contract signed on behalf of the partnership. This form of organization can be particularly risky if the group of owners is large and the partners do not know each other.

Daniel Matter knows firsthand about the risks of a partnership. A former partner in the accounting firm Pannell Kerr Foster, he thought he had heard the last of the firm when he resigned his partnership. He was wrong. Seven years later, he and 260 other former partners of the California firm were served with a 78-page lawsuit seeking $24 million in damages. The lawsuit alleged that Pannell Kerr had been negligent in preparing financial reports for a bankrupt Tennessee savings and loan. Although Daniel Matter had never worked for that particular client, he was potentially liable because he had been a partner when the audit was done. At age 53, Matter feared losing everything he owned.

> At age 53, Matter feared losing everything he owned.

FORMATION
Given this disadvantage, why does anyone do business as a partnership? Like sole proprietorships, partnerships are easy to form. Although, practically speaking, a partnership should have a written agreement, the UPA does not require anything in the way of forms or filings or agreements. If people act like partners—by sharing management and profits—the law will treat them as such, and if they do not act like partners, then nothing they say or write will make them a partnership.

For example, Kevin and Brenda formed an electrical contracting business. The business did so well that Kevin's first wife, Cynthia, asked the court to increase his child support payments. Kevin argued that, because he and Brenda were partners, he was entitled to only half of the business's profits. Therefore, his child support should not be increased.

---

[7] Uniform Partnership Act Section 6(1).

Cynthia claimed that Kevin and Brenda were not partners because Kevin had reported all the income from the business on his personal tax return while Brenda had reported none. Kevin had even put "sole proprietorship" in bold letters on the top of his return. No written partnership agreement existed. Kevin and Brenda never informed their accountant that they were a partnership. When Kevin answered interrogatories for Cynthia's lawsuit, he stated that he was sole owner and that Brenda worked for him. Nonetheless, the court held that Brenda and Kevin were partners because Brenda helped manage the business and shared in its profits.[8]

Partnership by Estoppel

Brenda and Kevin wanted to be partners so that they could share the *profits* of their business. In *partnership by estoppel*, non-partners are treated as if they were actually partners and are forced to share *liability*. **Partnership by estoppel applies if:**

- Participants tell other people that they are partners (even though they are not), or they allow other people to say, without contradiction, that they are partners;

- A third party relies on this assertion; and

- The third party suffers harm.

Dr. William Martin was held liable under a theory of partnership by estoppel because he told a patient that he and Dr. John Maceluch were partners (although they were not); the patient relied on this statement and made appointments to see Dr. Maceluch; and she was harmed by Dr. Maceluch's malpractice. He refused to come to the hospital when she was in labor and, as a result, her child was born with brain damage. Although Dr. Martin was out of the country at the time, he was as liable as if he had committed the malpractice himself.[9]

TRANSFER OF OWNERSHIP

Financing a partnership may be difficult because the firm cannot sell shares as a corporation does. The capital needs of the partnership must be provided by contributions from partners or by borrowing. Likewise, a partner only has the right to transfer the value of her partnership interest, not the interest itself. She cannot, for example, transfer the right to participate in firm management. Take the case of Evan and his mother. She is a partner in the immensely profitable McBain Consulting firm. She dies, leaving him an orphan with no siblings. He overcomes his grief as best he can and goes to her office on the next Monday to take over her job and her partnership. Imagine his surprise when her partners tell him that, as her sole heir, he can inherit the value of her partnership, but not the partnership itself. He is out on the sidewalk within the hour. The partners have promised him a check in the mail.

MANAGEMENT

The management of a partnership can be a significant challenge.

---

[8] *In Re Marriage of Cynthia Hassiepen*, 269 Ill. App. 3d 559, 646 N.E.2d 1348, 1995 Ill. App. LEXIS 101.
[9] *Haught v. Maceluch*, 681 F.2d 290, 1982 U.S. App. LEXIS 17123 (5th Cir. 1982).

Management Rights

Unless the partnership agrees otherwise, partners share both profits and losses equally, and each partner has an equal right to manage the business.[10] In a large partnership, with hundreds of partners, too many cooks can definitely spoil the firm's profitability. That is why large partnerships are almost always run by one or a few partners who are designated as **managing partners** or **members of the executive committee.** Some firms are run almost dictatorially by the partner who brings in the most business (called a "rainmaker"). Nonetheless, even in relatively autocratic firms, the atmosphere tends to be less hierarchical than in a corporation, where employees are accustomed to the concept of having a boss. Whatever the reality, partners by and large like to think of themselves as being the equal of every other partner.

Management Duties

Partners have a *fiduciary duty* to the partnership. This duty means that:

- *Partners are liable to the partnership for gross negligence or intentional misconduct.*

- *Partners cannot compete with the partnership.* Each partner must turn over to the partnership all earnings from any activity that is related to the partnership's business. Thus, law firms would typically expect a partner to turn over any fees he earned as a director of a company, but he could keep royalties from his novel on scuba diving.

- *A partner may not take an opportunity away from the partnership unless the other partners consent.* If the partnership wants to buy a private plane and a partner hears of one for sale, she must give the partnership an opportunity to buy it before she purchases it herself.

- *If a partner engages in a conflict of interest, he must turn over to the partnership any profits he earned from that activity.* In the following case, one partner bought partnership property secretly. Is that a conflict of interest?

MARSH V. GENTRY

642 S.W.2d 574, 1982 Ky. LEXIS 315
SUPREME COURT OF KENTUCKY, 1982

CASE SUMMARY

Facts: Tom Gentry and John Marsh were partners in a business that bought and sold racehorses. The partnership paid $155,000 for Champagne Woman, who subsequently had a foal named Excitable Lady. The partners decided to sell Champagne Woman at the annual Keeneland auction, the world's premier thoroughbred horse auction. On the day of the auction, Gentry decided to bid on the horse personally, without telling Marsh. Gentry bought Champagne Woman for $135,000. Later, he told Marsh that someone from California had approached him about buying Excitable Lady. Marsh agreed to the sale. Although he repeatedly asked Gentry the name of the purchaser, Gentry refused to tell him. Not until 11 months later, when Excitable Lady won a race at Churchill Downs, did Marsh learn that Gentry had been the purchaser. Marsh became the Excitable Man.

Issue: *Did Gentry violate his fiduciary duty when he bought partnership property without telling his partner?*

---

[10] Partnerships have the right to change internal management rules, but they cannot alter the rules governing their relationship with outsiders (such as the rules on liability).

Decision: Gentry violated his fiduciary duty to his partner.

Reasoning: Kentucky partnership law required Gentry to make full disclosure to his partner before buying partnership property. Although Gentry did not know that he would be the winning bidder at auction, he had an obligation to tell Marsh that he intended to bid.

As for the private sale, although Marsh had agreed to the price, he still had a right to know that his partner was the offeror. He would certainly have looked more carefully at an offer from a partner than from an unknown third party. Indeed, Marsh said later that he would not have agreed to either sale if he had known Gentry was the purchaser.

Gentry claims that partners frequently place secret bids at auctions of partnership property. Whether or not this is true, such behavior violates the law and is unacceptable. Partners owe each other a high degree of good faith.

TERMINATING A PARTNERSHIP

There are three steps in the process of terminating a partnership.

Dissolution

The dissolution process may depend upon the type of partnership involved.

Dissociation

When a partner leaves the partnership.

Partnership at will

A partnership with no fixed duration. Any of the partners may leave at any time, for any reason.

Partnership at Will   When a partner quits, that act is called a **dissociation**. If the partners have not agreed on how long the partnership will last, it is a **partnership at will**, which means that any of the partners can dissociate at any time, for any reason. Once a partner dissociates, the partnership has a choice: it can either buy out the departing partner(s) and continue in business or wind up the business and terminate the partnership. Exhibit 29.3 illustrates this process.

Exhibit 29.3

Term Partnership   If the partners have agreed in advance how long the partnership will last, it is a **term partnership**. A partnership is a personal relationship: each partner is personally liable for its debts. For this reason, courts will not force someone to remain in a partnership, no matter what the partnership agreement says. Even in a term partnership. a **partner always has the *power* to leave a partnership but may not have the *right*.** In other words, a partner can always dissociate, but she may have to pay damages for any harm that her departure causes.

Under the UPA, a term partnership dissolves if:

- A partner dissociates and half the remaining partners vote to wind up the partnership business.

- All the partners agree to dissolve.

- The term expires or the partnership achieves its goal (although partners can always decide by unanimous vote to continue the partnership).

All Partnerships   All partnerships dissolve if:

- An event occurs that the partners had agreed would cause dissolution (unless the partners vote unanimously to continue).

- The partnership business becomes illegal.

- A court determines that the partnership is unlikely to succeed. If the partners simply cannot get along or they cannot make a profit, any partner has the right to ask a court to dissolve the partnership. For example, two men formed a partnership to buy *The San Juan Star,* an English language newspaper in Puerto Rico. They ended up in court, each bitterly accusing the other of having violated the partnership agreement. Their hostility was so great that the judge ultimately decided he could not tell who was at fault and, furthermore, the two men could never run a business together. The court ordered one partner to buy out the other. If the partners could not agree on a buyout, the judge was prepared to order a sale of the newspaper to outsiders.[11]

Winding Up

During the winding up process, all debts of the partnership are paid, and the remaining proceeds are distributed to the partners.

Termination

After the sometimes lengthy and complex winding up, the actual termination of a partnership is anticlimactic. Termination happens automatically once the winding up is finished. The partnership is not required to do anything official; it can go out of the world even more quietly and simply than it came in.

---

[11] *Nemazee Capital Corp. v. Angulo Capital Corp.*, 1996 U.S. Dist. LEXIS 10750 (S. Dist. NY, 1996).

Term partnership
A partnership in which the partners agree in advance how long it will last.

LIMITED LIABILITY PARTNERSHIPS

A limited liability partnership (LLP) is a type of general partnership that most states now permit. There is a very important distinction, however, between these two forms of organization: **in an LLP, the partners are not liable for the debts of the partnership.**[12] They are, naturally, liable for their own misdeeds, just as if they were a member of an LLC or a shareholder of a corporation.

To form an LLP, the partners must file a statement of qualification with state officials. LLPs must also file annual reports. The other attributes of a partnership remain the same. Thus, an LLP is not a taxable entity and it has the right to choose its duration (that is, it can, but does not have to, survive the dissociation of a member).

Although an LLP can be much more advantageous for partners than a general partnership, the following case provides an important warning: it is essential to comply with all the technicalities of the LLP statute.

APCAR V. GAUS

2005 TEX. APP. LEXIS 379
COURT OF APPEALS OF TEXAS, 2005

CASE SUMMARY

Facts: Smith & West, LLP had two partners: Michael L. Gaus and John C. West. The partnership registered in Texas as a limited liability partnership. The Texas statute requires LLPs to renew their registrations each year, but Smith & West never did so. Four years after its initial registration, the partnership entered into a lease with MF Partners, which subsequently assigned the lease to Apcar. Three years into the lease, Smith & West stopped paying rent and abandoned the premises. Apcar filed suit against the two partners individually and against the partnership. Gaus, West, and Apcar each filed a motion for summary judgment. The trial court granted Gaus's and West's motions while denying Apcar's.

Issue: *Were Gaus and West personally liable for payments due under Smith & West's lease?*

Decision: Gaus and West were personally liable for the partnership's lease payments.

Reasoning: Under Texas law, an LLP must renew its registration within a year of making the initial application. Smith & West did not do so. Therefore, its status as an LLP expired on the first anniversary of its initial filing.

Smith & West signed a lease three years after its LLP status expired. Partners Gaus and West argue that they should be protected from personal liability on the lease even though the partnership had not complied strictly with the statute. But the statute makes no provision for substantial compliance, nor does it offer any grace period for filing a renewal application. Therefore, a partnership must comply with the precise terms of the statute for its partners to receive protection from individual liability. Smith and West failed to do that, and they are liable on the lease.

---

[12] UPA Section 306(c).

LIMITED PARTNERSHIPS AND LIMITED LIABILITY LIMITED PARTNERSHIPS

Although limited partnerships and limited liability limited partnerships sound confusingly similar to limited liability partnerships and general partnerships, like many siblings, they operate very differently. And truth to tell, limited partnerships and limited liability limited partnerships are relatively rare—they are generally used only for estate planning purposes (usually, to reduce estate taxes) and for highly sophisticated investment vehicles. You should be aware of their existence, but you may not see them very often in your business life. Here are the major features.

STRUCTURE

Limited partnerships must have at least one *limited* partner and one *general* partner.

LIABILITY

Limited partners are not *personally* liable, but general partners are. Like corporate shareholders, limited partners risk only their investment in the partnership (which is called their "capital contribution"). In contrast, general partners of the limited partnership are personally liable for the debts of the organization.

However, the revised version of the Uniform Limited Partnership Act permits a limited partnership, in its certificate of formation and partnership agreement, simply to declare itself a *limited liability* limited partnership.[13] **In a limited liability limited partnership, the general partner is not personally liable for the debts of the partnership.** This provision effectively removes the major disadvantage of limited partnerships. Although, at this writing, fewer than 20 states have actually passed the revised version of the Uniform Limited Partnership Act, this revision would seem to indicate the trend for the future.

TAXES

Limited partnerships are not taxable entities. Income is taxed only once before landing in a partner's pocket.

FORMATION

The general partners must file a **certificate of limited partnership** with their Secretary of State. Although most limited partnerships do have a partnership agreement, it is not required.

MANAGEMENT

General partners have the right to manage a limited partnership. Limited partners are essentially passive investors with few management rights beyond the right to be informed about the partnership business. Limited partnership agreements can, however, expand the rights of limited partners.

---

[13] ULPA Section 102(9).

TRANSFER OF OWNERSHIP

Limited partners have the right to transfer the *value* of their partnership interest, but they can sell or give away the interest itself only if the partnership agreement permits.

DURATION

Unless the partnership agreement provides otherwise, limited partnerships enjoy perpetual existence—they continue even as partners come and go.

EXAM *Strategy*

Question: In which one or more of the following forms of organization is it true that none of the partners are liable for the debts of the partnership?

(a) General partnership

(b) Limited liability partnership

(c) Limited partnership

(d) Limited liability limited partnership

Strategy: All these partnerships sound similar, but they are in fact very different, so it is important to keep them straight!

Result: In a general partnership, all the partners are liable. In a limited liability partnership, none are liable. In a limited partnership, the general partners are liable. In a limited liability limited partnership, none of the partners are liable. The correct answers are B and D.

PROFESSIONAL CORPORATIONS

Traditionally, most professionals (such as lawyers and doctors) were not permitted to incorporate their businesses, so they organized as partnerships. Now professionals are allowed to incorporate, but in a special way. These organizations are called "professional corporations" or "PCs." **PCs provide more liability protection than a general partnership.** If a member of a PC commits malpractice, the corporation's assets are at risk but not the personal assets of the innocent members. If Drs. Sharp, Payne, and Graves form a *partnership*, all the partners will be personally liable when Dr. Payne accidentally leaves her scalpel inside a patient. If the three doctors have formed a *PC* instead, Dr. Payne's Aspen condo and the assets of the PC will be at risk, but not the personal assets of the two other doctors.

Generally, the shareholders of a PC are not personally liable for the contract debts of the organization, such as leases or bank loans. Thus, if Sharp, Payne, & Graves, P.C. is unable to pay its rent, the landlord cannot recover from the personal assets of any of the doctors. As partners, the doctors would be personally liable.

PCs have some limitations. First, all shareholders of the corporation must be members of the same profession. For Sharp, Payne, & Graves, P.C., that means all shareholders must be licensed physicians. Other valued employees cannot own stock. Second, like other corporations, the required legal technicalities for forming and maintaining a PC are expensive and time-consuming. Third, tax issues can be complicated. A PC is a separate taxable entity, like any other corporation. It must pay tax on its profits, and then its shareholders pay tax on any dividends they receive. *Salaries*, however, are deductible from firm profits. Thus the PC can avoid paying taxes on its profits by paying out all the profits as salary. But any profits remaining in firm coffers *at the end of the year* are taxable. To avoid tax, PCs must be careful to calculate their profits accurately and pay them out before year's end. This chore can be time-consuming, and any error may cause unnecessary tax liability.

JOINT VENTURES

Imax Corp. recently announced that it would like to partner with cinema operators—it would supply its big screens in return for a share of the box office revenue. The arrangement that Imax is describing is not like the other partnerships we have discussed in this chapter—it is a joint venture. A **joint venture** is a partnership for a limited purpose. Imax and the cinema operators would not merge; they would simply work together. Each organization retains its own identity. Imax would be liable to an electrician whom the cinema operator had hired to install an Imax screen, but not to the cinema's popcorn supplier.

Joint venture
A partnership for a limited purpose.

OTHER FORMS OF ORGANIZATION

When starting a business, most entrepreneurs choose one of the forms of organization that we have discussed. There are, however, an assortment of other, less common forms that we must briefly cover—not so much because you are likely to use one of them yourself, but so that you will know what they are if you come across them in your business life or in reading the newspaper.

BUSINESS TRUSTS

A **business trust** is an unincorporated association run by trustees for the benefit of investors (who are called "beneficiaries"). This arrangement sounds like an unfavorable one for investors. They buy certificates in the trust, just as shareholders buy stock in a corporation, but they have fewer rights than shareholders. They do not elect the trustees; if a trustee resigns or dies, the other trustees choose a replacement. The trustees can take almost any action without approval of the investors and can issue an unlimited number of shares. The beneficiaries are not liable for the debts of the trust. Theoretically, the trustees are liable, but the trust agreement usually protects them from liability.

Business trust
An unincorporated association run by trustees for the benefit of investors.

Ordinary businesses usually do not consider this form of organization, but it does make sense for mutual funds and other investment management companies. Investors buy shares or certificates in the trust. The trustees, who are investment experts, invest the funds, paying out any returns to the investors, minus management fees. If investors are unhappy with a fund's performance, they do not have the right to vote out the trustees, but they can sell their shares and take their money elsewhere. It would be difficult to run an investment company if the beneficiaries were always changing trustees and investment style. A mutual fund is the one type of investment where it makes sense that investors *cannot* replace trustees.

COOPERATIVES

Cooperative

A group of individuals or businesses that join together to gain the advantages of volume purchases or sales.

Cooperatives are groups of individuals or businesses that join together to gain the advantages of volume purchases or sales. Profits are distributed to members using whatever formula they choose. Unincorporated cooperatives are generally subject to partnership law; incorporated cooperatives are governed by corporation law.

For example, the Harvard Cooperative Society is the oldest retail cooperative in the country. Founded in 1882 by Harvard students aiming to undercut price-gouging local merchants, the Coop (rhymes with "hoop") originally sold just textbooks and firewood. It has long since outgrown its first location—a five-foot shelf in a local tobacco store. Now the Coop is a landmark in Harvard Square, selling textbooks, clothing, and dorm supplies. Owned by its members, who are primarily students and alumni of Harvard and MIT, its annual sales are in the tens of millions of dollars.

FRANCHISES

This chapter has presented an overview of the various forms of organization. Franchises are not, strictly speaking, a separate form of organization. They are included here because they represent an important option for entrepreneurs. The United States has nearly 800,000 franchised businesses which employ more than 8 million people. Total sales are more than $1 trillion a year. Well-known franchises include Dunkin' Donuts, McDonald's, and Mail Boxes Etc. Most franchisors and franchisees are corporations, although they could legally choose to be any of the forms discussed in this chapter.

Buying a franchise is a compromise between starting one's own business as an entrepreneur and working for someone else as an employee. Franchisees are free to choose which franchise to buy, where to locate it, and how to staff it. But they are not completely on their own. They are buying an established business with all the kinks worked out. In case the owner has never boiled water before, the McDonald's operations manual explains everything from how to set the temperature controls on the stove, to the number of seconds that fries must cook, to the length of time they can be held in the rack before being discarded. And a well-known name like McDonald's or Mrs. Fields ought, by itself, to bring customers through the door.

There is, however, a fine line between being helpful and being oppressive. Franchisees sometimes complain that franchisor control is too tight—tips on cooking fries might be appreciated, but rules on how often to sweep the floor are not. Sometimes franchisors, in their zeal to maintain standards, prohibit innovation that appeals to regional tastes. Just because spicy biscuits are not popular in New England does not mean they should be banned in the South.

Franchises can be very costly to acquire, anywhere from several thousand dollars to several million. That fee is usually payable up front, whether or not a cookie or burger is ever sold. On top of the up-front fee, franchisees also typically pay an annual fee that is a percentage of *gross sales revenues*, not *profit*. Sometimes the fee seems to eat up all the profits. Franchisees also complain when they are forced to buy supplies from headquarters. In theory, the franchisors can purchase hamburger meat and paper plates more cheaply in bulk and also maintain quality controls. On the other hand, the franchisees are a captive audience, and they sometimes allege that headquarters has little incentive to keep prices low. Indeed, some franchisors make most of their profit from the products they sell to their store owners. Often the franchise agreement permits the company to change the terms of the agreement by raising fees or expenses. Franchisees also grumble when they are forced to contribute to expensive "co-op advertising" that benefits all the outlets in the region. The sandwich franchise Quiznos is currently involved in litigation with some of its franchisees, who claim that the company took their fees without finding a store location for them. Other litigants are seeking to void their contracts that require them to buy *everything* (including soap in the bathrooms and the piped-in music) from the company at inflated prices.

Originally, franchises were not regulated. But then abuses on the part of franchisors caused the North American Securities Administrators Association (NASAA) to enact franchise rules that some states then adopted. In particular, NASAA required franchisors to prepare a disclosure document called the Uniform Franchise Offering Circular (UFOC). Later, the Federal Trade Commission (FTC) also began to regulate franchises. At this writing, NASAA is on the verge of adopting the FTC's latest regulations as its own (with a few minor additions). Under FTC rules, a franchisor must deliver to a potential purchaser an offering circular at least 14 business days before any contract is signed or money is paid. The circular must include the following information:

- Any litigation against the company for the prior 10 years and any claims the company has made against franchisees during the prior year

- Whether it has gone through bankruptcy proceedings in the prior 10 years

- All fees

- Estimates of the required initial investment

- What goods must be purchased from the franchisor

- The number of franchisees in operation

- How many franchisees have gone out of business in the prior three years

- Any competition franchisees will face from other company-owned outlets, including through the Internet, catalog sales, and telemarketing

- Whether others can sell in the franchisee's territory and whether it can sell outside its territory

- A warning that franchisees should not rely on any earnings claims unless included in this document

- Audited financial statements, and

- A sample set of the contracts that a franchisee is expected to sign.

The purpose of the offering circular is to ensure that the franchisor discloses all relevant facts. It is not a guarantee of quality because the FTC does not investigate to make sure that the information is accurate. After the fact, if the FTC discovers the franchisor has violated the rules, it may sue on your behalf. (You do not have the right to bring suit personally against someone who violates FTC franchise rules, but you may be able to sue under state law.)

Suppose you obtain an offering circular for "Shrinking Cats," a franchise that offers psychiatric services for neurotic felines. The company has lost money on all the outlets it operates itself; it has sold only three franchises, two of which have gone out of business; and all the required contracts are ridiculously favorable to the franchisor. Nevertheless, the FTC will still permit sales so long as the franchisor discloses all the information required in the offering circular.

The following case illustrates some of the issues franchisees face.

KIELAND V. ROCKY MOUNTAIN CHOCOLATE FACTORY, INC.

2006 U.S. DIST. LEXIS 760578
UNITED STATES DISTRICT COURT FOR THE DISTRICT OF MINNESOTA, 2006

CASE SUMMARY

Facts: Rocky Mountain is a franchisor of stores that sell chocolate and other fancy candies. It gave Kristine and Scott Kieland and Kathleen and Scott Evavold a uniform franchise offering circular (UFOC) before they signed franchise agreements with the company.

Rocky Mountain required that its franchisees purchase an electronic point-of-sale cash register system (POS System). At the time the Kielands signed their agreement with Rocky Mountain, the company required a system that cost about $3,000 per register, with an annual maintenance fee of $773. The agreement stated, "We may require you to upgrade or update your POS Systems. No contractual limitation exists on the frequency or cost of this obligation."

Shortly after signing the agreement, the Kielands learned that they would have to purchase a different POS system (referred to as "AIM") that cost almost $20,000, with annual maintenance fees of almost $2,000. Their Rocky Mountain store failed four years after they purchased it.

Stanford Evavold emailed a pro forma budget to Kraig Carlson, a Rocky Mountain salesperson. The email said, "I am also attaching some of the numbers I put together. I don't believe you can state if these appear reasonable, but maybe you can tell me if it is a 'rainy day' or 'sunny day.'" Carlson responded that the numbers "did not raise any issues with him." Based on these assurances, the Evavolds signed an agreement that stated, "The Franchisee acknowledges and agrees that no representations have been made to it by the Franchisor regarding projected sales volumes, market potential, revenues, or profits of the Franchisee's Store."

The Evavolds' franchise was not as profitable as their budget had predicted.

The Kielands and the Evavolds sued Rocky Mountain for violating the Minnesota Franchise Act by failing to disclose the cost of the new AIM system and by approving Evavold's earnings estimate. Had they known all the relevant facts, the Kielands and the Evavolds would not have purchased a franchise. Rocky Mountain filed a motion for summary judgment.

Issue: *Did Rocky Mountain violate Minnesota franchise law?*

Decision: Rocky Mountain was not in violation of Minnesota law. Its motion for summary judgment is granted.

Reasoning: The Offering Circular specifically stated that the company had the right to require franchisees to upgrade their cash register systems an unlimited number of times at an unlimited cost. Although the new system cost $13,000 more to buy and $1,200 more to maintain than the old system, Rocky Mountain was completely within its rights. If this cost was going to be a problem for the Kielands, they should not have signed the agreement.

As for the Evavolds, it is not clear from the email exchanges that Carlson did, in fact, make any promises about earnings. But whether or not he had, the Offering Circular was very clear that sales people had no authority to do so. Therefore, the Evavolds had no right to recover from Rocky Mountain.

CHAPTER CONCLUSION

The process of starting a business is immensely time-consuming. Eighteen-hour days are the norm. Not surprisingly, entrepreneurs are sometimes reluctant to spend their valuable time on legal issues that, after all, do not contribute directly to the bottom line. No customer buys more biscuits because the franchise is a limited liability company instead of a corporation. Wise entrepreneurs know, however, that careful attention to legal issues is an essential component of success. The form of organization affects everything from taxes to liability to management control. The idea for the business may come first, but legal considerations occupy a close second place.

EXAM REVIEW

	Separate Taxable Entity	Personal Liability for Owners	Ease of Formation	Transferable Interests (Easily Bought and Sold)	Perpetual Existence	Other Features
Sole Proprietorship	No	Yes	Very easy	No, can only sell entire business	No	
Corporation	Yes	No	Difficult	Yes	Yes	
Close Corporation	Yes, for C corporation No, for S corporation	No	Difficult	Transfer restrictions	Yes	Protection of minority shareholders. No board of directors required
S Corporation	No	No	Difficult	Transfer restrictions	Yes	Only 100 shareholders. Only one class of stock. Shareholders must be individuals, estates, trusts, charities, or pension funds and be citizens or residents of the United States. All shareholders must agree to S status
Limited Liability Company	No	No	Difficult	Yes, if the operating agreement permits	Varies by state, but generally, yes	No limit on the number of shareholders, the number of classes of stock, or the type of shareholder
General Partnership	No	Yes	Easy	No	Depends on the partnership agreement	Management can be difficult
Limited Liability Partnership	No	No	Difficult	No	Depends on the partnership agreement	

(Continued)

	Separate Taxable Entity	Personal Liability for Owners	Ease of Formation	Transferable Interests (Easily Bought and Sold)	Perpetual Existence	Other Features
Limited Partnership	No	Yes, for general partner No, for limited partners	Difficult	Yes (for limited partners), if partnership agreement permits	Yes	
Limited Liability Limited Partnership	No	No	Difficult	Yes (for limited partners), if partnership agreement permits	Yes	
Professional Corporation	Yes	No	Difficult	Shareholders must all be members of same profession	Yes, as long as it has shareholders	Complex tax issues
Joint Venture	No	Yes	Easy	No	No	Partnership for a limited purpose
Business Trust	Yes	No	Difficult	Yes	Yes	Most commonly used by mutual funds and other investment companies
Cooperative	All these issues depend on the form of organization chosen by participants.					Groups of individuals or businesses that join together to gain the advantages of volume purchases or sales
Franchise	All these issues depend on the form of organization chosen by participants.					Established business. Name recognition. Management assistance. Loss of control. Fees may be high

ADDITIONAL QUESTIONS

1. ETHICS Lee McNeely told Hardee's officials that he was interested in purchasing multiple restaurants in Arkansas. A Hardee's officer assured him that any of the company-owned stores in Arkansas would be available for purchase. However, the company urged him to open a new store in Maumelle and sent him a letter estimating first-year sales at around $800,000. McNeely built the Maumelle restaurant, but gross sales the first year were only $508,000. When McNeely asked to buy an existing restaurant, a Hardee's officer refused, informing him that Hardee's rarely sold company-owned restaurants. The offering circular contained no misstatements, but McNeely brought suit alleging fraud in the sale of the Maumelle franchise. Does McNeely have a valid claim against Hardee's? Apart from the legal issues, did Hardee's officers be have ethically? Would they want their behavior to be publicized? Would they like to be treated this way themselves? Is all fair in love, war, and franchising?

EXAM Strategy

2. CPA Question: Assuming all other requirements are met, a corporation may elect to be treated as an S corporation under the Internal Revenue Code if it has:

(a) Both common and preferred stockholders

(b) A partnership as a stockholder

(c) One hundred or fewer stockholders

(d) The consent of a majority of the stockholders

Strategy: Review the list of requirements for an S corporation. (See the "Result" at the end of this section.)

3. Under Delaware law, a corporation cannot appear in court without a lawyer, but a partnership can. Fox Hollow Ventures, Ltd., was a limited liability company. One of its employees, who was not a lawyer, appeared in court to represent the company. Does an LLC more closely resemble a partnership, which may represent itself in court, or a corporation, which requires representation by a lawyer?

4. Glenleigh Falls Development Co. was a limited liability company that hired architects John and Marion Zaugg to design a residential golf course. The Zauggs were to receive partial payment for their services plus part ownership in the LLC. Although the articles of organization had been filed with the Secretary of State in Ohio, the operating agreement had not yet been signed by the members. The Zauggs signed the agreement, but two of the original four members did not. The agreement provided that no member could voluntarily withdraw. When the LLC refused to pay the Zauggs' bill for architectural services, they withdrew from the LLC and filed suit, seeking payment of their bill. The LLC counter-claimed, alleging that the Zauggs had wrongfully withdrawn. Did the Zauggs have the right to withdraw?

EXAM Strategy

5. Question: Alan Dershowitz, a law professor famous for his wealthy clients (O. J. Simpson, Claus von Bulow, Leona Helmsley), joined with other lawyers to open a kosher delicatessen, Maven's Court. Dershowitz met with greater success at the bar than in the kitchen—the deli failed after barely a year in business. One supplier sued for overdue bills. What form of organization would have been the best choice for Maven's Court?

Strategy: A sole proprietorship would not have worked, because there was more than one owner. A partnership would have been a disaster because of unlimited liability. They could have met all the requirements of an S Corporation or an LLC. (See the "Result" at the end of this section.)

6. ***CPA QUESTION*** A joint venture is a(n):

(a) Association limited to no more than two persons in business for profit

(b) Enterprise of numerous co-owners in a nonprofit undertaking

(c) Corporate enterprise for a single undertaking of limited duration

(d) Association of persons engaged as co-owners in a single undertaking for profit

---

EXAM Strategy

7. Question: Mrs. Meadows opened a biscuit shop called The Biscuit Bakery. The business was not incorporated. Whenever she ordered supplies, she was careful to sign the contract in the name of the business, not personally: The Biscuit Bakery by Daisy Meadows. Unfortunately, she had no money to pay her flour bill. When the vendor threatened to sue her, Mrs. Meadows told him that he could only sue the business, because all the contracts were in the business's name. Will Mrs. Meadows lose her dough?

Strategy: The first step is to figure out what type of organization her business is. Then recall what liability protection that organization offers. (See the "Result" at the end of this section.)

---

8. ***YOU BE THE JUDGE*** WRITING PROBLEM Cellwave was a limited partnership that applied to the Federal Communications Commission (FCC) for a license to operate cellular telephone systems. After the FCC awarded the license it discovered that, although all the limited partners had signed the limited partnership agreement, Cellwave had never filed its limited partnership certificate with the Secretary of State in Delaware. The FCC dismissed Cellwave's application on the grounds that the partnership did not exist when the application was filed. Did the FCC have the right to dismiss Cellwave's application? **Argument for Cellwave:** The limited partnership was effectively in existence as soon as the limited partners signed the agreement. The Secretary of State could not refuse to accept the certificate for filing; that was a mere formality. **Argument for the FCC:** When Cellwave applied for a license, it did not exist legally. Formalities matter.

9. Arnold and Judith Germain bought two franchises from My Pie International, Inc. They did not receive the franchise disclosure statement from My Pie until two years after the purchase. Did My Pie violate franchise law?

10. Leonard C. Blum, an attorney, was negligent in his representation of Louis Anthony, Sr. In settlement of Anthony's claim against him, Blum signed a promissory note for $10,400 on behalf of his law firm, an LLC. When the law firm did not pay, Anthony filed suit against Blum personally for payment of the note. Is a member personally liable for the debt of an LLC that was caused by his own negligence?

11. ***ROLE REVERSAL*** Draft a multiple-choice question that focuses on the difference between an LLC and an S corporation.

2. Result: An S corporation can have only one class of stock. A partnership cannot be a stockholder, and all the shareholders must consent to S corporation status. C is the correct answer.

5. Result: Maven's Court would have chosen an LLC or an S corporation.

7. Result: The Biscuit Bakery was a sole proprietorship. No matter how Mrs. Meadows signed the contracts, she is still personally liable for the debts of the business.

INTERNET RESEARCH PROBLEM

At **http://ftc.gov**, the Federal Trade Commission provides information on enforcement cases it has brought against franchisors who violate FTC rules. Do you see a pattern? Are some violations more common than others? How can you avoid falling prey to an unsuitable franchise offering?

You can find further practice problems at www.cengagebrain.com. See the preface of this book for website access details.

CORPORATIONS

Zuckerberg started TheFacebook in his dorm room at Harvard. Within 10 months, it had almost 1 million users.

On July 26, 2004, Mark Zuckerberg signed a Certificate of Incorporation for his company, which he called TheFacebook, Inc. At 11:34 A.M on July 29, 2004, that Certificate was filed with the Secretary of State for Delaware and TheFacebook began its life as a corporation. Zuckerberg had started this social networking Internet site the previous February in his dorm room at Harvard. By December of 2004, TheFacebook had almost 1 million users. By the beginning of 2006, the company was estimated to be worth between $750 million and $2 billion. As he built his company, what did Zuckerberg need to know about the law?

In this chapter, you will learn how to form a corporation. You will also learn about the rights and responsibilities of corporate managers and shareholders.

PROMOTER'S LIABILITY

Someone who organizes a corporation is called a **promoter. A promoter is personally liable on any contract he signs before the corporation is formed.** After formation, the corporation can **adopt** the contract, in which case, both it and the promoter are liable. The promoter can get off the hook personally only if the other party agrees to a **novation** —that is, a new contract with the corporation alone.

Novation
A new contract with different parties.

EXAM *Strategy*

Question: Dr. Warfield hired Wolfe, a young carpenter, to build his house. A week or so after they signed the contract, Wolfe filed Articles of Incorporation for Wolfe Construction, Inc. Warfield made payments to the corporation. Unfortunately, the work on the house was shoddy. The architect said he did not know whether to blow up the house or try and salvage what was there. Warfield sued Wolfe and Wolfe Construction, Inc. for damages. Wolfe argued that if he was liable as a promoter, then the corporation must be absolved and that, conversely, if the corporation was held liable, he, as an individual, must not be. Who is liable to Warfield? Does it matter if Wolfe signed the contract in his own name or in the name of the corporation?

Strategy: Wolfe's argument is wrong—Warfield does not have to choose between suing him individually or suing the corporation. He can certainly sue both.

Result: Wolfe is personally liable on any contract signed before the corporation is filed, no matter whose name is on the contract. The corporation is only liable if it adopts the contract. Did it do so here? The fact that the corporation cashed checks that were made out to it means that the corporation is also liable. So Warfield can sue both Wolfe and the corporation.

INCORPORATION PROCESS

The mechanics of incorporation are easy: simply download the online form and mail or fax it to the Secretary of State for your state. But do not let this easy process fool you; the incorporation document needs to be completed with some care. The corporate charter defines the corporation, including everything from the company's name to the number of shares it will issue. States use different terms to refer to a charter; some call it the "articles of incorporation," others use "articles of organization," and still others say "certificate" instead of "articles." All these terms mean the same thing. Similarly, some states use the term "shareholders," and others use "stockholders"; they are both the same.

There is no federal corporation code, which means that a company can incorporate only under state, not federal, law. No matter where a company actually does business, it may incorporate in any state. This decision is important because the organization must live by the laws of whichever state it chooses for incorporation. To encourage similarity among state corporation statutes, the American Bar Association drafted the Model Business Corporation Act (the Model

Act) as a guide. Many states do use the Model Act as a guide, although Delaware does not. Therefore, in this chapter we will give examples from both the Model Act and specific states, such as Delaware. Why Delaware? Despite its small size, it has a disproportionate influence on corporate law. Although only one third of 1 percent of the U.S. population lives in Delaware, more than half of all public companies have incorporated there, including 60 percent of Fortune 500 companies.

WHERE TO INCORPORATE?

A company is called a **domestic corporation** in the state where it incorporates and a **foreign corporation** everywhere else. Companies generally incorporate either in the state where they do most of their business or in Delaware. They typically must pay filing fees and franchise taxes in their state of incorporation, as well as in any state in which they do business. To avoid this double set of fees, a business that will be operating primarily in one state would probably select that state for incorporation rather than Delaware. But if a company is going to do business in several states, it might consider choosing Delaware (or, perhaps, Ohio, Pennsylvania, Nevada, or one of the other states with sophisticated corporate laws). Delaware offers corporations several advantages:

- *Laws that Favor Management.* For example, if the shareholders want to take a vote in writing instead of holding a meeting, many other states require the vote to be unanimous; Delaware requires only a majority to agree. The Delaware legislature also tries to keep up-to-date by changing its code to reflect new developments in corporate law.

- *An Efficient Court System.* Delaware has a special court (called "Chancery Court") that hears nothing but business cases and has judges who are experts in corporate law.

- *An Established Body of Precedent.* Because so many businesses incorporate in the state, its courts hear a vast number of corporate cases, creating a large body of precedent. Thus, lawyers feel they can more easily predict the outcome of a case in Delaware than in a state where few corporate disputes are tried each year.

THE CHARTER

Once a company has decided *where* to incorporate, the next step is to prepare and file the charter. The charter must always be filed with the Secretary of State; some jurisdictions also require that it be filed in a county office. Sample articles of incorporation for Delaware are available at the Division of Corporation's Web site.

Name

The Model Act imposes two requirements in selecting a name. First, all corporations must use one of the following words in their name: "corporation," "incorporated," "company," or "limited." Delaware also accepts some additional terms, such as "association" or "institute." Second, under both the Model Act and Delaware law, a new corporate name must be different from that of any corporation, limited liability company, or limited partnership that already exists in that state. If your name is Freddy Du Pont, you cannot name your corporation "Freddy Du Pont, Inc.," because Delaware already has a company named E. I. Du Pont de Nemours & Co. It does not matter that Freddy Du Pont is your real name or that the existing company is a large chemical business, whereas you want to open a video arcade. The names are too similar. TheFacebook was what Harvard students called their freshman directory.

Address and Registered Agent

A company must have an official address in the state in which it is incorporated so that the Secretary of State knows where to contact it and so that anyone who wants to sue the corporation can serve the complaint in-state. Because most companies incorporated in Delaware do not actually have an office there, they hire a registered agent to serve as their official presence in the state.

Incorporator

The incorporator signs the charter and delivers it to the Secretary of State. Incorporators are not required to buy stock, nor do they necessarily have any future relationship with the company. Oftentimes, the lawyer who forms the corporation serves as its incorporator. If no lawyer is involved, typically the promoter is also the incorporator. That is what happened with TheFacebook—Mark Zuckerberg served as incorporator.

Purpose

The corporation is required to give its purpose for existence. Most companies use a very broad purpose clause such as TheFacebook's:

> The purpose of the Corporation is to engage in any lawful act or activity for which corporations may be organized under the General Corporation Law of Delaware.

Stock

The charter must provide three items of information about the company's stock.

Par Value   The concept of par value was designed to protect investors. Originally, par value was supposed to be close to market price. A company could not issue stock at a price less than par, which meant that it could not sell to insiders at a sweetheart price well below market value. (Once the stock was issued, it could be traded at any price.) In modern times, par value does not relate to market value; it is usually some nominal figure such as 1¢ or $1 per share. Companies may even issue stock with no par value. TheFacebook stock has a par value of $0.0001 per share.

Number of Shares   Before stock can be sold, it must first be authorized in the charter. The corporation can authorize as many shares as the incorporators choose, but the more shares, the higher the filing fee. After incorporation, a company can add authorized shares by simply amending its charter and paying the additional fee. TheFacebook charter authorizes the creation of 10,000,000 shares.

Stock that has been authorized but not yet sold is called **authorized and unissued**. Stock that has been sold is termed **authorized and issued** or **outstanding.** Stock that the company has sold but later bought back is **treasury stock.**

Authorized and unissued
Stock that has been authorized, but not yet sold.

Authorized and issued
Stock that has been authorized and sold; another word for it is outstanding.

Treasury stock
Stock that a company has sold, but later bought back.

Classes and Series   Different shareholders often make different contributions to a company. Some may be involved in management, whereas others may simply contribute financially. Early investors may feel that they are entitled to more control than those who come along later (and who perhaps take less risk). Corporate structure can be infinitely flexible in defining the rights of these various shareholders. Stock can be divided into categories called **classes,** and these classes can be further divided into subcategories called **series.** All stock in a series has the same rights, and all series in a class are fundamentally the same, except for minor distinctions. For example, in a class of preferred stock, all shareholders may be entitled to a dividend, but the amount of the dividend may vary by series. Different classes of stock, however, may have very different rights—a class of preferred stock is different from a class of common stock. Exhibit 30.1 illustrates the concept of class and series.

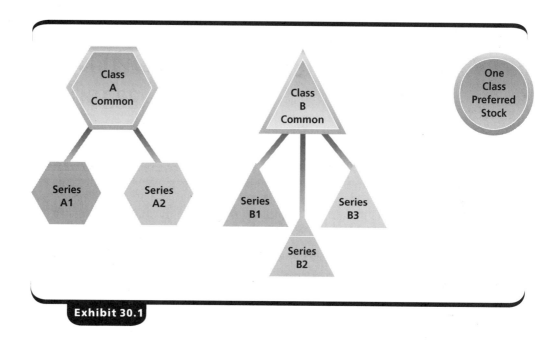

Exhibit 30.1

Defining the rights of a class or series of stock is like baking a cake—the stock can contain virtually any combination of the following ingredients (although the result may not be to everyone's taste):

- *Dividend Rights.* The charter establishes whether the shareholder is entitled to dividends and, if so, in what amount.

- *Voting Rights.* Shareholders are usually entitled to elect directors and vote on charter amendments, among other issues, but these rights can vary among different series and classes of stock. When Ford Motor Co. went public in 1956, it issued Class B common stock to members of the Ford family. This class of stock holds about 40 percent of the voting power and, thereby, effectively controls the company. Not surprisingly, the chairman of the company has often been named "Ford."

- *Liquidation Rights.* The charter specifies the order in which classes of stockholders will be paid upon dissolution of the company.

These are the ingredients for any class or series of stock. Some stock comes prepackaged like a cake mix. "Preferred" and "common" stock are two classic types. The Model Act does not use these terms, but many states still do.

Owners of *preferred stock* have preference on dividends and also, typically, in liquidation. If a class of preferred stock is entitled to dividends, then it must receive its dividends before common stockholders are paid theirs. If holders of ***cumulative*** **preferred stock** miss their dividend one year, common shareholders cannot receive a dividend until the cumulative preferred shareholders have been paid all that they are owed, no matter how long that takes. Alternatively, holders of ***non*-cumulative preferred stock** lose an annual dividend for good if the company cannot afford it in the year it is due. When a company dissolves, preferred stockholders typically have the right to receive their share of corporate assets before common shareholders. Exhibit 30.2 illustrates the order of payment for dividends.

Preferred stock

The owners of preferred stock have preference on dividends and also, typically, in liquidation.

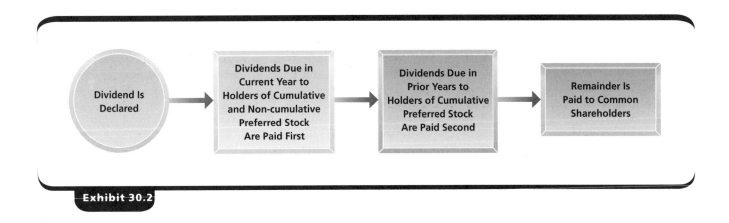

Exhibit 30.2

Common **stock is last in line for any corporate payouts, including dividends and liquidation payments.** If the company is liquidated, creditors of the company and preferred shareholders are paid before common shareholders.

AFTER INCORPORATION

DIRECTORS AND OFFICERS

Once the corporation is organized, the incorporators elect the first set of directors. Thereafter, shareholders elect directors. Under the Model Act, a corporation is required to have at least one director, unless (1) all the shareholders sign an agreement that eliminates the board, or (2) the corporation has 50 or fewer shareholders. To elect directors, the shareholders may hold a meeting, or, in the more typical case for a small company, they elect directors by **written consent.** A typical written consent looks like this:

Classic American Novels, Inc.
Written Consent

The undersigned shareholders of Classic American Novels, Inc., a corporation organized and existing under the General Corporation Law of the State of Wherever, hereby agree that the following action shall be taken with full force and effect as if voted at a validly called and held meeting of the shareholders of the corporation:

> Agreed: That the following people are elected to serve as directors for one year or until their successors have been duly elected and qualified:

> Herman Melville

> Louisa May Alcott

> Mark Twain

Dated: _____ Signed: _____
Willa Cather

Dated: _____ Signed: _____
Nathaniel Hawthorne

Dated: _____ Signed: _____
Harriet Beecher Stowe

Once the incorporators or shareholders have chosen the directors, the directors must elect the officers of the corporation. They can use a consent form if they wish. The Model Act is flexible. It simply requires a corporation to have whatever officers are described in the bylaws. The same person can hold more than one office.

The written consents and any records of actual meetings are kept in a **minute book**, which is the official record of the corporation. Entrepreneurs sometimes feel they are too busy to bother with all these details, but if a corporation is ever sold, the lawyers for the buyers will *insist* on a well-organized and complete minute book. In one case, a company that was seeking a $100,000 bank loan could not find all its minutes. Many of its early shareholders and directors were not available to re-authorize prior deeds. In the end, the company had to merge itself into a newly created corporation so it could start fresh with a new set of corporate records. The company spent $10,000 on this task, a large chunk out of the $100,000 loan.

Minute book
The official record of a corporation.

BYLAWS

The **bylaws** list all the "housekeeping" details for the corporation. For example, bylaws set the date of the annual shareholders' meeting, define what a quorum is (i.e., what percentage of stock must be represented for a meeting to count), indicate how many directors there will be, give titles to officers, and establish the fiscal (i.e., tax) year of the corporation.

Bylaws
A document that specifies the organizational rules of a corporation or other organization, such as the date of the annual meeting and the required number of directors.

ISSUING DEBT

Most startup companies begin with some combination of equity and debt. Equity (i.e., stock) is described in the charter; debt is not. Authorizing debt is often one of the first steps a new company takes. There are several types of debt:

- **Bonds** are long-term debt secured by company assets. If the company is unable to pay the debt, creditors have a right to specific assets, such as accounts receivable or inventory.

- **Debentures** are long-term *unsecured* debt. If the company cannot meet its obligations, the debenture holders are paid after bondholders but before stockholders.

- **Notes** are short-term debt, typically payable within five years. They may be either secured or unsecured.

Bonds
Long-term secured debt.

Debentures
Long-term unsecured debt.

Notes
When issued by a company, short-term debt, typically payable within five years.

DEATH OF THE CORPORATION

Sometimes, business ideas are not successful and the corporation fails. This death can be voluntary (the shareholders elect to terminate the corporation) or forced (by court order). Sometimes, a court takes a step that is much more damaging to shareholders than simply dissolving the corporation—it removes the shareholders' limited liability.

PIERCING THE CORPORATE VEIL

One of the major purposes of a corporation is to protect its owners—the shareholders—from personal liability for the debts of the organization. Sometimes, however, a court will **pierce the corporate veil**; that is, the court will hold shareholders personally liable for the debts of the corporation. Courts generally pierce a corporate veil in four circumstances:

Pierce the corporate veil
A court holds shareholders personally liable for the debts of the corporation.

- *Failure to Observe Formalities.* If an organization does not act like a corporation, it will not be treated like one. It must, for example, hold required shareholders' and directors' meetings (or sign consents), keep a minute book as a record of these meetings, and make all the required state filings. In addition, officers must be careful to sign all corporate documents with a corporate title, not as an individual. An officer should sign like this:

Classic American Novels, Inc.

By: _Stephen Crane_

Stephen Crane, President

- *Commingling of Assets.* Nothing makes a court more willing to pierce a corporate veil than evidence that shareholders have mixed their assets with those of the corporation. Sometimes, for example, shareholders may use corporate assets to pay their personal debts. If shareholders commingle assets, it is genuinely difficult for creditors to determine which assets belong to whom. This confusion is generally resolved in favor of the creditors—all assets are deemed to belong to the corporation.

- *Inadequate Capitalization.* If the founders of a corporation do not raise enough capital (either through debt or equity) to give the business a fighting chance of paying its debts, courts may require shareholders to pay corporate obligations. Therefore, if the corporation does not have sufficient capital, it needs to buy insurance, particularly to protect against tort liability. Judges are likelier to hold shareholders liable if the alternative is to send an injured tort victim away empty-handed. For example, Oriental Fireworks Co. had hundreds of thousands of dollars in annual sales, but only $13,000 in assets. The company did not bother to obtain any liability insurance, keep a minute book, or defend lawsuits. There was no need because the company had no money. But then a court pierced the corporate veil and found the owner of the company personally liable.[1]

- *Fraud.* If fraud is committed in the name of a corporation, victims can make a claim against the personal assets of the shareholders who profited from the fraud.

The following case is a good example of when a court should pierce the corporate veil.

BROOKS V. BECKER

2005 VA. CIR. LEXIS 13
CIRCUIT COURT OF FAIRFAX COUNTY, VIRGINIA, 2005

CASE SUMMARY

Facts: Ronald Becker was the sole shareholder, officer, and director of Becker Interiors. Becker and his companion, Robert LaPointe, used approximately $300,000 of Becker Interiors' funds to renovate their residence, pay their personal credit card bills, and invest in another company of which Becker was president. Becker sold a corporate car for $73,700 and deposited those funds into his personal account, along with the corporation's income tax refund check of $12,850.

Becker Interiors supervised the major renovation of a house in McLean, Virginia. The company hired Stephen

---

[1] *Rice v. Oriental Fireworks Co.*, 75 Or. App. 627, 707 P.2d 1250, 1985 Ore. App. LEXIS 3928.

Brooks as a subcontractor on the project. When the company refused to pay Brooks, he filed suit, winning a judgment against the company for $54,597.09. But it turned out that Becker Interiors had no assets.

Brooks then sued Ronald Becker in an attempt to pierce the corporate veil and hold Becker personally liable for the debts of the corporation.

Issues: *Can Brooks pierce the corporate veil? Is Becker personally liable for the debts of the corporation?*

Decision: The court allowed Brooks to pierce the corporate veil. Becker was held personally liable for the debts of Becker Interiors, Inc.

Reasoning: Courts are extremely reluctant to pierce a corporate veil and hold shareholders personally liable. Indeed, courts will take this extraordinary step only when necessary to promote justice, such as, for example, when a shareholder uses the corporation to evade personal debts, perpetrate

fraud or a crime, commit an injustice, or gain an unfair advantage. To hold a shareholder liable, the boundaries between the shareholder and the corporation must be so confused that, in effect, the business does not exist separately and to pretend that it does is unjust to the plaintiff.

In this case, the extraordinary remedy of piercing the corporate veil should be granted. Becker knowingly violated his duties as an officer, director, and shareholder of Becker Interiors by treating the corporation as his personal piggy bank. He testified that renovations to his personal residence were legitimate corporate expenses because he used the house as a showcase for his work. The court did not find this testimony credible. Nor did the court believe that Becker acted on his accountant's advice when he commingled personal and corporation funds. The court more easily believed his later testimony that his accountant was "mystified" by this commingling of funds. The court orders Becker to pay Brooks $54,597.09.

TERMINATION

Terminating a corporation is a three-step process:

- *Vote.* The directors recommend to the shareholders that the corporation be dissolved, and a majority of the shareholders agree.

- *Filing.* The corporation files "Articles of Dissolution" with the Secretary of State.

- *Winding Up.* The officers of the corporation pay its debts and distribute the remaining property to shareholders. When the winding up is completed, the corporation ceases to exist.

The Secretary of State may dissolve a corporation that violates state law by, for example, failing to pay the required annual fees. Indeed, many corporations, particularly small ones, do not bother with the formal dissolution process. They simply cease paying their annual fees and let the Secretary of State act. A court may dissolve a corporation if it is insolvent or if its directors and shareholders cannot resolve conflict over how the corporation should be managed. The court will then appoint a receiver to oversee the winding up.

THE ROLE OF CORPORATE MANAGEMENT

Now you know how to avoid some of the legal pitfalls that can ensnare the unwary entrepreneur when organizing a corporation. But what happens as the business grows? In the beginning, many entrepreneurs fund their startup themselves (with the aid of credit cards), but most expect that the business will ultimately attract outside investors. This concept of outside investors is, in historical terms, relatively new. Before the Industrial Revolution in the eighteenth and nineteenth centuries, a business owner typically supplied both capital and management. However, the capital needs of the great manufacturing enterprises spawned by the Industrial Revolution were larger than any small group of individuals could supply. To find capital, firms sought outside investors, who often had neither the knowledge nor the desire to manage the enterprise. Investors without management skills complemented managers without capital. ("Manager" includes both directors and officers.)

Modern businesses still have the same vast need for capital and the same division between managers and investors. As businesses grow, shareholders are too numerous and too uninformed to manage the enterprises they own. Therefore, they elect directors to manage for them. The directors set policy and then appoint officers to implement corporate goals. The Model Act describes the directors' role thus: "All corporate powers shall be exercised by or under the authority of, and the business and affairs of the corporation managed by or under the direction of, its board of directors...."

Directors have the authority to manage the corporate business, but they also have important responsibilities to shareholders and perhaps to other **stakeholders** who are affected by corporate decisions, such as employees, customers, creditors, suppliers, and neighbors. The interests of these various stakeholders often conflict. What are the rights—and responsibilities—of directors and officers to manage these conflicts?

Managers have a fiduciary duty to act in the best interests of the corporation's shareholders. Because shareholders are primarily concerned about their return on investment, managers must *maximize shareholder value*, which means providing shareholders with the highest possible financial return from dividends and stock price. However, reality is more complicated than this simple rule indicates. It is often difficult to determine which strategy will best maximize shareholder value. And what about stakeholders? A number of states have adopted statutes that permit directors to take into account the interests of stakeholders as well as stockholders. The Indiana Code, for example, permits directors to consider "both the short term and long term best interests of the corporation, taking into account, and weighing as the directors deem appropriate, the effects thereof on the corporation's shareholders and the other corporate constituent groups...."[2] The next section looks more closely at directors' responsibilities to their various constituencies.

Stakeholder
Anyone who is affected by the activities of a corporation, such as employees, customers, creditors, suppliers, shareholders, and neighbors.

THE BUSINESS JUDGMENT RULE

Officers and directors have a fiduciary duty to act in the best interests of their stockholders, but under the **business judgment rule**, the courts allow managers great leeway in carrying out this responsibility. The business judgment rule is a common law concept that virtually every court in the country recognizes. In addition, some states have enacted statutes that codify the business judgment rule. To be protected by the business judgment rule, managers must act in good faith:

Duty of Loyalty 1. Without a conflict of interest
Duty of Care 2. With the care that an ordinarily prudent person would take in a similar situation, and
3. In a manner they reasonably believe to be in the best interests of the corporation

[2] Indiana Code Section 23-1-35-1.

The business judgment rule is two shields in one: it protects both the manager and her decision. **If a manager has complied with the rule, a court will not hold her personally liable for any harm her decision has caused the company, nor will the court rescind her decision.** If the manager violates the business judgment rule, then she has the burden of proving that her decision was entirely fair to the shareholders. If it was not entirely fair, she may be held personally liable, and the decision can be rescinded.

The business judgment rule accomplishes three goals:

- *It permits directors to do their job.* If directors were afraid they would be liable for every decision that led to a loss, they would never make a decision, or at least not a risky one.

- *It keeps judges out of corporate management.* Without the business judgment rule, judges would be tempted, if not required, to second-guess managers' decisions.

- *It encourages directors to serve.* No one in his right mind would serve as a director if he knew that every decision was open to attack in the courtroom.

Analysis of the business judgment rule is divided into two parts. The obligation of a manager to act without a conflict of interest is called the **duty of loyalty**. The requirements that a manager act with care and in the best interests of the corporation are referred to as the **duty of care**.

Duty of loyalty

The obligation of a manager to act without a conflict of interest.

Duty of care

The requirement that a manager act with care and in the best interests of the corporation.

DUTY OF LOYALTY

The duty of loyalty prohibits managers from making a decision that benefits them at the expense of the corporation.

Self-Dealing

Self-dealing means that a manager makes a decision benefiting either himself or another company with which he has a relationship. While working at the Blue Moon restaurant, Zeke signs a contract on behalf of the restaurant to purchase bread from Rising Sun Bakery. Unbeknownst to anyone at Blue Moon, he is a part owner of Rising Sun. Zeke has engaged in self-dealing, which is a violation of the duty of loyalty.

Once a manager engages in self-dealing, the business judgment rule no longer applies. This does not mean the manager is automatically liable to the corporation or that his decision is automatically void. All it means is that the court will no longer presume that the transaction was acceptable. Instead, the court will scrutinize the deal more carefully. A self-dealing transaction is valid in any one of the following situations:

- **The disinterested members of the board of directors approve the transaction.** Disinterested directors are those who do not themselves benefit from the transaction.

- **The disinterested shareholders approve it.** The transaction is valid if the shareholders who do not benefit from it are willing to approve it.

- **The transaction was entirely fair to the corporation.** In determining fairness, the courts will consider the impact of the transaction on the corporation and whether the price was reasonable.

Exhibit 30.3 illustrates the rules on self-dealing.

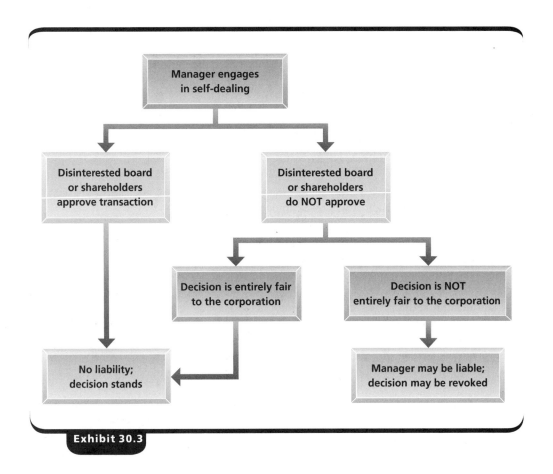

Exhibit 30.3

Corporate officers, especially in family businesses, sometimes forget that they do not have the right to do whatever they want. The following case illustrates the business judgment rule and also the enduring principle that litigation is a very sad method for resolving family disputes.

LIPPMAN v. SHAFFER

15 Misc. 3d 705; 836 N.Y.S.2d 766; 2006 N.Y. Misc. LEXIS 4212
SUPREME COURT OF NEW YORK, 2006

CASE SUMMARY

Facts: Harry Lippman's son, James, had two children, Wade and Amy. Years ago, Harry purchased Despatch Industries, Inc., which manufactured hardware for cabinets. James worked for the company until his retirement. In 1975, when Wade graduated from college, he joined the family business. Amy's husband, Alan Shaffer, went on the company payroll in 1982. In 1993, Wade and Alan both signed identical employment contracts with Despatch. In 1999, after Wade and his father, James, had a falling out, Wade quit his job with the company. The Despatch board agreed to pay $1.3 million to both Wade and Alan. Company tax returns referred to these as "severance" payments, although Alan continued to work for the company and receive a salary.

Wade filed suit against Alan and Despatch, alleging that the payments to Alan were improper and should be returned. The defendants argued that the payments were protected by the business judgment rule. Wade filed a motion for summary judgment.

Issue: *Were the payments to Alan protected by the business judgment rule?*

Decision: No, these payments were not protected and Wade's motion for summary judgment was granted.

Reasoning: The purpose of the business judgment rule is to prevent courts from second-guessing corporate decision making. But that does not mean managers can do whatever they want. The business judgment rule does not apply if (1) the directors were self-dealing and (2) the decision was not entirely fair to the corporation. Here, Alan engaged in self-dealing: not only was he on the board that approved the payment to himself, he signed the check. The decision was not fair because Alan had no right to receive the money—it was a "severance" payment, but he still worked for the company. The payment to Wade, on the other hand, was fair because he had left the company. Alan received something he was not entitled to, while Wade simply got what he was owed under his contract.

Corporate Opportunity

The self-dealing rules prevent managers from forcing their companies into unfair deals. The corporate opportunity doctrine is the reverse—it prohibits managers from excluding their company from favorable deals. **Managers are in violation of the corporate opportunity doctrine if they compete against the corporation without its consent.**

Charles Guth was president of Loft, Inc., which operated a chain of candy stores. These stores sold Coca-Cola. Guth purchased the Pepsi-Cola Co. personally, without offering the opportunity to Loft. The Delaware court found that Guth had violated the corporate opportunity doctrine and ordered him to transfer all his shares in Pepsi to Loft.[3] That was in 1939, and Pepsi-Cola was bankrupt; today, PepsiCo, Inc. is worth more than $100 billion.

In the following case, the manager felt that he had a good reason for taking a corporate opportunity. Unfortunately, the court disagreed.

ANDERSON V. BELLINO

265 Neb. 577, 658 N.W.2d 645, 2003 LEXIS 49
SUPREME COURT OF NEBRASKA, 2003

CASE SUMMARY

Facts: Richard Bellino and Robert Anderson formed LaVista Lottery, Inc. to operate a restaurant, lounge, and keno game in LaVista, Nevada.[4] They each owned 50 percent of the stock of Lottery, and both were officers and directors. During the next nine years, Lottery grossed more than $100 million. Bellino and Anderson each received over $4 million in salary and dividends. Although Bellino and Anderson were both involved in Lottery, Bellino spent more time, in part because of his personal relationship with Lottery's lounge manager. During this period, Bellino did not complain to Anderson about his lack of involvement in Lottery, and Anderson never refused to do anything that Bellino asked him to do.

Resentful of Anderson's work ethic, Bellino set up a meeting with LaVista's city administrator. Until that meeting, the city had been satisfied with Lottery's performance.

[3] *Guth v. Loft*, 5 A.2d 503, 23 Del. Ch. 255, 1939 Del. LEXIS 13 (Del. 1939).
[4] Keno is a game of chance similar to bingo except that in keno, the players choose the numbers on their ticket.

But after the meeting, the administrator recommended to the city council that the keno contract be put up for competitive bid. Bellino incorporated LaVista Keno, Inc., to bid on the contract.

Bellino wrote to Anderson complaining that he (Bellino) was doing too much work for Lottery at too little pay. (Evidently, $4 million is not as much as it used to be.) Therefore, Bellino intended to resign from Lottery and bid on the city contract himself. Anderson offered to do more work or whatever Bellino wanted, but Bellino refused any effort at reconciliation. He then submitted a bid on behalf of Keno. At the time he submitted the bid, he was still an officer of Lottery, as well as a director and a 50 percent shareholder. Anderson also bid on the contract on behalf of Lottery. The city awarded the new contract to Keno.

Anderson and Lottery filed suit against Bellino and Keno, alleging that they had usurped a corporate opportunity. The lower court found for Anderson and Lottery. It ordered Bellino to pay $644,992.63 but provided that Bellino could receive a credit of $172,514.63 against the judgment if Bellino transferred the stock of Keno to Lottery and

persuaded the city to relicense the keno contract from Keno to Lottery.

Issues: *Did Bellino usurp a corporate opportunity? Is he liable to Lottery?*

Decision: Affirmed. Bellino did usurp a corporate opportunity. He must comply with the lower court's order to pay Lottery.

Reasoning: Bellino argues that the corporate opportunity was simply the right to bid on the keno contract. But that is not true—the opportunity was the keno contract itself. The right to bid was simply a preliminary step toward obtaining the opportunity.

Because an officer or director has a fiduciary obligation, he must always act in good faith in his dealings with the corporation. He is liable if he causes harm to the corporation or deprives it of business.

By winning the keno contract, Bellino deprived Lottery of its only business. He should never have bid on the contract himself.

EXAM *Strategy*

Question: Uncle signed a lease with Landlord on a storefront in Georgetown, D.C. Uncle convinced Nephew to start a furniture store in the space. Uncle and Nephew formed a corporation to operate the store. Uncle owned 51 percent and Nephew 49 percent of the company's stock. Uncle signed a lease between himself and the store at a price that was 20 percent higher than the rent Uncle was paying Landlord. Uncle purchased a warehouse and then rented it to the corporation at a fair market rent. Nephew sued, alleging that the two leases were not valid. Were they?

Strategy: Under the business judgment rule, the courts will not second-guess a corporate action. However, if a manager engages in self-dealing, the business judgment rule does not apply.

Result: Uncle violated the duty of loyalty twice. The lease for the storefront was self-dealing—it directly benefited him. When he purchased the warehouse, he took a corporate opportunity that he should have offered first to the company. He is personally liable for any damages to the corporation. The company also has the right to cancel both leases and to purchase the warehouse from him.

DUTY OF CARE

In addition to the *duty of loyalty*, managers also owe a *duty of care*. **The duty of care requires officers and directors to act in the best interests of the corporation and to use the same care that an ordinarily prudent person would take in a similar situation.**

Rational Business Purpose

Courts generally agree in principle that directors and officers are liable for decisions that have no rational business purpose. In practice, however, these same courts have been extremely supportive of managerial decisions, looking hard to find some justification. For decades, the Chicago Cubs baseball team refused to install lights in Wrigley Field. Cubs' fans could only take themselves out to the ball game during the day. A shareholder sued on the grounds that the Cubs' revenues were peanuts and crackerjack compared with those generated by other teams that played at night. The Cubs defended their decision on the grounds that a large night crowd would cause the neighborhood to deteriorate, depressing the value of Wrigley Field (which was not owned by the Cubs). The court rooted for the home team and found that the Cubs' excuse was a "rational purpose" and a legitimate exercise of the business judgment rule.[5]

Legality

Courts are generally unsympathetic to managers who engage in illegal behavior, even if their goal is to help the company. For example, the managing director of an amusement park in New York State used corporate funds to purchase the silence of people who threatened to complain that the park was illegally operating on Sunday. The court ordered the director to repay the money he had spent on bribes, even though the company had earned large profits on Sundays.[6]

Informed Decision

Generally, courts will protect managers who make an *informed* decision, even if the decision ultimately harms the company. Making an informed decision means carefully investigating the facts. However, even if the decision is uninformed, the directors will not be held liable if the decision was entirely fair to the shareholders.

Exhibit 30.4 provides an overview of the duty of care.

EXAM *Strategy*

Question: You are the CEO of a software company. You will only allow your engineers to create software for Apple computers, not for PCs because you think Apple is cooler and you hate Microsoft. Some of your shareholders disagree with this policy. Is your decision protected by the business judgment rule?

Strategy: Remember that you owe a duty of care to the corporation. This means that you must have a rational business purpose for your decision.

Result: The courts are very generous in defining a rational business purpose. They would probably uphold your decision as long as it was not in some way personally benefiting you, e.g., as long as your name is not Steve Jobs (an Apple executive and major shareholder).

---

[5] *Shlensky v. Wrigley*, 95 Ill. App. 2d 173, 237 N.E.2d 776, 1968 Ill. App. LEXIS 1107 (Ill. App. Ct. 1968).
[6] *Roth v. Robertson*, 64 Misc. 343, 118 N.Y.S. 351, 1909 N.Y. Misc. LEXIS 279 (N.Y. 1909).

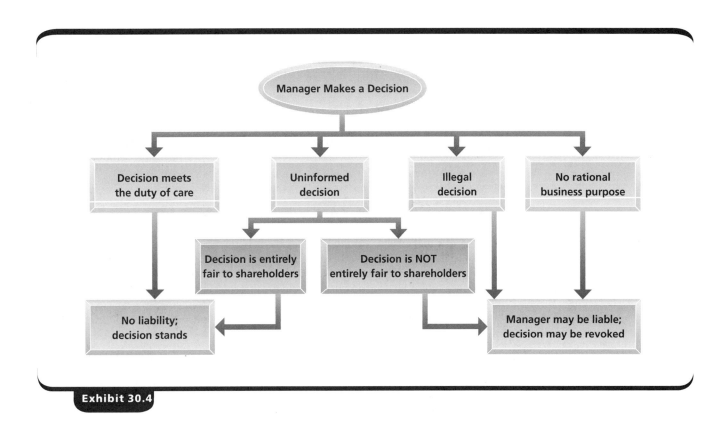

Exhibit 30.4

TAKEOVERS

The business judgment rule is an important guideline for officers and directors in the routine management of corporations. It also plays a crucial role in the regulation of hostile takeovers. In addition, both Congress and many state legislatures have passed statutes that define the roles of the various combatants in takeovers.

There are three ways to acquire control of a company:

- *Buy the company's assets.* Such a sale must be approved by both the shareholders and the board of directors of the acquired company.

- *Merge with the company.* In a merger, one company absorbs another. The acquired company ceases to exist. A merger must also be approved by the shareholders and the board of directors of the target company. If the current directors object, an acquiring company could buy enough stock to replace the board, but these battles are difficult and often end in defeat for the acquirer.

- *Buy stock from the shareholders.* This method is called a **tender offer** because the acquirer asks shareholders to "tender," or offer their stock for sale. Unlike the other methods of obtaining control, approval from the board of directors of the target company is not strictly necessary. As long as shareholders tender enough stock, the acquirer gains control. A tender offer is called a **hostile takeover** if the board of the target resists.

Tender offer
A public offer to buy a block of stock directly from shareholders.

Hostile takeover
An outsider buys a company in the face of opposition from the target company's board of directors.

As a shareholder, would you prefer for the law to favor the target or the bidder? Economic research suggests an answer.

> **ECONOMICS AND THE LAW**   Suppose you are thinking about buying stock in two companies. The directors and officers of Bright Future, Inc., own 25 percent of the company, whereas the managers of Dim Bulb Co. own virtually none. You might think that it would be better to invest in a company in which the managers own substantial amounts of stock. In such a case, managers have the same incentives as shareholders—you both benefit from higher stock prices. Moreover, you assume that managers who own lots of stock must have reason to believe that their company's future is promising. Because managers are likely to know more about the inner workings of a company than an ordinary shareholder would, you might legitimately conclude that Bright Future has, well, the brighter future.
>
> It turns out that reality is more complex. If managers own so much stock that they can defeat takeovers, then they tend to become complacent and care less about shareholder value. This phenomenon is called the "entrenchment effect." According to some estimates, the entrenchment effect is most pronounced in companies in which managers own between 5 and 25 percent of the stock.[7] Investors might be wise to investigate such companies carefully. Dim Bulb could be a better choice than Bright Future. ◆

FEDERAL REGULATION OF TENDER OFFERS: THE WILLIAMS ACT

The Williams Act applies only if the target company's stock is publicly traded. Under the Williams Act:

- Any individual or group who together acquire more than 5 percent of a company's stock must file a public disclosure document (called a "Schedule 13D") with the Securities and Exchange Commission (SEC);

- On the day a tender offer begins, a bidder must file a disclosure statement with the SEC;

- A bidder must keep a tender offer open for at least 20 business days initially and for at least 10 business days after any substantial change in the terms of the offer;

- Any shareholder may withdraw acceptance of the tender offer at any time while the offer is still open;

- If the bidder raises the price offered, all selling shareholders must be paid the higher price, regardless of when they tendered; and

- If the stockholders tender more shares than the bidder wants to buy, the bidder must purchase shares pro rata (i.e., it must buy the same proportion from everyone, not first come, first served).

---

[7] R. Morck, A. Schleifer, and R.W. Vishny, "Management Ownership and Market Valuation: An Empirical Analysis," Working Paper No. 23, Institute for Financial Research, Faculty of Business, University of Alberta, quoted in P.-O. Bjuggren, "Ownership and Efficiency in Companies Listed on Stockholm Stock Exchange 1985," in M. Faure and R. Van den Bergh, *Essays in Law and Economics* (MAKLU, Antwerp, 1985).

STATE REGULATION OF TAKEOVERS

Common Law of Takeovers

To protect themselves from hostile takeovers, companies adopt defensive measures known as **anti-takeover devices** or **shark repellents.** (The acquiring shareholder in a hostile takeover is sometimes referred to as a "shark.") **Shareholder rights plans (aka poison pills)** are among the most common anti-takeover devices. A target company will, for example, amend its charter to permit it to issue one share of preferred stock to each of its shareholders. If a shark purchases more than 20 percent of the target's stock and subsequently merges with the target, the preferred stock is convertible into 10 shares of the shark. This device makes a takeover much more expensive for the acquiring company.

Conventional wisdom views antitakeover devices as a mixed blessing—beneficial if used to ensure that shareholders receive the highest possible price for their stock in the event of a sale but harmful to shareholders if used only to protect management from being fired. However, recent research indicates that the stock prices of companies with few shark repellents significantly outperform those of companies that provide more protection to their managers.[8]

When establishing takeover defenses, shareholder welfare must be the board's primary concern. The directors may institute shark repellents, but they must do so to ensure that bids are high, not to protect their own jobs.

State Anti-takeover Statutes

When fighting takeover battles, companies have also found support in state governments. Legislators may not care if a group of directors is thrown into the unemployment line, but they do fear the impact on the local economy if a major employer leaves. When the Belzberg family threatened a hostile takeover of auto parts manufacturer Arvin Industries, the second largest employer in Columbus, Indiana, the state legislature quickly passed a tough anti-takeover bill that had been drafted by Arvin's own lawyers. Arvin and the Belzbergs promptly settled.

Most states have now passed laws to deter hostile takeovers. Among the common varieties:

- *Statutes that Automatically Impede Hostile Takeovers.* These statutes, for example, might ban hostile (but not friendly) mergers for five years after the acquirer buys 10 percent of a company.

- *Statutes that Authorize Companies to Fight Off Hostile Takeovers.* These statutes typically permit management, when responding to a hostile takeover, to consider the welfare of company stakeholders, such as the community, customers, suppliers, and employees. Some even go so far as to allow management to consider the regional or national economy.

Most of these statutes do not totally eliminate hostile takeovers. A determined, well-financed bidder can still be successful. But these state statutes do tip the playing field in favor of management. In the process they prevent some takeovers that shareholders might want, but they also ensure that shareholders receive a high price in those takeovers that are successful.

---

[8] P.A. Gompers, J. Ishii, A. Metrick, "Corporate Governance and Equity Prices,"*Quarterly Journal of Economics*, 118(1), Feb. 2003.

> **ETHICS** Supporters of these state statutes argue that large, publicly traded corporations owe a duty to all their constituencies. The loss of a large corporate presence can be immensely disruptive to a community. Perhaps a state should have the right to prevent economic upheaval within its borders.
>
> Opponents contend that shareholders own the company, and their interests ought to be paramount. Anti-takeover legislation entrenches management and prevents shareholders from obtaining the premium that accompanies a takeover. Opponents also argue that, if other stakeholders are so concerned with the well-being of the company, let them put their money where their mouths are and buy stock. And if current managers cannot offer shareholders as high a stock price as an outside raider, they ought to be replaced.
>
> What is that the ethical choice for directors? What guidance does the Chapter 2 ethics checklist offer? Who are the stakeholders? What values are important to a company director? If a director owned stock in another company, how would she wish the directors of that company to respond to a takeover? ◆

THE ROLE OF SHAREHOLDERS

As we have seen, *directors,* **not** *shareholders,* **have the right to manage the corporate business.** At one time corporate stock was primarily owned by individuals, but now institutional investors—pension plans, mutual funds, insurance companies, banks, foundations, and university endowments—own more than 50 percent of all shares publicly traded in the United States. Traditionally, unhappy shareholders could do little more than the "Wall Street walk"—they could sell their shares. The next section of this chapter explores the present day rights of shareholders.

RIGHTS OF SHAREHOLDERS

Shareholders have neither the right nor the obligation to manage the day-to-day business of the enterprise. If you own stock in Starbucks Corp., your share of stock plus $3.83 entitles you to a cup of Grande Vanilla Latte, the same as everyone else. By the same token, if the pipes freeze and the local Starbucks store floods, the manager has no right to call you, as a shareholder, to help clean up the mess. What rights do shareholders have?

RIGHT TO INFORMATION

Under the Model Act, shareholders acting in good faith and with a proper purpose have the right to inspect and copy the corporation's minute book, accounting records, and shareholder lists. A proper purpose is one that aids the shareholder in managing and protecting her investment. If, for example, Celeste is convinced that the directors of Devil Desserts, Inc., are mismanaging the company, she might demand a list of other shareholders so that she can ask them to join her in a lawsuit. This purpose is proper—although the company may not like it—and the company is required to give her the list. If, however, Celeste wants to use the shareholder list as a potential source for her new mail-order catalog featuring exercise equipment, the company could legitimately turn her down. The following case is typical: the court must decide if the shareholder is acting in his role as owner or competitor.

YOU *be the* JUDGE

CHOPRA v. HELIO SOLUTIONS, INC.

2007 Cal. App. Unpub. Lexis 5909
Court of Appeal of California, 2007

Facts: Paul Chopra was a minority shareholder and former director of Helio Solutions, Inc. Both he and Helio were in the business of reselling Sun Microsystems hardware and software. Chopra suspected that: (1) some of Helio's majority shareholders had purchased a building and leased it to Helio at an excessive rent; (2) the company had broken a lease so that it could rent this building; (3) some shareholders had used assets of the corporation to secure a personal loan; (4) Helio had permitted ex-employees to take away substantial business; and (5) the company had not collected a $1 million debt it was owed. In addition, he wanted to know if Helio was planning to issue stock and thereby dilute his ownership. Finally, he felt that his dividend of $1,952.55 was unreasonably low, given that Helio had $88 million in revenue.

Chopra hired a forensic accountant to help him investigate Helio's finances. At the accountant's request, Chopra asked Helio for these documents:

1. articles of incorporation

2. minutes for meetings of the board of directors and shareholders

3. all financial statements

4. all tax returns

5. the general ledger with accompanying journals

6. income and balance sheets

7. schedule of accounts payable and received and inventory

8. depreciation schedule for fixed assets

9. supporting documents including bank loans, lines of credit, accrued payroll liabilities, sales tax liabilities, other receivables, loans to officers and owners, significant prepayments or deposits, and equipment lease agreements

10. monthly bank statements

11. company credit card statements

12. compensation records

13. the following contracts: life insurance policies for officers and/or stockholders; pension plan and profit sharing plans; stock purchase plans; equipment and building leases; employment and bonus agreements for owners or key employees; covenants not to compete; loan agreements and credit information; documents connected with the company's real property; option grants and each owner's curriculum vitae

14. a list of patents

15. budget projections for the current year

16. company brochures and/or marketing information

17. a list of key management personnel with job title

18. an overview of company positions and objectives for each department manager

19. information regarding contingencies and lawsuits;

Helio Solutions gave Chopra items 1–6 but refused to turn over the other material. He filed suit.

You Be the Judge: Which of these documents must a company provide to its shareholders?

Argument for Chopra: These documents are necessary for assessing the value of Chopra's investment in the company and determining whether his interests as a minority shareholder are being protected. For example, without employee agreements and compensation information he cannot assess the current corporate financial situation, value the business, determine if the business is being properly managed, or discover whether the majority shareholders or directors are improperly diverting corporate funds for their own benefit. He needs the contracts and agreements related to equipment and building leases to determine whether the majority shareholders had purchased a building and leased it to Helio at an excessive rate.

Argument for Helio: Chopra is simply on a fishing expedition to find information that would help him compete

continued

against Helio. It seems as if he wants to use our budget projections and managerial objectives so that he can beat us to the punch on some of our new initiatives. Many of the requests relate to specific shareholders rather than to the company. Complying with these requests would be unreasonably burdensome to Helio. It would take weeks of work to pull these documents together and photocopy them.

Shareholders have some rights to corporate information, but they are not entitled to unlimited access to corporate confidences and secrets.

RIGHT TO VOTE
A corporation must have at least one class of stock with voting rights.

Proxies

Proxy

The person whom a shareholder appoints to vote for her at a meeting of the corporation. Also, the document a shareholder signs appointing this substitute voter.

Quorum

The percentage of voters who must be present for a meeting to count.

Annual report

A document that the SEC requires public companies to provide to their shareholders each year. It contains financial data.

Shareholders who do not wish to attend a shareholders' meeting may appoint someone else to vote for them. Confusingly, both this person and the document the shareholder signs to appoint the substitute voter are called a **proxy**. Under SEC rules, companies are not required to solicit proxies. However, a meeting is invalid without a certain percentage of shareholders in attendance, either in person or by proxy. This attendance requirement is referred to as a **quorum**. As a practical matter, if a public company with thousands of investors does not solicit proxies, it will not obtain a quorum. Therefore, virtually all public companies do solicit proxies. Along with the proxy, the company must also give shareholders a **proxy statement** and an **annual report**. The proxy statement provides information on everything from management compensation to a list of directors who miss too many meetings. The annual report contains detailed financial data. Under SEC rules, companies are required to post all of this information on their Web site. They must then mail to shareholders either hard copies of all the information, including ballots, or a card telling shareholders how to vote online. But shareholders always have the right to request hard copy versions.

Shareholder Proposals

Shareholders who oppose a particular company policy may use the proxy process to challenge that policy. **Under SEC rules, any shareholder who has continuously owned for one year at least 1 percent of the company or $2,000 of stock can require that one proposal be placed in the company's proxy statement to be voted on at the shareholder meeting.** In practice, many of these resolutions have a political agenda: cut greenhouse gases, withdraw from Myanmar, ban genetically modified ingredients. Others relate to corporate-governance issues such as secret ballots at shareholder meetings. One of the most popular proposals recently has been so-called "say on pay" votes in which shareholders ask for the right to approve or reject a company's compensation plans.. Over the last three years, public companies voted on 370 shareholder proposals. Prior to 1985, only two proposals had been approved—ever. Currently, about a quarter of all shareholder proposals receive a majority vote each year, a definite improvement (or deterioration, depending on your perspective). If a company refuses to include a shareholder proposal in its proxy material, shareholders can appeal to the SEC.

Despite the long history of shareholder proposals, an essential question remains unanswered: Are shareholder proposals binding on the company? The SEC recommends that proposals be couched in the form of a request or recommendation because state laws sometimes prohibit binding resolutions. Although shareholders traditionally followed this advice, many activists have been angered by companies that refuse to implement proposals that receive a majority vote from shareholders. Now, companies adopt about half of shareholder proposals that receive a majority vote. In response, some shareholders have begun to propose binding resolutions, but the number is still very small.

Ironically, companies sometimes implement shareholder proposals that have not received support from a majority of the shareholders. The pressure of shareholder proposals is credited with inducing many American companies to withdraw from South Africa in protest against its apartheid regime. Other companies implement shareholder proposals without even putting them up for a vote. Indeed, nearly half of all shareholder proposals are now withdrawn before a vote because the company capitulates. Many companies feel they have little choice but to negotiate, particularly with institutional investors over issues of corporate governance. For example, Colgate-Palmolive Co. agreed to a proposal by institutional investors to permit secret ballots at shareholder meetings.

Shareholder Meetings

Annual shareholder meetings are the norm for publicly traded companies. (Although technically not all states require public companies to hold an annual meeting of shareholders, the New York Stock Exchange [NYSE] requires companies listed with it to do so.) Companies whose stock is not publicly traded can either hold an annual meeting or use written consents from their shareholders. Everyone who owns stock on the **record date** must be sent notice of a meeting.

Election and Removal of Directors

The process of electing directors of a publicly traded company is different from what most people think. The nominating committee of the board of directors produces a slate of directors, with one name per opening. This slate is then sent to shareholders whose only choice is to vote in favor of a nominee or to withhold their vote (i.e., not vote at all). If a large number of shareholders withhold their votes, the nominee may be embarrassed a little, but the reality is that as long as he receives at least one vote (which can be his own), he is elected. Traditionally, if shareholders wanted to have a choice, they had to nominate their own slate, prepare and distribute a proxy statement to shareholders, and then communicate with shareholders why their slate is superior. This process is complex and expensive. Not surprisingly, each year only about one or two shareholder groups in the country undertook this effort. However, the SEC recently issued a rule that permits a shareholder who has owned three percent of a company for three years to propose nominees whom the board must include in its own proxy materials. At this writing, the SEC has stayed the rule, pending the outcome of a legal challenge.

The voting process would be fairer if the nominating committee of the board was independent. Although the NYSE does not permit the CEO of a listed company to serve on the board's nominating committee, these committees rarely, if ever, nominate someone to whom the CEO is opposed.

What are unhappy shareholders to do? In the waning years of Michael Eisner's rule at the Walt Disney Company, shareholders withheld 43 percent of their votes from him. But that vote of no confidence did not cause the board to fire him, nor did he resign, at least not immediately.[9] Some companies have adopted rules that require directors to resign if they do not receive a majority of the votes cast. But boards have been known to reappoint directors

---

[9] Ultimately, the Disney board did change its rules to require any directors receiving less than a majority of the votes cast to tender their resignation from the board. The board would then have the option of accepting or rejecting the resignation. Even under this new rule, however, Eisner would not have been forced to resign.

even after they resigned because of a negative shareholder vote. Other companies have set up advisory committees to allow shareholder input into the nomination process. Although shareholders theoretically elect directors who then choose the officers, the reality is that officers (particularly the CEO) choose the directors.

Compensation for Officers and Directors

Given the control that the CEO has over the selection process for the board of directors, it is not surprising that when the board sets the CEO's compensation, the results can sometimes appear to unfairly favor the CEO over the shareholders whose money is being used to compensate her.

Between 2001 and 2003, public companies spent 9.8% of their net income on compensation for top executives. Although there is much talk about "pay for performance" the reality is that luck (such as a favorable movement in exchange rates) is as important a determinant of executive compensation as good performance.[10] Here are some examples of executive compensation that particularly agitated shareholders:

- Michael Eisner was the head of Walt Disney Corporation for 20 years. At the beginning of his tenure, the company did very well and few complained when he was exceedingly well paid. But for the final 13 years, he earned $800 million while the stock performed worse than government bonds (a low-risk, low-return investment).

- During a five-year period in which Pfizer stock lost 43% of its value, its CEO received $65 million in compensation. He was also entitled to a pension of $83 million when he retired.

- The CEO of Fannie Mae earned $90 million during a time when the company's accounting system was so flawed that it overstated its earnings by $11 billion.

To many investors, sky-high executive salaries have become the symbol of all that is wrong with corporate governance. In many companies, salaries and bonus are the least of the compensation. Executives also receive:

- *Stock options.* Concerned about escalating executive salaries, shareholder activists began advocating "pay-for-performance" plans. The theory was that if executives received stock options instead of cash salaries, their incentives would be more closely aligned with those of shareholders. It was a good theory, but in practice, it did not work as intended.

    Stock options became a "heads, I win; tails, you lose" game. When stock prices soared in a bull market, options became unexpectedly valuable. In some cases, managers were richly rewarded even when their company had underperformed the (rising) market. However, when stock prices fell, boards lowered the price of the options.

    Options can be gamed. After the 9/11 terrorist attack, the stock market was closed for four days. When it reopened, stocks took a bigger plunge than they had in any week since Germany invaded France in 1940. In what appeared to be an unseemly exploitation of a national tragedy, 186 companies granted stock options to 511 executives during those few weeks. That is more than twice the number of companies that usually issued stock options in September.[11] These grants were at least legal; not so the backdated options that more

---

[10] See, for example, Marianne Bertrand and Sendhil Mullainathan "Are CEOs Rewarded for Luck? The Ones Without Principals Are," *The Quarterly Journal of Economics*, August 2001.

[11] Charles Forelle, James Bandler and Mark Maremont, "Executive Pay: The 9/11 Factor," *The Wall Street Journal,* July, 15, 2006, p. A1.

than 2,000 companies appear to have issued their executives. In granting options, companies claimed that they had been issued on an earlier date when the stock price was lower. This practice is fraud.

- *Termination, retirement plans and death benefits.* Most public companies provide their top executives with generous termination payments, no matter whether the person dies or is fired. Indeed, many CEO employment contracts provide that the employee is entitled to severance pay unless fired for committing a particular type of felony. Dying also pays. For example, Nabor Industries Ltd. will pay its 78-year-old CEO $263 million when he dies. The CEO of the Shaw Group is entitled to $17 million if he does not compete with the company after he dies.

- *Lavish perks.* Executives have long received perks such as country club memberships and cars, but the roster of options has expanded. One of the most popular perks now is use of the corporate jet. One study found a high correlation between the use of the company plane and membership in far-flung golf clubs. Unfortunately, the correlation is inverse: the more companies spend on private jets, the worse their stock performs.

How much more does a CEO earn than an average worker? In 1975, the answer for the top 100 CEOs was 39 times as much. By 2005, that ratio had risen to 475. (The ratio in Japan is 11 to 1, in Britain 22 to 1.) Or, to look at it another way, in 1960, the average salary of the CEO of a Fortune 500 company was twice that of the president of the United States. In 2006, the ratio was 30 to 1. Why has executive pay become so lavish?

- *Directors, not shareholders, set executive compensation.* Unless directors are major shareholders of the company (which is seldom the case), generous executive compensation has little impact on directors' income. It is easy to be generous with other people's money.

- *Executives have a great deal of influence over their own pay.* In principle, directors set executive compensation after arm's-length negotiations. However, in practice, these negotiations are not so neutral after all, almost always working to the advantage of the executive. For example:

    - *Compensation is rarely linked closely to individual performance, but instead to overall industry or stock market performance, which is defined in a way to favor executives.* Two-thirds of the largest 1,000 U.S. companies report that they performed better than their peers.[12] That is, in part, because these benchmarks can be manipulated. For example, Campbell Soup used one set of benchmark companies to determine executive compensation but another set to evaluate its total shareholder return. In all fairness, it seems that Campbell's ought to be consistent—presumably only one set of companies is the right comparison group.

    - *The busier the directors, the higher the executive pay.* Generally, executives are more likely to be overpaid if directors serve on many boards. These directors may be too busy to pay attention to such details. Such trophy directors may also be afraid that if they offend a chief executive at one company, word will get around, jeopardizing their position on other boards.

---

[11] Charles Forelle, James Bandler and Mark Maremont, "Executive Pay: The 9/11 Factor," *The Wall Street Journal,* July, 15, 2006, p. A1.

[12] Kevin J. Murphy, "Politics, Economics and Executive Compensation," reported in Lucian Bebchuk and Jesse Fried, *Pay Without Performance,* Harvard University Press, 2004, p. 71.

- *Most executives are above average.* Of course, not everyone can be above average, but most directors believe that their executives are. No one wants to admit to hiring incompetents. Suppose that you are on a company's compensation committee and have data about industry averages. If your executives are above average in performance, you should pay them above-average salaries. If they are not above average, you should fire them, which few boards want to do, except in the face of disaster. If *you* raise salaries, the industry average also rises. The next company that sets compensation has an even higher bar to jump. For example, Colgate-Palmolive awarded 2 million stock options to its CEO on the understanding that he would receive no further grants for five years. Three years later, however, when consultants found that the CEO's compensation had fallen below the median, the company immediately awarded him an additional 2.6 million options.

- *Compensation consultants often have conflicts of interest.* Many companies hire compensation consultants to offer advice on executive pay. These same consultants may also provide other services to the company—such as human resource management—for which the fees can be substantial. The consultants have every incentive to suggest generous packages. In any event, it is not their money.

To make matters even worse for shareholders, lavish compensation does not appear to improve a business's success. A study of the 58 companies that were most generous to their CEOs found that, on average, these companies significantly underperformed both the market generally and their industry in particular.[13]

The SEC recently amended its proxy rules to require more information about executive compensation. They wanted to know, for example, why option grants were approved and how much retirement benefits are worth. However, in the first year after this rule change, the SEC found that at least 350 companies had not adequately complied. Their disclosures were, in some cases, both too complex and incomplete.

Corporate executives are not the only people to earn fabulous salaries. Some athletes earn more even than CEOs. What is the difference between athletes and executives (besides a hook shot)? Athletes' salaries are indeed negotiated at arm's length. This negotiation process means that (1) their pay is not camouflaged; (2) they do not receive enormous severance packages on their way out the door; and (3) their retirement pay ranges from modest to nonexistent.[14] Also, an athlete's performance is transparent and easy to measure.

Shareholders' efforts to challenge executive compensation have met with little success. To be successful in such a challenge, shareholders must prove that the board was grossly uninformed or that the amount was so high that it had no relation to the value of the services performed and was really a gift. Courts tend to be unsympathetic to these lines of argument.

Fundamental Corporate Changes

A corporation must seek shareholder approval before undergoing any of the following fundamental changes: a merger, a sale of major assets, dissolution of the corporation, or an amendment to the charter.

---

[13] Reed Abelson, "Who Profits If the Boss Is Overfed?" *New York Times*, June 20, 1999, Business Section, p. 9.

[14] Some of the material in this section on executive compensation is drawn from Lucian Bebchuk and Jesse Fried, *Pay Without Performance*, Harvard University Press, 2004.

Right to Dissent

If a private corporation (i.e., one whose stock is not publicly traded) decides to undertake a fundamental change, the Model Act and many state laws require the company to buy back the stock of any shareholders who object. This process is referred to as dissenters' rights, and the company must pay "fair value" for the stock. Fundamental changes include a merger or a sale of most of the company's assets.

Right to Protection From Other Shareholders

Anyone who owns enough stock to control a corporation has a fiduciary duty to minority shareholders. (Minority shareholders are those with less than a controlling interest.) The courts have long recognized that minority shareholders are entitled to extra protection because it is easy (perhaps even natural) for controlling shareholders to take advantage of them. For example, a court refused to allow one brother, who was a majority shareholder of the family company, to force the other one (who held only a minority stake) to sell his shares. According to the court, a minority shareholder can be ejected only for a reason that is fair or has a business purpose.[15]

Corporate Governance in Publicly Traded Companies: Sarbanes-Oxley and Stock Exchange Rules

A spate of corporate scandals, involving such high-flying companies as Enron Corp., revealed that some boards of directors have not provided adequate oversight of their companies. In response, Congress passed the Sarbanes-Oxley Act of 2002 (SOX). This statute applies to public companies as well as to all foreign companies listed on a U.S. stock exchange. Under SOX:

- Rule 404 requires each company to adopt effective financial controls.

- CEOs and CFOs must personally certify their company's financial statements. They are subject to criminal penalties for violations.

- All members of a board's audit committee must be independent.

- A company cannot make personal loans to its directors or officers.

- If a company has to restate its earnings, its chief executive officer and chief financial officer must reimburse the company for any bonus or profits they have received from selling company stock within a year of the release of the flawed financials.

- Each company must disclose if it has an ethics code and, if it does not, why not.

- It is a felony to interfere with a federal investigation into fraud.

- Whistleblowing employees are protected.

- A new Public Accounting Oversight Board has been established to oversee the auditing of public companies.

The NYSE and NASDAQ have also established a new role for independent directors at listed companies:

---

[15] *Lerner v. Lerner*, 306 Md. 771, 511 A.2d 501, 1986 Md. LEXIS 264 (Md. 1986).

- Independent directors must comprise a majority of the board.

- They must meet regularly on their own without inside directors.

- Only independent directors can serve on compensation or nominating committees.

- Audit committees must have at least three independent directors who are financially literate.

The goal of these reforms was to prevent corporate abuses and restore investor confidence. Have the goals been achieved? Were they worth the cost? It has been estimated that in the first five years, public companies spent $26 billion on SOX compliance. There is also some consensus that, as a result of SOX, directors are more careful, financial accounting is more reliable and investor confidence is higher. And the annual cost of compliance seems to be declining.

It is difficult to quantify the benefit that investors gain from a reduction in accounting fraud. Only time will reveal whether SOX has given the boot to corporate scandals.

ENFORCING SHAREHOLDER RIGHTS

Shareholders in serious conflict with management have two different mechanisms for enforcing their rights: a derivative lawsuit or a direct lawsuit.

DERIVATIVE LAWSUITS

> The problem, of course, was that the shareholders were asking the board to approve a lawsuit against … itself.

A derivative lawsuit is brought by *shareholders* **to remedy a wrong to the** *corporation*. The suit is brought in the name of the corporation, and all proceeds of the litigation go to the corporation. For example, shareholders of Disney were upset when the board of directors approved a $130 million severance package for Michael Ovitz, who had served (unsuccessfully) as Disney's president for 14 months.[16] Because shareholders felt that that decision had harmed the company, they wanted to sue the directors. But they had no right to sue on their own behalf, because it was the *company* that had been harmed. Any injury to the shareholders was indirect. Thus, only the corporation could sue.

How could the shareholders force the company to sue the board? They had to **make demand** on the board, meaning they had to ask the board to bring suit. The problem, of course, was that the shareholders were asking the board to approve a lawsuit against … itself. The board has the right to turn down such a demand, and that is exactly what they generally do. There is one exception: the shareholders can file suit on behalf of the corporation without the approval of the board if *demand would be futile*. **Demand is considered to be futile if the directors violated the duty of care or the duty of loyalty that are required by the business judgment rule**. Showing a violation of the business judgment rule is, in essence, the only successful way to bring a derivative action. In the Disney case, the court decided that the decision to pay Michael Ovitz $130 million did not violate the business judgment rule. The board of directors had acted without a conflict of interest, had been informed, and had had a rational business purpose. Thus, the shareholders lost.

---

[16] *Brehm v. Eisner*, 2006 Del. LEXIS 307 (Del. 2006).

Alternatively, shareholders wanted to sue directors of eBay, Inc. who had received millions of dollars of stock from investment bank Goldman Sachs even as they were hiring Goldman to do work for eBay. The court held that the directors had had a conflict of interest which violated the business judgment rule. Therefore, the shareholders could bring suit against them in the name of the corporation without their permission.[17]

If shareholders are permitted to proceed with their derivative action, all damages go to the corporation; the individual shareholders benefit only to the extent that the settlement causes their stock to rise in value. Litigation is tremendously expensive. How can shareholders afford to sue if they are not entitled to damages? A corporation that loses a derivative suit must pay the legal fees of the victorious shareholders. (Losing shareholders are generally not required to pay the corporation's legal fees.) Most derivative lawsuits are brought by lawyers who seek out shareholders and persuade them to sue. Without this incentive, few shareholders would bring derivative suits, and much corporate wrongdoing would go unpunished.

Direct Lawsuits

Shareholders are permitted to sue the corporation directly only if their own rights have been harmed. If, for example, the corporation denies shareholders the right to inspect its books and records or to hold a shareholder meeting, they may sue in their own names and keep any damages awarded. The corporation is not required to pay the shareholders' legal fees; winning shareholders can use part of any damage award for this purpose.

CHAPTER CONCLUSION

Corporations first became prominent in the eighteenth and nineteenth centuries as a means for businesses to raise the outside capital needed for large-scale manufacturing. Shareholders without management skills complemented managers without capital. Although this separation between management and owners makes great economic sense and has contributed significantly to the rise of the American economy, it also creates complex legal issues. How can shareholders ensure that the corporation will operate in their best interest? How can managers make tough decisions without being second-guessed by shareholders? Balancing the interests of managers and shareholders is a complex problem the law has struggled to resolve, without completely satisfying either side.

EXAM REVIEW

1. **PROMOTERS** Promoters are personally liable for contracts they sign before the corporation is formed unless the corporation and the third party agree to a novation. (p. 753)

---

[17] *In re eBay, Inc. Shareholder Litigation*, 2004 Del. Ch. LEXIS 4 (Del. 2004).

EXAM Strategy

Question: Ajouelo signed an employment contract with Wilkerson. The contract stated: "Whatever company, partnership, or corporation that Wilkerson may form for the purpose of manufacturing shall succeed Wilkerson and exercise the rights and assume all of Wilkerson's obligations as fixed by this contract." Two months later, Wilkerson formed Auto-Soler Co. Ajouelo entered into a new contract with Auto-Soler providing that the company was liable for Wilkerson's obligations under the old contract. Neither Wilkerson nor the company ever paid Ajouelo. He sued Wilkerson personally. Does Wilkerson have any obligations to Ajouelo?

Strategy: A promoter is not liable for a contract he signed on behalf of a yet-to-be-formed corporation if the third party (in this case, Wilkinson) agrees to a novation. (See the "Result" at the end of this section.)

2. **STATE OF INCORPORATION** Companies generally incorporate in the state in which they will be doing business. However, if they intend to operate in several states, they may choose to incorporate in a jurisdiction known for its favorable corporate laws, such as Delaware or Nevada. (p. 754)

3. **THE CHARTER** A corporate charter must generally include the company's name, address, registered agent, purpose, and a description of its stock. (p. 754)

4. **PIERCING THE CORPORATE VEIL** A court may, under certain circumstances, pierce the corporate veil and hold shareholders personally liable for the debts of the corporation. (p. 758)

5. **TERMINATION** Termination of a corporation is a three-step process requiring a shareholder vote, the filing of "Articles of Dissolution," and the winding up of the enterprise's business. (p. 760)

6. **FIDUCIARY DUTY** Officers and directors have a fiduciary duty to act in the best interests of the shareholders of the corporation. (p. 761)

7. **BUSINESS JUDGMENT RULE** The business judgment rule protects managers from liability for their decisions as long as the managers observe the duty of care and the duty of loyalty. (p. 761)

8. **DUTY OF LOYALTY** Under the duty of loyalty, managers may not enter into an agreement on behalf of their corporation that benefits them personally, unless the board of directors or the shareholders have first approved it. If the manager does not seek the necessary approval, the business judgment rule no longer applies,

and the manager will be liable unless the transaction was entirely fair to the corporation. (p. 762)

9. **CORPORATE OPPORTUNITY** Under the duty of loyalty, managers may not take advantage of an opportunity that rightfully belongs to the corporation. (p. 764)

EXAM Strategy

Question: Vern Hayes owned 32 percent of Coast Oyster Co. and served as president and director. The company owned several large oyster beds, including two located in Washington State. Coast was struggling to pay its debts, so Hayes suggested that the company sell the Washington beds to Keypoint Co. After the sale, other officers at Coast discovered that Hayes owned 50 percent of Keypoint. They demanded that he give the Keypoint stock to Coast. Did Hayes violate his duty to Coast?

Strategy: Here, Hayes has violated the duty of loyalty not once, but twice. (See the "Result" at the end of this section.)

10. **DUTY OF CARE** Under the duty of care, managers must make honest, informed decisions that have a rational business purpose. (p. 766)

11. **WILLIAMS ACT** The Williams Act regulates the activities of a bidder in a tender offer for stock in a publicly traded corporation. (p. 768)

12. **PROXIES** Virtually all publicly held companies solicit proxies from their shareholders. A proxy authorizes someone else to vote in place of the shareholder. (p. 772)

13. **SHAREHOLDER PROPOSALS** Under certain circumstances public companies must include shareholder proposals in the proxy statement. (p. 772)

14. **DISSENTERS' RIGHTS** A shareholder of a privately held company who objects to a fundamental change in the corporation can insist that her shares be bought out at fair value. This protection is referred to as "dissenters' rights." (p. 777)

15. **MINORITY SHAREHOLDERS** Controlling shareholders have a fiduciary duty to minority shareholders. (p. 777)

16. **PROTECTION AGAINST MANAGEMENT ABUSES** Congress, the NYSE, and NASDAQ have all taken steps to prevent management abuses. These new regulations

require that companies adopt effective financial controls. They also require more independent directors on the board as a whole and on important subcommittees. (p. 777)

17. **DERIVATIVE LAWSUITS** A derivative lawsuit is brought by shareholders to remedy a wrong to the corporation. The suit is brought in the name of the corporation, and all proceeds of the litigation go to the corporation. (p. 778)

EXAM Strategy

Question: Daniel Cowin was a minority shareholder of Bresler & Reiner, Inc., a public company that developed real estate in Washington, D.C. He alleged numerous instances of corporate mismanagement, fraud, self-dealing, and breach of fiduciary duty by the board of directors. He sought damages for the diminished value of his stock. Could Cowin bring this suit as a direct action, or must it be a derivative suit?

Strategy: If the wrong was to the corporation, then Cowin must bring a derivative lawsuit. He can only bring a direct action if the harm was to him personally. (See the "Result" at the end of this section.)

1. Result: Wilkerson may have had an ethical obligation to Ajouelo but not a legal one. The court held that the second contract was a novation, which ended Wilkerson's obligations under the first contract.

9. Result: If the shareholders and directors did not know of Hayes's interest in Keypoint, they could not properly evaluate the contract. Hayes should have told them. Also, by purchasing stock in Keypoint, Hayes took a corporate opportunity. He had to turn over any profits he had earned on the transaction, as well as his stock in Keypoint.

17. Result: The court ruled that the injury had fallen equally on all the shareholders and therefore a derivative suit was appropriate.

ADDITIONAL QUESTIONS

1. Michael Ferns incorporated Erin Homes, Inc., to manufacture mobile homes. He issued himself a stock certificate for 100 shares for which he made no payment. He and his wife served as officers and directors of the organization, but, during the eight years of its existence, the corporation held only one meeting. Erin always had its own checking account, and all proceeds from the sales of mobile homes were deposited there. It filed federal income tax returns each year, using its own federal identification number. John and Thelma Laya paid $17,500 to purchase a mobile home from Erin, but the company never delivered it to them. The Layas sued Erin Homes and Michael Ferns, individually. Should the court "pierce the corporate veil" and hold Ferns personally liable?

2. **CPA QUESTION** A corporate stockholder is entitled to which of the following rights?

   (a) Elect officers

   (b) Receive annual dividends

   (c) Approve dissolution

   (d) Prevent corporate borrowing

3. An appraiser valued a subsidiary of Signal Co. at between $230 million and $260 million. Six months later, Burmah Oil offered to buy the subsidiary at $480 million, giving Signal only three days to respond. The board of directors accepted the offer without obtaining an updated valutation of the subsidiary or determining if other companies would offer a higher price. Members of the board were sophisticated, with a great deal of experience in the oil industry. A Signal Co. shareholder sued to prevent the sale. Is the Signal board protected by the business judgment rule?

4. **YOU BE THE JUDGE** WRITING PROBLEM Asher Hyman and Stephen Stahl formed a corporation named Ampersand to produce plays. Both men were employed by the corporation. After producing one play, Stahl decided to write *Phillys Beat*, focusing on the history of rock and roll in Philadelphia. As the play went into production, however, the two men quarreled over Hyman's repeated absences from work and the company's serious financial difficulties. Stahl resigned from Ampersand and formed another corporation to produce the play. Did the opportunity to produce *Phillys Beat* belong to Ampersand? **Argument for Stahl:** Ampersand was formed for the purpose of producing plays, not writing them. When Stahl wrote *Phillys Beat*, he was not competing against Ampersand. **Argument for Hyman:** Ampersand was in the business of producing plays, and it wanted *Phillys Beat*.

5. Angelica is planning to start a home security business in McGehee, Arkansas. She plans to start modestly but hopes to expand her business within 5 years to neighboring towns and, perhaps, within 10 years to neighboring states. Her inclination is to incorporate her business in Delaware. Is her inclination correct?

6. **ETHICS** Edgar Bronfman, Jr., dropped out of high school to go to Hollywood and write songs and produce movies. Eventually, he left Hollywood to work in the family business—the Bronfmans owned 36 percent of Seagram Co., a liquor and beverage conglomerate. Promoted to president of the company at the age of 32, Bronfman seized a second chance to live his dream. Seagram received 70 percent of its earnings from its 24 percent ownership of DuPont Co. Bronfman sold this stock at less than market value to purchase (at an inflated price) 80 percent of MCA, a movie and music company that had been a financial disaster for its prior owners. Some observers thought Bronfman had gone Hollywood; others that he had gone crazy. After the deal was announced, the price of Seagram shares fell 18 percent. Was there anything Seagram shareholders could have done to prevent what to them was not a dream but a nightmare? Apart from legal issues, was Bronfman's decision ethical? What ethical obligations did he owe Seagram's shareholders?

7. Klinicki and Lundgren started an air taxi service in Berlin, Germany, under the name Berlinair, Inc. Lundgren was approached by a group of travel agents who were interested in hiring an air charter business to take German tourists on vacation to warmer climes. Lundgren formed Air Berlin Charter Co. (ABC) and was its sole owner. On behalf of ABC, he entered into an air charter contract with the Berlin travel

agents. Lundgren concealed his negotiations from Klinicki, even though he used Berlinair working time, staff, money, and facilities. Lundgren defended his behavior on the grounds that Berlinair could not afford to enter into a contract with the travel agents. Has Lundgren violated the corporate opportunity doctrine?

8. ***CPA QUESTION*** Generally, a corporation's articles of incorporation must include all of the following except the:

   (a) Name of the corporation's registered agent.

   (b) Name of each incorporator.

   (c) Number of authorized shares.

   (d) Quorum requirements.

9. Two shareholders of Bruce Company, Harry and Yolan Gilbert, were fighting management for control of the company. They asked for permission to inspect Bruce's stockholder list so that they could either solicit support for their slate of directors at the upcoming stockholders' meeting, or attempt to buy additional stock from other stockholders, or both. Bruce's board refused to allow the Gilberts to see the shareholder list on the grounds that the Gilberts owned another corporation that competed with Bruce. Do the Gilberts have the right to see Bruce's shareholder list?

10. ***ROLE REVERSAL*** Write a short-answer question that deals with the duty of care under the business judgment rule.

INTERNET RESEARCH PROBLEMS

Think of an idea for a new company and prepare a corporate charter for your business. You can find sample charters online. For extra credit, do one charter for your state and one for Delaware.

Using the Internet, find information on a company's shareholder proposals in the last year. (You can, for example, type into Google: "shareholder proposals 2010.") What were these proposals about? What was the outcome of the shareholder vote? Can you find a proposal that shareholders supported?

You can find further practice problems at www.cengagebrain.com. See the preface of this book for website access details.

SECURITIES REGULATION

In 1926, America was gripped by a fever of stock market speculation. "Playing the market" became a national mania. The most engrossing news on any day's front page was the market. Up and up it soared. The cause of this psychological virus is uncertain, but the focus of the infection was the New York Stock Exchange. Between 1926 and 1929, annual volume leaped from 451 million to over 1.1 billion shares.

> **From the peak of the bull market in September to the debacle of October 29, over $32 billion of equity value simply vanished from the earth.**

Much of this feverish trading was done on margin. Customers put down only 10 or 20 percent of a stock's purchase price and then borrowed the rest from their broker. This easy-payment plan excited the gambling instinct of unwary amateurs and professional speculators alike. By September 1929, the volume of these margin loans was equal to about half the entire public debt of the United States.

On September 4, 1929, stock prices began to soften, and for the next month they slid gently. Over the weekend of October 19, brokers sent out thousands of margin calls, asking customers to pay down loans that now exceeded the value of their stock. If customers failed to pay, brokers dumped their stock on the market, causing prices to fall further and brokers to make more margin calls. Soon there was a mad scramble of selling as prices plunged in wild disorder. Tens of thousands of investors across the country were wiped out. On Tuesday, October 29, 1929, the speculative boom completely collapsed. That day, 4 million shares were traded, a record that stood for 30 years. From the peak of the bull market in September to the debacle of October 29, over $32 billion of equity value simply vanished from the earth.

The stock market crash spawned the Great Depression—the most pervasive, persistent, and destructive economic crisis the nation has ever faced. Retail trade fell by one-half, automobile production by two-thirds, steel by three-quarters. In 1933, more businesses failed than in any other year in history. Surviving businesses responded to the crisis by cutting dividends, reducing inventories, laying off workers, slashing wages, and canceling capital investments.

Unemployment statistics were the most poignant of all. In 1932, one in every five people in the labor force was out of a job. Millions of others were under-employed, working only two or three days a week for wages that could not support a family. Distress cut indiscriminately across all economic and social classes. Bankers, insurance agents, architects, and lawyers joined the throng of unemployed. Articles such as the following were common in newspapers across the land:

> *New York, Jan. 6, 1933 (AP)*—After vainly trying to get a stay of dispossession until Jan. 15 from his apartment in Brooklyn, yesterday, Peter J. Cornell, 48 years old, a former roofing contractor out of work and penniless, fell dead in the arms of his wife. A doctor gave the cause of his death as heart disease, and the police said it had at least partly been caused by the bitter disappointment of a long day's fruitless attempt to prevent himself and his family being put out on the streets.[1]

INTRODUCTION

At the time of the great stock market crash, there was no federal securities law, only state law. Congress recognized that the country needed a national securities system if it was to avoid another such catastrophe. In 1933, Congress passed the Securities Act of 1933 (1933 Act) to regulate the issuance of new securities. The next year, it passed the Securities Exchange Act of 1934 (1934 Act) to regulate companies with publicly traded securities. The 1934 Act also established the Securities and Exchange Commission (SEC), the regulatory agency that oversees the securities industry.

THE SECURITIES AND EXCHANGE COMMISSION
The SEC creates law in three different ways:

- **Rules.** The securities statutes are often little more than general guides. Through its rules, the SEC fills in the crucial details.

- **Releases.** These are informal pronouncements from the SEC on current issues. Releases often operate as two-way communication. When the SEC issues a release to announce a proposed change in the rules, it also asks for comments on the proposal.

---

[1] The material in this section is adapted from Cabell Phillips, *From the Crash to the Blitz* (Toronto: Macmillan, 1969).

- **No-Action Letters.** Anyone who is in doubt about whether a particular transaction complies with the securities laws can ask the SEC directly. The response is called a no-action letter because it states that "the staff will recommend that the Commission take no action" if the transaction is done in a specified manner.

In addition to creating laws, the SEC has the power to enforce them. It can bring **cease and desist orders** against those who violate the securities laws, and it can also levy fines or confiscate profits from illegal transactions. Those accused of wrongdoing can appeal these sanctions to the courts. The SEC does not have the authority to bring a criminal action; it refers criminal cases to the Justice Department.

WHAT IS A SECURITY?

Both the 1933 and the 1934 Acts regulate securities. The official definition of a security includes a note, stock, treasury stock, bond, debenture, evidence of indebtedness, certificate of interest or participation in any profit-sharing agreement, and 17 other equivalents. Courts have interpreted this definition to mean that a **security** is any transaction in which the buyer (1) invests money in a common enterprise and (2) expects to earn a profit predominantly from the efforts of others.

Security
Any transaction in which the buyer invests money in a common enterprise and expects to earn a profit predominantly from the efforts of others.

This definition covers investments that are not necessarily called *securities*. For example, they may be called orange trees. W. J. Howey Co. owned large citrus groves in Florida. It sold these trees to investors, most of whom were from out of state and knew nothing about farming. Purchasers were expected to hire someone to take care of their trees. Someone like Howey-in-the-Hills, Inc., a related company that just happened to be in the service business. Customers were free to hire any service company, but 85 percent of the acreage was covered by service contracts with Howey-in-the-Hills. The court held that Howey was selling a security (no matter how orange or tart), because the purchaser was investing in a common enterprise (the orange grove) expecting to earn a profit from Howey's farmwork.

Other courts have interpreted the term "security" to include animal breeding arrangements (chinchillas, silver foxes, or beavers, take your pick); condominium purchases in which the developer promises the owner a certain level of income from rentals; and even investments in whiskey.

SECURITIES ACT OF 1933

The 1933 Act requires that, before offering or selling securities, the issuer must register the securities with the SEC, unless the securities qualify for an exemption. An issuer is the company that sells the stock initially. Registering securities with the SEC in a public offering is a major undertaking, but the 1933 Act exempts some securities and also some particular types of securities transactions from the full-blown registration requirements of a public offering.

Issuer
A company that sells its own stock.

It is also important to remember that **when an issuer registers securities, the SEC does not investigate the quality of the offering.** Permission from the SEC to sell securities does not mean that the company has a good product or will be successful. SEC approval simply means that, on the surface, the company has provided all required information about itself and its major products. The guiding principle of the federal securities laws is that investors can make a reasoned decision on whether to buy or sell securities if they have full and accurate information about a company and the security it is selling. For example, the Green Bay

Packers football team sold an offering of stock to finance stadium improvements. The prospectus admitted:

> IT IS VIRTUALLY IMPOSSIBLE that any investor will ever make a profit on the stock purchase. The company will pay no dividends, and the shares cannot be sold.

This does not sound like a stock you want in your retirement fund; on the other hand, the SEC will not prevent Green Bay from selling it, or you from buying it, so long as you understand what the risks are.

One last point: **the 1933 Act prohibits fraud in *any* securities transaction.** Anyone who issues fraudulent securities is in violation of the 1933 Act, whether or not the securities are registered. Both the SEC and any purchasers of the stock can sue the issuer.

Companies must deliver certain documents to investors and also file them with the SEC. Almost all filings with the SEC must be made electronically, using the EDGAR (Electronic Data Gathering, Analysis, and Retrieval) system. Once filed with the SEC, this information is available online (at **http://www.sec.gov**).

GENERAL EXEMPTION

Before offering securities for sale, the issuer must determine whether they are exempt from registration under the 1933 Act. Typically, exemptions are based on two factors: the type of security and the type of transaction.

EXEMPT SECURITIES

The 1933 Act exempts some types of securities from registration because they (1) are inherently low risk, (2) are regulated by other statutes, or (3) are not really investments. The following securities are exempt from registration:

- **Government securities,** which include any security issued or guaranteed by federal or state government

- **Bank securities,** which include any security issued or guaranteed by a bank

- **Short-term notes,** which are high-quality negotiable notes or drafts that are due within nine months of issuance and are not sold to the general public

- **Nonprofit issues,** which include any security issued by a nonprofit religious, educational, or charitable organization

- **Insurance policies and annuity contracts,** which are governed by insurance regulations

EXEMPT TRANSACTIONS

Section 4(2) of the 1933 Act exempts from registration "transactions by an issuer not involving any public offering." These are simple words to define a complex problem. In effect, the 1933 Act says that an issuer is not required to register securities that are sold in a private offering, that is, an offering with only a few investors or a relatively small amount of money involved. In private offerings, the full-blown disclosure of a public offering is neither necessary nor appropriate. For instance, a group of sophisticated investors who know an industry well do not need full disclosure. Or, if the amount at stake is relatively small, it would not make economic sense for the issuer to incur the heavy expense of a public offering.

There is an important distinction between exempt *securities* and exempt *transactions*. Exempt *securities* are always exempt, throughout their lives, no matter how many times they are sold. Stock sold in an exempt *transaction* is exempt only that one time, not necessarily in any subsequent sale. Suppose that County Bank sells stock to the public. Under the 1933 Act, the bank is never required to register these securities, no matter how many times they are sold. On the other hand, suppose that Tumbleweed, Inc., a quilt maker, sells $5 million worth of stock in a private offering that is exempt from registration. Shamika buys 100 shares of this stock. Seven years later, the company decides to sell stock in a public offering that must be registered. As part of this public offering, Shamika sells her 100 shares. This time, the shares must be registered because they are being sold in a *public offering*.

Most small companies use private, not public, offerings to raise capital. There are three different types of private offerings—intrastate, Regulation D, and Regulation A—each with its own set of rules.

Intrastate Offering Exemption

Under SEC Rule 147, an issuer is not required to register securities that are *offered* and *sold* only to residents of the state in which the issuer is incorporated and does business. This exemption was designed to provide local financing for local businesses. To qualify under Rule 147, 80 percent of the issuer's revenues and assets must be in-state, and it must also intend to spend 80 percent of the offering's proceeds in-state. Neither the issuer nor any purchaser can sell the securities outside the state for nine months after the offering.

Rule 147 is a **safe harbor**—if an issuer totally complies with it, the offering definitely qualifies as intrastate. But even if the issuer does not comply absolutely with the rule, the SEC or the courts may still consider the offering to be intrastate; however, the issuer cannot be sure in advance how the decision will come out. Sonic was a Utah corporation that sold stock to Utah residents. *Seven* months later, the company sold stock to an Illinois company. Although Sonic violated Rule 147 by making the second sale too early, the court held that the company had nonetheless qualified for an intrastate offering because it had not intended, at the time of the original offering, to sell stock outside Utah.[2] Although Sonic had not totally complied with Rule 147, it had come close enough to avoid liability. A safe harbor is less dangerous, but a voyage outside its boundaries does not necessarily end in disaster.

Regulation D

Three different types of private offerings can be made under Regulation D (often referred to as Reg D) under Rules 504, 505, and 506.

Rule 504   Under this rule (known as the "seed capital" rule), a company:

- May sell up to $1 million in securities during each 12-month period.

- May advertise the stock and solicit an unlimited number of investors if:

  - The transaction is registered under a state law with disclosure requirements, or

  - Sales are limited to accredited investors. **Accredited investors** are institutions (such as banks and insurance companies) or wealthy individuals (with a net worth of more than $1 million or an annual income of more than $200,000).

Accredited investors
Are institutions (such as banks and insurance companies) or wealthy individuals (with a net worth of more than $1 million or an annual income of more than $200,000).

---

[2] *Busch v. Carpenter*, 827 F.2d 653, 1987 U.S. App. LEXIS 11034 (10th Cir. 1987).

Restricted stock

Securities purchased strictly for investment purposes.

If the securities are neither registered under state law nor sold exclusively to accredited investors, they are **restricted stock**, which means they must be purchased for investment purposes. As a general rule, the buyer cannot resell restricted securities, either publicly or privately, for one year.

Rule 505   This rule permits a company to sell up to $5 million of stock during each 12-month period, subject to the following restrictions:

- The company may not advertise the stock publicly.

- The issuer can sell to as many accredited investors as it wants, but is limited to only 35 unaccredited investors.

- The company need not provide information to accredited investors but must make some disclosure to unaccredited investors. This requirement provides issuers with a serious incentive to avoid unaccredited investors because the disclosure requirements, although less demanding than for a public offering, are nonetheless burdensome.

- Stock purchased under this rule is restricted.

Rule 506   This rule is similar to Rule 505. The differences are that:

- There is no limit on the amount of stock a company can sell.

- If an unaccredited purchaser is unsophisticated, he must have a **purchaser representative** to help him evaluate the investment. Is an *unsophisticated* investor someone who does not care for opera? No, it is someone who is unable to assess the risks of the offering himself.

The following table sets out the menu of choices under Reg D:

	Maximum Value of Securities Sold in a 12-Month Period	Maximum Number of Investors		Is Disclosure Required?	Is Public Advertising Permitted?	Are Securities Restricted?
Rule 504 Option 1:	$1 million	No limit on accredited investors	Or	Disclosure under state law	Yes	No
Option 2:	$1 million	No limit	and	No	No	Yes
Rule 505	$5 million	No limit on accredited investors; no more than 35 unaccredited investors		Only for unaccredited investors	No	Yes
Rule 506	No limit	No limit on accredited investors; no more than 35 unaccredited investors, who must be either be sophisticated or have a purchaser representative		Only for unaccredited investors	No	Yes

Regulation A

Although an offering under Regulation A is *called* a private offering, it really is a small public offering. **Reg A permits an issuer to sell $5 million of securities *publicly* in any 12-month period.** The issuer must give each purchaser an offering circular that provides the same disclosure required for unaccredited investors under Reg D. The following table compares a public offering, Reg A, and Reg D:

	Initial Public Offering	Regulation A	Regulation D
Maximum Value of Securities Sold	No limit	$5 million	$1 million, $5 million, or no limit, depending on the rule
Public Solicitation of Purchasers	Permitted	Permitted	Permitted only under Rule 504
Suitability Requirements for Purchasers	No requirements	No requirements	Must determine if investors are accredited or sophisticated
Disclosure Requirements	Elaborate registration statement, audited financials	Offering circular that is less detailed than a registration statement	Rule 504: may require disclosure under state law Rules 505 and 506: none for accredited investors, the same requirements as Reg A for unaccredited investors
Resale of Securities	Permitted	Permitted	Sometimes permitted under Rule 504, otherwise not permitted for one year
Number of Offerings per year	209	34	27,843

Direct Public Offerings

Traditionally, a small company either sold stock to people it knew well or hired an investment banker to place the securities with a wider public. But now, instead of going through Wall Street, many companies trying to raise capital for the first time sell stock to the public themselves through a direct public offering (DPO). In a DPO, the issuer typically sells shares to its stakeholders: customers, employees, suppliers, or the community. The issuer makes a DPO offering under Rule 147, Regulation D or Regulation A.

The advantages of a DPO are

- It is much cheaper and faster than a regular public offering done through an underwriter.
- It can be an effective marketing tool—shareholders tend to become even more loyal customers.

The downside:

- Each investor must receive written information about the company. The cost of this disclosure can be prohibitive when dealing with many small investors. Mailing a $10 disclosure document to hundreds of investors who only want to buy $50 worth of stock each may not be an efficient means of raising money.
- Although shareholders are warned that they should view their purchases as long-term investments, some will inevitably want to sell their shares. Setting up a system to permit these trades can be tricky and time consuming.

Although the companies featured in the following article found their DPOs worthwhile, the process consumed significant management time.

In 1995, Spring Street Brewery, a New York microbrewery, became the first company to conduct an offering on the Internet. It established a home page that allowed potential investors to examine and download its offering documents. In the end, it raised $1.6 million.

Thanksgiving Coffee Co. of Fort Bragg, California, used both cyber technology and the old-fashioned face-to-face approach. It had originally planned simply to sell to its loyal customer base. "You think that everybody who knows about you will line up around the block to buy stock, but you have to put the offering in front of potential investors' faces seven times to get them to take action," says Thanksgiving general manager Rick Moon. He did just that. He put offering notices on coffee-bean bags; he hung announcements on bean dispensers. Vendors got the advertisements, as did mail-order customers. Information about the stock sale appeared on the company's Web site, in its catalog, and in advertisements in targeted magazines. Anyone who called about the stock got regular updates on the offering. In the end, the huge effort paid off. By the time the offering closed, Thanksgiving Coffee had sold 20 percent of its stock for $1.25 million.[3]

EXAM *Strategy*

Question: As a pitcher for the Cleveland Indians farm team, Randy Newsom had dreams of glory but a paycheck that was a nightmare—$8,000 for the season. Newsom came up with a clever solution: He set up a Web site that offered fans the opportunity to buy a share of his future. For only $20, the buyer was entitled to .002 percent of his career pay. Any problems with this plan?

Strategy: Remember that even orange trees can be securities.

Result: Newsom was selling securities: buyers were investing in him, hoping that they could earn a profit from his efforts. He had neither registered the securities nor qualified for an exemption, so his plan was illegal.

Initial public offering (IPO)

A company's first public sale of securities.

Secondary offering

Any public sale of securities by a company after the initial public offering.

Firm commitment underwriting

The underwriter buys stock from the issuer and sells it to the public.

Best efforts underwriting

The underwriter does not buy the stock but instead acts as the company's agent in selling it.

PUBLIC OFFERINGS

When a company wishes to raise significant amounts of capital from a large number of people, it has to do a public offering. A company's first public sale of securities is called **an initial public offering** or an **IPO.** Any subsequent public sale is called a **secondary offering.** This is the process an issuer follows for either type of sale:

1. *Underwriting.* For a public offering, companies hire an investment bank to serve as underwriter. In a **firm commitment underwriting**, the underwriter buys the stock from the issuer and resells it to the public. The underwriter bears the risk that the stock may sell at a lower price than expected. In a **best efforts underwriting**, the underwriter does not buy the stock but instead acts as the company's agent in selling it. If the stock sells at a low price, the company, not the underwriter, is the loser.

---

[3] Stephanie Gruner, "When Mom & Pop Go Public," *INC.*, Dec. 1996, p. 66. Copyright 1996 by Mansueto Ventures LLC. Reproduced with permission of Mansueto Ventures LLC via Copyright Clearance Center, Inc.

2. *Registration Statement*. The **registration statement** has two purposes: to notify the SEC that a sale of securities is pending and to disclose information to prospective purchasers. The registration statement typically must include detailed information about the issuer and its business, a description of the stock, the proposed use of the proceeds from the offering, and audited balance sheets and income statements. But the amount of required disclosure depends on the issuer—more disclosure is required for an IPO than for an offering by a so-called "well-known seasoned issuer." Preparing a registration statement is neither quick nor inexpensive—it can cost as much as $1 million for an IPO.

3. *Prospectus*. Typically, buyers never see the registration statement; they are given the **prospectus** instead. (The prospectus is also included in the registration statement that is sent to the SEC.) The prospectus includes the important disclosures about the company, while the registration statement includes additional information that is of interest to the SEC but not to the typical investor, such as the names and addresses of the lawyers for the issuer and underwriter. All investors must receive a copy of the prospectus before purchasing the stock.

4. *Sales Effort*. Even before the final registration statement and prospectus are completed, the investment bank begins its sales effort. It cannot actually make sales during this period, but it can solicit offers. The SEC closely regulates an issuer's sales effort to make sure that no one is unduly hyping the stock.

5. *Going Effective*. Once its review of the preliminary registration statement is complete, the SEC sends the issuer a **comment letter**, listing changes that must be made to the registration statement. An issuer almost always amends the registration statement at least once, and sometimes more than once. Remember that the SEC does not assess the value of the stock or the merit of the investment. Its role is to ensure that the company has disclosed enough to enable investors to make an informed decision. After the SEC has approved a final registration statement (which includes, of course, the final prospectus), the issuer and underwriter agree on a price for the stock and the date to **go effective**, that is, to begin the sale.

In the following case, eToys sued its underwriter, Goldman Sachs, for underpricing its stock offering. Should Goldman be liable? You be the judge.

YOU *be the* JUDGE

EBC I, INC. v. GOLDMAN SACHS & CO.
2005 N.Y. LEXIS 1178
COURT OF APPEALS OF NEW YORK, 2005

Facts: Goldman Sachs was the lead underwriter for eToys' initial public offering. eToys agreed to sell 8,320,000 shares of its stock to Goldman at a price of $18.65 per share, for resale to the public at $20. (Goldman had the option to buy an additional 1,248,000 shares at the same price.) The bank's potential profit was $1.35 per share, for a maximum of $12,916,800.

On the first day of the offering, the price of eToys' stock rose as high as $85 and closed at $76.56. Within a year, however, the price had fallen below $20. eToys ultimately filed for bankruptcy protection.

eToys alleged that Goldman made side deals with other clients allowing them to purchase shares in eToys' offering in exchange for kickbacks to Goldman of a portion of their profits on the stock. This arrangement would have created an incentive for Goldman to underprice the stock. eToys also alleged that Goldman had a fiduciary duty to eToys that it violated by not disclosing this conflict of interest.

continued

Goldman filed a motion to dismiss denying that it had a fiduciary relationship to eToys.

You Be the Judge: Did Goldman have a fiduciary duty to eToys? Did it violate this duty?

Argument for eToys: A fiduciary relationship exists between two parties if one of them is under a duty to act for or to give advice for the benefit of the other. eToys hired Goldman for its expertise and paid handsomely for its advice about many aspects of going public. The company would never have relied on this advice had it known about the side deals with other clients—deals that could harm eToys.

eToys trusted Goldman, the bank betrayed that trust, and eToys suffered an enormous financial penalty as a result.

Argument for Goldman Sachs: This is a simple case: eToys sold stock, Goldman bought it. Goldman negotiated the best price it could. If eToys was unhappy with this deal, it had no one to blame but itself.

If eToys expected Goldman to act as a fiduciary, the agreement should have stated so explicitly. The company always knew that its interests were different from Goldman's. eToys sought the highest price; Goldman had to ensure that it could resell the shares at a profit. The lower the price to eToys, the lower the risk to Goldman. Goldman took a substantial risk buying this stock, and in this case the risk paid off. It does not always do so.

eToys was a sophisticated company with sophisticated advisors. Its stockholders included well-known venture-capital firms. Its largest single stockholder, Idealab, was an incubator for successful technology companies (see **http://www.idealab.com**). eToys' law firm—the Venture Law Group, P.C.—specialized in representing high-tech companies. During one year, this law firm was fourth on the list of firms that handled the most initial public offerings for technology companies.

In short, the offering price was not "set" by Goldman; it was negotiated by two sophisticated parties.

SALES OF RESTRICTED SECURITIES

The SEC wants to ensure that the public sale of stock takes place in an orderly manner. Therefore, it imposes some restrictions on the sale of stock, even after a company has gone public. **Rule 144 limits the resale of two types of securities issued by public companies:** *control securities* and *restricted securities.*

Restricted security
Any stock purchased from the issuer in a private offering.

A **restricted security** is any stock purchased from the issuer in a private offering (such as Regulation D). These securities may not be sold within six months of the private offering. After six months, restricted securities can be sold freely, unless they are also control securities, in which case those restrictions still apply. (As noted previously, if the issuer is not public, restricted securities must be held one year before any sale.)

Control security
Stock held by any shareholder who owns more than 10 percent of a class of stock or by any officer or director of the company.

A **control security** is stock held by any shareholder who owns more than 10 percent of a class of stock or by any officer or director of the company. In any three-month period, such an insider can sell only an amount of stock equal to the average weekly trading volume for the prior four weeks or 1 percent of the number of shares outstanding, whichever is greater. The purpose of this rule is to protect other investors from precipitous declines in stock price. If company insiders sold all of their stock in one day, the price would plunge, causing losses to the other shareholders.

EXAM *Strategy*

Question: You are the CEO of Calmm.com, Inc. The company's board has decided to sell $2 million in stock. You have 40 wealthy friends who would like to invest a total of $1 million. What would be the best way to raise these funds? Would a public offering work?

Strategy: Review the options for both private and public offerings.

Result: A public offering is not a good idea—it would cost as much as $1 million. Rule 504 is not suitable because it would limit you to raising only $1 million. Under Rule 505, you could sell to all your wealthy friends (if they are accredited investors), and as many as 35 unaccredited investors. Rule 506 is more complicated (and therefore more expensive), so Rule 505 would be a better choice.

....

LIABILITY UNDER THE 1933 ACT

Liability for Selling Unregistered Securities

Section 12(a)(1) of the 1933 Act imposes liability on anyone who sells a security that is not registered and not exempt. The purchaser of the security can demand rescission—a return of his money in exchange for the stock—or, if he no longer owns the stock, he can ask for damages.

Fraud

Under Section 12(a)(2) of the 1933 Act, **the seller of a security is liable for making any material misstatement or omission, either oral or written, in connection with the offer or sale of a security.** This provision applies to both *public* and *private* offerings if there is some use of interstate commerce, such as the mails, telephone (even for an *intra*state call), or check (which clears). It is difficult to imagine a securities transaction that does not involve interstate commerce.

Criminal Liability

Under Section 24 of the 1933 Act, the Justice Department can prosecute anyone who willfully violates the Act.

Liability for the Registration Statement

Section 11 of the 1933 Act establishes the penalties for any errors in a registration statement. **If a final registration statement contains a material misstatement or omission, the purchaser of the security can recover from everyone who signed the registration statement.** This list of signatories includes the issuer, its directors, and chief officers; experts (such as auditors[4], engineers, or lawyers); and the underwriters. Everyone who signed the registration statement is jointly and severally liable for any error, except the experts, who are liable only for misstatements in the part of the registration statement for which they were responsible.[5] Thus an auditor is liable for misstatements in the financials but not, say, for omissions about the CEO's criminal past.

Damages To prevail under Section 11, the plaintiff need only prove that there was a material misstatement or omission and that she lost money. **Material** means important enough to affect an investor's decision. The plaintiff does not have to prove that she relied on (or even

Material
Important enough to affect an investor's decision.

---

[4] Large accounting firms may have the deepest pockets among the possible defendants, so they are often sued for the full amount of plaintiffs' losses in Section 11 cases.
[5] Joint and several liability means that all members of a group are liable. The plaintiff can sue them as a group or anyone of them individually for the full amount owing. The plaintiff cannot, however, recover more than the total amount of the damages owing.

read) the registration statement, that she bought the stock from the issuer, or that the defendant was negligent. The plaintiff can recover the difference between what she paid for the stock and its value on the date of the lawsuit.

Suppose that Pet Detective, Inc., does an IPO at $10 per share. A week later, Ace Investora buys 1,000 shares at $10 each. He knows nothing about the company, but he likes the name. This stock turns out to be a dog—Pet Detective has only two agencies, not the 200 stated in the registration statement. After Investora sells the stock at 10 cents a share, he can sue under Section 11 for $9,900.

Due Diligence   All is not hopeless, however, for those who have signed the registration statement. If the statement contains a material misstatement or omission, the company is liable and has no defense. But everyone else who signed the registration statement can avoid liability by showing that he investigated the registration statement as thoroughly as a "prudent person in the management of his own property." This investigation is called **due diligence**. Its importance cannot be overstated. The SEC does not conduct its own investigation to ensure that the registration statement is accurate. It can only ensure that, on the surface, the issuer has supplied all relevant information. If an issuer chooses to lie, the SEC has no way of knowing. It is the job of the underwriters to check the accuracy of the filing. Thus underwriters typically spend two or three weeks visiting the company, reading all its corporate documents (including minutes back to the beginning), and calling its bankers, customers, suppliers, and competitors to ensure that the registration statement is accurate and no skeletons have been overlooked.

When Section 11 was first passed, investment bankers were outraged. Some predicted that this liability provision would cause capital in America to dry up, that grass would grow on Wall Street. In fact, the first case under Section 11 arose 35 years and 27,000 registration statements later. In this case—*Escott v. Barchris Construction Corp.*—the registration statement was seriously flawed.[6] The underwriter failed to read the minutes of the executive committee meetings that revealed the company to be in serious financial condition. Much of the company's alleged backlog of orders was from nonexistent corporations. Proceeds of the offering were earmarked to pay off debt, not to buy new plant and equipment, as the registration statement had indicated. The company's directors, underwriters, and underwriters' counsel were held liable.

Although *Barchris* still strikes fear in the hearts of underwriters, some commentators now argue that underwriters do not take their due diligence obligations seriously enough. Was there adequate disclosure in the following case?

Due diligence

An investigation of the registration statement by someone who signs it.

ROMBACH V. CHANG

355 F.3d 164, 2004 U.S. APP. LEXIS 778
UNITED STATES COURT OF APPEALS FOR THE SECOND CIRCUIT, 2004

CASE SUMMARY

Facts: Family Golf Centers, Inc. was a public company that owned and operated 119 golf courses nationwide. To raise funds for the purchase of additional courses, it sold shares in a second public offering. During the year following that sec- ond offering, Family Golf had lower than expected earnings and its stock price plummeted by more than 43 percent. Within two years of the offering, the company filed for bankruptcy protection.

---

[6] 283 F. Supp. 643, 1968 U.S. Dist. LEXIS 3853 (S.D.N.Y. 1968).

The plaintiffs purchased stock from the company in the second public offering. They filed suit against the company's officers and underwriters, alleging that the registration statement contained misrepresentations about Family Golf's financial performance and projected income. The district court granted defendants' motion to dismiss, and the plaintiffs appealed.

Issue: *Did the defendants violate Section 11 by issuing a false or misleading registration statement?*

Decision: Family Golf did not violate Section 11. Affirmed.

Reasoning: Plaintiffs do not allege that the registration statement contained false or misleading information. Instead, they argue that the document was missing information that should have been included. In particular, plaintiffs assert that the registration statement should have explicitly disclosed that (1) Family Golf's lenders were pressuring it to raise money

and (2) the company was having a hard time integrating its new golf courses into the existing operational structure.

While the registration statement did not make those explicit statements, it did say:

1. Both the company and some individual courses had lost money in the prior year;

2. Cash reserves were declining;

3. The company might not be able to raise all the money it needed;

4. Integrating new courses into the company's operational structure could be difficult; and

5. The company might not perform as well in the future as it had done in the past.

It is true that some of this language sounds like nothing more than boilerplate. Nonetheless, taken together, it provided adequate warning to investors.

SECURITIES EXCHANGE ACT OF 1934

Most buyers do not purchase new securities from the issuer in an initial public offering. Rather they buy stock that is publicly traded in the open market. This stock is, in a sense, *secondhand* because others, perhaps many others, have already owned it. The purpose of the 1934 Act is to maintain the integrity of this secondary market.

GENERAL PROVISIONS OF THE 1934 ACT

Registration Requirements

As we have seen, the 1933 Act requires an issuer to register securities before selling them. That is a onetime effort for the company. The 1933 Act does not require the issuer to provide shareholders with any additional information in later years. Suppose that an automobile company registered and sold securities for the first time in 1946. Purchasers of those securities knew a lot about the firm—in 1946. But how can current investors assess the company? The 1934 Act plugs this hole. It requires issuers with publicly traded stock to continue to make information available to the public so that current—and potential—shareholders can evaluate the company. It is often said that the 1933 Act registers securities, and the 1934 Act registers companies.

Under the 1934 Act, an issuer must register with the SEC if (1) it completes a public offering under the 1933 Act, or (2) its securities are traded on a national exchange (such as the New York Stock Exchange), or (3) it has at least 500 shareholders and total assets that exceed $10 million. A company can *de*register if its number of shareholders falls below 300 or if it has fewer than 500 shareholders and assets of less than $10 million.

Disclosure Requirements—Section 13

Like the 1933 Act, the 1934 Act focuses on disclosure. The difference is that the 1933 Act requires onetime disclosure when a company sells stock to the public. The 1934 Act requires *ongoing*, regular disclosure for any company with a class of stock that is publicly traded. Companies that are required to register under the 1934 Act are called **reporting companies.** **Section 13 requires reporting companies to file the following documents:**

- An initial, detailed information statement when the company first registers (similar to the filing required under the 1933 Act)

- Annual reports on Form 10-K, containing audited financial statements, a detailed analysis of the company's performance, and information about officers and directors

- Quarterly reports on Form 10-Q, which are less detailed than 10-Ks and contain unaudited financials

- Form 8-Ks to report any significant developments, such as bankruptcy, a change in control, a purchase or sale of significant assets, the resignation of a director as a result of a policy dispute, a change in fiscal year, or a change in auditing firms

In response to corporate scandals, Congress passed the Sarbanes-Oxley Act of 2002. It requires each company's CEO and CFO to certify that:

- The information in the quarterly and annual reports is true;

- The company has effective internal controls; and

- The officers have informed the company's audit committee and its auditors of any concerns that they have about the internal control system.

A reporting company must send its annual report to shareholders. All annual reports and other 1934 Act filings are available on the SEC Web site (**http://www.sec.gov**).

Proxy Requirements—Section 14

As discussed in Chapter 30, most shareholders of public corporations do not attend annual shareholder meetings. Instead, the company solicits their proxies, permitting them to vote by mail rather than in person. If a company solicits proxies, it is required to supply shareholders with a proxy statement that is intended to give them enough information to make informed decisions about the company. The proxy statement contains detailed information about officers and directors, including their experience, relationship with the company, and compensation. (The annual report provides financial information.) Proxy statements must also be filed with the SEC. Proxy contests and shareholder proposals are discussed in Chapter 30.

Under SEC rules, a company is not *required* to solicit proxies from shareholders, but if it does not, it is unlikely to obtain the quorum needed for the meeting to be held. In any event, a company cannot avoid its responsibility to inform shareholders. Whether or not it solicits proxies, it is still required to furnish shareholders with an information statement that contains essentially the same material as a proxy statement.

Short-Swing Trading—Section 16

During congressional hearings after the 1929 stock market crash, witnesses testified that insiders had manipulated the stock market. For example, insiders would buy a large block of stock, announce a substantial dividend, and then divest before the dividend was reduced.

Section 16 was designed to prevent corporate insiders—officers, directors, and shareholders who own more than 10 percent of the company—from taking unfair advantage of privileged information to manipulate the market.

Section 16 takes a two-pronged approach:

- First, insiders must **report** their trades within two business days. This report must also reveal their total stock holdings in the company. The filings must be made to the SEC electronically, and both the SEC and the company are required to post them on their respective Web sites within one business day after they are made.

- Second, insiders must **turn over to the corporation** any profits they make from the purchase and sale or sale and purchase of company securities in a six-month period. Section 16 is a strict liability provision. It applies even if the insider did not actually take advantage of secret information or try to manipulate the market; if she bought and sold or sold and bought stock in a six-month period, she is liable.

Suppose that Manuela buys 20,000 shares of her company's stock in June at $10 a share. In September, her (uninsured) summer house in Florida is destroyed by a hurricane. To raise money for rebuilding, she sells the stock at $12 per share, making a profit of $40,000. Her house will have to remain in ruins because she has violated Section 16 and must turn over the profit to her company.

LIABILITY UNDER THE 1934 ACT

Section 18

Under Section 18, anyone who makes a false or misleading statement in a filing under the 1934 Act is liable to buyers or sellers who (1) acted in reliance on the statement and (2) can prove that the price at which they bought or sold was affected by the false filing. Section 18 applies to all filings under the 1934 Act, including proxy statements and annual reports.

Section 10(b)

Section 18 applies only to *filings* under the 1934 Act. What happens if a company executive makes a false public *statement* about the company? Or writes an untrue statement somewhere other than in a filing? In one case, a corporate officer bought up shares of his company's stock even as he made pessimistic public statements about the company. That is the type of behavior that Section 10(b) is designed to prevent. **Section 10(b) prohibits fraud in connection with the purchase and sale of any security, whether or not the security is registered under the 1934 Act.**

The SEC adopted Rule 10b-5 to clarify Section 10(b), but the rule is still a relatively vague, catch-all provision designed to fill any holes left by other sections of the securities laws.[7] Interpretation has largely been left to the courts, which generally have interpreted Rule 10b-5 to require:

---

[7] Rule 10b-5 prohibits any person, in connection with a purchase or sale of any security, from (1) employing any device, scheme, or artifice to defraud; (2) making any untrue statement of a material fact or omitting to state a material fact necessary in order to make the statements made, in light of the circumstances under which they were made, not misleading; or (3) engaging in any act, practice, or course of business that operates or would operate as a fraud or deceit upon any person.

- **A Misstatement or Omission of a Material Fact.** Anyone who fails to disclose material information, or makes incomplete or inaccurate disclosure, is liable. **Material** has the same meaning as under the 1933 Act: important enough to affect an investor's decision. For example, a company repeatedly and falsely denied that it was involved in merger negotiations. It was liable even though the negotiations had only been in a preliminary stage.[8]

- **Scienter.** This is a legal term meaning *willfully, knowingly, or recklessly*. To be liable under Rule 10b-5, the defendant must have (1) known (or been reckless in not knowing) that the statement was inaccurate and (2) intended for the plaintiff to rely on the statement. Negligence is not enough. A group of shareholders sued the accounting firm Ernst & Ernst because it had failed to discover, during the course of an audit, that a company's chief executive was stealing funds. According to the shareholders, the auditors should have discovered that the executive refused to allow anyone else to open his mail and, therefore, should have been suspicious of wrongdoing. The court found Ernst & Ernst not liable. Although it may have been negligent, it had not *intentionally* or even *recklessly* facilitated fraud.[9]

- **Purchase or Sale.** Rule 10b-5 covers both buyers and sellers. It does not include, however, someone who failed to purchase stock because of a material misstatement. In the case of the company executive who spread negative rumors about his company while he bought stock, those who sold because of his false rumors could sue under Rule 10b-5, but not those who simply failed to buy.

- **Reliance.** To bring suit, a plaintiff must show that she relied on the misstatement or omission. In the case of open-market trades, reliance is difficult to prove, so the courts are willing to assume it.

- **Economic Loss.** The plaintiffs must suffer a loss in the value of their investment. For example, a couple sold their pharmaceutical business to another company in exchange for stock of the purchaser. Some time later, they discovered that the purchaser had lied about its financial condition. However, the court held that the couple could not recover because, by the time they sold their stock in the purchaser, it was worth substantially more than when they acquired it. Thus, they had not suffered an economic loss.

- **Loss Causation.** The economic loss must have been caused by the misstatement of a material fact. For example, a group of investors bought stock in Dura Pharmaceuticals. They alleged that, when making the purchase, they had relied on statements by company executives that (1) its drug sales would be profitable and (2) the Food and Drug Administration would approve its new asthma spray device. Neither of these statements turned out to be true and the company's stock price fell. Plaintiffs argued that, if it had not been for the misrepresentations, the stock price would have been lower when they purchased stock and then would not have fallen as far (or at all) when the truth came out.

The Supreme Court ruled, however, that the plaintiffs could not recover because there was no proof that the misstatements had *caused* the decline in stock price. The price drop could have been the result of other factors, such as changes in the industry or in the economy as a whole.[10]

The following case resolves one of the most important 10(b) issues in recent history: are those who aid and abet fraud also liable?

---

[8] *Basic Inc. v. Levinson*, 485 U.S. 224, 108 S.Ct. 978, 1988 U.S. LEXIS 1197 (1988).

[9] *Ernst & Ernst v. Hochfelder*, 425 U.S. 185, 96 S.Ct. 1375, 1976 U.S. LEXIS 2 (1976).

[10] *Dura Pharmaceuticals, Inc. v. Broudo*, 125 S.Ct. 1627, 2005 U.S. LEXIS 3478 (2005).

STONERIDGE INVESTMENT PARTNERS, LLC v. SCIENTIFIC-ATLANTA, INC.

28 S.Ct. 761; 2008 U.S. LEXIS 1091
SUPREME COURT OF THE UNITED STATES, 2008

CASE SUMMARY

Facts: Charter Communications, Inc., a cable operator, engaged in a variety of fraudulent practices to pump up its financial statements so they would meet Wall Street expectations. When these efforts fell short, Charter approached two of its suppliers—Scientific-Atlanta and Motorola—for help in furthering the fraud. These two companies supplied Charter with the digital cable converter (set top) boxes that Charter furnished its customers. Charter arranged to overpay the suppliers $20 for each set top box it purchased, with the understanding that they would return the overpayment by purchasing advertising from Charter. These transactions had no economic purpose other than inflating Charter's revenue and operating cash flow numbers by $17 million. They violated generally accepted accounting principles. The plan was successful—Charter did manage to fool its auditors.

The inflated numbers were included in financial statements filed with the SEC and reported to the public. Purchasers of Charter stock sued the two suppliers, alleging that they had violated Section 10(b) and Rule 10b-5. The District Court granted defendants' motion to dismiss. The U.S. Court of Appeals for the Eighth Circuit affirmed. The Supreme Court granted certiorari.

Issue: *Were the two suppliers liable under Section 10(b) for their role in Charter's fraud?*

Decision: No, the suppliers were not liable. Affirmed.

Reasoning: While it is true that the two suppliers engaged in unconventional behavior that may even have been fraudulent, they did not violate federal securities laws. A lawsuit for common-law fraud in a state court would be a more appropriate remedy.

To win a lawsuit under Section 10(b), plaintiffs must show that they relied on the defendants' behavior. But none of the investors knew what the two suppliers had done, so they could hardly have relied on it.

A free economy works best if all participants show integrity. However, federal power should not intervene in a realm already governed by state law. Furthermore, if federal securities laws did apply in situations such as this, plaintiffs with weak claims could use threats of a lawsuit to extort settlements from innocent companies. Fear of such litigation might raise the cost of doing business in this country and even deter overseas firms from operating here. Companies might decide to shift their securities offerings to foreign capital markets.

The Private Securities Litigation Reform Act of 1995

The Private Securities Litigation Reform Act is an amendment to the 1934 Act intended to discourage fraud suits by shareholders. Under this amendment, companies are liable to shareholders for so-called forward-looking statements (that is, financial projections or statements about future plans) *only if* (1) the company fails to include a warning that the predictions may not come to pass, *and* (2) the shareholders can show that company executives knew the predictions were false. Suppose a pharmaceutical company predicts that a new drug will generate billions in sales, but two years later the drug is a total failure. Before 1995, shareholders would have had a strong case, but now the company would not be liable so long as it had disclosed, at the time of making the prediction, reasons why the drug might not be a success. Even if the company failed to mention these reasons, it would be liable only if executives knew the prediction to be false when they made it.

INSIDER TRADING

Insider trading is immensely tempting. Anyone with reliable secret information can earn millions of dollars overnight. Costandi Nasser bought shares of Santa Fe International, Inc., after learning that Kuwait Petroleum Co. was set to acquire the company. His profit? $4.6 million in three weeks. The downside? Insider trading is a crime punishable by fines and imprisonment. The guilty party may also be forced to turn over to the SEC three times the profit made. Ivan Boesky paid $100 million and spent two years in prison. Dennis Levine suffered an $11.6 million penalty and three years in prison.

> Insider trading is a crime punishable by fines and imprisonment.

Why is insider trading a crime? Who is harmed? After all, if you buy or sell stock in a company, presumably you are reasonably content with the price or you would not have traded. Insider trading is illegal because:

- It offends our fundamental sense of fairness. No one wants to be in a poker game with marked cards.

- Investors will lose confidence in the market if they feel that insiders have an unfair advantage.

- Investment banks typically "make a market" in stocks, meaning that they hold extra shares so that orders can be filled smoothly. If an insider buys stock because she knows the company is about to sign an important contract, she earns the profit on that information at the expense of the market maker who sold her the stock. These market makers expect to earn a certain profit. If they do not earn it from normal stock appreciation, they simply raise the commission they charge for being a market maker. As a result, everyone who buys and sells stock pays a slightly higher price because insider trading skims off some of the profits.

Economists argue that there is another reason insider trading is illegal.

ECONOMICS AND THE LAW

Generally, economists think that society benefits when financial information spreads widely and quickly. Investors are thereby able to make more informed decisions. However, insider trading is an exception to this rule. When someone trades on inside information, she can quickly earn vast profits—but she has effectively stolen these profits from uninformed shareholders. The benefit that society gains from having this hidden information indirectly revealed to the market (via her purchase or sale of stock) is less than the harm to the shareholders who trade in ignorance. True, everyone now knows that the stock is more or less valuable than the market thought, but they have learned this information at a high price. Thus, the government prohibits insider trading to prevent society from "paying too much" for this private information.

Recent research supports the view that insider trading harms securities markets. In comparing returns in all 103 stock markets in the world, two economists found that markets in those countries that enforced insider trading laws earned 5 percent higher returns than did markets in countries with no laws or with lax enforcement. Five percent of the world's stock market capitalization amounts to $1.75 trillion.[11] ◆

As noted, Rule 10b-5 is a vaguely worded rule that generally prohibits fraud. The language of the rule never explicitly mentions insider trading, but courts have interpreted it to prohibit this activity. Although the courts are nominally *interpreting* the rule, in fact, they are more or less fashioning this crime out of whole cloth. Insider trading has been described as

---

[11] Hazem Daouk and Utpal Bhattacharya, "The World Price of Insider Trading," *Journal of Finance*, 2002, vol. 57, pp. 75–108. Discussed as a working paper in *The Economist*, Jan. 22, 2000, p. 75.

"the judicial oak that has grown from little more than a legislative acorn." The current rules on insider trading are as follows:

- **Strangers.** The SEC has argued many times that anyone in possession of nonpublic material information must disclose it or refrain from trading. The courts, however, have definitively rejected this approach. The Supreme Court has held that **someone who trades on inside information is liable only if he breaches a fiduciary duty.** Suppose that, while looking in a dumpster, Harry finds correspondence indicating that MediSearch, Inc., will shortly announce a major breakthrough in the treatment of AIDS. Harry buys the stock, which promptly quadruples in value. Harry will be dining at the Ritz, not in the dumpster nor in federal prison, because he has no fiduciary duty to MediSearch.

- **Fiduciaries.** Anyone who works for a company is a fiduciary. **A fiduciary violates Rule 10b-5 if she trades stock of her company while in possession of nonpublic material information.** If the director of research for MediSearch learns of the promising new treatment for AIDS and buys stock in the company before the information is public, she has violated Rule 10b-5. This rule applies not only to employees who work for the company, but also to **constructive insiders**—others who have an indirect employment relationship, such as employees of the company's auditors or law firm. Thus, if a lawyer who works at the firm that is patenting MediSearch's new discovery buys stock before the information is public, she has violated Rule 10b-5.

- *Possession* **versus** *use* **of information.** Suppose that an insider sells stock just after learning that her company is about to report lower earnings but before this information is public. When challenged by the SEC, she argues that she sold her stock for other reasons—say, to buy a new house, or set her son up in business. To deal with this type of situation, the SEC issued **Rule 10b5-1, which provides that an insider violates Rule 10b-5 if she trades while in possession of material, nonpublic information, unless she has committed in advance to a plan to sell those securities.** Thus, if an insider knows that she will want to sell stock to pay college tuition, she can establish such a sales plan in advance. (And, then, despite any change in circumstances, she must sell according to the plan.) She will then not be liable for the sales, no matter what inside information she ultimately learns.

- **Tippers.** Now things become really complicated. **Insiders who pass on nonpublic, material information are liable under Rule 10b-5, even if they do not trade themselves, so long as (1) they know the information is confidential and (2) they expect some personal gain.** Personal gain is loosely defined. Essentially, any gift to a friend counts as personal gain. W. Paul Thayer was a corporate director, deputy secretary of defense, and former fighter pilot ace who gave stock tips to his girlfriend in lieu of paying her rent. That counted as personal gain, and he spent a year and a half in prison.

- **Tippees. Those who receive tips—tippees—are liable for trading on inside information, even if they do not have a fiduciary relationship to the company, so long as (1) they know the information is confidential, (2) they know that it came from an insider who was violating his fiduciary duty, and (3) the insider expected some personal gain.** Barry Switzer, then head football coach at the University of Oklahoma, went to a track meet to see his son compete. While sunbathing on the bleachers, he overheard someone talking about a company that was going to be acquired. Switzer bought the stock but was acquitted of insider trading charges, because the insider had not breached his fiduciary duty. He had not tipped anyone on purpose—he had simply been careless. Also, Switzer did not know that the insider was breaching a fiduciary duty, and the insider expected no personal gain.[12]

Constructive insider
Anyone who has an indirect employment relationship with a company, such as employees of the company's auditors or law firm.

---

[12] *SEC v. Switzer*, 590 F. Supp. 756, 1984 U.S. Dist. LEXIS 15303 (W.D. Okla. 1984).

- **Takeovers.** Frustrated by its lack of success under Rule 10b-5, the SEC adopted Rule 14e-3. **This rule prohibits trading on inside information during a tender offer if the trader knows the information was obtained from either the bidder or the target company.** The trader or tipper need not have violated a fiduciary duty.

- **Misappropriation.** In an effort to tighten the insider trading noose further, the SEC developed a new theory—misappropriation. Under this theory, **a person is liable if he trades in securities (1) for personal profit, (2) using confidential information, and (3) in breach of a fiduciary duty to the source of the information.** This theory applies even if that source was not the company whose stock was traded. In the following case, the Supreme Court explains the logic underlying the principle of misappropriation.

UNITED STATES V. O'HAGAN

521 U.S. 642, 117 S.Ct. 2199, 1997 U.S. LEXIS 4033
SUPREME COURT OF THE UNITED STATES, 1997

CASE SUMMARY

Facts: Grand Metropolitan PLC (Grand Met) hired the law firm of Dorsey & Whitney to represent it in a takeover of Pillsbury Co. James O'Hagan, a partner in Dorsey & Whitney, did not work for Grand Met, but he found out about the deal and purchased significant amounts of Pillsbury stock. After Grand Met publicly announced its takeover attempt, the price of Pillsbury stock rose dramatically. O'Hagan sold his stock at a profit of more than $4.3 million. A jury convicted O'Hagan of misappropriation in violation of Section 10(b), and he was sentenced to prison.[13] The appeals court reversed, ruling that misappropriation is not a violation of Section 10(b). The Supreme Court granted *certiorari*.

Issue: *Did O'Hagan violate insider trading laws?*

Decision: O'Hagan was guilty of misappropriation, which is illegal under insider trading laws.

Reasoning: Under the traditional law of insider trading, a corporate insider cannot use important, secret information to trade in the securities of his corporation. The traditional theory applies not only to officers, directors, and other employees of a corporation, but also to attorneys, accountants, and others who *temporarily* become fiduciaries of a corporation.

The misappropriation theory applies to someone who is not a corporate insider, but nonetheless owes a fiduciary duty to the source of the information. Thus, in this case, O'Hagan did not work for Pillsbury, the company whose stock he bought, but he did violate his fiduciary duty to his law firm. The theft of such information is the same thing as embezzlement. It makes no sense to find a lawyer like O'Hagan guilty if he works for a law firm representing the target of a tender offer, but not if he works for a law firm representing the bidder.

After the *O'Hagan* case established the principle of misappropriation, it was still not clear how this rule applied to family members. If a wife told her husband that her company was about to be taken over and he then sold company stock as a result, was he in violation of 10b-5? Did he have a fiduciary duty to her? Rule 10b-5-2 establishes that anyone who receives non-public, material information from a spouse, parent, child or sibling, has a fiduciary duty unless the trader can prove that he did not have a duty of trust or confidence to the family member in question.

---

[13] O'Hagan used the profits that he gained through this trading to conceal his previous embezzlement of client funds. There is a moral here.

EXAM *Strategy*

Question: Paul was an investment banker who sometimes bragged about deals he was working on. One night he told a bartender, Ryanne, about an upcoming deal. Ryanne bought stock in the company Paul had mentioned. Both were prosecuted for insider trading. Ryanne was acquitted but Paul was convicted, even though Ryanne was the one who made money. How is that possible?

Strategy: Note that there are different standards for tippers and tippees.

Result: Paul is liable if he knew the information was confidential and he expected some personal gain. A gift counts as personal gain. (The courts have an expansive definition of "gift"—practically anything counts. Here the information could be interpreted as a tip to the bartender.) Ryanne was not liable because she did not know the information was confidential and that it came from an insider who was violating his fiduciary duty.

FOREIGN CORRUPT PRACTICES ACT

In the 1970s, more than 450 major U.S. corporations paid millions of dollars in foreign bribes. The Japanese premier and the Italian president both resigned after it was revealed that Lockheed had paid them off. In the Netherlands, members of the royal family were implicated in the scandal. Many of these payments had been labeled "commissions" or other legitimate business expenses and then illegally deducted from the company's income tax. In response, Congress passed the Foreign Corrupt Practices Act as an amendment to the 1934 Act.

Under the Foreign Corrupt Practices Act (FCPA), it is a crime for *any American company* (whether reporting under the 1934 Act or not) to make or promise to make payments or gifts to foreign officials, political candidates, or parties in order to influence a governmental decision. There is one exception: it is legal for a company to make payments to a foreign official to expedite a "routine governmental action." Anyone who violates the law is subject to fines and imprisonment. For more on enforcement of the FCPA, google "doj fcpa."

Congress believed that the ready availability of corporate "slush funds" had facilitated the payment of bribes. Therefore, it also tightened accounting standards for companies that report under the 1934 Act. It requires *reporting companies* to (1) keep books that accurately and fairly reflect the transactions of the issuer, and (2) maintain a system of internal controls that ensures transactions are executed only "in accordance with management's authorization."

ETHICS What's wrong with bribery anyway? Many businesspeople think it is relatively harmless, just a cost of doing business, like New York City's high taxes or Germany's high labor costs. Corruption is not a victimless crime. Poor people in poor countries are the losers when officials are on the take: corruption means that good projects are squeezed out by bad ones. And corruption can reduce a country's entire administration to a state of decay. Honest officials give up. Bribes grow ever bigger and more ubiquitous. The trough becomes less well stocked; the snouts plunge deeper.[14] Worldwide about $400 billion is lost each year to corruption in government procurement. The anticorruption czar in Mexico estimated that bribes reduce Mexico's GDP annually by 9.5 percent. This sum is twice the country's education budget. From the Chapter 2 ethics checklist: Who are the stakeholders? What are the consequences of corruption? ◆

---

[14] "Who Will Listen to Mr. Clean?" *The Economist*, Aug. 2, 1997, p. 52.

BLUE SKY LAWS

At the end of the nineteenth century, years before the great stock market crash, states had already begun to regulate the sale of securities. These statutes are called **blue sky laws** (because crooks were willing to sell naive investors a "piece of the great blue sky"). Currently, all states and the District of Columbia have blue sky laws.

EXEMPTION FROM STATE REGULATION

To make life easier for issuers of stock, Congress passed the **National Securities Markets Improvement Act (NSMIA) of 1996.** Essentially, states may no longer regulate offerings of securities that are:

- Traded on a national exchange
- Exempt under Rule 506, or
- Sold to "qualified purchasers."

STATE REGULATION

Any securities offerings not covered by the NSMIA must comply with state securities laws. Easier said than done. The 50 states have exhibited great creativity in crafting their securities laws and, as a result, have caused many headaches for issuers of securities. To begin, the 1933 Act is primarily concerned with disclosure, but many state statutes focus on the quality of the investment and require a so-called *merit review*. For example, in 1981, the Massachusetts securities commissioner refused to allow Apple Computer Co. to sell its initial public offering in Massachusetts because he believed the stock, selling at 92 times earnings, was too risky. He "protected" Massachusetts residents from this investment.

Typically, states take one of the following approaches to securities offerings:

- *Registration by notification.* Some states permit issuers with an established track record simply to file a notice before offering their securities.

- *Registration by coordination.* Some states permit issuers that have registered with the SEC simply to file copies of the federal registration statement (and perhaps some additional documents) with the state.

- *Registration by qualification.* Some states require issuers to undergo a full-blown registration, complete with a merit review.

FACILITATING STATE REGULATION

All is not bleak, however. There are three options that ease the process of complying with state securities requirements.

Coordinated Equity Review (CER)

For offerings over $5 million that are registered with the SEC, the issuer might be able to take advantage of the **Coordinated Equity Review (CER)** program. Under this program, the issuer deals with only one state, which takes responsibility for coordinating the comments from all other states. The process is simpler, but state officials still have the right to conduct a merit review.

Small Company Offering Registration (SCOR)

Most states permit a so-called **SCOR (small company offering registration)** for use in offerings of up to $1 million over any 12-month period. The issuer has the right to advertise publicly (even on the Internet) and can sell any amount of securities to any number of investors (as long as the total offering does not exceed $1 million). The relatively simple form (U-7) is in a question-and-answer format. It is designed to be filled out by company executives without the assistance of lawyers or accountants who are securities experts. Any company using a SCOR form can request a coordinated review from the states in which it has filed. Under this system, a designated lead state takes responsibility for coordinating the process with all other states. The result is a faster, simpler process. States do have the right to conduct a merit review, although it tends to be less burdensome than the usual merit examination. SCOR registration is designed to be used with

- Rule 147
- Rule 504
- Regulation A

Uniform Limited Offering Exemption

Under the **Uniform Limited Offering Exemption,** most states largely exempt from registration any offerings under Rule 505.

The moral of the story? Securities offerings are exceedingly complex and require professional supervision. Do not attempt this at home!

CHAPTER CONCLUSION

The 1929 stock market crash and the Great Depression that followed were an economic catastrophe for the United States. The Securities Act of 1933 and the Securities Exchange Act of 1934 were designed to prevent such disasters from ever occurring again. Whether or not they achieve that goal, they undoubtedly enhance the reliability and stability of the securities markets.

EXAM REVIEW

1. **SECURITY** A security is any transaction in which the buyer invests money in a common enterprise and expects to earn a profit predominantly from the efforts of others. (p. 787)

EXAM Strategy

Question: Christopher Stenger bought 12 Impressionist paintings from R.H. Love Galleries for $1.5 million. Love told Stenger that art investment would produce a safe profit. The two men agreed that Stenger could exchange any painting within five years for any one or two other paintings with the same or greater value. When Stenger's paintings did not increase in value, he sued Love, arguing that the right to trade paintings made them securities. Is Stenger correct?

Strategy: Are all three elements of a security present here? (See the "Result" at the end of this section.)

2. **REGISTRATION** Before any offer or sale, an issuer must register securities with the SEC, unless the securities qualify for an exemption. (p. 787)

3. **EXEMPTIONS** These securities are exempt from the registration requirement: government securities, bank securities, short-term notes, nonprofit issues, insurance policies, and annuity contracts. (p. 788)

4. **SECURITIES OFFERINGS** The following table compares the different types of securities offerings:

	Public Offering	Intrastate Offering	Regulation A	Regulation D: Rule 504	Regulation D: Rule 505	Regulation D: Rule 506
Maximum Value of Securities Sold	Unlimited	Unlimited	$5 million	$1 million	$5 million	Unlimited
Public Solicitation of Purchasers	Permitted	Permitted	Permitted	Sometimes permitted	Not permitted	Not permitted
Suitability Requirements for Purchasers	No requirements	Must reside in issuer's state	No requirements	May be limited to accredited investors	No limit on accredited investors; no more than 35 unaccredited investors	No limit on accredited investors; no more than 35 unaccredited investors who, if unsophisticated, must have a purchaser representative
Disclosure Requirements	Elaborate registration statement; audited financials	None	Offering circular that is less detailed than a registration statement	May be required under state law	Same requirements as Reg A for unaccredited investors; no disclosure to accredited investors	Same requirements as Reg A for unaccredited investors; no disclosure to accredited investors
Resale of Securities	Permitted	Permitted, but may not be made out of state for nine months	Permitted	Sometimes permitted	Not permitted for one year	Not permitted for one year

EXAM Strategy

CPA Question: Hamilton Corp. makes a $4.5 million securities offering under Rule 505 of Regulation D of the Securities Act of 1933. Under this regulation, Hamilton is:

(a) Required to provide full financial information to accredited investors only

(b) Allowed to make the offering through a general solicitation

(c) Limited to selling to no more than 35 nonaccredited investors

(d) Allowed to sell to an unlimited number of investors, both accredited and nonaccredited

Strategy: The answer is not (a), because accredited investors are never entitled to *more* disclosure than other investors. The answer is not (b) because Rule 505 does not permit a general solicitation. The answer is not (d) because Rule 505 is limited to only 35 unaccredited investors. (See the "Result" at the end of this section.)

5. **LIABILITY UNDER THE 1933 ACT** If a final registration statement contains a material misstatement or omission, the purchaser of a security offered under that statement can recover from everyone who signed it. (p. 795)

6. **THE 1934 ACT** The 1934 Act requires public companies to make regular filings with the SEC. (p. 797)

7. **SECTION 16** Under Section 16, insiders who buy and sell or sell and buy company stock within a six-month period must turn over to the corporation any profits from the trades. They must also disclose any trades they make in company stock. (p. 799)

EXAM Strategy

Question: You are the president of Turbocharge, Inc., a publicly traded company. You have been buying stock recently because you think the company's product—a more efficient hybrid engine—is very promising. One day, you show up at work and find your desk in the hallway. The CEO has fired you. In a huff, you sell all your company stock. The only silver lining to your cloud is that you make a large profit. Or is this a silver lining?

Strategy: You can be in violation of Section 16 even if you did not have any inside information when you trade. (See the "Result" at the end of this section.)

8. **SECTION 10(B)** Section 10(b) prohibits fraud in connection with the purchase and sale of any security, whether or not the issuer is registered under the 1934 Act. (p. 799)

9. **INSIDER TRADING** Section 10(b) also prohibits insider trading. (p. 802)

10. **FOREIGN CORRUPT PRACTICES ACT** Under the Foreign Corrupt Practices Act, it is a crime for any U.S. company to make payments to foreign officials to influence a government decision unless the purpose of that payment is to expedite a routine governmental action. (p. 805)

11. **THE NSMIA** The NSMIA prohibits states from regulating securities offerings that are:
   • Traded on a national exchange
   • Exempt under Rule 506, or
   • Sold to "qualified purchasers." (p. 806)

12. **BLUE SKY LAWS** Any securities offerings not covered by the NSMIA must comply with state securities laws, which are varied and complex. (p. 806)

1. Result: The painting was not a security because there was no "common enterprise." The investors did not pool funds or share profits with other investors. Nor did Stenger share in any profits earned on Love's paintings.

4. Result: The answer is (c).

7. Result: You are in violation of Section 16. Even though you acted without any bad intent, you must turn over all your profits to the company.

ADDITIONAL QUESTIONS

1. **CPA QUESTION** When a common stock offering requires registration under the Securities Act of 1933:
   (a) The registration statement is automatically effective when filed with the SEC.
   (b) The issuer would act unlawfully if it were to sell the common stock without providing the investor with a prospectus.
   (c) The SEC will determine the investment value of the common stock before approving the offering.
   (d) The issuer may make sales 10 days after filing the registration statement.

2. Fluor, an engineering and construction company, was awarded a $1 billion project to build a coal gasification plant in South Africa. Fluor signed an agreement with a South African client that prohibited them both from announcing the agreement until March 10. Accordingly, Fluor denied all rumors that a major transaction was pending. Between March 3 and March 6, the State Teachers Retirement Board pension fund sold 288,257 shares of Fluor stock. After the contract was announced, the stock price went up. Did Fluor violate Rule 10b-5?

3. Do you love ice cream? Here is an opportunity for you! For only $800, you can buy a cow from Berkshire Ice Cream. The company gets milk from the cow and you get to share in the profits from the sale of ice cream. Just last month, Berkshire mailed $32,000 worth of checks to investors—who are expecting a 20 percent annual rate of return. Are there any problems with this plan?

4. **ETHICS** ETS Payphones, Inc., sold pay phones to the public. The company then leased back the pay phones from the purchaser, promising a fixed 14 percent annual return on their investment. Although ETS's marketing materials trumpeted the "incomparable pay phone" as "an exciting business opportunity," the pay phones did not generate enough revenue for ETS to make the required payments, so the company depended on funds from new investors to meet its obligations to its existing customers. After ETS filed for bankruptcy protection, the SEC sued, alleging that ETS had been selling unregistered securities. Were the pay phone contracts securities under the 1933 Act? ETS advertised this investment as low-risk (offering a "guaranteed" fixed return). These sorts of advertisements are particularly attractive to individuals more vulnerable to investment fraud, including older and less sophisticated investors. Whether or not the pay phone contracts were securities, was it ethical to pitch what was, in fact, a high risk investment to vulnerable investors who were unable to assess the risks accurately? Were these actions right? How would the CEO of ETS have felt if someone had sold such an investment to his poor, elderly mother?

5. **CPA QUESTION** Pace Corp. previously issued 300,000 shares of its common stock. The shares are now actively traded on a national securities exchange. The original offering was exempt from registration under the Securities Act of 1933. Pace has $2.5 million in assets and 425 shareholders. With regard to the Securities Exchange Act of 1934, Pace is:

   (a) Required to file a registration statement because its assets exceed $2 million in value

   (b) Required to file a registration statement even though it has fewer than 500 shareholders

   (c) Not required to file a registration statement because the original offering of its stock was exempt from registration

   (d) Not required to file a registration statement unless insiders own at least 5 percent of its outstanding shares of stock

6. **YOU BE THE JUDGE** WRITING PROBLEM World-Wide Coin Investments Ltd. sold rare coins, precious metals, camera equipment, and Coca-Cola collector items. Its stock was registered with the SEC under the 1934 Act. Joseph Hale was the controlling shareholder, chairman of the board, CEO, and president. World-Wide's independent auditor warned Hale that the company's faulty system of accounting procedures was causing problems with inventory control. Furthermore, the auditor could not document transactions, and it had found that the books and records of the company were inaccurate. Is World-Wide in violation of the Foreign Corrupt Practices Act? **Argument for the SEC:** Without exception, all reporting companies are required to maintain accurate books and records. **Argument for World-Wide:** This is a small company, and the cost of such an elaborate internal control system would bankrupt it.

7. Suppose that, while waiting in line at the grocery store, you overhear a stranger saying that the FDA is going to approve a new drug tomorrow—one that will be a huge success for Alpha Pharmaceuticals. Is it legal for you to buy stock in Alpha?

8. Malaga Arabian Limited Partnership sold investments in the Spanish Arabian horse industry under Rule 506. James E. Mark, who purchased one of the partnership interests, alleged that the partnership violated Rule 506 because it never gave him any disclosure about the risks of the investment. He was not an accredited investor. At trial, the partnership said that it had surveyed investors to ensure that they were either accredited or sophisticated but had not actually read the surveys and did not have them available for the trial court. Is this offering exempt from registration under the 1933 Act?

9. **ROLE REVERSAL** Prepare a multiple-choice question that focuses on an issue involving Rule 504, restricted securities, or insider trading.

INTERNET RESEARCH PROBLEM

Choose a company, go to the EDGAR database at the SEC, and look at all filings this company has made during the last year. What filings has it made and why? Extra credit: search EDGAR for a prospectus for an initial public offering.

You can find further practice problems at www.cengagebrain.com. See the preface of this book for website access details.

PROPERTY

Charley lives in retirement in his modest bungalow, counting pennies to make his meager savings last. Then everything changes—or does it? He is playing bridge with three friends: a rabbi, a bishop, and a banker. As rain beats against the roof and everyone murmurs about possible flooding, the banker suddenly announces to the astonished group that he is obscenely rich and is going to give $100,000 to everyone at the table. "Meet me at the bank tomorrow at 10:00, and the money is yours." Shouts! Hugs! Tears!

> As rain beats against the roof and everyone murmurs about possible flooding, the banker suddenly announces to the astonished group that he is obscenely rich and is going to give $100,000 to everyone at the table.

That night, as rain continues to lash the house, Charley smiles in his sleep, dreaming that he is floating in a tropical paradise. He awakens to discover that he is floating—literally. His bedroom is filled with water, and Charley's head is now pressing against the ceiling. To avoid a catastrophe, the Power Company has released a nearby dam, inundating 150 acres. The water level on Charley's property is 16 feet and rising. Charley squirms through a broken window and escapes from his uninsured house just as it disappears into the roiling, black floodwaters.

The next morning, Charley, sneezing, arrives at the bank, where the bishop and rabbi grimly announce that the banker died before he could sign the three cashier's checks. There is no money. Charley, dazed and distraught, sues the Power Company for the damage to his house compensation and recovers—nothing. The company was legally entitled to destroy his house! Desperate, he seeks his $100,000 from the bank. Read on for the result.

A bewildering two days for Charley, but instructive for us, as we have glimpsed two issues of property law. The Power Company was entitled to destroy his house if it chose, because it owned an *easement*. The banker's promise will be settled according to the law of *gifts*. Our survey will focus on three primary topics: real property, landlord-tenant law, and personal property.

REAL PROPERTY

NATURE OF REAL PROPERTY

We need to define a few terms. A **grantor** is an owner who conveys his property, or some interest in it, to someone else, called the **grantee**. If you sell your house to Veronica, you are the grantor and she is the grantee. Real property may be any of the following:

- **Land.** Land is the most common and important form of real property. In England, land was historically the greatest source of wealth and social status, far more important than industrial or commercial enterprises. As a result, the law of real property has been of paramount importance for nearly 1,000 years, developing very gradually to reflect changing conditions. Some real property terms sound medieval for the simple reason that they are medieval.

- **Buildings.** Buildings are real property. Houses, office buildings, and factories all fall (or stand) in this category.

- **Subsurface Rights.** In most states, the owner of the land also owns anything under the surface, down to the center of the earth. In some cases the subsurface rights may be worth far more than the surface land, for example, if there is oil or gold underfoot. Although the landowner generally owns these rights, she may sell them while retaining ownership of the surface land.

- **Air Rights.** The owner of land owns the air space above the land. Suppose you own an urban parking lot. The owner of an adjacent office building wishes to build a walkway across your parking lot to join her building with a neighboring skyscraper. The office owner needs your permission to build across the air space and will expect to pay you a handsome fee for the privilege.

- **Plants.** Plant life growing on land is real property, whether the plants are naturally occurring, such as trees, or cultivated crops.

- **Fixtures.** Fixtures are goods that have become permanently attached to real property. A house (which is real property) contains many fixtures. The furnace and heating ducts were goods when they were manufactured and when they were sold to the builder, because they were movable. But when the builder attached them to the house, the items became fixtures. By contrast, neither the refrigerator nor the grand piano is a fixture.

When an owner sells real property, the buyer normally takes the fixtures, unless the parties specify otherwise. Sometimes it is difficult to determine whether something is a fixture. The general rule is this: **an object is a fixture if a reasonable person would consider the item to be a permanent part of the property**. What would a reasonable person think of this dispute?

Grantor
An owner who conveys an interest in his property to someone else.

Grantee
A person who receives an interest in property from a grantor.

FREEMAN V. BARRS

237 S.W.3d 285
MISSOURI COURT OF APPEALS, 2007

CASE SUMMARY

Facts: Mary Ann Barrs paid $3.5 million to Francis Freeman for 4,000 acres of ranch land, including a covered "pole-barn," which had open sides, a large cattle scale, and an enclosed veterinarian's office. The parties used a form contract, which stated that all fixtures were included with the sale. The document offered space for the parties to specify items that were included or excluded with the sale, but neither party listed the cattle scale as either in or out of the deal. After the agreement went through, Barrs and Freeman got into a beef over who owned the scale. The trial judge grilled numerous witnesses and ultimately weighed in on the side of Barrs, declaring the scale a fixture that belonged to the real estate. Broiling, Freeman appealed.

Issue: *Was the cattle scale a fixture?*

Decision: Yes, the scale was a fixture. Affirmed.

Reasoning: The scale's maker testified that it was designed to be portable. It would only take him an hour to cut away a welded metal fence and then fifteen minutes to move the scale itself.

On the other hand, the scale weighs 6,500 pounds. It is inside a covered barn that also includes a vet's office. To install the scale, a fence and gates within the barn had to be cut. There were concrete ramps and fencing around the scale to direct cattle onto it. The fence posts were set in concrete. No one had moved the scale since its installation.

A 6,500-pound scale placed inside a structure on a specially sized concrete pad and surrounded by metal pole fencing is annexed to the real estate. The scale was a fixture, and was included in the sale of the real estate.

ESTATES IN REAL PROPERTY

Use and ownership of real estate can take many different legal forms. A person may own property outright, having the unrestricted use of the land and an unlimited right to sell it. However, someone may also own a lesser interest in real property. For example, you could inherit the use of a parcel of land during your lifetime but have no power to leave the land to your heirs. Or you could retain ownership and possession of some land yet allow a corporation to explore for oil and drill wells. The different rights that someone can hold in real property are known as **estates** or **interests**. Both terms simply indicate specified rights in property.

Freehold Estates
The owner of a freehold estate has the present right to possess the property and to use it in any lawful way she wants. The three most important freehold estates are (1) fee simple absolute, (2) fee simple defeasible, and (3) life estate.

Fee Simple Absolute. A fee simple absolute **provides the owner with the greatest possible control of the property. This is the most common form of land ownership.** Suppose Cecily inherits a fee simple interest in a 30-acre vineyard. She may use the land for any purpose that the law allows. She may continue to raise grapes, or, if she hates wine, she may rip up the vines and

Fee simple absolute
Full and total ownership of a property.

build a condominium complex. Although zoning laws may regulate her use, nothing in Cecily's estate itself limits her use of the land. Cecily may pass on to her heirs her entire estate—that is, her full fee simple absolute.

Fee Simple Defeasible.   Other estates contain more limited rights than the fee simple absolute. Wily establishes the Wily Church of Perfection. Upon his death, Wily leaves a 100-acre estate to the church for as long as it keeps the name "Wily Church of Perfection." Wily has included a significant limitation in the church's ownership. The church has a fee simple defeasible.

Fee simple defeasible

Ownership of a property that can be terminated upon the occurrence of a limiting event.

   A fee simple defeasible may terminate upon the occurrence of some limiting event. If the congregation decides to rename itself the Happy Valley Church of Perfection, the church automatically loses its estate in the 100 acres. Ownership of the land then **reverts** to Wily's heirs, meaning title goes back to them. Because the heirs might someday inherit the land, they are said to have a *future interest* in the 100 acres. A land owner may create a fee simple defeasible to ensure that property is used in a particular way or is not used in a specified manner. In the following case, a California city was surprised to learn that this ancient doctrine still has plenty of life.

WALTON v. CITY OF RED BLUFF

2 CAL. APP. 4TH 117, 3 CAL. RPTR. 2d 275, 1991 Cal. APP. LEXIS 1474
CALIFORNIA COURT OF APPEAL, 1991

CASE SUMMARY

Facts: In 1908 and 1916, Mrs. Elizabeth Kraft and her son, Edward Kraft, granted to the city of Red Bluff two adjoining properties, with buildings, for use as a public library. The grants from the Krafts required continuous use as a public library and stated that the property would return to the Kraft family if the city ever used it for other purposes.

   In 1986, Red Bluff decided that the buildings were too small for its needs and moved all the books to a new building nearby. The city used the Kraft property for other civic purposes such as town meetings, social gatherings, and school tutoring. Herbert Kraft Walton, a descendant and heir, filed suit seeking to have the property reconveyed to him. The trial court found for Red Bluff, and Walton appealed.

Issue: *Did Red Bluff violate the terms of the grants, so the property must now revert to Walton?*

Decision: The property reverts to Walton. Reversed.

Reasoning: The grant stated that if the property was used for anything but "library purposes," it would revert immediately to the Kraft family. The document defined "library purposes" broadly. However, once the books were removed, there is no evidence that Red Bluff conducted any of the described activities.

   Red Bluff focused its argument on the "changed conditions" doctrine, which states that a power of termination expires when it becomes obsolete. For example, in one important case, a grant restricted property to residential use. Because the neighborhood had changed dramatically and was no longer residential, the court ruled that it would be unjust to enforce the reversionary clause.

   Here, though, the change is simply that the city needs more space. Red Bluff does not claim that the present building cannot be used as a library, or that neighborhood changes have made such use impractical. There is nothing unfair about enforcing the restriction in this grant, and Walton is entitled to the property.

Life Estate.   A life estate is exactly what you would think: **an estate for the life of some named person.** For example, Aretha owns Respect Farm, and in her will, she leaves it to Max, for his lifetime. Max is the **life tenant** He is entitled to live on the property and work it as a normal farm during his lifetime, though he is obligated to maintain it properly. The moment Max dies, the farm reverts to Aretha or her heirs.

Concurrent Estates

When two or more people own real property at the same time, they have concurrent estates. In a **tenancy in common**, the owners have an equal interest in the entire property. Each co-tenant has the right to sell her interest to someone else, or to leave it to her heirs upon her death. A **joint tenancy** is similar, except that upon the death of one joint tenant (owner), his interest passes *to the surviving joint tenants*, not to his heirs.

To provide special rights for married couples, some states have created **tenancy by the entirety** and **community property**. These forms of ownership allow one spouse to protect some property from the other, and from the other's creditors.

Condominiums and **cooperatives** are most common in apartment buildings with multiple units, though they can be used in other settings, such as a cluster of houses on a single parcel of land. In a condominium, the owner of the apartment typically has a fee simple absolute in his particular unit. He is normally entitled to sell or lease the unit, must pay taxes on it, and may receive the normal tax deduction if he is carrying a mortgage. All unit owners belong to a condominium association, which manages the common areas. In a cooperative, the residents generally do not own their particular unit. Instead, they are shareholders in a corporation that owns the building and leases specified units to the shareholders.

NONPOSSESSORY INTERESTS

All the estates and interests that we have examined thus far focused on one thing: possession of the land. Now we look at interests that *never* involve possession. These interests may be very valuable, even though the holder never lives on the land.

Easements

The Alabama Power Co. drove a flatbed truck over land owned by Thomas Burgess, damaging the property. The power company did this to reach its power lines and wooden transmission poles. Burgess had never given Alabama Power permission to enter his land, and he sued for the damage that the heavy trucks caused. He recovered—nothing. Alabama Power had an easement to use Burgess's land.

An easement gives one person the right to enter land belonging to another and make a limited use of it, without taking anything away. Burgess had bought his land from a man named Denton, who years earlier had sold an easement to Alabama Power. The easement gave the power company the right to construct several transmission poles on one section of Denton's land and to use reasonable means to reach the poles. Alabama Power owned that easement forever, and when Burgess bought the land, he took it subject to the easement. Burgess is stuck with his uninvited guest as long as he owns the land.[1]

Property owners normally create easements in one of two ways. A **grant** occurs when a landowner expressly intends to convey an easement to someone else. This is how Alabama Power acquired its easement. A **reservation** occurs when an owner sells land but keeps some

---

[1] *Burgess v. Alabama Power Co.*, 658 So.2d 435, 1995 Ala. LEXIS 119 (Ala. 1995).

Life estate
Ownership of property for the lifetime of a particular person.

Life tenant
A person who has the use of a property during his lifetime only.

Concurrent estate
Two or more people owning property at the same time.

Tenancy in common
Two or more people holding equal interest in a property, but with no right of survivorship.

Joint tenancy
Two or more people holding equal interest in a property, with the right of survivorship.

Easement
The right to enter land belonging to another and make limited use of it.

right to enter the property. A farmer might sell 40 acres to a developer but reserve an easement giving him the right to drive his equipment across a specified strip of the land.

Although many easements involve walking or driving across property, some are dramatically different. In the chapter's opening scenario, based on a real case, extraordinarily heavy rainfall presented the Power Company with a potential catastrophe. To control the water level of its lake, the company opened a dam. But this prudent move came with a terrible cost, as the surging flood inundated many acres and destroyed Charley's house. Could that possibly be legal? Yes. The Power Company had a *flood easement*, meaning the right to send an unlimited amount of water onto specified neighboring land, including Charley's modest property. The easement was recorded in the state's registry of deeds, and Charley—or any prospective buyer—should have considered it before buying affected property.

How did the Power Company obtain such an extraordinary easement? By purchasing it, long ago, from whoever owned Charley's property at that time. Why would anyone buy a house with a flood easement on it? First, the price will be cheaper. Second, the buyer may assume that since the power company never *had* used its easement, it never *would* do so. That was Charley's guess—but Charley guessed wrong.

Profit

Profit
The right to enter land belonging to another and take something from it.

A *profit* gives one person the right to enter land belonging to another and take something away. You own 100 acres of vacation property, and suddenly a mining company informs you that the land contains valuable nickel deposits. You may choose to sell a profit to the mining company, allowing it to enter your land and take away the nickel. You receive cash up front, and the company earns money from the sale of the mineral.

License

License
The right to enter land belonging to another temporarily.

A license gives the holder temporary permission to enter upon another's property. Unlike an easement or profit, a license is a *temporary* right. When you attend a basketball game by buying a ticket, the basketball club that sells you the ticket is the licensor and you are the licensee. You are entitled to enter the licensor's premises, namely the basketball arena, and to remain during the game, though the club can revoke the license if you behave unacceptably.

Mortgage

Mortgage
A security interest in real property.

Mortgagor
An owner who gives a security interest in property in order to obtain a loan.

Mortgagee
The party acquiring a security interest in property.

Generally, in order to buy a house, a prospective owner must borrow money. The bank or other lender will require security before it hands over its money, and the most common form of security for a real estate loan is a mortgage. **A mortgage is a security interest in real property.** The homeowner who borrows money is the **mortgagor**, because she is *giving* the mortgage to the lender. The lender, in turn, is the **mortgagee**, the party acquiring a security interest. The mortgagee in most cases obtains a **lien** on the house, meaning the right to foreclose on the property if the mortgagor fails to pay back the money borrowed.

EXAM *Strategy*

Question: Madison owns 160 acres of unused land in Montana. To make some money from the property, she has recently sold an easement, a profit, and a license. Give examples that show how Madison might have done that, and how the three interests differ from each other.

Strategy: An easement gives someone the right to enter land belonging to another and make a limited use of it, without taking anything away. A profit gives a person the right to enter land belonging to another and take something away. A license gives the holder temporary permission to enter upon another's property.

Result: Madison sold an easement to an adjacent property owner, allowing him to drive "all farm equipment" straight across her property on a designated road. To a mineral company, she sold the right to extract silver from 80 specified acres. For a local Fourth of July celebration, she charged a hot-air balloon company a one-time fee, allowing the outfit to give rides from her property, at the same time selling tickets to park on the land.

SALE OF REAL PROPERTY

For most people, buying or selling a house is the biggest, most important financial transaction they will make. Here we consider several of the key issues that may arise.

Seller's Obligations Concerning the Property

Historically, the common law recognized the rule of caveat emptor in the sale of real property—that is, let the buyer beware. If a buyer walked into his new living room and fell through the floor into a lake of toxic waste, it was his tough luck. But the common law changes with the times, and today courts place an increasing burden of fairness on the sellers of real estate. Two of the most significant obligations are the implied warranty of habitability and the duty to disclose defects.

Implied Warranty of Habitability.   **Most states now impose an implied warranty of habitability on a builder who sells a new home.** This means that, whether he wants to or not, the builder is guaranteeing that the new house contains **adequate materials and good workmanship.** The law implies this warranty because of the inherently unequal position of builder and buyer. Some defects might be obvious to a lay observer, such as a room with no roof or a front porch that sways whenever the neighbors sneeze. But only the builder will know if he made the frame with proper wood, if the heating system was second rate, the electrical work shabby, and so forth. Note that in most states the law implies this warranty to protect buyers of residential, but not commercial, property.

Duty to Disclose Defects.   **The seller of a home must disclose facts that a buyer does not know and cannot readily observe, if they materially affect the property's value.** Roy and Charlyne Terrell owned a house in the Florida Keys, where zoning codes required all living areas to be 15 feet above sea level. They knew that their house violated the code because a bedroom and bathroom were on the ground floor. They offered to sell the house to Robert Revitz, assuring him that the property complied with all codes and that flood insurance would cost about $350 per year. Revitz bought the house, moved in, and later learned that because of the code violations, flood insurance would be slightly more expensive—costing just over *$36,000 per year.* He sued and won. The court declared that the Terrells had a duty to disclose the code violations; it ordered a rescission of the contract, meaning that Revitz got his money back. The court mentioned that the duty to disclose was wide ranging and included leaking roofs, insect infestation, cracks in walls and foundations, and any other problems that a buyer might be unable to discern.[2]

---

[2] *Revitz v. Terrell*, 572 So.2d 996, 1990 Fla. App. LEXIS 9655 (Fla. Dist. Ct. App. 1990).

EXAM *Strategy*

Question: Grace bought a lakefront lot, intending to build a summer cottage. Then she learned that the soil was unsuitable for a septic system. She would have to hire an engineer at substantial expense to determine if it was even possible to construct an alternative waste disposal system. Instead, she put the land up for sale. Luis walked around the property with Grace, and the two discussed what a fine site it would be for a summer home. Luis never asked about septic issues, and Grace never mentioned her problem. After the deal went through, Luis discovered that a septic system was prohibitively expensive, and he sued. Did Grace have a duty to disclose the septic problems?

Strategy: Review the seller's obligation to disclose latent defects.

Result: A seller generally must report any latent defect he knows about that the buyer should not be expected to discover himself. Grace was obligated to disclose that a septic system would be unusually expensive or even impossible. Yes, it would have been wise for Luis to ask about septic issues. However, the obligation lies with the seller to disclose an important problem that is not readily visible to a buyer. Grace loses.

Sales Contract and Title Examination

The statute of frauds requires that an agreement to sell real property must be in writing to be enforceable. A contract for the sale of a house is often several pages of dense legal reading, in which the lawyers for the buyer and seller attempt to allocate risks for every problem that might go wrong. However, the contract need not be so thorough. A written contract for the sale of land is generally valid if it includes the names of all parties, a precise description of the property being sold, the price, and signatures.

Once the parties have agreed to the terms and signed a contract, the buyer's lawyer performs a **title examination,** which means that she, or someone she hires, searches through the local land registry for all documents that relate to the property. The purpose is to ensure that the seller actually has valid title to this land, because it is dispiriting to give someone half a million dollars for property and then discover that he never owned it and neither do you. Even if the seller owns the land, his title may be subject to other claims, such as an easement or a mortgage.

Closing and Deeds

Deed
A document that proves ownership of property.

While the buyer is checking the seller's title, she also probably needs to arrange financing, as described earlier in the section on mortgages. When the title work is complete and the buyer has arranged financing, the parties arrange a **closing**, a meeting at which the property is actually sold. The seller brings to the closing a **deed**, which is the document proving ownership of the land. The seller signs the deed over to the buyer in exchange for the purchase price. The buyer pays the price either with a certified check and/or by having her lender pay. If a lender pays part or all of the price, the buyer executes a mortgage to the lender as part of the closing.

Recording

Recording the deed means filing it with the official state registry. The registry clerk places a photocopy of the deed in the agency's bound volumes and indexes the deed by the name of the grantor and the grantee. Recording is a critical step in the sale of land, because it puts all the world on notice that the grantor has sold the land. It has little effect between grantor and grantee: once the deed and money are exchanged, the sale is generally final between those two. But recording is vital to protect the general public.

LAND USE REGULATION

Zoning

Zoning statutes are state laws that permit local communities to regulate building and land use. The local communities, whether cities, towns, or counties, then pass zoning ordinances that control many aspects of land development. For example, a town's zoning ordinance may divide the community into an industrial zone where factories may be built, a commercial zone in which stores of a certain size are allowed, and several residential zones in which only houses may be constructed. Within the residential zones, there may be further divisions, for example, permitting two-family houses in certain areas and requiring larger lots in others.

An owner prohibited by an ordinance from erecting a certain kind of building, or adding on to his present building, may seek a **variance** from the zoning board, meaning an exception granted for special reasons unique to the property. Whether a board will grant a variance generally depends upon the type of the proposed building, the nature of the community, the reason the owner claims he is harmed by the ordinance, and the reaction of neighbors.

Eminent Domain

Eminent domain is the power of the government to take private property for public use. A government may need land to construct a highway, an airport, a university, or public housing. All levels of government—federal, state, and local—have this power. But the Fifth Amendment to the United States Constitution states: "… nor shall private property be taken for public use, without just compensation." The Supreme Court has held that this clause, the Takings Clause, applies not only to the federal government but also to state and local governments. So, although all levels of government have the power to take property, they must pay the owner a fair price.

A "fair price" generally means the reasonable market value of the land. Generally, if the property owner refuses the government's offer, the government will file suit seeking **condemnation** of the land—that is, a court order specifying what compensation is just and awarding title to the government.

Eminent domain
The power of the government to take private property for public use.

LANDLORD-TENANT LAW

On a January morning in Studio City, California, Alpha Donchin took her small shih tzu for a walk. Suddenly, less than a block from her house, two large rottweilers attacked Donchin and her pet. The heavy animals mauled the 14-pound shih tzu, and when Donchin picked up her dog, the rottweilers knocked her down, breaking her hip and causing other serious injuries.

Ubal do Guerrero, who lived in a rented house nearby, owned the two rottweilers, and Donchin sued him. But she also sued Guerrero's *landlord*, David Swift, who lived four blocks away from the rental property. Donchin claimed that the landlord was liable for her injuries because he knew of the dogs' vicious nature and permitted them to escape from the property he rented to Guerrero. Should the landlord be liable for injuries caused by his tenant's dogs?

As is typical of many landlord-tenant issues, the law in this area is in flux. Under the common law, a landlord had no liability for injuries caused by animals belonging to a tenant,

> **If Donchin could prove that Swift knew the dogs were dangerous and allowed them to escape through a defective fence, the landlord would be liable for her injuries.**

Landlord
The owner of a freehold estate who allows another person temporarily to live on his property.

Tenant
A person given temporary possession of the landlord's property.

Tenancy for years
A lease for a stated, fixed period.

and many states adhere to that rule. But some states are expanding the landlord's liability for injuries caused on or near his property. The California court ruled that Donchin could maintain her suit against Swift. If Donchin could prove that Swift knew the dogs were dangerous and allowed them to escape through a defective fence, the landlord would be liable for her injuries.[3]

One reason for the erratic evolution of landlord-tenant law is that it is really a combination of three venerable areas of law: property, contract, and negligence. The confluence of these legal theories produces results that are unpredictable but interesting and important. We begin our examination of landlord-tenant law with an analysis of the different types of tenancy.

Recall that a freehold estate is the right to possess real property and use it in any lawful manner. **When an owner of a freehold estate allows another person temporary, exclusive possession of the property, the parties have created a landlord-tenant relationship.** The freehold owner is the **landlord**, and the person allowed to possess the property is the tenant. The landlord has conveyed a **leasehold** interest to the **tenant**, meaning the right to temporary possession. Courts also use the word **"tenancy"** to describe the tenant's right to possession. A leasehold may be commercial or residential.

Lease

The statute of frauds generally requires that a lease be in writing. Some states will enforce an oral lease if it is for a short term, such as one year or less, but even when an oral lease is permitted, it is wiser for the parties to put their agreement in writing, because a written lease avoids many misunderstandings. At a minimum, a lease must state the names of the parties, the premises being leased, the duration of the agreement, and the rent. But a well-drafted lease generally includes many provisions, called covenants. A **covenant** is simply a promise by either the landlord or the tenant to do something or refrain from doing something. For example, most leases include a covenant concerning the tenant's payment of a security deposit and the landlord's return of the deposit, a covenant describing how the tenant may use the premises, and several covenants about who must maintain and repair the property, who is liable for damage, and so forth. The parties should also agree about how the lease may be terminated and whether the parties have the right to renew it.

TYPES OF TENANCY

There are four types of tenancy: a tenancy for years, a periodic tenancy, a tenancy at will, and a tenancy at sufferance. The most important feature distinguishing one from the other is how each tenancy terminates. In some cases, a tenancy terminates automatically, while in others, one party must take certain steps to end the agreement.

Tenancy for Years

Any lease for a stated, fixed period is a tenancy for years. If a landlord rents a summer apartment for the months of June, July, and August of next year, that is a tenancy for years. A company that rents retail space in a mall beginning January 1, 2009, and ending December 31, 2012, also has a tenancy for years. A tenancy for years terminates automatically when the agreed period ends.

[3] *Donchin v. Guerrero*, 34 Cal. App. 4th 1832, 1995 Cal. App. LEXIS 462 (Cal. Ct. App. 1995).

Periodic Tenancy

A periodic tenancy is created for a fixed period and then automatically continues for additional periods until either party notifies the other of termination. This is probably the most common variety of tenancy. Suppose a landlord agrees to rent you an apartment "from month to month, rent payable on the first." That is a periodic tenancy. The tenancy automatically renews itself every month, unless either party gives adequate notice to the other that she wishes to terminate. A periodic tenancy could also be for one-year periods—in which case it automatically renews for an additional year if neither party terminates—or for any other period.

Periodic tenancy
A lease for a fixed period, automatically renewable unless terminated.

Tenancy at Will

A tenancy at will has no fixed duration and may be terminated by either party at any time. Tenancies at will are unusual tenancies.[4] Typically, the agreement is vague, with no specified rental period and with payment, perhaps, to be made in kind. The parties might agree, for example, that a tenant farmer could use a portion of his crop as rent. Since either party can end the agreement at any time, it provides no security for either landlord or tenant.

Tenancy at will
A tenancy with no fixed duration, which may be terminated by either party at any time.

Tenancy at Sufferance

A tenancy at sufferance occurs when a tenant remains on the premises, against the wishes of the landlord, after the expiration of a true tenancy. Thus, a tenancy at sufferance is not a true tenancy because the tenant is staying without the landlord's agreement. The landlord has the option of seeking to evict the tenant or of forcing the tenant to pay rent for a new rental period.

Tenancy at sufferance
A tenancy that exists without the permission of the landlord, after the expiration of a true tenancy.

LANDLORD'S DUTIES

DUTY TO DELIVER POSSESSION

The landlord's first important duty is to deliver possession of the premises at the beginning of the tenancy—that is, to make the rented space available to the tenant. In most cases, this presents no problems and the new tenant moves in. But what happens if the previous tenant has refused to leave when the new tenancy begins? In most states, the landlord is legally required to remove the previous tenant. In some states, it is up to the new tenant either to evict the existing occupant or begin charging him rent.

Quiet Enjoyment

All tenants are entitled to quiet enjoyment of the premises, meaning the right to use the property without the interference of the landlord. Most leases expressly state this covenant of quiet enjoyment. And if a lease includes no such covenant, the law implies the right of quiet enjoyment anyway, so all tenants are protected. If a landlord interferes with the tenant's quiet enjoyment, he has breached the lease, entitling the tenant to damages.

---

[4] The courts of some states, annoyingly, use the term "tenancy at will" for what are, in reality, parperiodic tenancies. They do this to bewilder law students and even lawyers, a goal at which they are quite successful. This text uses "tenancy at will" in its more widely known sense, meaning a tenancy terminable at any time.

Eviction
An act that forces a tenant to
abandon the property.

The most common interference with quiet enjoyment is an **eviction**, meaning some act that forces the tenant to abandon the premises. Of course, some evictions are legal, as when a tenant fails to pay the rent. But some evictions are illegal. There are two types of eviction: actual and constructive.

Actual Eviction.   **If a landlord prevents the tenant from possessing the premises, he has actually evicted her.** Suppose a landlord decides that a group of students are "troublemakers." Without going through lawful eviction procedures in court, the landlord simply waits until the students are out of the apartment and changes the locks. By denying the students access to the premises, the landlord has actually evicted them and has breached their right of quiet enjoyment.

Constructive Eviction.   **If a landlord substantially interferes with the tenant's use and enjoyment of the premises, he has constructively evicted her.** Courts construe certain behavior as the equivalent of an eviction. In these cases, the landlord has not actually prevented the tenant from possessing the premises but has instead interfered so greatly with her use and enjoyment that the law regards the landlord's actions as equivalent to an eviction. Suppose the heating system in an apartment house in Juneau, Alaska, fails during January. The landlord, an avid sled-dog racer, tells the tenants he is too busy to fix the problem. If the tenants move out, the landlord has constructively evicted them and is liable for all expenses they suffer.

To claim a constructive eviction, the tenant must vacate the premises. The tenant must also prove that the interference was sufficiently serious and lasted long enough that she was forced to move out. A lack of hot water for two days is not fatal, but lack of any water for two weeks creates a constructive eviction.

Duty to Maintain Premises

In most states, a landlord has a duty to deliver the premises in a habitable condition and a continuing duty to maintain the habitable condition. This duty overlaps with the quiet enjoyment obligation, but it is not identical. The tenant's right to quiet enjoyment focuses primarily on the tenant's *ability to use* the rented property. The landlord's duty to maintain the property focuses on whether the property *meets a particular legal standard.* The required standard may be stated in the lease, created by a state statute, or implied by law.

Lease. The lease itself generally obligates the landlord to maintain the exterior of any buildings and the common areas. If a lease does not do so, state law may imply the obligation.

Building Codes. Many state and local governments have passed building codes, which mandate minimum standards for commercial and/or residential property. The codes are likely to be stricter for residential property and may demand such things as minimum room size, sufficient hot water, secure locks, proper working kitchens and bathrooms, absence of insects and rodents, and other basics of decent housing. Generally, all rental property must comply with the building code, whether the lease mentions the code or not.

Implied Warranty of Habitability. Students Maria Ivanow, Thomas Tecza, and Kenneth Gearin rented a house from Les and Martha Vanlandingham. The monthly rent was $900. But the roommates failed to pay any rent for the final five months of the tenancy. After they moved out, the Vanlandinghams sued. How much did the landlords recover? Nothing. The landlords had breached the implied warranty of habitability.

The implied warranty of habitability requires that a landlord meet all standards set by the local building code, or that the premises be fit for human habitation. Most states, though not all, *imply* this warranty of habitability, meaning that the landlord must meet this standard whether the lease includes it or not.

The Vanlandinghams breached the implied warranty. The students had complained repeatedly about a variety of problems. The washer and dryer, which were included in the lease, frequently failed. A severe roof leak caused water damage in one of the bedrooms. Defective pipes flooded the bathroom. The refrigerator frequently malfunctioned, and the roommates repaired it several times. The basement often flooded, and when it was dry, rats and opossums lived in it. The heat sometimes failed.

In warranty of habitability cases, a court normally considers the severity of the problems and their duration. In the case of Maria Ivanow and friends, the court reduced the rent 50 percent. The students had already paid more than the reduced rent to the landlord, so they owed nothing for the last five months.[5]

Tenant Remedies for Defective Conditions.   Different states allow various remedies for defective conditions. You can find the tenant rights for your state online. Many states allow a tenant to withhold rent, representing the decreased value of the premises. In some states, if a tenant notifies the landlord of a serious defect and the landlord fails to remedy the problem, the tenant may deduct a reasonable amount of money from the rental payment and have the repair made himself. Also, a landlord who refuses to repair significant defects is breaching the lease and/or state law, and the tenant may simply sue for damages.

Duty to Return Security Deposit

Most landlords require tenants to pay a security deposit, in case the tenant damages the premises. In many states, a landlord must either return the security deposit soon after the tenant has moved out or notify the tenant of the damage and the cost of the repairs. A landlord who fails to do so may owe more than he anticipates, as the following case demonstrates.

MISHKIN V. YOUNG

107 P.3d 393, 2005 WL 452168
SUPREME COURT OF COLORADO, 2005

CASE SUMMARY

Facts: A Colorado statute required a landlord either to return a security deposit or provide an accounting of why money was being withheld. The landlord had to do this within 30 days of the tenant's surrender of the property, or up to 60 days if the lease permitted. If the landlord failed to refund the money, the tenant, after giving seven days' notice, could sue for treble damages. The landlord could avoid the treble damages by refunding the deposit within those seven days.

Marc Mishkin leased an apartment from Dean Young, paying a security deposit of $1,625. The lease stated that the deposit would be returned no later than 45 days after the

tenant moved out. After Mishkin left, Young did not return the money. Forty-eight days after leaving, Mishkin sent a demand for the deposit, notifying Young that in seven days he would sue for treble damages. Six days later, Young gave Mishkin a statement detailing $1,574.60 worth of property damage, along with a check for $50.40.

Mishkin sued. The trial court ruled that Young was entitled to withhold the money because of the damages. Mishkin appealed. The appellate court ruled that the Colorado statute required the landlord to return the full security deposit within the seven-day period. Young appealed.

---

[5] *Vanlandingham v. Ivanow,* 246 Ill. App. 3d 348, 615 N.E.2d 1361, 1993 Ill. App. LEXIS 985 (Ill. Ct. App. 1993).

Issue: *May a landlord avoid the treble damages by accounting for the security deposit within seven days of the tenant's notice to sue?*

Decision: No, a landlord may avoid treble damages during the seven-day period only by refunding the full deposit. Affirmed.

Reasoning: Landlords may withhold security deposits only if they account for all deductions within 30 days. The language in Mishkin's lease legally extended this deadline

to 45 days. Young failed to make an accounting within 45 days, and therefore he forfeited the right to retain any portion of Mishkin's security deposit.

The notice period creates only two possibilities. A landlord may refund every penny of a former tenant's security deposit within seven days. If he fails to do so, he is liable to the tenant for treble damages. The law is strict, and it acts as a significant deterrent to landlords who choose to keep deposits wrongfully.

TENANT'S DUTIES

Duty to Pay Rent

> My landlord said he's gonna raise the rent. "Good," I said, " 'cause I can't raise it."
>
> *Slappy White*, comedian, 1921–1995

Rent

Compensation paid by a tenant to a landlord.

Rent is the compensation the tenant pays the landlord for use of the premises, and paying the rent, despite Mr. White's wistful hope, is the tenant's foremost obligation. The lease normally specifies the amount of rent and when it must be paid. Typically, the landlord requires that rent be paid at the beginning of each rental period, whether that is monthly, annually, or otherwise.

If the tenant fails to pay rent on time, the landlord has several remedies. She is entitled to apply the security deposit to the unpaid rent. She may also sue the tenant for nonpayment of rent, demanding the unpaid sums, cost of collection, and interest. Finally, the landlord may evict a tenant who has failed to pay rent.

State statutes prescribe the steps a landlord must take to evict a tenant for nonpayment. Typically, the landlord must serve a termination notice on the tenant and wait for a court hearing. At the hearing, the landlord must prove that the tenant has failed to pay rent on time. If the tenant has no excuse for the nonpayment, the court grants an order evicting him. The order authorizes a sheriff to remove the tenant's goods and place them in storage, at the tenant's expense. However, if the tenant was withholding rent because of unlivable conditions, the court may refuse to evict.

Duty to Use Premises Properly

A lease normally lists what a tenant may do in the premises and prohibits other activities. For example, a residential lease allows the tenant to use the property for normal living purposes, but not for any retail, commercial, or industrial purpose.

A tenant is liable to the landlord for any significant damage he causes to the property. The tenant is not liable for normal wear and tear. If, however, he knocks a hole in a wall or damages the plumbing, the landlord may collect the cost of repairs, either by using the security deposit or by suing if necessary.

INJURIES

Tenant's Liability

A tenant is generally liable for injuries occurring within the premises she is leasing, whether that is an apartment, a store, or otherwise. If a tenant permits grease to accumulate on a kitchen floor and a guest slips and falls, the tenant is liable. If a merchant negligently installs display shelving that tips onto a customer, the merchant pays for the harm. Generally, a tenant is not liable for injuries occurring in common areas over which she has no control, such as exterior walkways. If a tenant's dinner guest falls because the building's common stairway has loose steps, the landlord is probably liable.

Landlord's Liability

Historically, the common law held a landlord responsible only for injuries that occurred in the common areas or due to the landlord's negligent maintenance of the property. Increasingly, though, the law holds landlords liable under the normal rules of negligence law. **In many states, a landlord must use reasonable care to maintain safe premises and is liable for foreseeable harm.** For example, most states now have building codes that require a landlord to maintain structural elements in safe condition. States further imply a warranty of habitability, which mandates reasonably safe living conditions.

Crime.   Landlords may be liable in negligence to tenants or their guests for criminal attacks that occur on the premises. Courts have struggled with this issue and have reached opposing results in similar cases. The very prevalence of crime sharpens the debate. What must a landlord do to protect a tenant? Courts typically answer the question by looking at four factors.

- *Nature of the Crime.* How did the crime occur? Could the landlord have prevented it?

- *Reasonable Person Standard.* What would a reasonable landlord have done to prevent this type of crime? What did the landlord actually do?

- *Foreseeability.* Was it reasonably foreseeable that such a crime might occur? Were there earlier incidents or warnings?

- *Prevalence of Crime in the Area.* If the general area, or the particular premises, has a high crime rate, courts are more likely to hold that the crime was foreseeable and the landlord responsible.

The following case highlights some of the issues facing courts as they apply changing mores to a tragic loss.

DICKINSON ARMS-REO, L.P. v. CAMPBELL

4 S.W.3d 333
TEXAS COURT OF APPEALS, 1999

CASE SUMMARY

Facts: About midnight, Joe Campbell and his girlfriend, Jenny Cady, left a club in separate cars, agreeing to meet at her apartment. Campbell parked his pickup truck in a space at the Dickinson Arms Apartments, where Cady lived.

Meanwhile, two sixteen-year-olds, Jeremy Gartrell and Donald Nichols, members of the Assassins, were visiting a fellow gang member who lived at the apartments. Gartrell approached Campbell, demanded the truck, and shot Campbell with a .22-caliber pistol, killing him. Gartrell was convicted of murder and sentenced to 50 years.

Campbell's parents sued the Dickinson Arms, claiming that the landlord's neglect of security had permitted the killing. Testimony indicated that over a three-year period, there had been 184 reported criminal offenses at the apartments. The property manager testified that no one told her gang members lived in the complex; company policy required her to check with police for possible preventive safety programs, but she had never done so; and she had never performed a security survey of the complex. The plaintiffs' expert witness testified that because of the high crime rates, the Dickinson Arms should have been protected with a perimeter fence, gates, and a security guard.

The jury found that the landlord failed to provide adequate security, and gave a judgment of $341,000 for the plaintiffs. The Dickinson Arms appealed.

Issue: *Was the landlord liable for the death?*

Decision: The Dickinson Arms was liable. Affirmed.

Reasoning: A landlord may be liable for criminal conduct on his property. However, the injured party must demonstrate that other crimes had occurred on the property recently, and that the earlier acts were so similar to the new incident that a landlord could have foreseen the harm that did occur.

The Campbells' evidence demonstrated that 184 crimes had occurred at the Dickinson Arms, including 20 burglaries, 13 auto thefts, 11 assaults, and 8 thefts. These crimes made it reasonably foreseeable that a confrontation on the property might lead to murder.

The Dickinson Arms' expert witness testified that a security guard, perimeter fencing, and limited access gates would not have stopped an impulsive offender like Gartrell, whom he described as a time bomb waiting to explode. Gartrell's former high school principal and his peers confirmed his violent nature, lack of respect for authority, and obduracy.

The Campbells' evidence showed that Gartrell had wanted to do a carjacking all day. Before going to the Dickinson Arms, Gartrell and Nichols walked to a nearby Taco Bell. Gartrell told Nichols he was going to carjack a green Mustang that pulled up. But there were customers present, and the Taco Bell was well lit. Nichols said, "Don't be stupid," and the pair walked next door to a Kroger's. That parking lot was also well lit, and again Gartrell did nothing.

The two arrived at the Dickinson Arms Apartments. Nichols testified that the parking lot was dark, and that they knew there was no security guard or access control gates. A tenant, though, said that the lighting in the parking lot was good enough for her to see Joe Campbell's body and truck from her apartment window. The parents' expert testified that if the apartment complex had provided access control gates, a night security guard, and perimeter fencing, this offense probably would never have occurred.

It is the role of the jury to resolve conflicts in the testimony. This evidence is legally and factually sufficient to support the jury's verdict of liability.

PERSONAL PROPERTY

Personal property
All property other than real property.

Gift
A voluntary transfer of property from one person to another, without consideration.

Donor
A person who gives property away.

Donee
A person who receives a gift of property.

Personal property means all property other than real property. Real property, as we know, refers to land and things firmly attached to it. All other property is personal: a bus, a toothbrush, a share of stock. Most personal property is goods, meaning something that can be moved. We have already examined the purchase and sale of goods, which are governed by the Uniform Commercial Code (UCC). Now we look at two important aspects of personal property: gifts and bailments.

GIFTS

A gift is a voluntary transfer of property from one person to another without any consideration. It is the lack of consideration that distinguishes a gift from a contract. Contracts usually consist of mutual promises to do something in the future. Each promise is consideration for the other one, and the mutual consideration makes each promise enforceable. But a gift is a one-way transaction, without consideration. The person who gives property away is the **donor** and the one who receives it is the **donee**.

A gift involves three elements:

- The donor intends to transfer ownership of the property to the donee immediately.

- The donor delivers the property to the donee.

- The donee accepts the property.

INTENTION TO TRANSFER OWNERSHIP

The donor must intend to transfer ownership to the property right away, immediately giving up all control of the item. Notice the two important parts of this element. First, the donor's intention must be to transfer ownership—that is, to give title to the donee. Merely proving that the owner handed you property does not guarantee that you have received a gift; if the owner only intended that you use the item, there is no gift and she can demand it back.

Second, the donor must also intend the property to transfer *immediately.* A promise to make a gift in the future is unenforceable. Promises about future behavior are governed by contract law, and a contract is unenforceable without consideration. That is why poor Charley, at the beginning of this chapter, will never collect his $100,000 from the banker. If the banker had handed Charley the cash as he gushed his extravagant words, Charley could keep the money. However, the banker's promise to make the gift the next day is legally worthless. Nor does Charley have an enforceable contract, since there was no consideration for the banker's promise.

A *revocable gift* is a contradiction in terms, because it violates the rule just discussed. It is not a gift, and the donee keeps nothing.[6] Suppose Harold tells his daughter Faith, "The mule is yours from now on, but if you start acting stupid again, I'm taking her back." Harold has retained some control over the animal, which means he has not intended to transfer ownership. There is no gift, and Harold still owns the mule.

Delivery

Physical Delivery.   **The donor must deliver the property to the donee.** Generally, this involves physical delivery. If Anna hands Eddie a Rembrandt drawing, saying, "I want you to have this forever," she has satisfied the delivery requirement. This is the element missing from the banker's "gift" to Charley.

Constructive Delivery.   Physical delivery is the most common and the surest way to make a gift, but it is not always necessary. **A donor makes constructive delivery by transferring ownership without a physical delivery.** Most courts permit constructive delivery only when physical delivery is impossible or extremely in convenient. Suppose Anna wants to give her niece Jen a blimp, which is parked in a hangar at the airport. The blimp will not fit through the doorway of Jen's dorm. Instead of flying the aircraft to the university, Anna may simply deliver to Jen the certificate of title and the keys to the blimp. When she has done that, Jen owns the aircraft.

---

[6] The only exception to this rule is a gift *causa mortis,* discussed in a later section.

Inter Vivo Gifts and Gifts Causa Mortis.   A gift can be either *inter vivos* or *causa mortis*. An *inter vivos* gift means a gift made during life—that is, when the donor is not under any fear of impending death. The vast majority of gifts are *inter vivos*, involving a healthy donor and donee. Shirley, age 30 and in good health, gives her husband Terry an eraser for his birthday. This is an *inter vivos* gift, which is absolute. The gift becomes final upon delivery, and the donor may not revoke it. If Shirley and Terry have a fight the next day, Shirley has no power to erase her gift.

A gift *causa mortis* is one made in contemplation of approaching death. The gift is valid if the donor dies as expected but is revoked if he recovers. Suppose Lance's doctors have told him he will probably die of a liver ailment within a month. Lance calls Jane to his bedside and hands her a fistful of emeralds, saying, "I'm dying; these are yours." Jane sheds a tear, then sprints to the bank. If Lance dies of the liver ailment within a few weeks, Jane gets to keep the emeralds. The law permits the gift *causa mortis* to act as a substitute for a will because the donor's delivery of the property clearly indicates his intentions. But note that this kind of gift is revocable. Since a gift *causa mortis* is conditional (upon the donor's death), the donor has the right to revoke it at any time before he dies. If Lance telephones Jane the next day and says that he has changed his mind, he gets the jewels back. Further, if the donor recovers and does not die as expected, the gift is automatically revoked.

Inter vivos gift
A gift made during the donor's life, with no fear of impending death.

Gift *causa mortis*
A gift made in contemplation of approaching death.

EXAM *Strategy*

Question: Julie does good deeds for countless people, and many are deeply grateful. On Monday, Wilson tells Julie, "You are a wonderful person, and I have a present for you. I am giving you this baseball, which was the 500th home run hit by one of the great players of all time." He hands her the ball, which is in fact worth nearly half a million dollars. On Tuesday, Cassandra tells Julie, "I only have a few weeks to live. I want you to have this signed first edition of *Ulysses*. It is priceless and it is yours." The book is worth about $200,000. On Wednesday, both Wilson and Cassandra decide they have been foolhardy, and demand that Julie return the items. Must she do so?

Strategy: Both of these donors are attempting to revoke their gifts. An *inter vivos* gift cannot be revoked, but a gift *causa mortis* can be. To answer the question, you must know what kind of gifts these were.

Result: A gift *causa mortis* is one made in fear of approaching death, and this rule applies to Cassandra. Such a gift is revocable any time before the donor dies, so Cassandra gets her book back. A gift *inter vivos* is one made without any such fear of death. Most gifts fall in this category, and they are irrevocable. Wilson was not anticipating his demise, so his was a gift *inter vivos*. Julie keeps the baseball.

Acceptance
The donee must accept the gift. This rarely leads to disputes, but if a donee should refuse a gift and then change her mind, she is out of luck. Her repudiation of the donor's offer means there is no gift, and she has no rights in the property.

The following case offers a combination of love and anger, alcohol and diamonds—always a volatile mix.

YOU *be the* JUDGE

ALBINGER v. HARRIS
2002 Mont. 118, 2002 WL 1226858
MONTANA SUPREME COURT, 2002

Facts: Michelle Harris and Michael Albinger lived together, on and off, for three years. Their roller-coaster relationship was marred by alcohol abuse and violence. When they announced their engagement, Albinger gave Harris a $29,000 diamond ring, but the couple broke off their wedding plans because of emotional and physical turmoil. Harris returned the ring. Later, they reconciled and resumed their marriage plans, and Albinger gave his fiancee the ring again. This cycle repeated several times over the three years. Each time they broke off their relationship, Harris returned the ring to Albinger, and each time they made up, he gave it back to her.

On one occasion, Albinger held a knife over Harris as she lay in bed, threatening to chop off her finger if she didn't remove the ring. He beat her and forcibly removed the ring. Criminal charges were brought but then dropped when, inevitably, the couple reconciled. Another time, Albinger told her to "take the car, the horse, the dog, and the ring and get the hell out." Finally, mercifully, they ended their stormy affair, and Harris moved to Kentucky—keeping the ring.

Albinger sued for the value of the ring. The trial court found that the ring was a conditional gift, made in contemplation of marriage, and ordered Harris to pay its full value. She appealed. The Montana Supreme Court had to decide, in a case of first impression, whether an engagement ring was given in contemplation of marriage. (In Montana and in many states, neither party to a broken engagement may sue for breach of contract, because it is impossible to determine who is responsible for ending the relationship.)

You Be the Judge: Who owns the ring?

Argument for Harris: The main problem with calling the ring a "conditional gift" is that there is no such thing. The elements of a gift are intent, delivery, and acceptance, and Harris has proven all three. A gift is not a contract, nor is it a loan. Once a gift has been accepted, the donor has no more rights in the property and may not demand its return. Hundreds of years of litigation have resulted in only one exception to this rule—a gift *causa mortis*—and despite some cynical claims to the contrary, marriage is not death. If this court carves a new exception to the long-standing rule, other unhappy donors will dream up more "conditions" that supposedly entitle them to their property. What is more, to create a special rule for engagement rings would be blatant gender bias, because the exception would only benefit men. This court should stick to settled law, and permit the recipient of a gift to keep it.

Argument for Albinger: The symbolism of an engagement ring is not exactly news. For decades, Americans have given rings—frequently diamond—in contemplation of marriage. All parties understand why the gift is made and what is expected if the engagement is called off: the ring must be returned. Albinger's intent, to focus on one element, was conditional—and Michelle Harris understood that. Each time the couple separated, she gave the ring back. She knew that she could wear this beautiful ring in anticipation of their marriage, but that custom and decency required its return if the wedding was off. She knew it, that is, until greed got the better of her and she fled to Kentucky, attempting to profit at the expense of Albinger's generosity. We are not asking for new law, but for confirmation of what everyone has known for generations: there is no wedding ring when there is no wedding.

The following chart distinguishes between a contract and a gift:

A Contract and a Gift Distinguished

A Contract:

Lou: I will pay you $2,000 to paint the house if you promise to finish by July 3.	Abby: I agreed to paint the house by July 3 for $2,000.

Lou and Abby have a contract. Each promise is consideration in support of the other promise. Lou and Abby can each enforce the other's promise.

A Gift:

Lou hands Phil two opera tickets, while saying:

Lou: I want you to have these two tickets to *Rigoletto*.	Phil: Hey, thanks.

This is a valid *inter vivos* gift. Lou intended to transfer ownership immediately and deliver the property to Phil, who now owns the tickets.

Neither Contract nor Gift:

Lou: You're a great guy. Next week, I'm going to give you two tickets to *Rigoletto*.	Jason: Hey, thanks.

There is no gift because Lou did not intend to transfer ownership immediately, and he did not deliver the tickets. There is no contract because Jason has given no consideration to support Lou's promise.

Bailment

Bailment

The rightful possession of goods by one who is not the owner, usually by mutual agreement between the bailor and bailee.

A bailment is the rightful possession of goods by one who is not the owner. The one who delivers the goods is the **bailor** and the one in possession is the **bailee**. Bailments are common. Suppose you are going out of town for the weekend and loan your motorcycle to Stan. You are the bailor and your friend is the bailee. When you check your suitcase with the airline, you are again the bailor and the airline is the bailee. If you rent a car at your destination, you become the bailee while the rental agency is the bailor. In each case, someone other than the true owner has rightful, temporary possession of personal property.

The parties generally—but not always—create a bailment by agreement. In each of the examples, the parties agreed to the bailment. In two cases, the agreement included payment, which is common but not essential. When you buy your airline ticket, you pay for your ticket, and the price includes the airline's agreement, as bailee, to transport your suitcase. When you rent a car, you pay the bailor for the privilege of using it. By loaning your motorcycle, you engage in a bailment without either party paying compensation.

A bailment without any agreement is called a constructive, or involuntary, bailment. Suppose you find a wristwatch in your house that you know belongs to a friend. You are obligated to return the watch to the true owner, and until you do so, you are the bailee, liable for harm to the property. This is called a constructive bailment because, with no agreement between the parties, the law is *construing* a bailment.

Because the bailor is the one who delivers the goods to another, the bailor is typically the owner, but he need not be. Suppose that Stan, who borrowed your motorcycle, allows his girlfriend Sheila to try out the bike, and she takes it to a mall where she jumps over a row of six parked cars. Stan, the bailee from you, has become a bailor, and Sheila is his bailee.

Control

To create a bailment, the bailee must assume physical control with intent to possess. A bailee may be liable for loss or damage to the property. But it is not fair to hold him liable unless he has taken physical control of the goods, intending to possess them.

Disputes about whether someone has taken control often arise in parking lot cases. When a car is damaged or stolen, the lot's owner may try to avoid liability by claiming it lacked control of the parked auto and therefore was not a bailee. If the lot is a "park and lock" facility, where the car's owner retains the key and the lot owner exercises no control at all, then there may be no bailment, and no liability for damage. By contrast, when a driver leaves her keys with a parking attendant, the lot clearly is exercising control of the auto, and the parties have created a bailment. The lot is probably liable for loss or damage. What about cases in the middle, where the driver keeps her keys but the lot owner exercises *some other control?* There is no uniform rule, but the trend is probably toward liability for the lot owner.

Rights of the Bailee

The bailee's primary right is possession of the property. Anyone who interferes with the bailee's rightful possession is liable to her. **The bailee is typically, though not always, permitted to use the property.** Obviously, a customer is permitted to drive a car rented from an agency. But some bailees have no authority to use the goods. If you store your furniture in a warehouse, the storage company is your bailee, but it has no right to curl up in your bed. The bailee may or may not be entitled to compensation, depending on the parties' agreement.

Duties of the Bailee

The bailee is strictly liable to redeliver the goods on time to the bailor or to whomever the bailor designates. Strict liability means there are virtually no exceptions. Rudy stores his $6,000 drum set with Melissa's Warehouse while he is on vacation. Blake arrives at the warehouse and shows a forged letter, supposedly from Rudy, granting Blake permission to remove the drums. If Melissa permits Blake to take the drums, she will owe Rudy $6,000, even if the forgery was a high-quality job.

Due Care

The bailee is obligated to exercise due care. **The level of care required depends upon who receives the benefit of the bailment.** There are three possibilities:

- *Sole Benefit of Bailee.* If the bailment is for the sole benefit of the bailee, the bailee is required to use **extraordinary care** with the property. Generally, in these cases, the bailor loans something for free to the bailee. If your neighbor loans you a power lawn mower, the bailment is probably for your sole benefit. You are liable if you are even slightly inattentive in handling the lawn mower and can expect to pay for virtually any harm done.

- *Mutual Benefit.* When the bailment is for the mutual benefit of bailor and bailee, the bailee must use **ordinary care** with the property. Ordinary care is what a reasonably prudent person would use under the circumstances. When you rent a car, you benefit from the use of the car, and the agency profits from the fee you pay. Most bailments benefit both parties, and courts decide the majority of bailment disputes under this standard.

- *Sole Benefit of Bailor.* When the bailment benefits only the bailor, the bailee must use only **slight care.** This kind of bailment is called a **gratuitous bailment,** and the bailee is liable only for **gross negligence.** Sheila enters a greased-pig contest and asks you to hold her $140,000 diamond engagement ring while she competes. You put the ring in your pocket. Sheila wins the $20 first prize, but the ring has disappeared. This was a gratuitous bailment, and you are not liable to Sheila unless she can prove gross negligence on your part. If the ring dropped from your pocket or was stolen, you are not liable. If you used the ring to play catch with friends, you are liable.

Burden of Proof.   In an ordinary negligence case, the plaintiff has the burden of proof to demonstrate that the defendant was negligent and caused the alleged harm. In bailment cases, the burden of proof is reversed. **Once the bailor has proven the existence of a bailment and loss or harm to the goods, a presumption of negligence arises, and the burden shifts to the bailee to prove adequate care.** This is a major change from ordinary negligence cases. Georgina's car is struck by another auto. If Georgina sues for negligence, it is her burden to prove that the defendant was driving unreasonably and caused the harm. By comparison, assume that Georgina rents Sam her sailboat for a month. At the end of the month, Sam announces that the boat is at the bottom of Lake Michigan. If Georgina sues Sam, she only needs to demonstrate that the parties had a bailment and that he failed to return the boat. The burden then shifts to Sam to prove that the boat was lost through no fault of his own. If he cannot meet that burden, Georgina recovers the full value of the boat.

The parties may use a contract to specify whether they have created a bailment, hoping to protect their rights. But even then things do not always go smoothly, as the following case demonstrates.

MITCHELL v. BANK OF AMERICA NATIONAL ASSOCIATION

2002 WL 31139375
COURT OF APPEALS OF TEXAS, 2002

CASE SUMMARY

Facts: Donna and Timothy Mitchell rented a safe deposit box from a Dallas branch of the Bank of America. The lease agreement stated that the bank "had no possession or custody of, nor control over, the contents of the Box, and the Lessee [the couple] assumes all risks in connection with the depositing of such content." The lease also permitted the bank to remove the box's contents if the rental fee went unpaid.

Bank officers, believing the Mitchells were behind in their rental fees, drilled into the box and removed the contents, which they inventoried and sent to a central vault elsewhere. When the Mitchells learned of this, they were very upset and "loudly discussed the value of the contents" in the lobby of the Dallas branch.

A week later, the bank informed the Mitchells the contents were back at the Dallas branch. The couple placed the contents into a bag, which they put under the front seat of their car. Shortly after leaving the bank, the Mitchells had a

flat tire. A stranger offered assistance. While they were all changing the tire, the bag disappeared.

The Mitchells sued the bank, claiming that its negligence enabled bank employees to learn of the box's contents. In a well-prepared scam, an employee or his accomplice let the air out of the couple's tire, offered roadside assistance, and stole the bag.

The trial court gave summary judgment for the bank, finding that the contract language quoted above meant that there was no bailment and no possible negligence. The Mitchells appealed.

Issue: *Was there a bailment?*

Decision: Yes, there was a bailment. Reversed.

Reasoning: The common law establishes rules for liability in bailments, but the parties can use an express written contract to change legal responsibility. Here, the parties signed a lease for the safe deposit box, and to the extent it applies, the lease controls the bank's liability.

The lease stated that so long as the Mitchells' property was in the box, there was no delivery to the bank. That provision is valid, and it means that when the Mitchells placed their possessions in the safe deposit box, the parties created no bailment.

However, the lease also authorized the bank to remove the contents of the box if the Mitchells failed to pay the rental fee. The parties thus contemplated a delivery of the property to the bank under certain circumstances, and they did *not* change the common law duties once the bank took control of the box's contents.

The trial court granted summary judgment for the bank on the grounds that the contract precluded a bailment, and hence liability. That was in error. Once the bank took the property, the contract, by its own terms, no longer applied. The parties had entered into a bailment, and the common-law rules of liability controlled their conduct.

Rights and Duties of the Bailor.   The bailor's rights and duties are the reverse of the bailee's. The bailor is entitled to the return of his property on the agreed-upon date. He is also entitled to receive the property in good condition and to recover damages for harm to the property if the bailee failed to use adequate care.

CHAPTER CONCLUSION

Real property law is ancient but forceful, as Charley discovered when a power company flooded his land and an old-fashioned easement deprived him of compensation. Had Charley understood nonpossessory interests, he might have declined to buy the property. Landlord-tenant law, by contrast, is new and rapidly changing, especially as to liability for injuries. Personal property law affects most of us every day, as we leave goods with a repair shop or accept a diamond engagement ring. Understanding property law can be worth a lot of money, even if the wedding is cancelled.

EXAM REVIEW

1. **REAL PROPERTY** Real property includes land, buildings, air and subsurface rights, plant life, and fixtures. A fixture is any good that has become attached to other real property. (p. 814)

EXAM Strategy

Question: Paul and Shelly Higgins had two wood stoves in their home. Each rested on, but was not attached to, a built-in brick platform. The downstairs wood stove was connected to the chimney flue and was used as part of the main heating system for the house. The upstairs stove, in the master bedroom, was purely decorative. It had no stovepipe connecting it to the chimney. The Higginses sold their house to Jack Everitt, and neither party said anything about the two stoves. Is Everitt entitled to either stove? Both stoves?

Strategy: An object is a fixture if a reasonable person would consider the item to be a permanent part of the property, taking into account attachment, adaptation, and other objective manifestations of permanence. (See the "Result" at the end of this section.)

2. **ESTATES** A fee simple absolute provides the owner with the greatest possible control of the property, including the right to make any lawful use of it and to sell it. A fee simple defeasible may terminate upon the occurrence of some limiting event. A life estate permits the owner to possess the property during her life but not to sell it or leave it to heirs. (pp. 815–816)

3. **EASEMENT** An easement gives a person the right to enter land belonging to another and make a limited use of it, without taking anything away. (p. 817)

4. **HABITABILITY** The implied warranty of habitability means that a builder selling a new home guarantees the adequacy of materials and workmanship. (p. 819)

5. **DISCLOSURE** The seller of a home must disclose facts that a buyer does not know and cannot readily observe if they materially affect the property's value. (p. 819)

6. **LANDLORD-TENANT** When an owner of a freehold estate allows another person temporary, exclusive possession of the property, the parties have created a landlord-tenant relationship. (p. 821)

7. **TENANCIES** Any lease for a stated, fixed period is a tenancy for years. A periodic tenancy is created for a fixed period and then automatically continues for additional periods until either party notifies the other of termination. A tenancy at will has no fixed duration and may be terminated by either party at any time. A tenancy at sufferance occurs when a tenant remains, against the wishes of the landlord, after the expiration of a true tenancy. (p. 822)

8. **CONSTRUCTIVE EVICTION** A landlord may be liable for constructive eviction if he substantially interferes with the tenant's use and enjoyment of the premises. (p. 824)

9. **IMPLIED WARRANTY OF HABITABILITY** The implied warranty of habitability requires that a landlord meet all standards set by the local building code and/or that the premises be fit for human habitation. (p. 824)

10. **TENANT'S OBLIGATIONS** The tenant is obligated to pay the rent and must pay the landlord for any significant damage he causes to the property. (pp. 826)

11. **LANDLORD'S LIABILITY** At common law, a landlord had very limited liability for injuries on the premises, but today many courts require a landlord to use reasonable care and hold her liable for foreseeable harm. (p. 827)

EXAM Strategy

Question: Hank rents an apartment in a rental housing community called Mountain Garden, a middle-class development of five buildings. Crime on the estate is about 15 percent lower than in the surrounding community, and violent crime is 25 percent lower. A guard at the entry booth monitors who is allowed to enter. The parking lots are poorly lit.

Hank invites his friend Sheila for dinner. They get into an argument, first about whether Hank put marijuana in the chicken pasta, and second about Hank's relationship with another woman. The row grows violent, Hank rushes at Sheila, and she stabs him with a kitchen knife. Hank dies, and his estate sues Mountain Garden for negligence. Who is likely to win?

Strategy: The court will apply four factors to its analysis: the nature of the crime, the reasonable person standard, foreseeability, and prevalence of crime in the area.

---

12. **GIFT** A gift is a voluntary transfer of property from one person to another without consideration. The elements of a gift are intention to transfer ownership immediately, delivery, and acceptance. (p. 828)

---

13. **BAILMENT** A bailment is the rightful possession of goods by one who is not the owner. The one who delivers the goods is the bailor and the one in possession is the bailee. To create a bailment, the bailee must assume physical control with intent to possess. (p. 832)

---

14. **BAILEE** The bailee is obligated to exercise due care. The level of care required depends upon who receives the benefit of the bailment: if the bailee is the sole beneficiary, she must use extraordinary care; if the parties mutually benefit, the bailee must use ordinary care; and if the bailor is the sole beneficiary of the bailment, the bailee must use only slight care. The bailee is strictly liable to redeliver the goods. (p. 833)

EXAM Strategy

Question: Shannon borrows Marty's car, but when she returns the auto, she hands the keys to Scott, who claims he is Marty's brother. Scott offers a driver's license and passport to reassure Shannon. Scott is actually a con artist. Marty sues Shannon. Outcome?

(a) Marty will win.

(b) Marty will win only if a *reasonable person* would have spotted the fraud.

(c) Marty will win only if he in fact has no brother named Scott.

(d) Marty will lose, because Scott offered reasonable identification.

Strategy: Make sure you know the standard a bailee must meet for redelivering goods. (See the "Result" at the end of this section.)

1. Result: A buyer normally takes all fixtures. The downstairs stove was permanently attached to the house and used as part of the heating system. The owner who installed it *intended* that it remain, and it was a fixture; Everitt got it. The upstairs stove was not permanently attached and was not a fixture; the sellers could take it with them.

11. Result: Mountain Garden is likely to win. This crime was committed by an invited guest, not an intruder who entered because of sloppy security. A reasonable manager would have permitted Sheila to enter the property. There was no reason for Mountain Garden to anticipate the fight that led to the killing. Finally, Mountain Garden is safer than the surrounding community, and its manager could not expect a dinner date to lead to homicide.

14. Result: The bailee is strictly liable to redeliver the goods to the bailor. There are no excuses. The "reasonable person" standard does not apply. The correct answer is (a).

ADDITIONAL QUESTIONS

1. In 1944, W. E. Collins conveyed land to the Church of God of Prophecy. The deed said: "This deed is made with the full understanding that should the property fail to be used for the Church of God, it is to be null and void and property to revert to W. E. Collins or heirs." In the late 1980s, the church wished to move to another property and sought a judicial ruling that it had the right to sell the land. The trial court ruled that the church owned a fee simple absolute and had the right to sell the property. Comment.

2. *CPA QUESTION* On July 1, 1992, Quick, Onyx, and Nash were deeded a piece of land as tenants in common. The deed provided that Quick owned half the property and Onyx and Nash owned one quarter each. If Nash dies, the property will be owned as follows:

   a. Quick 1/2, Onyx 1/2

   b. Quick 5/8, Onyx 3/8

   c. Quick 1/3, Onyx 1/3, Nash's heirs 1/3

   d. Quick 1/2, Onyx 1/4, Nash's heirs 1/4

3. Summey Building Systems built a condominium project in Myrtle Beach, South Carolina. The project included an adjacent parking deck. Shortly after Summey relinquished control to the condominium association, the deck began to experience problems. Water and caustic materials leaked through the upper deck and dripped onto cars parked underneath. Cracks appeared, and an expert concluded that the bond between the top deck and the structural supports was insufficient. Repairs would cost about $205,000. Summey had never warranted that the deck would be free of all problems. Is the company liable for the repairs?

4. Kenmart Realty sued to evict Mr. and Ms. Alghalabio for nonpayment of rent and sought the unpaid monies, totaling several thousand dollars. In defense, the Alghalabios claimed that their apartment was infested with rats. They testified that there were numerous rat holes in the walls of the living room, bedroom, and kitchen, that there were rat droppings all over the apartment, and that on one occasion they saw

their toddler holding a live rat. They testified that the landlord had refused numerous requests to exterminate. Please rule on the landlord's suit.

5. ***YOU BE THE JUDGE*** WRITING PROBLEM Dominion Bank owned a large office building in Washington, D.C. Because it planned to sell the building, the bank stopped leasing new space and five of the 13 floors became vacant. Tenants complained to the bank that vagrants were using the empty spaces for drug deals and prostitution. Jane Doe, a secretary who worked in the building, was dragged to an empty, unlocked floor and raped. She sued the bank. A security expert testified that all vacant offices and floors should have been sealed off. Is the bank liable for Doe's injuries? **Argument for Jane Doe:** The bank created a dangerous situation by gradually abandoning a commercial building. The bank should be held to a "reasonable person" standard, one that it clearly failed to meet. **Argument for Dominion Bank:** The bank is not a police force. The bank's obligation was to keep the rented premises in good working order, which it did.

6. While in her second year at the Juilliard School of Music in New York City, Ann Rylands had a chance to borrow for one month a rare Guadagnini violin, made in 1768. She returned the violin to the owner in Philadelphia but telephoned her father to ask if he would buy it for her. He borrowed money from his pension fund and paid the owner. Ann traveled to Philadelphia to pick up the violin. She had exclusive possession of the violin for the next 20 years, using it in her professional career. Unfortunately, she became an alcoholic, and during one period when she was in a treatment center, she entrusted the violin to her mother for safekeeping. At about that time, her father died. When Ann was released from the center, she requested return of the violin, but her mother refused. Who owns the violin?

7. ***ETHICS*** Jane says to Cody, "If you will agree to work as my yard man, I'll pay you $1,000 per week for a normal work week. You can start on Monday, and I'll guarantee you eight months' work." Cody is elated at his good fortune and agrees to start work on Monday. Later that day, Cody, still rejoicing, says to Beth, his girlfriend, "You know those sapphire earrings in the jewelry store that you're wild about? At the end of next week I'm going to buy them for you." On Monday, Jane realizes what a foolish thing she said and refuses to hire Cody. Cody, in turn, refuses to buy the earrings for Beth. Cody sues Jane and wins; Beth sues Cody and loses. Why the opposite outcomes? What basic ideas of fairness underlie the two results?

8. Ronald Armstead worked for First American Bank as a courier. His duties included making deliveries between the bank's branches in Washington, D.C. Armstead parked the bank's station wagon near the entrance of one branch in violation of a sign that read "No Parking Rush Hour Zone." In the rear luggage section of the station wagon were four locked bank dispatch bags containing checks and other valuable documents. Armstead had received tickets for illegal parking at this spot on five occasions. Shortly after Armstead entered the bank, a tow truck arrived and its operator prepared to tow the station wagon. Transportation Management, Inc., operated the towing service on behalf of the District of Columbia. Armstead ran out to the vehicle and told the tow truck operator that he was prepared to drive the vehicle away immediately. But the operator drove away with the station wagon in tow. One and one-half hours later, a bank employee paid for the car's release, but one dispatch bag, containing documents worth $107,000, was missing. First American sued Transportation Management and the District of Columbia. The defendants sought summary judgment, claiming they could not be liable. Were they correct?

9. **YOU BE THE JUDGE** WRITING PROBLEM Eileen Murphy often cared for her elderly neighbor, Thomas Kenney. He paid her $25 per day for her help and once gave her a bank certificate of deposit worth $25,000. Murphy alleged that shortly before his death, Kenney gave her a large block of shares in three corporations. He called his broker to instruct him to transfer the shares to Murphy's name, but the broker was unavailable. So Kenney told Murphy to write her name on the shares and keep them, which she did. Two weeks later Kenney died. When Murphy presented the shares to Kenney's broker to transfer ownership to her, the broker refused because Kenney had never signed them over to Murphy. Was Murphy entitled to the $25,000? To the shares? **Argument for Murphy:** The purpose of the law is to do what a donor intended, and it is obvious that Kenney intended Murphy to have the $25,000 and the shares. **Argument for the Estate:** Murphy is not entitled to the $25,000 because we have no way of knowing what Kenney's intentions were when he gave her the money. She is not entitled to the shares of stock because Kenney's failure to endorse them over to her meant he never delivered them.

10. **ROLE REVERSAL** Write a short-answer question focusing on one of the following: a fixture, an easement, or adverse possession.

11. **ROLE REVERSAL** Write a multiple-choice question highlighting the difference between any two of the following: a contract, an *inter vivos* gift, or a gift *causa mortis*.

INTERNET RESEARCH PROBLEM

On the Internet, search for the law of your state concerning a landlord's obligation to provide a habitable apartment. Now assume that you are living in a rental unit with serious defects. Write a letter to the landlord asking for prompt repairs. If you want help, look online for a form letter to guide you.

You can find further practice problems at www.cengagebrain.com. See the preface of this book for website access details.

CYBERLAW

Garrett always said that his computer was his best friend. He was online all the time, sending instant messages to his friends, listening to music, doing research for his courses, and, okay, maybe playing a few games now and again. Occasionally, the computer could be annoying. It would crash once in a while, trashing part of a paper before he saved it. And there was the time that a copy of an e-mail he sent Lizzie complaining about Caroline somehow ended up in Caroline's inbox. He was pretty irritated when the White Sox tickets he bought in an online auction turned out to be for a Little League team. And he was tired of all the spam advertising pornographic Web sites. But these things happen and, despite the petty annoyances, his computer was an important part of his life.

> **Garrett eagerly clicked on the Web site and discovered, to his horror, that *he* was featured—in the nude.**

Then one day, Garrett received a panicked instant message from a teammate on the college wrestling squad telling him to click on a certain Web site pronto to see someone they knew. Garrett eagerly clicked on the Web site and discovered, to his horror, that *he* was featured—in the nude. The Web site was selling DVDs showing him and other members of the wrestling team in the locker room in various states of undress. Other DVDs, from other locker and shower rooms, were for sale, too, showing football players and wrestlers from dozens of universities. The DVDs had titles like "Straight Off the Mat" and "Voyeur Time." No longer trusting technology, Garrett pulled on his running shoes and dashed over to the office of his business law professor.

Computers and the Internet—cyberspace—together comprise one of the great technological developments of modern times.[1] Inevitably, new technologies create the need for new law. In the thirteenth century, England was one of the first countries to develop passable roads. Like the Internet, these roadways greatly enhanced communication, creating social and business opportunities, but also enabled new crimes. Good roads meant that bad guys could sneak out of town without paying their bills. Parliament responded with laws to facilitate the collection of out-of-town debts. Similarly, while the Internet has opened up enormous opportunities in both our business and personal lives, it has also created the need for new laws, both to pave the way for these opportunities and to limit their dangers.

The process of lawmaking never stops. Judges sit and legislatures meet—all in an effort to create better rules and a better society. However, in an established area of law, such as contracts, the basic structure changes little. Cyberlaw is different because it is still very much in its infancy. Not only are new laws being created almost daily but whole areas of regulation are, as yet, unpaved roads. Although the process of rule making has progressed well, much debate still surrounds cyberspace law and much work remains to be done. This chapter focuses on the existing rules and also discusses the areas of regulation that are still incomplete and in debate.

Cyberlaw affects many areas of our lives. This chapter, however, deals with issues that are unique to the cyber world, such as online privacy, hacking, and spam.

Before beginning the chapter in earnest, let's return briefly to Garrett, the wrestler. What recourse does Garrett have for his Internet injuries? The nude video incident happened at Illinois State University and seven other colleges. Approximately 30 athletes filed suit against GTE and PSINet for selling the DVDs online, but the two Web hosts were found not liable under the Communications Decency Act because they had not produced the DVDs themselves—they had simply permitted the sale of someone else's content. What about Garrett's other computer injuries? Lizzie was not being a good friend, but it was perfectly legal for her to forward Garrett's e-mail to Caroline. The seller of the White Sox tickets violated both federal and state fraud statutes. The federal CAN-SPAM Act prohibits spam—unsolicited commercial e-mail—but a lawsuit is a slow and awkward tool for killing such a flourishing weed. Thus far, the available legal tools have been relatively ineffectual (as you can tell from your e-mail inbox).

PRIVACY

The Internet has vastly increased our ability to communicate quickly and widely. In the pre-Internet era, setting up a meeting required days of phone tag. Intraoffice memos were typed, photocopied, and then hand-delivered by messengers. Catalog orders were sent via regular mail, a slow, inefficient, and costly method.

As wonderful as computerized communication can be, though, it is not without its dangers. Consumers enter the most personal data—credit card numbers, bank accounts, lists

---

[1] The term "Internet" means "the international computer network of both Federal and non-Federal interoperable packet switched data networks." 47 U.S. Section 230 (f)(1). It began in the 1960s as a project to link military contractors and universities. Now, it is a giant network that connects smaller groups of linked computer networks. The World Wide Web was created in 1991 by Tim Berners-Lee as a subnetwork of the Internet. It is a decentralized collection of documents containing text, pictures, and sound. Users can move from document to document using links that form a "web" of information.

of friends, medical information, product preferences—on the Internet. Who will have access to this data? Who can see it, use it, sell it? Many people fear that the Internet is a very large window through which the government, employers, business, and criminals can find out more than they should about you and your money, habits, beliefs and health. Even e-mail has its dangers: Who has not been embarrassed by an e-mail that ended up in the wrong mailbox?

Many commentators argue that, without significant changes in the law, our privacy will be obliterated. At the moment, however, privacy on the Internet is very much like the weather—everyone talks about it, but (so far) no one has done much about it.

OF COOKIES AND CACHES

If you order a book from Amazon.com, you may notice that the next time you log on, you are greeted with the message, "Hello, [Your Name]. We have recommendations for you." Click on the link and you may find that, because you previously bought a GMAT study guide, Amazon will entice you with other guides for standardized tests. However did Amazon know? Many Web sites automatically place a cookie on the hard drive of your computer when you visit them. **A cookie is a small file that includes an identification number and may also include personal data such as your address, phone and credit card numbers, and searches you have made or advertisements you have clicked on.**[2]

Some cookies are designed to follow a user from site to site, along the entire Internet trail. Indeed, a whole industry of Internet marketing firms knows how to target Web banners to individual surfers. Thus, if you visit Web sites for hotels in Togo you might, without your knowledge, be invisibly linked to an Internet marketing company that will automatically record this site visit in a cookie on your hard drive. Then, when you visit a travel site, in less time than it takes you to say "click," the marketing company can automatically retrieve your cookie, realize you are interested in Togo, and show you banner ads for travel there. You, meanwhile, are blissfully unaware that you have a dossier in cyberspace.

Other cookies can be used to authenticate who you are, storing such information as your name, address, and credit card number. Amazon.com has patented its so-called "One-Click" system that permits a shopper to buy an item by clicking once on the button. What could be easier than that? One-click buying would not be possible without cookies. No doubt, cookies are convenient. And not just for one-click shopping. Consumers benefit from targeted advertisements—for instance, long-distance runners see ads for running shoes, not cigarettes. Industry representatives also argue that, without the revenue from cookie-based ads, many Internet sites would not be free to consumers.

But there is no such thing as a free lunch, or even a free snack. Cookies raise privacy issues. When you traipse around the Internet, cookies create a dossier that could come back to haunt you. Although much of the information gathered is anonymous (that is, the consumer is identified only by a computer identification number), this anonymous information can be linked to **personally identifiable information (PII)**, such as name and address. One company markets a databank with the names of 150 million registered voters. Anyone can buy a list of voters that is sliced and diced however they want, say, Republicans between the ages of 45 and 60 with Hispanic surnames and incomes greater than $50,000. This company can also transmit

Personally identifiable information (PII)
Data, such as name and address, that identify a user of a Web site.

---

[2] Legend has it that the term "cookie" refers to the Hansel and Gretel fairy tale. An evil stepmother forced her husband to take his two young children out into the woods and lose them. Anticipating such a plan, the children left a trail of bread crumbs to follow home. Legend does not reveal why these files are called cookies rather than crumbs.

specially tailored banner ads to voters surfing the Web.[3] If marketers can put together a databank of Hispanic Republican voters, they can also find out that you have visited a Web site for recovering alcoholics or unrecovered gamblers or Nazi sympathizers. Do you want information about every Web site you visit to be public? So far, consumers have not generally complained about Web data collection because it all happens so secretly that they are not aware of it. And besides, cookies make life easier. Who wants to have to enter a login name and password every time you return to your favorite sites?

Even without cookies, your computer creates a dossier about you. When you surf the Web, your computer stores a copy of the Web pages you visit in a cache file on your hard drive. Thus, anyone with access to your hard drive could get a good idea of your regular stopping places. Would you be concerned if your boss knew that you were visiting sites that specialized in job searches, cancer, or, for that matter, *any* non-job-related site? (For advice on how to protect your privacy, slip over to **http://www.consumerprivacyguide.org.**)

GOVERNMENT REGULATION OF ONLINE PRIVACY

Members of Congress have filed many bills to regulate online privacy. So intense, however, is the debate between industry and consumer advocates that no consensus—and little law—has emerged. There has, however, been some government regulation.

The First Amendment

How would you like to be called a cockroach, mega scumbag, and crook in front of thousands of people? Or be accused of having a fake medical degree, fat thighs, and poor feminine hygiene? What would you think if your ex-wife told 55,000 people that your insensitivity made her so sick she was throwing up every day? **The First Amendment to the Constitution protects free speech,** and that includes these postings and worse, which have appeared on Internet message boards and blogs. As upsetting as they may be, they are protected as free speech under the First Amendment as long as the poster is not committing defamation. In these cases, the courts ruled that the statements were opinion, not fact, and therefore were not defamatory.

Explaining its ruling in one of the cases, the court said:

> Users [of the Internet] are able to engage freely in informal debate and criticism, leading many to substitute gossip for accurate reporting and often to adopt a provocative, even combative tone. Hyperbole and exaggeration are common, and 'venting' is at least as common as careful and considered argumentation. Some commentators have likened cyberspace to a frontier society free from the conventions and constraints that limit discourse in the real world.
>
> It hardly need be said that this [court does not] condone [these] rude and childish posts; indeed, [the] intemperate, insulting, and often disgusting remarks understandably offended plaintiff and possibly many other readers. Nevertheless, the fact that society may find speech offensive is not a sufficient reason for suppressing it. Indeed, if it is the speaker's opinion that gives offense, that consequence is a reason for according it constitutional protection.[4]

---

[3] For example, during the 2000 Republican presidential primaries, time was running short for John McCain to obtain enough voter signatures to get his name on the Virginia ballot. For $5,000, his campaign hired a company to send Internet advertisements to registered Republican voters in Virginia. When people in this database went online, they would see a McCain banner asking them to sign his petition.

[4] *Krinsky v. Doe*, 6159 Cal. App. 4th 1154, 2008 Cal. App. LEXIS 180.

The Fourth Amendment

The Fourth Amendment to the Constitution prohibits unreasonable searches and seizures by the government. In enforcing this provision of the Constitution, the courts ask: Did the person being searched have a legitimate expectation of privacy in the place searched or the item seized? If yes, then the government must obtain a warrant from a court before conducting the search. (For more on this topic, investigate Chapter 7, on crime.) The Fourth Amendment applies to computers.

The architecture professor in the following case would have benefited from a course in business law and perhaps in computer science, too.

UNITED STATES OF AMERICA V. ANGEVINE

281 F.3d 1130, 2002 U.S. APP. LEXIS 2746
UNITED STATES COURT OF APPEALS FOR THE TENTH CIRCUIT, 2002

CASE SUMMARY

Facts: Professor Eric Angevine taught architecture at Oklahoma State University. The university provided him with a computer that was linked to the university network, and through it to the Internet. Professor Angevine used this computer to download more than 3,000 pornographic images of young boys. After viewing the images and printing some of them, he deleted the files. Tipped off by Professor Angevine's wife, police officers seized the computer without first obtaining a search warrant. They then turned the machine over to a police computer expert, who retrieved the pornographic files that the professor had deleted.

The Oklahoma State University computer policy stated that:

- The contents of all storage media owned or stored on university computing facilities are the property of the university.

- Employees cannot use university computers to access obscene material.

- The university reserves the right to view or scan any file or software stored on a computer or passing through the network, and will do so periodically to audit the use of university resources. The university cannot guarantee confidentiality of stored data.

- System administrators keep logs of file names that may indicate why a particular data file is being erased, when it was erased, and what user identification has erased it.

The trial court held that federal agents did not need a warrant to search Professor Angevine's office computer because he had no expectation of privacy. He was sentenced to 51 months in prison for "knowing possession of child pornography." The professor appealed.

Issue: *Did Professor Angevine have a reasonable expectation of privacy in his office computer?*

Decision: Professor Angevine could not have a reasonable expectation of privacy. Affirmed.

Reasoning: The university's computer-use policy reserved the right to audit Internet use by employees and to monitor individuals suspected of misusing their computers. The policy explicitly cautions computer users that information flowing through the university network is not confidential, either in transit or in storage on a computer. As a result, employees cannot have a reasonable expectation of privacy in downloaded data.

Professor Angevine made a careless effort to protect his privacy. Although the university policy revealed that network administrators actively audit transmissions, Professor Angevine downloaded child pornography. Later, he did attempt to erase the pornography, but the university computer policy also warned that system administrators kept logs recording when and by whom files were deleted. In any event, having transmitted pornographic data through a monitored university network, Professor Angevine could not create a reasonable expectation of privacy merely by deleting the files.

The FTC

Section 5 of the FTC Act prohibits unfair and deceptive acts or practices. The FTC applies this statute to online privacy policies: It does not require Web sites to have a privacy policy, but if they do have one, they must follow it. For example, Gateway Learning Corporation sold *Hooked on Phonics* products online. The privacy policy on its Web site sounded good: it promised that the company would not give PII to third parties without the customer's consent and would not change its privacy policy without first notifying customers. Wrong on both counts—the company changed its policy, gave PII to third parties, and never told its customers. Gateway admitted that it was in violation of the FTC Act and agreed to discontinue its illegal practices.

Electronic Communications Privacy Act of 1986

The Electronic Communications Privacy Act of 1986 (ECPA) is a federal statute that prohibits unauthorized interception or disclosure of wire and electronic communications or unauthorized access to stored communications. The definition of electronic communication includes e-mail and transmissions from pagers and cellular phones. Violators are subject to both criminal and civil penalties. An action does not violate the ECPA if it is unintentional or if either party consents. Also, the USA Patriot Act, passed after the September 11th attacks, has broadened the *government's* right to monitor electronic communications.

Under the ECPA:

1. **Any intended recipient of an electronic communication has the right to disclose it.** Thus, if you sound off in an e-mail to a friend about your boss, the (erstwhile) friend may legally forward that e-mail to the boss or anyone else.

2. **Internet service providers (ISPs) are generally prohibited from disclosing electronic messages to anyone other than the addressee,** unless this disclosure is necessary for the performance of their service or for the protection of their own rights or property.

3. **An employer has the right to monitor workers' electronic communications if (1) the employee consents, (2) the monitoring occurs in the ordinary course of business, or (3) the employer provides the computer system (in the case of e-mail).** Note that an employer has the right to monitor electronic communication even if it does not relate to work activities.

4. **To access electronic communications that have been stored for 180 days or less, the government must obtain a search warrant. Once the communications have been stored for more than 180 days, the government can access it by obtaining a search warrant, subpoena, or court order.**

One lesson from the ECPA: e-mail is not private and it is dangerous. The majority of employers monitor their employees' e-mail. In the event of litigation, the opposing party can access e-mail, even messages that have in theory been deleted. Many people who should have known better have been caught in the e-mail trap. Merrill Lynch stock analyst Henry Blodget praised stocks to the public even as he was referring to them in e-mails as a "piece of s***." He has been banned for life from the securities industry. Then there was Harry Stonecipher, the CEO of Boeing, who sent explicit e-mails to the employee with whom he was having an extramarital affair. When copies of the e-mails were sent to the board of directors, he was fired.

In the following case, two important principles are at stake. Which one should win?

YOU *be the* JUDGE

SCOTT v. BETH ISRAEL MEDICAL CENTER INC.
2007 N.Y. Misc. LEXIS
SUPREME COURT of NEW YORK, 2007

Facts: Beth Israel Medical Center (BI)'s e-mail policy stated: All information and documents created, received, saved, or sent on the Medical Center's computer or communications systems are the property of the Medical Center. Employees have no personal privacy right in any material created, received, saved, or sent using Medical Center communication or computer systems. The Medical Center reserves the right to access and disclose such material at any time without prior notice.

Dr. Norman Scott was head of the orthopedics department at BI. His contract with the hospital provided for $14 million in severance pay if he was fired without cause. BI did fire him, and the question was whether it was for cause or not. In preparation for a lawsuit against BI, Scott used the hospital's computer system to send e-mails to his lawyer. Each of these e-mails included the following notice:

> This message is intended only for the use of the Addressee and may contain information that is privileged and confidential. If you are not the intended recipient, you are hereby notified that any dissemination of this communication is strictly prohibited. If you have received this communication in error, please erase all copies of the message and its attachments and notify us immediately.

BI obtained copies of all of Scott's e-mails. It notified him that it had copies of the e-mails to his lawyer. No one at BI had read the e-mails yet, but they intended to do so. Communications between a client and lawyer are generally protected, but a client waives this privilege if he publicly discloses the information. When Scott requested that the e-mails be returned to him unread, BI refused. Scott filed a motion seeking the return of the documents.

You Be the Judge: Did Scott have a right to privacy in e-mails he sent to his lawyer using the BI system?

Argument for Scott: Despite BI's policy, all the e-mails Scott sent asserted that they were confidential. That should be enough to protect them. The attorney-client privilege is a foundation of our legal system. It is absolutely crucial for justice that clients be able to communicate with their lawyers in confidence. In a test between a core principle such as attorney-client privilege and a private entity's e-mail policy, the privilege must win. The hospital should not be allowed to read Scott's e-mails.

Argument for BI: Scott was aware of BI's policy and knew that e-mails were the property of the hospital. Therefore, when he sent the e-mails, he was disclosing them publicly. If the communications were that important, he should have made a greater effort to protect them. BI has the right to read them.

Children's Online Privacy Protection Act of 1998

The Children's Online Privacy Protection Act of 1998 (COPPA) prohibits Internet operators from collecting information from children under 13 without parental permission. It also requires sites to disclose how they will use any information they acquire. Enforcement is in the hands of the FTC. The Web site for Mrs. Fields cookies offered birthday coupons for free cookies to children under 13. Although the company did not share information with outsiders, it did collect PII without parental consent from 84,000 children. This information included name, home address, and birthdate. Mrs. Fields paid a penalty of $100,000 and agreed not to violate the law again.

Gramm-Leach-Bliley Privacy Act of 1999

The Gramm-Leach-Bliley Privacy Act of 1999 (GLB) requires banks and other financial institutions to disclose to consumers any non-public information they wish to reveal to third parties.[5] A financial institution cannot disclose this private information if the consumer opts out (that is, denies permission). Advice on how to opt out is available at **http://www. privacyrights.org**; search the site for "opt out."

GLB also prohibits *pretexting*, a process by which so-called *information brokers* use deception to find out private financial information. Thus, an FTC investigator contacted a Web site that was offering to sell private financial information. She offered to pay for information about her "fiancé's" bank balances. Someone working for the Web site successfully obtained this information by calling the bank and pretending to be the fiancé. The Web site settled with the FTC and agreed not to violate the GLB in future.

State Regulation

A few states have passed their own online privacy statutes. For instance, the California Online Privacy Act of 2003 requires any Web site that collects PII from California residents to post a privacy policy conspicuously and then abide by its terms.

The European Directive

The European Union (EU) has established strict privacy rules for the collection of personal data. This directive could have far-reaching impact outside of Europe because it prohibits the transfer of personal data to any countries that do not provide adequate privacy protection. Canada, South America, Australia, New Zealand, and parts of Asia have passed legislation to comply with the directive. Because the United States has not done so, the Department of Commerce reached agreement with the EU on so-called *safe harbor principles*. Any company that complies with the safe harbor rules will be permitted to receive data from European companies.

To be in compliance with the safe harbor principles, a company must:

1. Tell consumers how it intends to use their data and how they can limit its use.

2. Provide consumers with the opportunity to prevent disclosure of their personal data (in other words, to opt out). If the data are particularly sensitive (involving, for example, health or sex), then the data cannot be used unless the consumer opts in.

3. Provide adequate security for the data.

4. Provide customers with reasonable access to their data.

5. Establish a procedure for resolving disputes with customers.

Most American companies have not complied with the safe harbor principles because:

- The rules are cumbersome and require major changes in how companies manage customer data.

- European countries are not aggressively enforcing the rules, even against their own companies.

- If a U.S. company announces that it will comply with the safe harbor principles and then does not, the FTC has the authority to sanction the company. Therefore, companies may be better off complying with a weak policy rather than violating a strict one.

---

[5] 15 U.S.C. Section 6801.

Spyware

Is your computer running sluggishly? Does it crash frequently? Has the home page on your Web browser suddenly changed without your consent? Is there a program in your systems tray that you do not recognize? You might have **spyware** on your computer. Spyware is a computer program that slips onto your computer without your permission—through e-mails, Internet downloads, or software installations. These programs monitor your activities, log your keystrokes and can report e-mail addresses, passwords and credit card numbers to outsiders.

Congress has considered legislation to control spyware, but has not taken final action. California has enacted the Consumer Protection Against Computer Spyware Act, which makes spyware illegal.

Spyware
A computer program that enters a user's computer without permission and monitors and reports the user's activities.

SPAM

Spam is officially known as unsolicited commercial e-mail (UCE) or unsolicited bulk e-mail (UBE). Whatever it is called, it can be annoying as millions of these messages clog ISP computers and consumer mailboxes. As much as 80 percent of all e-mail is spam. It is estimated that roughly half of all spam is fraudulent—either in content (promoting a scam) or in packaging (the headers or return address are false). At a minimum, bulk e-mail adds to the cost of connecting to the Internet. ISPs must, for example, increase server capacity to handle the millions of spam e-mails. Moreover, both consumers and ISPs must endure the cost of outages caused by an overload of bulk e-mail. ISPs also argue that their reputations as service providers are harmed when consumers blame them for unsolicited advertisements. ISPs typically use filters to block this unwanted mail, but these programs are not foolproof and much spam sneaks through. The average worker spends ten business days a year dealing with spam. This lost productivity costs business $50 billion worldwide.

> As much as 80 percent of all e-mail is spam.

The Controlling the Assault of Non-Solicited Pornography and Marketing Act (CAN-SPAM) is a federal statute regulating spam. This statute applies to virtually all promotional e-mails, whether or not the sender has a pre-existing relationship with the recipient. E-mails covered by CAN-SPAM must:

- Provide an opt-out system that permits the recipient to unsubscribe

- Clearly indicate that the e-mail is an advertisement

- Provide a valid physical return address (not a post office box)

- Clearly indicate the nature of pornographic messages

A company can avoid these requirements by obtaining advance permission from the recipients.

Although one can only applaud the effort, the CAN-SPAM Act has not in truth noticeably decreased the amount of spam. Spammers operate in the netherworld of cyberspace where they are difficult to identify and locate. It may be, too, that the opt-out provision is having a perverse effect—instead of inspiring a spammer to remove e-mail addresses from his list, an opt-out request simply confirms to him that a live person is receiving his e-mails. But the statute does provide a new tool for fighting spam and ISPs have filed hundreds of lawsuits against spammers.

The following case addresses an important spam issue: Which of the many players should be liable?

YOU *be the* JUDGE

UNITED STATES OF AMERICA v. CYBERHEAT, INC.

2007 U.S. Dist. LEXIS 15448 United States District Court for the District of Arizona, 2007

Facts: Cyberheat, Inc., ran sexually explicit Web sites for consenting adults. It hired other companies (which it called "affiliates") to drive potential subscribers to its sites. The affiliates were paid a fee for each subscriber they generated. The contract that Cyberheat signed with its affiliates explicitly prohibited them from violating the CAN-SPAM Act. It also discouraged e-mail promotions. But Cyberheat did not investigate affiliates before signing a contract with them, nor did it actively monitor them to determine if they were complying with the contract. Cyberheat provided affiliates with hyperlinks to use in e-mails, so that when clicked, these links went directly to the sexually explicit Web sites being advertised.

The FTC alleged that ten of these affiliates violated the CAN-SPAM Act by sending 642 unwelcome, sexually explicit spam e-mails for which they were paid $209,120 in commissions. In some cases, the pornographic spam had fake subject lines, which meant that unsuspecting recipients—from an eight-year-old studying for a history test to an 80-year-old great-aunt trying to send a greeting card—opened e-mails with seemingly benign subject lines that, in fact, contained pornographic images.

Cyberheat received about 400 complaints from computer users, which it ignored or handled belatedly—oftentimes the affiliate in question was allowed to continue for more than a year, and in other cases the affiliate was never terminated.

The Justice Department, on behalf of the FTC, filed suit against Cyberheat, seeking civil penalties of up to $11,000 for each violation and an injunction to prohibit further violations of the Act. Both the FTC and Cyberheat filed motions for summary judgment.

You Be the Judge: Did Cyberheat violate the CAN-SPAM Act?

Argument for the FTC: Spam has become one of the most pervasive intrusions in the lives of Americans. Much of it is pornographic. The purpose of the Act is to protect those who do not want to view sexually explicit material.

Anyone who supplies this pornographic material should be held to a high standard—they must be responsible for ensuring that it is not sent to innocent and unwilling recipients. Cyberheat certainly could have foreseen that when it supplied pornographic materials to its affiliates, violations of the Act would result. It might not be fair to hold Cyberheat responsible for an accidental or mistaken violation, immediately attended to and corrected. But that is not what happened here—Cyberheat kept paying any number of violators. It cannot insulate itself from liability for the actions of the affiliates on its ultimate behalf and for its financial benefit purely by putting on blinders. It has a duty that it can only delegate at its own peril.

Cyberheat profited from violations of the Act, and now it must pay.

Argument for Cyberheat: Let's be clear about two important points: Cyberheat did not send any of these sexually explicit e-mails. Nor did it pay anyone to send e-mails. It simply paid affiliates who attracted new subscribers to its Web sites. The company did not expressly, implicitly, or otherwise authorize any violations of the Act. There is no evidence either that Cyberheat intended to violate the Act or that it intended that the affiliates violate it. The affiliates were independent companies, and Cyberheat had no control over what they did. In fact, Cyberheat insisted that the affiliates *not* violate the Act and discouraged them from using e-mail. It is not right to hold Cyberheat liable for something it had explicitly forbidden.

EXAM *Strategy*

Question: Cruise.com operated a Web site selling cruise vacations. It sent unsolicited e-mail advertisements—dubbed "E-deals"—to prospective customers. Eleven of these "E-deals" went to inbox@webguy.net. Each message offered the recipient an opportunity to be removed from the mailing list by clicking on a line of text or by writing to a specific postal address. Has Cruise.com violated the CAN-SPAM Act?

Strategy: Remember that this Act does not prohibit all unsolicited e-mails.

Result: Cruise.com was not in violation because it offered the recipients a way to unsubscribe. Also, it provided a valid physical return address.

INTERNET SERVICE PROVIDERS AND WEB HOSTS: COMMUNICATIONS DECENCY ACT OF 1996

ISPs are companies, such as Earthlink, that provide connection to the Internet. Web hosts post Web pages on the Internet. Both play important roles in cyberspace. As the legal structure that supports the Internet develops, so have legal issues involving these players.

The Internet is an enormously powerful tool for disseminating information. But what if some of this information happens to be false or in violation of our privacy rights? Is an ISP liable for transmitting it to the world? In 1995, a trial judge in New York held that an ISP, Prodigy Services Company, was potentially liable for defamatory statements that an unidentified person posted on one of its bulletin boards.[6] The message alleged that the president of an investment bank had committed "criminal and fraudulent acts." It was not only a false statement, it was posted on the most widely read financial computer bulletin board in the country. Although one can only feel sympathy for the target of this slur, the decision nonetheless alarmed many observers who argued that there was no way ISPs could review every piece of information that hurtles through their portals. The next year, Congress overruled the Prodigy case by passing the Communications Decency Act of 1996 (CDA).[7] **Under the CDA, ISPs and Web hosts are not liable for information that is provided by someone else. Only content providers are liable.** The following case lays out the arguments in favor of the CDA, but also illustrates some of the costs of the statute (and of the Internet).

[6] *Stratton Oakmont, Inc. v. Prodigy Services Company*, 1995 N.Y. Misc. LEXIS 229.
[7] 47 U.S.C. 230.

CARAFANO V. METROSPLASH.COM, INC.[8]

339 F.3d 1119, 2003 U.S. APP. LEXIS 16548
UNITED STATES COURT OF APPEALS FOR THE NINTH CIRCUIT, 2003

CASE SUMMARY

Facts: Matchmaker.com is an Internet dating service that permits members to post profiles of themselves and to view the profiles of other members. Matchmaker reviews photos for impropriety before posting them but does not examine the profiles.

Christianne Carafano is an actor who uses the stage name Chase Masterson. She has appeared in numerous films and television shows, such as *Star Trek: Deep Space Nine* and *General Hospital.* Without her knowledge, someone in Berlin posted a profile of her in the Los Angeles section of Matchmaker. In answer to the question "Main source of current events?" the person posting the profile put "*Playboy Playgirl*" and for "Why did you call?" responded "Looking for a one-night stand." In addition, the essays indicated that she was looking for a "hard and dominant" man with "a strong sexual appetite" and that she "liked sort of being controlled by a man, in and out of bed." Pictures of the actor taken off the Internet were included with the profile. The profile also provided her home address and an e-mail address, which, when contacted, produced an automatic e-mail reply stating, "You think you are the right one? Proof it!!" [sic], and providing Carafano's home address and telephone number.

Unaware of the improper posting, Carafano began receiving sexually explicit messages on her home voice mail as well as a sexually explicit fax that threatened her and her son. She received numerous phone calls, letters, and e-mail from male fans, expressing concern that she had given out her address and phone number (but simultaneously indicating an interest in meeting her). Feeling unsafe, Carafano and her son moved out of their home for several months.

One Saturday a week or two after the profile was first posted, Carafano's assistant, Siouxzan Perry, learned of the false profile through a message from "Jeff." Acting on Carafano's instructions, Perry contacted Matchmaker, demanding that the profile be removed immediately. The Matchmaker employee did not remove it then because Perry herself had not posted it, but on Monday morning the company blocked the profile from public view and then deleted it the following day.

Carafano filed suit against Matchmaker alleging invasion of privacy, misappropriation of the right of publicity, defamation, and negligence. The district court rejected Matchmaker's argument for immunity under the CDA on the grounds that the company provided part of the profile content.

Issue: *Does the CDA protect Matchmaker from liability?*

Decision: Matchmaker is not liable.

Reasoning: Under the CDA, Internet publishers are not liable for false or defamatory material if someone else provided the information. In this way, Internet publishers are different from print, television, and radio publishers.

Interactive computer services have millions of users. It would be impossible for these services to screen each of their millions of postings. If they were liable for content, they might choose to severely limit the number and type of messages. To avoid any restriction on free speech, Congress chose to protect computer services from liability if someone else provided the content.

The fact that some of the content in Carafano's fake profile was provided in response to Matchmaker's questionnaire does not make the company liable. The answers to the questions were provided exclusively by the user. No profile has any content until a user actively creates it. In this case, Carafano's home address and the e-mail address that revealed her phone number were transmitted unaltered to profile viewers. Thus, Matchmaker did not play a significant role in creating, developing, or transforming the relevant information.

Despite the serious and utterly deplorable consequences in this case, Matchmaker cannot be held liable under the CDA.

---

[8] Matchmaker.com, Inc. changed its legal name to Metrosplash.com, Inc. but continued to do business as Matchmaker.com.

EXAM *Strategy*

Question: Craigslist, Inc., runs a Web site for classified ads, including ads for the sale and rental of houses and apartments. Some of the posted ads were discriminatory (although not consistent), containing text such as: "Neighborhood is predominantly Caucasian, Polish and Hispanic," "NO MINORITIES," "Non-Women of Color NEED NOT APPLY." Was Craigslist liable for these ads?

Strategy: Remember that only content providers are liable.

Result: Craigslist was not liable because it was only a conduit for information, not a provider itself.

CRIME ON THE INTERNET

Despite its great benefits, the Internet has also opened new frontiers in crime for the dishonest and unscrupulous.

HACKING

Gaining unauthorized access to a computer system is called *hacking*. The Pentagon reports that hackers make more than 250,000 attempts annually on its computers. The goal of hackers is varied; some do it for little more than the thrill of the challenge. The objective for other hackers may be industrial espionage, extortion, or theft of credit card information. Whatever the motive, hacking is a major crime. The Federal Bureau of Investigation ranks cybercrime as its third highest priority, right behind terrorism and spying.

Hacking is a crime under the federal Computer Fraud and Abuse Act of 1986 (CFAA).[9] This statute applies to any computer attached to the Internet.

The CFAA prohibits:

- Computer espionage
- Theft of financial information
- Theft of information from the U.S. government
- Theft from a computer
- Computer trespass
- Computer fraud
- Intentional, reckless, and negligent damage to a computer
- Trafficking in computer passwords
- Computer extortion

There are two problems with the CFAA. First, while the statute prohibits the use of a virus to harm a computer, it does not ban the creation of viruses that someone else could use for hacking. Thus, it is legal for Web sites to sell source code for viruses—codes that even beginners can use destructively.

---

[9] 18 U.S.C. Section 1030.

Second, the CFAA applies only to U.S. criminals. Because the Internet is truly international, cybercriminals do not always fall within the jurisdiction of American laws. For example, a computer virus called ILOVEYOU caused an estimated $7 billion worth of damage worldwide. Although the perpetrator would have been subject to prosecution under the CFAA in the United States, he lived in the Philippines, which did not have laws prohibiting cybercrime. Nor could the suspect be extradited automatically to the United States because the extradition treaty only applied if both nations had the same law. The Philippines ultimately dropped all charges against the suspect.

FRAUD

Fraud is a growth business on the Internet. The Internet's anonymity and speed facilitate fraud, and computers help criminals identify and contact victims. Common scams include the sale of merchandise that is either defective or nonexistent, the so-called Nigerian letter scam,[10] billing for services that are touted as "free," fake scholarship search services, business opportunity scams (for a small investment, you will get rich), romance fraud (you meet someone online who wants to visit you but needs money for travel expenses), and credit card scams (for a fee, you can get a credit card, even with a poor credit rating). One of the new scams involves *over* payment. You are renting out a house, selling a pet, or accepting a job, and "by accident," you are sent too much money. You wire the excess back, only to find out that the initial check or funds transfer was no good. To protect yourself from Internet fraud, steal over to **http://www.lookstoogood-tobetrue.com.**

Fraud is the deception of another person for the purpose of obtaining money or property from him. It can be prosecuted under state law or the Computer Fraud and Abuse Act. In addition, federal mail and wire fraud statutes prohibit the use of mail or wire communication in furtherance of a fraudulent scheme.[11] The FTC can bring civil cases under Section 5 of the FTC act. (Chapter 7, on crime, discusses fraud.)

Auctions

Internet auctions are the number one source of consumer complaints about online fraud. Wrongdoers either sell goods they do not own, provide defective goods, or offer fakes. Fewer than 1 percent of online auctions involve fraud, but with upwards of $9 billion worth of goods being auctioned on the Internet each year, even 1 percent begins to add up. In a recent case—which will not reduce the amount of auction fraud—a court held that eBay, the Internet auction site, was not liable to Tiffany & Company for the counterfeit Tiffany products sold on the site. The jewelry company had sued after discovering that most items advertised on eBay as Tiffany products were, in fact, fakes. The court held that eBay's only legal obligation was to remove products once told that they were counterfeit.[12]

Shilling is an increasingly popular online auction fraud. **Shilling means that a seller either bids on his own goods or agrees to cross-bid with a group of other sellers.** Shilling is prohibited because the owner drives up the price of his own item by bidding on it. Thus, for example, Kenneth Walton, a San Francisco lawyer, put up for auction on eBay an abstract painting

---

[10] Victims receive an e-mail from someone alleging to be a Nigerian government official who has stolen money from the government. He needs some place safe to park the money for a short time. The official promises that, if the victim will permit her account to be used for this purpose, she will be allowed to keep a percentage of the stolen money. Instead, of course, once the "official" has the victim's bank information, he cleans out the account.

[11] U.S.C. Sections 1341–1346.

[12] *Tiffany Inc. v. eBay, Inc.*, 2008 U.S. Dist. LEXIS 53359.

purportedly by famous artist Richard Diebenkorn. A bidder offered $135,805 before eBay withdrew the item in response to charges that Walton had placed a bid on the painting himself and had also engaged in cross-bidding with a group of other eBay users. Although Walton claimed that he had placed the bids for friends, he ultimately pleaded guilty to charges of federal wire and mail fraud. He was sentenced to almost four years in prison and paid almost $100,000 in restitution to those who overpaid for the items he bid on.

To date, eBay has generally responded to shillers by suspending them. Shillers are also subject to suit under general anti-fraud statutes. In addition, some states explicitly prohibit shilling.[13]

Identity Theft

Identity theft is one of the scariest crimes against property. Thieves steal the victim's social security number and other personal information such as bank account numbers and mother's maiden name, which they use to obtain loans and credit cards. The money owed is never repaid, leaving victims to prove that they were not responsible for the debts. The thieves may even commit (additional) crimes under their new identities. Meanwhile, the victim may find himself unable to obtain a credit card, loan, or job. One victim spent several nights in jail after he was arrested for a crime that his alter ego had committed.

Although identity fraud existed before computers, the Internet has made it much easier. For example, consumer activists were able to purchase the social security numbers of the director of the CIA, the Attorney General of the United States, and other top administration officials. The cost? $26 each. No surprise then that 8 million Americans are victims of this crime each year.

Responding to these concerns, Congress passed the Identity Theft and Assumption Deterrence Act of 1998.[14] **This statute prohibits the use of false identification to commit fraud or other crime and it also permits the victim to seek restitution in court.** In addition, the owner of a credit card must generally pay only the first $50 that is stolen. Nonetheless, the time and effort required to undo the damage can be substantial.

A number of states have also passed identity theft statutes. California, for example, prohibits the use of Social Security numbers on ID cards or on bank statements or other documents sent by mail. California is the only state with a law requiring companies to notify consumers when their personal information has been stolen. Congress is considering similar legislation.

What can you do to prevent the theft of your identity?

1. Check your credit reports at least once a year. (Consumers are entitled by law to one free credit report every year from each of the three major reporting agencies. You can order these reports at **https://www.annualcreditreport.com.**)

2. Place a freeze on your credit report so that anyone who is about to issue a loan or credit card will double-check with you first.

3. If you suspect that your identity has been stolen, contact the FTC at 877-IDTHEFT, 877-438-4338, or google "ftc identity theft" to get to the FTC's identity theft site. Also, file a police report immediately and keep a copy to show creditors. Notify the three credit agencies.

---

[13] For example, New Mexico law provides that "It shall be unlawful to employ shills or puffers at any such auction sale or to offer or to make or to procure to be offered or made any false bid or offer any false bid to buy or pretend to buy any article sold or offered for sale." N.M. Stat. Section 61-16-14.

[14] 18 U.S. Section 1028.

Phishing

Have you ever received an e-mail like this:

> We regret to inform you that your eBay account could be suspended if you don't re-update your account information. To resolve this problems [sic] please use the link below and re-enter your account information. If your problems could not be resolved your account will be suspended for a period of 24 hours, after this period your account will be terminated.

This e-mail is not from eBay, but rather from a fraudster hoping to lure the recipient into revealing her eBay account information, including credit card numbers and passwords. It is part of one of the most rapidly growing areas of Internet fraud: **phishing. In this crime, a fraudster sends an e-mail directing the recipient to enter personal information on a Web site that is an illegal imitation of a legitimate site**. Prosecutors can bring criminal charges against phishers for fraud. The targeted companies have sued these criminals for fraud, trademark infringement, false advertising and cybersquatting (discussed in Chapter 34, on intellectual property).

No reputable company will ask customers to respond to an e-mail with personal information. When in doubt, close down the suspicious e-mail, re-launch your Web browser, and then go to the company's main Web site. If the legitimate company needs information from you, it will so indicate on the site.

EXAM *Strategy*

Question: TruePrint sent e-mails to thousands of consumers, advertising its business card service. The subject line said, "FREE GIFT!" Consumers who opened the e-mail, were then asked to click on a link, which led to a Web page that asked for personal information. After filling in the information and clicking a "continue" button, they landed on a second Web page. In the fine print at the bottom of this page was the following statement, "Printing is free. Pay only for shipping and processing. Please see our Free Offer Details for more information." Finally, at the end of the process on the next Web page, consumers learned that shipping the free gift would cost $5.67, payable by credit card or check. The e-mail did not make any reference to TruePrint. Has TruePrint violated the law?

Strategy: Indeed, TruePrint has violated two laws.

Result: First, it has advertised a "free gift" when, in fact, the gift costs $5.67. That is fraud. Second, it has violated the CAN-SPAM act because the subject line of the e-mail is untrue – the gift is not free. It has further violated CAN-SPAM by its failure to provide TruePrint's valid physical return address.

CHAPTER CONCLUSION

The Internet has changed our lives in ways that were inconceivable a generation ago, and the law is rushing to catch up. Old laws will be applied in new ways, other laws will need to change completely and, as legislators and courts learn from experience, new laws will be enacted.

Inevitably, the law of cyberspace will become increasingly international. What does Europe accomplish by regulating Internet privacy if its citizens spend a good portion of their time on American Web sites? What will the FTC do if scam artists, or spammers, operate offshore?

Effective regulation of cyberspace will require cooperation among nations and between government and industry.

EXAM REVIEW

1. **THE FIRST AMENDMENT** The First Amendment to the Constitution protects speech on the Internet as long as the speech is not defamatory. (p. 844)

2. **THE FOURTH AMENDMENT** The Fourth Amendment to the Constitution prohibits unreasonable searches and seizures by the government. This provision applies to computers. (p. 845)

Question: Three travel agents used fictitious accounts to steal 61 million frequent flyer miles from American Airlines. As evidence in the criminal trial, prosecutors used electronic communications from the agents on SABRE, American's computerized travel reservations system. The agents alleged that this search was illegal. Do you agree?

Strategy: There are two laws that are relevant to this case: the ECPA and the Fourth Amendment. (See the "Result" at the end of this section.)

3. **THE FTC ACT** Section 5 of the FTC Act prohibits unfair and deceptive practices. The FTC does not require Web sites to have a privacy policy, but if they do have one, they must follow it. (p. 846)

4. **THE ECPA** The Electronic Communications Privacy Act of 1986 is a federal statute that prohibits unauthorized interception or disclosure of wire and electronic communications or unauthorized access to stored communications. However, it permits an employer to monitor workers' electronic communications if (1) the employee consents, (2) the monitoring occurs in the ordinary course of business, or (3) the employer provides the computer system (in the case of e-mail). (p. 846)

5. **COPPA** The Children's Online Privacy Protection Act of 1998 prohibits Internet operators from collecting information from children under 13 without parental permission. It also requires sites to disclose how they will use any information they acquire. (p. 847)

6. **GLB** The Gramm-Leach-Bliley Privacy Act of 1999 requires banks and other financial institutions to disclose to consumers any non-public information they wish to reveal to third parties. The financial institution cannot disclose this private information if the consumer opts out. (p. 848)

7. **SAFE HARBOR PRINCIPLES** The U.S. Department of Commerce and the European Union have established safe harbor principles for the collection of personal data. (p. 848)

8. **SPYWARE** Spyware is a computer program that slips onto your computer without your permission—through e-mails, Internet downloads, or software installations. Congress has considered legislation to control spyware, but has not taken final action. California has enacted the Consumer Protection Against Computer Spyware Act, which makes spyware illegal. (pp. 849)

9. **CAN-SPAM** Controlling the Assault of Non-Solicited Pornography and Marketing Act (CAN-SPAM) is a federal statute regulating spam. This statute applies to virtually all promotional e-mails, whether or not the sender has a pre-existing relationship with the recipient. E-mails covered by CAN-SPAM must:

   - Provide an opt-out system that permits the recipient to unsubscribe
   - Clearly indicate that the e-mail is an advertisement
   - Provide a valid physical return address (not a post office box)
   - Clearly indicate the nature of pornographic messages (p. 849)

10. **THE CDA** Under the Communications Decency Act of 1996, ISPs and Web hosts are not liable for information that is provided by someone else. (p. 851)

EXAM Strategy

Question: Ton Cremers was the director of security at Amsterdam's famous Rijksmuseum and the operator of the Museum Security Network (the Network) Web site. Robert Smith, a handyman working for Ellen Batzel in North Carolina, sent an e-mail to the Network alleging that Batzel was the granddaughter of Heinrich Himmler (one of Hitler's henchmen) and that she had art that Himmler had stolen. These allegations were completely untrue. Cremers posted Smith's e-mail on the Network's Web site and sent it to the Network's subscribers. Cremers exercised some editorial discretion in choosing which e-mails to send to subscribers, generally omitting any that were unrelated to stolen art. Is Cremers liable to Batzel for the harm that this inaccurate information caused?

Strategy: Cremers is liable only if he is a content provider. (See the "Result" at the end of this section.)

---

11. **THE CFAA** Hacking is a crime under the federal Computer Fraud and Abuse Act of 1986. The CFAA prohibits:

   - Computer espionage
   - Theft of financial information
   - Theft of information from the U.S. government
   - Theft from a computer
   - Computer trespass
   - Computer fraud
   - Intentional, reckless, and negligent damage to a computer
   - Trafficking in computer passwords
   - Computer extortion (p. 853)

EXAM Strategy

Question: To demonstrate the inadequacies of existing computer security systems, Cornell student Robert Morris created a computer virus. His plan, however, went awry, as plans sometimes do. He thought his virus would be relatively harmless, but it ran amok, crashing scores of computers at universities, military sites, and medical research sites. Has he committed a crime, or is he liable only for civil penalties? Does it matter that he did not intend to cause damage?

Strategy: Review the provisions of the CFAA. (See the "Result" at the end of this section.)

12. **FRAUD** Fraud is the deception of another person for the purpose of obtaining money or property from him. (p. 854)

13. **IDENTITY THEFT** The Identity Theft and Assumption Deterrence Act of 1998 prohibits the use of false identification to commit fraud or other crime. (p. 855)

2. **Result:** Under the ECPA, American had a right to disclose any electronic communications sent on its system (it owned SABRE). The agents did not have a reasonable expectation of privacy on the American system.

10. **Result:** The court found that he was not liable.

11. **Result:** Morris was convicted of a crime under the CFAA. He intended to trespass on a computer, so it did not matter that he had no intent to cause harm.

ADDITIONAL QUESTIONS

1. **ETHICS** Matt Drudge published a report on his Web site (**http://www.drudgereport.com**) that White House aide Sidney Blumenthal "has a spousal abuse past that has been effectively covered up.... There are court records of Blumenthal's violence against his wife." The Drudge Report is an electronic publication focusing on Hollywood and Washington gossip. AOL paid Drudge $3,000 a month to make the Drudge Report available to AOL subscribers. Drudge e-mailed his reports to AOL, which then posted them. Before posting, however, AOL had the right to edit content. Drudge ultimately retracted his allegations against Blumenthal, who sued AOL. He alleged that under the Communications Decency Act of 1996, AOL was a "content provider" because it paid Drudge and edited what he wrote. Do you agree? Putting liability aside, what moral obligation did AOL have to its members? To Blumenthal? Should AOL be liable for content it bought and provided to its members?

2. **YOU BE THE JUDGE** WRITING PROBLEM Jerome Schneider wrote several books on how to avoid taxes. These books were sold on Amazon.com. Amazon permits visitors to post comments about items for sale. Amazon's policy suggests that these

comments should be civil (e.g., no profanity or spiteful remarks). The comments about Schneider's books were not so kind. One person alleged Schneider was a felon. When Schneider complained, an Amazon representative agreed that some of the postings violated its guidelines and promised that they would be removed within one to two business days. Two days later, the posting had not been removed. Schneider filed suit. **Argument for Schneider:** Amazon has editorial discretion over the posted comments: It both establishes guidelines and then monitors the comments to ensure that they comply with the guidelines. These activities make Amazon an information content provider, not protected by the Communications Decency Act. **Argument for Amazon:** The right to edit material is not the same thing as creating the material in the first place.

3. During the course of 10 months, Joseph Melle sent more than 60 million unsolicited e-mail advertisements to AOL members. What charges could be brought against him?

4. Anthony Davis operated a computer bulletin board system that permitted users to send and receive e-mail, access the Internet, and download software. Davis's system had one attribute that distinguished it from, say, AOL. It specialized in pornography. Alerted by an anonymous tip, the Oklahoma City Police Department obtained a warrant to search his premises for "equipment, order materials, papers, membership lists and other paraphernalia pertaining to the distribution or display of pornographic material." During their raid, the officers seized computer equipment that contained 150,000 e-mails in electronic storage, some of which had not been retrieved by the recipients. Alleging that the e-mails had not been included in the warrant, Davis filed suit against the police officers for violations of the Electronic Communications Privacy Act. Does Davis have a valid claim?

5. What can you do to protect your privacy online? Draw up a concrete list of steps that you might reasonably consider. Are there some actions that you would not be willing to take, either because they are not worth the effort or because they are too sneaky?

6. Craig Hare offered computers and related equipment for sale on various Internet auction Web sites. He accepted payment but not responsibility—he never shipped the goods. Both the FTC and the U.S. attorney general in Florida (that is, the prosecutor for the federal government) brought charges against him. What charges did they bring? Why would these two separate agencies of the federal government both bring suit?

7. **ROLE REVERSAL** Write a short-answer question that deals with an issue involving crime in cyberspace.

INTERNET RESEARCH PROBLEM

1. The FTC offers advice to Web site operators about how to comply with the Children's Online Privacy Protection Act. To find the relevant part of the FTC Web site, google "ftc coppa guidelines facts for business." Choose a Web site and evaluate whether or not it complies with the statute.

2. The Web site **http://www.onguardonline.gov** provides suggestions on how you can protect yourself against Internet fraud. Have you ever violated this advice?

You can find further practice problems at www.cengagebrain.com. See the preface of this book for website access details.

Cooper is a producer at a small indie film company in Los Angeles. He puts together packages that have a script, a director, and actors. He then finds investors who pay to make the movie and distributors who purchase the right to release it in cinemas, on TV, and on DVD. (Although most people think that box office results are what count, the reality is that over half of most movies' revenue comes from DVD rentals and sales.)

Cooper is pretty excited about two packages he has put together: one stars established actor Robert De Niro, and the other features an up-and-coming director working with movie star Clive Owen. But his excitement has turned to disappointment: shockingly, he cannot find anyone willing to invest in either movie. Cooper hears the same thing from everyone: "DVD sales are way down, so we know we won't get the payback we used to. We simply can't afford to invest in as many movies."

On a flight to New York in search of investors, Cooper finds himself sitting next to a man who is watching a movie on his computer. Cooper knows this movie has not even been released to DVD yet. Clearly the man has downloaded it from an illegal Web site. Cooper slowly crushes the plastic cup in his hand. What's wrong with that guy? Doesn't he know that movies cost money to make? Doesn't he realize people like him are killing an industry?

> On a flight to New York in search of investors, Cooper finds himself sitting next to a man who is watching a movie on his computer.... Clearly the man has downloaded it from an illegal Web site.

INTRODUCTION

For much of history, land was the most valuable form of property. It was the primary source of wealth and social status. Today, intellectual property is a major source of wealth. New ideas—for manufacturing processes, computer programs, medicines, books—bring both affluence and influence.

ECONOMICS AND THE LAW   Although both can be valuable assets, land and intellectual property are fundamentally different. The value of land lies in the owner's right to exclude, to prevent others from entering it. Intellectual property, however, has little economic value unless others use it. This ability to share intellectual property is both good news and bad. On the one hand, the owner can produce and sell unlimited copies of, say, a software program, but on the other hand, the owner has no easy way to determine if someone is using the program for free. The high cost of developing intellectual property, combined with the low cost of reproducing it, makes it particularly vulnerable to theft. And because intellectual property is nonexclusive, many people see no problem with using it for free. But when consumers take intellectual property—movies, songs, and books—without paying for it, they ensure that fewer of these items will be produced.

Some commentators suggest that the United States has been a technological leader partly because its laws have always provided strong protection for intellectual property. The Constitution provided for patent protection early in the country's history. In contrast, one of the oldest civilizations in the world, China, has been relatively slow in developing new technology. It did not institute a patent system until 1985. ◆

The conflict between those who have intellectual property and those who want to use it has taken on a global dimension. Developing countries argue that American intellectual property laws increase the price of medicines, such as AIDS drugs and vaccines, that could save lives if only they were cheaper and, therefore, more readily available. "Patents kill" is their slogan. The United States responds that, without patent protection, there would be no innovation, no miracle drugs.

But even U.S. drug companies admit that patents can sometimes stifle innovation. The pharmaceutical company Bristol-Meyers Squibb says that it cannot conduct research on many cancer-fighting drugs because of patents held by its competitors. Information technology firms make a similar complaint. In a study of the American semiconductor business, researchers found that more patents did not necessarily mean there was more innovation. Instead, some companies were simply more aggressive about patenting every possible aspect of their research. Nor was there any evidence that innovation increased as patent rights were enhanced.

The role of intellectual property law is to balance the rights of those who create intellectual property and those who would enjoy it. And as this chapter reveals, such a balancing act is no easy feat.

PATENTS

Patent
A grant by the government permitting the inventor exclusive use of an invention for a specified period.

A **patent** is a grant by the government permitting the inventor exclusive use of an invention for 20 years (or 14 years in the case of design patents). During this period, no one may make, use, or sell the invention without permission. In return, the inventor publicly discloses information about the invention that anyone can use upon expiration of the patent.

TYPES OF PATENTS

There are three types of patents: utility patents, design patents, and plant patents.

Utility Patent

Whenever people use the word "patent" by itself, they are referring to a utility patent. This type of patent is available to those who invent (or significantly improve) any of the following:

Type of Invention	Example
Mechanical invention	A hydraulic jack used to lift heavy aircraft
Electrical invention	A prewired, portable wall panel for use in large, open-plan offices
Chemical invention	The chemical 2-chloroethylphosphonic acid used as a plant growth regulator
Process	A method for applying a chemical compound to an established plant such as rice in order to inhibit the growth of weeds selectively; the application can be patented separately from the actual chemical
Machine	A device that enables a helicopter pilot to control all flight functions (pitch, roll, and heave) with one hand
Composition of matter	A sludge used as an explosive at construction sites; the patent specifies the water content, the density, and the types of solids contained in the mixture

What about an electronic signal—is that patentable? In a recent case, an inventor filed a patent application for a method of encoding additional information on electronic signals emitted from digital audio files. The process was very useful, but the court ruled that it was not patentable because the signal is not a mechanical, electrical, or chemical invention, a process, a machine, or the composition of matter.[1]

A patent is not available solely for an idea, but only for its tangible application. Thus patents are not available for laws of nature, scientific principles, mathematical algorithms, or formulas such as $a^2 + b^2 = c^2$.

In recent years, so-called "business method patents" have been controversial. These patents involve data processing or mathematical calculations used in business. For instance, a patent has been issued on a type of trust that reduces taxes on stock options. Business method patents have been particularly common in e-commerce. For example, Amazon.com patented its One-Click method of instant ordering. The company then obtained an injunction to prevent barnesandnoble.com from using its Express Lane service that was similar to One-Click. The judge directed barnesandnoble.com to add another step to its ordering process.

In a recent case—*Bilski v. Kappos*—the Supreme Court ruled that business methods are *generally* patentable, even as it held that the *particular* patent in the case (a method for hedging risk in commodities trading) was too abstract to be acceptable.[2] In the same case, the Supreme Court encouraged lower courts to narrow the scope of business method patents, but did not offer guidance as to what these limits should be. For the time being, it seems that inventors will continue to apply for business method patents while waiting for a lower court to develop standards that meet the approval of the Supreme Court. This could

---

[1] *In re Nuijten*, 500 F.3d 1346; 2007 U.S. App. LEXIS 22426.
[2] 130 S.Ct. 3218; 2010 U.S. LEXIS 5521 (U.S. S.Ct. 2010).

be a lengthy wait—in the *Bilski* case, 13 years elapsed from the filing of the patent application until the Supreme Court decision.

Design Patent

A design patent protects the appearance, not the function, of an item. It is granted to anyone who invents a new, original, and ornamental design for an article. For example, Braun, Inc., patented the look of its handheld electric blenders. Design patents last only 14 years, not 20.

Plant Patent

Anyone who creates a new type of plant can patent it, *provided that* the inventor is able to reproduce it asexually—through grafting, for instance, not by planting its seeds. For example, one company patented its unique heather plant.

REQUIREMENTS FOR A PATENT

To obtain a patent, the inventor must show that her invention meets all of the following tests:

- **Novel**. An invention is not patentable if it (1) is known or has already been used in this country, or (2) has been described in a publication here or overseas. For example, an inventor discovered a new use for existing chemical compounds but was not permitted to patent it because the compounds had already been described in prior publications, though the new uses had not.[3]

- **Nonobvious**. An invention is not patentable if it is obvious to a person with ordinary skill in that particular area. An inventor was not allowed to patent a waterflush system designed to remove cow manure from the floor of a barn because it was obvious.[4]

- **Useful**. To be patented, an invention must be useful. It need not necessarily be commercially valuable, but it must have some current use. Being merely of scientific interest is not enough. Thus a company was denied a patent for a novel process for making steroids because they had no therapeutic value.[5]

EXAM *Strategy*

Question: In 1572, during the reign of Queen Elizabeth I of England, a patent application was filed for a knife with a bone handle rather than a wooden one. Would this patent be granted under current U.S. law?

Strategy: Was a bone handle novel, nonobvious, and useful?

Result: It was useful—no splinters from a bone handle. It was novel—no one had ever done it before. But the patent was denied because it was obvious.

---

[3] *In re Schoenwald*, 964 F.2d 1122, 1992 U.S. App. LEXIS 10181 (Fed. Cir. 1992).
[4] *Sakraida v. Ag Pro, Inc.*, 425 U.S. 273, 96 S.Ct. 1532, 1976 U.S. LEXIS 146 (1976).
[5] *Brenner v. Manson*, 383 U.S. 519, 86 S.Ct. 1033, 1966 U.S. LEXIS 2907 (1966).

PATENT APPLICATION AND ISSUANCE

To obtain a patent, the inventor must file a complex application with the Patent and Trademark Office (PTO) in Washington, D.C. If a patent examiner determines that the application meets all legal requirements, the PTO will issue the patent. Traditionally, patent examiners relied on their (often substantial) expertise, their reading of scientific papers, and database searches to evaluate patents. More complex technology and a huge increase in the number of applications have challenged the ability of any one human being to keep up with latest developments. The PTO has begun a pilot project—called Peer to Patent—it hopes will make the approval process quicker and more accurate. Taking a page from Wikipedia, the online encyclopedia, the PTO will post selected applications on the Web. Anyone may participate in the review process, but participants will rate contributions and only the most valuable will go to the patent examiner.

If an examiner denies a patent application for any reason, the inventor can appeal that decision to the PTO Board of Appeals and from there to the Court of Appeals for the Federal Circuit in Washington.[6] Alternatively, upon denial of the application, the inventor can file suit against the PTO in the federal district court in Washington.

Priority between Two Inventors

When two people invent the same product, who is entitled to a patent—the first to invent or the first to file an application? Generally, the person who invents and *puts the invention into practice* has priority over the first filer. Having the idea is not enough—the inventor must actually use the product.

Prior Sale

However, an inventor must apply for a patent within one year of selling the product commercially. The purpose of this rule is to encourage prompt disclosure of inventions. It prevents someone from inventing a product, selling it for years, and then obtaining a 20-year monopoly with a patent.

Provisional Patent Application

Inventors who are unable to assess the market value of their ideas sometimes hesitate to file a patent application because the process is expensive and cumbersome. To solve this problem, the PTO now permits inventors to file a **provisional patent application (PPA)**. The PPA is a simpler, shorter, cheaper application that gives inventors the opportunity to show their ideas to potential investors without incurring the full expense of a patent application. PPA protection lasts only one year. To maintain protection after that time, the inventor must file a regular patent application.

Duration of a Patent

Patents are valid for 20 years from the date of *filing* the application (except design patents, which are valid for 14 years from date of *issuance*). Currently, approval of a patent takes about 30 months from the date of filing, which means that patent holders effectively receive less than 18 years of protection (although in the case of exceptional delays, it is possible to request an extension).

---

[6] Recall from Chapter 3 that the Court of Appeals for the Federal Circuit is the thirteenth United States Court of Appeals. It hears appeals from specialized trial courts.

ECONOMICS AND THE LAW How long should patents last? Holders enjoy a monopoly that protects them from competition and permits them to charge higher prices. But these monopoly profits are not all bad—they also provide inventors with the incentive to spend large sums hoping to develop new products. In theory, the duration of a patent should be individually tailored to each product. The goal is to ensure that a patent creates the right incentive for each product. Take, for example, a complex, life-saving drug that costs $400 million to develop. No drug company would undertake such a project without assurance that it could recoup its costs. But if the company can make $300 million in the first year of sale, it needs only a short patent life to recoup its costs. On the other hand, if the company could only make $25 million a year, it should have at least a 16-year patent. Likewise, if a product has little value to society, its patent should be of short duration.

Of course, the PTO would be in chaos if examiners had to decide how much protection each individual patent deserved, but Germany has gone some distance along this path. It awards a standard patent for important inventions. Less important products receive a so-called petty patent that lasts only three years. Moreover, all patent owners pay an annual maintenance fee. At the beginning, this fee is low, but it increases so much each year that only 5 percent of German patents are maintained for a full term. Most owners abandon ship in less than eight years.[7] ◆

Infringement

A patent holder has the exclusive right to use the invention during the term of the patent. A holder can prohibit others from using any product that is substantially the same, license the product to others for a fee, and recover damages from anyone who uses the product without permission.

International Patent Treaties

Suppose you have a great idea that you want to protect around the world. It used to be that filing an application in other countries was a logistical nightmare because almost every country had its own unique filing procedures and standards. Several treaties now facilitate this process, although it is still not the one-stop (or one-click) effort that inventors desire. These treaties were drafted by the World Intellectual Property Organization (WIPO) of the United Nations.

The Paris Convention for the Protection of Industrial Property (Paris Convention) requires each member country to grant to citizens of other member countries the same rights under patent law as its own citizens enjoy. Thus, the patent office in each member country must accept and recognize all patent and trademark applications filed with it by anyone who lives in any member country. For example, the French patent office cannot refuse to accept an application from an American, as long as the American has complied with French law.

The Patent Law Treaty requires that countries use the same standards for the form and content of patent applications (whether submitted on paper or electronically). This treaty reduces the procedural conflicts over issues such as translations and fees. In short, it takes an important first step in standardizing the application *process*. Still to be worked out, however, is an international standard for the *substance* of patent laws. For instance, the U.S. "first to invent" rule conflicts with the "first to file" rule used in most other countries. Also countries often have very different definitions of what constitutes "novelty" under patent law.

In addition to these treaties, any country that joins the World Trade Organization must agree to TRIPS (trade-related aspects of intellectual property rights). This agreement does

---

[7] R. Cooter and T. Ulen, *Law and Economics*, 2d ed. (Reading, Mass.: Addison-Wesley, 1997).

not create an international patent system but it does require all participants to meet minimum standards for the protection of intellectual property. How individual countries achieve that goal is left to them.

COPYRIGHTS

The holder of a copyright owns the *particular tangible expression* **of an idea, but not the underlying idea or method of operation**. Abner Doubleday could copyright a book setting out his particular version of the rules of baseball, but he could not copyright the rules themselves nor could he require players to pay him a royalty. Similarly, the inventor of double-entry bookkeeping could copyright a pamphlet explaining his system but not the system itself.

Unlike patents, the ideas underlying copyrighted material need not be novel. For example, three movies—*Like Father Like Son*, *Vice Versa*, and *Freaky Friday*—were about a parent and child who switch bodies. The movies all had the same plot, but there was no copyright violation because their *expressions* of the basic idea were different.

The Copyright Act protects literature, music, drama, choreography, pictures, sculpture, movies, recordings, architectural works, and "computer data bases, and computer programs to the extent that they incorporate authorship in the programmer's expression of original ideas, as distinguished from the ideas themselves."

Originally, copyrights lasted only 14 years, with the right to one 14-year extension. But copyright holders have aggressively fought to lengthen the copyright period. These efforts have been led by the Walt Disney Company, which wants to protect its rights in Mickey Mouse. Now, a copyright is valid until 70 years after the death of the work's only or last living author or, in the case of works owned by a corporation, the copyright lasts 95 years from publication or 120 years from creation. Once a copyright expires, anyone may use the material. Mark Twain died in 1910, so anyone may now publish *Tom Sawyer* without permission and without paying a copyright fee.

A work is automatically copyrighted once it is in tangible form. For example, once a songwriter puts notes on paper, the work is copyrighted without further ado. But if she whistles a happy tune without writing it down, the song is not copyrighted, and anyone else can use it without permission. Registration with the Copyright Office of the Library of Congress is necessary only if the holder wishes to bring suit to enforce the copyright. Although authors still routinely place the copyright symbol (©) on their works, such a precaution is not necessary in the United States. However, some lawyers still recommend using the copyright symbol because other countries recognize it. Also, the penalties for intentional copyright infringement are heavier than for unintentional violations, and the presence of a copyright notice is evidence that the infringer's actions were intentional.

INFRINGEMENT

Anyone who uses copyrighted material without permission is violating the Copyright Act. **To prove a violation, the plaintiff must present evidence that the work was original** and that either:

- The infringer actually copied the work, or

- The infringer had access to the original and the two works are substantially similar.

A court may (1) prohibit the infringer from committing further violations, (2) order destruction of the infringing material, and (3) require the infringer to pay damages, profits earned, and attorney's fees.

FIRST SALE DOCTRINE

Suppose you buy a CD that, in the end, you do not like. Under the *first sale doctrine*, you have the legal right to sell that CD. **The first sale doctrine permits a person who owns a lawfully made copy of a copyrighted work to sell or otherwise dispose of the copy.** Note, however, that the first sale doctrine does not permit the owner to *make a copy*. If you listen to a CD and then decide to sell it, that is legal. But it is not legal to copy the CD onto your iPod and then sell the original or any copy of it.

FAIR USE

Because the period of copyright protection is so long, it has become even more important to uphold the exceptions to the law. Bear in mind that the point of copyright laws is to encourage creative work. A writer who can control, and profit from, artistic work will be inclined to produce more. If enforced oppressively, however, the copyright laws could stifle creativity by denying access to copyrighted work. **The fair use doctrine** permits limited use of copyrighted material without permission of the author for purposes such as criticism, comment, news reporting, scholarship, or research. Courts generally do not permit a use that will decrease revenues from the original work by, say, competing with it. A reviewer is permitted, for example, to quote from a book without the author's permission, but could not reproduce so much that the review was competing with the book itself.

Fair use doctrine
Permits limited use of copyrighted material without permission of the author.

Fair use has become a highly controversial issue in this age of the Internet. For example, Universal Music demanded that YouTube remove a home video of a toddler dancing to a Prince song. A director making a documentary on torture was denied permission to use a short clip showing torture on the TV show *24*. Then J. K. Rowling, the author of the *Harry Potter* series of books, sued to prevent the publication of the *Harry Potter Lexicon*—an unauthorized reference guide to the books that contained direct quotations, paraphrases and plot summaries. The court ruled that although such a guide can be fair use, this one was not because the author had copied too much of Rowling's distinctive original language.

Also under the fair use doctrine, faculty members are permitted to photocopy and distribute copyrighted materials to students, so long as the materials are brief and the teacher's action is spontaneous. If, over his breakfast coffee one morning, Professor Learned spots a terrific article in *Mad Magazine* that perfectly illustrates a point he intends to make in class that day, the fair use doctrine permits him to photocopy the page and distribute it to his class. However, under a misinterpretation of the fair use doctrine, some faculty had been in the habit of routinely preparing lengthy course packets of copyrighted material without permission of the authors. In *Basic Books, Inc. v. Kinkos Graphic Corp.*[8] a federal court held that this practice violated the copyright laws because the material was more than one short passage and because it was sold to students. Now, when professors put together course packets, they (or the copy shop) must obtain permission and pay a royalty for the use of copyrighted material. Likewise, it is illegal for students to make photocopies of a classmate's course packet or textbook.

---

[8] 758 F. Supp. 1522, 1991 U.S. Dist. LEXIS 3804 (S.D.N.Y. 1991). A federal appeals court reached the same result in *Princeton University Press v. Michigan Document Services, Inc.*, 99 F.3d 1381, 1996 U.S. App. LEXIS 29132 (6th Cir. 1996).

Parody

Parody has a long history in the United States—some of our most cherished songs have been the basis of parodies. Before Francis Scott Key wrote the words to "The Star-Spangled Banner," other lyrics that mocked colonial governors had been set to the same music. (The tune was well known as a drinking song.)

Because of the political and social commentary that is inherent in many parodies, courts have long granted them special respect. In a case involving a 2 Live Crew parody of the song *Pretty Woman* the Supreme Court decided in favor of 2 Live Crew, holding that **parody is a fair use of copyrighted material so long as the use of the original is not excessive.**[9] The parody may copy enough to remind the audience of the original work, but not so much that the parody harms the market for the original.

The following e-mail exchange between Richard Saperstein, a movie producer, and Tom Strickler, a talent agent, which recently zapped around Hollywood, illustrates the importance of the 2 Live Crew case (to which Strickler refers).

> [From Saperstein to Strickler:]
> Tom—

Please give me a call about a spec script Elia Infascelli-Smith has gone out with called $40,000 MAN. As you know, along with Universal, we control the rights to SIX MILLION DOLLAR MAN. My understanding is this spec includes characters we own.

> Best—Richard

> [Strickler's response:]

> Richard:

Good news. As you may know, The United States Supreme Court has affirmed the right of Parody as an unassailable First Amendment Right. This has enabled you to make movies like *Scream* and *Scary Movie* in which you parody many films which Dimension does not own or control.

The script is a parody and if you have any problems I suggest you hire a Constitutional lawyer and file a brief with the US Supreme Court. This will be an uphill battle—the court voted 9 to 0 when this last hit the docket and those stubborn justices all believe in Stare Decisis.

And if you succeed at the Supreme Court—you will have to stop making *Scream* and *Scary Movie*.

This will take about 5 to 7 years … and lawyers are an expensive breed, but I wish you good luck on your journey to deny our First Amendment rights.

> All the best,
> Tom

> # I wish you good luck on your journey to deny our First Amendment rights.

Internet Searching

Copyright protection is as old as the country itself, having been included in the Constitution. But intellectual property has changed dramatically in the last 250 years, and legal protections suitable for the eighteenth century do not work as well today. Now Congress and the courts are playing catch-up, trying to mend and patch the laws to cover the digital world.

---

[9] *Campbell v. Acuff-Rose Music, Inc.*, 510 U.S. 569, 114 S.Ct. 1164, 1994 U.S. LEXIS 2052 (1994).

Internet searching has created a new issue of copyright law and fair use. In the following case, the court is asked to decide if the mighty Google search engine violates copyright law. You be the judge.

YOU *be the* JUDGE

PERFECT 10, INC. v. GOOGLE INC.

487 F.3d 701; 2007 U.S. App. LEXIS 11420
United States Court of Appeals for the Ninth Circuit, 2007

Facts: Perfect 10, Inc. has a Web site on which it sells copyrighted images of nude models. Subscribers pay a monthly fee to view these photos. Perfect 10 also sells smaller images for use on cell phones. Sometimes, Google's image search engine displays thumbnails of Perfect 10's photos. (Thumbnails are low-resolution images measuring roughly 2 inches × 1.5 inches.) In theory, these thumbnails could also be used on cell phones, although there was no evidence that they had been so far.

Perfect 10 filed suit alleging that Google was violating copyright law by reproducing the thumbnail images. The district court issued an injunction prohibiting Google from displaying Perfect 10's photos. Google appealed, alleging that the thumbnails were a fair use.

You Be the Judge: Do Google's thumbnail displays of Perfect 10's photos violate copyright law? Are they a fair use?

Argument for Perfect 10: When Google makes and displays copies of Perfect 10's photographs, it is in direct violation of copyright law. Perfect 10 owns the images and Google is displaying them without permission. Although the photos are small, they can be enlarged. They can also be used on cell phones in direct competition with Perfect 10's own business. The fact that these thumbnails have not yet been downloaded to cellphones does not mean that it will not happen in the future.

Google is not some charitable organization doing searches for the public good. It is a hugely profitable business. If it wants to make a profit from copyrighted works, it should pay for the privilege.

Argument for Google: The goal of the copyright law is to protect original work but also to support the development of new ideas that build on earlier ones. Courts have long acknowledged that they must avoid an application of this statute that is so rigid it would stifle the very creativity the law is designed to foster. Hence the fair use exception. These thumbnails are a fair use.

Although the images were created originally to serve an entertainment or aesthetic function, a search engine transforms them into a research tool, directing users to a source of information. As an electronic reference tool, search engines provide an enormous social benefit. They are a crucial part of the way we all live and work. If Perfect 10 prevails in this case, and search engines either cannot display copyrighted material or have to pay for it, Internet searching will be crippled. It is more important that the public have access to information on the Internet than it is to protect Perfect 10's right to its images.

As for the cell phone issue, there is no evidence that Google's thumbnails have in fact been used on cell phones.

In short, Google's search engine promotes the purposes of copyright and serves the interests of the public.

DIGITAL MUSIC AND MOVIES

As we have seen with the *Google* case, one of the major challenges for legal institutions in regulating copyrights is simply that modern intellectual property is so easy to copy. Many consumers have been in the habit of violating the law by downloading copyrighted material—both music and movies—for free. The entertainment world used to turn a blind eye, but recording companies and movie studios have come to believe that illegal downloading is hurting profitability. For the first time, CD sales actually declined nationally. One study found that the decline was particularly sharp in areas around college campuses. Perhaps even more insidious, a whole generation has grown up believing that music and even movies were, and should be, free. Although at least one study seemed to indicate that downloading does not harm CD sales, the entertainment industry remains convinced that it does.[10] Arguably, it is irrelevant whether free downloading is harmful because copyright holders have the legal right to determine how their property will be distributed.

The Recording Industry Association of America (RIAA) began aggressively suing those who downloaded music illegally. Then a coalition of entertainment businesses sued two companies that distributed the software used by many consumers to violate copyright law. So important was this issue that the Supreme Court waded into these murky waters.

METRO-GOLDWYN-MAYER STUDIOS INC. v. GROKSTER, LTD.

125 S.Ct. 2764, 2005 U.S. LEXIS 5212
SUPREME COURT OF THE UNITED STATES, 2005

CASE SUMMARY

Facts: Grokster, Ltd., and StreamCast Networks, Inc., distributed free software that allowed computer users to share electronic files through peer-to-peer networks, so called because users' computers communicated directly with each other, not through central servers. The Grokster and StreamCast software could be used for legal purposes. Indeed, peer-to-peer networks were utilized by universities, government agencies, corporations, libraries, and individuals, among others. Even the briefs in this very case could be downloaded legally with the StreamCast software.

Nonetheless, nearly 90 percent of the files available for download through Grokster or StreamCast were copyrighted. Billions of files were shared each month—the probable scope of copyright infringement was staggering. The two companies encouraged the illegal uses of their software. For example, the chief technology officer of StreamCast said that "the goal is to get in trouble with the law and get sued. It's the best way to get in the news."

A group of copyright holders (MGM and others) sued Grokster and StreamCast alleging that they were violating the copyright law by knowingly and intentionally distributing their software to users who would reproduce and distribute copyrighted works illegally. Both parties moved for summary judgment. The trial court held for Grokster and

StreamCast; the appeals court affirmed. The Supreme Court granted *certiorari.*

Issue: *Were Grokster and StreamCast violating copyright law?*

Decision: Grokster and StreamCast did violate copyright law.

Reasoning: This case presents a trade-off between protecting artistic expression and inhibiting technological innovation. It is important not to discourage the development of technologies that could have both lawful and unlawful potential. Accordingly, mere knowledge that a product *could* be used to infringe copyrights is not enough to create liability. But when users can use Grokster software to copy songs or movies easily, they develop a disdain for copyright protection. If a product is widely used to commit infringement, copyright holders may not be able to enforce their rights effectively unless they go against the distributor of the copying device. To balance these competing interests, we hold that distributors are liable only if they deliberately encourage copyright violation.

Grokster distributed an electronic newsletter containing links to articles promoting its software's ability to access popular copyrighted music. Both Grokster and StreamCast

---

[10] Felix Oberholzer-Gee and Koleman Strumpf, "The Effect of File Sharing on Record Sales," 2004, available at http://www.unc.edu/~cigar/papers/FileSharing_March2004.pdf.

helped customers locate and play copyrighted materials. Neither company attempted to develop filtering tools or other mechanisms to reduce the illegal use of their software. There is evidence of infringement on a gigantic scale.

These companies made money by selling advertisements that were sent to the screens of computers using their software. The more the software was used, the more ads they could send out and the greater their advertising revenue became. The success of the defendant's business model hinged on high-volume use, which infringed copyrights. The unlawful objective is unmistakable.

Anyone who distributes a product or software and then promotes its use for the purpose of infringing copyrights is liable for the resulting acts of infringement by third parties.

The No Electronic Theft Act

Enacted in 1997, the **No Electronic Theft Act** is intended to deter the downloading of copyrighted material. It provides for criminal penalties for the reproduction or distribution of copyrighted material that has a retail value greater than $1,000, even if the offender has no profit motive. Thus, for instance, if a student photocopied for ten of her friends a textbook that is worth $150, she could be subject to criminal penalties, including a prison term of one year. Originally, the Justice Department did not enforce this statute, but it has now begun to do so, particularly against those who set up networks to trade games, movies and music.

The Family Entertainment and Copyright Act

Under the **Family Entertainment and Copyright Act,** it is a criminal offense to use a camcorder to film a movie in the theater. This statute also establishes criminal penalties for willful copyright infringement that involves distributing software, music, or film on a computer network.

The Digital Millennium Copyright Act

The good news is that Mary Schmich wrote an influential article in the *Chicago Tribune*. The bad news is that people deleted her name, attributed the article to Kurt Vonnegut, and sent it around the world via e-mail. Tom Tomorrow's cartoon was syndicated to 100 newspapers, but, by the time the last papers received it, the cartoon had already gone zapping around cyberspace. Because his name had been deleted from the original, some editors thought he had plagiarized it.

In response to such incidents, Congress passed the **Digital Millennium Copyright Act** (DMCA), which provides that:

- **It is illegal to delete copyright information, such as the name of the author or the title of the article**. It is also illegal to distribute false copyright information. Thus, anyone who e-mailed Schmich's article without her name on it, or who claimed it was his own work, would be violating the law.

- **It is illegal to circumvent encryption or scrambling devices that protect copyrighted works**. For example, some software programs are designed so that they can only be copied once. Anyone who overrides this protective device to make another copy is violating the law. (The statute does permit purchasers of copyrighted software to make one backup copy.) If you buy a Disney DVD that prevents you from fastforwarding through commercials, you are violating the DMCA if you figure out how to do it anyway.

- **It is illegal to distribute tools and technologies used to circumvent encryption devices.** If you tell others how to fast-forward through the Disney commercials, you have violated the statute.

The DMCA has been controversial. Its goal was laudable: to protect legitimate businesses from copyright pirates. However, opponents allege that:

- The DMCA interferes with legal activities. For instance, copy-protected CDs prevent consumers from making copies for their own use. These copies are legal under the fair use doctrine.

- The DMCA interferes with legitimate scientific research. An organization called the Secure Digital Music Initiative (SDMI) developed a technology to encrypt digital music. It issued a public challenge to see if anyone could override the encryption. Edward Felten, a Princeton professor, did manage to circumvent the technology, but when he tried to present his results at an academic conference, the SDMI threatened him with suit for violating the DMCA. He ultimately was able to publish part of his research, but only after filing suit against SDMI.

INTERNATIONAL COPYRIGHT TREATIES

The Berne Convention requires member countries to provide automatic copyright protection to any works created in another member country. The protection does not expire until 50 years after the death of the author.[11] The WIPO Copyright Treaty and the WIPO Performances and Phonograms Treaty add computer programs, movies, and music to the list of copyrightable materials.

In 2004, Congress enacted a law that permits the president to appoint a copyright law enforcement officer charged with the responsibility of stopping copyright infringement overseas. Also, for the first time, Congress funded the National Intellectual Property Law Enforcement Coordination Council, which was established to protect American intellectual property internationally.

EXAM *Strategy*

Question: Timothy has sold his used textbooks and CDs to the college bookstore. Are these sales legal?

Strategy: What is the difference between a used textbook and a used CD? What additional facts would you need to know to determine if the sales are legal?

Result: Under the First Sale Doctrine, it is legal for Timothy to sell his one and only copy to the bookstore. Thus, the sale of used textbooks and CDS is legal so long as he did not first copy them. To answer the question you would need to know if he had made copies – more likely with a CD than a textbook.

---

[11] Under U.S. law, copyrights last 70 years. The United States must grant works created in other signatory countries a copyright that lasts either 50 years or the length of time granted in that country, whichever is longer, but in no case longer than 70 years.

TRADEMARKS

Trademark
Any combination of words and symbols that a business uses to identify its products or services and distinguish them from others.

A **trademark** is any combination of words and symbols that a business uses to identify its products or services and distinguish them from others. Trademarks are important to both consumers and businesses. Consumers use trademarks to distinguish between competing products. People who feel that Nike shoes fit their feet best can rely on the Nike trademark to know they are buying the shoe they want. A business with a high-quality product can use a trademark to develop a loyal base of customers who are able to distinguish its product from another.

TYPES OF MARKS

There are four different types of marks:

- **Trademarks** are affixed to *goods* in interstate commerce.

- **Service marks** are used to identify services, not products. Fitness First, Burger King, and Weight Watchers are service marks. In this chapter, the terms "trademark" and "mark" are used to refer to both trademarks and service marks.

- **Certification marks** are words or symbols used by a person or organization to attest that products and services produced by others meet certain standards. The Good House-keeping Seal of Approval means that the Good Housekeeping organization has determined that a product meets its standards.

- **Collective marks** are used to identify members of an organization. The Lions Club, the Girls Scouts of America, and the Masons are examples of collective marks.

OWNERSHIP AND REGISTRATION

Under common law, the first person to use a mark in trade owns it. Registration with the federal government is not necessary. However, under the federal Lanham Act, the owner of a mark may register it on the Lanham Act Principal Register. A trademark owner may use the symbol ™ at any time, even before registering it, but not until the mark is registered can the symbol ® be placed next to it. Registration has several advantages:

- Even if a mark has been used in only one or two states, registration makes it valid nationally.

- Registration notifies the public that a mark is in use because anyone who applies for registration first searches the Public Register to ensure that no one else has rights to the mark.

- Five years after registration, a mark becomes virtually incontestable because most challenges are barred.

- The damages available under the Lanham Act are higher than under common law.

- The holder of a registered trademark generally has the right to use it as an Internet domain name.

Under the Lanham Act, the owner files an application with the PTO. The PTO will accept an application only if the owner has already used the mark attached to a product in interstate commerce or promises to use the mark within six months after the filing. In addition, the applicant must be the *first* to use the mark in interstate commerce. Initially, the trademark is valid for 10 years, but the owner can renew it for an unlimited number of 10-year terms as long as the mark is still in use.

VALID TRADEMARKS

Words (Reebok), symbols (Microsoft's flying window logo), phrases (Nike's "Just do it"), shapes (Apple's iPod), sounds (NBC's three chimes), colors (Owens Corning's pink insulation), and even scents (plumeria blossoms on sewing thread) can be trademarked. **To be valid, a trademark must be distinctive**—that is, the mark must clearly distinguish one product from another. There are five basic categories of distinctive marks:

- **Fanciful marks** are made-up words such as Converse or Saucony.

- **Arbitrary marks** use existing words that do *not* describe the product—Prince tennis racquets, for example. No one really thinks that these racquets are designed by or for royalty.

- **Suggestive marks** *indirectly* describe the product's function. Greyhound implies that the bus line is swift, and Coppertone suggests what customers will look like after applying the product.

- Marks with **secondary meaning** cannot, by themselves, be trademarked, unless they have been used so long that they are now associated with the product in the public's mind. When a film company released a movie called *Ape*, it used as an illustration a picture that looked like a scene from *King Kong*—a gigantic gorilla astride the World Trade Center in New York City. The court held that the movie posters of *King Kong* had acquired a secondary meaning in the mind of the public, so the *Ape* producers were forced to change their poster.[12]

- **Trade dress** is the image and overall appearance of a business or product. It may include size, shape, color, or texture. The Supreme Court held that a Mexican restaurant was entitled to protection under the Lanham Act for the shape and general appearance of the exterior of its building as well as the decor, menu, servers' uniforms, and other features reflecting the total image of the restaurant.[13]

The following categories are not distinctive and *cannot* be trademarked:

- **Similar to an Existing Mark**. To avoid confusion, the PTO will not grant a trademark that is similar to one already in existence on a similar product. Once the PTO had granted a trademark for "Pledge" furniture polish, it refused to trademark "Promise" for the same product. "Chat noir" and "black cat" were also too similar because one is simply a translation of the other. Houghton-Mifflin Co. sued to prevent a punk rock band from calling itself Furious George because the name is too similar to Curious George, the star of a series of children's books.

- **Generic Trademarks**. No one is permitted to trademark an item's ordinary name—"shoe" or "book," for example. Sometimes, however, a word begins as a trademark and later

---

[12] *Paramount Pictures Corp. v. Worldwide Entertainment Corp.*, 2 Media L. Rep. 1311, 195 U.S.P.Q. (BNA) 539, 1977 U.S. Dist. LEXIS 17931 (S.D.N.Y. 1977).

[13] *Two Pesos, Inc. v. Taco Cabana, Inc.*, 505 U.S. 763, 112 S.Ct. 2753, 1992 U.S. LEXIS 4533 (1992).

becomes a generic name. Zipper, escalator, aspirin, linoleum, thermos, yo-yo, band-aid, ping-pong, and nylon all started out as trademarks but became generic. Once a name is generic, the owner loses the trademark because the name can no longer be used to distinguish one product from another—all products are called the same thing. That is why, in advertisements for Sanka, people ask for "a cup of Sanka-brand decaffeinated coffee." And why Xerox Corp. encourages people to say, "I'll photocopy this document," rather than "I'll xerox it." Jeep, Rollerblade, and TiVo are trademarks that seem destined for generic status.

- **Descriptive Marks**. Words cannot be trademarked if they simply describe the product— such as "low-fat," "green," or "crunchy." Descriptive words can, however, be trademarked if they do *not* describe that particular product because they then become distinctive rather than descriptive. "Blue Diamond" is an acceptable trademark for nuts as long as the nuts are neither blue nor diamond shaped.

- **Names.** The PTO generally will not grant a trademark in a surname because other people are already using it and have the right to continue. No one could register "Jefferson" as a trademark. However, a surname can be used as part of a longer title—"Jefferson Home Tours," for instance. Similarly, no one can register a geographical name such as "Boston" unless it is also associated with another word, such as "Boston Ale."

- **Deceptive Marks**. The PTO will not register a mark that is deceptive. It refused to register a trademark with the words "National Collection and Credit Control" and an eagle superimposed on a map of the United States because this trademark gave the false impression that the organization was an official government agency.

- **Scandalous or Immoral Trademarks**. The PTO refused to register a mark that featured a nude man and woman embracing. In upholding the PTO's decision, the court was unsympathetic to arguments that this was the perfect trademark for a newsletter on sex.[14]

INFRINGEMENT

To win an infringement suit, the trademark owner must show that the defendant's trademark is likely to deceive customers about who has made the goods or provided the services. The rightful owner is entitled to (1) an injunction prohibiting further violations, (2) destruction of the infringing material, (3) up to three times actual damages, (4) any profits the infringer earned on the product, and (5) attorney's fees.

What about a perfume for dogs? Would a reasonable consumer confuse Pucci with Gucci, Bono Sports with Ralph Lauren Polo Sports, or Miss Claybone for Liz Claiborne? None of these companies challenged the parody use of their names for a dog perfume. But Tommy Hilfiger Licensing, Inc. did not see the humor in the name Timmy Holedigger. The court, however, advised Hilfiger "to chill," pointing out that there was no evidence of actual confusion.[15] On the other hand, auction Web site eBay did prevent a seller of perfumes from using the name Perfumebay. The court ruled that the use of "ebay" confused consumers.[16]

---

[14] *In re McGinley*, 660 F.2d 481, 211 U.S.P.Q. (BNA) 668, 1981 CCPA LEXIS 177 (C.C.P.A. 1981).

[15] *Tommy Hilfiger Licensing, Inc. v. Nature Labs, LLC*, 221 F. Supp. 2d 410; 2002 U.S. Dist. LEXIS 14841 (2002).

[16] *Perfumebay.com Inc. v. eBay Inc.*, 506 F.3d 1165, 2007 U.S. App. LEXIS 25726.

FEDERAL TRADEMARK DILUTION ACT OF 1995

Before Congress passed the Federal Trademark Dilution Act of 1995 (FTDA), a trademark owner could win an infringement lawsuit only by proving that consumers would be deceived about who had really made the product. **This statute prevents others from using a trademark in a way that (1) dilutes its value, even though consumers are not confused about the origin of the product; or (2) tarnishes it by association with unwholesome goods or services**. For example, Barbie's Playhouse was a Web site with a font and colors similar to those used by Mattel for its copyrighted Barbie doll. Also, the doll at the bottom of the Web site looked like a Barbie doll. The court found that Barbie's Playhouse had violated the FTDA.[17]

DOMAIN NAMES

Roughly 50 million Internet addresses, known as domain names, have been registered, so it is often difficult to find a distinctive name for a new business. Domain names can be immensely valuable as they are an important component of doing business. Suppose you want to buy a new pair of jeans. Without thinking twice, you type in **http://www.jcrew.com** and there you are, ready to order. What if that address took you to a different site altogether, say, the personal site of one Jackie Crew? The store might lose out on a sale. Companies not only want to own their own domain name, they want to prevent complaint sites such as **http://www.untied.com** (about United Airlines), **http://www.ihatestarbucks.com**, or the always popular variation on the "sucks" theme, such as **http://www.aolsucks.org.** Generic domain names can be valuable, too. Shopping.com paid $750,000 to acquire its domain name from the previous (lucky) owner.

Who has the right to a domain name? In the beginning, the National Science Foundation, which maintained the Internet, granted Network Solutions, Inc. (NSI), a private company, the right to allocate domain names. NSI charged no fee for domain names and the rule was "first come, first served." Then so-called "cybersquatters" began to register domain names, not to use, but to sell to others. Someone, for example, tried to sell the name "Bill Gates" for $1 million.

In response to complaints, NSI began suspending any domain name that was challenged by the holder of a registered trademark. For instance, NSI would not allow Princeton Review to keep kaplan.com, which Princeton had acquired simply to inconvenience its arch rival in the test preparation business. Congress then passed the **Anticybersquatting Consumer Protection Act, which permits both trademark owners and famous people to sue anyone who registers their name as a domain name in "bad faith."** The rightful owner of a trademark is entitled to damages of up to $100,000.

As both the value and the number of domain names soared, the U.S. government transferred management of the Internet, including the allocation of names, to a private, nonprofit, international organization, the Internet Corporation for Assigned Names and Numbers (ICANN). Disputes over domain names can be decided by arbitration under ICANN's Uniform Domain Name Dispute Resolution Policy (UDRP) rather than by litigation under the Anticybersquatting Consumer Protection Act.

If a domain name is confusingly similar to a trademark, the owner has the right to bring a UDRP proceeding. To bring such a case, the complainant (i.e., the plaintiff) must allege that:

- The domain name creates confusion because it is similar to a registered trademark.

- The respondent (i.e., the defendant) has no legitimate reason to use the domain name.

---

[17] *Mattel, Inc. v. Jcom, Inc.*, 1998 U.S. Dist. LEXIS 16195.

- The respondent registered the domain name in bad faith. If the respondent is a competitor of the complainant and has acquired the domain name to disrupt the complainant's business (à la Princeton Review), that is evidence of bad faith. So is an attempt by the respondent to sell the name to the complainant.

If the complainant wins, it is entitled either to take over the domain name or to cancel it.

For example, in a dispute over wal-martsucks.com, the WIPO arbitrator ordered that the name be transferred to Wal-Mart. The respondent had demonstrated his bad faith by attempting to sell the name for $530,000. In a similar case, however, the WIPO arbitrator found for a respondent who had registered Wallmartcanadasucks.com. In this case, the respondent had not tried to sell the name and was using the Web site to criticize Wal-Mart. As the arbitrator stated in his opinion: "Posting defamatory material on a Web site would not justify revocation of a domain name. The Policy should not be used to shut down robust debate and criticism." Either party has the option before or after an ICANN arbitration to litigate the issue in court.

Our discussion thus far has been about registering a trademark as a domain name. Sometimes businesses want to do the opposite—trademark a domain name. The PTO will issue such a trademark only for services offered via the Internet. Thus it trademarked "eBay" for "on-line trading services in which seller posts items to be auctioned and bidding is done electronically." The PTO will not trademark a domain name that is merely an address and does not identify the service provided.

INTERNATIONAL TRADEMARK TREATIES

Under the **Paris Convention**, if someone registers a trademark in one country, then he has a grace period of six months during which he can file in any other country using the same original filing date. Under the **Madrid Agreement**, any trademark registered with the international registry is valid in all signatory countries. (The United States is a signatory.) The **Trademark Law Treaty** simplifies and harmonizes the process of applying for trademarks around the world. Now, a U.S. firm seeking international trademark protection need only file one application, in English, with the PTO, which sends the application to the WIPO, which transmits it to each country in which the applicant would like trademark protection.

EXAM *Strategy*

Question: Jerry Falwell was a nationally known Baptist minister. You can read about him on falwell.com. You can read about his views on homosexuality at fallwell.com—a site critical of his views. This site has a disclaimer indicating that it is not affiliated with Reverend Falwell. The minister sued fallwell.com, alleging a violation of trademark law and the anti-cybersquatting statute. Was there a violation?

Strategy: To win a trademark claim, the reverend had to show that there was some confusion between the two sites. To win the cybersquatting claim, he had to show bad faith on the part of fallwell.com.

Result: The reverend lost on both counts. The court ruled that there was no confusion—fallwell.com had a clear disclaimer. Also, there was no indication of bad faith. The court was reluctant to censor political commentary.

TRADE SECRETS

What do the formulas for Coke and motor oil have in common with computer circuitry, a machine for making adhesive tape, and a procedure for applying hair dye? They are all trade secrets. **A trade secret is a formula, device, process, method, or compilation of information that, when used in business, gives the owner an advantage over competitors who do not know it.** In determining if information is a trade secret, courts consider:

Trade secret

A formula, device, process, method, or compilation of information that, when used in business, gives the owner an advantage over competitors.

- How difficult (and expensive) was the information to obtain? Was it readily available from other sources?

- Does the information create an important competitive advantage?

- Did the company make a reasonable effort to protect it?

It has been estimated that the theft of trade secrets costs U.S. businesses $100 billion a year. In response, most states have now adopted the Uniform Trade Secrets Act (UTSA). Anyone who misappropriates a trade secret is liable to the owner for (1) actual damages, (2) unjust enrichment, or (3) a reasonable royalty. If the misappropriation was willful or malicious, the court may award attorney's fees and double damages. A jury awarded Avery Dennison Corp. $40 million in damages from a competitor that had misappropriated secret information about the adhesives used in self-stick stamps.

Although a company can patent some types of trade secrets, it may be reluctant to do so because patent registration requires that the formula be disclosed publicly. In addition, patent protection expires after 20 years. Some types of trade secrets cannot be patented—customer lists, business plans, manufacturing processes, and marketing strategies.

The following case deals with a typical issue: How much information can employees take with them when they start their own, competing business?

POLLACK v. SKINSMART DERMATOLOGY AND AESTHETIC CENTER P.C.

2004 Pa. Dist. & Cnty. Dec. LEXIS 214
COMMON PLEAS COURT OF PHILADELPHIA COUNTY, PENNSYLVANIA, 2004

CASE SUMMARY

Facts: Dr. Andrew Pollack owned the Philadelphia Institute of Dermatology (PID), a dermatology practice. Drs. Toby Shawe and Samy Badawy worked for PID as independent contractors, receiving a certain percentage of the revenues from each patient they treated. Natalie Wilson was Dr. Pollack's medical assistant.

Pollack tentatively agreed to sell the practice to Shawe and Badawy. But instead of buying his practice, the two doctors decided to start their own, which they called Skinsmart. They executed a lease for the Skinsmart office space, offered Wilson a job, and instructed PID staff members to make copies of their appointment books and printouts of the patient list. Then they abruptly resigned from PID. Wilson called PID patients to reschedule procedures at Skinsmart. The two doctors also called patients and sent out a mailing to patients and referring physicians to tell them about Skinsmart.

Pollack filed suit, alleging that the two doctors had misappropriated trade secrets.

Issue: *Did Shawe and Badawy misappropriate trade secrets from PID?*

Decision: The two doctors did misappropriate trade secrets.

Reasoning: The right to protect trade secrets must be balanced against the right of individuals to pursue whatever occupation they choose. For this reason, secrets will be protected only if they are the particular information of the employer, not general secrets of the trade. To win his case, Pollack must demonstrate that:

1. The trade secrets have value.
2. They are important to his business.
3. He owned them.
4. He took reasonable steps to protect them.

Against this backdrop, it is clear the patient list is a trade secret, worthy of protection. Patient information is confidential and is not known to anyone outside the practice. Pollack relied upon the patient list as the core component of his practice. For this reason, it is valuable. He made substantial effort to compile the list over a number of years. It contained 20,000 names with related information. Pollack spent money on computers, software, and employees to keep and maintain the list. He also sought to protect the secrecy of the information. Within PID's offices, the information was not universally known or accessible. Not every staff member, including the practicing physicians, could pull the records. Wilson did not have access to them, and the doctors relied on other PID employees to access the patient list.

Only civil penalties are available under the Uniform Trade Secrets Act. To safeguard national security and maintain the nation's industrial and economic edge, Congress passed the **Economic Espionage Act of 1996, which makes it a *criminal* offense to steal (or attempt to steal) trade secrets for the benefit of someone other than the owner, including for the benefit of any foreign government.** Xiaodong Sheldon Meng was convicted of violating this statute after he was caught stealing computer code used in military weapons. He had committed the theft on behalf of the government of China. Meng was sentenced to twenty-four months in prison. Timothy Kissane received the same sentence for stealing computer source code from an employer. He planned to sell it to the company's competitors.

CHAPTER CONCLUSION

Intellectual property takes many different forms. It can be an Internet domain name, a software program, a cartoon character, a formula for motor oil, or a process for making drugs. Because of its great variety, intellectual property is difficult to protect. Yet, for many individuals and companies, intellectual property is the most valuable asset they will ever own. As its economic value increases, so does the need to understand the rules of intellectual property law.

EXAM REVIEW

	Patent	Copyright	Trademark	Trade Secrets
Protects:	Mechanical, electrical, chemical inventions; processes; machines; composition of matter; designs, plants	The tangible expression of an idea, but not the idea itself	Words and symbols that a business uses to identify its products or services	A formula, device, process, method, or compilation of information that, when used in business, gives the owner an advantage over competitors who do not know it
Requirements for Legal Protection:	Application approved by PTO	An item is automatically copyrighted once it is in tangible form	Use is the only requirement; registration is not necessary but does offer some benefits	Must be kept confidential
Duration:	20 years after the application is filed (14 years from date of issuance for a design patent)	70 years after the death of the work's only or last living author or, for a corporation, 95 years from publication or 120 years from creation	Valid for 10 years but the owner can renew for an unlimited number of terms as long as the mark is still being used	As long as it is kept confidential

ADDITIONAL QUESTIONS

1. ***ETHICS*** Virtually any TV show, movie, or song can be downloaded for free on the Internet. Most of this material is copyrighted and was very expensive to produce. Most of it is also available for a fee through such legitimate sites as iTunes. What is your ethical obligation? Should you pay $1.99 to download an episode of *The Office* from iTunes or take it for free from an illegal site?

2. In the documentary movie *Expelled: No Intelligence Allowed* there is a 15-second clip of "Imagine," a song by John Lennon. His wife and sons, who held the copyright, sued to block this use of the song. The movie is sympathetic to "intelligent design"—the theory that the universe is too complex to have been created by evolution alone. There must have been a god involved. Who will win this suit?

3. For many years, the jacket design for Webster's Ninth New Collegiate Dictionary featured a bright red background. The front was dominated by a "bull's-eye" logo. The center of the bull's-eye was white with the title of the book in blue. Merriam-Webster registered this logo as a trademark. Random House published a dictionary with a red dust jacket, the title in large black and white letters, and Random House's "house" logo—an angular drawing of a house—in white. What claim might Merriam-Webster make against Random House? Would it be successful?

EXAM Strategy

4. Question: Hey, Paula," a pop hit that spent months on the music charts, was back on the radio 30 years later, but in a form the song's author never intended. Talk-show host Rush Limbaugh played a version with the same music as the original but with lyrics that poked fun at President Bill Clinton's alleged sexual misconduct with Paula Jones. Has Limbaugh violated the author's copyright?

Strategy: Although this example may look like a copyright violation, it falls under an exception. (See the "Result" at the end of this section.)

5. After Edward Miller left his job as a salesperson at the New England Insurance Agency, Inc., he took some of his New England customers to his new employer. At New England, the customer lists had been kept in file cabinets. Although the company did not restrict access to these files, it claimed there was a "You do not peruse my files and I do not peruse yours" understanding. The lists were not marked "confidential" or "not to be disclosed." Did Miller steal New England's trade secrets?

6. Rebecca Reyher wrote (and copyrighted) a children's book entitled *My Mother Is the Most Beautiful Woman in the World*. The story was based on a Russian folktale told to her by her own mother. Years later, the children's TV show *Sesame Street* televised a skit entitled "The Most Beautiful Woman in the World." The *Sesame Street* version took place in a different locale and had fewer frills, but the sequence of events in both stories was identical. The author of the *Sesame Street* script denied he had ever seen Reyher's book but said his skit was based on a story told to his sister some 20 years before. Has *Sesame Street* infringed Reyher's copyright?

7. Roger Schlafly applied for a patent for two prime numbers. (A prime number cannot be evenly divided by any number other than itself and 1. For example: 1, 2, 3, 5, 7, 11, 13.) Schlafly's numbers are a bit longer—one is 150 digits, the other is 300. His numbers, when used together, can help perform the type of mathematical operation necessary for exchanging coded messages by computer. Should the PTO issue this patent?

EXAM Strategy

8. Question: DatagraphiX manufactured and sold computer graphics equipment that allowed users to transfer large volumes of information directly from computers to microfilm. Customers were required to keep maintenance documentation on-site for the DatagraphiX service personnel. The service manual carried this legend: "No other use, direct or indirect, of this document or of any information derived there from is authorized. No copies of any part of this document shall be made without written approval by DatagraphiX." Additionally, on every page of the maintenance manual the company placed warnings that the information was proprietary and not to be duplicated. Frederick J. Lennen left DatagraphiX to start his own company that serviced DatagraphiX equipment. Can DatagraphiX prevent Lennen from using its manuals?

Strategy: With trade secrets, the key is that the owner has made a reasonable effort to protect them. (See the "Result" at the end of this section.)

EXAM Strategy

9. Question: A man asked a question of the advice columnist at his local newspaper. His wife had thought of a clever name for an automobile. He wanted to know if there was any way they could own or register the name so that no one else could use it. If you were the columnist, how would you respond?

Strategy: The couple wants to trademark this name. Can they do so? (See the "Result" at the end of this section.).

10. Babe Ruth was one of the greatest baseball players of all time. After Ruth's death, his daughters registered the words "Babe Ruth" as a trademark. MacMillan, Inc., published a baseball calendar that contained three Babe Ruth photos. Ruth's daughters did not own the specific photographs, but they objected to the use of Ruth's likeness. As holders of the Babe Ruth trademark, do his daughters have the right to prevent others from publishing pictures of Ruth without their permission?

11. Harper & Row signed a contract with former President Gerald Ford to publish his memoirs. As part of the deal, the two agreed that *Time* magazine could print an excerpt from the memoirs shortly before the book was published. *Time* was to pay $25,000 for this right. Before *Time* published its version, *Nation* magazine published an unauthorized excerpt. *Time* canceled its article and refused to pay the $25,000. Harper sued *Nation* for copyright infringement. What was *Nation*'s defense? Was it successful?

12. Frank B. McMahon wrote one of the first psychology textbooks to feature a light and easily readable style. He also included many colloquialisms and examples that appealed to a youthful student market. Charles G. Morris wrote a psychology textbook that copied McMahon's style. Has Morris infringed McMahon's copyright?

13. **ROLE REVERSAL** Draft a multiple-choice question that focuses on an issue of copyright law.

4. Result: Parody (especially about politics!) is a fair use of copyrighted material as long as use of the original is not excessive.

8. Result: The court held that these manuals were DatagraphiX's trade secrets.

9. Result: The couple could not trademark the name unless they had already or were intending to attach it to a product used in interstate commerce. So unless they had plans to manufacture a car, they could not trademark the name.

INTERNET RESEARCH PROBLEM

Think of a name for an interesting new product. Check online to see if this name is available as a trademark. Also check to see if it is available as an Internet domain name.

You can find further practice problems at www.cengagebrain.com. See the preface of this book for website access details.

Preamble

We the People of the United States, in Order to form a more perfect Union, establish Justice, insure domestic Tranquility, provide for the common defense, promote the general Welfare, and secure the Blessings of Liberty to ourselves and our Posterity, do ordain and establish this Constitution for the United States of America.

ARTICLE I

Section 1.

All legislative Powers herein granted shall be vested in a Congress of the United States, which shall consist of a Senate and House of Representatives.

Section 2.

The House of Representatives shall be composed of Members chosen every second Year by the People of the several States, and the Electors in each State shall have the Qualifications requisite for Electors of the most numerous Branch of the State Legislature.

No Person shall be a Representative who shall not have attained to the Age of twenty five Years, and been seven Years a Citizen of the United States, and who shall not, when elected, be an Inhabitant of that State in which he shall be chosen.

Representatives and direct Taxes shall be apportioned among the several States which may be included within this Union, according to their respective Numbers, which shall be determined by adding to the whole Number of free Persons, including those bound to Service for a Term of Years, and excluding Indians not taxed, three fifths of all other Persons. The actual Enumeration shall be made within three Years after the first Meeting of the Congress of the United States, and within every subsequent Term of ten Years, in such Manner as they shall by Law direct. The number of Representatives shall not exceed one for every thirty Thousand, but each State shall have at Least one Representative; and until such enumeration shall be made, the State of New Hampshire shall be entitled to chuse three, Massachusetts eight, Rhode Island and Providence Plantations one, Connecticut five, New-York six, New Jersey four, Pennsylvania eight, Delaware one, Maryland six, Virginia ten, North Carolina five, South Carolina five, and Georgia three.

When vacancies happen in the Representation from any State, the Executive Authority thereof shall issue Writs of Election to fill such vacancies.

The House of Representatives shall chuse their Speaker and other Officers; and shall have the sole Power of Impeachment.

Section 3.   The Senate of the United States shall be composed of two Senators from each State, chosen by the Legislature thereof, for six Years; and each Senator shall have one Vote.

Immediately after they shall be assembled in Consequence of the first Election, they shall be divided as equally as may be into three Classes. The Seats of the Senators of the first Class shall be vacated at the Expiration of the second Year, of the second Class at the Expiration of the fourth Year, and of the third Class at the Expiration of the sixth Year, so that one third may be chosen every second Year; and if Vacancies happen by Resignation or otherwise, during the Recess of the Legislature of any State, the Executive thereof may make temporary Appointments until the next Meeting of the Legislature, which shall then fill such Vacancies.

No Person shall be a Senator who shall not have attained to the Age of thirty Years, and been nine Years a Citizen of the United States, and who shall not, when elected, be an Inhabitant of that State for which he shall be chosen.

The Vice President of the United States shall be President of the Senate, but shall have no Vote, unless they be equally divided.

The Senate shall chuse their other Officers, and also a President pro tempore, in the Absence of the Vice President, or when he shall exercise the Office of President of the United States.

The Senate shall have the sole power to try all Impeachments. When sitting for that Purpose, they shall be an Oath or Affirmation. When the President of the United States is tried, the Chief Justice shall preside: And no Person shall be convicted without the Concurrence of two thirds of the Members present.

Judgment in Cases of Impeachment shall not extend further than to removal from Office, and disqualification to hold and enjoy any Office of honor, Trust or Profit under the United States: but the Party convicted shall nevertheless be liable and subject to Indictment, Trial, Judgment and Punishment, according to Law.

Section 4.   The Times, Places and Manner of holding Elections for Senators and Representatives, shall be prescribed in each State by the Legislature thereof: but the Congress may at any time by Law make or alter such Regulations, except as to the Places of chusing Senators.

The Congress shall assemble at least once in every Year, and such Meeting shall be on the first Monday in December, unless they shall by Law appoint a different Day.

Section 5.   Each House shall be the Judge of the Elections, Returns and Qualifications of its own Members, and a Majority of each shall constitute a Quorum to do Business; but a smaller Number may adjourn from day to day, and may be authorized to compel the Attendance of absent Members, in such Manner, and under such Penalties as each House may provide.

Each House may determine the Rules of its Proceedings, punish its Members for disorderly Behaviour, and, with the Concurrence of two thirds, expel a Member.

Each House shall keep a Journal of its Proceedings, and from time to time publish the same, excepting such Parts as may in their Judgment require Secrecy; and the Yeas and Nays of the Members of either House on any question shall, at the Desire of one fifth of those Present, be entered on the Journal.

Neither House, during the Session of Congress, shall, without the Consent of the other, adjourn for more than three days, nor to any other Place than that in which the two Houses shall be sitting.

The Senators and Representatives shall receive a Compensation for their Services, to be ascertained by Law, and paid out of the Treasury of the United States. They shall in all Cases, except Treason, Felony and Breach of the Peace, be privileged from Arrest during their Attendance at the Session of their respective Houses, and in going to and returning from the same; and for any Speech or Debate in either House, they shall not be questioned in any other Place.

No Senator or Representative shall, during the Time for which he was elected, be appointed to any civil Office under the Authority of the United States, which shall have been created, or the Emoluments whereof shall have been encreased during such time; and no Person holding any Office under the United States, shall be a Member of either House during his Continuance in Office.

Section 6.

All Bills for raising Revenue shall originate in the House of Representatives; but the Senate may propose or concur with Amendments as on other Bills.

Every Bill which shall have passed the House of Representatives and the Senate, shall, before it become a Law, be presented to the President of the United States; If he approve he shall sign it, but if not he shall return it, with his Objections to that House in which it shall have originated, who shall enter the Objections at large on their Journal, and proceed to reconsider it. If after such Reconsideration two thirds of that House shall agree to pass the Bill, it shall be sent, together with the Objections, to the other House, by which it shall likewise be reconsidered, and if approved by two thirds of that House, it shall become a Law. But in all such Cases the Votes of both Houses shall be determined by Yeas and Nays, and the Names of the Persons voting for and against the Bill shall be entered on the Journal of each House respectively. If any Bill shall not be returned by the President within ten Days (Sundays excepted) after it shall have been presented to him, the Same shall be a Law, in like Manner as if he had signed it, unless the Congress by their Adjournment prevent its Return, in which Case it shall not be a Law.

Every Order, Resolution, or Vote to which the Concurrence of the Senate and House of Representatives may be necessary (except on a question of Adjournment) shall be presented to the President of the United States; and before the Same shall take Effect, shall be approved by him, or being disapproved by him, shall be repassed by two thirds of the Senate and House of Representatives, according to the Rules and Limitations prescribed in the Case of a Bill.

Section 7.

The Congress shall have Power to lay and collect Taxes, Duties, Imposts and Excises, to pay the Debts and provide for the common Defence and general Welfare of the United States; but all Duties, Imposts and Excises shall be uniform throughout the United States;

To borrow Money on the credit of the United States;

To regulate Commerce with foreign Nations, and among the several States, and with the Indian Tribes;

To establish an uniform Rule of Naturalization, and uniform Laws on the subject of Bankruptcies throughout the United States;

To coin Money, regulate the Value thereof, and of foreign Coin, and fix the Standard of Weights and Measures;

To provide for the Punishment of counterfeiting the Securities and current Coin of the United States;

To establish Post Offices and post Roads;

Section 8.

To promote the Progress of Science and useful Arts, by securing for limited Times to Authors and Inventors the exclusive Right to their respective Writings and Discoveries;

To constitute Tribunals inferior to the supreme Court;

To define and punish Piracies and Felonies committed on the high Seas, and Offenses against the Law of Nations;

To declare War, grant Letters of Marque and Reprisal, and make Rules concerning Captures on Land and Water;

To raise and support Armies, but no Appropriation of Money to that Use shall be for a longer Term than two Years;

To provide and maintain a Navy;

To make Rules for the Government and Regulation of the land and naval Forces;

To provide for calling forth the Militia to execute the Laws of the Union, suppress Insurrections and repel Invasions;

To provide for organizing, arming, and disciplining, the Militia, and for governing such Part of them as may be employed in the Service of the United States, reserving to the States respectively, the Appointment of the Officers, and the Authority of training the Militia according to the discipline described by Congress;

To exercise exclusive Legislation in all Cases whatsoever, over such District (not exceeding ten Miles square) as may, by Cession of particular States, and the Acceptance of Congress, become the Seat of the Government of the United States, and to exercise like Authority over all Places purchased by the Consent of the Legislature of the State in which the Same shall be, for the Erection of Forts, Magazines, Arsenals, dock-Yards, and other needful Buildings;—And

To make all Laws which shall be necessary and proper for carrying into Execution the foregoing Powers, and all other Powers vested by this Constitution in the Government of the United States, or in any Department or Officer thereof.

Section 9.

The Migration or Importation of such Persons as any of the States now existing shall think proper to admit, shall not be prohibited by the Congress prior to the Year one thousand eight hundred and eight, but a Tax or Duty may be imposed on such Importation, not exceeding ten dollars for each Person.

The Privilege of the Writ of Habeas Corpus shall not be suspended, unless when in Cases of Rebellion or Invasion the public Safety may require it.

No Bill of Attainder or ex post facto Law shall be passed.

No Capitation, or other direct, Tax shall be laid, unless in Proportion to the Census or Enumeration herein before directed to be taken.

No Tax or Duty shall be laid on Articles exported from any State.

No Preference shall be given by any Regulation of Commerce or Revenue to the Ports of one State over those of another; nor shall Vessels bound to, or from, one State, be obliged to enter, clear, or pay Duties in another.

No Money shall be drawn from the Treasury, but in Consequence of Appropriations made by Laws; and a regular Statement and Account of the Receipts and Expenditures of all public Money shall be published from time to time.

No Title of Nobility shall be granted by the United States: And no Person holding any Office of Profit or Trust under them, shall, without the Consent of the Congress, accept of any present, Emolument, Office, or Title, of any kind whatever, from any King, Prince, or foreign State.

Section 10.

No State shall enter into any Treaty, Alliance, or Confederation; grant Letters of Marque and Reprisal; coin Money; emit Bills of Credit; make any Thing but gold and silver Coin a Tender in Payment of Debts; pass any Bill of Attainder, ex post facto Law, or Law impairing the Obligation of Contracts, or grant any Title of Nobility.

No State shall, without the Consent of the Congress, lay any Imposts or Duties on Imports or Exports, except what may be absolutely necessary for executing its inspection Laws: and the net Produce of all Duties and Imposts, laid by any State on Imports or Exports, shall be for the Use of the Treasury of the United States; and all such Laws shall be subject to the Revision and Controul of the Congress.

No State shall, without the Consent of Congress, lay any Duty of Tonnage, keep Troops, or Ships of War in time of Peace, enter into any Agreement or Compact with another State, or with a foreign Power, or engage in War, unless actually invaded, or in such imminent Danger as will not admit of delay.

ARTICLE II

Section 1.

The executive Power shall be vested in a President of the United States of America. He shall hold his Office during the Term of four Years, and, together with the Vice President, chosen for the same Term, be elected, as follows:

Each State shall appoint, in such Manner as the Legislature thereof may direct, a Number of Electors, equal to the whole Number of Senators and Representatives to which the State may be entitled in the Congress: but no Senator or Representative, or Person holding an Office of Trust or Profit under the United States, shall be appointed an Elector.

The Electors shall meet in their respective States, and vote by Ballot for two Persons, of whom one at least shall not be an Inhabitant of the same State with themselves. And they shall make a list of all the Persons voted for, and of the Number of Votes for each; which List they shall sign and certify, and transmit sealed to the Seat of the Government of the United States, directed to the President of the Senate. The President of the Senate shall, in the presence of the Senate and House of Representatives, open all the Certificates, and the Votes shall be counted. The Person having the greatest Number of Votes shall be the President, if such Number be a Majority of the whole Number of Electors appointed; and if there be more than one who have such Majority, and have an equal Number of Votes, then the House of Representatives shall immediately chuse by Ballot one of them for President; and if no Person have a Majority, then from the five highest on the List the said House shall in like Manner chuse the President. But in chusing the President, the Votes shall be taken by States, the Representation from each State having one Vote; A quorum for this Purpose shall consist of a Member or Members from two thirds of the States, and a Majority of all the States shall be necessary to a Choice. In every Case, after the Choice of the President, the Person having the greatest Number of Votes of the Electors shall be the Vice President. But if there should remain two or more who have equal Votes, the Senate shall chuse from them by Ballot the Vice President.

The Congress may determine the Time of Chusing the Electors, and the Day on which they shall give their Votes; which Day shall be the same throughout the United States.

No Person except a natural born Citizen, or a Citizen of the United States, at the time of the Adoption of this Constitution, shall be eligible to the Office of President; neither shall any Person be eligible to that Office who shall not have attained to the Age of thirty five Years, and been fourteen Years a Resident within the United States.

In Case of the Removal of the President from Office, or of his Death, Resignation, or Inability to discharge the Powers and Duties of the said Office, the Same shall devolve on the Vice President, and the Congress may by Law provide for the Case of Removal, Death, Resignation or Inability, both of the President and Vice President, declaring what Officer shall then act as President, and such Officer shall act accordingly, until the Disability be removed, or a President shall be elected.

The President shall, at stated Times, receive for his Services, a Compensation, which shall neither be encreased nor diminished during the Period for which he shall have been elected, and he shall not receive within that Period any other Emolument from the United States, or any of them.

Before he enter on the Execution of his Office, he shall take the following Oath or Affirmation:—"I do solemnly swear (or affirm) that I will faithfully execute the Office of President of the United States, and will to the best of my Ability, preserve, protect and defend the Constitution of the United States."

Section 2.   The President shall be Commander in Chief of the Army and Navy of the United States, and of the Militia of the several States, when called into the actual Service of the United States; he may require the Opinion, in writing, of the principal Officer in each of the executive Departments, upon any Subject relating to the Duties of their respective Offices, and he shall have Power to grant Reprieves and Pardons for Offenses against the United States, except in Cases of Impeachment.

He shall have Power, by and with the Advice and Consent of the Senate, to make Treaties, providing two thirds of the Senators present concur; and he shall nominate, and by and with the Advice and Consent of the Senate, shall appoint Ambassadors, other public Ministers and Consuls, Judges of the supreme Court, and all other Officers of the United States, whose Appointments are not herein otherwise provided for, and which shall be established by Law: but the Congress may by Law vest the Appointment of such inferior Officers, as they think proper, in the President alone, in the Courts of Law, or in the Heads of Departments.

The President shall have Power to fill up all Vacancies that may happen during the Recess of the Senate, by granting Commissions which shall expire at the End of their next Session.

Section 3.   He shall from time to time give to the Congress Information of the State of the Union, and recommend to their Consideration such Measures as he shall judge necessary and expedient; he may, on extraordinary Occasions, convene both Houses, or either of them, and in Case of Disagreement between them, with Respect to the Time of Adjournment, he may adjourn them to such Time as he shall think proper, he shall receive Ambassadors and other public Ministers; he shall take Care that the Laws be faithfully executed, and shall Commission all the Officers of the United States.

Section 4.   The President, Vice President and all civil Officers of the United States, shall be removed from Office on Impeachment for, and Conviction of, Treason, Bribery, or other high Crimes and Misdemeanors.

ARTICLE III

Section 1.

The judicial Power of the United States, shall be vested in one supreme Court, and in such inferior Courts as the Congress may from time to time ordain and establish. The Judges, both of the supreme and inferior Courts, shall hold their Offices during good Behaviour, and shall, at Times, receive for their Services, a Compensation, which shall not be diminished during their Continuance in Office.

Section 2.

The judicial Power shall extend to all Cases, in Law and Equity, arising under this Constitution, the Laws of the United States, and Treaties made, or which shall be made, under their Authority;—to all Cases affecting Ambassadors, other public Ministers and Consuls;—to all Cases of admiralty and maritime Jurisdiction;—to Controversies to which the United States shall be a Party;—to controversies between two or more States;—between a State and Citizens of another State;—between Citizens of different States;—between Citizens of the same State claiming Lands under Grants of different States; and between a State, or the Citizens thereof, and foreign States, Citizens or Subjects.

In all Cases affecting Ambassadors, other public Ministers and Consuls, and those in which a State shall be Party, the supreme Court shall have original Jurisdiction. In all the other Cases before mentioned, the supreme Court shall have appellate Jurisdiction, both as to Law and Fact, with such Exceptions, and under such Regulations as the Congress shall make.

The Trial of all Crimes, except in Cases of Impeachment, shall be by Jury; and such Trial shall be held in the State where the said Crimes shall have been committed; but when not committed within any State, the Trial shall be at such Place or Places as the Congress may by Law have directed.

Section 3.

Treason against the United States, shall consist only in levying War against them, or in adhering to their Enemies, giving them Aid and Comfort. No Person shall be convicted of Treason unless on the Testimony of two Witnesses to the same overt Act, or on Confession in open Court.

The Congress shall have Power to declare the Punishment of Treason, but no Attainder of Treason shall work Corruption of Blood, or Forfeiture except during the Life of the Person attainted.

ARTICLE IV

Section 1.

Full Faith and Credit shall be given in each State to the public Acts, Records, and judicial Proceedings of every other State. And the Congress may by general Laws prescribe the Manner in which such Acts, Records and Proceedings shall be proved, and the Effect thereof.

Section 2.

The Citizens of each State shall be entitled to all Privileges and Immunities of Citizens in the several States.

A Person charged in any State with Treason, Felony, or other Crime, who shall flee from Justice, and be found in another State, shall on Demand of the executive Authority of the State from which he fled, be delivered up, to be removed to the State having Jurisdiction of the Crime.

No Person held to Service or Labour in one State, under the Laws thereof, escaping into another, shall, in Consequence of any Law or Regulation therein, be discharged from such Service or Labour, but shall be delivered up on Claim of the Party to whom such Service or Labour may be due.

Section 3.   New States may be admitted by the Congress into this Union; but no new State shall be formed or erected within the Jurisdiction of any other State; nor any State be formed by the Junction of two or more States, or Parts of States, without the Consent of the Legislatures of the States concerned as well as the Congress.

The Congress shall have Power to dispose of and make all needful Rules and Regulations respecting the Territory or other Property belonging to the United States; and nothing in this Constitution shall be so construed as to Prejudice any Claims of the United States, or of any particular State.

Section 4.   The United States shall guarantee to every State in this Union a Republican Form of Government, and shall protect each of them against Invasion; and on Application of the Legislature, or of the Executive (when the Legislature cannot be convened) against domestic Violence.

ARTICLE V

The Congress, whenever two thirds of both Houses shall deem it necessary, shall propose Amendments to this Constitution, or, on the Application of the Legislatures of two thirds of the several States, shall call a Convention for proposing Amendments, which, in either Case, shall be valid to all Intents and Purposes, as Part of this Constitution, when ratified by the Legislatures of three fourths of the several States, or by Conventions in three fourths thereof, as the one or the other Mode of Ratification may be proposed by the Congress; Provided that no Amendment which may be made prior to the Year One thousand eight hundred and eight shall in any Manner affect the first and fourth Clauses in the Ninth Section of the first Article; and that no State, without its Consent, shall be deprived of its equal Suffrage in the Senate.

ARTICLE VI

All Debts contracted and Engagements entered into, before the Adoption of this Constitution, shall be as valid against the United States under this Constitution, as under the Confederation.

This Constitution, and the Laws of the United States which shall be made in Pursuance thereof; and all Treaties made, or which shall be made, under the Authority of the United States, shall be the supreme Law of the Land; and the Judges in every State shall be bound thereby, any Thing in the Constitution or Laws of any State to the Contrary notwithstanding.

The Senators and Representatives before mentioned, and the Members of the several State Legislatures, and all executive and judicial Officers, both of the United States and of the Several States, shall be bound by Oath or Affirmation, to support this Constitution; but no religious Test shall ever be required as a Qualification to any Office or public Trust under the United States.

ARTICLE VII

The Ratification of the Conventions of nine States, shall be sufficient for the Establishment of this Constitution between the States so ratifying the Same.

Amendment I [1791].

Congress shall make no law respecting an establishment of religion, or prohibiting the free exercise thereof; or abridging the freedom of speech, or the press; or the right of the people peaceably to assemble, and to petition the Government for a redress of grievances.

Amendment II [1791].

A well regulated Militia, being necessary to the security for a free State, the right of the people to keep and bear Arms, shall not be infringed.

Amendment III [1791].

No Soldier shall, in time of peace be quartered in any house, without the consent of the Owner, nor in time of war, but in a manner to be prescribed by law.

Amendment IV [1791].

The right of the people to be secure in their persons, houses, papers, and effects, against unreasonable searches and seizures, shall not be violated, and no Warrants shall issue, but upon probable cause, supported by Oath or Affirmation, and particularly describing the place to be searched, and the persons or things to be seized.

Amendment V [1791].

No person shall be held to answer for a capital, or otherwise infamous crime, unless on a presentment or indictment of a Grand Jury, except in cases arising in the land or naval forces, or in the Militia, when in actual service in time of War or public danger; nor shall any person be subject for the same offense to be twice put in jeopardy of life or limb; nor shall be compelled in any criminal case to be a witness against himself, nor be deprived of life, liberty, or property, without due process of law; nor shall private property be taken for public use, without just compensation.

Amendment VI [1791].

In all criminal prosecutions, the accused shall enjoy the right to a speedy and public trial, by an impartial jury of the State and district wherein the crime shall have been committed, which district shall have been previously ascertained by law, and to be informed of the nature and cause of the accusation; to be confronted with the Witnesses against him; to have compulsory process for obtaining witnesses in his favor, and to have the Assistance of counsel for his defence.

Amendment VII [1791].

In suits at common law, where the value in controversy shall exceed twenty dollars, the right of trial by jury shall be preserved, and no fact tried by a jury, shall be otherwise re-examined in any Court of the United States, than according to the rules of the common law.

Amendment VIII [1791].

Excessive bail shall not be required, no excessive fines imposed, nor cruel and unusual punishments inflicted.

Amendment IX [1791].   The enumeration in the Constitution, of certain rights, shall not be construed to deny or disparage others retained by the people.

Amendment X [1791].   The powers not delegated to the United States by the Constitution, nor prohibited by it to the States, are reserved to the States respectively, or to the people.

Amendment XI [1798].   The judicial power of the United States shall not be construed to extend to any suit in law or equity, commenced or prosecuted against one of the United States by Citizens of another State, or by Citizens or Subjects of any Foreign State.

Amendment XII [1804].   The Electors shall meet in their respective states and vote by ballot for President and Vice-President, one of whom, at least, shall not be an inhabitant of the same state with themselves; they shall name in their ballots the person voted for as President, and in distinct ballots the person voted for as Vice-President, and they shall make distinct lists of all persons voted for as President, and of all persons voted for as Vice-President, and of the number of votes for each, which lists they shall sign and certify, and transmit sealed to the seat of the government of the United States, directed to the President of the Senate;—The President of the Senate shall, in the presence of the Senate and House of Representatives, open all the certificates and the votes shall then be counted;—The person having the greatest number of votes for President, shall be the President, if such number be a majority of the whole number of Electors appointed; and if no person have such majority, then from the persons having the highest numbers not exceeding three on the list of those voted for as President, the House of Representatives shall choose immediately, by ballot, the President. But in choosing the President, the votes shall be taken by states, the representation from each state having one vote; a quorum for this purpose shall consist of a member or members from two-thirds of the states, and a majority of all the states shall be necessary to a choice. And if the House of Representatives shall not choose a President whenever the right of choice shall devolve upon them, before the fourth day of March next following, then the Vice-President shall act as President, as in the case of the death or other constitutional disability of the President. The person having the greatest number of votes as Vice-President, shall be the Vice-President, if such number be a majority of the whole number of Electors appointed, and if no person have a majority, then from the two highest numbers on the list, the Senate shall choose the Vice-President; a quorum for the purpose shall consist of two-thirds of the whole number of Senators, and a majority of the whole number shall be necessary to a choice. But no person constitutionally ineligible to the office of President shall be eligible to that of the Vice-President of the United States.

Amendment XIII [1865].   **Section 1.**   Neither slavery nor involuntary servitude, except as a punishment for crime whereof the party shall have been duly convicted, shall exist within the United States, or any place subject to their jurisdiction.

Section 2.   Congress shall have power to enforce this article by appropriate legislation.

Amendment XIV [1868].   **Section 1.**   All persons born or naturalized in the United States, and subject to the jurisdiction thereof, are citizens of the United States and of the State wherein they reside. No State shall make or enforce any law which shall abridge the privileges or immunities of citizens of the United States; nor shall any State deprive any person of life, liberty, or property, without due process of law; nor deny to any person within its jurisdiction the equal protection of the laws.

Section 2. Representatives shall be appointed among the several States according to their respective numbers, counting the whole number of persons in each State, excluding Indians not taxed. But when the right to vote at any election for the choice of electors for President and Vice President of the United States, Representatives in Congress, the Executive and Judicial officers of a State, or the members of the Legislature thereof, is denied to any of the male inhabitants of such State, being twenty-one years of age, and citizens of the United States, or in any way abridged, except for participation in rebellion, or other crime, the basis of representation therein shall be reduced in the proportion which the number of such male citizens shall bear the whole number of male citizens twenty-one years of age in such State.

Section 3. No person shall be a Senator or Representative in Congress, or elector of President and Vice President, or hold any office, civil or military, under the United States, or under any State, who, having previously taken an oath, as a member of Congress, or as an officer of the United States, or as a member of any State legislature, or as an executive or judicial officer of any State, to support the Constitution of the United States, shall have engaged in insurrection or rebellion against the same, or given aid or comfort to the enemies thereof. But Congress may by a vote of two-thirds of each House, remove such disability.

Section 4. The validity of the public debt of the United States, authorized by law, including debts incurred for payment of pensions and bounties for services in suppressing insurrection or rebellion, shall not be questioned. But neither the United States nor any State shall assume or pay any debt or obligation incurred in aid of insurrection of rebellion against the United States, or any claim for the loss or emancipation of any slave; but all such debts, obligations and claims shall be held illegal and void.

Section 5. The Congress shall have power to enforce, by appropriate legislation, the provisions of this article.

Section 1. The right of citizens of the United States to vote shall not be denied or abridged by the United States or by any State on account of race, color, or previous condition of servitude.

Amendment XV [1870].

Section 2. The Congress shall have power to enforce this article by appropriate legislation.

The Congress shall have power to lay and collect taxes on incomes, from whatever source derived, without apportionment among the several States, and without regard to any census or enumeration.

Amendment XVI [1913].

The Senate of the United States shall be composed of two Senators from each State, elected by the people thereof, for six years; and each Senator shall have one

Amendment XVII [1913].

vote. The electors in each State shall have the qualifications requisite for electors of the most numerous branch of the State legislatures.

When vacancies happen in the representation of any State in the Senate, the executive authority of each State shall issue writs of election to fill such vacancies; *Provided,* That the legislature of any State may empower the executive thereof to make temporary appointments until the people fill the vacancies by election as the legislature may direct.

This amendment shall not be construed as to affect the election or term of any Senator chosen before it becomes valid as part of the Constitution.

Amendment XVIII [1919].

Section 1.   After one year from the ratification of this article the manufacture, sale, or transportation of intoxicating liquors within, the importation thereof into, or the exportation thereof from the United States and all territory subject to the jurisdiction thereof for beverage purposes is hereby prohibited.

Section 2.   The Congress and the several States shall have concurrent power to enforce this article by appropriate legislation.

Section 3.   This article shall be inoperative unless it shall have been ratified as an amendment to the Constitution by the legislatures of the several States, as provided in the Constitution, within seven years from the date of the submission hereof to the States by the Congress.

Amendment XIX [1920].

The right of citizens of the United States to vote shall not be denied or abridged by the United States or by any State on account of sex.

Congress shall have power to enforce this article by appropriate legislation.

Amendment XX [1933].

Section 1.   The terms of the President and Vice President shall end at noon on the 20th day of January, and the terms of Senators and Representatives at noon on the 3d day of January, of the years in which such terms would have ended if this article had not been ratified; and the terms of their successors shall then begin.

Section 2.   The Congress shall assemble at least once in every year, and such meeting shall begin at noon on the 3d day of January, unless they shall by law appoint a different day.

Section 3.   If, at the time fixed for the beginning of the term of the President, the President elect shall have died, the Vice President elect shall become President. If a President shall not have been chosen before the time fixed for the beginning of his term, or if the President elect shall have failed to qualify, then the Vice President elect shall act as President until a President shall have qualified; and the Congress may by law provide for the case wherein neither a President elect nor a Vice President elect shall have qualified, declaring who shall then act as President, or the manner in which one who is to act shall be selected, and such person shall act accordingly until a President or Vice President shall have qualified.

Section 4.   The Congress may by law provide for the case of the death of any of the persons from whom the House of Representatives may choose a President whenever the right of choice shall have devolved upon them, and for the case of the death of any of the persons from whom the Senate may choose a Vice President whenever the right of choice shall have devolved upon them.

Section 5.   Sections 1 and 2 shall take effect on the 15th day of October following the ratification of this article.

Section 6.   This article shall be inoperative unless it shall have been ratified as an amendment to the Constitution by the legislatures of three-fourths of the several States within seven years from the date of its submission.

Section 1.   The eighteenth article of amendment to the Constitution of the United States is hereby repealed.

Amendment XXI [1933].

Section 2.   The transportation or importation into any State, Territory, or possession of the United States for delivery or use therein of intoxicating liquors, in violation of the laws thereof, is hereby prohibited.

Section 3.   This article shall be inoperative unless it shall have been ratified as an amendment to the Constitution by conventions in the several States, as provided in the Constitution, within seven years from the date of the submission hereof to the States by the Congress.

Section 1.   No person shall be elected to the office of the President more than twice, and no person who has held the office of President, or acted as President, for more than two years of a term to which some other person was elected President shall be elected to the office of the President more than once. But this Article shall not apply to any person holding the office of President when this Article was proposed by the Congress, and shall not prevent any person who may be holding the office of President, or acting as President, during the term within which this Article becomes operative from holding the office of President, or acting as President during the remainder of such term.

Amendment XXII [1951].

Section 2.   This article shall be inoperative unless it shall have been ratified as an amendment to the Constitution by the legislatures of three-fourths of the several States within seven years from the date of its submission to the States by the Congress.

Section 1.   The District constituting the seat of Government of the United States shall appoint in such manner as the Congress may direct:

Amendment XXIII [1961].

A number of electors of President and Vice President equal to the whole number of Senators and Representatives in Congress to which the District would be entitled if it were a State, but in no event more than the least populous State; they shall be in addition to those appointed by the States, but they shall be considered, for the purposes of the election of President and Vice President, to be electors appointed by a State; and they shall meet in the District and perform such duties as provided by the twelfth article of amendment.

Section 2.   The Congress shall have power to enforce this article by appropriate legislation.

Amendment XXIV [1964].

Section 1.   The right of citizens of the United States to vote in any primary or other election for President or Vice President, for electors for President or Vice President, or for Senator or Representative in Congress, shall not be denied or abridged by the United States or any State by reason of failure to pay any poll tax or other tax.

Section 2.   The Congress shall have power to enforce this article by appropriate legislation.

Amendment XXV [1967].

Section 1.   In case of the removal of the President from office or of his death or resignation, the Vice President shall become President.

Section 2.   Whenever there is a vacancy in the office of the Vice President, the President shall nominate a Vice President who shall take office upon confirmation by a majority vote of both Houses of Congress.

Section 3.   Whenever the President transmits to the President pro tempore of the Senate and the Speaker of the House of Representatives his written declaration that he is unable to discharge the powers and duties of his office, and until he transmits to them a written declaration to the contrary, such powers and duties shall be discharged by the Vice President as Acting President.

Section 4.   Whenever the Vice President and a majority of either the principal officers of the executive departments or of such other body as Congress may by law provide, transmit to the President pro tempore of the Senate and the Speaker of the House of Representatives their written declaration that the President is unable to discharge the powers and duties of his office, the Vice President shall immediately assume the powers and duties of the office as Acting President.

Thereafter, when the President transmits to the President pro tempore of the Senate and the Speaker of the House of Representatives his written declaration that no inability exists, he shall resume the powers and duties of his office unless the Vice President and a majority of either the principal officers of the executive department or of such other body as Congress may by law provide, transmit within four days to the President pro tempore of the Senate and the Speaker of the House of Representatives their written declaration that the President is unable to discharge the powers and duties of his office. Thereupon Congress shall decide the issue, assembling within forty-eight hours for that purpose if not in session. If the Congress, within twenty-one days after receipt of the latter written declaration, or, if Congress is not in session, within twenty-one days after Congress is required to assemble, determines by two-thirds vote of both Houses that the President is unable to discharge the powers and duties of his office, the Vice President shall continue to discharge the same as Acting President; otherwise, the President shall resume the powers and duties of his office.

Amendment XXVI [1971].

Section 1.   The right of citizens of the United States, who are eighteen years of age or older, to vote shall not be denied or abridged by the United States or by any State on account of age.

Section 2.   The Congress shall have power to enforce this article by appropriate legislation.

No law, varying the compensation for the services of the Senators and Representatives, shall take effect, until an election of Representatives shall have intervened.

Amendment XXVII [1992].

APPENDIX B

UNIFORM COMMERCIAL CODE (SELECTED PROVISIONS)

ARTICLE 1

GENERAL PROVISIONS

PART 1 **Short Title, Construction, Application and Subject Matter of the Act**

§1–101.　Short Title.

This Act shall be known and may be cited as Uniform Commercial Code.

§1–102.　Purposes; Rules of Construction; Variation by Agreement.

(1)　This Act shall be liberally construed and applied to promote its underlying purposes and policies.

(2)　Underlying purposes and policies of this Act are

(a)　to simplify, clarify and modernize the law governing commercial transactions;

(b)　to permit the continued expansion of commercial practices through custom, usage and agreement of the parties;

(c)　to make uniform the law among the various jurisdictions.

(3)　The effect of provisions of this Act may be varied by agreement, except as otherwise provided in this Act and except that the obligations of good faith, diligence, reasonableness and care prescribed by this Act may not be disclaimed by agreement but the parties may by agreement determine the standards by which the performance of such obligations is to be measured if such standards are not manifestly unreasonable.

(4)　The presence in certain provisions of this Act of the words "unless otherwise agreed" or words of similar import does not imply that the effect of other provisions may not be varied by agreement under subsection (3).

(5)　In this Act unless the context otherwise requires

(a)　words in the singular number include the plural, and in the plural include the singular;

(b)　words of the masculine gender include the feminine and the neuter, and when the sense so indicates words of the neuter gender may refer to any gender.

§1–103.　Supplementary General Principles of Law Applicable.

Unless displaced by the particular provisions of this Act, the principles of law and equity, including the law merchant and the law relative to capacity to contract, principal and agent, estoppel, fraud, misrepresentation, duress, coercion, mistake, bankruptcy, or other validating or invalidating cause shall supplement its provisions.

§1–104.　Construction Against Implicit Repeal.

This Act being a general act intended as a unified coverage of its subject matter, no part of it shall be deemed to be impliedly repealed by subsequent legislation if such construction can reasonably be avoided.

§1–105.　Territorial Application of the Act; Parties' Power to Choose Applicable Law.

(1)　Except as provided hereafter in this section, when a transaction bears a reasonable relation to this state and also to another state or nation the parties may agree that the law either of this state or of such other state or nation shall govern their rights and duties. Failing such agreement this Act applies to transactions bearing an appropriate relation to this state.

(2)　Where one of the following provisions of this Act specifies the applicable law, that provision governs and a contrary agreement is effective only to the extent permitted by the law (including the conflict of laws rules) so specified:

Rights of creditors against sold goods. Section 2–402.

Applicability of the Article on Leases. Sections 2A–105 and 2A–106.

Applicability of the Article on Bank Deposits and Collections. Section 4–102.

Governing law in the Article on Funds Transfers. Section 4A–507.

Letters of Credit, Section 5–116.

Bulk sales subject to the Article on Bulk Sales. Section 6–103.

Applicability of the Article on Investment Securities. Section 8–106.

Law governing perfection, the effect of perfection or nonperfection, and the priority of security interests and agricultural liens. Sections 9–301 through 9–307.

As amended in 1972, 1987, 1988, 1989, 1994, 1995, and 1999.

§1–106.   Remedies to Be Liberally Administered.

(1) The remedies provided by this Act shall be liberally administered to the end that the aggrieved party may be put in as good a position as if the other party had fully performed but neither consequential or special nor penal damages may be had except as specifically provided in this Act or by other rule of law.

(2) Any right or obligation declared by this Act is enforceable by action unless the provision declaring it specifies a different and limited effect.

§1–107.   Waiver or Renunciation of Claim or Right After Breach.

Any claim or right arising out of an alleged breach can be discharged in whole or in part without consideration by a written waiver or renunciation signed and delivered by the aggrieved party.

§1–108.   Severability.

If any provision or clause of this Act or application thereof to any person or circumstances is held invalid, such invalidity shall not affect other provisions or applications of the Act which can be given effect without the invalid provision or application, and to this end the provisions of this Act are declared to be severable.

§1–109.   Section Captions.

Section captions are parts of this Act.

PART 2   General Definitions and Principles of Interpretation

§1–201.   General Definitions.

Subject to additional definitions contained in the subsequent Articles of this Act which are applicable to specific Articles or Parts thereof, and unless the context otherwise requires, in this Act:

(1) "Action" in the sense of a judicial proceeding includes recoupment, counterclaim, set-off, suit in equity and any other proceedings in which rights are determined.

(2) "Aggrieved party" means a party entitled to resort to a remedy.

(3) "Agreement" means the bargain of the parties in fact as found in their language or by implication from other circumstances including course of dealing or usage of trade or course of performance as provided in this Act (Sections 1–205 and 2–208). Whether an agreement has legal consequences is determined by the provi-

sions of this Act, if applicable; otherwise by the law of contracts (Section 1–103). (Compare "Contract".)

(4) "Bank" means any person engaged in the business of banking.

(5) "Bearer" means the person in possession of an instrument, document of title, or certificated security payable to bearer or indorsed in blank.

(6) "Bill of lading" means a document evidencing the receipt of goods for shipment issued by a person engaged in the business of transporting or forwarding goods, and includes an airbill. "Airbill" means a document serving for air transportation as a bill of lading does for marine or rail transportation, and includes an air consignment note or air waybill.

(7) "Branch" includes a separately incorporated foreign branch of a bank.

(8) "Burden of establishing" a fact means the burden of persuading the triers of fact that the existence of the fact is more probable than its non-existence.

(9) "Buyer in ordinary course of business" means a person that buys goods in good faith, without knowledge that the sale violates the rights of another person in the goods, and in the ordinary course from a person, other than a pawnbroker, in the business of selling goods of that kind. A person buys goods in the ordinary course if the sale to the person comports with the usual or customary practices in the kind of business in which the seller is engaged or with the seller's own usual or customary practices. A person that sells oil, gas, or other minerals at the wellhead or minehead is a person in the business of selling goods of that kind. A buyer in ordinary course of business may buy for cash, by exchange of other property, or on secured or unsecured credit, and may acquire goods or documents of title under a pre-existing contract for sale. Only a buyer that takes possession of the goods or has a right to recover the goods from the seller under Article 2 may be a buyer in ordinary course of business. A person that acquires goods in a transfer in bulk or as security for or in total or partial satisfaction of a money debt is not a buyer in ordinary course of business.

(10) "Conspicuous": A term or clause is conspicuous when it is so written that a reasonable person against whom it is to operate ought to have noticed it. A printed heading in capitals (as: NON-NEGOTIABLE BILL OF LADING) is conspicuous. Language in the body of a form is "conspicuous" if it is in larger or other contrasting type or color. But in a telegram any stated term is "conspicuous". Whether a term or clause is "conspicuous" or not is for decision by the court.

(11) "Contract" means the total legal obligation which results from the parties' agreement as affected by this Act and any other applicable rules of law. (Compare "Agreement".)

(12) "Creditor" includes a general creditor, a secured creditor, a lien creditor and any representative of creditors, including an assignee for the benefit of creditors, a trustee in bankruptcy, a receiver in equity and an executor or administrator of an insolvent debtor's or assignor's estate.

(13) "Defendant" includes a person in the position of defendant in a cross-action or counterclaim.

(14) "Delivery" with respect to instruments, documents of title, chattel paper, or certificated securities means voluntary transfer of possession.

(15) "Document of title" includes bill of lading, dock warrant, dock receipt, warehouse receipt or order for the delivery of goods, and also any other document which in the regular course of business or financing is treated as adequately evidencing that the person in possession of it is entitled to receive, hold and dispose of the document and the goods it covers. To be a document of title a document must purport to be issued by or addressed to a bailee and purport to cover goods in the bailee's possession which are either identified or are fungible portions of an identified mass.

(16) "Fault" means wrongful act, omission or breach.

(17) "Fungible" with respect to goods or securities means goods or securities of which any unit is, by nature or usage of trade, the equivalent of any other like unit. Goods which are not fungible shall be deemed fungible for the purposes of this Act to the extent that under a particular agreement or document unlike units are treated as equivalents.

(18) "Genuine" means free of forgery or counterfeiting.

(19) "Good faith" means honesty in fact in the conduct or transaction concerned.

(20) "Holder" with respect to a negotiable instrument, means the person in possession if the instrument is payable to bearer or, in the cases of an instrument payable to an identified person, if the identified person is in possession. "Holder" with respect to a document of title means the person in possession if the goods are deliverable to bearer or to the order of the person in possession.

(21) To "honor" is to pay or to accept and pay, or where a credit so engages to purchase or discount a draft complying with the terms of the credit.

(22) "Insolvency proceedings" includes any assignment for the benefit of creditors or other proceedings intended to liquidate or rehabilitate the estate of the person involved.

(23) A person is "insolvent" who either has ceased to pay his debts in the ordinary course of business or cannot pay his debts as they become due or is insolvent within the meaning of the federal bankruptcy law.

(24) "Money" means a medium of exchange authorized or adopted by a domestic or foreign government and includes a monetary unit of account established by an intergovernmental organization or by agreement between two or more nations.

(25) A person has "notice" of a fact when

(a) he has actual knowledge of it; or

(b) he has received a notice or notification of it; or

(c) from all the facts and circumstances known to him at the time in question he has reason to know that it exists.

A person "knows" or has "knowledge" of a fact when he has actual knowledge of it. "Discover" or "learn" or a word or phrase of similar import refers to knowledge rather than to reason to know. The time and circumstances under which a notice or notification may cease to be effective are not determined by this Act.

(26) A person "notifies" or "gives" a notice or notification to another by taking such steps as may be reasonably required to inform the other in ordinary course whether or not such other actually comes to know of it. A person "receives" a notice or notification when

(a) it comes to his attention; or

(b) it is duly delivered at the place of business through which the contract was made or at any other place held out by him as the place for receipt of such communications.

(27) Notice, knowledge or a notice or notification received by an organization is effective for a particular transaction from the time when it is brought to the attention of the individual conducting that transaction, and in any event from the time when it would have been brought to his attention if the organization had exercised due diligence. An organization exercises due diligence if it maintains reasonable routines for communicating significant information to the person conducting the transaction and there is reasonable compliance with the routines. Due diligence does not require an individual acting for the organization to communicate information unless such communication is part of his regular duties or unless he has reason to know of the transaction and that the transaction would be materially affected by the information.

(28) "Organization" includes a corporation, government or governmental subdivision or agency, business trust, estate, trust, partnership or association, two or more persons having a joint or common interest, or any other legal or commercial entity.

(29) "Party", as distinct from "third party", means a person who has engaged in a transaction or made an agreement within this Act.

(30) "Person" includes an individual or an organization (See Section 1–102).

(31) "Presumption" or "presumed" means that the trier of fact must find the existence of the fact presumed unless and until evidence is introduced which would support a finding of its nonexistence.

(32) "Purchase" includes taking by sale, discount, negotiation, mortgage, pledge, lien, issue or re-issue, gift or any other voluntary transaction creating an interest in property.

(33) "Purchaser" means a person who takes by purchase.

(34) "Remedy" means any remedial right to which an aggrieved party is entitled with or without resort to a tribunal.

(35) "Representative" includes an agent, an officer of a corporation or association, and a trustee, executor or administrator of an estate, or any other person empowered to act for another.

(36) "Rights" includes remedies.

(37) "Security interest" means an interest in personal property or fixtures which secures payment or performance of an obligation. The term also includes any interest of a consignor and a buyer of accounts, chattel paper, a payment intangible, or a promissory note in a transaction that is subject to Article 9. The special property interest of a buyer of goods on identification of those goods to a contract for sale under Section 2–401 is not a "security interest", but a buyer may also acquire a "security interest" by complying with Article 9. Except as otherwise provided in Section 2–505, the right of a seller or lessor of goods under Article 2 or 2A to retain or acquire possession of the goods is not a "security interest", but a seller or lessor may also acquire a "security interest" by complying with Article 9. The retention or reservation of title by a seller of goods notwithstanding shipment or delivery to the buyer (Section 2–401) is limited in effect to a reservation of a "security interest".

Whether a transaction creates a lease or security interest is determined by the facts of each case; however, a transaction creates a security interest if the consideration the lessee is to pay the lessor for the right to possession and use of the goods is an obligation for the term of the lease not subject to termination by the lessee, and

(a) the original term of the lease is equal to or greater than the remaining economic life of the goods,

(b) the lessee is bound to renew the lease for the remaining economic life of the goods or is bound to become the owner of the goods,

(c) the lessee has an option to renew the lease for the remaining economic life of the goods for no additional consideration or nominal additional consideration upon compliance with the lease agreement, or

(d) the lessee has an option to become the owner of the goods for no additional consideration or nominal additional consideration upon compliance with the lease agreement.

A transaction does not create a security interest merely because it provides that

(a) the present value of the consideration the lessee is obligated to pay the lessor for the right to possession and use of the goods is substantially equal to or is greater than the fair market value of the goods at the time the lease is entered into,

(b) the lessee assumes risk of loss of the goods, or agrees to pay taxes, insurance, filing, recording, or registration fees, or service or maintenance costs with respect to the goods,

(c) the lessee has an option to renew the lease or to become the owner of the goods,

(d) the lessee has an option to renew the lease for a fixed rent that is equal to or greater than the reasonably predictable fair market rent for the use of the goods for the term of the renewal at the time the option is to be performed, or

(e) the lessee has an option to become the owner of the goods for a fixed price that is equal to or greater than the reasonably predictable fair market value of the goods at the time the option is to be performed.

For purposes of this subsection (37):

(x) Additional consideration is not nominal if (i) when the option to renew the lease is granted to the lessee the rent is stated to be the fair market rent for the use of the goods for the term of the renewal determined at the time the option is to be performed, or (ii) when the option to become the owner of the goods is granted to the lessee the price is stated to be the fair market value of the goods determined at the time the option is to be performed. Additional consideration is nominal if it is less than the lessee's reasonably predictable cost of performing under the lease agreement if the option is not exercised;

(y) "Reasonably predictable" and "remaining economic life of the goods" are to be determined with reference to the facts and circumstances at the time the transaction is entered into; and

(z) "Present value" means the amount as of a date certain of one or more sums payable in the future, discounted to the date certain. The discount is determined by the interest rate specified by the parties if the rate is not manifestly unreasonable at the time the transaction is entered into; otherwise, the discount is determined

by a commercially reasonable rate that takes into account the facts and circumstances of each case at the time the transaction was entered into.

(38) "Send" in connection with any writing or notice means to deposit in the mail or deliver for transmission by any other usual means of communication with postage or cost of transmission provided for and properly addressed and in the case of an instrument to an address specified thereon or otherwise agreed, or if there be none to any address reasonable under the circumstances. The receipt of any writing or notice within the time at which it would have arrived if properly sent has the effect of a proper sending.

(39) "Signed" includes any symbol executed or adopted by a party with present intention to authenticate a writing.

(40) "Surety" includes guarantor.

(41) "Telegram" includes a message transmitted by radio, teletype, cable, any mechanical method of transmission, or the like.

(42) "Term" means that portion of an agreement which relates to a particular matter.

(43) "Unauthorized" signature means one made without actual, implied or apparent authority and includes a forgery.

(44) "Value". Except as otherwise provided with respect to negotiable instruments and bank collections (Sections 3–303, 4–210 and 4–211) a person gives "value" for rights if he acquires them

(a) in return for a binding commitment to extend credit or for the extension of immediately available credit whether or not drawn upon and whether or not a chargeback is provided for in the event of difficulties in collection; or

(b) as security for or in total or partial satisfaction of a preexisting claim; or

(c) by accepting delivery pursuant to a preexisting contract for purchase; or

(d) generally, in return for any consideration sufficient to support a simple contract.

(45) "Warehouse receipt" means a receipt issued by a person engaged in the business of storing goods for hire.

(46) "Written" or "writing" includes printing, typewriting or any other intentional reduction to tangible form.

§1–202. Prima Facie Evidence by Third Party Documents.

A document in due form purporting to be a bill of lading, policy or certificate of insurance, official weigher's or inspector's certificate, consular invoice, or any other document authorized or required by the contract to be issued by a third party shall be prima facie evidence of its own authenticity and genuineness and of the facts stated in the document by the third party.

§1–203. Obligation of Good Faith.

Every contract or duty within this Act imposes an obligation of good faith in its performance or enforcement.

§1–204. Time; Reasonable Time; "Seasonably".

(1) Whenever this Act requires any action to be taken within a reasonable time, any time which is not manifestly unreasonable may be fixed by agreement.

(2) What is a reasonable time for taking any action depends on the nature, purpose and circumstances of such action.

(3) An action is taken "seasonably" when it is taken at or within the time agreed or if no time is agreed at or within a reasonable time.

§1–205. Course of Dealing and Usage of Trade.

(1) A course of dealing is a sequence of previous conduct between the parties to a particular transaction which is fairly to be regarded as establishing a common basis of understanding for interpreting their expressions and other conduct.

(2) A usage of trade is any practice or method of dealing having such regularity of observance in a place, vocation or trade as to justify an expectation that it will be observed with respect to the transaction in question. The existence and scope of such a usage are to be proved as facts. If it is established that such a usage is embodied in a written trade code or similar writing the interpretation of the writing is for the court.

(3) A course of dealing between parties and any usage of trade in the vocation or trade in which they are engaged or of which they are or should be aware give particular meaning to and supplement or qualify terms of an agreement.

(4) The express terms of an agreement and an applicable course of dealing or usage of trade shall be construed wherever reasonable as consistent with each other; but when such construction is unreasonable express terms control both course of dealing and usage of trade and course of dealing controls usage trade.

(5) An applicable usage of trade in the place where any part of performance is to occur shall be used in interpreting the agreement as to that part of the performance.

(6) Evidence of a relevant usage of trade offered by one party is not admissible unless and until he has given the other party such notice as the court finds sufficient to prevent unfair surprise to the latter.

§1–206. Statute of Frauds for Kinds of Personal Property Not Otherwise Covered.

(1) Except in the cases described in subsection (2) of this section a contract for the sale of personal property is not enforceable by way of action or defense beyond five thousand dollars in amount or value of remedy unless there is some writing which indicates that a contract for sale has been made between the parties at a defined or stated price, reasonably identifies the subject matter, and is signed by the party against whom enforcement is sought or by his authorized agent.

(2) Subsection (1) of this section does not apply to contracts for the sale of goods (Section 2–201) nor of securities (Section 8–113) nor to security agreements (Section 9–203).

As amended in 1994.

§1–207. Performance or Acceptance Under Reservation of Rights.

(1) A party who with explicit reservation of rights performs or promises performance or assents to performance in a manner demanded or offered by the other party does not thereby prejudice the rights reserved. Such words as "without prejudice", "under protest" or the like are sufficient.

(2) Subsection (1) does not apply to an accord and satisfaction. As amended in 1990.

§1–208. Option to Accelerate at Will.

A term providing that one party or his successor in interest may accelerate payment or performance or require collateral or additional collateral "at will" or "when he deems himself insecure" or in words of similar import shall be construed to mean that he shall have power to do so only if he in good faith believes that the prospect of payment or performance is impaired. The burden of establishing lack of good faith is on the party against whom the power has been exercised.

§1–209. Subordinated Obligations.

An obligation may be issued as subordinated to payment of another obligation of the person obligated, or a creditor may subordinate his right to payment of an obligation by agreement with either the person obligated or another creditor of the person obligated. Such a subordination does not create a security interest as against either the common debtor or a subordinated creditor. This section shall be construed as declaring the law as it existed prior to the enactment of this section and not as modifying it. Added 1966.

Note: *This new section is proposed as an optional provision to make it clear that a subordination agreement does not create a security interest unless so intended.*

ARTICLE 2

SALES

PART 1 Short Title, General Construction and Subject Matter

§2–101. Short Title.

This Article shall be known and may be cited as Uniform Commercial Code—Sales.

§2–102. Scope; Certain Security and Other Transactions Excluded From This Article.

Unless the context otherwise requires, this Article applies to transactions in goods; it does not apply to any transaction which although in the form of an unconditional contract to sell or present sale is intended to operate only as a security transaction nor does this Article impair or repeal any statute regulating sales to consumers, farmers or other specified classes of buyers.

§2–103.   Definitions and Index of Definitions.

(1) In this Article unless the context otherwise requires

(a) "Buyer" means a person who buys or contracts to buy goods.

(b) "Good faith" in the case of a merchant means honesty in fact and the observance of reasonable commercial standards of fair dealing in the trade.

(c) "Receipt" of goods means taking physical possession of them.

(d) "Seller" means a person who sells or contracts to sell goods.

(2) Other definitions applying to this Article or to specified Parts thereof, and the sections in which they appear are:

"Acceptance". Section 2–606.

"Banker's credit". Section 2–325.

"Between merchants". Section 2–104.

"Cancellation". Section 2–106(4).

"Commercial unit". Section 2–105.

"Confirmed credit". Section 2–325.

"Conforming to contract". Section 2–106.

"Contract for sale". Section 2–106.

"Cover". Section 2–712.

"Entrusting". Section 2–403.

"Financing agency". Section 2–104.

"Future goods". Section 2–105.

"Goods". Section 2–105.

"Identification". Section 2–501.

"Installment contract". Section 2–612.

"Letter of Credit". Section 2–325.

"Lot". Section 2–105

"Merchant". Section 2–104.

"Overseas". Section 2–323.

"Person in position of seller". Section 2–707.

"Present sale". Section 2–106.

"Sale". Section 2–106.

"Sale on approval". Section 2–326.

"Sale or return". Section 2–326.

"Termination". Section 2–106.

(3) The following definitions in other Articles apply to this Article:

"Check". Section 3–104.

"Consignee". Section 7–102.

"Consignor". Section 7–102.

"Consumer goods". Section 9–109.

"Dishonor". Section 3–507.

"Draft". Section 3–104.

(4) In addition Article 1 contains general definitions and principles of construction and interpretation applicable throughout this Article.

As amended in 1994 and 1999.

§2–104.   Definitions: "Merchant"; "Between Merchants"; "Financing Agency".

(1) "Merchant" means a person who deals in goods of the kind or otherwise by his occupation holds himself out as having knowledge or skill peculiar to the practices or goods involved in the transaction or to whom such knowledge or skill may be attributed by his employment of an agent or broker or other intermediary who by his occupation holds himself out as having such knowledge or skill.

(2) "Financing agency" means a bank, finance company or other person who in the ordinary course of business makes advances against goods or documents of title or who by arrangement with either the seller or the buyer intervenes in ordinary course to make or collect payment due or claimed under the contract for sale, as by purchasing or paying the seller's draft or making advances against it or by merely taking it for collection whether or not documents of title accompany the draft. "Financing agency" includes also a bank or other person who similarly intervenes between persons who are in the position of seller and buyer in respect to the goods (Section 2–707).

(3) "Between merchants" means in any transaction with respect to which both parties are chargeable with the knowledge or skill of merchants.

§2–105.   Definitions: Transferability; "Goods"; "Future" Goods; "Lot"; "Commercial Unit".

(1) "Goods" means all things (including specially manufactured goods) which are movable at the time of identification to the contract for sale other than the money in which the price is to be paid, investment securities (Article 8) and things in action. "Goods" also includes the unborn young of animals and growing crops and other identified things attached to realty as described in the section on goods to be severed from realty (Section 2–107).

(2) Goods must be both existing and identified before any interest in them can pass. Goods which are not both existing and identified are "future" goods. A purported present sale of future goods or of any interest therein operates as a contract to sell.

(3) There may be a sale of a part interest in existing identified goods.

(4) An undivided share in an identified bulk of fungible goods is sufficiently identified to be sold although the quantity of the bulk is not determined. Any agreed proportion of such a bulk or any quantity thereof agreed upon by number, weight or other measure may to the extent of the seller's interest in the bulk be sold to the buyer who then becomes an owner in common.

(5) "Lot" means a parcel or a single article which is the subject matter of a separate sale or delivery, whether or not it is sufficient to perform the contract.

(6) "Commercial unit" means such a unit of goods as by commercial usage is a single whole for purposes of sale and division of which materially impairs its character or value on the market or in use. A commercial unit may be a single article (as a machine) or a set of articles (as a suite of furniture or an assortment of sizes) or a quantity (as a bale, gross, or carload) or any other unit treated in use or in the relevant market as a single whole.

§2–106. Definitions: "Contract"; "Agreement"; "Contract for Sale"; "Sale"; "Present Sale"; "Conforming" to Contract; "Termination"; "Cancellation".

(1) In this Article unless the context otherwise requires "contract" and "agreement" are limited to those relating to the present or future sale of goods. "Contract for sale" includes both a present sale of goods and a contract to sell goods at a future time. A "sale" consists in the passing of title from the seller to the buyer for a price (Section 2–401). A "present sale" means a sale which is accomplished by the making of the contract.

(2) Goods or conduct including any part of a performance are "conforming" or conform to the contract when they are in accordance with the obligations under the contract.

(3) "Termination" occurs when either party pursuant to a power created by agreement or law puts an end to the contract otherwise than for its breach. On "termination" all obligations which are still executory on both sides are discharged but any right based on prior breach or performance survives.

(4) "Cancellation" occurs when either party puts an end to the contract for breach by the other and its effect is the same as that of "termination" except that the cancelling party also retains any remedy for breach of the whole contract or any unperformed balance.

§2–107. Goods to Be Severed From Realty: Recording.

(1) A contract for the sale of minerals or the like (including oil and gas) or a structure or its materials to be removed from realty is a contract for the sale of goods within this Article if they are to be severed by the seller but until severance a purported present sale thereof which is not effective as a transfer of an interest in land is effective only as a contract to sell.

(2) A contract for the sale apart from the land of growing crops or other things attached to realty and capable of severance without material harm thereto but not described in subsection (1) or of timber to be cut is a contract for the sale of goods within this Article whether the subject matter is to be severed by the buyer or by the seller even though it forms part of the realty at the time of contracting, and the parties can by identification effect a present sale before severance.

(3) The provisions of this section are subject to any third party rights provided by the law relating to realty records, and the contract for sale may be executed and recorded as a document transferring an interest in land and shall then constitute notice to third parties of the buyer's rights under the contract for sale.

As amended in 1972.

PART 2 Form, Formation and Readjustment of Contract

§2–201. Formal Requirements; Statute of Frauds.

(1) Except as otherwise provided in this section a contract for the sale of goods for the price of $500 or more is not enforceable by way of action or defense unless there is some writing sufficient to indicate that a contract for sale has been made between the parties and signed by the party against whom enforcement is sought or by his authorized agent or broker. A writing is not insufficient because it omits or incorrectly states a term agreed upon but the contract is not enforceable under this paragraph beyond the quantity of goods shown in such writing.

(2) Between merchants if within a reasonable time a writing in confirmation of the contract and sufficient against the sender is received and the party receiving it has reason to know its contents, its satisfies the requirements of subsection (1) against such party unless written notice of objection to its contents is given within ten days after it is received.

(3) A contract which does not satisfy the requirements of subsection (1) but which is valid in other respects is enforceable

(a) if the goods are to be specially manufactured for the buyer and are not suitable for sale to others in the ordinary course of the seller's business and the seller, before notice of repudiation is received and under circumstances which reasonably indicate that the goods are for the buyer, has made either a substantial beginning of their manufacture or commitments for their procurement; or

(b) if the party against whom enforcement is sought admits in his pleading, testimony or otherwise in court that a contract for sale was made, but the contract is not enforceable under this provision beyond the quantity of goods admitted; or

(c) with respect to goods for which payment has been made and accepted or which have been received and accepted (Sec. 2–606).

§2–202. Final Written Expression: Parol or Extrinsic Evidence.

Terms with respect to which the confirmatory memoranda of the parties agree or which are otherwise set forth in a writing intended by the parties as a final expression of their agreement with respect to such terms as are included therein may not be contradicted by evidence of any prior agreement or of a contemporaneous oral agreement but may be explained or supplemented

(a) by course of dealing or usage of trade (Section 1–205) or by course of performance (Section 2–208); and

(b) by evidence of consistent additional terms unless the court finds the writing to have been intended also as a complete and exclusive statement of the terms of the agreement.

§2–203.   Seals Inoperative.

The affixing of a seal to a writing evidencing a contract for sale or an offer to buy or sell goods does not constitute the writing a sealed instrument and the law with respect to sealed instruments does not apply to such a contract or offer.

§2–204.   Formation in General.

(1) A contract for sale of goods may be made in any manner sufficient to show agreement, including conduct by both parties which recognizes the existence of such a contract.

(2) An agreement sufficient to constitute a contract for sale may be found even though the moment of its making is undetermined.

(3) Even though one or more terms are left open a contract for sale does not fail for indefiniteness if the parties have intended to make a contract and there is a reasonably certain basis for giving an appropriate remedy.

§2–205.   Firm Offers.

An offer by a merchant to buy or sell goods in a signed writing which by its terms gives assurance that it will be held open is not revocable, for lack of consideration, during the time stated or if no time is stated for a reasonable time, but in no event may such period of irrevocability exceed three months; but any such term of assurance on a form supplied by the offeree must be separately signed by the offeror.

§2–206.   Offer and Acceptance in Formation of Contract.

(1) Unless other unambiguously indicated by the language or circumstances

(a) an offer to make a contract shall be construed as inviting acceptance in any manner and by any medium reasonable in the circumstances;

(b) an order or other offer to buy goods for prompt or current shipment shall be construed as inviting acceptance either by a prompt promise to ship or by the prompt or current shipment of conforming or nonconforming goods, but such a shipment of nonconforming goods does not constitute an acceptance if the seller seasonably notifies the buyer that the shipment is offered only as an accommodation to the buyer.

(2) Where the beginning of a requested performance is a reasonable mode of acceptance an offeror who is not notified of acceptance within a reasonable time may treat the offer as having lapsed before acceptance.

§2–207.   Additional Terms in Acceptance or Confirmation.

(1) A definite and seasonable expression of acceptance or a written confirmation which is sent within a reasonable time operates as an acceptance even though it states terms additional to or different from those offered or agreed upon, unless acceptance is expressly made conditional on assent to the additional or different terms.

(2) The additional terms are to be construed as proposals for addition to the contract. Between merchants such terms become part of the contract unless:

(a) the offer expressly limits acceptance to the terms of the offer;

(b) they materially alter it; or

(c) notification of objection to them has already been given or is given within a reasonable time after notice of them is received.

(3) Conduct by both parties which recognizes the existence of a contract is sufficient to establish a contract for sale although the writings of the parties do not otherwise establish a contract. In such case the terms of the particular contract consist of those terms on which the writings of the parties agree, together with any supplementary terms incorporated under any other provisions of this Act.

§2–208.   Course of Performance or Practical Construction.

(1) Where the contract for sale involves repeated occasions for performance by either party with knowledge of the nature of the performance and opportunity for objection to it by the other, any course of performance accepted or acquiesced in without objection shall be relevant to determine the meaning of the agreement.

(2) The express terms of the agreement and any such course of performance, as well as any course of dealing and usage of trade, shall be construed whenever reasonable as consistent with each other; but when such construction is unreasonable, express terms shall control course of performance and course of performance shall control both course of dealing and usage of trade (Section 1–205).

(3) Subject to the provisions of the next section on modification and waiver, such course of performance shall be relevant to show a waiver or modification of any term inconsistent with such course of performance.

§2–209.   Modification, Rescission and Waiver.

(1) An agreement modifying a contract within this Article needs no consideration to be binding.

(2) A signed agreement which excludes modification or rescission except by a signed writing cannot be otherwise modified or rescinded, but except as between merchants such a requirement on a form supplied by the merchant must be separately signed by the other party.

(3) The requirements of the statute of frauds section of this Article (Section 2–201) must be satisfied if the contract as modified is within its provisions.

(4) Although an attempt at modification or rescission does not satisfy the requirements of subsection (2) or (3) it can operate as a waiver.

(5) A party who has made a waiver affecting an executory portion of the contract may retract the waiver by reasonable notification received by the other party that strict performance will be required of any term waived, unless the retraction would be unjust in view of a material change of position in reliance on the waiver.

§2–210. Delegation of Performance; Assignment of Rights.

(1) A party may perform his duty through a delegate unless otherwise agreed or unless the other party has a substantial interest in having his original promisor perform or control the acts required by the contract. No delegation of performance relieves the party delegating of any duty to perform or any liability for breach.

(2) Except as otherwise provided in Section 9–406, unless otherwise agreed, all rights of either seller or buyer can be assigned except where the assignment would materially change the duty of the other party, or increase materially the burden or risk imposed on him by his contract, or impair materially his chance of obtaining return performance. A right to damages for breach of the whole contract or a right arising out of the assignor's due performance of his entire obligation can be assigned despite agreement otherwise.

(3) The creation, attachment, perfection, or enforcement of a security interest in the seller's interest under a contract is not a transfer that materially changes the duty of or increases materially the burden or risk imposed on the buyer or impairs materially the buyer's chance of obtaining return performance within the purview of subsection (2) unless, and then only to the extent that, enforcement actually results in a delegation of material performance of the seller. Even in that event, the creation, attachment, perfection, and enforcement of the security interest remain effective, but (i) the seller is liable to the buyer for damages caused by the delegation to the extent that the damages could not reasonably by prevented by the buyer, and (ii) a court having jurisdiction may grant other appropriate relief, including cancellation of the contract for sale or an injunction against enforcement of the security interest or consummation of the enforcement.

(4) Unless the circumstances indicate the contrary a prohibition of assignment of "the contract" is to be construed as barring only the delegation to the assignee of the assignor's performance.

(5) An assignment of "the contract" or of "all my rights under the contract" or an assignment in similar general terms is an assignment of rights and unless the language or the circumstances (as in an assignment for security) indicate the contrary, it is a delegation of performance of the duties of the assignor and its acceptance by the assignee constitutes a promise by him to perform those duties. This promise is enforceable by either the assignor or the other party to the original contract.

(6) The other party may treat any assignment which delegates performance as creating reasonable grounds for insecurity and may without prejudice to his rights against the assignor demand assurances from the assignee (Section 2–609).

As amended in 1999.

PART 3 General Obligation and Construction of Contract

§2–301. General Obligations of Parties.

The obligation of the seller is to transfer and deliver and that of the buyer is to accept and pay in accordance with the contract.

§2–302. Unconscionable Contract or Clause.

(1) If the court as a matter of law finds the contract or any clause of the contract to have been unconscionable at the time it was made the court may refuse to enforce the contract, or it may enforce the remainder of the contract without the unconscionable clause, or it may so limit the application of any unconscionable clause as to avoid any unconscionable result.

(2) When it is claimed or appears to the court that the contract or any clause thereof may be unconscionable the parties shall be afforded a reasonable opportunity to present evidence as to its commercial setting, purpose and effect to aid the court in making the determination.

§2–303. Allocations or Division of Risks.

Where this Article allocates a risk or a burden as between the parties "unless otherwise agreed", the agreement may not only shift the allocation but may also divide the risk or burden.

§2–304. Price Payable in Money, Goods, Realty, or Otherwise.

(1) The price can be made payable in money or otherwise. If it is payable in whole or in part in goods each party is a seller of the goods which he is to transfer.

(2) Even though all or part of the price is payable in an interest in realty the transfer of the goods and the seller's obligations with reference to them are subject to this Article, but not the transfer of the interest in realty or the transferor's obligations in connection therewith.

§2–305. Open Price Term.

(1) The parties if they so intend can conclude a contract for sale even though the price is not settled. In such a case the price is a reasonable price at the time for delivery if

  (a) nothing is said as to price; or

  (b) the price is left to be agreed by the parties and they fail to agree; or

(c)   the price is to be fixed in terms of some agreed market or other standard as set or recorded by a third person or agency and it is not so set or recorded.

(2)   A price to be fixed by the seller or by the buyer means a price for him to fix in good faith.

(3)   When a price left to be fixed otherwise than by agreement of the parties fails to be fixed through fault of one party the other may at his option treat the contract as cancelled or himself fix a reasonable price.

(4)   Where, however, the parties intend not to be bound unless the price be fixed or agreed and it is not fixed or agreed there is no contract. In such a case the buyer must return any goods already received or if unable so to do must pay their reasonable value at the time of delivery and the seller must return any portion of the price paid on account.

§2–306.   Output, Requirements and Exclusive Dealings.

(1)   A term which measures the quantity by the output of the seller or the requirements of the buyer means such actual output or requirements as may occur in good faith, except that no quantity unreasonably disproportionate to any stated estimate or in the absence of a stated estimate to any normal or otherwise comparable prior output or requirements may be tendered or demanded.

(2)   A lawful agreement by either the seller or the buyer for exclusive dealing in the kind of goods concerned imposes unless otherwise agreed an obligation by the seller to use best efforts to supply the goods and by the buyer to use best efforts to promote their sale.

§2–307.   Delivery in Single Lot or Several Lots.

Unless otherwise agreed all goods called for by a contract for sale must be tendered in a single delivery and payment is due only on such tender but where the circumstances give either party the right to make or demand delivery in lots the price if it can be apportioned may be demanded for each lot.

§2–308.   Absence of Specified Place for Delivery.

Unless otherwise agreed

(a)   the place for delivery of goods is the seller's place of business or if he has none his residence; but

(b)   in a contract for sale of identified goods which to the knowledge of the parties at the time of contracting are in some other place, that place is the place for their delivery; and

(c)   documents of title may be delivered through customary banking channels.

§2–309.   Absence of Specific Time Provisions; Notice of Termination.

(1)   The time for shipment or delivery or any other action under a contract if not provided in this Article or agreed upon shall be a reasonable time.

(2)   Where the contract provides for successive performances but is indefinite in duration it is valid for a reasonable time but unless otherwise agreed may be terminated at any time by either party.

(3)   Termination of a contract by one party except on the happening of an agreed event requires that reasonable notification be received by the other party and an agreement dispensing with notification is invalid if its operation would be unconscionable.

§2–310.   Open Time for Payment or Running of Credit; Authority to Ship Under Reservation.

Unless otherwise agreed

(a)   payment is due at the time and place at which the buyer is to receive the goods even though the place of shipment is the place of delivery; and

(b)   if the seller is authorized to send the goods he may ship them under reservation, and may tender the documents of title, but the buyer may inspect the goods after their arrival before payment is due unless such inspection is inconsistent with the terms of the contract (Section 2–513); and

(c)   if delivery is authorized and made by way of documents of title otherwise than by subsection (b) then payment is due at the time and place at which the buyer is to receive the documents regardless of where the goods are to be received; and

(d)   where the seller is required or authorized to ship the goods on credit the credit period runs from the time of shipment but post-dating the invoice or delaying its dispatch will correspondingly delay the starting of the credit period.

§2–311.   Options and Cooperation Respecting Performance.

(1)   An agreement for sale which is otherwise sufficiently definite (subsection (3) of Section 2–204) to be a contract is not made invalid by the fact that it leaves particulars of performance to be specified by one of the parties. Any such specification must be made in good faith and within limits set by commercial reason-ableness.

(2)   Unless otherwise agreed specifications relating to assortment of the goods are at the buyer's option and except as otherwise provided in subsections (1)(c) and (3) of Section 2–319 specifications or arrangements relating to shipment are at the seller's option.

(3)   Where such specification would materially affect the other party's performance but is not seasonably made or where one party's cooperation is necessary to the agreed performance of the other but is not seasonably forthcoming, the other party in addition to all other remedies

(a)   is excused for any resulting delay in his own performance; and

(b)   may also either proceed to perform in any reasonable manner or after the time for a material part of his own performance treat the failure to specify or to cooperate as a breach by failure to deliver or accept the goods.

§2–312. Warranty of Title and Against Infringement; Buyer's Obligation Against Infringement.

(1) Subject to subsection (2) there is in a contract for sale a warranty by the seller that

(a) the title conveyed shall be good, and its transfer rightful; and

(b) the goods shall be delivered free from any security interest or other lien or encumbrance of which the buyer at the time of contracting has no knowledge.

(2) A warranty under subsection (1) will be excluded or modified only by specific language or by circumstances which give the buyer reason to know that the person selling does not claim title in himself or that he is purporting to sell only such right or title as he or a third person may have.

(3) Unless otherwise agreed a seller who is a merchant regularly dealing in goods of the kind warrants that the goods shall be delivered free of the rightful claim of any third person by way of infringement or the like but a buyer who furnishes specifications to the seller must hold the seller harmless against any such claim which arises out of compliance with the specifications.

§2–313. Express Warranties by Affirmation, Promise, Description, Sample.

(1) Express warranties by the seller are created as follows:

(a) Any affirmation of fact or promise made by the seller to the buyer which relates to the goods and becomes part of the basis of the bargain creates an express warranty that the goods shall conform to the affirmation or promise.

(b) Any description of the goods which is made part of the basis of the bargain creates an express warranty that the goods shall conform to the description.

(c) Any sample or model which is made part of the basis of the bargain creates an express warranty that the whole of the goods shall conform to the sample or model.

(2) It is not necessary to the creation of an express warranty that the seller use formal words such as "warrant" or "guarantee" or that he have a specific intention to make a warranty, but an affirmation merely of the value of the goods or a statement purporting to be merely the seller's opinion or commendation of the goods does not create a warranty.

§2–314. Implied Warranty: Merchantability; Usage of Trade.

(1) Unless excluded or modified (Section 2–316), a warranty that the goods shall be merchantable is implied in a contract for their sale if the seller is a merchant with respect to goods of that kind. Under this section the serving for value of food or drink to be consumed either on the premises or elsewhere is a sale.

(2) Goods to be merchantable must be at least such as

(a) pass without objection in the trade under the contract description; and

(b) in the case of fungible goods, are of fair average quality within the description; and

(c) are fit for the ordinary purposes for which such goods are used; and

(d) run, within the variations permitted by the agreement, of even kind, quality and quantity within each unit and among all units involved; and

(e) are adequately contained, packaged, and labeled as the agreement may require; and

(f) conform to the promises or affirmations of fact made on the container or label if any.

(3) Unless excluded or modified (Section 2–316) other implied warranties may arise from course of dealing or usage of trade.

§2–315. Implied Warranty: Fitness for Particular Purpose.

Where the seller at the time of contracting has reason to know any particular purpose for which the goods are required and that the buyer is relying on the seller's skill or judgment to select or furnish suitable goods, there is unless excluded or modified under the next section an implied warranty that the goods shall be fit for such purpose.

§2–316. Exclusion or Modification of Warranties.

(1) Words or conduct relevant to the creation of an express warranty and words or conduct tending to negate or limit warranty shall be construed wherever reasonable as consistent with each other; but subject to the provisions of this Article on parol or extrinsic evidence (Section 2–202) negation or limitation is inoperative to the extent that such construction is unreasonable.

(2) Subject to subsection (3), to exclude or modify the implied warranty of merchantability or any part of it the language must mention merchantability and in case of a writing must be conspicuous, and to exclude or modify any implied warranty of fitness the exclusion must be by a writing and conspicuous. Language to exclude all implied warranties of fitness is sufficient if it states, for example, that "There are no warranties which extend beyond the description on the face hereof."

(3) Notwithstanding subsection (2)

(a) unless the circumstances indicate otherwise, all implied warranties are excluded by expressions like "as is", "with all faults" or other language which in common understanding calls the buyer's attention to the exclusion of warranties and makes plain that there is no implied warranty; and

(b) when the buyer before entering into the contract has examined the goods or the sample or model as fully as he desired or has refused to examine the goods there is no implied warranty with regard to defects which an examination ought in the circumstances to have revealed to him; and

(c) an implied warranty can also be excluded or modified by course of dealing or course of performance or usage of trade.

(4) Remedies for breach of warranty can be limited in accordance with the provisions of this Article on liquidation or limitation of damages and on contractual modification of remedy (Sections 2–718 and 2–719).

§2–317.   Cumulation and Conflict of Warranties Express or Implied.

Warranties whether express or implied shall be construed as consistent with each other and as cumulative, but if such construction is unreasonable the intention of the parties shall determine which warranty is dominant. In ascertaining that intention the following rules apply:

(a) Exact or technical specifications displace an inconsistent sample or model or general language of description.

(b) A sample from an existing bulk displaces inconsistent general language of description.

(c) Express warranties displace inconsistent implied warranties other than an implied warranty of fitness for a particular purpose.

§2–318.   Third Party Beneficiaries of Warranties Express or Implied.

Note: If this Act is introduced in the Congress of the United States this section should be omitted. (States to select one alternative.)

Alternative A A seller's warranty whether express or implied extends to any natural person who is in the family or household of his buyer or who is a guest in his home if it is reasonable to expect that such person may use, consume or be affected by the goods and who is injured in person by breach of the warranty. A seller may not exclude or limit the operation of this section.

Alternative B A seller's warranty whether express or implied extends to any natural person who may reasonably be expected to use, consume or be affected by the goods and who is injured in person by breach of the warranty. A seller may not exclude or limit the operation of this section.

Alternative C A seller's warranty whether express or implied extends to any person who may reasonably be expected to use, consume or be affected by the goods and who is injured by breach of the warranty. A seller may not exclude or limit the operation of this section with respect to injury to the person of an individual to whom the warranty extends.

As amended 1966.

§2–319.   F.O.B. and F.A.S. Terms.

(1) Unless otherwise agreed the term F.O.B. (which means "free on board") at a named place, even though used only in connection with the stated price, is a delivery term under which

(a) when the term is F.O.B. the place of shipment, the seller must at that place ship the goods in the manner provided in this Article (Section 2–504) and bear the expense and risk of putting them into the possession of the carrier; or

(b) when the term is F.O.B. the place of destination, the seller must at his own expense and risk transport the goods to that place and there tender delivery of them in the manner provided in this Article (Section 2–503);

(c) when under either (a) or (b) the term is also F.O.B. vessel, car or other vehicle, the seller must in addition at his own expense and risk load the goods on board. If the term is F.O.B. vessel the buyer must name the vessel and in an appropriate case the seller must comply with the provisions of this Article on the form of bill of lading (Section 2–323).

(2) Unless otherwise agreed the term F.A.S. vessel (which means "free alongside") at a named port, even though used only in connection with the stated price, is a delivery term under which the seller must

(a) at his own expense and risk deliver the goods alongside the vessel in the manner usual in that port or on a dock designated and provided by the buyer; and

(b) obtain and tender a receipt for the goods in exchange for which the carrier is under a duty to issue a bill of lading.

(3) Unless otherwise agreed in any case falling within subsection (1)(a) or (c) or subsection (2) the buyer must seasonably give any needed instructions for making delivery, including when the term is F.A.S. or F.O.B. the loading berth of the vessel and in an appropriate case its name and sailing date. The seller may treat the failure of needed instructions as a failure of cooperation under this Article (Section 2–311). He may also at his option move the goods in any reasonable manner preparatory to delivery or shipment.

(4) Under the term F.O.B. vessel or F.A.S. unless otherwise agreed the buyer must make payment against tender of the required documents and the seller may not tender nor the buyer demand delivery of the goods in substitution for the documents.

§2–320.   C.I.F. and C. & F. Terms.

(1) The term C.I.F. means that the price includes in a lump sum the cost of the goods and the insurance and freight to the named destination. The term C. & F. or C.F. means that the price so includes cost and freight to the named destination.

(2) Unless otherwise agreed and even though used only in connection with the stated price and destination, the term C.I.F. destination or its equivalent requires the seller at his own expense and risk to

(a) put the goods into the possession of a carrier at the port for shipment and obtain a negotiable bill or bills of lading covering the entire transportation to the named destination; and

(b) load the goods and obtain a receipt from the carrier (which may be contained in the bill of lading) showing that the freight has been paid or provided for; and

(c) obtain a policy or certificate of insurance, including any war risk insurance, of a kind and on terms then current at the port of shipment in the usual amount, in the currency of the contract, shown to cover the same goods covered by the bill of lading and providing for payment of loss to the order of the buyer or for the account of whom it may concern; but the seller may add to the price the amount of the premium for any such war risk insurance; and

(d) prepare an invoice of the goods and procure any other documents required to effect shipment or to comply with the contract; and

(e) forward and tender with commercial promptness all the documents in due form and with any indorsement necessary to perfect the buyer's rights.

(3) Unless otherwise agreed the term C. & F. or its equivalent has the same effect and imposes upon the seller the same obligations and risks as a C.I.F. term except the obligation as to insurance.

(4) Under the term C.I.F. or C. & F. unless otherwise agreed the buyer must make payment against tender of the required documents and the seller may not tender nor the buyer demand delivery of the goods in substitution for the documents.

§2–321. C.I.F. or C. & F.: "Net Landed Weights"; "Payment on Arrival"; Warranty of Condition on Arrival.

Under a contract containing a term C.I.F. or C. & F.

(1) Where the price is based on or is to be adjusted according to "net landed weights", "delivered weights", "out turn" quantity or quality or the like, unless otherwise agreed the seller must reasonably estimate the price. The payment due on tender of the documents called for by the contract is the amount so estimated, but after final adjustment of the price a settlement must be made with commercial promptness.

(2) An agreement described in subsection (1) or any warranty of quality or condition of the goods on arrival places upon the seller the risk of ordinary deterioration, shrinkage and the like in transportation but has no effect on the place or time of identification to the contract for sale or delivery or on the passing of the risk of loss.

(3) Unless otherwise agreed where the contract provides for payment on or after arrival of the goods the seller must before payment allow such preliminary inspection as is feasible; but if the goods are lost delivery of the documents and payment are due when the goods should have arrived.

§2–322. Delivery "Ex-Ship".

(1) Unless otherwise agreed a term for delivery of goods "ex-ship" (which means from the carrying vessel) or in equivalent language is not restricted to a particular ship and requires delivery from a ship which has reached a place at the named port of destination where goods of the kind are usually discharged.

(2) Under such a term unless otherwise agreed

(a) the seller must discharge all liens arising out of the carriage and furnish the buyer with a direction which puts the carrier under a duty to deliver the goods; and

(b) the risk of loss does not pass to the buyer until the goods leave the ship's tackle or are otherwise properly unloaded.

§2–323. Form of Bill of Lading Required in Overseas Shipment; "Overseas".

(1) Where the contract contemplates overseas shipment and contains a term C.I.F. or C. & F. or F.O.B. vessel, the seller unless otherwise agreed must obtain a negotiable bill of lading stating that the goods have been loaded on board or, in the case of a term C.I.F. or C. & F., received for shipment.

(2) Where in a case within subsection (1) a bill of lading has been issued in a set of parts, unless otherwise agreed if the documents are not to be sent from abroad the buyer may demand tender of the full set; otherwise only one part of the bill of lading need be tendered. Even if the agreement expressly requires a full set

(a) due tender of a single part is acceptable within the provisions of this Article on cure of improper delivery (subsection (1) of Section 2–508); and

(b) even though the full set is demanded, if the documents are sent from abroad the person tendering an incomplete set may nevertheless require payment upon furnishing an indemnity which the buyer in good faith deems adequate.

(3) A shipment by water or by air or a contract contemplating such shipment is "overseas" insofar as by usage of trade or agreement it is subject to the commercial, financing or shipping practices characteristic of international deep water commerce.

§2–324. "No Arrival, No Sale" Term.

Under a term "no arrival, no sale" or terms of like meaning, unless otherwise agreed,

(a) the seller must properly ship conforming goods and if they arrive by any means he must tender them on arrival but he assumes no obligation that the goods will arrive unless he has caused the non-arrival; and

(b) where without fault of the seller the goods are in part lost or have so deteriorated as no longer to conform to the contract or arrive after the contract time, the buyer may proceed as if there had been casualty to identified goods (Section 2–613).

§2–325. "Letter of Credit" Term; "Confirmed Credit".

(1) Failure of the buyer seasonably to furnish an agreed letter of credit is a breach of the contract for sale.

(2) The delivery to seller of a proper letter of credit suspends the buyer's obligation to pay. If the letter of credit is dishonored, the seller may on seasonable notification to the buyer require payment directly from him.

(3) Unless otherwise agreed the term "letter of credit" or "banker's credit" in a contract for sale means an irrevocable credit issued by a financing agency of good repute and, where the shipment is overseas, of good international repute. The term "confirmed credit" means that the credit must also carry the direct obligation of such an agency which does business in the seller's financial market.

§2–326.   Sale on Approval and Sale or Return; Rights of Creditors.

(1) Unless otherwise agreed, if delivered goods may be returned by the buyer even though they conform to the contract, the transaction is

  (a) a "sale on approval" if the goods are delivered primarily for use, and

  (b) a "sale or return" if the goods are delivered primarily for resale.

(2) Goods held on approval are not subject to the claims of the buyer's creditors until acceptance; goods held on sale or return are subject to such claims while in the buyer's possession.

(3) Any "or return" term of a contract for sale is to be treated as a separate contract for sale within the statute of frauds section of this Article (Section 2–201) and as contradicting the sale aspect of the contract within the provisions of this Article or on parol or extrinsic evidence (Section 2–202).

As amended in 1999.

§2–327.   Special Incidents of Sale on Approval and Sale or Return.

(1) Under a sale on approval unless otherwise agreed

  (a) although the goods are identified to the contract the risk of loss and the title do not pass to the buyer until acceptance; and

  (b) use of the goods consistent with the purpose of trial is not acceptance but failure seasonably to notify the seller of election to return the goods is acceptance, and if the goods conform to the contract acceptance of any part is acceptance of the whole; and

  (c) after due notification of election to return, the return is at the seller's risk and expense but a merchant buyer must follow any reasonable instructions.

(2) Under a sale or return unless otherwise agreed

  (a) the option to return extends to the whole or any commercial unit of the goods while in substantially their original condition, but must be exercised seasonably; and

  (b) the return is at the buyer's risk and expense.

§2–328.   Sale by Auction.

(1) In a sale by auction if goods are put up in lots each lot is the subject of a separate sale.

(2) A sale by auction is complete when the auctioneer so announces by the fall of the hammer or in other customary manner. Where a bid is made while the hammer is falling in acceptance of a prior bid the auctioneer may in his discretion reopen the bidding or declare the goods sold under the bid on which the hammer was falling.

(3) Such a sale is with reserve unless the goods are in explicit terms put up without reserve. In an auction with reserve the auctioneer may withdraw the goods at any time until he announces completion of the sale. In an auction without reserve, after the auctioneer calls for bids on an article or lot, that article or lot cannot be withdrawn unless no bid is made within a reasonable time. In either case a bidder may retract his bid until the auctioneer's announcement of completion of the sale, but a bidder's retraction does not revive any previous bid.

(4) If the auctioneer knowingly receives a bid on the seller's behalf or the seller makes or procures such as bid, and notice has not been given that liberty for such bidding is reserved, the buyer may at his option avoid the sale or take the goods at the price of the last good faith bid prior to the completion of the sale. This subsection shall not apply to any bid at a forced sale.

PART 4   Title, Creditors and Good Faith Purchasers

§2–401.   Passing of Title; Reservation for Security; Limited Application of This Section.

Each provision of this Article with regard to the rights, obligations and remedies of the seller, the buyer, purchasers or other third parties applies irrespective of title to the goods except where the provision refers to such title. Insofar as situations are not covered by the other provisions of this Article and matters concerning title became material the following rules apply:

(1) Title to goods cannot pass under a contract for sale prior to their identification to the contract (Section 2–501), and unless otherwise explicitly agreed the buyer acquires by their identification a special property as limited by this Act. Any retention or reservation by the seller of the title (property) in goods shipped or delivered to the buyer is limited in effect to a reservation of a security interest. Subject to these provisions and to the provisions of the Article on Secured Transactions (Article 9), title to goods passes from the seller to the buyer in any manner and on any conditions explicitly agreed on by the parties.

(2) Unless otherwise explicitly agreed title passes to the buyer at the time and place at which the seller completes his performance with reference to the physical delivery of the goods, despite any reservation of a security interest and even though a document of title is to be delivered at a different time or place; and in particular and despite any reservation of a security interest by the bill of lading

  (a) if the contract requires or authorizes the seller to send the goods to the buyer but does not require him to deliver them at destination, title passes to the buyer at the time and place of shipment; but

  (b) if the contract requires delivery at destination, title passes on tender there.

(3) Unless otherwise explicitly agreed where delivery is to be made without moving the goods,

  (a) if the seller is to deliver a document of title, title passes at the time when and the place where he delivers such documents; or

  (b) if the goods are at the time of contracting already identified and no documents are to be delivered, title passes at the time and place of contracting.

(4) A rejection or other refusal by the buyer to receive or retain the goods, whether or not justified, or a justified revocation of

acceptance revests title to the goods in the seller. Such revesting occurs by operation of law and is not a "sale".

§2–402. Rights of Seller's Creditors Against Sold Goods.

(1) Except as provided in subsections (2) and (3), rights of unsecured creditors of the seller with respect to goods which have been identified to a contract for sale are subject to the buyer's rights to recover the goods under this Article (Sections 2–502 and 2–716).

(2) A creditor of the seller may treat a sale or an identification of goods to a contract for sale as void if as against him a retention of possession by the seller is fraudulent under any rule of law of the state where the goods are situated, except that retention of possession in good faith and current course of trade by a merchant-seller for a commercially reasonable time after a sale or identification is not fraudulent.

(3) Nothing in this Article shall be deemed to impair the rights of creditors of the seller

(a) under the provisions of the Article on Secured Transactions (Article 9); or

(b) where identification to the contract or delivery is made not in current course of trade but in satisfaction of or as security for a pre-existing claim for money, security or the like and is made under circumstances which under any rule of law of the state where the goods are situated would apart from this Article constitute the transaction a fraudulent transfer or voidable preference.

§2–403. Power to Transfer; Good Faith Purchase of Goods; "Entrusting".

(1) A purchaser of goods acquires all title which his transferor had or had power to transfer except that a purchaser of a limited interest acquires rights only to the extent of the interest purchased. A person with voidable title has power to transfer a good title to a good faith purchaser for value. When goods have been delivered under a transaction of purchase the purchaser has such power even though

(a) the transferor was deceived as to the identity of the purchaser, or

(b) the delivery was in exchange for a check which is later dishonored, or

(c) it was agreed that the transaction was to be a "cash sale", or

(d) the delivery was procured through fraud punishable as larcenous under the criminal law.

(2) Any entrusting of possession of goods to a merchant who deals in goods of that kind gives him power to transfer all rights of the entruster to a buyer in ordinary course of business.

(3) "Entrusting" includes any delivery and any acquiescence in retention of possession regardless of any condition expressed between the parties to the delivery or acquiescence and regardless of whether the procurement of the entrusting or the possessor's disposition of the goods have been such as to be larcenous under the criminal law.

(4) The rights of other purchasers of goods and of lien creditors are governed by the Articles on Secured Transactions (Article 9), Bulk Transfers (Article 6) and Documents of Title (Article 7).

As amended in 1988.

PART 5 Performance

§2–501. Insurable Interest in Goods; Manner of Identification of Goods.

(1) The buyer obtains a special property and an insurable interest in goods by identification of existing goods as goods to which the contract refers even though the goods so identified are non-conforming and he has an option to return or reject them. Such identification can be made at any time and in any manner explicitly agreed to by the parties. In the absence of explicit agreement identification occurs

(a) when the contract is made if it is for the sale of goods already existing and identified;

(b) if the contract is for the sale of future goods other than those described in paragraph (c), when goods are shipped, marked or otherwise designated by the seller as goods to which the contract refers;

(c) when the crops are planted or otherwise become growing crops or the young are conceived if the contract is for the sale of unborn young to be born within twelve months after contracting or for the sale of crops to be harvested within twelve months or the next normal harvest season after contracting whichever is longer.

(2) The seller retains an insurable interest in goods so long as title to or any security interest in the goods remains in him and where the identification is by the seller alone he may until default or insolvency or notification to the buyer that the identification is final substitute other goods for those identified.

(3) Nothing in this section impairs any insurable interest recognized under any other statute or rule of law.

§2–502. Buyer's Right to Goods on Seller's Insolvency.

(1) Subject to subsections (2) and (3) and even though the goods have not been shipped a buyer who has paid a part or all of the price of goods in which he has a special property under the provisions of the immediately preceding section may on making and keeping good a tender of any unpaid portion of their price recover them from the seller if:

(a) in the case of goods bought for personal, family, or household purposes, the seller repudiates or fails to deliver as required by the contract; or

(b) in all cases, the seller becomes insolvent within ten days after receipt of the first installment on their price.

(2) The buyer's right to recover the goods under subsection (1)(a) vests upon acquisition of a special property, even if the seller had not then repudiated or failed to deliver.

(3) If the identification creating his special property has been made by the buyer he acquires the right to recover the goods only if they conform to the contract for sale.

As amended in 1999.

§2–503.   Manner of Seller's Tender of Delivery.

(1) Tender of delivery requires that the seller put and hold conforming goods at the buyer's disposition and give the buyer any notification reasonably necessary to enable him to take delivery. The manner, time and place for tender are determined by the agreement and this Article, and in particular

(a) tender must be at a reasonable hour, and if it is of goods they must be kept available for the period reasonably necessary to enable the buyer to take possession; but

(b) unless otherwise agreed the buyer must furnish facilities reasonably suited to the receipt of the goods.

(2) Where the case is within the next section respecting shipment tender requires that the seller comply with its provisions.

(3) Where the seller is required to deliver at a particular destination tender requires that he comply with subsection (1) and also in any appropriate case tender documents as described in subsections (4) and (5) of this section.

(4) Where goods are in the possession of a bailee and are to be delivered without being moved

(a) tender requires that the seller either tender a negotiable document of title covering such goods or procure acknowledgment by the bailee of the buyer's right to possession of the goods; but

(b) tender to the buyer of a non-negotiable document of title or of a written direction to the bailee to deliver is sufficient tender unless the buyer seasonably objects, and receipt by the bailee of notification of the buyer's rights fixes those rights as against the bailee and all third persons; but risk of loss of the goods and of any failure by the bailee to honor the non-negotiable document of title or to obey the direction remains on the seller until the buyer has had a reasonable time to present the document or direction, and a refusal by the bailee to honor the document or to obey the direction defeats the tender.

(5) Where the contract requires the seller to deliver documents

(a) he must tender all such documents in correct form, except as provided in this Article with respect to bills of lading in a set (subsection (2) of Section 2–323); and

(b) tender through customary banking channels is sufficient and dishonor of a draft accompanying the documents constitutes non-acceptance or rejection.

§2–504.   Shipment by Seller.

Where the seller is required or authorized to send the goods to the buyer and the contract does not require him to deliver them at a particular destination, then unless otherwise agreed he must

(a) put the goods in the possession of such a carrier and make such a contract for their transportation as may be reasonable having regard to the nature of the goods and other circumstances of the case; and

(b) obtain and promptly deliver or tender in due form any document necessary to enable the buyer to obtain possession of the goods or otherwise required by the agreement or by usage of trade; and

(c) promptly notify the buyer of the shipment.

Failure to notify the buyer under paragraph (c) or to make a proper contract under paragraph (a) is a ground for rejection only if material delay or loss ensues.

§2–505.   Seller's Shipment under Reservation.

(1) Where the seller has identified goods to the contract by or before shipment:

(a) his procurement of a negotiable bill of lading to his own order or otherwise reserves in him a security interest in the goods. His procurement of the bill to the order of a financing agency or of the buyer indicates in addition only the seller's expectation of transferring that interest to the person named.

(b) a non-negotiable bill of lading to himself or his nominee reserves possession of the goods as security but except in a case of conditional delivery (subsection (2) of Section 2–507) a non-negotiable bill of lading naming the buyer as consignee reserves no security interest even though the seller retains possession of the bill of lading.

(2) When shipment by the seller with reservation of a security interest is in violation of the contract for sale it constitutes an improper contract for transportation within the preceding section but impairs neither the rights given to the buyer by shipment and identification of the goods to the contract nor the seller's powers as a holder of a negotiable document.

§2–506.   Rights of Financing Agency.

(1) A financing agency by paying or purchasing for value a draft which relates to a shipment of goods acquires to the extent of the payment or purchase and in addition to its own rights under the draft and any document of title securing it any rights of the shipper in the goods including the right to stop delivery and the shipper's right to have the draft honored by the buyer.

(2) The right to reimbursement of a financing agency which has in good faith honored or purchased the draft under commitment to or authority from the buyer is not impaired by subsequent discovery of defects with reference to any relevant document which was apparently regular on its face.

§2–507.   Effect of Seller's Tender; Delivery on Condition.

(1) Tender of delivery is a condition to the buyer's duty to accept the goods and, unless otherwise agreed, to his duty to pay for them. Tender entitles the seller to acceptance of the goods and to payment according to the contract.

(2) Where payment is due and demanded on the delivery to the buyer of goods or documents of title, his right as against the seller to

retain or dispose of them is conditional upon his making the payment due.

§2–508. Cure by Seller of Improper Tender or Delivery; Replacement.

(1) Where any tender or delivery by the seller is rejected because non-conforming and the time for performance has not yet expired, the seller may seasonably notify the buyer of his intention to cure and may then within the contract time make a conforming delivery.

(2) Where the buyer rejects a non-conforming tender which the seller had reasonable grounds to believe would be acceptable with or without money allowance the seller may if he seasonably notifies the buyer have a further reasonable time to substitute a conforming tender.

§2–509. Risk of Loss in the Absence of Breach.

(1) Where the contract requires or authorizes the seller to ship the goods by carrier

(a) if it does not require him to deliver them at a particular destination, the risk of loss passes to the buyer when the goods are duly delivered to the carrier even though the shipment is under reservation (Section 2–505); but

(b) if it does require him to deliver them at a particular destination and the goods are there duly tendered while in the possession of the carrier, the risk of loss passes to the buyer when the goods are there duly so tendered as to enable the buyer to take delivery.

(2) Where the goods are held by a bailee to be delivered without being moved, the risk of loss passes to the buyer

(a) on his receipt of a negotiable document of title covering the goods; or

(b) on acknowledgment by the bailee of the buyer's right to possession of the goods; or

(c) after his receipt of a non-negotiable document of title or other written direction to deliver, as provided in subsection (4)(b) of Section 2–503.

(3) In any case not within subsection (1) or (2), the risk of loss passes to the buyer on his receipt of the goods if the seller is a merchant; otherwise the risk passes to the buyer on tender of delivery.

(4) The provisions of this section are subject to contrary agreement of the parties and to the provisions of this Article on sale on approval (Section 2–327) and on effect of breach on risk of loss (Section 2–510).

§2–510. Effect of Breach on Risk of Loss.

(1) Where a tender or delivery of goods so fails to conform to the contract as to give a right of rejection the risk of their loss remains on the seller until cure or acceptance.

(2) Where the buyer rightfully revokes acceptance he may to the extent of any deficiency in his effective insurance coverage treat the risk of loss as having rested on the seller from the beginning.

(3) Where the buyer as to conforming goods already identified to the contract for sale repudiates or is otherwise in breach before risk of their loss has passed to him, the seller may to the extent of any deficiency in his effective insurance coverage treat the risk of loss as resting on the buyer for a commercially reasonable time.

§2–511. Tender of Payment by Buyer; Payment by Check.

(1) Unless otherwise agreed tender of payment is a condition to the seller's duty to tender and complete any delivery.

(2) Tender of payment is sufficient when made by any means or in any manner current in the ordinary course of business unless the seller demands payment in legal tender and gives any extension of time reasonably necessary to procure it.

(3) Subject to the provisions of this Act on the effect of an instrument on an obligation (Section 3–310), payment by check is conditional and is defeated as between the parties by dishonor of the check on due presentment.

As amended in 1994.

§2–512. Payment by Buyer Before Inspection.

(1) Where the contract requires payment before inspection non-conformity of the goods does not excuse the buyer from so making payment unless

(a) the non-conformity appears without inspection; or

(b) despite tender of the required documents the circumstances would justify injunction against honor under this Act (Section 5–109(b)).

(2) Payment pursuant to subsection (1) does not constitute an acceptance of goods or impair the buyer's right to inspect or any of his remedies.

As amended in 1995.

§2–513. Buyer's Right to Inspection of Goods.

(1) Unless otherwise agreed and subject to subsection (3), where goods are tendered or delivered or identified to the contract for sale, the buyer has a right before payment or acceptance to inspect them at any reasonable place and time and in any reasonable manner. When the seller is required or authorized to send the goods to the buyer, the inspection may be after their arrival.

(2) Expenses of inspection must be borne by the buyer but may be recovered from the seller if the goods do not conform and are rejected.

(3) Unless otherwise agreed and subject to the provisions of this Article on C.I.F. contracts (subsection (3) of Section 2–321), the buyer is not entitled to inspect the goods before payment of the price when the contract provides

(a) for delivery "C.O.D." or on other like terms; or

(b) for payment against documents of title, except where such payment is due only after the goods are to become available for inspection.

(4) A place or method of inspection fixed by the parties is presumed to be exclusive but unless otherwise expressly agreed it does not postpone identification or shift the place for delivery or for passing the risk of loss. If compliance becomes impossible, inspection shall be as provided in this section unless the place or method fixed was clearly intended as an indispensable condition failure of which avoids the contract.

§2–514. When Documents Deliverable on Acceptance; When on Payment.

Unless otherwise agreed documents against which a draft is drawn are to be delivered to the drawee on acceptance of the draft if it is payable more than three days after presentment; otherwise, only on payment.

§2–515. Preserving Evidence of Goods in Dispute.

In furtherance of the adjustment of any claim or dispute

(a) either party on reasonable notification to the other and for the purpose of ascertaining the facts and preserving evidence has the right to inspect, test and sample the goods including such of them as may be in the possession or control of the other; and

(b) the parties may agree to a third party inspection or survey to determine the conformity or condition of the goods and may agree that the findings shall be binding upon them in any subsequent litigation or adjustment.

PART 6   Breach, Repudiation and Excuse

§2–601. Buyer's Rights on Improper Delivery.

Subject to the provisions of this Article on breach in installment contracts (Section 2–612) and unless otherwise agreed under the sections on contractual limitations of remedy (Sections 2–718 and 2–719), if the goods or the tender of delivery fail in any respect to conform to the contract, the buyer may

(a) reject the whole; or

(b) accept the whole; or

(c) accept any commercial unit or units and reject the rest.

§2–602. Manner and Effect of Rightful Rejection.

(1) Rejection of goods must be within a reasonable time after their delivery or tender. It is ineffective unless the buyer seasonably notifies the seller.

(2) Subject to the provisions of the two following sections on rejected goods (Sections 2–603 and 2–604),

(a) after rejection any exercise of ownership by the buyer with respect to any commercial unit is wrongful as against the seller; and

(b) if the buyer has before rejection taken physical possession of goods in which he does not have a security interest under the provisions of this Article (subsection (3) of Section 2–711), he is

under a duty after rejection to hold them with reasonable care at the seller's disposition for a time sufficient to permit the seller to remove them; but

(c) the buyer has no further obligations with regard to goods rightfully rejected.

(3) The seller's rights with respect to goods wrongfully rejected are governed by the provisions of this Article on Seller's remedies in general (Section 2–703).

§2–603. Merchant Buyer's Duties as to Rightfully Rejected Goods.

(1) Subject to any security interest in the buyer (subsection (3) of Section 2–711), when the seller has no agent or place of business at the market of rejection a merchant buyer is under a duty after rejection of goods in his possession or control to follow any reasonable instructions received from the seller with respect to the goods and in the absence of such instructions to make reasonable efforts to sell them for the seller's account if they are perishable or threaten to decline in value speedily. Instructions are not reasonable if on demand indemnity for expenses is not forthcoming.

(2) When the buyer sells goods under subsection (1), he is entitled to reimbursement from the seller or out of the proceeds for reasonable expenses of caring for and selling them, and if the expenses include no selling commission then to such commission as is usual in the trade or if there is none to a reasonable sum not exceeding ten per cent on the gross proceeds.

(3) In complying with this section the buyer is held only to good faith and good faith conduct hereunder is neither acceptance nor conversion nor the basis of an action for damages.

§2–604. Buyer's Options as to Salvage of Rightfully Rejected Goods.

Subject to the provisions of the immediately preceding section on perishables if the seller gives no instructions within a reasonable time after notification of rejection the buyer may store the rejected goods for the seller's account or reship them to him or resell them for the seller's account with reimbursement as provided in the preceding section. Such action is not acceptance or conversion.

§2–605. Waiver of Buyer's Objections by Failure to Particularize.

(1) The buyer's failure to state in connection with rejection a particular defect which is ascertainable by reasonable inspection precludes him from relying on the unstated defect to justify rejection or to establish breach

(a) where the seller could have cured it if stated seasonably; or

(b) between merchants when the seller has after rejection made a request in writing for a full and final written statement of all defects on which the buyer proposes to rely.

(2) Payment against documents made without reservation of rights precludes recovery of the payment for defects apparent on the face of the documents.

§2–606. What Constitutes Acceptance of Goods.

(1) Acceptance of goods occurs when the buyer

(a) after a reasonable opportunity to inspect the goods signifies to the seller that the goods are conforming or that he will take or retain them in spite of their nonconformity; or

(b) fails to make an effective rejection (subsection (1) of Section 2–602), but such acceptance does not occur until the buyer has had a reasonable opportunity to inspect them; or

(c) does any act inconsistent with the seller's ownership; but if such act is wrongful as against the seller it is an acceptance only if ratified by him.

(2) Acceptance of a part of any commercial unit is acceptance of that entire unit.

§2–607. Effect of Acceptance; Notice of Breach; Burden of Establishing Breach After Acceptance; Notice of Claim or Litigation to Person Answerable Over.

(1) The buyer must pay at the contract rate for any goods accepted.

(2) Acceptance of goods by the buyer precludes rejection of the goods accepted and if made with knowledge of a non-conformity cannot be revoked because of it unless the acceptance was on the reasonable assumption that the non-conformity would be seasonably cured but acceptance does not of itself impair any other remedy provided by this Article for non-conformity.

(3) Where a tender has been accepted

(a) the buyer must within a reasonable time after he discovers or should have discovered any breach notify the seller of breach or be barred from any remedy; and

(b) if the claim is one for infringement or the like (subsection (3) of Section 2–312) and the buyer is sued as a result of such a breach he must so notify the seller within a reasonable time after he receives notice of the litigation or be barred from any remedy over for liability established by the litigation.

(4) The burden is on the buyer to establish any breach with respect to the goods accepted.

(5) Where the buyer is sued for breach of a warranty or other obligation for which his seller is answerable over

(a) he may give his seller written notice of the litigation. If the notice states that the seller may come in and defend and that if the seller does not do so he will be bound in any action against him by his buyer by any determination of fact common to the two litigations, then unless the seller after seasonable receipt of the notice does come in and defend he is so bound.

(b) if the claim is one for infringement or the like (subsection (3) of Section 2–312) the original seller may demand in writing that his buyer turn over to him control of the litigation including settlement or else be barred from any remedy over and if he also agrees to bear all expense and to satisfy any adverse judgment, then unless the buyer after seasonable receipt of the demand does turn over control the buyer is so barred.

(6) The provisions of subsections (3), (4) and (5) apply to any obligation of a buyer to hold the seller harmless against infringement or the like (subsection (3) of Section 2–312).

§2–608. Revocation of Acceptance in Whole or in Part.

(1) The buyer may revoke his acceptance of a lot or commercial unit whose non-conformity substantially impairs its value to him if he has accepted it

(a) on the reasonable assumption that its nonconformity would be cured and it has not been seasonably cured; or

(b) without discovery of such non-conformity if his acceptance was reasonably induced either by the difficulty of discovery before acceptance or by the seller's assurances.

(2) Revocation of acceptance must occur within a reasonable time after the buyer discovers or should have discovered the ground for it and before any substantial change in condition of the goods which is not caused by their own defects. It is not effective until the buyer notifies the seller of it.

(3) A buyer who so revokes has the same rights and duties with regard to the goods involved as if he had rejected them.

§2–609. Right to Adequate Assurance of Performance.

(1) A contract for sale imposes an obligation on each party that the other's expectation of receiving due performance will not be impaired. When reasonable grounds for insecurity arise with respect to the performance of either party the other may in writing demand adequate assurance of due performance and until he receives such assurance may if commercially reasonable suspend any performance for which he has not already received the agreed return.

(2) Between merchants the reasonableness of grounds for insecurity and the adequacy of any assurance offered shall be determined according to commercial standards.

(3) Acceptance of any improper delivery or payment does not prejudice the party's right to demand adequate assurance of future performance.

(4) After receipt of a justified demand failure to provide within a reasonable time not exceeding thirty days such assurance of due performance as is adequate under the circumstances of the particular case is a repudiation of the contract.

§2–610. Anticipatory Repudiation.

When either party repudiates the contract with respect to a performance not yet due the loss of which will substantially impair the value of the contract to the other, the aggrieved party may

(a) for a commercially reasonable time await performance by the repudiating party; or

(b) resort to any remedy for breach (Section 2–703 or Section 2–711), even though he has notified the repudiating party that he would await the latter's performance and has urged retraction; and

(c) in either case suspend his own performance or proceed in accordance with the provisions of this Article on the seller's right to identify goods to the contract notwithstanding breach or to salvage unfinished goods (Section 2–704).

§2–611.   Retraction of Anticipatory Repudiation.

(1) Until the repudiating party's next performance is due he can retract his repudiation unless the aggrieved party has since the repudiation cancelled or materially changed his position or otherwise indicated that he considers the repudiation final.

(2) Retraction may be by any method which clearly indicates to the aggrieved party that the repudiating party intends to perform, but must include any assurance justifiably demanded under the provisions of this Article (Section 2–609).

(3) Retraction reinstates the repudiating party's rights under the contract with due excuse and allowance to the aggrieved party for any delay occasioned by the repudiation.

§2–612.   "Installment Contract"; Breach.

(1) An "installment contract" is one which requires or authorizes the delivery of goods in separate lots to be separately accepted, even though the contract contains a clause "each delivery is a separate contract" or its equivalent.

(2) The buyer may reject any installment which is non-conforming if the non-conformity substantially impairs the value of that installment and cannot be cured or if the non-conformity is a defect in the required documents; but if the non-conformity does not fall within subsection (3) and the seller gives adequate assurance of its cure the buyer must accept that installment.

(3) Whenever non-conformity or default with respect to one or more installments substantially impairs the value of the whole contract there is a breach of the whole. But the aggrieved party reinstates the contract if he accepts a non-conforming installment without seasonably notifying of cancellation or if he brings an action with respect only to past installments or demands performance as to future installments.

§2–613.   Casualty to Identified Goods.

Where the contract requires for its performance goods identified when the contract is made, and the goods suffer casualty without fault of either party before the risk of loss passes to the buyer, or in a proper case under a "no arrival, no sale" term (Section 2–324) then

(a) if the loss is total the contract is avoided; and

(b) if the loss is partial or the goods have so deteriorated as no longer to conform to the contract the buyer may nevertheless demand inspection and at his option either treat the contract as voided or accept the goods with due allowance from the contract price for the deterioration or the deficiency in quantity but without further right against the seller.

§2–614.   Substituted Performance.

(1) Where without fault of either party the agreed berthing, loading, or unloading facilities fail or an agreed type of carrier becomes unavailable or the agreed manner of delivery otherwise becomes commercially impracticable but a commercially reasonable substitute is available, such substitute performance must be tendered and accepted.

(2) If the agreed means or manner of payment fails because of domestic or foreign governmental regulation, the seller may withhold or stop delivery unless the buyer provides a means or manner of payment which is commercially a substantial equivalent. If delivery has already been taken, payment by the means or in the manner provided by the regulation discharges the buyer's obligation unless the regulation is discriminatory, oppressive or predatory.

§2–615.   Excuse by Failure of Presupposed Conditions.

Except so far as a seller may have assumed a greater obligation and subject to the preceding section on substituted performance:

(a) Delay in delivery or non-delivery in whole or in part by a seller who complies with paragraphs (b) and (c) is not a breach of his duty under a contract for sale if performance as agreed has been made impracticable by the occurrence of a contingency the non-occurrence of which was a basic assumption on which the contract was made or by compliance in good faith with any applicable foreign or domestic governmental regulation or order whether or not it later proves to be invalid.

(b) Where the causes mentioned in paragraph (a) affect only a part of the seller's capacity to perform, he must allocate production and deliveries among his customers but may at his option include regular customers not then under contract as well as his own requirements for further manufacture. He may so allocate in any manner which is fair and reasonable.

(c) The seller must notify the buyer seasonably that there will be delay or non-delivery and, when allocation is required under paragraph (b), of the estimated quota thus made available for the buyer.

§2–616.   Procedure on Notice Claiming Excuse.

(1) Where the buyer receives notification of a material or indefinite delay or an allocation justified under the preceding section he may by written notification to the seller as to any delivery concerned, and where the prospective deficiency substantially impairs the value of the whole contract under the provisions of this Article relating to breach of installment contracts (Section 2–612), then also as to the whole,

(a) terminate and thereby discharge any unexecuted portion of the contract; or

(b) modify the contract by agreeing to take his available quota in substitution.

(2) If after receipt of such notification from the seller the buyer fails so to modify the contract within a reasonable time not exceeding thirty days the contract lapses with respect to any deliveries affected.

(3) The provisions of this section may not be negated by agreement except in so far as the seller has assumed a greater obligation under the preceding section.

PART 7   Remedies

§2–701.   Remedies for Breach of Collateral Contracts Not Impaired.

Remedies for breach of any obligation or promise collateral or ancillary to a contract for sale are not impaired by the provisions of this Article.

§2–702.   Seller's Remedies on Discovery of Buyer's Insolvency.

(1) Where the seller discovers the buyer to be insolvent he may refuse delivery except for cash including payment for all goods theretofore delivered under the contract, and stop delivery under this Article (Section 2–705).

(2) Where the seller discovers that the buyer has received goods on credit while insolvent he may reclaim the goods upon demand made within ten days after the receipt, but if misrepresentation of solvency has been made to the particular seller in writing within three months before delivery the ten day limitation does not apply. Except as provided in this subsection the seller may not base a right to reclaim goods on the buyer's fraudulent or innocent misrepresentation of solvency or of intent to pay.

(3) The seller's right to reclaim under subsection (2) is subject to the rights of a buyer in ordinary course or other good faith purchaser under this Article (Section 2–403). Successful reclamation of goods excludes all other remedies with respect to them.

§2–703.   Seller's Remedies in General.

Where the buyer wrongfully rejects or revokes acceptance of goods or fails to make a payment due on or before delivery or repudiates with respect to a part or the whole, then with respect to any goods directly affected and, if the breach is of the whole contract (Section 2–612), then also with respect to the whole undelivered balance, the aggrieved seller may

(a) withhold delivery of such goods;

(b) stop delivery by any bailee as hereafter provided (Section 2–705);

(c) proceed under the next section respecting goods still unidentified to the contract;

(d) resell and recover damages as hereafter provided (Section 2–706);

(e) recover damages for non-acceptance (Section 2–708) or in a proper case the price (Section 2–709);

(f) cancel.

§2–704.   Seller's Right to Identify Goods to the Contract Notwithstanding Breach or to Salvage Unfinished Goods.

(1) An aggrieved seller under the preceding section may

(a) identify to the contract conforming goods not already identified if at the time he learned of the breach they are in his possession or control;

(b) treat as the subject of resale goods which have demonstrably been intended for the particular contract even though those goods are unfinished.

(2) Where the goods are unfinished an aggrieved seller may in the exercise of reasonable commercial judgment for the purposes of avoiding loss and of effective realization either complete the manufacture and wholly identify the goods to the contract or cease manufacture and resell for scrap or salvage value or proceed in any other reasonable manner.

§2–705.   Seller's Stoppage of Delivery in Transit or Otherwise.

(1) The seller may stop delivery of goods in the possession of a carrier or other bailee when he discovers the buyer to be insolvent (Section 2–702) and may stop delivery of carload, truckload, planeload or larger shipments of express or freight when the buyer repudiates or fails to make a payment due before delivery or if for any other reason the seller has a right to withhold or reclaim the goods.

(2) As against such buyer the seller may stop delivery until

(a) receipt of the goods by the buyer; or

(b) acknowledgment to the buyer by any bailee of the goods except a carrier that the bailee holds the goods for the buyer; or

(c) such acknowledgment to the buyer by a carrier by reshipment or as warehouseman; or

(d) negotiation to the buyer of any negotiable document of title covering the goods.

(3) (a) To stop delivery the seller must so notify as to enable the bailee by reasonable diligence to prevent delivery of the goods.

(b) After such notification the bailee must hold and deliver the goods according to the directions of the seller but the seller is liable to the bailee for any ensuing charges or damages.

(c) If a negotiable document of title has been issued for goods the bailee is not obliged to obey a notification to stop until surrender of the document.

(d) A carrier who has issued a non-negotiable bill of lading is not obliged to obey a notification to stop received from a person other than the consignor.

§2–706.   Seller's Resale Including Contract for Resale.

(1) Under the conditions stated in Section 2–703 on seller's remedies, the seller may resell the goods concerned or the undelivered balance thereof. Where the resale is made in good faith and in a commercially reasonable manner the seller may recover the difference between the resale price and the contract price together with any incidental damages allowed under the provisions of this Article (Section 2–710), but less expenses saved in consequence of the buyer's breach.

(2) Except as otherwise provided in subsection (3) or unless otherwise agreed resale may be at public or private sale including sale by way of one or more contracts to sell or of identification to an existing contract of the seller. Sale may be as a unit or in parcels and at any time and place and on any terms but every aspect of the sale including the method, manner, time, place and terms must be commercially reasonable. The resale must be reasonably identified as referring to the broken contract, but it is not necessary that the goods be in existence or that any or all of them have been identified to the contract before the breach.

(3) Where the resale is at private sale the seller must give the buyer reasonable notification of his intention to resell.

(4) Where the resale is at public sale

(a) only identified goods can be sold except where there is a recognized market for a public sale of futures in goods of the kind; and

(b) it must be made at a usual place or market for public sale if one is reasonably available and except in the case of goods which are perishable or threaten to decline in value speedily the seller must give the buyer reasonable notice of the time and place of the resale; and

(c) if the goods are not to be within the view of those attending the sale the notification of sale must state the place where the goods are located and provide for their reasonable inspection by prospective bidders; and

(d) the seller may buy.

(5) A purchaser who buys in good faith at a resale takes the goods free of any rights of the original buyer even though the seller fails to comply with one or more of the requirements of this section.

(6) The seller is not accountable to the buyer for any profit made on any resale. A person in the position of a seller (Section 2–707) or a buyer who has rightfully rejected or justifiably revoked acceptance must account for any excess over the amount of his security interest, as hereinafter defined (subsection (3) of Section 2–711).

§2–707.   "Person in the Position of a Seller".

(1) A "person in the position of a seller" includes as against a principal an agent who has paid or become responsible for the price of goods on behalf of his principal or anyone who otherwise holds a security interest or other right in goods similar to that of a seller.

(2) A person in the position of a seller may as provided in this Article withhold or stop delivery (Section 2–705) and resell (Section 2–706) and recover incidental damages (Section 2–710).

§2–708.   Seller's Damages for Non-Acceptance or Repudiation.

(1) Subject to subsection (2) and to the provisions of this Article with respect to proof of market price (Section 2–723), the measure of damages for non-acceptance or repudiation by the buyer is the difference between the market price at the time and place for tender and the unpaid contract price together with any incidental damages provided in this Article (Section 2–710), but less expenses saved in consequence of the buyer's breach.

(2) If the measure of damages provided in subsection (1) is inadequate to put the seller in as good a position as performance would have done then the measure of damages is the profit (including reasonable overhead) which the seller would have made from full performance by the buyer, together with any incidental damages provided in this Article (Section 2–710), due allowance for costs reasonably incurred and due credit for payments or proceeds of resale.

§2–709.   Action for the Price.

(1) When the buyer fails to pay the price as it becomes due the seller may recover, together with any incidental damages under the next section, the price

(a) of goods accepted or of conforming goods lost or damaged within a commercially reasonable time after risk of their loss has passed to the buyer; and

(b) of goods identified to the contract if the seller is unable after reasonable effort to resell them at a reasonable price or the circumstances reasonably indicate that such effort will be unavailing.

(2) Where the seller sues for the price he must hold for the buyer any goods which have been identified to the contract and are still in his control except that if resale becomes possible he may resell them at any time prior to the collection of the judgment. The net proceeds of any such resale must be credited to the buyer and payment of the judgment entitles him to any goods not resold.

(3) After the buyer has wrongfully rejected or revoked acceptance of the goods or has failed to make a payment due or has repudiated (Section 2–610), a seller who is held not entitled to the price under this section shall nevertheless be awarded damages for non-acceptance under the preceding section.

§2–710.   Seller's Incidental Damages.

Incidental damages to an aggrieved seller include any commercially reasonable charges, expenses or commissions incurred in stopping delivery, in the transportation, care and custody of goods after the buyer's breach, in connection with return or resale of the goods or otherwise resulting from the breach.

§2–711.   Buyer's Remedies in General; Buyer's Security Interest in Rejected Goods.

(1) Where the seller fails to make delivery or repudiates or the buyer rightfully rejects or justifiably revokes acceptance then with respect to any goods involved, and with respect to the whole if the

breach goes to the whole contract (Section 2–612), the buyer may cancel and whether or not he has done so may in addition to recovering so much of the price as has been paid

(a) "cover" and have damages under the next section as to all the goods affected whether or not they have been identified to the contract; or

(b) recover damages for non-delivery as provided in this Article (Section 2–713).

(2) Where the seller fails to deliver or repudiates the buyer may also

(a) if the goods have been identified recover them as provided in this Article (Section 2–502); or

(b) in a proper case obtain specific performance or replevy the goods as provided in this Article (Section 2–716).

(3) On rightful rejection or justifiable revocation of acceptance a buyer has a security interest in goods in his possession or control for any payments made on their price and any expenses reasonably incurred in their inspection, receipt, transportation, care and custody and may hold such goods and resell them in like manner as an aggrieved seller (Section 2–706).

§2–712." Cover"; Buyer's Procurement of Substitute Goods.

(1) After a breach within the preceding section the buyer may "cover" by making in good faith and without unreasonable delay any reasonable purchase of or contract to purchase goods in substitution for those due from the seller.

(2) The buyer may recover from the seller as damages the difference between the cost of cover and the contract price together with any incidental or consequential damages as hereinafter defined (Section 2–715), but less expenses saved in consequence of the seller's breach.

(3) Failure of the buyer to effect cover within this section does not bar him from any other remedy.

§2–713. Buyer's Damages for Non-Delivery or Repudiation.

(1) Subject to the provisions of this Article with respect to proof of market price (Section 2–723), the measure of damages for non-delivery or repudiation by the seller is the difference between the market price at the time when the buyer learned of the breach and the contract price together with any incidental and consequential damages provided in this Article (Section 2–715), but less expenses saved in consequence of the seller's breach.

(2) Market price is to be determined as of the place for tender or, in cases of rejection after arrival or revocation of acceptance, as of the place of arrival.

§2–714. Buyer's Damages for Breach in Regard to Accepted Goods.

(1) Where the buyer has accepted goods and given notification (subsection (3) of Section 2–607) he may recover as damages for

any non-conformity of tender the loss resulting in the ordinary course of events from the seller's breach as determined in any manner which is reasonable.

(2) The measure of damages for breach of warranty is the difference at the time and place of acceptance between the value of the goods accepted and the value they would have had if they had been as warranted, unless special circumstances show proximate damages of a different amount.

(3) In a proper case any incidental and consequential damages under the next section may also be recovered.

§2–715. Buyer's Incidental and Consequential Damages.

(1) Incidental damages resulting from the seller's breach include expenses reasonably incurred in inspection, receipt, transportation and care and custody of goods rightfully rejected, any commercially reasonable charges, expenses or commissions in connection with effecting cover and any other reasonable expense incident to the delay or other breach.

(2) Consequential damages resulting from the seller's breach include

(a) any loss resulting from general or particular requirements and needs of which the seller at the time of contracting had reason to know and which could not reasonably be prevented by cover or otherwise; and

(b) injury to person or property proximately resulting from any breach of warranty.

§2–716. Buyer's Right to Specific Performance or Replevin.

(1) Specific performance may be decreed where the goods are unique or in other proper circumstances.

(2) The decree for specific performance may include such terms and conditions as to payment of the price, damages, or other relief as the court may deem just.

(3) The buyer has a right of replevin for goods identified to the contract if after reasonable effort he is unable to effect cover for such goods or the circumstances reasonably indicate that such effort will be unavailing or if the goods have been shipped under reservation and satisfaction of the security interest in them has been made or tendered. In the case of goods bought for personal, family, or household purposes, the buyer's right of replevin vests upon acquisition of a special property, even if the seller had not then repudiated or failed to deliver.

As amended in 1999.

§2–717. Deduction of Damages From the Price.

The buyer on notifying the seller of his intention to do so may deduct all or any part of the damages resulting from any breach of the contract from any part of the price still due under the same contract.

§2–718. Liquidation or Limitation of Damages; Deposits.

(1) Damages for breach by either party may be liquidated in the agreement but only at an amount which is reasonable in the light of the anticipated or actual harm caused by the breach, the difficulties of proof of loss, and the inconvenience or nonfeasibility of otherwise obtaining an adequate remedy. A term fixing unreasonably large liquidated damages is void as a penalty.

(2) Where the seller justifiably withholds delivery of goods because of the buyer's breach, the buyer is entitled to restitution of any amount by which the sum of his payments exceeds

(a) the amount to which the seller is entitled by virtue of terms liquidating the seller's damages in accordance with subsection (1), or

(b) in the absence of such terms, twenty per cent of the value of the total performance for which the buyer is obligated under the contract or $500, whichever is smaller.

(3) The buyer's right to restitution under subsection (2) is subject to offset to the extent that the seller establishes

(a) a right to recover damages under the provisions of this Article other than subsection (1), and

(b) the amount or value of any benefits received by the buyer directly or indirectly by reason of the contract.

(4) Where a seller has received payment in goods their reasonable value or the proceeds of their resale shall be treated as payments for the purposes of subsection (2); but if the seller has notice of the buyer's breach before reselling goods received in part performance, his resale is subject to the conditions laid down in this Article on resale by an aggrieved seller (Section 2–706).

§2–719. Contractual Modification or Limitation of Remedy.

(1) Subject to the provisions of subsections (2) and (3) of this section and of the preceding section on liquidation and limitation of damages,

(a) the agreement may provide for remedies in addition to or in substitution for those provided in this Article and may limit or alter the measure of damages recoverable under this Article, as by limiting the buyer's remedies to return of the goods and repayment of the price or to repair and replacement of nonconforming goods or parts; and

(b) resort to a remedy as provided is optional unless the remedy is expressly agreed to be exclusive, in which case it is the sole remedy.

(2) Where circumstances cause an exclusive or limited remedy to fail of its essential purpose, remedy may be had as provided in this Act.

(3) Consequential damages may be limited or excluded unless the limitation or exclusion is unconscionable. Limitation of consequential damages for injury to the person in the case of consumer goods is prima facie unconscionable but limitation of damages where the loss is commercial is not.

§2–720. Effect of "Cancellation" or "Rescission" on Claims for Antecedent Breach.

Unless the contrary intention clearly appears, expressions of "cancellation" or "rescission" of the contract or the like shall not be construed as a renunciation or discharge of any claim in damages for an antecedent breach.

§2–721. Remedies for Fraud.

Remedies for material misrepresentation or fraud include all remedies available under this Article for non-fraudulent breach. Neither rescission or a claim for rescission of the contract for sale nor rejection or return of the goods shall bar or be deemed inconsistent with a claim for damages or other remedy.

§2–722. Who Can Sue Third Parties for Injury to Goods.

Where a third party so deals with goods which have been identified to a contract for sale as to cause actionable injury to a party to that contract

(a) a right of action against the third party is in either party to the contract for sale who has title to or a security interest or a special property or an insurable interest in the goods; and if the goods have been destroyed or converted a right of action is also in the party who either bore the risk of loss under the contract for sale or has since the injury assumed that risk as against the other;

(b) if at the time of the injury the party plaintiff did not bear the risk of loss as against the other party to the contract for sale and there is no arrangement between them for disposition of the recovery, his suit or settlement is, subject to his own interest, as a fiduciary for the other party to the contract;

(c) either party may with the consent of the other sue for the benefit of whom it may concern.

§2–723. Proof of Market Price: Time and Place.

(1) If an action based on anticipatory repudiation comes to trial before the time for performance with respect to some or all of the goods, any damages based on market price (Section 2–708 or Section 2–713) shall be determined according to the price of such goods prevailing at the time when the aggrieved party learned of the repudiation.

(2) If evidence of a price prevailing at the times or places described in this Article is not readily available the price prevailing within any reasonable time before or after the time described or at any other place which in commercial judgment or under usage of trade would serve as a reasonable substitute for the one described may be used, making any proper allowance for the cost of transporting the goods to or from such other place.

(3) Evidence of a relevant price prevailing at a time or place other than the one described in this Article offered by one party is not admissible unless and until he has given the other party such notice as the court finds sufficient to prevent unfair surprise.

§2–724. Admissibility of Market Quotations.

Whenever the prevailing price or value of any goods regularly bought and sold in any established commodity market is in issue, reports in official publications or trade journals or in newspapers or periodicals of general circulation published as the reports of such market shall be admissible in evidence. The circumstances of the preparation of such a report may be shown to affect its weight but not its admissibility.

§2–725. Statute of Limitations in Contracts for Sale.

(1) An action for breach of any contract for sale must be commenced within four years after the cause of action has accrued. By the original agreement the parties may reduce the period of limitation to not less than one year but may not extend it.

(2) A cause of action accrues when the breach occurs, regardless of the aggrieved party's lack of knowledge of the breach. A breach of warranty occurs when tender of delivery is made, except that where a warranty explicitly extends to future performance of the goods and discovery of the breach must await the time of such performance the cause of action accrues when the breach is or should have been discovered.

(3) Where an action commenced within the time limited by subsection (1) is so terminated as to leave available a remedy by another action for the same breach such other action may be commenced after the expiration of the time limited and within six months after the termination of the first action unless the termination resulted from voluntary discontinuance or from dismissal for failure or neglect to prosecute.

(4) This section does not alter the law on tolling of the statute of limitations nor does it apply to causes of action which have accrued before this Act becomes effective.

REVISED ARTICLE 9

SECURED TRANSACTIONS

PART 1   General Provisions

[Subpart 1. Short Title, Definitions, and General Concepts]

§9–101. Short Title.

This article may be cited as Uniform Commercial Code—Secured Transactions.

§9–102. Definitions and Index of Definitions.

(a) In this article:

(1) "Accession" means goods that are physically united with other goods in such a manner that the identity of the original goods is not lost.

(2) "Account", except as used in "account for", means a right to payment of a monetary obligation, whether or not earned by performance, (i) for property that has been or is to be sold, leased, licensed, assigned, or otherwise disposed of, (ii) for services rendered or to be rendered, (iii) for a policy of insurance issued or to be issued, (iv) for a secondary obligation incurred or to be incurred, (v) for energy provided or to be provided, (vi) for the use or hire of a vessel under a charter or other contract, (vii) arising out of the use of a credit or charge card or information contained on or for use with the card, or (viii) as winnings in a lottery or other game of chance operated or sponsored by a State, governmental unit of a State, or person licensed or authorized to operate the game by a State or governmental unit of a State. The term includes health-care insurance receivables. The term does not include (i) rights to payment evidenced by chattel paper or an instrument, (ii) commercial tort claims, (iii) deposit accounts, (iv) investment property, (v) letter-of-credit rights or letters of credit, or (vi) rights to payment for money or funds advanced or sold, other than rights arising out of the use of a credit or charge card or information contained on or for use with the card.

(3) "Account debtor" means a person obligated on an account, chattel paper, or general intangible. The term does not include persons obligated to pay a negotiable instrument, even if the instrument constitutes part of chattel paper.

(4) "Accounting", except as used in "accounting for", means a record:

(A) authenticated by a secured party;

(B) indicating the aggregate unpaid secured obligations as of a date not more than 35 days earlier or 35 days later than the date of the record; and

(C) identifying the components of the obligations in reasonable detail.

(5) "Agricultural lien" means an interest, other than a security interest, in farm products:

(A) which secures payment or performance of an obligation for:

(i) goods or services furnished in connection with a debtor's farming operation; or

(ii) rent on real property leased by a debtor in connection with its farming operation;

(B) which is created by statute in favor of a person that:

(i) in the ordinary course of its business furnished goods or services to a debtor in connection with a debtor's farming operation; or

(ii) leased real property to a debtor in connection with the debtor's farming operation; and

(C) whose effectiveness does not depend on the person's possession of the personal property.

(6) "As-extracted collateral" means:

(A) oil, gas, or other minerals that are subject to a security interest that:

(i) is created by a debtor having an interest in the minerals before extraction; and

(ii) attaches to the minerals as extracted; or

(B) accounts arising out of the sale at the wellhead or minehead of oil, gas, or other minerals in which the debtor had an interest before extraction.

(7) "Authenticate" means:

(A) to sign; or

(B) to execute or otherwise adopt a symbol, or encrypt or similarly process a record in whole or in part, with the present intent of the authenticating person to identify the person and adopt or accept a record.

(8) "Bank" means an organization that is engaged in the business of banking. The term includes savings banks, savings and loan associations, credit unions, and trust companies.

(9) "Cash proceeds" means proceeds that are money, checks, deposit accounts, or the like.

(10) "Certificate of title" means a certificate of title with respect to which a statute provides for the security interest in question to be indicated on the certificate as a condition or result of the security interest's obtaining priority over the rights of a lien creditor with respect to the collateral.

(11) "Chattel paper" means a record or records that evidence both a monetary obligation and a security interest in specific goods, a security interest in specific goods and software used in the goods, a security interest in specific goods and license of software used in the goods, a lease of specific goods, or a lease of specific goods and license of software used in the goods. In this paragraph, "monetary obligation" means a monetary obligation secured by the goods or owed under a lease of the goods and includes a monetary obligation with respect to software used in the goods. The term does not include (i) charters or other contracts involving the use or hire of a vessel or (ii) records that evidence a right to payment arising out of the use of a credit or charge card or information contained on or for use with the card. If a transaction is evidenced by records that include an instrument or series of instruments, the group of records taken together constitutes chattel paper.

(12) "Collateral" means the property subject to a security interest or agricultural lien. The term includes:

(A) proceeds to which a security interest attaches;

(B) accounts, chattel paper, payment intangibles, and promissory notes that have been sold; and

(C) goods that are the subject of a consignment.

(13) "Commercial tort claim" means a claim arising in tort with respect to which:

(A) the claimant is an organization; or

(B) the claimant is an individual and the claim:

(i) arose in the course of the claimant's business or profession; and

(ii) does not include damages arising out of personal injury to or the death of an individual.

(14) "Commodity account" means an account maintained by a commodity intermediary in which a commodity contract is carried for a commodity customer.

(15) "Commodity contract" means a commodity futures contract, an option on a commodity futures contract, a commodity option, or another contract if the contract or option is:

(A) traded on or subject to the rules of a board of trade that has been designated as a contract market for such a contract pursuant to federal commodities laws; or

(B) traded on a foreign commodity board of trade, exchange, or market, and is carried on the books of a commodity intermediary for a commodity customer.

(16) "Commodity customer" means a person for which a commodity intermediary carries a commodity contract on its books.

(17) "Commodity intermediary" means a person that:

(A) is registered as a futures commission merchant under federal commodities law; or

(B) in the ordinary course of its business provides clearance or settlement services for a board of trade that has been designated as a contract market pursuant to federal commodities law.

(18) "Communicate" means:

(A) to send a written or other tangible record;

(B) to transmit a record by any means agreed upon by the persons sending and receiving the record; or

(C) in the case of transmission of a record to or by a filing office, to transmit a record by any means prescribed by filing-office rule.

(19) "Consignee" means a merchant to which goods are delivered in a consignment.

(20) "Consignment" means a transaction, regardless of its form, in which a person delivers goods to a merchant for the purpose of sale and:

(A) the merchant:

(i) deals in goods of that kind under a name other than the name of the person making delivery;

(ii) is not an auctioneer; and

(iii) is not generally known by its creditors to be substantially engaged in selling the goods of others;

(B) with respect to each delivery, the aggregate value of the goods is $1,000 or more at the time of delivery;

(C) the goods are not consumer goods immediately before delivery; and

(D) the transaction does not create a security interest that secures an obligation.

(21) "Consignor" means a person that delivers goods to a consignee in a consignment.

(22) "Consumer debtor" means a debtor in a consumer transaction.

(23) "Consumer goods" means goods that are used or bought for use primarily for personal, family, or household purposes.

(24) "Consumer goods transaction" means a consumer transaction in which:

(A) an individual incurs an obligation primarily for personal, family, or household purposes; and

(B) a security interest in consumer goods secures the obligation.

(25) "Consumer obligor" means an obligor who is an individual and who incurred the obligation as part of a transaction entered into primarily for personal, family, or household purposes.

(26) "Consumer transaction" means a transaction in which (i) an individual incurs an obligation primarily for personal, family, or household purposes, (ii) a security interest secures the obligation,

and (iii) the collateral is held or acquired primarily for personal, family, or household purposes. The term includes consumer-goods transactions.

(27) "Continuation statement" means an amendment of a financing statement which:

(A) identifies, by its file number, the initial financing statement to which it relates; and

(B) indicates that it is a continuation statement for, or that it is filed to continue the effectiveness of, the identified financing statement.

(28) "Debtor" means:

(A) a person having an interest, other than a security interest or other lien, in the collateral, whether or not the person is an obligor;

(B) a seller of accounts, chattel paper, payment intangibles, or promissory notes; or

(C) a consignee.

(29) "Deposit account" means a demand, time, savings, pass-book, or similar account maintained with a bank. The term does not include investment property or accounts evidenced by an instrument.

(30) "Document" means a document of title or a receipt of the type described in Section 7–201(2).

(31) "Electronic chattel paper" means chattel paper evidenced by a record or records consisting of information stored in an electronic medium.

(32) "Encumbrance" means a right, other than an ownership interest, in real property. The term includes mortgages and other liens on real property.

(33) "Equipment" means goods other than inventory, farm products, or consumer goods.

(34) "Farm products" means goods, other than standing timber, with respect to which the debtor is engaged in a farming operation and which are:

(A) crops grown, growing, or to be grown, including:

(i) crops produced on trees, vines, and bushes; and

(ii) aquatic goods produced in aquacultural operations;

(B) livestock, born or unborn, including aquatic goods produced in aquacultural operations;

(C) supplies used or produced in a farming operation; or

(D) products of crops or livestock in their unmanufactured states.

(35) "Farming operation" means raising, cultivating, propagating, fattening, grazing, or any other farming, livestock, or aquacultural operation.

(36) "File number" means the number assigned to an initial financing statement pursuant to Section 9–519(a).

(37) "Filing office" means an office designated in Section 9–501 as the place to file a financing statement.

(38) "Filing-office rule" means a rule adopted pursuant to Section 9–526.

(39) "Financing statement" means a record or records composed of an initial financing statement and any filed record relating to the initial financing statement.

(40) "Fixture filing" means the filing of a financing statement covering goods that are or are to become fixtures and satisfying Section 9–502(a) and (b). The term includes the filing of a financing statement covering goods of a transmitting utility which are or are to become fixtures.

(41) "Fixtures" means goods that have become so related to particular real property that an interest in them arises under real property law.

(42) "General intangible" means any personal property, including things in action, other than accounts, chattel paper, commercial tort claims, deposit accounts, documents, goods, instruments, investment property, letter-of-credit rights, letters of credit, money, and oil, gas, or other minerals before extraction. The term includes payment intangibles and software.

(43) "Good faith" means honesty in fact and the observance of reasonable commercial standards of fair dealing.

(44) "Goods" means all things that are movable when a security interest attaches. The term includes (i) fixtures, (ii) standing timber that is to be cut and removed under a conveyance or contract for sale, (iii) the unborn young of animals, (iv) crops grown, growing, or to be grown, even if the crops are produced on trees, vines, or bushes, and (v) manufactured homes. The term also includes a computer program embedded in goods and any supporting information provided in connection with a transaction relating to the program if (i) the program is associated with the goods in such a manner that it customarily is considered part of the goods, or (ii) by becoming the owner of the goods, a person acquires a right to use the program in connection with the goods. The term does not include a computer program embedded in goods that consist solely of the medium in which the program is embedded. The term also does not include accounts, chattel paper, commercial tort claims, deposit accounts, documents, general intangibles, instruments, investment property, letter-of-credit rights, letters of credit, money, or oil, gas, or other minerals before extraction.

(45) "Governmental unit" means a subdivision, agency, department, county, parish, municipality, or other unit of the government of the United States, a State, or a foreign country. The term includes an organization having a separate corporate existence if the organization is eligible to issue debt on which interest is exempt from income taxation under the laws of the United States.

(46) "Health-care-insurance receivable" means an interest in or claim under a policy of insurance which is a right to payment of a monetary obligation for health-care goods or servies provided.

(47) "Instrument" means a negotiable instrument or any other writing that evidences a right to the payment of a monetary obligation, is not itself a security agreement or lease, and is of a type that in ordinary course of business is transferred by delivery with any necessary indorsement or assignment. The term does not include (i) investment property, (ii) letters of credit, or (iii) writings that evidence a right to payment arising out of the use of a credit or charge card or information contained on or for use with the card.

(48) "Inventory" means goods, other than farm products, which:

(A) are leased by a person as lessor;

(B) are held by a person for sale or lease or to be furnished under a contract of service;

(C) are furnished by a person under a contract of service; or

(D) consist of raw materials, work in process, or materials used or consumed in a business.

(49) "Investment property" means a security, whether certificated or uncertificated, security entitlement, securities account, commodity contract, or commodity account.

(50) "Jurisdiction of organization", with respect to a registered organization, means the jurisdiction under whose law the organization is organized.

(51) "Letter-of-credit right" means a right to payment or performance under a letter of credit, whether or not the beneficiary has demanded or is at the time entitled to demand payment or performance. The term does not include the right of a beneficiary to demand payment or performance under a letter of credit.

(52) "Lien creditor" means:

(A) a creditor that has acquired a lien on the property involved by attachment, levy, or the like;

(B) an assignee for benefit of creditors from the time of assignment;

(C) a trustee in bankruptcy from the date of the filing of the petition; or

(D) a receiver in equity from the time of appointment.

(53) "Manufactured home" means a structure, transportable in one or more sections, which, in the traveling mode, is eight body feet or more in width or 40 body feet or more in length, or, when erected on site, is 320 or more square feet, and which is built on a permanent chassis and designed to be used as a dwelling with or without a permanent foundation when connected to the required utilities, and includes the plumbing, heating, air-conditioning, and electrical systems contained therein. The term includes any structure that meets all of the requirements of this paragraph except the size requirements and with respect to which the manufacturer voluntarily files a certification required by the United States Secretary of Housing and Urban Development and complies with the standards established under Title 42 of the United States Code.

(54) "Manufactured-home transaction" means a secured transaction:

(A) that creates a purchase-money security interest in a manufactured home, other than a manufactured home held as inventory; or

(B) in which a manufactured home, other than a manufactured home held as inventory, is the primary collateral.

(55) "Mortgage" means a consensual interest in real property, including fixtures, which secures payment or performance of an obligation.

(56) "New debtor" means a person that becomes bound as debtor under Section 9–203(d) by a security agreement previously entered into by another person.

(57) "New value" means (i) money, (ii) money's worth in property, services, or new credit, or (iii) release by a transferee of an interest in property previously transferred to the transferee.

The term does not include an obligation substituted for another obligation.

(58) "Noncash proceeds" means proceeds other than cash proceeds.

(59) "Obligor" means a person that, with respect to an obligation secured by a security interest in or an agricultural lien on the collateral, (i) owes payment or other performance of the obligation, (ii) has provided property other than the collateral to secure payment or other performance of the obligation, or (iii) is otherwise accountable in whole or in part for payment or other performance of the obligation. The term does not include issuers or nominated persons under a letter of credit.

(60) "Original debtor", except as used in Section 9–310(c), means a person that, as debtor, entered into a security agreement to which a new debtor has become bound under Section 9–203(d).

(61) "Payment intangible" means a general intangible under which the account debtor's principal obligation is a monetary obligation.

(62) "Person related to", with respect to an individual, means:

(A) the spouse of the individual;

(B) a brother, brother-in-law, sister, or sister-in-law of the individual;

(C) an ancestor or lineal descendant of the individual or the individual's spouse; or

(D) any other relative, by blood or marriage, of the individual or the individual's spouse who shares the same home with the individual.

(63) "Person related to", with respect to an organization, means:

(A) a person directly or indirectly controlling, controlled by, or under common control with the organization;

(B) an officer or director of, or a person performing similar functions with respect to, the organization;

(C) an officer or director of, or a person performing similar functions with respect to, a person described in subparagraph (A);

(D) the spouse of an individual described in subparagraph (A), (B), or (C); or

(E) an individual who is related by blood or marriage to an individual described in subparagraph (A), (B), (C), or (D) and shares the same home with the individual.

(64) "Proceeds", except as used in Section 9–609(b), means the following property:

(A) whatever is acquired upon the sale, lease, license, exchange, or other disposition of collateral;

(B) whatever is collected on, or distributed on account of, collateral;

(C) rights arising out of collateral;

(D) to the extent of the value of collateral, claims arising out of the loss, nonconformity, or interference with the use of, defects or infringement of rights in, or damage to, the collateral; or (E) to the extent of the value of collateral and to the extent payable to the debtor or the secured party, insurance payable by reason of the loss or nonconformity of, defects or infringement of rights in, or damage to, the collateral.

(65) "Promissory note" means an instrument that evidences a promise to pay a monetary obligation, does not evidence an order to pay, and does not contain an acknowledgment by a bank that the bank has received for deposit a sum of money or funds.

(66) "Proposal" means a record authenticated by a secured party which includes the terms on which the secured party is willing to accept collateral in full or partial satisfaction of the obligation it secures pursuant to Sections 9–620, 9–621, and 9–622.

(67) "Public-finance transaction" means a secured transaction in connection with which:

(A) debt securities are issued;

(B) all or a portion of the securities issued have an initial stated maturity of at least 20 years; and

(C) the debtor, obligor, secured party, account debtor or other person obligated on collateral, assignor or assignee of a secured obligation, or assignor or assignee of a security interest is a State or a governmental unit of a State.

(68) "Pursuant to commitment", with respect to an advance made or other value given by a secured party, means pursuant to the secured party's obligation, whether or not a subsequent event of default or other event not within the secured party's control has relieved or may relieve the secured party from its obligation.

(69) "Record", except as used in "for record", "of record", "record or legal title", and "record owner", means information that is inscribed on a tangible medium or which is stored in an electronic or other medium and is retrievable in perceivable form.

(70) "Registered organization" means an organization organized solely under the law of a single State or the United States and as to which the State or the United States must maintain a public record showing the organization to have been organized.

(71) "Secondary obligor" means an obligor to the extent that:

(A) the obligor's obligation is secondary; or

(B) the obligor has a right of recourse with respect to an obligation secured by collateral against the debtor, another obligor, or property of either.

(72) "Secured party" means:

(A) a person in whose favor a security interest is created or provided for under a security agreement, whether or not any obligation to be secured is outstanding;

(B) a person that holds an agricultural lien;

(C) a consignor;

(D) a person to which accounts, chattel paper, payment intangibles, or promissory notes have been sold;

(E) a trustee, indenture trustee, agent, collateral agent, or other representative in whose favor a security interest or agricultural lien is created or provided for; or

(F) a person that holds a security interest arising under Section 2–401, 2–505, 2–711(3), 2A–508(5), 4–210, or 5–118.

(73) "Security agreement" means an agreement that creates or provides for a security interest.

(74) "Send", in connection with a record or notification, means:

(A) to deposit in the mail, deliver for transmission, or transmit by any other usual means of communication, with postage or cost of transmission provided for, addressed to any address reasonable under the circumstances; or

(B) to cause the record or notification to be received within the timce that it would have been received if properly sent under subparagraph (A).

(75) "Software" means a computer program and any supporting information provided in connection with a transaction relating to the program. The term does not include a computer program that is included in the definition of goods.

(76) "State" means a State of the United States, the District of Columbia, Puerto Rico, the United States Virgin Islands, or any territory or insular possession subject to the jurisdiction of the United States.

(77) "Supporting obligation" means a letter-of-credit right or secondary obligation that supports the payment or performance of an account, chattel paper, a document, a general intangible, an instrument, or investment property.

(78) "Tangible chattel paper" means chattel paper evidenced by a record or records consisting of information that is inscribed on a tangible medium.

(79) "Termination statement" means an amendment of a financing statement which:

(A) identifies, by its file number, the initial financing statement to which it relates; and

(B) indicates either that it is a termination statement or that the identified financing statement is no longer effective.

(80) "Transmitting utility" means a person primarily engaged in the business of:

(A) operating a railroad, subway, street railway, or trolley bus;

(B) transmitting communications electrically, electromagnetically, or by light;

(C) transmitting goods by pipeline or sewer; or

(D) transmitting or producing and transmitting electricity, steam, gas, or water.

(b) The following definitions in other articles apply to this article:

"Applicant." Section 5–102

"Beneficiary." Section 5–102

"Broker." Section 8–102

"Certificated security." Section 8–102

"Check." Section 3–104

"Clearing corporation." Section 8–102

"Contract for sale." Section 2–106

"Customer." Section 4–104

"Entitlement holder." Section 8–102

"Financial asset." Section 8–102

"Holder in due course." Section 3–302

"Issuer" (with respect to a letter of credit or letter-of-credit right). Section 5–102

"Issuer" (with respect to a security). Section 8–201

"Lease." Section 2A–103

"Lease agreement." Section 2A–103

"Lease contract." Section 2A–103

"Leasehold interest." Section 2A–103

"Lessee." Section 2A–103

"Lessee in ordinary course of business." Section 2A–103

"Lessor." Section 2A–103

"Lessor's residual interest." Section 2A–103

"Letter of credit." Section 5–102

"Merchant." Section 2–104

"Negotiable instrument." Section 3–104

"Nominated person." Section 5–102

"Note." Section 3–104

"Proceeds of a letter of credit." Section 5–114

"Prove." Section 3–103

"Sale." Section 2–106

"Securities account." Section 8–501

"Securities intermediary." Section 8–102

"Security." Section 8–102

"Security certificate." Section 8–102

"Security entitlement." Section 8–102

"Uncertificated security." Section 8–102

(c) Article 1 contains general definitions and principles of construction and interpretation applicable throughout this article.

Amended in 1999 and 2000.

§9–103. Purchase-Money Security Interest; Application of Payments; Burden of Establishing.

(a) In this section:

(1) "purchase-money collateral" means goods or software that secures a purchase-money obligation incurred with respect to that collateral; and

(2) "purchase-money obligation" means an obligation of an obligor incurred as all or part of the price of the collateral or for value given to enable the debtor to acquire rights in or the use of the collateral if the value is in fact so used.

(b) A security interest in goods is a purchase-money security interest:

(1) to the extent that the goods are purchase-money collateral with respect to that security interest;

(2) if the security interest is in inventory that is or was purchase-money collateral, also to the extent that the security interest secures a purchase-money obligation incurred with respect to other inventory in which the secured party holds or held a purchase-money security interest; and

(3) also to the extent that the security interest secures a purchase-money obligation incurred with respect to software in which the secured party holds or held a purchase-money security interest.

(c) A security interest in software is a purchase-money security interest to the extent that the security interest also secures a purchase-money obligation incurred with respect to goods in which the secured party holds or held a purchase-money security interest if:

(1) the debtor acquired its interest in the software in an integrated transaction in which it acquired an interest in the goods; and

(2) the debtor acquired its interest in the software for the principal purpose of using the software in the goods.

(d) The security interest of a consignor in goods that are the subject of a consignment is a purchase-money security interest in inventory.

(e) In a transaction other than a consumer-goods transaction, if the extent to which a security interest is a purchase-money security interest depends on the application of a payment to a particular obligation, the payment must be applied:

(1) in accordance with any reasonable method of application to which the parties agree;

(2) in the absence of the parties' agreement to a reasonable method, in accordance with any intention of the obligor manifested at or before the time of payment; or

(3) in the absence of an agreement to a reasonable method and a timely manifestation of the obligor's intention, in the following order:

(A) to obligations that are not secured; and

(B) if more than one obligation is secured, to obligations secured by purchase-money security interests in the order in which those obligations were incurred.

(f) In a transaction other than a consumer-goods transaction, a purchase-money security interest does not lose its status as such, even if:

(1) the purchase-money collateral also secures an obligation that is not a purchase-money obligation;

(2) collateral that is not purchase-money collateral also secures the purchase-money obligation; or

(3) the purchase-money obligation has been renewed, refinanced, consolidated, or restructured.

(g) In a transaction other than a consumer-goods transaction, a secured party claiming a purchase-money security interest has the burden of establishing the extent to which the security interest is a purchase-money security interest.

(h) The limitation of the rules in subsections (e), (f), and (g) to transactions other than consumer-goods transactions is intended to leave to the court the determination of the proper rules in consumer-goods transactions. The court may not infer from that limitation the nature of the proper rule in consumer-goods transactions and may continue to apply established approaches.

§9–104. Control of Deposit Account.

(a) A secured party has control of a deposit account if:

(1) the secured party is the bank with which the deposit account is maintained;

(2) the debtor, secured party, and bank have agreed in an authenticated record that the bank will comply with instructions originated by the secured party directing disposition of the funds in the deposit account without further consent by the debtor; or

(3) the secured party becomes the bank's customer with respect to the deposit account.

(b) A secured party that has satisfied subsection (a) has control, even if the debtor retains the right to direct the disposition of funds from the deposit account.

§9–105. Control of Electronic Chattel Paper.

A secured party has control of electronic chattel paper if the record or records comprising the chattel paper are created, stored, and assigned in such a manner that:

(1) a single authoritative copy of the record or records exists which is unique, identifiable and, except as otherwise provided in paragraphs (4), (5), and (6), unalterable;

(2) the authoritative copy identifies the secured party as the assignee of the record or records;

(3) the authoritative copy is communicated to and maintained by the secured party or its designated custodian;

(4) copies or revisions that add or change an identified assignee of the authoritative copy can be made only with the participation of the secured party;

(5) each copy of the authoritative copy and any copy of a copy is readily identifiable as a copy that is not the authoritative copy; and

(6) any revision of the authoritative copy is readily identifiable as an authorized or unauthorized revision.

§9–106. Control of Investment Property.

(a) A person has control of a certificated security, uncertificated security, or security entitlement as provided in Section 8–106.

(b) A secured party has control of a commodity contract if:

(1) the secured party is the commodity intermediary with which the commodity contract is carried; or

(2) the commodity customer, secured party, and commodity intermediary have agreed that the commodity intermediary will apply any value distributed on account of the commodity contract as directed by the secured party without further consent by the commodity customer.

(c) A secured party having control of all security entitlements or commodity contracts carried in a securities account or commodity account has control over the securities account or commodity account.

§9–107. Control of Letter-of-Credit Right.

A secured party has control of a letter-of-credit right to the extent of any right to payment or performance by the issuer or any nominated person if the issuer or nominated person has consented to an assignment of proceeds of the letter of credit under Section 5–114 (c) or otherwise applicable law or practice.

§9–108. Sufficiency of Description.

(a) Except as otherwise provided in subsections (c), (d), and (e), a description of personal or real property is sufficient, whether or not it is specific, if it reasonably identifies what is described.

(b) Except as otherwise provided in subsection (d), a description of collateral reasonably identifies the collateral if it identifies the collateral by:

(1) specific listing;

(2) category;

(3) except as otherwise provided in subsection (e), a type of collateral defined in [the Uniform Commercial Code];

(4) quantity;

(5) computational or allocational formula or procedure; or

(6) except as otherwise provided in subsection (c), any other method, if the identity of the collateral is objectively determinable.

(c) A description of collateral as "all the debtor's assets" or "all the debtor's personal property" or using words of similar import does not reasonably identify the collateral.

(d) Except as otherwise provided in subsection (e), a description of a security entitlement, securities account, or commodity account is sufficient if it describes:

(1) the collateral by those terms or as investment property; or

(2) the underlying financial asset or commodity contract.

(e) A description only by type of collateral defined in [the Uniform Commercial Code] is an insufficient description of:

(1) a commercial tort claim; or

(2) in a consumer transaction, consumer goods, a security entitlement, a securities account, or a commodity account.

[Subpart 2. Applicability of Article]

§9–109. Scope.

(a) Except as otherwise provided in subsections (c) and (d), this article applies to:

(1) a transaction, regardless of its form, that creates a security interest in personal property or fixtures by contract;

(2) an agricultural lien;

(3) a sale of accounts, chattel paper, payment intangibles, or promissory notes;

(4) a consignment;

(5) a security interest arising under Section 2–401, 2–505, 2–711 (3), or 2A–508(5), as provided in Section 9–110; and

(6) a security interest arising under Section 4–210 or 5–118.

(b) The application of this article to a security interest in a secured obligation is not affected by the fact that the obligation is itself secured by a transaction or interest to which this article does not apply.

(c) This article does not apply to the extent that:

(1) a statute, regulation, or treaty of the United States preempts this article;

(2) another statute of this State expressly governs the creation, perfection, priority, or enforcement of a security interest created by this State or a governmental unit of this State;

(3) a statute of another State, a foreign country, or a governmental unit of another State or a foreign country, other than a statute generally applicable to security interests, expressly governs creation, perfection, priority, or enforcement of a security interest created by the State, country, or governmental unit; or

(4) the rights of a transferee beneficiary or nominated person under a letter of credit are independent and superior under Section 5–114.

(d) This article does not apply to:

(1) a landlord's lien, other than an agricultural lien;

(2) a lien, other than an agricultural lien, given by statute or other rule of law for services or materials, but Section 9–333 applies with respect to priority of the lien;

(3) an assignment of a claim for wages, salary, or other compensation of an employee;

(4) a sale of accounts, chattel paper, payment intangibles, or promissory notes as part of a sale of the business out of which they arose;

(5) an assignment of accounts, chattel paper, payment intangibles, or promissory notes which is for the purpose of collection only;

(6) an assignment of a right to payment under a contract to an assignee that is also obligated to perform under the contract;

(7) an assignment of a single account, payment intangible, or promissory note to an assignee in full or partial satisfaction of a preexisting indebtedness;

(8) a transfer of an interest in or an assignment of a claim under a policy of insurance, other than an assignment by or to a health-care provider of a health-care-insurance receivable and any subsequent assignment of the right to payment, but Sections 9–315 and 9–322 apply with respect to proceeds and priorities in proceeds;

(9) an assignment of a right represented by a judgment, other than a judgment taken on a right to payment that was collateral;

(10) a right of recoupment or set-off, but:

(A) Section 9–340 applies with respect to the effectiveness of rights of recoupment or set-off against deposit accounts; and

(B) Section 9–404 applies with respect to defenses or claims of an account debtor;

(11) the creation or transfer of an interest in or lien on real property, including a lease or rents thereunder, except to the extent that provision is made for:

(A) liens on real property in Sections 9–203 and 9–308;

(B) fixtures in Section 9–334;

(C) fixture filings in Sections 9–501, 9–502, 9–512, 9–516, and 9–519; and

(D) security agreements covering personal and real property in Section 9–604;

(12) an assignment of a claim arising in tort, other than a commercial tort claim, but Sections 9–315 and 9–322 apply with respect to proceeds and priorities in proceeds; or

(13) an assignment of a deposit account in a consumer transaction, but Sections 9–315 and 9–322 apply with respect to proceeds and priorities in proceeds.

§9–110. Security Interests Arising under Article 2 or 2A.

A security interest arising under Section 2–401, 2–505, 2–711(3), or 2A–508(5) is subject to this article. However, until the debtor obtains possession of the goods:

(1) the security interest is enforceable, even if Section 9–203(b)(3) has not been satisfied;

(2) filing is not required to perfect the security interest;

(3) the rights of the secured party after default by the debtor are governed by Article 2 or 2A; and

(4) the security interest has priority over a conflicting security interest created by the debtor.

PART 2   Effectiveness of Security Agreement; Attachment of Security Interest; Rights of Parties to Security Agreement

[Subpart 1. Effectiveness and Attachment]

§9–201. General Effectiveness of Security Agreement.

(a) Except as otherwise provided in [the Uniform Commercial Code], a security agreement is effective according to its terms between the parties, against purchasers of the collateral, and against creditors.

(b) A transaction subject to this article is subject to any applicable rule of law which establishes a different rule for consumers and [insert reference to (i) any other statute or regulation that regulates the rates, charges, agreements, and practices for loans, credit sales, or other extensions of credit and (ii) any consumer-protection statute or regulation].

(c) In case of conflict between this article and a rule of law, statute, or regulation described in subsection (b), the rule of law, statute, or regulation controls. Failure to comply with a statute or regulation described in subsection (b) has only the effect the statute or regulation specifies.

(d) This article does not:

(1) validate any rate, charge, agreement, or practice that violates a rule of law, statute, or regulation described in subsection (b); or

(2) extend the application of the rule of law, statute, or regulation to a transaction not otherwise subject to it.

§9–202. Title to Collateral Immaterial.

Except as otherwise provided with respect to consignments or sales of accounts, chattel paper, payment intangibles, or promissory notes, the provisions of this article with regard to rights and obligations apply whether title to collateral is in the secured party or the debtor.

§9–203. Attachment and Enforceability of Security Interest; Proceeds; Supporting Obligations; Formal Requisites.

(a) A security interest attaches to collateral when it becomes enforceable against the debtor with respect to the collateral, unless an agreement expressly postpones the time of attachment.

(b) Except as otherwise provided in subsections (c) through (i), a security interest is enforceable against the debtor and third parties with respect to the collateral only if:

(1) value has been given;

(2) the debtor has rights in the collateral or the power to transfer rights in the collateral to a secured party; and

(3) one of the following conditions is met:

(A) the debtor has authenticated a security agreement that provides a description of the collateral and, if the security interest covers timber to be cut, a description of the land concerned;

(B) the collateral is not a certificated security and is in the possession of the secured party under Section 9–313 pursuant to the debtor's security agreement;

(C) the collateral is a certificated security in registered form and the security certificate has been delivered to the secured party under Section 8–301 pursuant to the debtor's security agreement; or

(D) the collateral is deposit accounts, electronic chattel paper, investment property, or letter-of-credit rights, and the secured party has control under Section 9–104, 9–105, 9–106, or 9–107 pursuant to the debtor's security agreement.

(c) Subsection (b) is subject to Section 4–210 on the security interest of a collecting bank, Section 5–118 on the security interest of a letter-of-credit issuer or nominated person, Section 9–110 on a security interest arising under Article 2 or 2A, and Section 9–206 on security interests in investment property.

(d) A person becomes bound as debtor by a security agreement entered into by another person if, by operation of law other than this article or by contract:

(1) the security agreement becomes effective to create a security interest in the person's property; or

(2) the person becomes generally obligated for the obligations of the other person, including the obligation secured under the security agreement, and acquires or succeeds to all or substantially all of the assets of the other person.

(e) If a new debtor becomes bound as debtor by a security agreement entered into by another person:

(1) the agreement satisfies subsection (b)(3) with respect to existing or after-acquired property of the new debtor to the extent the property is described in the agreement; and

(2) another agreement is not necessary to make a security interest in the property enforceable.

(f) The attachment of a security interest in collateral gives the secured party the rights to proceeds provided by Section 9–315 and is also attachment of a security interest in a supporting obligation for the collateral.

(g) The attachment of a security interest in a right to payment or performance secured by a security interest or other lien on personal or real property is also attachment of a security interest in the security interest, mortgage, or other lien.

(h) The attachment of a security interest in a securities account is also attachment of a security interest in the security entitlements carried in the securities account.

(i) The attachment of a security interest in a commodity account is also attachment of a security interest in the commodity contracts carried in the commodity account.

§9–204. After-Acquired Property; Future Advances.

(a) Except as otherwise provided in subsection (b), a security agreement may create or provide for a security interest in after-acquired collateral.

(b) A security interest does not attach under a term constituting an after-acquired property clause to:

(1) consumer goods, other than an accession when given as additional security, unless the debtor acquires rights in them within 10 days after the secured party gives value; or

(2) a commercial tort claim.

(c) A security agreement may provide that collateral secures, or that accounts, chattel paper, payment intangibles, or promissory notes are sold in connection with, future advances or other value, whether or not the advances or value are given pursuant to commitment.

§9–205. Use or Disposition of Collateral Permissible.

(a) A security interest is not invalid or fraudulent against creditors solely because:

(1) the debtor has the right or ability to:

(A) use, commingle, or dispose of all or part of the collateral, including returned or repossessed goods;

(B) collect, compromise, enforce, or otherwise deal with collateral;

(C) accept the return of collateral or make repossessions; or

(D) use, commingle, or dispose of proceeds; or

(2) the secured party fails to require the debtor to account for proceeds or replace collateral.

(b) This section does not relax the requirements of possession if attachment, perfection, or enforcement of a security interest depends upon possession of the collateral by the secured party.

§9–206.   Security Interest Arising in Purchase or Delivery of Financial Asset.

(a) A security interest in favor of a securities intermediary attaches to a person's security entitlement if:

(1) the person buys a financial asset through the securities intermediary in a transaction in which the person is obligated to pay the purchase price to the securities intermediary at the time of the purchase; and

(2) the securities intermediary credits the financial asset to the buyer's securities account before the buyer pays the securities intermediary.

(b) The security interest described in subsection (a) secures the person's obligation to pay for the financial asset.

(c) A security interest in favor of a person that delivers a certificated security or other financial asset represented by a writing attaches to the security or other financial asset if:

(1) the security or other financial asset:

(A) in the ordinary course of business is transferred by delivery with any necessary indorsement or assignment; and

(B) is delivered under an agreement between persons in the business of dealing with such securities or financial assets; and

(2) the agreement calls for delivery against payment.

(d) The security interest described in subsection (c) secures the obligation to make payment for the delivery.

[Subpart 2. Rights and Duties]

§9–207.   Rights and Duties of Secured Party Having Possession or Control of Collateral.

(a) Except as otherwise provided in subsection (d), a secured party shall use reasonable care in the custody and preservation of collateral in the secured party's possession. In the case of chattel paper or an instrument, reasonable care includes taking necessary steps to preserve rights against prior parties unless otherwise agreed.

(b) Except as otherwise provided in subsection (d), if a secured party has possession of collateral:

(1) reasonable expenses, including the cost of insurance and payment of taxes or other charges, incurred in the custody, preservation, use, or operation of the collateral are chargeable to the debtor and are secured by the collateral;

(2) the risk of accidental loss or damage is on the debtor to the extent of a deficiency in any effective insurance coverage;

(3) the secured party shall keep the collateral identifiable, but fungible collateral may be commingled; and

(4) the secured party may use or operate the collateral:

(A) for the purpose of preserving the collateral or its value;

(B) as permitted by an order of a court having competent jurisdiction; or

(C) except in the case of consumer goods, in the manner and to the extent agreed by the debtor.

(c) Except as otherwise provided in subsection (d), a secured party having possession of collateral or control of collateral under Section 9–104, 9–105, 9–106, or 9–107:

(1) may hold as additional security any proceeds, except money or funds, received from the collateral;

(2) shall apply money or funds received from the collateral to reduce the secured obligation, unless remitted to the debtor; and

(3) may create a security interest in the collateral.

(d) If the secured party is a buyer of accounts, chattel paper, payment intangibles, or promissory notes or a consignor:

(1) subsection (a) does not apply unless the secured party is entitled under an agreement:

(A) to charge back uncollected collateral; or

(B) otherwise to full or limited recourse against the debtor or a secondary obligor based on the nonpayment or other default of an account debtor or other obligor on the collateral; and

(2) subsections (b) and (c) do not apply.

§9–208.   Additional Duties of Secured Party Having Control of Collateral.

(a) This section applies to cases in which there is no outstanding secured obligation and the secured party is not committed to make advances, incur obligations, or otherwise give value.

(b) Within 10 days after receiving an authenticated demand by the debtor:

(1) a secured party having control of a deposit account under Section 9–104(a)(2) shall send to the bank with which the deposit account is maintained an authenticated statement that releases the bank from any further obligation to comply with instructions originated by the secured party;

(2) a secured party having control of a deposit account under Section 9–104(a)(3) shall:

(A) pay the debtor the balance on deposit in the deposit account; or

(B) transfer the balance on deposit into a deposit account in the debtor's name;

(3) a secured party, other than a buyer, having control of electronic chattel paper under Section 9–105 shall:

(A) communicate the authoritative copy of the electronic chattel paper to the debtor or its designated custodian;

(B) if the debtor designates a custodian that is the designated custodian with which the authoritative copy of the electronic chattel paper is maintained for the secured party, communicate to the custodian an authenticated record releasing the designated custodian from any further obligation to comply with instructions originated by the secured party and instructing the custodian to comply with instructions originated by the debtor; and

(C) take appropriate action to enable the debtor or its designated custodian to make copies of or revisions to the authoritative copy which add or change an identified assignee of the authoritative copy without the consent of the secured party;

(4) a secured party having control of investment property under Section 8–106(d)(2) or 9–106(b) shall send to the securities intermediary or commodity intermediary with which the security entitlement or commodity contract is maintained an authenticated record that releases the securities intermediary or commodity intermediary from any further obligation to comply with entitlement orders or directions originated by the secured party; and

(5) a secured party having control of a letter-of-credit right under Section 9–107 shall send to each person having an unfulfilled obligation to pay or deliver proceeds of the letter of credit to the secured party an authenticated release from any further obligation to pay or deliver proceeds of the letter of credit to the secured party.

§9–209.   Duties of Secured Party If Account Debtor Has Been Notified of Assignment.

(a) Except as otherwise provided in subsection (c), this section applies if:

(1) there is no outstanding secured obligation; and

(2) the secured party is not committed to make advances, incur obligations, or otherwise give value.

(b) Within 10 days after receiving an authenticated demand by the debtor, a secured party shall send to an account debtor that has received notification of an assignment to the secured party as assignee under Section 9–406(a) an authenticated record that releases the account debtor from any further obligation to the secured party.

(c) This section does not apply to an assignment constituting the sale of an account, chattel paper, or payment intangible.

§9–210.   Request for Accounting; Request Regarding List of Collateral or Statement of Account.

(a) In this section:

(1) "Request" means a record of a type described in paragraph (2), (3), or (4).

(2) "Request for an accounting" means a record authenticated by a debtor requesting that the recipient provide an accounting of the unpaid obligations secured by collateral and reasonably identifying the transaction or relationship that is the subject of the request.

(3) "Request regarding a list of collateral" means a record authenticated by a debtor requesting that the recipient approve or correct a list of what the debtor believes to be the collateral securing an obligation and reasonably identifying the transaction or relationship that is the subject of the request.

(4) "Request regarding a statement of account" means a record authenticated by a debtor requesting that the recipient approve or correct a statement indicating what the debtor believes to be the aggregate amount of unpaid obligations secured by collateral as of a specified date and reasonably identifying the transaction or relationship that is the subject of the request.

(b) Subject to subsections (c), (d), (e), and (f), a secured party, other than a buyer of accounts, chattel paper, payment intangibles, or promissory notes or a consignor, shall comply with a request within 14 days after receipt:

(1) in the case of a request for an accounting, by authenticating and sending to the debtor an accounting; and

(2) in the case of a request regarding a list of collateral or a request regarding a statement of account, by authenticating and sending to the debtor an approval or correction.

(c) A secured party that claims a security interest in all of a particular type of collateral owned by the debtor may comply with a request regarding a list of collateral by sending to the debtor an authenticated record including a statement to that effect within 14 days after receipt.

(d) A person that receives a request regarding a list of collateral, claims no interest in the collateral when it receives the request, and claimed an interest in the collateral at an earlier time shall comply with the request within 14 days after receipt by sending to the debtor an authenticated record:

(1) disclaiming any interest in the collateral; and

(2) if known to the recipient, providing the name and mailing address of any assignee of or successor to the recipient's interest in the collateral.

(e) A person that receives a request for an accounting or a request regarding a statement of account, claims no interest in the obligations when it receives the request, and claimed an interest in the obligations at an earlier time shall comply with the request within 14 days after receipt by sending to the debtor an authenticated record:

(1) disclaiming any interest in the obligations; and

(2) if known to the recipient, providing the name and mailing address of any assignee of or successor to the recipient's interest in the obligations.

(f) A debtor is entitled without charge to one response to a request under this section during any six-month period. The secured party may require payment of a charge not exceeding $25 for each additional response.

As amended in 1999.

PART 3   Perfection and Priority

[Subpart 1. Law Governing Perfection and Priority]

§9–301.   Law Governing Perfection and Priority of Security Interests.

Except as otherwise provided in Sections 9–303 through 9–306, the following rules determine the law governing perfection, the effect of perfection or nonperfection, and the priority of a security interest in collateral:

(1) Except as otherwise provided in this section, while a debtor is located in a jurisdiction, the local law of that jurisdiction governs perfection, the effect of perfection or nonperfection, and the priority of a security interest in collateral.

(2) While collateral is located in a jurisdiction, the local law of that jurisdiction governs perfection, the effect of perfection or nonperfection, and the priority of a possessory security interest in that collateral.

(3) Except as otherwise provided in paragraph (4), while negotiable documents, goods, instruments, money, or tangible chattel paper is located in a jurisdiction, the local law of that jurisdiction governs:

(A) perfection of a security interest in the goods by filing a fixture filing;

(B) perfection of a security interest in timber to be cut; and

(C) the effect of perfection or nonperfection and the priority of a nonpossessory security interest in the collateral.

(4) The local law of the jurisdiction in which the wellhead or minehead is located governs perfection, the effect of perfection or nonperfection, and the priority of a security interest in as-extracted collateral.

§9–302. Law Governing Perfection and Priority of Agricultural Liens.

While farm products are located in a jurisdiction, the local law of that jurisdiction governs perfection, the effect of perfection or nonperfection, and the priority of an agricultural lien on the farm products.

§9–303. Law Governing Perfection and Priority of Security Interests in Goods Covered by a Certificate of Title.

(a) This section applies to goods covered by a certificate of title, even if there is no other relationship between the jurisdiction under whose certificate of title the goods are covered and the goods or the debtor.

(b) Goods become covered by a certificate of title when a valid application for the certificate of title and the applicable fee are delivered to the appropriate authority. Goods cease to be covered by a certificate of title at the earlier of the time the certificate of title ceases to be effective under the law of the issuing jurisdiction or the time the goods become covered subsequently by a certificate of title issued by another jurisdiction.

(c) The local law of the jurisdiction under whose certificate of title the goods are covered governs perfection, the effect of perfection or nonperfection, and the priority of a security interest in goods covered by a certificate of title from the time the goods become covered by the certificate of title until the goods cease to be covered by the certificate of title.

§9–304. Law Governing Perfection and Priority of Security Interests in Deposit Accounts.

(a) The local law of a bank's jurisdiction governs perfection, the effect of perfection or nonperfection, and the priority of a security interest in a deposit account maintained with that bank.

(b) The following rules determine a bank's jurisdiction for purposes of this part:

(1) If an agreement between the bank and the debtor governing the deposit account expressly provides that a particular jurisdiction is the bank's jurisdiction for purposes of this part, this article, or [the Uniform Commercial Code], that jurisdiction is the bank's jurisdiction.

(2) If paragraph (1) does not apply and an agreement between the bank and its customer governing the deposit account expressly provides that the agreement is governed by the law of a particular jurisdiction, that jurisdiction is the bank's jurisdiction.

(3) If neither paragraph (1) nor paragraph (2) applies and an agreement between the bank and its customer governing the deposit account expressly provides that the deposit account is maintained at an office in a particular jurisdiction, that jurisdiction is the bank's jurisdiction.

(4) If none of the preceding paragraphs applies, the bank's jurisdiction is the jurisdiction in which the office identified in an account statement as the office serving the customer's account is located.

(5) If none of the preceding paragraphs applies, the bank's jurisdiction is the jurisdiction in which the chief executive office of the bank is located.

§9–305. Law Governing Perfection and Priority of Security Interests in Investment Property.

(a) Except as otherwise provided in subsection (c), the following rules apply:

(1) While a security certificate is located in a jurisdiction, the local law of that jurisdiction governs perfection, the effect of perfection or nonperfection, and the priority of a security interest in the certificated security represented thereby.

(2) The local law of the issuer's jurisdiction as specified in Section 8–110(d) governs perfection, the effect of perfection or nonperfection, and the priority of a security interest in an uncertificated security.

(3) The local law of the securities intermediary's jurisdiction as specified in Section 8–110(e) governs perfection, the effect of perfection or nonperfection, and the priority of a security interest in a security entitlement or securities account.

(4) The local law of the commodity intermediary's jurisdiction governs perfection, the effect of perfection or nonperfection, and the priority of a security interest in a commodity contract or commodity account.

(b) The following rules determine a commodity intermediary's jurisdiction for purposes of this part:

(1) If an agreement between the commodity intermediary and commodity customer governing the commodity account expressly provides that a particular jurisdiction is the commodity intermediary's jurisdiction for purposes of this part, this article, or [the Uniform Commercial Code], that jurisdiction is the commodity intermediary's jurisdiction.

(2) If paragraph (1) does not apply and an agreement between the commodity intermediary and commodity customer governing the commodity account expressly provides that the agreement is governed by the law of a particular jurisdiction, that jurisdiction is the commodity intermediary's jurisdiction.

(3) If neither paragraph (1) nor paragraph (2) applies and an agreement between the commodity intermediary and commodity customer governing the commodity account expressly provides that the commodity account is maintained at an office in a particular jurisdiction, that jurisdiction is the commodity intermediary's jurisdiction.

(4) If none of the preceding paragraphs applies, the commodity intermediary's jurisdiction is the jurisdiction in which the office identified in an account statement as the office serving the commodity customer's account is located.

(5) If none of the preceding paragraphs applies, the commodity intermediary's jurisdiction is the jurisdiction in which the chief executive office of the commodity intermediary is located.

(c) The local law of the jurisdiction in which the debtor is located governs:

(1) perfection of a security interest in investment property by filing;

(2) automatic perfection of a security interest in investment property created by a broker or securities intermediary; and

(3) automatic perfection of a security interest in a commodity contract or commodity account created by a commodity intermediary.

§9–306. Law Governing Perfection and Priority of Security Interests in Letter-of-Credit Rights.

(a) Subject to subsection (c), the local law of the issuer's jurisdiction or a nominated person's jurisdiction governs perfection, the effect of perfection or nonperfection, and the priority of a security interest in a letter-of-credit right if the issuer's jurisdiction or nominated person's jurisdiction is a State.

(b) For purposes of this part, an issuer's jurisdiction or nominated person's jurisdiction is the jurisdiction whose law governs the liability of the issuer or nominated person with respect to the letter-of-credit right as provided in Section 5–116.

(c) This section does not apply to a security interest that is perfected only under Section 9–308(d).

§9–307. Location of Debtor.

(a) In this section, "place of business" means a place where a debtor conducts its affairs.

(b) Except as otherwise provided in this section, the following rules determine a debtor's location:

(1) A debtor who is an individual is located at the individual's principal residence.

(2) A debtor that is an organization and has only one place of business is located at its place of business.

(3) A debtor that is an organization and has more than one place of business is located at its chief executive office.

(c) Subsection (b) applies only if a debtor's residence, place of business, or chief executive office, as applicable, is located in a jurisdiction whose law generally requires information concerning the existence of a nonpossessory security interest to be made generally available in a filing, recording, or registration system as a condition or result of the security interest's obtaining priority over the rights of a lien creditor with respect to the collateral. If subsection (b) does not apply, the debtor is located in the District of Columbia.

(d) A person that ceases to exist, have a residence, or have a place of business continues to be located in the jurisdiction specified by subsections (b) and (c).

(e) A registered organization that is organized under the law of a State is located in that State.

(f) Except as otherwise provided in subsection (i), a registered organization that is organized under the law of the United States and a branch or agency of a bank that is not organized under the law of the United States or a State are located:

(1) in the State that the law of the United States designates, if the law designates a State of location;

(2) in the State that the registered organization, branch, or agency designates, if the law of the United States authorizes the registered organization, branch, or agency to designate its State of location; or

(3) in the District of Columbia, if neither paragraph (1) nor paragraph (2) applies.

(g) A registered organization continues to be located in the jurisdiction specified by subsection (e) or (f) notwithstanding:

(1) the suspension, revocation, forfeiture, or lapse of the registered organization's status as such in its jurisdiction of organization; or

(2) the dissolution, winding up, or cancellation of the existence of the registered organization.

(h) The United States is located in the District of Columbia.

(i) A branch or agency of a bank that is not organized under the law of the United States or a State is located in the State in which the branch or agency is licensed, if all branches and agencies of the bank are licensed in only one State.

(j) A foreign air carrier under the Federal Aviation Act of 1958, as amended, is located at the designated office of the agent upon which service of process may be made on behalf of the carrier.

(k) This section applies only for purposes of this part.

[Subpart 2. Perfection]

§9–308. When Security Interest or Agricultural Lien Is Perfected; Continuity of Perfection.

(a) Except as otherwise provided in this section and Section 9–309, a security interest is perfected if it has attached and all of the applicable requirements for perfection in Sections 9–310 through 9–316 have been satisfied. A security interest is perfected when it attaches if the applicable requirements are satisfied before the security interest attaches.

(b) An agricultural lien is perfected if it has become effective and all of the applicable requirements for perfection in Section 9–310 have been satisfied. An agricultural lien is perfected when it becomes effective if the applicable requirements are satisfied before the agricultural lien becomes effective.

(c) A security interest or agricultural lien is perfected continuously if it is originally perfected by one method under this article and is later perfected by another method under this article, without an intermediate period when it was unperfected.

(d) Perfection of a security interest in collateral also perfects a security interest in a supporting obligation for the collateral.

(e) Perfection of a security interest in a right to payment or performance also perfects a security interest in a security interest, mortgage, or other lien on personal or real property securing the right.

(f) Perfection of a security interest in a securities account also perfects a security interest in the security entitlements carried in the securities account.

(g) Perfection of a security interest in a commodity account also perfects a security interest in the commodity contracts carried in the commodity account.

Legislative Note: Any statute conflicting with subsection (e) must be made expressly subject to that subsection.

§9–309. Security Interest Perfected upon Attachment.

The following security interests are perfected when they attach:

(1) a purchase-money security interest in consumer goods, except as otherwise provided in Section 9–311(b) with respect to consumer goods that are subject to a statute or treaty described in Section 9–311(a);

(2) an assignment of accounts or payment intangibles which does not by itself or in conjunction with other assignments to the same assignee transfer a significant part of the assignor's outstanding accounts or payment intangibles;

(3) a sale of a payment intangible;

(4) a sale of a promissory note;

(5) a security interest created by the assignment of a health-care-insurance receivable to the provider of the health-care goods or services;

(6) a security interest arising under Section 2–401, 2–505, 2–711(3), or 2A–508(5), until the debtor obtains possession of the collateral;

(7) a security interest of a collecting bank arising under Section 4–210;

(8) a security interest of an issuer or nominated person arising under Section 5–118;

(9) a security interest arising in the delivery of a financial asset under Section 9–206(c);

(10) a security interest in investment property created by a broker or securities intermediary;

(11) a security interest in a commodity contract or a commodity account created by a commodity intermediary;

(12) an assignment for the benefit of all creditors of the transferor and subsequent transfers by the assignee thereunder; and

(13) a security interest created by an assignment of a beneficial interest in a decedent's estate; and

(14) a sale by an individual of an account that is a right to payment of winnings in a lottery or other game of chance.

§9–310. When Filing Required to Perfect Security Interest or Agricultural Lien; Security Interests and Agricultural Liens to Which Filing Provisions Do Not Apply.

(a) Except as otherwise provided in subsection (b) and Section 9–312(b), a financing statement must be filed to perfect all security interests and agricultural liens.

(b) The filing of a financing statement is not necessary to perfect a security interest:

(1) that is perfected under Section 9–308(d), (e), (f), or (g);

(2) that is perfected under Section 9–309 when it attaches;

(3) in property subject to a statute, regulation, or treaty described in Section 9–311(a);

(4) in goods in possession of a bailee which is perfected under Section 9–312(d)(1) or (2);

(5) in certificated securities, documents, goods, or instruments which is perfected without filing or possession under Section 9–312 (e), (f), or (g);

(6) in collateral in the secured party's possession under Section 9–313;

(7) in a certificated security which is perfected by delivery of the security certificate to the secured party under Section 9–313;

(8) in deposit accounts, electronic chattel paper, investment property, or letter-of-credit rights which is perfected by control under Section 9–314;

(9) in proceeds which is perfected under Section 9–315; or

(10) that is perfected under Section 9–316.

(c) If a secured party assigns a perfected security interest or agricultural lien, a filing under this article is not required to continue the perfected status of the security interest against creditors of and transferees from the original debtor.

§9–311. Perfection of Security Interests in Property Subject to Certain Statutes, Regulations, and Treaties.

(a) Except as otherwise provided in subsection (d), the filing of a financing statement is not necessary or effective to perfect a security interest in property subject to:

(1) a statute, regulation, or treaty of the United States whose requirements for a security interest's obtaining priority over the rights of a lien creditor with respect to the property preempt Section 9–310(a);

(2) [list any certificate-of-title statute covering automobiles, trailers, mobile homes, boats, farm tractors, or the like, which provides for a security interest to be indicated on the certificate as a condition or result of perfection, and any non-Uniform Commercial Code central filing statute]; or

(3) a certificate-of-title statute of another jurisdiction which provides for a security interest to be indicated on the certificate as a condition or result of the security interest's obtaining priority over the rights of a lien creditor with respect to the property.

(b) Compliance with the requirements of a statute, regulation, or treaty described in subsection (a) for obtaining priority over the rights of a lien creditor is equivalent to the filing of a financing statement under this article. Except as otherwise provided in subsection (d) and Sections 9–313 and 9–316(d) and (e) for goods covered by a certificate of title, a security interest in property subject to a statute, regulation, or treaty described in subsection (a) may be perfected only by compliance with those requirements, and a security interest so perfected remains perfected notwithstanding a change in the use or transfer of possession of the collateral.

(c) Except as otherwise provided in subsection (d) and Section 9–316(d) and (e), duration and renewal of perfection of a security interest perfected by compliance with the requirements prescribed by a statute, regulation, or treaty described in subsection (a) are governed by the statute, regulation, or treaty. In other respects, the security interest is subject to this article.

(d) During any period in which collateral subject to a statute specified in subsection (a)(2) is inventory held for sale or lease by a person or leased by that person as lessor and that person is in the business of selling goods of that kind, this section does not apply to a security interest in that collateral created by that person.

Legislative Note: This Article contemplates that perfection of a security interest in goods covered by a certificate of title occurs upon receipt by appropriate State officials of a properly tendered application for a certificate of title on which the security interest is to be indicated, without a relation back to an earlier time. States whose certificate-of-title statutes provide for perfection at a different time or contain a relation-back provision should amend the statutes accordingly.

§9–312. Perfection of Security Interests in Chattel Paper, Deposit Accounts, Documents, Goods Covered by Documents, Instruments, Investment Property, Letter-of-Credit Rights, and Money; Perfection by Permissive Filing; Temporary Perfection without Filing or Transfer of Possession.

(a) A security interest in chattel paper, negotiable documents, instruments, or investment property may be perfected by filing.

(b) Except as otherwise provided in Section 9–315(c) and (d) for proceeds:

(1) a security interest in a deposit account may be perfected only by control under Section 9–314;

(2) and except as otherwise provided in Section 9–308(d), a security interest in a letter-of-credit right may be perfected only by control under Section 9–314; and

(3) a security interest in money may be perfected only by the secured party's taking possession under Section 9–313.

(c) While goods are in the possession of a bailee that has issued a negotiable document covering the goods:

(1) a security interest in the goods may be perfected by perfecting a security interest in the document; and

(2) a security interest perfected in the document has priority over any security interest that becomes perfected in the goods by another method during that time.

(d) While goods are in the possession of a bailee that has issued a nonnegotiable document covering the goods, a security interest in the goods may be perfected by:

(1) issuance of a document in the name of the secured party;

(2) the bailee's receipt of notification of the secured party's interest; or

(3) filing as to the goods.

(e) A security interest in certificated securities, negotiable documents, or instruments is perfected without filing or the taking of possession for a period of 20 days from the time it attaches to the extent that it arises for new value given under an authenticated security agreement.

(f) A perfected security interest in a negotiable document or goods in possession of a bailee, other than one that has issued a negotiable document for the goods, remains perfected for 20 days without filing if the secured party makes available to the debtor the goods or documents representing the goods for the purpose of:

(1) ultimate sale or exchange; or

(2) loading, unloading, storing, shipping, transshipping, manufacturing, processing, or otherwise dealing with them in a manner preliminary to their sale or exchange.

(g) A perfected security interest in a certificated security or instrument remains perfected for 20 days without filing if the secured party delivers the security certificate or instrument to the debtor for the purpose of:

(1) ultimate sale or exchange; or

(2) presentation, collection, enforcement, renewal, or registration of transfer.

(h) After the 20-day period specified in subsection (e), (f), or (g) expires, perfection depends upon compliance with this article.

§9–313. When Possession by or Delivery to Secured Party Perfects Security Interest without Filing.

(a) Except as otherwise provided in subsection (b), a secured party may perfect a security interest in negotiable documents, goods, instruments, money, or tangible chattel paper by taking possession of the collateral. A secured party may perfect a security interest in certificated securities by taking delivery of the certificated securities under Section 8–301.

(b) With respect to goods covered by a certificate of title issued by this State, a secured party may perfect a security interest in the goods by taking possession of the goods only in the circumstances described in Section 9–316(d).

(c) With respect to collateral other than certificated securities and goods covered by a document, a secured party takes possession of collateral in the possession of a person other than the debtor, the secured party, or a lessee of the collateral from the debtor in the ordinary course of the debtor's business, when:

(1) the person in possession authenticates a record acknowledging that it holds possession of the collateral for the secured party's benefit; or

(2) the person takes possession of the collateral after having authenticated a record acknowledging that it will hold possession of collateral for the secured party's benefit.

(d) If perfection of a security interest depends upon possession of the collateral by a secured party, perfection occurs no earlier than the time the secured party takes possession and continues only while the secured party retains possession.

(e) A security interest in a certificated security in registered form is perfected by delivery when delivery of the certificated security occurs under Section 8–301 and remains perfected by delivery until the debtor obtains possession of the security certificate.

(f) A person in possession of collateral is not required to acknowledge that it holds possession for a secured party's benefit.

(g) If a person acknowledges that it holds possession for the secured party's benefit:

(1) the acknowledgment is effective under subsection (c) or Section 8–301(a), even if the acknowledgment violates the rights of a debtor; and

(2) unless the person otherwise agrees or law other than this article otherwise provides, the person does not owe any duty to the secured party and is not required to confirm the acknowledgment to another person.

(h) A secured party having possession of collateral does not relinquish possession by delivering the collateral to a person other than the debtor or a lessee of the collateral from the debtor in the ordinary course of the debtor's business if the person was instructed before the delivery or is instructed contemporaneously with the delivery:

(1) to hold possession of the collateral for the secured party's benefit; or

(2) to redeliver the collateral to the secured party.

(i) A secured party does not relinquish possession, even if a delivery under subsection (h) violates the rights of a debtor. A person to which collateral is delivered under subsection (h) does not owe any duty to the secured party and is not required to confirm the delivery to another person unless the person otherwise agrees or law other than this article otherwise provides.

§9–314. Perfection by Control.

(a) A security interest in investment property, deposit accounts, letter-of-credit rights, or electronic chattel paper may be perfected by control of the collateral under Section 9–104, 9–105, 9–106, or 9–107.

(b) A security interest in deposit accounts, electronic chattel paper, or letter-of-credit rights is perfected by control under Section 9–104, 9–105, or 9–107 when the secured party obtains control and remains perfected by control only while the secured party retains control.

(c) A security interest in investment property is perfected by control under Section 9–106 from the time the secured party obtains control and remains perfected by control until:

(1) the secured party does not have control; and

(2) one of the following occurs:

(A) if the collateral is a certificated security, the debtor has or acquires possession of the security certificate;

(B) if the collateral is an uncertificated security, the issuer has registered or registers the debtor as the registered owner; or

(C) if the collateral is a security entitlement, the debtor is or becomes the entitlement holder.

§9–315. Secured Party's Rights on Disposition of Collateral and in Proceeds.

(a) Except as otherwise provided in this article and in Section 2–403(2):

(1) a security interest or agricultural lien continues in collateral notwithstanding sale, lease, license, exchange, or other disposition thereof unless the secured party authorized the disposition free of the security interest or agricultural lien; and

(2) a security interest attaches to any identifiable proceeds of collateral.

(b) Proceeds that are commingled with other property are identifiable proceeds:

(1) if the proceeds are goods, to the extent provided by Section 9–336; and

(2) if the proceeds are not goods, to the extent that the secured party identifies the proceeds by a method of tracing, including application of equitable principles, that is permitted under law other than this article with respect to commingled property of the type involved.

(c) A security interest in proceeds is a perfected security interest if the security interest in the original collateral was perfected.

(d) A perfected security interest in proceeds becomes unperfected on the 21st day after the security interest attaches to the proceeds unless:

(1) the following conditions are satisfied:

(A) a filed financing statement covers the original collateral;

(B) the proceeds are collateral in which a security interest may be perfected by filing in the office in which the financing statement has been filed; and

(C) the proceeds are not acquired with cash proceeds;

(2) the proceeds are identifiable cash proceeds; or

(3) the security interest in the proceeds is perfected other than under subsection (c) when the security interest attaches to the proceeds or within 20 days thereafter.

(e) If a filed financing statement covers the original collateral, a security interest in proceeds which remains perfected under subsection (d)(1) becomes unperfected at the later of:

(1) when the effectiveness of the filed financing statement lapses under Section 9–515 or is terminated under Section 9–513; or

(2) the 21st day after the security interest attaches to the proceeds.

§9–316.   Continued Perfection of Security Interest Following Change in Governing Law.

(a) A security interest perfected pursuant to the law of the jurisdiction designated in Section 9–301(1) or 9–305(c) remains perfected until the earliest of:

(1) the time perfection would have ceased under the law of that jurisdiction;

(2) the expiration of four months after a change of the debtor's location to another jurisdiction; or

(3) the expiration of one year after a transfer of collateral to a person that thereby becomes a debtor and is located in another jurisdiction.

(b) If a security interest described in subsection (a) becomes perfected under the law of the other jurisdiction before the earliest time or event described in that subsection, it remains perfected thereafter. If the security interest does not become perfected under the law of the other jurisdiction before the earliest time or event, it becomes unperfected and is deemed never to have been perfected as against a purchaser of the collateral for value.

(c) A possessory security interest in collateral, other than goods covered by a certificate of title and as-extracted collateral consisting of goods, remains continuously perfected if:

(1) the collateral is located in one jurisdiction and subject to a security interest perfected under the law of that jurisdiction;

(2) thereafter the collateral is brought into another jurisdiction; and

(3) upon entry into the other jurisdiction, the security interest is perfected under the law of the other jurisdiction.

(d) Except as otherwise provided in subsection (e), a security interest in goods covered by a certificate of title which is perfected by any method under the law of another jurisdiction when the goods become covered by a certificate of title from this State remains perfected until the security interest would have become unperfected under the law of the other jurisdiction had the goods not become so covered.

(e) A security interest described in subsection (d) becomes unperfected as against a purchaser of the goods for value and is deemed never to have been perfected as against a purchaser of the goods for value if the applicable requirements for perfection under Section 9–311(b) or 9–313 are not satisfied before the earlier of:

(1) the time the security interest would have become unperfected under the law of the other jurisdiction had the goods not become covered by a certificate of title from this State; or

(2) the expiration of four months after the goods had become so covered.

(f) A security interest in deposit accounts, letter-of-credit rights, or investment property which is perfected under the law of the bank's jurisdiction, the issuer's jurisdiction, a nominated person's jurisdiction, the securities intermediary's jurisdiction, or the commodity intermediary's jurisdiction, as applicable, remains perfected until the earlier of:

(1) the time the security interest would have become unperfected under the law of that jurisdiction; or

(2) the expiration of four months after a change of the applicable jurisdiction to another jurisdiction.

(g) If a security interest described in subsection (f) becomes perfected under the law of the other jurisdiction before the earlier of the time or the end of the period described in that subsection, it remains perfected thereafter. If the security interest does not become perfected under the law of the other jurisdiction before the earlier of that time or the end of that period, it becomes unperfected and is deemed never to have been perfected as against a purchaser of the collateral for value.

[Subpart 3. Priority]

§9–317.   Interests That Take Priority over or Take Free of Security Interest or Agricultural Lien.

(a) A security interest or agricultural lien is subordinate to the rights of:

(1) a person entitled to priority under Section 9–322; and

(2) except as otherwise provided in subsection (e), a person that becomes a lien creditor before the earlier of the time:

(A) the security interest or agricultural lien is perfected; or

(B) one of the conditions specified in Section 9–203(b)(3) is met and a financing statement covering the collateral is filed.

(b) Except as otherwise provided in subsection (e), a buyer, other than a secured party, of tangible chattel paper, documents, goods, instruments, or a security certificate takes free of a security interest or agricultural lien if the buyer gives value and receives delivery of the collateral without knowledge of the security interest or agricultural lien and before it is perfected.

(c) Except as otherwise provided in subsection (e), a lessee of goods takes free of a security interest or agricultural lien if the lessee gives value and receives delivery of the collateral without knowledge of the security interest or agricultural lien and before it is perfected.

(d) A licensee of a general intangible or a buyer, other than a secured party, of accounts, electronic chattel paper, general intangibles, or investment property other than a certificated security takes free of a security interest if the licensee or buyer gives value without knowledge of the security interest and before it is perfected.

(e) Except as otherwise provided in Sections 9–320 and 9–321, if a person files a financing statement with respect to a purchase-money security interest before or within 20 days after the debtor receives delivery of the collateral, the security interest takes priority over the rights of a buyer, lessee, or lien creditor which arise between the time the security interest attaches and the time of filing.

As amended in 2000.

§9–318. No Interest Retained in Right to Payment That Is Sold; Rights and Title of Seller of Account or Chattel Paper with Respect to Creditors and Purchasers.

(a) A debtor that has sold an account, chattel paper, payment intangible, or promissory note does not retain a legal or equitable interest in the collateral sold.

(b) For purposes of determining the rights of creditors of, and purchasers for value of an account or chattel paper from, a debtor that has sold an account or chattel paper, while the buyer's security interest is unperfected, the debtor is deemed to have rights and title to the account or chattel paper identical to those the debtor sold.

§9–319. Rights and Title of Consignee with Respect to Creditors and Purchasers.

(a) Except as otherwise provided in subsection (b), for purposes of determining the rights of creditors of, and purchasers for value of goods from, a consignee, while the goods are in the possession of the consignee, the consignee is deemed to have rights and title to the goods identical to those the consignor had or had power to transfer.

(b) For purposes of determining the rights of a creditor of a consignee, law other than this article determines the rights and title of a consignee while goods are in the consignee's possession if, under this part, a perfected security interest held by the consignor would have priority over the rights of the creditor.

§9–320. Buyer of Goods.

(a) Except as otherwise provided in subsection (e), a buyer in ordinary course of business, other than a person buying farm products from a person engaged in farming operations, takes free of a security interest created by the buyer's seller, even if the security interest is perfected and the buyer knows of its existence.

(b) Except as otherwise provided in subsection (e), a buyer of goods from a person who used or bought the goods for use primarily for personal, family, or household purposes takes free of a security interest, even if perfected, if the buyer buys:

(1) without knowledge of the security interest;

(2) for value;

(3) primarily for the buyer's personal, family, or household purposes; and

(4) before the filing of a financing statement covering the goods.

(c) To the extent that it affects the priority of a security interest over a buyer of goods under subsection (b), the period of effectiveness of a filing made in the jurisdiction in which the seller is located is governed by Section 9–316(a) and (b).

(d) A buyer in ordinary course of business buying oil, gas, or other minerals at the wellhead or minehead or after extraction takes free of an interest arising out of an encumbrance.

(e) Subsections (a) and (b) do not affect a security interest in goods in the possession of the secured party under Section 9–313.

§9–321. Licensee of General Intangible and Lessee of Goods in Ordinary Course of Business.

(a) In this section, "licensee in ordinary course of business" means a person that becomes a licensee of a general intangible in good faith, without knowledge that the license violates the rights of another person in the general intangible, and in the ordinary course from a person in the business of licensing general intangibles of that kind. A person becomes a licensee in the ordinary course if the license to the person comports with the usual or customary practices in the kind of business in which the licensor is engaged or with the licensor's own usual or customary practices.

(b) A licensee in ordinary course of business takes its rights under a nonexclusive license free of a security interest in the general intangible created by the licensor, even if the security interest is perfected and the licensee knows of its existence.

(c) A lessee in ordinary course of business takes its leasehold interest free of a security interest in the goods created by the lessor, even if the security interest is perfected and the lessee knows of its existence.

§9–322. Priorities among Conflicting Security Interests in and Agricultural Liens on Same Collateral.

(a) Except as otherwise provided in this section, priority among conflicting security interests and agricultural liens in the same collateral is determined according to the following rules:

(1) Conflicting perfected security interests and agricultural liens rank according to priority in time of filing or perfection. Priority dates from the earlier of the time a filing covering the collateral is first made or the security interest or agricultural lien is first perfected, if there is no period thereafter when there is neither filing nor perfection.

(2) A perfected security interest or agricultural lien has priority over a conflicting unperfected security interest or agricultural lien.

(3) The first security interest or agricultural lien to attach or become effective has priority if conflicting security interests and agricultural liens are unperfected.

(b) For the purposes of subsection (a)(1):

(1) the time of filing or perfection as to a security interest in collateral is also the time of filing or perfection as to a security interest in proceeds; and

(2) the time of filing or perfection as to a security interest in collateral supported by a supporting obligation is also the time of filing or perfection as to a security interest in the supporting obligation.

(c) Except as otherwise provided in subsection (f), a security interest in collateral which qualifies for priority over a conflicting security interest under Section 9–327, 9–328, 9–329, 9–330, or 9–331 also has priority over a conflicting security interest in:

(1) any supporting obligation for the collateral; and

(2) proceeds of the collateral if:

(A) the security interest in proceeds is perfected;

(B) the proceeds are cash proceeds or of the same type as the collateral; and

(C) in the case of proceeds that are proceeds of proceeds, all intervening proceeds are cash proceeds, proceeds of the same type as the collateral, or an account relating to the collateral.

(d) Subject to subsection (e) and except as otherwise provided in subsection (f), if a security interest in chattel paper, deposit accounts, negotiable documents, instruments, investment property, or letter-of-credit rights is perfected by a method other than filing, conflicting perfected security interests in proceeds of the collateral rank according to priority in time of filing.

(e) Subsection (d) applies only if the proceeds of the collateral are not cash proceeds, chattel paper, negotiable documents, instruments, investment property, or letter-of-credit rights.

(f) Subsections (a) through (e) are subject to:

(1) subsection (g) and the other provisions of this part;

(2) Section 4–210 with respect to a security interest of a collecting bank;

(3) Section 5–118 with respect to a security interest of an issuer or nominated person; and

(4) Section 9–110 with respect to a security interest arising under Article 2 or 2A.

(g) A perfected agricultural lien on collateral has priority over a conflicting security interest in or agricultural lien on the same collateral if the statute creating the agricultural lien so provides.

§9–323. Future Advances.

(a) Except as otherwise provided in subsection (c), for purposes of determining the priority of a perfected security interest under Section 9–322(a)(1), perfection of the security interest dates from the time an advance is made to the extent that the security interest secures an advance that:

(1) is made while the security interest is perfected only:

(A) under Section 9–309 when it attaches; or

(B) temporarily under Section 9–312(e), (f), or (g); and

(2) is not made pursuant to a commitment entered into before or while the security interest is perfected by a method other than under Section 9–309 or 9–312(e), (f), or (g).

(b) Except as otherwise provided in subsection (c), a security interest is subordinate to the rights of a person that becomes a lien creditor to the extent that the security interest secures an advance made more than 45 days after the person becomes a lien creditor unless the advance is made:

(1) without knowledge of the lien; or

(2) pursuant to a commitment entered into without knowledge of the lien.

(c) Subsections (a) and (b) do not apply to a security interest held by a secured party that is a buyer of accounts, chattel paper, payment intangibles, or promissory notes or a consignor.

(d) Except as otherwise provided in subsection (e), a buyer of goods other than a buyer in ordinary course of business takes free of a security interest to the extent that it secures advances made after the earlier of:

(1) the time the secured party acquires knowledge of the buyer's purchase; or

(2) 45 days after the purchase.

(e) Subsection (d) does not apply if the advance is made pursuant to a commitment entered into without knowledge of the buyer's purchase and before the expiration of the 45-day period.

(f) Except as otherwise provided in subsection (g), a lessee of goods, other than a lessee in ordinary course of business, takes the leasehold interest free of a security interest to the extent that it secures advances made after the earlier of:

(1) the time the secured party acquires knowledge of the lease; or

(2) 45 days after the lease contract becomes enforceable.

(g) Subsection (f) does not apply if the advance is made pursuant to a commitment entered into without knowledge of the lease and before the expiration of the 45-day period.

As amended in 1999.

§9–324. Priority of Purchase-Money Security Interests.

(a) Except as otherwise provided in subsection (g), a perfected purchase-money security interest in goods other than inventory or livestock has priority over a conflicting security interest in the same goods, and, except as otherwise provided in Section 9–327, a perfected security interest in its identifiable proceeds also has priority, if the purchase-money security interest is perfected when the debtor receives possession of the collateral or within 20 days thereafter.

(b) Subject to subsection (c) and except as otherwise provided in subsection (g), a perfected purchase-money security interest in inventory has priority over a conflicting security interest in the same inventory, has priority over a conflicting security interest in chattel paper or an instrument constituting proceeds of the inventory and in proceeds of the chattel paper, if so provided in Section 9–330, and, except as otherwise provided in Section 9–327, also has priority in identifiable cash proceeds of the inventory to the extent the identifiable cash proceeds are received on or before the delivery of the inventory to a buyer, if:

(1) the purchase-money security interest is perfected when the debtor receives possession of the inventory;

(2) the purchase-money secured party sends an authenticated notification to the holder of the conflicting security interest;

(3) the holder of the conflicting security interest receives the notification within five years before the debtor receives possession of the inventory; and

(4) the notification states that the person sending the notification has or expects to acquire a purchase-money security interest in inventory of the debtor and describes the inventory.

(c) Subsections (b)(2) through (4) apply only if the holder of the conflicting security interest had filed a financing statement covering the same types of inventory:

(1) if the purchase-money security interest is perfected by filing, before the date of the filing; or

(2) if the purchase-money security interest is temporarily perfected without filing or possession under Section 9–312(f), before the beginning of the 20-day period thereunder.

(d) Subject to subsection (e) and except as otherwise provided in subsection (g), a perfected purchase-money security interest in livestock that are farm products has priority over a conflicting security interest in the same livestock, and, except as otherwise provided in Section 9–327, a perfected security interest in their identifiable proceeds and identifiable products in their unmanufactured states also has priority, if:

(1) the purchase-money security interest is perfected when the debtor receives possession of the livestock;

(2) the purchase-money secured party sends an authenticated notification to the holder of the conflicting security interest;

(3) the holder of the conflicting security interest receives the notification within six months before the debtor receives possession of the livestock; and

(4) the notification states that the person sending the notification has or expects to acquire a purchase-money security interest in livestock of the debtor and describes the livestock.

(e) Subsections (d)(2) through (4) apply only if the holder of the conflicting security interest had filed a financing statement covering the same types of livestock:

(1) if the purchase-money security interest is perfected by filing, before the date of the filing; or

(2) if the purchase-money security interest is temporarily perfected without filing or possession under Section 9–312(f), before the beginning of the 20-day period thereunder.

(f) Except as otherwise provided in subsection (g), a perfected purchase-money security interest in software has priority over a conflicting security interest in the same collateral, and, except as otherwise provided in Section 9–327, a perfected security interest in its identifiable proceeds also has priority, to the extent that the purchase-money security interest in the goods in which the software was acquired for use has priority in the goods and proceeds of the goods under this section.

(g) If more than one security interest qualifies for priority in the same collateral under subsection (a), (b), (d), or (f):

(1) a security interest securing an obligation incurred as all or part of the price of the collateral has priority over a security interest securing an obligation incurred for value given to enable the debtor to acquire rights in or the use of collateral; and

(2) in all other cases, Section 9–322(a) applies to the qualifying security interests.

§9–325. Priority of Security Interests in Transferred Collateral.

(a) Except as otherwise provided in subsection (b), a security interest created by a debtor is subordinate to a security interest in the same collateral created by another person if:

(1) the debtor acquired the collateral subject to the security interest created by the other person;

(2) the security interest created by the other person was perfected when the debtor acquired the collateral; and

(3) there is no period thereafter when the security interest is unperfected.

(b) Subsection (a) subordinates a security interest only if the security interest:

(1) otherwise would have priority solely under Section 9–322(a) or 9–324; or

(2) arose solely under Section 2–711(3) or 2A–508(5).

§9–326. Priority of Security Interests Created by New Debtor.

(a) Subject to subsection (b), a security interest created by a new debtor which is perfected by a filed financing statement that is effective solely under Section 9–508 in collateral in which a new debtor has or acquires rights is subordinate to a security interest in the same collateral which is perfected other than by a filed financing statement that is effective solely under Section 9–508.

(b) The other provisions of this part determine the priority among conflicting security interests in the same collateral perfected by filed financing statements that are effective solely under Section 9–508. However, if the security agreements to which a new debtor became bound as debtor were not entered into by the same original debtor, the conflicting security interests rank according to priority in time of the new debtor's having become bound.

§9–327. Priority of Security Interests in Deposit Account.

The following rules govern priority among conflicting security interests in the same deposit account:

(1) A security interest held by a secured party having control of the deposit account under Section 9–104 has priority over a conflicting security interest held by a secured party that does not have control.

(2) Except as otherwise provided in paragraphs (3) and (4), security interests perfected by control under Section 9–314 rank according to priority in time of obtaining control.

(3) Except as otherwise provided in paragraph (4), a security interest held by the bank with which the deposit account is

maintained has priority over a conflicting security interest held by another secured party.

(4) A security interest perfected by control under Section 9–104 (a)(3) has priority over a security interest held by the bank with which the deposit account is maintained.

§9–328. Priority of Security Interests in Investment Property.

The following rules govern priority among conflicting security interests in the same investment property:

(1) A security interest held by a secured party having control of investment property under Section 9–106 has priority over a security interest held by a secured party that does not have control of the investment property.

(2) Except as otherwise provided in paragraphs (3) and (4), conflicting security interests held by secured parties each of which has control under Section 9–106 rank according to priority in time of:

  (A) if the collateral is a security, obtaining control;

  (B) if the collateral is a security entitlement carried in a securities account and:

    (i) if the secured party obtained control under Section 8–106 (d)(1), the secured party's becoming the person for which the securities account is maintained;

    (ii) if the secured party obtained control under Section 8–106 (d)(2), the securities intermediary's agreement to comply with the secured party's entitlement orders with respect to security entitlements carried or to be carried in the securities account; or

    (iii) if the secured party obtained control through another person under Section 8–106(d)(3), the time on which priority would be based under this paragraph if the other person were the secured party; or

  (C) if the collateral is a commodity contract carried with a commodity intermediary, the satisfaction of the requirement for control specified in Section 9–106(b)(2) with respect to commodity contracts carried or to be carried with the commodity intermediary.

(3) A security interest held by a securities intermediary in a security entitlement or a securities account maintained with the securities intermediary has priority over a conflicting security interest held by another secured party.

(4) A security interest held by a commodity intermediary in a commodity contract or a commodity account maintained with the commodity intermediary has priority over a conflicting security interest held by another secured party.

(5) A security interest in a certificated security in registered form which is perfected by taking delivery under Section 9–313(a) and not by control under Section 9–314 has priority over a conflicting security interest perfected by a method other than control.

(6) Conflicting security interests created by a broker, securities intermediary, or commodity intermediary which are perfected without control under Section 9–106 rank equally.

(7) In all other cases, priority among conflicting security interests in investment property is governed by Sections 9–322 and 9–323.

§9–329. Priority of Security Interests in Letter-of-Credit Right.

The following rules govern priority among conflicting security interests in the same letter-of-credit right:

(1) A security interest held by a secured party having control of the letter-of-credit right under Section 9–107 has priority to the extent of its control over a conflicting security interest held by a secured party that does not have control.

(2) Security interests perfected by control under Section 9–314 rank according to priority in time of obtaining control.

§9–330. Priority of Purchaser of Chattel Paper or Instrument.

(a) A purchaser of chattel paper has priority over a security interest in the chattel paper which is claimed merely as proceeds of inventory subject to a security interest if:

  (1) in good faith and in the ordinary course of the purchaser's business, the purchaser gives new value and takes possession of the chattel paper or obtains control of the chattel paper under Section 9–105; and

  (2) the chattel paper does not indicate that it has been assigned to an identified assignee other than the purchaser.

(b) A purchaser of chattel paper has priority over a security interest in the chattel paper which is claimed other than merely as proceeds of inventory subject to a security interest if the purchaser gives new value and takes possession of the chattel paper or obtains control of the chattel paper under Section 9–105 in good faith, in the ordinary course of the purchaser's business, and without knowledge that the purchase violates the rights of the secured party.

(c) Except as otherwise provided in Section 9–327, a purchaser having priority in chattel paper under subsection (a) or (b) also has priority in proceeds of the chattel paper to the extent that:

  (1) Section 9–322 provides for priority in the proceeds; or

  (2) the proceeds consist of the specific goods covered by the chattel paper or cash proceeds of the specific goods, even if the purchaser's security interest in the proceeds is unperfected.

(d) Except as otherwise provided in Section 9–331(a), a purchaser of an instrument has priority over a security interest in the instrument perfected by a method other than possession if the purchaser gives value and takes possession of the instrument in good faith and without knowledge that the purchase violates the rights of the secured party.

(e) For purposes of subsections (a) and (b), the holder of a purchase-money security interest in inventory gives new value for chattel paper constituting proceeds of the inventory.

(f) For purposes of subsections (b) and (d), if chattel paper or an instrument indicates that it has been assigned to an identified secured party other than the purchaser, a purchaser of the chattel paper or instrument has knowledge that the purchase violates the rights of the secured party.

§9–331. Priority of Rights of Purchasers of Instruments, Documents, and Securities under Other Articles; Priority of Interests in Financial Assets and Security Entitlements under Article 8.

(a) This article does not limit the rights of a holder in due course of a negotiable instrument, a holder to which a negotiable document of title has been duly negotiated, or a protected purchaser of a security. These holders or purchasers take priority over an earlier security interest, even if perfected, to the extent provided in Articles 3, 7, and 8.

(b) This article does not limit the rights of or impose liability on a person to the extent that the person is protected against the assertion of a claim under Article 8.

(c) Filing under this article does not constitute notice of a claim or defense to the holders, or purchasers, or persons described in subsections (a) and (b).

§9–332. Transfer of Money; Transfer of Funds from Deposit Account.

(a) A transferee of money takes the money free of a security interest unless the transferee acts in collusion with the debtor in violating the rights of the secured party.

(b) A transferee of funds from a deposit account takes the funds free of a security interest in the deposit account unless the transferee acts in collusion with the debtor in violating the rights of the secured party.

§9–333. Priority of Certain Liens Arising by Operation of Law.

(a) In this section, "possessory lien" means an interest, other than a security interest or an agricultural lien:

(1) which secures payment or performance of an obligation for services or materials furnished with respect to goods by a person in the ordinary course of the person's business;

(2) which is created by statute or rule of law in favor of the person; and

(3) whose effectiveness depends on the person's possession of the goods.

(b) A possessory lien on goods has priority over a security interest in the goods unless the lien is created by a statute that expressly provides otherwise.

§9–334. Priority of Security Interests in Fixtures and Crops.

(a) A security interest under this article may be created in goods that are fixtures or may continue in goods that become fixtures. A security interest does not exist under this article in ordinary building materials incorporated into an improvement on land.

(b) This article does not prevent creation of an encumbrance upon fixtures under real property law.

(c) In cases not governed by subsections (d) through (h), a security interest in fixtures is subordinate to a conflicting interest of an encumbrancer or owner of the related real property other than the debtor.

(d) Except as otherwise provided in subsection (h), a perfected security interest in fixtures has priority over a conflicting interest of an encumbrancer or owner of the real property if the debtor has an interest of record in or is in possession of the real property and:

(1) the security interest is a purchase-money security interest;

(2) the interest of the encumbrancer or owner arises before the goods become fixtures; and

(3) the security interest is perfected by a fixture filing before the goods become fixtures or within 20 days thereafter.

(e) A perfected security interest in fixtures has priority over a conflicting interest of an encumbrancer or owner of the real property if:

(1) the debtor has an interest of record in the real property or is in possession of the real property and the security interest:

(A) is perfected by a fixture filing before the interest of the encumbrancer or owner is of record; and

(B) has priority over any conflicting interest of a predecessor in title of the encumbrancer or owner;

(2) before the goods become fixtures, the security interest is perfected by any method permitted by this article and the fixtures are readily removable:

(A) factory or office machines;

(B) equipment that is not primarily used or leased for use in the operation of the real property; or

(C) replacements of domestic appliances that are consumer goods;

(3) the conflicting interest is a lien on the real property obtained by legal or equitable proceedings after the security interest was perfected by any method permitted by this article; or

(4) the security interest is:

(A) created in a manufactured home in a manufactured-home transaction; and

(B) perfected pursuant to a statute described in Section 9–311(a)(2).

(f) A security interest in fixtures, whether or not perfected, has priority over a conflicting interest of an encumbrancer or owner of the real property if:

(1) the encumbrancer or owner has, in an authenticated record, consented to the security interest or disclaimed an interest in the goods as fixtures; or

(2) the debtor has a right to remove the goods as against the encumbrancer or owner.

(g) The priority of the security interest under paragraph (f)(2) continues for a reasonable time if the debtor's right to remove the goods as against the encumbrancer or owner terminates.

(h) A mortgage is a construction mortgage to the extent that it secures an obligation incurred for the construction of an improvement on land, including the acquisition cost of the land, if a recorded record of the mortgage so indicates. Except as otherwise provided in subsections (e) and (f), a security interest in fixtures is subordinate to a construction mortgage if a record of the mortgage is recorded before the goods become fixtures and the goods become fixtures before the completion of the construction. A mortgage has this priority to the same extent as a construction mortgage to the extent that it is given to refinance a construction mortgage.

(i) A perfected security interest in crops growing on real property has priority over a conflicting interest of an encumbrancer or owner of the real property if the debtor has an interest of record in or is in possession of the real property.

(j) Subsection (i) prevails over any inconsistent provisions of the following statutes:

[List here any statutes containing provisions inconsistent with subsection (i).]

Legislative Note: States that amend statutes to remove provisions inconsistent with subsection (i) need not enact subsection (j).

§9–335. Accessions.

(a) A security interest may be created in an accession and continues in collateral that becomes an accession.

(b) If a security interest is perfected when the collateral becomes an accession, the security interest remains perfected in the collateral.

(c) Except as otherwise provided in subsection (d), the other provisions of this part determine the priority of a security interest in an accession.

(d) A security interest in an accession is subordinate to a security interest in the whole which is perfected by compliance with the requirements of a certificate-of-title statute under Section 9–311(b).

(e) After default, subject to Part 6, a secured party may remove an accession from other goods if the security interest in the accession has priority over the claims of every person having an interest in the whole.

(f) A secured party that removes an accession from other goods under subsection (e) shall promptly reimburse any holder of a security interest or other lien on, or owner of, the whole or of the other goods, other than the debtor, for the cost of repair of any physical injury to the whole or the other goods. The secured party need not reimburse the holder or owner for any diminution in value of the whole or the other goods caused by the absence of the accession removed or by any necessity for replacing it. A person entitled to reimbursement may refuse permission to remove until the secured party gives adequate assurance for the performance of the obligation to reimburse.

§9–336. Commingled Goods.

(a) In this section, "commingled goods" means goods that are physically united with other goods in such a manner that their identity is lost in a product or mass.

(b) A security interest does not exist in commingled goods as such. However, a security interest may attach to a product or mass that results when goods become commingled goods.

(c) If collateral becomes commingled goods, a security interest attaches to the product or mass.

(d) If a security interest in collateral is perfected before the collateral becomes commingled goods, the security interest that attaches to the product or mass under subsection (c) is perfected.

(e) Except as otherwise provided in subsection (f), the other provisions of this part determine the priority of a security interest that attaches to the product or mass under subsection (c).

(f) If more than one security interest attaches to the product or mass under subsection (c), the following rules determine priority:

(1) A security interest that is perfected under subsection (d) has priority over a security interest that is unperfected at the time the collateral becomes commingled goods.

(2) If more than one security interest is perfected under subsection (d), the security interests rank equally in proportion to the value of the collateral at the time it became commingled goods.

§9–337. Priority of Security Interests in Goods Covered by Certificate of Title.

If, while a security interest in goods is perfected by any method under the law of another jurisdiction, this State issues a certificate of title that does not show that the goods are subject to the security interest or contain a statement that they may be subject to security interests not shown on the certificate:

(1) a buyer of the goods, other than a person in the business of selling goods of that kind, takes free of the security interest if the buyer gives value and receives delivery of the goods after issuance of the certificate and without knowledge of the security interest; and

(2) the security interest is subordinate to a conflicting security interest in the goods that attaches, and is perfected under Section 9–311(b), after issuance of the certificate and without the conflicting secured party's knowledge of the security interest.

§9–338. Priority of Security Interest or Agricultural Lien Perfected by Filed Financing Statement Providing Certain Incorrect Information.

If a security interest or agricultural lien is perfected by a filed financing statement providing information described in Section 9–516(b)(5) which is incorrect at the time the financing statement is filed:

(1) the security interest or agricultural lien is subordinate to a conflicting perfected security interest in the collateral to the extent that the holder of the conflicting security interest gives value in reasonable reliance upon the incorrect information; and

(2) a purchaser, other than a secured party, of the collateral takes free of the security interest or agricultural lien to the extent that, in reasonable reliance upon the incorrect information, the purchaser gives value and, in the case of chattel paper, documents, goods, instruments, or a security certificate, receives delivery of the collateral.

§9–339.   Priority Subject to Subordination.

This article does not preclude subordination by agreement by a person entitled to priority.

[Subpart 4. Rights of Bank]

§9–340.   Effectiveness of Right of Recoupment or Set-Off against Deposit Account.

(a) Except as otherwise provided in subsection (c), a bank with which a deposit account is maintained may exercise any right of recoupment or set-off against a secured party that holds a security interest in the deposit account.

(b) Except as otherwise provided in subsection (c), the application of this article to a security interest in a deposit account does not affect a right of recoupment or set-off of the secured party as to a deposit account maintained with the secured party.

(c) The exercise by a bank of a set-off against a deposit account is ineffective against a secured party that holds a security interest in the deposit account which is perfected by control under Section 9–104(a)(3), if the set-off is based on a claim against the debtor.

§9–341.   Bank's Rights and Duties with Respect to Deposit Account.

Except as otherwise provided in Section 9–340(c), and unless the bank otherwise agrees in an authenticated record, a bank's rights and duties with respect to a deposit account maintained with the bank are not terminated, suspended, or modified by:

(1) the creation, attachment, or perfection of a security interest in the deposit account;

(2) the bank's knowledge of the security interest; or

(3) the bank's receipt of instructions from the secured party.

§9–342.   Bank's Right to Refuse to Enter into or Disclose Existence of Control Agreement.

This article does not require a bank to enter into an agreement of the kind described in Section 9–104(a)(2), even if its customer so requests or directs. A bank that has entered into such an agreement is not required to confirm the existence of the agreement to another person unless requested to do so by its customer.

PART 4   Rights of Third Parties

§9–401.   Alienability of Debtor's Rights.

(a) Except as otherwise provided in subsection (b) and Sections 9–406, 9–407, 9–408, and 9–409, whether a debtor's rights in collateral may be voluntarily or involuntarily transferred is governed by law other than this article.

(b) An agreement between the debtor and secured party which prohibits a transfer of the debtor's rights in collateral or makes the transfer a default does not prevent the transfer from taking effect.

§9–402.   Secured Party Not Obligated on Contract of Debtor or in Tort.

The existence of a security interest, agricultural lien, or authority given to a debtor to dispose of or use collateral, without more, does not subject a secured party to liability in contract or tort for the debtor's acts or omissions.

§9–403.   Agreement Not to Assert Defenses against Assignee.

(a) In this section, "value" has the meaning provided in Section 3–303(a).

(b) Except as otherwise provided in this section, an agreement between an account debtor and an assignor not to assert against an assignee any claim or defense that the account debtor may have against the assignor is enforceable by an assignee that takes an assignment:

(1) for value;

(2) in good faith;

(3) without notice of a claim of a property or possessory right to the property assigned; and

(4) without notice of a defense or claim in recoupment of the type that may be asserted against a person entitled to enforce a negotiable instrument under Section 3–305(a).

(c) Subsection (b) does not apply to defenses of a type that may be asserted against a holder in due course of a negotiable instrument under Section 3–305(b).

(d) In a consumer transaction, if a record evidences the account debtor's obligation, law other than this article requires that the record include a statement to the effect that the rights of an assignee are subject to claims or defenses that the account debtor could assert against the original obligee, and the record does not include such a statement:

(1) the record has the same effect as if the record included such a statement; and

(2) the account debtor may assert against an assignee those claims and defenses that would have been available if the record included such a statement.

(e) This section is subject to law other than this article which establishes a different rule for an account debtor who is an individual and who incurred the obligation primarily for personal, family, or household purposes.

(f) Except as otherwise provided in subsection (d), this section does not displace law other than this article which gives effect to an agreement by an account debtor not to assert a claim or defense against an assignee.

§9–404. Rights Acquired by Assignee; Claims and Defenses against Assignee.

(a) Unless an account debtor has made an enforceable agreement not to assert defenses or claims, and subject to subsections (b) through (e), the rights of an assignee are subject to:

(1) all terms of the agreement between the account debtor and assignor and any defense or claim in recoupment arising from the transaction that gave rise to the contract; and

(2) any other defense or claim of the account debtor against the assignor which accrues before the account debtor receives a notification of the assignment authenticated by the assignor or the assignee.

(b) Subject to subsection (c) and except as otherwise provided in subsection (d), the claim of an account debtor against an assignor may be asserted against an assignee under subsection (a) only to reduce the amount the account debtor owes.

(c) This section is subject to law other than this article which establishes a different rule for an account debtor who is an individual and who incurred the obligation primarily for personal, family, or household purposes.

(d) In a consumer transaction, if a record evidences the account debtor's obligation, law other than this article requires that the record include a statement to the effect that the account debtor's recovery against an assignee with respect to claims and defenses against the assignor may not exceed amounts paid by the account debtor under the record, and the record does not include such a statement, the extent to which a claim of an account debtor against the assignor may be asserted against an assignee is determined as if the record included such a statement.

(e) This section does not apply to an assignment of a health-care-insurance receivable.

§9–405. Modification of Assigned Contract.

(a) A modification of or substitution for an assigned contract is effective against an assignee if made in good faith. The assignee acquires corresponding rights under the modified or substituted contract. The assignment may provide that the modification or substitution is a breach of contract by the assignor. This subsection is subject to subsections (b) through (d).

(b) Subsection (a) applies to the extent that:

(1) the right to payment or a part thereof under an assigned contract has not been fully earned by performance; or

(2) the right to payment or a part thereof has been fully earned by performance and the account debtor has not received notification of the assignment under Section 9–406(a).

(c) This section is subject to law other than this article which establishes a different rule for an account debtor who is an individual and who incurred the obligation primarily for personal, family, or household purposes.

(d) This section does not apply to an assignment of a health-care-insurance receivable.

§9–406. Discharge of Account Debtor; Notification of Assignment; Identification and Proof of Assignment; Restrictions on Assignment of Accounts, Chattel Paper, Payment Intangibles, and Promissory Notes Ineffective.

(a) Subject to subsections (b) through (i), an account debtor on an account, chattel paper, or a payment intangible may discharge its obligation by paying the assignor until, but not after, the account debtor receives a notification, authenticated by the assignor or the assignee, that the amount due or to become due has been assigned and that payment is to be made to the assignee. After receipt of the notification, the account debtor may discharge its obligation by paying the assignee and may not discharge the obligation by paying the assignor.

(b) Subject to subsection (h), notification is ineffective under subsection (a):

(1) if it does not reasonably identify the rights assigned;

(2) to the extent that an agreement between an account debtor and a seller of a payment intangible limits the account debtor's duty to pay a person other than the seller and the limitation is effective under law other than this article; or

(3) at the option of an account debtor, if the notification notifies the account debtor to make less than the full amount of any installment or other periodic payment to the assignee, even if:

(A) only a portion of the account, chattel paper, or payment intangible has been assigned to that assignee;

(B) a portion has been assigned to another assignee; or

(C) the account debtor knows that the assignment to that assignee is limited.

(c) Subject to subsection (h), if requested by the account debtor, an assignee shall seasonably furnish reasonable proof that the assignment has been made. Unless the assignee complies, the account debtor may discharge its obligation by paying the assignor, even if the account debtor has received a notification under subsection (a).

(d) Except as otherwise provided in subsection (e) and Sections 2A–303 and 9–407, and subject to subsection (h), a term in an agreement between an account debtor and an assignor or in a promissory note is ineffective to the extent that it:

(1) prohibits, restricts, or requires the consent of the account debtor or person obligated on the promissory note to the assignment or transfer of, or the creation, attachment, perfection, or enforcement of a security interest in, the account, chattel paper, payment intangible, or promissory note; or

(2) provides that the assignment or transfer or the creation, attachment, perfection, or enforcement of the security interest may give rise to a default, breach, right of recoupment, claim, defense, termination, right of termination, or remedy under the account, chattel paper, payment intangible, or promissory note.

(e) Subsection (d) does not apply to the sale of a payment intangible or promissory note.

(f) Except as otherwise provided in Sections 2A–303 and 9–407 and subject to subsections (h) and (i), a rule of law, statute, or regulation that prohibits, restricts, or requires the consent of a government, governmental body or official, or account debtor to the assignment or transfer of, or creation of a security interest in, an account or chattel paper is ineffective to the extent that the rule of law, statute, or regulation:

(1) prohibits, restricts, or requires the consent of the government, governmental body or official, or account debtor to the assignment or transfer of, or the creation, attachment, perfection, or enforcement of a security interest in the account or chattel paper; or

(2) provides that the assignment or transfer or the creation, attachment, perfection, or enforcement of the security interest may give rise to a default, breach, right of recoupment, claim, defense, termination, right of termination, or remedy under the account or chattel paper.

(g) Subject to subsection (h), an account debtor may not waive or vary its option under subsection (b)(3).

(h) This section is subject to law other than this article which establishes a different rule for an account debtor who is an individual and who incurred the obligation primarily for personal, family, or household purposes.

(i) This section does not apply to an assignment of a health-care-insurance receivable.

(j) This section prevails over any inconsistent provisions of the following statutes, rules, and regulations:

[List here any statutes, rules, and regulations containing provisions inconsistent with this section.]

Legislative Note: States that amend statutes, rules, and regulations to remove provisions inconsistent with this section need not enact subsection (j).

As amended in 1999 and 2000.

§9–407. Restrictions on Creation or Enforcement of Security Interest in Leasehold Interest or in Lessor's Residual Interest.

(a) Except as otherwise provided in subsection (b), a term in a lease agreement is ineffective to the extent that it:

(1) prohibits, restricts, or requires the consent of a party to the lease to the assignment or transfer of, or the creation, attachment, perfection, or enforcement of a security interest in an interest of a party under the lease contract or in the lessor's residual interest in the goods; or

(2) provides that the assignment or transfer or the creation, attachment, perfection, or enforcement of the security interest may give rise to a default, breach, right of recoupment, claim, defense, termination, right of termination, or remedy under the lease.

(b) Except as otherwise provided in Section 2A–303(7), a term described in subsection (a)(2) is effective to the extent that there is:

(1) a transfer by the lessee of the lessee's right of possession or use of the goods in violation of the term; or

(2) a delegation of a material performance of either party to the lease contract in violation of the term.

(c) The creation, attachment, perfection, or enforcement of a security interest in the lessor's interest under the lease contract or the lessor's residual interest in the goods is not a transfer that materially impairs the lessee's prospect of obtaining return performance or materially changes the duty of or materially increases the burden or risk imposed on the lessee within the purview of Section 2A–303(4) unless, and then only to the extent that, enforcement actually results in a delegation of material performance of the lessor.

As amended in 1999.

§9–408. Restrictions on Assignment of Promissory Notes, Health-Care-Insurance Receivables, and Certain General Intangibles Ineffective.

(a) Except as otherwise provided in subsection (b), a term in a promissory note or in an agreement between an account debtor and a debtor which relates to a health-care-insurance receivable or a general intangible, including a contract, permit, license, or franchise, and which term prohibits, restricts, or requires the consent of the person obligated on the promissory note or the account debtor to, the assignment or transfer of, or creation, attachment, or perfection of a security interest in, the promissory note, health-care-insurance receivable, or general intangible, is ineffective to the extent that the term:

(1) would impair the creation, attachment, or perfection of a security interest; or

(2) provides that the assignment or transfer or the creation, attachment, or perfection of the security interest may give rise to a default, breach, right of recoupment, claim, defense, termination, right of termination, or remedy under the promissory note, health-care-insurance receivable, or general intangible.

(b) Subsection (a) applies to a security interest in a payment intangible or promissory note only if the security interest arises out of a sale of the payment intangible or promissory note.

(c) A rule of law, statute, or regulation that prohibits, restricts, or requires the consent of a government, governmental body or official, person obligated on a promissory note, or account debtor to the assignment or transfer of, or creation of a security interest in, a promissory note, health-care-insurance receivable, or general intangible, including a contract, permit, license, or franchise between an account debtor and a debtor, is ineffective to the extent that the rule of law, statute, or regulation:

(1) would impair the creation, attachment, or perfection of a security interest; or

(2) provides that the assignment or transfer or the creation, attachment, or perfection of the security interest may give rise to a default, breach, right of recoupment, claim, defense, termination, right of termination, or remedy under the promissory note, health-care-insurance receivable, or general intangible.

(d) To the extent that a term in a promissory note or in an agreement between an account debtor and a debtor which relates to a health-care-insurance receivable or general intangible or a rule of law, statute, or regulation described in subsection (c) would be effective under law other than this article but is ineffective under subsection (a) or (c), the creation, attachment, or perfection of a security interest in the promissory note, health-care-insurance receivable, or general intangible:

(1) is not enforceable against the person obligated on the promissory note or the account debtor;

(2) does not impose a duty or obligation on the person obligated on the promissory note or the account debtor;

(3) does not require the person obligated on the promissory note or the account debtor to recognize the security interest, pay or render performance to the secured party, or accept payment or performance from the secured party;

(4) does not entitle the secured party to use or assign the debtor's rights under the promissory note, health-care-insurance receivable, or general intangible, including any related information or materials furnished to the debtor in the transaction giving rise to the promissory note, health-care-insurance receivable, or general intangible;

(5) does not entitle the secured party to use, assign, possess, or have access to any trade secrets or confidential information of the person obligated on the promissory note or the account debtor; and

(6) does not entitle the secured party to enforce the security interest in the promissory note, health-care-insurance receivable, or general intangible.

(e) This section prevails over any inconsistent provisions of the following statutes, rules, and regulations:

[List here any statutes, rules, and regulations containing provisions inconsistent with this section.]

Legislative Note: States that amend statutes, rules, and regulations to remove provisions inconsistent with this section need not enact subsection (e).

As amended in 1999.

§9–409. Restrictions on Assignment of Letter-of-Credit Rights Ineffective.

(a) A term in a letter of credit or a rule of law, statute, regulation, custom, or practice applicable to the letter of credit which prohibits, restricts, or requires the consent of an applicant, issuer, or nominated person to a beneficiary's assignment of or creation of a security interest in a letter-of-credit right is ineffective to the extent that the term or rule of law, statute, regulation, custom, or practice:

(1) would impair the creation, attachment, or perfection of a security interest in the letter-of-credit right; or

(2) provides that the assignment or the creation, attachment, or perfection of the security interest may give rise to a default, breach, right of recoupment, claim, defense, termination, right of termination, or remedy under the letter-of-credit right.

(b) To the extent that a term in a letter of credit is ineffective under subsection (a) but would be effective under law other than this article or a custom or practice applicable to the letter of credit, to the transfer of a right to draw or otherwise demand performance under the letter of credit, or to the assignment of a right to proceeds of the letter of credit, the creation, attachment, or perfection of a security interest in the letter-of-credit right:

(1) is not enforceable against the applicant, issuer, nominated person, or transferee beneficiary;

(2) imposes no duties or obligations on the applicant, issuer, nominated person, or transferee beneficiary; and

(3) does not require the applicant, issuer, nominated person, or transferee beneficiary to recognize the security interest, pay or render performance to the secured party, or accept payment or other performance from the secured party.

As amended in 1999.

PART 5 Filing

[Subpart 1. Filing Office; Contents and Effectiveness of Financing Statement]

§9–501. Filing Office.

(a) Except as otherwise provided in subsection (b), if the local law of this State governs perfection of a security interest or agricultural lien, the office in which to file a financing statement to perfect the security interest or agricultural lien is:

(1) the office designated for the filing or recording of a record of a mortgage on the related real property, if:

(A) the collateral is as-extracted collateral or timber to be cut; or

(B) the financing statement is filed as a fixture filing and the collateral is goods that are or are to become fixtures; or

(2) the office of [ ] [or any office duly authorized by [ ]], in all other cases, including a case in which the collateral is goods that are or are to become fixtures and the financing statement is not filed as a fixture filing.

(b) The office in which to file a financing statement to perfect a security interest in collateral, including fixtures, of a transmitting utility is the office of [ ]. The financing statement also constitutes a fixture filing as to the collateral indicated in the financing statement which is or is to become fixtures.

Legislative Note: The State should designate the filing office where the brackets appear. The filing office may be that of a governmental official (e.g., the Secretary of State) or a private party that maintains the States filing system.

§9–502. Contents of Financing Statement; Record of Mortgage as Financing Statement; Time of Filing Financing Statement.

(a) Subject to subsection (b), a financing statement is sufficient only if it:

(1) provides the name of the debtor;

(2) provides the name of the secured party or a representative of the secured party; and

(3) indicates the collateral covered by the financing statement.

(b) Except as otherwise provided in Section 9–501(b), to be sufficient, a financing statement that covers as-extracted collateral or timber to be cut, or which is filed as a fixture filing and covers goods that are or are to become fixtures, must satisfy subsection (a) and also:

(1) indicate that it covers this type of collateral;

(2) indicate that it is to be filed [for record] in the real property records;

(3) provide a description of the real property to which the collateral is related [sufficient to give constructive notice of a mortgage under the law of this State if the description were contained in a record of the mortgage of the real property]; and

(4) if the debtor does not have an interest of record in the real property, provide the name of a record owner.

(c) A record of a mortgage is effective, from the date of recording, as a financing statement filed as a fixture filing or as a financing statement covering as-extracted collateral or timber to be cut only if:

(1) the record indicates the goods or accounts that it covers;

(2) the goods are or are to become fixtures related to the real property described in the record or the collateral is related to the real property described in the record and is as-extracted collateral or timber to be cut;

(3) the record satisfies the requirements for a financing statement in this section other than an indication that it is to be filed in the real property records; and

(4) the record is [duly] recorded.

(d) A financing statement may be filed before a security agreement is made or a security interest otherwise attaches.

Legislative Note: Language in brackets is optional. Where the State has any special recording system for real property other than the usual grantor-grantee index (as, for instance, a tract system or a title registration or Torrens system) local adaptations of subsection (b) and Section 9–519(d) and (e) may be necessary. See, e.g., Mass. Gen. Laws Chapter 106, Section 9–410.

§9–503.   Name of Debtor and Secured Party.

(a) A financing statement sufficiently provides the name of the debtor:

(1) if the debtor is a registered organization, only if the financing statement provides the name of the debtor indicated on the public record of the debtor's jurisdiction of organization which shows the debtor to have been organized;

(2) if the debtor is a decedent's estate, only if the financing statement provides the name of the decedent and indicates that the debtor is an estate;

(3) if the debtor is a trust or a trustee acting with respect to property held in trust, only if the financing statement:

(A) provides the name specified for the trust in its organic documents or, if no name is specified, provides the name of the settlor and additional information sufficient to distinguish the debtor from other trusts having one or more of the same settlors; and

(B) indicates, in the debtor's name or otherwise, that the debtor is a trust or is a trustee acting with respect to property held in trust; and

(4) in other cases:

(A) if the debtor has a name, only if it provides the individual or organizational name of the debtor; and

(B) if the debtor does not have a name, only if it provides the names of the partners, members, associates, or other persons comprising the debtor.

(b) A financing statement that provides the name of the debtor in accordance with subsection (a) is not rendered ineffective by the absence of:

(1) a trade name or other name of the debtor; or

(2) unless required under subsection (a)(4)(B), names of partners, members, associates, or other persons comprising the debtor.

(c) A financing statement that provides only the debtor's trade name does not sufficiently provide the name of the debtor.

(d) Failure to indicate the representative capacity of a secured party or representative of a secured party does not affect the sufficiency of a financing statement.

(e) A financing statement may provide the name of more than one debtor and the name of more than one secured party.

§9–504.   Indication of Collateral.

A financing statement sufficiently indicates the collateral that it covers if the financing statement provides:

(1) a description of the collateral pursuant to Section 9–108; or

(2) an indication that the financing statement covers all assets or all personal property.

As amended in 1999.

§9–505.   Filing and Compliance with Other Statutes and Treaties for Consignments, Leases, Other Bailments, and Other Transactions.

(a) A consignor, lessor, or other bailor of goods, a licensor, or a buyer of a payment intangible or promissory note may file a financing statement, or may comply with a statute or treaty described in Section 9–311(a), using the terms "consignor", "consignee", "lessor", "lessee", "bailor", "bailee", "licensor", "licensee", "owner", "registered owner", "buyer", "seller", or words of similar import, instead of the terms "secured party" and "debtor".

(b) This part applies to the filing of a financing statement under subsection (a) and, as appropriate, to compliance that is equivalent to filing a financing statement under Section 9–311(b), but the filing or compliance is not of itself a factor in determining whether the collateral secures an obligation. If it is determined for another reason that the collateral secures an obligation, a security interest held by the consignor, lessor, bailor, licensor, owner, or buyer which attaches to the collateral is perfected by the filing or compliance.

§9–506.   Effect of Errors or Omissions.

(a) A financing statement substantially satisfying the requirements of this part is effective, even if it has minor errors or omissions, unless the errors or omissions make the financing statement seriously misleading.

(b) Except as otherwise provided in subsection (c), a financing statement that fails sufficiently to provide the name of the debtor in accordance with Section 9–503(a) is seriously misleading.

(c) If a search of the records of the filing office under the debtor's correct name, using the filing office's standard search logic, if any, would disclose a financing statement that fails sufficiently to provide the name of the debtor in accordance with Section 9–503(a), the name provided does not make the financing statement seriously misleading.

(d) For purposes of Section 9–508(b), the "debtor's correct name" in subsection (c) means the correct name of the new debtor.

§9–507. Effect of Certain Events on Effectiveness of Financing Statement.

(a) A filed financing statement remains effective with respect to collateral that is sold, exchanged, leased, licensed, or otherwise disposed of and in which a security interest or agricultural lien continues, even if the secured party knows of or consents to the disposition.

(b) Except as otherwise provided in subsection (c) and Section 9–508, a financing statement is not rendered ineffective if, after the financing statement is filed, the information provided in the financing statement becomes seriously misleading under Section 9–506.

(c) If a debtor so changes its name that a filed financing statement becomes seriously misleading under Section 9–506:

(1) the financing statement is effective to perfect a security interest in collateral acquired by the debtor before, or within four months after, the change; and

(2) the financing statement is not effective to perfect a security interest in collateral acquired by the debtor more than four months after the change, unless an amendment to the financing statement which renders the financing statement not seriously misleading is filed within four months after the change.

§9–508. Effectiveness of Financing Statement If New Debtor Becomes Bound by Security Agreement.

(a) Except as otherwise provided in this section, a filed financing statement naming an original debtor is effective to perfect a security interest in collateral in which a new debtor has or acquires rights to the extent that the financing statement would have been effective had the original debtor acquired rights in the collateral.

(b) If the difference between the name of the original debtor and that of the new debtor causes a filed financing statement that is effective under subsection (a) to be seriously misleading under Section 9–506:

(1) the financing statement is effective to perfect a security interest in collateral acquired by the new debtor before, and within

four months after, the new debtor becomes bound under Section 9B–203(d); and

(2) the financing statement is not effective to perfect a security interest in collateral acquired by the new debtor more than four months after the new debtor becomes bound under Section 9–203 (d) unless an initial financing statement providing the name of the new debtor is filed before the expiration of that time.

(c) This section does not apply to collateral as to which a filed financing statement remains effective against the new debtor under Section 9–507(a).

§9–509. Persons Entitled to File a Record.

(a) A person may file an initial financing statement, amendment that adds collateral covered by a financing statement, or amendment that adds a debtor to a financing statement only if:

(1) the debtor authorizes the filing in an authenticated record or pursuant to subsection (b) or (c); or

(2) the person holds an agricultural lien that has become effective at the time of filing and the financing statement covers only collateral in which the person holds an agricultural lien.

(b) By authenticating or becoming bound as debtor by a security agreement, a debtor or new debtor authorizes the filing of an initial financing statement, and an amendment, covering:

(1) the collateral described in the security agreement; and

(2) property that becomes collateral under Section 9–315(a)(2), whether or not the security agreement expressly covers proceeds.

(c) By acquiring collateral in which a security interest or agricultural lien continues under Section 9–315(a)(1), a debtor authorizes the filing of an initial financing statement, and an amendment, covering the collateral and property that becomes collateral under Section 9–315(a)(2).

(d) A person may file an amendment other than an amendment that adds collateral covered by a financing statement or an amendment that adds a debtor to a financing statement only if:

(1) the secured party of record authorizes the filing; or

(2) the amendment is a termination statement for a financing statement as to which the secured party of record has failed to file or send a termination statement as required by Section 9–513(a) or (c), the debtor authorizes the filing, and the termination statement indicates that the debtor authorized it to be filed.

(e) If there is more than one secured party of record for a financing statement, each secured party of record may authorize the filing of an amendment under subsection (d).

As amended in 2000.

§9–510. Effectiveness of Filed Record.

(a) A filed record is effective only to the extent that it was filed by a person that may file it under Section 9–509.

(b) A record authorized by one secured party of record does not affect the financing statement with respect to another secured party of record.

(c) A continuation statement that is not filed within the six-month period prescribed by Section 9–515(d) is ineffective.

§9–511.   Secured Party of Record.

(a) A secured party of record with respect to a financing statement is a person whose name is provided as the name of the secured party or a representative of the secured party in an initial financing statement that has been filed. If an initial financing statement is filed under Section 9–514(a), the assignee named in the initial financing statement is the secured party of record with respect to the financing statement.

(b) If an amendment of a financing statement which provides the name of a person as a secured party or a representative of a secured party is filed, the person named in the amendment is a secured party of record. If an amendment is filed under Section 9–514(b), the assignee named in the amendment is a secured party of record.

(c) A person remains a secured party of record until the filing of an amendment of the financing statement which deletes the person.

§9–512.   Amendment of Financing Statement.

[Alternative A]

(a) Subject to Section 9–509, a person may add or delete collateral covered by, continue or terminate the effectiveness of, or, subject to subsection (e), otherwise amend the information provided in, a financing statement by filing an amendment that:

(1) identifies, by its file number, the initial financing statement to which the amendment relates; and

(2) if the amendment relates to an initial financing statement filed [or recorded] in a filing office described in Section 9–501(a)(1), provides the information specified in Section 9–502(b).

[Alternative B]

(a) Subject to Section 9–509, a person may add or delete collateral covered by, continue or terminate the effectiveness of, or, subject to subsection (e), otherwise amend the information provided in, a financing statement by filing an amendment that:

(1) identifies, by its file number, the initial financing statement to which the amendment relates; and

(2) if the amendment relates to an initial financing statement filed [or recorded] in a filing office described in Section 9–501(a)(1), provides the date [and time] that the initial financing statement was filed [or recorded] and the information specified in Section 9–502(b).

[End of Alternatives]

(b) Except as otherwise provided in Section 9–515, the filing of an amendment does not extend the period of effectiveness of the financing statement.

(c) A financing statement that is amended by an amendment that adds collateral is effective as to the added collateral only from the date of the filing of the amendment.

(d) A financing statement that is amended by an amendment that adds a debtor is effective as to the added debtor only from the date of the filing of the amendment.

(e) An amendment is ineffective to the extent it:

(1) purports to delete all debtors and fails to provide the name of a debtor to be covered by the financing statement; or

(2) purports to delete all secured parties of record and fails to provide the name of a new secured party of record.

Legislative Note: States whose real-estate filing offices require additional information in amendments and cannot search their records by both the name of the debtor and the file number should enact Alternative B to Sections 9–512(a), 9–518(b), 9–519(f), and 9–522(a).

§9–513.   Termination Statement.

(a) A secured party shall cause the secured party of record for a financing statement to file a termination statement for the financing statement if the financing statement covers consumer goods and:

(1) there is no obligation secured by the collateral covered by the financing statement and no commitment to make an advance, incur an obligation, or otherwise give value; or

(2) the debtor did not authorize the filing of the initial financing statement.

(b) To comply with subsection (a), a secured party shall cause the secured party of record to file the termination statement:

(1) within one month after there is no obligation secured by the collateral covered by the financing statement and no commitment to make an advance, incur an obligation, or otherwise give value; or

(2) if earlier, within 20 days after the secured party receives an authenticated demand from a debtor.

(c) In cases not governed by subsection (a), within 20 days after a secured party receives an authenticated demand from a debtor, the secured party shall cause the secured party of record for a financing statement to send to the debtor a termination statement for the financing statement or file the termination statement in the filing office if:

(1) except in the case of a financing statement covering accounts or chattel paper that has been sold or goods that are the subject of a consignment, there is no obligation secured by the collateral covered by the financing statement and no commitment to make an advance, incur an obligation, or otherwise give value;

(2) the financing statement covers accounts or chattel paper that has been sold but as to which the account debtor or other person obligated has discharged its obligation;

(3) the financing statement covers goods that were the subject of a consignment to the debtor but are not in the debtor's possession; or

(4) the debtor did not authorize the filing of the initial financing statement.

(d) Except as otherwise provided in Section 9–510, upon the filing of a termination statement with the filing office, the financing statement to which the termination statement relates ceases to be effective. Except as otherwise provided in Section 9–510, for purposes of Sections 9–519(g), 9–522(a), and 9–523(c), the filing with the filing office of a termination statement relating to a financing statement that indicates that the debtor is a transmitting utility also causes the effectiveness of the financing statement to lapse.

As amended in 2000.

§9–514. Assignment of Powers of Secured Party of Record.

(a) Except as otherwise provided in subsection (c), an initial financing statement may reflect an assignment of all of the secured party's power to authorize an amendment to the financing statement by providing the name and mailing address of the assignee as the name and address of the secured party.

(b) Except as otherwise provided in subsection (c), a secured party of record may assign of record all or part of its power to authorize an amendment to a financing statement by filing in the filing office an amendment of the financing statement which:

(1) identifies, by its file number, the initial financing statement to which it relates;

(2) provides the name of the assignor; and

(3) provides the name and mailing address of the assignee.

(c) An assignment of record of a security interest in a fixture covered by a record of a mortgage which is effective as a financing statement filed as a fixture filing under Section 9–502(c) may be made only by an assignment of record of the mortgage in the manner provided by law of this State other than [the Uniform Commercial Code].

§9–515. Duration and Effectiveness of Financing Statement; Effect of Lapsed Financing Statement.

(a) Except as otherwise provided in subsections (b), (e), (f), and (g), a filed financing statement is effective for a period of five years after the date of filing.

(b) Except as otherwise provided in subsections (e), (f), and (g), an initial financing statement filed in connection with a public-finance transaction or manufactured-home transaction is effective for a period of 30 years after the date of filing if it indicates that it is filed in connection with a public-finance transaction or manufactured-home transaction.

(c) The effectiveness of a filed financing statement lapses on the expiration of the period of its effectiveness unless before the lapse a continuation statement is filed pursuant to subsection (d). Upon lapse, a financing statement ceases to be effective and any security interest or agricultural lien that was perfected by the financing statement becomes unperfected, unless the security interest is perfected otherwise. If the security interest or agricultural lien becomes unperfected upon lapse, it is deemed never to have been perfected as against a purchaser of the collateral for value.

(d) A continuation statement may be filed only within six months before the expiration of the five-year period specified in subsection

(a) or the 30-year period specified in subsection (b), whichever is applicable.

(e) Except as otherwise provided in Section 9–510, upon timely filing of a continuation statement, the effectiveness of the initial financing statement continues for a period of five years commencing on the day on which the financing statement would have become ineffective in the absence of the filing. Upon the expiration of the five-year period, the financing statement lapses in the same manner as provided in subsection (c), unless, before the lapse, another continuation statement is filed pursuant to subsection (d). Succeeding continuation statements may be filed in the same manner to continue the effectiveness of the initial financing statement.

(f) If a debtor is a transmitting utility and a filed financing statement so indicates, the financing statement is effective until a termination statement is filed.

(g) A record of a mortgage that is effective as a financing statement filed as a fixture filing under Section 9–502(c) remains effective as a financing statement filed as a fixture filing until the mortgage is released or satisfied of record or its effectiveness otherwise terminates as to the real property.

§9–516. What Constitutes Filing; Effectiveness of Filing.

(a) Except as otherwise provided in subsection (b), communication of a record to a filing office and tender of the filing fee or acceptance of the record by the filing office constitutes filing.

(b) Filing does not occur with respect to a record that a filing office refuses to accept because:

(1) the record is not communicated by a method or medium of communication authorized by the filing office;

(2) an amount equal to or greater than the applicable filing fee is not tendered;

(3) the filing office is unable to index the record because:

(A) in the case of an initial financing statement, the record does not provide a name for the debtor;

(B) in the case of an amendment or correction statement, the record:

(i) does not identify the initial financing statement as required by Section 9–512 or 9–518, as applicable; or

(ii) identifies an initial financing statement whose effectiveness has lapsed under Section 9–515;

(C) in the case of an initial financing statement that provides the name of a debtor identified as an individual or an amendment that provides a name of a debtor identified as an individual which was not previously provided in the financing statement to which the record relates, the record does not identify the debtor's last name; or

(D) in the case of a record filed [or recorded] in the filing office described in Section 9–501(a)(1), the record does not provide a sufficient description of the real property to which it relates;

(4) in the case of an initial financing statement or an amendment that adds a secured party of record, the record does not provide a name and mailing address for the secured party of record;

(5) in the case of an initial financing statement or an amendment that provides a name of a debtor which was not previously provided in the financing statement to which the amendment relates, the record does not:

(A) provide a mailing address for the debtor;

(B) indicate whether the debtor is an individual or an organization; or

(C) if the financing statement indicates that the debtor is an organization, provide:

(i) a type of organization for the debtor;

(ii) a jurisdiction of organization for the debtor; or

(iii) an organizational identification number for the debtor or indicate that the debtor has none;

(6) in the case of an assignment reflected in an initial financing statement under Section 9–514(a) or an amendment filed under Section 9–514(b), the record does not provide a name and mailing address for the assignee; or

(7) in the case of a continuation statement, the record is not filed within the six-month period prescribed by Section 9–515(d).

(c) For purposes of subsection (b):

(1) a record does not provide information if the filing office is unable to read or decipher the information; and

(2) a record that does not indicate that it is an amendment or identify an initial financing statement to which it relates, as required by Section 9–512, 9–514, or 9–518, is an initial financing statement.

(d) A record that is communicated to the filing office with tender of the filing fee, but which the filing office refuses to accept for a reason other than one set forth in subsection (b), is effective as a filed record except as against a purchaser of the collateral which gives value in reasonable reliance upon the absence of the record from the files.

§9–517.   Effect of Indexing Errors.

The failure of the filing office to index a record correctly does not affect the effectiveness of the filed record.

§9–518.   Claim Concerning Inaccurate or Wrongfully Filed Record.

(a) A person may file in the filing office a correction statement with respect to a record indexed there under the person's name if the person believes that the record is inaccurate or was wrongfully filed.

[Alternative A]

(b) A correction statement must:

(1) identify the record to which it relates by the file number assigned to the initial financing statement to which the record relates;

(2) indicate that it is a correction statement; and

(3) provide the basis for the person's belief that the record is inaccurate and indicate the manner in which the person believes the record should be amended to cure any inaccuracy or provide the basis for the person's belief that the record was wrongfully filed.

[Alternative B]

(b) A correction statement must:

(1) identify the record to which it relates by:

(A) the file number assigned to the initial financing statement to which the record relates; and

(B) if the correction statement relates to a record filed [or recorded] in a filing office described in Section 9–501(a)(1), the date [and time] that the initial financing statement was filed [or recorded] and the information specified in Section 9–502(b);

(2) indicate that it is a correction statement; and

(3) provide the basis for the person's belief that the record is inaccurate and indicate the manner in which the person believes the record should be amended to cure any inaccuracy or provide the basis for the person's belief that the record was wrongfully filed.

[End of Alternatives]

(c) The filing of a correction statement does not affect the effectiveness of an initial financing statement or other filed record.

Legislative Note: States whose real-estate filing offices require additional information in amendments and cannot search their records by both the name of the debtor and the file number should enact Alternative B to Sections 9–512(a), 9–518(b), 9–519(f), and 9–522(a).

[Subpart 2. Duties and Operation of Filing Office]

§9–519.   Numbering, Maintaining, and Indexing Records; Communicating Information Provided in Records.

(a) For each record filed in a filing office, the filing office shall:

(1) assign a unique number to the filed record;

(2) create a record that bears the number assigned to the filed record and the date and time of filing;

(3) maintain the filed record for public inspection; and

(4) index the filed record in accordance with subsections (c), (d), and (e).

(b) A file number [assigned after January 1, 2002,] must include a digit that:

(1) is mathematically derived from or related to the other digits of the file number; and

(2) aids the filing office in determining whether a number communicated as the file number includes a single-digit or transpositional error.

(c) Except as otherwise provided in subsections (d) and (e), the filing office shall:

(1) index an initial financing statement according to the name of the debtor and index all filed records relating to the initial financing statement in a manner that associates with one another an initial financing statement and all filed records relating to the initial financing statement; and

(2) index a record that provides a name of a debtor which was not previously provided in the financing statement to which the record relates also according to the name that was not previously provided.

(d) If a financing statement is filed as a fixture filing or covers as-extracted collateral or timber to be cut, [it must be filed for record and] the filing office shall index it:

(1) under the names of the debtor and of each owner of record shown on the financing statement as if they were the mortgagors under a mortgage of the real property described; and

(2) to the extent that the law of this State provides for indexing of records of mortgages under the name of the mortgagee, under the name of the secured party as if the secured party were the mortgagee thereunder, or, if indexing is by description, as if the financing statement were a record of a mortgage of the real property described.

(e) If a financing statement is filed as a fixture filing or covers as-extracted collateral or timber to be cut, the filing office shall index an assignment filed under Section 9–514(a) or an amendment filed under Section 9–514(b):

(1) under the name of the assignor as grantor; and

(2) to the extent that the law of this State provides for indexing a record of the assignment of a mortgage under the name of the assignee, under the name of the assignee.

[Alternative A]

(f) The filing office shall maintain a capability:

(1) to retrieve a record by the name of the debtor and by the file number assigned to the initial financing statement to which the record relates; and

(2) to associate and retrieve with one another an initial financing statement and each filed record relating to the initial financing statement.

[Alternative B]

(f) The filing office shall maintain a capability:

(1) to retrieve a record by the name of the debtor and:

(A) if the filing office is described in Section 9–501(a)(1), by the file number assigned to the initial financing statement to which the record relates and the date [and time] that the record was filed [or recorded]; or

(B) if the filing office is described in Section 9–501(a)(2), by the file number assigned to the initial financing statement to which the record relates; and

(2) to associate and retrieve with one another an initial financing statement and each filed record relating to the initial financing statement.

[End of Alternatives]

(g) The filing office may not remove a debtor's name from the index until one year after the effectiveness of a financing statement naming the debtor lapses under Section 9–515 with respect to all secured parties of record.

(h) The filing office shall perform the acts required by subsections (a) through (e) at the time and in the manner prescribed by filing-office rule, but not later than two business days after the filing office receives the record in question.

[(i) Subsection[s] [(b)] [and] [(h)] do[es] not apply to a filing office described in Section 9–501(a)(1).]

Legislative Notes:

1. States whose filing offices currently assign file numbers that include a verification number, commonly known as a check digit, or can implement this requirement before the effective date of this Article should omit the bracketed language in subsection (b).

2. In States in which writings will not appear in the real property records and indices unless actually recorded the bracketed language in subsection (d) should be used.

3. States whose real-estate filing offices require additional information in amendments and cannot search their records by both the name of the debtor and the file number should enact Alternative B to Sections 9–512 (a), 9–518(b), 9–519(f), and 9–522(a).

4. A State that elects not to require real-estate filing offices to comply with either or both of subsections (b) and (h) may adopt an applicable variation of subsection (i) and add Except as otherwise provided in subsection (i), to the appropriate subsection or subsections.

§9–520.   Acceptance and Refusal to Accept Record.

(a) A filing office shall refuse to accept a record for filing for a reason set forth in Section 9–516(b) and may refuse to accept a record for filing only for a reason set forth in Section 9–516(b).

(b) If a filing office refuses to accept a record for filing, it shall communicate to the person that presented the record the fact of and reason for the refusal and the date and time the record would have been filed had the filing office accepted it. The communication must be made at the time and in the manner prescribed by filing-office rule but [, in the case of a filing office described in Section 9–501(a)(2),] in no event more than two business days after the filing office receives the record.

(c) A filed financing statement satisfying Section 9–502(a) and (b) is effective, even if the filing office is required to refuse to accept it for filing under subsection (a). However, Section 9–338 applies to a filed financing statement providing information described in Section 9–516(b)(5) which is incorrect at the time the financing statement is filed.

(d) If a record communicated to a filing office provides information that relates to more than one debtor, this part applies as to each debtor separately.

Legislative Note: A State that elects not to require real-property filing offices to comply with subsection (b) should include the bracketed language.

§9–521.   Uniform Form of Written Financing Statement and Amendment.

(a) A filing office that accepts written records may not refuse to accept a written initial financing statement in the following form and format except for a reason set forth in Section 9–516(b):

[NATIONAL UCC FINANCING STATEMENT (FORM UCC1)(REV. 7/29/98)]

[NATIONAL UCC FINANCING STATEMENT ADDEN-
DUM (FORM UCC1Ad)(REV. 07/29/98)]

(b) A filing office that accepts written records may not refuse to
accept a written record in the following form and format except for a
reason set forth in Section 9–516(b):

[NATIONAL UCC FINANCING STATEMENT AMEND-
MENT (FORM UCC3)(REV. 07/29/98)]

[NATIONAL UCC FINANCING STATEMENT AMEND-
MENT ADDENDUM (FORM UCC3Ad)(REV. 07/29/98)]

§9–522.   Maintenance and Destruction of Records.

[Alternative A]

(a) The filing office shall maintain a record of the information
provided in a filed financing statement for at least one year after the
effectiveness of the financing statement has lapsed under Section
9–515 with respect to all secured parties of record. The record must
be retrievable by using the name of the debtor and by using the file
number assigned to the initial financing statement to which the
record relates.

[Alternative B]

(a) The filing office shall maintain a record of the information
provided in a filed financing statement for at least one year after the
effectiveness of the financing statement has lapsed under Section
9–515 with respect to all secured parties of record. The record must
be retrievable by using the name of the debtor and:

(1) if the record was filed [or recorded] in the filing office
described in Section 9–501(a)(1), by using the file number assigned
to the initial financing statement to which the record relates and the
date [and time] that the record was filed [or recorded]; or

(2) if the record was filed in the filing office described in Section
9–501(a)(2), by using the file number assigned to the initial
financing statement to which the record relates.

[End of Alternatives]

(b) Except to the extent that a statute governing disposition of
public records provides otherwise, the filing office immediately
may destroy any written record evidencing a financing statement.
However, if the filing office destroys a written record, it shall
maintain another record of the financing statement which complies
with subsection (a).

*Legislative Note: States whose real-estate filing offices require additional
information in amendments and cannot search their records by both the
name of the debtor and the file number should enact Alternative B to
Sections 9–512(a), 9–518(b), 9–519(f), and 9–522(a).*

§9–523.   Information from Filing Office; Sale or License of Records.

(a) If a person that files a written record requests an acknowledgment of the filing, the filing office shall send to the person an
image of the record showing the number assigned to the record
pursuant to Section 9–519(a)(1) and the date and time of the filing
of the record. However, if the person furnishes a copy of the record
to the filing office, the filing office may instead:

(1) note upon the copy the number assigned to the record
pursuant to Section 9–519(a)(1) and the date and time of the filing
of the record; and

(2) send the copy to the person.

(b) If a person files a record other than a written record, the filing
office shall communicate to the person an acknowledgment that
provides:

(1) the information in the record;

(2) the number assigned to the record pursuant to Section 9–
519(a)(1); and

(3) the date and time of the filing of the record.

(c) The filing office shall communicate or otherwise make available
in a record the following information to any person that requests it:

(1) whether there is on file on a date and time specified by the
filing office, but not a date earlier than three business days before
the filing office receives the request, any financing statement that:

(A) designates a particular debtor [or, if the request so states,
designates a particular debtor at the address specified in the request];

(B) has not lapsed under Section 9–515 with respect to all
secured parties of record; and

(C) if the request so states, has lapsed under Section 9–515
and a record of which is maintained by the filing office under
Section 9–522(a);

(2) the date and time of filing of each financing statement; and

(3) the information provided in each financing statement.

(d) In complying with its duty under subsection (c), the filing
office may communicate information in any medium. However, if
requested, the filing office shall communicate information by issuing
[its written certificate] [a record that can be admitted into evidence in
the courts of this State without extrinsic evidence of its authenticity].

(e) The filing office shall perform the acts required by subsections
(a) through (d) at the time and in the manner prescribed by filing-
office rule, but not later than two business days after the filing office
receives the request.

(f) At least weekly, the [insert appropriate official or governmental
agency] [filing office] shall offer to sell or license to the public on a
nonexclusive basis, in bulk, copies of all records filed in it under this
part, in every medium from time to time available to the filing office.

Legislative Notes:

*1. States whose filing office does not offer the additional service of
responding to search requests limited to a particular address should omit
the bracketed language in subsection (c)(1)(A).*

*2. A State that elects not to require real-estate filing offices to comply with
either or both of subsections (e) and (f) should specify in the appropriate
subsection(s) only the filing office described in Section 9–501(a)(2).*

§9–524.   Delay by Filing Office.

Delay by the filing office beyond a time limit prescribed by this part
is excused if:

(1) the delay is caused by interruption of communication or
computer facilities, war, emergency conditions, failure of equipment, or other circumstances beyond control of the filing office; and

(2) the filing office exercises reasonable diligence under the circumstances.

§9–525.   Fees.

(a) Except as otherwise provided in subsection (e), the fee for filing and indexing a record under this part, other than an initial financing statement of the kind described in subsection (b), is [the amount specified in subsection (c), if applicable, plus]:

(1) $[X] if the record is communicated in writing and consists of one or two pages;

(2) $[2X] if the record is communicated in writing and consists of more than two pages; and

(3) $[1/2X] if the record is communicated by another medium authorized by filing-office rule.

(b) Except as otherwise provided in subsection (e), the fee for filing and indexing an initial financing statement of the following kind is [the amount specified in subsection (c), if applicable, plus]:

(1) $——— if the financing statement indicates that it is filed in connection with a public-finance transaction;

(2) $——— if the financing statement indicates that it is filed in connection with a manufactured-home transaction.

[Alternative A]

(c) The number of names required to be indexed does not affect the amount of the fee in subsections (a) and (b).

[Alternative B]

(c) Except as otherwise provided in subsection (e), if a record is communicated in writing, the fee for each name more than two required to be indexed is $———.

[End of Alternatives]

(d) The fee for responding to a request for information from the filing office, including for [issuing a certificate showing] [communicating] whether there is on file any financing statement naming a particular debtor, is:

(1) $——— if the request is communicated in writing; and

(2) $——— if the request is communicated by another medium authorized by filing-office rule.

(e) This section does not require a fee with respect to a record of a mortgage which is effective as a financing statement filed as a fixture filing or as a financing statement covering as-extracted collateral or timber to be cut under Section 9–502(c). However, the recording and satisfaction fees that otherwise would be applicable to the record of the mortgage apply.

Legislative Notes:

1. To preserve uniformity, a State that places the provisions of this section together with statutes setting fees for other services should do so without modification.

2. A State should enact subsection (c), Alternative A, and omit the bracketed language in subsections (a) and (b) unless its indexing system entails a substantial additional cost when indexing additional names.

As amended in 2000.

§9–526.   Filing-Office Rules.

(a) The [insert appropriate governmental official or agency] shall adopt and publish rules to implement this article. The filing-office rules must be[:

(1) consistent with this article[; and

(2) adopted and published in accordance with the [insert any applicable state administrative procedure act]].

(b) To keep the filing-office rules and practices of the filing office in harmony with the rules and practices of filing offices in other jurisdictions that enact substantially this part, and to keep the technology used by the filing office compatible with the technology used by filing offices in other jurisdictions that enact substantially this part, the [insert appropriate governmental official or agency], so far as is consistent with the purposes, policies, and provisions of this article, in adopting, amending, and repealing filing-office rules, shall:

(1) consult with filing offices in other jurisdictions that enact substantially this part; and

(2) consult the most recent version of the Model Rules promulgated by the International Association of Corporate Administrators or any successor organization; and

(3) take into consideration the rules and practices of, and the technology used by, filing offices in other jurisdictions that enact substantially this part.

§9–527.   Duty to Report.

The [insert appropriate governmental official or agency] shall report [annually on or before ———] to the [Governor and Legislature] on the operation of the filing office. The report must contain a statement of the extent to which:

(1) the filing-office rules are not in harmony with the rules of filing offices in other jurisdictions that enact substantially this part and the reasons for these variations; and

(2) the filing-office rules are not in harmony with the most recent version of the Model Rules promulgated by the International Association of Corporate Administrators, or any successor organization, and the reasons for these variations.

PART 6   Default

[Subpart 1. Default and Enforcement of Security Interest]

§9–601.   Rights after Default; Judicial Enforcement; Consignor or Buyer of Accounts, Chattel Paper, Payment Intangibles, or Promissory Notes.

(a) After default, a secured party has the rights provided in this part and, except as otherwise provided in Section 9–602, those provided by agreement of the parties. A secured party:

(1) may reduce a claim to judgment, foreclose, or otherwise enforce the claim, security interest, or agricultural lien by any available judicial procedure; and

(2) if the collateral is documents, may proceed either as to the documents or as to the goods they cover.

(b) A secured party in possession of collateral or control of collateral under Section 9–104, 9–105, 9–106, or 9–107 has the rights and duties provided in Section 9–207.

(c) The rights under subsections (a) and (b) are cumulative and may be exercised simultaneously.

(d) Except as otherwise provided in subsection (g) and Section 9–605, after default, a debtor and an obligor have the rights provided in this part and by agreement of the parties.

(e) If a secured party has reduced its claim to judgment, the lien of any levy that may be made upon the collateral by virtue of an execution based upon the judgment relates back to the earliest of:

(1) the date of perfection of the security interest or agricultural lien in the collateral;

(2) the date of filing a financing statement covering the collateral; or

(3) any date specified in a statute under which the agricultural lien was created.

(f) A sale pursuant to an execution is a foreclosure of the security interest or agricultural lien by judicial procedure within the meaning of this section. A secured party may purchase at the sale and thereafter hold the collateral free of any other requirements of this article.

(g) Except as otherwise provided in Section 9–607(c), this part imposes no duties upon a secured party that is a consignor or is a buyer of accounts, chattel paper, payment intangibles, or promissory notes.

§9–602.   Waiver and Variance of Rights and Duties.

Except as otherwise provided in Section 9–624, to the extent that they give rights to a debtor or obligor and impose duties on a secured party, the debtor or obligor may not waive or vary the rules stated in the following listed sections:

(1) Section 9–207(b)(4)(C), which deals with use and operation of the collateral by the secured party;

(2) Section 9–210, which deals with requests for an accounting and requests concerning a list of collateral and statement of account;

(3) Section 9–607(c), which deals with collection and enforcement of collateral;

(4) Sections 9–608(a) and 9–615(c) to the extent that they deal with application or payment of noncash proceeds of collection, enforcement, or disposition;

(5) Sections 9–608(a) and 9–615(d) to the extent that they require accounting for or payment of surplus proceeds of collateral;

(6) Section 9–609 to the extent that it imposes upon a secured party that takes possession of collateral without judicial process the duty to do so without breach of the peace;

(7) Sections 9–610(b), 9–611, 9–613, and 9–614, which deal with disposition of collateral;

(8) Section 9–615(f), which deals with calculation of a deficiency or surplus when a disposition is made to the secured party, a person related to the secured party, or a secondary obligor;

(9) Section 9–616, which deals with explanation of the calculation of a surplus or deficiency;

(10) Sections 9–620, 9–621, and 9–622, which deal with acceptance of collateral in satisfaction of obligation;

(11) Section 9–623, which deals with redemption of collateral;

(12) Section 9–624, which deals with permissible waivers; and

(13) Sections 9–625 and 9–626, which deal with the secured party's liability for failure to comply with this article.

§9–603.   Agreement on Standards Concerning Rights and Duties.

(a) The parties may determine by agreement the standards measuring the fulfillment of the rights of a debtor or obligor and the duties of a secured party under a rule stated in Section 9–602 if the standards are not manifestly unreasonable.

(b) Subsection (a) does not apply to the duty under Section 9–609 to refrain from breaching the peace.

§9–604.   Procedure If Security Agreement Covers Real Property or Fixtures.

(a) If a security agreement covers both personal and real property, a secured party may proceed:

(1) under this part as to the personal property without prejudicing any rights with respect to the real property; or

(2) as to both the personal property and the real property in accordance with the rights with respect to the real property, in which case the other provisions of this part do not apply.

(b) Subject to subsection (c), if a security agreement covers goods that are or become fixtures, a secured party may proceed:

(1) under this part; or

(2) in accordance with the rights with respect to real property, in which case the other provisions of this part do not apply.

(c) Subject to the other provisions of this part, if a secured party holding a security interest in fixtures has priority over all owners and encumbrancers of the real property, the secured party, after default, may remove the collateral from the real property.

(d) A secured party that removes collateral shall promptly reimburse any encumbrancer or owner of the real property, other than the debtor, for the cost of repair of any physical injury caused by the removal. The secured party need not reimburse the encumbrancer or owner for any diminution in value of the real property caused by the absence of the goods removed or by any necessity of replacing them. A person entitled to reimbursement may refuse permission to remove until the secured party gives adequate assurance for the performance of the obligation to reimburse.

§9–605. Unknown Debtor or Secondary Obligor.

A secured party does not owe a duty based on its status as secured party:

(1) to a person that is a debtor or obligor, unless the secured party knows:

(A) that the person is a debtor or obligor;

(B) the identity of the person; and

(C) how to communicate with the person; or

(2) to a secured party or lienholder that has filed a financing statement against a person, unless the secured party knows:

(A) that the person is a debtor; and

(B) the identity of the person.

§9–606. Time of Default for Agricultural Lien.

For purposes of this part, a default occurs in connection with an agricultural lien at the time the secured party becomes entitled to enforce the lien in accordance with the statute under which it was created.

§9–607. Collection and Enforcement by Secured Party.

(a) If so agreed, and in any event after default, a secured party:

(1) may notify an account debtor or other person obligated on collateral to make payment or otherwise render performance to or for the benefit of the secured party;

(2) may take any proceeds to which the secured party is entitled under Section 9–315;

(3) may enforce the obligations of an account debtor or other person obligated on collateral and exercise the rights of the debtor with respect to the obligation of the account debtor or other person obligated on collateral to make payment or otherwise render performance to the debtor, and with respect to any property that secures the obligations of the account debtor or other person obligated on the collateral;

(4) if it holds a security interest in a deposit account perfected by control under Section 9–104(a)(1), may apply the balance of the deposit account to the obligation secured by the deposit account; and

(5) if it holds a security interest in a deposit account perfected by control under Section 9–104(a)(2) or (3), may instruct the bank to pay the balance of the deposit account to or for the benefit of the secured party.

(b) If necessary to enable a secured party to exercise under subsection (a)(3) the right of a debtor to enforce a mortgage nonjudicially, the secured party may record in the office in which a record of the mortgage is recorded:

(1) a copy of the security agreement that creates or provides for a security interest in the obligation secured by the mortgage; and

(2) the secured party's sworn affidavit in recordable form stating that:

(A) a default has occurred; and

(B) the secured party is entitled to enforce the mortgage nonjudicially.

(c) A secured party shall proceed in a commercially reasonable manner if the secured party:

(1) undertakes to collect from or enforce an obligation of an account debtor or other person obligated on collateral; and

(2) is entitled to charge back uncollected collateral or otherwise to full or limited recourse against the debtor or a secondary obligor.

(d) A secured party may deduct from the collections made pursuant to subsection (c) reasonable expenses of collection and enforcement, including reasonable attorney's fees and legal expenses incurred by the secured party.

(e) This section does not determine whether an account debtor, bank, or other person obligated on collateral owes a duty to a secured party.

As amended in 2000.

§9–608. Application of Proceeds of Collection or Enforcement; Liability for Deficiency and Right to Surplus.

(a) If a security interest or agricultural lien secures payment or performance of an obligation, the following rules apply:

(1) A secured party shall apply or pay over for application the cash proceeds of collection or enforcement under Section 9–607 in the following order to:

(A) the reasonable expenses of collection and enforcement and, to the extent provided for by agreement and not prohibited by law, reasonable attorney's fees and legal expenses incurred by the secured party;

(B) the satisfaction of obligations secured by the security interest or agricultural lien under which the collection or enforcement is made; and

(C) the satisfaction of obligations secured by any subordinate security interest in or other lien on the collateral subject to the security interest or agricultural lien under which the collection or enforcement is made if the secured party receives an authenticated demand for proceeds before distribution of the proceeds is completed.

(2) If requested by a secured party, a holder of a subordinate security interest or other lien shall furnish reasonable proof of the interest or lien within a reasonable time. Unless the holder complies, the secured party need not comply with the holder's demand under paragraph (1)(C).

(3) A secured party need not apply or pay over for application noncash proceeds of collection and enforcement under Section 9–607 unless the failure to do so would be commercially unreasonable. A secured party that applies or pays over for application noncash proceeds shall do so in a commercially reasonable manner.

(4) A secured party shall account to and pay a debtor for any surplus, and the obligor is liable for any deficiency.

(b) If the underlying transaction is a sale of accounts, chattel paper, payment intangibles, or promissory notes, the debtor is not entitled to any surplus, and the obligor is not liable for any deficiency.

As amended in 2000.

§9–609. Secured Party's Right to Take Possession after Default.

(a) After default, a secured party:

(1) may take possession of the collateral; and

(2) without removal, may render equipment unusable and dispose of collateral on a debtor's premises under Section 9–610.

(b) A secured party may proceed under subsection (a):

(1) pursuant to judicial process; or

(2) without judicial process, if it proceeds without breach of the peace.

(c) If so agreed, and in any event after default, a secured party may require the debtor to assemble the collateral and make it available to the secured party at a place to be designated by the secured party which is reasonably convenient to both parties.

§9–610. Disposition of Collateral after Default.

(a) After default, a secured party may sell, lease, license, or otherwise dispose of any or all of the collateral in its present condition or following any commercially reasonable preparation or processing.

(b) Every aspect of a disposition of collateral, including the method, manner, time, place, and other terms, must be commercially reasonable. If commercially reasonable, a secured party may dispose of collateral by public or private proceedings, by one or more contracts, as a unit or in parcels, and at any time and place and on any terms.

(c) A secured party may purchase collateral:

(1) at a public disposition; or

(2) at a private disposition only if the collateral is of a kind that is customarily sold on a recognized market or the subject of widely distributed standard price quotations.

(d) A contract for sale, lease, license, or other disposition includes the warranties relating to title, possession, quiet enjoyment, and the like which by operation of law accompany a voluntary disposition of property of the kind subject to the contract.

(e) A secured party may disclaim or modify warranties under subsection (d):

(1) in a manner that would be effective to disclaim or modify the warranties in a voluntary disposition of property of the kind subject to the contract of disposition; or

(2) by communicating to the purchaser a record evidencing the contract for disposition and including an express disclaimer or modification of the warranties.

(f) A record is sufficient to disclaim warranties under subsection (e) if it indicates "There is no warranty relating to title, possession, quiet enjoyment, or the like in this disposition" or uses words of similar import.

§9–611. Notification before Disposition of Collateral.

(a) In this section, "notification date" means the earlier of the date on which:

(1) a secured party sends to the debtor and any secondary obligor an authenticated notification of disposition; or

(2) the debtor and any secondary obligor waive the right to notification.

(b) Except as otherwise provided in subsection (d), a secured party that disposes of collateral under Section 9–610 shall send to the persons specified in subsection (c) a reasonable authenticated notification of disposition.

(c) To comply with subsection (b), the secured party shall send an authenticated notification of disposition to:

(1) the debtor;

(2) any secondary obligor; and

(3) if the collateral is other than consumer goods:

(A) any other person from which the secured party has received, before the notification date, an authenticated notification of a claim of an interest in the collateral;

(B) any other secured party or lienholder that, 10 days before the notification date, held a security interest in or other lien on the collateral perfected by the filing of a financing statement that:

(i) identified the collateral;

(ii) was indexed under the debtor's name as of that date; and

(iii) was filed in the office in which to file a financing statement against the debtor covering the collateral as of that date; and

(C) any other secured party that, 10 days before the notification date, held a security interest in the collateral perfected by compliance with a statute, regulation, or treaty described in Section 9–311(a).

(d) Subsection (b) does not apply if the collateral is perishable or threatens to decline speedily in value or is of a type customarily sold on a recognized market.

(e) A secured party complies with the requirement for notification prescribed by subsection (c)(3)(B) if:

(1) not later than 20 days or earlier than 30 days before the notification date, the secured party requests, in a commercially reasonable manner, information concerning financing statements indexed under the debtor's name in the office indicated in subsection (c)(3)(B); and

(2) before the notification date, the secured party:

(A) did not receive a response to the request for information; or

(B) received a response to the request for information and sent an authenticated notification of disposition to each secured party or other lienholder named in that response whose financing statement covered the collateral.

§9–612.   Timeliness of Notification before Disposition of Collateral.

(a) Except as otherwise provided in subsection (b), whether a notification is sent within a reasonable time is a question of fact.

(b) In a transaction other than a consumer transaction, a notification of disposition sent after default and 10 days or more before the earliest time of disposition set forth in the notification is sent within a reasonable time before the disposition.

§9–613.   Contents and Form of Notification before Disposition of Collateral: General.

Except in a consumer-goods transaction, the following rules apply:

(1) The contents of a notification of disposition are sufficient if the notification:

(A) describes the debtor and the secured party;

(B) describes the collateral that is the subject of the intended disposition;

(C) states the method of intended disposition;

(D) states that the debtor is entitled to an accounting of the unpaid indebtedness and states the charge, if any, for an accounting; and

(E) states the time and place of a public disposition or the time after which any other disposition is to be made.

(2) Whether the contents of a notification that lacks any of the information specified in paragraph (1) are nevertheless sufficient is a question of fact.

(3) The contents of a notification providing substantially the information specified in paragraph (1) are sufficient, even if the notification includes:

(A) information not specified by that paragraph; or

(b) minor errors that are not seriously misleading.

(4) A particular phrasing of the notification is not required.

(5) The following form of notification and the form appearing in Section 9–614(3), when completed, each provides sufficient information:

NOTIFICATION OF DISPOSITION OF COLLATERAL

To: [*Name of debtor, obligor, or other person to which the notification is sent*]

From: [*Name, address, and telephone number of secured party*]

Name of Debtor(s): [*Include only if debtor(s) are not an addressee*]

[*For a public disposition:*]

We will sell [or lease or license, *as applicable*] the [*describe collateral*] [to the highest qualified bidder] in public as follows:

Day and Date: ————

Time: ————

Place: ————

[*For a private disposition:*]

We will sell [or lease or license, *as applicable*] the [*describe collateral*] privately sometime after [*day and date*].

You are entitled to an accounting of the unpaid indebtedness secured by the property that we intend to sell [or lease or license *as applicable*] [for a charge of $————]. You may request an accounting by calling us at [*telephone number*].

[End of Form]

As amended in 2000.

§9–614.   Contents and Form of Notification before Disposition of Collateral: Consumer-Goods Transaction.

In a consumer-goods transaction, the following rules apply:

(1) A notification of disposition must provide the following information:

(A) the information specified in Section 9–613(1);

(B) a description of any liability for a deficiency of the person to which the notification is sent;

(C) a telephone number from which the amount that must be paid to the secured party to redeem the collateral under Section 9–623 is available; and

(D) a telephone number or mailing address from which additional information concerning the disposition and the obligation secured is available.

(2) A particular phrasing of the notification is not required.

(3) The following form of notification, when completed, provides sufficient information:

[*Name and address of secured party*]

[*Date*]

NOTICE OF OUR PLAN TO SELL PROPERTY

[*Name and address of any obligor who is also a debtor*]

Subject: [*Identification of Transaction*]

We have your [*describe collateral*], because you broke promises in our agreement.

[*For a public disposition:*]

We will sell [*describe collateral*] at public sale. A sale could include a lease or license. The sale will be held as follows:

Date:————

Time: ————

Place: ————

You may attend the sale and bring bidders if you want.

[*For a private disposition:*]

We will sell [*describe collateral*] at private sale sometime after

[*date*]. A sale could include a lease or license.

The money that we get from the sale (after paying our costs) will reduce the amount you owe. If we get less money than you owe, you [*will or will not, as applicable*] still owe us the difference. If we get more money than you owe, you will get the extra money, unless we must pay it to someone else.

You can get the property back at any time before we sell it by paying us the full amount you owe (not just the past due payments), including our expenses. To learn the exact amount you must pay, call us at [*telephone number*].

If you want us to explain to you in writing how we have figured the amount that you owe us, you may call us at [*telephone number*] [or write us at [*secured party's address*]] and request a written explanation. [We will charge you $——— for the explanation if we sent you another written explanation of the amount you owe us within the last six months.]

If you need more information about the sale call us at [*telephone number*] [or write us at [*secured party's address*]].

We are sending this notice to the following other people who have an interest in [*describe collateral*] or who owe money under your agreement:

[*Names of all other debtors and obligors, if any*]

[End of Form]

(4) A notification in the form of paragraph (3) is sufficient, even if additional information appears at the end of the form.

(5) A notification in the form of paragraph (3) is sufficient, even if it includes errors in information not required by paragraph (1), unless the error is misleading with respect to rights arising under this article.

(6) If a notification under this section is not in the form of paragraph (3), law other than this article determines the effect of including information not required by paragraph (1).

§9–615. **Application of Proceeds of Disposition; Liability for Deficiency and Right to Surplus.**

(a) A secured party shall apply or pay over for application the cash proceeds of disposition under Section 9–610 in the following order to:

(1) the reasonable expenses of retaking, holding, preparing for disposition, processing, and disposing, and, to the extent provided for by agreement and not prohibited by law, reasonable attorney's fees and legal expenses incurred by the secured party;

(2) the satisfaction of obligations secured by the security interest or agricultural lien under which the disposition is made;

(3) the satisfaction of obligations secured by any subordinate security interest in or other subordinate lien on the collateral if:

(A) the secured party receives from the holder of the subordinate security interest or other lien an authenticated demand for proceeds before distribution of the proceeds is completed; and

(B) in a case in which a consignor has an interest in the collateral, the subordinate security interest or other lien is senior to the interest of the consignor; and

(4) a secured party that is a consignor of the collateral if the secured party receives from the consignor an authenticated demand for proceeds before distribution of the proceeds is completed.

(b) If requested by a secured party, a holder of a subordinate security interest or other lien shall furnish reasonable proof of the interest or lien within a reasonable time. Unless the holder does so, the secured party need not comply with the holder's demand under subsection (a)(3).

(c) A secured party need not apply or pay over for application noncash proceeds of disposition under Section 9–610 unless the failure to do so would be commercially unreasonable. A secured party that applies or pays over for application noncash proceeds shall do so in a commercially reasonable manner.

(d) If the security interest under which a disposition is made secures payment or performance of an obligation, after making the payments and applications required by subsection (a) and permitted by subsection (c):

(1) unless subsection (a)(4) requires the secured party to apply or pay over cash proceeds to a consignor, the secured party shall account to and pay a debtor for any surplus; and

(2) the obligor is liable for any deficiency.

(e) If the underlying transaction is a sale of accounts, chattel paper, payment intangibles, or promissory notes:

(1) the debtor is not entitled to any surplus; and

(2) the obligor is not liable for any deficiency.

(f) The surplus or deficiency following a disposition is calculated based on the amount of proceeds that would have been realized in a disposition complying with this part to a transferee other than the secured party, a person related to the secured party, or a secondary obligor if:

(1) the transferee in the disposition is the secured party, a person related to the secured party, or a secondary obligor; and

(2) the amount of proceeds of the disposition is significantly below the range of proceeds that a complying disposition to a person other than the secured party, a person related to the secured party, or a secondary obligor would have brought.

(g) A secured party that receives cash proceeds of a disposition in good faith and without knowledge that the receipt violates the rights of the holder of a security interest or other lien that is not subordinate to the security interest or agricultural lien under which the disposition is made:

(1) takes the cash proceeds free of the security interest or other lien;

(2) is not obligated to apply the proceeds of the disposition to the satisfaction of obligations secured by the security interest or other lien; and

(3) is not obligated to account to or pay the holder of the security interest or other lien for any surplus.

As amended in 2000.

§9–616. **Explanation of Calculation of Surplus or Deficiency.**

(a) In this section:

(1) "Explanation" means1 a writing that:

(A) states the amount of the surplus or deficiency;

(B) provides an explanation in accordance with subsection (c) of how the secured party calculated the surplus or deficiency;

(C) states, if applicable, that future debits, credits, charges, including additional credit service charges or interest, rebates, and expenses may affect the amount of the surplus or deficiency; and

(D)   provides a telephone number or mailing address from which additional information concerning the transaction is available.

(2)   "Request" means a record:

(A)   authenticated by a debtor or consumer obligor;

(B)   requesting that the recipient provide an explanation; and

(C)   sent after disposition of the collateral under Section 9–610.

(b)   In a consumer-goods transaction in which the debtor is entitled to a surplus or a consumer obligor is liable for a deficiency under Section 9–615, the secured party shall:

(1)   send an explanation to the debtor or consumer obligor, as applicable, after the disposition and:

(A)   before or when the secured party accounts to the debtor and pays any surplus or first makes written demand on the consumer obligor after the disposition for payment of the deficiency; and

(B)   within 14 days after receipt of a request; or

(2)   in the case of a consumer obligor who is liable for a deficiency, within 14 days after receipt of a request, send to the consumer obligor a record waiving the secured party's right to a deficiency.

(c)   To comply with subsection (a)(1)(B), a writing must provide the following information in the following order:

(1)   the aggregate amount of obligations secured by the security interest under which the disposition was made, and, if the amount reflects a rebate of unearned interest or credit service charge, an indication of that fact, calculated as of a specified date:

(A)   if the secured party takes or receives possession of the collateral after default, not more than 35 days before the secured party takes or receives possession; or

(B)   if the secured party takes or receives possession of the collateral before default or does not take possession of the collateral, not more than 35 days before the disposition;

(2)   the amount of proceeds of the disposition;

(3)   the aggregate amount of the obligations after deducting the amount of proceeds;

(4)   the amount, in the aggregate or by type, and types of expenses, including expenses of retaking, holding, preparing for disposition, processing, and disposing of the collateral, and attorney's fees secured by the collateral which are known to the secured party and relate to the current disposition;

(5)   the amount, in the aggregate or by type, and types of credits, including rebates of interest or credit service charges, to which the obligor is known to be entitled and which are not reflected in the amount in paragraph (1); and

(6)   the amount of the surplus or deficiency.

(d)   A particular phrasing of the explanation is not required. An explanation complying substantially with the requirements of subsection (a) is sufficient, even if it includes minor errors that are not seriously misleading.

(e)   A debtor or consumer obligor is entitled without charge to one response to a request under this section during any six-month period in which the secured party did not send to the debtor or consumer obligor an explanation pursuant to subsection (b)(1).

The secured party may require payment of a charge not exceeding $25 for each additional response

§9–617.   Rights of Transferee of Collateral.

(a)   A secured party's disposition of collateral after default:

(1)   transfers to a transferee for value all of the debtor's rights in the collateral;

(2)   discharges the security interest under which the disposition is made; and

(3)   discharges any subordinate security interest or other subordinate lien [other than liens created under [cite acts or statutes providing for liens, if any, that are not to be discharged]].

(b)   A transferee that acts in good faith takes free of the rights and interests described in subsection (a), even if the secured party fails to comply with this article or the requirements of any judicial proceeding.

(c)   If a transferee does not take free of the rights and interests described in subsection (a), the transferee takes the collateral subject to:

(1)   the debtor's rights in the collateral;

(2)   the security interest or agricultural lien under which the disposition is made; and

(3)   any other security interest or other lien.

§9–618.   Rights and Duties of Certain Secondary Obligors.

(a)   A secondary obligor acquires the rights and becomes obligated to perform the duties of the secured party after the secondary obligor:

(1)   receives an assignment of a secured obligation from the secured party;

(2)   receives a transfer of collateral from the secured party and agrees to accept the rights and assume the duties of the secured party; or

(3)   is subrogated to the rights of a secured party with respect to collateral.

(b)   An assignment, transfer, or subrogation described in subsection (a):

(1)   is not a disposition of collateral under Section 9–610; and

(2)   relieves the secured party of further duties under this article.

§9–619.   Transfer of Record or Legal Title.

(a)   In this section, "transfer statement" means a record authenticated by a secured party stating:

(1)   that the debtor has defaulted in connection with an obligation secured by specified collateral;

(2)   that the secured party has exercised its post-default remedies with respect to the collateral;

(3)   that, by reason of the exercise, a transferee has acquired the rights of the debtor in the collateral; and

(4) the name and mailing address of the secured party, debtor, and transferee.

(b) A transfer statement entitles the transferee to the transfer of record of all rights of the debtor in the collateral specified in the statement in any official filing, recording, registration, or certificate-of-title system covering the collateral. If a transfer statement is presented with the applicable fee and request form to the official or office responsible for maintaining the system, the official or office shall:

(1) accept the transfer statement;

(2) promptly amend its records to reflect the transfer; and

(3) if applicable, issue a new appropriate certificate of title in the name of the transferee.

(c) A transfer of the record or legal title to collateral to a secured party under subsection (b) or otherwise is not of itself a disposition of collateral under this article and does not of itself relieve the secured party of its duties under this article.

§9–620.   Acceptance of Collateral in Full or Partial Satisfaction of Obligation; Compulsory Disposition of Collateral.

(a) Except as otherwise provided in subsection (g), a secured party may accept collateral in full or partial satisfaction of the obligation it secures only if:

(1) the debtor consents to the acceptance under subsection (c);

(2) the secured party does not receive, within the time set forth in subsection (d), a notification of objection to the proposal authenticated by:

(A) a person to which the secured party was required to send a proposal under Section 9–621; or

(B) any other person, other than the debtor, holding an interest in the collateral subordinate to the security interest that is the subject of the proposal;

(3) if the collateral is consumer goods, the collateral is not in the possession of the debtor when the debtor consents to the acceptance; and

(4) subsection (e) does not require the secured party to dispose of the collateral or the debtor waives the requirement pursuant to Section 9–624.

(b) A purported or apparent acceptance of collateral under this section is ineffective unless:

(1) the secured party consents to the acceptance in an authenticated record or sends a proposal to the debtor; and

(2) the conditions of subsection (a) are met.

(c) For purposes of this section:

(1) a debtor consents to an acceptance of collateral in partial satisfaction of the obligation it secures only if the debtor agrees to the terms of the acceptance in a record authenticated after default; and

(2) a debtor consents to an acceptance of collateral in full satisfaction of the obligation it secures only if the debtor agrees to the terms of the acceptance in a record authenticated after default or the secured party:

(A) sends to the debtor after default a proposal that is unconditional or subject only to a condition that collateral not in the possession of the secured party be preserved or maintained;

(B) in the proposal, proposes to accept collateral in full satisfaction of the obligation it secures; and

(C) does not receive a notification of objection authenticated by the debtor within 20 days after the proposal is sent.

(d) To be effective under subsection (a)(2), a notification of objection must be received by the secured party:

(1) in the case of a person to which the proposal was sent pursuant to Section 9–621, within 20 days after notification was sent to that person; and

(2) in other cases:

(A) within 20 days after the last notification was sent pursuant to Section 9–621; or

(B) if a notification was not sent, before the debtor consents to the acceptance under subsection (c).

(e) A secured party that has taken possession of collateral shall dispose of the collateral pursuant to Section 9–610 within the time specified in subsection (f) if:

(1) 60 percent of the cash price has been paid in the case of a purchase-money security interest in consumer goods; or

(2) 60 percent of the principal amount of the obligation secured has been paid in the case of a non-purchase-money security interest in consumer goods.

(f) To comply with subsection (e), the secured party shall dispose of the collateral:

(1) within 90 days after taking possession; or

(2) within any longer period to which the debtor and all secondary obligors have agreed in an agreement to that effect entered into and authenticated after default.

(g) In a consumer transaction, a secured party may not accept collateral in partial satisfaction of the obligation it secures.

§9–621.   Notification of Proposal to Accept Collateral.

(a) A secured party that desires to accept collateral in full or partial satisfaction of the obligation it secures shall send its proposal to:

(1) any person from which the secured party has received, before the debtor consented to the acceptance, an authenticated notification of a claim of an interest in the collateral;

(2) any other secured party or lienholder that, 10 days before the debtor consented to the acceptance, held a security interest in or other lien on the collateral perfected by the filing of a financing statement that:

(A) identified the collateral;

(B) was indexed under the debtor's name as of that date; and

(C) was filed in the office or offices in which to file a financing statement against the debtor covering the collateral as of that date; and

(3) any other secured party that, 10 days before the debtor consented to the acceptance, held a security interest in the collateral perfected by compliance with a statute, regulation, or treaty described in Section 9–311(a).

(b) A secured party that desires to accept collateral in partial satisfaction of the obligation it secures shall send its proposal to any secondary obligor in addition to the persons described in subsection (a).

§9–622.   Effect of Acceptance of Collateral.

(a) A secured party's acceptance of collateral in full or partial satisfaction of the obligation it secures:

(1) discharges the obligation to the extent consented to by the debtor;

(2) transfers to the secured party all of a debtor's rights in the collateral;

(3) discharges the security interest or agricultural lien that is the subject of the debtor's consent and any subordinate security interest or other subordinate lien; and

(4) terminates any other subordinate interest.

(b) A subordinate interest is discharged or terminated under subsection (a), even if the secured party fails to comply with this article.

§9–623.   Right to Redeem Collateral.

(a) A debtor, any secondary obligor, or any other secured party or lienholder may redeem collateral.

(b) To redeem collateral, a person shall tender:

(1) fulfillment of all obligations secured by the collateral; and

(2) the reasonable expenses and attorney's fees described in Section 9–615(a)(1).

(c) A redemption may occur at any time before a secured party:

(1) has collected collateral under Section 9–607;

(2) has disposed of collateral or entered into a contract for its disposition under Section 9–610; or

(3) has accepted collateral in full or partial satisfaction of the obligation it secures under Section 9–622.

§9–624.   Waiver.

(a) A debtor or secondary obligor may waive the right to notification of disposition of collateral under Section 9–611 only by an agreement to that effect entered into and authenticated after default.

(b) A debtor may waive the right to require disposition of collateral under Section 9–620(e) only by an agreement to that effect entered into and authenticated after default.

(c) Except in a consumer-goods transaction, a debtor or secondary obligor may waive the right to redeem collateral under Section 9–623 only by an agreement to that effect entered into and authenticated after default.

[Subpart 2. Noncompliance with Article]

§9–625.   Remedies for Secured Party's Failure to Comply with Article.

(a) If it is established that a secured party is not proceeding in accordance with this article, a court may order or restrain collection, enforcement, or disposition of collateral on appropriate terms and conditions.

(b) Subject to subsections (c), (d), and (f), a person is liable for damages in the amount of any loss caused by a failure to comply with this article. Loss caused by a failure to comply may include loss resulting from the debtor's inability to obtain, or increased costs of, alternative financing.

(c) Except as otherwise provided in Section 9–628:

(1) a person that, at the time of the failure, was a debtor, was an obligor, or held a security interest in or other lien on the collateral may recover damages under subsection (b) for its loss; and

(2) if the collateral is consumer goods, a person that was a debtor or a secondary obligor at the time a secured party failed to comply with this part may recover for that failure in any event an amount not less than the credit service charge plus 10 percent of the principal amount of the obligation or the time-price differential plus 10 percent of the cash price.

(d) A debtor whose deficiency is eliminated under Section 9–626 may recover damages for the loss of any surplus. However, a debtor or secondary obligor whose deficiency is eliminated or reduced under Section 9–626 may not otherwise recover under subsection (b) for noncompliance with the provisions of this part relating to collection, enforcement, disposition, or acceptance.

(e) In addition to any damages recoverable under subsection (b), the debtor, consumer obligor, or person named as a debtor in a filed record, as applicable, may recover $500 in each case from a person that:

(1) fails to comply with Section 9–208;

(2) fails to comply with Section 9–209;

(3) files a record that the person is not entitled to file under Section 9–509(a);

(4) fails to cause the secured party of record to file or send a termination statement as required by Section 9–513(a) or (c);

(5) fails to comply with Section 9–616(b)(1) and whose failure is part of a pattern, or consistent with a practice, of noncompliance; or

(6) fails to comply with Section 9–616(b)(2).

(f) A debtor or consumer obligor may recover damages under subsection (b) and, in addition, $500 in each case from a person that, without reasonable cause, fails to comply with a request under Section 9–210. A recipient of a request under Section 9–210 which never claimed an interest in the collateral or obligations that are the subject of a request under that section has a reasonable excuse for failure to comply with the request within the meaning of this subsection.

(g) If a secured party fails to comply with a request regarding a list of collateral or a statement of account under Section 9–210, the secured party may claim a security interest only as shown in the list or statement included in the request as against a person that is reasonably misled by the failure.

As amended in 2000.

§9–626.   Action in Which Deficiency or Surplus Is in Issue.

(a) In an action arising from a transaction, other than a consumer transaction, in which the amount of a deficiency or surplus is in issue, the following rules apply:

(1) A secured party need not prove compliance with the provisions of this part relating to collection, enforcement, disposition, or acceptance unless the debtor or a secondary obligor places the secured party's compliance in issue.

(2) If the secured party's compliance is placed in issue, the secured party has the burden of establishing that the collection, enforcement, disposition, or acceptance was conducted in accordance with this part.

(3) Except as otherwise provided in Section 9–628, if a secured party fails to prove that the collection, enforcement, disposition, or acceptance was conducted in accordance with the provisions of this part relating to collection, enforcement, disposition, or acceptance, the liability of a debtor or a secondary obligor for a deficiency is limited to an amount by which the sum of the secured obligation, expenses, and attorney's fees exceeds the greater of:

(A) the proceeds of the collection, enforcement, disposition, or acceptance; or

(B) the amount of proceeds that would have been realized had the noncomplying secured party proceeded in accordance with the provisions of this part relating to collection, enforcement, disposition, or acceptance.

(4) For purposes of paragraph (3)(B), the amount of proceeds that would have been realized is equal to the sum of the secured obligation, expenses, and attorney's fees unless the secured party proves that the amount is less than that sum.

(5) If a deficiency or surplus is calculated under Section 9–615 (f), the debtor or obligor has the burden of establishing that the amount of proceeds of the disposition is significantly below the range of prices that a complying disposition to a person other than the secured party, a person related to the secured party, or a secondary obligor would have brought.

(b) The limitation of the rules in subsection (a) to transactions other than consumer transactions is intended to leave to the court the determination of the proper rules in consumer transactions. The court may not infer from that limitation the nature of the proper rule in consumer transactions and may continue to apply established approaches.

§9–627.   Determination of Whether Conduct Was Commercially Reasonable.

(a) The fact that a greater amount could have been obtained by a collection, enforcement, disposition, or acceptance at a different time or in a different method from that selected by the secured party is not of itself sufficient to preclude the secured party from establishing that the collection, enforcement, disposition, or acceptance was made in a commercially reasonable manner.

(b) A disposition of collateral is made in a commercially reasonable manner if the disposition is made:

(1) in the usual manner on any recognized market;

(2) at the price current in any recognized market at the time of the disposition; or

(3) otherwise in conformity with reasonable commercial practices among dealers in the type of property that was the subject of the disposition.

(c) A collection, enforcement, disposition, or acceptance is commercially reasonable if it has been approved:

(1) in a judicial proceeding;

(2) by a bona fide creditors' committee;

(3) by a representative of creditors; or

(4) by an assignee for the benefit of creditors.

(d) Approval under subsection (c) need not be obtained, and lack of approval does not mean that the collection, enforcement, disposition, or acceptance is not commercially reasonable.

§9–628.   Nonliability and Limitation on Liability of Secured Party; Liability of Secondary Obligor.

(a) Unless a secured party knows that a person is a debtor or obligor, knows the identity of the person, and knows how to communicate with the person:

(1) the secured party is not liable to the person, or to a secured party or lienholder that has filed a financing statement against the person, for failure to comply with this article; and

(2) the secured party's failure to comply with this article does not affect the liability of the person for a deficiency.

(b) A secured party is not liable because of its status as secured party:

(1) to a person that is a debtor or obligor, unless the secured party knows:

(A) that the person is a debtor or obligor;

(B) the identity of the person; and

(C) how to communicate with the person; or

(2) to a secured party or lienholder that has filed a financing statement against a person, unless the secured party knows:

(A) that the person is a debtor; and

(B) the identity of the person.

(c) A secured party is not liable to any person, and a person's liability for a deficiency is not affected, because of any act or omission arising out of the secured party's reasonable belief that a transaction is not a consumer-goods transaction or a consumer transaction or that goods are not consumer goods, if the secured party's belief is based on its reasonable reliance on:

(1) a debtor's representation concerning the purpose for which collateral was to be used, acquired, or held; or

(2) an obligor's representation concerning the purpose for which a secured obligation was incurred.

(d) A secured party is not liable to any person under Section 9–625 (c)(2) for its failure to comply with Section 9–616.

(e) A secured party is not liable under Section 9–625(c)(2) more than once with respect to any one secured obligation.

PART 7 Transition

§9–701. Effective Date.

This [Act] takes effect on July 1, 2001.

§9–702. Savings Clause.

(a) Except as otherwise provided in this part, this [Act] applies to a transaction or lien within its scope, even if the transaction or lien was entered into or created before this [Act] takes effect.

(b) Except as otherwise provided in subsection (c) and Sections 9–703 through 9–709:

(1) transactions and liens that were not governed by [former Article 9], were validly entered into or created before this [Act] takes effect, and would be subject to this [Act] if they had been entered into or created after this [Act] takes effect, and the rights, duties, and interests flowing from those transactions and liens remain valid after this [Act] takes effect; and

(2) the transactions and liens may be terminated, completed, consummated, and enforced as required or permitted by this [Act] or by the law that otherwise would apply if this [Act] had not taken effect.

(c) This [Act] does not affect an action, case, or proceeding commenced before this [Act] takes effect.

As amended in 2000.

§9–703. Security Interest Perfected before Effective Date.

(a) A security interest that is enforceable immediately before this [Act] takes effect and would have priority over the rights of a person that becomes a lien creditor at that time is a perfected security interest under this [Act] if, when this [Act] takes effect, the applicable requirements for enforceability and perfection under this [Act] are satisfied without further action.

(b) Except as otherwise provided in Section 9–705, if, immediately before this [Act] takes effect, a security interest is enforceable

and would have priority over the rights of a person that becomes a lien creditor at that time, but the applicable requirements for enforceability or perfection under this [Act] are not satisfied when this [Act] takes effect, the security interest:

(1) is a perfected security interest for one year after this [Act] takes effect;

(2) remains enforceable thereafter only if the security interest becomes enforceable under Section 9–203 before the year expires; and

(3) remains perfected thereafter only if the applicable requirements for perfection under this [Act] are satisfied before the year expires.

§9–704. Security Interest Unperfected before Effective Date.

A security interest that is enforceable immediately before this [Act] takes effect but which would be subordinate to the rights of a person that becomes a lien creditor at that time:

(1) remains an enforceable security interest for one year after this [Act] takes effect;

(2) remains enforceable thereafter if the security interest becomes enforceable under Section 9–203 when this [Act] takes effect or within one year thereafter; and

(3) becomes perfected:

(A) without further action, when this [Act] takes effect if the applicable requirements for perfection under this [Act] are satisfied before or at that time; or

(B) when the applicable requirements for perfection are satisfied if the requirements are satisfied after that time.

§9–705. Effectiveness of Action Taken before Effective Date.

(a) If action, other than the filing of a financing statement, is taken before this [Act] takes effect and the action would have resulted in priority of a security interest over the rights of a person that becomes a lien creditor had the security interest become enforceable before this [Act] takes effect, the action is effective to perfect a security interest that attaches under this [Act] within one year after this [Act] takes effect. An attached security interest becomes unperfected one year after this [Act] takes effect unless the security interest becomes a perfected security interest under this [Act] before the expiration of that period.

(b) The filing of a financing statement before this [Act] takes effect is effective to perfect a security interest to the extent the filing would satisfy the applicable requirements for perfection under this [Act].

(c) This [Act] does not render ineffective an effective financing statement that, before this [Act] takes effect, is filed and satisfies the applicable requirements for perfection under the law of the jurisdiction governing perfection as provided in [former Section 9–103]. However, except as otherwise provided in subsections (d) and (e) and Section 9–706, the financing statement ceases to be effective at the earlier of:

(1) the time the financing statement would have ceased to be effective under the law of the jurisdiction in which it is filed; or

(2) June 30, 2006.

(d) The filing of a continuation statement after this [Act] takes effect does not continue the effectiveness of the financing statement filed before this [Act] takes effect. However, upon the timely filing of a continuation statement after this [Act] takes effect and in accordance with the law of the jurisdiction governing perfection as provided in Part 3, the effectiveness of a financing statement filed in the same office in that jurisdiction before this [Act] takes effect continues for the period provided by the law of that jurisdiction.

(e) Subsection (c)(2) applies to a financing statement that, before this [Act] takes effect, is filed against a transmitting utility and satisfies the applicable requirements for perfection under the law of the jurisdiction governing perfection as provided in [former Section 9–103] only to the extent that Part 3 provides that the law of a jurisdiction other than the jurisdiction in which the financing statement is filed governs perfection of a security interest in collateral covered by the financing statement.

(f) A financing statement that includes a financing statement filed before this [Act] takes effect and a continuation statement filed after this [Act] takes effect is effective only to the extent that it satisfies the requirements of Part 5 for an initial financing statement.

§9–706. When Initial Financing Statement Suffices to Continue Effectiveness of Financing Statement.

(a) The filing of an initial financing statement in the office specified in Section 9–501 continues the effectiveness of a financing statement filed before this [Act] takes effect if:

(1) the filing of an initial financing statement in that office would be effective to perfect a security interest under this [Act];

(2) the pre-effective-date financing statement was filed in an office in another State or another office in this State; and

(3) the initial financing statement satisfies subsection (c).

(b) The filing of an initial financing statement under subsection (a) continues the effectiveness of the pre-effective-date financing statement:

(1) if the initial financing statement is filed before this [Act] takes effect, for the period provided in [former Section 9–403] with respect to a financing statement; and

(2) if the initial financing statement is filed after this [Act] takes effect, for the period provided in Section 9–515 with respect to an initial financing statement.

(c) To be effective for purposes of subsection (a), an initial financing statement must:

(1) satisfy the requirements of Part 5 for an initial financing statement;

(2) identify the pre-effective-date financing statement by indicating the office in which the financing statement was filed and providing the dates of filing and file numbers, if any, of the financing statement and of the most recent continuation statement filed with respect to the financing statement; and

(3) indicate that the pre-effective-date financing statement remains effective.

§9–707. Amendment of Pre-Effective-Date Financing Statement.

(a) In this section, "Pre-effective-date financing statement" means a financing statement filed before this [Act] takes effect.

(b) After this [Act] takes effect, a person may add or delete collateral covered by, continue or terminate the effectiveness of, or otherwise amend the information provided in, a pre-effective-date financing statement only in accordance with the law of the jurisdiction governing perfection as provided in Part 3. However, the effectiveness of a pre-effective-date financing statement also may be terminated in accordance with the law of the jurisdiction in which the financing statement is filed.

(c) Except as otherwise provided in subsection (d), if the law of this State governs perfection of a security interest, the information in a pre-effective-date financing statement may be amended after this [Act] takes effect only if:

(1) the pre-effective-date financing statement and an amendment are filed in the office specified in Section 9–501;

(2) an amendment is filed in the office specified in Section 9–501 concurrently with, or after the filing in that office of, an initial financing statement that satisfies Section 9–706(c); or

(3) an initial financing statement that provides the information as amended and satisfies Section 9–706(c) is filed in the office specified in Section 9–501.

(d) If the law of this State governs perfection of a security interest, the effectiveness of a pre-effective-date financing statement may be continued only under Section 9–705(d) and (f) or 9–706.

(e) Whether or not the law of this State governs perfection of a security interest, the effectiveness of a pre-effective-date financing statement filed in this State may be terminated after this [Act] takes effect by filing a termination statement in the office in which the pre-effective-date financing statement is filed, unless an initial financing statement that satisfies Section 9–706(c) has been filed in the office specified by the law of the jurisdiction governing perfection as provided in Part 3 as the office in which to file a financing statement.

As amended in 2000.

§9–708.   Persons Entitled to File Initial Financing Statement or Continuation Statement.

A person may file an initial financing statement or a continuation statement under this part if:

(1) the secured party of record authorizes the filing; and

(2) the filing is necessary under this part:

(A) to continue the effectiveness of a financing statement filed before this [Act] takes effect; or

(B) to perfect or continue the perfection of a security interest.

As amended in 2000.

§9–709.   Priority.

(a) This [Act] determines the priority of conflicting claims to collateral. However, if the relative priorities of the claims were established before this [Act] takes effect, [former Article 9] determines priority.

(b) For purposes of Section 9–322(a), the priority of a security interest that becomes enforceable under Section 9–203 of this [Act] dates from the time this [Act] takes effect if the security interest is perfected under this [Act] by the filing of a financing statement before this [Act] takes effect which would not have been effective to perfect the security interest under [former Article 9]. This subsection does not apply to conflicting security interests each of which is perfected by the filing of such a financing statement.

The Code consists of the following articles:

Art.

1. General Provisions

2. Sales

2A. Leases

3. Negotiable Instruments

4. Bank Deposits and Collections

4A. Fund Transfers

5. Letters of Credit

6. Repealer of Article 6 Bulk Transfers and [Revised] Article 6 Bulk Sales

7. Warehouse Receipts, Bills of Lading and Other Documents of Title

8. Investment Securities

9. Secured Transactions

10. Effective Date and Repealer

11. Effective Date and Transmission Provisions

GLOSSARY

A

Abatement An order to the owner of a property to eliminate a nuisance.

Absolute privilege Exists in courtrooms and legislative hearings. Anyone speaking there, such as a witness in a court, can say anything and never be sued for defamation. (Chapter 6)

Accept To sign a check. (Chapter 22)

Acceptance Retention of the collateral by a secured party as full or partial satisfaction of a debt. (Chapter 25)

Accepted check A check that the drawee bank has signed. This signature is a promise that the bank will pay the check out of its own funds.

Accession The use of labor and/or materials to add value to the personal property of another.

Accommodation party Someone who does not benefit from an instrument but agrees to guarantee its payment.

Accord and satisfaction An agreement to settle a debt for less than the sum claimed. (Chapter 11)

Accounts Any right to receive payment for goods sold or leased, other than rights covered by chattel paper or instruments.

Accredited investor Under the Securities Act of 1933, an accredited investor is an institution (such as a bank or insurance company) or any individual with a net worth of more than $1 million or an annual income of more than $200,000. (Chapter 31)

Acquit To find the defendant not guilty of the crime for which he was tried.

Act of State doctrine A rule requiring American courts to abstain from cases if a court order would interfere with the ability of the President or Congress to conduct foreign policy.

Actual authority An agent is authorized to act for a principal.

Actus reus The guilty act. The prosecution must show that a criminal defendant committed some proscribed act. In a murder prosecution, taking another person's life is the *actus reus*.

Ad valorem According to the value of the goods. (Chapter 8)

Additional terms Those terms that raise issues not covered in an offer. (Chapter 18)

Adhesion contract A standard form contract prepared by one party and presented to the other on a "take it or leave it" basis. (Chapter 12)

Adjudicate To hold a formal hearing in a disputed matter and issue an official decision. (Chapter 4)

Administrative law Concerns all agencies, boards, commissions, and other entities created by a federal or state legislature and charged with investigating, regulating, and adjudicating a particular industry or issue.

Administrative law judge An agency employee who acts as an impartial decision-maker. (Chapter 4)

Administrator A person appointed by the court to oversee the probate process for someone who has died intestate (that is, without a will).

Administratrix A female administrator.

Adverse possession A means of gaining ownership of land belonging to another by entering upon the property, openly and notoriously, and claiming exclusive use of it for a period of years.

Affidavit A written statement signed under oath.

Affirm An appellate court issues a decision upholding the judgment of a lower court. (Chapter 3)

Affirmative action A plan introduced in a workplace for the purpose of either remedying the effects of past discrimination or achieving equitable representation of minorities and women.

After-acquired property Items that a debtor obtains after making a security agreement with the secured party. (Chapter 25)

Agent A person who acts for a principal. (Chapter 27)

Alternative dispute resolution Any method of resolving a legal conflict other than litigation, such as negotiation, arbitration, mediation, mini-trials, and summary jury trials. (Chapter 3)

Amendment Any addition to a legal document. The constitutional amendments, the first ten of which are known collectively as the Bill of Rights, secure numerous liberties and protections directly for the people.

Annual report Each year, public companies must send their shareholders a document that contains detailed financial data. (Chapter 30)

Annuity Payment to a beneficiary during his lifetime.

Answer The pleading, filed by the defendant in court and served on the plaintiff, which responds to each allegation in the plaintiff's complaint.

Antitrust laws Make it illegal to destroy competition and capture an entire market. (Chapter 8)

Apparent authority A situation in which conduct of a principal causes a third party to believe that the principal consents to have an act done on his behalf by a person purporting to act for him when, in fact, that person is not acting for the principal.

Appeals court Any court in a state or federal system that reviews cases that have already been tried. (Chapter 3)

Appellant The party who appeals a lower court decision to a higher court. (Chapter 3)

Appellee The party opposing an appeal from a lower court to a higher court. (Chapter 3)

Arbitration A form of alternative dispute resolution in which the parties hire a neutral third party to hear their respective arguments, receive evidence, and then make a binding decision.

Arson Malicious use of fire or explosives to damage or destroy real estate or personal property.

Artisan's lien A security interest in personal property. (Chapter 25)

Assault An intentional act that causes the plaintiff to fear an imminent battery. (Chapter 6)

Assignee The party who receives an assignment of contract rights from a party to the contract.

Assignment The act by which a party transfers contract rights to a third person. (Chapter 15)

Assignor The party who assigns contract rights to a third person.

Assisted suicide The process of hastening death for a terminally ill patient at the request of this patient.

Attachment A court order seizing property of a party to a civil action, so that there will be sufficient assets available to pay the judgment. (Chapter 25)

Authorized and unissued stock Stock that has been approved by the corporation's charter but has not yet been sold. (Chapter 30)

Authorized and issued stock Stock that has been approved by the corporation's charter and subsequently sold. (Chapter 30)

Automatic stay Prohibits creditors from collecting debts that the bankrupt incurred before the bankruptcy petition was filed. (Chapter 26)

B

Bailee A person who rightfully possesses goods belonging to another. (Chapter 12, 19)

Bailment Giving possession and control of personal property to another person. (Chapter 12, 32)

Bailor One who creates a bailment by delivering goods to another. (Chapter 12, 19)

Bait and switch A practice where sellers advertise products that are not generally available but are being used to draw interested parties in so that they will buy other products.

Bankrupt Another term for debtor. (Chapter 26)

Bankruptcy estate The new legal entity created when a debtor files a bankruptcy petition. All of the debtor's existing assets pass into the estate. (Chapter 26)

Battery The intentional touching of another person in a way that is unwanted or offensive. (Chapter 6)

Bearer paper An instrument payable "to bearer." Any holder in due course can demand payment. (Chapter 22)

Best efforts underwriting When the underwriter does not buy the stock but instead acts as the company's agent in selling it. (Chapter 31)

Beyond a reasonable doubt The government's burden in a criminal prosecution. (Chapter 3)

Bilateral contract A binding agreement in which each party has made a promise to the other.

Bilateral mistake Occurs when both parties negotiate based on the same factual error. (Chapter 13)

Bill A proposed statute that has been submitted for consideration to Congress or a state legislature. (Chapter 4)

Bill of lading A receipt for goods, given by a carrier such as a ship, that minutely describes the merchandise being shipped. A negotiable bill of lading may be transferred to other parties, and entitles any holder to collect the goods.

Bill of Rights The first ten amendments to the Constitution.

Blue sky laws State securities laws.

Bona fide occupational qualification (BFOQ) A job requirement that would otherwise be discriminatory is permitted in situations in which it is *essential* to the position in question. (Chapter 28)

Bona fide purchaser Someone who buys goods in good faith, for value, typically from a seller who has merely voidable title.

Bonds Long-term debt secured by some of the issuing company's assets. (Chapter 30)

Brief The written legal argument that an attorney files with an appeal court. (Chapter 3)

Bulk sale A transfer of most or all of a merchant's assets.

Burden of proof The allocation of which party must prove its case. In a civil case, the plaintiff has the burden of proof to persuade the fact finder of every element of her case. In a criminal case, the government has the burden of proof.

Business judgment rule A common law rule that protects managers from liability if they are acting without a conflict of interest and make informed decisions that have a rational business purpose.

Business trust An unincorporated association run by trustees for the benefit of investors. (Chapter 29)

Buyer in ordinary course of business (BIOC) Someone who buys goods in good faith from a seller who routinely deals in such goods. (Chapter 19, 25)

Bylaws A document that specifies the organizational rules of a corporation or other organization, such as the date of the annual meeting and the required number of directors. (Chapter 30)

C

Cap and trade A market-based system for reducing emissions.

Capacity The legal ability to enter into a contract.

Cashier's check A check that is drawn by a bank on itself. (Chapter 22)

Certificate of deposit An instrument issued by a bank which promises to repay a deposit, with interest, on a specified date. (Chapter 22)

Certified check A check that the drawee bank has signed. This signature is a promise that the bank will pay the check out of its own funds.

Certiorari, writ of Formal notice from the United States Supreme Court that it will accept a case for review.

Challenge for cause An attorney's request, during *voir dire*, to excuse a prospective juror because of apparent bias. (Chapter 3)

Chancery, court of In medieval England, the court originally operated by the Chancellor.

Charging order A court order granting the creditor of a partner the right to receive that partner's share of partnership profits.

Chattel paper Any writing that indicates two things: (1) a debtor owes money and (2) a secured party has a security interest in specific goods. The most common chattel paper is a document indicating a consumer sale on credit.

Check An instrument in which the drawer orders the drawee bank to pay money to the payee. (Chapter 22)

Chicago School A theory of antitrust law first developed at the University of Chicago. Adherents to this theory believe that antitrust enforcement should focus on promoting efficiency and should not generally be concerned about the size or number of competitors in any market.

CISG See Convention on Contracts for the International Sale of Goods (CISG).

Civil law The large body of law concerning the rights and duties between parties. It is distinguished from criminal law, which concerns behavior outlawed by a government. (Chapter 1)

Claim in recoupment An issuer subtracts (i.e., "sets off") any other claims that he has against the initial payee from the amount that he owes on an instrument. (Chapter 22)

Class action A method of litigating a civil lawsuit in which one or more plaintiffs (or occasionally defendants) seek to represent an entire group of people with similar claims against a common opponent. (Chapter 3)

Classification The process by which the Customs Service decides what label to attach to imported merchandise, and therefore what level of tariff to impose. (Chapter 8)

Close corporation A corporation with a small number of shareholders. Its stock is not publicly traded. Also known as a *closely held corporation*. (Chapter 29)

Codicil An amendment to a will.

Collateral The property subject to a security interest. (Chapter 25)

Collateral promise A promise to pay the debt of another person, as a favor to the debtor.

Collective bargaining Contract negotiations between an employer and a union.

Collective bargaining agreement (CBA) A contract between a union and management.

Collective bargaining unit The precisely defined group of employees who are represented by a particular union.

Comity A doctrine that requires a court to abstain from hearing a case out of respect for another court that also has jurisdiction. *International comity* demands that a U.S. court refuse to hear a case in which a foreign court shares jurisdiction if there is a conflict between the laws and if it is more logical for the foreign court to take the case. (Chapter 8)

Commerce clause One of the powers granted by Article I, Section 8 of the Constitution, it gives Congress exclusive power to regulate international commerce and concurrent power with the states to regulate domestic commerce. (Chapter 5)

Commercial impracticability After the creation of a contract, an entirely unforeseen event occurs which makes enforcement of the contract extraordinarily unfair.

Commercial paper Instruments such as checks and promissory notes that contain a promise to pay money. Commercial paper includes both negotiable and non-negotiable instruments.

Commercial speech Communication, such as television advertisements, that has the dominant theme of proposing a commercial transaction. (Chapter 5)

Common carrier A transportation company that makes its services available on a regular basis to the general public.

Common law Judge-made law, that is, the body of all decisions made by appellate courts over the years. (Chapter 1, 4)

Common stock Certificates that reflect ownership in a corporation. Owners of this equity security are last in line for corporate pay-outs such as dividends and liquidation proceeds.

Comparative negligence A rule of tort law that permits a plaintiff to recover even when the defendant can show that the plaintiff's own conduct contributed in some way to her harm.

Compensatory damages The amount of money that the court thinks will restore the plaintiff to the position he was in before the defendant's conduct caused an injury. (Chapter 6, 17)

Complaint A pleading, filed by the plaintiff, providing a short statement of the claim. (Chapter 3)

Concerted action Tactics, such as a strike, used by a union to gain a bargaining advantage.

Concurrent estate Two or more people owning property at the same time. (Chapter 32)

Condition A condition is an event that must occur in order for a party to be obligated under a contract. (Chapter 16)

Condition precedent A condition that must occur before a particular contract duty arises.

Condition subsequent A condition that must occur after a particular contract duty arises, or the duty will be discharged.

Confiscation Expropriation without adequate compensation of property owned by foreigners. (Chapter 8)

Conforming goods Items that satisfy the contract terms. If a contract calls for blue sailboats, then green sailboats are non-conforming.

Consent order An agreement entered into by a wrongdoer and an administrative agency (such as the Securities and Exchange Commission or the Federal Trade Commission) in which the wrongdoer agrees not to violate the law in the future.

Consequential damages Those resulting from the unique circumstances of *this injured party*. (Chapter 17)

Consideration In contract law, something of legal value that has been bargained for and given in exchange by the parties.

Constitution The supreme law of a political entity. The United States Constitution is the highest law in the country.

Consumer Any natural person, that is, not a corporation or business. (Chapter 24)

Consumer credit contract A contract in which a consumer borrows money from a lender to purchase goods and services from a seller who is affiliated with the lender. (Chapter 22)

Contract A legally enforceable promise or set of promises.

Contract carrier A transportation company that does not make its services available to the general public but engages in continuing agreements with particular customers.

Contributory negligence A rule of tort law that permits a negligent defendant to escape liability if she can demonstrate that the plaintiff's own conduct contributed in any way to the plaintiff's harm.

Control security Stock owned by any officer or director of the issuer, or by any shareholder who holds more than 10 percent of a class of stock of the issuer. (Chapter 31)

Convention on Contracts for the International Sale of Goods (CISG) A United Nations–sponsored agreement that creates a neutral body of law for sale of goods contracts between companies from different countries.

Conversion (1) A tort committed by taking or using someone else's personal property without his permission. (2) A bank has paid a check that has a forged indorsement. (Chapter 23)

Cookie A small computer file that identifies the user of a computer. Internet sites typically place cookies on a computer's hard drive to track visitors to their site.

Cooperative A group of individuals or businesses that join together to gain the advantages of volume purchases or sales. (Chapter 29)

Copyright Under federal law, the holder of a copyright owns a particular expression of an idea, but not the idea itself. This ownership right applies to creative activities such as literature, music, drama, and software.

Corporation by estoppel Even if a corporation has not actually been formed, courts will sometimes enforce contracts entered into in the belief that the corporation did indeed exist.

Compliance program A plan to prevent and detect criminal conduct at all levels of the company.

Constructive insider Anyone who has an indirect employment relationship with a company, such as employees of the company's auditors or law firm. (Chapter 31)

Counter-claim A claim made by the defendant against the plaintiff. (Chapter 3)

Cover The buyer's right to obtain substitute goods when a seller has breached a contract. (Chapter 17)

Creditor beneficiary When one party to a contract intends to benefit a third party to whom he owes a debt, that third party is referred to as a creditor beneficiary.

Criminal law Rules that permit a government to punish certain behavior by fine or imprisonment. (Chapter 1, 7)

Criminal procedure The process of investigating, interrogating, and trying a criminal defendant.

Cross-examine During a hearing, when a lawyer questions an opposing witness. (Chapter 3)

Cure The seller's right to respond to a buyer's rejection of nonconforming goods; the seller accomplishes this by delivering conforming goods before the contract deadline.

D

Damages (1) The harm that a plaintiff complains of at trial, such as an injury to her person, or money lost because of a contract breach. (2) Money awarded by a trial court for injury suffered.

De facto **corporation** Occurs when a promoter makes a good faith effort to incorporate (although fails to complete the process entirely) and uses the corporation to conduct business. The state can challenge the validity of the corporation, but a third party cannot.

***De jure* corporation** The promoter of the corporation has substantially complied with the requirements for incorporation, but has made some minor error. No one has the right to challenge the validity of the corporation.

***De novo* decision** The power of an appellate court or appellate agency to make a new decision in a matter under appeal, entirely ignoring the findings and conclusions of the lower court or agency official. (Chapter 4)

Debentures Long-term, unsecured debt, typically issued by a corporation. (Chapter 30)

Debtor A person who owes money or some other obligation to another party. (Chapter 25, 26)

Decedent A person who has died.

Deed A document that proves ownership of property. (Chapter 32)

Defamation The act of injuring someone's reputation by stating something false about her to a third person. *Libel* is defamation done either in writing or by broadcast. *Slander* is defamation done orally. (Chapter 6)

Default The failure to perform an obligation, such as the failure to pay money when due. (Chapter 25)

Default judgment A court order awarding one party everything it requested because the opposing party failed to respond in time. (Chapter 3)

Default rules Under the Uniform Partnership Act, these rules govern the relationship among the partners unless the partners explicitly make a different agreement.

Defendant The person being sued. (Chapter 1)

Deficiency Having insufficient funds to pay off a debt. (Chapter 25)

Definiteness A doctrine holding that a contract will only be enforced if its terms are sufficiently precise that a court can determine what the parties meant.

Delegation The act by which a party to a contract transfers duties to a third person who is not a party to the contract. (Chapter 15)

Deponent The person being questioned in a deposition. (Chapter 3)

Deposition A form of discovery in which a party's attorney has the right to ask oral questions of the other party or of a witness. Answers are given under oath.

Derivative action A lawsuit brought by shareholders in the name of the corporation to enforce a right of the corporation.

Deterrence Using punishment, such as imprisonment, to discourage criminal behavior.

Devisee Someone who inherits under a will.

Different terms Terms that contradict those in an offer. (Chapter 18)

Direct examination During a hearing, when a lawyer asks questions of his own witness. (Chapter 3)

Directed verdict The decision by a court to instruct a jury that it must find in favor of a particular party because, in the judge's opinion, no reasonable person could disagree on the outcome. (Chapter 3)

Disabled person Someone with a physical or mental impairment that substantially limits a major life activity, or someone who is regarded as having such an impairment. (Chapter 28)

Disability insurance Replaces the insured's income if he becomes unable to work because of illness or injury.

Disaffirm To give notice to the other party to a contract that the party giving the notice refuses to be bound by the agreement. (Chapter 13)

Discharge (1) A party to a contract has no more duties. (2) A party to an instrument is released from liability. (Chapter 16, 23, 26)

Disclaimer A statement that a particular warranty does not apply. (Chapter 20)

Discovery A stage in litigation, after all pleadings have been served, in which each party seeks as much relevant information as possible about the opposing party's case. (Chapter 3)

Dishonor An obligor refuses to pay an instrument that is due. (Chapter 23)

Dismiss To terminate a lawsuit, often on procedural grounds, without reaching the merits of the case.

Dissociation A dissociation occurs when a partner leaves a partnership. (Chapter 29)

Diversity jurisdiction One of the two main types of civil cases that a U.S. district court has the power to hear. It involves a lawsuit between citizens of different states, in which at least one party makes a claim for more than $75,000. (Chapter 3)

Domestic corporation A corporation is a domestic corporation in the state in which it was formed.

Donee A person who receives a gift. (Chapter 32)

Donee beneficiary When one party to a contract intends to make a gift to a third party, that third party is referred to as a donee beneficiary.

Donor A person who makes a gift to another. (Chapter 32)

Double jeopardy A criminal defendant may be prosecuted only once for a particular criminal offense.

Draft The drawer of this instrument orders someone else to pay money. Checks are the most common form of draft. The drawer of a check orders a bank to pay money. (Chapter 22)

Dram acts Make businesses liable for serving drinks to intoxicated customers who later cause harm.

Drawee The person who pays a draft. In the case of a check, the bank is the drawee. (Chapter 22, 23)

Drawer The person who issues a draft. (Chapter 22)

Due diligence An investigation of the registration statement by someone who signs it. (Chapter 31)

Due Process Clause Part of the Fifth Amendment. *Procedural due process* ensures that before depriving anyone of liberty or property, the government must go through procedures which ensure that the deprivation is fair. *Substantive due process* holds that certain rights, such as privacy, are so fundamental that the government may not eliminate them. (Chapter 5)

Dumping Selling merchandise at one price in the domestic market and at a cheaper, unfair price in an international market. (Chapter 8)

Durable power of attorney An instrument that permits an attorney-in-fact to act for a principal. A durable power is effective until the principal revokes it or dies. It continues in effect even if the principal becomes incapacitated.

Duress (1) A criminal defense in which the defendant shows that she committed the wrongful act because a third person threatened her with imminent physical harm. (2) An improper threat made to force another party to enter into a contract. (Chapter 13)

Duty A tax imposed on imported items.

Duty of care The requirement that a manager act with care and in the best interests of the corporation. (Chapter 30)

Duty of loyalty The obligation of a manager to act without a conflict of interest. (Chapter 30)

E

Easement The right to enter land belonging to another and make a limited use of it, without taking anything away. (Chapter 32)

Economic loss doctrine A common-law rule holding that when an injury is purely economic, and it arises from a contract made between two businesses, the injured party may sue only under the Universal Commercial Code (UCC). (Chapter 20)

Electronic funds Moneys that are moved between accounts by means of a computer, an ATM, or a wire transfer. (Chapter 24)

Element A fact that a party to a lawsuit must prove in order to prevail. (Chapter 6)

Embezzlement Fraudulent conversion of property already in the defendant's possession.

Eminent domain The power of the government to take private property for public use. (Chapter 5, 32)

Employee at will A worker whose job does not have a specified duration.

Enabling legislation A statute authorizing the creation of a new administrative agency and specifying its powers and duties.

Engagement letter A written contract by which a client hires an accountant.

Entrapment A criminal defense in which the defendant demonstrates that the government induced him to break the law.

Equal dignities rule If an agent is empowered to enter into a contract that must be in writing, then the appointment of the agent must also be written. (Chapter 27)

Equal Protection Clause Part of the Fourteenth Amendment, it generally requires the government to treat equally situated people the same. (Chapter 5)

Equity The broad powers of a court to fashion a remedy where justice demands it and no common law remedy exists. An injunction is an example of an equitable remedy. (Chapter 1)

Error of law A mistake made by a trial judge that concerns a legal issue as opposed to a factual matter. Permitting too many leading questions is a legal error; choosing to believe one witness rather than another is a factual matter. (Chapter 3)

Escalator clause A lease clause allowing the landlord to raise the rent for specified reasons.

Estate The legal entity that holds title to assets after the owner dies and before the property is distributed.

Estoppel Out of fairness, a person is denied the right to assert a claim.

Ethics The study of how people ought to act. (Chapter 2)

Eviction An act that forces a tenant to abandon the property. (Chapter 32)

Evidence, rules of Law governing the proof offered during a trial or formal hearing. These rules limit the questions that may be asked of witnesses and the introduction of physical objects.

Exclusionary rule In a criminal trial, a ban on the use of evidence obtained in violation of the Constitution.

Exclusive dealing contract A contract in which a distributor or retailer agrees with a supplier not to carry the products of any other supplier.

Exculpatory clause A contract provision that attempts to release one party from liability in the event the other party is injured. (Chapter 12)

Executed contract A binding agreement in which all parties have fulfilled all obligations.

Executive agency An administrative agency within the executive branch of government.

Executive order An order by a president or governor, having the full force of law.

Executor A person chosen by the decedent to oversee the probate process.

Executory contract A binding agreement in which one or more of the parties has not fulfilled its obligations.

Executrix A female executor.

Exhaustion of remedies A principle of administrative law that no party may appeal an agency action to a court until she has utilized all available appeals within the agency itself.

Expectation interest A remedy in a contract case that puts the injured party in the position he would have been in had both sides fully performed. (Chapter 1)

Expert witness A witness in a court case who has special training or qualifications to discuss a specific issue, and who is generally permitted to state an opinion.

Export To transport goods or services out of a country. (Chapter 8)

Express authority Conduct of a principal that, reasonably interpreted, causes the agent to believe that the principal desires him to do a specific act.

Express contract A binding agreement in which the parties explicitly state all important terms.

Express warranty A guarantee, created by the words or actions of the seller, that goods will meet certain standards. (Chapter 20)

Expropriation A government's seizure of property or companies owned by foreigners. (Chapter 8)

F

Factfinder The one responsible, during a trial, for deciding what occurred, that is, who did what to whom, when, how, and why. It is either the jury or, in a jury-waived case, the judge.

Fair representation, duty of The union's obligation to act on behalf of all members impartially and in good faith.

Fair use doctrine Permits limited use of copyrighted material without permission of the author. (Chapter 34)

False imprisonment The intentional restraint of another person without reasonable cause and without her consent. (Chapter 6)

Federal question One of the two main types of civil cases that a U.S. district court has the power to hear. It involves a federal statute or a constitutional provision. (Chapter 3)

Federal Sentencing Guidelines Detailed rules that judges must follow when sentencing defendants convicted of crimes in federal court.

Federalism A form of national government in which power is shared between one central authority and numerous local authorities.

Fee simple absolute The greatest possible ownership right in real property, including the right to possess, use, and dispose of the property in any lawful manner. (Chapter 32)

Fee simple defeasible Ownership interest in real property that may terminate upon the occurrence of some limiting event. (Chapter 32)

Felony The most serious crimes, typically those for which the defendant could be imprisoned for more than a year.

Fiduciary duty An obligation to behave in a trustworthy and confidential fashion toward the object of that duty.

Financing statement A document that a secured party files to give the general public notice that the secured party has a secured interest in the collateral. (Chapter 25)

Finding statutes Laws that govern found property. Also known as *estray statutes.*

Firm commitment underwriting The underwriter buys stock from the issuer and sells it to the public. (Chapter 31)

Firm offer A contract offer that cannot be withdrawn during a stated period. (Chapter 10)

Fixtures Goods that are attached to real estate. (Chapter 25)

Forced share The percentage of a decedent's estate that a spouse is entitled to claim under state law. Also known as statutory share.

Foreign corporation A corporation formed in another state.

Foreign Sovereign Immunity Act (FSIA) A federal statute that protects other nations from suit in courts of the United States, except under specified circumstances. (Chapter 8)

Formal rulemaking The process whereby an administrative agency notifies the public of a proposed new rule and then permits a formal hearing, with opportunity for evidence and cross-examination, before promulgating the final rule.

Founding Fathers The authors of the U.S. Constitution, who participated in the Constitutional Convention in Philadelphia in 1787.

Framers *See* Founding Fathers.

Franchise An arrangement in which the franchisee buys from a franchiser the right to establish a business using the franchiser's trade name and selling the franchiser's products. Typically the franchiser also trains the franchisee in the proper operation of the business.

Fraud Deception of another person to obtain money or property. (Chapter 6, 7)

Freedom of Information Act (FOIA) A federal statute giving private citizens and corporations access to many of the documents possessed by an administrative agency.

Freehold estate The present right to possess property and to use it in any lawful manner.

Fresh start After the termination of a bankruptcy case, creditors cannot make a claim against the debtor for money owed before the initial bankruptcy petition was filed. (Chapter 26)

Frustration of purpose After the creation of a contract, an entirely unforeseen event occurs that eliminates the value of the contract for one of the parties.

Fully disclosed principal If the third party in an agency relationship knows the identity of the principal, that principal is fully disclosed.

Fundamental rights In constitutional law, those rights that are so basic that any governmental interference with them is suspect and likely to be unconstitutional.

G

GAAP Generally accepted accounting principles. Rules set by the Financial Accounting Standards Board to be used in preparing financial statements.

GAAS Generally accepted auditing standards. Rules set by the American Institute of Certified Public Accountants (AICPA) to be used in conducting audits.

Gap-filler provisions Uniform Commercial Code (UCC) rules for supplying missing terms. (Chapter 10)

Gap period The period between the time that creditors file an involuntary petition and the court issues the order for relief. (Chapter 26)

GATT *See* General Agreement on Tariffs and Trade. (Chapter 8)

General Agreement on Tariffs and Trade (GATT) A massive international treaty, negotiated in stages between the 1940s and 1994 and signed by over 130 nations. (Chapter 8)

General deterrence *See* Deterrence.

General intangibles Potential sources of income such as copyrights, patents, trademarks, goodwill and certain other rights to payment.

General intent The defendant intended to do the prohibited physical action (the *actus reus*).

Gift A voluntary transfer of property from one person to another without consideration. (Chapter 32)

Gift *causa mortis* A gift made in contemplation of approaching death. (Chapter 32)

Goods Anything movable, except for money, securities, and certain legal rights. (Chapter 8, 18, 25)

Grand jury A group of ordinary citizens that decides whether there is probable cause the defendant committed the crime and should be tried.

Grantee The person who receives property, or some interest in it, from the owner. (Chapter 32)

Grantor (1) An owner who conveys property, or some interest in it. (2) Someone who creates a trust. (Chapter 32)

Gratuitous assignment An assignment made as a gift, for no consideration. (Chapter 15)

Greenmail If a company is threatened with a hostile takeover, its board of directors may offer to buy the stock of the attacker at an above-market price with the hope that the attacker will take her profits and leave the company alone.

Grievance A formal complaint alleging a contract violation.

Guilty A court's finding that a defendant has committed a crime.

H

Hacking Gaining unauthorized access to a computer system.

Harmless error A ruling made by a trial court which an appeals court determines was legally wrong but not fatal to the decision. (Chapter 3)

Heir Someone who inherits from a decedent who died intestate (that is, without a will).

Holder For order paper, anyone in possession of the instrument if it is payable to or indorsed to her. For bearer paper, anyone in possession. (Chapter 22)

Holder in due course Someone who has given value for an instrument, in good faith, without notice of outstanding claims or other defenses. (Chapter 22)

Holographic will A handwritten will that has not been witnessed.

Horizontal agreement or merger An agreement or merger between two potential competitors.

Hostile takeover An outsider buys a company in the face of opposition from the target company's board of directors. (Chapter 30)

Hybrid rulemaking A method of administrative agency procedure incorporating some elements of formal and some elements of informal rulemaking, typically involving a limited public hearing with restricted rights of testimony and cross-examination.

I

Identify In sales law, to designate the specific goods that are the subject of a contract.

IFRS "International Financial Reporting Standards" is a new set of international standard accounting rules, used by over 100 countries, currently being proposed for U.S. companies to follow.

Illegal contract An agreement that is void because it violates a statute or public policy.

Illusory promise An apparent promise that is unenforceable because the promisor makes no firm commitment.

Implied authority When a principal directs an agent to undertake a transaction, the agent has the right to do acts that are incidental to it, usually accompany it, or are reasonably necessary to accomplish it.

Implied contract A binding agreement created not by explicit language but by the informal words and conduct of the parties.

Implied warranty Guarantees created by the Uniform Commercial Code and imposed on the seller of goods.

Implied warranty of fitness for a particular purpose If the seller knows that the buyer plans to use the goods for a particular purpose, the seller generally is held to warrant that the goods are in fact fit for that purpose. (Chapter 10)

Implied warranty of habitability A landlord must meet all standards set by the local building code, or otherwise ensure that the premises are fit for human habitation.

Implied warranty of merchantability Requires that goods must be of at least average, passable quality in the trade. (Chapter 10)

Import To transport goods or services into a country. (Chapter 8)

Import ban A prohibition of certain goods.

In camera "In the judge's chambers," meaning that the judge does something out of view of the jury and the public.

Incidental beneficiary Someone who might have benefited from a contract between two others but has no right to enforce that agreement. (Chapter 15)

Incidental damages The relatively minor costs, such as storage and advertising, that the injured party suffered when responding to a contract breach. (Chapter 17)

Incorporator The person who signs a corporate charter.

Indemnification A promise to pay someone else's obligations.

Independent agency An administrative agency outside the executive branch of government, such as the Interstate Commerce Commission.

Independent contractor Someone who undertakes tasks for others and whose work is not closely controlled.

Indictment The government's formal charge that a defendant has committed a crime.

Indorser Anyone, other than the issuer or acceptor, who signs an instrument. (Chapter 23)

Indorsement The signature of a payee. (Chapter 22)

Infliction of emotional distress A tort. It can be the *intentional infliction of emotional distress*, meaning that the defendant behaved outrageously and deliberately caused the plaintiff severe psychological injury, or it can be the *negligent infliction of emotional distress*, meaning that the defendant's conduct violated the rules of negligence.

Informal rulemaking The process whereby an administrative agency notifies the public of a proposed new rule and permits comment but is then free to promulgate the final rule without a public hearing.

Initial public offering (IPO) A company's first public sale of securities. (Chapter 31)

Injunction A court order that a person either do or stop doing something. (Chapter 17)

Inside directors Members of the board of directors who are also officers of the corporation.

Insider Family members of an individual debtor, officers and directors of a corporation, or partners of a partnership. (Chapter 26)

Instructions or charge The explanation given by a judge to a jury, outlining the jury's task in deciding a lawsuit and the underlying rules of law the jury should use in reaching its decision.

Instruments Drafts, checks, certificates of deposit and notes.

Insurable interest A person has an insurable interest if she would be harmed by the danger that she has insured against.

Insured A person whose loss is the subject of an insurance policy.

Insurer The person who issues an insurance policy.

Integrated contract A writing that the parties intend as the complete and final expression of their agreement. (Chapter 14)

Intended beneficiary Someone who may enforce a contract made between two other parties. (Chapter 15)

Intentional infliction of emotional distress Results from extreme and outrageous conduct that causes serious emotional harm. (Chapter 6)

Intentional tort An act deliberately performed that violates a legally imposed duty and injures someone. (Chapter 6)

Inter vivos gift A gift made "during life," that is, when the donor is not under any fear of impending death. (Chapter 32)

Inter vivos trust A trust established while the grantor is still living.

Interest A legal right in something, such as ownership or a mortgage or a tenancy. (Chapter 17)

Interference with a contract *See* Tortious interference with a contract. (Chapter 6)

Interference with a prospective advantage *See* Tortious interference with a prospective advantage. (Chapter 6)

International comity Requires one court to reject a lawsuit that would more logically be resolved in another nation.

Internet An international computer network that connects smaller groups of linked computer networks.

Interpretive rules A formal statement by an administrative agency expressing its view of what existing statutes or regulations mean.

Interrogatory A form of discovery in which one party sends to an opposing party written questions that must be answered under oath.

Intestate Without a will.

Intrusion A tort if a reasonable person would find the invasion of her private life offensive. (Chapter 6)

Inventory Goods that the seller is holding for sale or lease in the ordinary course of its business. (Chapter 25)

Involuntary bailment A bailment that occurs without an agreement between the bailor and bailee.

Invitee Someone who has the right to be on property, such as a customer in a shop.

Issue All direct descendants such as children, grandchildren, and so on.

Issuer The maker of a promissory note or the drawer of a draft. (Chapter 22, 31)

J

Joint and several liability All members of a group are liable. They can be sued as a group, or any one of them can be sued individually for the full amount owing.

Joint liability All members of a group are liable and must be sued together.

Joint tenancy Two or more people holding equal interest in a property, with the right of survivorship. (Chapter 32)

Joint venture A partnership for a limited purpose. (Chapter 32)

Judgment *non obstante veredicto (JNOV)* "Judgment notwithstanding the verdict." A trial judge overturns the verdict of the jury and enters a judgment in favor of the opposing party. (Chapter 3)

Judgment rate The interest rate that courts use on court-ordered judgments. (Chapter 22)

Judicial activism The willingness shown by certain courts (and not by others) to decide issues of public policy, such as constitutional questions (free speech, equal protection, etc.) and matters of contract fairness (promissory estoppel, unconscionability, etc.). (Chapter 5)

Judicial restraint A court's preference to abstain from adjudicating major social issues and to leave such matters to legislatures. (Chapter 5, 9)

Judicial review The power of the judicial system to examine, interpret, and even nullify actions taken by another branch of government.

Jurisdiction The power of a court to hear a particular dispute, civil or criminal, and to make a binding decision. (Chapter 3)

Jurisprudence The study of the purposes and philosophies of the law, as opposed to particular provisions of the law. (Chapter 1)

Justification A criminal defense in which the defendant establishes that he broke the law to avoid a greater harm.

L

Labor-Management Relations Act Designed to curb union abuses.

Landlord The owner of a freehold estate who allows another person to live on his property temporarily. (Chapter 32)

Larceny Taking personal property with the intention of preventing the owner from ever using it.

Law merchant The body of rules and customs developed by traders and businesspersons throughout Europe from roughly the fifteenth to the eighteenth century. (Chapter 18)

Lease A contract creating a landlord-tenant relationship.

Legal positivism The legal philosophy holding that law is what the sovereign says it is, regardless of its moral content.

Legal realism The legal philosophy holding that what really influences law is who makes and enforces it, not what is put in writing.

Legal remedy Generally, money damages. It is distinguished from equitable remedy, which includes injunctions and other nonmonetary relief.

Legislative history Used by courts to interpret the meaning of a statute, this is the record of hearings, speeches, and explanations that accompanied a statute as it made its way from newly proposed bill to final law.

Legislative rules Regulations issued by an administrative agency.

Letter of credit A commercial device used to guarantee payment in international trade, usually between parties that have not previously worked together. (Chapter 8)

Letter of intent A letter that summarizes negotiating progress. (Chapter 10)

Liability insurance Reimburses the insured for any liability she incurs by accidentally harming someone else.

Libel The act of injuring someone's reputation by stating (in writing or by broadcast) something false about her to a third person. (Chapter 6)

License To grant permission to another person (1) to make or sell something or (2) to enter on property. (Chapter 32)

Licensee A person who is on the property of another for her own purposes, but with the owner's permission. A social guest is a typical licensee.

Lien A security interest created by rule of law, often based on labor that the secured party has expended on the collateral. (Chapter 25)

Life estate An ownership interest in real property entitling the holder to use the property during his lifetime, but which terminates upon his death. (Chapter 32)

Life insurance Provides for payments to a beneficiary upon the death of the insured.

Life tenant A person who has the use of a property during his lifetime only. (Chapter 32)

Limited liability company An organization that has the limited liability of a corporation but is not a taxable entity.

Limited liability limited partnership In a limited liability limited partnership, the general partner is not personally liable for the debts of the partnership.

Limited partnership A partnership with two types of partners: (1) limited partners who have no personal liability for the debts of the enterprise nor any right to manage the business, and (2) general partners who are responsible for management and personally liable for all debts.

Liquidated damages clause A contract clause specifying how much a party must pay upon breach. (Chapter 17)

Liquidated debt The amount of the indebtedness is not in dispute. (Chapter 11)

Litigation The process of resolving disputes through formal court proceedings. (Chapter 3)

Living trust A trust established while the grantor is alive. *See inter vivos* trust.

Living will An instrument that permits adults to refuse medical treatment. It can also appoint a health care proxy to make medical decisions for a person who has become incompetent.

Local A regional union that represents workers at a particular company.

Lockout A management tactic, designed to gain a bargaining advantage, in which the company refuses to allow union members to work (and hence deprives them of their pay).

M

Mailbox rule A contract doctrine holding that acceptance is effective upon dispatch, that is, when it is mailed or otherwise taken out of the control of the offeree. (Chapter 10)

Maker The issuer of a promissory note. (Chapter 22)

Marital trust A legal entity created for the purpose of reducing a married couple's estate taxes.

Material Important or significant. Information that would affect a person's decision if he knew it. (Chapter 31)

Mechanic's lien A security created when a worker improves real property. (Chapter 25)

Mediation The process of using a neutral person to aid in the settlement of a legal dispute. A mediator's decision is non-binding.

Meeting of the minds The parties understood each other and intended to reach an agreement. (Chapter 10)

Mens rea Guilty state of mind.

Merchant Someone who routinely deals in the particular goods involved, or who appears to have special knowledge or skill in those goods, or who uses agents with special knowledge or skill in those goods. (Chapter 18)

Merchantable The goods are fit for the ordinary purposes for which they are used. (Chapter 20)

Merger An acquisition of one company by another.

Midnight deadline A rule that each bank in the collection process must pass a check along before midnight of the next banking day after it receives the check. (Chapter 24)

Minor A person under the age of 18.

Minority shareholders Shareholders who do not own enough stock to control their corporation.

Minute book Records of shareholder meetings and directors' meetings are kept in the corporation's minute book. (Chapter 30)

Mirror image rule A contract doctrine that requires acceptance to be on exactly the same terms as the offer. (Chapter 10)

Misdemeanor A less serious crime, typically one for which the maximum penalty is incarceration for less than a year, often in a jail, as opposed to a prison.

Misrepresentation A factually incorrect statement made during contract negotiations. (Chapter 13)

Mitigation One party acts to minimize its losses when the other party breaches a contract. (Chapter 17)

Modify An appellate court issues an order changing a lower court ruling. (Chapter 3)

Money laundering Taking the profits of criminal acts and either (1) using the money to promote more crime or (2) attempting to conceal the money's source.

Monopolization A company acquires or maintains a monopoly through the commission of unacceptably aggressive acts. A violation of Section 2 of the Sherman Act.

Mortgage A security interest in real property. (Chapter 32)

Mortgagee A creditor who obtains a security interest in real property, typically in exchange for money given to the mortgagor to buy the property. (Chapter 32)

Mortgagor A debtor who gives a mortgage (security interest) in real property to a creditor, typically in exchange for money used to buy the property. (Chapter 32)

Motion A formal request that a court take some specified step during litigation. A motion to compel discovery is a request that a trial judge order the other party to respond to discovery. (Chapter 3)

Motion for a protective order A request that the court limit discovery. (Chapter 3)

Motion to suppress A request that the court exclude evidence because it was obtained in violation of the Constitution.

Multinational enterprise A corporation that is doing business in more than one country simultaneously.

N

NAFTA *See* North American Free Trade Agreement (NAFTA). (Chapter 8)

National Labor Relations Act (NLRA) Ensures the right of workers to form unions and encourages management and unions to bargain collectively.

National Labor Relations Board (NLRB) The administrative agency charged with overseeing labor law.

Nationalization A government's seizure of property or companies. (Chapter 8)

Natural law The theory that an unjust law is no law at all, and that a rule is only legitimate if based on an immutable morality.

Negative or dormant aspect of the Commerce Clause The doctrine that prohibits a state from any action that interferes with or discriminates against interstate commerce.

Negligence and strict liability Injuries caused by neglect and oversight rather than by deliberate conduct. (Chapter 6)

Negligence per se Violation of a standard of care set by statute. Driving while intoxicated is illegal; thus, if a drunk driver injures a pedestrian, he has committed negligence per se.

Negotiable instrument A type of commercial paper that is freely transferable.

Negotiation The transfer of an instrument. To be negotiated, order paper must be indorsed and then delivered to the transferee. For bearer paper, no indorsement is required—it must simply be delivered to the transferee.

No-strike clause A clause in a CBA that prohibits the union from striking while the CBA is in force.

Nominal damages A token sum, such as one dollar, given to a plaintiff who demonstrates that the defendant breached the contract but cannot prove serious injury. (Chapter 17)

Noncompetition agreement A contract in which one party agrees not to compete with another in a stated type of business.

Nonconforming goods Merchandise that differs from that specified in the contract. (Chapter 19)

Non-point source When pollutants are released simultaneously from more than one source.

Norris-LaGuardia Act Prohibits federal court injunctions in peaceful labor disputes.

North American Free Trade Agreement A commercial association among Canada, the United States, and Mexico designed to eliminate almost all trade barriers. (Chapter 8)

Note An unconditional, written promise that the maker of the instrument will pay a specific amount of money on demand or at a definite time. When issued by a corporation, a note refers to short-term debt, typically payable within five years. (Chapter 30)

Notice to quit A landlord's notice terminating a tenancy.

Novation A three-way agreement in which the obligor transfers all rights and duties to a third party. (Chapter 15, 30)

Nuisance An unprivileged interference with a person's use and enjoyment of property.

Nuncupative will An oral will.

O

Obligee The party to a contract who is entitled to receive performance from the other party. (Chapter 15)

Obligor The party to a contract who is required to do something for the benefit of the other party. (Chapter 15, 25)

Obscenity Constitutional law doctrine holding that some works will receive no First Amendment protection because a court determines they depict sexual matters in an offensive way.

Offer In contract law, an act or statement that proposes definite terms and permits the other party to create a contract by accepting those terms. (Chapter 10)

Offeree The party in contract negotiations who receives the first offer. (Chapter 10)

Offeror The party in contract negotiations who makes the first offer. (Chapter 10)

Opinion Because it cannot be proven right or wrong, an opinion is generally a valid defense in defamation cases. (Chapter 6)

Oppression One party uses its superior power to force a contract on the weaker party. (Chapter 12)

Order for relief An official acknowledgment that a debtor is under the jurisdiction of the bankruptcy court. (Chapter 26)

Order paper An instrument that includes the words "pay to the order of" or their equivalent. (Chapter 22)

Output contract An agreement that obligates the seller of goods to sell everything he produces during a stated period to a particular buyer. (Chapter 10)

Outside directors Members of the board of directors who are not employees of the corporation. Also known as *independent directors*.

Override The power of Congress or a state legislature to pass legislation despite a veto by a president or governor. A congressional override requires a two-thirds vote in each house.

P

Parol evidence Written or oral evidence, outside the language of a contract, offered by one party to clarify interpretation of the agreement.

Parol evidence rule In the case of an integrated contract, neither party may use evidence outside the writing to contradict, vary, or add to its terms.

Part performance An exception to the statute of frauds permitting a buyer of real estate to enforce an oral contract if she paid part of the price, entered the property, and made improvements, with the owner's knowledge.

Partially disclosed principal If the third party in an agency relationship knows that the agent is acting for a principal, but does not know the identity of the principal, that principal is partially disclosed.

Partnership An association of two or more persons to carry on as co-owners of a business for profit. (Chapter 29)

Partnership at will A partnership that has no fixed duration. A partner has the right to resign from the partnership at any time. (Chapter 29)

Partnership by estoppel If a person who is not a partner implies that he is a partner or does not object when other people imply it, he is liable as if he really were a partner.

Patent The right to the exclusive use of an invention for 20 years. (Chapter 32)

Payable on demand The holder of an instrument is entitled to be paid whenever she asks. (Chapter 22)

Payee Someone who is owed money under the terms of an instrument. (Chapter 22)

Payment order A transfer money from the issuer's account into the payee's. (Chapter 24)

Per se **violation of an antitrust law** An automatic breach. Courts will generally not consider mitigating factors.

Peremptory challenge During *voir dire*, a request by one attorney that a prospective juror be excused for an unstated reason. (Chapter 3)

Perfect tender rule A rule permitting the buyer to reject goods if they fail in any respect to conform to the contract.

Perfection A series of steps a secured party must take to protect its rights in collateral against people other than the debtor. (Chapter 25)

Periodic tenancy A lease for a fixed period, automatically renewable unless terminated. (Chapter 32)

Period for years A lease for a fixed period, automatically renewable unless terminated.

Perpetual trust A trust that lasts forever. Also known as a dynasty trust.

Personal property All property other than real property. (Chapter 32)

Personally identifiable information (PII) Data that identifies a user of a Web site, such as name and address. (Chapter 33)

Personal services contracts Permits the promisee to make a subjective evaluation of the promisor's performance. (Chapter 16)

Pierce the corporate veil When the court holds shareholders personally liable for the debts of the corporation. (Chapter 30)

Plain meaning rule In statutory interpretation, the premise that words with an ordinary, everyday significance will be so interpreted, unless there is some apparent reason not to.

Plaintiff The person who is suing. (Chapter 1)

Plea bargain An agreement in which the defendant pleads guilty to a reduced charge and the prosecution recommends to the judge a relatively lenient sentence.

Pleadings The documents that begin a lawsuit: the complaint, the answer, the counter-claim, and the reply. (Chapter 3)

Pledge A secured transaction in which a debtor gives collateral to the secured party. (Chapter 25)

Point source A single producer of pollution.

Political speech Protected unless it is intended and likely to create imminent lawless action. (Chapter 5)

Positive aspect of the Commerce Clause The power granted to Congress to regulate commerce between the states.

Precedent An earlier case that decided the same legal issue as that presently in dispute, and which therefore will control the outcome of the current case. (Chapter 1, 3, 4)

Predatory pricing A violation of Section 2 of the Sherman Act in which a company lowers its prices below cost to drive competitors out of business.

Preemption The doctrine, based on the Supremacy Clause, by which any federal statute takes priority whenever (1) a state statute conflicts or (2) there is no conflict but Congress indicated an intention to control the issue involved.

Preference When a debtor unfairly pays creditors immediately before filing a bankruptcy petition. (Chapter 26)

Preferred stock Owners of preferred stock have a right to receive dividends and liquidation proceeds of the company before common shareholders. (Chapter 30)

Preponderance of the evidence The level of proof that a plaintiff must meet to prevail in a civil lawsuit. It means that the plaintiff must offer evidence that, in sum, is slightly more persuasive than the defendant's evidence. (Chapter 3)

Presentment A holder of an instrument makes a demand for payment. (Chapter 23)

Pretermitted child A child omitted from a parent's will.

Prima facie "At first sight." A fact or conclusion that is presumed to be true unless someone presents evidence to disprove it.

Principal In an agency relationship, the principal is the person for whom the agent is acting. (Chapter 27)

Privacy Act A federal statute prohibiting federal agencies from divulging to other agencies or organizations information about private citizens.

Privity The relationship that exists between two parties who make a contract, as opposed to a third party who, though affected by the contract, is not a party to it.

Probable cause In a search and seizure case, it means that the information available indicates that it is more likely than not that a search will uncover particular criminal evidence.

Probate The process of carrying out the terms of a will.

Procedural due process *See* Due Process Clause. (Chapter 5)

Procedural law The rules establishing how the legal system itself is to operate in a particular kind of case. (Chapter 1)

Proceeds Anything that a debtor obtains from the sale or disposition of collateral. Normally, the term *proceeds* refers to cash obtained from the sale of the secured property.

Production of documents and things A form of discovery in which one party demands that the other furnish original documents or physical things, relating to the suit, for inspection and copying.

Product liability The potential responsibility that a manufacturer or seller has for injuries caused by defective goods.

Professional corporation A form of organization that permits professionals (such as doctors, lawyers, and accountants) to incorporate. Shareholders are not personally liable for the torts of other shareholders, or for the contract debts of the organization.

Profit The right to enter land belonging to another and take something away, such as minerals or timber. (Chapter 32)

Promisee The person to whom a promise is made. (Chapter 11, 15)

Promisor A person who makes a promise. (Chapter 11, 15)

Promissory estoppel A doctrine in which a court may enforce a promise made by the defendant even when there is no contract, if the defendant knew that the plaintiff was likely to rely on the promise, the plaintiff did in fact rely, and enforcement of it is the only way to avoid injustice.

Promissory note The maker of the instrument promises to pay a specific amount of money. (Chapter 22)

Promoter The person who creates a corporation by raising capital and undertaking the legal steps necessary for formation.

Promulgate To issue a new rule.

Proof of claim A form stating the name of an unsecured creditor and the amount of the claim against the debtor. (Chapter 26)

Property insurance Covers physical damage to real estate, personal property, or inventory from causes such as fire, smoke, lightning, wind, riot, vandalism, or theft.

Prosecution The government's attempt to convict a defendant of a crime by charging him, trying the case, and forcing him to defend himself.

Prospectus Under the Securities Act of 1933, an issuer must provide this document to anyone who purchases a security in a public transaction. The prospectus contains detailed information about the issuer and its business, a description of the stock, and audited financial statements.

Protective order A court order limiting one party's discovery.

Proxy (1) A person whom the shareholder designates to vote in his place. (2) The written form (typically a card) that the shareholder uses to appoint a designated voter. (Chapter 30)

Proxy statement When a public company seeks proxy votes from its shareholders, it must include a proxy statement. This statement contains information about the company, such as a detailed description of management compensation.

Publicly traded corporation A company that (1) has completed a public offering under the Securities Act of 1933, or (2) has securities traded on a national exchange, or (3) has 500 shareholders and $10 million in assets.

Punitive damages Money awarded at trial not to compensate the plaintiff for harm but to punish the defendant for conduct that the factfinder considers extreme and outrageous. (Chapter 6)

Purchase money security interest (PMSI) A security interest taken by the person who sells the collateral to the debtor, or by a person who advances money so that the debtor may buy the collateral. (Chapter 25)

Q

Qualified privilege When providing a reference about a former employee, an employer is liable for false statements only if he knows them to be false or if he is primarily motivated by ill will between two people who have a legitimate need to exchange information. (Chapter 6, 28)

Qualifying to do business Registering a corporation in a state in which it is not organized but in which it has an ongoing presence.

Quantum meruit "As much as she deserves." The damages awarded in a quasi-contract case.

Quasi-contract A legal fiction in which, to avoid injustice, the court awards damages as if a contract had existed, although one did not.

Quid pro quo A Latin phrase meaning "this for that." It refers to a form of sexual harassment in which some aspect of a job is made contingent upon sexual activity. (Chapter 28)

Quiet enjoyment A tenant's right to use property without the interference of the landlord.

Quota A limit on the quantity of a particular good that may enter a nation. (Chapter 8)

Quorum The number of voters that must be present for a meeting to count. (Chapter 30)

R

Racketeer Influenced and Corrupt Organizations Act (RICO) A powerful federal statute, originally aimed at organized crime, now used in many criminal prosecutions and civil lawsuits.

Racketeering acts Any of a long list of specified crimes, such as embezzlement, arson, mail fraud, wire fraud, and so forth.

Ratification When someone accepts the benefit of an unauthorized transaction or fails to repudiate it once he has learned of it, he is then bound by it. (Chapter 8, 13)

Reaffirm To promise to pay a debt even after it is discharged. (Chapter 26)

Real property Land, together with certain things associated with it, such as buildings, subsurface rights, air rights, plant life and fixtures.

Reasonable doubt The level of proof that the government must meet to convict the defendant in a criminal case. The factfinder must be persuaded to a very high degree of certainty that the defendant did what the government alleges.

Reciprocal dealing agreement An agreement under which Company A will purchase from Company B only if Company B also buys from Company A. These agreements are rule of reason violations of the Sherman Act.

Record Information written on paper or stored in an electronic or other medium. (Chapter 25)

Record date To vote at a shareholders meeting, a shareholder must own stock on the record date.

Red herring A preliminary prospectus.

Redeem To pay the full value of a debt to get the collateral back. (Chapter 25)

Reformation The process by which a court rewrites a contract to ensure its accuracy or viability. (Chapter 17)

Refusal to deal An agreement among competitors that they will not trade with a particular supplier or buyer. Such an agreement is a rule of reason violation of the Sherman Act.

Registration statement A document filed with the Securities and Exchange Commission under the Securities Act of 1933 by an issuer seeking to sell securities in a public transaction.

Reliance interest A remedy in a contract case that puts the injured party in the position he would have been in had the parties never entered into a contract. (Chapter 17)

Remand The power of an appellate court to return a case to a lower court for additional action.

Rent Compensation paid by a tenant to a landlord. (Chapter 32)

Reply A pleading, filed by the plaintiff in response to a defendant's counter-claim. (Chapter 3)

Repossession A secured party takes collateral because the debtor has defaulted on payments. (Chapter 25)

Repudiation An indication made by one contracting party to the other that it will not perform.

Request for admission A form of discovery in which one party demands that the opposing party either admit or deny particular factual or legal allegations.

Requirements contract An agreement that obligates a buyer of specified goods to purchase all of the goods she needs during a stated period from a particular seller. (Chapter 10)

Res ipsa loquitur A doctrine of tort law holding that the facts may imply negligence when the defendant had exclusive control of the thing that caused the harm, the accident would not normally have occurred without negligence, and the plaintiff played no role in causing the injury.

Resale price maintenance A *per se* violation of the Sherman Act in which a manufacturer enters into an agreement with retailers about the prices they will charge.

Rescind To cancel a contract. (Chapter 13, 16)

Rescission To "undo" a contract and put the parties where they were before they made their agreement. (Chapter 17).

Respondeat superior A rule of agency law holding that a principal is liable when a servant acting within the scope of employment commits a tort that causes physical harm to a person or property.

Restitution Restoring an injured party to its original position. (Chapter 13)

Restitution interest A remedy in a contract case that returns to the injured party a benefit that he has conferred on the other party, which would be unjust to leave with that person. (Chapter 17)

Restricted security Any stock purchased in a private offering (such as one under Regulation D). (Chapter 31)

Restricted stock Securities purchased strictly for investment purposes. (Chapter 31)

Retribution Giving a criminal defendant the punishment he deserves.

Reverse An appellate court issues an order overruling a lower court and granting judgment for the party that had lost in the lower court. (Chapter 3)

Reverse and remand To nullify the lower decision and return the case for reconsideration or retrial. (Chapter 3)

Reversion The right of an owner (or her heirs) to property upon the death of a life tenant.

Revocable trust A trust that can be undone or changed at any time.

Revocation The act of disavowing a contract offer, so that the offeree no longer has the power to accept.

Rule of reason violation An action that breaches the antitrust laws only if it has an anticompetitive impact.

Rulemaking The power of an administrative agency to issue regulations.

S

S corporation A corporation that is not a taxable entity.

Sale on approval A transfer in which a buyer takes goods intending to use them herself, but has the right to return the goods to the seller. (Chapter 19)

Sale or return A transfer in which the buyer takes the goods intending to resell them, but has the right to return the goods to the original owner. (Chapter 19)

Scienter In a case of securities fraud, the plaintiff must prove that the defendant acted willfully, knowingly, or recklessly.

Secondary boycott Picketing, directed by a union against a company, designed to force that company to stop doing business with the union's employer.

Secondary offering Any public sale of securities by a company after the initial public offering. (Chapter 31)

Secured party A person or company that holds a security interest. (Chapter 25)

Security Any purchase in which the buyer invests money in a common enterprise and expects to earn a profit predominantly from the efforts of others. (Chapter 31)

Security agreement A contract in which the debtor gives a security interest to the secured party. (Chapter 25)

Security interest An interest in personal property or fixtures that secures the performance of some obligation. (Chapter 15, 25)

Separation of powers The principle, established by the first three articles of the Constitution, that authority should be divided among the legislative, executive, and judicial branches.

Servant An agent whose work is closely controlled by the principal.

Service mark A type of trademark used to identify services, not products.

Settlor Someone who creates a trust.

Sexual harassment Unwanted sexual advances, comments or touching, sufficiently severe to violate Title VII of the 1964 Civil Rights Act. (Chapter 28)

Shilling A seller at auction either bids on his own goods or agrees to cross-bid with a group of other sellers.

Short-swing trading Under Section 16 of the Securities Exchange Act, insiders must turn over to the corporation any profits they make from the purchase and sale or sale and purchase of company securities in a six-month period.

Signatory A person, company, or nation that has signed a legal document, such as a contract, agreement, or treaty. (Chapter 8)

Signature liability The liability of someone who signs an instrument. (Chapter 23)

Sight draft An order directing someone else to pay money on demand. (Chapter 22)

Single-recovery principle A rule of tort litigation that requires a plaintiff to claim all damages, present and future, at the time of trial, not afterwards. (Chapter 6)

Slander *See* Defamation. (Chapter 6)

Sole proprietorship An unincorporated business owned by a single person. (Chapter 29)

Sovereign The recognized political power, whom citizens obey. (Chapter 1)

Sovereign immunity The right of a national government to be free of lawsuits brought in foreign courts.

Spam Unsolicited commercial or bulk e-mail. ("To spam" is to send such e-mail.)

Specific deterrence *See* Deterrence.

Specific performance A contract remedy requiring the breaching party to perform the contract, by conveying land or some unique asset, rather than by paying money damages. (Chapter 17)

Spyware A computer program that enters a user's computer without permission and monitors and reports the user's activities. (Chapter 32)

Sole proprietorship An unincorporated business owned by one person.

Stakeholder Anyone who is affected by the activities of a corporation, such as employees, customers, creditors, suppliers, shareholders, and neighbors. (Chapter 30)

Stale check A check presented more than six months after its due date.

Stare decisis "Let the decision stand." A basic principle of the common law, it means that precedent is usually binding. (Chapter 4)

Statute A law passed by a legislative body, such as Congress. (Chapter 1)

Statute of frauds This law provides that certain contracts are not enforceable unless in writing.

Statute of limitations A statute that determines the period within which a particular kind of lawsuit must be filed. (Chapter 16)

Statute of repose A law that places an absolute limit on when a lawsuit may be filed, regardless of when the defect was discovered.

Statutory interpretation A court's power to give meaning to new legislation by clarifying ambiguities, providing limits, and ultimately applying it to a specific fact pattern in litigation.

Straight bankruptcy Also known as *liquidation*, this form of bankruptcy mandates that the bankrupt's assets be sold to pay creditors but the creditor has no obligation to share future earnings. (Chapter 26)

Strict liability A tort doctrine holding to a very high standard all those who engage in ultrahazardous activity (e.g., using explosives) or who manufacture certain products.

Strict performance Requires one party to perform its obligations precisely, with no deviation from the contract terms. (Chapter 17)

Strike The ultimate weapon of a labor union, it occurs when all or most employees of a particular plant or employer walk off the job and refuse to work.

Strike suit A lawsuit without merit that defendants sometimes settle simply to avoid the nuisance of litigation.

Sublease A tenant's transfer of *some* of his legal interest in a property.

Subpoena An order to appear, issued by a court or government body.

Subpoena *duces tecum* An order to produce certain documents or things before a court or government body.

Subprime loan A loan that has an above-market interest rate because the borrower is high-risk.

Subrogated to The bank can substitute for, or take the place of, a party. (Chapter 24)

Substantial performance The promisor performs contract duties well enough to be entitled to his full contract price, minus the value of any defects. (Chapter 16)

Substantive due process *See* Due Process Clause. (Chapter 5)

Substantive law Rules that establish the rights of parties. For example, the prohibition against slander is substantive law, as opposed to procedural law. (Chapter 1)

Substitute check A paper printout of the electronic version of a check, which is legally the same as the original. (Chapter 24)

Summary judgment The power of a trial court to terminate a lawsuit before a trial has begun, on the grounds that no essential facts are in dispute. (Chapter 3)

Supermajority voting Typically, shareholders can approve charter amendments by a majority vote. However, sometimes corporations require more than a majority of shareholders (e.g., 80 percent) to approve certain charter amendments, such as a merger. These provisions are designed to discourage hostile takeovers.

Superseding cause An event that interrupts the chain of causation and relieves a defendant from liability based on her own act.

Supremacy Clause From Article VI of the Constitution, it declares that federal statutes and treaties take priority over any state law, if there is a conflict between the two or, even absent a conflict, if Congress manifests an intent to preempt the field. (Chapter 5)

Surplus A sum of money greater than the debt incurred. (Chapter 25)

T

Takings Clause Part of the Fifth Amendment, it ensures that when any governmental unit takes private property for public use, it must compensate the owner. (Chapter 5)

Tariff A duty imposed on imported goods by the government of the importing nation.

Tenancy at sufferance A tenancy that exists without the permission of the landlord, after the expiration of a true tenancy. (Chapter 32)

Tenancy at will A tenancy with no fixed duration, which may be terminated by either party at any time. (Chapter 32)

Tenancy by the entirety A form of joint ownership available only to married couples. If one member of the couple dies, the property goes automatically to the survivor. Creditors cannot attach the property, nor can one owner sell the property without the other's permission.

Tenancy for years A lease for a stated, fixed period. (Chapter 32)

Tenancy in common Two or more people holding equal interest in a property, but with no right of survivorship. (Chapter 32)

Tenant A person given temporary possession of the landlord's property. (Chapter 32)

Tender To make conforming goods available to the buyer.

Tender offer A public offer to buy a block of stock directly from shareholders. (Chapter 30)

Term partnership When the partners agree in advance on the duration of a partnership. (Chapter 29)

Termination statement A document indicating that a secured party no longer claims a security interest in the collateral. (Chapter 25)

Testamentary trust A trust created by the grantor's will.

Testator Someone who dies having executed a will.

Testatrix A female testator.

Third party beneficiary Someone who stands to benefit from a contract to which she is not a party. An *intended* beneficiary may enforce such a contract; an *incidental* beneficiary may not.

Three-Fifths Clause A clause in Article 1, section 2 of the United States Constitution, now void and regarded as racist, which required that for purposes of taxation and representation, a slave should be counted as three-fifths of a person.

Tied product In a tying arrangement, the product that a buyer must purchase as the condition for being allowed to buy another product.

Time draft An order directing someone else to pay money in the future. (Chapter 22)

Time of the essence clause A clause that generally makes contract dates strictly enforceable. (Chapter 16)

Tort A civil wrong, committed in violation of a duty that the law imposes. (Chapter 6)

Tortious interference with a contract A tort in which the defendant deliberately impedes an existing contract between the plaintiff and another entity. (Chapter 6)

Tortious interference with a prospective advantage A tort in which the defendant deliberately obstructs a developing venture or advantage that the plaintiff has created. (Chapter 6)

Tracing When an auditor takes an item of original data and tracks it forward to ensure that it has been properly recorded throughout the bookkeeping process.

Trade acceptance A draft drawn by a seller of goods on the buyer and payable to the seller or some third party. (Chapter 22)

Trade secret A formula, device, process, method, or compilation of information that, when used in business, gives the owner an advantage over competitors who do not know it. (Chapter 34)

Trademark Any combination of words and symbols that a business uses to identify its products or services and that federal law will protect. (Chapter 32)

Treasury stock Stock that has been bought back by its issuing corporation. (Chapter 30)

Trespass A tort committed by intentionally entering land that belongs to someone else, or remaining on the land after being asked to leave.

Trespasser Anyone on a property without consent.

Trial court Any court in a state or federal system that holds formal hearings to determine the facts in a civil or criminal case. (Chapter 3)

Trust An entity that separates legal and beneficial ownership.

Tying a product In a tying arrangement, the product offered for sale on the condition that another product be purchased as well.

Tying arrangement A violation of the Sherman and Clayton Acts in which a seller requires that two distinct products be purchased together. The seller uses its significant power in the market for the tying product to shut out a substantial part of the market for the tied product.

U

Ultra vires An activity that is not permitted by a corporation's charter.

Ultrahazardous activity Conduct that is lawful yet unusual and much more likely to cause injury than normal commercial activity.

Unconscionable contract An agreement that a court refuses to enforce because it is fundamentally unfair as a result of unequal bargaining power by one party. (Chapter 18)

Undisclosed principal If a third party in an agency relationship does not know that the agent is acting for a principal, that principal is undisclosed.

Undue influence One party so dominates the thinking of another party to a contract that the dominant party cannot truly consent to the agreement.

Unfair labor practice An act, committed by either a union or an employer, that violates the National Labor Relations Act, such as failing to bargain in good faith.

Unilateral contract A binding agreement in which one party has made an offer that the other can accept only by action, not words.

Unilateral mistake Occurs when only one party enters a contract under a mistaken assumption. (Chapter 13)

Unliquidated debt A claimed debt that is disputed, either because the parties disagree over whether there is in fact a debt or because they disagree over the amount. (Chapter 11)

U.S. Trustee, The Oversees the administration of bankruptcy law in a region. (Chapter 26)

Usury Charging interest at a rate that exceeds legal limits.

Utter To pass on an instrument that one knows to be forged. (Chapter 23)

V

Value The holder has *already* done something in exchange for the instrument. (Chapter 22)

Valuation A process by which the Customs Service determines the fair value of goods being imported, for purposes of imposing a duty.

Verdict The decision of the factfinder in a case.

Vertical agreement or merger An agreement or merger between two companies at different stages of the production process, such as when a company acquires one of its suppliers or distributors.

Veto The power of the president to reject legislation passed by Congress, terminating the bill unless Congress votes by a 2/3 majority to override. (Chapter 4)

Vouching Auditors choose a transaction listed in a company's books and check backwards for original data to support it.

Void agreement An agreement that neither party may legally enforce, usually because the purpose of the bargain was illegal or because one of the parties lacked capacity to make it.

Voidable contract An agreement that, because of some defect, may be terminated by one party, such as a minor, but not by both parties.

Voidable title Limited rights in goods, inferior to those of the owner. (Chapter 19)

Voir dire The process of selecting a jury. Attorneys for the parties and the judge may inquire of prospective jurors whether they are biased or incapable of rendering a fair and impartial verdict. (Chapter 3)

W

Warrant liability The liability of someone who receives payment on an instrument.

Warranty A guarantee that goods will meet certain standards. (Chapter 20)

Warranty of fitness for a particular purpose An assurance under the Uniform Commercial Code that the goods are fit for the special purpose for which the buyer intends them and of which the seller is aware.

Warranty liability The liability of someone who receives payment on an instrument. (Chapter 23)

Warranty of merchantability An assurance under the Uniform Commercial Code that the goods are fit for their ordinary purpose.

Whistleblower Someone who discloses wrongful behavior.

Winding up The process whereby the assets of a partnership are sold and the proceeds distributed.

World Trade Organization (WTO) Created by GATT to stimulate international commerce and resolve trade disputes. (Chapter 8)

World Wide Web A decentralized collection of documents containing text, pictures and sound that is accessible from Internet sites. It is a sub-network of the Internet.

Writ An order from a government compelling someone to do a particular thing.

Writ of certiorari A petition asking the Supreme Court to hear a case. (Chapter 3)

Wrongful discharge An employer may not fire a worker for a reason that violates basic social rights, duties, or responsibilities. (Chapter 28)

TABLE OF CASES

INDEX